Psychopathology

BPS Textbooks in Psychology

BPS Blackwell presents a comprehensive and authoritative series covering everything a student needs in order to complete an undergraduate degree in psychology. Refreshingly written to consider more than North American research, this series is the first to give a truly international perspective. Written by the very best names in the field, the series offers an extensive range of titles from introductory level through to final year optional modules, and every text fully complies with the BPS syllabus in that topic. No other series bears the BPS seal of approval!

Each book is supported by a companion website, featuring additional resource materials for both instructors and students, designed to encourage critical thinking, and providing for all your course lecturing and testing needs.

Published

Psychology edited by Miles Hewstone, Frank Fincham and Jonathan Foster

Personality and Individual Differences Tomas Chamorro-Premuzic

Introduction to Social Psychology, *4th edition* edited by Miles Hewstone, Wolfgang Stroebe and Klaus Jonas

Psychopathology Graham Davey

Forthcoming

Judgment and Decision Making David Hardman

An Introduction to Reading Development and Reading Difficulties Kate Cain

Memory Chris Moulin and Martin Conway

Cognition John Groeger and Benjamin Clegg

Group Processes and Intergroup Relations Rhiannon Turner and Richard Crisp

An Introduction to Developmental Psychology, 2nd edition Alan Slater and Gavin Bremner

Community Psychology Carolyn Kagen, Mark Burton, Paul Duckett, Rebecca Lawthom and Asiya Siddiquee

Psychobiology Chris Chandler

GRAHAM DAVEY

PSYCHOPATHOLOGY
Research, Assessment and Treatment in Clinical Psychology

BPS TEXTBOOKS IN PSYCHOLOGY

The British Psychological Society

BPS Blackwell

This edition first published 2008 by the British Psychological Society and Blackwell Publishing Ltd
© 2008 Graham Davey

BPS Blackwell is an imprint of Blackwell Publishing, which was acquired by John Wiley & Sons in February 2007. Blackwell's publishing program has been merged with Wiley's global Scientific, Technical, and Medical business to form Wiley-Blackwell.

Registered Office
John Wiley & Sons Ltd, The Atrium, Southern Gate, Chichester, West Sussex, PO19 8SQ, UK

Editorial Offices
350 Main Street, Malden, MA 02148-5020, USA
9600 Garsington Road, Oxford, OX4 2DQ, UK
The Atrium, Southern Gate, Chichester, West Sussex, PO19 8SQ, UK

For details of our global editorial offices, for customer services, and for information about how to apply for permission to reuse the copyright material in this book please see our website at www.wiley.com/wiley-blackwell.

The right of Graham Davey to be identified as the author of this work has been asserted in accordance with the Copyright, Designs and Patents Act 1988.

Library of Congress Cataloging-in-Publication Data

Davey, Graham.
    Psychopathology: Research, assessment and treatment in clinical psychology / Graham Davey.
        p.   cm. – (BPS textbooks in psychology)
    Includes bibliographical references and index.
    ISBN 978-1-4051-3224-4 (pbk.: alk. paper)   1. Psychology, Pathological–Textbooks.   I. Title.
    RC454.D275   2008
    616.89–dc22

                                                                                     2008009305

A catalogue record for this book is available from the British Library.

Set in 9.5 / 11.5 pt Dante by Graphicraft Limited, Hong Kong
Printed in Spain by Graphy Cems

The British Psychological Society's free Research Digest e-mail service rounds up the latest research and relates it to your syllabus in a user-friendly way. To subscribe go to www.researchdigest.org.uk or send a blank e-mail to subscribe-rd@lists.bps.org.uk.

4   2013

Commissioning Editor:	Andrew McAleer
Development Editor:	Elizabeth Johnston
Marketing Managers:	Darren Reed and Leann Fowler
Production Editors:	Jenny Phillips and Hannah Rolls
Project Manager / Copy Editor:	Brigitte Lee
Proofreader:	Caroline Morris
Indexer:	Marie Lorimer
Picture Editor:	Leanda Shrimpton
Picture Researcher:	Helen Nash

Brief Contents

Contents

7 Experiencing Psychosis: Schizophrenia and its Symptoms

8 Substance Abuse and Dependency

11 Personality Disorders   390

PART III DEVELOPMENTAL PSYCHOPATHOLOGY

15 Childhood Psychological Problems

16 Learning, Intellectual and Developmental Disabilities   570

ACKNOWLEDGEMENTS

This textbook has been a major project, and as such could not have been completed without the help, understanding and support of a lot of people. I should begin by thanking Andrew McAleer, Elizabeth Johnston and Philip Carpenter at Blackwell for their unquestioning support for this project over the years, and for their help and assistance whenever I needed it. Catherine Flack has also advised extensively on the teaching and learning features of the book, and I have benefited considerably from her sound and expert advice. Many people have contributed in specific but highly practical ways by providing me with materials, information, feedback on draft chapters, advice on terminology and clinical practice, and contributing directly to some of the features. These people include Miranda Blayney, Alison Brown, Kate Cavanagh, Roger Cocks, Rudi Dallos, Andy Field, Daniel Freeman, Theresa Gannon, David Green, Richard Hastings, Marko Jelicic, Jo Johnson, Fergal Jones, Ruth Mann, Charlie Martin, Lance McCracken, Benie MacDonald, Fran Meeten, Michael Morgan, Peter Muris, Ben Smith, Helen Startup, Emma Veitch, Brendan Weekes and Leonora Wilkinson.

I also need to express my deepest gratitude to my partner Benie who has supported me emotionally and practically through this lengthy project; to my children Kate and Lizzie, who have endured my ramblings about this project for so long that they have now both eschewed psychology for academic careers in the arts and humanities; to our dog, Megan, who unwittingly (but maybe wittingly!) accompanied me on many of the long walks required to consolidate some of the ideas that contributed to this book; and finally, to all those family members who endured this obsession, including Emily, Doon, Lucy, Simon, Cathy and my mother Betty. Thanks must go to The Roundhill in Brighton for regularly providing me with an internet connection when I needed a beer, and to Andy and Dave for providing me with those beers on a regular basis. Thanks also to La Trata bar on Naxos for providing cold beers and regular stunning sunsets while I was finalizing these last few pages. Finally, I must also thank my late father, Ray. Without his support and encouragement during my academic career I could now be doing shift work in a hosiery factory in the East Midlands – God bless!

Despite all these invaluable forms of help and support, I am – of course – still responsible for the accuracy and quality of the contents of this book. I hope you enjoy it.

Graham Davey
Brighton, August 2007

PREFACE

Psychopathology and the associated profession of clinical psychology have become established topics of study on undergraduate psychology degree programmes. This is hardly surprising given that a substantial proportion of students entering degree programmes in psychology do so with a career in applied psychology firmly in mind. This text has been designed to provide those students with a comprehensive coverage of both psychopathology and clinical practice, and is written to serve as a textbook accessible at all undergraduate levels and as a source book for more in-depth study at postgraduate masters level. The emphasis in the book is on providing students with a thorough academic knowledge of psychopathology, based on current research in a range of relevant areas – especially knowledge of the assessment, aetiology and effective treatments for a range of common and less common mental health problems.

In addition to establishing a working academic knowledge of psychopathology, the book attempts to convey some of the issues and challenges that face clinical practitioners, as well as to provide readers with a realistic insight into what clinical psychologists do and how they do it. To this end, each chapter ends with a list of *clinical issues* that confront the practising clinical psychologist across each of the psychopathologies discussed. In addition, *Treatment in Practice* features explain how specific treatments are applied in practice, many chapters contain discussions of how clinical services are structured, and there are also features describing the kinds of activities undertaken by clinical psychologists in a typical week. To be sure, this is not a textbook designed for students undergoing clinical training, but it is hoped that it will provide a much-needed insight for undergraduate students into psychopathology and how it is assessed and treated.

The first four chapters cover basic conceptual issues in psychopathology, including the thorny topic of *defining* psychopathology, the tools used to *assess* psychopathology, the methods used to *research* psychopathology and the techniques used to *treat* psychopathology. Chapters 5 to 16 cover a range of specific psychopathology categories, including a majority of those likely to be encountered by practising clinical psychologists.

Each chapter covering a specific psychopathology is organized in a similar fashion. Readers are initially provided with a personal account of the psychopathology, which is used to introduce a discussion of the main features of the problem including any relevant diagnostic issues. Chapters then continue with an in-depth discussion of research into the aetiology and origins of the psychopathology, followed by a broad coverage of the treatments and interventions commonly applied to that psychopathology.

The diagnostic classification scheme described in this text is DSM-IV-TR – a diagnostic scheme widely adopted by clinical psychologists involved in both practice and research. It is acknowledged that there is currently an extensive debate about the value of diagnosis in clinical practice, and these issues are covered in the text, from the considerable limitations of diagnostic classification as currently conceived (see Chapter 1) to issues associated with the application of individual diagnostic criteria (see Chapters 5 to 16).

The text is supplemented by a range of features designed to facilitate effective teaching and learning. They include:

- **Focus Point Boxes**: These provide more in-depth discussion of particular topics that are conceptually important, controversial or simply of contemporary interest. Whenever possible, these are linked to everyday examples – such as high-profile news items – that allow readers to consider the issues in a contemporary, everyday context.

- **Activity Boxes**: Activity boxes offer readers an opportunity to engage in active learning about a topic by completing a task or activity. Examples of such activities include simple experiments designed to demonstrate a particular phenomenon, opportunities for further reading and research, or topics and questions suitable for small group discussion. Instructors or teachers may want to make use of these activities when structuring their class teaching. Access to these activities based on the type of activity, suitability of class size, skills development, learning objectives and time requirement can be found on the book's associated website.

- **Research Methods Boxes**: These features contain detailed descriptions of methods utilized in psychopathology research, describing the pros and cons of individual methods and their potential uses. These examples act to supplement the general material provided on research methods in Chapter 3. Like most researchers, those involved in clinical psychology research are often imaginative in their use of research methods, and many of the examples provided in research methods boxes attempt to convey how methods from other areas of psychology and science generally can be adapted to study issues relevant to psychopathology.

- **Case Histories**: Most chapters contain example case histories describing the symptoms, experiences and life circumstances encountered by individuals experiencing particular psychopathologies. Each of these examples concludes with a *clinical commentary* that is designed to link the detail of that specific case history to the general facts to be learned in the text.

- **Client's Perspective Boxes**: Many chapters also contain examples of an individual's own descriptions of the experience of psychopathology. These are designed to provide readers with an insight into the phenomenology of different psychopathologies, and the way that symptoms affect moods, experiences and everyday living – including social, occupational and educational functioning. These descriptions supplement the *personal accounts* of psychopathologies that begin each chapter. As with case histories, client's perspective features usually conclude with a *clinical commentary* that links the personal experiences of the psychopathology to the academic content of the text.

- **Treatment in Practice Boxes**: These boxes attempt to provide readers with a more detailed insight into how individual treatments are conducted in practice. It is often difficult for a student to understand, for example, how a therapy is conducted in practice from descriptions given in academic texts. These boxes provide some specific examples of how practitioners might implement the principles of a treatment in a specific case.

- **Self-Test Questions**: Throughout each chapter readers will encounter *self-test questions*. These are designed to test readers' absorption of basic factual and conceptual knowledge. Instructors and teachers can also use these questions as a basis for discussing key material in class or in small group discussions.

- **Summary Tables**: Each chapter that covers specific psychopathology categories (i.e. Chapters 5 to 16) contains a full summary table of the information covered in the chapter. In all cases this is organized into a list of specific diagnostic categories, details of prevalence rates, the defining characteristics of the psychopathology, the DSM-IV-TR diagnostic criteria, key features of the psychopathology, the main theories of its aetiology and the main forms of treatment. These summary tables are located at the beginning of chapters to provide readers with an overview of the material to be covered. Additionally, having completed a chapter, readers can refer back to the summary table to remind themselves of the structure and content of the material they have covered.

- **Learning Outcomes and Section Summaries**: At the end of each chapter is a list of the main learning outcomes for the chapter. These are couched in terms of the knowledge that students are expected to acquire during the course of learning from the chapter, and the analytical and critical skills they are expected to achieve in describing and evaluating material in the chapter. Also, within each chapter there are section summaries designed to provide a clear overview of the key points within each main section. Students can use these summaries as revision aids, while teachers and instructors can use them to assess the knowledge that should be acquired from each section.

- **Links to Journal Articles and Further Reading**: All chapters have an extensive bibliography of further reading for interested readers or advanced-level students who need further detail on specific topics. These are organized into *links to journal articles* and *texts for further reading*. A list of relevant journal articles is provided covering reviews of specific topics, seminal discussion of critical conceptual and theoretical issues, studies describing important research in an area, or discussions and descriptions relevant to clinical practice. Nowadays, students in higher education have regular free electronic access to many journal articles via their HE institution, and this was one of the main reasons for including a full and extensive list of journal articles for students to pursue – hopefully at minimal cost to themselves. When articles on the list are encountered in the text, they are highlighted in blue to draw the reader's attention to them. I have also tried to make the list of texts for further reading as broad and up-to-date as possible, but there will be an inevitable passage of time between writing these lists and publication, which may mean some very recent and topical texts have been omitted.

- **Research Questions and Clinical Issues**: At the end of each chapter are two lists. One is a list of *research questions* that arise from the content of the chapter. These are often questions that address research issues that have yet to be resolved, and provide readers with some insight into the direction in which current research on a topic may be evolving (or perhaps more pertinently, should be evolving!). The second is a list of *clinical issues* that describe some of the clinical problems or questions facing practitioners. These may be issues to do with clinical practice or may cover ethical and moral questions that confront clinical psychologists when dealing with clients. The lists of both research questions and clinical issues can be used either as a source of essay titles, or as the basis for class or small group discussions. In all cases, there should be material in the body of the chapter to help readers or students address these questions.

- **Glossary**: At the end of each chapter is a list of key terms used in the chapter. When each term first appears in the text, it is highlighted in bold and italic and is either described or defined at that point. Highlighting these terms makes them easy to locate, and the list of key terms can serve as a revision checklist – especially for students due to take multiple-choice questionnaire assessments. There is also a full and comprehensive glossary of concepts at the end of the book, which readers can refer to for quick and ready definitions of key terms.

- **DVD**: Every copy of this book comes with an associated DVD. This contains two important sources of material. The first consists of video clips representing interviews with individuals exhibiting symptoms of specific psychopathologies. There are 18 interviews provided on the DVD, allowing readers to learn how an interview can reveal information about symptoms associated with specific types of psychopathology. These interviews should be viewed in conjunction with the assessment and diagnostic information provided in the text. The availability of an interview clip to supplement the text is signalled by the presence of this symbol next to the text. For reasons of confidentiality, all of these interviews are re-enacted using actors, but the dialogue was constructed from the clinical observations of trained practitioners with considerable experience and expertise in conducting clinical interviews. These video excerpts have been kindly made available by the the University of Sheffield and Dr Stephen Peters. The second block of material on the DVD represents an introduction to clinical psychology and clinical psychology training for readers and students who may be interested in pursuing a career in this area. This consists of a video originally commissioned by the British Psychological Society Division of Clinical Psychology.

I am indebted to David Green for his help in allowing this video to be reproduced as part of the material associated with this book.

- **Associated Website**: The companion website available at www.blackwellpublishing.com/psychopathology features a wide range of resources to support both instructors and students, including thousands of multiple choice questions available for both students and instructors, sample chapters, seminar activities, study skills material, PowerPoint slides, and much more.

Finally, I hope you find this book readable, accessible, enlightening, clear in structure, sufficient and accurate in detail, and an effective instrument to enable teachers to teach and learners to learn. If not – it is entirely my fault!

I | General Concepts, Processes and Procedures

1 | Psychopathology: Concepts and Classification

ROUTE MAP OF THE CHAPTER

This first chapter introduces a number of basic issues concerned with the definition, explanation and classification of psychopathology. The first section describes how behaviour that was often labelled as 'mad' has been explained over the ages, and how our modern-day conceptions of 'madness' and psychopathology have developed. We then look at modern methods of explaining psychopathology and discuss a number of psychological approaches to explanation. The chapter then proceeds to a discussion of how psychopathology should be defined, and how we identify behaviour that is in need of support and treatment. Finally, we look at how psychopathology is classified, and review in detail the structure and pros and cons of the DSM method of classification.

Am I crazy? I don't know what is wrong with me. I did have depression in the past and what I am going through doesn't feel a lot like what I had before. My moods change every 30 minutes at times. I have been like this for a while. It started out about once a week when I would have a day where I was going from one extreme to the next. In the past few weeks it has gotten worse. It seems like my moods change for no reason at all. There are times that I will just lay down and cry for what appears to be no reason at all and then 2 hours later I will be happy. I find myself yelling at my son for stupid reasons and then shortly after I am fine again. I truly feel that I am going crazy and the more I think about it the worse I get. I am not sleeping or eating much and when I do eat I feel like I will be sick.

JOAN'S STORY

For the last ten months serving in Iraq I've told myself not to think about all that's going on around me. I've forced myself to go about my daily activities in some sort of normal manner. I knew that if I thought too much about the fact that mortars could hit me at any time. Or if I laid in bed every night knowing that a mortar could drop through the ceiling while I slept. Or if I focused too much on the randomness of death here, I'd go crazy.

And for the last ten months, I've managed to put these things out of my head for the most part. I've managed to try to live a normal life here while people die around me. But for some reason, since I got back from leave, I can't seem to shake the jitters, the nervousness, the just plain uneasiness I feel walking around or driving through the city streets.

Everywhere I walk I'm constantly thinking about where I'm going to go if a mortar lands. I'm always looking for the next bunker. When I leave the relative safety of the base, I'm constantly running scenarios through my head of the worst case situations.

There comes a point where living in fear is not living at all.

GREG'S STORY

When I was a child I regularly experienced dreams in which there was an awful buzzing noise, at the same time I could see what I can only describe as the needle from a machine such as a lie detector test drawing lines. I had a dream where an older alien cloaked in orange took me on a ship and told me things that I can't remember yet. He took me over an island (I think it was Australia), everything was dead and there was a mushroom cloud over it. Then there were 5 or 6 aliens, one was holding a clear ball. I knew that inside there was an embryo, they put it inside me. About one and a half weeks later I was confirmed pregnant. Then, when we were driving on the motorway, I seem to have lost 2 hours before seeing a brilliant flash above the car. I got pains in my left temple, behind my left eye and in my left cheekbone. There is a scar on my right leg which I can't explain. Some people think I'm crazy, but I know it happened.

BETTY'S STORY

I started using cocaine at thirteen. Before, I was using marijuana and alcohol and it didn't really work for me, so I wanted to step it up a level. I started using heroin when I was fifteen. I began using it to come down from cocaine and get some sleep. But I started liking the heroin high and started using it straight. Everyday, after awhile. Along with cocaine, I also began taking prescription drugs when I was thirteen. They were so easy to get. I never had to buy them or get them from a doctor. I would just get them from friends who had gone through their parent's medicine cabinet. I also thought that prescription drugs were 'safer' than other drugs. I figured that it was okay for people to take them, and if they were legal, I was fine. Like I said, prescription drugs were incredibly easy to get from friends, and it always seemed to be a last-minute thing. Heroin was also easy to get – all I had to do was go into town and buy it. My heroin use started spiralling out of control. I stopped going to school. I was leaving home for days at a time. My whole life revolved around getting and using drugs – I felt like I was going crazy.

ERICA'S STORY

Introduction

We begin this book with personal accounts from four very different individuals. Possibly the only common link between these four accounts is that they each use the word 'crazy' in relating their story. *Joan* questions whether she is going crazy, *Greg* tells us how he tries to prevent himself from going crazy, other people think *Betty* is crazy, and *Erica's* life gets so out of control that she too felt like she was 'going crazy'. We tend to use words like 'crazy', 'madness' and 'insanity' regularly – as if we knew what we meant by those terms. However, we do tend to use these terms in a number of different circumstances – for example, (1) when someone's behaviour deviates from expected norms, (2) when we are unclear about the reasons for someone's actions, (3) when a behaviour seems to be irrational, or (4) when a behaviour or action appears to be maladaptive or harmful to the individual or others. You can try to see whether these different uses of the term 'crazy' or 'mad' apply to each of our personal accounts, but they probably still won't capture the full meaning of why each individual used the word 'crazy' in their vignettes. Trying to define our use of everyday words like 'crazy', 'madness' and 'insanity' leads us on to thinking about those areas of thinking and behaving that seem to deviate from normal or everyday modes of functioning. For psychologists, the study of these deviations from normal or everyday functioning is known as *psychopathology*, and the branch of psychology responsible for understanding and treating psychopathology is known as *clinical psychology*.

Psychopathology   The study of deviations from normal or everyday psychological functioning.

Clinical psychology   The branch of psychology responsible for understanding and treating psychopathology.

Let's examine our four personal accounts a little more closely. *Joan* is distressed because she appears to have no control over her moods. She feels depressed; she shouts at her son, she feels sick when she eats. *Greg* feels anxious about the dangers of his daily life serving in Iraq. He feels nervous and jittery. *Betty* doesn't think she's crazy – but other people do. They think that her story about being abducted by aliens is a sign of psychosis or disordered thinking – she thinks it seems perfectly logical. Finally, *Erica's* behaviour has become controlled by her need for drugs. She feels out of control and all other activities in her life – such as her education – are suffering severely because of this.

These four cases are all ones that are likely to be encountered by clinical psychologists. Although very different in their detail, they do all possess some commonalities that might help us to define what represents psychopathology. For example, (1) both *Joan* and *Greg* experience debilitating distress, (2) both *Joan* and *Erica* feel that important aspects of their life (such as their moods or cravings) are out of their control and they cannot cope, (3) both *Joan* and *Erica* find that their conditions have resulted in them failing to function properly in certain spheres of their life (e.g. as a mother or as a student), and (4) *Betty's* life appears to be controlled by thoughts and memories which are probably not real. As we shall see later, these are all important aspects of psychopathology, and define to some extent what will be the subject matter of clinical practice.

However, deciding what are proper and appropriate examples of psychopathology is not easy. Just because someone's behaviour deviates from accepted norms or patterns does not mean he or she is suffering from a mental or psychiatric illness, and just because we might use the term 'crazy' to describe someone's behaviour does not mean that it is the product of disordered thinking. Similarly, we cannot attempt to define psychopathology on the basis that some 'normal' functioning (psychological, neurological or biological) has gone wrong. This is because (1) we are still some way from understanding the various processes that contribute to psychopathology, and (2) many forms of behaviour that require treatment by clinical psychologists are merely extreme forms of what we would call 'normal' or 'adaptive' behaviour. For example, we all worry and we all get depressed at some times, but these activities do not significantly interfere with our everyday living. However, for some other people, their experience of these activities may be so extreme as to cause them significant distress and to prevent them from undertaking normal daily living. Before we continue to discuss individual psychopathologies in detail, it is important to discuss how we define and classify psychopathology and mental health problems generally.

1.1 EXPLAINING PSYCHOPATHOLOGY

Throughout history, we have been willing to label behaviour as 'mad', 'crazy' or 'insane' if it appears unpredictable, irrational, harmful, or if it simply deviates from accepted contemporary social norms. Characters from history who have been labelled in such a way include the Roman Emperor Caligula, King George III, Vincent Van Gogh, King Saul of Israel and Virginia Woolf, to name just a few. But the term 'madness' does not imply a cause – it simply redescribes the behaviour as something that is odd. Views about what *causes* 'mad' behaviour have changed significantly over the course of history, and it is instructive to understand how the way we attribute the causes of mental health problems have developed over time. The following models provide some examples of how we attempt to *explain* psychopathology. We will begin by looking at a historical perspective on explaining psychopathology, which is known as demonic possession. We will then look at more contemporary models of explanation such as the *medical model* and *psychological models*.

Medical model   An explanation of psychopathology in terms of underlying biological or medical causes.

Psychological models   Models which view psychopathology as caused primarily by psychological rather than biological processes.

1.1.1 Demonic Possession

Many forms of psychopathology are accompanied by what appear to be changes in the individual's personality, and these changes in personality or behaviour are some of the first symptoms that are noticed. The reserved person may become manic and outgoing, and the gregarious person withdrawn and sombre. They may start behaving in ways which mean they neglect important daily activities (such as parenting or going to work), or may be harmful to themselves or others. The fact that an individual's personality seems to have changed (and may do so very suddenly) has historically tended people towards describing those exhibiting symptoms of psychopathology as being 'possessed' in some way. That is, their behaviour has changed in such a way that their personality appears to have been taken over and replaced by the persona of someone or something else.

Explanations of psychopathology in terms of 'possession' have taken many forms over the course of history, and it is a form of explanation that has meant that many who have been suffering debilitating and distressing psychological problems have been persecuted and physically abused rather than offered the support and treatment they need. Many ancient civilizations, such as those in Egypt, China, Babylon and Greece, believed that those exhibiting symptoms of psychopathology were possessed by bad spirits (this is known as **demonology**), and the only way to exorcise these bad spirits was with elaborate, ritualized ceremonies that frequently involved direct physical attacks on the sufferer's body in an attempt to force out the demons (e.g. through torture, flogging or starvation). Not surprisingly, such actions usually had the effect of increasing the distress and suffering of the victim.

Demonology   The belief that those exhibiting symptoms of psychopathology are possessed by bad spirits.

Demonology survived as an explanation of psychopathology and mental health problems right up until the eighteenth century, when witchcraft and demonic possession were common explanations for psychopathology. This contrasts with the Middle Ages in England when individuals were often treated in a relatively civilized fashion. When someone exhibited symptoms typical of psychopathology, a 'lunacy trial' was held to determine the individual's sanity, and if the person was found to be insane, he or she was given the protection of the law (Neugebauer, 1979). Nevertheless, demonic possession is still a common explanation of psychopathology in some less developed areas of the world – especially where witchcraft and voodoo are still important features of the local culture such as Haiti and some areas of Western Africa (Desrosiers & Fleurose, 2002).

1.1.2 The Medical or Disease Model

As cultures develop, so too do the types of causes to which they attribute behaviour. In particular, as we began to understand some of the biological causes of physical disease and illness, then our conception of 'madness' moved very slowly towards treating it as a disease (hence the term 'mental illness'). The impetus for this change in conception came in the nineteenth century when it became apparent that many forms of behaviour typical of psychopathology were the result of physical illnesses, such as strokes or viral infections. For example, without proper treatment, the later stages of the sexually transmitted disease *syphilis* are characterized by the inability to coordinate muscle movements, paralysis, numbness, gradual blindness and dementia – and many of these symptoms caused radical changes in the individual's personality. The discovery that syphilis had a biological cause, and was also an important contributor to the mental disorder known as **general paresis**, implied that many other examples of mental or psychological illness might also have medical or biological explanations. This became known as the **somatogenic hypothesis**, which advocated that the causes or explanations of psychological problems could be found in physical or biological impairments.

General paresis   A brain disease occurring as a late consequence of syphilis, characterized by dementia, progressive muscular weakness and paralysis.

Somatogenic hypothesis   The hypothesis that the causes or explanations of psychological problems can be found in physical or biological impairments.

The medical model of psychopathology that was fostered by the somatogenic hypothesis was an important development because it introduced scientific thinking into our attempts to understand psychopathology, and shifted explanations away from those associated with cultural and religious beliefs. The medical model has given rise to a large body of scientific knowledge about psychopathology that is based on medicine. This profession is known as **psychiatry**, and the primary approach of the medical model is to identify the biological causes of psychopathology and treat them with medication or surgery. As we shall see in later chapters, there are many explanations of psychopathology that allude to biological causes, and these attempt to explain symptoms in terms of such factors as brain abnormalities (e.g. in dementia, autism), biochemical imbalances (especially imbalances of brain neurotransmitters) (e.g. major depression, bipolar disorder, schizophrenia), genetic factors (e.g. learning disabilities, autism, schizophrenia), chromosome disorders (e.g. intellectual disabilities), congenital risk factors (such as maternal infections during pregnancy) (e.g. intellectual disorders, ADHD), abnormal physical development (e.g. autism), and the physical effects of pathological activities (e.g. the effect of hyperventilation in panic disorder), amongst others. However, while such biological factors may play a role in the aetiology of some psychopathologies, biological explanations are not the only way in which psychopathology can be explained, and nor is biological dysfunction necessarily a factor underlying all psychopathology. As we shall see later, it is often a person's experiences that are dysfunctional, not their biological substrates.

Psychiatry   A scientific method of treatment that is based on medicine, the primary approach of which is to identify the biological causes of psychopathology and treat them with medication or surgery.

However, despite its obvious importance in developing a scientific view of psychopathology and providing some influential treatments, the medical model of psychopathology has some significant implications for the way we conceive mental health problems. First, an obvious implication is that it implies that medical or biological causes underlie psychopathology. This is by no means always the case, and bizarre behaviour can be developed by perfectly normal learning processes. For example, in Chapter 7 we describe the example of the schizophrenic sufferer who learned through perfectly normal learning processes to carry a broom around with her for 24 hours a day (see Focus Point 7.6). Similarly, children with autism or intellectual disabilities often learn disruptive, challenging or self-harming behaviours through normal learning processes that have nothing to do with their intellectual deficits (see Treatment in Practice Box 16.1). Furthermore, in contrast to the medical model, both psychodynamic and contemporary cognitive accounts of psychopathology argue that many psychological problems are the result of the individual acquiring dysfunctional ways of thinking and acting, and acquiring these characteristics through normal, functional learning processes. In this sense, it is not the individual or any part of their biology that is dysfunctional, it is the *experiences* they have had that are dysfunctional and have led to them thinking and acting in the way they do.

Secondly, the medical model adopts what is basically a reductionist approach by attempting to reduce the complex psychological and emotional features of psychopathology to simple biology. If you look at the personal accounts provided at the beginning of this chapter, it is arguable whether the phenomenology (i.e. the personal experience of psychopathology) or the complex cognitive factors involved in many psychological problems can be reduced to simple biological descriptions. Biological reductionism cannot easily encapsulate the distress felt by sufferers, nor can it easily explain the dysfunctional beliefs and forms of thinking that are characteristic of many psychopathologies.

Thirdly, as we have mentioned already, there is an implicit assumption in the medical model that psychopathology is caused by 'something not working properly'. For example, this type of explanation may allude to brain processes not functioning normally, brain or body biochemistry being imbalanced, or normal physical development being impaired. This 'something is broken and needs to be fixed' view of psychopathology is problematic for a number of reasons. (1) Rather than reflecting a dysfunction, psychopathology might just represent a more extreme form of normal behaviour. We all get anxious, we all worry and we all get depressed. Yet anxiety, worry and depression in their extreme forms provide the basis of many of the mental health problems we will cover in this book. If we take the example of worry, we can all testify to the fact that we worry about something at some time. However, for some of us it may become such a prevalent and regular activity that it becomes disabling, and may lead to a diagnosis of generalized anxiety disorder (GAD, see Chapter 4). Nevertheless, there is no reason to suppose that the cognitive mechanisms that generate the occasional worry bout in all of us are not the same ones that generate chronic worry in others (Davey, 2003). In this sense, psychopathology can be viewed as being on a dimension rather than being a discrete phenomenon that is separate from normal experience, and we will discuss this aspect of psychopathology in more detail in section 1.3. (2) By implying that psychopathology is caused by a normal process that is broken, imperfect or dysfunctional, the medical model may have an important influence on how we view people suffering from mental health problems, and indeed, how they might

view themselves. (See Focus Point 1.1.) At the very least it can be stigmatizing to be labelled as someone who is biologically or psychologically imperfect, and people with mental health problems are often viewed as second-class citizens – even when their symptoms are really only more prominent and persistent versions of characteristics that we all possess. Client's Perspective 1.1 shows how different people's reactions can be to someone with a mental health problem, and how this can lead to loss of respect and consideration when they perceive that individual as no longer being a properly functioning member of society.

Even so, we cannot lay all the blame for the stigma attached to mental health problems at the feet of the medical model, and there are still attitudes within most societies that view symptoms of psychopathology as threatening and uncomfortable. Some sectors of the popular media bear some responsibility for propagating the stigma attached to mental health problems, and Focus Point 1.2 describes a recent example. Furthermore, studies have suggested that stigmatizing attitudes towards people with mental health problems are widespread and commonly held (Crisp, Gelder, Rix, Meltzer et al., 2000; Byrne, 1997; Heginbotham, 1998). In a survey of over 1,700 adults in the UK, Crisp et al. (2000) found that (1) the most commonly held belief was that people with mental health problems were dangerous – especially those with schizophrenia, alcoholism and drug dependency; (2) people believed that some mental health problems such as eating disorders and substance abuse were self-inflicted; and (3) respondents believed that people with mental health problems were generally hard to talk to. People tended to hold these negative beliefs regardless of their age, regardless of what knowledge they had of mental health problems, and regardless of whether they knew someone who had a mental health problem. The fact that such negative attitudes appear to be so entrenched suggests that campaigns to change these beliefs will have to be multifaceted, will have to do more than just impart knowledge about mental health problems, and will need to challenge existing negative stereotypes especially as they are portrayed in the general media (Pinfold, Toulmin, Thornicroft, Huxley et al., 2003). Activity Box 1.1 provides an opportunity to assess your own awareness about mental health by seeing how well you can answer the 12 questions posed in this Mental Health Awareness Quiz.

1.1.3 Psychological Models

By its very nature, the medical model tends us towards thinking of mental health problems as 'illness', and this can have quite important ramifications for how people suffering mental health problems might view themselves and their future. For example, Focus Point 1.1 describes how easy it is to medicalize everyday emotions such as depression and low mood. When such experiences are seen as a condition that requires visits to a GP or treatment with drugs, they become viewed as pathological and no longer part of normal, everyday experience. Client's Perspective 1.2 provides an insight into how the medical model of mental health

Psychological models   Models which view psychopathology as caused primarily by psychological rather than biological processes.

'Creating' mental health problems through the medicalization of everyday problems of living

It is worth considering when an everyday 'problem in living' becomes something that should be categorized as a mental health problem. It is a fact of life that we all have to deal with difficult life situations. Sometimes these may make us anxious or depressed, sometimes we might feel as though we are 'unable to cope' with these difficulties. But they are still problems that almost everyone encounters. Many people have their own strategies for coping with these problems: some get help and support from friends and family, and in more severe cases perhaps seek help from their doctor or GP. However, at what point do problems of living cease to be everyday problems and become mental health problems? In particular, we must be wary about 'medicalizing' problems in daily living so that they become viewed as 'abnormal', symptoms of illness or disease, or even as characteristics of individuals who are 'ill' or in some way 'second class'.

Below are two useful examples of how everyday problems in living might become medicalized to the point where they are viewed as representing illness or disease rather than normal events of everyday living.

First, experiencing *depression* is the third most common reason for consulting a doctor or GP in the UK (Singleton, Bumpstead, O'Brien et al., 2001). In order for GPs to be able to provide treatment for such individuals, there is a tendency for them to overdiagnose mild or moderate depression (Middleton, Shaw, Hull & Feder, 2005). This may have contributed to the common view expressed by lay people that depression is a disease rather than a normal consequence of everyday life stress (Lauber, Falcato, Nordt & Rossler, 2003). If lay people already view depression as a disease or biological illness, and GPs are more than willing to diagnose it, then we run the risk of the medicalization of normal everyday negative emotions such as mild distress or even unhappiness (Shaw & Woodward, 2004).

Second, some clinical researchers have argued that the medical pharmaceutical industry in particular has attempted to manipulate women's beliefs about their sexuality in order to sell their products (Moynihan, 2006). Some drug companies claim that *sexual desire problems* affect up to 43 per cent of American women (Moynihan, 2003), and can be successfully treated with, for example, hormone patches. However, others claim that this figure is highly improbable and includes women who are quite happy with their reduced level of sexual interest (Bancroft, Loftus & Long, 2003). Tiefer (2006) lists a number of processes that have been used either wittingly or unwittingly in the past to medicalize what many see as normal sexual functioning – especially the normal lowering of sexual desire found in women during the menopause. These include:

1 taking a normal function and implying that there is something wrong with it and that it should be treated (e.g. implying that there is something abnormal about the female menopause, when it is a perfectly normal biological process);

2 imputing suffering that is not necessarily there (i.e. implying that individuals who lack sexual desire are 'suffering' as a result);

3 defining as large a proportion of the population as possible as suffering from the 'disease';

4 defining a condition as a 'deficiency', disease or disease of hormonal imbalance (e.g. implying that women experiencing the menopause have a 'deficiency' of sexual hormones); and

5 taking a common symptom that could mean anything and making it sound as if it is a sign of a serious disease (e.g. implying that lack of sexual desire is a symptom of underlying dysfunction).

While sexual dysfunctions are sometimes caused by medical conditions, lack of sexual desire and interest is itself often portrayed as a medical condition in need of treatment. Yet a reduction in sexual interest and desire can be a healthy and adaptive response to normal changes in body chemistry or a normal reaction to adverse life stressors or relationship changes. Medicalizing symptoms in this way leads to our viewing what are normal everyday symptoms and experiences as examples of dysfunction or psychopathology.

problems can cause sufferers to experience a lack of control over their condition, leading to a sense that they are victims of their condition that affects their ability to view themselves as individuals with a fulfilling and productive future. Indeed, many individuals experience depressed mood and low self-esteem after receiving a psychiatric diagnosis and feel socially excluded (Warner, Taylor, Powers & Hyman, 1989; Farina, Gliha, Boudreau, Allen et al., 1971). At the very least, this implies that diagnosis and treatment should take place in a context that allows sufferers to fully

Depression   A mood disorder involving emotional, motivational, behavioural, physical and cognitive symptoms.

understand their symptoms, to appreciate their own self-worth and social inclusion, and to discuss their symptoms within their own frame of reference – depending on whether individuals see their mental health problems primarily as medical, psychological or perhaps even spiritual (British Psychological Society, 2000).

Moving away from the medical model of psychopathology, some approaches to understanding and explaining mental health problems still see them as symptoms produced by an underlying cause that is psychological rather than biological or medical (what is known as the pathology model). Such approaches often view the cause of mental health problems as a perfectly normal and

CLIENT'S PERSPECTIVE 1.1

A question of dignity – written by Louise from her own experience with depression

'During an episode of depression accompanied by anxiety, I shared my illness with a large number of people. In retrospect, now that the depression is lifting, I realize that this was a grave mistake, at least in light of the way society functions . . . What has occurred?

When I was deeply depressed, I noticed that some friends departed. I understand now that they could not cope with depression and withdrew. In a few cases the rejection was rude and cruel and those who had seemed to be friends were found not to be so. Other friends stayed and offered their help.

In some cases I became a "second-class citizen". I could be treated with a briskness and dismissive air that had never been present before. I could be rudely dismissed and ignored on special occasions. My presence was clearly thought to be potentially threatening. Perhaps I wouldn't be happy enough or introduce inappropriate topics. I had laid bare my weakness and others were not about to forget it. These people, like all human beings, probably thought that they were doing the right thing. They were saving others from my presence. They also probably thought that they were treating me as my merits deserved. I had permanently lost the respect and consideration that I had once received.

It is no wonder that people conceal serious illness, whether cancer, heart disease, or mental illness. Once exposed, these illnesses prove to be unforgettable to others. People never walk with the same dignity again. To some this weakness justifies treatment that shows no respect to the person as a human being. Somehow the person is seen to be responsible for the weakness and therefore appropriately blamed. The person has lost the right to be treated with honour. This honour is accorded only to those who are strong, healthy and successful.'

Source: www.mentalhealth.com/story/p52–dp11.hmtl

FOCUS POINT 1.2

The popular press can often present mental illness in a way which propagates the stigmas attached to mental illness. In September 2003, the ex-heavyweight champion boxer Frank Bruno was treated for depression at a psychiatric hospital. Unsympathetic coverage of his illness in the media was subsequently criticized by the mental health charity Sane (www.sane.org.uk).

The BBC News website reported that an early edition of the *Sun* newspaper carried the front page headline 'Bonkers Bruno Locked Up', which was later changed to 'Sad Bruno in Mental Home'.

Sane chief executive Marjorie Wallace said: 'It is both an insult to Mr Bruno and damaging to many thousands of people who endure mental illness to label him as "bonkers" or "a nutter" and having to be "put in a mental home"' (news.bbc.co.uk/1/hi/uk/3130376.stm).

adaptive reaction to difficult or stressful life conditions (such as the psychoanalytic view that psychopathology is a consequence of perfectly normal psychodynamic processes that are attempting to deal with conflict). As such, psychological models of psychopathology tend to view mental health symptoms as normal reactions medi-ated by intact psychological or cognitive mechanisms, and not the result of processes that are 'broken' or malfunctioning.

The following sections describe in brief some of the main psychological approaches to understanding and explaining psychopathology.

ACTIVITY BOX 1.1

A Mental Health Awareness Quiz

See how many of the following questions you can answer correctly to test your own awareness of mental health issues.

1 Are mental health problems inherited?

2 Violence towards others is a symptom of which mental illness?

3 35- to 50-year-olds show the highest incidence of suicide – True or False?

4 People who talk about suicide are not likely to go on to do it – True or False?

5 Men are more likely than women to attempt suicide – True or False?

6 What proportion of people are known to experience mental health problems? Is it (a) 1 in 8, (b) 1 in 4 or (c) 1 in 6?

7 What percentage of GP consultations are for mental health problems? Is it (a) 30%, (b) 50% or (c) 25%?

8 Drugs such as cannabis and ecstasy can increase the risk of panic attacks, anxiety disorders and psychotic episodes – True or False?

9 At what age are mental health problems most likely to occur?

10 In a MIND survey of people who currently have or have previously experienced a mental health problem:

   (a) What percentage of these people said that they had been abused or harassed in public?

   (b) What percentage of these people claim to have been harassed, intimidated or teased at work because of a psychiatric history?

11 Mental Health Media (a campaigning organization) has identified three major stereotypes of how people with a mental illness are portrayed by the media. One of these is sad and pitiable. What are the other two?

Answers

1 They can be, but not always.

2 None. Violence towards others is not on any diagnostic criteria. For every person killed by someone with a mental illness there are roughly 70 deaths on the road and 10 alcohol-related deaths. We are far more likely to be assaulted by someone we know, in our own homes, than by a random stranger with a mental illness. People with mental health problems are more likely to be victims than perpetrators of violence. Interestingly, approximately 70 per cent of media coverage links mental distress to violence.

3 False – the highest risk group is 18–25 years.

4 False – most people who commit suicide usually tell someone of their intentions within the prior 2 months.

5 False.

6 **(b)** 1 in 4. However, this is only the number of people we know about, who have sought help. The associated stigma means that many will be too embarrassed to seek help.

7 **(c)** 25% (source: National Service Framework for Mental Health, Department of Health).

8 True.

9 16–25 years and over 65 years.

10 **(a)** 47%

   (b) 38%

11 **(a)** Comical and **(b)** violent to themselves and others. These stereotypes are found in fictional accounts and 'factual' reporting. This means that the key messages from the media are that if someone has a mental illness we should:

- feel sorry for them
- be afraid of them
- laugh at them

50 per cent of people surveyed by Mind said that media coverage had a negative effect on their mental health. Effects included feeling more anxious or depressed and experiencing hostility from neighbours. A third of respondents said family or friends reacted to them differently because of recent media coverage.

Source: adapted from Student Psychological Health Project, Educational Development and Support Centre, University of Leicester (www.le.ac.uk/edsc/sphp) and 'Looniversity Challenge', a mental health awareness quiz provided by mental health awareness group Fifteen Training and Development, Brighton, UK

1.1.3.1 The Psychoanalytical or Psychodynamic Model

This approach was first formulated and pioneered by the Viennese neurologist *Sigmund Freud* (1856–1939). He collaborated with the physician Josef Breuer in an attempt to understand the causes of mysterious physical symptoms such as hysteria and spontaneous paralysis – symptoms that appeared to have no obvious medical causes. Freud and Breuer first tried to use hypnosis as a means of understanding and treating these conditions, but during these cases clients often began talking about earlier traumatic experiences and highly stressful emotions. In many cases, simply talking about these repressed experiences and emotions under hypnosis led to an easing of symptoms. Freud built on these cases to develop his influential theory of *psychoanalysis*, which was an

Sigmund Freud An Austrian neurologist and psychiatrist who founded the psychoanalytic school of psychology.

Psychoanalysis An influential psychological model of psychopathology based on the theoretical works of Sigmund Freud.

CLIENT'S PERSPECTIVE 1.2

'Loss of control, whether truly lost or merely removed by others, and the attempt to re-establish that control have been central elements in my life since the age of 18. My argument is that the psychiatric system, as currently established, does too little to help people retain control of their lives through periods of emotional distress, and does far too much to frustrate their subsequent efforts to regain self-control. To live 18 years with a diagnosed illness is not incentive for a positive self-image. Illness is a one-way street, especially when the experts toss the concept of cure out of the window and congratulate themselves on candour. The idea of illness, of illness that can never go away, is not a dynamic, liberating force. Illness creates victims. While we harbour thoughts of emotional distress as some kind of deadly plague, it is not unrealistic to expect that many so-called victims will lead limited, powerless and unfulfilled lives.'

Peter Campbell (1996)

attempt to explain both normal and abnormal psychological functioning in terms of how various psychological mechanisms help to defend against anxiety and depression by repressing memories and thoughts that may cause conflict and stress. Freud argued that three psychological forces shape an individual's personality and may also generate psychopathology. These are the id (instinctual needs), the ego (rational thinking) and the superego (moral standards).

Id   In psychoanalysis, the concept used to describe innate instinctual needs – especially sexual needs.

The concept of the *id* was used to describe innate instinctual needs – especially sexual needs. He noted that from a very early age, children obtained pleasure from nursing, defecating, masturbating and other 'sexually' related activities and that many forms of behaviour were driven by the need to satisfy the needs of the id.

As we grow up, Freud argued that it becomes apparent to us that the environment itself will not satisfy all our instinctual needs, and we develop a separate part of our psychology known as the *ego*. This is a rational part of the psyche that attempts to control the impulses of the id, and *ego defence mechanisms* develop by which the ego attempts to control unacceptable id impulses and reduce the anxiety that id impulses may arouse.

Ego   In psychoanalysis, a rational part of the psyche that attempts to control the impulses of the id.

Ego defence mechanisms   Means by which the ego attempts to control unacceptable id impulses and reduce the anxiety that id impulses may arouse.

Superego   In psychoanalysis, a development from both the id and ego which represents our attempts to integrate 'values' that we learn from our parents or society.

The *superego* develops out of both the id and ego, and represents our attempts to integrate 'values' that we learn from our parents or society. Freud argued that we will often judge ourselves by the values that we assimilate, and if we think our behaviour does not meet the standards implicit in those values, we will feel guilty and stressed.

According to Freud, the id, ego and superego are often in conflict, and psychological health is maintained only when they are in balance. However, if these three factors are in conflict, then behaviour may begin to exhibit signs of psychopathology. Individuals attempt to control conflict between these factors and also reduce stress and conflict from external events by developing *defence mechanisms*. Table 1.1 describes some of these defence mechanisms together with some examples of how they are presumed to prevent the experience of stress and anxiety.

Defence mechanisms   In psychoanalysis, the means by which individuals attempt to control conflict between the id, ego and superego and also reduce stress and conflict from external events.

A further factor that Freud believed could cause psychopathology was the way in which children negotiated various *stages of development* from infancy to maturity. He defined a number of important stages through which childhood development progressed, and each of these stages was named after a body area or erogenous zone. If the child successfully negotiated each stage, then this led to personal growth and a psychologically healthy person. If, however, adjustment to a particular stage was not successful, then the individual would become fixated on that early stage of development. For example, Freud labelled the first 18 months of life as the *oral stage* because of the child's need for food from the mother. If the mother fails to satisfy these oral needs, the child may become fixated at this stage and in later life display 'oral stage characteristics' such as extreme dependence on others. Other stages of development include the anal stage (18 months to 3 years), the phallic stage (3 to 5 years), the latency stage (5–12 years) and the genital stage (12 years to adulthood).

Stages of development   Progressive periods of development from infancy to maturity.

Oral stage   According to Freud, the first 18 months of life based on the child's need for food from the mother. If the mother fails to satisfy these oral needs, the child may become fixated at this stage and in later life display 'oral stage characteristics' such as extreme dependence on others.

There is no doubt that the psychoanalytical model has been extremely influential, both in its attempts to provide explanations for psychopathology and in the treatments it has helped to develop. Psychoanalysis was arguably the first of the 'talking

Table 1.1 *Defence mechanisms in psychoanalytic theory*

Each of the Freudian defence mechanisms described below functions to reduce the amount of stress or conflict that might be caused by specific experiences.

Denial

The individual denies the source of the anxiety exists (e.g. I didn't fail my exam, it must be a mistake).

Repression

Suppressing bad memories, or even current thoughts that cause anxiety (e.g. repressing thoughts about liking someone because you are frightened that you may be rejected if you approach them).

Regression

Moving back to an earlier developmental stage (e.g. when highly stressed you abandon normal coping strategies and return to an early developmental stage, for example by smoking if you are fixated at the oral stage).

Reaction formation

Doing or thinking the opposite to how you feel (e.g. a person who is angry with their boss may go out of their way to be kind and courteous to them).

Projection

Ascribing unwanted impulses to someone else (e.g. the unfaithful husband who is extremely jealous of his wife might always suspect that she is being unfaithful).

Rationalization

Finding a rational explanation for something you've done wrong (e.g. you didn't fail the exam because you didn't study hard enough but because the questions were unfair).

Displacement

Moving an impulse from one object (target) to another (e.g. if you've been told off by your boss at work, you go home and shout at your partner or kick the dog).

Sublimation

Transforming impulses into something constructive (e.g. redecorating the bedroom when you're feeling angry about something).

therapies' and as many as 20 per cent of modern practising clinical psychologists identify themselves, at least in part, with a psychoanalytical or psychodynamic approach to psychopathology (Prochaska & Norcross, 2003). Psychoanalysis was also the first approach to introduce a number of perspectives on psychopathology that are still important today, including (1) the view that psychopathology can have its origins in early experiences

rather than being a manifestation of biological dysfunction, and (2) the possibility that psychopathology may often represent the operation of 'defence mechanisms' that reflect attempts by the individual to suppress stressful thoughts and memories (see, for example, cognitive theories of chronic worrying in Chapter 5 and theories of dissociative disorders in Chapter 13).

Theorists in the psychoanalytic tradition have elaborated on Freud's original theory, and we will see many examples of psychodynamic explanations applied to specific psychopathologies presented later in this book. However, psychoanalytic theory does have many shortcomings, and it is arguably no longer the explanation or treatment of choice for most psychological problems, nor is it a paradigm in which modern-day evidence-based researchers attempt to understand psychopathology. This is largely because the central concepts in psychoanalytic theory are hard to objectively define and measure. Because concepts such as the id, ego and superego are difficult to observe and measure, it is therefore difficult to conduct objective research on them to see if they are actually related to symptoms of psychopathology in the way that Freud and his associates describe (Erdelyi, 1992).

1.1.3.2 The Behavioural Model

Most psychological models have in common the view that psychopathology is caused by how we assimilate our experiences and how this is reflected in thinking and behaviour. The *behavioural model* adopts the broad view that many examples of psychopathology reflect our learned reactions to life experiences. That is, psychopathology can be explained as learned reactions to environmental experiences, and this approach was promoted primarily by the behaviourist school of psychology.

> **Behavioural model** An influential psychological model of psychopathology based on explaining behaviour.

During the 1950s and 1960s, many clinical psychologists became disillusioned by psychoanalytic approaches to psychopathology and sought an approach that was more scientific and objective. They turned to that area of psychology known as *learning theory*, and argued that just as adaptive behaviour can be acquired through learning, then so can many forms of dysfunctional behaviour. The two important principles of learning on which this approach was based are classical conditioning and operant conditioning. *Classical conditioning* represents the learning of an association between two stimuli, the first of which (the conditioned stimulus, CS) predicts the occurrence of the second (the unconditioned stimulus, UCS).

> **Learning theory** The body of knowledge encompassing principles of classical and operant conditioning (and which is frequently applied to explaining and treating psychopathology).

> **Classical conditioning** The learning of an association between two stimuli, the first of which (the conditioned stimulus, CS) predicts the occurrence of the second (the unconditioned stimulus, UCS).

The prototypical example of this form of learning is Pavlov's experiment in which a hungry dog learns to salivate to a bell (the CS) that predicts subsequent delivery of food (the UCS). This is

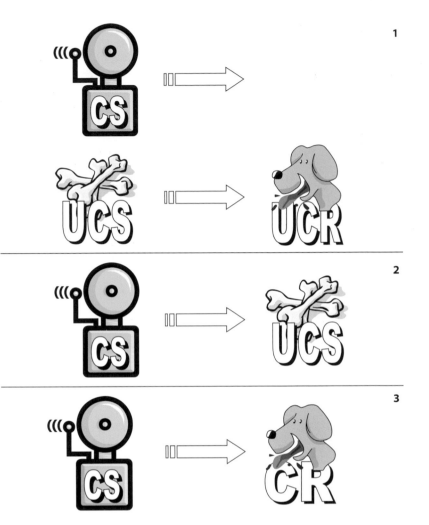

Figure 1.1 *Classical conditioning*
(1) Before conditioning takes place, Pavlov's dog salivates only to the presentation of food and not to the presentation of the bell; (2) pairing the bell with food then enables the dog to learn to predict food whenever it hears the bell, and (3) this results in the dog subsequently salivating whenever it hears the bell. This type of learning has frequently been used to explain psychopathology, and one such example is the acquisition of specific phobias where the phobic stimulus (the CS) elicits fear because it has been paired with some kind of trauma (the UCS) (see Figure 5.1).

Operant conditioning The learning of a specific behaviour or response because that behaviour has certain consequences.

represented schematically in Figure 1.1. In contrast, *operant conditioning* represents the learning of a specific behaviour or response because that behaviour has certain rewarding or reinforcing consequences. A prototypical example of operant conditioning is a hungry rat learning to press a lever to obtain food in an experimental chamber called a Skinner Box (see Figure 1.2).

These two forms of learning have been used to explain a number of examples of psychopathology. For example, classical conditioning has been used to explain the acquisition of emotional disorders including many of those with anxiety-based symptoms (see Chapter 5). Some forms of specific phobias appear to be acquired when the sufferer experiences the phobic stimulus (the CS) in association with a traumatic event (the UCS). Such experiences might account for the acquisition of dog phobia (in which dogs have become associated with, for example, being bitten or chased),

accident phobia (in which travelling in cars has become associated with being in a traumatic car accident) and dental phobia (when being at the dentist has become associated with a traumatic dental experience) (Davey, 1989; Kuch, 1997; Doogan & Thomas, 1992).

Classical conditioning processes have also been implicated in a number of other forms of psychopathology, including the acquisition of post-traumatic stress disorder (PTSD) (see Chapter 5), the acquisition of paraphilias (see Chapter 10) and substance dependency (see Chapter 8). Operant conditioning has been used extensively to explain why a range of psychopathology-relevant behaviours may have been acquired and maintained. Examples you will find in this book include learning approaches to understanding the acquisition of bizarre behaviours in schizophrenia (Ullman & Krasner, 1975), how the stress-reducing or stimulant effects of nicotine, alcohol and many illegal drugs may lead to substance dependency (e.g. Schachter, 1982), how hypochondriacal tendencies and somatoform disorders may be acquired when a child's illness

Figure 1.2 *Operant conditioning*
In operant conditioning, the rat learns to press the lever in this Skinner Box because it delivers food, and food acts to reinforce that behaviour so that it occurs more frequently in the future (known as operant reinforcement). Operant reinforcement has been used to explain how many behaviours that are typical of psychopathology are acquired and maintained. That is, many bizarre and disruptive behaviours may be acquired because they actually have positive or rewarding outcomes (see Focus Point 7.6 as an example).

symptoms are reinforced by attention from parents (Latimer, 1981) and how the disruptive, self-harming or challenging behaviour exhibited by individuals with intellectual or developmental disabilities may be maintained by attention from family and carers (Mazaleski, Iwata, Vollmer, Zarcone & Smith, 1993).

Behaviour therapy Therapies based mainly on the principles of classical and operant conditioning.

Behaviour modification A set of therapies based on the principles of operant conditioning.

The behavioural approach led to the development of important behavioural treatment methods, including *behaviour therapy* and *behaviour modification*. For example, if psychopathology is learned through normal learning processes, then it should be possible to use those same learning processes to help the individual 'unlearn' any maladaptive behaviours or emotions. This view enabled the development of treatment methods based on classical conditioning principles (such as flooding, systematic desensitization and aversion therapy; see Chapter 4) and operant conditioning principles (e.g. functional analysis, token economies; see Chapters 4, 7 and 16). Furthermore, learning principles could be used to alter psychopathology symptoms even if the original symptoms were not necessarily acquired through conditioning processes themselves, and so the behavioural approach to treatment had a broad appeal across a very wide range of symptoms and disorders.

As influential as the behavioural approach has been over the years, it too has some limitations. For example, many psychopathologies are complex and symptoms are acquired gradually over many years (e.g. obsessive-compulsive disorder, substance dependency,

Plate 1.1

somatoform disorders, etc.). It would be almost impossible to trace the reinforcement history of such symptoms across time in an attempt to verify that reinforcement processes had shaped these psychopathologies. Secondly, learning paradigms may simply not represent the most ideal conceptual framework in which to describe and understand some quite complex psychopathologies. For example, many psychopathologies are characterized by a range of cognitive factors such as information processing biases, belief schemas and dysfunctional ways of thinking, and learning theory jargon is probably not the best framework in which to accurately and inclusively describe these phenomena. The cognitive approaches we will describe next are probably more suited to describing and explaining these aspects of psychopathology.

1.1.3.3 The Cognitive Model

Perhaps the most widely adopted current psychological model of psychopathology is the *cognitive model*, and one

Cognitive model An influential psychological model of psychopathology

in four of all present-day clinical psychologists would describe their approach as cognitive (Prochaska & Norcross, 2003). Primarily, this approach considers psychopathology to be the result of individuals acquiring irrational beliefs, developing dysfunctional ways of thinking and processing information in biased ways. It was an approach first pioneered by Albert Ellis (1962) and Aaron Beck (1967). Albert Ellis argued that emotional distress (such as anxiety or depression) is caused primarily because people develop a set of irrational beliefs by which they need to judge their behaviour. Some people become anxious, for example, because they make unrealistic demands on themselves. The anxious individual may have developed unrealistic beliefs such as 'I must be loved by everyone', and the depressed individual may believe 'I am incapable of doing anything worthwhile'. Judging their behaviour against such 'dysfunctional' beliefs causes distress. Aaron Beck developed a highly successful cognitive therapy for depression based on the view that depressed individuals have developed unrealistic distortions in the way they perceive themselves, the world and their future (see Chapter 6). For example, the cognitive approach argues that depression results from individuals having developed negative beliefs about themselves (e.g. 'I am worthless'), the world (e.g. 'bad things always happen') and their future (e.g. 'I am never going to achieve anything'), and these beliefs act to maintain depressive thinking.

The view that dysfunctional ways of thinking generate and maintain symptoms of psychopathology has been applied across a broad range of psychological problems, including both anxiety disorders and mood disorders, and has also been applied to the explanation of specific symptoms, such as paranoid thinking in schizophrenia (Morrison, 2001a), antisocial and impulsive behaviour in personality disorders (Young, Klosko & Weishaar, 2003), dysfunctional sexual behaviour in sex offenders and paedophiles (Ward, Hudson, Johnston & Marshall, 1997) and illness reporting in hypochondriasis and somatoform disorders (Warwick, 1995), to name but a few.

The cognitive approach has also been highly successful in generating an influential approach to treatment. If dysfunctional thoughts and beliefs maintain the symptoms of psychopathology, then these dysfunctional thoughts and beliefs can be identified, challenged and replaced by more functional cognitions. This has given rise to a broad-ranging therapeutic approach known as *cognitive behaviour therapy (CBT)*, and many examples of the use of this approach will be encountered in this book.

Cognitive behaviour therapy (CBT)
An intervention for changing both thoughts and behaviour. CBT represents an umbrella term for many different therapies that share the common aim of changing both cognitions and behaviour.

As successful as the cognitive approach seems to have been in recent years, it too has some limitations. For example, rather than being a cause of psychopathology, it has to be considered that dysfunctional thoughts and beliefs may themselves simply be just another symptom of psychopathology. For example, we have very little knowledge at present about how dysfunctional thoughts and beliefs develop. Are they the product of childhood experiences? Do they develop from the behavioural and emotional symptoms of psychopathology (i.e. do depressed people think they are worthless because of their feelings of depression)? Or are they merely *post hoc* constructions that function to help individuals rationalize the way they feel? These are all potentially fruitful areas for future research.

1.1.3.4 The Humanist-Existential Approach

Some approaches to psychopathology believe that insights into emotional and behavioural problems cannot be achieved unless individuals are able to gain insight into their lives from a broad range of perspectives. People not only acquire psychological conflicts and experience emotional distress, they also have the ability to acquire self-awareness, develop important values and a sense of meaning in life, and pursue freedom of choice. If these latter abilities are positively developed and encouraged, then conflict, emotional distress and psychopathology can often be resolved. This is the general approach adopted by *humanistic* and *existential* models of psychopathology, and the aim is to resolve psychological problems through insight, personal development and self-actualization.

Humanist-existential approach
Approach that aims to resolve psychological problems through insight, personal development and self-actualization.

Because such approaches are concerned primarily with insight and personal growth when dealing with psychopathology, they are interested less in the aetiology and origins of psychopathology than in ameliorating psychopathological symptoms through encouraging personal development. An influential example of the humanistic-existential approach is *client-centred therapy*, developed by Carl Rogers (1951, 1987). This approach stresses the goodness of human nature and assumes that if individuals are unrestricted by fears and conflicts, they will develop into well-adjusted, happy individuals. The client-centred therapist will try to create a supportive climate in which the client is helped to acquire positive self-worth. The therapist will use *empathy* to help her to understand the client's feelings, and *unconditional positive regard*, by which the therapist expresses her willingness to totally accept the client for who he or she is.

Client-centred therapy An approach to psychopathology stressing the goodness of human nature, assuming that if individuals are unrestricted by fears and conflicts, they will develop into well-adjusted, happy individuals.

Empathy An ability to understand and experience a client's own feelings and personal meanings, and a willingness to demonstrate unconditional positive regard for the client.

Unconditional positive regard Valuing clients for who they are without judging them.

As we said earlier, this type of approach to psychopathology does not put much emphasis on how psychopathology is acquired, but does try to eradicate psychopathology by moving the individual from one phenomenological perspective (e.g. one that contains fears and conflicts) to another (e.g. one that enables clients to view themselves as worthy, respected and achieving individuals). Approaches such as humanistic and existentialist ones are difficult to evaluate. For example, most controlled studies have indicated that clients undergoing client-centred therapy tend to fare no better than those undergoing non-therapeutic control treatments (Patterson, 2000; Greenberg, Watson & Lietaer, 1998). Similarly, exponents of existential therapies believe that experimental methodologies are inappropriate for estimating the effectiveness of such therapies, because experimental methods either dehumanize the individuals involved or are incapable of measuring the kinds of existential benefits that such approaches claim to bestow (Walsh & McElwain, 2002; May & Yalom, 1995). Nevertheless, such approaches to treatment are still accepted as having some value and are used at least in part by clinical psychologists, counselling psychologists and psychotherapists (see Table 1.2).

SELF-TEST QUESTIONS

- Why was demonic possession such a popular way of explaining psychopathology in historical times?
- What are the pros and cons of the medical model of psychopathology?
- Can you describe the basic concepts underlying psychoanalytic and psychodynamic approaches to psychopathology?
- What are the learning principles on which the behavioural approach to psychopathology is based?
- Who were the main founders of the cognitive approach to psychopathology, and what were their main contributions?
- How do humanistic-existential approaches to psychopathology differ from most of the others?

Table 1.2 *Mental health practitioners in the UK*

Title	Description
CHARTERED CLINICAL PSYCHOLOGIST	Anyone who has been awarded a degree in psychology (most in the UK are accredited by the *British Psychological Society*) can call himself or herself a psychologist. However, there are many different types of psychologists, and those who are qualified to offer therapy and undertake clinical assessments have undertaken an extra 3 years specialized training. The UK government is intending to introduce statutory regulation of practising psychologists in 2008, when the term 'clinical psychologist' will become a protected title that can be used only by those with accredited training.
PSYCHIATRIST	Psychiatrists are medically trained doctors who have undergone the normal medical training but have chosen to specialize in mental illness. Their approach to mental illness is primarily medical, but some do offer some forms of psychotherapy. They are the only practitioner group qualified to prescribe medication.
PSYCHOTHERAPIST	Psychotherapy is an umbrella term that covers almost all forms of therapy, but psychotherapists tend to specialize in only one type of therapy (e.g. psychodynamic, humanistic). Psychotherapists do not necessarily have a basic training in psychology. Many other professionals may also have training in psychotherapy, including clinical psychologists, psychiatrists, nurses and social workers.
COUNSELLOR	Counsellors are individuals who have been trained specifically in counselling skills, and may be skilled in the use of one or more forms of psychotherapy (see section 4.1.2).
SOCIAL WORKER	This is a fully trained social worker who has received further training that enables him or her to undertake certain forms of psychotherapy.
OTHER MENTAL HEALTH PROFESSIONALS	Under the UK Mental Health Act, many other professionals have a role to play in providing mental health services and care. They include mental health nurses, community psychiatric nurses, approved social workers, occupational therapists and community support workers.

SECTION SUMMARY

1.1 Explaining Psychopathology

- Historical explanations of psychopathology often alluded to the fact that the individual had been 'possessed' in some way.

- The **medical model** attempts to explain psychopathology in terms of underlying biological or medical causes.

- **Psychological models** view psychopathology as caused primarily by psychological rather than biological processes.

- Influential psychological models of psychopathology include the **psychoanalytical model**, the **behavioural model**, the **cognitive model** and the **humanist-existential model**.

1.2 DEFINING PSYCHOPATHOLOGY

The models of psychopathology we have discussed in the previous sections represent different ways of trying to *explain* unusual or maladaptive behaviour, but they do not necessarily help us to *define* exactly what kinds of symptoms or behaviour should be considered as examples of psychopathology. In the personal accounts that we have included at the beginning of this chapter, it is not hard to believe that the experiences reported by *Joan*, *Greg* and even *Erica* are ones for which they would be happy to receive some structured help and support. Interestingly, even though her behaviour may seem the most bizarre of each of these introductory accounts, *Betty* is the one who doesn't believe she has a problem. So how do we define what is a problem that should be considered suitable for support and treatment, and what is not? Unlike medicine, we can't simply base our definitions on the existence of a pathological cause. This is because we have already argued that psychological problems often do not have underlying physical or biological causes; and secondly, knowledge of the aetiology of many psychopathologies is still very much in its infancy, so we are not yet in a position to provide a classification of psychopathologies that is based on causal factors. This leads us to try to define psychopathology in ways that are independent of the possible causes of such problems – and, as we shall see, many attempts to do this have important ethical and practical implications. For example, most of us would find the murder of one human being by another an abhorrent act – yet, are all murderers mentally ill and suffering from a form of psychopathology that may need treatment?

The problems of defining psychopathology revolve not only around what criteria we use to define it, but also around what terminology we use. For example, numerous psychopathology courses and textbooks still use the title *Abnormal Psychology*. Merely using this title implies that people suffering from mental health problems are in some way 'abnormal', either in the statistical or in the functional sense – neither of which is necessarily true because we have already suggested that many forms of psychopathology (1) are common rather than unusual (e.g. depression, worrying) and (2) do not imply that any biological or psychological system is malfunctioning. But the term 'abnormal' also has more important ramifications because it implies that those people suffering psychopathology are in some way 'not normal' or are inferior members of society. In this sense, the 'abnormal' label may affect our willingness to fully include such individuals in everyday activities and may lead to us treating such individuals with suspicion rather than respect (see Client's Perspectives 1.1 and 1.2, and Focus Point 1.2). Individuals with mental health problems have become increasingly vocal about how psychopathology and those who suffer from it are labelled and perceived by others. Examples of groups set up to communicate these views include *service user groups* (groups of individuals who are end users of the mental health services provided by, for example, government agencies such as the NHS) and organizations such as *Mad Pride* (www.ctono.freeserve.co.uk/), dedicated to changing the way in which society views people with mental health problems.

So, when considering how to define psychopathology, we must consider not only whether a definition is useful in the scientific and professional sense, but also whether it provides a definition that will minimize the stigma experienced by sufferers, and facilitate the support they need to function as inclusive members of society. Let us bear this in mind as we look at some potential ways of identifying and defining psychopathology.

> **Abnormal psychology**   An alternative definition of psychopathology, albeit with negative connotations in regard to being 'not normal'.

> **Service user groups**   Groups of individuals who are end users of the mental health services provided by, for example, government agencies such as the NHS.

> **Mad Pride**   A UK organization dedicated to changing the way in which society views people with mental health problems.

1.2.1 Deviation from the Statistical Norm

We can use statistical definitions to decide whether an activity or a psychological attribute deviates substantially from the *statistical norm*, and in some areas of clinical psychology this is used as a means of deciding whether a particular disorder

> **Statistical norm**   The mean, average or modal example of a behaviour.

meets diagnostic criteria. For example, in the area of intellectual disability, if an IQ score is significantly below the norm of 100, this is currently used as one criterion for diagnosing mental retardation (see Chapter 16, Table 16.3). Figure 1.3 shows the distribution of IQ scores in a standard population, and this indicates that the percentage of individuals with IQ scores below 70 would be relatively rare (i.e. around 2.5–3 per cent of the population). However, there are at least two important problems with using deviations from statistical norms as indications of psychopathology. First, in the intellectual disability case, an IQ of less than 70 may be statistically rare, but rather than simply forcing the individual into a diagnostic category, a better approach would be to evaluate the specific needs of individuals with intellectual disabilities in a way that allows us to suggest strategies, services and supports that will optimize individual functioning. Secondly, as we can see from Figure 1.3, substantial deviation from the norm does not necessarily imply psychopathology because individuals with exceptionally high IQs are also statistically rare – yet we would not necessarily be willing to consider this group of individuals as candidates for psychological intervention.

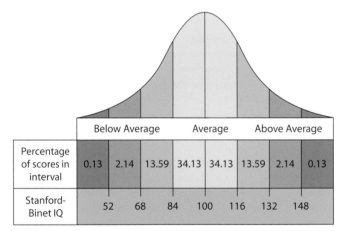

	Below Average			Average		Above Average	
Percentage of scores in interval	0.13	2.14	13.59	34.13	34.13	13.59	2.14	0.13
Stanford-Binet IQ	52	68	84	100	116	132	148

Figure 1.3
This figure represents a normal distribution curve for IQ scores. From this distribution it can be seen that 68 per cent of people score between 84 and 116 points, while only 2.27 per cent of people have an IQ score below 68 points. This graph suggests that around 2–3 per cent of the population will have IQs lower than the 70 points that is the diagnostic criterion for Mental Retardation. However, the problem for basing a definition of psychopathology on scores that deviate substantially from the norm is that high IQ also is very rare. Only 2.27 per cent of the population have an IQ score greater than 132 points.

1.2.2 Deviation from Social Norms

There is often a tendency within individual societies for the members of that society to label a behaviour or activity as indicative of psychopathology if it is far removed from what we consider to be the social norms for that culture. We assume (perhaps quite wrongly) that socially normal and acceptable behaviours have evolved to represent adaptive ways of behaving, and that anyone who deviates from these norms is exhibiting psychopathology. However, it is very difficult to use deviation from social norms as a way of defining psychopathology.

First, different cultures often differ significantly in what they consider to be socially normal and acceptable. For example, in the Soviet Union during the 1970s and 1980s, political dissidents who were active against the communist regime were regularly diagnosed with schizophrenia and incarcerated in psychiatric hospitals. At first we might think that this is a cynical method of political repression used to control dissent, but amongst many in the Soviet Union at the time it represented a genuine belief that anti-Soviet activity was indeed a manifestation of psychopathology (for example, anyone who wanted to protest against the perfect social system must be suffering from mental health problems!). Soviet psychiatrists even added to the official symptoms of schizophrenia by including '*reformist delusions*: a belief that an improvement in social conditions can be achieved only through the revision of people's attitudes, in accordance with the individual's own ideas for the transformation of reality', and '*litigation mania*: a conviction, which does not have any basis in fact, that the individual's own rights as a human being are being violated and flouted' (Goldacre, 2002). However, since the collapse of the Soviet system, few would suspect that these kinds of beliefs and activities are representative of psychopathology.

Second, it is difficult to use cultural norms to define psychopathology because cultural factors seem to significantly affect how psychopathology manifests itself. For example, (1) social and cultural factors will affect the vulnerability of an individual to causal factors (e.g. poor mental health is more prevalent in low-income countries) (Desjarlais, Eisenberg, Good & Kleinman, 1996). (2) Culture can produce 'culture-bound' symptoms of psychopathology which seem confined to specific cultures and can influence how stress, anxiety and depression manifest themselves. Two examples of such 'culture-bound' effects are described in Focus Point 1.3. These are known as **Ataque de Nervios**, a form of panic disorder found in Latinos from the Caribbean (Salman, Liebowitz, Guarnaccia, Jusino et al., 1998), and **Seizisman**, a state of psychological paralysis found in the Haitian community (Nicolas, DeSilva, Grey & Gonzalez-Eastep, 2006). Finally, (3) society or culture can influence the course of psychopathology; for example, schizophrenia in developing countries has a more favourable course and outcome than in developed countries (Weisman, 1997).

Ataque de Nervios   A form of panic disorder found in Latinos from the Caribbean.

Seizisman   A state of psychological paralysis found in the Haitian community.

1.2.3 Maladaptive Behaviour

It is often tempting to define psychopathology in terms of whether it renders the individual incapable of adapting to what most of us would consider normal daily living. That is, whether a person can undertake and hold down a job, cope with the demands of being a parent, develop loving relationships or function socially. In its extreme form, maladaptive behaviour might involve behaving in a way that is a threat to the health and well-being of the individual and to others. It is certainly the case that current diagnostic criteria, such as DSM-IV-TR, do use deficits in social, occupational and educational functioning as one criterion for defining many psychological disorders, but it is by no means the only criterion by which those disorders are defined.

The problem with defining psychopathology solely in terms of maladaptive behaviour is also apparent when we discuss forms of behaviour that we might call maladaptive but that we would not necessarily want to label as psychopathological. The behaviour of many people convicted of murder or terrorist acts, for example, is maladaptive in the sense that it is harmful to others, but it is by no means the case that all murderers or terrorists commit their crimes because they have mental health problems (for an interesting contemporary example of this discussion, see Focus Point 12.1). On the other side of the coin, it can be argued that many forms of psychopathology may not be representative of maladaptive behaviour but instead serve a protective or adaptive function. For example, a case can be made for suggesting that specific phobias such as height phobia, water phobia, or snake and spider phobia are adaptive responses which protect us from exposure to potentially life-threatening situations (e.g. Seligman, 1971; see Chapter 5).

1.2.4 Distress and Impairment

Later in this chapter we will look at some of the ways in which psychologists and psychiatrists have attempted to classify psychopathology. In order to be diagnosed as a psychological disorder, one of the most common requirements is that the symptoms must cause 'clinically significant distress or impairment in social, academic or occupational functioning'. It is clearly the case that many individuals with severe symptoms of psychopathology do suffer considerable personal distress – often to the point of wanting to take their own lives. Defining psychopathology in terms of the degree of distress and impairment expressed by the sufferer is useful in a number of ways. First, it allows people to judge their own 'normality' rather than subjecting them to judgements about their 'normality' made by others in society such as psychologists or psychiatrists. Many people who are diagnosed with psychological disorders originally present themselves for treatment because of the distress and impairment caused by their symptoms, and to some degree this makes them judges of their own needs. Secondly, defining psychopathology in terms of the degree of distress and impairment experienced can be independent of the type of lifestyle chosen by the individual. This means we do not judge whether someone has a psychopathology purely on the basis of whether

Psychopathology and culture

Psychopathology can manifest itself in different forms in different cultures, and this can lead to some disorders that are culture-specific (i.e. have a set of symptoms which are found only in that particular culture). Two such examples are *Ataque de Nervios*, which is an anxiety-based disorder found almost exclusively amongst Latinos from the Caribbean (Salman, Liebowitz, Guarnaccia, Jusino et al., 1998), and *Seizisman*, a state of psychological paralysis found in the Haitian community (Nicolas, DeSilva, Grey & Gonzalez-Eastep, 2006).

Ataque de Nervios

Its literal translation is 'attack of nerves', and symptoms include trembling, attacks of crying, screaming uncontrollably, and becoming verbally or physically aggressive. In some cases these primary symptoms are accompanied by fainting bouts, dissociative experiences and suicide attempts.

Research on *Ataque de Nervios* has begun to show that it is found predominantly in women, people over 45 years of age, and people from low socioeconomic backgrounds and disrupted marriages (Guarnaccia, De La Cancela & Carrillo, 1989). The symptoms appear to resemble many of those found in panic disorder, but with a coexisting affective disorder characterized by emotional lability and anger (Salman et al., 1998).

From this research, it appears that *Ataque de Nervios* may be a form of panic disorder brought on by stressful life events (such as economic or marital difficulties), but whose expression is determined by the social and cultural norms within that cultural group. In particular, Latino cultures place less emphasis on self-control and emotional restraint than other Western cultures, and so the distress of panic disorder in Latinos tends to be externalized in the form of screaming, uncontrolled behaviour and aggression. In contrast, in Western cultures the distress of panic disorder is usually coped with by adopting avoidance and withdrawal strategies – hence the common diagnosis of panic disorder with agoraphobia.

Seizisman

The term literally means 'seized-up-ness' and refers to a state of paralysis usually brought on by rage, anger or sadness, and in rare cases happiness. Events that can cause *Seizisman* include a traumatic event (such as receiving bad news), a family crisis and verbal insults from others. Individuals affected by the syndrome become completely dysfunctional, disorganized and confused, and unresponsive to their surroundings (Laguerre, 1981). The following quote illustrates how viewing traumatic events while working within a Haitian community that is attuned to the symptoms of this syndrome can actually give rise to these culture-bound symptoms:

> I remember over and over, when I was a UN Human Rights Monitor and I was down there in Port-au-Prince viewing cadaver after cadaver left by the Haitian army, people would say, 'Now go home and lie down or you will have *Seizisman*'. And I never really had a problem, you know? I never threw up or fainted no matter what I saw, but I started to feel 'stressed', which is an American illness defined in an American way. After viewing one particularly vile massacre scene, I went home and followed the cultural model I had been shown. I lay down, curled up, and went incommunicado. 'Ah-hah! *Seizisman*!' said the people of my household.

> (Nicola et al., 2006, p. 705)

he or she is perceived as productively contributing to society or not, but on the basis of how that person is able to cope with his or her lifestyle (e.g. we often tend to think of reclusive characters as eccentric oddballs, but they may be perfectly happy with their self-chosen lifestyle).

As attractive as this definition for defining psychopathology seems, it does have a number of difficulties. First, this approach does not provide any standards by which we should judge behaviour itself. For example, in our introductory personal accounts, *Betty*'s behaviour and thoughts do not entirely seem to be based in reality, and they could be manifestations of the thought-disordered behaviour that is sometimes characteristic of those developing schizophrenia (see Chapter 7). But *Betty* does not express any feelings of distress or impairment. Similarly, *Erica* does admit that her substance dependency is beginning to cause her some distress, but should we consider that a teenager's drug addiction is in need of treatment only if the individual expresses unhappiness about her situation?

Finally, psychopathology classification schemes include so-called 'disorders' in which diagnosis does not require the sufferer necessarily to report any personal distress or impairment. A good example of this is that group of disorders known as *personality disorders* (see Chapter 11). For example, individuals diagnosed with borderline personality disorder or antisocial personality disorder frequently exhibit behaviour that is impulsive, emotional, threatening and harmful to themselves and others. Yet they are rarely willing to admit that their behaviour is unusual or problematic.

SUMMARY

None of these individual ways of defining psychopathology is ideal. They may fail to include examples of behaviour that we intuitively believe are representative of mental health problems (the distress and impairment approach); they may include examples we intuitively feel are *not* examples of psychopathology (e.g. the statistical approach, the deviation from social norms approach); or they may represent forms of categorization that would lead us simply to impose stigmatizing labels on people rather then considering their individual needs (e.g. the statistical approach). In practice, classification schemes tend to use an amalgamation of all these approaches, with emphasis being placed on individual approaches depending on the nature of the symptoms and disorder being classified.

SELF-TEST QUESTIONS

● What are the problems with using the normal curve to define psychopathology?
● How do cultural factors make it difficult to define psychopathology in terms of deviations from social norms?
● What are the pros and cons of using maladaptive behaviour or distress and impairment as means of defining psychopathology?

SECTION SUMMARY

1.2 Defining Psychopathology

● Potential ways of defining psychopathology include **deviation from the statistical norm**, **deviation from social norms**, exhibiting **maladaptive behaviour** and experiencing **distress and impairment**.

1.3 CLASSIFYING PSYCHOPATHOLOGY

At this point you may be saying to yourself, 'why try to define and classify psychopathology at all?' Nevertheless, there are some good reasons for wanting to do this. First, as a social and biological science, psychology will want to try to understand the causes of mental health problems. This is important so that we can develop both effective treatments that address the root causes of psychopathology and prevention strategies designed to reduce the risk of individuals developing symptoms of psychopathology.

Most sciences use classification to group phenomena into categories according to their similarities. Categorization and classification is thus an important first stage in the pursuit of knowledge about causes and aetiology, and it would be difficult to discuss aetiology in this book if there were not some form of classification that enabled us to understand how different causes relate to different symptoms. Secondly, classification is necessary if we are to organize services and support for sufferers effectively. For example, the needs of individuals with intellectual disabilities, major depression, an anxiety-based disorder or substance dependency are all very different and require different approaches and means of support and intervention. Thirdly, how do we decide if our interventions and support for sufferers have been effective unless we have some objective way of defining what constitute the symptoms of psychopathology? One important and objective way of determining whether an individual is responding to treatment is to see if there has been any improvement in objectively defined and measurable symptoms. Finally, whether we like it or not, modern-day society requires that we assess and classify people for a number of reasons, and this is also the case with psychopathology. For example, we might want to know whether a person is psychologically fit to stand trial for a criminal offence, whether a child has disabilities that will require special educational needs, or whether financial compensation or damages should be awarded to an individual because of psychological symptoms caused by the actions of others. All of these requirements of modern society necessitate a form of assessment and classification that can adequately and objectively deal with these kinds of issues.

1.3.1 The Development of Classification Systems

Arguably the first person to develop a comprehensive classification system for psychopathology was the German psychiatrist Emil Kraepelin (1883–1923). He suggested that psychopathology, like physical illness, could be classified into different and separate pathologies, each of which had a different cause and could be described by a distinct set of symptoms which he called a *syndrome*. Kraepelin's work provided some hope that mental illness could be described and successfully treated in much the same way as other medical illnesses.

Syndrome   A distinct set of symptoms.

Following on from Kraepelin's scheme, the first extensive system for classifying psychopathology was developed by the World Health Organization (WHO), who added psychological disorders to the *International List of Causes of Death (ICD)* in 1939. Despite this development, the mental disorders section in the ICD was not widely accepted, and in 1952 the *American Psychiatric Association (APA)* published

International List of Causes of Death (ICD)
The international standard diagnostic classification developed by the World Health Organization (WHO).

American Psychiatric Association (APA)
A scientific and professional organization that represents psychiatry in the United States.

Diagnostic and Statistical Manual (DSM)
An American Psychiatric Association handbook for mental health professionals that lists different categories of mental disorders and the criteria for diagnosing them.

its first ***Diagnostic and Statistical Manual (DSM)***. In 1968 the APA produced a second version of its diagnostic manual (DSM-II). In 1969, the WHO published a new classification system, which was more widely accepted, and in the UK a glossary of definitions was produced to accompany the WHO system (General Register Office, 1968). However, the WHO system was simply a listing of diagnostic categories, and while DSM-II and the British Glossary of Mental Disorders provided more information on which to base diagnoses, the actual practice of diagnosing psychopathology varied widely. In 1980, the APA produced a substantially revised and expanded DSM-III, which has come to be accepted as the most influential diagnostic system. The most recent version that is used in this book is ***DSM-IV-TR*** (TR means 'text revision'), published in 2000. APA task forces are already working on the next revision, DSM-V, which is due to be published in 2011. The ICD system is currently in its tenth edition (ICD-10), and most revisions of the DSM have been coordinated with the ICD to ensure some consistency of diagnosis across systems. For convenience and consistency, we will be using only the DSM diagnostic system in this book (see Cooper, 1994, for a guide to the ICD-10 classification system).

DSM-IV-TR   The most recent version of the *Diagnostic and Statistical Manual*, currently the most widely adopted psychopathology classification system.

1.3.2 *DSM-IV-TR*

1.3.2.1 **Defining and Diagnosing Psychopathology**

Before attempting to classify psychopathology, it was necessary for DSM to define what it considers to be a mental disorder. As we have already seen in section 1.2, this is not a simple matter. However, DSM does make some attempt to rule out behaviours that are simply socially deviant as examples of psychopathology, and puts the emphasis on distress and disability as important defining characteristics. Focus Point 1.4 shows the relevant section from DSM-IV-TR that attempts to define what should be classified as a mental disorder. It is also important to try to define at this point what exactly the DSM system is designed to do. Wakefield (1997) argues that DSM has four basic objectives: (1) it must provide necessary and sufficient criteria for correct differential diagnosis; (2) it should provide a means of distinguishing 'true' psychopathology (in the medical sense) from non-disordered human conditions that are often labelled as 'problems in living'; (3) it should provide diagnostic criteria in a way that allows them to be applied systematically by different clinicians in different settings; and (4) the diagnostic criteria it provides should be theoretically neutral, in the sense that they do not favour one theoretical approach to psychopathology over another. Whether DSM can achieve these four objectives will be to some extent the measure of its success.

DSM-IV-TR also provides the following information: (1) *essential features* of the disorder (those that 'define' the disorder), (2) *associated features* (i.e. those that are usually, but not always, present), (3) *diagnostic criteria* (a list of symptoms that must be present for the patient to be given this diagnostic label) and (4) information on *differential diagnosis* (i.e. information on how to differentiate this disorder from other, similar disorders). Finally, as we mentioned earlier, an important feature of DSM is that it avoids any suggestion about the cause of a disorder unless the cause has been definitely established. This means that diagnosis is made almost entirely on the basis of observable behavioural symptoms rather than on any supposition about the underlying cause of the symptoms.

1.3.2.2 **The Dimensions of Classification**

DSM-IV-TR encourages clinicians to rate individuals on five separate dimensions, or axes, and these are listed in Table 1.3. Axes I and II cover the classification of psychopathology, with Axis I comprising the majority of common diagnostic categories such as anxiety disorders, depression, schizophrenia, etc. Axis II consists of personality disorders and intellectual disabilities, and covers psychopathologies that may be more chronic and long term. These

FOCUS POINT 1.4

The DSM-IV-TR definition of psychopathology

'In DSM-IV-TR, each of the mental disorders is conceptualized as a clinically significant behavioral or psychological syndrome or pattern that occurs in an individual and that is associated with present distress (e.g. a painful symptom) or disability (i.e., impairment in one or more important areas of functioning) or with a significantly increased risk of suffering death, pain, disability, or an important loss of freedom. In addition, this syndrome or pattern must not be merely an expectable and culturally sanctioned response to a particular event, for example, the death of a loved one. Whatever its original cause, it must currently be considered a manifestation of a behavioral, psychological, or biological dysfunction in the individual. Neither deviant behavior (e.g. political, religious, or sexual) nor conflicts that are primarily between the individual and society are mental disorders unless the deviance or conflict is a symptom of a dysfunction in the individual.'

(APA, 2000, pp. xxi–xxii)

Table 1.3 *The five dimensions of classification in DSM-IV-TR*

AXIS I	Clinical Disorders (e.g. anxiety disorders, mood disorders, schizophrenia and other psychotic disorders, etc.). Other conditions that may be a focus of clinical attention.
AXIS II	Personality Disorders (e.g. antisocial personality disorder, schizotypical personality disorder, etc.). Mental Retardation.
AXIS III	General Medical Conditions (e.g. infectious and parasitic diseases, diseases of the circulatory system, injury and poisoning, etc.).
AXIS IV	Psychosocial and Environmental problems (e.g. problems with primary support group, educational problems, economic problems).
AXIS V	Global Assessment of Functioning.

disorders are separated onto two different axes to encourage clinicians to explore the possibility that some shorter-term disorders (e.g. a diagnosed anxiety disorder) may also be concurrent with a longer-term disorder (such as a personality disorder). Axes III, IV and V are included so that the clinician can acquire a fuller appreciation of an individual's life situation. For example, a chronic physical illness, such as cancer or a cardiac disorder, may be a source of psychopathology symptoms (e.g. depression) and may affect what kinds of treatment interventions can be made. For example, it may be that certain forms of medication for depression should not be used if the client has a heart condition. In addition, Axis IV allows the clinician to note any psychosocial, environmental, financial or family factors that might be influencing psychopathology. Finally, Axis V allows the clinician to take a broader look at the client's level of psychological and social functioning, and assess the client's ability in the longer term to cope with any symptoms of psychopathology.

1.3.2.3 Problems with Classification

While DSM-IV-TR provides an objective and reliable set of criteria by which psychopathology symptoms can be diagnosed, it is in many senses imperfect.

First, we have already mentioned that it does not classify psychopathology according to its causes, but does so merely on the basis of symptoms. This can be problematic in a number of different ways. For example, psychopathologies that look the same on the surface may have different causes, and as a consequence require different forms of treatment. Also, diagnosis on the basis of symptoms gives the illusion of explanation, when it is nothing more than a redescription of the symptoms (Carson, 1996). So, to say that the client 'hears voices because she has schizophrenia' sounds like an explanation, but within DSM, schizophrenia is merely a collective term for the defining symptoms.

Second, simply using DSM criteria to label people with a disorder can be stigmatizing and harmful. We have already seen in section 1.2 that individuals with a psychopathology diagnosis tend to be viewed and treated differently within society. In addition, diagnostic labels actually encourage individuals to adopt a 'sick' role and can result in people adopting a long-term role as someone with what they perceive as a debilitating psychopathology (Scheff, 1975; see Client's Perspective 1.2).

Thirdly, DSM diagnostic classification tends to define disorders as **discrete entities** (i.e. after being assessed, you will either be diagnosed with a disorder or you will not). However, much recent evidence has begun to suggest that psychopathology may be **dimensional** rather than discrete (Krueger & Piasecki, 2002). That is, symptoms diagnosed as a disorder may just be more extreme versions of everyday behaviour. For example, at times we all worry about our own life problems – some more than others. In extreme cases this activity can become so regular and persistent that it will interfere with our daily living and may meet DSM-IV-TR criteria for diagnosis as a disorder (e.g. generalized anxiety disorder, GAD; see Chapter 5). In such circumstances, the cut-off point for defining an activity such as worrying as a disorder becomes relatively arbitrary.

> **Defining disorders as discrete entities** The tendency to define individuals as either having a particular disorder or not.

> **Dimensional approach to classification** The idea that symptoms diagnosed as a disorder may just be more extreme versions of everyday behaviour.

In an attempt to deal with this criticism, a clinical significance criterion was added to many diagnostic categories in DSM-IV-TR which requires that symptoms cause 'significant distress or impairment in social, occupational, or other important areas of functioning' (Spitzer & Wakefield, 1999). The purpose of this is to try to differentiate symptoms that reflect normal reactions to stress with which the individual may be able to cope from those that may require intervention and treatment to restore functioning. The fact that most psychopathology is dimensional rather than categorical is likely to be reflected in revisions in DSM-V and will enable disorders to be diagnosed at different levels of severity.

Fourthly, DSM conceptualizes psychopathology as a collection of hundreds of distinct categories of disorders, but what happens in practice provides quite a different picture. For example, the discrete, differentially defined disorders listed in DSM regularly co-occur. This is known as **comorbidity**, where an individual client will often be diagnosed with two or more distinct disorders (e.g. an anxiety disorder such as obsessive-compulsive disorder and major depression). What is interesting is that comorbidity is so common that it is the norm rather than the exception. For example, surveys suggest that up to 79 per cent of individuals diagnosed with a disorder at some point during their lifetime will have a history of more than one disorder (Kessler, McGonagle, Zhao, Nelson et al., 1994).

> **Comorbidity** The co-occurrence of two or more distinct disorders.

The frequency of comorbidity suggests that most disorders as defined by DSM may indeed not be independent discrete disorders but may represent symptoms of either **hybrid disorders**

> **Hybrid disorders** Disorders that contain elements of a number of different disorders.

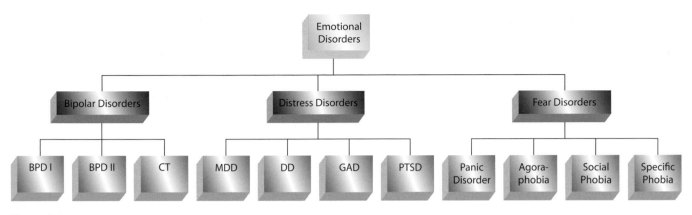

Figure 1.4
More detailed research on anxiety and depressive disorders can help reveal the way in which individual disorders are related and why many diagnosable disorders are frequently comorbid. This figure shows a proposed spectrum of emotional disorders which indicates how anxiety and depression may be related. For example, the fact that MDD and GAD are both classified as distress disorders provides some indication of why these two apparently different DSM disorders are frequently comorbid. Only the bottom line of the figure represents the individual disorders defined in DSM-IV-TR. BPD I = bipolar I disorder; BPD II = bipolar II disorder; CT = cyclothymia; MDD = major depressive disorder; DD = dysthymic disorder; GAD = generalized anxiety disorder; PTSD = post-traumatic stress disorder.
Source: Watson (2005).

(e.g. a disorder that contains elements of a number of different disorders) or a more broad-ranging *syndrome* or *disorder spectrum* that represents a higher-order categorical class of symptoms (Krueger, Watson & Barlow, 2005; Widiger & Samuel, 2005). An example of a hybrid disorder is **mixed anxiety-depressive disorder**. Many people exhibit symptoms of both anxiety and depression, yet do not meet the threshold for either an anxiety or a depression diagnosis (Barlow & Campbell, 2000). Examples such as this suggest that because DSM defines disorders as numerous discrete entities, it fails to recognize cases where discrete symptoms, although individually not reaching a level significant enough for diagnosis, may collectively be causing considerable distress.

Mixed anxiety-depressive disorder
A hybrid disorder exhibiting symptoms of both anxiety and depression.

There is also a broader theoretical implication to the fact that comorbidity is so common. This is that psychopathology may occur in a spectrum that has a hierarchical structure rather than consisting merely of numerous discrete disorders. For example, Watson (2005) argues that anxiety and depression (which are both diagnosed as separate disorders in DSM-IV-TR) may both be members of a larger spectrum of emotional disorders. This is based on the facts that (1) 58 per cent of individuals with major depression also meet DSM criteria for a comorbid anxiety disorder (Kessler, Nelson, McGonagle, Liu et al., 1996), (2) various anxiety disorders are highly comorbid with each other (Brown, Campbell, Lehman, Grisham et al., 2001) and (3) depression and anxiety are together both highly comorbid with other psychopathologies, such as substance abuse, eating disorders, somatoform disorders and personality disorders (Mineka, Watson & Clark, 1998; Widiger & Clark, 2000).

Figure 1.4 provides a schematic representation of this proposed spectrum of emotional disorders, indicating its hierarchical structure and showing how individual disorders defined in DSM may only represent the bottom level of this hierarchy. Defining psychopathology in such hierarchical structures rather than as discrete independent entities has the benefit of explaining and predicting comorbidity and begins to provide some theoretical insight into how different symptoms may be related.

One final problem with DSM-IV-TR as it is currently constructed is that the diagnostic criteria often allow for extensive within-category heterogeneity (Krueger, Watson & Barlow, 2005). For example, the DSM diagnostic criteria for a personality disorder often specify that the individual must meet the criteria for only five of nine specified symptoms; thus, individuals who are diagnosed with a personality disorder may share no more than one common feature. In some cases (e.g. obsessive-compulsive personality disorder; see Chapter 11), it is theoretically possible for two different diagnosed cases to have no shared features at all. This means that there can be great variability in the symptoms displayed by different individuals diagnosed with the same disorder.

SUMMARY

While DSM-IV-TR is not ideal, it is the most comprehensive classification system we have available. While we have just listed a number of criticisms of DSM, we must also remember that classification in and of itself does have some advantages. We must also remember that DSM is an evolving classification system that takes into account criticisms of previous versions and develops to incorporate recent research. Thus, when DSM-V is published in 2011, it is likely to have attempted to address some of the problems with diagnosis that we have listed above.

- Can you briefly describe the history of the development of psychopathology classification systems?
- What is the DSM classification system primarily designed to do?
- What are the five axes or dimensions of classification in DSM?
- DSM is not an ideal classification system. Can you describe at least four problems associated with this method of classification?

SECTION SUMMARY

1.3 Classifying Psychopathology

- The two most influential classification systems are the **American Psychiatric Association (APA)** *Diagnostic and Statistical Manual* (DSM) and the **World Health Organization (WHO)** *International List of Causes of Death* (ICD).

- Currently, the most widely adopted classification system is **DSM-IV-TR**.

- DSM-IV-TR encourages clinicians to rate clients on five separate **axes**.

1.4 GOOD PSYCHOLOGICAL HEALTH

So far in this chapter we have focused on psychopathology, mental health problems and diagnosable psychological disorders, but we must remember that it is often useful when defining psychopathology to view it in the context of what we would normally consider to be criteria for *good psychological health*. Table 1.3 shows that Axis V of DSM-IV-TR attempts to measure the individual's current level of adaptive functioning in areas of social relationships, employment and use of leisure time. In most cases, good psychological health can be indicated by the presence of most of the following attributes: (1) an efficient perception of reality, (2) good self-knowledge and awareness of one's own feelings, (3) the ability to exercise voluntary control over behaviour, (4) good self-esteem and an appreciation of one's own worth, (5) an ability to form and maintain affectionate relationships with others and (6) productivity – a positive and planned approach to life. Table 1.4 shows the *Global Assessment of Functioning Scale (GAF)* that is used to assess adaptive functioning, and this acts as a measure of psychological health that can be contrasted with measures of psychopathology.

Good psychological health   A measure of an individual's current level of adaptive functioning in areas of social relationships, employment and use of leisure time.

Global Assessment of Functioning Scale (GAF)   A scale used to assess adaptive functioning which acts as a measure of psychological health that can be contrasted with measures of psychopathology.

Table 1.4   *The Global Assessment of Functioning (GAF) Scale*

Score	Criteria
100–91	Superior functioning in a wide range of activities, life's problems never seem to get out of hand, is sought out by others because of his or her many positive qualities. No symptoms.
90–81	Absent or minimal symptoms (e.g. mild anxiety before an exam), good functioning in all areas, interested and involved in a wide range of activities, socially effective, generally satisfied with life, no more than everyday problems or concerns (e.g. an occasional argument with family members).
71–80	If symptoms are present, they are transient and expectable reactions to psychosocial stressors (e.g. difficulty concentrating after family argument); no more than slight impairment in social, occupational or school functioning (e.g. temporarily falling behind in schoolwork).
61–70	Some mild symptoms (e.g. depressed mood and mild insomnia) OR some difficulty in social, occupational or school functioning (e.g. occasional truancy, or theft within the household), but generally functioning pretty well, has some meaningful interpersonal relationships.
51–60	Moderate symptoms (e.g. flat affect and circumstantial speech, occasional panic attacks) OR moderate difficulty in social, occupational or school functioning (e.g. no friends, conflicts with peers or co-workers).
41–50	Serious symptoms (e.g. suicidal ideation, severe obsessional rituals, frequent shoplifting) OR any serious impairment in social, occupational or school functioning (e.g. no friends, unable to keep a job).
31–40	Some impairment in reality testing or communication (e.g. speech is at times illogical, obscure or irrelevant) OR major impairment in several areas, such as work or school, family relations, judgement, thinking or mood (e.g. depressed man avoids friends, neglects family and is unable to work; child frequently beats up younger children, is defiant at home and is failing at school).

Table 1.4 *(Cont'd)*

21–30	Behaviour is considerably influenced by delusions or hallucinations OR serious impairments in communication or judgement (e.g. sometimes incoherent, acts grossly inappropriately, suicidal preoccupations) OR inability to function in almost all areas (e.g. stays in bed all day, no job, home or friends).
11–20	Some danger of hurting self or others (e.g. suicide attempts without clear expectation of death, frequently violent, manic excitement) OR occasionally fails to maintain minimal personal hygiene (e.g. smears faeces) OR gross impairment in communication (e.g. largely incoherent or mute).
1–10	Persistent danger of severely hurting self or others (e.g. recurrent violence) OR persistent inability to maintain minimal personal hygiene OR serious suicidal acts with clear expectation of death.
0	Inadequate information.

Source: taken from DSM-IV-TR (APA, 2000), p. 34.

SECTION SUMMARY

1.4 Good Psychological Health

- Criteria for good psychological health can be found in the **Global Assessment of Functioning Scale (GAF)**.

1.5 CONCEPTUAL AND CLASSIFICATION ISSUES REVIEWED

This chapter has introduced the important conceptual and classification issues that surround psychopathology. We have discussed how methods of explaining psychopathology have developed over the ages and moved on to a more scientific basis with the advent of medical and psychological models of psychopathology. The medical model proved to be an important stepping stone towards objective explanations of psychopathology, but still has significant limitations, including the fact that it implies an underlying medical cause for psychopathology – which is not always true – and that psychopathology is caused by 'something biological or psychological not working properly' – again, an implication which is not always correct. The four main psychological approaches, psychodynamic, behavioural, cognitive and humanistic-existential, all provide a rather different means of explaining psychopathology, and all four approaches are still influential today.

Defining exactly what kinds of symptoms or behaviour should be considered as examples of psychopathology is also problematic. The four types of definition that we discussed (deviation from the statistical norm, deviation from social norms, maladaptive behaviour and distress and impairment) all have limitations. Some fail to cover examples of behaviour that we would intuitively believe to be representative of mental health problems, while others may cover examples that we intuitively feel are not examples of psychopathology, or they may represent forms of categorization that would lead us to impose stigmatizing labels on people suffering from psychopathology. In practice, classification schemes end up using an amalgamation of these different approaches to definition.

Finally, we discussed the pros and cons of classification schemes for psychopathology and how these schemes developed. The most commonly accepted form of classification is the APA *Diagnostic and Statistical Manual* (DSM), whose current version is DSM-IV-TR. This is the version we will be referring to throughout this text.

LEARNING OUTCOMES

When you have completed this chapter, you should be able to:

1 Compare and contrast approaches to the explanation of psychopathology, including historical approaches, the medical model and psychological models.

2 Discuss the pros and cons of a number of different approaches to defining psychopathology.

3 Describe the history of the development of psychopathology classification systems.

4 Compare and contrast the pros and cons of DSM as a means of classifying and diagnosing psychopathology.

KEY TERMS

Abnormal psychology 17
American Psychiatric Association (APA) 20
Ataque de Nervios 18
Behaviour modification 14
Behaviour therapy 14
Behavioural model 12
Classical conditioning 12
Client-centred therapy 15
Clinical psychology 5
Cognitive behaviour therapy (CBT) 15
Cognitive model 14
Comorbidity 22
Defence mechanisms 11
Demonology 6
Diagnostic and Statistical Manual (DSM) 21
Dimensional approach to classification 22
Defining disorders as discrete entities 22
DSM-IV-TR 21
Ego 11
Ego defence mechanisms 11
Empathy 15
General paresis 6
Global Assessment of Functioning Scale (GAF) 24
Good psychological health 24

Humanist-existentialist approach 15
Hybrid disorders 22
Id 11
International List of Causes of Death (ICD) 20
Learning theory 12
Mad Pride 17
Medical model 5
Mixed anxiety-depressive disorder 23
Operant conditioning 13
Oral stage 11
Psychiatry 6
Psychoanalysis 10
Psychological models 7
Psychopathology 5
Seizisman 18
Service user groups 17
Sigmund Freud 10
Somatogenic hypothesis 6
Stages of development 11
Statistical norm 17
Superego 11
Syndrome 20
Unconditional positive regard 15

REVIEWS, THEORIES AND SEMINAL STUDIES

Links to Journal Articles

1.1 Explaining Psychopathology

Crisp, A.H., Gelder, M.G., Rix, S., Meltzer, H.I. & Rowlands, O.J. (2000). Stigmatization of people with mental illness. *British Journal of Psychiatry, 177,* 4–7.

1.2 Defining Psychopathology

British Psychological Society (2000). *Recent advances in understanding mental illness and psychotic experiences.* London: British Psychological Society.

Desrosiers, A. & Fleurose, S.S. (2002). Treating Haitian patients: Key cultural aspects. *American Journal of Psychotherapy, 56,* 508–521.

Nicolas, G., DeSilva, A.M., Grey, K.S. & Gonzalez-Eastep, D. (2006). Using a multicultural lens to understand illness among Haitians living in America. *Professional Psychology: Research and Practice, 37,* 702–707.

1.3 Classifying Psychopathology

Krueger, R.F. & Piasecki, T.M. (2002). Toward a dimensional and psychometrically informed approach to conceptualizing psychopathology. *Behaviour Research and Therapy, 40,* 485–499.

Krueger, R.F., Watson, D. & Barlow, D.H. (2005). Introduction to the special section: Towards a dimensionally based taxonomy of psychopathology. *Journal of Abnormal Psychology, 114,* 491–493.

McNally, R.J. (2001). On Wakefield's harmful dysfunction analysis of mental disorder. *Behaviour Research and Therapy, 39,* 309–314.

Wakefield, J.C. (1997). Diagnosing DSM-IV. Part I. DSM-IV and the concept of disorder. *Behaviour Research and Therapy, 35,* 633–649.

Watson, D. (2005). Rethinking the mood and anxiety disorders: A quantitative hierarchical model for DSM-V. *Journal of Abnormal Psychology, 114,* 522–536.

Widiger, T.A. & Samuel, D.B. (2005). Diagnostic categories or dimensions? A question for the Diagnostic and Statistical Manual of Mental Disorders: Fifth Edition. *Journal of Abnormal Psychology, 114*, 494–504.

Texts for Further Reading

American Psychiatric Association (2000). *Diagnostic and statistical manual of mental disorders* (4th ed., Text Revision). Washington, DC: American Psychiatric Association.

Cave, S. (2002). *Classification and diagnosis of psychological abnormality*. Hove: Psychology Press.

Cooper, J.E. (1994). *Pocket guide to ICD-10 classification of mental and behavioural disorders*. New York: Churchill Livingstone.

Helzer, J.E. & Hudziak, J.J. (2002). *Defining psychopathology in the 21st Century: DSM-V and beyond*. Washington, DC: American Psychiatric Press.

Maj, M., Gaebel, W., Lopez-Ibor, J. & Sartorius, N. (Eds.) (2002). *Psychiatric diagnosis and classification*. New York: Wiley.

RESEARCH QUESTIONS

- Psychoanalytic and psychodynamic approaches to psychopathology are still very influential, but can the central concepts in this approach be objectively defined and measured as part of an attempt to assess the validity of the approach?

- Behavioural approaches often stress the importance of reinforcement histories in psychopathology, but are there any objective and systematic ways in which reinforcement histories can be traced?

- Can the efficacy of humanistic-existentialist therapies ever be objectively measured and compared with the efficacy of other therapies?

- Can research on the causes of psychopathology provide a basis for the classification of psychopathology?

- How can psychopathology research contribute to an understanding of comorbidity?

- Can psychopathology research provide an insight into the way in which different diagnostic disorders are related?

CLINICAL ISSUES

1.1 Explaining Psychopathology

- Should clinical psychologists be looking for physical or biological impairments as the causes of psychopathology?
- Is 'bizarre' behaviour always a good indication of underlying psychopathology?
- Is psychopathology simply a more extreme form of normal behaviour?
- What do clinical psychologists need to do in order to challenge existing negative stereotypes of individuals with mental health problems?
- Depressed or low mood is often associated with receiving a psychiatric diagnosis. What can clinical practitioners do to minimize this?

1.2 Defining Psychopathology

- Psychopathology textbooks and courses still use the title 'Abnormal Psychology'. What effect might this title have on conceptions of psychopathology, and what can clinical practitioners do to influence the use of this and similar titles?
- How do cultural factors affect both our definition of psychopathology and our attempts at diagnosis?
- Is the presence of personal distress and impairment necessary for identifying symptoms as examples of psychopathology?

1.3 Classifying Psychopathology

- Do clinical psychologists need psychopathology classification systems in order to do their job properly?
- What are the basic functions of a classification scheme such as DSM?
- What are the problems for the practising clinician of using a diagnostic system that does not classify psychopathology according to its causes?
- Does giving clients a diagnostic label tend them towards adopting a 'sick role'?
- Should only individuals who have been diagnosed with a DSM-classified disorder be provided with access to structured treatment?
- Are the DSM diagnostic criteria so heterogeneous in some cases that it is possible to diagnose two people with the same disorder, although in fact they have no symptoms in common?

2 Clinical Assessment

ROUTE MAP OF THE CHAPTER

This chapter describes the various ways in which clinicians gather information about a client's problems. This information can then be used to help them classify the person's problems, understand the causes of those problems and treat the problems. The chapter discusses the benefits and limitations of clinical interviews, psychological tests, biologically based assessments and clinical observation, and introduces the concepts of reliability and validity. The chapter ends by discussing cultural biases in clinical assessments and the popular use of case formulations as a means of understanding clients' problems and developing a strategy for treatment.

I saw Mrs Ann Smith, aged 39, in my clinic today. She met the criteria for depression, with a five-month history of low mood. This was triggered by an argument with her husband during the Christmas period. Despite receiving a lot of support from her husband, Ann continues to experience 'black spells', which can go on for five days per episode. In March she expressed some suicidal thoughts, which precipitated her referral to psychiatric services.

At interview Ann was well presented, clear and articulate. However, both her eye contact and concentration were poor, and she reported having lost 10lbs in weight. This is the first time she has been referred to psychiatric services, but has been prescribed antidepressant medication on three previous occasions by her GP. She states that she has experienced low times throughout her life.

She is the middle child of three and stated that she missed a lot of schooling due to the combination of having chronic asthma and an overprotective mother. She left school without qualifications, feeling she has not realized her potential in any area. She married Michael 14 years ago. Owing to his job as a vicar, they entertain frequently. She finds the entertaining difficult. I would welcome your assessment of this case, with a view of taking her on for therapy.

ANN'S STORY (IN BLACKBURN, JAMES & FLITCROFT, 2006)

Introduction

Ann has low mood. She has been prescribed anti-depressant medication by her GP, who subsequently referred her to a psychiatrist. Following an interview with the psychiatrist, the latter sent the above referral letter on to a clinical psychologist. The referral letter immediately raises a number of questions, the main one being 'Can we help this person?' But this question itself raises a number of other questions that will need answering. These questions include: (1) Are Ann's symptoms typical of a specific psychological problem (e.g. depression)? (2) What has led her to have these problems? (3) Are there specific events that trigger her symptoms? (4) How can we help her? and (5) By what criteria will we judge that we have successfully helped her? These are all questions that the clinical psychologist must answer by gathering a variety of information about the client. This information is often acquired using a range of different clinical tools and techniques. Clinical assessment procedures are formal ways of finding answers to these questions, especially: 'Precisely what problems does this person have?', 'What has caused the problems?', 'What is the best way to treat the problems?' and 'Did the treatment work?'

Clinicians use a wide range of assessment procedures to gather this information. In many cases the types of techniques they use will depend on their theoretical orientation to psychopathology. For example, the cognitive-behavioural clinician may want to find out quite different information to a psychodynamic clinician – largely because his conceptions of the causes of psychopathology are different, and because the kinds of therapeutic techniques he employs are different. The cognitive therapist will want to know what kinds of cognitions may trigger symptoms so that these cognitions can be addressed in therapy, whereas a psychodynamic therapist may want to explore the client's history of conflicts and defence mechanisms in order to assess the individual's suitability for psychodynamic therapy (Marzillier & Marzillier, 2008).

In this chapter we will describe the range of assessment techniques available to clinicians that enable them to answer the basic questions about a case that we have just raised. These techniques are an aid to diagnosis, an aid to determining the best intervention for a client, and a help in establishing whether treatment has successfully dealt with the client's symptoms. We will discuss these assessment types individually, but to gain a complete picture of the client's condition, the clinician will usually use a range of different assessments (Meyer, Finn, Eyde, Kay et al., 2001). The chapter begins by discussing different types of assessment, including the interview, psychological tests, biologically based tests and observation. We will then look at how the validity and reliability of these tests are determined, and finally discuss some issues relating to diagnosis and how diagnosis is related to the development of a treatment plan (known as formulation).

2.1 METHODS OF ASSESSMENT

2.1.1 Clinical Interviews

2.1.1.1 The Nature of Clinical Interviews

We have all probably been interviewed at some point in our lives. It may be for a job, a place at university, or by our GP who is enquiring about symptoms of an illness. An interview usually represents an informal, relatively unstructured conversation between two or more people, the purpose of which is to gather some information about one or more of those people in the interview. The clinical interview is probably the first form of contact that a client will have with a clinician, and the clinical psychologist will usually be trying to gain a broad insight into the client and his or her problems. Questions may relate to the nature of the symptoms the client experiences, the client's past history, and his or her current living and working circumstances. The type of questions that will be asked in a clinical interview will depend very much on the theoretical orientation of the clinician. For example, psychodynamic clinicians are likely to want to ask questions about the client's childhood history and memories of past events, and to take note of any strong emotional responses that may indicate unconscious processes (see Chapter 1). In contrast, the behavioural interviewer will want to explore any relationships between the client's symptoms and environmental events, such as the consequences of symptoms that may reinforce them. Finally, the cognitive clinician will want to try to discover whether the client holds any assumptions or beliefs that may maintain or influence his or her problems.

In general, those conducting clinical interviews must be skilful in guiding the client towards revealing the kinds of information they are looking for. They must be able to establish a good rapport with their clients, they must gain their trust, they must be able to convince clients of the value of the theoretical approach they are taking, and in most cases they must be able to empathize with their clients in order to encourage them to elaborate on their concerns and to provide information that they may otherwise be reluctant to give. The clinical interviewer can encounter a number of difficulties when conducting an interview which will often require all their experience and skill to overcome. For example, (1) many clients will want to withhold information about themselves, especially if it involves painful or embarrassing memories, or if the information concerns illegal or unsocial activities (such as illegal drug use or illegal sexual activities), and (2) clients may well have poor self-knowledge and so be unable to answer questions accurately or with any real insight into why they behave or feel the way they do. It is the skilled interviewer's job to find ways to deal with these problems and to reveal the reliable information that he or she needs to form a diagnosis, to understand the causes of the client's problems, and to formulate a treatment programme.

2.1.1.2 Structured Interviews

Clinicians can also use the interview method to acquire the kinds of standardized information they need to make a diagnosis or to construct a case formulation (see section 2.2), but this requires them to conduct the interview in a **structured** way. The normal clinical interview would probably contain many open questions such as 'Tell me

> **Structured interview** An interview in which questions to be asked, their sequence and detailed information to be gathered are all predetermined.

something about yourself and what you do', and the direction of the interview will be to some extent determined by the client's responses to these open questions. However, structured interviews can be used to enable clinicians to make decisions about diagnosis and functioning. One such structured interview technique is known as the *Structured Clinical Interview for DSM-IV-TR (SCID)* (Spitzer, Gibbon & Williams, 1986), which can be used for determining diagnoses on Axis I of DSM-IV-TR. The SCID is a branching, structured interview in which the client's response to one question will determine the next question to be asked. This enables the clinician to establish the main symptoms exhibited by a client, their severity (on a scale of 1–3), and whether a combination of these symptoms and severity meet DSM-IV-TR criteria for a particular disorder. The SCID has been shown to provide highly reliable diagnoses for most Axis I disorders (Segal, Hersen & Van Hasselt, 1994), with one study indicating 85.7 per cent agreement on diagnosis between different clinicians using the SCID (Miller, Dasher, Collins, Griffiths et al., 2001).

> **Structured Clinical Interview for DSM-IV-TR (SCID)**   A branching, structured interview in which the client's response to one question will determine the next question to be asked.

Structured interviews can also be used to determine overall levels of psychological and intellectual functioning, especially in older people who may be suffering from degenerative disorders such as dementia. One such structured interview is the *Mini Mental State Examination (MMSE)*, which is a structured test that takes 10 minutes to administer and can provide reliable information on the client's overall levels of cognitive and mental functioning. A fuller description of this structured interview is given in Chapter 14 (see Focus Point 14.2).

2.1.1.3 Limitations of the Clinical Interview

The clinical interview is usually a good way of beginning the process of assessment and can provide a range of useful information for the clinician. However, there are limitations to this method. First, the reliability of clinical interviews is probably quite low. That is, no matter how skilled they may be, two different clinicians are quite likely to end up with rather different information from an unstructured interview. For example, clients are likely to give different information to an interviewer who is 'cold' and unresponsive than to one who is 'warm' and supportive (Eisenthal, Koopman & Lazare, 1983), and a teenage client is likely to respond differently to a young interviewer who is dressed casually than to an older interviewer who is dressed formally. There is also significant evidence that an interviewer's race and sex will influence a client's responses (Paurohit, Dowd & Cottingham, 1982). As we have already mentioned, many clients may have quite poor self-awareness, so only a skilled interviewer will be able to glean the information he or she requires by inferring information from the client's responses. Interviewers are also prone to biases that may affect the conclusions they draw from an interview. For

> **Unstructured interview**   A free-flowing interview in which questions to be asked, their sequence and detailed information to be gathered are not predetermined.

example, they may rely too heavily on first impressions (the primacy effect), or give priority only to negative information (Meehl, 1996), and may be influenced by irrelevant details such as the client's biological sex, race, skin colour or sexual orientation. Finally, there are some psychological disorders in which sufferers may intentionally mislead the interviewer or lie to them, and these can mean that the client can manipulate the interview or deliberately provide misleading information. This can often occur with personality disorders, such as borderline personality disorder or anti-social personality disorder, or in the case of sexual disorders such as paedophilia (see Chapters 10 and 11).

2.1.2 Psychological Tests

Psychological tests represent highly structured ways of gathering information about an individual. They usually take the form of a written questionnaire in which the client has to respond to a series of questions or stimuli. However, they can be given verbally by the clinician or even completed on a computer. The psychological test is one of the most common forms of assessment in clinical psychology and is considerably more structured than the interview method. Psychological tests have a number of advantages as methods of assessment. (1) They usually assess the client on one or more specific characteristics or traits (e.g. levels of anxiety, depression, IQ, cognitive functioning, or individual psychopathology traits such as hypochondriasis, paranoia, conversion hysteria, etc.). (2) They will usually (but not always) have very rigid response requirements so that the questions can be scored according to a pre-conceived scoring system. Table 2.1 provides an example of the question format for a measure of trait anxiety – the State-Trait Anxiety Inventory (STAI) (Spielberger, Gorsuch, Lushene, Vagg & Jacobs, 1983) – which is a test format common to many psychometric tests. (3) Once data from these tests have been collected from large numbers of participants, statistical norms for the tests can be established. This is known as *standardization*, and allows the clinician to see where an individual client's score on the test falls in relation to the normal distribution of scores for that test (see, for example, Figure 1.3). It also means that the clinician may be able to use the score on a particular test to estimate whether a client might meet the diagnostic criteria for a psychological disorder. For example, scores on a test such as the Clark-Beck Obsessive Compulsive Inventory (CBOCI) (Clark & Beck, 2003) can be used to estimate the probability with which a client might meet DSM-IV-TR diagnostic criteria for OCD. Finally, (4) unlike the *ad hoc* quizzes and questionnaires you might find in popular magazines, most structured psychological tests are rigorously tested to ensure that they are both valid and reliable (see section 2.1.5). That is, they are tested to ensure that they are a valid measure of what they claim to be measuring (e.g. that scores on a written psychological test claiming to measure anxiety actually correlate with behavioural measures of anxiety) and that the test is reliable in the sense that it yields consistent scores when it is given to the same person on different occasions.

> **Standardization**   Statistical norms taken from data that have been collected from large numbers of participants of psychological tests.

Table 2.1 *Measuring state and trait anxiety using a questionnaire*

The Spielbeger STAI-Y2 is a well-known psychometric test for measuring levels of state and trait anxiety. Its questions take the following format, and this format is one that is regularly used in psychological tests of this kind (Spielberger, Gorsuch, Lushene, Vagg & Jacobs, 1983).

A number of statements which people have used to describe themselves are given below. Read each statement and then circle the appropriate number to the right of the statement to indicate how you *generally* feel. There are no right or wrong answers. Do not spend too much time on any one statement but give the answer which seems to describe how you generally feel.

1 = Almost never
2 = Sometimes
3 = Often
4 = Almost always

1	I feel pleasant	1	2	3	4
2	I feel nervous and restless	1	2	3	4
3	I feel satisfied with myself	1	2	3	4
4	I wish I could be as happy as others seem to be	1	2	3	4
5	I feel like a failure	1	2	3	4
6	I feel rested	1	2	3	4

The scale of 1 to 4 is known as a **Likert scale** where clients have to specify their level of agreement with each statement. Some items will be reversed so that respondents cannot simply endorse each item in the same way (for example, Q3 is a reversed item in which the anxious individual would endorse a low number rather than a high number). Clinicians can then create a total score for a client by adding together the individual scores that the client has circled (but remembering to reverse score any reversed items – e.g. on Q3, 4 would be scored as 1, 3 as 2, and so on). When data have been collected from a large number of participants from differing age groups and demographic backgrounds, statistical norms for the test can be established. This is known as **standardization**. This allows clinicians to compare the score of their client with the normal distribution of scores that occur in the population in general.

Psychometric approach   The idea that a psychological test assumes that there are stable underlying characteristics or traits (e.g. anxiety, depression, compulsiveness, worry) that exist at different levels in everyone.

Most psychological tests are based on the *psychometric approach*. That is, the test assumes that there are stable underlying characteristics or traits (e.g. anxiety, depression, compulsiveness, worry, etc.) that exist at different levels in everyone. The psychological tests we will discuss below can take a number of different forms and serve a number of different functions. For example, some tests stick rather rigidly to the structured question, response and scoring format similar to that shown in Table 2.1 (personality inventories, specific symptom inventories), while others (such as projective tests) may closely define the questions or stimuli to be presented to the client, but allow a much wider range of potential responses. The clinical psychologist will use psychological tests for a variety of different purposes, including the assessment of psychopathology symptoms, intelligence and neurological or cognitive deficits.

2.1.2.1 Personality Inventories

The most well known of the personality inventories used by clinical psychologists and psychiatrists is the *Minnesota Multiphasic Personality Inventory (MMPI)*. Originally developed in the 1940s by Hathaway and McKinley (1943), it has recently been updated by Butcher, Dahlstrom, Graham, Tellegen et al. (1989) and is now known as the MMPI-2. The MMPI-2 consists of 567 self-statements to which clients have to respond on a 3-point scale by replying either 'true', 'false' or 'cannot say'. The questions cover topics such as mood, physical concerns, social attitudes, psychological symptoms and feelings of well-being. The original authors asked around 800 psychiatric patients to indicate whether the questions were true for them, and compared their responses with those from 800 non-psychiatric patients. They then included in the inventory only those questions that differentiated between the two groups. The test now has 4 validity scales and 10 clinical scales, examples of which are shown in Table 2.2. The test provides scores for each scale between 0 and 120, and scores above 70 on a scale are considered to be indicative of psychopathology. The scores from the various scales can be displayed on a graph to give a distinctive profile indicating the client's general personality features, potential psychopathology and emotional needs.

Minnesota Multiphasic Personality Inventory (MMPI)   The most well-known of the personality inventories used by clinical psychologists and psychiatrists.

An example of an *MMPI profile* is shown in Figure 2.1. The validity scales are particularly useful because they allow the clinician to estimate whether a client has been providing false information on the test. Clients might provide false information for a number of reasons: (1) because they want to 'look good' and so respond in a socially acceptable way (measured by the lie scale); (2) because they may want to fake psychopathology symptoms in order to receive attention and treatment (measured by the F scale) (Rogers, Sewell, Martin & Vitacco, 2003); (3) because they are being evasive or simply having difficulty reading or interpreting the questions (measured by the ? scale); or (4) because they are defensive and want to avoid appearing incompetent (measured by the K scale).

MMPI profile   A graph providing a distinctive profile indicating the client's general personality features, potential psychopathology and emotional needs taken from the results of the Minnesota Multiphasic Personality Inventory.

Clinical research has indicated that the MMPI has good internal reliability, and scores on the MMPI appear to have excellent

Table 2.2 *Sub-scales and sample items from the MMPI*

SUB-SCALE	WHAT THE SCALE MEASURES	SAMPLE ITEM
?	Evasiveness or difficulty interpreting the question	(number of items left unanswered)
L (lie scale)	Tendency of respondent to respond in a socially acceptable way	'I approve of every person I meet'
F	Respondent is trying to fake psychopathology symptoms	'Everything tastes sweet'
K	Respondent is defensive and trying not to look incompetent	'Things couldn't be going any better for me'
Hypochondriasis (HS)	Abnormal concern with bodily sensations	'I am often aware of tingling feelings in my body'
Depression (D)	Pessimism and hopelessness	'Life never feels worthwhile to me'
Conversion Hysteria (Hy)	Uses physical symptoms to avoid conflicts and responsibilities	'My muscles often twitch for no apparent reason'
Psychopathy (Pd)	Emotional shallowness and disregard for social norms	'I don't care about what people think of me'
Masculinity–Femininity (Mf)	Identifies respondents with non-traditional gender characteristics	'I like to arrange flowers'
Paranoia (Pa)	Pathological suspiciousness or delusions of grandeur or persecution	'There are evil people trying to influence my mind'
Psychasthenia (Pt)	Identifies respondents with obsessions, compulsions, guilt, and irrational fears	'I save everything I buy, even after I have no use for it'
Schizophrenia (Sc)	Identifies bizarre sensory experiences and beliefs	'Things around me do not seem real'
Hypomania (Ma)	Identifies emotional excitement, hyperactivity and impatience	'Sometimes I have a strong impulse to do something that others will find appalling'
Social Introversion (Si)	Identifies someone who is shy, modest and prefers solitary activities	'I am easily embarrassed'

clinical validity by corresponding accurately with clinical diagnoses and ratings of symptoms made by both clinicians and members of the client's own family (Ganellan, 1996; Graham, 1990; Vacha-Hasse, Kogan, Tani & Woodall, 2001). One limitation of the MMPI is the time that it takes to administer: answering 567 questions requires some stamina on the part of both the client and the overworked clinician. However, shortened versions of the MMPI-2 are available that show both good reliability and validity (Dahlstrom & Archer, 2000).

2.1.2.2 Specific Trait Inventories

While personality inventories such as the MMPI assess characteristics of the client across a range of different traits and domains, other inventories have been developed simply to measure functioning in one specific area or one specific psychopathology. Such tests may measure emotional functioning, such as levels of anxiety, depression or anger, or they may measure aspects of behaviour such as social skills. More recently, other tests have been developed

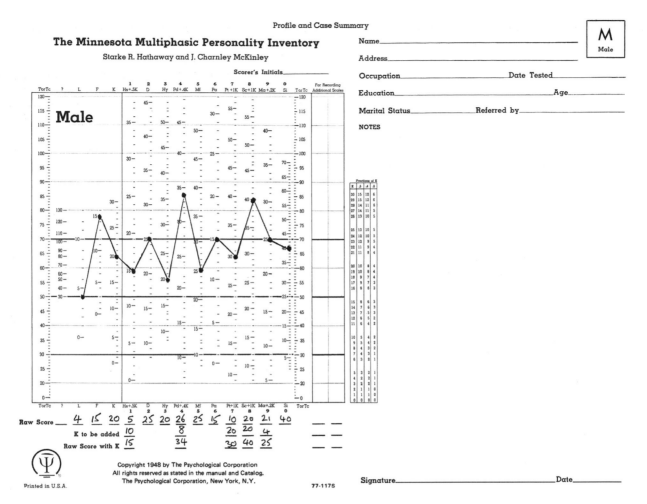

Figure 2.1 *MMPI profile*
The scores on each scale of the MMPI can be displayed on a graph to give a distinctive profile indicating the client's general personality features, potential psychopathology (scores on scales that extend beyond the horizontal line) and emotional needs.

Source: Form completed by the author. Original © The Psychological Corporation.

in an attempt to measure cognitive functioning or cognitive constructs that are relevant to psychopathology. One such example is the Obsessive Belief Questionnaire (OBQ) (Steketee, Frost, Bhar, Bouvard et al., 2005), which was designed to assess beliefs and appraisals considered critical to the acquisition and maintenance of obsessions. This measures six cognitive constructs thought to play a role in obsessive-compulsive disorder (OCD) including (1) intolerance of uncertainty, (2) overestimation of threat, (3) control of thoughts, (4) importance of thoughts, (5) beliefs about inflated responsibility and (6) perfectionism. You may want to look at section 5.5 to understand how these cognitive constructs are relevant to the aetiology of OCD. Specific tests such as these can be used to measure variables that are directly observable and measurable, such as characteristics found in observable behaviour. But they are becoming increasingly used to measure *hypothetical constructs* that are not necessarily directly observable but have to be inferred from the answers given to a range of questions. For example, the degree to which

Hypothetical constructs Constructs that are not necessarily directly observable but have to be inferred from other data.

an individual cannot tolerate uncertainty (a factor that has been implicated in the acquisition and maintenance of a number of anxiety disorders) is assessed on the OBQ by asking respondents to endorse statements such as 'I am uncertain there is something wrong with me' or 'I should be 100% certain that everything around me is safe'. Taken together, such questions provide an estimate of how much the individual is able to tolerate uncertainty.

Because of their potential diagnostic and theoretical value (such inventories can also be used as research tools to help us understand the causes of psychopathology), the number of specific trait inventories available to clinicians and researchers has burgeoned in the past 10–15 years. While some are very valuable and have good face validity, many others are relatively underdeveloped. For example, unlike the MMPI, a majority of specific trait inventories fail to include any questions to indicate whether respondents are faking responses or are merely being careless with their answers, and many are not subjected to stringent standardization, validation and reliability tests. There is even a view that researchers may simply create a specific trait inventory to serve their own theoretical purposes and to give their theoretical perspective a façade of objective credibility (i.e. they may create an inventory simply to 'measure' a construct that they themselves have invented) (Davey, 2003).

2.1.2.3 Projective Tests

Projective tests A group of tests usually consisting of a standard fixed set of stimuli that are presented to clients, but which are ambiguous enough for clients to put their own interpretation on what the stimuli represent.

This group of tests usually consists of a standard fixed set of stimuli that are presented to clients but are ambiguous enough for clients to put their own interpretation on what the stimuli represent. This often allows for considerable variation in responses between clients, as well as considerable variation between clinicians in how the responses should be interpreted. The most widely used of the projective tests are the Rorschach Inkblot Test, the Thematic Apperception Test (TAT) and the Sentence Completion Test. Projective tests were originally based on the psychodynamic view that people's intentions and desires are largely unconscious and must be inferred indirectly (Dosajh, 1996). Most projective tests were designed during the mid-twentieth century and were extremely popular for assessment purposes right up to the turn of the century. However, as we shall see below, because they are open-ended tests that allow considerable variation in client responding, they are significantly less reliable and valid than more structured tests. Nevertheless, even though their popularity has declined in recent years (Piotrowski, Belter & Keller, 1998), many clinicians still use these types of tests to give them some first impressions of a client's symptoms or as part of a larger battery of assessment procedures.

Rorschach Inkblot Test A projective personality test using inkblots by dropping ink onto paper and then folding the paper in half to create a symmetrical image.

The *Rorschach Inkblot Test* was originally developed by the Swiss psychiatrist Hermann Rorschach. He created numerous inkblots by dropping ink onto paper and then folding the paper in half to create a symmetrical image. He discovered that everyone he showed them to saw designs and shapes in the blots, and he assumed that their responses revealed information about the individual's psychological condition. Most versions of the Rorschach Inkblot Test now use around 10 official inkblots of which five are black ink on white, two are black and red ink on white, and three are multicoloured; examples of a black and white and multicoloured inkblot are given in Figure 2.2. Clinicians will have available a highly structured scoring system (e.g. Exner & Weiner, 1995) that allows them to compare the scores clients provide with a set of standardized personality norms, which may provide indications of underlying psychopathology. However, if the test is used as a formal assessment procedure, it is still heavily dependent on the clinician's interpretation of the client's responses. For example, if certain themes keep appearing in the client's responses, they may provide evidence of underlying conflicts, such as the repeated perception of eyes on the inkblots perhaps providing evidence of paranoia the clinician may want to explore further. Nevertheless, the Rorschach Test can be a valid and reliable test for the detection of thought disorders that may

be indicative of schizophrenia or people at risk of developing schizophrenia (Lilienfeld, Wood & Garb, 2000; Viglione, 1999).

The *Thematic Apperception Test (TAT)* is a projective personality test consisting of 30 black and white pictures of people in vague or ambiguous situations (Morgan & Murray,

Thematic Apperception Test (TAT) A projective personality test consisting of 30 black and white pictures of people in vague or ambiguous situations.

1935). Clients are asked to create a dramatic story around the picture, describing what they think is happening in the picture, what events preceded it, what the individuals in the picture are saying, thinking or feeling, and what the outcome of the situation is likely to be. Many clinicians claim that this test is particularly useful for eliciting information about whether the client is depressed, has suicidal thoughts or strong aggressive impulses (Rapaport, Gill & Shaefer, 1968). Clients usually identify with one of the characters in the pictures (known as the 'hero'), and the picture then serves as a vehicle for clients to describe their own feelings and emotions as if they were involved in the ambiguous scene. The TAT may also allow clinicians to determine clients' expectations about relationships with peers, parents, other authority figures and romantic partners. It can also be a useful tool after a client has been formally diagnosed in matching him or her with a suitable form of psychotherapy. The TAT has also been used to evaluate the motivations and attitudes of individuals who have been accused of violent crimes (Kim, Cogan, Carter & Porcerelli, 2005).

Finally, the *Sentence Completion Test* is a useful open-ended assessment test that was first developed in the 1920s. It provides clients with the first part of an uncompleted sentence, such as 'I like . . .',

Sentence completion test An open-ended projective personality test that provides clients with the first part of an uncompleted sentence which they complete with words of their own.

'I think of myself as . . .', 'I feel guilty when . . .', which clients then complete with words of their own. This test allows clinicians to identify topics that can be further explored with clients, and can also help to identify ways in which an individual's psychopathology might bias his or her thinking and the way he or she processes information. Research Methods in Clinical Psychology Box 2.1 shows how the Sentence Completion Test has been used to identify trauma-relevant thinking biases in combat veterans with post-traumatic stress disorder (Kimble, Kaufman, Leonard, Nestor et al., 2002). Such thinking biases help to maintain emotional problems, and using the sentence completion task can help the clinician to identify ways of thinking that can be targeted during treatment.

As we mentioned earlier, the popularity of projective tests has declined steadily over the years. There are a number of reasons for this. (1) Such tests are mainly based on revealing information that is relevant to psychodynamic approaches to psychopathology, and the role of psychodynamic approaches in the assessment and treatment of psychopathology has itself declined over the past 30 years. (2) Even though standardized procedures for scoring projective tests have developed over recent years, the reliability of such tests is still disappointingly low (Lilienfeld, Wood & Garb, 2000), and different clinicians will often interpret the same responses in quite different ways. (3) Even with highly standardized scoring methods, some projective tests such as the Rorschach

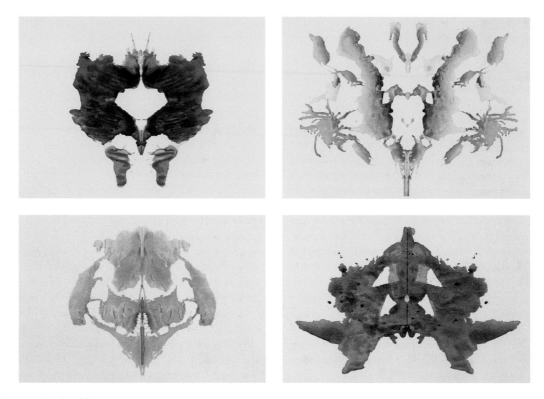

Figure 2.2 *The Rorschach Inkblot Test*
The Rorschach Inkblot Test usually consists of ten official inkblots. Five inkblots are black ink on white. Two are black and red ink on white. Three are multicoloured. The pictures above give examples of a black and white inkblot, a black and red inkblot and two multicoloured inkblots. The clinician shows the inkblots in a particular order and asks the client: 'What might this be?' (a free association phase). After the patient has seen and responded to all the inkblots, the clinician then presents them again one by one to study (the inquiry phase). The client is asked to list everything they see in each blot, where they see it, and what there is in the blot that makes it look like that. The blot can also be rotated. The clinician also times the patient, which then factors into the overall assessment.

Methods of interpretation differ. The most widely used method in the United States is based on the work of John E. Exner (Exner & Weiner, 1995). In this system, responses are scored systematically with reference to their level of vagueness or synthesis of multiple images in the blot, the location of the response, which of a variety of determinants is used to produce the response (for example, whether the shape of the inkblot, its colour, or its texture is primary in making it look like what it is said to resemble), the form quality of the response (to what extent a response is faithful to how the actual inkblot looks), the contents of the response (what the respondent actually sees in the blot), the degree of mental organizing activity that is involved in producing the response, and any illogical, incongruous or incoherent aspects of responses.

Test often result in psychopathology being inferred when other evidence for such a conclusion is sparse. For example, Hamel, Shaffer and Erdberg (2000) administered the Rorschach Test to 100 schoolchildren, none of whom had any history of mental health problems. However, the results of the test were interpreted in almost all cases as evidence of faulty reasoning that might be indicative of schizophrenia or mood disorder. (4) Projective tests such as the TAT have intrinsic cultural biases. For instance, in the traditional set of TAT pictures, there are no ethnic minority

Figure 2.3 *(left) The Thematic Apperception Test (TAT)*
The Thematic Apperception Test consists of 30 black and white pictures similar to the one shown left. The client is asked to create a dramatic story around the picture. Clients will usually identify with one of the characters in the picture, which enables them to express their own feelings and emotions as if they were involved in the scene.

RESEARCH METHODS IN CLINICAL PSYCHOLOGY BOX 2.1

The Sentence Completion Test

The sentence completion task is an open-ended assessment test that provides clients with the first part of a sentence which they have to complete in their own words. This is a useful projective test that allows clinicians to identify topics that are important to the client, and to identify any biases in the way that a client tends to think about things. For example, incomplete sentences such as 'My greatest fear . . .', 'I feel . . .', 'I need . . .' etc. can give the clinician an insight into some of the client's emotional responses. Similarly, questions such as 'My father . . .', 'Other pupils . . .', 'Most girls . . .' will provide some insight into the client's feelings about others.

The sentence completion task can also be used successfully as an important research tool. For example, Kimble, Kaufman, Leonard, Nestor et al. (2002) used a sentence completion task to assess interpretation biases in combat veterans who were diagnosed with post-traumatic stress disorder (PTSD) (see Chapter 5, section 5.6). They gave their participants 33 sentences to complete. Each item was generated so that it could be completed with words of military or non-military content. Examples included:

'He was almost hit by a . . .'
'The night sky was full of . . .'
'The air was heavy with the smell of . . .'
'The silence was broken by the . . .'

For example, 'He was almost hit by a . . .' could be completed with the word 'rock' or the word 'bullet'. Figure 1 shows that

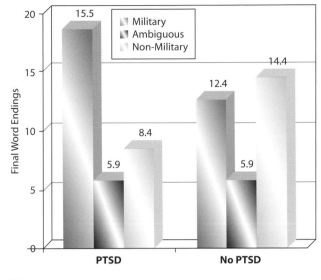

Figure 1

veterans with PTSD completed sentences with significantly more 'war' or trauma-relevant words than veterans without PTSD. These findings suggest that individuals diagnosed with PTSD have biases in the accessibility, encoding and retrieval of trauma-relevant information, and that sentence completion tasks of this kind might help to differentiate individuals with a diagnosable mental health condition from those without.

characters even though clients are expected to identify with one of the characters in the picture. In some cases this limitation has been overcome by developing more contemporary TAT pictures that contain figures for ethnic minorities (Costantino, Flanagan & Malgady, 2001). Finally, (5) most projective tests are labour-intensive for the limited amount of objective information they provide. Clinicians need extensive training in order to administer tests such as the Rorschach and TAT, and they are time-consuming to administer, interpret and score. Given the development of more objective and easily scored inventories, this has inevitably led to a decline in the popularity of projective tests.

2.1.2.4 Intelligence Tests

Intelligence tests are regularly used by clinicians in a variety of settings and for a variety of reasons. *IQ (intelligence quotient) tests*, as they are

IQ (intelligence quotient) tests
Intelligence tests used as a means of estimating intellectual ability.

now generally known, were first devised in the early part of the twentieth century as a means of comparing intellectual ability in specific groups of people (e.g. army recruits). Arguably the first IQ test was that produced by the French psychologist Alfred Binet in 1905, which was a test that purported to measure intelligence across a number of verbal and non-verbal skills. From early tests such as this there are now over 100 tests of intelligence available, most of which are standardized to have a score of 100 as the mean and a score of 15 or 16 as the standard deviation (see Figure 1.3). As you can see from Figure 1.3, 68 per cent of the population will score between 84 and 116 (one standard deviation from the mean) on IQ tests, and around 2–3 per cent of the population will have IQ scores less than 2 standard deviations from the mean (e.g. less than 70). Because of their continued development over the previous 100 years, IQ tests have *high internal consistency* (i.e. a client will score roughly the same on different items that measure the same ability), *high test-retest reliability* (i.e. a client who takes the same test twice but some months or years apart will achieve roughly the same score both times) and *good validity* (i.e. the tests are good at predicting intellectual ability or future educational performance) (Sparrow & Davis, 2000).

Intelligence tests are used by clinicians in a number of contexts. For example, (1) they are used with other measures of ability to diagnose intellectual and learning disabilities. The cardinal DSM-IV-TR diagnostic criterion for Mental Retardation is based primarily on an IQ score two standard deviations below the mean (i.e. an IQ score of less than 70; see Chapter 16). (2) IQ tests are also used to try to assess the needs of individuals with learning, developmental or intellectual disabilities so that support can be provided in any specific areas of need. Tests that provide scores on a range of different ability scales are best suited for this purpose, and one such example is the *Wechsler Adult Intelligence Scale*, now in its third edition (WAIS-III) (Wechsler, 2004). This contains scales that measure vocabulary, arithmetic ability, digit span, information comprehension, letter–number sequencing, picture completion ability, reasoning ability, symbol search and object assembly ability. Tests such as the WAIS-III can also be used as part of a battery of tests to assess whether an individual is eligible for special educational needs and provides information that will suggest strategies, services and supports to optimize the individual's functioning within society. (3) Intelligence tests are frequently used as part of a battery of assessments used in neurological evaluations (see Chapter 14, section 14.1.2). They can help to detect when a client has brain damage caused by traumatic injury or cerebral infection or a degenerative brain disorder such as Alzheimer's disease.

Wechsler Adult Intelligence Scale (WAIS)
An intelligence test containing scales that measure vocabulary, arithmetic ability, digit span, information comprehension, letter–number sequencing, picture completion ability, reasoning ability, symbol search and object assembly ability.

However, despite their practical benefits across a range of clinical contexts, intelligence tests still have a number of limitations.

First, intelligence is an inferred construct. That is, it does not objectively exist in the same way that physical attributes such as heart rate or blood pressure exist, but is a hypothetical construct that has been developed by psychologists to help us try to understand how well individuals can adapt to various problems. This has led some sceptical psychologists to suggest that there is no clear definition of intelligence but that 'intelligence is merely what IQ tests measure'!

Secondly, if that latter statement is true, then our conception of whether someone is intelligent or not will depend on the reliability and validity of the individual IQ test we use to measure his or her intelligence, and this can raise some difficulties. For example, many IQ tests are culturally biased and appear to be based on middle-class, majority ethnic background views of what is adaptive (Gopaul-McNichol & Armour-Thomas, 2002), so they will disadvantage those from lower socioeconomic backgrounds or from ethnic minorities. While attempts have been made over the years to eradicate cultural bias of this kind, it is difficult to eliminate it entirely. For instance, a test question may ask whether a cup goes with a bowl, a spoon or a saucer, but children from a low socioeconomic background may never have drunk from a cup with a saucer, and may be more likely to associate a cup or mug with a spoon. Even so, because it is widely known that some ethnic minorities perform relatively poorly on IQ tests, this knowledge alone can interfere with test performance in that group (Spencer, Steele & Quinn, 1999).

Thirdly, intelligence tests mainly tend to be rather 'static' tests of intellectual ability and provide a snapshot of ability at any point in time. What they do not usually appear to measure is individuals' capacity to learn or their potential to acquire new cognitive abilities (Grigorenko & Sternberg, 1998).

Fourthly, many researchers argue that our current conception of intelligence as measured by IQ tests is too narrow. There are many other skills that are not usually included in our conceptions of and measures of intelligence, and these include music ability,

Plate 2.1 *The Wechsler Adult Intelligence Scale (WAIS-III)*
The WAIS-III is one of the tests of intellectual ability most commonly used by clinicians. It comprises a range of verbal and performance tests that measure intellectual ability on a variety of sub-scales including vocabulary, arithmetic ability, digit span, information comprehension, letter–number sequencing, picture completion ability, reasoning ability, symbol search and object assembly ability.

Plate 2.2 *Bend it like Beckham*
Is David Beckham's ability to bend a free kick over a defensive wall and past a goalkeeper as much an intelligent skill as arithmetic or verbal ability?

physical skill, the ability to perceive, understand and express emotion (known as 'emotional intelligence') and the ability to implement solutions to real-world problems (Gardner, 1998; Mayer, Salovey & Caruso, 2000). For example, is David Beckham's ability to bend a free kick over a wall of defenders and past a goalkeeper as much an intelligent skill as arithmetic or verbal ability?

2.1.2.5 Neurological Impairment Tests

Many psychological and cognitive problems are caused not by problematic life experiences or by dysfunctional ways of thinking but by damage to the structure and functioning of the brain. Such damage to the brain can be caused by traumatic injury (such as might be received in a car accident), cardiovascular accidents such as a stroke, cerebral infection (such as meningitis), a brain tumour, or they can be the result of a degenerative brain disorder such as Alzheimer's disease. In such cases damage to the brain can cause both changes in personality (e.g. change someone from a passive into an aggressive individual) and deficits in cognitive functioning depending on the areas of the brain that are affected. These issues are discussed more thoroughly in Chapter 14, but at this point we will mention the value of neurological assessment tests in enabling clinicians to determine the nature of any cognitive deficits (e.g. memory deficits, deficits in language skills), to identify whether such deficits are the result of brain damage, and in many cases to identify the area of the brain that has been affected.

Clinicians will usually employ a battery of tests when assessing for possible neurological deficits. These may include EEG analyses, brain scans such as PET scans and fMRI scans (see next section), blood tests (to assess potential inherited or genetic components to a disorder) and chemical analyses of cerebrospinal fluids. But of equal importance in this overall assessment is the use of neurological tests that measure cognitive, perceptual and motor performance as indicators of underlying brain dysfunction (Rao, 2000). The rationale behind the use of such neurological tests is that different psychological functions (such as motor skills, memory, language, planning and executive functioning) are localized in different areas of the brain (see Table 14.2), so discovering a specific cognitive deficit can help to identify the area of the brain where any damage may be localized.

In addition, collecting such information is also crucial for identifying the focus of rehabilitation strategies and in patient care and planning for the client (Veitch & Oddy, 2008). Tests that are commonly used by clinical neuropsychologists in this respect are the *Adult Memory and Information Processing Battery (AMIPB)* (Coughlan & Hollows, 1985), the *Halstead-Reitan Neuropsychological Test Battery*

> **Adult Memory and Information Processing Battery (AMIPB)**   An assessment method comprising two tests of speed of information processing, verbal memory tests (list learning and story recall), and visual memory tests (design learning and figure recall).

> **Halstead-Reitan Neuropsychological Test Battery**   A common neuropsychological test used in the USA which has been compiled to evaluate brain and nervous system functioning across a fixed set of eight tests. The tests evaluate function across visual, auditory and tactile input, verbal communication, spatial and sequential perception, the ability to analyse information, and the ability to form mental concepts, make judgements, control motor output and to attend to and memorize stimuli.

(Broshek & Barth, 2000) and the *Mini Mental State Examination (MMSE)*. Each of these tests is described in more detail in Chapter 14 (section 14.1.2). Their administration and scoring are an important part of the day-to-day tasks undertaken by clinical neuropsychologists (Veitch & Oddy, 2008; see 'A Week in the Life of a Clinical Psychologist', Chapter 14, p. 519).

> **Mini Mental State Examination (MMSE)**
> A structured test that takes 10 minutes to administer and can provide reliable information on a client's overall levels of cognitive and mental functioning.

2.1.3 Biologically Based Assessments

In many cases information about biological structures and biological functioning can help to inform the assessment and diagnosis of psychological problems. There are two main types of biologically based assessment that we will describe here, psychophysiological tests and brain imaging.

2.1.3.1 Psychophysiological Tests

There are a number of psychophysiological tests that can be used to provide information about potential psychological problems. For example, anxiety causes increased activity in the sympathetic nervous system and is regularly accompanied by changes in physiological measures such as heart rate, blood pressure, body temperature and electrodermal responding. Similarly, anger is usually associated with physiological changes in blood pressure and heart rate. So, psychophysiological tests can provide useful information related to emotionally based psychological problems.

One important measure of physiological activity is *electrodermal responding*, sometimes known as the galvanic skin response (GSR) or skin conductance response (SCR). Emotional responses such as anxiety, fear or anger increase sweat-gland activity, and changes in this activity can be recorded with the use of electrodes that would normally be attached to the fingers of the participant. Changes in skin conductance caused by sweat-gland activity can then be measured as changes on a polygraph – a pen that records changes in skin conductance on a continually moving roll of graph paper (see Plate 2.3). Skin conductance measures have been used in a variety of contexts to assess: (1) the kinds of stimuli or events that elicit anxiety in a client (Cuthbert, Lang, Strauss, Drobes et al., 2003; Alpers, Wilhelm & Roth, 2005); (2) autonomic or physiological reactivity in certain diagnostic groups (e.g. individuals diagnosed with antisocial personality disorder tend to have less reactive autonomic nervous systems than non-clinical samples) (Lykken, 1995); (3) the ability of clients to cope following treatment interventions (Bobadilla & Taylor, 2007; Grillon, Cordova, Morgan, Charney & Davis, 2004); and (4) whether autonomic indices of anxiety or arousal correspond with appropriate changes in behaviour (e.g. in panic disorder, avoidance responses may be triggered by physiological changes indicative of anxiety) (Karekla, Forsyth & Kelly, 2004).

> **Electrodermal responding**
> A psychophysiological measure which uses electrodes attached to the fingers of participants to test emotional responses such as anxiety, fear or anger by measuring changes in sweat gland activity.

Plate 2.3
The polygraph is a device used to measure changes in physiological responding that may indicate emotional changes such as anxiety, fear or anger. The polygraph works by recording physiological measures (such as skin conductance or heart rate) on a continually moving roll of graph paper. In more recent times, these measures can be analysed directly by computer and the output displayed on the computer screen.

specific preset questions. This technique has often been used in criminal prosecutions and employment screening – especially in the US (Krapohi, 2002). However, while a polygraph may detect anxiety or arousal caused by the participant lying, it is also likely to detect changes in arousal caused by factors other than lying (e.g. the question simply being a stressful or unusual one), and so may represent an anxious – but innocent – participant as one who may appear to be guilty (Raskin & Honts, 2002). As a result, findings from lie detector tests in the US are now used significantly less as evidence of criminal guilt (Daniels, 2002).

Finally, another important psychophysiological assessment measure is the *electroencephalogram (EEG)*. This involves electrodes being attached to the scalp that record underlying electrical activity and can help to localize unusual brain patterns in different areas of the brain. Abnormal electrical patterns detected by EEG can indicate a number of problems, including epilepsy, brain tumours or brain injury (Cuthill & Espie, 2005).

> **Electroencephalogram (EEG)**
> A psychophysiological assessment measure which involves electrodes being attached to the scalp that record underlying electrical activity and can help to localize unusual brain patterns in different areas of the brain.

2.1.3.2 Neuroimaging Techniques

Many behavioural, cognitive and psychological problems may be linked to abnormalities in brain functioning. While neurological tests can indicate that possible brain dysfunction may be involved, we will usually need to use techniques that provide images of the brain to confirm this. There are a range of neuroimaging or brain imaging techniques now available. Some provide the clinician with anatomical and structural information about the brain (e.g. whether a brain tumour is present), while others provide information about brain activity and brain functioning (e.g. whether specific brain areas are fully functioning).

Computerized axial tomography or *CAT* scan machines are sophisticated versions of X-ray machines that can be used to form a 3-dimensional picture of the brain. Figure 2.4 shows a CAT scan machine. The patient lies down on a platform which then moves through a large doughnut-like ring. The ring turns so that with each turn a narrow 'slice' of the brain is X-rayed, and a computer uses this information to construct 2-dimensional cross-sections of the brain. These many separate images can also be combined to provide a 3-dimensional image of the brain. CAT scan images can help to detect abnormal growths in the brain such as tumours or enlargement of the ventricles in the brain that can indicate tissue degeneration typical of dementia or schizophrenia.

> **Computerized axial tomography (CAT)**
> A neuroimaging technique which uses sophisticated versions of X-ray machines and can be used to form a three-dimensional picture of the brain.

Positron emission tomography or *PET* scans allow measurement of both brain structure and function. A PET scan can provide pictures of

> **Positron emission tomography (PET)**
> A neuroimaging technique which scans to allow measurement of both brain structure and function by utilizing radiation emitted from the participant to develop images.

> **Electromyogram (EMG)**
> A psychophysiological measurement technique that measures the electrical activity in muscles.

> **Electrocardiogram (ECG)**
> A psychophysiological measurement technique used for measuring heart rate.

Other useful examples of psychophysiological measurement techniques include the *electromyogram (EMG)*, which measures the electrical activity in muscles, and the *electrocardiogram (ECG)* for measuring heart rate. Although measures such as electrodermal responding can indicate emotional changes indicative of anxiety, fear or anger, they are not always foolproof. Rather than specifically indicating the presence of these discrete emotions, skin conductance is more properly an indicator of general physiological arousal, and this can be caused by a variety of factors, including simply orienting towards or attending to an event (Siddle, 1983). This issue is nowhere better illustrated than in the history of the use of lie detectors. *Lie detectors* use changes in autonomic responding in an attempt to identify whether an individual is lying in response to

> **Lie detector** A psychophysiological test which uses changes in autonomic responding in an attempt to identify whether an individual is lying in response to specific preset questions.

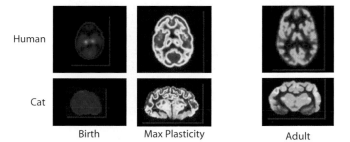

Figure 2.5 *Using PET scans to identify the metabolic maturation of human and cat brains*
The top row provides PET images of glucose metabolism at birth (left), at 6 years of age (middle), and in the young adult (right). Red is the highest metabolic rate with lower values in orange, yellow, green, blue and purple. This sequence shows that the highest metabolic rate occurs at 6 years. The buttom row shows the same temporal sequence in the metabolic maturation of the cat brain.

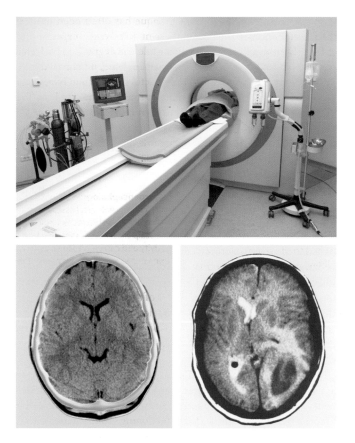

Figure 2.4 *Computerized axial tomography or 'CAT' scan*
The top picture shows a CAT scan machine. The client lies down on the platform with their head positioned within the large doughnut-like ring. The ring turns to X-ray individual thin 'slices' of the brain, and a computer is used to turn these individual images into either a 2-dimensional or 3-dimensional picture of the brain. The lower picture shows an example CAT scan of a 'slice' of a normal brain next to one that reveals a large brain tumour (the darker area).

tool for assessing cognitive functioning and provides information about brain functioning both in degenerative diseases such as Alzheimer's disease and in intellectual disabilities such as Down's Syndrome. In Chapter 7, Figure 7.2 provides an example of the use of PET scans in assessing brain functioning in schizophrenia.

One further imaging technique that has been developed is known as ***magnetic resonance imaging***, or ***MRI***. MRI scanning involves the participant being placed inside a large circular magnet which causes the hydrogen atoms in the body to move. This produces an electromagnetic signal that is converted by the scanner's computer into visual pictures of the brain. Pictures of the brain produced by MRI scanning are highly detailed and allow the detection of even the smallest of lesions or tumours. A more recent development of MRI technology is known as ***functional magnetic resonance imaging***, or ***fMRI***. This allows the clinician to take brain images so quickly that tiny changes in brain metabolism can be detected and can provide minute-to-minute information about actual brain activity. This technology is now being used to study and compare the characteristics of normal, diseased and injured brains, and to assess the risks involved in surgery or other invasive treatments. Figure 14.2 in Chapter 14 provides an example of fMRI scans showing brain activation during a motor task in individuals with HIV-associated dementia and non-clinical control participants.

Magnetic resonance imaging (MRI)
A neuroimaging technique which involves the participant being placed inside a large circular magnet that causes the hydrogen atoms in the body to move. This produces an electromagnetic signal that is converted by the scanner's computer into visual pictures of the brain.

Functional magnetic resonance imaging (fMRI)   A development of MRI technology which allows the clinician to take brain images so quickly that tiny changes in brain metabolism can be detected and can provide minute-to-minute information about actual brain activity.

chemical activity in the brain either at rest or when the participant is undertaking cognitive tasks such as language, learning, remembering or sensory processing. The PET scanner utilizes radiation emitted from the participant to develop images. Participants are given a minute amount of a radioactive drug that closely resembles a natural substance used by the body. Gamma radiation produced by the radioactive drug is detected by the PET scanner and shows in fine detail the metabolism of glucose in the brain. The PET scanner's computer uses this detail to produce colour pictures of the functioning brain. Brightly coloured areas represent areas of the brain where metabolic rates are high and represent high levels of brain activity.

Figure 2.5 shows how PET scans highlight areas of brain activity. Because the PET scan provides images of the brain indicating both levels of activity and areas of activity, it is a useful

As you can see from this section, the use of modern brain imaging technology has been invaluable in providing detailed evidence of brain abnormalities and dysfunction in relation to a whole range of psychopathology problems.

2.1.4 Clinical Observation

A further method of collecting useful clinical information is by direct observation of a client's behaviour. This can supplement information from interviews and psychological tests and often allows an assessment of behaviour in its natural context, such as the home, school classroom or community setting. Direct observation can provide an objective assessment of the *frequency* of particular behaviours (e.g. aggressive behaviours) when this may not be so easily obtained from reports given by clients themselves, their family or carers. It also allows behaviour to be assessed in the context of events that *precede* the behaviour (and so may trigger the problem behaviour) and events that immediately *follow* the behaviour (and may represent the consequences of the behaviour that reinforce its occurrence). In Chapter 16, Treatment in Practice Box 16.1 provides a detailed example of how an observational technique can be used to identify what factors might be triggering and maintaining challenging behaviour in an individual with intellectual disabilities. This example used an *ABC chart* that requires the observer to note what happens before the

ABC chart An observation method that requires the observer to note what happens before the target behaviour occurs (A), what the individual did (B), and what the consequences of the behaviour were (C).

target behaviour occurs (**A**), what the individual did (**B**) and what the consequences of the behaviour were (**C**). Focus Point 2.1 provides some examples of how behaviours and events can be coded when undertaking a clinical observation (Nock & Kurtz, 2005). Which type of coding method you use will depend largely on what you want to find out (e.g. do you just want to find out how frequently a behaviour occurs, or do you want to know more about the context in which a behaviour is emitted?).

There are a number of advantages to using observational techniques. First, if the observer is appropriately trained, observation can provide important objective measures of the frequency of behaviours and those events that precede and follow them. The latter information will often provide an insight into the purpose the problematic behaviour serves (e.g. in Treatment in Practice Box 16.1, systematic observation reveals that the purpose of Andy's self-injurious behaviour is to enable him to be removed from noisy and crowded situations) (Kazdin, 2001; Miltenberger, 1997). Second, observational data have greater external or **ecological validity** than self-reports or other forms of testing because such data provide a measurement of the behaviour as it is actu-

Ecological validity The extent to which conditions simulated in the laboratory reflect real-life conditions.

ally occurring in a context. Third, observation of behaviour in a context can often suggest workable answers to problem behaviour, as can clearly be seen in Treatment in Practice Box 16.1. Once it was established that Andy's self-injurious behaviour was functioning to get him removed from a stressful environment, staff could look out for signs that he was becoming

FOCUS POINT **2.1**

Observational coding forms

Below are four different types of observational coding forms. The one that a clinician would use would depend on the type of data he or she wants to collect.

Figure 1 is a simple coding scheme in which the observer merely describes the behaviours she observes plus the antecedents and consequences of these behaviours. Because the observer is describing the behaviours in her own words, there is likely to be poor inter-rater reliability using this scheme.

Situation	Behaviour	Antecedents	Consequences
Sitting in circle time 9:00 am	Slapped peer sitting immediately to his left with open hand	None observed	Peer and teacher both ignored
9:03 am	Yelled 'NO!' at teacher and remained seated	Teacher gave specific command for all students to return to their seats	Teacher ignored, students laughed
9:05 am	Got up and sat in seat	Peer came over to him and whispered in his ear	Teacher gave specific, labelled praise to target child

Figure 1 *Sample descriptive coding form*

Behaviour	Frequency
Fidgeting in seat	IIIII
Getting out of seat	III
Running around classroom	I
Interrupting others	IIII
Physical aggression toward peers	I
Physical aggression toward teachers	
Verbal threats of aggression toward peers	II
Verbal threat of aggression toward teachers	I

Figure 2 *Sample checklist for coding child behaviour*

Behaviours	30″	1′ 30″	2′ 30″	3′ 30″	4′ 30″	5′ 30″	6′ 30″	7′ 30″	8′ 30″	9′ 30″	10′
Inappropriate Movement	✓			✓																	
Inattention			✓	✓					✓	✓							✓	✓	✓	✓	✓
Physical Aggression	✓	✓																			
Self-Injurious Behaviour						✓	✓								✓						
(continued)																					

Figure 3 *Sample interval coding form*

Target Behaviour	Antecedents	Consequences						Comments
		Teacher +	Teacher −	Teacher 0	Peer +	Peer −	Peer 0	
Physical Aggression	Teacher left room Child took his toy		I	IIIIII	IIIIII I			
	None observed			I	I			
Positive Social Interaction	Teacher specific prompt			IIIII			IIIII	
	None observed			III			III	
(continued)								

Figure 4 *Sample interval coding form with antecedents, behaviours and consequences*

Figure 2 provides a coding system that simply measures the frequency of selected behaviours. **Figure 3** extends this by providing the frequency of selected behaviours over a period of time. This will allow the clinician to see if there is anything interesting in the sequence or order that behaviours are emitted.

Finally, **Figure 4** provides a coding scheme that allows the recording of quite complex information, including the behaviour of the client in relation to others in the situation, such as teacher and peers.

Source: Nock & Kurtz (2005).

overstimulated and remove him from the room before he began to injure himself.

Having listed the advantages of clinical observation, its drawbacks should now be mentioned. First, it is one of the more time-consuming forms of assessment, not just in terms of the amount of time required to simply observe behaviour, but also in terms of the amount of time needed to properly train observers in the use of the various coding systems (e.g. Abikoff, Gittelman & Klein, 1980) (see Focus Point 2.1). This is especially so if members of the client's family need to be trained to make systematic observations in the home setting. Secondly, observation will usually take place in a specific setting (e.g. the school classroom or the home), and behaviour in this specific context may not be typical of behaviour in other contexts (Nock & Kurtz, 2005). Thirdly, the presence of an observer may lead those involved in the observation setting to behave differently to how they would normally behave (Kazdin, 1978; Skinner, Dittmer & Howell, 2000), and this may often be the case with children, who will show dramatic improvements in behaviour when they are aware they are being observed. This problem can often be overcome by video-recording behaviour without an observer present and then analysing this at a later time.

Analogue observations Clinical observations carried out in a controlled environment that allows surreptitious observation of the client.

Similarly, the clinician may want to undertake *analogue observations* in a controlled environment that allows surreptitious observation of the client. For example, children can be observed interacting in a playroom while the observer is situated behind a two-way mirror. Fourthly, unless observers are properly trained in the coding methods used, there may be poor inter-observer reliability (Kamphaus & Frick, 2002). That is, two different observers assessing the same participant may focus on quite different aspects of behaviour and context, and arrive at quite different conclusions about the frequency and causes of behaviour. Fifthly, as in all observational procedures, the data can be influenced by the observer's expectations. Observer expectations can cause biases in the way that information is viewed and recorded, and this can be caused by the theoretical orientation of the observer and what he or she already knows about the person being observed.

Self-observation A form of clinical observation that involves asking clients to observe and record their own behaviour, perhaps by using a diary or a palmtop computer to note when certain behaviours or thoughts occur and in what contexts they occur.

Self-monitoring A form of clinical observation which involves asking clients to observe and record their own behaviour, to note when certain behaviours or thoughts occur, and in what contexts they occur.

One final form of clinical observation that is frequently used is known as *self-observation* or *self-monitoring*. This involves asking clients to observe and record their own behaviour, perhaps by using a diary or a palm-top computer to note when certain behaviours or thoughts occur and in what contexts they occur. This has the benefit of collecting data in real time and overcomes problems associated with poor and biased recall of behaviour and events when using retrospective recall methods (Strongman & Russell, 1986). The increasing use of electronic diaries for self-observation

has come to be known as *ecological momentary assessment (EMA)* (Stone & Shiffman, 1994). Such methods have been used to gather information about client's day-to-day experiences, to aid diagnosis, to plan treatment and to evaluate the effectiveness of treatment (Piasecki, Hufford, Solham & Trull, 2007).

In addition, self-monitoring itself can have beneficial effects on behaviour even prior to any attempts at intervention. For example, many problematic behaviours (e.g. smoking, illicit drug use, excessive eating) can occur without the individual being aware of how frequently they happen and in what circumstances they happen, and self-monitoring can begin to provide some self-knowledge that can be acted on by the individual. As a result, self-monitoring often has the effect of increasing the frequency of desirable behaviours and decreasing the frequency of undesirable behaviours (McFall & Hammen, 1971). This is known as *reactivity*, and clinicians can often take advantage of this process to facilitate behaviour change.

Ecological momentary assessment (EMA) The use of diaries for self-observation or self-monitoring, perhaps by using an electronic diary or a palmtop computer.

Reactivity The effect of increasing the frequency of desirable behaviours and decreasing the frequency of undesirable behaviours as a result of self-monitoring.

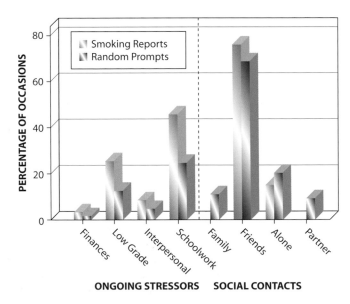

Figure 2.6 *Self-monitoring of smoking behaviour*
This figure shows the results of a smoking self-monitoring task undertaken by a college student. The student was asked to record what they were doing each time a cigarette was smoked and each time they were given random prompts by a palm-top computer. Comparing the base rates (random prompts) with smoking rates when in various situations allows the clinician to see whether certain situations are triggers for smoking. In this case comparisons suggest that low grades and doing schoolwork represent triggers for smoking, whereas being with family or partner usually elicits no cigarette smoking.
Source: Piasecki, Hufford, Solham & Trull (2007).

2.1.5 The Reliability and Validity of Assessment Methods

In order for assessment methods to provide objective information about clients, we need to be sure about two things. First, we need to be sure that the method has high *reliability*. That is, that the method will still provide the same result when used by different clinicians on different occasions. Second, we need to be sure that the assessment has *validity*. That is, that it actually does measure what it claims to measure (e.g. if it is a test measuring anxiety, then scores on the test should correlate well with other ways of measuring anxiety).

Reliability The extent that an assessment method will still provide the same result when used by different clinicians on different occasions.

Validity The extent that an assessment method actually does measure what it claims to be measuring.

2.1.5.1 Reliability

Reliability refers to how consistently an assessment method will produce the same results, and reliability can be affected by a number of different factors. First, *test-retest reliability* refers to the extent that the test will produce roughly similar results when the test is given to the same person several weeks or even months apart (as long as no treatments or interventions have occurred in between). As we indicated earlier, most psychological tests are based on the assumption that most traits and personal characteristics are relatively stable and can be reliably measured. If the test has high test-retest reliability, when an individual is given the test on two separate occasions, the two scores should be highly correlated.

Test-retest reliability The extent that a test will produce roughly similar results when the test is given to the same person several weeks or even months apart (as long as no treatments or interventions have occurred in between).

Second, *inter-rater reliability* refers to the degree to which two independent clinicians will actually agree when interpreting or scoring a particular test. Most highly structured tests, such as personality inventories, will have high inter-rater validity because the scoring system is clearly defined and there is little room for individual clinician judgements when interpreting the test. However, some other tests have much lower inter-rater reliability, especially where scoring schemes are not rigidly defined: projective tests are one example of this (see above, section 2.1.2.3).

Inter-rater reliability The degree to which two independent clinicians actually agree when interpreting or scoring a particular test.

Thirdly, many assessment tests have multiple items (e.g. personality and trait inventories), and internal consistency within such tests is important. *Internal consistency* refers to the extent to which all the items in the test consistently relate to each other. For example, if there are 20 items in a test, then we would expect scores on each of those 20 items to correlate highly with each other. If one item

Internal consistency The extent to which all the items in a test consistently relate to one another.

doesn't correlate highly with the others, then it may lower the internal consistency of the test. The internal consistency of a questionnaire or inventory can usually be assessed by using a statistical test called *Cronbach's α*. This test will also indicate whether any individual item in the test is significantly reducing the internal consistency of the test (Field, 2005b, pp. 667–676).

Cronbach's α A statistical test which indicates whether any individual item in an assessment test is significantly reducing the internal consistency of the test.

2.1.5.2 Validity

It is important to be sure that an assessment method actually measures what it claims to be measuring, and this is covered by the concept of *test validity*. However, validity is a complex concept, and we will begin by discussing some of the more obvious issues surrounding this problem.

Test validity The extent that an assessment method actually measures what it claims to be measuring.

To determine whether a test actually measures what it claims to measure, we need to establish the *concurrent validity* of the test. That is, we need to see if scores on that test correlate highly with scores from other types of assessment that we know also measure that attribute. For example, the Spider Phobia Questionnaire (SPQ) purports to be a measure of the spider phobic's anxious reaction to spiders (Watts & Sharrock, 1984). In order to establish the concurrent validity of this questionnaire, we might need to be sure that scores actually correlate highly with other measures of spider fear such as the magnitude of physiological anxiety measures taken while the individual is viewing a spider.

Concurrent validity A measure of how highly correlated scores of one test are with scores from other types of assessment that we know also measure that attribute.

A particular assessment method may appear to be valid simply because it has questions which intuitively seem relevant to the trait or characteristic being measured. This is known as *face validity*, but just because a test has items that seem intuitively sensible does not mean that the test is a valid measure of what it claims to be. For example, a questionnaire measuring health anxiety may ask about how frequently the respondent visits a doctor. Although this would be a characteristic of health anxiety, it is also a characteristic of individuals who are genuinely ill or have chronic health problems.

Face validity The idea that a particular assessment method may appear to be valid simply because it has questions which intuitively seem relevant to the trait or characteristic being measured.

For an assessment method to have high *predictive validity* it must be able to help the clinician to predict future behaviour and future symptoms, and so be valuable enough to help with the planning of care, support or treatment for that individual. For example, a good measure of depression would predict that certain types of antidepressant medication will help to alleviate the symptoms. Some assessment measures are predictive in the sense that they help us to understand the kinds of factors

Predictive validity The degree to which an assessment method is able to help the clinician predict future behaviour and future symptoms.

that might pose as risk factors for subsequent psychopathology. For example, assessments that allow us to gather reliable information about childhood abuse and neglect will indicate that such individuals are likely to suffer a range of possible psychopathologies in later life (see Table 15.2).

Finally, **construct validity** is also an important concept in clinical assessment. A construct is a hypothetical or inferred attribute that may not be directly observable or directly measurable. Hypothetical constructs are used frequently in the study of psychopathology to help understand some of the cognitive factors that may cause or maintain mental health problems, and so being able to measure them is a useful tool in diagnosis and subsequent treatment. For example, individuals with obsessive-compulsive disorder (OCD) tend to have inflated conceptions of their own responsibility for preventing harm, and this **inflated responsibility** appears to be an important vulnerability factor in developing OCD (Salkovkis, 1985; Rachman, 1998; see Chapter 5). However, inflated responsibility is not directly observable, but has to be inferred from indirect measures of the individual's behaviour, and so questionnaires such as the Obsessive Beliefs Questionnaire (OBQ) have been developed to measure beliefs about inflated responsibility (see above, p. 34). The more independent evidence that can be gathered to show that a measure of a construct like inflated responsibility is related to other similar measures (e.g. compulsive perseveration at checking tasks, or higher scores in groups diagnosed with OCD than non-clinical control participants), the greater the construct validity of the measure.

> **Construct validity**   Independent evidence showing that a measure of a construct is related to other similar measures.

> **Inflated responsibility**   The belief that one has power which is pivotal to bring about or prevent subjectively crucial negative outcomes. These outcomes are perceived as essential to prevent. They may be actual, that is, having consequences in the real world and/or at a moral level.

2.1.6 Cultural Bias in Assessment

A majority of the most widely used assessment methods have been developed on populations consisting largely of people from a single cultural background and with a limited ethnic profile – that is, most tests have been developed on white European or white American populations. Because of this fact, many tests and assessment methods may be **culturally biased** and provide a less than accurate picture of the mental health of individuals from different cultural backgrounds. As we shall see below, these biases can manifest in many different ways, and clinicians must be aware that such biases may affect both their judgements and their diagnoses.

> **Cultural bias**   The phenomenon of interpreting and judging phenomena in terms particular to one's own culture.

2.1.6.1 Examples of Cultural Anomalies in Assessment and Diagnosis

Cultural anomalies can be identified in a number of different ways. First, some ethnic groups score differently on assessment tests than others. For example, American Asians tend to score significantly higher on most scales of the MMPI than white Americans (McNulty, Graham, Ben-Porath & Stein, 1997). Second, black Americans have a higher rate of diagnosis of disorders such as alcoholism or schizophrenia, whereas white Americans are more likely to be given the less stigmatizing diagnosis of major depression (Garb, 1998). Similarly, it was clear during the 1970s that West Indian immigrants to the UK were significantly more likely to be hospitalized with a diagnosis of schizophrenia than non-immigrants or immigrants from other areas of the world (Cochrane, 1977). While this latter finding might be considered as an ethnic difference in susceptibility to some psychiatric disorders, subsequent studies suggested that many West Indian immigrants who had been hospitalized with a diagnosis of schizophrenia lacked the symptoms commonly regarded as primary indicators of the disorder (Littlewood, 1992). Similar studies suggested that alcoholism was preferentially diagnosed in Irish immigrants to the UK – often independently of a proper assessment of symptoms – and this suggested that popular ethnic stereotypes were often carried over into medical and psychiatric practice (Bagley & Binitie, 1970). As well as the apparent bias in assessment and diagnosis in ethnic minorities, individuals from low socioeconomic groups may also experience bias. For example, many clinicians tend to view clients from lower socioeconomic backgrounds as more disturbed than those from higher socioeconomic groups (Bentacourt & Lopez, 1993; Robins & Regier, 1991), and this may result from clinicians' stereotypes of different socioeconomic groups being able to influence judgements made during unstructured interviews (Garb, 1997).

2.1.6.2 Causes of Cultural Anomalies in Assessment and Diagnosis

The reasons for cultural differences in assessment and diagnosis are multifaceted and not simply due to the fact that most structured assessment tools were developed without regard to cultural diversity. We will discuss some of the factors below. They include: (1) the fact that mental health symptoms may manifest differently in different cultures; (2) language differences between client and clinician; (3) the effect of cultural differences in religion and spiritual beliefs on the expression and perception of psychopathology; (4) the way that cultural differences affect client–clinician relationships; and (5) the role of cultural stereotypes in the perception of 'normality' and 'abnormality' in ethnic groups.

First, we saw in Chapter 1 that stress and mental health problems can actually manifest quite differently in different cultures. Focus Point 1.3 provides two examples of this. Since the diagnosis of psychopathology is based almost entirely on the presence of observable symptoms (especially in DSM-IV-TR), then this will complicate and confuse the process of diagnosis when assessing clients from different cultural backgrounds.

Second, language differences and difficulties can also create biases in assessment and diagnosis. For example, a number of studies have suggested that the diagnosis that a client receives may depend critically on whether that person is assessed in his or her first or second language. Interestingly, when clients are interviewed in their second language, their symptoms are often assessed as significantly *less* severe than if they are interviewed in their first language (Malgady & Constantino, 1998). This appears to be because undertaking an interview in a second language requires clients to organize their thoughts better and therefore appear more coherent. However, this is not the only distortion that can affect assessment and diagnosis. Some other studies have suggested that undertaking a diagnostic interview in the client's second language can also result in symptoms being assessed as significantly *more* severe than if it was in the client's first language. This distortion seems to be caused by the client's misuse of words, hesitations and misunderstanding of questions suggesting a lack of coherent thought (Cuellar, 1998). Even the misunderstanding of colloquialisms when client and clinician are both using their first language can affect assessment. For example, Turner, Hersen and Heiser (2003) point to the use by African Americans of the phrase 'That's all right' when asked about their motives for engaging in certain behaviours. A white American clinician might see this response as the individual condoning what might be seen as pathological behaviour, but in African American speech this phrase is used to mean 'Although I know exactly how to answer you, I have no intention of doing so'.

Third, differences in spiritual or religious beliefs between cultures can affect assessment and diagnosis. For example, behaviour that may be considered as a symptom of psychopathology in one culture may be seen as relatively normal or to have nonpsychological causes in other cultures. We saw in Chapter 1 that some cultural beliefs view unusual behaviour as evidence that the individual is possessed by evil spirits rather than suffering mental health problems. Similarly, in some other cultures visual or auditory hallucinations with a religious content may be considered to be a normal part of religious experience rather than a sign of psychopathology, and the clinician may be faced with a client who is not necessarily exhibiting the early symptoms of schizophrenia but is merely indulging in religious experiences common to his or her culture.

Fourth, when facing a clinician who is a member of an ethnic majority, clients from an ethnic minority are quite likely to experience apprehension and timidity which can affect the way they present themselves at interview as well as the clinician's view of their symptoms (Terrell & Terrell, 1984; Whaley, 1998). For example, apprehension and timidity can often make clients seem incoherent or withdrawn, and this would need to be disentangled from any similar symptoms that were a true manifestation of psychopathology. In more extreme examples, clients from an ethnic minority may be distrustful of clinicians from an ethnic majority. Clinicians in such a position need to be flexible in their approach to assessment and diagnosis and to build a helpful therapeutic relationship by candidly exploring issues of apprehension, timidity and distrust (Whaley, 1997).

Finally, just like any other social interaction, a discussion between a client and clinician can be influenced by racial and ethnic stereotypes. For example, stereotypes can significantly affect how ambiguous information in an interview or a case report is interpreted. In an analogue study, Rosenthal and Berven (1999) gave white American students a vignette providing unfavourable information about a hypothetical client. For half the participants the client was described as white American, for the other half he was described as African American. Subsequently, participants were given more favourable information about the client. For those who believed the client to be white American, the more favourable information influenced their final judgement, but for those who thought he was a black American, the positive information failed to change their original negative view. Common stereotypes held about African American and Hispanic clients by clinicians are that they are violent, hostile and unmotivated for treatment (Pavkov, Lewis & Lyons, 1989; Whaley, 1998), and these perceptions undoubtedly affect their clinical judgements. Garb (1997) called this a ***confirmatory bias***, whereby clinicians ignore information that does not support their initial hypotheses or stereotypes and interpret ambiguous information as supporting their hypotheses. In some cases these biased judgements are the result of direct racism, but more often they are probably manifestations of indirect racism in which clinicians are unaware of their stereotype biases. Whether direct or indirect racism is involved, clinicians have a responsibility to learn about and eradicate their own stereotypes and prejudices, and to provide an honest and unbiased assessment process for clients from ethnic minorities (Hollar, 2001; Adebimpe, 1994).

> **Confirmatory bias**   A clinical bias whereby clinicians ignore information that does not support their initial hypotheses or stereotypes and they interpret ambiguous information as supporting their hypotheses.

2.1.6.3 Addressing Cultural Anomalies in Assessment and Diagnosis

Clinicians need to work hard to eliminate cultural bias from their assessment and diagnostic processes. This issue needs to be addressed at a number of levels, including eradicating bias from existing assessment tools, developing new culture-free assessments, adopting assessment procedures that minimize cultural bias, and training clinicians to identify cultural and racial bias in their own thinking and in the assessment processes that they use.

DSM-IV-TR has made some attempt to identify potential cultural anomalies in diagnosis by including a specific section on culture, age and gender factors within most diagnostic categories. For example, we note in Chapter 15 that when diagnosing conduct disorder, the clinician is asked to take account of the social background of the client. In certain deprived inner-city areas, behaviours characteristic of conduct disorder may be seen as being protective and may represent the norm for that environment. They may also serve an adaptive function in dealing with poverty and the threatening behaviour of others rather than being symptoms of an underlying pathology.

In addition to this, clinicians need proper education and training when required to assess and diagnose minority persons (Hall, 1997; Aklin & Turner, 2006). They would need to understand minorities' construction of self, their understanding of illness and their attitudes to mental health provision and medicine in general (Littlewood, 1992). Sadly, clinicians from minority groups are often as ill-equipped to deal with the diagnosis of clients from minority groups as their non-minority colleagues, largely because they have been trained in the same programmes (Turner, Hersen & Heiser, 2003).

Finally, we can attempt to aspire to culture-free assessment methods by making tests and assessments more valid and reliable. Aklin and Turner (2006) advocate the development of structured interviews to replace the current unstructured interview that is frequently the main vehicle for diagnosis. Support for this view comes from studies indicating there are fewer problems with the assessment of ethnic minorities when structured rather than unstructured methods of interviewing are used (Widiger, 1997).

SUMMARY

You can see from the preceding sections that cultural bias in assessment and diagnosis is a complex and pervasive phenomenon. Clinicians need to be aware of the sources of any cultural bias in these processes, and should be reflective about their own potential stereotypes of ethnic minorities and the effect this might have on their clinical judgements.

SELF-TEST QUESTIONS

- What are the main benefits and limitations of the clinical interview?
- What is a structured interview? Can you provide an example of one?
- What are the advantages of psychological tests as methods of assessment?
- Can you describe a detailed example of a personality inventory?
- How do projective tests differ from other types of psychological test?
- Can you describe the features of at least one projective test?
- What are the benefits and limitations of intelligence tests?
- Can you name and describe at least two psychophysiological tests that might be used for clinical assessment?
- Can you name and describe three different neuroimaging techniques?
- What are the benefits and limitations of clinical observation techniques?
- What is ecological momentary assessment (EMA)?
- Can you define what is meant by test-retest reliability, inter-rater reliability and internal reliability?
- Can you define what is meant by concurrent validity, face validity, predictive validity and construct validity?
- Can you provide at least three examples of cultural bias in assessment and diagnosis?
- Can you describe at least two studies that have identified some of the causes of cultural bias in assessment and diagnosis?

SECTION SUMMARY

2.1 Methods of Assessment

- An **unstructured clinical interview** is probably the first contact a client will have with a clinician.

- **Structured interviews** can be used to help make decisions about diagnosis and functioning. One such example is the **Structured Clinical Interview for DSM-IV-TR (SCID)**.

- **Psychological tests** are a highly structured way of gathering information about the client.

- The most well-known personality inventory is the **Minnesota Multiphasic Personality Inventory (MMPI)**.

- **Specific trait inventories** are used to measure functioning in one specific area (e.g. depression).

- **Projective tests** include the **Rorschach Inkblot Test**, the **Thematic Apperception Test (TAT)** and the **Sentence Completion Test**.

- Both **IQ tests** and tests of general ability, such as the **Wechsler Adult Intelligence Scale (WAIS)**, are regularly used by clinicians.

- **Neurological impairment tests** are used to measure deficits in cognitive functioning that may be caused by abnormalities in brain functioning.

- **Psychophysiological tests** can be used to measure emotional responding.

- **Neuroimaging techniques** generate images of the brain that provide information on any abnormalities in brain functioning.

- Important neuroimaging techniques include **computerized axial tomography (CAT)**, **positron emission tomography (PET)** and **magnetic resonance imaging (MRI)**.

- **Clinical observation** techniques can be used to gather objective information about the frequency of behaviours or the contexts in which behaviours occur.

- **Test reliability** measures whether the test will provide the same result when used by different clinicians on different occasions.

- **Test validity** measures whether an assessment method actually measures what it claims to measure.

- Because assessment methods have usually been developed on populations from a single cultural background, they often result in biased assessments when applied to individuals from a different cultural background.

2.2 CASE FORMULATION

The various forms of assessment we have described in the previous section are all used by clinicians to gather useful information about clients and their problems. Some clinicians use this information to establish a psychiatric diagnosis (e.g. to determine whether the client's symptoms meet DSM-IV-TR criteria for a specific disorder), whereas others use this information to draw up a psychological explanation of the client's problems and to develop a plan for therapy. This latter approach is known as

Case formulation The use of clinical information to draw up a psychological explanation of the client's problems and to develop a plan for therapy.

case formulation and is one that has been increasingly adopted over the past 20 years by clinicians who consider that each client's problems are uniquely different, and so require an individualized approach (Persons, 1989). It is an approach also championed by those who view the psychiatric diagnostic model of psychopathology as unhelpful in practice and stigmatizing to clients (Boyle, 2007; May, 2007) (see Chapter 1, section 1.1.2).

Most practising clinical psychologists will usually develop a case formulation when dealing with a client. This is an attempt to work towards explaining the client's problems in established theoretical terms. In most cases the explanation developed will also suggest interventions that may be successful in resolving those problems. It will be a precise account of the patient's problems that is a collaborative exercise with the client, not one that is imposed on the client (as psychiatric diagnosis might be). Persons (1989) has described case formulation as having six components: (1) creating a list of the client's problems; (2) identifying and describing the underlying psychological mechanisms that might be mediating these problems (and the nature of the mechanisms described will depend on the theoretical orientation of the clinical psychologist – see below); (3) understanding the way in which the psychological mechanisms generate the client's problems; (4) identifying the kinds of events that may have precipitated the client's problems; (5) identifying how these precipitating events may have caused the current problems through the proposed psychological mechanisms; and (6) developing a scheme of treatment based on these explanations and predicting any obstacles to treatment.

How a case formulation is constructed will depend on the theoretical orientation of the clinical psychologist and, within an individual formulation, explanation of the client's problems will be couched in terms of the psychologist's own preferred theoretical approach. For example, those who work within a cognitive or behavioural model of psychopathology (see Chapter 1, section 1.1.3) will attempt to find explanations for the client's problems based on cognitive and behavioural causes – sometimes known as an **ABC** approach. That is, they will attempt to identify the **antecedents** (**A**) to the problems, describe the **beliefs** (**B**) or cognitive factors that are triggered by these antecedents, and the **consequences** (**C**) of these events. For example, if a client suffers from panic attacks, the case formulation may discover that (1) these occur in situations where there are crowds of people (antecedents), (2) the client believes that feeling hot, sweaty and faint are signals for an impending heart attack (beliefs), and (3) the client indulges in certain 'safety' behaviours designed to keep her 'safe' – such as avoiding going out of the house – but which reinforce the symptoms and beliefs (consequences) (Marzillier & Marzillier, 2008). Based on this knowledge, the clinical psychologist can begin to understand the factors that are causing and maintaining these problems (e.g. the faulty beliefs and the 'safety' behaviours) and develop therapeutic interventions to try to deal with them.

In contrast, psychologists who hold a psychodynamic perspective use formulations to address the way that current problems reflect underlying unconscious conflicts and early developmental experiences, and will couch their formulations in these kinds of ways. For those psychologists who believe that a holistic or sys-

JACK
Tries to help, fails, drinks, takes drugs, feels angry – feels rejected so takes drink/drugs to feel better.

MOTHER AND SISTERS
Helpful and concerned about Jack's abuse, but then feel let down, angry, rejecting.

Figure 2.7 *A systemic case formulation*
Jack has problems with both drugs and drink. He later became involved in petty crime, and was diagnosed as depressed. He also began to exhibit paranoia and delusional ideation. This simple formulation shows how the reactions of Jack and his mother and sisters reinforce Jack's feelings of rejection and his abuse of drink and drugs.
Source: Dallos & Stedmon (2006).

temic view of a person's problems is important (e.g. an individual's problems can only be fully understood within a family or social context), the formulation will be developed in terms of the important relationships between the client and significant other people in his or her life. For example, within the context of the family, someone with a psychological problem may be seen as a weak and dependent person, and this may influence how other members of the family treat the client, and determine what demands the client may make on his or her family. Thus, the client's problems can be formulated as interactions between various 'actors' (the family members) which may maintain the client's problems (Marzillier & Marzillier, 2008; Dallos & Draper, 2005). Figure 2.7 provides a simple example of a systemic formulation which attempts to explain how a client's problems are maintained by the relationships between him and other members of his family.

In many cases clinicians prefer to represent their formulations in a diagrammatic form that permits easy identification of factors that may be causing the client's problems and which also enables them to clearly explain the formulation to the client. Activity Box 2.1 provides a detailed and structured example of how a formulation based on a cognitive-behavioural approach could be attempted, and offers an example of a formulation interview that readers can attempt to interpret in terms of the theoretical model provided. This example shows how the case formulation for a client suffering panic disorder would be interpreted by a cognitive-behavioural psychologist in terms of existing cognitive models of panic disorder (see Chapter 5, p. 133). Once the diagram is completed it should suggest some possible targets for interventions (e.g. using CBT to change misinterpretations of bodily sensations and to prevent the use of safety behaviours; see Chapter 5, section 5.3).

ACTIVITY BOX 2.1

A cognitive-behavioural formulation for panic disorder

This activity should be attempted with the help and advice of your instructor or teacher. It consists of four stages: (1) a description of the cognitive theoretical model of panic disorder in which the formulation is to be attempted (see Chapter 5, section 5.3); (2) a template for the formulation interview that a clinician would undertake to gain the information required; (3) a template formulation diagram to be completed following the interview; and (4) an illustrative interview that you can use to gather the information required to complete the formulation diagram. All these examples are taken from Wells (2006, pp. 56–59).

Part 1: The cognitive model of panic disorder

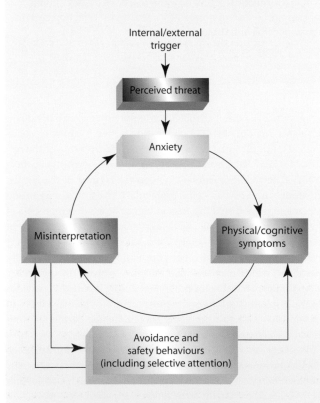

Part 2: The template panic disorder formulation interview

Introduction: I'm going to ask you about a recent typical panic attack so that we may begin to map out what happened. When was your most recent panic attack?

1 Thinking about just before you panicked: what was the very first thing that you noticed that indicated that

you might panic? Was it a thought, a sensation, or an emotion?
(Answer = thought, go to Q3; Answer = sensation, go to Q2; Answer = emotion, if anxiety go to Q4 and if other emotion ask: 'When you had that emotion, what sensations did you have?' Then proceed with Q2.)

2 When you noticed that sensation, what thought went through your mind?

3 When you noticed that thought, how did that make you feel emotionally?

4 When you noticed that emotion, what sensations did you have?

5 When you had those sensations, what thought went through your mind?

6 How much did you believe [insert catastrophic thought] at that time?

7 What happened to your anxiety when you thought that?

8 Did you do anything to prevent [insert catastrophic thought]? What was that?

9 Did you do anything to lower anxiety? What was that?

10 Since you have developed panic, do you focus attention on your body/thoughts? In what way?

Part 3: The template formulation diagram
Try to fill this in with the appropriate details once you have read the illustrative interview in Part 4.

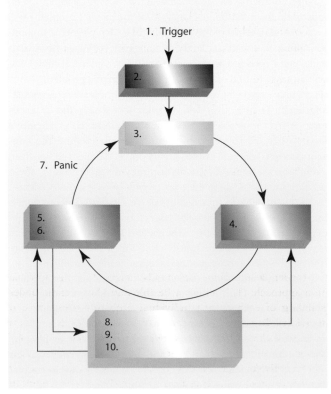

Part 4: An illustrative interview

Clinician: Thinking about just before you panicked. What was the very first thing that you noticed that indicated that you might panic? Was it a thought, a sensation or an emotion?

Client: It was an emotion, frustration.

Clinician: When you had that emotion, what sensations did you have?

Client: I felt dizzy, vertigo I suppose you'd call it.

Clinician: When you noticed that sensation, what thought went through your mind?

Client: I thought it's going to bring it on.

Clinician: When you had that thought, how did that make you feel emotionally?

Client: I felt scared and anxious.

Clinician: When you noticed that emotion, what sensations did you have?

Client: I got the lot, dizziness, choking, chest tight, sweating, nausea.

Clinician: When you had those sensations, what thought went through your mind?

Client: I thought I was dying of a heart attack or something.

Clinician: How much did you believe you were having a heart attack on a scale of zero to 100%?

Client: I was convinced, 70%.

Clinician: What happened to your anxiety when you thought that?

Client: I panicked very quickly.

Clinician: Did you do anything to prevent a heart attack?

Client: Yes, I had a drink of alcohol and tried to calm down. I also took an aspirin.

Clinician: How did you try to calm down?

Client: I took deep breaths and tried to slow my pulse down.

Clinician: Since you developed panic, do you focus more attention on your body/thoughts?

Client: I take my pulse and try to listen to my heart beating when I'm falling asleep.

Tarrier (2006) lists the various advantages of the case formulation approach: (1) it allows a flexible and idiosyncratic understanding of each client's individual problems irrespective of individual diagnoses clients may have been given (i.e. in clinical practice, a client's problems do not usually fall into simple diagnostic categories but may reflect a range of problems unique to that individual); (2) it is collaborative and treats the client with regard; (3) it is firmly based on a theoretical understanding of

psychopathology (unlike diagnosis, which is based entirely on a description of symptoms); (4) it can include information about a client's past history (e.g. exposure to risk factors) and the client's personal, social and family history; and (5) it allows the development of treatment strategies that can be moulded to the specific needs of that individual client, and is especially advantageous in treating complex cases that do not easily conform to standard diagnostic categories.

> **SELF-TEST QUESTIONS**
>
> ● What are the main components of a case formulation?
> ● Can you describe how a cognitive-behavioural clinician and a psychodynamic clinician might approach case formulation differently?

SECTION SUMMARY

2.2 Case Formulation

● A **case formulation** is used by clinicians to draw up a psychological explanation of a client's problems and to develop a plan for therapy.

● The clinicians' theoretical approach will determine how they explain the client's problems and what information they require during the case formulation process.

2.3 CLINICAL ASSESSMENT ISSUES REVIEWED

This chapter has reviewed the diverse and varied ways in which clinicians gather information by which they can classify, understand and treat the mental health problems brought to them by their clients. This information is used to address a number of questions, including: 'Precisely what problems does this person have?', 'What has caused her problems?', 'What is the best way to treat her problems?' and 'Did the treatment work?' By far the most common assessment method is the clinical interview. This may be entirely unstructured or may have a very rigid structure depending on the nature of the information the clinician wants to gather (Activity Box 2.1 provides a good example of a structured interview designed to gather very specific information about a client). However, as well as benefits, the clinical interview has many limitations. Its reliability is quite low, depends on clients' willingness to provide valid information about themselves and their problems, and is prone to cultural bias when clinician and client are from differing ethnic backgrounds.

More structured ways of gathering information include psychological tests. Under this heading we reviewed personality inventories, specific trait inventories, projective tests and intelligence tests. Biologically based assessments such as psychophysiological tests and brain neuroimaging techniques can be valuable for confirming the validity of interview or pencil and paper tests, and can often identify whether any impairments in brain functioning may be underlying the client's problems.

Finally, we discussed the use of case formulations, which have become a popular tool for clinicians of most theoretical persuasions. The case formulation allows the clinician to draw up a psychological explanation of the client's problems and to develop a plan for therapy, which allows a flexible and personal understanding of each client's individual problems.

 # LEARNING OUTCOMES

When you have completed this chapter, you should be able to:

1 Describe a range of clinical assessment methods and evaluate the benefits and limitations of each.

2 Describe the concepts of reliability and validity as applied to clinical assessment methods.

3 Critically analyse some of the sources of cultural bias that may influence the process of clinical assessment.

4 Explain what a case formulation is and provide some examples from different psychological approaches.

KEY TERMS

ABC chart 42
Adult Memory and Information Processing Battery (AMIPB) 39
Analogue observations 44
Case formulation 49
Computerized axial tomography (CAT) 40
Concurrent validity 45
Confirmatory bias 47
Construct validity 46
Cronbach's α 45
Cultural bias 46
Ecological momentary assessment (EMA) 44
Ecological validity 42
Electrocardiogram (ECG) 40
Electrodermal responding 39
Electroencephalogram (EEG) 40
Electromyogram (EMG) 40
Face validity 45
Functional magnetic resonance imaging (fMRI) 41
Halstead-Reitan Neuropsychological Test Battery 39
Hypothetical constructs 34
Internal consistency 45
Inter-rater reliability 45

IQ (intelligence quotient) tests 37
Lie detectors 40
Magnetic resonance imaging (MRI) 41
Mini Mental State Examination (MMSE) 39
Minnesota Multiphasic Personality Inventory (MMPI) 32
MMPI profile 32
Positron emission tomography (PET) 40
Predictive validity 45
Projective tests 35
Psychometric approach 32
Reliability 45
Rorschach Inkblot Test 35
Self-monitoring 44
Self-observation 44
Sentence completion test 35
Standardization 31
Structured Clinical Interview for DSM-IV-TR (SCID) 31
Structured interview 30
Test-retest reliability 45
Thematic Apperception Test (TAT) 35
Unstructured interview 31
Validity 45
Wechsler Adult Intelligence Scale (WAIS) 38

REVIEWS, THEORIES AND SEMINAL STUDIES

Links to Journal Articles

2.1 Methods of Assessment

Aklin, W.M. & Turner, S.M. (2006). Toward understanding ethnic and cultural factors in the interviewing process. *Psychotherapy, 43*, 50–64.

Boyle, M. (2007). The problem with diagnosis. *The Psychologist, 20,* 290–292.

Dahlstrom, W.G. & Archer, R.P. (2000). A shortened version of the MMPI-2. *Assessment, 7,* 131.

Garb, H.N. (1997). Race bias, social class bias, and gender bias in clinical judgment. *Clinical Psychology: Science and Practice, 4,* 99–120.

Lilienfeld, S.O., Wood, J.M. & Garb, H.N. (2000). The scientific status of projective techniques. *Psychological Science in the Public Interest, 1,* 27–66.

Littlewood, R. (1992). Psychiatric-diagnosis and racial bias: Empirical and interpretative approaches. *Social Science and Medicine, 34,* 141–149.

Meyer, G.J., Finn, S.E., Eyde, L.D., Kay, G.G. et al. (2001). Psychological testing and psychological assessment: A review of evidence and issues. *American Psychologist, 56,* 128–165.

Miller, P.R., Dasher, R., Collins, R., Griffiths, P. & Brown, F. (2001). Inpatient diagnostic assessments. 1. Accuracy of structured vs. unstructured interviews. *Psychiatry Research, 105,* 255–264.

Nock, M.K. & Kurtz, S.M.S. (2005). Direct behavioural observation in school settings: Bringing science to practice. *Cognitive and Behavioral Practice, 12,* 359–370.

Piasecki, T.M., Hufford, M.R., Solham, M. & Trull, T.J. (2007). Assessing clients in their natural environments with electronic diaries: Rationale, benefits, limitations, and barriers. *Psychological Assessment, 19,* 25–43.

Sparrow, S.S. & Davis, S.M. (2000). Recent advances in the assessment of intelligence and cognition. *Journal of Child Psychology and Psychiatry, 41,* 117–131.

Texts for Further Reading

Eells, T.D. (Ed.) (2006). *Handbook of psychotherapy case formulation.* New York: Guilford Press.

Exner, J.E. & Erdberg, P. (2005). *The Rorschach: A comprehensive system: Advanced interpretation.* Chichester: Wiley.

Groth-Marnat, G. (2006). *Psychological testing and assessment,* 12th ed. New York: Academic Internet Publishers.

Group for the Advancement of Psychiatry (2002). *Cultural assessment in clinical psychiatry.* Washington, DC: American Psychiatric Press.

Hersen, M. & Turner, S.M. (Eds.) (2003). *Diagnostic interviewing.* Kluwer Academic/Plenum Press.

Johnstone, L. & Dallos, R. (Eds.) (2006). *Formulation in psychology and psychotherapy: Making sense of people's problems.* London: Routledge.

Nicols, D.S. (2001). *Essentials of MMPI-2 assessment.* Chichester: Wiley.

Saccuzzo, D. & Kaplan, R. (2004). *Psychological testing: Principles, applications and issues,* 6th ed. London: Wadsworth.

Sommers-Flanagan, J. & Sommers-Flanagan, R. (1999). *Clinical interviewing.* Chichester: Wiley.

Tarrier, N. (Ed.) (2006). *Case formulation in cognitive behaviour therapy: The treatment of challenging and complex cases.* London: Routledge.

RESEARCH QUESTIONS

2.1 Methods of Assessment

- Are there stable underlying characteristics or traits that exist in everyone and that can be measured by psychological tests?

- Should all specific trait inventories include items that measure the faking of answers?

- Is it acceptable from a theoretical perspective for researchers to create an inventory to measure a hypothetical construct that they themselves have developed?

- Can research help to improve the reliability of projective tests?

- Can psychological research help to define whether the hypothetical construct of 'intelligence' actually exists?

CLINICAL ISSUES

2.1 Methods of Assessment

- What methods can clinicians use for developing a rapport with a client and gaining the client's trust?

- In a clinical interview, how do clinicians help clients to reveal information that they may want to withhold?

- How does a clinician deal with a client who has poor self-knowledge?

- How might the age of a clinician or the way he or she is dressed affect the course of a clinical interview?

- How do clinicians prevent themselves from relying too heavily on first impressions or giving priority to negative information in a clinical interview?

- A test such as the MMPI can take several hours for clients to complete. Can clinicians do anything to prevent fatigue affecting clients' responding?

- How can projective tests be used to help match a client with a suitable form of psychotherapy?

- Can only clinicians with a psychodynamic approach usefully employ projective tests?

- Are there any IQ tests that clinicians can use that will measure an individual's capacity to learn or his or her potential to acquire new cognitive abilities?

- Are psychophysiological measures, such as electrodermal responding, useful measures of emotional responding for the clinician?

- Will clinical neuropsychologists always need evidence from neuroimaging techniques to confirm a diagnosis indicating neurological deficits?

- Observational methods are time-consuming, so are they a good use of the clinician's time?

- How can clinicians be sure that the observational methods they are using are reliable and not affected by observer bias?

- Self-monitoring techniques facilitate behaviour change without active intervention. How can the clinician take advantage of this process when developing a treatment programme?

- Studies suggest that many clinicians view clients from low socioeconomic backgrounds as more disturbed than those from higher socioeconomic backgrounds. How can clinicians actively avoid such biases?

- What things should the clinician take into account when an interview is conducted in the client's second language?

- Clients from ethnic minority groups often feel apprehensive and timid when being interviewed by a clinician. How can the clinician identify and overcome these feelings?

- How can clinicians learn about and eradicate direct and indirect racism in the clinical assessment process?

2.2 Case Formulation

- How might a clinician's theoretical approach affect the way he or she conducts a case formulation?

- How important for the success of a case formulation is the collaboration of the client?

3 Research Methods in Clinical Psychology

ROUTE MAP OF THE CHAPTER

This chapter begins by describing what research is before discussing a number of ways in which research can be conducted, with special attention being paid to the role of scientific method in clinical psychology research. The chapter then describes why clinical psychologists might want training in research and examines what kinds of questions they are interested in addressing. The bulk of the chapter is concerned with describing and evaluating a range of research designs used by clinical psychology researchers. Finally, a chapter on research would not be complete without a full discussion of the ethical issues that clinical psychologists are likely to encounter while undertaking research.

I am a clinical psychologist. Among the health care professions, clinical psychology is one of the few to provide extensive research training, and a clinical psychologist can be involved in both basic and applied research. Because of the breadth of their training in research methods, clinical psychologists are well suited to design, implement, and evaluate research, and to conduct evaluations of the services provided by mental health care agencies. When you are a practising clinical psychologist, finding time to conduct research of any kind is difficult. But when I am involved it helps me to satisfy my curiosity, to generate new knowledge on which more effective treatments may be based, and to evaluate whether the current services we offer are effective.

SARAH'S STORY

Introduction

Why might a profession whose main aim is arguably to alleviate mental health problems want to do research or be involved in research? Why are clinical psychologists given such a rigorous training in research methods anyway – shouldn't they simply be taught how to treat people? The personal account above goes some way towards answering these questions. Even if they are simply offering a treatment-based service, clinical psychologists should be able to evaluate whether their services are effective and successful. To do this with any degree of objectivity requires a knowledge of *scientific method*. *Sarah's Story* reflects a widely held view that the clinical psychologist should be thought of as a *scientist-practitioner* or an *applied scientist* – someone who is competent as both a researcher and a practitioner. This view arose in the early twentieth century when psychology was thought of as an experimental science. However, as the discipline of psychology developed from being a pure research subject to an applied profession, clinical psychology maintained its links with universities and the academic world. Indeed, in the UK, almost all clinical psychology training courses are based in university psychology departments and have substantial research training components to them.

The current view of the link between research and practice that is held in the UK tends to be one in which scientific method is systematically integrated into clinical work (Barker, Pistrang & Elliott, 2002). Shapiro (1985) defines this applied scientist

Scientific method   A research method which espouses the pursuit of knowledge through systematic observation and requires that research findings are replicable and testable.

Scientist-practitioner   Someone who is competent as both a researcher and a practitioner.

Applied scientist   Someone who is competent as both a researcher and a practitioner.

view of clinical psychologists as (1) applying the findings of general psychology to the area of mental health, (2) using only methods of assessment that have been scientifically validated and (3) doing clinical work within the framework of scientific method. However, this view of clinical psychologists, their approach to research and how they use research is not as clear-cut as it sounds. In order to understand how research is used by clinicians and integrated into their role as mental health professionals, we need to spend a little time understanding what is meant by (1) research and (2) scientific method. We also need to look at what value research might have within the broader scope of psychopathology. For example, some researchers simply want to understand what causes psychopathology, others want to know whether there is empirical evidence supporting the efficacy of specific treatments, and others simply want a systematic way of classifying and interpreting the symptoms of their clients.

3.1 RESEARCH AND SCIENCE

3.1.1 What is Research?

If you are a psychology student, you have probably already encountered a course designed to teach you about research. You will probably have undertaken some practical classes designed to teach you about research methods, and you will also have learned about the role that statistics play in interpreting research data. But did anyone actually tell you what research is in the first place? In general, psychology considers itself to be either a biological or a social science, so the emphasis is on using scientific method to understand human behaviour. But research can mean much more than this. In its broadest sense, research is a form of investigation aimed at discovering some facts about a topic or about furthering understanding of that topic through careful consideration or study. In this respect, research does not necessarily have to adhere to scientific principles, and understanding of a topic may be enhanced in many other ways. For example, we can learn a lot about human behaviour and human nature from literature and the way that many classical authors describe everyday experiences and their consequences.

Many clinicians and psychotherapists claim that they gain understanding and knowledge from their own clinical experiences which they can use systematically and successfully when treating their clients (Morrow-Bradley & Elliott, 1986). Even historical research can be used to further understanding of psychopathology. In a systematic search of the historical literature on spiders and how humans have perceived them over the centuries, Davey (1994b) found that spiders had been traditionally linked with the spread of disease and illness – a finding which may help us to understand why spider fear is so prevalent in Western societies today. What is common to these different approaches is that they are attempts to understand an issue through systematic and careful consideration of the relevant facts. However, how we collect the facts that are relevant to our considerations can vary considerably. Literature collects facts usually through the author's observations of life and everyday living which are then presented within an unfolding story; historical research collects facts by accumulating evidence from historical documents or artefacts; and the practising clinician gathers facts from his or her everyday experiences with clients. In each case, these facts can then be considered systematically in an attempt to enhance our understanding.

In contrast, scientific method advocates that facts are collected in rather specific ways. Usually this means that we should collect our facts for consideration in a systematic way defined by objectivity and precise measurement (usually so that our collecting of facts can be replicated by others and our conclusions verified by them). Because the scientific method is used predominantly in psychological research and clinical psychology research, we will discuss this approach in detail below.

3.1.2 Scientific Method

Scientific method espouses the pursuit of knowledge through systematic and thorough observation. It also requires that research findings are replicable and testable.

By *replicable*, we mean that the results of the research have been collected under controlled conditions that will allow any other researcher to reproduce those exact same

> **Replicable** Results of research which have been collected under controlled conditions that will allow any other researcher to reproduce those exact same findings.

findings. Researchers using the scientific method attempt to achieve this by precise measurement of stimuli and behaviour and accurate and complete description of the methods by which the data were collected. Replicability is essential to the progress of scientific knowledge because it means that different researchers can be sure that a research finding is a legitimate fact that can be relied upon when developing explanations of a phenomenon. This is especially true in the case of human behaviour, where the subject matter is often complex and may differ significantly from situation to situation. Activity Box 3.1 provides a discussion of one of the seminal research papers in human psychopathology – the attempt by Watson & Rayner (1920) to condition a phobia in an 11-month-old infant (see Chapter 5, p. 123). You will see from this discussion that although this paper is often considered to be one of the founding pieces of scientific research in psychopathology, the ability of other contemporary researchers to replicate it was limited – largely

ACTIVITY BOX 3.1

How *not* to report research findings: The example of Watson & Rayner (1920)

In 1920 J.B. Watson and Rosalie Rayner reported the findings of a study that has come to be known as the **'Little Albert' study**, which is often cited as one of the founding pieces of scientific research in psychopathology. However, despite being quoted in almost every clinical psychology textbook since that time, the original report of this research is not as clearly written as we might wish, and many subsequent studies were unable to replicate it.

After reading the Watson and Rayner (1920) article:

1   Can you accurately describe what they did?

2   Can you describe exactly what they found?

3   Can you describe the procedures you would use in a study designed to try to replicate their findings?

Two other articles that are instructive here are:

> Delprato, D.J. (1980). Hereditary determinants of fears and phobias: A critical review. *Behavior Therapy, 11*, 79–103.

> Harris, B. (1979). Whatever happened to Little Albert? *American Psychologist, 34*, 151–160.

Harris (1979) describes how the Watson and Rayner (1920) study has become a well-known piece of psychological 'folklore' with many textbooks misquoting the details of the research because their authors have relied on secondary sources rather than reading the original article. Even Watson himself misrepresented and distorted this research in later writings.

Delprato (1980) describes a number of studies conducted in the 10–15 years after 1920 that attempted to replicate the 'Little Albert' findings. Many of these failed in their attempts, and as a consequence are rarely mentioned in clinical psychology textbooks.

Conclusion

Accurate descriptions of research and accurate reporting of research are essential for proper understanding. If research reports lack necessary detail or are confusing, they are not only difficult to replicate, they may also give rise to misreporting of findings.

---

because Watson and Rayner were less than systematic in the way they collected their data and reported it.

Testable   A scientific explanation that is couched in such a way that it clearly suggests ways in which it can be tested and potentially falsified.

By *testable*, we mean that a scientific explanation is couched in such a manner that it clearly suggests ways in which it can be tested and potentially falsified. Scientific method often relies on the construction of theories to explain phenomena. A *theory* is a set of propositions that usually attempt to explain a phenomenon by describing the cause–effect relationships that contribute to that phenomenon. Theories are expected to be able to take into account all relevant research findings on a phenomenon, and be articulated in such a way that they will also have predictive value. That is, they should be able to predict what might happen in as yet untested situations. Thus, a good theory will allow the researcher to generate *hypotheses* about what might happen, and to test these hypotheses in other research studies. If the hypotheses are confirmed in these other studies the theory is upheld, but if the hypotheses are disconfirmed then the theory is either wrong or needs to be changed in detail to explain the new facts.

Theory   A set of propositions that usually attempt to explain a phenomenon by describing the cause–effect relationships that contribute to that phenomenon.

Hypothesis   A tentative explanation for a phenomenon used as a basis for further investigation.

This process illustrates one of the important distinctions between science and so-called non-science. Karl Popper (1959) proposed that science must be able to formulate hypotheses that are capable of refutation or falsification. If it is not possible to falsify a theory by generating testable hypotheses, then that theory is not scientific and in Popper's view is of little explanatory value. Activity Box 3.2 provides an example of a psychological theory that attempts to explain why some people develop panic disorder (see Chapter 5, section 5.3). This is a theory that can be represented schematically as a series of cause–effect relationships. The sequence of cause–effect relationships described in this theory are assumed to precipitate regular panic attacks in those diagnosed with panic disorder. This relatively simple theory is constructed in such a way that we can generate a number of testable hypotheses from it, and so we could potentially falsify the theory according to Popper's criteria. Alternatively, consider the following:

> The self in Gestalt Theory is a process, constantly changing according to needs and environmental stimuli. It does not exist prior to and apart from relationships. Self-experience is constituted exclusively in and by relationships. There is no self independent of contact, it is rather 'something given in contact' that comes to life in the encounter with the world. As such it is the agent of growth and the product of relational experiences.
> (adapted from www.g-gej.org)

This certainly seems to be a kind of psychological theory attempting to explain our concept of self, but can this be considered a scientific theory in Popper's sense? What hypotheses could you generate from this theory? How would you test them?

3.1.3 Scientific Method as a Model for Clinical Psychology Research: The Pros and Cons

We have described what the scientific method is, but is it the best model by which to conduct clinical psychology research? In many countries of the world, clinical psychology has either explicitly or implicitly adopted the scientist practitioner model described earlier,

ACTIVITY BOX 3.2

Testing a theory of panic disorder

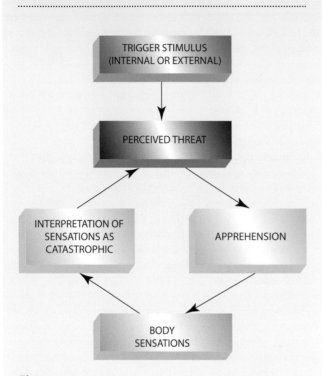

Figure 1

This is a schematic (diagrammatic) representation of Clark's (1986) theory (or model) of panic disorder. In this theory, perception of a threat triggers apprehension followed by a focusing on bodily sensations caused by that apprehension. Finally, these bodily sensations are catastrophically mis-interpreted as threatening. This then creates a vicious cycle of cause–effect events that precipitates a panic attack.

If this theory meets Popper's criteria as a scientific theory, then we should be able to generate testable hypotheses from it which will either confirm the theory or falsify it. Below are a few examples of testable hypotheses from this theory. See if you can think up any more.

Testable hypotheses

In individuals diagnosed with panic disorder:

1 Perceiving a threat should lead to increased appre-hension (as measured by increased levels of anxiety).

2 Perceiving a threat should eventually lead to enhanced discrimination of body sensations.

3 Increasing discrimination of body sensations should trigger catastrophizing.

4 Inducing catastrophic interpretations of bodily sensations should lead to increased perception of threat.

with the implication that practising clinical psychologists are willing to at least call themselves scientists by training even if they do not regularly practise as scientists. Nevertheless, in many countries there is a growing pressure for mental health services to provide scientific evidence that treatments and therapies are effective and economical. In the UK, one such agency that attempts to assess and recommend effective forms of treatment for mental health problems is the *National Institute for Health and Clinical Excellence* (known as *NICE*, www.nice.org.uk). It does this primarily by recommending treatments whose efficacy can be labelled as *evidence-based*, that is, whose efficacy has been proven through research using the scientific method.

> **National Institute for Health and Clinical Excellence (NICE)** An independent UK organization responsible for providing national guidance on promoting good health and preventing and treating ill health.

> **Evidence-based treatments** Treatments whose efficacy has been proven through research using the scientific method.

There is thus some pressure from these agencies for clinical psychologists to accept the scientific method – at least as a way of assessing the effectiveness of therapies. However, as we shall see on numerous occasions throughout this book, many forms of therapy are not couched in ways that make them amenable to assessment through a scientific approach (e.g. psychoanalysis). As a result, at least some clinicians view processes designed to scientifically assess treatments (such as those conducted by NICE) as being ways in which those clinicians who support therapies derived from traditional scientific approaches can impose their own view of what treatments are effective (Elliott, 1998; Roth & Fonagy, 1996). Let us look at some of the benefits and costs of clinical psychology adopting the scientific method in its research.

There are a number of apparent benefits to clinical psychology using the scientific method as a model for research. First, there is probably no doubt that clinical psychology has used its scientific status as a means of acquiring prestige and establishing its status as an independent discipline within the field of mental health (Lavender, 1996). There was no greater proponent of this approach than one of the founders of British clinical psychology, H.J. Eysenck, who was a vigorous supporter of science and scientific method in clinical psychology research.

Secondly, some writers have argued that clinical psychologists often consistently fail to use research evidence to inform their treatments and instead rely on anecdotal clinical experience (Dawes, 1994). If this is so, there is a thin line between a clinician basing his interventions on unvalidated experience and a bogus psychotherapist inventing a so-called therapy whose basic tenets are not amenable to objective assessment. Keeping abreast of recent developments in evidence-based research is therefore an important component of good practice for clinical psychologists, and scientific method provides the theoretical and empirical develop-ments by which the clinician can achieve this (Singer, 1980).

Thirdly, Belar and Perry (1992) have argued that scientific method provides a useful framework for theory building (see previous section), which allows clinicians to test out their clinical observations and assess their efficacy. Otherwise, they argue, clinical experiences are in danger of becoming simply a set of random observations which clinicians are unable to categorize into effective and ineffective interventions.

In contrast, at least some clinicians have argued that the scientific method in its strictest form may not be suitable for clinical psychology research or practice. First, some writers claim that to base clinical psychology research on strict scientific method aligns it too closely to the medical model of psychopathology and invites many of the problems associated with that model (see Chapter 1, section 1.1.2) (Corrie & Callahan, 2000). Secondly, while the scientist-practitioner model is often seen as the model for clinical psychology, it is seldom an ideal that is fulfilled in practice (Barlow, Hayes & Nelson, 1984). For the clinical psychologist, the need to alleviate a client's psychological problems is often more pressing than the need to be scientifically rigorous. Similarly, the demands placed on overworked clinicians in under-resourced mental health services rarely give them time to engage in any meaningful research independently of their clinical practice (Head & Harmon, 1990), and they will certainly rank research as a priority significantly lower than their service commitment (Allen, 1985; Corrie & Callahan, 2000). The pressures of their work mean that they will often view the research literature (whether based on scientific method or not) as irrelevant to their professional practice (Barlow, Hayes & Nelson, 1984).

Thirdly, in contrast to scientific method, an alternative approach to research in clinical psychology is one based on *social constructionism* (Burr, 1995). This approach emphasizes that reality is a social construction, and so there are no basic 'truths' of the kind that we seek to discover using the scientific method. Instead, knowledge consists of multiple realities that are constructed by people and may be historically and culturally specific. It is claimed this approach has particular relevance in clinical psychology because psychopathology frequently involves individuals creating their own realities (e.g. paranoid individuals create a reality in which everyone is against them, and depressed individuals create a reality in which they view themselves as worthless). These various realities can be accessed through analysing language and social interactions, and so those who advocate a social constructionist approach argue that the study of language and discourse is the only means of understanding human experience and, as a consequence, human psychopathology.

This discussion has looked at some of the pros and cons of adopting scientific method as the model for research in clinical psychology. Despite the fact that at least some clinicians have adopted alternative frameworks (e.g. the social constructionist approach), scientific method is still the most favoured model for research in most areas of clinical psychology, including research on the causes of psychopathology (aetiology), research pursuing the development of new forms of treatment, and research assessing the efficacy of treatments. Even though each person may develop his or her own individual psychological reality, the fact that human beings are evolved biological organisms means that there are almost certain to be general 'truths' or processes common to all humans that can be discovered using scientific method. As a consequence, there are also likely to be a set of general 'truths' or processes common to psychopathology across all individuals.

Social constructionism An approach to research in clinical psychology emphasizing that reality is a social construction, and so there are no basic 'truths' of the kind that we seek to discover using the scientific method.

SELF-TEST QUESTIONS

● Can you describe the main principles of the scientific method?
● What is the difference between a theory and a hypothesis?
● What do we mean when we say that decisions about the effectiveness of an intervention should be evidence-based?
● What are the benefits and drawbacks of clinical psychology using the scientific method as a model for research?
● What is social constructionism and how does it offer a different research approach to the scientific method?

SECTION SUMMARY

3.1 Research and Science

● **Research** is about furthering understanding of a topic through careful consideration or study.

● **Scientific method** espouses the pursuit of knowledge through systematic observation, and requires that research findings are **replicable** and **testable**.

● A **theory** is a set of propositions that attempt to explain a phenomenon.

● There is growing pressure for mental health services to recommend treatments whose efficacy is **evidence-based**.

● **Social constructionism** is one research approach in clinical psychology that is an alternative to the scientific method.

3.2 CLINICAL PSYCHOLOGY RESEARCH: WHAT DO WE WANT TO FIND OUT?

3.2.1 How Does Clinical Psychology Research Help Us To Understand Psychopathology?

Clinical psychology researchers use research methods in a variety of different ways to answer a number of different questions. We will describe the range of research methods available to clinical psychologists in the next section, but first let's briefly look at how research can help us understand psychopathology.

Research can have a number of immediate goals. These goals include description, prediction, control and understanding (explanation), and clinical psychology researchers may be using research methods to achieve any one or more of these goals.

Description The defining and categorizing of events and relationships relevant to psychopathology.

For example, *description* involves the defining and categorizing of events and relationships, and researchers may simply want to find suitable ways of describing and categorizing psychopathology. To some extent this is what is represented in DSM-IV-TR (the categorizing of psychopathology), but other researchers have used research methods to discover whether different symptoms are related or co-occur (e.g. Watson, 2005). For example, Figure 1.4 in Chapter 1 provides an example of how research methods have been used to understand how symptoms of anxiety and depression are related. Such categorization of symptoms is a first step towards defining the biological or psychological mechanisms that link anxiety and depression.

Once we have been able to describe and categorize psychopathology, then we are one step away from *prediction*. A logical next stage

Prediction A statement (usually quantitative) about what will happen under specific conditions, as a logical consequence of scientific theories.

is to use these descriptions and categorizations to help us predict psychopathology. For example, we may know that certain childhood or developmental experiences may increase the risk of developing psychopathology later in life. One such list of these risk factors is provided in Table 15.2 in Chapter 15. This table indicates how various forms of childhood abuse or neglect can raise the risk of developing a range of psychopathologies (as one example, childhood physical and sexual abuse increases the risk of developing adolescent eating disorders). However, while research may have iden-

Risk factors Factors which may increase the risk of developing psychopathology later in life.

tified such experiences as *risk factors*, this does not imply a direct causal relationship between the risk factor and the psychopathology – it merely indicates that the early experience in some as yet unknown way increases the possibility that a psychopathology will occur.

The next aim of research would move beyond describing and categorizing events to actually trying to *control* them in a way that

Control Using our knowledge of the causal relationships between events to manipulate behaviour or cognitions.

(1) provides us with a clear picture of the causal relationships involved and (2) allows us to develop methods of changing events for the better. In the case of psychopathology, this latter aim would include using our knowledge of the causal relationships between events to control behaviour so that we could change it – the basic tenet of many forms of treatment and psychotherapy. One of the main tools for discovering causal relationships between events is the experimental method, which we will describe in more detail in section 3.3. For example, a number of studies have indicated that experimentally inducing a bias to interpret ambiguous events as threatening causes an increase in experienced anxiety (Wilson, MacLeod, Mathews & Rutherford, 2006). As a consequence this research suggests that if we can decrease this interpretation bias in anxious individuals, it should significantly reduce the anxiety they experience.

The final aim of research is *understanding*. That is, once we have described and categorized psychopathology, and once we have begun to identify some of the causal factors affecting psychopathology, we are probably at a point where we want to describe how all these factors interact. This will provide us with a theory or *model* of the phenomenon we are trying to explain. Activity Box 3.2 provides a useful example of how researchers believe the various causal factors involved in panic disorder interact. It is the development of models such as this (describing the interrelationships between events) that can add significantly to our understanding of psychopathology and suggest practical ways of alleviating and treating symptoms.

Understanding A full description of how the causal factors affecting psychopathology interact.

Model A hypothetical description of a process or mechanism (such as a process or psychological mechanism involved in psychopathology).

3.2.2 What Questions Do Clinical Psychologists Use Research To Try And Answer?

Potentially we can use research methods to try to understand any aspect of psychopathology that might interest us. Arguably, the primary aim of clinical psychology research is to further our knowledge and understanding of psychopathology and its treatment. One important aspect of this is an understanding of the causes of psychopathology, and especially an understanding of the aetiology of psychological problems and disorders. Although the term *aetiology* is mainly used in medical settings to refer to the causes of

Aetiology A term widely used in psychopathology to describe the causes or origins of psychological symptoms.

diseases or pathologies, it is also widely used in psychopathology to describe the causes or origins of psychological symptoms. We will discuss in detail research that has led to an understanding of aetiology in sections specifically set aside for this in later chapters.

One practical implication of research into the aetiology of mental health problems is that understanding the causes of psychopathology will inevitably suggest methods of intervention that might be used to alleviate those problems. Once again, Activity Box 3.2 provides a useful example illustrating this. The model of panic disorder displayed there describes the causal factors generating a panic attack that have been identified using controlled research methods (Clark, 1986). Clearly, in this model, panic attacks are precipitated by the individual catastrophically misinterpreting ambiguous bodily sensations. This implies that attempting to control and change this tendency to catastrophically misinterpret bodily sensations should help to reduce the frequency and intensity of panic attacks in panic disorder. Over the years, interventions of this kind have been refined to a point where they offer successful treatment for many suffering panic disorder (Wells, 2006; Fisher, 2008).

To be useful in helping to understand psychopathology, research does not necessarily have to be carried out on those who have mental health problems or who display symptoms of psychopathology. In Chapter 1 we discussed the possibility that much of what is labelled as psychopathology is often just an extreme form of common and accepted behaviours. That is, symptoms diagnosed as a psychological disorder may just be more extreme versions of everyday behaviour. One good example is worrying. Worrying is usually viewed as a perfectly normal reaction to the challenges and stressors in life and the activity of worrying may often help us to cope with these problems by enabling us to think them through. However, once uncontrollable worrying becomes a chronic reaction to even minor stressors, it then begins to cause distress and interfere with normal daily living. Because symptoms diagnosed as a disorder may just be more extreme versions of everyday behaviour, then what we find out about activities such as worrying in non-clinical populations will probably provide some insights into the aetiology of pathological worrying when it is a significant indicator of a psychological disorder such as generalized anxiety disorder (GAD) (see Chapter 5, section 5.4). Undertaking research on healthy, non-clinical populations in order

Analogue research   Research on healthy, non-clinical populations in order to shed light on the aetiology of psychopathology.

to shed light on the aetiology of psychopathology is known as *analogue research*, and such research makes an important contribution to the understanding of psychopathology (Davey, 2003; Vredenburg, Flett & Krames, 1993).

Another important function of clinical psychology research is to determine the efficacy of treatments and interventions. This includes testing the effectiveness of newly developed drug, surgical or psychological treatments. Research may even try to compare the effectiveness of two different types of treatment for a psychological disorder (e.g. comparing a drug treatment for depression with a psychological treatment for depression). Such studies are not quite as simple as they may initially seem because researchers will have to compare those who undergo the treatment with those who do not, and they will also have to control for extraneous factors that might influence improvement that are not directly due to the therapy being tested (e.g. how attentive the therapist is, or the

degree to which the client participating in the study 'expects' to get better). We will discuss therapy outcome research of this kind in more detail in Chapter 5, but interested readers may want to have a look at Sloane, Staples, Cristol, Yorkston et al. (1975), Shapiro, Barkham, Rees, Hardy et al. (1994) or Clark, Ehlers, Hackmann, McManus et al. (2006) as examples of how intervention outcome research is conducted.

Finally, practising clinical psychologists often have pressing questions that, for various reasons, they need to answer. Very often these are questions of a practical nature related to their employment as mental health professionals working in organizations that provide mental health services. For example, in the UK, most NHS service providers will want to ensure that the service they are offering is effective. This research is known as *evaluation research* or *clinical audit*. Clinical audit uses research methods to determine whether existing clinical knowledge, skills and resources are effec-

Clinical audit   The use of research methods to determine whether existing clinical knowledge, skills and resources are effective and are being properly used. Also known as **evaluation research**.

tive and are being properly used. The kinds of questions addressed will include 'what is the service trying to achieve?' and 'how will we know if the service has achieved what it is trying to achieve?' (Barker, Pistrang & Elliott, 2002). In this sense, clinical audit does not add to the body of knowledge about psychopathology but is an attempt to ensure that current knowledge is being effectively used. In particular, clinical audit is intended to influence the activities of a local team of clinicians rather than clinical practice generally (Cooper, Turpin, Bucks & Kent, 2005). It uses research methods to assess how much end users value the services on offer, their satisfaction with these services, and what is perceived as good and bad about the services offered (see Tulett, Jones & Lavender, 2006, for an example). Focus Point 3.1 provides a summary of how clinical audit differs from other types of fundamental psychopathology research.

These, then, are some of the reasons why clinical psychologists do research. They include attempts to answer pressing practical problems (e.g. what treatments are effective?) and attempts to

FOCUS POINT 3.1

The distinction between research and audit

The primary aim of research is to add to the existing body of knowledge about psychopathology in such a way that it may influence clinical practice generally. The primary aim of clinical audit is to improve the delivery of health care by comparing current practice with standards of care.

Features of clinical psychology research

1 May involve experiments on human participants, whether patients, patients as volunteers or healthy volunteers.

2 Is a systematic investigation which aims to increase the sum of knowledge.

3 May involve allocating patients randomly to different treatment groups.

4 May involve a completely new treatment.

5 May involve work or input for patients and staff beyond that required for normal clinical management.

6 Usually involves an attempt to test a hypothesis.

7 May involve the application of strict selection criteria to patients with the same problem before they are entered into the research study.

8 Usually will be sufficiently statistically powered.

Features of clinical audit/service evaluation

1 Never involves experiments, whether on healthy volunteers or patients as volunteers.

2 Never involves allocating patients randomly to different treatment groups.

3 Never involves a completely new treatment.

4 Places demands on patients and staff that do not significantly exceed those required for normal clinical management.

5 May involve patients with the same problem being given different treatments, but only after full discussion of the known advantages and disadvantages of each treatment. The patients are allowed to choose freely which treatment they get.

Source: Cooper, Turpin, Bucks & Kent (2005)

SELF-TEST QUESTIONS

- Can you name four main goals of research?
- What does the term aetiology mean?
- What is analogue research?
- What is a clinical audit?

add to the body of knowledge about psychopathology (e.g. what causes specific psychopathologies?). The next section introduces some of the research methods that can be used to answer such questions.

SECTION SUMMARY

3.2 Clinical Psychology Research: What Do We Want To Find Out?

- The main goals of research are **description**, **prediction**, **control** and **understanding**.

- Clinical psychology research is often aimed at understanding the **aetiology** or causes of psychopathology.

- **Analogue research** involves using healthy non-clinical participants or non-human animal studies to understand psychopathology.

3.3 RESEARCH DESIGNS IN CLINICAL PSYCHOLOGY

There is a whole range of research designs that are relevant to clinical psychology research and the type of method you choose will be determined by a number of factors, including (1) the nature of

the question you are asking (e.g. do you want to find out whether one event causes another or whether these events are merely correlated?), (2) the nature of the population you are studying (e.g. is the psychopathology you are studying rare, and so you only have access to a few participants?), and (3) whether your research is at an early or advanced stage (e.g. you may simply want to be able to describe some of the phenomena associated with a psychopathology rather than to explain its causes in detail). The following represent examples of the main research designs used in clinical psychology research. Other more specific examples can be found in the specialized Research Methods in Clinical Psychology boxes found in individual chapters.

3.3.1 Correlational Designs

Correlational designs are among those most commonly used in clinical psychology research. The aim of this methodology is to try to

> **Correlational designs**   Research designs which enable a researcher to determine if there is a relationship between two or more variables.

determine whether there is a relationship between two or more variables. For example, is trait anxiety associated with worrying? Is body dissatisfaction associated with excessive dieting in eating disorders? Is the availability of drugs associated with substance abuse in adolescents? As long as we have valid and reliable ways of measuring the variables we want to study (see Chapter 2, section 2.1.5), then we can undertake a correlational analysis. Basically, a correlational analysis will tell you whether two variables co-vary. That is, if you increase the value of one measure, then does the value of the other also increase? In the examples we have just given, a positive correlation between trait anxiety and worrying would indicate that, as trait anxiety increased, worry would also increase, and a positive correlation between body dissatisfaction and dieting would indicate that as body dissatisfaction increased, so too would dieting behaviour. Note that this does not imply a causal relationship between the two variables and does not explain why they are related, it only indicates that scores on one variable co-vary with scores on the other variable. So, for example, a positive correlation between trait anxiety and worrying could mean that (1) increases in worrying cause an increase in trait anxiety, (2) increases in trait anxiety cause an increase in worrying, or (3) that some other variable causes similar changes in both worry and trait anxiety (for example, increases in depression could cause both increases in worrying *and* increases in trait anxiety). A correlational analysis is often a method that is used at the very beginning of a research programme to simply try to map out how the relevant variables involved in a particular phenomenon interrelate.

To undertake a correlational analysis, researchers need to obtain pairs of scores on the variables being studied. For example, if you are interested in whether there is a relationship between trait anxiety and worrying, you can ask participants to complete questionnaires measuring worry and trait anxiety. You will then have two scores for each participant, and these scores can be entered into a spreadsheet for a computer statistical package such as *Statistical Package for the Social Sciences (SPSS)* (Field, 2005a). This will compute a correlation coefficient (denoted by the symbol *r*) which measures the degree of relationship between the two variables. The correlation coefficient can range from +1.00 through 0.00 to −1.00, with 1.00 denoting a perfect *positive correlation* between the two variables (i.e. as scores on one variable increase, then scores on the other variable will increase), and −1.00 denoting a perfect *negative correlation* between the two variables (i.e. as scores on one variable increase, then scores on the other variable will decrease). A correlation coefficient of 0.00 indicates that the two variables are completely unrelated. The relationship between two variables can also be represented graphically in what is known as a *scattergram*. Figure 3.1 provides three examples of scattergrams representing three different types of relationships between variables. These scattergrams show how the *line of best fit* differs with the nature of the relationship between the two variables concerned. The statistical package that calculates the correlation coefficient and prints out the scattergram will also provide you with an indication of the *statistical significance* of your results. Researchers will want to know the degree to which their results occurred by chance. If the probability of their results occurring by chance is low, then they can be relatively assured that the finding is a reliable one. Traditionally, a correlation is considered statistically significant if the probability of it

Statistical Package for the Social Sciences (SPSS)   A computer program specifically developed for statistical analysis for the social sciences.

Positive correlation   A relationship between two variables in which a high score on one measure is accompanied by a high score on the other.

Negative correlation   A relationship between two variables in which a high score on one measure is accompanied by a low score on the other.

Scattergram   A graphical representation showing the relationship between two variables.

Line of best fit   A straight line used as a best approximation of a summary of all the points in a scattergram.

Statistical significance   The degree to which the outcome of a study is greater or smaller than would be expected by chance.

A

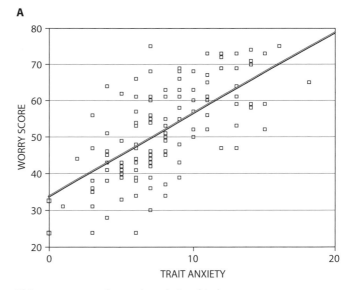

This scattergram shows the relationship between worry scores and trait anxiety scores for the 132 participants. This exhibits a positive correlation, and the **line of best fit** (the straight line) indicates this by showing an increasing trend. The correlation coefficient calculated by SPSS was $r = 0.66$, and this was significant at $p < 0.001$.

B

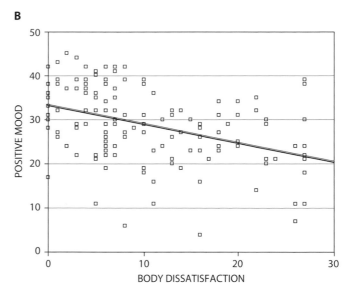

This scattergram shows the relationship between measures of positive mood and body dissatisfaction for the 132 participants. This exhibits a negative correlation, and the **line of best fit** (the straight line) indicates this by showing a decreasing trend. The correlation coefficient calculated by SPSS was $r = -0.40$, and this was significant at $p < 0.001$.

Figure 3.1 *Correlation scattergrams*
In a questionnaire study, 132 female college student participants were asked to fill in valid and reliable questionnaires measuring (1) the extent to which they worried, (2) their level of trait anxiety, (3) the degree of positive mood they exhibited over the past 6 months, (4) their level of dissatisfaction with their body shape, (5) their current level of depression and (6) their height.

C

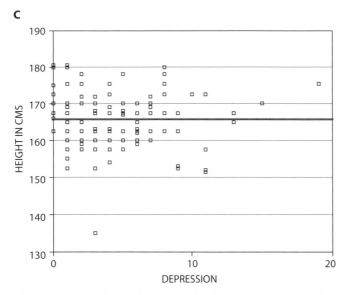

This scattergram shows the relationship between measures of height and depression for the 132 participants. This indicates that these variables are unrelated with the **line of best fit** (the straight line) showing neither an increasing nor decreasing trend. The correlation coefficient calculated by SPSS was $r = 0.01$, with $p > 0.80$, and this was non-significant.

Figure 3.1 *(Cont'd)*

'Correlation Street'

Plate 3.1

occurring by chance is less than 5 in 100: this is written as $p < 0.05$ (*p* stands for probability). From the examples given in Figure 3.1, you can see that the correlations in both parts A and B are statistically significant (because the *p* values are less than 0.05). However, the correlation in part C is not significant (because the *p* value is higher than 0.05), meaning there is probably no important relationship between the two variables.

Correlational designs are valuable for clinical psychology researchers in a variety of ways. First, they allow researchers to begin to understand what variables may be interrelated, and this provides a useful first step towards understanding a particular phenomenon. Second, correlational designs are useful for researching how individual differences and personality factors may relate to psychopathology. For example, it would allow us to determine whether a personality factor such as perfectionism was related to a psychopathology such as obsessive-compulsive disorder (e.g. Tolin, Woods & Abramowitz, 2003). Thirdly, it would also allow us to determine whether certain experiences were associated with specific psychopathologies, such as whether the experience of stressful events is associated with depression (e.g. Brown & Harris, 1978).

However, as we indicated earlier, correlational designs are limited. They certainly do not allow us to draw any conclusions about causality, and they usually provide very little insight into the mechanism or process that might mediate the relationship between the two variables that are correlated. (See Focus Point 3.2.) We need to use other designs (such as the experimental design) to help us answer the question of *how* the two variables are related.

3.3.2 Longitudinal Studies and Prospective Designs

An alternative form of correlational design is known as the **longitudinal study** or **prospective design**. In the traditional correlational design, all measures are taken at the same point in time (known as a **cross-sectional design**, because the study simply takes a sample of measures as a 'cross-section' of ongoing behaviour). However, in longitudinal or prospective designs, measures are taken at two or more different times. In a longitudinal study, measures are taken from the same participants on different occasions usually over a period of time. This may extend over many years, or in more long-term studies, over a participant's whole lifetime. Prospective studies take measures of the relevant variables at a particular point in time (usually called time 1), and then go back to the same participants at some future time and take the same or similar measures again (usually called time 2). Both longitudinal and prospective designs enable researchers to specify more precisely the time-order relationships between variables that are correlated. That is, because measures are taken from the same participant at both times 1 and 2, researchers can not only see whether there are correlations between variables X and Y, but also whether variable X measured at time 1 predicts *changes* in measures of variable Y that occurred between times 1 and 2. A detailed example of

Longitudinal studies Research which takes measures from the same participants at two or more different times in order to specify the time relationships between variables. This may extend over many years or over a participant's whole lifetime.

Prospective designs Research which takes measures from the same participants at two or more different times in order to specify the time relationships between variables.

Cross-sectional design A research design that involves the collection of data from a sample at just one point in time.

Correlation and causation

A significant positive correlation between two variables does not imply causation, nor does it provide any real insight into why or how the two variables are related. Take the following example.

There is a significant positive correlation between body piercings and measures of negative mood (Skegg, Nada-Raja, Paul & Skegg, 2007). Does this mean that body piercing causes negative mood, or that negative mood causes a person to have body piercings? We certainly can't tell from the correlation alone. However, the significant relationship between these two variables may not even represent a causal relationship between them at all: they may both be caused by some other *third variable* that was not measured in the correlational study. In this case, both having body piercings and negative mood may be caused by some other variable, such as (1) *being young*, and so being more likely to indulge in body piercing and experience adolescent depression (Caliendo, Armstrong & Roberts, 2005); (2) *a tendency to indulge in risk-taking behaviours*, and thus being more likely to be less socially conformist but negatively affected by unusual experiences (Carroll, Riffenburgh, Roberts & Myhre, 2002); or (3) *substance abuse*, and so being likely to be

drawn to socially nonconformist cultures that might include body piercing as a fashion statement as well as experiencing the negative emotions that are associated with substance abuse (Forbes, 2001).

a prospective design is give in Research Methods Box 6.1 (Chapter 6), where a measure of negative attributional style at time 1 was shown to predict increases in depression scores between times 1 and 2. This type of design enables researchers to understand the time course of relationships between two variables, and to determine whether one variable predicts changes in a second variable. In the case given in Research Methods Box 6.1, a negative attributional style predicts future increases in depression, and can therefore be identified as a risk factor for depression.

One example of a longitudinal study is the Dunedin Multidisciplinary Health and Development Study, a longitudinal investigation of health and behaviour in a complete birth cohort (Moffitt, Caspi, Rutter & Silva, 2001). Participants in the study were born in Dunedin, New Zealand, between April 1972 and March 1973, and over 1,000 of these individuals then participated in follow-up assessments at age 3, 5, 7, 9, 11, 13, 15, 18, 21 and 26 years. The study has enabled researchers to understand the time-order relationships between variables associated with health and psychopathology, and to understand how some variables can be identified as predictors or risk factors for later behaviour. For example, using prospective data from the Dunedin study, Trzesniewski, Donnellan, Moffitt, Robins et al. (2006) found that low self-esteem in adolescents was a predictor in later life of poorer mental and physical health, poor economic prospects and high levels of criminality.

3.3.3 Epidemiological Studies

Epidemiology is the study of the frequency and distribution of disorders within specific populations over a specified period of time. In this sense, epidemiological research usually takes the form of a large-scale survey, and tends to be *descriptive* in the sense that it attempts to provide details primarily about the *prevalence* of psychological disorders. However, it can also be used to gather information about the factors that correlate with psychological disorders, and this can provide information about how a specific disorder affects people, whether it is more prevalent in young people or old people, men or women, and so on. It can also help us to understand what some of the risk factors are for a specific psychological disorder, and whether the incidence of a disorder is increasing or decreasing over time. *Epidemiological studies* are usually large-scale ones, and need to have enough respondents in the survey to ensure that the sample is representative of all types of person in the population being studied. One of the largest epidemiological studies

> **Prevalence** The number of instances of a given disease or psychopathology in a given population at a designated time.

> **Epidemiological studies** Research which takes the form of a large-scale survey used to study the frequency and distribution of disorders within specific populations over a specified period of time.

in the world is in the US and is called the NIMH Epidemiologic Catchment Area Study (Regier, Myers, Kramer, Robins et al., 1984; Narrow, Rae, Robins & Regier, 2002). This survey has interviewed over 20,000 respondents and has collected data on the prevalence rates of an extensive range of psychological disorders, many of which are described in the prevalence sections of later chapters.

> **Prevalence rates**   The representation of incidence by duration of a particular disorder.

Prevalence rates can be described in a number of different ways. For example, respondents in an epidemiological study can be asked: (1) 'Have you ever experienced symptoms of a specific psychopathology in your lifetime?' (providing information on the *lifetime prevalence* rate of a disorder),

> **Lifetime prevalence**   The frequency of a disorder within a lifetime.

(2) 'Have you experienced symptoms of a specific psychopathology in the last month?' (providing information on the *one-month prevalence* rate of a disorder; e.g. Regier, Farmer, Rae, Myers et al.,

> **One-month prevalence**   The frequency of a disorder within the last month.

1993), or (3) 'Are you experiencing symptoms of a specific psychopathology at the present time?' (providing information on what is known as the *point prevalence* of a disorder, i.e. the frequency of a disorder in the population at any one point in time). You can see from

> **Point prevalence**   The frequency of a disorder in the population at any one point in time.

these examples that prevalence rates represent *incidence × duration*. It is important to view prevalence in this way because some disorders are of high incidence but low duration (e.g. bouts of depression), and some others are of low incidence but long duration (e.g. schizophrenia). DSM-IV-TR usually provides information on either the lifetime prevalence rates of a disorder or its point prevalence, and these are the kinds of statistics we will be using when considering specific disorders in later chapters.

The benefits of epidemiological studies are that they provide information about the frequency of mental health problems that can be used for planning health care services. They may also provide information about the risk factors for various psychological disorders, which will help health service providers to identify those who may be at risk of developing a mental health problem and so introduce programmes designed to help prevent those problems. For example, excessive alcohol consumption in pregnant mothers is a risk factor for infant foetal alcohol syndrome in the offspring, and prevention programmes aim to identify those women at risk of alcohol abuse during pregnancy and to provide interventions or alcohol-reduction counselling (Floyd, O'Connor, Sokol, Bertrand et al., 2005).

However, like all research approaches, there are some limitations to epidemiological studies. For example, to provide valid descriptions of the prevalence rates of psychological disorders in a particular population, the sample used must be truly representative of that population. This is often difficult to achieve because such studies will never attain a 100 per cent response rate, and many respondents will often refuse to take part. Studies suggest that those who are most likely to refuse to take part in an epidemiological survey are men, individuals of low socioeconomic status

and individuals from ethnic minority populations (Fischer, Dornelas & Goethe, 2001), and this is likely to mean that the samples used in most epidemiological studies are not fully representative of the population being studied.

3.3.4 Experimental Designs

Arguably one of the most powerful research designs is the *experiment*. This is a design in which the researcher manipulates a particular variable and observes the effect of

> **Experiment**   A design in which the researcher manipulates a particular variable and observes the effect of this manipulation on some outcome, such as the participant's behaviour.

this manipulation on some outcome, such as the participant's behaviour. For example, if we want to know whether negative mood makes people worry, we can experimentally manipulate participants' moods and see if this changes the extent to which they worry in the way we predicted. One important advantage of the experimental design over many of the other research designs we will discuss is that it does allow researchers to determine whether there is a *causal relationship* between variables, and to identify the direction of the causal effect. This is an important step in developing theories and models about the aetiology of psychopathologies (Field & Davey, 2005).

3.3.4.1 Basic Features of the Experimental Method

In most experiments the researcher manipulates one particular variable to assess its effects on a particular outcome. Usually the experimenter begins with an *experimental hypothesis* or *experimental prediction* about what will happen. For example, we may predict that if we increase negative mood,

> **Experimental hypothesis**   A prediction about what the outcome of an experimental manipulation might be (also known as **experimental prediction**).

our participants will worry more, and this hypothesis is derived either from (1) an existing academic theory about worrying, (2) our observations of worrying in everyday life, (3) the existing research literature on worrying or (4) the outcomes of other studies we have conducted on worrying. The variable we are manipulating (in this case mood) is known as the *independent variable*, and the

> **Independent variable (IV)**   The variable that is manipulated in an experiment.

outcome variable we are measuring (in this case worrying) is known as the *dependent variable*.

> **Dependent variable (DV)**   The outcome variable that is measured in an experiment.

However, imagine that our experiment involves simply increasing negative mood and finding out that this increases the participants' tendency to worry. This is not as informative as it seems because (1) simply changing participants' mood in any direction (positive or negative) may cause them to worry more; (2) if we use sad music to put our participants into a negative mood, maybe it is just listening to music that makes them worry more (regardless of whether it is sad music); or, more radically, (3) any participant taking part in any experiment may simply worry more. This clearly indicates that to be able to make some valid conclusions about the effect of our manipulation, we will have to compare our manipulation with some other conditions that control for any confounding effects. These comparisons are known as *control conditions*.

Control conditions   Conditions within an experiment that control for any effects other than that produced by the independent variable.

For example, suitable control conditions in our example experiment would be to have a group of participants who undergo a mood manipulation that increases positive rather than negative mood, and perhaps a third group who undergo a similar manipulation that does not change mood at all. So, our *experimental group* may listen to sad music that makes their mood more negative, our first *control group* may listen to happy music that makes their mood more positive, and our second control group may listen to neutral music that does not change their mood in either direction.

Experimental group   A group of participants who experience the independent variable in an experimental study.

Control group   A group of participants who experience manipulations other than the independent variable being investigated.

Suppose now that, after the music manipulation, participants in our experimental group worry significantly more than participants in both the positive and neutral control groups. This allows us to conclude that negative mood causes an increase in worrying, and allows us to discount our other potential confounding explanations. For example, the increase in worrying in the negative group is *not* a result of (1) a change in mood in any direction (because the positive mood group did not show a similar increase in worrying), (2) simply listening to music (because all three groups listened to music, but only the negative group showed an increase in worry), or (3) simply being in an experiment (because our positive and neutral mood groups did not increase their worry as much as the negative mood group).

It is still possible, however, that the differences in worrying between our three groups have occurred by chance. Just as the researcher using correlational designs needs to conduct a statistical analysis to rule this out, so does the researcher using experimental designs. This means that we need to have an objective way of measuring the outcome (dependent variable) so that the data from the experiment can be subjected to a statistical analysis and we can be assured that our findings are statistically significant (see section 3.3.1). In this case we need to find a way of objectively measuring the amount of worrying that each participant indulges in after the mood manipulation.

One other feature of designing experiments is in the assignment of participants to the various conditions or groups in the experiment. Typically, researchers use *random assignment* of participants to experimental conditions. This is to ensure that at the outset of the experiment,

Random assignment   Assignment of participants to different treatments, interventions or conditions according to chance.

all groups have participants with similar characteristics. In our example experiment, the findings of our study would be compromised if we happened to have participants in our negative mood group who naturally worried more than the participants in the other two control groups – even before we had completed our experimental manipulations. This can usually be prevented by the random assignment of participants to groups, and this should normally ensure that there are no statistical differences between the groups at the outset of the experiment on characteristics that may influence the dependent variable.

Finally, both the experimenter and the participant may introduce bias into an experiment that can affect the validity of the findings. For example, during an experiment, a participant may begin to think about the purpose of the experiment and behave in a way which is consistent with these thoughts. When this occurs, the participant is said to be responding according to the *demand characteristics* of the experiment (i.e. what he or she thinks the experiment is about) rather than to the stimuli and events in the experiment. Equally, the experimenter may unwittingly bias the results of an experiment. Because the experimenter may know which of the experimental conditions a participant is in, and also knows what the experimental predictions are for these conditions, the experimenter may provide subtle cues which lead the participant to behave in the predicted way. To avoid experimenter bias of this kind, a *double-blind* procedure can be used in which neither the experimenter nor the participant is aware of which group the participant is in (i.e. a second experimenter may be employed simply to assign participants to experimental conditions without the first experimenter knowing).

Demand characteristics   The features of an experiment which are the result of participants acting according to what they believe is expected of them.

Double-blind   An experimental procedure in which neither the experimenter nor the participant is aware of which experimental condition the participant is in.

Activity Box 3.3 introduces the kinds of questions that researchers undertaking an experimental study need to ask when designing and analysing their experiment. You should ensure you understand the various concepts described in this section before attempting this activity.

3.3.4.2 Uses of the Experiment in Clinical Psychology Research

Experimental designs are used extensively in research into the aetiology of psychopathology. This is because the experiment is a powerful technique that allows researchers to establish the direction of causal relationships between events, and this is critical for our understanding of the causes of psychopathology. Many research methods do allow us to say that two variables may be significantly associated, but that is all – they do not tell us whether there is a causal relationship between these events. For example, we know that depression is associated with low levels of the brain neurotransmitter serotonin. But do low levels of serotonin cause depression, or does depression cause a reduction in brain serotonin levels, or is some third factor involved in affecting both?

ACTIVITY BOX 3.3

Questions to ask when designing an experiment

Below is a series of questions that you can ask yourself as you go through the process of designing an experiment. The example answers to these questions are based on a researcher who wants to find out whether negative mood significantly increases worrying (see Johnston & Davey, 1997, for one example of how this question has been tackled experimentally).

1 What is my experimental hypothesis and what prediction can I derive from it?

Hypothesis: That negative mood makes people worry more.

Prediction: That inducing a negative mood in participants will make them worry more.

2 What existing evidence am I using to justify my experimental hypothesis?

That there is a significant positive correlation between worry and anxious and depressed mood (e.g. Meyer, Miller, Metzger & Borkovec, 1990)

3 What is my experimental manipulation, and what materials and procedures will I need to practically implement it in the experiment?

The manipulation is to induce negative mood in the experimental group. I could do this by playing them sad music or getting them to watch stressful videos.

4 Am I sure that my experiment is manipulating only one independent variable? (NB never try to manipulate more than one variable in a single experiment because you will not know which one caused any effects you observe – manipulate the second variable in a different experiment.)

Yes.

5 What possible confounding variables do I need to control for?

A change of mood in any direction could increase worrying, as could just listening to music or watching a video regardless of its content.

6 What control groups do I need to control for these confounding variables?

I need to have control groups that experience a change in mood other than an increase in negative mood – perhaps a group that listen to music or watch a video that increases positive mood; and I need a group that listens to music or watches videos that do not cause any change in mood.

7 Does my experimental group differ from my control groups only on the one single factor that I am trying to manipulate?

Yes – my experimental group listen to music or watch videos: they differ only to the extent that they are the only group to experience an increase in negative mood.

8 Am I sure that there is a random assignment of participants to the various groups in my experiment?

Yes – I will allocate each participant to a group by drawing lots.

9 Prior to undertaking the experimental manipulation, can I be sure that my groups do not differ on important characteristics that may spuriously affect the outcome of the study?

Prior to the experimental manipulation I need to be sure that each group does not differ on levels of positive or negative mood or on the frequency with which they normally worry. I will give them validated questionnaires that measure these attributes prior to the experiment to check that participants in each group do not differ significantly on the scores on these questionnaires.

10 How can I check that my experimental manipulation is effective enough?

I need to be sure that the music/video causes an increase in negative mood in my experimental group, an increase in positive mood in my first control group and no change in mood in my second control group. I will take a measure of their mood before and after they experience the manipulation and see if their moods change as predicted.

11 How can I objectively measure my dependent variable?

My dependent variable has to be a measure of the frequency of worry. I could ask them to think about something that is worrying them at present and time how long they do this for. Alternatively, I could get them to write down what they are worrying about and count how many sentences this amounts to (see Davey, 2006, for an example).

12 Is my experimental design one that lends itself easily to statistical analysis so that I can ascertain whether my findings are statistically significant?

Yes – it represents a simple one-way ANOVA comparing worry scores across the three groups in the study. See Field (2005a).

13 Are there any ethical issues that I need to consider about subjecting my participants to this kind of procedure?

With any experiment that manipulates mood or asks the participant to think about stressful material, such as their current worries, there are likely to be ethical issues. You should consider how you can minimize these issues and send participants out of the experiment in a physical and mental state similar to those they were in when they started the experiment. See section 3.4 for more about ethical issues.

14 Do I have the means to obtain the informed consent of my participants?

See section 3.4.1 and Figure 3.4.

15 Is there any way that I might introduce some experimenter bias that will affect the way in which participants may respond in each of the groups in my experiment?

I must be sure to give the participants their experimental instructions in exactly the same way. I could also conduct the experiment blind, by asking someone else to conduct the mood induction so that I am unaware what condition participants are in when I ask them to worry.

16 Is there any way that I, as the experimenter, might bias the way that the dependent variable is measured?

Worrying is a fairly subjective phenomenon. I must be very sure that the method of measuring this is objective and fair and involves no subjective judgements on my part.

Now you have looked through these examples, attempt to answer these same questions when designing an experiment to tackle one or more of the following research issues:

(1) Do uncontrollable stressful experiences make people feel sad and depressed?

(2) Does actively suppressing an unpleasant thought cause the thought to occur more frequently once the person has stopped suppressing it?

(3) When people are anxious, do they have a tendency to interpret ambiguous stimuli as threats (see Activity Box 5.2)?

(4) Does reading poetry make people feel less anxious?

(5) Does feeling sad or depressed increase a person's body dissatisfaction?

(6) Do people remember threatening words better when they are in an anxious mood?

(7) Does an increase in feelings of anxiety also cause an increase in feelings of sadness and depression?

Only properly controlled experiments can answer some of these questions. Having said this, it is often difficult to do experiments with individuals with mental health problems. Experiments involve manipulating critical variables, and this may mean exposing already vulnerable and distressed individuals to even greater distress. Imagine doing our experiment on the effect of negative mood on worrying with individuals diagnosed with generalized anxiety disorder. These are people who already suffer chronic uncontrollable worry at distressing levels, and our negative mood manipulation could make this even worse. In order to avoid these ethical difficulties, many clinical psychology researchers carry out their research in what are known as *analogue experiments* using *analogue populations* (see Davey, 2003; Vredenburg, Flett & Krames, 1993). Analogue populations are usually participants without any mental health problems and often consist of a normal sample of healthy, student participants. However, for experiments on psychopathology undertaken with analogue populations to be valuable, we need to consider what makes them valid analogues of psychopathology processes. There are at least three ways in which we can argue that analogue studies are valid.

> **Analogue populations** Populations that are usually participants without any mental health problems, which may be human or non-human animals.

1 It is being increasingly argued that psychopathology is dimensional rather than discrete. That is, symptoms diagnosed as a psychological disorder may just be extreme versions of normal, everyday behaviours and reactions (Krueger & Piasecki, 2002). If so, then what we find out about these behaviours and reactions in non-clinical populations will tell us something about the processes that cause the more severe reactions found in clinical populations.

2 In the laboratory, we can use experimental manipulations to create psychopathology in non-clinical participants. For example, in Chapter 5, Research Methods Box 5.2 describes experimental manipulations that allow us to cause panic attacks in non-clinical participants. We can use these manipulations to study a participant's reaction to a panic attack under controlled conditions.

3 Non-clinical participants can be selected for an experimental study because they are similar to individuals with psychopathology. For example, a good deal of research has been carried out on college students who score high on measures of depression (Vredenburg, Flett & Krames, 1993). Such participants do not usually have levels of depression that are clinically significant, but this does allow an experimenter to compare how college students scoring high or low on measures of depression might react to an experimental manipulation.

Analogue populations do not even have to be human to provide valuable information about psychopathology. Animal studies are also a valuable source of information about basic processes that might underlie psychopathology, especially when attempting to

Animal models The use of laboratory animals in research to simulate processes comparable to those occurring in humans.

understand how brain function may influence psychopathology. *Animal models* allow researchers to experimentally investigate such factors as the genetics of a psychopathology (using intensive breeding programmes), changes in brain biochemistry associated with specific psychopathologies (such as changes in brain neurotransmitter levels associated with psychotic-like symptoms), and the effects of drugs on psychopathology (such as the effect of antidepressants on brain biochemistry and behaviour) (e.g. Porsolt, Lepichon & Jalfre, 1977; Lavi-Avnon, Yadid, Overstreet & Weller, 2005). Animal studies have the advantage of providing complete control over the organism's developmental history (and so controlling genetic factors and factors affected by feeding and living experiences), and permit the use of some experimental methods that would be considered too intrusive to use with human participants (such as assessing the effects of electrical stimulation of the brain, and the sampling of brain neurotransmitters). Nevertheless, even though many types of animal research are legally licensed by governments, it is an area of research that has become increasingly controversial because of changing views on the ethical implications of using non-human animals in scientific experiments (Rollin, 2006; Rowan, 1997).

Another important use of the experimental design in psychopathology research is in studies testing the effectiveness of treatments for mental health problems. These types of studies are

Clinical trials Experimental research studies used to test the effectiveness of treatments for mental health problems.

often known as *clinical trials*, and attempt to test whether (1) a treatment is more effective than no treatment; (2) whether treatment A is more effective than treatment B; or (3) whether a newly developed treatment is more effective than existing treatments. In a standard treatment efficacy experiment, researchers will allocate clients or patients with a specific psychopathology (e.g. depression) to different experimental conditions. The experimental group will receive the treatment manipulation whose efficacy is being tested (e.g. a form of psychotherapy), and control groups will undergo other manipulations depending on what comparisons need to be made. For example, if the researchers want to discover if the psychotherapy treatment is more effective than a drug treatment, then a control group will receive the drug instead of psychotherapy. The researchers will then measure symptoms at various points in time after the two treatments to assess which is more effective (e.g. Ward, King, Lloyd, Bower et al., 2000; Leff, Vearnals, Brewin, Wolff et al., 2000).

Sometimes, researchers may want to assess whether a particular intervention is more effective than simply doing nothing. However, this is not as simple a comparison as it sounds. Logically, you would imagine that a researcher would subject half the participants to the intervention and allocate the other half to a control condition in which they receive no treatment. Suppose the researcher wants to assess the effectiveness of a drug treatment for depression. Just giving the experimental group a pill containing the drug and giving the control group nothing has a number of problems. First, the experimental group may get better simply because they are being giving a pill and this leads them to *expect* to

get better. This is known as a *placebo effect*, where a participant may improve simply because the procedure she is undergoing leads her to believe she should get better. To control for this possibility, a control group should be included in which the participants are given a pill that contains an inactive substance (such as a sugar pill). This is known as a *placebo control condition*, which controls for the possibility that participants may improve simply because they are being given a pill regardless of what is in it. Nevertheless, suffice it to say here that the experimental method does provide a useful paradigm for assessing the effectiveness of different interventions. We will discuss the complexities and limitations of this approach when we discuss treatment methods more thoroughly in Chapter 4.

Placebo effect The effect when participants in a clinical trial show improvement even though they are not being given a theoretically structured treatment.

Placebo control condition A control group that is included in a clinical trial to assess the effects of participant expectations.

SUMMARY

The experiment is arguably the most powerful research tool that we have because it allows us to draw conclusions about the direction of causality between variables, and this is the first step towards putting together theories and models of how psychopathology is caused. However, in order to provide valid results, experiments must be carefully designed and well controlled. Experiments are more than just data collection exercises, and the experimenter needs to *manipulate* important variables in order to discover causal relationships between events and behaviour. This means that in some cases the experiment can be too intrusive for use with clients suffering psychopathology. Thus, many of our studies investigating psychopathology need to be conducted on analogue populations such as healthy volunteers and non-human participants.

3.3.5 Mixed Designs

One of the basic principles of experimental design is that participants must be assigned to different groups on a random basis. However, this principle can be set aside if the research question being tackled requires a *mixed design*. For example, suppose we wanted to see whether negative mood caused anxious individuals to worry more than depressed individuals. In an experiment of this kind, we would still be experimentally inducing negative mood (the experimental manipulation), but we would not be assigning participants randomly to the experimental groups: rather, we would want to

Mixed designs Research which uses the non-random assignment of participants to groups in an experiment.

ensure that in one experimental group we had only anxious individuals and in a second experimental group we had only depressed individuals. We would select the participants pre-experimentally on the basis of these attributes and assign them non-randomly to each group. This is known as a mixed design because (1) we are adopting elements from the experimental approach (i.e. we are manipulating an independent variable), but (2) we are assigning our participants non-randomly to the experimental groups. This is a design that is used quite frequently in psychopathology research because the clinical psychology researcher may often want to know if a particular variable will affect individuals with different psychopathologies in similar or different ways.

An example of a mixed design is a study by Sanderson, Rapee and Barlow (1989) investigating the effects of expectations on panic disorder. They pre-selected two groups of participants, one group consisting of individuals diagnosed with panic disorder and the other group consisting of individuals with no psychiatric diagnosis. They then subjected both groups to an experimental manipulation. In this case, they asked all participants to inhale compressed air but told them they were inhaling CO_2, which could induce a panic attack (see Chapter 5, p. 137). Even though the compressed air itself could not have induced a panic attack, participants diagnosed with panic disorder were significantly more likely to have a panic attack after the manipulation, suggesting that in such individuals the mere expectation of a panic attack is likely to induce one.

Mixed designs are frequently used in treatment outcome studies, where the effectiveness of a particular intervention is being assessed on individuals with different psychiatric diagnoses or with different severity of symptoms. Figure 3.2 shows the results of a mixed design study carried out by Huppert, Schultz, Foa and Barlow (2004) designed to assess the effects of administering a placebo pill to three different groups of participants, each diagnosed with a different psychiatric disorder. In this study the researchers found that their experimental manipulation (the administration of a placebo pill) significantly reduced the severity of reported symptoms in individuals diagnosed with social phobia and panic disorder, but not in individuals diagnosed with OCD.

This example illustrates how useful the mixed design can be when attempting to assess how individuals with different diagnoses or groups of symptoms will react to an experimental manipulation (such as a treatment intervention). However, we must always be aware of the fact that one of the variables in a mixed design (in this case the diagnostic groups) is not manipulated, so we cannot infer a direct *causal* relationship between the diagnostic category and the effects of the manipulation. For example, in Figure 3.2, we cannot infer that the failure of the OCD group to improve after being given a placebo is caused by the specific fact that they are suffering from OCD because we have not explicitly manipulated that variable. It could be that some other variable related to OCD is causing the failure to respond, such as having less faith in drug treatments generally, or that individuals with OCD may be more resistant to any treatment than those in the other groups.

3.3.6 Natural Experiments

Most experiments are the result of a deliberate manipulation carried out under controlled conditions by an experimenter. However, in the case of clinical psychology research, nature may sometimes provide us with the opportunity to observe the effects on behaviour of a natural manipulation. ***Natural experiments*** usually allow us to collect data on the effects of events that we would not usually be able to manipulate

> **Natural experiments**   Research which allows researchers to observe the effects on behaviour of a naturally occurring 'manipulation' (such as an earthquake).

in the laboratory. Such events include natural disasters such as earthquakes and floods, traumatic disasters or accidents such as the King's Cross tube station fire, or terrorist attacks such as those on the New York Trade Centre of 11 September 2001. For example, van Griensven, Chakkraband, Thienkrua, Pengjuntr et al. (2006) studied survivors of the 2004 tsunami in southern Thailand and found that the event had caused elevated rates of symptoms of PTSD, anxiety and depression in survivors. Other studies have used naturally occurring disasters as a tool to assess whether such events increase psychopathology only in individuals with particular characteristics. For instance, Weems, Pina, Costa, Watts et al. (2007) found that PTSD symptoms in children following the devastation caused by Hurricane Katrina in the southern USA in 2005 was highest in those children who had high levels of trait anxiety prior to the disaster.

Other variables that may play a part in the development of psychopathology include poverty and social deprivation, and these are clearly factors that we could not easily manipulate in

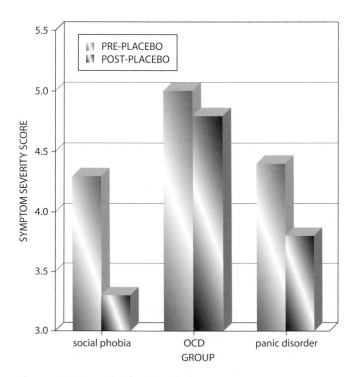

Figure 3.2 *Example of a mixed design*
Source: Huppert, Schultz, Foa and Barlow (2004).

Plate 3.2 *The King's Cross tube station fire, 1987*
Natural disasters and accidents – such as the King's Cross tube station fire of 1987, can be used as 'natural' experiments, allowing clinical psychology researchers to collect data on the effects of events that we would not easily be able to manipulate in the laboratory.

a controlled experiment. However, Costello, Compton, Keeler and Angold (2003) took advantage of the opening of a casino in a Native American reservation to study how poverty and conduct disorder in children might be linked (see Chapter 15, p. 547). The introduction of the casino provided income that moved many of the local families out of poverty, and Costello et al. found that this resulted in a significant decrease in the symptoms of conduct disorder in local children – but only in those children whose families had benefited financially from the introduction of the casino, suggesting either a direct or indirect link between poverty and symptoms of childhood conduct disorder.

3.3.7 Single Case Studies

For a variety of reasons, clinical psychology researchers may study just one individual and gather the information and knowledge they require from detailed description and analysis of a single case. This may take the form of a comprehensive *case study* in which the clinician gathers detailed information about the individual, including details of symptoms, family history, medical history, personal experiences, educational background, and so on, and then attempts to ascertain what light these details may cast on an understanding of the individual's psychopathology. In some respects, the case formulation that clinical practitioners undertake when conducting therapy is a form of case study, in which they attempt to understand the causes of an individual client's symptoms in terms of that person's cognitions, experiential history or

Case study An in-depth investigation of an individual participant.

personal relationships (see Chapter 2, section 2.2). An alternative form of the single case study is the *single-case experiment*, in which a participant's behaviour is observed and measured both before and after an experimental manipulation. The researcher can then make some assumptions about what is happening by comparing the participant's behaviour before the manipulation with her behaviour after the manipulation. The individual thus acts as both experimental participant and control participant.

Single-case experiment A single case study in which a participant's behaviour is observed and measured both before and after an experimental manipulation.

3.3.7.1 Case Studies

Before the development of sophisticated research designs, the case study was one of the most widely used methods of collecting information about psychopathology, and knowledge collected in this way often served as the basis for the development of early theories. One famous exponent of the case study was Sigmund Freud himself. Many important features of psychoanalytic theory were based on Freud's detailed observation and analysis of individual cases. One such example is the famous case of Little Hans, a 5-year-old boy who had a fear of horses. In Chapter 5, Focus Point 5.1 describes how Freud studied this single case in detail, and how it enabled him to develop his view that many childhood fears were caused by a subconscious Oedipus complex. In a different example in the 1940s, case studies of disturbed children provided the Austrian psychiatrist Leo Kanner with a set of observations indicating a consistent set of symptoms that he called *infantile autism*, which gave rise to the symptom classification that we currently know as autistic spectrum disorder (see Chapter 16, section 16.4).

Case studies are valuable in a number of different circumstances. (1) They are useful when there are only a few instances of a particular psychopathology available for study. This was the case when dissociative identity disorder (DID) (multiple personalities) was first reported as a specific disorder in the 1950s and 1960s: an example of the use of case histories in the first descriptions of this disorder is provided in Case History 13.1 in Chapter 13. (2) Case studies are also valuable for providing new insights into existing psychopathologies. The detailed information that a case study can offer may often provide new ways of looking at a particular problem and new facts that can subsequently be subjected to more rigorous research methods (Davison & Lazarus, 1995). The example of Kanner's discovery of infantile autism through meticulous case studies of individual children is one such example. (3) The case study can provide detailed information that may *disprove* existing theories. We saw in section 3.1.2 that scientific hypotheses can often be refuted or falsified by a single finding. Case histories are capable of providing individual findings that are inconsistent with existing theories or explanations of a psychopathology. For example, some theories of eating disorders such as anorexia nervosa propose that dissatisfaction with body shape is a critical factor in developing an eating disorder. However, it would only take one case history describing an individual who developed anorexia *without* exhibiting any body dissatisfaction to question the universality of this theory.

Despite these benefits, the case study also has a significant number of limitations. First, and most important, case studies lack the objectivity and control provided by many other research methods. For example, the information collected by a clinical researcher in a case study is likely to be significantly influenced by that clinician's theoretical orientation. Arguably, the detailed information on Little Hans collected by Freud was significantly influenced by Freud's own theoretical views on psychopathology, and it was quite likely that he collected and used only that information that was consistent with his existing views. Freud clearly spent much time finding out about Little Hans's childhood, whereas more cognitively or behaviourally oriented psychologists would focus on current cognitions or those current environmental factors that might be maintaining Little Hans's behaviour (see Chapter 1, section 1.1.3). Secondly, case studies are usually low on *external validity*. That is, the findings from one case are rarely generalizable to other cases. For instance, because of the subjective nature of the information collected by a clinician in a case study, how can we be sure the supposed causes of psychopathology in that case study will also be true for other individuals with similar psychopathologies? Finally, we have just argued that the case study can be valuable in providing evidence that could disprove a theory. However, because of the uncontrolled way in which case studies are collected, it is not a particularly useful method for providing evidence to support theories. For example, a case study may indicate that a young woman with an eating disorder is dissatisfied with her body shape. This is information that is *consistent* with theories of eating disorders that assume a role for body dissatisfaction, but it is not evidence that differentially favours that theory because the case study does not (1) rule out other explanations or (2) indicate that body dissatisfaction plays a critical role in causing the eating disorder.

External validity   The extent to which the results of a study can be extrapolated to other situations.

3.3.7.2 Single-Case Experiments

The single-case experiment has a particular value in psychopathology research and is used relatively frequently. The main value of this method is that it enables the researcher (1) to undertake an experimental manipulation (and so potentially make some inferences about causal relationships between variables) and (2) to use one individual as both experimental and control participant. There is a particular advantage in using a single participant and subjecting that individual to both experimental and control conditions. First, in many psychopathology studies, the use of a control group may mean denying individual participants a treatment that they need. For example, if a researcher is attempting to assess the efficacy of a particular treatment, she would have to compare the treatment with a control group that did not receive that treatment. This obviously raises ethical issues about withholding treatment from participants who may benefit from it. Secondly, some psychopathologies are quite rare, and it can be difficult to gather enough participants to form groups of experimental and control participants. Thus, conducting an experiment on a single participant may be a necessity.

The single-case experiment allows the experimenter to take some baseline measures of behaviour (the control condition) before introducing the experimental manipulation (the experimental condition), and behaviour during baseline can then be compared with behaviour following the manipulation. Most single-case experiments use variations of what are known as the ABA or ABAB design. In the *ABA design*, an initial baseline stage involves the observation and measurement of behaviour without any intervention (A). This is then followed by a treatment or manipulation stage where the experimental manipulation is introduced and its effect on behaviour observed and measured (B). Subsequently a final return-to-baseline stage is introduced (A) in which behaviour is once more observed in the absence of the treatment or manipulation. The second baseline stage is included to ensure that any behaviour change that occurs in stage B is caused by the manipulation and not by any confounding factor such as a natural drift in behaviour over time. In the *ABAB design* (sometimes known as a *reversal design*), a second treatment or manipulation stage is introduced and provides extra power in demonstrating that any changes in behaviour are explicitly due to the manipulation or treatment.

ABA design   A single-case experiment which involves an initial baseline stage of observation and measurement of behaviour without any intervention (A), followed by a treatment or manipulation stage where the experimental manipulation is introduced and its effect on behaviour observed and measured (B). A final return-to-baseline stage is then introduced (A) in which behaviour is once more observed in the absence of the treatment or manipulation.

ABAB design   A single-case experiment, similar to the ABA design, with the addition of a second treatment or manipulation stage, providing extra power in demonstrating that any changes in behaviour are explicitly due to the manipulation or treatment.

Figure 3.3 provides an example of the use of an ABAB design. This demonstrates the effectiveness of providing a social story conveying information about appropriate mealtime behaviour for an individual with Asperger's syndrome (Bledisoe, Smith Myles & Simpson, 2007). In this example, the effectiveness of the manipulation was demonstrated by the fact that behaviours returned to baseline levels following the withdrawal of the manipulation (the second A stage), and across all four stages the frequency of the measured behaviour fluctuated in accordance with whether the experimental manipulation was present (B) or not (A).

One disadvantage of the ABAB design is that it alternates periods of treatment with non-treatment. This may be problematic if the study is assessing the effectiveness of a treatment that has important benefits for the participant (e.g. it prevents self-injurious behaviour or alleviates distress). This problem can be overcome by using a *multiple-baseline design*. There are two variations to this procedure. (1) Using a single participant, the researcher can select two or more behaviours to measure and can target the treatment or manipulation on one behaviour but allow the other behaviours to act as control

Multiple-baseline design   An experimental design in which the researcher studies several behaviours at a time.

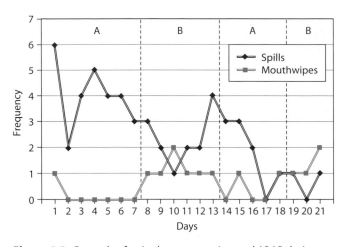

Figure 3.3 *Example of a single-case experimental ABAB design*
The participant in this study was a 13-year-old male with Asperger's syndrome and attention deficit hyperactivity disorder (ADHD) (see Chapter 15) who exhibited a number of eating-related problems (e.g. talking with mouth full, spilling food, talking in a loud voice). Days 1–7 show the baseline levels of spills (a 'bad' response) and mouthwipes (a 'good' response) (the first A phase). The intervention used (phase B) was a social story provided to the participant to help him improve his eating habits. The figure shows how good eating behaviours tended to increase and bad behaviours tended to decrease in frequency during the intervention phases, but return to normal during baseline phases.

Source: Bledisoe, Smith Myles & Simpson (2007).

comparisons. (2) The researcher can use multiple participants by first taking baseline measures from each (stage A), then introducing the treatment or manipulation (B) successively across the participants. The multiple-baseline design means that each individual within the study can receive the treatment for a maximum amount of time without compromising the experimental balance of the study (e.g. Thompson, Kearns & Edmonds, 2006).

While the single-case experiment has a number of significant benefits, it too also has some limitations. Most importantly, it is still a single case study, so it may be difficult to generalize the results to other individuals with similar psychopathologies: because a treatment works for one person does not necessarily mean it will work for another. Group designs overcome this problem by using statistical inference across a number of participants to determine the probability that the findings from the study will be generalizable to a larger population. However, the problem of generalizability can be overcome to some extent by using more than one participant. If the treatment or manipulation is effective across more than one participant, then this increases the chances that it will be generalizable to other individuals.

3.3.8 Meta-analyses

Many different researchers frequently conduct studies investigating the same or similar phenomena, so it is usually the case that we end up with many studies providing information on the same issue. For example, we may want to know whether cognitive behaviour therapy (CBT) is a successful treatment for depression, and many different researchers may end up conducting studies and experiments to this end. Some of these studies may convincingly demonstrate that CBT is effective, some others may suggest that its effectiveness is marginal, and still others may fail to provide any evidence for its effectiveness. How do we decide which studies to believe, and how do we try to make an informed decision about the effectiveness of CBT in treating depression? Traditionally, this task would have been undertaken in review articles in which the reviewer would collect together all the relevant studies, and try to make an informed judgement across the whole range of studies and their results (e.g. Marcotte, 1997; Laidlaw, 2001; Brewin, 1996). However, this approach is likely to be highly subjective: one reviewer may significantly disagree with another about the importance of individual studies, and some researchers with vested interests in particular types of treatment may consciously or unconsciously bias the way they interpret findings (e.g. those favouring drug treatments for depression are likely to be less convinced by studies demonstrating the effectiveness of CBT than others) (Field, 2005b).

These problems with subjective reviews have led to attempts to develop more objective reviews using statistical methods. **_Meta-analyses_** are the outcome of this process, and are now becoming accepted ways of objectively assessing the strength of findings across different studies. A meta-analysis attempts to detect trends across studies that may have used different procedures, different numbers of participants, different types of control procedures and different forms of measurement, and it does this by comparing effect sizes across studies. An **_effect size_** is an objective and standardized measure of the magnitude of the effect observed in a study (i.e. the difference in measured outcome between participants in a treatment or experimental group and those in appropriate control conditions), and the fact that it is standardized means that we can use this measure to compare the outcomes of studies that may have used different forms of measurement. Meta-analyses are now an almost accepted way of overviewing studies that address the same or a similar research issue and are particularly popular as a statistical tool for assessing the effectiveness of interventions for psychopathology (for examples see Cuijpers, van Straten & Warmerdam, 2007; Cuijpers, van Straten & Smit, 2006; de Maat, Dekker, Schoevers & de Jonghe, 2006).

While many meta-analyses have been carried out specifically on the effectiveness of individual treatments and interventions, the basis of comparison can be other factors such as type of psychopathology

Meta-analyses Statistically accepted ways of assessing the strength of a particular finding across a number of different studies.

Effect size An objective and standardized measure of the magnitude of the effect observed in a research study.

being treated or the comparison of drug treatments generally versus psychotherapy interventions. One of the earliest meta-analyses was a large-scale study carried out by Smith and Glass (1977) assessing whether psychotherapies were more effective than no treatment at all. From the results of their meta-analyses they concluded (1) that a very wide range of psychotherapies were more effective at reducing symptoms of psychopathology than no treatment at all, and perhaps more controversially, (2) that effect sizes did not differ significantly across different types of psychotherapies, implying that all psychotherapies were equally effective!

Nevertheless, while a meta-analysis may seem like an objective solution to the problem of reviewing the findings from groups of studies, this method too has its limitations. First, meta-analyses rely almost entirely on analysing the results of published studies, and published studies are much more likely to have significant results than non-significant results (Dickersin, Min & Meinert, 1992). This means that meta-analyses are likely to overestimate mean effect sizes because they are unlikely to include unpublished studies that are probably non-significant. The result is that they are probably biased towards claiming that a variable or treatment is effective when it may not be (Field, 2005b). Secondly, effect sizes will be influenced by the quality of the research (e.g. whether the control conditions are adequate or whether outcome measures are accurate and sensitive), but meta-analyses include all studies equally and do not take into account the quality of individual studies. The researcher undertaking a meta-analysis can overcome this problem by comparing effect sizes in 'well-conducted' and 'badly conducted' studies (Field, 2005b), but this then involves the researcher in making some subjective judgements about what is 'good' and 'bad' research (Eysenck, 1994). There is even the possibility that meta-analyses might become a self-perpetuating form of analysis, with at least some studies now attempting meta-analyses of meta-analyses (e.g. Butler, Chapman, Forman & Beck, 2006)!

3.3.9 Qualitative Methods

So far we have mainly discussed those research methods that place an important emphasis on accurate and valid measurement of behaviour and attempt to draw conclusions from their studies on the basis of statistical inference. These methods tend to be collectively known as *quantitative methods*. However, there is a growing body of research methodologies in clinical psychology that place less emphasis on exact measurement and statistical analysis, and these are known as *qualitative methods*. Instead of emphasizing mathematical analyses of data, the raw material for qualitative research is ordinary language, and any analysis is verbal rather than statistical. The raw data in qualitative studies are usually participants's own descriptions of themselves, their experiences, their feelings and thoughts, their ways of communicating with others and their ways of understanding the world. Study samples are often small, and data are collected using unstructured or semi-structured interview techniques that can be analysed in a variety of non-statistical ways. Qualitative methods are particularly suited to clinical psychology research because they enable the researcher to gain an insight into the full experience of psychopathology, including the sufferer's feelings, ways of coping, and the specific ramifications that the psychopathology has on everyday life (see Research Methods Box 3.1, p. 78). In recent years qualitative methods have provided information relevant to scale development, informed theories of psychopathology and offered explanations for unusual research findings and unusual case histories (Hill, Thompson & Williams, 1997; Rennie, Watson & Monteiro, 2002; Nelson & Quintana, 2005; Miller & Crabtree, 2000).

Barker, Pistrang and Elliot (2002) provide a succinct illustration of the difference between qualitative and quantitative research:

> A simplified illustration of the difference between the quantitative and the qualitative approach is shown in the differing responses to the question 'How are you feeling today?' A quantitative oriented researcher might ask the participant to respond on a seven-point scale, ranging from 1 = 'very unhappy' to 7 = 'very happy', and receive an answer of 5, signifying 'somewhat happy'. A qualitative researcher might ask the same person the same question, 'How are you feeling today?', but request an open-ended answer, which could run something like 'Not too bad, although my knee is hurting me a little, and I've just had an argument with my boyfriend. On the other hand, I think I might be up for promotion at work, so I'm excited about that.' In other words, the quantitative approach yields data which are relatively simple to process, but are limited in depth and hide ambiguities; the qualitative approach yields a potentially large quantity of rich, complex data which may be difficult and time consuming to analyse.
>
> (Barker, Pistrang & Elliot, 2002, p. 73)

This example shows how qualitative methods are non-quantitative, usually open-ended (in the sense that researchers do not know before the study exactly what data they may collect) and enable researchers to begin to understand an individual's lived experiences, the feelings he has about his experiences and the perceptions and meaning he gives to them (Nelson & Poulin, 1997; Polkinghorne, 1983). Given these characteristics, a typical qualitative study will involve detailed interviewing of participants to identify themes involving feelings and the meaning that those participants give to their feelings.

The advantages of using qualitative methods are: (1) some aspects of psychopathology are difficult to express numerically, and a qualitative approach allows data to be collected about more complex aspects of experience; (2) they permit intensive and in-depth study of individuals or small groups of individuals; (3) because interviewing techniques are usually open-ended, researchers may discover interesting things about a psychopathology that they were not originally looking for; and (4) they can be an extremely valuable source of information at the outset of a research programme and provide a rich source of information which may lead the researcher to construct hypotheses suitable for study using quantitative methods.

Quantitative methods   Research methods that place an important emphasis on accurate and valid measurement of behaviour and attempt to draw conclusions from their studies on the basis of statistical inference.

Qualitative methods   Research methods that rely on the analysis of verbal reports rather than on statistical analyses of quantifiable data.

RESEARCH METHODS IN CLINICAL PSYCHOLOGY BOX 3.1

A qualitative study of dental phobia

This example is based on a paper by Abrahamsson, Hallberg and Carlsson (2007) and gives an insight into how qualitative methods might be used in clinical psychology research. The following sections describe the aims of the study, how it was conducted and how the results were analysed to provide a theoretical perspective on the experience of dental phobia.

Aims

To explore the situation of dental phobic patients and to investigate (1) how their dental phobia interferes with their normal routines, their daily functioning and their social activities and relationships; (2) what factors contribute to the maintenance of their phobia; and (3) how they cope with their fear.

Study sample

18 patients applying for treatment at a specialized dental fear clinic in Göteborg, Sweden. All patients were currently refusing dental treatment because of their phobia.

In-depth interviews

Audiotaped, open-ended interviews were conducted with each participant. The purpose of using open-ended interviews was to explore the situation of dental phobics as expressed by the participants themselves. An interview guide was used as a basic checklist to make sure that relevant topics were covered. These included onset of dental fear, family, experiences in dental care, health and effects on everyday life and coping strategies. Interviews were introduced with questions such as 'Does your dental fear have an impact on your daily life?', 'In what way?', 'What do you do/feel?' and so on.

Ethical issues

It was stressed that participation was voluntary, all data collected would be confidential and the participant had the right to end participation at any time. All participants completed and signed an informed consent form.

Analysis of data

Interview transcripts were analysed using grounded theory (see p. 79). The aim of this method is to focus on different qualities of phenomena in order to generate a model or a theory. Different qualities of phenomena might include psychosocial processes, existing problems caused by dental phobia, how participants coped with their problems, and so on. This process should be conducted with the original aims of the study clearly in mind. The interviews were analysed line-by-line and broken down into segments reflecting their content. Segments with similar contents were then grouped together to form more abstract categories.

Examples of forming abstract categories

One participant expressed the following: 'What I'm most afraid of is that infections will spread . . . I've had a lot of colds in the last year . . . I don't know if it has anything to do with my teeth. I only know that I've waited much too long.' Another participant said: 'The idea of having false teeth at 45, then I'd be at rock bottom . . . I don't know if I could handle it psychologically.' Similar comments made by a number of participants led the researchers to create the abstract category **Threat to own health** to describe this group of responses.

Similarly, participants also provided responses of the following kind: 'My worries about going to the dentist are a matter for me and me alone . . . maybe I could tell someone but they probably wouldn't care at all' and 'A friend said he had booked an appointment for me [at the dentist] and I went completely cold. When the time got nearer [for the appointment] I saw the date couldn't be right and understood that it was a joke.' These and similar responses were grouped into the abstract category of **Lack of social support and understanding**.

Conclusions

This analysis allowed the researchers to construct a model or theory of the experience of dental phobia which is represented schematically in Figure 1 below. Four main categories of experience were developed: threat to self-respect and well-being, avoidance, readiness to act and ambivalence in coping. This provides a rich description of how dental fear affects the daily lives of these individuals and how social and psychological factors interact to determine how they cope with this fear.

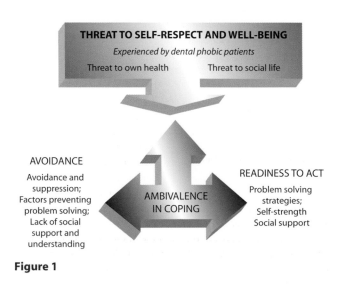

Figure 1

Source: Abrahamsson, Hallberg & Carlsson (2007)

3.3.9.1 Conducting and Analysing Qualitative Studies

Qualitative studies are not entirely unstructured, and qualitative techniques specify ways in which data should be collected and analysed. First, unlike quantitative methods that tend to emphasize the random selection of participants and allocation to experimental groups, qualitative methods tend to deliberately specify groups of participants for sampling depending on the phenomenon or psychopathology the researcher is interested in. For example, these may include individuals who have suffered childhood abuse, families with a member who is suffering a mental health problem, parents of autistic children and so on (Cresswell, 1998). Once selected, participants will then usually take part in a semi-structured, open-ended interview in a relaxed and comfortable interaction (Kvale, 1996). All interview questions would normally be related back to the original research question(s) posed prior to the study. For instance, a research question might be: 'How do individuals with panic disorder cope with day-to-day living?' In this example, the interviewer can ask very general questions or more specific questions that are derived from the original research question. A general question might be: 'What problems do you encounter each day because of your panic attacks, and how do you cope with them?' A more specific question might be: 'How do you feel about not being able to leave the house because of the possibility you might have a panic attack?' In this kind of structure, participants have the opportunity to respond to both general and specific questions. The general questions allow participants to create their own picture of their experiences, and the specific questions allow the researcher to obtain detailed information that is relevant to the original research question.

Once detailed responses from the interview have been collected, the researcher has the task of making sense of the data, picking out consistent themes that emerge in the participant's responding, and deciding how these themes might relate to the original research question that was posed. The first step is to break up the interview transcript into manageable and meaningful units. There are a number of ways to do this (Giorgi, 1985; Merleau-Ponty, 1962), but for simplicity we will describe a commonly used approach known as grounded theory.

Grounded theory is an approach to qualitative analysis that was developed by Glaser and Strauss (1967). It involves identifying consistent categories or themes within the data, and then building on these to provide more abstract theoretical insights into the phenomenon being studied. Research Methods Box 3.1 provides a detailed, specific example of how grounded theory has been used to understand how dental phobics cope with their psychopathology and how it affects their day-to-day living. As we can see, this study was able to identify a number of consistent themes that emerged from the interview data and provide a rich insight into the everyday experiences and feelings of individuals with dental phobia. The study also provided some higher-level theoretical insights by suggesting how several psy-

Grounded theory An approach to qualitative analysis which involves identifying consistent categories or themes within the data, then building on these to provide more abstract theoretical insights into the phenomenon being studied.

chological and social factors interact to determine how dental phobics cope with their fear (Abrahamsson, Hallberg & Carlsson, 2007). Grounded theory can be used with data collected in a number of forms, including interviews, focus groups, observation of participants and diary material. It is also an approach that allows a constant dynamic interaction between research and theory. For example, the study reported in Research Methods Box 3.1 provided some theoretical insights into how dental phobics coped with their fear. This theoretical insight can then provide the basis of a refined research question and a subsequent qualitative study pursuing this issue in further detail.

3.3.9.2 Summary of Qualitative Methods

Qualitative methods lend themselves particularly well to understanding and describing many aspects of psychopathology and are becoming increasingly used in clinical psychology research (Barker, Pistrang & Elliot, 2002). They are useful for collecting data on everyday feelings and experiences associated with psychopathology, and data collected in this way can make a significant contribution to theory. In this section it has not been possible to convey either the full range of qualitative methods available to the researcher or the important philosophical and epistemological underpinnings of many of these techniques (see Willig, 2001; Henwood & Pidgeon, 1992). However, qualitative methods are not just an alternative to quantitative methods: the two can be combined in a useful and productive way in clinical psychology research. Examples include using qualitative data to clarify quantitative findings, beginning research in a new area with qualitative research but moving this on using quantitative methods, or using qualitative data to develop quantitative measures (Barker, Pistrang & Elliot, 2002).

SUMMARY

This section has reviewed the various research methodologies that are available to clinical psychology researchers. All of these methodologies include ways of collecting information and, in many cases, ways of interpreting that information. As we indicated at the outset of this section, the type of research method you adopt will depend very much on: (1) the nature of the research question you are asking (do I want to discover whether there are causal relationships between variables, or do I just want to know if two variables are related in some way?); (2) the nature of the population you are studying (e.g. do you have lots of participants available or just a few?); and (3) whether your research is at an early or advanced stage (if it is the former, you may want to use qualitative methods, if the latter, then quantitative methods may be more appropriate).

SELF-TEST QUESTIONS

- What are the main aims of correlational designs?
- What is the difference between a positive and negative correlation?
- Can you identify how a scattergram can tell us how two variables are related (see Figure 3.1)?
- How do longitudinal and prospective studies differ from correlational studies?
- Can you describe the different ways in which prevalence rates can be measured?
- Which research design is the most effective for identifying causal relationships between variables?
- Can you describe what an independent variable (IV) and a dependent variable (DV) are?
- Experimental designs use control groups. What are they and how would you design one?
- What are the demand characteristics of an experiment?
- What are clinical trials?
- What is a placebo control condition?
- Can you describe what a mixed design is?
- What are the advantages and drawbacks of using case studies in research?
- What is an ABAB design?
- How do multiple-baseline designs differ from ABAB designs?
- How is effect size used to overview studies in a meta-analysis?
- What are the main differences between quantitative and qualitative research methods?
- What is grounded theory?

- A **placebo effect** is when participants in a clinical trial show improvement even though they are not being given an effective treatment.
- **Mixed designs** use the non-random assignment of participants to groups in an experiment.
- **Natural experiments** allow researchers to observe the effects on behaviour of a naturally occurring 'manipulation' (such as an earthquake).
- **Single case studies** allow researchers to collect data from just one individual.
- The **single-case experiment** uses **ABA, ABAB** or **multiple-baseline designs** to carry out controlled experiments on individual participants.
- **Meta-analyses** are statistically accepted ways of assessing the strength of a particular finding across a number of different studies.
- **Qualitative methods** use ordinary language as their raw material, and adopt verbal rather than statistical analyses.
- **Grounded theory** is one particular example of a qualitative method that is used extensively in clinical psychology research.

SECTION SUMMARY

3.3 Research Designs in Clinical Psychology

- **Correlational designs** enable the researcher to determine if there is a relationship between two or more variables.
- A correlation coefficient can range from +1.00 through 0.00 to −1.00, with +1.00 referring to a perfect **positive correlation** between two variables and −1.00 denoting a perfect **negative correlation**.
- Both **longitudinal** and **prospective studies** take measures from the same participants at two or more different times in order to specify the time relationships between variables.
- **Epidemiological studies** provide details about the **prevalence** of psychological disorders.
- **Experiments** involve the researcher manipulating one of the variables (the **independent variable**) and then measuring the effect of this on behaviour (the **dependent variable**).
- To be valid, experimental studies need to use appropriately designed **control conditions**.
- **Clinical trials** are types of experiments that are used to test the effectiveness of treatments.

3.4 ETHICAL ISSUES IN CLINICAL PSYCHOLOGY RESEARCH

It would be almost impossible to do psychological research in general, and clinical psychology research in particular, without those individuals who are needed to act as participants. However, the people that we recruit as participants have rights that need to be protected, they have a dignity that needs to be preserved, and their well-being needs to be maintained. These issues all form part of the ethical deliberations that need to be fully considered before we begin a particular piece of research. Examples of ethical issues that might be encountered in clinical psychology research include: 'Is it harmful to induce panic attacks in an experiment?', 'What will be the effect of inducing a negative mood in my participants and how can I ensure this doesn't affect them after the experiment?', 'Is giving a participant a placebo pill instead of an active drug tantamount to withholding treatment?', 'Does my experiment involve deceiving the participants in any way?' and 'How can I be sure that my participants' involvement in the study is truly voluntary?' Most organizations that host clinical psychology research (such as universities or hospitals) now have ethical committees that are required to vet all research proposals to see that they meet basic ethical standards and protect the participants in the research. Ethical issues in clinical psychology research fall under three main headings: (1) informed consent; (2) causing distress or withholding benefits; and (3) privacy and confidentiality.

3.4.1 Informed Consent

Informed consent   Detailed information about an experiment given to participants in order to enable them to make an informed decision about participation.

Researchers should always properly inform participants about what it is they will be participating in, what they will be asked to do, and what experiences they might have while taking part in the study. This information needs to be detailed enough for the researcher to be sure that the potential participant can make a rational and informed decision about whether to participate or not. This means that the information provided about the study should be as detailed as possible and – importantly – couched in language that the participant will understand and does not include technical jargon that is only likely to be comprehensible to the researcher. This information should also include (1) details of the purpose of the experiment, (2) a description of the procedures the participant will encounter, (3) the duration of the study, (4) who will know about the participant's involvement in the study and whether confidentiality will be maintained, (5) whether participation is voluntary or a payment is being offered and (6) clear indication to participants that they can withdraw from the study at any time and without prejudice if they so wish. Participants should also be given the opportunity to ask questions about the study in order to enable them to make an informed decision about participation, and they should also be given sufficient time to reflect on this information.

Informed consent form   A from giving detailed information about an experiment which participants must sign to acknowledge that they understand what the study involves and that they formally consent to take part in the study.

All of this information is usually provided in a written *informed consent form* which participants must then sign to acknowledge that they understand what the study involves and that they formally consent to take part in it. A simple example of an informed consent form is provided in Figure 3.4. Consent forms may be more or less detailed depending on the complexity of the study and the nature of the participants required. For example, if the study is one that requires the participation of individuals already undergoing treatment for mental health problems, then participants may need to know how their involvement in the study might affect their treatment and whether it might have an adverse effect on their existing mental health condition. In such circumstances, informed consent forms might also want to include further details such as (1) the identity of the researchers and their contact details, (2) a clear description of any complex procedures (e.g. any procedures that may be invasive), (3) the identity of others who might be directly or indirectly associated with the research (e.g. organizations that might be funding the research, such as drug companies or mental health charities), (4) reasons why the participant has been selected (in case the participant may feel stigmatized by being approached to participate), (5) the possible harms and benefits of the procedure (especially if the participant

---

Consent Form

This experiment will take approximately 15–20 minutes and consists of listening to music, reading vignettes on a computer screen and taking part in a short task.

Thank you for agreeing to take part in this experiment. Your formal consent is required to confirm that your participation is voluntary and that you have the right to withdraw at any time.

I confirm that the experimental procedure has been fully explained to me and I understand what I am required to do.

I understand that I am free to ask questions and that I am free to leave the experiment at any time.

I understand that all information I give is confidential and will be used only for the purposes of this experiment.

Male/Female

Age:

1 SIGNED   Date: / /

Figure 3.4 *Informed consent form*
Above is an example of a simple informed consent form that would be used in an experiment looking at the effect of music-induced mood changes on a simple written task.

has an existing mental health problem) and (6) details of any future use of the data collected from the study.

The issue of informed consent becomes problematic when an individual's understanding of the information provided in a consent form is limited. This is particularly so with children and certain categories of adults – for example, those who have learning disabilities or exhibit psychotic symptoms (Bersoff & Bersoff, 1999; Fisher, Cea, Davidson & Fried, 2006). In the case of children and adolescents below the age of 17 years, the written consent of a parent or guardian is required as well as either the verbal or written agreement of the child.

Obtaining the full informed consent of a participant also becomes somewhat problematic if informing the participant of all the details of the study is likely to significantly affect the results. For example, participants in many drug treatment studies are given placebo pills to assess what improvement might occur if they *believe* they are receiving a drug but in fact are not. This involves some *deception* on the part of researchers in the sense that they have not told those taking the placebo

Deception   The act of deceiving.

that it is not an active drug. At the very least this means that the participant is not being given *all* the information about what is happening in a study, and if this is the case, can he or she make an informed decision about whether to participate? This is a moot point, and is important because many psychological studies depend for the validity of their findings on deceptions of this kind. Many researchers overcome this problem by withholding some information from participants if providing that information is likely to affect the outcome of the study. They will then offer the participant a full debriefing at the end of the study, explaining any deception and offering any withheld information. If participants are unhappy about this, the researcher can then offer them the opportunity to withdraw their consent to use their data (Bersoff & Bersoff, 1999).

Finally, it is worth reiterating that all efforts should be made to ensure that a participant's involvement in a study should be truly *voluntary*. There should be no explicit or implicit coercion. How often has a student trying to finish off his undergraduate project gone into the corridor or tea bar and tried to persuade someone to take part in his experiment – 'I only need half a dozen more people', they plead. Is anyone approached in this way a genuine volunteer if they agree to take part? Probably not, because at least some will feel obliged to participate in order to 'help' the student out. Similar problems in obtaining truly voluntary consent are found in many other situations, such as studies that involve hospital inpatients, prisoners and even undergraduate psychology students who have to take part in research studies to gain course credits for their degree programme! Some service providers (such as the NHS) have developed a more imaginative and inclusive way of seeking participant involvement in clinical research by involving end-users (e.g. clients and patients) in the design and development of research. INVOLVE (www.involve.org.uk) is the NHS website that promotes public involvement in NHS research. The site lists a range of important reasons for involving end-users and service consumers in research.

> **Voluntary** Of one's own free will or design; not forced or compelled.

3.4.2 Causing Distress or Withholding Benefits

In many cases it is difficult to do clinical psychology research without asking someone with a psychopathology to describe or experience their symptoms during the study. In other cases we intentionally try to recreate the conditions that cause psychopathology symptoms in order to understand the causes of that psychopathology. Both of these cases involve the researcher in important ethical considerations. In clinical psychology research, distress to participants can be caused in a number of ways, for instance by (1) asking them to relate or relive distressing memories or experiences (e.g. in a study looking retrospectively at experiences that may have preceded a psychopathology), (2) subjecting them to experimental manipulations that may cause stress, anxiety or negative feelings generally (e.g. a mood induction procedure), (3) requiring them to reveal information about themselves that may be embarrassing or humiliating (e.g. in questionnaire studies investigating sexual behaviour), (4) presenting physically aversive stimuli such as electric shocks or loud noises (e.g. in fear conditioning studies) or (5) subjecting participants to circumstances and situations that may be threatening to their self-image or self-esteem (e.g. in situations where participants may be given real or false feedback suggesting their performance on a task is poor or sub-standard). Even asking a participant to complete a validated questionnaire measuring trait characteristics such as anxiety or depression might be distressing. For example, answering questions

about the frequency of suicidal ideation in a questionnaire such as the Beck Depression Inventory (BDI) may trigger distressing thoughts for someone who is either currently depressed or knows someone who has attempted suicide.

Because of these potential harms that could affect participants, researchers have an obligation to be vigilant throughout a study for any indication that participants might be experiencing distress. If researchers do notice indications of distress, they should terminate the study or suspend data collection until the participant feels able to continue. A basic rule is that at the end of the study, the participant should certainly be in no worse a psychological or physical state than when he or she started it. In experimental studies that are likely to cause stress (such as fear conditioning studies, negative mood manipulations, studies involving negative or threatening materials), the experimenter should always ask participants at the end of the study how they are feeling. If they claim they feel distressed, stressed, anxious, sad or have other negative feelings, then the experimenter should be able to offer some active means of dealing with these feelings. This may include offering the opportunity to listen to a relaxation tape or music designed to induce positive mood, or in more severe cases the experimenter may want to provide information about counselling services that can be made available to the participant (e.g. if it is a study taking place on a university campus, the experimenter may be able to provide the location and phone number of the university counselling service). Clearly, making people distressed in a research study is not an acceptable end in itself, and the researcher must always weigh up whether the potential benefits of his or her research (in terms of its contribution to knowledge) outweigh the potential distress that may be caused to some participants.

On the other side of the coin, a study may not cause distress but may involve actively withholding benefits for the participant. This is especially the case with studies attempting to assess the effectiveness of treatments for psychopathology. For example, let us assume a researcher is attempting to find out if a new psychotherapy is effective for treating depression. The study would involve participants diagnosed with depression. Some of them would be allocated to the experimental condition and receive the new psychotherapy, while for comparison purposes others would need to be allocated to control conditions that did *not* receive the new psychotherapy. This raises a significant ethical issue. Should we withhold effective treatment for someone suffering depression simply because we need to allocate them to a *no treatment control condition*? A similar issue is that such studies also have very *narrow inclusion criteria*. That is, to be able to interpret her results clearly, the researcher would want to ensure that the study only included participants who had a simple diagnosis of depression. Interpreting the data would be complicated if the study also included participants who were diagnosed with other disorders that were comorbid with depression. This means that those with more complex psychopathologies are likely to be excluded from

> **No treatment control** In treatment outcome studies, a condition in which participants receive no treatment in order to control for the effects of spontaneous remission.

> **Narrow inclusion criteria** The use in psychopathology research only of individuals with a very specific diagnosis.

treatment outcome studies and so denied access to the treatment programme associated with the study. Researchers tend to try to overcome the ethical issues involved in allocating a patient to a no treatment condition by adopting what are called *waiting-list controls*. That is, they use patients who are on a waiting list for treatment as their no treatment control condition. Such individuals would not be receiving treatment anyway during the time that they are on the waiting list. This may be a suitable way out of this particular ethical dilemma, but as readers are probably aware, it is a solution that paradoxically is available only as long as service providers are unable to offer immediate treatment!

> **Waiting-list controls** The use of patients who are on a waiting list for treatment as a no treatment control condition in treatment outcome studies.

3.4.3 Privacy and Confidentiality

> **Privacy** The right of participants to decide not to provide some forms of information to the researcher if they so wish (e.g. their age or sexual orientation).

> **Confidentiality** The right of participants in psychological research to expect that information they provide will be treated in confidence.

All participants in psychological research have a right to privacy and confidentiality. *Privacy* means that participants can decide not to provide some forms of information to the researcher if they so wish (e.g. their age or sexual orientation), and *confidentiality* means participants in psychological research have a right to expect that information they provide will be treated confidentially. For example, if a piece of research is eventually published in a scientific journal, participants who contributed to the study should not be identifiable. In the event that confidentiality and/or anonymity cannot be guaranteed, the participant must be warned of this in advance of agreeing to participate. Indeed, according to legislation in many countries (such as the Data Protection Act in the UK), information obtained about a participant during a study is confidential unless otherwise agreed in advance.

In many cases, such as questionnaire studies, researchers will ensure that all data collected are anonymous, and participants will usually only have to provide basic demographic information (e.g. sex, age) that will not usually allow them to be identified. In some other circumstances (such as longitudinal studies, where participants may have to be contacted to provide data on more than one occasion) it may be necessary to retain some information that will identify the participant over the course of the study, but this can be erased once all the data are collected. In studies where personal or sensitive information is being collected (such as studies involving participants with mental health problems), the informed consent form should clearly state who will have access to the data and the findings of the study. If interviews with participants are audiotaped or videotaped, it should be clear to the participant who will hold those tapes and how long they will be retained before being destroyed.

However, issues of confidentiality and anonymity become problematic when the participant discloses information about illegal activities or events or circumstances that may be detrimental to an individual's psychological or physical health. For example, what should a researcher do if a participant tells him about suicidal intentions, serious drug abuse, criminal activities, physical or sexual abuse, and so on? Certainly, researchers have a legal and moral obligation to consider appropriate action if they believe a crime has been committed or is intended, and in some countries it is mandatory by law, for example, to report information about criminal activities such as child abuse (Becker-Blease & Freyd, 2006). Perhaps it is important to be clear that confidentiality is not the same as secrecy, and is therefore not absolute. If the researcher believes that a study might reveal information about illegal or immoral activities, then she might inform participants at the outset of the study that (1) confidentiality is not absolute and (2) she will inform the participant if confidentiality is broken. However, providing such information at the outset of a study is likely to mean that participants will be significantly less willing to provide sensitive information (Bersoff & Bersoff, 1999).

Finally, what should a researcher do when participants provide information that they are likely to harm themselves or others or are seriously distressed? This obviously requires a judgement on the part of the researcher, and no one can morally turn a blind eye knowing that others may be harmed or an individual is in a state of life-threatening distress. Because of their knowledge of psychopathology and the provision of treatments, most clinical psychology researchers are usually in the privileged position of being able to offer at least some kind of support and guidance to those disclosing information indicating serious distress. As a consequence, researchers may be able to suggest treatment or referral to an appropriate support service immediately after the study.

SUMMARY

No description of research using human participants is complete without a thorough discussion of ethical issues. Proper ethical procedures are designed to protect the rights, dignity and well-being of participants in research, and are a necessary part of any clinical psychology research project. Ethical issues can be grouped under three broader headings, namely (1) informed consent (e.g. 'Are participants fully informed about the study and can they freely and voluntarily give their informed consent to participate?'), (2) causing distress or withholding benefits (e.g. 'What is the risk that a research procedure will cause a participant harm or distress, and how can we avoid this?') and (3) privacy and confidentiality (e.g. 'Are the participants' rights to privacy and confidentiality being properly respected?').

SELF-TEST QUESTIONS

- What is informed consent?
- What ethical issues need to be considered when a research study may cause distress to a participant or lead to the withholding of benefits?
- How should issues of privacy and confidentiality be considered when designing and conducting a research study?

SECTION SUMMARY

3.4 Ethical Issues in Clinical Psychology Research

- Participants in clinical psychology research have **rights** that need to be protected, **dignity** that needs to be preserved and **well-being** that needs to be maintained.

- The **informed consent** of participants should always be obtained before they take part in a study.

- Participation in any research study should be **voluntary**.

- Researchers have an obligation to be vigilant throughout a study for any indication that the participant might be experiencing **distress**.

- All participants in psychological research have a right to **privacy** and **confidentiality**.

3.5 RESEARCH METHODS IN CLINICAL PSYCHOLOGY REVIEWED

Research is an important and central feature of clinical psychology. Research techniques allow us to (1) describe the symptoms of psychopathologies and the feelings and experiences of those who suffer with mental health problems, (2) understand the causes of psychopathologies, (3) assess the efficacy of interventions developed to treat psychopathology and (4) assess the effectiveness of services provided to treat and support those with mental health problems (known as evaluation research or clinical audit). Different research methods may be based on different theories of knowledge, and a theory of knowledge represents a way of trying to understand the world. Many of the research methods we have described in this chapter are based on the scientific method espoused by Karl Popper, which requires that research results should be replicable and theories should be experimentally testable. However, even within the realm of clinical psychology there are many who feel that the scientific method is not well suited to exploring many of the important aspects of psychopathology such as the phenomenology of psychopathology.

We then described in detail a range of research methods that are available to the clinical psychology researcher. The type of method adopted will usually depend very much on the nature of the research question being asked. For example, correlational and longitudinal methods are useful for determining if there is a rela-

tionship between two or more variables, the experimental method is useful for identifying causal relationships between variables, case studies provide important ways of studying a phenomenon when the number of available participants is restricted, and qualitative methods are useful for gaining an insight into the full experience of psychopathology or beginning new research in an area. The final and essential part of a description of research methods in clinical psychology is a discussion of ethical issues, which are vital in the protection of the rights, dignity and well-being of those who participate in clinical psychology research.

LEARNING OUTCOMES

When you have completed this chapter, you should be able to:

1 Describe and evaluate a range of research methods that can be used in clinical psychology research.

2 Describe the types of research questions that are central to clinical psychology research.

3 Critically evaluate the ethical issues relevant to clinical psychology research.

KEY TERMS

ABA design 75
ABAB design 75
Aetiology 62
Analogue populations 71
Analogue research 63
Animal models 72
Applied scientist 57
Case study 74
Clinical audit 63
Clinical trials 72
Confidentiality 83
Control 62
Control conditions 69
Control group 69
Correlational designs 64
Cross-sectional design 66
Deception 81
Demand characteristics 69
Dependent variable (DV) 68
Description 62
Double-blind 69

REVIEWS, THEORIES AND SEMINAL STUDIES

Links to Journal Articles

3.1 Research and Science

Belar, C.D. & Perry, N.W. (1992). National conference on scientist-practitioner education and training for professional practice of psychology. *American Psychologist, 47,* 71–75.

Corrie, S. & Callahan, M.M. (2000). A review of the scientist-practitioner model: Reflections on its potential contribution to counselling psychology within the context of current health care trends. *British Journal of Medical Psychology, 73,* 413–427.

Davey, G.C.L. (2003). Doing clinical psychology research: What is interesting isn't always useful. *Psychologist, 16,* 412–416.

Shapiro, D.A. (1996). Validated treatments and evidence-based services. *Clinical Psychology: Science and Practice, 3,* 256–259.

Watson, J.B. & Rayner, R. (1920). Conditioned emotional reactions. *Journal of Experimental Psychology, 3,* 1–14.

3.2 Clinical Psychology Research: What Do We Want To Find Out?

Cooper, M., Turpin, G., Bucks, R. & Kent, G. (2005). *Good practice guidelines for the conduct of psychological research within the NHS.* London: British Psychological Society.

3.3 Research Designs in Clinical Psychology

Clark, D.M., Ehlers, A., Hackmann, A., McManus, F. et al. (2006). Cognitive therapy versus exposure and applied relaxation in social phobia: A randomized controlled trial. *Journal of Consulting and Clinical Psychology, 74,* 568–578.

De Maat, S., Dekker, J., Schoevers, R. & de Jonghe, F. (2006). Relative efficacy of psychotherapy and pharmacotherapy in the treatment of depression: A meta-analysis. *Psychotherapy Research, 16,* 562–572.

Henwood, K.L. & Pidgeon, N.F. (1992). Qualitative research and psychological theorizing. *British Journal of Psychology, 83,* 97–111.

Huppert, J.D., Schultz, L.T., Foa, E.B. & Barlow, D.H. (2004). Differential response to placebo among patients with social phobia, panic disorder, and obsessive-compulsive disorder. *American Journal of Psychiatry, 161,* 1485–1487.

Nelson, M.L. & Quintana, S.M. (2005). Qualitative clinical research with children and adolescents. *Journal of Clinical Child and Adolescent Psychology, 34,* 344–356.

Regier, D.A., Myers, J.K., Kramer, M., Robins, L.N. et al. (1984). The NIMH Epidemiologic Catchment Area Program: Historical context, major objectives, and study population characteristics. *Archives of General Psychiatry, 41,* 934–941.

Vredenburg, K., Flett, G.L. & Krames, L. (1993). Analog versus clinical depression: A critical reappraisal. *Psychological Bulletin, 113,* 327–344.

Weems, C.F., Pina, A.A., Costa, N.M., Watts, S.E. et al. (2007). Predisaster trait anxiety and negative affect predict post-traumatic stress in youths after Hurricane Katrina. *Journal of Consulting and Clinical Psychology, 75,* 154–159.

3.4 Ethical Issues in Clinical Psychology Research

Becker-Blease, K.A. & Freyd, J.J. (2006). Research participants telling the truth about their lives. *American Psychologist, 61*, 218–226.

Davison, G.C. & Stuart, R.B. (1975). Behavior therapy and civil liberties. *American Psychologist,* 755–763.

Fisher, C.B., Hoagwood, K., Boyce, C., Duster, T. et al. (2002). Research ethics for mental health science involving ethnic minority children and youths. *American Psychologist, 57*, 1024–1040.

Rollin, B.E. (2006). The regulation of animal research and the emergence of animal ethics: A conceptual history. *Theoretical Medicine and Bioethics, 27*, 285–304.

Texts for Further Reading

Barker, C., Pistrang, N. & Elliott, R. (2002). *Research methods in clinical psychology* (2nd ed.). New York: Wiley.

Kendall, P.C., Butcher, J.N. & Holmbeck, G.N. (Eds.) (1999) *Handbook of research methods in clinical psychology* (2nd ed.). New York: Wiley.

Marks, D.F. & Yardley, L. (Eds.) (2003) *Research methods for clinical and health psychology.* London: Sage.

Miles, J. & Gilbert, P. (Eds.) (2005) *A handbook of research methods for clinical and health psychology.* Oxford: Oxford University Press.

Morgan, G.A., Gliner, J.A. & Harmon, R.J. (2005) *Understanding and evaluating research in applied and clinical settings.* Hillsdale, NJ: Lawrence Erlbaum.

Roberts, M. & Ilardi, S.S. (Eds.) (2005) *Handbook of research methods in clinical psychology.* Oxford: Blackwell Publishing.

RESEARCH QUESTIONS

3.1 Research and Science

- The 1920 paper by Watson and Rayner on conditioning a phobia in an 8-month-old infant is considered to be one of the founding pieces of scientific research in psychopathology – but what are its weaknesses?

- Because all human beings are different, are there likely to be any general 'truths' or processes about psychopathology that can be discovered using scientific method?

3.2 Clinical Psychology Research: What Do We Want To Find Out?

- Can we ever discover whether early experiences have a direct *causal* effect on later psychopathology?

- Is an understanding of the causes of psychopathology the primary aim of clinical psychology research?

- Can doing research on healthy volunteers tell us anything about the causes and symptoms of psychopathology?

3.3 Research Designs in Clinical Psychology

- Can epidemiological studies ever be valid and valuable unless they attain a 100 per cent response rate?

- Is some research on psychopathology impossible to carry out because of the distress it may cause to participants who already have mental health problems?

- Can we ever imply causality from the results of a mixed design study?

- Are meta-analyses so flawed in their application that they are no better at providing valid overviews of an area than a discursive review?

3.4 Ethical Issues in Clinical Psychology Research

- Are all psychopathology studies that involve deception unethical?

- Is it ethically acceptable to recreate the conditions that cause psychopathology in the laboratory?

- Can clinical trials ever provide valid findings unless they use a no treatment control condition?

CLINICAL ISSUES

3.1 Research and Science

- Can a practising clinician's everyday experiences with clients provide the basis for an understanding of psychopathology?

- Are theories of psychopathology that are not scientifically verifiable useful in clinical practice? Can it ever be proven that they are useful?

- What is the difference between a clinician who bases his interventions on unvalidated experience and a bogus psychotherapist who invents a so-called therapy whose basic tenets are not amenable to objective assessment?

- Does basing clinical psychology research on scientific method align it too closely to the medical model of psychopathology?

- Is the clinical psychologist's need to alleviate a client's psychological problems more pressing than the need to be scientifically rigorous?

- Is it acceptable for practising clinical psychologists to view the research literature as irrelevant to their professional practice?

3.2 Clinical Psychology Research: What Do We Want To Find Out?

- Will understanding of the causes of psychopathology always suggest methods of therapeutic intervention?

3.3 Research Designs in Clinical Psychology

- Do single case studies have any value if their findings can only rarely be generalized to other cases?

3.4 Ethical Issues in Clinical Psychology Research

- What should a clinical psychology researcher do if a participant in a study provides information that she is likely to harm herself or others or is seriously distressed?

4 | Treating Psychopathology

ROUTE MAP OF THE CHAPTER

This chapter discusses the reasons for treating psychopathology, the different theoretical approaches to treatment and how we attempt to evaluate whether treatment is successful or not. The first section describes six different theoretical approaches to treatment and the basic principles on which each of these approaches is based. We then discuss some of the modes of treatment delivery, many of which have been developed in recent years. Finally, we discuss ways of evaluating treatment and cover issues about what constitutes a therapeutic gain, how long it may take to achieve a successful outcome and how therapeutic gains should be measured. We end the chapter by describing some of the methodologies that are currently used to objectively assess the effectiveness of treatments for psychopathology.

I was a 22-year-old trainee working for a publishing company in London, and I was obsessed with food. I made a pact with myself to limit myself to less than 700 calories a day. This worked well for a while, but then I started binge eating, and my fear of gaining weight led me to make myself sick. Sometimes up to 5 or 6 times a day. This left me totally drained – both emotionally and physically, and my relationship with my partner began to go downhill rapidly. I really hated myself, and I felt fat and disgusting most days. If only I felt thinner I would feel better about myself. My GP eventually referred me to a clinical psychologist, who helped me to understand how my thinking was just plain wrong. He explained to me how I evaluated my self-worth purely on the basis of my weight and body shape. My thinking was also 'black and white' – I believed that foods were either 'good' or if not, they were 'bad'. During therapy I learned to identify and challenge my irrational thoughts about food and eating; this helped me to begin to eat relatively normally again, and I began to feel less anxious and worthless. What amazed me most was that eating normally didn't mean I put on weight, and I felt in control again – the first time for years. All this was so wonderful that I became anxious about the possibility of therapy ending and that I'd simply go back to starving and bingeing. But I was encouraged to practise a number of coping strategies and learned what I should do in circumstances where I felt I might relapse back into my old ways.

ELLY'S STORY

Introduction

Psychopathology can take many forms and involve anxiety, depression, feelings of worthlessness, guilt and lack of control, amongst others. For many people these feelings become so intense that they cause personal distress and significantly impair normal daily functioning. Some people are able to deploy adaptive coping strategies that allow them to successfully negotiate such periods in their life (e.g. by seeking help and support from friends and family, or using problem-solving strategies to deal with life problems that may be causing their symptoms). Others may be less able to cope constructively and choose less adaptive means of dealing with their symptoms, such as resorting to substance abuse and dependency or deliberate self-harm. Whatever route individuals may take, the distress and disruption that symptoms of psychopathology cause will often lead them to seek professional help and support for their problems. The first port of call is usually the doctor or GP, who may be able to offer sufficient help to deal with acute bouts of psychopathology such as those involving depression, stress and anxiety-based problems. In most cases this support will usually be in the form of suitable medication, but it may also take the form of access to stress management courses, short-term counselling or psychotherapy, access to self-help information or even computerized cognitive behaviour therapy (CBT) (e.g. van Boeijen, van Oppen, van Balkom, Visser et al., 2005). In other cases it may be necessary for an individual to be referred for more specific and specialized treatment, the nature of which may often depend on the type and severity of that person's symptoms. This is a fairly standardized route by which individuals suffering psychopathology come into contact with the treatment methods required to alleviate their symptoms and distress. Others may simply decide to bypass the health services available in their community and directly approach an accredited counsellor or psychotherapist who can privately supply the treatment services they require. Whichever route is followed, the aim is to find a suitable specialist who can successfully alleviate the symptoms of psychopathology and ease the distress that is experienced.

4.1 THE NATURE AND FUNCTION OF TREATMENTS FOR PSYCHOPATHOLOGY

Elly's Story provides her personal account of how therapy helped to alleviate her eating problems, how it provided her with insight into the thought patterns that gave rise to her psychopathology and how she learned to cope with situations that might give rise to relapse. Based on the example in *Elly's Story*, treatments for psychopathology will usually possess some, if not all, of the following characteristics: (1) they can provide relief from the distress caused by symptoms; (2) they can provide clients with self-awareness and insight into their problems; (3) they enable clients to acquire coping and problem-solving skills that will prevent similar problems occurring in the future; and (4) they attempt to identify and resolve the causes of the psychopathology, whether those causes are recognized as problematic ways of behaving, problematic ways of thinking or problematic ways of dealing with or assimilating life experiences. Many treatments possess only some of these characteristics. For example, many drug treatments for psychopathology will have a *palliative effect* (i.e. reduce the severity of symptoms and so alleviate distress), but they may only rarely provide clients with insight into their problems. Some other therapies may serve the primary purpose of helping clients to achieve insight into their

Palliative effect The reduction of the severity of symptoms and alleviation of distress.

problems (e.g. psychodynamic psychotherapies), but it does not always follow that this insight will bring about behaviour change or provide suitable coping skills (Prochaska & Norcross, 2001). Still other therapies may provide effective ways of changing behaviour (such as many behaviour therapies), but do not necessarily provide clients with insight into the causes of their problems.

The treatment that is provided for a psychopathology will depend on at least two factors: (1) the theoretical orientation and training of the therapist and (2) the nature of the psychopathology. First, a therapist will tend to adopt those treatment practices that he or she has most experience with and was originally trained to use. This will often involve therapies with a specific theoretical approach (e.g. a psychodynamic approach, a client-centred approach, a cognitive approach or a behavioural approach – see section 1.1.3 in Chapter 1). These theoretical approaches will not only advocate different treatment procedures, they will also promote quite different approaches to understanding and explaining psychopathology. Most accredited therapists will now also have to demonstrate that they have periodically engaged in *continuing professional development (CPD)*. That is, they must demonstrate that they regularly update their knowledge of recent developments in treatment techniques. If a therapist is unable to demonstrate that she is actively engaged in CPD, then she may be in danger of losing her status as a legally registered practitioner. This has meant that practitioners have become much more eclectic in the types of treatment they will offer as they learn new treatment methods through the need to demonstrate their continuing professional development. While some practising therapists may also use the research literature as a way of updating their therapeutic skills, most rely on information

Continuing professional development (CPD) The demonstration by accredited therapists that they regularly update their knowledge of recent developments in treatment techniques.

from less formal sources, such as colleagues, professional news-letters, workshops and conferences (Goldfried & Wolfe, 1996).

Secondly, treatments may be chosen largely on the basis that they are effective at treating a certain type of psychopathology. In the UK, the National Institute for Health and Clinical Excellence (NICE) recommends treatments for specific psychopathologies on the basis that their effectiveness is evidence-based and empirically supported by scientifically rigorous research (see also a discussion of NICE in section 3.1.3 of Chapter 3). We will discuss some of these recommendations in later chapters when we examine treatment programmes for specific psychopathologies. Nowadays, most types of theoretical approach have been adapted to treat most psychopathologies, or at least some aspect of most psychopathologies, and these will be discussed in detail in the treatment sections of each ensuing chapter.

4.1.1 Theoretical Approaches to Treatment

Traditionally, popular therapies have been developed around a relatively small number of important theoretical approaches. We discussed these theoretical approaches in some detail in Chapter 1 (section 1.1.3), and you may want to return to this section in order to refresh your memory about how these different theoretical models conceptualize and explain psychopathology. This section continues with a summary of how these theoretical approaches are adapted to treat psychopathology.

4.1.1.1 Psychodynamic Approaches

The aim of most psychodynamic therapies is to reveal unconscious conflicts that may be causing symptoms of psychopathology. Most **psychodynamic approaches** assume that unconscious conflicts develop early in life, and part of the therapy is designed to identify life events that may have caused these unconscious conflicts. Once these important developmental life events and unconscious conflicts have been identified, the therapist will help the client to acknowledge the existence of these conflicts, bring the conflicts into conscious awareness, and work with the client to develop strategies for change. One important form of psychodynamic therapy is **psychoanalysis**, based on the theoretical works of Sigmund Freud (1856–1939). The aim of psychoanalysis is to bring any unconscious conflicts into awareness, to help the individual understand the source of these conflicts (perhaps by identifying past experiences or discussing the nature of important relationships) and to help the individual towards a sense of control over behaviour, feelings and attitudes. There are a number of basic techniques used by psychoanalysts to achieve these goals.

> **Psychodynamic approaches**   Theories which assume that unconscious conflicts develop early in life. Part of the therapy is designed to identify life events that may have caused these unconscious conflicts.

> **Psychoanalysis**   The method of psychological therapy originated by Sigmund Freud in which free association, dream interpretation and analysis of transference are used to explore repressed or unconscious impulses, anxieties and internal conflicts.

1 *Free association*: Here clients are encouraged to verbalize all thoughts, feelings and images that come to mind while the analyst is normally seated behind them. This process functions to bring into awareness any unconscious conflicts or associations between thoughts and feelings.

> **Free association**   A technique used in psychoanalysis where the client is encouraged to verbalize all thoughts, feelings and images that come to mind.

2 *Transference*: Here the analyst is used as a target for emotional responses: clients behave or feel towards the analyst as they would have behaved or felt towards an important person in their life. This allows clients to achieve understanding of their feelings by acting out any feelings or neuroses that they have towards that person.

> **Transference**   A technique used in psychoanalysis where the analyst is used as a target for emotional responses: clients behave towards the analyst as they would have behaved towards an important person in their lives.

3 *Dream analysis*: Freud believed that unconscious conflicts often revealed themselves in symbolic forms in dreams. The analysis of dream content is an important means of accessing unconscious beliefs and conflicts.

> **Dream analysis**   The analysis of dream content as a means of accessing unconscious beliefs and conflicts.

4 *Interpretation*: Finally, the skilled psycho-analyst has to interpret information from all of the above sources and help clients to identify important underlying conflicts as well as to develop ways of dealing with these conflicts.

> **Interpretation**   In psychoanalysis, helping the client to identify important underlying conflicts.

As a form of treatment, psychoanalysis may take up to 3–5 sessions a week and change is expected to take place at a normal maturational rate, so it may require anything between 3 and 7 years for the full therapeutic benefits of the therapy to be recognized. Other forms of psychodynamic therapy may be briefer and less intensive than psychoanalysis, and may draw on techniques from other sources such as family therapy (see section 4.1.1.5). Psychoanalysis represents a quest for self-knowledge, where an individual's problems are viewed in the context of the whole person and, in particular, any conflicts he or she may have repressed. It can be an effective treatment for many people with moderate to severe anxiety or depression-based problems, especially when other, more conventional, therapies have failed.

4.1.1.2 Behaviour Therapy

In the 1940s and 1950s there was a growing dissatisfaction with the medical or disease model of psychopathology as well as with the unscientific approaches to psychopathology being generated by many psychodynamic theories. These dissatisfactions led psychologists to look towards the developing area of experimental psychology for

> **Behaviour therapy**   A form of treatment based mainly on the principles of classical and operant conditioning.

objective knowledge that might be used to inform treatment and therapy. The body of knowledge that psychologists turned to was that of *conditioning* (see section 1.1.3.2 in Chapter 1), and this gave rise to the development of what came to be known as *behaviour therapies*. First, such therapies stressed the need to treat symptoms of psychopathology as *bona fide* behavioural problems rather than the mere symptoms of some other hidden, underlying cause. Secondly, at the time, many psychologists believed that numerous psychological disorders were the result of what was called *faulty learning*, and that symptoms were acquired through simple conditioning processes. For example, it was believed that anxiety symptoms could be acquired through classical conditioning (see Figure 5.1), and behavioural problems might be acquired through processes of operant conditioning – e.g. bizarre and inappropriate behaviours might be acquired because they have been reinforced or rewarded in the past (see Focus Point 7.6). The reasoning here was that if psychological problems were acquired through learning, then conditioning principles could be used to develop therapies that effectively helped the individual to 'unlearn' those problematic associations. Two distinctive strands of behaviour therapy developed from these assumptions. The first was a set of therapies based on the principles of classical conditioning, and the second a set of therapies based on the principles of operant conditioning. While the former group of therapies continues to be known as behaviour therapy, the latter group has also come to be known as *behaviour modification* or *behaviour analysis*.

The term behaviour therapy is often used even more eclectically nowadays to refer to any treatment that attempts to directly change behaviour (rather than, say, cognitions), whether the underlying principles are based on conditioning or not.

Conditioning   A form of learning in which an organism learns to associate events with one another (e.g. classical conditioning or operant conditioning).

Faulty learning   A view that the symptoms of psychological disorders are acquired through the learning of pathological responses.

Behaviour analysis   An approach to psychopathology based on the principles of operant conditioning (also known as **behaviour modification**).

Therapies Based on Classical Conditioning Principles

Behaviour therapy effectively originates from the writings of Wolpe (1958), who argued that many forms of emotional disorder could be treated using the classical conditioning principle of *extinction*. The assumption was that if emotional problems such as anxiety disorders were learned through classical conditioning, they could be 'unlearned' by disrupting the association between the anxiety-provoking cues or situations and the threat or traumatic outcomes that they have become associated with. In practice, this means ensuring that the anxiety-provoking stimulus, event or situation is experienced in the absence of accompanying trauma so that the former no longer

Extinction   The classical conditioning principle which assumes emotional problems can be 'unlearned' by disrupting the association between the anxiety-provoking cues or situations and the threat or traumatic outcomes with which they have become associated.

comes to evoke the latter. The most famous behaviour therapy techniques to apply extinction principles are *flooding*, *counterconditioning* and *systematic desensitization*, which have collectively come to be known as *exposure therapies* (Richard & Lauterbach, 2007) because they are all based on the need to expose clients to the events and situations that evoke their distress and anxiety in order that they can learn that they are no longer threatening (see Davey, 1998). Wolpe (1958) also introduced the principle of *reciprocal inhibition*, in which an emotional response is eliminated not just by extinguishing the relationship between the emotion-inducing cue and the threatening consequence, but also by attaching a response to the emotion-inducing cue which is incompatible with anxiety (e.g. relaxation). It has often been assumed that these techniques can only be applied to the treatment of emotional problems such as anxiety disorders, but they have in fact been applied to a range of disorders including addictive disorders (O'Leary & Wilson, 1975), marital conflict (Jacobson & Weiss, 1978) and sexual dysfunction (Mathews et al., 1976).

Aversion therapy is another treatment based on classical conditioning, but it is rather different from the preceding therapies because it attempts to condition an aversion to a stimulus or event to which the individual is inappropriately attracted. For example, aversion therapy is most widely used in the treatment of addictive behaviours such as alcoholism, and in these procedures the taste of alcohol is paired with aversive outcomes (e.g. sickness-inducing drugs) in order to condition an aversive reaction to alcohol (e.g. Voegtlin & Lemere, 1942; Lemere & Voegtlin, 1950) (see Chapters 8 and 10 for discussion of the use of aversion therapy in the treatment of substance abuse and paraphilias). Since the 1950s and 1960s, this type of procedure has been used to treat a wide variety of problems, including inappropriate or distressing sexual activities (e.g. Feldman & MacCulloch, 1965), drug and alcohol addiction (McRae, Budney & Brady, 2003) and even obsessions and compulsions associated with anxiety (Lam & Steketee, 2001). Aversion therapy was popularized in the 1971 cult film *A Clockwork Orange*, where the lead character's excessive violence was treated by 'conditioning' him to vomit whenever he saw

Flooding   A form of desensitization for the treatment of phobias and related disorders in which the patient is repeatedly exposed to highly distressing stimuli.

Counterconditioning   A behaviour therapy technique designed to use conditioning techniques to establish a response that is antagonistic to the psychopathology.

Systematic desensitization   An exposure therapy based on the need to expose clients to the events and situations that evoke their distress and anxiety in a graduated and progressive way.

Exposure therapy   Treatment in which sufferers are helped by the therapist to confront and experience events and stimuli relevant to their trauma and their symptoms.

Reciprocal inhibition   A principle of behaviour therapy in which an emotional response is eliminated not just by extinguishing the relationship between the emotion-inducing cue and the threatening consequence, but also by attaching a response to the emotion-inducing cue which is incompatible with anxiety (e.g. relaxation).

Aversion therapy   A treatment based on classical conditioning which attempts to condition an aversion to a stimulus or event to which the individual is inappropriately attracted.

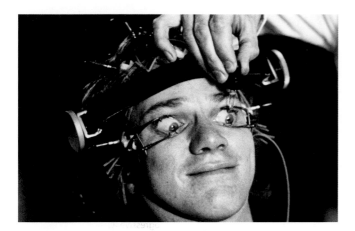

Plate 4.1
Alex (Malcolm McDowell), the leading character in Stanley Kubrick's 1971 film *A Clockwork Orange*, undergoes aversion therapy to cure his violent tendencies.

a violent act. However, while aversion therapy for some problems (e.g. alcoholism) has been shown to have some therapeutic gains when used in conjunction with broader community support programmes (Azrin, 1976), addictive responses are often very resistant to this form of treatment, and there is very little evidence that aversion therapy alone has anything other than short-lived effects (e.g. Wilson, 1978).

Therapies Based on Operant Conditioning Principles

The principles of operant conditioning offer some rather different approaches to treatment and therapy than do those of classical conditioning. Operant conditioning is concerned with influencing the frequency of a behaviour by manipulating the consequences of that behaviour. For example, if a behaviour is followed by rewarding or reinforcing consequences, it will *increase* in frequency. If it is followed by punishing or negative consequences, it will *decrease* in frequency (Davey, 1989). Operant conditioning principles have mainly been used in therapy in three specific ways: (1) to try to understand what rewarding or reinforcing factors might be maintaining an inappropriate or maladaptive behaviour: this is known as functional analysis (e.g. trying to understand what factors might be maintaining challenging or aggressive behaviours in individuals with intellectual disabilities); (2) to use reinforcers and rewards to try to establish new or appropriate behaviours (e.g. to establish self-help or social behaviours in individuals who have become withdrawn because of their psychopathology); and (3) to use negative or punishing consequences to try to suppress or eliminate problematic behaviours in need of urgent attention (e.g. to eliminate or suppress self-injurious behaviours in individuals with intellectual disabilities or severe autistic symptoms) (see section 16.3.4.2 in Chapter 16).

A *functional analysis* is where the therapist attempts to identify consistencies between problematic behaviours and their consequences – especially to try to discover whether there might be a consistent event or consequence that appears

Functional analysis   A systematic analysis of the consistencies between problematic behaviours and their consequences.

to be maintaining the behaviour by rewarding it. For example, self-injurious or challenging behaviours may be maintained by a range of reinforcing consequences, such as the attention the behaviour may attract or the sensory stimulation it provides (see Treatment in Practice Box 16.1). Identifying the nature of the consequence allows the therapist to disrupt the reinforcement contingency and, if necessary, reduce the frequency of that behaviour through extinction (Mazaleski, Iwata, Vollmer, Zarcone et al., 1993; Wacker et al., 1990). Functional analysis has been adopted across a range of clinical settings and has been successfully applied to controlling aggressive/challenging behaviour (O'Reilly, 1995), tantrums (Derby, Wacker, Sasso, Steege et al., 1992), ADHD (Northrup et al., 1995), depression (Ferster, 1985), eating problems (Slade, 1982) and self-injurious behaviour (Iwata et al., 1985).

Other influential interventions based on operant conditioning principles include the token economy, response shaping and behavioural self-control. In the psychiatric setting, a *token economy* involves participants receiving tokens (a generalized reinforcer) for engaging in behaviours defined by the programme: at a later time,

Token economy   A reward system which involves participants receiving tokens for engaging in certain behaviours which at a later time can be exchanged for a variety of reinforcing or desired items.

these tokens can be exchanged for a variety of reinforcing or desired items (e.g. access to the hospital grounds, a visit to the cinema). In psychiatric care, the token economy was first used to foster prosocial or self-help behaviours (e.g. combing hair, bathing, brushing teeth) in previously withdrawn patients, although its use and popularity have declined significantly over the past 20 years (for a fuller discussion of this decline, see Focus Point 7.9).

Response shaping is a procedure that can be used to encourage new behaviours that are not already occurring at a reasonable frequency.

Response shaping   A reinforcement procedure that is used to develop new behaviours.

This may be especially a problem with withdrawn individuals or individuals with restricted behavioural repertoires (such as those with severe intellectual disabilities). However, the technique of response shaping by successive approximations is a way around this problem. Here, the therapist will first reinforce a behaviour that does occur quite frequently and is an approximation to the specific target response. Once this general response is established, reinforcement is given only for closer and closer approximations to the target response. An example of the use of response shaping is provided in Treatment in Practice Box 4.1.

Finally, the use of operant conditioning principles for behaviour change purposes does not have to be overseen or administered by a therapist. The principles are quite clear and can be used by any individual to control and manage his or her own behaviour. This personal use of operant conditioning principles has come to be known as *behavioural self-control* (e.g. Thoresen & Mahoney, 1974) and has since been developed into multifaceted behavioural pro-

Behavioural self-control   The personal use of operant conditioning principles to change or control one's own behaviour.

grammes to deal with a variety of personal problems, including addiction, habits, obsessions and other behavioural problems

CLINICAL PERSPECTIVE: TREATMENT IN PRACTICE BOX 4.1

An example of response shaping

Response shaping is a useful procedure for strengthening rarely occurring behaviours or building up complex response repertoires, and this method is utilized regularly in behaviour modification programmes. An early study by Isaacs, Thomas and Goldiamond (1960) serves to illustrate this method. They attempted to reinstate verbal behaviour in a psychiatric inpatient who had been mute for over 19 years. In this example, the target behaviour occurs relatively infrequently, and thus has to be approached via the reinforcement of successive approximations to the behaviour. The researchers discovered that although the patient was withdrawn, he did appear to respond to chewing gum, which they considered would act as an effective reinforcer. They then broke down the target behaviour so that it could be reached by reinforcing a series of approximations to verbal behaviour. The first responses to be reinforced were fairly simple, discrete responses whose baseline levels were high enough for them to occur spontaneously within a training session. The shaping program went as follows:

1   When the patient moved his eyes towards the chewing gum, he was reinforced by being given the gum; after 2 weeks the probability of this response was relatively high.

2   The experimenters then gave the patient gum only when he moved his mouth and lips; by the end of week 3, these behaviours were relatively frequent.

3   The experimenters then withheld gum until the patient made vocalizations of some sort; by the end of the fourth week the patient was moving his eyes and lips and making audible 'croaking' noises.

4   During weeks 4 and 5, the experimenters asked the patient to 'say gum', repeating this each time the patient vocalized. At the end of week 6, the patient spontaneously said 'gum please'.

5   In later sessions the patient verbally responded to questions from the experimenters, but only in the therapeutic situation.

6   To enable verbal behaviour to generalize beyond the experimental setting, the patient was placed back on the ward and the nursing staff were asked to attend to his needs – but only if he verbalized them.

This example demonstrates a number of features of the response-shaping procedure in clinical settings. First, it provides an example of how response shaping can be a powerful and effective means of establishing complex response repertoires relatively quickly. Second, it illustrates the distinction between 'arbitrary' and 'natural' reinforcers in behaviour modification. In this case, chewing gum was an effective reinforcer for the behaviours being shaped – but it is an 'arbitrary' one in that it is not a normal reinforcer for verbal behaviour. Thus, while chewing gum may have acted as an effective reinforcer during the shaping process, in order to be maintained in any way, verbalizations need to be transferred to a more 'natural' reinforcer for those behaviours. This was the aim of stage 6 in the study where the patient's needs were met only if he verbalized them.

Finally, there was no apparent follow-up analysis of the gains achieved in this study, and one suspects that, once back in the unstructured setting of the ward, the patient in the Isaacs et al. study would have reverted to his previous mute state. However, this study does emphasize two things. First, behaviour change has to be subsequently supported by stable and structured changes to the individual's environment which will maintain the therapeutic gains achieved in the behaviour modification programme. Secondly, whether or not the patient in this study did revert to a mute state, the usefulness of response-shaping procedures in swiftly developing relatively complex behaviour repertoires cannot be denied. The problem of response maintenance, however, usually requires other considerations (cf. Glynn, 1990; Stokes & Baer, 1977; Stokes & Osnes, 1988).

Source: Davey (1998)

(Lutzker & Martin, 1981; Stuart & Davis, 1972). A programme developed by Stuart (1967) provides a good example of a multifaceted behavioural self-control scheme designed to address obesity by controlling behaviours contributing to overeating. The main elements of this programme were: (1) recording the time and quantity of food consumption (self-observation); (2) weighing in before each meal and before bedtime (helping the individual to discriminate how eating might have contributed to weight gain); (3) removal of food from all places in the house except the kitchen (so that only the kitchen comes to act as a cue for eating); (4) pairing eating with no other activity that might make eating enjoyable and so reinforce it (e.g. eating should *not* occur while watching an enjoyable TV programme); (5) setting a weight loss goal of

1–2 pounds/week (setting clearly attainable goals); (6) slowing down the pace of eating (defining appropriate responses); and (7) substituting other activities for between-meal eating (programming acceptable competing responses). These principles are relatively easy to apply to your own behaviour, and Activity Box 4.1 provides some suggestions as to how you might develop your own behavioural self-control programme to promote an activity such as studying.

4.1.1.3 Cognitive Therapies

In the past 25 years one of the most impressive developments in our understanding of psychopathology has been our evolving

ACTIVITY BOX 4.1

Developing your own behavioural-self control programme: Promoting studying behaviour

How often do you sit down to write an essay or a lab report or do some reading for a seminar, only for your attention to begin to wander almost immediately? After just a few minutes you are up making a cup of coffee to distract yourself from the difficulty of concentrating on the task in hand.

Below are some examples of how you might apply behavioural self-control principles to help you concentrate more easily when you are studying. All of these principles are based on operant or classical conditioning. When you have read these principles, sit down and write a behavioural self-control programme for your own studying behaviour that takes into account your own learning environment and your personal circumstances.

Reinforcement/punishment

Always try to find some way of rewarding yourself whenever you have achieved a study goal, and make sure that you take this reward immediately on completion of the task. It may be something as simple as a refreshing cup of coffee, a chat with friends, a trip to the cinema, or just listening to your favourite song on your iPod.

Response-reinforcer contiguity/contingency

While many people claim to be aware of the principle of operant reinforcement, most rarely apply it consistently. For instance, you may decide to spend two hours in the library writing an essay and then reward yourself for this effort by going and having a coffee and a chat with friends. However, you may find that you are working so well that you continue writing until your concentration and motivation begin to wane – then you go off for coffee. With all the good intentions in the world, what has happened is that you have inadvertently reinforced behaviours consistent with falling levels of concentration and motivation rather than the two hours of focused work that preceded this. Always ensure that the things you like doing (i.e. rewards) occur *immediately after* the behaviour you want to foster (i.e. concentrating).

Stimulus control (environmental planning)

If you study in an environment that also controls other behaviours, then you will inevitably find it difficult to concentrate solely on studying. For example, if you try to write an essay in your kitchen, that could be very difficult because a kitchen will also have come to elicit other competing behaviours such as eating or putting on the kettle. To study effectively, you need to do this in an environment that does not control alternatives to studying (a library is a good example).

Response shaping and the setting of attainable targets

All behavioural programmes set attainment targets of some kind, and it is extremely important that any sub-goals in the programme are attainable. For example, if studying, you must set yourself a goal that you are certain you can achieve (e.g. reading a textbook for 15 minutes rather than 6 hours!). It is critical that goals are attainable: if they are not met because they are over-ambitious, then this is tantamount to punishing the effort that was expended in attempting to meet the goal.

Response discrimination/feedback

Can you recall accurately how many hours you have spent studying in the last week? Probably not, and this is because most people have poor recall of the frequency of behaviours they are trying to develop or reinforce. This being the case, it is perhaps not surprising that you may have difficulty controlling your studying – because you are unable to accurately discriminate it or to remember it. One way in which this can be overcome is by including in the programme a period of self-observation, where you record or chart information relevant to studying behaviour (e.g. how many hours you studied each day, what you achieved and where you studied). This will give you an idea of the baseline frequency with which you study and will allow you to set some future goals that can increase this baseline level.

Source: Davey (2004)

---

insight into the cognitive factors that play important roles in causing and maintaining psychopathology. For example, some psychopathologies are caused by dysfunctional 'ways of thinking' – either about the self or about the world (e.g. in major depression). In other cases psychopathologies are characterized by dysfunctional ways of processing and interpreting incoming information. For example, many anxiety disorders are characterized by a bias towards processing threatening or anxiety-relevant information (e.g. generalized anxiety disorder; see Research Methods Box 5.2) or to interpreting ambiguous information negatively (e.g. panic disorder; see Figure 5.3). In both cases these biases act to develop and maintain anxiety. If such cognitive factors are maintaining psychopathology, then developing treatments that try to address and change these dysfunctional cognitive features is important. Two early forms of *cognitive therapy* based on these assumptions were rational emotive therapy (RET) and Beck's cognitive therapy.

How people construe themselves, their life and the world is likely to be a major determinant of their feelings. *Rational emotive therapy (RET)*, developed by Albert Ellis (1962), was one of the first cognitive therapies to address these factors. In

Cognitive therapy A form of psychotherapy based on the belief that psychological problems are the products of faulty ways of thinking about the world.

Rational emotive therapy (RET) A cognitive technique developed by Albert Ellis (1962) which addresses how people construe themselves, their life and the world.

particular, Ellis believed that people carry around with them a set of implicit assumptions that determine how they judge themselves and others, and that many of these implicit assumptions may be irrational and cause emotional distress. For example, two irrational beliefs include (1) demanding perfection from oneself and from others and (2) expecting approval from others for everything one does. Clearly, there will be many occasions when these goals are not met, and this will cause anxiety, depression and emotional discomfort. RET attempts to challenge these irrational beliefs and to persuade the individual to set more attainable life goals. As such, RET is a good example of a group of therapies which attempt to change a set of core beliefs about the world that may be dysfunctional (i.e. either fallacious or a source of conflict and emotional distress). However, make no mistake about it, changing an individual's core beliefs – which have been developed and refined over a period of many years – is no easy thing. This is why highly structured cognitive therapies are required for successful treatment. These therapies will normally go through a process of challenging existing dysfunctional beliefs, replacing them with more rational beliefs, and then getting the individual to test out this new set of beliefs in structured behavioural exercises.

Aaron Beck's cognitive theory of depression is outlined in more detail in Chapter 6. From this theory he developed a cognitive therapy for depression. Beck argues that depression results when individuals develop a set of cognitive schemas (or beliefs) that bias them towards negative interpretations of the self, the world and the future. Any therapy for depression must therefore address these schemas, deconstruct them and replace them with more rational schemas that do not always lead to negative interpretations. *Beck's cognitive therapy* does this by engaging the depressed individual in an objective assessment of her beliefs, and requires her to provide evidence for her biased views of the world.

> **Beck's cognitive therapy**   Theory that argues that depression is maintained by a 'negative schema' that leads depressed individuals to hold negative views about themselves, their future and the world (the 'negative triad').

This enables the individual to perceive her existing schemas as biased, irrational and overgeneralized (see Chapter 6, section 6.4.2).

Out of these early pioneering cognitive therapies developed what is now known as *cognitive behaviour therapy (CBT)*, which is an intervention for changing both thoughts and behaviour and represents an umbrella term for many different therapies that share these common aims. A CBT intervention usually possesses most of the following characteristics:

> **Cognitive behaviour therapy (CBT)**   A psychotherapy based on modifying cognitions, assumptions, beliefs and behaviours, with the aim of influencing disturbed emotions.

1 The client is encouraged to keep a diary noting the occurrence of significant events and associated feelings, moods and thoughts in order to demonstrate how events, moods and thoughts might be interlinked.

2 With the help of the therapist, the client is urged to identify and challenge irrational, dysfunctional or biased thoughts or assumptions.

3 Clients are given homework in the form of 'behavioural experiments' to test whether their thoughts and assumptions are accurate and rational.

4 Clients are trained in news ways of thinking, behaving and reacting in situations that may evoke their psychopathology.

As an example, Treatment in Practice Box 5.3 in Chapter 5 demonstrates how a cognitive behaviour therapist would conduct an interview designed to identify and challenge irrational and dysfunctional beliefs in an individual diagnosed with panic disorder.

CBT is generally perceived as an evidence-based and cost-effective form of treatment that can be successfully applied to a very broad range of psychopathologies (Butler, Chapman, Forman & Beck, 2006). Table 4.1 provides a list of further reading if you wish to discover how CBT has been applied across a range of mental health problems.

4.1.1.4 Humanistic Therapies

Throughout the twentieth century, many psychotherapists felt that psychological therapy was becoming too focused on psychological and behavioural mechanisms or on psychological structures (such as personality), and was losing sight of both individuals' feelings and the individuals themselves. As a consequence, a number of what are called *'humanistic' therapies* developed, including gestalt therapy (Perls, 1969), existential therapies (Cooper, 2003), primal therapy (Janov, 1973), narrative therapy (Freedman & Combs, 1996), transpersonal therapy (Wellings, Wilde & McCormick, 2000) and – arguably the most successful – client-centred therapy (Rogers, 1951).

> **Humanistic therapies**   Therapies that attempt to consider the 'whole' person and not just the symptoms of psychopathology.

These therapies have a number of factors in common: (1) they espouse the need for therapists to develop a more personal relationship with clients in order to help clients reach a state of realization that they can help themselves; (2) they are *holistic therapies* in that they emphasize the need to consider the 'whole' person, not just those 'bits' of the person that manifest psychopathology; (3) therapy should be seen as a way of enabling individuals to make their own decisions and solve their own problems rather than imposing structured treatments or ways of thinking on them; (4) the therapist–client relationship has to be a genuinely reciprocal and empathetic one, rather than the limited skilled professional–referred client relationship that exists in many forms of psychological therapy; and (5) increasing emotional awareness is a critical factor in alleviating psychological distress and is necessary before clients can begin to resolve life problems.

> **Holistic therapies**   Therapies which emphasize the need to consider the 'whole' person, not just those 'bits' of the person that manifest psychopathology.

Client-centred therapy focuses on the individual's immediate conscious experience. Critical to this form of humanistic therapy is the creation of a therapeutic climate that allows clients to progress from a state of rigid self-perception to one that encourages independence, self-direction and the pursuit of self-growth. For Carl

> **Client-centred therapy**   An approach to psychopathology stressing the goodness of human nature, assuming that if individuals are unrestricted by fears and conflicts, they will develop into well-adjusted, happy individuals.

Table 4.1 *Further reading on CBT as applied to specific psychopathologies*

Psychopathology or client group	Reference
Cognitive Therapy for Bipolar Disorder	Lam, Hayward & Bright (1999)
Cognitive Therapy for Delusions, Voices and Paranoia	Chadwick, Birchwood & Trower (1996)
Cognitive Therapy for Psychosis	Fowler, Garety & Kuipers (1995)
Cognitive Behaviour Therapy with Older People	Laidlaw, Thompson, Siskin & Gallagher-Thompson (2003)
Cognitive Behavioural Therapy in the Treatment of Addiction	Koumimtsidis, Reynolds, Drummond, Davis, Sell & Tarrier (2007)
Cognitive Therapy for Depression	Bjorgvinsson & Rosqvist (2008)
Cognitive Behavioural Therapy for Chronic Fatigue Syndrome	Kinsella (2007)
Cognitive Behaviour Therapy with Children and Adolescents	Reinecke, Dattilio & Freeman (2006)
Cognitive Behavioural Therapy for Adult Asperger's Syndrome	Gaus (2007)
Cognitive Behavioural Therapy for OCD	Clark (2006)
Cognitive Therapy for Personality Disorders	Davidson (2007)
Cognitive Behavioural Therapy for Trauma	Follette & Ruzek (2006)
Cognitive Behavioural Therapy for PTSD	Zayfert & Becker (2007)
Cognitive Behaviour Therapy for Social Phobia	Hofman & Otto (2008)
Cognitive Behavioural Therapy for Adult ADHD	Ramsay & Rostain (2007)
Cognitive Behavioural Therapy for Generalized Anxiety Disorder (GAD)	Dugas & Robichaud (2006)
Cognitive Behavioural Treatment of Obesity	Cooper, Fairburn & Hawker (2004)
Cognitive Behavioural Treatment of Borderline Personality Disorder	Linehan (1993)
Cognitive Therapy for Schizophrenia and Psychotic Disorders	Kingdon & Turkington (2004); Haddock & Slade (1995); Morrison, Renton, Dunn, Williams & Bentall (2003)
Cognitive Behavioural Therapy for People with Learning and Intellectual Disabilities	Kroese, Dagnan & Loumidis (1997)

Empathy   An ability to understand and experience a client's own feelings and personal meanings, and a willingness to demonstrate unconditional positive regard for the client.

Rogers (1902–87), **empathy** ('putting yourself in someone else's shoes') was the central important feature of any therapist–client relationship and is essential in guiding clients towards resolving their own life problems. Empathy has at least two main components in this context: (1) an ability to understand and experience the client's own feelings and personal meanings and (2) a willingness to demonstrate **unconditional positive regard**

Unconditional positive regard   Valuing clients for who they are without judging them.

for the client. This latter feature involves valuing clients for who they are and refraining from judging them. Another important feature of client-centred therapy is that it is not directive. The therapist acts primarily as an understanding listener who assists the client by offering advice only when asked. The overriding goal is to develop individuals through empathy, congruence and unconditional positive regard to a point where they are successful in experiencing and accepting themselves and are able to resolve their own conflicts and difficulties.

In much the same way that psychoanalysis has evolved, client-centred therapy has developed not just as a therapy but also as a process for fostering personal self-growth. The general approach places relatively little emphasis on how the psychopathology was acquired, but attempts to eliminate symptoms by moving the client from one phenomenological state (e.g. a state of anxiety, depression) to another (e.g. one that enables clients to view themselves as worthy and respected individuals).

4.1.1.5 Family and Systemic Therapies

Family therapy A form of intervention involving family members that is helpful as a means of dealing with psychopathology that may result from the relationship dynamics within the family.

Family therapy is a form of intervention which is becoming increasingly helpful as a means of dealing with psychopathology that may result from the relationship dynamics within the family (Dallos & Draper, 2005). Family therapy has a number of purposes: (1) it helps to improve communications between members of the family – especially where communication between individuals might be the cause of psychopathology in one or more family members; (2) it can resolve specific conflicts – for example between adolescents and their parents; and (3) it

Systems theory Approach that attempts to understand the family as a social system.

may apply *systems theory* (attempting to understand the family as a social system) to treatment by trying to understand the complex relationships and alliances that exist between family members, and then attempting to remould these relationships into those expected in a well-functioning family (the latter may usually involve ensuring that the primary relationship in the family – between the two parents – is strong and functional) (Minuchin, 1985).

In family therapy the therapist or family therapy team meets with those members of the family willing to participate in discussion about a topic or problem raised by one or more members of the family. In the case of an adolescent eating disorder, the parents may have raised the issue of how their child's eating disorder affects family functioning, and this may be explored with the family over a series of meetings. Family therapists are usually quite eclectic in the range of approaches they may bring to family therapy. These may include cognitive behavioural methods, psychodynamic approaches or systemic analyses depending on the nature of the problem and its underlying causes. In many cases family therapists may focus on how patterns of interaction within the family maintain the problem (e.g. an eating disorder) rather than trying to identify the cause (the latter may be seen as trying to allocate blame for the problem within the family). Over a period of between 5 and 20 sessions, the family therapist will attempt to identify family interaction patterns that the family may not be aware of, and to suggest to family members different ways of responding to each other. A case example of the use of family therapy with an adolescent with an eating disorder is provided in Treatment in Practice Box 9.1 in Chapter 9.

4.1.1.6 Drug Treatments

Pharmacological or drug treatments are regularly used to alleviate some of the symptoms of psychopathologies. They are often the first line of treatment provided by GPs and doctors to tackle anxiety and mood-based problems, and may be sufficient to enable an individual to see through an acute bout of anxiety or depression. Some of the most commonly used drug treatments include *antidepressant drugs* to deal with symptoms of depression and mood disorder, *anxiolytic drugs* to treat symptoms of anxiety and stress, and *antipsychotic drugs* prescribed for symptoms of psychosis and schizophrenia.

Antidepressant drugs Drug treatments intended to treat symptoms of depression and mood disorder.

Drug treatments for depression were first successfully developed in the 1960s. The drugs that were first developed were called *tricyclic antidepressants* (because of their chemical structure) and have an effect by increasing the amount of norepinephrine and serotonin available for synaptic transmission. Other antidepressants introduced during this period were *monoamine oxidase (MAO) inhibitors* (such as phenelzine and tranylcypromine). MAOIs

Anxiolytic drugs Drug treatments intended to treat symptoms of anxiety and stress.

Antipsychotic drugs Drug treatments intended to treat symptoms of psychosis and schizophrenia.

Tricyclic antidepressants Antidepressant drugs developed in the 1960s which have their effect by increasing the amount of norepinephrine and serotonin available for synaptic transmission.

Monoamine oxidase (MAO) inhibitors A group of antidepressant drugs which have their effects by increasing levels of both serotonin and norepinephrine in the brain.

are effective for some people with major depression who do not respond to other antidepressants. They are also effective for the treatment of panic disorder and bipolar depression. Most recently, we have seen the development of the first 'designer drugs' for depression, including fluoxetine (Prozac), sertraline (Zoloft), paroxetine (Paxil) and citalopram (Celexa). These newer drugs are collectively called *selective serotonin reuptake inhibitors* or *SSRIs*, because they selectively affect the uptake of only one neurotransmitter – usually serotonin.

Selective serotonin reuptake inhibitors (SSRIs) A recent group of antidepressant drugs that selectively affect the uptake of only one neurotransmitter – usually serotonin.

SSRIs can reduce the symptoms of depression as rapidly as tricyclic antidepressants and have far fewer side effects. SSRIs – especially Prozac – have often been viewed as the miracle drug for depression. However, it too can cause some side effects (such as a loss of sexual desire in up to 30 per cent of users; Montgomery, 1995), and is perhaps at the point where it is becoming over-prescribed by GPs who may be failing to look further for more structured psychological treatment for their patients (Olfson & Klerman, 1993).

There are a number of psychological disorders that are characterized by chronic, high levels of anxiety. The more prevalent of these include clinically diagnosable specific phobias, panic disorder, generalized anxiety disorder (GAD), obsessive-compulsive disorder (OCD) and post-traumatic stress disorder (PTSD) (see Chapter 5). The symptoms of these disorders can usually be treated with anxiolytics (tranquillizers) such as the **benzodiazepines** (which include the well-known tranquillizer, valium), and they have their effect by increasing the level of the neurotransmitter GABA at synapses in the brain. Benzodiazepines are usually prescribed for only short periods because they can encourage dependency if taken over a longer period, and can also be abused if available in large doses. However, it is important to be aware that anxiolytics will usually offer only symptom relief and do not address the psychological and cognitive factors that may be maintaining the anxiety.

Benzodiazepines A group of anxiolytics which have their effect by increasing the level of the neurotransmitter GABA at synapses in the brain.

Drug treatments for psychosis and schizophrenia have radically revolutionized the way that schizophrenia sufferers are treated and cared for. The use of effective antipsychotic drugs became common in the 1960s and 1970s. This had the effect of drastically reducing the number of individuals with psychotic symptoms who needed long-term institutionalized care and has enabled many experiencing such symptoms to achieve relatively normal day-to-day functioning. Prior to the 1980s it was estimated that two out of three schizophrenia sufferers would spend most of their lives in a psychiatric institution; beyond the 1980s the average length of stay is down to as little as two months (Lamb, 1984).

Antipsychotics (such as chlorpromazine and haloperidol) have their effects by blocking dopamine receptors and help to reduce the high levels of dopamine in the brain (see Chapter 7). This not only reduces the major positive symptoms (such as thought disorder and hallucinations), but can also reduce the major negative symptoms (such as social withdrawal). However, while these drugs have had a remarkable effect on reducing the symptoms of psychosis, and, as a consequence, reducing the burden of institutionalized care for sufferers, there are some negative factors to consider. For example, most antipsychotics do have some undesirable side effects for some people (such as blurred vision, muscle spasms, blood disorders, cardiac problems), and these side effects can cause relapse or make sufferers unwilling to take their medication on a regular basis (requiring constant monitoring if the individual is being cared for in the community).

Despite the fact that appropriate medication can often provide relief from the symptoms of psychopathology, there is a view that interventions using drugs alone may be problematic for a number of reasons. First, prescribing drugs for some mild psychopathology symptoms may effectively 'medicalize' what are merely everyday problems of living and lead people to believe that acute bouts of anxiety or depression are 'diseases' that will not be alleviated until medical treatment has been sought (Shaw & Woodward, 2004; see Focus Point 1.1 in Chapter 1). Secondly, long-term prescription of drugs for a psychopathology may lead sufferers to believe that their symptoms are unchangeable and that their psychological and social functioning will depend on their continuing to take their medication. This can often prevent such individuals from trying to

understand their symptoms and from gaining insight into symptoms that may be primarily psychological rather than medical in nature (Bentall, 2003; see Activity Box 7.2 in Chapter 7 for an example related to drug interventions for psychotic symptoms). Finally, there is some evidence that while drug treatment of psychopathology may alleviate the immediate symptoms, it may worsen the long-term course of a disorder. For example, while antidepressant drugs may alleviate the immediate symptoms of depression, there is evidence that they may also increase vulnerability to relapse over the longer term (Fava, 2003). This may be due to drug tolerance effects as a result of continued drug use plus the fact that drug treatment alone may not facilitate the kinds of beneficial insights into the psychopathology that psychological therapies may provide. This account is consistent with the fact that when drug treatments are successful over the longer term, this is more likely to be the case if they are combined with psychological treatment (e.g. CBT) (Hollon & Beck, 1994; Thase, Greenhouse, Frank, Reynolds et al., 1997).

SUMMARY

Each of the treatment approaches we have discussed in this section can be used to treat a range of different psychopathologies, and we will look more closely at how to evaluate their success later in this chapter. These approaches differ not only in the basic intervention procedures they use, but also in the way each attempts to explain psychopathology (see Chapter 1). Contemporary practitioners may well be skilled in using more than one of these approaches, and, indeed, a combination of approaches may be used to address specific psychopathologies (e.g. the use of both drug treatment and CBT to treat depression). Table 4.2 provides a summary of the specific treatments covered in this book grouped according to their main theoretical approach.

4.1.2 Modes of Treatment Delivery

The standard and traditional mode of psychotherapy delivery is in one-to-one, face-to-face meetings or sessions between a therapist and a client, and this is still the most prevalent mode of delivery today. However, with the pressing need to treat ever-increasing numbers of individuals referred with symptoms of psychopathology, over-stretched clinicians and service providers often look to find more cost-effective and efficient ways to deliver treatment interventions. The following section looks briefly at some of the modes of delivery that have been developed to supplement the traditional one-to-one therapist–client model.

4.1.2.1 Group Therapy

Therapy can be undertaken in a group and not just on a one-to-one basis between therapist and client. **Group therapy** can

Group therapy Therapy taken in the form of a group, usually when individuals share similar problems or psychopathologies.

Table 4.2 *Common specific treatments for psychopathology and psychological disorders grouped by generic treatment type*

GENERIC TREATMENT TYPE	SPECIFIC PSYCHOPATHOLOGY OR PSYCHOLOGICAL DISORDER	SPECIFIC TREATMENT SUB-TYPE	CHAPTER IN THIS BOOK (For fuller details)
PSYCHODYNAMIC/ PSYCHOANALYTIC THERAPY	Major depression	Psychoanalysis	Chapter 6
	Paranoid, schizoid, antisocial, narcissistic, histrionic and avoidant personality disorders		Chapter 11
	Borderline personality disorder	Object relations psychotherapy; dialectical behaviour therapy	Chapter 11
	Dependent personality disorder	Object relations psychotherapy	Chapter 11
	Conversion disorder; somatization disorder; body dysmorphic disorder; hypochondriasis	Psychodynamic therapy and hypnotherapy	Chapter 12
	Dissociative disorders		Chapter 13
COGNITIVE BEHAVIOUR THERAPY (CBT)	Social phobia		Chapter 5
	Panic disorder		Chapter 5
	Generalized anxiety disorder (GAD)	Self-monitoring and cognitive restructuring	Chapter 5
	Obsessive-compulsive disorder (OCD)		Chapter 5
	Post-traumatic stress disorder (PTSD)	Cognitive restructuring	Chapter 5
	Major depression	Cognitive restructuring and mindfulness-based cognitive therapy (MBCT)	Chapter 6
	Psychosis and schizophrenia		Chapter 7
	Substance abuse and dependency		Chapter 8
	Bulimia nervosa		Chapter 9
	Binge-eating disorder		Chapter 9
	Paraphilias		Chapter 10
	Gender identity disorder (GID)	Cognitive treatment designed to change gender identity beliefs	Chapter 10
	Narcissistic, histrionic, avoidant, dependent and obsessive-compulsive personality disorder		Chapter 11
	Antisocial and borderline personality disorder	Schema therapy	Chapter 11
	Somatoform disorders		Chapter 12
	Childhood psychological problems	CBT for childhood anxiety and depression	Chapter 15
BEHAVIOUR THERAPY	Specific phobia	Exposure therapy; systematic desensitization; flooding	Chapter 5
	Panic disorder	Exposure-based treatments	Chapter 5
	Generalized anxiety disorder (GAD)	Stimulus control treatment	Chapter 5
	Obsessive-compulsive disorder (OCD)	Exposure and ritual prevention treatments (EPR)	Chapter 5

Table 4.2 *(Cont'd)*

GENERIC TREATMENT TYPE	SPECIFIC PSYCHOPATHOLOGY OR PSYCHOLOGICAL DISORDER	SPECIFIC TREATMENT SUB-TYPE	CHAPTER IN THIS BOOK (For fuller details)
BEHAVIOUR THERAPY (cont'd)	Post-traumatic stress disorder (PTSD)	Exposure therapy; eye-movement desensitization and reprocessing (EMDR)	Chapter 5
	Major depression	Social skills training; behavioural activation therapy	Chapter 5
	Psychosis and schizophrenia	Social skills training	Chapter 6
	Substance abuse and dependency	Aversion therapy; behavioural self-control training (BSCT); controlled drinking	Chapter 8
	Sexual dysfunctions	Stop-start technique; squeeze technique; tease technique; directed masturbation training	Chapter 10
	Paraphilias	Aversion therapy; covert conditioning; masturbatory satiation; orgasmic reorientation	Chapter 10
	Somatoform disorders	Changing reinforcement contingencies; behavioural stress management; exposure and response prevention	Chapter 12
	Childhood psychological problems	Systematic desensitization; reinforcement techniques; behaviour management techniques	Chapter 15
	Intellectual disabilities	Behavioural training procedures	Chapter 16
	Autistic spectrum disorder (ASD)	Behavioural training methods	Chapter 16
CLIENT-CENTRED/ HUMANISTIC THERAPY	Post-traumatic stress disorder (PTSD)	Psychological debriefing	Chapter 5
	Anorexia nervosa	Interpersonal psychotherapy	Chapter 9
DRUG TREATMENTS	Social phobia	Monoamine-oxidase inhibitors (MAOIs) and serotonin reuptake inhibitors (SSRIs)	Chapter 5
	Panic disorder	Tricyclic antidepressants and benziodiazepines	Chapter 5
	Generalized anxiety disorder (GAD)	Anxiolytics such as benzodiazepines	Chapter 5
	Obsessive-compulsive disorder (OCD)	SSRIs	Chapter 5
	Major depression	Tricyclic drugs, MAOIs and SSRIs	Chapter 6
	Bipolar disorder	Lithium carbonate	Chapter 6
	Psychosis and schizophrenia	Antipsychotic drugs	Chapter 7
	Substance abuse and dependency	Detoxification and drug maintenance therapy	Chapter 8
	Anorexia nervosa	SSRIs	Chapter 9
	Bulimia nervosa	Antidepressant drugs (e.g. SSRIs)	Chapter 9

Table 4.2 *(Cont'd)*

GENERIC TREATMENT TYPE	SPECIFIC PSYCHOPATHOLOGY OR PSYCHOLOGICAL DISORDER	SPECIFIC TREATMENT SUB-TYPE	CHAPTER IN THIS BOOK (For fuller details)
DRUG TREATMENTS (cont'd)	Binge-eating disorder	Antidepressant drugs (e.g. SSRIs)	Chapter 9
	Sexual dysfunctions	Drug and hormone treatments	Chapter 10
	Paraphilias	Hormonal and drug treatments	Chapter 10
	Paranoid, schizoid, schizotypical and antisocial personality disorders	Antipsychotic drugs	Chapter 11
	Borderline personality disorder	Antidepressants	Chapter 11
	Dissociative disorders	Antidepressants	Chapter 13
	Childhood psychological problems	SSRIs for depression; Ritalin and other stimulants for ADHD	Chapter 15
	Autistic spectrum disorder (ASD)	Haloperidol, Rispiridone, Naltrexone	Chapter 16
FAMILY THERAPY AND SYSTEMIC APPROACHES	Psychosis and schizophrenia		Chapter 7
	Substance abuse and dependency		Chapter 8
	Anorexia nervosa		Chapter 9
	Sexual dysfunctions	Couples therapy	Chapter 10
	Childhood psychological problems	Systemic family therapy; parent training programmes; functional family therapy (FFT)	Chapter 15

be useful (1) when a group of individuals share similar problems or psychopathologies (e.g. self-help groups) or (2) when there is a need to treat an individual in the presence of others who might have a role in influencing the psychopathology (e.g. family therapy). Group therapies can have a number of advantages, especially when individuals (1) may need to work out their problems in the presence of others (e.g. in the case of emotional problems relating to relationships, feelings of isolation, loneliness and rejection); (2) may need comfort and support from others; and (3) may acquire therapeutic benefit from observing and watching others. There are now many different types of group therapy (Bloch & Crouch, 1987), including *experiential groups* and *encounter groups* (which encourage therapy and self-growth through disclosure and interaction) and *self-help groups* (which bring together people who have a common problem in an attempt to share information and help and offer mutual support – e.g. Alcoholics Anonymous, www.alcoholics-anonymous.org.uk; see Focus Point 8.2 in Chapter 8).

Experiential groups   Group therapy which encourages therapy and self-growth through disclosure and interaction.

Encounter groups   Group therapy which encourages therapy and self-growth through disclosure and interaction.

Self-help groups   Group therapy which brings together people who share a common problem in an attempt to share information and help and support one another.

4.1.2.2 Counselling

Counselling is still a developing and evolving profession that has burgeoned in the past 20–30 years. Its expansion has partly resulted from the increasing demand for trained specialists able to provide immediate support and treatment across a broad range of problems and client groups. Counsellors receive specialized training in a range of support, guidance and intervention techniques, and their levels of training are monitored and accredited by professional bodies such as the British Association for Counselling and Psychotherapy (BACP) in the UK, or Division 17 (Counselling Psychology) of the American Psychological Association. Arguably, the primary task for counselling is to give clients an opportunity to explore, discover and clarify ways of living more satisfyingly and resourcefully and to help them to 'understand and

Counselling   A profession that aims both to promote personal growth and productivity and to alleviate any personal problems that may reflect underlying psychopathology.

clarify their views of their lifespace, and to learn to reach their self-determined goals through meaningful, well-informed choices and through resolution of problems of an emotional or interpersonal nature' (Burks & Stefflre, 1979, p. 14).

These definitions indicate that counselling is a profession that aims both to promote personal growth and productivity and to alleviate any personal problems that may reflect underlying psychopathology. In order to achieve these aims, counsellors tend to adopt a range of theoretical approaches, with the main ones being psychodynamic, cognitive behavioural and humanistic (MacLeod, 2003). Counsellors with different theoretical orientations may often focus on different outcomes. Humanistic counsellors tend to promote self-acceptance and personal freedom, psychodynamic counsellors focus primarily on insight, and cognitive behavioural counsellors are mainly concerned with the management and control of behaviour and symptoms of psychopathology (MacLeod, 2003). Some counsellors specialize in areas such as marital breakdown, rape, bereavement or addictions, and their specialized roles may be recognized by the use of titles such as *mental health counsellor*, *marriage counsellor* or *student counsellor*.

> **Mental health counsellor** A counsellor who specializes in mental health problems.

> **Marriage counsellor** A counsellor who specializes in marriage problems.

> **Student counsellor** A counsellor who specializes in students' problems.

Counselling agencies have been established in a range of organizations to supplement community mental health services and provide more direct and immediate access to support for vulnerable or needy individuals. Counselling services may be directed towards people with particular medical conditions such as AIDS and cancer, and also to the carers of individuals suffering these illnesses, and these services are often provided by voluntary and charitable organizations set up specifically for these purposes. Even individual companies and organizations may have set up their own in-house counselling services to help people through difficulties and anxieties associated with their work.

4.1.2.3 Computerized CBT (CCBT)

Because a treatment such as CBT has a highly organized structure, it lends itself well to delivery by other modes and as a package that might be used independently by clients. In recent years, *computerized CBT (CCBT)* has been developed as an alternative to therapist-delivered CBT. It consists of highly developed software packages that can be delivered via an interactive computer interface on a personal computer, over the Internet or via the telephone using interactive voice response (IVR) systems. The UK Department of Health has recommended the use of two CCBT packages. The first, *Beating the Blues*, is an option for delivering computer-based CBT in the management of mild and moderate depression, while the second, *Fear Fighter*, is an option for delivering computer-based CBT in the management of panic and phobia (Department of Health, 2007).

> **Computerized CBT (CCBT)** An alternative to therapist-delivered CBT which consists of highly developed software packages that can be delivered via an interactive computer interface on a personal computer, over the internet or via the telephone using interactive voice response (IVR) systems.

Beating the Blues consists of a 15-minute introductory video and eight 1-hour interactive sessions, including homework to be completed between sessions. The programme helps clients identify thinking errors, challenge negative thoughts and recognize core negative beliefs, and provides help and advice on more adaptive thinking styles (www.ultrasis; see also Treatment in Practice Box 6.1, Chapter 6). *Fear Fighter* is a CBT-based package for phobic, panic and anxiety disorders and is divided into nine steps with support available from trained helpers via telephone calls or emails throughout treatment. The package helps clients identify specific problems, develop realistic treatment goals and monitor achievement through self-exposure (www.fearfighter.com).

> **Beating the Blues** A computer-based CBT programme used in the management of mild and moderate depression.

> **Fear Fighter** A computer-based CBT used in the management of panic and phobia.

Studies comparing CCBT with other forms of support and intervention are still in their infancy, but those available are relatively supportive. For example, Proudfoot, Ryden, Everitt, Shapiro et al. (2004) found that *Beating the Blues* provided a more effective treatment for depression and anxiety than GP treatment as usual. In a review of 16 studies exploring the efficacy of CCBT, Kaltenthaler, Parry and Beverley (2004) found that five studies showed CCBT to have equivalent outcomes to therapist-led CBT, and four studies found CCBT to be more effective than GP treatment as usual.

4.1.2.4 E-therapy

The rapid growth of the Internet over the past 10–15 years has meant that people now have almost immediate access to information about mental health problems, and email provides another potential form of communication between therapists and clients. As a result, more and more therapists and practitioners are using email as an integral part of the treatment they provide (Hsiung, 2002). Email is a useful adjunct to face-to-face sessions in a number of ways.

> **E-therapy** A treatment method which involves the use of email and internet technology.

1 It may be used to enhance weekly sessions, monitor treatment from a distance, monitor behaviour daily, communicate with the client's family members or intervene in a crisis (Yellowlees, 2002; Yager, 2002).

2 It allows clients to initiate contact with therapists more easily, which may make them feel safer and, because the communication is online, more secure (Ainsworth, 2002).

3 It allows clients who may be withdrawn or shy in personal face-to-face interviews (such as adolescents with eating disorders) to be more open and compliant (Yager, 2002).

4 It enables clients to contact therapists more regularly in areas where resources are more difficult to access in person, or when clients are living in remote and inaccessible areas (Gibson, Morley & Romeo-Wolff, 2002).

A study by Stroh (1999) indicated that in a survey of 10,000 physicians in the US, about 85 per cent used the Internet and about 35 per cent exchanged emails with clients. However, at present there is very little research on the effectiveness of online services or the potential beneficial effects of email communication between therapists and clients. There are also a number of limitations to email communication, including miscommunication, because neither party is able to see the non-verbal cues being given by the other; it is very difficult to ensure the confidentiality of online communications; and online communication makes it very difficult to intervene effectively in severe emergencies when, for example, a client may have suicidal intentions.

4.1.2.5 Therapy by Telephone

Telephone therapy   Treatment and support conducted over the telephone.

Most clients telephone their therapists, if only to schedule an appointment, but the telephone can also provide a means of facilitating and conducting treatment. For example, Ludman, Simon, Tutty and von Korff (2007) report an evaluation of a telephone-based CBT programme for depression in which clients were given eight core sessions in which standard CBT procedures were adapted for use over the telephone. This was supplemented by homework exercises for clients, and regular assessments were also conducted over the phone. Figure 4.1 shows that CBT conducted over the phone was more successful in reducing depression scores than usual care (clients receiving antidepressants) up to 12–18 months post-treatment. This finding supplements results of other outcome studies suggesting that telephone therapy is both acceptable and effective (Leach & Christensen, 2006; Lynch, Tamburrino & Nagel, 1997; Mohr, Hart, Julian, Catledge et al., 2005). Telephone therapy may prove to be an effective form of intervention when clients live in remote or inaccessible areas, and it is a mode of delivery that can save time and reduce travel costs.

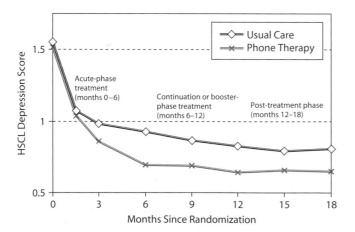

Figure 4.1
Improvement in depression scores as a function of therapy by telephone (CBT) or care as usual (pharmacotherapy). CBT by telephone results in a marked improvement in depression scores over pharmacotherapy in the first 6 months of treatment and gains are maintained up to 18 months after the start of treatment. (HSCL = Hopkins Symptom Checklist, a measure of the remission of depression.)

Source: Ludman, Simon, Tutty & von Korff (2007).

Plate 4.2
Many therapists are increasingly using the telephone to conduct treatment, and recent studies suggest that therapies such as CBT can be just as effective when administered by phone (Leach & Christensen, 2006).

SUMMARY

With the average waiting time for conventional treatments provided by community mental health services in the UK sometimes as long as 1–2 years – especially for popular and specialized treatments such as CBT – practitioners and service providers are under pressure to provide more cost-effective and immediate forms of interventions for people with mental health problems (Layard, 2007). We have reviewed some of the modes of delivery that may prove to be more immediate and cost effective, although most of them represent relatively new innovations that have yet to be fully and properly evaluated.

SELF-TEST QUESTIONS

- What are the main principles of psychodynamic therapy?
- Can you describe some of the basic techniques used by psychoanalysts?
- Can you describe the behaviour therapy techniques that are based on classical conditioning?
- Can you describe some of the treatment techniques that have been developed based on principles of operant reinforcement?
- Can you describe at least two types of cognitive therapy?
- What are the main theoretical principles on which humanistic therapies are based?
- What are the main principles used in client-centred therapy?
- What is family therapy and how is it conducted?
- Can you name the main types of drug treatments for psychopathology?
- Can you describe 2–3 types of group therapy?
- What are the main characteristics of counselling?
- Can you describe the main features of computerized CBT (CCBT), e-therapy and therapy by telephone?

SECTION SUMMARY

4.1 The Nature and Function of Treatments for Psychopathology

- The treatment provided for a psychopathology will depend on the theoretical orientation of the therapist and the nature of the psychopathology.

- **Psychodynamic approaches** to therapy attempt to reveal unconscious conflicts that may be causing psychopathology.

- **Behaviour therapies** are mainly based on the principles of classical and operant conditioning.

- Behaviour therapies based on classical conditioning include **flooding, counterconditioning, systematic desensitization** and **aversion therapy**.

- Therapies based on operant conditioning include **functional analysis, token economy, response shaping** and **behavioural self-control**.

- Important **cognitive therapies** include **rational emotive therapy (RET)**, Beck's cognitive therapy and **cognitive behaviour therapy (CBT)**.

- **Humanistic therapies** attempt to consider the 'whole' person and not just the symptoms of psychopathology.

- **Family therapy** attempts to deal with psychopathology by addressing relationship dynamics within the family.

- **Drug treatments** have been developed to alleviate some of the symptoms of psychopathology.

- Important drug treatments include **antidepressant drugs, anxiolytic drugs** and **antipsychotic drugs**.

- Recently developed modes of treatment delivery include **group therapy, counselling, computerized CBT (CCBT), e-therapy** and **therapy by telephone**.

4.2 EVALUATING TREATMENT

All of the therapies and treatments we have discussed in previous sections of this chapter have at least some degree of intuitive plausibility as treatments for psychological problems. Nevertheless, how do we assess how effective a treatment is? This is not as simple as it sounds. First, we often have to try to compare the efficacy of therapies that have quite different assumptions about what 'successful therapy' is (e.g. cognitive therapies would expect to see some significant improvement after a few weeks or months,

whereas psychoanalytic and humanistic therapies are seen as developmental, life-long processes promoting self-growth). Secondly, we have to decide on what constitutes a therapeutic gain (i.e. on what particular measures we are expecting to see improvement). For example, Erwin (2000) describes how different theoretical approaches to treatment use radically different criteria for judging outcomes. Therapists using CBT typically use elimination of psychopathology symptoms as the main criterion of success; behaviour therapists view the modification of maladaptive behaviours as important; psychodynamic therapists view the elimination of unconscious conflicts as critical to therapeutic success; and humanistic psychotherapists see enhancement of personal autonomy as their main therapeutic objective. Erwin concludes that, at the end of the day, what constitutes a successful therapeutic intervention is often a subjective judgement and may boil down to little more than that the outcome was beneficial in some way to the client – or at least to someone!

Despite these difficulties in deciding on a common set of criteria for gauging success across different treatment types, there are some good reasons for wanting to try to objectively assess how successful therapies are. (1) Psychological disorders are distressing to the individual and we have a moral and professional obligation to try to find ways of alleviating this distress rapidly and effectively. (2) Some treatments may have short-term gains but are significantly less effective over the longer term, which may leave the individual open to relapse. We thus need to be sure that therapies have lasting therapeutic effects. Finally, (3) individuals with psychological problems are a very vulnerable group of people. We need to ensure that they are not exploited financially or psychologically by what is a growing industry of essentially bogus therapies with shallow – though often beguiling – rationales and little or no medium-term therapeutic benefit.

4.2.1 Factors Affecting the Evaluation of Treatments

On what basis do therapists decide whether their treatments are successful? Focus Point 4.1 provides an interesting example of this. The therapist that Davey (2002) describes in this example assumed that her treatment was effective because no one ever returned to complain about it! But there may be many reasons why individuals may not complain, and the client in this example is quite happy to return for more therapy even though her first session was not as successful as she was led to believe it should be. Such is the enmeshed relationship between some therapists and their clients that they may well satisfy the needs of each other (the client helps the therapist earn a living, and the therapist provides the client with some care and attention) without necessarily achieving any substantial therapeutic gain for the client in those areas that were originally intended. The moral of this story is that a client simply saying he or she is satisfied with the outcome of the therapy does not mean either (1) that any objective therapeutic gain has been achieved, or (2), if some therapeutic gain was achieved, that it was due explicitly to the type of therapy used. Determining whether a treatment works because of the principles it contains is known as

FOCUS POINT 4.1

Stop smoking in one session!

'As I was passing a local "holistic" health clinic, I noticed a sign outside which – in large letters – implored "STOP SMOKING IN ONE SESSION" (which session – surely not the first one?!). Having interests in both clinical and health psychology areas, I was intrigued to find out more. As it turns out, a friend of mine had just recently visited the clinic and had received a single one-hour session of hypnotherapy in an attempt to stop smoking – cost £50. Knowing the literature on psychological treatments for smoking and how difficult it is to achieve abstinence, I decided to find out a little more about these treatment claims. I emailed the hypnotherapists offering services at the clinic asking if stopping smoking in one session of hypnotherapy was achievable, and what their success rates were like. I did get a reply from one of the practitioners, who had worked as a hypnotherapist for seven years. She replied: "I did not do follow-up calls as I thought this would be intrusive so therefore I did not have stats on my success rates. However, I knew I had a high success rate as people referred others to me and came back to me for help on other issues." Interestingly, my friend who had attended the clinic was smoking regularly again within three days of the hypnotherapy session, and – despite having long discussions with me about the validity of the treatment and its lack of success – said she was thinking of attending again (this time in relation to other aspects of her life) because the hypnotherapist had been so caring, understanding and interested in her problems!'

Source: Davey (2002)

Internal validity Determining whether a treatment works because of the principles it contains.

assessing its *internal validity*, and it is issues such as this that makes assessing the efficacy of therapies difficult. The sections below describe some of the factors that can confound the assessment of therapeutic effectiveness.

4.2.1.1 Spontaneous Remission

Just because someone exhibits objective improvement in symptoms after treatment does not necessarily mean that the treatment was effective. The famous British psychologist Hans Eysenck argued that many people who have psychological disorders will simply get better anyway over a period of time – even without therapy (Eysenck, 1961). This is known as *spontaneous remission*, and the current estimate is that around 30 per cent of those diagnosed with anxiety and depression-based disorders will get better without structured treatment (Jacobson & Christenson, 1996). So, if we are assessing the effectiveness of a therapy, we would expect to see improvement rates *significantly greater* than 30 per cent in order to take into account the fact that many of those undertaking the

Spontaneous remission The fact that many people who have psychological disorders will simply get better anyway over a period of time, even without therapy.

therapy would have a spontaneous improvement in symptoms anyway.

4.2.1.2 Placebo Effects

If individuals suffering with anxiety symptoms are given a sugar pill but are told that it is an anxiolytic medication, they often report significant improvements in those symptoms. This suggests that individuals will often get better because they *expect* to get better – even though the actual treatment they have been given is effectively useless (Paul, 1966). This is known as the *placebo effect* (Paul, 1966; see also section 3.4.2 in chapter 3). Thus, it may be the case that many psychological treatments have beneficial effects because the client *expects* them to work – and *not* because they are treatments that are effective in tackling the factors maintaining the psychopathology. Unfortunately, the positive gains produced by placebo effects are short-lived and comparative studies of placebo effects with actual structured psychotherapies strongly suggest that the latter lead to greater improvement than placebo control conditions (Robinson, Berman & Neimeyer, 1990; Andrews & Harvey, 1981).

Placebo effect The effect when participants in a clinical trial show improvement even though they are not being given a theoretically structured treatment.

4.2.1.3 Unstructured Attention, Understanding and Caring

We know that people with psychological problems also show some improvement in symptoms when they can simply talk about their problems in an unstructured way with either a professional therapist or a friend or relative (Lambert, Shapiro & Bergin, 1986). This suggests that many forms of social support may have a therapeutic effect in and of themselves (Borkovec & Costello, 1993), and this factor must be taken into account when judging how effective a structured therapy is. One of the important things that we want to find out about therapies is not just whether they are effective in making people better, but whether they make people better specifically because of the principles they contain (e.g. does psychoanalysis work because of the psychodynamic principles on which that form of therapy is based, and does CBT work because of the structured way that it attempts to identify and challenge dysfunctional beliefs?). One recently developed form of control condition for attention, understanding and caring is known as *befriending*. This is a control condition designed to provide participants with approximately the same amount of therapist contact as the treatment conditions being tested, with sessions spaced at similar intervals. In the befriending condition the therapist aims to be empathetic and non-directive, and does not attempt to directly tackle symptoms. The session is normally focused on discussion of neutral topics such as hobbies, sport and current affairs (Sensky, Turkington, Kingdon, Scott et al., 2000; Bendall, Jackson, Killackey, Allott et al., 2006).

Befriending A form of control condition for attention, understanding and caring used in treatment outcome studies.

4.2.2 Methods of Assessing the Effectiveness of Treatments

We have to begin this section by acknowledging that the advocates of some therapeutic approaches do not believe that the success or otherwise of their approaches can be assessed using objective or quantitative methods (e.g. Marzillier, 2004). This is because those therapists view their treatments not as attempts to eliminate symptoms of psychopathology but as attempts to reconstruct a client's meaning of the world, or to move the client from one phenomenological state to another (e.g. humanistic approaches). In each case these changes are not easy to measure objectively, and there are no particularly well-defined criteria for when these goals have been reached.

Nevertheless, there are still many compelling reasons for wanting to assess in some formal way whether a treatment is effective and successful. Some of the moral and compassionate reasons for wanting to do so were outlined at the beginning of section 4.2. In addition to these reasons, mental health service providers have a duty to ensure that the services they are offering are effective. They will thus need some benchmark by which to measure whether the treatments they propose are successful or at least provide satisfaction for the end-users they are providing for (see section 3.3.2 on clinical audit in Chapter 3, and the discussion of the National Institute for Health and Clinical Excellence in section 4.1 of this chapter).

Two popular methodologies for assessing the effectiveness of treatments are randomized controlled trials (RCTs) and meta-analyses.

4.2.2.1 Randomized Controlled Trials (RCTs)

The current methodology of choice for assessing the effectiveness of therapies is the *randomized controlled trial (RCT)* (e.g. Barker, Pistrang & Elliott, 2002, pp. 153–159). This procedure compares the effectiveness of the treatment being assessed (across a range of objective measures) with a variety of control conditions and with other forms of therapy and treatment (if necessary). Participants in the study are assigned *randomly* to each of these conditions. Apart from the treatment being assessed, the control conditions used in RCTs are those that will control for the kinds of effects described in section 4.2.1. These include (1) a *no treatment or a waiting-list control group* of participants who will receive no treatment (to control for the effects of spontaneous remission); this condition is often difficult to achieve because of the ethical issues involved in withholding treatment from clinically distressed individuals (see section 3.4.2 in Chapter 3); (2) an expectancy and relationship control group, to control for placebo effects and for the beneficial effects of contact with a therapist (e.g. 'befriending' – see section 4.2.1.3); and (3) a comparative treatment group, in which the original therapy can be compared with a plausible alternative therapy that is known to have beneficial effects. For the original therapy to be deemed effective and possess internal validity, participants receiving that therapy must show greater improvement than those in both the no treatment and the expectancy and relationship control conditions, and improvement that is at least equivalent to that exhibited by the comparative treatment group.

Randomized controlled trials (RCTs) A procedure for assessing the effectiveness of therapies by comparing the effectiveness of the treatment being assessed (across a range of objective measures) with a variety of control conditions, and with other forms of therapy and treatment (if necessary).

No treatment or a waiting-list control group A group of participants in a randomized controlled trial who control for the effects of spontaneous remission.

Figure 4.2 provides a schematic example of an RCT study comparing the efficacy of cognitive therapy and exposure plus applied relaxation treatments for social phobia. This shows how the original 116 participants in the study were assessed, the reasons why 54 were excluded from the study, how they were randomly allocated to one of three treatment conditions, how many dropped out of the study before completion, and when the outcome assessments were taken. The graph below the flowchart shows that the cognitive therapy condition was significantly more effective at reducing symptoms of social phobia than both exposure and applied relaxation and those in a waiting-list control condition.

While RCTs provide an objective way of assessing the effectiveness of therapies, they do have a number of practical limitations: (1) participants drop out of these studies and may do so more from some conditions – e.g. the no treatment conditions – more than others; (2) RCTs are costly and time-consuming to undertake; and (3) because participants are assigned randomly to conditions, this does not take account of the fact that some participants may prefer some types of therapy to others (Brewin & Bradley, 1989).

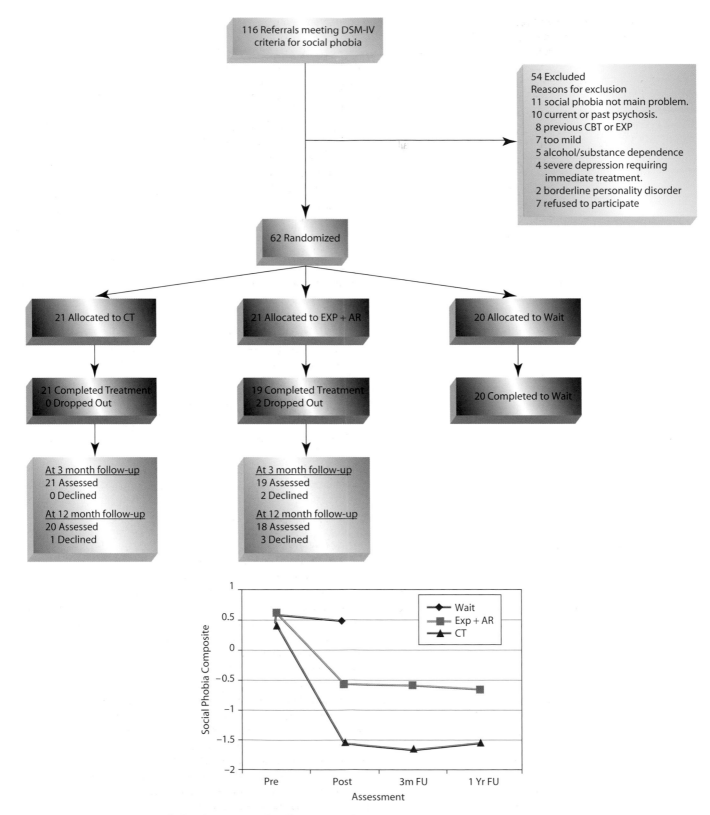

Figure 4.2 *A random controlled trial comparing the effectiveness of CBT and applied relaxation for social phobia.*
The flowchart shows how the 116 participants in the study were allocated to experimental conditions and assessed. The graph beneath the flowchart shows that the CBT condition (CT) was more effective at reducing the symptoms of social phobia than applied relaxation (Exp + AR) and a waiting-list control (Wait).

Source: Clark, Ehlers, Hackmann, McManus et al. (2006).

Table 4.3 *Good practice features that would normally be expected in a well-designed and conducted RCT*

- The study should use randomized assignments of participants to experimental and control conditions.

- The interventions used need to be clearly specified so that delivery is consistent across therapists and can be repeated by other researchers if necessary. This is usually achieved by providing the treatment protocol in a manual to ensure that therapists faithfully replicate the therapeutic procedure.

- Appropriate control groups should be used (e.g. waiting-list controls, treatment as usual or other comparative treatment groups).

- Participants in all groups should be treated equivalently apart from the experimental variable being manipulated (e.g. they should have had the same length of treatment, equivalent therapists, the same assessments, etc.)

- Those conducting the post-treatment ratings and assessments of participants should be blind to the experimental condition participants were in.

- Participants in the study should form a specific homogeneous group (e.g. by all meeting the criteria for a single DSM-IV-TR diagnosis – participants with comorbid diagnoses are usually excluded).

- There needs to be a low attrition rate for the study (the results may be invalid if lots of participants drop out of the study before the end, or if significantly more participants drop out of one particular group).

- The participants should be followed up and reassessed either 6 months or 12 months after the end of treatment (to ensure that any effects found at the end of the study are relatively long-lasting).

- Demonstrations of the effectiveness of a particular treatment need to be replicated by independent teams of researchers, thus demonstrating the generalizability of the findings across research settings.

Source: Barker, Pistrang & Elliot (2002).

Nevertheless, despite these drawbacks, RCTs have remained a popular method for assessing the relative effectiveness of treatments. Table 4.3 provides a list of good practice features that would normally be expected in a well-designed and conducted RCT.

4.2.2.2 Meta-analyses

We have already discussed *meta-analyses* as a research method in Chapter 3 (section 3.3.8), and readers are referred back to this section in the first instance. The benefit of meta-analyses is that they can be used to compare the effectiveness of studies that may have employed different procedures, numbers of participants, types of control procedures and forms of measurement by comparing effect sizes across studies. One important use of meta-analyses has been to try to answer an enduring question in psychotherapy: are psychotherapies more effective than no treatment at all? An early large-scale meta-analysis carried out by Smith, Glass and Miller (1980) concluded that psychotherapies were more effective than no treatment, but that effect sizes did not differ across different psychotherapies, suggesting that all different psychotherapies were equally effective.

> **Meta-analyses** Statistically accepted ways of assessing the strength of a particular finding across a number of different studies.

4.2.3 What Treatments are Effective?

4.2.3.1 Is Treatment More Effective Than No Treatment?

We have identified a couple of objective ways of assessing whether therapies are effective, but what do these studies using such methods tell us? Comparative studies tend to suggest that most of the accepted therapies are all more effective than no treatment or expectancy control conditions, but that the therapies themselves do not differ in their relative effectiveness. For example, in a study of depressed individuals, Gibbons, Hedeker, Elkin, Waternaux et al. (1993) found that cognitive therapy, interpersonal therapy and antidepressant medication were all as effective as each other, but all more effective than a placebo control condition (after 16 weeks of treatment). Similarly, the meta-analysis conducted by Smith, Glass and Miller (1980) indicated that psychotherapies were all more effective than no treatment, but none was significantly more effective than another. This has led clinicians to attempt to discover if there are any common features across treatments that contribute to their effectiveness. At least some studies have indicated that regardless of their theoretical orientation and the treatments they offer, successful therapists often have characteristics in common that may contribute to their effective treatment of clients. These include providing good feedback, helping clients to focus on and understand their own thoughts, attempting to promote autonomy and self-efficacy in their clients, and helping clients with their existing relationships (Korchin & Sands, 1983).

Rather than conducting objective and well-controlled outcome studies, others have approached the issue of the effectiveness of treatments by viewing clients as consumers and canvassing their views on how satisfied they have been with the treatment 'product' that they received. Seligman (1995) reported the results of a large-scale survey of individuals in the USA who had undergone psychotherapy and concluded that: (1) respondents claimed they benefited significantly from psychotherapy; (2) psychotherapy alone did not differ in effectiveness from medication plus psychotherapy; (3) psychologists, psychiatrists, social workers and counsellors did not differ in their effectiveness as therapists; and (4) the longer the duration of their treatment, the larger the positive gains respondents reported. While the empirical rigour of this consumer-based study falls far short of that expected in well-controlled outcome studies, it does provide some information about how the recipients of psychotherapy view their treatment and its effects. But as we noted in Focus Point 4.1, asking clients how satisfied they are following treatment may not be the best way to judge the treatment's effectiveness and may reflect the involvement of psychological factors that extend beyond the original purpose of the treatment.

SUMMARY

In this section we have described some of the methods that have been developed to try to evaluate the effectiveness of treatments for psychopathology. Over the past 10–20 years a large number of studies assessing the efficacy of therapies for psychological disorders have been carried out, and there is now good empirical evidence to support the effectiveness and internal validity of many of these therapies. There are too many to mention here, but interested readers are referred to Chambless and Ollendick (2001) for a review and analysis of many of these studies; to Butler, Chapman, Forman and Beck (2006) for a review of the effectiveness of CBT for a range of psychopathologies; and to Westen, Novotny and Thompson-Brenner (2004) for a review of the pros and cons of the RCT method for assessing the effectiveness of treatments. Readers are also referred to the treatment sections of individual psychopathology chapters in this book for a review of the most effective treatments for individual psychopathologies.

SELF-TEST QUESTIONS

- What kinds of factors can affect the evaluation of treatments and need to be controlled for in treatment outcome studies?
- What are the two most popular methodologies for assessing the effectiveness of treatments?
- Are structured treatments for psychopathology effective?

SECTION SUMMARY

4.2 Evaluating Treatment

- Factors affecting the evaluation of treatments include **spontaneous remission, placebo effects** and **attentional factors** provided by the therapist's relationship with the client.

- Popular methods for assessing the effectiveness of treatments are **randomized controlled trials (RCTs)** and **meta-analyses**.

- Most large-scale studies suggest that treatment in general is significantly more effective than no treatment.

4.3 TREATING PSYCHOPATHOLOGY REVIEWED

Treatments for psychopathology have developed significantly over the last 50–60 years. The main aims of treatments are to provide relief from the distress of symptoms, to equip clients with insight into their problems, and to provide them with a means of coping with life problems and psychological distress. Most treatments for psychopathology consist of either drug treatments or psychotherapy. Psychotherapy can be divided into five main theoretical approaches: psychodynamic approaches, behaviour therapy, cognitive therapy, humanistic therapies and family or systemic therapies. Because of the demands placed on over-stretched clinicians and service providers, a number of different cost-effective modes of delivery have been developed in recent years. These include group therapy, counselling, computerized CBT (CCBT), e-therapy and therapy by telephone. Evaluating the effectiveness of treatments for psychopathology is still a difficult and disputed process, with disagreements about what constitutes a therapeutic gain, how long it may take to achieve a successful outcome and how therapeutic gains should be measured (if they can be measured at all). The practical need for objective methods for assessing the relative success of treatments has given rise to the adoption of randomized controlled trials (RCTs) and meta-analyses as important methods for assessing treatments. Most large-scale studies indicate that psychotherapies generally are more effective than no treatment, but there is little convincing evidence that one psychotherapy method is necessarily more effective than another. Nevertheless, the last 20 years have seen a significant increase in the number of treatment outcome studies published, and many of these indicate that certain types of treatments may be more effective than others at treating individual specific psychopathologies. (See also the treatment sections in the chapters covering individual psychopathologies.)

 LEARNING OUTCOMES

When you have completed this chapter, you should be able to:

1 Describe some of the reasons for wanting to treat psychopathology.

2 Describe, compare and contrast the basic theoretical principles on which at least four different types of psychotherapy are based.

3 Describe and evaluate at least 3–4 different modes of delivery for treatments of psychopathology.

4 Critically assess methods for determining the effectiveness of treatments for psychopathology.

KEY TERMS

Antidepressant drugs *98*
Antipsychotic drugs *98*
Anxiolytic drugs *98*
Aversion therapy *92*
Beating the Blues *103*
Beck's cognitive therapy *96*
Befriending *107*
Behaviour analysis *92*
Behaviour modification *92*
Behaviour therapy *91*
Behavioural self-control *93*
Benzodiazepines *99*
Client-centred therapy *96*
Cognitive behaviour therapy (CBT) *96*
Cognitive therapy *95*
Computerized CBT (CCBT) *103*
Conditioning *92*
Continuing professional development (CPD) *90*
Counselling *102*
Counterconditioning *92*
Dream analysis *91*
Empathy *97*
Encounter groups *102*
E-therapy *103*
Experiential groups *102*
Exposure therapies *92*
Extinction *92*
Family therapy *98*
Faulty learning *92*
Fear Fighter *103*
Flooding *92*

Free association *91*
Functional analysis *93*
Group therapy *99*
Holistic therapies *96*
Humanistic therapies *96*
Internal validity *106*
Interpretation *91*
Marriage counsellor *103*
Mental health counsellor *103*
Meta-analyses *109*
Monoamine oxidase inhibitors (MAOIs) *98*
No treatment or a waiting-list control group *107*
Palliative effect *90*
Placebo effect *106*
Psychoanalysis *91*
Psychodynamic approaches *91*
Randomized controlled trials (RCTs) *107*
Rational emotive therapy (RET) *95*
Reciprocal inhibition *92*
Response shaping *93*
Selective serotonin reuptake inhibitors (SSRIs) *98*
Self-help groups *102*
Spontaneous remission *106*
Student counsellor *103*
Systematic desensitization *92*
Systems theory *98*
Telephone therapy *104*
Token economy *93*
Transference *91*
Tricyclic antidepressants *98*
Unconditional positive regard *97*

REVIEWS, THEORIES AND SEMINAL STUDIES

Links to Journal Articles

4.1 The Nature and Function of Treatments for Psychopathology

Erwin, E. (2000). Is a science of psychotherapy possible? *American Psychologist, 55*, 1133–1138.

Fava, G.A. (2003). Can long-term treatment with antidepressant drugs worsen the course of depression? *Journal of Clinical Psychiatry, 64*, 123–133.

Kaltenthaler, E., Parry, G. & Beverley, C. (2004). Computerized cognitive behaviour therapy: A systematic review. *Behavioural and Cognitive Psychotherapy, 32*, 31–55.

Leach, L.S. & Christensen, H. (2006). A systematic review of telephone-based interventions for mental disorders. *Journal of Telemedicine and Telecare, 12*, 122–129.

Marzillier, J. (2004). The myth of evidence-based psychotherapy. *Psychologist, 17*, 392–395.

Prochaska, J.O. & Norcross, J.C. (2001). Stages of change. *Psychotherapy, 38*, 443–448.

4.2 Evaluating Treatments

Butler, A.C., Chapman, J.E., Forman, E.M. & Beck, A.T. (2006). The empirical status of cognitive-behavioral therapy: A review of meta-analyses. *Clinical Psychology Review, 26*, 17–31.

Chambless, D.L. & Ollendick, T.H. (2001). Empirically supported psychological interventions: Controversies and evidence. *Annual Review of Psychology, 52*, 685–716.

Clark, D.M., Ehlers, A., Hackmann, A., McManus, F. et al. (2006). Cognitive therapy versus exposure and applied relaxation in social phobia: A randomized controlled trial. *Journal of Consulting and Clinical Psychology, 74,* 568–578.

Seligman, M.E.P. (1995). The effectiveness of psychotherapy: The Consumer Reports study. *American Psychologist, 50,* 965–974.

Shapiro, D.A., Barkham, M., Rees, A., Hardy, G.E., Reynolds, S. & Startup, M. (1994). Effects of treatment duration and severity of depression on the effectiveness of cognitive-behavioral and psychodynamic-interpersonal psychotherapy. *Journal of Consulting and Clinical Psychology, 62,* 522–534.

Smith, M.L. & Glass, G.V. (1977). Meta-analysis of psychotherapy outcome studies. *American Psychologist, 32,* 752–760.

Westen, D., Novotny, C.A. & Thompson-Brenner, H. (2004). The empirical status of empirically supported psychotherapies: Assumptions, findings, and reporting in controlled clinical trials. *Psychological Bulletin, 130,* 631–663.

Texts for Further Reading

Barker, C., Pistrang, N. & Elliott, R. (2002). *Research methods in clinical psychology* (2nd ed.). New York: Wiley.

Carr, A. (2006). *Family therapy: Concepts, process and practice* (2nd ed.). Chichester: Wiley.

Cone, J.D. (2001). *Evaluating outcomes: Empirical tools for effective practice.* Washington, DC: American Psychological Association.

Dallos, R. & Draper, R. (2005). *Introduction to family therapy: Systemic theory and practice* (2nd ed.). Maidenhead: Open University Press.

Dobson, K.S. (2002). *Handbook of cognitive-behavioural therapies.* New York: Guilford Press.

Fall, K.A., Holden, J.M. & Marquis, A. (2003). *Theoretical models of counselling and psychotherapy.* London: Routledge.

Hsiung, R.C. (Ed.) (2002). *E-therapy: Case studies, guiding principles, and the clinical potential of the internet.* New York: W.W. Norton.

Lemma-Wright, A. (1995). *Invitation to psychodynamic psychology.* Chichester: Wiley.

Miltenberger, R.G. (2003). *Behavior modification: Principles and procedures.* Belmont, CA: Wadsworth.

Nelson-Jones, R. (2006). *Theory and practice of counselling and therapy* (4th ed.). Thousand Oaks, CA: Sage.

O'Donohue, W., Fisher, J.E. & Hayes, S.C. (2003). *Cognitive behaviour therapy: Applying empirically supported techniques in your practice.* Chichester: Wiley.

Richard, D.C.S. & Lauterbach, D.L. (2007). *Handbook of exposure therapies.* New York: Academic Press.

Rogers, C.R. (2003). *Client-centred therapy: Its current practice, implications and theory.* New York: Constable & Robinson.

RESEARCH QUESTIONS

4.1 The Nature and Function of Treatments for Psychopathology

- Do behaviour therapies work because they contain conditioning principles?

- To what extent is the therapist–client relationship a critical factor in successful treatment?

- Do drug treatments for depression make clients vulnerable to relapse over the longer term?

- Is computerized CBT (CCBT) as effective as other forms of treatment for psychopathology?

- Is e-therapy as effective as other forms of treatment for psychopathology?

4.2 Evaluating Treatments

- How do researchers investigating the effectiveness of treatments decide on what a 'therapeutic gain' is, and how it is to be measured?

- When assessing the effectiveness of treatments, how do researchers take into account the fact that a therapist–client relationship alone may contribute to improvement?

- Advocates of some therapeutic approaches claim their therapeutic approaches cannot be assessed using objective or quantitative methods. How can the scientific researcher address this fact?

- Randomized controlled trials (RCTs) are adversely affected by participants dropping out of studies before completion. How can researchers address this problem?

- Are all psychotherapies equally effective?

- Are there any common features across different psychotherapies that contribute to the success of treatment?

- Is asking clients how satisfied they are with their treatment a good way of assessing the effectiveness of that treatment?

CLINICAL ISSUES

4.1 The Nature and Function of Treatments for Psychopathology

- How important to the success of treatment is helping the client to achieve insight into their problems?

- Practising clinicians have a professional duty to update their therapeutic skills. What is the best way to achieve this?

- How can therapists be sure that their treatment will have long-term benefits and will generalize to environments other than the therapy situation?

- How important to the success of treatment is the personal relationship between therapist and client?

- Is there any therapeutic advantage to be gained from the therapist acting solely as an understanding listener?

- Under what circumstances might successful treatment be facilitated by trying to understand the relationships and alliances that exist between the client's family members?

- Do GPs over-prescribe medications to their patients who present with psychopathology symptoms?

- In what ways might the long-term prescription of drugs for mental health problems be counterproductive to long-term recovery?

- Is the cost-effectiveness of a treatment a good reason for advocating its use?

- Are there circumstances in which trained counsellors are better suited to treat psychopathology than trained clinical psychologists?

- Under what circumstances might a therapist decide to use email or therapy by telephone as an alternative to face-to-face sessions?

4.2 Evaluating Treatments

- How should an individual therapist make decisions about whether his or her treatment of a client is effective or not?

- If therapists are unable to objectively assess that their treatment approach is effective, are they therefore no better than charlatans offering bogus therapies?

- How might a therapist's relationship with a client adversely affect the course of treatment?

- Are there moral and compassionate reasons for wanting to objectively assess whether a treatment is effective?

- How can therapists develop characteristics that contribute to successful therapy across all treatments regardless of their theoretical orientation?

II | Adult Mental Health

5 | Anxiety-Based Problems

ROUTE MAP OF THE CHAPTER

This chapter describes some of the main anxiety-based problems. It discusses contemporary accounts of their causes (aetiology) and describes a range of relevant and effective treatments for each. It is divided into six main sections covering specific phobias, social phobia, panic disorder, generalized anxiety disorder, obsessive-compulsive disorder and post-traumatic stress disorder. These topics are chosen because they represent some of the most prevalent anxiety-based problems (e.g. panic disorder, generalized anxiety disorder) as well as some of the most thoroughly researched, and our understanding of their causes has become relatively well developed.

I am a baritone soloist and have performed serious music, in public, for some thirty years. The first time was for my entire high school class at graduation where I did the Coronation scene from Boris Godounov.

For the first fifteen years, it was not always a pleasant experience. I got nauseous and shook like a leaf before, during and after nearly every performance. At one point, during a Messiah performance in the middle of 'But Who May Abide', I asked myself why I was doing this. Even though scared half to death, my heart in my throat, blood pounding in my ears, I continued, almost compulsively. . . . It was always worst when I tried to achieve perfection. This was usually in front of other students at weekly recitals in graduate school, when I knew they were taking exquisite note of every mistake.

TOBIAS'S STORY

Introduction

This example of performance anxiety displays a number of features that are characteristic of the experience of anxiety, whether the everyday experiences of anxiety that we all encounter or the more debilitating and chronic experience of anxiety that is suffered by those diagnosed with clinical problems. Firstly, there are the physical symptoms of anxiety, such as muscle tension, dry mouth, perspiring, trembling and difficulty swallowing. In its more chronic form, anxiety may also be accompanied by dizziness, chronic fatigue, sleeping difficulties, rapid or irregular heartbeat, diarrhoea or a persistent need to urinate, sexual problems and nightmares. Secondly, *Tobias's Story* gives a good insight into the cognitive characteristics of anxiety. These include a feeling of apprehension or fear, usually resulting from the anticipation of a threatening event or situation. Usually accompanying anxiety are intrusive thoughts about the threat, catastrophic bouts of worrying about the possible negative outcomes associated with the threat and, in some specific types of problems, uncontrollable flashbacks about past traumas and anxiety-provoking experiences. Overly anxious people also find it hard to stop thinking negative and threatening thoughts, and this is in part due to the cognitive biases that have developed with the experience of anxiety. Interestingly, *Tobias's Story* also highlights the role that some personality (or dispositional factors) play in the development of anxiety and may act as vulnerability factors – in this case, the desire to achieve perfection.

We all experience feelings of anxiety quite naturally in many situations – such as just before an important exam, while making a presentation at college or work, at an interview or on a first date. Most anxiety reactions are perfectly natural, and they have evolved as adaptive responses that are essential for us to perform effectively in challenging circumstances. However, anxiety can often become so intense or attached to inappropriate events or situations that it becomes maladaptive and problematic for the individual (Lepine, 2002). This is when an anxiety disorder may develop. An *anxiety disorder* is an excessive or aroused state characterized by feelings of apprehension, uncertainty and fear. In a sufferer of an anxiety disorder the anxiety response:

Anxiety disorder An excessive or aroused state characterized by feelings of apprehension, uncertainty and fear.

1 may be out of proportion to the threat posed by the situation or event (e.g. in specific phobias);

2 may be a state that individuals constantly find themselves in and may not be easily attributable to any specific threat (e.g. in generalized anxiety disorder or some forms of panic disorder);

3 may persist chronically and be so disabling that it causes constant emotional distress to the individual, who is unable to plan and conduct normal day-to-day living. This can result in an inability to hold down a regular job or maintain long-term relationships with friends, partners and family.

Anxiety-based problems are relatively common, and around 30–40 per cent of individuals in Western societies will develop a problem that is anxiety related at some point in their lives (Shepherd, Cooper, Brown & Kalton, 1996). As a result, pathological anxiety imposes a high individual and social burden, tends to be more chronic than many other psychological problems, and can be as disabling as physical illness. In both Europe and the USA, the cost of treating anxiety-based problems runs into many billions of pounds annually, making them more economically expensive than any other psychological problem (Rovner, 1993). These economic costs include psychiatric, psychological and emergency care, hospitalization, prescription drugs, reduced productivity, absenteeism from work and suicide (Lepine, 2002).

In this chapter we will discuss in detail six of the main anxiety disorders. The details of these disorders are summarized at the outset in Table 5.1, and readers may want to refer back to this table when they have read and digested the information on each separate disorder. The six disorders are:

● specific phobias

● social phobia

● panic disorder

● generalized anxiety disorder (GAD)

● obsessive-compulsive disorder (OCD)

● post-traumatic stress disorder (PTSD)

Anxiety disorders are diagnosed when subjectively experienced anxiety is present and recurs on such a regular and chronic basis that it disrupts normal daily living. Many of the symptoms of anxiety are common to a number of different anxiety disorders, and this can lead to comorbidity (see Chapter 1, section 1.3.2.3). Comorbidity is not unusual in the diagnosis of anxiety disorders (Rodriguez, Weisberg, Pagano, Machan et al., 2004), and may occur because a number of basic psychological processes or similar developmental experiences may be common to different diagnostic categories. Some common aspects are:

Comorbidity The co-occurrence of two or more distinct disorders.

1 Physiological symptoms of panic are found not only in panic disorder, but also in the reactions to phobic stimuli in specific phobias.

Table 5.1 *Anxiety disorders: summary*

DISORDER AND LIFETIME PREVALENCE RATES	DEFINITION	MAIN DSM-IV-TR DIAGNOSTIC FEATURES	KEY FEATURES	THEORIES OF AETIOLOGY	MAIN FORMS OF TREATMENT
SPECIFIC PHOBIA (7.2%–11.3%)	Excessive, unreasonable, persistent fear triggered by a specific object or situation	Marked and specific fear trigger by a specific object or situation Exposure evokes immediate anxiety Individual recognizes the fear is excessive The phobic situation is always avoided The fear interferes significantly with daily functioning	Clinical phobias are usually restricted to a small group of objects and situations (e.g. animals, heights, water, blood and injury) Twice as many females as males develop specific phobias Phobics acquire a set of threat-relevant beliefs that maintain their phobia	Psychoanalytic accounts Classical conditioning Biological preparedness Non-associative fear acquisition Disease-avoidance model	Exposure therapy Systematic desensitization Flooding One-session rapid treatments

Table 5.1 *(Cont'd)*

DISORDER AND LIFETIME PREVALENCE RATES	DEFINITION	MAIN DSM-IV-TR DIAGNOSTIC FEATURES	KEY FEATURES	THEORIES OF AETIOLOGY	MAIN FORMS OF TREATMENT
SOCIAL PHOBIA *(7%–13%)*	A severe and persistent fear of social or performance situations	Persistent fear of social or performance situations Exposure to social situations provokes anxiety Individual recognizes that fear is excessive Avoidance and anxiety significantly interferes with daily functioning	Anxiety of socially based situations is so pervasive it has been labelled 'social anxiety disorder' Social phobia is sometimes associated with panic attacks Social phobics appear to have developed an information processing and interpretation bias which causes them to make excessively negative predictions about future social events	Genetic factors Role of behavioural inhibition in childhood Information processing biases (e.g. negative processing of ambiguous information) Self-focused attention	CBT Medication (e.g. MAOIs and SSRIs)
PANIC DISORDER *(1.5%–3.5%)*	The experience of repeated and uncontrollable panic attacks	Recurrent, persistent panic attacks At least 1 month of persistent concern or worry about these attacks Panic attacks cannot be accounted for by the physical effects of a substance or a general medical condition	Onset is common in adolescence or early adulthood, and normally following a period of stress Frequency of panic attacks can vary between one attack per week to frequent daily attacks Associated with fear of serious underlying medical condition or that the individual is losing control or 'going crazy'	Hyperventilation model Suffocation alarm theories Noradrenergic overactivity Classical conditioning Anxiety sensitivity Catastrophic misinterpretation of bodily sensations	Tricyclic antidepressants and benzodiazepines Exposure-based treatments CBT
GENERALIZED ANXIETY DISORDER (GAD) *(5%)*	The experience of continual apprehension and anxiety about future events, leading to chronic and pathological worry	Excessive anxiety and worry occurring more days than not for 6 months Worry is uncontrollable Associated with 3 or more physical symptoms The anxiety or worry causes significant distress or impairment of daily functioning	Pathological worry is the cardinal diagnostic feature of GAD GAD is twice as common in women as in men 12% of those who attend anxiety clinics will present with GAD Highly comorbid with a range of other anxiety disorders and major depression	Genetic factors Information processing biases Dysfunctional beliefs about worrying The role of dispositional factors	Anxiolytics such as benzodiazepines Stimulus control treatment CBT (including self-monitoring, relaxation training and cognitive restructuring)

Table 5.1 *(Cont'd)*

DISORDER AND LIFETIME PREVALENCE RATES	DEFINITION	MAIN DSM-IV-TR DIAGNOSTIC FEATURES	KEY FEATURES	THEORIES OF AETIOLOGY	MAIN FORMS OF TREATMENT
OBSESSIVE-COMPULSIVE DISORDER (OCD) (2.5%)	Recurrent obsessions or compulsions that are severe enough to be time-consuming or cause distress	Recurrent thoughts, impulses, images experienced as intrusive and inappropriate Repetitive behaviours or mental acts that the person feels driven to perform The person recognizes that these obsessions or compulsions are excessive or unreasonable The obsessions or compulsions cause marked distress	OCD onset is gradual and begins to manifest in early adolescence or adulthood – normally following a stressful life event Affects women more frequently than men The main compulsions are checking and washing behaviours – although these rarely occur together in the same individual Sometimes comorbid with other disorders such as major depression and eating disorders	Role of brain deficits in the frontal lobes and basal ganglia Memory deficits Inflated responsibility Thought–action fusion Perseveration and the role of negative mood	Exposure and ritual prevention treatments (EPR) CBT Drug treatment (SSRIs) Cingulatomy
POST-TRAUMATIC STRESS DISORDER (PTSD) (3%–8%)	A set of persistent, anxiety-related symptoms that occur after experiencing or witnessing an extremely traumatic event	Experience of events involving death or threatened death Response involves intense fear, helplessness or horror The traumatic event is persistently re-experienced The individual persistently avoids stimuli associated with the trauma Physical symptoms indicating increased arousal Duration of the disturbance is more than 1 month The disturbance causes significant distress or impairment	Following a severe traumatic event, women are significantly more likely to develop PTSD than men Experiences that are likely to cause PTSD include physical assault and rape, torture, POW and combat experiences, natural disasters such as floods and earthquakes, and motor vehicle accidents Main symptoms include increased arousal, avoidance and numbing of emotions, and re-experiencing of the traumatic event	Theory of shattered assumptions Classical conditioning Emotional processing theory Mental defeat Dual representation theory	Psychological debriefing Exposure therapy Eye-movement desensitization and reprocessing (EMDR) Cognitive restructuring

2 Cognitive biases – such as information processing biases that tend anxious people to selectively attend to threatening stimuli (Mathews & McLeod, 1994) – are common to almost all anxiety disorders.

3 A number of prominent psychopathologies are characterized by the dysfunctional and uncontrollable perseveration of certain thoughts, behaviours or activities (e.g. pathological worrying in generalized anxiety disorder, perseverative compulsions in obsessive-compulsive disorder and rumination during periods of depression), and the psychological mechanism that underlies dysfunctional perseveration may be similar across all these disorders (Davey, 2006b).

4   Certain specific early experiences can be found in the aetiology of a number of different anxiety disorders (e.g. physical or sexual abuse during childhood), and experiences such as these may increase an individual's risk of developing several anxiety-based problems.

Let's look at each of the anxiety diagnostic categories in turn, starting with a closer look at specific phobias.

5.1 SPECIFIC PHOBIAS

Specific phobia   An excessive, unreasonable, persistent fear triggered by a specific object or situation.

Specific phobias (SP) are defined as an excessive, unreasonable, persistent fear triggered by a specific object or situation. The DSM-IV-TR criteria for Specific Phobia are presented in Table 5.2. The phobic trigger usually elicits extreme fear and often panic, which usually means that the phobic individual develops avoidance strategies designed to minimize the possibility of contact with that phobic trigger. Phobics are normally aware that their fear of the phobic situation or event is excessive or unreasonable (in comparison either with the actual threat it represents or with the less fearful responses of other people), but they do acquire a strong set of *phobic beliefs* that appear to control their fear (Thorpe & Salkovskis, 1997). These beliefs normally contain information about why they think the phobia is threatening and how to react when they are in the phobic situation (e.g. avoid contact). Many contemporary psychological treatments for specific phobias are designed to challenge these dysfunctional phobic beliefs and replace them with more functional beliefs that foster approach and contact with the phobic stimulus.

Phobic beliefs   Beliefs about phobic stimuli that maintain the phobic's fear and avoidance of that stimulus or situation.

Table 5.2 *DSM-IV-TR criteria for specific phobia*

A   Marked and persistent fear that is excessive or unreasonable, cued by the presence or anticipation of a specific object or situation (e.g. flying, heights, animals).

B   Exposure to the phobic stimulus almost inevitably provokes an immediate anxiety response, which may take the form of a situationally bound or situationally predisposed panic attack.

C   The person recognizes that the fear is excessive or unreasonable.

D   The phobic situation(s) is avoided or else is endured with intense anxiety or distress.

E   The avoidance, anxious anticipation or distress in the feared situation(s) interferes significantly with the person's normal routine, occupational (or academic) functioning, or social activities or relationships, or there is marked distress about having the phobia.

F   In individuals under 18 years, the duration is at least 6 months.

G   The anxiety, panic attacks or phobic avoidance associated with the specific object or situation are not better accounted for by another mental disorder, such as OCD (e.g. fear of dirt in someone with obsessions about contamination), PTSD (e.g. avoidance of stimuli associated with a severe stressor), separation anxiety disorder (e.g. avoidance of school), social phobia (e.g. avoidance of social situations because of fear of embarrassment), panic disorder with agoraphobia, or agoraphobia without history of panic disorder.

5.1.1 Prevalence

Specific phobias are extraordinarily common, with surveys suggesting that a clear majority of the general population (60.2 per cent) experience 'unreasonable fears' (Chapman, 1997) – although in most cases these fears are rarely severe enough to result in impairment or distress. Around 10 per cent of people will meet DSM-IV-TR criteria for a specific phobia within their lifetime, which suggests that severe and disruptive phobic symptoms can be quite common. Table 5.4 shows the prevalence rates for some of the more common forms of specific phobia. There is also a clear gender difference in the prevalence of specific phobias, with a lifetime prevalence rate of around 7 per cent for men and 16 per cent for women (Kessler, McGonagle, Zhao, Nelson et al., 1994).

5.1.2 Common Phobias

Interestingly, common phobias tend to focus on a relatively small group of objects and situations, the main ones being animal phobias (including fear of snakes, spiders, rats, mice, creepy-crawlies such as cockroaches, invertebrates such as maggots and slugs), social phobia, dental phobia, water phobia, height phobia, claustrophobia and a cluster of blood, injury and inoculation fears (known as BII). Most other types of phobias are less common and can be thought of as quite unusual given the degree of threat they might realistically pose – such phobias include fear of cotton wool, buttons, chocolate, dolls and vegetables (McNally, 1997)! DSM-IV-TR subdivides specific phobias according to the source of the fear into four groups: (1) blood, injuries and injections (BII); (2) situational fears (e.g. aeroplanes, lifts, enclosed spaces); (3) animals; and (4) the natural

Table 5.3 *The phobic beliefs of spider phobics*

Phobics develop a set of dysfunctional beliefs about their phobic stimulus or event. These beliefs are very rarely challenged because the phobic avoids all circumstances where such beliefs might be disconfirmed. These beliefs maintain phobic fear and serve to motivate responses designed to avoid contact with the phobic stimulus. Below are some examples of phobic beliefs held by spider phobics. Such beliefs are the kinds that are challenged in both exposure therapy and cognitive therapy procedures.

Harm Beliefs

When a spider is in my vicinity I believe that the spider will:

(a) bite me

(b) crawl towards my private parts

(c) do things on purpose to tease me

(d) get on to parts of me that I cannot reach

Chaser and Prey Beliefs

When I encounter a spider it will:

(a) run towards me

(b) stare at me

(c) settle on my face

(d) not be shaken off once it is on me

Unpredictability and Speed Beliefs

When I encounter a spider:

(a) its behaviour will be very unpredictable

(b) it will be very quick

(c) it will run in an elusive way

Invasiveness Beliefs

When I encounter a spider it will:

(a) crawl into my clothes

(b) walk over me during the night

(c) will hide in places I do not want, such as my bed

Response Beliefs

When I encounter a spider I will:

(a) feel faint

(b) lose control of myself

(c) go hysterical

(d) scream

Source: adapted from Arntz, Lavy, van den Berg & van Rijsoort, 1993; Thorpe & Salkovskis, 1995.

Table 5.4 *Lifetime prevalence rates for common specific phobias*

SPECIFIC PHOBIA	LIFETIME PREVALENCE RATES
Social phobia	3.2%[a]
Blood-injury-injection phobia	3.5%[c]
Animal phobias generally	1.1%[a]
Dental phobia	3–5%[b]
Water phobia	3.3%[a]
Height phobia	4.7%[a]
Claustrophobia/enclosed spaces	2.4%[a]

[a] Taken from the Epidemiologic Catchment Area (ECA) study (see Chapman, 1997).
[b] Kent (1997).
[c] Bienvenu & Eaton (1998).

environment (e.g. heights, water). There is some evidence that if you suffer from a specific phobia in one of these categories, you are more likely to suffer a phobia of one or more of the others in that category (e.g. Davey, 1992b; Fredrikson, Annas, Fischer & Wik, 1996), and thus phobias within each category can have a higher incidence of comorbidity (Kendler, Myers, Prescott & Neale, 2001).

There are also important cultural differences in the kinds of stimuli and events that can become the focus of clinical phobias. For example, Taijin-kyofu-sho (TKS) is a common Japanese syndrome characterized by a fear of embarrassing or offending other people (Prince & Tchenglaroche, 1987). This is rather different from the Western syndrome of social phobia, where the fear is based on the public embarrassment experienced by the phobic individual himself or herself. Davey, McDonald, Hirisave, Prabhu et al. (1998) also found a number of important cross-cultural differences in animal fears. For example, while fear of spiders is a common phobic reaction in most Western cultures, spiders were significantly less feared in the Indian sample used in the study. This kind of cross-cultural variability suggests that 'fear-relevance' may at least in part be determined and developed by factors that are specific to individual cultures, and this should be contrasted with more biologically oriented views which argue that fear-responses have been universally pre-wired by evolutionary selection pressures (Davey, 1995; see section 5.1.3.3 below on evolutionary accounts of phobias).

5.1.3 The Aetiology of Specific Phobias

Attempts to explain specific phobias have a long history, dating back to the early days of the psychoanalytic approaches pioneered by Freud and the conditioning views developed by the behaviourist

Plate 5.1
A majority of people claim to have a phobia of some kind, although most are not severe enough to cause distress or to disrupt normal daily life. Some phobias are unusual, such as phobia of cotton wool or buttons – but they are much more common than you think.

J.B. Watson. Originally, there was a tendency to try to explain all types of phobias with just one explanatory theory (e.g. classical conditioning), but this approach has now given way to the view that different types of phobias might be acquired in quite different ways (a multifaceted approach). Over the years, an intriguing debate has taken place about whether phobias are biologically determined through evolutionary processes or whether they are responses learned during the lifetime of the individual. This debate will be an important feature of what follows.

5.1.3.1 Psychoanalytic Accounts

Phobias have intrigued psychologists for more than a century. This may be because they manifest as irrational fears of things that usually pose little if any realistic threat, and their acquisition more often than not cannot be explained by recourse to simple learning experiences such as a specific traumatic event. This has led at least some approaches to psychopathology to view phobias as symbolic of other, more deep-rooted psychological difficulties. For example, psychoanalytic theory as developed by Freud saw phobias as a defence against the anxiety produced by repressed id impulses, and

this fear became associated with external events or situations that had a symbolic relevance to that repressed id impulse. Focus Point 5.1 describes the classic case of Little Hans, a 5-year-old boy who developed a severe phobia of horses. Within Freud's psychoanalytic theory, the function of phobias was to avoid confrontation with the real, underlying issues (in this case, a repressed childhood conflict). However, because of the nature of psychoanalytical theorizing, there is little in the way of objective evidence to support such accounts of phobias. Nevertheless, there is often an element of insight that can be drawn from the symbolic interpretations of case histories provided by psychoanalysis, and many anxiety disorders may indeed function for the sufferer as a way of avoiding confrontation with more challenging life issues and difficulties.

5.1.3.2 Classical Conditioning and Phobias

Attempts to explain phobias in terms of classical conditioning (see Chapter 1, section 1.1.3.2) date back to the famous 'Little Albert' study reported by Watson and Rayner in 1920. Albert was an 11-month-old infant, and Watson and Rayner attempted to condition in him a fear of his pet white rat. They did this by pairing the rat – the *conditioned stimulus* (CS) – with the frightening event of a loud noise produced by striking an iron bar – the *unconditioned stimulus* (UCS), which distressed Albert (the *unconditioned response*, UCR). After several pairings of the rat with the noise, Albert began to cry (the *conditioned response*, CR) whenever the rat was introduced into the room. This type of explanation has been popular over the past 50 years, and more sophisticated contemporary conditioning models of specific phobias have been developed (Davey, 1992a, 1997). However, it is difficult to generally explain the range of features possessed by specific phobias with conditioning theories. These criticisms include:

1 Traumatic experiences are essential for conditioning accounts, yet many phobics appear unable to recall any trauma or aversive conditioning experience at the time of the onset of their phobia (Rachman, 1977; Marks, 1969; Emmelkamp, 1982). This appears to be particularly true of some animal phobics such as snake and spider phobics (Davey, 1992b; Murray & Foote, 1979), and also height and water phobics (Menzies & Clarke, 1993a,b).

2 Not all people who have pain or trauma paired with a situation develop a phobia. For example, not everyone who has a traumatic experience undergoing dental treatment acquires a dental phobia (Lautch, 1971), not everyone who experiences a violent thunderstorm acquires a thunderstorm phobia (Liddell & Lyons, 1978) and not all fliers who experience a traumatic flying accident express a subsequent anxiety of flying (Aitken, Lister & Main, 1981; Goorney, 1970). This suggests that a potential conditioning experience is itself insufficient to cause a phobia.

3 Simple conditioning models treat all stimuli as equally likely to enter into association with aversive consequences, yet fears and phobias are not evenly distributed across stimuli and experiences. People appear to develop phobias of animals (snakes, spiders), heights, water, death, thunder and fire more readily than fears of, for example, hammers, electric outlets, knives or guns, even though the latter

FOCUS POINT **5.1**

Little Hans: The psychoanalytic interpretation of a specific phobia

One of the most famous cases in the history of psychoanalysis is that of 'Little Hans', a 5-year-old boy who revealed many of his perceptions, fantasies and fears to his physician father, who, in turn, reported them to Sigmund Freud. Hans began to have a fear of horses, which eventually grew to the point that he refused to leave the house. The immediate event that precipitated this phobia was seeing a big, heavy horse fall down. Freud interpreted this to mean that Hans at that moment perceived his own wish that his father would fall down. Then Hans, a little Oedipus, could take his father's place with his beautiful mother. Another part of the fear derived from the large size of horses, which Hans unconsciously identified with the great power of his father. He expressed the fear that a horse would come into his room. He also became afraid not only of horses biting him, but also of carts, furniture vans and buses. This revealed, to the psychoanalyst, still another aspect of Hans's unconscious fantasies, namely that the falling-down horse stood not only for his father, but also for his mother in childbirth, the box-like carts and vehicles representing the womb. All these complicated, repressed feelings and perception were thus incorporated in a single phobia.

It is important to note that Little Hans was basically a straightforward, cheerful child who experienced normal psychosexual development marred only by the episode of the phobia, from which he recovered rather promptly. Fourteen years later, 19-year-old Hans came to see Freud. He had continued to develop well and had survived, without unusual difficulty, the divorce and remarriage of both parents. The problems of his childhood were used by Freud to illustrate the normal process of psychosexual development – the complex, intense, erotic drama of early childhood.

Source: www.webschooling.com/edupsy.html

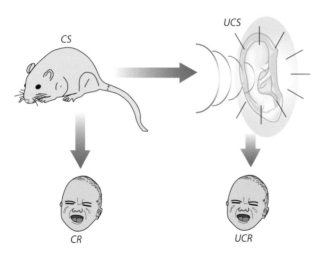

Figure 5.1
The 'Little Albert' classical conditioning study by Watson and Rayner (1920) demonstrated the acquisition of a phobia by pairing Little Albert's pet rat (the conditioned stimulus, CS) with a loud noise (unconditioned stimulus, UCS).

group of stimuli seem to have a high likelihood of being associated with pain or trauma (Seligman, 1971).

4 A simple conditioning model does not appear to account for the common clinical phenomenon of *incubation*.

Incubation is where fear increases in magnitude over successive encounters with the phobic stimulus, even though it is not followed by a traumatic consequence

> **Incubation**   A common clinical phenomenon where fear increases in magnitude over successive encounters with the phobic stimulus – even though it is not followed by a traumatic consequence.

(Eysenck, 1979). Incubation is a phenomenon that is frequently observed clinically, but according to conditioning theory it should lead to extinction rather than enhancement of the fear response.

Due to these features it is problematic for a classical conditioning account to explain the acquisition of *all* phobias as resulting from traumatic conditioning episodes, but there is strong evidence that traumatic conditioning experiences are responsible for the acquisition of at least *some* phobias. These include dental phobia (Davey, 1988), choking phobia (Greenberg, Stern & Weilberg, 1988), accident phobia (Kuch, 1997), and most dog phobias (DiNardo, Guzy & Bak, 1988; Doogan & Thomas, 1992).

5.1.3.3 Evolutionary Accounts of Phobias

The fact that phobias tend to be focused on a limited set of fears that have evolutionary significance has led some researchers to suggest that we may be biologically prepared or pre-wired to acquire certain phobias. For instance, clinical phobias tend to cluster around things such as heights, water, spiders, snakes, blood and injury, all of which can be considered to have a real life-threatening significance that has been present for many thousands of years. In contrast, we rarely develop clinical phobias of life-threatening stimuli that have only appeared more recently in our phylogenetic past – such as guns and electricity. There are two predominant evolutionary theories of phobias.

First, Seligman (1971) argued that evolutionary selection pressures have evolved in us a biological predisposition to learn to associate fear with stimuli that have been hazardous for our pretechnological ancestors. That is, we tend to have a built-in predisposition to learn to fear things such as snakes, spiders, heights and water because these have been life-threatening to our ancestors, and those of our ancestors that evolved a biological predisposition to fear these kinds of stimuli will have been more likely to survive and pass that fear predisposition on to future generations. This account is

Biological preparedness   A theory which argues that we have a built-in predisposition to learn to fear things such as snakes, spiders, heights and water because these have been life-threatening to our ancestors.

known as *biological preparedness*, and has been supported by two lines of evidence.

Firstly, if participants in a classical conditioning experiment are shown pictures of 'fear-relevant' stimuli such as snakes and spiders (conditioned stimuli, CSs) paired with electric shock (unconditioned stimuli, UCSs), they develop fear of the CSs more quickly and show a greater resistance to extinction than if pictures of fear-irrelevant stimuli are used as CSs (e.g. pictures of houses) (Ohman, Erixon & Lofberg, 1975).

Also Cook and Mineka (1990) found that laboratory-reared rhesus monkeys that had never before seen a snake rapidly acquired fear reactions to snakes after being shown a demonstration of another monkey being frightened in the presence of a snake. They did not acquire fear reactions after watching a demonstration of another monkey being frightened in the presence of a stimulus such as a rabbit or a flower. Both studies suggest that humans and primates such as rhesus monkeys have an unlearned predisposition to rapidly acquire fear responses to some types of stimuli and not others (see Ohman & Mineka, 2001).

Secondly, Poulton and Menzies (2002) have argued for the existence of a limited number of innate, evolutionary-relevant

Non-associative fear acquisition
A model which argues that fear of a set of biologically relevant stimuli develops naturally after very early encounters given normal maturational processes and normal background experiences, and no specific traumatic experiences with these stimuli are necessary to evoke this fear.

fears. This *non-associative fear acquisition* model argues that fear of a set of biologically relevant stimuli develops naturally after very early encounters given normal maturational processes and normal background experiences, and no

specific traumatic experiences with these stimuli are necessary to evoke this fear. Following repeated exposure to these stimuli, the innate fear reaction will habituate and should eventually disappear. Poulton and Menzies (2002) claim that this account explains why most children go through a discrete developmental period when they appear to be frightened of potential life-threatening stimuli such as heights and water (Graham & Gaffan, 1997), and why there is little evidence in retrospective studies for phobias such as height and water phobia being caused by specific traumatic experiences (Menzies & Clarke, 1993a,b, 1995a,b). This account then goes on to explain adult phobias as instances where these developmental phobias have failed to habituate properly.

While evolutionary accounts are appealing and appear to have at least some face validity, we must be cautious about accepting them on the basis of existing evidence (Delprato, 1980). First, such accounts depend on the fact that current phobic stimuli have actually acted as important selection pressures over our evolutionary past. But this is very difficult to verify empirically. For example, do we tend to have phobic reactions to spiders because they once constituted an important life-threatening pressure on our pre-technological ancestors? There is no convincing evidence to suggest this. Secondly, evolutionary accounts can be constructed in a *post hoc* manner and are at risk of being either 'adaptive stories' (McNally, 1995) or

'imaginative reconstructions' (Lewontin, 1979) (cf. Merckelbach & de Jong, 1997). This view argues that it is possible to construct, *post hoc*, an adaptive scenario for the fear and avoidance of almost any stimulus or event (McNally, 1995) – see Activity Box 5.1. This

ACTIVITY BOX 5.1

Assessing evolutionary explanations of specific phobias

Some explanations of specific phobias argue that the rather limited set of fears that become the focus for clinical phobias (e.g. spiders, snakes, heights, water, blood and injury, confined spaces) are the result of evolutionary selection pressures. They argue that those of our ancestors that feared and avoided these stimuli survived and so passed their fear and avoidance tendencies on to their offspring. Evolutionary-based accounts such as these assume that those things that are the focus of phobias today did pose a real threat to the survival of our ancestors.

Have a look at what is displayed in the following pictures before taking a few minutes to write down as many reasons

as you can think of why each one might be a threat to the survival of a human being. Then read on.

You were probably able to think of a number of reasons why each of these might be a threat to the survival of a human being. Of these six stimuli, 1 and 2 are typical phobic stimuli, 3 and 4 are potentially life-threatening but are rarely the focus for phobias, and we would not normally consider 5 and 6 to be any threat to survival at all. Yet it is still not difficult to think of reasons why 5 and 6 *might* be dangerous if we are pressed to do so. This is know as the **adaptive fallacy** (McNally, 1995) – that is, you can usually think up reasons why any stimulus or event might be dangerous. Given that you were able to do this with all six of these stimuli:

1 Why is it that only two of them are the focus for phobias?

2 Why are two of them clearly dangerous, yet not the focus for phobias?

These are questions that evolutionary accounts of phobias need to address.

Adaptive fallacy   The view that it is possible to think up a threatening or dangerous consequence for encountering any stimulus or situation.

does not mean that evolutionary accounts are wrong (see Ohman & Mineka, 2001, for a contemporary evolutionary account of phobias), merely that they are tantalizingly easy to propose but very difficult to substantiate.

5.1.3.4 Multiple Pathways to Phobias

There is no reason why the acquisition of all phobias should be explained by just a single process – and evidence is now accumulating to suggest that different types of phobias are acquired in quite different ways (Merckelbach, de Jong, Muris & van den Hout, 1996). We have already suggested that some phobias, such as dog phobia, dental phobia, choking phobia and accident phobia, are caused by traumatic conditioning experiences. In contrast, many other common phobias do not appear to be characterized by a traumatic experience at their outset – in fact, sufferers often cannot recall the exact onset of their phobia, which suggests that the onset may be gradual and precipitated by factors that are not immediately obvious to the individual. Phobias that fit this description include most animal phobias (including snake and spider phobia) (Murray & Foote, 1979; Merckelbach, Muris & Schouten, 1996), and height and water phobia (Menzies & Clarke, 1993a,b).

Recent evidence suggests that at least some phobias are closely associated with the emotion of *disgust*. High levels of disgust sensitivity have been found to be associated with small animal pho-

Disgust   A food-rejection emotion whose purpose is to prevent the transmission of illness and disease through the oral incorporation of contaminated items.

bias in general (Ware, Jain, Burgess & Davey, 1994; Davey, 1994b), spider phobia specifically (Mulkens, de Jong & Merckelbach, 1996),

and has been hypothesized to play a role in mediating blood-injury-injection phobia (Page, 1994; but see de Jong & Merckelbach, 1998; Kleinknecht, Kleinknecht & Thorndike, 1997). Disgust is a food-rejection emotion whose purpose is to prevent the transmission of illness and disease through the oral incorporation of contaminated items (Davey, 1994c; Rozin & Fallon, 1987), and elevated disgust sensitivity implies increased avoidance of disgust-relevant objects (such as faeces or mucus). In the case of animal phobias, Davey (1992a) has argued that many animals that become the focus for phobic responding do so because they have disgust relevance. Specifically, they may have acquired a disgust relevance (1) by directly spreading disease and being a source of contamination (e.g. rats, cockroaches), (2) by possessing features which mimic primary disgust-relevant stimuli (by resembling, for example, faeces or mucus; e.g. slugs or animals that are perceived as slimy such as snakes, snails or lizards), or (3) by having contemporary or historical significance as stimuli that signalled disease, illness or contamination (e.g. maggots, spiders; cf. Davey, 1994a). This *disease-avoidance model* of animal phobias (Matchett & Davey, 1991) is supported by the findings that a high level of disgust sensitivity is a

Disease-avoidance model   The view that animal phobias are caused by attempts to avoid disease or illness that might be transmitted by these animals.

vulnerability factor for animal phobias (such as spider phobia), and can mitigate against successful therapy if it is not directly addressed in treatment (de Jong, Andrea & Muris, 1997; Mulkens, de Jong & Merckelbach, 1996).

Alternatively, there is evidence that factors closely associated with *panic* and panic disorder (see section 5.3) are also linked to a number of specific phobias. First, there is a fairly high co-morbidity rate between panic disorder and some specific

Panic   A sudden uncontrollable fear or anxiety.

phobias. Studies have identified comorbidity rates of between 40 and 65 per cent (de Ruiter, Rijken, Garssen, van Schaik & Kraaimaat, 1989; Starcevic, Uhlenhuth, Kellner, & Pathak, 1992), suggesting that panic is common in people suffering from many different types of specific phobia. Second, some categories of specific phobia – especially situational phobias – share important characteristics with panic disorder. For example, situational phobias appear to have a preponderance of spontaneous onsets typical of panic disorder (Himle, Crystal, Curtis & Fluent, 1991), have a significantly higher rate of comorbidity with panic disorder than do other types of phobias, such as animal phobias (Starcevic & Bogojevic, 1997), and frequently have uncontrollable panic attacks as one of the symptoms of phobic responding (e.g. height phobia: Antony, Brown & Barlow, 1997; flying phobia: McNally & Louro, 1992; claustrophobia: McIsaac, 1995). Similarly, both claustrophobia and height phobia have aetiological factors in common with panic disorder. For instance, subjective fear in claustrophobia is focused not just on external dangers but on anxiety expectancies and bodily sensations (Craske, Mohlman, Yi, Glover & Valeri, 1995), and spontaneous panic attacks are found significantly more often in claustrophobics than in other types of phobias (Rachman & Levitt, 1985; Craske & Sipsas, 1992). Height phobia is associated not only with heightened discrimination of bodily sensations, but also with a bias towards interpreting ambiguous bodily sensations

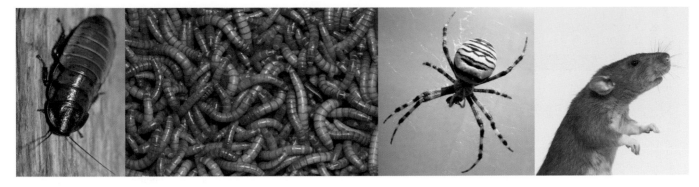

Plate 5.2
Small animal phobias are very common and include creepy-crawlies, insects, molluscs, rodents, spiders, snakes and lizards. Interestingly, if you are fearful of one of these types of animals, you are more likely to be fearful of others in this group. Fear of such animals may be related more to the emotion of disgust rather than to anxiety.

as threatening – a characteristic which is central to the aetiology of panic disorder (Davey, Menzies & Gallardo, 1997) (see section 5.3.2.2).

These examples suggest that specific phobias may have a number of different causes – depending on the nature of the phobic stimulus or event – and the aetiologies appear to involve quite different vulnerability factors and psychological processes. This being so, specific phobias are a coherent category only on the basis of their defining symptoms, and therapists may need to look more closely at the different aetiologies to construct successful treatments.

5.1.4 The Treatment of Phobias

Traditionally, successful treatment for specific phobias has tended to revolve around some form of exposure to the phobic stimulus or situation. In the past, behavioural treatments of choice for specific phobias have included systematic desensitization, flooding and counterconditioning (see Chapter 4, section 4.1.1.2). One important issue in therapy for specific phobias is to address the phobic beliefs that sufferers hold about their phobic event or situation (see Table 5.3). These beliefs are often dysfunctional in that they do not match with the reality of the threat (or lack of it) posed by the phobic stimulus, and they also maintain fear and avoidance responses. Because of their strong avoidance of any contact with their phobic situation, sufferers rarely find themselves in a situation where they encounter evidence that disconfirms their phobic beliefs (e.g. continually avoiding spiders never helps spider phobics to disconfirm their belief that, for example, 'I would come to physical harm in the presence of a spider') (Thorpe & Salkovskis, 1995, 1997). One important feature of **exposure therapy** is that it does put phobic individuals in situations where they can experience evidence that is contrary to their dysfunctional beliefs. More recently, specific behavioural treatments have been combined with cognitive therapy techniques to produce integrated short-term therapies that involve cognitive restructuring, intensive exposure to the phobic event or stimulus, and modelling, which can be

Plate 5.3
Exposure therapy is one of the most successful treatments for specific phobias. For many sufferers, however, the thought of having to encounter a real spider is severely distressing. Instead, therapists have developed virtual reality exposure treatments, in which the client can first encounter spiders in a controlled virtual environment. Photo courtesy Hunter Hoffman (Spider2007a6008in.jpg).

effective in as little time as one 3-hour session (Ost, 1997) (see Treatment in Practice Box 5.1).

In conclusion, it must be remembered that many people can live with their phobias – either because the phobias are sub-clinical in intensity or people's fears are so specific that they do not interfere substantially with their daily lives. So only people with the most distressing or disabling phobias are the ones who seek treatment. In general, recently developed therapies for specific phobias have been shown to be extremely effective and successful (Ost, 1997). These therapies are usually multi-faceted and combine aspects of exposure therapy with cognitive restructuring.

SELF-TEST QUESTIONS

- What are the main diagnostic criteria for specific phobias?
- What are the most common phobias, and what are the kinds of *phobic beliefs* that accompany them?
- How do classical conditioning and evolutionary theories attempt to explain the acquisition of phobias? What are their similarities and differences?
- Why is exposure such an important feature of treatment for specific phobias?

CLINICAL PERSPECTIVE: TREATMENT IN PRACTICE BOX 5.1

One-session rapid treatment of spider phobia

One-session treatments for specific phobias were developed during the 1990s and are remarkably successful as effective and long-lasting treatments for many specific phobias (Ost, 1997; Koch, Spates & Himle, 2004; Ost, Alm, Brandberg & Breitholtz, 2001). One-session treatments usually include a combination of graduated *in vivo* exposure and modelling. Below is an example of a one-session treatment procedure for spider phobia.

Step 1: Catching a small spider in a plastic bowl

The therapist first models how the client should pick up the spider by putting a bowl over it, sliding a card underneath to trap the spider, then picking up the bowl using the card as a lid. This is repeated 3–4 times. On the last occasion the client is instructed to hold the bowl in the palm of her hand. At this point a brief role-play can be carried out. The therapist plays the part of a person born blind, and the client has to describe what is happening, thus forcing the client to look at the spider in the bowl.

Step 2: Touching the spider

The therapist asks the client what she thinks will happen if she touches the spider. Most spider phobics say the spider will climb up their arm. This is a prediction that can be tested by the therapist who then touches the spider. This is repeated up to 10 times to show the client that the spider's reaction is almost always to run away. This is followed by the client touching the spider, usually with some physical guidance from the therapist.

Step 3: Holding the spider in the hand

The therapist takes the spider on her hand, letting it walk from one hand to another. The client is then encouraged to put her index finger on the therapist's hand so that the spider can walk across the finger and back to the therapist's hand. This is repeated a number of times until the spider walks across all the client's fingers. Gradually, the therapist withdraws physical support and the client allows the spider to walk from one hand to another.

These three steps are repeated with spiders of increasingly larger size. Throughout the session, the client is taught that she can acquire control over the spider by gradually being able to predict what the spider will do. The goal of the therapy is to ensure that at the end of the session, the client can handle two spiders with low or no anxiety and no longer believe her catastrophic cognitions about spiders.

Source: Ost (1997)

SECTION SUMMARY

5.1 Specific Phobias

- Specific phobias are defined as an excessive, unreasonable, persistent fear triggered by a specific object or situation.

- Around 10 per cent of people will meet DSM-IV-TR criteria for a specific phobia within their lifetime.

- **Common phobias** include small animal phobias (insects, rodents, spiders, snakes), social phobia, dental phobia, water phobia, height phobia, claustrophobia and blood-injury-inoculation (BII) phobia.

- The famous **'Little Albert'** study by Watson and Rayner (1920) is an example of how phobias can be acquired through classical conditioning.

- **Evolutionary accounts** of phobias suggest that we have an inbuilt biological predisposition to fear certain stimuli and events (e.g. heights, water, snakes), because these stimuli were life-threatening to our pre-technological ancestors. Evolutionary accounts of phobias include biological preparedness theory and the non-associative fear acquisition model.

- There is now strong evidence that different phobias may be caused by quite different processes: some involve classical conditioning, some are caused by high disgust sensitivity, while others appear to be caused by processes similar to those that cause panic disorder.

- Successful **treatment** for phobias tends to depend on some kind of exposure to the phobic stimulus or situation. Exposure therapies that are combined with cognitive behaviour therapy can be effective in as little time as one 3-hour session.

5.2 SOCIAL PHOBIA

Social phobia is distinguished by a severe and persistent fear of social or performance situations. Social phobics try to avoid any kind of social situation in which they believe they may behave in an embarrassing way or in which they believe they may be negatively evaluated. So pervasive

> **Social phobia** A severe and persistent fear of social or performance situations.

is anxiety of these socially based situations that it has been more generally labelled as 'social anxiety disorder' (Liebowitz, Heimberg, Fresco, Travers & Stein, 2000) and is a predictor of several other debilitating problems such as depression and substance abuse (Rapee & Spence, 2004).

DSM-IV-TR describes some of the defining features of social phobia:

> individuals with social phobia experience concerns about embarrassment and are afraid that others will judge them to be anxious, weak, 'crazy', or stupid. They may fear public speaking because of concern that others will notice their trembling hands or voice. Or they may experience extreme anxiety when conversing with others because of fear they will appear inarticulate. They may avoid eating, drinking, or writing in public because of fear of being embarrassed by having others see their hands shake. Individuals with social phobia almost always experience symptoms of anxiety (e.g. palpitations, tremors, sweating, gastrointestinal discomfort, diarrhea, muscle tension, blushing, confusion) in the feared social situations, and, in severe cases, these symptoms may meet the criteria for a panic attack.
>
> (APA, 1994, p. 412)

Table 5.5 lists the DSM-IV-TR criteria for the diagnosis of social phobia.

5.2.1 Prevalence

Social phobia has a lifetime prevalence rate of between 7 and 13 per cent in Western societies and afflicts females significantly more often than males (Furmark, 2002). Age of onset is considerably earlier than for many of the other anxiety disorders, typically occurring in early to mid-teens and usually prior to 18 years of age (Rapee, 1995; Otto, Pollack, Maki, Gould et al., 2001). It is also a particularly persistent disorder and has the lowest overall remission rate of the main anxiety disorders (Massion, Dyck, Shea, Phillips et al., 2002). Cross-cultural studies have shown that prevalence rates are significantly lower in Southeast Asian countries (e.g. Korea and Taiwan) than in Western societies (Furmark, 2002), but this may be due at least in part to the fact that the expression of social anxiety differs across cultures. For example, in Japan, Taijin-kyofu-sho (TKS) is a form of social phobia in which the main fear is of offending others (see section 5.1). In Western cultures, social anxiety manifests itself primarily as fear of embarrassing oneself.

5.2.2 The Aetiology of Social Phobia

Although it is a phobia in its own right, social phobia is considered separately from simple phobias in DSM-IV-TR. There are a number of reasons for this. First, it is a highly prevalent disorder and compares with generalized anxiety disorder (GAD) as the most common of the anxiety disorders. Secondly, as we will see below, theories of social phobia suggest that factors rather specific to social anxiety are important in the aetiology of social phobia. In particular, social phobics possess a range of information processing and interpretation biases that cause them to make excessively negative predictions about future social events. We discuss these various types of bias in the following sections, after first considering genetic and developmental factors.

Table 5.5 *DSM-IV-TR criteria for diagnosis of social phobia*

A A marked persistent fear of one or more social or performance situations in which the person is exposed to unfamiliar people or to possible scrutiny by others. The individual fears that he or she will act in a way that will be humiliating or embarrassing.

B Exposure to the feared social situation almost invariably provokes anxiety, which may take the form of a situationally bound or situationally predisposed panic attack.

C The person recognizes that the fear is excessive or unreasonable.

D The feared social or performance situations are avoided or else are endured with intense anxiety or distress.

E The avoidance or anxious anticipation of the feared social or performance situation(s) interferes significantly with the person's normal routine, occupational (academic) functioning, or social activities or relationships.

F In individuals under 18 years, the duration is at least 6 months.

G The fear or avoidance is not due to the direct physiological effects of a substance or a general medical condition, and is not better accounted for by another mental disorder.

H If a general medical condition or another mental disorder is present, the fear in Criterion A is unrelated to it, e.g. the fear is not of stuttering, trembling in Parkinson's disease, or exhibiting abnormal eating behaviour in anorexia nervosa or bulimia nervosa.

5.2.2.1 Genetic Factors

Evidence is accruing that there is an underlying genetic component to social phobia. For example, children with social phobia are more likely to have parents with social phobia than non-phobic children (Lieb, Wittchen, Hoefler, Fuetsch et al., 2000; Mancini, van Ameringen, Szatmari, Fugere et al., 1996), and twin studies also suggest that there is a significant but moderate genetic influence on the development of social phobia (Beatty, Heisel, Hall, Levine et al., 2002; Ollendick & Hirschfeld Becker, 2002). While indicating the importance of genetic influences, such studies do beg the question of what aspect of social phobia is inherited. However, some studies have been able to identify specific constructs related to social phobia that appear to have a genetic component. These include submissiveness, anxiousness, social avoidance and behavioural inhibition (Warren, Schmitz & Emde,

CLIENT'S PERSPECTIVE 5.1

Social phobia

'You have to be a sufferer of social phobia (SP) to understand the pure terror that a victim of this illness feels. It's the sort of blind panic dread and fear that one would feel facing a firing squad or if you fell into a lion's cage. You shake like a leaf, you blush, your mouth goes dry, you can't speak, you break out in a cold sweat, your legs feel so weak you think you're going to fall. Your thoughts become confused and disorientated. Forget butterflies in the stomach – your guts are twisted inside out with FEAR.

SP made me sink so low I ended up cleaning public toilets for a living. I never married (no, I'm not gay), I had no children, I never owned my own house. I rent a small flat in a very poor part of London all because of SEVERE SP. My parents were cold reserved people unable to show their emotions. I was never abused in any way but I look back on my childhood as a lonely unhappy time. Maybe that was the root cause of my phobia. I mention that because we can all think of something that may have been the cause. My SP started in my last year at school when I became very self-conscious and developed a fearful dread of being asked to read in front of the class. This extreme anxiety moved on with me into my working life. I was a smart looking young man so I got some good jobs, but because of SP no way could I hold them. Would you buy from a salesman who went a deep red, stammered, couldn't look you in the eye, and shook so much that even his head trembled? No – nor would the boss who in the end would say get lost, you're bad for business.

Over the years I slid down and down the social ladder with long spells out of work and, of course, no money. By the time I was thirty I could only do work where I did not have to deal with people like road sweep, night work in factories and in the end cleaning public toilets when closed at night. SP was now so bad

I couldn't face going into a shop to buy something. To pass a queue of people waiting for a bus was hell. I was sure they were all staring at me. I couldn't sit facing other passengers on a train unless I had a newspaper to hide behind. If I attempted going into a restaurant or café, I'd pick a table facing the wall and if anyone sat at my table my hands would shake so much I couldn't get the food into my mouth. I became the ultimate night person, only going out late to walk the streets.'

Source: www.social-phobia.co.uk/

Clinical Commentary

This client's perspective highlights the extreme fear experienced by many social phobics in a range of social and performance situations, and the impact this can have on social functioning specifically and life planning more generally. This description highlights a number of important features of social phobia, including: (1) the biased interpretations that social phobics have of the reactions of others to them (e.g. 'To pass a queue of people waiting for a bus was hell. I was sure they were all staring at me'); (2) the belief that there are obvious physical signs of their nervousness which observers interpret judgementally (e.g. 'Would you buy from a salesman who went a deep red, stammered, couldn't look you in the eye?'); and (3) the tendency of social phobics to focus attention on themselves and their own reactions to the possible detriment of their own performance (e.g. 'My SP started in my last year at school when I became very self-conscious and developed a fearful dread of being asked to read in front of the class').

1999; Robinson, Reznick, Kagan & Corley, 1992). Other studies indicate that social phobia contains an inherited component that is shared with other anxiety disorders, which suggests that what might be inherited is a vulnerability to anxiety disorders generally rather than social phobia specifically (Kendler, Walters, Neale, Kessler et al., 1995; Nelson, Grant, Bucholz, Glowinski et al., 2000). Nevertheless, there may still be a modest inherited element that is specific to social phobia, and this has been estimated to account for as much as 13 per cent of the variance in social fears generally (Kendler, Myers, Prescott & Neale, 2001).

5.2.2.2 Developmental Factors

Because social phobia appears at a relatively early age compared to other anxiety disorders, it has been argued that various developmental factors and early experiences may precipitate the disorder

(Neal & Edelmann, 2003). For example, there is considerable evidence that children who exhibit a behaviourally inhibited temperament style are at increased risk for subsequent social phobia (Neal, Edelmann & Glachan, 2002; Kagan, Reznick, Clarke, Snidman et al., 1984). However, it is also the case that a significant proportion of children who are highly behaviourally inhibited in early life do *not* subsequently develop social phobia – so childhood behavioural inhibition is not a sufficient condition for social phobia (Schwartz, Snidman & Kagan, 1999). Early parent–child interaction styles may also play a role in the development of social anxiety. Studies of parent–child interactions suggest that the parents of social phobics exert greater control over their children, show less warmth, are less sociable than the parents of individuals without social phobia and also use shame as a method of discipline (Rapee & Melville, 1997; Siqueland, Kendall & Steinberg, 1996; Bruch & Heimberg, 1994). While these factors seem to be important predictors of subsequent social phobia, it is impossible to determine at present whether they represent actual causal factors.

5.2.2.3 Cognitive Factors

There appear to be a number of cognitive processes that are characteristic of social phobia and which may all act in some way to maintain fear of social situations (Stravynski, Bond & Amando, 2004). First, social phobics possess an information processing and interpretation bias in which they make excessively negative predictions about future social events (Heinrichs & Hofmann, 2001; Hirsch & Clark, 2004). For example, individuals with social phobia rate the probability of negative social events occurring as higher than either non-clinical controls or individuals with other anxiety disorders (Foa, Franklin, Perry & Herbert, 1996; Gilboa-Schechtman, Franklin & Foa, 2000), and this negative evaluation is likely to maintain their avoidance of social situations.

Secondly, individuals with social phobia interpret their performance in social situations significantly more critically than non-sufferers and independent assessors who have observed their behaviour (Stopa & Clark, 1993; Rapee & Lim, 1992). Social phobics also find it very difficult to process positive social feedback (Alden, Mellings & Laposa, 2004). This focus on negative aspects of the social situation, and the relative inability to take anything 'good' from a social performance, are likely to maintain the social phobic's dysfunctional beliefs that social situations are threatening and that their own performance is likely to be flawed.

Thirdly, some theories of social phobia argue that sufferers show a strong tendency to shift their attention inwards onto themselves and their own anxiety responses during social performance – especially when they fear they will be negatively evaluated (Clark & Wells, 1995; Rapee & Heimberg, 1997). This is known as *self-focused attention* (Spurr & Stopa, 2002; Bogels & Mansell, 2004) and has the effect of leading socially anxious individuals to believe they may look as anxious as they feel inside. This prevents objective processing of the social situation, leads them to engage in critical self-evaluation and may well adversely affect their actual performance in the social situation. Studies have shown that social phobics do indeed display higher levels of self-reported self-focused attention than non-clinical populations (Bogels & Lamers, 2002) and that they recall social memories more often from an observer perspective than from a personal perspective (suggesting that they do indeed 'observe' themselves while performing socially) (Wells, Clark & Ahmad, 1998). Self-focused attention therefore appears to have the effect of reinforcing individuals' perception of their own anxiety in the social situation, can distract individuals from focusing on the social task at hand and lead to unskilled performance, and result in avoidance of future social situations (Alden, Teschuk & Tee, 1992).

Finally, individuals with social phobia also indulge in excessive post-event processing of social events that includes critical self-appraisal of performance and assessment of symptom severity.

Self-focused attention   A theory of social phobia arguing that sufferers show a strong tendency to shift their attention inwards onto themselves and their own anxiety responses during social performance – especially when they fear they will be negatively evaluated.

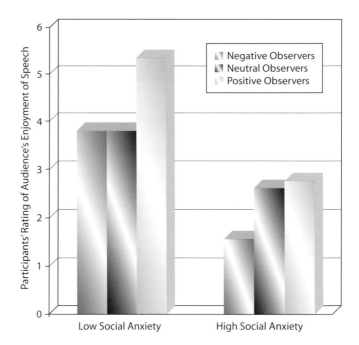

Figure 5.2
High and low socially anxious participants were asked to give a speech to a group of observers. After giving the speech, the high socially anxious participants rated observers' enjoyment of their speech significantly lower than low socially anxious participants. The high socially anxious participants do this even when the observers have been instructed to provide positive feedback, suggesting that socially phobic individuals do not attend to positive feedback cues given by an audience.

Source: Perowne & Mansell (2002).

Such post-event rumination has the effect of maintaining negative appraisals of performance over time and maintaining social anxiety (Abbott & Rapee, 2004; Rachman, Gruter-Andrew & Shafran, 2000).

5.2.3 The Treatment of Social Phobia

Both pharmacological treatments and cognitive behaviour therapies (CBT) have been shown to be effective in alleviating the symptoms of social phobia (Rodebaugh, Holaway & Heimberg, 2004; Davidson, 2003), and both are used widely to treat the disorder.

Successful CBT treatments include elements of the following:

- Exposure therapy, where the client remains in a feared social situation despite distress, either *in vivo* or through the therapist taking on the role of a stranger in a social situation (Heimberg & Becker, 2002). (See Treatment in Practice Box 5.2.)

- Social skills training, consisting of modelling, behavioural rehearsal, corrective feedback and positive reinforcement. This training addresses the social skills deficits often characteristic of social phobics.

CLINICAL PERSPECTIVE: TREATMENT IN PRACTICE BOX 5.2

Cognitive therapy for social phobia

The following is a step-by-step account of the cognitive therapy for social phobia devised by Clark and Wells (1995). The aims of this procedure are: (1) to decrease self-focused attention; (2) to reduce the level of negative interpretations of internal information (e.g. sweating as a sign of poor performance); (3) to eliminate the use of safety behaviours which maintain negative beliefs (e.g. if the phobic believes he is trembling and that this may be visible, he may grip objects tightly in order to conceal it: this response merely maintains the phobic's belief that he is anxious and trembling); and (4) to reduce negative post-event processing (see section 5.2.2.3).

Step 1: The initial phase is designed to inform clients about those factors that are maintaining their social phobia (see above), and that these are the factors that the therapy is specifically designed to target.

Step 2: The second phase attempts to manipulate safety behaviours. Here clients have to role-play a social situation and observe their own responses and identify key safety behaviours. Clients will then attempt to drop these safety behaviours during subsequent role-playing.

Step 3: Clients are trained to shift their attention externally and away from their own internal responses and cognitions.

Step 4: Video feedback of performance can be used to modify distorted self-imagery.

Step 5: Clients are provided with some behavioural experiments in which they specify their fears of particular social situations and then test out whether they occurred during role-play sessions.

Step 6: Problematic post-event processing is identified and modified using focused cognitive restructuring techniques.

Source: Stangier, Heidenreich, Peitz, Lauterbach & Clark (2003)

- Cognitive restructuring, designed to challenge and replace the negative biases in information processing and the dysfunctional negative self-evaluations of social performance, and to reduce self-focused attention (Rodebaugh & Chambless, 2004).

Each of these elements used alone does show therapeutic gains, but an integrated CBT programme appears to result in maintenance of gains over 6- to 12-month follow-up periods (Feske & Chambless, 1995).

Drugs such as monoamine oxidase inhibitors (MAOIs) and, more recently, serotonin reuptake inhibitors (SSRIs) (see Chapter 4, section 4.1.1.6) have been shown to cause improvement in measures of social anxiety (Blanco, Schneier, Schmidt, Blanco-Jerez et al., 2003; van der Linden, Stein & van Balkom, 2000). Comparative outcome studies have suggested that both pharmacological and CBT treatments are more effective than non-treatment controls (Gould, Buckminster, Pollock, Otto & Yap, 1997), but that the two types of therapy may offer complementary benefits, drug therapy offering a more immediate benefit than CBT, but CBT helping clients to maintain their therapeutic gains over time (Liebowitz, Heimberg, Schneier, Hope et al., 1999).

SELF-TEST QUESTIONS

- What are the main diagnostic criteria for social phobia and how does this disorder manifest itself?
- Can you describe the various cognitive factors that appear to play an important role in maintaining social phobia?
- How do cognitive behaviour therapies (CBT) and drug treatments complement each other in the treatment of social phobia?

SECTION SUMMARY

5.2 Social Phobia

- Social phobia is distinguished by a severe and persistent fear of social or performance situations.

- Social phobia has a lifetime prevalence rate of between 7 and 13 per cent in Western societies.

- There is evidence for a **genetic** component to social phobia, but this may be a predisposition to develop anxiety disorders generally rather than social phobia specifically.

- There are a number of **cognitive** factors that are characteristic of social phobics. These include a tendency to: (1) make excessively negative predictions about future social events; (2) over-critically evaluate their own social performance; (3) shift their attention inwards on to themselves; and (4) indulge in post-event critical appraisal of their own performance.

- Both **monoamine oxidase inhibitors** and **serotonin reuptake inhibitors** have been shown to be successful pharmacological treatments for social phobia, as well as **cognitive behaviour therapy** (CBT).

5.3 PANIC DISORDER

Panic disorder An anxiety disorder characterized by repeated panic or anxiety attacks.

As the name suggests, *panic disorder* is characterized by repeated panic or anxiety attacks. These attacks are associated with a variety of physical symptoms, including heart palpitations, perspiring, dizziness, hyperventilating, nausea and trembling (see Case History 5.1). In addition, the individual may experience real feelings of terror or severe apprehension and depersonalization (a feeling of not being connected to your own body or in real contact with what is happening around you). Most people will experience at least one panic attack in their lifetime, but panic disorder is diagnosed when recurrent, unexpected panic attacks keep occurring and are followed by at least one month of persistent concerns about having a further attack. For some individuals panic attacks are unpredictable, but for others they may become associated (perhaps through classical conditioning: see Chapter 1, section 1.1.3.2) to specific situations or events (e.g. riding on public transport).

DSM-IV-TR defines a panic attack as a discrete period of intense fear or discomfort in which four or more of a list of symptoms develop suddenly and reach a peak within 10 minutes (see Table 5.6). The criteria for panic disorder state that individuals must experience recurrent panic attacks, and in addition they must develop a persistent concern that future panic attacks will occur (see Table 5.7). The frequency of panic attacks in panic disorder can vary considerably between individuals from one attack per week to frequent daily attacks. Panic disorder is associated with a number of fears and apprehensions that the sufferer develops. These include fears that the attacks indicate an underlying serious medical condition (e.g. cardiac disease, seizure disorder), even though repeated medical tests indicate no life-threatening illness. Others feel they are losing control or simply 'going crazy'. Sufferers often make significant changes to their behaviour and their life as a result of the disorder. For example, they may ensure

CASE HISTORY 5.1

Panic disorder

Marilyn is a 33-year-old single woman who works at a local telephone company and lives alone in her apartment. She has panic disorder with agoraphobia and her first panic attack occurred 3 years ago when driving over a bridge on a very rainy day. She experienced dizziness, pounding heart, trembling and difficulty breathing. She was terrified her symptoms meant she was about to pass out and lose control of her car. Since that time she has experienced eight unexpected panic attacks during which she feared she was about to pass out and lose control of herself. She frequently experiences limited symptom attacks (e.g. feels dizzy and fears she may pass out). As a result of her intense fear of having another panic attack she avoids the following situations: waiting in line, drinking alcohol, elevators, movie theatres, driving over bridges, driving on the freeway, flying by plane, and heights (e.g. she will not go out on her tenth floor balcony). She is often late for work because of taking a route that doesn't require her to take the freeway. She also finds herself avoiding more and more activities. She frequently feels tearful and on guard. Sometimes she gets very angry at herself as she does not understand why she has become so fearful and avoidant.

Sharon is a 38-year-old single mother of two teenage daughters who works as a fitness instructor at a local gym. She experienced her first panic attack during her teens when watching a horror movie with friends at a local movie theatre. Since that time she has experienced one to two full panic attacks per year that come out of the blue in a variety of situations (e.g. while waiting in line at the bank, at a shopping mall, walking alone at the park). The panic attacks recurred out of the blue when she was 29 while eating a hot and spicy meal at a local restaurant. Her panic attacks always include dizziness, feeling of choking, dry mouth, unreality, feeling detached from her body and feeling as if she may lose bowel control. Her main fear is that she is dying due to a stroke, although medical problems have been ruled out. Sharon does not avoid anything to prevent the panic attacks and there has not been a huge negative impact of the panic attacks upon her work, family or social functioning.

Source: www.anxietybc.com/disorders/PANIC.html

Clinical Commentary

Both Marilyn and Sharon exhibit a number of physical symptoms typical of panic attacks, although these examples show that not everyone experiences similar symptoms. Panic attacks often come 'out of the blue' and are unpredictable, which adds to their frightening nature. In both examples the individual believes that the symptoms are signs of impending physical illness or loss of control (catastrophic misinterpretation). The pervasive fear of further attacks means that Marilyn has developed avoidance responses in an attempt to minimize future attacks. These avoidance responses interfere with her normal daily life (causing further stress), and inadvertently help to maintain dysfunctional catastrophic beliefs.

Table 5.6 *DSM-IV-TR criteria for a panic attack*

A discrete period of intense fear or discomfort, in which four (or more) of the following symptoms develop abruptly and reach a peak within 10 minutes:

(1) Palpitations, pounding heart, or accelerated heart rate

(2) Sweating

(3) Trembling or shaking

(4) Sensations of shortness of breath or smothering

(5) Feeling of choking

(6) Chest pain or discomfort

(7) Nausea or abdominal distress

(8) Feeling dizzy, unsteady, lightheaded, or faint

(9) Derealization (feelings of unreality) or depersonalization (being detached from oneself)

(10) Fear of losing control or going crazy

(11) Fear of dying

(12) Paresthesias (numbness or tingling sensations)

(13) Chills or hot flushes

Table 5.7 *DSM-IV-TR criteria for diagnosing panic disorder*

A Both (1) and (2):

  (1) recurrent unexpected panic attacks

  (2) at least one of the attacks has been followed by 1 month (or more) of one (or more) of the following:

    (a) persistent concern about having additional attacks

    (b) worry about the implications of the attacks or their consequences (e.g. losing control, having a heart attack)

    (c) a significant change in behaviour related to the attacks

B The panic attacks are not due to the direct physiological effects of a substance (e.g. a drug of abuse, a medication) or a general medical condition.

C The panic attacks are not better accounted for by another mental disorder, such as social phobia, specific phobia, OCD, PTSD, or separation anxiety disorder.

NB Panic disorder will normally be diagnosed 'with' or 'without' agoraphobia, depending on whether the individual exhibits anxiety about being in places or situations from which escape might be difficult.

that there is always a 'safe' place available in case they have an attack, and this may cause them to avoid social situations and even quit their job. Concerns about future attacks often result in the development of avoidant behaviour; sufferers may find it difficult to leave the 'safety' of their own home, in which case panic disorder with agoraphobia is a common diagnosis.

5.3.1 Prevalence

The lifetime prevalence of panic disorder is between 1.5 and 3.5 per cent (DSM-IV-TR) and is experienced more by women than men (relative lifetime prevalence rates of 5 per cent and 2 per cent respectively; Kessler et al., 1994). Onset is common in adolescence or early adulthood and can often be associated with a period of stress in the individual's life (Pollard, Pollard & Corn, 1989). There is some evidence for culturally determined variance in both the prevalence of panic disorder and in the way that panic disorder may manifest itself. For example, in some Asian societies, prevalence is particularly low, possibly because of the stigma related to admitting and reporting psychological disorders (e.g. in Taiwan; Weissman, Bland, Canino, Faravelli et al., 1997). However, in other cultures, panic disorder may be expressed in the form of quite different symptoms. For example, *Ataque de Nervios* is an anxiety-based disorder found almost exclusively in Latinos in the Caribbean. This appears to be a form of panic disorder brought on by stressful life events (such as economic or marital difficulties) but whose expression is determined by the social and cultural norms within that cultural group (see Chapter 1, Focus Point 1.3). In particular, Latino cultures place less emphasis on self-control and emotional restraint than other Western cultures, and so the distress of panic disorder in Latinos tends to be externalized in the form of screaming, uncontrolled behaviour and aggression (Salman et al., 1998). In contrast, in Western cultures the distress of panic disorder is usually coped with by adopting avoidance and withdrawal strategies – hence the common diagnosis of panic disorder with agoraphobia.

It is important to remember that panic attacks may be a feature of the symptoms in a number of the anxiety disorders (e.g. specific phobias and social phobia). However, panic disorder itself is characterized by frequent uncontrollable panic attacks, and an important aspect of this anxiety-based problem is the individual's intense fear of experiencing panic attacks. As we shall see, it is this latter feature of panic disorder that plays a central role in theories of the disorder.

5.3.2 The Aetiology of Panic Disorder

Because of the intense nature of the physical symptoms of panic disorder, many researchers have looked towards biological causes. However, it has become clear that there are also important psychological and cognitive factors that contribute to the aetiology and maintenance of panic disorder.

5.3.2.1 Biological Theories of Panic Disorder

The Role of Hyperventilation *Hyperventilation* is a common feature of panic attacks, and Ley (1987) has suggested that dysfunctional breathing patterns may trigger a series of autonomic reactions that precipitate a full-blown panic attack. Hyperventilation is defined as a 'minute ventilation that exceeds metabolic

> **Hyperventilation**   A rapid form of breathing that results in ventilation exceeding metabolic demand and has an end result of raising blood pH level. A common feature of panic attacks.

demand' and has an end result of raising blood pH level. Oxygen is then delivered less efficiently to body cells, which can lead to cardiovascular changes that try to help compensate for the lack of oxygen in the cells, and in turn can produce the symptoms of panic attacks that are recognized as anxiety (Zvolensky & Eifert, 2001).

This type of explanation has been partially supported by evidence from what are called **biological challenge tests** (see Figure 5.3),

> **Biological challenge tests**   Research in which panic attacks are induced by administering carbon dioxide-enriched air (CO_2) or by encouraging hyperventilation.

where panic attacks have been induced by administering carbon dioxide-enriched air (CO_2) or by encouraging hyperventilation (Ley & Walker, 1973). Similarly, sensitivity to increases in CO_2 have been suggested as a risk factor for panic disorder (Papp, Klein & Gorman, 1993),

> **Suffocation alarm theories**   Models of panic disorder in which a combination of increased CO_2 intake may activate an oversensitive suffocation alarm system and give rise to the intense terror and anxiety experienced during a panic attack.

and have given rise to what are known as **suffocation alarm theories** of panic disorder, where a combination of increased CO_2 intake may activate an over-sensitive suffocation alarm system and give rise to the intense terror and anxiety experience during a panic attack (Klein, 1993). In support of this account, panic disorder patients do report significantly more symptoms of shortness of breath when anxious, and more frequent frightening suffocation experiences than other anxiety patients. However, when panic disorder patients are asked to participate in periods of breath-holding, they do not report any greater levels of anxiety than non-anxious controls, suggesting that they do not necessarily possess a more sensitive suffocation alarm system (Roth, Wilhelm & Trabert, 1998).

One further intriguing feature of the hyperventilation account is that, while biological challenge tests produce physiological changes that often provoke full-blown panic attacks, they only tend to do so in individuals with a history of panic attacks or panic disorder (Margraf, Ehlers & Roth, 1986). This is the case even though the physiological changes caused by biological challenge tests are the same in people diagnosed with panic disorder and those who have no anxiety disorder (Gorman, Kent, Martinez et al., 2001). This evidence quite strongly suggests that an important causal factor in panic disorder is the way that individuals *interpret* the physiological changes caused by the biological challenge, and this gives rise to the psychological accounts of panic disorder that have been developed over the past 25 years.

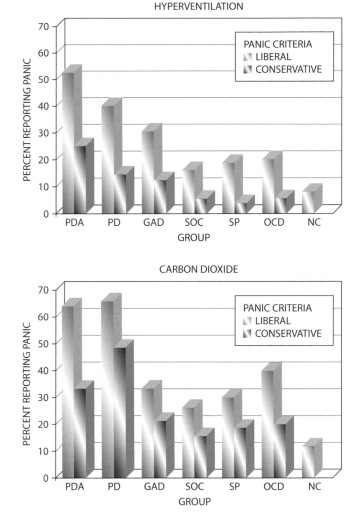

Figure 5.3
Proportion of participants with a range of anxiety disorders who report a panic attack after either (a) being asked to hyperventilate or (b) receiving a CO_2 challenge.
(PDA = panic disorder with agoraphobia; PD = panic disorder; GAD = generalized anxiety disorder; SOC = social phobia; SP = simple phobia; OCD = obsessive-compulsive disorder; NC = non-anxious controls).

Source: Rapee, Brown, Antony & Barlow (1992).

Noradrenergic Overactivity A further account of panic disorder that alludes to biological differences between those who suffer panic disorder and those who do not is that the disorder may be caused by overactivity in the noradrenergic neurotransmitter system (Redmond, 1977). There is certainly evidence that the noradrenaline network may mediate the effects of biological challenges in producing panic attacks (Bailey, Argyropoulos, Lightman & Nutt, 2003), and that norepinephrine is implicated in the symptomatology of panic disorder (Sand, Mori, Godau, Stober et al., 2002). One particular view related to putative overactivity in the noradrenergic system is that patients with panic disorder are deficient in the gamma-aminobutyric (GABA) neurons that inhibit

RESEARCH METHODS IN CLINICAL PSYCHOLOGY BOX 5.1

Biological challenge procedures and panic disorder

A number of provocative agents can be used to induce panic attacks. In research on panic disorder, they have been used to investigate whether individuals with panic disorder have a greater sensitivity to such agents. Indeed, all of the agents listed below induce panic attacks more readily in panic disorder sufferers than in normal controls. This suggests that individuals with panic disorder may be biologically or psychologically sensitive to the effects of these agents.

Agent	Biological mechanism for causing panic	Effect on panic disorder sufferers and non-clinical controls	References
Sodium lactate	Possibly through alkalinization of the blood	Tends to induce panic attacks in panic disorder sufferers but not in normal controls	Bourin et al. (1998) Krystal et al. (1996)
Carbon dioxide (CO_2)	Increased breathing and hyperventilation in order to remove CO_2 causes respiratory alkalosis	Produces an increase in subjective anxiety in panic disorder sufferers including symptoms of panic	Gorman et al. (1984) Perna et al. (1995)
Yohimbine	Increases central noradrenergic activity in the locus ceruleus (an area of the brain implicated in panic)	Tends to induce panic attacks in a majority of panic disorder sufferers, and greater levels of self-reported anxiety than controls	Charney et al. (1984) Charney et al. (1987)
Caffeine	Indirectly increases norepinephrine and increases arousal	Tends to cause panic symptoms in panic disorder sufferers but not in normal controls	Charney et al. (1985) Beck & Berisford (1992)

noradrenergic activity, and PET scan studies have tended to support this view (Malizia, Cunningham, Bell, Liddle et al., 1998). Nevertheless, it is still unclear whether the role of the noradrenergic system is to mediate the symptoms of panic attacks when they occur, or whether noradrenergic overactivity represents a vulnerability factor in the aetiology of panic disorder.

5.3.2.2 Psychological Theories of Panic Disorder

Classical Conditioning Goldstein and Chambless (1978) were the first to suggest that an important feature of panic disorder was the sufferer's 'fear of fear'. That is, when they detected what they thought were any internal signs of a panic attack (e.g. mild dizziness), sufferers would immediately become fearful of the possible consequences. This would then precipitate a full-blown attack. Goldstein and Chambless (1978) interpreted this as a form of interoceptive classical conditioning, in which the internal cue (such as dizziness) had become established as an internal conditioned stimulus (CS) predicting a panic attack (the unconditioned stimulus, UCS). However, while this account has intuitive appeal,

it is not clear in conditioning terms what is the CS and what is the UCS. For example, is a skipped heartbeat a CS that precipitates a panic attack, or is it a symptom of the panic attack itself (the UCS) (McNally, 1990)? Bouton, Mineka and Barlow (2001) have attempted to address these conceptual difficulties by suggesting that anxiety and panic are separable aspects of panic disorder. They suggest that anxiety is anticipatory and prepares the system for a trauma, whereas panic deals with a trauma that is already in progress. In this conditioning account, anxiety is the learned reaction, called conditioned response (CR), to the detection of cues, the conditioned stimulus (CS), that might predict a panic attack, and once conditioned anxiety develops it will exacerbate subsequent panic attacks and lead to the development of panic disorder. As predicted by this model, studies confirm that panic attacks are regularly preceded by anxiety in individuals with panic disorder (Barlow, 1988; Kenardy & Taylor, 1999).

Anxiety Sensitivity What is clear about the phenomenology of panic disorder is that sufferers become extremely anxious when they detect any cues (internal or external) that may be indicative of a panic attack. So any theory of panic disorder needs to explain why sufferers are made anxious by the detection of these cues, and how this subsequently leads to a full-blown panic attack. Individuals who do *not* suffer panic disorder report a number of interoceptive and affective responses in biological challenge tests, but they are only rarely made anxious by these symptoms and hardly ever panic (Bass & Gardner, 1985; Starkman, Zelnik, Nesse & Cameron, 1985). So, what determines whether someone will panic in response to unusual bodily sensations? Reiss and McNally (1985) proposed that some individuals have pre-existing beliefs that bodily sensations may predict harmful consequences. They developed the construct of ***anxiety sensitivity***, which refers to fears of anxiety symptoms that are based on beliefs that such symptoms have harmful consequences (e.g. that a rapid heartbeat predicts an impending heart attack). In order to measure this construct, Reiss, Peterson, Gursky and McNally (1986) developed the *Anxiety Sensitivity Index* (ASI) (see also the Revised Anxiety Sensitivity Index, ASI-R: Taylor & Cox, 1998), which contains items such as 'Unusual body sensations scare me' and 'It scares me when I feel faint' (see Table 5.8). Studies have shown that individuals with panic disorder score significantly higher on the ASI than either non-clinical controls or individuals diagnosed with other anxiety disorders (Taylor & Cox, 1998; Rapee, Ancis & Barlow, 1988). Furthermore, in a prospective study, high ASI scores predicted the occurrence of subsequent panic attacks in army recruits undergoing a stressful period of training (Schmidt, Lerew & Jackson, 1997), which suggests that elevated anxiety sensitivity may be a risk factor for panic and perhaps panic disorder (McNally, 2002).

Anxiety sensitivity   Fears of anxiety symptoms based on beliefs that such symptoms have harmful consequences (e.g. that a rapid heart beat predicts an impending heart attack).

Anxiety Sensitivity Index   A measure, developed by Reiss, Peterson, Gursky & McNally (1986), to measure anxiety sensitivity.

Catastrophic Misinterpretation of Bodily Sensations

Based on the fact that panic disorder sufferers are clearly anxious about the possible consequences of bodily symptoms, Clark (1986, 1988) developed an influential model of panic disorder in which he hypothesized that panic attacks are precipitated by individuals catastrophically misinterpreting their bodily sensations as threatening. Many body sensations are ambiguous: for example, the heart skipping a beat could mean either an imminent heart attack (negative interpretation) or that someone you like has just walked into the room (positive interpretation). However, individuals who tend to develop panic disorder appear to ***catastrophically misinterpret bodily sensations***, that is, they have a cognitive bias towards accepting the more threatening interpretation of their sensations (Clark, Salkovskis, Ost, Breitholz et al., 1997; see Austin & Richards, 2001, for a review). Clark argues that this leads to a vicious cycle where any apprehension is interpreted threateningly and increases the perceived threat, which leads to an escalation of anxiety symptoms that then precipitate a panic attack. This is represented schemati-

Catastrophic misinterpretation of bodily sensations   A feature of panic disorders where there is a cognitive bias towards accepting the more threatening interpretation of an individual's own sensations.

Table 5.8 *Example items from the Anxiety Sensitivity Index (ASI-R) (Taylor & Cox, 1998)*

The ASI-R measures anxiety sensitivity, which is a measure of an individual's fear of anxiety. Anxiety sensitivity is one of the best predictors of future panic attacks and may be a risk factor for panic disorder.

1 When I feel like I'm not getting enough air I get scared that I might suffocate.
2 When my chest feels tight, I get scared I won't be able to breathe properly.
3 It scares me when I feel faint.
4 When my throat feels tight, I worry that I could choke to death.
5 It scares me when my heart beats rapidly.
6 It scares me when I feel shaky (trembly).
7 When I have trouble swallowing, I worry that I could choke.
8 It scares me when my body feels strange or different in some way.
9 I think it would be horrible for me to faint in public.
10 When I tremble in the presence of others I fear what people might think of me.
11 When I feel a strong pain in my stomach, I worry it could be cancer.
12 When my heart is beating rapidly, I worry that I might be having a stroke.
13 When I feel dizzy, I worry there is something wrong with my brain.
14 When my stomach is upset, I worry that I might be seriously ill.
15 It scares me when I feel tingling or prickling sensations in my hands.
16 When I feel 'spacey' or spaced out I worry that I may be mentally ill.

cally in Figure 5.4. There is a good deal of evidence to support this psychological account. Individuals with panic disorder have been shown to attend to and discriminate their bodily sensations more closely than individuals without panic disorder (Ehlers & Breuer, 1992), and panic disorder sufferers report that thoughts of imminent danger typically accompany their attacks (Hibbert, 1984; Ottaviani & Beck, 1987). In addition, individuals with panic disorder will experience a panic attack when they have been told they will receive a CO_2 challenge, but in fact are given only *compressed air* (Sanderson, Rapee & Barlow, 1989), suggesting that just the *expectancy* of an attack is enough to trigger one.

All of these accounts suggest there is likely to be an important psychological component to the development of panic disorder that involves a negatively valenced bias in how individuals interpret and react to their own bodily sensations. This interpretation

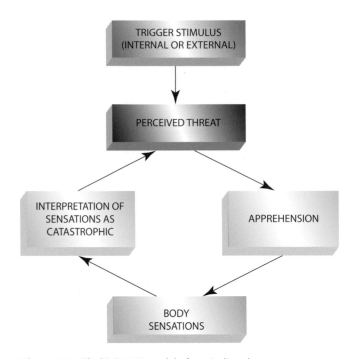

Figure 5.4 *Clark's (1986) model of panic disorder*
Perception of a threat triggers apprehension and then bodily sensations associated with that apprehension are interpreted catastrophically. This causes further anxiety, which feeds into a vicious cycle that triggers a full-blown panic attack.

bias appears to trigger anxiety, which in turn triggers a panic attack. The issues that remain to be resolved in these accounts are (1) exactly how the anxiety elicited by catastrophic misinterpretation of bodily sensations leads to panic, and (2) why some individuals have acquired high levels of anxiety sensitivity and catastrophic beliefs in the first place.

5.3.3 The Treatment of Panic Disorder

Because of the distressing physical symptoms experienced in panic disorder, psychoactive medication is usually the first line of treatment provided for sufferers, and both tricyclic antidepressants and benzodiazepines may be effective in controlling symptoms (Roy-Byrne & Cowley, 1998) (see Chapter 4, section 4.1.1.6). However, there is good evidence that structured exposure therapy or cognitive behaviour therapy (CBT) is as effective, if not superior, to drug treatments over the longer term (e.g. Craske, Brown & Barlow, 1991).

In exposure-based treatments, the client is persuaded to experience the conditions that precipitate a panic attack in the controlled environment of the therapy situation (Craske & Barlow, 2001). For example, someone whose attacks are preceded by bouts of dizziness may be asked to spin around in a chair, or if hyperventilation is a trigger, the individual will be asked to breathe rapidly for a period of time. At the first bodily signs of the symptoms

 CLINICAL PERSPECTIVE: TREATMENT IN PRACTICE BOX 5.3

Cognitive therapy for panic disorder

The following transcript gives an example of how a cognitive therapist (T) would try to challenge the catastrophic beliefs of a panic disorder sufferer (P) who believes that signs of an impending panic attack are signals for an imminent heart attack.

P: When I'm panicking, it's terrible, I can feel my heart pounding; it's so bad I think it could burst through my chest.

T: What thoughts go through your mind when your heart is pounding like that?

P: Well, I'll tell you what I think; it's so bad that I think I'm going to have a heart attack. It can't be good for your heart beating like that.

T: So you're concerned that anxiety can damage your heart or cause a heart attack.

P: Yes, it must do you some damage. You hear of people dropping down dead from heart attacks caused by stress.

T: Do you think more people have stress in their lives than die of heart attacks?

P: Yes, I suppose so.

T: How can that be if stress causes heart attacks?

P: Well, I suppose it doesn't always cause problems. Maybe it does only in some people.

T: Yes, that's right; stress can cause some problems in some people. It tends to be people who have something wrong with their hearts in the first place. But stress is not necessarily the same as sudden anxiety or panic. When you panic your body releases adrenalin which causes the heart to speed up and your body to work faster. It's a way of preparing you to deal better with danger. If adrenalin damaged the heart or body, how would people have evolved from dangerous primitive times? Wouldn't we all have been wiped out?

P: Yes, I suppose so.

T: So maybe panic itself doesn't cause heart attacks, there has to be something physically wrong for that to happen. When people have had heart attacks they are often given an injection of adrenalin directly into the heart in order to help start it again. Do you think they would do that if it damaged the heart even more?

P: No, I'm sure they wouldn't.

T: So, how much do you now believe that anxiety and panic will damage your heart?

Source: Wells (1997), pp. 123–124

associated with panic, the client is then asked to apply cognitive and physical techniques designed to manage the attack (such as applying relaxation techniques). This enables the client to manage the attack under relatively 'safe' conditions, and to learn to exercise control over the cues that would normally predict panic (Craske, Maidenberg & Bystritsky, 1995).

Clearly, an important distinguishing feature of individuals with panic disorder is their fear of bodily sensations, their catastrophic misinterpretation of these sensations, and the effect these cognitions have in triggering a panic attack. The development of CBT for panic disorder has therefore focused specifically on providing clients with challenges to these beliefs in the form of both corrective information and experiences designed to eliminate faulty emotional responding (e.g. Clark, Salkovskis, Hackmann, Middleton et al., 1994; Telch, Lucas, Schmidt, Hanna et al., 1993; Luermans, De Cort, Scruers & Griez, 2004). A typical treatment programme would include:

1 Education about the nature and physiology of panic attacks.

2 Breathing training designed to control hyperventilation.

3 Cognitive restructuring therapy to identify and challenge faulty threat perceptions.

4 Interoceptive exposure to reduce fear of harmless bodily sensations.

5 Prevention of 'safety' behaviours that may maintain attacks and avoid disconfirmation of maladaptive threat beliefs.

SELF-TEST QUESTIONS

● Can you describe the main symptoms of a panic attack, and the diagnostic criteria for panic disorder?
● How does hyperventilation cause a panic attack?
● What role does the catastrophic misinterpretation of bodily sensations play in the acquisition and maintenance of panic disorder?
● Can psychological explanations of panic disorder explain more of the facts of panic disorder than biological explanations?
● What are the important features of cognitive behaviour therapy for panic disorder?

Such programmes have been shown to produce a durable reduction in symptoms and a significant increase in quality of life for panic disorder sufferers (Barlow, Gorman, Shear & Woods, 2000; Telch, Schmidt, Jaimez, Jacquin & Harrington, 1995). More recent studies have also suggested that such CBT programmes may be effective specifically because they significantly reduce the tendency to react fearfully to benign bodily sensations (Smits, Powers, Cho & Telch, 2004).

● The lifetime prevalence rate for panic disorder is between 1.5 and 3.5 per cent, although prevalence rates do differ between different cultures.

● **Hyperventilation** is a common feature of panic disorder, and some theorists have argued that the effect of hyperventilation on body CO_2 levels is a causal factor in the development of a panic attack.

● Individuals with panic disorder have high levels of **anxiety sensitivity**, which is a fear of anxiety symptoms.

● Individuals who develop panic disorder tend to **catastrophically misinterpret** bodily sensations and interpret them as signs of an imminent physical threat (e.g. an imminent heart attack signalled by a missed heartbeat). This cognitive bias leads to a vicious cycle which increases the anxiety symptoms that precipitate a panic attack.

● **Tricyclic antidepressants** and **benzodiazepines** are an effective first line treatment for panic disorder, but structured **exposure therapy** or **cognitive behaviour therapy** (CBT) is as effective, if not superior, to drug treatments over the longer term.

5.4 GENERALIZED ANXIETY DISORDER (GAD)

Generalized anxiety disorder (GAD) is a pervasive condition in which the sufferer experiences continual apprehension and anxiety about future events, which leads to chronic and pathological worrying about those events. We all worry about things to some degree – and, indeed, many people find it beneficial to think about how they might deal with challenging future events. However, worrying for the individual with GAD has a number of features that make it disabling and a source of extreme emotional discomfort. For example:

> **Generalised anxiety disorder (GAD)**
> A pervasive condition in which the sufferer experiences continual apprehension and anxiety about future events, which leads to chronic and pathological worrying about those events.

1 Worrying is a chronic and pathological activity that is directed not only to major life issues (e.g. health, finances, relationships, work-related matters), but also to many minor day-to-day issues and hassles that others would not perceive as threatening (Craske, Rapee, Jackel & Barlow, 1989; Tallis, Davey & Capuzzo, 1994).

2 Worrying is perceived as uncontrollable – individuals with GAD feel they cannot control either the onset or termination of a worry bout.

SECTION SUMMARY

5.3 Panic Disorder

● Panic disorder is characterized by repeated panic or anxiety attacks associated with a variety of physical symptoms, including heart palpitations, dizziness, perspiring, hyperventilation, nausea, trembling and depersonalization.

Table 5.9 *DSM-IV-TR criteria for diagnosing generalized anxiety disorder (GAD)*

A Excessive anxiety and worry (apprehensive expectation) occurring more days than not for at least 6 months, about a number of events or activities (such as work or school performance).

B The person finds it difficult to control the worry.

C The anxiety and worry are associated with three (or more) of the following six symptoms (with at least some symptoms present for more days than not for the past 6 months):

   (1) restlessness or feeling keyed up or on edge

   (2) being easily fatigued

   (3) difficulty concentrating or mind going blank

   (4) irritability

   (5) muscle tension

   (6) sleep disturbance

D The focus of the anxiety or worry is not confined to features of an Axis I disorder, e.g. the anxiety or worry is not about symptoms of other mental or physical disorders (e.g. having a panic attack in panic disorder).

E The anxiety, worry, or physical symptoms cause clinically significant distress or impairment in social, occupational, or other important areas of functioning.

F The disturbance is not due to the direct physiological effects of a substance or a general medical condition, and does not occur exclusively during a mood disorder, a psychotic disorder, or a pervasive developmental disorder.

Table 5.10 *Catastrophizing in worriers and non-worriers*

These catastrophizing sequences generated by a chronic worrier (top) and a non-worrier (bottom) were produced using the catastrophic interview procedure. The individual is first asked, 'What is your main worry at the moment?' In this case both participants replied, 'Getting good grades in school'. The interviewer then passes this response back to the participant by saying, 'What is it that worries you about getting good grades in school?' Each time the participant responds, the interviewer passes the response back by asking what it is about the response that worries the participant. The interview continues until the participant can no longer think of any reasons.

By looking at the catastrophizing sequences below, we can deduce a number of things about chronic worriers: (1) they produce significantly more catastrophizing steps than non-worriers; (2) they experience increasing emotional

Table 5.10 (Cont'd)

distress as catastrophizing continues, as evidenced by their 'discomfort' scores; and (3) the content of their catastrophizing steps becomes more and more threatening and catastrophic, as evidenced by their increasing 'likelihood' scores as catastrophizing progresses.

CHRONIC WORRIER

Topic: Getting good grades in school

Catastrophizing step	Discomfort	likelihood
I won't live up to my expectations.	50	30
I'd be disappointed in myself.	60	100
I'd lose my self-confidence.	70	50
My loss of self-confidence would spread to other areas of my life.	70	50
I wouldn't have as much control as I'd like.	75	80
I'd be afraid of facing the unknown.	75	100
I'd become very anxious.	75	100
Anxiety would lead to further loss of self-confidence.	75	80
I wouldn't get my confidence back.	75	50
I'd feel like I wouldn't have any control over my life.	75	80
I'd be susceptible to things that normally wouldn't bother me.	75	80
I'd become more and more anxious.	80	80
I'd have no control at all and I'd become mentally ill.	85	30
I'd become dependent on drugs and therapy.	50	30
I'd always remain dependent on drugs.	85	50
They'd deteriorate my body.	85	100
I'd be in pain.	85	100
I'd die.	90	80
I'd end up in hell.	95	80

NON-WORRIER

Topic: Getting good grades in school

Catastrophizing step		
I might do poorly on a test.	3	20
I'd get a bad grade in the class.	3	100
That would lower my grade-point average.	2	100
I'd have less of a chance of getting a good job.	2	60
I'd end up in a bad job.	2	80
I'd get a low salary.		
I'd have less money to spend on what I want.	2	100
	2	100
I'd be unhappy.	2	35
It would be a strain on me.	2	10
I'd worry more.	2	5

Source: Vasey & Borkovec (1992).

PEARLS BEFORE SWINE   **BY STEPHAN PASTIS**

Plate 5.4

Catastrophizing An example of magnification, in which the individual takes a single fact to its extreme (e.g. a scratch on a new car means the car is wrecked and needs replacing).

3 Worrying is closely associated with the **catastrophizing** of worries – that is, worry bouts persist for longer in GAD, they are associated with increasing levels of anxiety and distress as the bout continues, and worrying seems to make the problem *worse* rather than better (see Table 5.10). While pathological and chronic worrying is the cardinal diagnostic feature of GAD, it may also be accompanied by physical symptoms such as fatigue, trembling, muscle tension, headache and nausea.

GAD is diagnosed if:

- excessive anxiety and worry occur more days than not for a period of at least 6 months;
- the individual reports difficulty in controlling the worry;
- worry is accompanied by at least three additional symptoms from a list including irritability, muscle tension, being easily fatigued, difficulty concentrating, restlessness and disturbed sleep;
- finally, a consequence of these symptoms will be clinically significant distress or impairment in social, occupational or other important areas of functioning. (See Table 5.9.)

GAD is twice as common in women as in men, and can often persist from adolescence to old age (Barlow, Blanchard, Vermilyea, Vermilyea & DiNardo, 1986). Over 5 per cent of the population will be diagnosed with GAD at some point in their lifetime (Wittchen & Hoyer, 2001), and over 12 per cent of those who attend anxiety disorder clinics will present with symptoms typical of GAD (Kessler, Keller & Wittchen, 2001). GAD is also highly comorbid with a range of other anxiety disorders and with depression (Brown, O'Leary & Barlow, 2001).

5.4.1 The Aetiology of Generalized Anxiety Disorder (GAD)

The challenge in explaining GAD is to understand why some individuals worry chronically and pathologically, while many other individuals – often with more stressful lifestyles – worry significantly less. Theories will therefore have to explain why GAD sufferers persist with their worrying even when it causes them significant distress.

5.4.1.1 Biological Theories

There is some evidence for a genetic component in both anxiety generally and GAD specifically (Noyes, Woodman, Garvey, Cook et al., 1992), which suggests that GAD has an inherited component. However, although there is a familial component to GAD, the evidence of a specific genetic component is modest (Hettema, Neale & Kendler, 2001), and it is doubtful that the claim of GAD sufferers that they are 'born worriers' is defensible. Given this, the main theories of GAD have focused on psychological and cognitive features of the pathological worrier.

Information Processing Biases in GAD A good deal of research has now indicated that anxious individuals, and especially

Information processing biases Biases in interpreting, attending to, storing or recalling information which may give rise to dysfunctional thinking and behaving.

those suffering GAD, have a series of *information processing biases* which appear to maintain their hypervigilance for threat, create further sources for worry and maintain anxiety. For example, experimental evidence has demonstrated that individuals with GAD preferentially allocate attention to threatening stimuli and threatening information (Mogg & Bradley, 1998; Mathews & MacLeod, 1994). These types of studies have indicated that:

- Preferential allocation of attention to threatening stimuli occurs pre-attentively (i.e. prior to the anxious individual becoming consciously aware of the threat) (Mogg, Bradley, Williams & Mathews, 1993; Mogg, Bradley & Halliwell, 1994). (See Figure 5.5.)

- Preferential allocation occurs to both verbal stimuli and to pictures of threatening emotional faces (Bradley, Mogg, Falla & Hamilton, 1998; Bradley, Mogg, Millar, Bonham-Carter et al., 1997).

- The bias towards attending to threatening stimuli in anxious individuals is mirrored by the tendency of non-anxious individuals to attentionally *avoid* threat, i.e. to shift attention *away from* threatening stimuli (Bradley, Mogg, White et al., 1999; Mogg & Bradley, 1998).

There is accumulating evidence that attentional biases to threat may actually *cause* anxiety (rather than being simply an outcome or consequence of being anxious). For example, studies that have attempted to experimentally induce information processing biases in non-clinical populations have suggested that attentional and

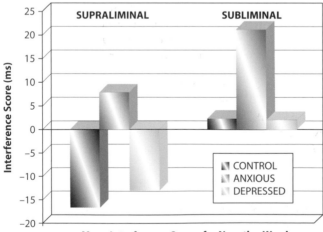

Mean Interference Scores for Negative Words

Figure 5.5
Anxious participants show the longest reaction times to name the colour of a threat word (the Emotional Stroop procedure – see Research Methods Box 5.2), suggesting that they have a tendency to prioritize the meaning of threat words. This is also the case when threat words are presented subliminally (right-hand figure), suggesting that this attentional bias occurs before the anxious individual is consciously aware of the meaning of the word.
Source: Mogg, Bradley, Williams & Mathews (1993).

ACTIVITY BOX 5.2

Interpretation biases and anxiety: The homophone spelling task

Homophones are words that sound the same but have different meanings. These types of words have been used to detect interpretation biases for threat in anxious individuals. For example, the homophones *Die/Dye* have different meanings, one of which is potentially negative or threatening. If anxious individuals are given auditory presentations of threat/neutral homophones and asked to spell the words they hear, they are more likely to write down the threatening rather than the neutral interpretation (Blanchette & Richards, 2003). This is evidence of a bias towards interpreting ambiguous information as threatening that is related to anxiety, and this bias can be found in most of the anxiety disorders.

Read out the following list of homophones to a fellow student (at the rate of about one every 2 seconds), and get him or her to spell the words as he or she hears them. How many does your participant spell in the threatening way? If your participant is anxious – perhaps because of an imminent exam – he or she is likely to respond with mainly threatening spellings.

Die/Dye
Pain/Pane
Patients/Patience
Mourn/Morn
Weak/Week
Bury/Berry
Groan/Grown
Flu/Flew
Slay/Sleigh
Tense/Tents
Tied/Tide
Ail/Ale
Wail/Whale
War/Wore
Flee/Flea

interpretative biases for threat may indeed have a causal effect on experienced anxiety and the processing of future information (Wilson, MacLeod, Mathews & Rutherford, 2006). These studies use a computer-based task to train participants to choose the threatening interpretations of ambiguous statements (see Activity Box 5.2). They have shown that experimentally induced processing biases for threat will not only cause corresponding changes in state anxiety, but also tend the individual to interpret new information in a threatening way (Mathews & MacLeod, 2002; Hertel, Mathews, Peterson & Kintner, 2003; Mathews & Mackintosh, 2000). These attentional biases in GAD appear to be part of a wider set of cognitive biases in anxious individuals, all of which appear to

RESEARCH METHODS IN CLINICAL PSYCHOLOGY BOX 5.2

The Emotional Stroop Procedure

During the 1980s and 1990s, clinical psychology borrowed a number of very useful experimental techniques from cognitive psychology that allowed researchers to investigate some of the important cognitive processes involved in anxiety and depression.

The Emotional Stroop is one such example. This procedure allows researchers to determine whether individuals with anxiety or depression have a bias towards attending to and processing anxiety-relevant or depression-relevant information (e.g. Mogg, Bradley, Williams & Mathews, 1993) – a factor that may maintain their anxious state.

In this procedure, participants are presented with individual words in coloured ink. Some of the words are anxiety- (or depression-) relevant words, and others are emotionally neutral words. For example:

DEATH (an anxiety-relevant word)
or
CARPET (a neutral word)

Participants have to name the *colour of the ink* as quickly as possible, and their reaction time is recorded.

The implication of this procedure is that if individuals automatically attend to the meaning of threatening words (such as death), then this will delay their processing the colour and responding to it. So, if there is an attentional bias to anxiety-relevant words, then reaction times to name the *colour* of the word will be slower with anxiety-related words than with neutral, control words.

Most Emotional Stroop studies and their associated procedures do indicate that individuals suffering anxiety have an attentional bias towards anxiety-relevant words and stimuli (including anxiety-relevant faces; Mogg, Millar & Bradley, 2000), and that this attentional bias occurs pre-attentively (i.e. before the individual becomes consciously aware of the meaning of the word).

---

facilitate threatening interpretations of on-going and future events, focus attention on threat-related events and make this information processing bias resistant to change (Davey, 2006c).

Cognitions, Beliefs and the Function of Worrying

We mentioned earlier that individuals with GAD persist chronically with their worrying even though it causes them considerable distress and generates symptoms that disrupt normal day-to-day living. This suggests that worrying may serve a particular *function* for such individuals, and this functionality may outweigh the negative effects of their worrying. Some theories of GAD emphasize this functional aspect of worrying. First, both pathological worriers and individuals diagnosed with GAD hold strong beliefs that worrying is a necessary process that must be undertaken fully and properly in order to avoid future catastrophes (Davey, Tallis & Capuzzo, 1996; Wells, 2006b; Borkovec, Hazlett-Stevens & Diaz, 1999). These dysfunctional beliefs about the utility of worrying appear to motivate worriers to persist with their worrying (see Table 5.11). Secondly, there is growing evidence that worrying may indeed be reinforced because it distracts the worrier from experiencing other negative emotions and processing even more stressful phobic images. That is, worry is an internal narrative process that prevents the individual from processing other – often more stressful – information (Borkovec, 1994; Borkovec & Lyonfields, 1993). Evidence to support this view comes from the fact that worry produces very little physiological or emotional arousal (Hoehn-Saric & McLeod, 1988) and appears to block the processing of emotional images (Borkovec, Lyonfields, Wiser & Diehl, 1993).

Dispositional Characteristics of Worrying

While there is still some way to go in understanding the psychological and developmental processes that lead to individuals becoming pathological worriers, there is a good deal of knowledge available about what kinds of psychological features they possess. For example, worriers are intolerant of uncertainty (Ladouceur, Talbot & Dugas, 1997), are high on perfectionism (Pratt, Tallis & Eysenck, 1997) and have feelings of responsibility for negative outcomes (Startup & Davey, 2003; Wells & Papageorgiou, 1998). All of this suggests that they possess characteristics that will drive them to attempt to think about resolving problematic issues. However, worriers also have poor problem-solving confidence (Davey, 1994c) and couch their worries in ways that reflect personal inadequacies and insecurities (Davey & Levy, 1998). This contrasting combination of characteristics appears to drive individuals to try to resolve problems, but the process is thwarted by their personal doubt about their own ability to solve them successfully (Davey, 1994d).

5.4.2 The Treatment of Generalized Anxiety Disorder (GAD)

As with most of the anxiety disorders, GAD can be treated either with drugs or with structured psychological therapy such as CBT, or with a combination of both. However, deciding what type of treatment to use is often the most important decision for service

Table 5.11 *Dysfunctional beliefs in pathological worriers*

A number of studies indicate that pathological worriers and individuals with GAD possess a very strong and stable set of beliefs about worry as an important activity to indulge in – largely because they believe that if they do *not* worry, then bad things will happen to them.

The following are some of the positive beliefs that individuals diagnosed with GAD hold about worry as a necessary thing to do:

- 'Worry helps to motivate me to get things done that I need to get done.' (Motivation)

- 'Worrying is an effective way to problem solve.' (Problem solving)

- 'If I worry about something, when something bad does happen, I'll be better prepared for it.' (Preparation)

- 'If I worry about something, I am more likely to actually figure out how to avoid or prevent something bad from happening.' (Avoidance/Prevention)

- 'Worrying about most of the things I worry about is a way to distract myself from worrying about even more emotional things, things that I don't want to think about.' (Distraction from more emotional topics)

- 'Although it may not actually be true, it feels like if I worry about something, the worrying makes it less likely that something bad will happen.' (Superstition)

Individuals with GAD hold these beliefs more strongly than non-anxious individuals, and they drive the individual with GAD to worry chronically (Borkovec, Hazlett-Stevens & Diaz, 1999).

Source: Borkovec & Roemer (1995).

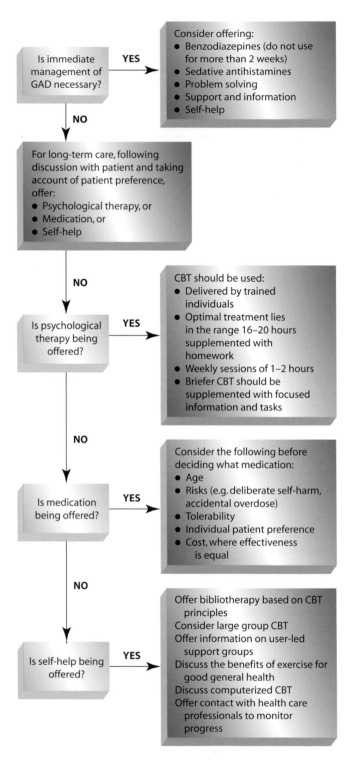

Figure 5.6
Primary care management of individuals with GAD.

providers and therapists – especially for a disorder that is as prevalent as GAD. The UK National Institute for Clinical Excellence (NICE) has made some recommendations about how decisions should be made for treating GAD in primary care. These are outlined in Figure 5.6. Medication is recommended if immediate management of the problem is important (if the patient is experiencing extreme distress or has suicidal ideation). Otherwise, longer-term structured psychological therapy (such as CBT) or self-help programmes should be offered. This decision tree shows that comparisons of different types of therapy (e.g. drug vs. psychological therapy) are not just about their relative effectiveness over the long term, but also concern their value at various points in treatment, taking into account the patient's preferences and the severity of the symptoms.

5.4.2.1 Pharmacological Treatment

Because GAD involves chronic daily anxiety and emotional discomfort, anxiolytics – such as the benzodiazepines – are usually the first line of treatment for sufferers. Studies show that they are a more effective treatment for sufferers than placebo controls (Apter & Allen, 1999).

5.4.2.2 Stimulus Control Treatment

One of the earliest behavioural interventions for worry in GAD adopted the principle of stimulus control. This is based on the conditioning principle that the environments in which behaviours are enacted come to control the future occurrence of those

CLINICAL PERSPECTIVE: TREATMENT IN PRACTICE BOX 5.4

Stimulus control treatment for GAD

Stimulus control treatment for GAD is an effective treatment for reducing the frequency of worry by controlling the range of contexts in which the activity occurs (see section 5.4.2.2).

There are four basic instructions underpinning this procedure:

1 Learn to identify worrisome thoughts and other thoughts that are unnecessary or unpleasant. Distinguish these from necessary or pleasant thoughts related to the present moment.

2 Establish a half-hour worry period to take place at the same time and in the same location each day.

3 When you catch yourself worrying, postpone the worry to the worry period and replace it with attending to present-moment experience.

4 Make use of the half-hour worry period to worry about your concerns and to engage in problem solving to eliminate those concerns.

Source: Borkovec (2005); Borkovec, Wilkinson, Folensbee & Lerman (1983)

---

behaviours, and can act to elicit them (the principle of stimulus control). Because worrying can occur almost anywhere, and so come under the control of a vast range of contexts, the first aim of *stimulus control treatment* is to limit the contexts in which worrying occurs. This is achieved by telling clients that they can worry – but only for a specific period in a particular location each day (Borkovec, Wilkinson, Folensbee & Lerman, 1983). For example, they are instructed to worry at a specific time (e.g. between waking and the end of breakfast) or in a particular location (the living room).

> **Stimulus control treatment** An early behavioural intervention for worry in GAD which adopted the principle of stimulus control. This is based on the conditioning principle that the environments in which behaviours are enacted come to control their future occurrence and can act to elicit those behaviours (the principle of stimulus control).

5.4.2.3 Cognitive Behaviour Therapy

In the previous section we reviewed a number of psychological theories of GAD which suggest that cognitive biases and dysfunctional beliefs about the function of worrying may be central to the development and maintenance of the disorder. This being so, integrated cognitive behavioural therapy seems a suitable method to tackle GAD. CBT for GAD normally consists of a number of elements, the main ones being:

- self-monitoring
- relaxation training
- cognitive restructuring
- behavioural rehearsal

Self-monitoring involves making clients aware of their fixed patterns of behaviour and the triggers that may precipitate worry. These triggers are often thoughts about future events that have very low probabilities of happening (e.g. the accidental death of a loved one while driving to work), and the client's attention is drawn to the fact that these are cognitively constructed rather than real events. *Relaxation training* is an obvious way of dealing with the chronic stress experienced by GAD sufferers. The specific technique of progressive muscular relaxation is often used (Bernstein, Borkovec & Hazlett-Stevens, 2000), and relaxation is found to be as effective as some forms of cognitive therapy (Arntz, 2003).

Cognitive restructuring methods are used to challenge the biases that GAD sufferers hold about how frequently bad events might happen (Beck, Emery & Greenberg, 1985) and to generate thoughts that are more accurate (Borkovec, 2005). One way of doing this is by using an outcome diary in which clients write down on a daily basis their worries and how likely they think the focus of their worries will actually happen. Clients can then compare their own inflated estimate of the likelihood of the event with subsequent reality (Borkovec, Hazlett-Stevens & Diaz, 1999). Other types of cognitive restructuring involve the challenging and replacement of dysfunctional beliefs about the advantages of worrying (Wells, 1999) or the belief held by pathological worriers that uncertainty has to be resolved by thinking through every possible scenario (Dugas, Ladouceur, Leger, Freeston et al., 2003).

Finally, *behavioural rehearsal* involves either the actual or imagined rehearsal of adaptive coping responses that need to be deployed when a worry trigger is encountered. These coping strategies may involve the deployment of relaxation

> **Relaxation training** A method of dealing with the chronic stress experienced by psychopathology sufferers. A specific technique of progressive muscular relaxation is often used, and relaxation is found to be as effective as some forms of cognitive therapy.

> **Cognitive restructuring** Methods used to challenge the biases that a client might hold about how frequently bad events might happen and to generate thoughts that are more accurate.

> **Behavioural rehearsal** A coping strategy that involves either the actual or imagined rehearsal of adaptive coping responses that need to be deployed when a worry trigger is encountered.

> **Self-monitoring** A form of clinical observation which involves asking clients to observe and record their own behaviour, to note when certain behaviours or thoughts occur, and in what contexts they occur.

SELF-TEST QUESTIONS

- What is the cardinal diagnostic feature of GAD?
- What are the features of worry in GAD that make it a distressing experience for the sufferer?
- How do information processing biases and cognitive factors contribute to the acquisition, maintenance and experience of anxiety in GAD?
- How do psychological treatments of GAD attempt to bring the activity of worrying under control?

exercises or pleasant distracting activities designed to avoid worry (Butler, Fennell, Robson & Gelder, 1991). CBT for GAD has been shown to be effective with or without the use of pharmacological treatments (Lang, 2004) and has long-term effectiveness for a significant proportion of clients (Durham, Chambers, MacDonald, Power & Major, 2003).

SECTION SUMMARY

5.4 Generalized Anxiety Disorder (GAD)

- The cardinal diagnostic characteristic of GAD is chronic uncontrollable worrying, which is accompanied by physical symptoms such as irritability, muscle tension, fatigue, poor concentration, restlessness and disturbed sleep.

- Over 5 per cent of the population will be diagnosed with GAD in their lifetime, and 12 per cent of those who attend anxiety disorder clinics will present with GAD.

- Individuals with GAD possess an **information processing bias** which appears to maintain their hypervigilance for threat and create the opportunity to catastrophically worry about events. There is evidence that these information processing biases may actually cause anxiety generally.

- Worrying in GAD appears to be maintained by **dysfunctional beliefs** about the utility of worrying which appear to motivate individuals with GAD to persist with their worrying.

- **Anxiolytics** are useful for dealing with the anxiety symptoms exhibited by individuals with GAD, but treatments based on controlling the process of worrying and challenging dysfunctional beliefs about worrying appear to have more longer-term benefit.

5.5 OBSESSIVE-COMPULSIVE DISORDER (OCD)

We have all occasionally gone back to check whether we locked a door or have experienced a sudden, intrusive thought that we find disturbing and out of place (e.g. harming our own child). However, for the person with *obsessive-compulsive disorder (OCD)*, such thoughts and actions are repeated often and result in a distressing and disabling way of life (see Client's Perspective Box 5.2). OCD has two important and sometimes independent characteristics, obsessions and compulsions.

Obsessions are intrusive and recurring thoughts that the individual finds disturbing and uncontrollable. These obsessive thoughts frequently take the form of causing some harm or distress to oneself or to some important other person (such as a partner or offspring). Common obsessions take the form of fear of contamination (i.e. contaminating oneself or important others), fear of directly or indirectly causing physical harm to others, and fears of expressing some immoral, sexual or aggressive impulse. Obsessive thoughts can also take the form of pathological doubting and indecision, and this may lead to sufferers developing repetitive behaviour patterns such as compulsive checking or washing.

Compulsions represent repetitive or ritualized behaviour patterns that the individual feels driven to perform in order to prevent some negative outcome happening. This can take the form of ritualized and persistent checking of doors and windows (to ensure that the house is safe), or ritualized washing activities designed to prevent infection and contamination. Ritualized compulsions such as these also act to reduce the stress and anxiety caused by the sufferer's obsessive fears. Whilst the main compulsions are usually related to checking or washing, OCD can also manifest itself less regularly as compulsive hoarding (Steketee, Frost & Kyrios, 2003), superstitious ritualized movements or the systematic arranging of objects (Radomsky & Rachman, 2004). In most cases compulsions are clearly excessive, and are usually recognized as such by the sufferer. Rituals can become rigid, stereotyped sequences of behaviours which the individual is driven to perform as a result of cognitive triggers such as intrusive thoughts related to the individual's specific fears. For example, individuals distressed by unwanted immoral or blasphemous thoughts can attempt to suppress the thought and reduce anxiety by indulging in compulsive acts such as counting backwards from a number until the thought has gone.

Table 5.12 shows the main DSM-IV-TR diagnostic criteria for OCD. Diagnosis is dependent on the obsessions or compulsions causing marked distress, being time consuming or significantly interfering with the person's normal daily living. This latter diagnostic criterion delineates OCD compulsions from other urges, such as the uncontrollable desire to eat, drink or gamble, because the latter are often engaged in with pleasure (see Chapters 8 and 9 for discussions of these alternative types of compulsions).

Obsessive-compulsive disorder (OCD) A disorder characterized either by obsessions (intrusive and recurring thoughts that the individual finds disturbing and uncontrollable) or by compulsions (ritualized behaviour patterns that the individual feels driven to perform in order to prevent some negative outcome happening).

Obsessions Intrusive and recurring thoughts that an individual finds disturbing and uncontrollable.

Compulsions Repetitive or ritualized behaviour patterns that an individual feels driven to perform in order to prevent some negative outcome happening.

CLIENT'S PERSPECTIVE 5.2

Obsessive-compulsive disorder (OCD)

The following accounts describe the experiences of two individuals who have suffered different forms of obsessive-compulsive disorder. The first exhibits washing compulsions and superstitious avoidance rituals, while the second experiences persistent obsessive and intrusive thoughts that cause considerable distress.

'I first remember hand washing when I was about 4. My mother had died of cancer the year before – also my cousin and playmate, and my dog. I think that gave me some sense of having to DO something to ward off death. Then I had nose twitching for a while at about 11.

Then in school a guy I despised sneezed on me at 44 minutes after the hour and I thought I changed identity with him. Ever since I've had a superstitious avoidance of 44. It has popped up and frozen me in fear. Then I started to say my best friend's name like a mantra to offset anything bad. In the navy I didn't want to stand on the centerline of the ship. Thus began my avoidance of symmetry. It happens all day. I look like I've seen a ghost – the fear is so great.'

'Basically what I'm dealing with right now are these weird thoughts. I'll be sitting with someone, like my mum for instance, who I am very close to, and just think "I wish she would die, or I wish you would die" when I don't think I mean it. But then what happens is I start wondering if I really do mean it. Another thing, someone will say something horrible, like "I just found out my mum has cancer" and I'll immediately think "I wish my mum had cancer" when of course I don't wish that. Recently I had a huge breakdown. I started believing I actually wanted to harm my mother. I thought I was going to stab her with a knife and actually thought I might do it. At one point I even said to myself in my head, you should just do it. I got so scared I went straight to the doctor that day. This thought made me so sick I lost all this weight, couldn't sleep. All because I couldn't figure out how you know if you really want to kill someone. It sounds so crazy but I actually thought, how do I know if I really love her or if I don't? How do I know I won't just pick up a knife and stab her? I thought I had become a sociopath or something.'

Source: www.stuckinadoorway.co.uk/

Table 5.12 *The main DSM-IV-TR diagnostic criteria for obsessive-compulsive disorder*

Obsessions are defined as:

(1) Recurrent and persistent thoughts, impulses, or images that are experienced, at some time during the disturbance, as intrusive and inappropriate and that cause marked anxiety or distress.

(2) The thoughts, impulses, or images are not simply excessive worries about real-life problems.

(3) The person attempts to ignore or suppress such thoughts, impulses, or images, or to neutralize them with some other thought or action.

(4) The person recognizes that the obsessional thoughts, impulses, or images are a product of his or her own mind (not imposed from without as in thought insertion).

Compulsions are defined as:

(1) Repetitive behaviours (e.g. hand washing, ordering, checking) or mental acts (e.g. praying, counting, repeating words silently) that the person feels driven to perform in response to an obsession, or according to rules that must be applied rigidly.

(2) The behaviours or mental acts are aimed at preventing or reducing distress or preventing some dreaded event or situation; however, these behaviours or mental acts either are not connected in a realistic way with what they are designed to neutralize or prevent or are clearly excessive.

Plate 5.5
Film star Leonardo DiCaprio has revealed he suffers from obsessive-compulsive disorder. The *Titanic* star says he has to force himself not to step on every chewing gum stain when walking along and fight urges to walk through a doorway several times, because he doesn't want his condition taking over his life.

CASE HISTORY 5.2

Obsessive-compulsive disorder

Catherine was 28 years old. It was a week before her wedding. The alarm went off at 7.00 a.m. as usual. She turned to switch it off, and was immediately overwhelmed by the feeling of dread that had been her constant companion for the past 6 months.

She went to the bathroom and washed her hands. She stepped inside the shower and started to wash herself, washing her hands repeatedly between washing different parts of her body. Three-quarters of an hour later she emerged, gathered up her nightwear and towel and dumped them in the washing machine. Her hands felt dirty again so she returned to the bathroom to clean them. By now her hands were washed red raw so she rubbed in some moisturizer. They didn't feel as clean and she felt a strong urge to wash them once more. She looked at her reflection in the mirror and told herself not to be so stupid, that she would be late for work again if she didn't get a move on. But she couldn't resist the urge. She quickly washed her hands and hurried into the kitchen, kicking the door open to avoid contact with the germ-ridden doorknob.

After breakfast – and several more hand washes – she systematically went from room to room locking and checking all the doors and windows. Finally she stepped outside the house. By now she was already late for work but thought she'd better go back inside and check everything one more time, just to be sure. When this was done, she got into her car and drove down the street. Before she reached the end of the road she wondered if she had locked the front door properly. Back she went and checked the handle five more times.

She had almost reached her workplace when she was suddenly plagued by the idea that she might have accidentally hit a cyclist. She mentally retraced her steps. She remembered driving past a few cyclists but certainly didn't notice that she had hit any of them at the time. However, just to be on the safe side, she decided to drive round the block again. It came as no surprise when she didn't see any injured cyclists lying on the road and she cursed herself for giving in to such an irrational idea.

When she finally pulled up outside her place of work she looked at her watch and saw that, yet again, she was unacceptably late. Work started at 8.30 a.m. not 10.30 a.m.

Catherine was diagnosed as having obsessive-compulsive disorder in 1994. Her diagnosis came as a relief. At least now she knew she wasn't going crazy and that the behaviour that had inexplicably taken over her life had a name and was treatable. While her family was generally supportive she said the majority of people didn't understand. 'A lot of people around me were shocked but felt I should just get over it, they couldn't see any logical reason for the behaviour or the distress.'

Source: www.ocd.org.nz/personal_story.htm

Clinical Commentary

This example shows how obsessions and compulsions in OCD are often compelling and difficult for the sufferer to resist – even when the individual is aware that these thoughts and actions are 'stupid' or irrational. Catherine's compulsions are fuelled by the 'feelings of dread' that she experiences most mornings when she wakes up, and this provides the highly anxious state under which compulsions (such as compulsive washing) are performed. 'Doubting' is also a common feature of OCD, and Catherine experiences this more than once on her way to work (in the form of doubting whether the door is locked or whether she may have hit a cyclist on her way to work). The high levels of inflated responsibility usually possessed by OCD sufferers such as Catherine means that they are driven to continually check that their doubts are unfounded.

5.5.1 Prevalence

OCD onset is usually gradual and frequently begins to manifest itself in early adolescence or early adulthood following a stressful event such as pregnancy, childbirth, relationship or work problems (Kringlen, 1970). Lifetime prevalence is around 2.5 per cent, with a 1-year prevalence rate of 1.5–2.1 per cent, and women are marginally more frequently affected than men (Stein, Forde, Anderson et al., 1997). Few studies have investigated the effect of cultural factors on the prevalence and manifestation of OCD symptoms. However, a cross-cultural study reported by Fontenelle, Mendlowicz, Marques and Versiani (2004) concluded that universal characteristics of sufferers regardless of cultural background included a predominance of females, a relatively early age of onset and a preponderance of mixed obsessions and compulsions. The exception to this was the apparent content of obsessions, with Brazilian and Middle Eastern samples exhibiting a predominance of aggressive or religious obsessions (compared with North America, Europe and Africa).

5.5.2 The Aetiology of Obsessive-Compulsive Disorder

When considering the aetiology of OCD, readers should be aware that it represents a psychological problem that possesses a number of quite different, and often independent, features. For example, obsessions do not always occur with compulsions, and the two main types of compulsions (washing and checking) rarely occur together in the same individual. This means that many theories of the aetiology of OCD have been developed to address only some of its features (e.g. thought suppression accounts are relevant to explaining only obsessive thoughts) and are not meant to be universal explanations of OCD. Bear this in mind when reading through the following sections.

5.5.2.1 Biological Factors

Onset of OCD can be associated with traumatic brain injury or encephalitis (Jenike, 1986), which suggests that there may be a neurophysiological deficit in some forms of OCD. This neurophysiological deficit may give rise to the 'doubting' that things have been done properly that is a central feature of many forms of OCD. Areas of the brain that have been identified as important in this respect include the frontal lobes and the basal ganglia. When sufferers are shown stimuli representative of their obsession or compulsion (e.g. an unlocked door), blood flow increases in both the frontal lobes and the basal ganglia, suggesting that these areas may have at least some role in OCD (Rauch, Jenike, Alpert, Baer et al., 1994).

In other neuropsychological studies OCD sufferers appear to demonstrate a variety of basic information processing and executive functioning deficits (the latter refers to processes that are involved in planning and attentional control), including deficits in spatial working memory, spatial recognition, visual attention, visual memory and motor response initiation (Greisberg & McKay, 2003). However, while such executive deficits may contribute to 'doubting' that something has been done properly, they do not necessarily indicate that neurophysiological deficits play a causal role in OCD.

Traditional neuropsychological studies have tended to rely on intensive study of individuals with known brain lesions and investigated the effect of these lesions on executive functions related to OCD. However, because such lesions may result in symptoms similar to those found in OCD, it does not mean that all OCD sufferers possess such lesions. An alternative view of brain dysfunction and OCD is based on findings from neuroimaging studies. For example, Rapoport (1989) has argued that obsessions and compulsions are genetically stored and learned behaviours that are involuntarily triggered by the brain. Baxter, Ackerman, Swerdlow, Brody et al. (2000) have developed this approach by suggesting that uncontrollable compulsions in OCD result from the brain being unable to inhibit these genetically stored behaviours. In particular, they use evidence from neuroimaging studies to argue that OCD compulsions result from the failure of inhibitory pathways projecting via the basal ganglia to inhibit innate behaviour patterns (Saxena, Brody, Schwartz et al., 1998). While this hypothesis can account for the rather restricted set of behaviours that manifest as compulsions (i.e. it is argued that only certain behaviours have been genetically stored), it still represents an oversimplification of how brain structures such as the basal ganglia might be involved in OCD (Frampton, 2003).

5.5.2.2 Psychological Factors

Memory Deficits 'Doubting' is a central feature of OCD, and especially the compulsions associated with the disorder. As a result, it has been suggested that OCD may be characterized by memory deficits that give rise to the doubting that, for example, doors have been locked or hands have been washed properly. Memory deficit models take a number of different forms. It has been suggested that OCD sufferers may have:

- a general memory deficit (Sher, Mann & Frost, 1984);
- less confidence in the validity of their memories (Sheffler-Rubenstein, Peynircioglu, Chambless & Pigott, 1993); or
- a deficit in the ability to distinguish between the memory of real and imagined actions (Brown, Kosslyn, Breiter, Baer & Jenike, 1994).

However, while OCD sufferers do claim to have doubts about their recollection of having either checked or washed properly, recent evidence suggests that lack of confidence in recall may be a *consequence* of compulsive checking or washing rather than a cause of it (van den Hout & Kindt, 2003; Tolin et al., 2001). In effect, the more someone checks, the less confident that person will be about what he or she has checked.

Inflated Responsibility Everyone experiences uncontrollable intrusive thoughts on almost a daily basis (Rachman & DeSilva, 1978). However, what differentiates these normal intrusive thoughts from the distressing and obsessive thoughts experienced in OCD is the meaning attached to them by OCD sufferers. Individuals diagnosed with OCD appear to have developed a series of dysfunctional beliefs about their obsessional thoughts. For example:

1 Because they had the thought, they feel responsible for its content – so, if a sufferer thinks of murdering his child, he believes he may be going crazy and *will* murder his child (Salkovskis, 1985).

2 Sufferers appraise obsessional thoughts as having potentially harmful consequences. This causes intense anxiety and triggers compulsive actions designed to eradicate the thought or to make sure that the perceived harm does not occur (e.g. compulsive thought suppression strategies such as counting backwards or checking and rechecking locks and windows to ensure that the home is safe).

3 Individuals with OCD tend to have inflated conceptions of their own responsibility for preventing harm. This *inflated responsibility* appears to be an important vulnerability factor in developing OCD (Salkovkis, 1985; Rachman, 1998).

> **Inflated responsibility** The belief that one has power to bring about or prevent subjectively crucial negative outcomes. These outcomes are perceived as essential to prevent. They may be actual, that is, having consequences in the real world, and/or at a moral level.

Salkovskis, Rachman, Ladouceur, Freeston et al. (1996) have defined inflated responsibility as 'the belief that one has power which is pivotal to bring about or prevent subjectively crucial

Table 5.13 *Inflated responsibility and the Responsibility Attitude Scale*

Inflated responsibility is a central characteristic of individuals diagnosed with OCD and appears to be an important precipitating factor in the disorder. Below are some items from the Responsibility Attitude Scale (RAS) (Salkovskis et al., 2000) designed to measure responsibility-related beliefs as they apply to OCD. This will give you some idea of the beliefs that make up the construct of inflated responsibility.

1 I often feel responsible for things that go wrong.

2 If I don't act when I can foresee danger, then I am to blame for any consequences if it happens.

3 If I think bad things, this is as bad as DOING bad things.

4 I worry a great deal about the effects of things that I do or don't do.

5 To me, not acting to prevent disaster is as bad as making disasters happen.

6 I must always think through the consequences of even the smallest actions.

7 I often take responsibility for things that other people do not think are my fault.

8 Everything I do can cause serious problems.

9 I must protect others from harm.

10 If I can have even a slight influence on things going wrong, then I must act to prevent it.

11 For me, even slight carelessness is inexcusable when it might affect others.

12 Even if harm is a very unlikely possibility, I should always try to prevent it at any cost.

13 I have to make sure other people are protected from all of the consequences of things I do.

14 If I take sufficient care, then I can prevent any harmful accidents.

15 I often think that bad things will happen if I am not careful enough.

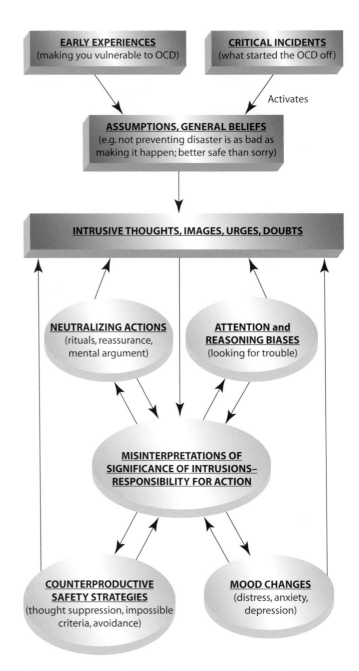

Figure 5.7 *A cognitive model of OCD proposed by Salkovskis, Wroe, Gledhill, Morrison et al. (2000).*
This model highlights the importance of a number of factors in maintaining obsessive-compulsive symptoms. These include (1) misinterpreting the importance and meaning of intrusive thoughts, (2) inflated responsibility for negative outcomes and (3) the role of rituals and neutralizing actions in maintaining obsessive thoughts and compulsive actions.

negative outcomes. These outcomes are perceived as essential to prevent. They may be actual, that is having consequences in the real world, and/or at a moral level.' (See Table 5.13.) There is considerable evidence that inflated responsibility is a characteristic that is a central causal feature of obsessive-compulsive disorder generally (Salkovskis, Shafran, Rachman & Freeston, 1999; Salkovskis, Wroe, Gledhill, Morrison et al., 2000) and compulsive checking specifically (Rachman, 2002; Bouchard, Rheaume & Ladouceur, 1999). Experimental studies that have manipulated inflated responsibility have shown that it *causes* increases in perseverative activities such as compulsive checking (Lopatka & Rachman, 1995; Bouchard, Rheaume & Ladouceur, 1999).

Figure 5.7 shows a schematic representation of a cognitive behavioural model of OCD which incorporates both the misinterpretation of the significance of intrusions by sufferers and their

perceived responsibility for any negative or harmful outcomes (Salkovskis, Shafran, Rachman & Freeston, 1999). This model assumes that the dysfunctional beliefs that characterize OCD patients are learned over long periods from childhood onwards, and may be formed as a result of extreme events or circumstances. The dysfunctional assumptions held by OCD sufferers include the following:

Thought-action fusion A dysfunctional assumption held by OCD sufferers that having a thought about an action is like performing it.

1 having a thought about an action is like performing it (this is known as ***thought–action fusion***; Shafran & Rachman, 2004);

2 failing to prevent harm to oneself or others is the same as having caused the harm in the first place;

3 responsibility is not reduced by other factors such as something being improbable;

4 not trying to neutralize or suppress an intrusive thought is equivalent to wanting the harm involved in the thought to happen; and

5 one should always try to exercise control over one's thoughts (Salkovskis & McGuire, 2003).

The fact that such dysfunctional beliefs are held by OCD sufferers and that they appear to contribute significantly to the symptoms of the disorder makes them a promising target for cognitive behavioural treatment interventions (see below).

Thought Suppression Because individuals with obsessive thoughts find these intrusions aversive and distressing, they may try to actively suppress them (using either ***thought suppression*** or distraction techniques). However, there is good evidence that actively suppressing an unwanted thought will actually cause it to occur more frequently once the period of suppression or inhibition is over (known as a 'rebound' effect; see Figure 5.8). This may account to some degree for the fact that OCD sufferers experience significantly more intrusions than non-clinical populations (Wenzlaff & Wegner, 2000). Wenzlaff, Klein and Wegner (1991) have also argued that suppressing an unpleasant thought induces a strong negative emotional state that results in the suppressed thought becoming associated with that negative mood state. Whenever that negative mood state occurs in the future, it is therefore more likely to elicit the unwanted and aversive thought, and this may also contribute to the OCD sufferer's experiencing regular, uncontrollable intrusions.

Thought suppression A defence mechanism used by individuals with obsessive thoughts to actively suppress them (using either thought suppression or distraction techniques).

Perseveration and the Role of Mood OCD is one example of a number of perseverative psychopathologies, each of which is characterized by the dysfunctional perseveration of certain thoughts, behaviours or activities (others include pathological worrying and chronic rumination in depression). In almost all examples of these psychopathologies, the perseveration (e.g. compulsive checking, washing) is viewed as excessive, out of proportion to the functional purpose that it serves, and a source of emotional discomfort for the individual concerned. In this context, some theories have attempted to explain why OCD sufferers *persevere* at an activity for significantly longer than non-sufferers. One such account is the ***mood-as-input hypothesis***

Mood-as-input hypothesis A hypothesis claiming that people use their concurrent mood as information about whether they have successfully completed a task or not.

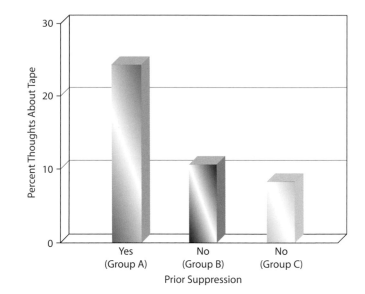

Figure 5.8 *The 'rebound' effect.*
After listening to a tape of a recorded story, participants were asked to verbalize their stream of conscious. However, participants in one group (Group A) were asked to suppress their thoughts of the tape during this period, while other participants were not (Groups B and C). In the final period, all participants were asked to think about anything. The figure shows that participants in the suppression condition subsequently reported more thoughts about the tape than participants in the other groups (a 'rebound' effect).
Source: Clark, Ball & Pape (1991).

(Martin & Davies, 1998; Davey, 2006b; MacDonald & Davey, 2005a). This model states that OCD sufferers persevere with their compulsive activities because (1) they use an implicit 'stop rule' for the compulsive activity which says they must only stop when they are sure they have completed the task fully and properly (known as an 'as many as can' stop rule); and (2) they undertake the task in a strong negative mood (usually an anxious mood). The mood-as-input account claims that OCD sufferers use their concurrent mood as 'information' to assess whether they have met their strict stop rule criteria. However, their endemic negative mood is interpreted as providing information that they have *not* completed the task properly – so they persevere (i.e. a negative mood implies all is not well and the criteria have not been met). This model is supported by the fact that the inflated responsibility that OCD sufferers possess is likely to give rise to deployed 'as many as can' stop rules (to ensure that, for example, checking or washing is done properly so that no harm will ensue) (Startup & Davey, 2003). Interestingly, and consistent with the mood-as-input account, inflated responsibility is not a *sufficient* condition for an individual to persevere at a compulsive activity – it has to be accompanied by negative mood (MacDonald & Davey, 2005b). This is because a negative mood is continually being interpreted as providing feedback that the important goals of the compulsive activity have not been met, so the activity needs to be continued.

SUMMARY

As we mentioned at the outset of this section on aetiology, many of these theories are designed to address only specific features of OCD rather than represent universal explanations of the disorder. For example, some theories try to explain why 'doubting' is a central feature of OCD (these include both neurophysiological and memory deficit models), others address why intrusive thoughts become so aversive and uncontrollable (e.g. inflated responsibility and thought suppression accounts), and yet others try to explain why individuals with OCD show dysfunctional perseveration at activities such as checking or washing (e.g. the mood-as-input model). Undoubtedly, a full account of OCD will contain at least some, if not all, of these different elements of explanation.

5.5.3 The Treatment of Obsessive-Compulsive Disorder

5.5.3.1 Exposure and Ritual Prevention Treatments (EPR)

The most common, and arguably the most successful, treatment for OCD is *exposure and ritual prevention* (ERP, also known as exposure and response prevention) (Meyer, 1966; Kyrios, 2003). This therapy consists of two components. The first is graded exposure to the situations and thoughts that trigger distress – for example, for someone with compulsive washing, this may involve touching a dirty dish or imagining touching a dirty dish (the latter is called imaginal exposure). Clients will encounter their triggers in a graded and planned way until distress levels have significantly decreased. The second component is ritual or response prevention, which involves strategies such as practising competing behaviours, habit reversal or modification of compulsive rituals (see Treatment in Practice Box 5.5). Preventing clients from engaging in their rituals:

Exposure and ritual prevention treatments A means of treatment for obsessive-compulsive disorder (OCD) which involves graded exposure to the thoughts that trigger distress, followed by the development of behaviours designed to prevent the individual's compulsive rituals.

1 allows anxiety to extinguish by habituating the links between obsessions and their associated distress;

2 eliminates ritualistic behaviours that may negatively reinforce anxiety (Steketee, 1993);

3 contributes to the disconfirmation of dysfunctional beliefs (e.g. 'I will catch an infectious disease if I touch a dirty cup') by forcing clients to encounter feared situations and experiencing the reality of the outcomes associated with that action.

ERP is a highly flexible therapy that can be adapted to group, self-help, inpatient, outpatient, family therapy and computer-guided interventions (Fischer, Himle & Hanna, 1998; Grayson, 1999; Wetzel, Bents & Florin, 1999; Hand, 1998; Nakagawa, Marks, Park, Bachofen et al., 2000). Controlled outcome studies suggest that ERP is a long-term effective treatment for around 75 per cent of clients treated with ERP (Franklin & Foa, 1998; Kyrios, 2003).

5.5.3.2 Cognitive Behaviour Therapy (CBT)

Although ERP has been the treatment of choice for OCD for over 20 years, it is often a difficult treatment for many sufferers to enter. This is because sufferers may feel unable to expose themselves to their fear triggers and find it impossible to prevent themselves acting out their rituals. As many as 30 per cent of clients drop out of ERP before completing treatment (Wilhelm, 2000). An alternative form of therapy for such individuals is cognitive behaviour therapy (CBT), based on targeting and modifying the dysfunctional beliefs that OCD sufferers hold about their fears, thoughts and the significance of their rituals (Abramowitz, Brigidi & Roche, 2001; Salkovskis, 1999; Wilhelm, 2000; Marks, 2003; see section 5.5.2.2, inflated responsibility). Dysfunctional beliefs that are usually challenged in cognitive therapy for OCD include:

- *responsibility appraisals*, where sufferers believe they are solely responsible for preventing any harmful outcomes;

- the *over-importance of thoughts*, where sufferers believe that having a thought about an action is like performing the action (thought–action fusion) (see Figure 5.7);

- *exaggerated perception of threat*, where sufferers have highly inflated estimates of the likelihood of harmful outcomes (van Oppen & Arntz, 1994).

An integrated cognitive therapy for OCD would thus consist of:

- educating clients that intrusive thoughts are quite normal, and that having a thought about an action is not the same as performing it (Salkovskis, 1999);

- focusing on changing clients' abnormal risk assessment – perhaps by working through the probabilities associated with feared outcomes (van Oppen & Arntz, 1994);

- providing clients with behavioural exercises that will disconfirm their dysfunctional beliefs (e.g. a client who fears shouting out blasphemous thoughts in church would be asked to go to church and see if this happens) (Salkovskis, 1999).

5.5.3.3 Pharmacological and Neurosurgical Treatments

Pharmacological treatments have proved to be a short-term effective and cheap way of treating OCD, although relapse tends to be common on discontinuation of the drug treatment (McDonough, 2003; Pato, Zohar-Kadouch, Zohar & Murphy, 1988). Serotonin and serotonin reuptake inhibitors (SSRIs) are the most commonly prescribed drugs and have the effect of increasing

Exposure hierarchies and response prevention in ERP treatments of OCD

Arguably the most effective therapies for OCD are exposure and ritual prevention treatments (ERP) (see section 5.5.3.1). Table 1 gives examples of a graded exposure regime for fear of contamination from germs and distressing thoughts about sexual abuse. Table 2 provides some examples of response prevention techniques.

Table 1

Example 1 *Fear of contamination* (distress level/100)	*Example 2* *Teacher's distressing intrusive thoughts about sexually abusing students* (distress level/100)
1 Touch rim of own unwashed coffee cup. (30)	1 Watch video or listen to audio tape of expert discussing sexual abuse of children. (40)
2 Touch rim of partner's unwashed coffee cup. (40)	2 Listen to tape of expert while looking at class photo. (50)
3 Eat snack from dish in cupboard after touching partner's unwashed coffee cup. (45)	3 Listen to loop tape of own distressing thoughts about sexually abusing students in general. (60)
4 Drink water from partner's glass. (55)	4 Listen to loop tape about students in general looking at class photo. (65)
5 Eat snack straight from unwashed table top. (65)	5 Listen to loop tape of distressing thought about sexually abusing specific student. (70)
6 Have coffee at a café. (70)	6 Listen to loop tape about specific student looking at class photo. (75)
7 Have meal at a restaurant. (80)	7 Listen to loop tape holding specific student's homework. (80)
8 Touch toilet seat at home without washing hands for 15 mins. (85)	8 Stand in front of class repeating statement on loop tape to self. (90)
9 Touch toilet seat at home without washing hands for 30 mins. (90)	9 Stand close to specific student repeating statement on loop tape to self. (95)
10 Use public toilet. (100)	10 Stand next to specific student repeating statement on loop tape to self. (100)

Table 2

OCD Symptom	*Response Prevention Strategy*
Hand washing or cleaning rituals	Response delay (i.e. extending period between 'contamination' and cleaning or washing); use of ritual restrictions (e.g. decreasing cleaning or washing time); clenching fists; extension strategies to undermine avoidance (e.g. touch self, clothes)
Checking lights, switches, oven, appliances, etc.	Response delay; use of ritual restrictions (e.g. restrict number of checks); turning and walking away; extension strategies (whistle a happy tune)
Counting (e.g. bricks, words)	Refocusing techniques; singing a song; going 'blank'; meditation

Source: Kyrios (2003)

brain serotonin levels (see Chapter 4, section 4.1.1.6). However, there is still no consensus view on a model of serotonin dysfunction in OCD (Delgado & Moreno, 1998), and it has been suggested that the beneficial effects of SSRIs may be restricted simply to their non-specific ameliorative effect on dysfunctional brain circuits. Tricyclic antidepressants can have beneficial effects across some specific symptoms of OCD (such as reducing the persistence and frequency of compulsive rituals), but seem to have their effect only when OCD is comorbid with depression (Hohagen, Winkelmann, Rasche-Rauchle, Hand et al., 1998). Comparative studies have suggested that both SSRIs and tricyclic drugs are less effective than standard psychological therapies such as exposure and ritual prevention (ERP) (Greist, 1998). In general, ERP is equally as effective as drug treatments in the short term, free from physical and psychological side effects, and associated with greater long-term gains (Greist, 1998; Marks, 1997). When pharmacological and psychological treatments have failed, neurosurgery has become an intervention of last resort in OCD. The most common procedure is *cingulatomy*, which involves destroying cells in the cingulum, close to the corpus callosum. These treatments do report some improvement in OCD symptoms (Dougherty, Baer, Cosgrove, Cassem et al., 2002), but there is a lack of evidence on the longer-term gains of neurosurgical treatments and their possible side effects (McDonough, 2003).

> **Cingulatomy** A neurosurgical treatment involving destroying cells in the cingulum, close to the corpus callosum.

SELF-TEST QUESTIONS

- Can you describe what *obsessions* and *compulsions* are, and provide some examples of each?
- How have biological theories attempted to explain the obsessions and compulsions found in OCD?
- How does the construct of 'inflated responsibility' help to explain how OCD is acquired and maintained?
- What are the similarities and differences between exposure and ritual prevention treatment (EPR) and cognitive behaviour therapy (CBT) for OCD?

give rise to the typical 'doubting' behaviour common in the disorder, or result in an inability to inhibit certain behaviour patterns (such as checking).

- OCD tends to be associated with a number of **dysfunctional beliefs**. The most prominent is sufferers' inflated conception of their own responsibility for preventing harm, and this **inflated responsibility** appears to be an important vulnerability factor in developing OCD.

- **Exposure and ritual prevention** (EPR) treatments are the most common, and arguably the most successful, means of treatment for OCD. These involve graded exposure to the thoughts that trigger distress, followed by the development of behaviours designed to prevent the individual's compulsive ritual.

- **Pharmacological treatments** for OCD can also be effective (e.g. serotonin and serotonin reuptake inhibitors), and psychosurgery is sometimes a treatment of last resort (e.g. **cingulatomy**).

SECTION SUMMARY

5.5 Obsessive-Compulsive Disorder (OCD)

- OCD is characterized by either **obsessions** – which are intrusive and recurring thoughts that the individual finds disturbing and uncontrollable – or **compulsions** – which are ritualized behaviour patterns that the individual feels driven to perform in order to prevent some negative outcome happening.

- Common compulsions include washing, checking and, to a lesser degree, hoarding and the systematic arrangement of objects.

- OCD onset is usually gradual and has a lifetime prevalence rate of around 2.5 per cent.

- **Biological theories** of OCD argue that there may be neurological deficits underlying OCD which either

5.6 POST-TRAUMATIC STRESS DISORDER (PTSD)

Post-traumatic stress disorder (PTSD) was not recognized as a specific category of psychopathology until 1980, when it was included for the first time in DSM-III. PTSD is somewhat different from the other anxiety-based disorders because its definition and diagnosis include identifying exposure to a specific fear-evoking event as a cause of the symptoms (see Table 5.14). PTSD is a set of persistent symptoms that occur after experiencing or witnessing an extremely fear-evoking traumatic event (see Client's Perspective 5.3). Such events include combat during a war, rape or other types of physical assault, child abuse, car or aeroplane crashes, or natural or human-caused disasters. The symptoms of PTSD are also somewhat different from those experienced in other anxiety disorders, and can be grouped into three main categories:

> **Post-traumatic stress disorder (PTSD)** A set of persistent anxiety-based symptoms that occur after experiencing or witnessing an extremely fear-evoking traumatic event.

- *increased arousal*, which includes an exaggerated startle response (Shalev, Peri, Brandes, Freedman et al., 2000), difficulty sleeping, hypervigilance and difficulty concentrating;

- *avoidance and numbing of emotions*: the individual will attempt to avoid all situations or events that might trigger memories of the traumatic event, and there is a sense of detachment and lack of feelings of positive emotion;

Table 5.14 *DSM-IV-TR criteria for the diagnosis of PTSD*

A The person has been exposed to a traumatic event in which both of the following were present:

   (1) The person experienced, witnessed, or was confronted with an event or events that involved actual or threatened death or serious injury, or a threat to the physical integrity of self or others.

   (2) The person's response involved intense fear, helplessness, or horror.

B The traumatic event is persistently re-experienced in one (or more) of the following ways:

   (1) Recurrent and intrusive distressing recollections of the event, including images, thoughts, or perceptions.

   (2) Recurrent distressing dreams of the event

   (3) Acting or feeling as if the traumatic event were recurring (includes a sense of reliving the experience, illusions, hallucinations, and dissociative flashback episodes).

   (4) Intense psychological distress at exposure to internal or external cues that symbolize or resemble an aspect of the traumatic event.

   (5) Physiological reactivity on exposure to internal or external cues that symbolize or resemble an aspect of the traumatic event.

C Persistent avoidance of stimuli associated with the trauma and numbing of general responsiveness (not present before the trauma), as indicated by three (or more) of the following:

   (1) efforts to avoid thoughts, feelings, or conversations associated with the trauma

   (2) efforts to avoid activities, places, or people that arouse recollections of the trauma

   (3) inability to recall an important aspect of the trauma

   (4) markedly diminished interest or participation in significant activities

   (5) feeling of detachment or estrangement from others

   (6) restricted range of affect (e.g. unable to have loving feelings)

   (7) sense of foreshortened future (e.g. does not expect to have a career)

D Persistent symptoms of increased arousal (not present before the trauma), as indicated by two (or more) of the following:

   (1) difficulty falling or staying asleep

   (2) irritability or outbursts of anger

   (3) difficulty concentrating

   (4) hypervigilance

   (5) exaggerated startle response

E Duration of the disturbance is more than 1 month.

F The disturbance causes clinically significant distress or impairment in social, occupational, or other important areas of functioning.

CLIENT'S PERSPECTIVE 5.3

Post-traumatic stress disorder

'It's been 8 months since my experience and I still deal with these feelings. I'm doing a lot better but throughout the week, I can feel myself getting worse and worse until I break down. The worst part is the irritability and rage I have inside of me. I don't know why I'm so mad at life but the littlest things will set me off. I don't have the "flashbacks" anymore . . . just the feelings I had when I was going through the ordeal. It's a very dark and depressing place and it's getting harder to come out of it each time it happens. I almost feel blinded and out of control when I get these attacks. It scares me to think of what I'm capable of doing. The worst part about this is that I don't know what triggers these feelings. I can be fine all day and then my mood will change for the worse. I generally feel very depressed and it's hard to deal with at times. Just when I think I don't have to worry about it anymore, it hits ten times harder. I've tried just about every remedy there is. I've seen 4 therapists and have been on 3 SSRIs . . . all of which made me worse. I feel very discouraged with life. I don't know if this even has to do with PTSD because I thought I was over it.'

Clinical Commentary

This description is typical of many PTSD sufferers and highlights feelings of depression, lack of control and anger. Some theories of PTSD (such as 'mental defeat') emphasize that those who develop PTSD after a severe trauma tend to view themselves as victims, process all information about the trauma negatively and view themselves as unable to act effectively. Such individuals believe they are unable to influence their own fate and do not have the necessary skills to protect themselves from future trauma. Ehlers and Clark (2000) suggest that such individuals only partially process their memory of the trauma because of their perceived lack of control over it, and so they do not integrate that event fully into their own autobiographical knowledge.

Source: www.healthboards.com/

- *re-experiencing*: the individual regularly recalls very vivid flashbacks of events experienced during the trauma, and these images often occur in recurrent nightmares. Associated problems and symptoms include depression, guilt, shame, anger, marital problems, physical illness, sexual dysfunction, substance abuse, suicidal thoughts and stress-related violence (Jacobsen, Southwick & Kosten, 2001; Zatzick, Marmar, Weiss, Browner et al., 1997; Hobfoll, Spielberger, Breznitz, Figley et al., 1991).

The kinds of traumatic events that precipitate PTSD are often life-threatening in their severity. Studies suggest that PTSD symptoms are developed by up to 90 per cent of rape victims (Rothbaum, Foa, Riggs, Murdock et al., 1992), between 70 and 90 per cent of torture victims (Moisander & Edston, 2003), over 50 per cent of prisoners of war (POWS) (Engdahl, Dikel, Eberly & Blank, 1997), between 20 and 25 per cent of earthquake and flood survivors (Basoglu, Kilic, Salcioglu & Livanou 2004; North, Kawasaki, Spitznagel & Hong, 2004) and around 15 per cent of motor vehicle accident victims (Bryant & Harvey, 1998). More

recently, *severe stress* has been included in DSM-IV-TR as a possible causal factor in PTSD, and this has led to the inclusion in this category of cases where the stressor has not been life-threatening to the sufferer (e.g. suffering PTSD after the loss of a loved one; Breslau, Davis, Andreski & Peterson, 1991) or has involved simply viewing stressful images of life-threatening traumas (e.g. watching images of the 9/11 terrorist attacks on TV; Piotrowski & Brannen, 2002). This extension of the diagnostic criteria for PTSD has generated controversy, either because it makes the symptoms of PTSD easier to fake in those who might benefit financially from a diagnosis (Rosen, 2004), or because it confuses PTSD with merely experiencing stress (McNally, 2003a). Some of the controversial issues are listed in Focus Point 5.2.

The DSM-IV-TR diagnostic criteria for PTSD are:

1 The person has been exposed to a traumatic event in which the person experienced or witnessed actual or threatening death to the self or others, or his or her response involved intense fear, helplessness or horror.

FOCUS POINT 5.2

Controversies in the study of PTSD

In many ways, post-traumatic stress disorder is a controversial topic. Controversy has arisen because of the way it is diagnosed; the potential that individuals have to fake the disorder (especially when they are involved in lawsuits to secure financial compensation for involvement in a disaster or accident); and the issue of whether repressed and then recovered memories of sexual abuse play a role in PTSD. Harvard psychologist Richard McNally (2003a) has reviewed some of these controversial issues in an article in the *Annual Review of Psychology*. They are considered below.

'Conceptual bracket creep' in the definition of trauma
Recent changes in the criteria for diagnosis of post-traumatic stress disorder mean that PTSD can be diagnosed if 'the person experienced, witnessed, or was confronted with an event or events that involved actual or threatened death or serious injury, or *a threat to the integrity of self or others*'. McNally points out that PTSD could now be attributed to someone who merely learns about someone else being threatened with harm, or to a range of non-life-threatening stressors, such as exposure to sexual jokes in the workplace (Avina & O'Donohue, 2002).

Erroneously equating PTSD with merely experiencing stress
After the terrorist attacks on the World Trade Centre on 11 September 2001, surveys suggested that a majority of Americans were suffering substantial levels of stress as a result of the attack. Technically this would allow almost anyone to claim

to have developed PTSD according to the broadened diagnostic criteria, yet this clearly fails to distinguish between normal stress and a psychological disorder.

Faking symptoms of PTSD
It is notoriously easy to fake most of the symptoms of PTSD. Because it is a diagnosis linked to explicit traumatic experiences, there are many cases of individuals faking the disorder in order to obtain financial compensation or damages against those who might have been involved in causing the trauma, or to obtain disability payments (McGrath & Frueh, 2002). Indeed, it is estimated that around 75 per cent of Vietnam war veterans who are currently claiming PTSD compensation are either faking symptoms or never actually saw combat (Burkett & Whitley, 1998).

Recovered memories of trauma
A highly controversial debate has waged for many years now about whether disorders such as PTSD may be caused by traumatic experiences (such as childhood sexual abuse) that are repressed in memory, but then subsequently recovered using contentious techniques like hypnosis (Brown, Scheflin & Hammond, 1998). The jury is still out on this issue, but as McNally points out, there is accumulating evidence that those individuals who claim to have recovered memories of previous trauma are prone to exhibit false memory effects (i.e. in laboratory tests of memory, they claim to recall and recognize items that they have not previously been shown). Clancy, McNally, Schacter, Lenzenweger et al. (2002) found that individuals who had reported being abducted by space aliens also exhibited these false memory effects in the laboratory! (See also Chapter 13, Focus Point 13.2.)

2 The traumatic event is re-experienced in intrusive thoughts and images, nightmares, the vivid reliving of events or dissociative flashbacks.

3 The persistent avoidance of stimuli associated with the trauma (e.g. avoiding thoughts and feelings associated with the trauma, or avoiding activities, places or people associated with the trauma).

4 Persistent symptoms of increased arousal, including difficulty sleeping, anger outbursts, difficulty concentrating, hypervigilance and an exaggerated startle response. For diagnosis, the duration of the symptoms should be more than 1 month and should cause significant distress or impairment in social or occupational functioning. (See Table 5.14.)

The lifetime prevalence rate for PTSD is between 1 and 3 per cent (Helzer, Robins & McEvoy, 1987). However, around 50 per cent of adults experience at least one event in their lifetime that might qualify as a PTSD-causing trauma (Ozer & Weiss, 2004). Following such events, women are significantly more likely than men to develop PTSD (by a factor of 2.4:1), and this is not explained simply by differences in the perceived threat to life from the experience (Holbrook, Hoyt, Stein & Sieber, 2002). Apart from gender differences in prevalence rates, there is also some emerging evidence on the role that cultural variables play in PTSD. Ethnic groups can differ quite significantly in the prevalence of PTSD – Caucasian disaster victims show lower prevalence rates than Latinos or African Americans – and these differences cannot be entirely explained simply by differences in the frequency of exposure to traumatic experiences (Perilla, Norris & Lavizzo, 2002; Norris, Perilla, Ibanez & Murphy, 2001).

5.6.1 The Aetiology of Post-Traumatic Stress Disorder

The diagnostic criteria for PTSD specify either a life-threatening trauma or severe stress as a causal factor in the disorder. However, not everyone who has these kinds of experiences develops PTSD. This is the main challenge for any theory of the aetiology of PTSD – why do some people develop PTSD symptoms after these experiences, but not others? The answer must lie either in psychological or biological vulnerability factors, or in the psychological strategies that individuals have developed to deal with events like trauma and stress (e.g. differences in learned coping strategies). Also, because PTSD has many different symptom features, some theories address specific features of the symptomatology (e.g. the flashbacks), and others address the time course of the disorder and how it is emotionally experienced (Brewin & Holmes, 2003). We will explore these various possibilities below when we look at the five main theories of the aetiology of PTSD:

- theory of shattered assumptions
- conditioning theory
- emotional processing theory
- 'mental defeat'
- dual representation theory

5.6.1.1 Vulnerability Factors

As not everyone who experiences a life-threatening trauma develops PTSD, there must be factors that make some people more vulnerable than others. A number of factors have been identified that characterize those individuals likely to develop PTSD after trauma. These include:

- a tendency to take personal responsibility for the traumatic event and the misfortunes of others involved in the event (Mikhliner & Solomon, 1988);
- developmental factors such as early separation from parents or an unstable family life during early childhood (King, King, Foy & Gudanowski, 1996);
- a family history of PTSD (Foy, Resnick, Sipprelle & Carroll, 1987);
- existing high levels of anxiety or a pre-existing psychological disorder (Breslau, Davis, Andreski, Peterson et al., 1997).

Interestingly, low intelligence is also a vulnerability factor (VasterlingDuke, Brailey, Constans et al., 2002), and high IQ is the best predictor of resistance to the development of PTSD (Silva, Alpert, Munoz et al., 2000). This may be because there is a link between IQ level and the development of coping strategies to deal with experienced trauma or stress. Other important predictors of PTSD development are the experiences reported by trauma victims at the time of the trauma. These include the reporting of dissociative symptoms at the time of the trauma (e.g. feelings of depersonalization, out-of-body experiences, time-slowing and amnesia) (Ehlers, Mayou & Bryant, 1998; Candel & Merckelbach, 2004) and a belief that one is about to die (McNally, 2003b). These types of experiences may be important in that they may relate to how the individual processes and stores information about the trauma at the time, and this is significant in some specific theories of PTSD symptoms.

5.6.1.2 Theory of Shattered Assumptions

Many people develop schemas of the world that portray it as a benevolent, safe place, the people who live in it as good, moral and well-meaning, and they view themselves as being worthy people (Janoff-Bulman, 1992). Therefore, when a traumatic event occurs which severely challenges these beliefs (e.g. being assaulted by a stranger or involved in a serious traffic accident while oneself obeying all the driving laws), the individual is left in a state of disbelief, shock and conflict. This challenges the individual's core beliefs, leaves him or her in a state of 'unreality', and – because the trauma survivor has had to update his or her assumptions about the world in a negative way – may adversely affect long-term adjustment to the trauma (Bolton & Hill, 1996; Janoff-Bulman, 1992). However, while this may sound like a reasonable explanation of why some individuals exhibit shock and numbing following trauma, the facts do not entirely support it. Paradoxically, it is those who have already experienced the world as an unsafe place (i.e. have experienced previous trauma) who are most likely to develop PTSD, not those who have a core belief that the world is safe and benevolent (Resick, 2001).

> **Theory of shattered assumptions**
> A theory of PTSD that argues that a severe traumatic experience will shatter a person's belief in the world as a safe and benign place, resulting in the symptoms typical of PTSD.

5.6.1.3 Conditioning Theory

Because there is always an identifiable traumatic experience in the history of PTSD, it is quite reasonable to suppose that many of the symptoms of PTSD may be due to classical conditioning (see Chapter 1, section 1.1.3.2). That is, trauma (the unconditioned stimulus, UCS) becomes associated at the time of the trauma with situational cues associated with the place and time of the trauma (the conditioned stimulus, CS) (Keane, Zimering & Caddell, 1985). When these cues (or similar cues) are encountered in the future, they elicit the arousal and fear that was experienced during the trauma. For example, seeing a pile of bricks on the ground may elicit strong arousal, fear and startle responses for an earthquake survivor, because such cues had become associated with the fear experienced during the traumatic earthquake experience. The conditioning model would further argue that such conditioned fear responses do not extinguish because sufferers develop both cognitive and physical avoidance responses which distract them from fully processing such cues and therefore do not allow the associations between cues and trauma to extinguish. The reduction in fear resulting from these avoidance responses reinforces those responses and maintains PTSD symptoms. There is probably an element of classical conditioning in the development of PTSD, largely because formally neutral cues do come to elicit PTSD symptoms. There is also evidence that individuals suffering PTSD will more readily develop conditioned responses in laboratory-based experiments than non-sufferers (Orr, Metzger, Lasko, Macklin et al., 2000). However, classical conditioning does not provide a full explanation of PTSD. It does not explain why some individuals who experience trauma develop PTSD and others do not, and it cannot easily explain the range of symptoms that are peculiar to PTSD and rarely found in other anxiety disorders, such as re-experiencing symptoms, dissociative experiences, and so on.

5.6.1.4 Emotional Processing Theory

Foa, Steketee and Rothbaum (1989) have suggested that the intense nature of the trauma in PTSD creates a representation of the trauma in memory that becomes strongly associated with other contextual details of the event (e.g. if a person has been badly injured in a serious traffic accident, cues to do with roads, cars, hospitals and even travelling generally will come to selectively activate the fear network in memory). The avoidance of any contexts that might activate this fear network means that there is little opportunity for the PTSD sufferer to weaken these associations between fear and the everyday cues that will activate that fear. This account has elements in common with classical conditioning models of PTSD, but it differs in some significant ways. First,

Emotional processing theory
Theory that claims that severe traumatic experiences are of such major significance to an individual that they lead to the formation of representations and associations in memory that are quite different to those formed as a result of everyday experience.

emotional processing theory claims that severe traumatic experiences are of such major significance to the individual that they lead to the formation of representations and associations in memory that are quite different from those

formed as a result of everyday experience. For example, if severe trauma has become associated with certain cues (e.g. after being assaulted in an alleyway), this experience will now override any other positive associations formed as a result of previous experience with that cue (the alleyway). Secondly, severe trauma not only results in cues eliciting very strong fear responses, it also changes the individual's previous assumptions about how safe the world is, so many more cues than previously will come to elicit responses related to fear, startle and hypervigilance (Foa & Rothbaum, 1998).

The emotional processing theory is an example of those theories of PTSD that have attempted to include explanations about how fear responses are learned, stored and triggered, and about how the traumatic event changes individuals' assumptions and beliefs about themselves and the world. These types of theories have come to be known as information processing models because they specify how fear memories are laid down and activated in fear networks. They have also given rise to some successful therapeutic procedures for PTSD which address how the fear network resulting from traumatic experience can be modified (Foa & Rothbaum, 1998). In addition, this account of PTSD has been elaborated more recently to take account of the fact that individuals who prior to the trauma have relatively fixed views about themselves and the world are actually more vulnerable to PTSD (Foa & Riggs, 1993).

5.6.1.5 'Mental Defeat'

Ehlers and Clark (2000) have suggested that there is a specific psychological factor that is important in making an individual vulnerable to PTSD. This is a specific frame of mind called *'mental defeat'*, in which individuals see themselves as victims: they process all information about the trauma

'Mental defeat' A theoretical view of PTSD in which individuals see themselves as victims, process information about the trauma negatively, and view themselves as unable to act effectively.

negatively, and view themselves as unable to act effectively. This negative approach to the traumatic event and its consequences simply adds to the distress, influences the way the individual recalls the trauma, and may give rise to maladaptive behavioural and cognitive strategies that maintain the disorder. In effect, these individuals believe they are unable to influence their own fate and do not have the necessary skills to protect themselves from future trauma. Ehlers and Clark suggest that such individuals only partially process their memory of the trauma because of their perceived lack of control over it, and so they do not integrate that event fully into their own autobiographical knowledge. This leads to symptoms such as re-experiencing the trauma in the present (outside of a temporal context), difficulty in recalling events from the trauma, and dissociation between the experience of fear responses and their meaning. The 'mental defeat' model is supported by evidence suggesting that PTSD sufferers do indeed have negative views of the self and the world, including negative interpretations of the trauma (Dunmore, Clark & Ehlers, 1999), negative interpretations of PTSD symptoms (Clohessy & Ehlers, 1999; Mayou, Bryant & Ehlers, 2001), negative interpretations of the responses of others (Dunmore, Clark & Ehlers, 1999) and a belief that the trauma has permanently changed their life (Dunmore, Clark & Ehlers, 1999; Ehlers, Maercker & Boos, 2000).

5.6.1.6 Dual Representation Theory

> **Dual representation theory** An approach to explaining post-traumatic stress disorder (PTSD) suggesting that it may be a hybrid disorder involving two separate memory systems.

A rather different approach to explaining PTSD, called *dual representation theory*, is that it may be a hybrid disorder consisting of the involvement of two separate memory systems (Brewin, 2001; Brewin, Dalgleish & Joseph, 1996). The *verbally accessible memory* (VAM) system registers memories of the trauma that are consciously processed at the time. These memories are narrative in nature and contain information about the event, its context and personal evaluations of the experience. They are integrated with other autobiographical memories and can be readily retrieved. The *situationally accessible memory* (SAM) system, however, records information from the trauma that may have been too brief to apprehend or take in consciously, and this includes information about sights and sounds, and extreme bodily reactions to trauma. The SAM system is thus responsible for the vivid, uncontrollable flashbacks experienced by PTSD sufferers which are difficult to communicate to others (because these memories are not stored in a narrative form).

There is good neuropsychological evidence for the existence of these two separate memory systems and their links with the brain centre associated with fear (the amygdala) (Brewin, 2001). There is also evidence that is consistent with predictions from the dual representation theory. For example, Hellawell and Brewin (2004) found that, when describing their memories, PTSD sufferers characterized flashback periods with greater use of detail, particularly perceptual detail, by more mentions of death, greater use of the present tense and more mention of fear, helplessness and horror. In contrast, ordinary memories were characterized by greater mentions of secondary emotions such as guilt and anger. These findings are consistent with the view that flashbacks are the result of sensory and response information stored in the SAM system.

SUMMARY

Once again, it is clear that PTSD has a number of different features, each of which requires explanation. Some theories have tried to explain some of the specific features of PTSD (such as dual representation theory's attempt to explain specific features such as flashbacks), while others have tried to identify the dispositional features that make some individuals vulnerable to developing PTSD while others do not (e.g. theory of shattered assumptions and 'mental defeat'). Others attempt to describe why severe trauma causes the symptoms that it does, and why these anxiety-based symptoms persist for such long periods (e.g. conditioning theory and emotional processing theory).

5.6.2 The Treatment of Post-Traumatic Stress Disorder

The treatment of PTSD has two main aims. The first is to try to prevent the development of PTSD after an individual has experienced a severe trauma. The second is to treat the symptoms of PTSD once these symptoms have developed. Rapid psychological debriefing has usually been the accepted way of intervening immediately after trauma in order to try to prevent the development of PTSD, although there is now some doubt about whether this kind of rapid intervention provides any therapeutic gains. Once symptoms have developed, most psychological therapies rely on some form of exposure therapy (usually involving clients imagining events during their traumatic experience) in an attempt to extinguish fear symptoms. Therapies that possess this exposure element include imaginal flooding, eye-movement desensitization and reprocessing (EMDR) and cognitive restructuring.

5.6.2.1 Psychological Debriefing

Over the past 20 years or so there has been a growing belief amongst mental health professionals that PTSD can be prevented by immediate and rapid *debriefing* of trauma victims within 24–72 hours after the traumatic event (Caplan, 1964; Bisson, 2003). The exact

> **Psychological debriefing** A structured way of trying to intervene immediately after trauma in order to try to prevent the development of PTSD.

form of the intervention can vary, with the most widely used techniques referred to as crisis intervention or critical incident stress management (CISM) (Everly, Flannery & Mitchell, 2000). The purpose of these interventions is to reassure the participants that they are normal people who have experienced an abnormal event, to encourage them to review what has happened to them, to express their feelings about the event, and to discuss and review support and coping strategies in the immediate post-trauma period. Psychological debriefing has been used with survivors, victims, relatives, emergency care workers and providers of mental health care (Bisson, 2003). The scale of this type of intervention can be gauged by reactions to the 9/11 terrorist attacks on the World Trade Centre, when more than 9,000 counsellors went to New York to offer immediate aid to victims and families of the attack (McNally, Bryant & Ehlers, 2003). Critical incident stress debriefing comprises a number of components, including:

- explanation of the purpose of the intervention;
- asking participants to describe their experiences;
- discussion of the participants' feelings about the event;
- discussion of any trauma-related symptoms participants may be experiencing;
- encouraging participants to view their symptoms as normal reactions to trauma;
- discussing the participants' needs for the future (Mitchell & Everly, 1993)

As laudable as immediate professional help may seem in these circumstances, there is much criticism of psychological debriefing

Plate 5.6
The psychological impact of the devastating Asian tsunami of December 2004 is difficult to calculate. Over the past 20 years it was felt that immediate counselling of victims was the best way to prevent the development of PTSD. However, more recent research has suggested that such immediate interventions may not be helpful, and in many cases may impede natural recovery.

and its value as an intervention for PTSD. First, it is not clear whether victims will gain any benefit from being counselled by strangers and possibly 'coerced' into revealing thoughts and memories that in the immediate wake of the trauma may be difficult to express. Secondly, many of the survivors of severe trauma do not display symptoms of psychological disorders, nor will they develop PTSD. Psychological debriefing techniques make little attempt to differentiate these survivors from those who may genuinely need longer-term guidance and treatment. Thirdly, controlled comparative studies that have attempted to evaluate the effects of psychological debriefing techniques suggest there is little convincing evidence that debriefing reduces the incidence of PTSD – and indeed, in some cases it may *impede* natural recovery following trauma (Bisson, 2003; McNally, Bryant & Ehlers, 2003).

5.6.2.2 Exposure Therapies

Arguably the most effective form of treatment for PTSD is exposure therapy, in which sufferers are helped by the therapist to confront and experience events and stimuli relevant to their trauma and their symptoms. The rationale behind exposure therapy is that (1) it will help to extinguish associations between trauma cues and fear responses (Foa & Rothbaum, 1998), and (2) it will help individuals to disconfirm any symptom-maintaining dysfunctional beliefs that have developed as a result of the trauma (e.g. 'I can't handle any stress') (Foa & Rauch, 2004).

For individuals suffering PTSD, exposure to their fear triggers is often a difficult step to take, and may even make symptoms worse in the early stages of treatment (Keane, Gerardi, Quinn & Litz, 1992). This being the case, exposure can be tackled in a number of different forms – especially in various imaginal forms. This can be achieved (1) by asking clients to provide a detailed written narrative of their traumatic experiences (Resick & Schnicke, 1992); (2) with the assistance of virtual reality technology using computer-generated imagery (Rothbaum, Hodges, Ready,

Graap & Alarcon, 2001); or (3) by simply asking clients to visualize feared, trauma-related scenes for extended periods of time (known as *imaginal flooding*) (Keane, Fairbank, Caddell & Zimering, 1989). Such imaginal treatments are usually then supplemented with subsequent *in vivo* exposure that would require graded exposure to real trauma-related cues. Comparative studies generally indicate that exposure-based therapies provide therapeutic gains that are superior to medication and social support (Foa & Meadows, 1997; Marks, Lovell, Noshirvani & Livanou, 1998).

> **Imaginal flooding** A technique whereby a client is asked to visualize feared, trauma-related scenes for extended periods of time.

A recently developed and controversial form of exposure therapy for PTSD is known as *eye-movement desensitization and reprocessing* (EMDR) (Shapiro, 1989, 1995). In this form of treatment, clients are required to focus their attention on a traumatic image or memory while simultaneously visually following the therapist's finger moving backwards and forwards in front of their eyes. This continues until clients report a significant decrease in anxiety to the image or memory. The therapist then encourages clients to restructure the memory positively, by thinking positive thoughts in relation to that image (e.g. 'I can deal with this'). The rationale for this procedure is that combining eye movements with attention to fearful images encourages rapid deconditioning and restructuring of the feared image (Shapiro, 1995, 1999).

> **Eye-movement desensitization and reprocessing** A form of exposure therapy for PTSD in which clients are required to focus their attention on a traumatic image or memory while simultaneously visually following the therapist's finger moving backwards and forwards before their eyes.

There is evidence that EMDR is more effective than no treatment, supportive listening and relaxation (McNally, 1999), but some studies have shown that it has a higher relapse rate than cognitive behaviour therapy (Devilly & Spence, 1999). Critics of EMDR argue that, although it does have some success in treating the symptoms of PTSD, it is little more than just another form of exposure therapy. Indeed, there is growing evidence that the eye movement component of EMDR is not necessary for improvement (McNally, 1999; Cahill, Carrigan & Frueh, 1999), and this has led McNally (1999, p. 2) to conclude that 'what is effective in EMDR (imaginal exposure) is not new, and what is new (eye movements) is not effective'.

5.6.2.3 Cognitive Restructuring

There are various forms of cognitive restructuring therapy for PTSD, but most attempt to help clients do two things: evaluate and replace intrusive or negative automatic thoughts; and evaluate and change dysfunctional beliefs about the world, themselves and their future that have developed as a result of the trauma (Marks, Lovell, Noshirvani & Livanou, 1998; Foa & Rothbaum, 1998). For example, Foa and Rothbaum (1998) suggested that two basic dysfunctional beliefs mediate the development and maintenance of PTSD. These are (1) 'the world is a dangerous place' and (2) 'I am totally incompetent'. Foa and Cahill (2001) argued that immediately after a severe trauma, all victims develop a negative view of the world and themselves, but for most individuals these beliefs become disconfirmed through daily experience. However, those who avoid trauma-related thoughts will also avoid disconfirming these extreme views, and this will foster the development of chronic PTSD. While exposure therapy alone may encourage experiences that disconfirm these dysfunctional beliefs, cognitive therapists have proposed that procedures that directly attempt to alter PTSD-related cognitions should also be included in the treatment (Resick & Schnicke, 1992; Steil & Ehlers, 2000). However, studies that have analysed treatments that contain both exposure and cognitive restructuring components suggest that cognitive restructuring does not significantly augment exposure therapy in producing changes in dysfunctional cognitions (Foa & Rauch, 2004).

SELF-TEST QUESTIONS

- Can you describe the main symptoms of PTSD and how they may differ from the symptoms found in other anxiety disorders?
- Can you list some of the important risk factors for PTSD, and describe how they might contribute to the development of PTSD?
- We discussed five main theories of the aetiology of PTSD (theory of shattered assumptions, conditioning theory, emotional processing theory, 'mental defeat', and dual representation theory), can you describe the main features of at least two of these and discuss their similarities and differences?
- What are the main treatments for PTSD, and how have these been derived from theories of the aetiology of PTSD?

SECTION SUMMARY

5.6 Post-Traumatic Stress Disorder (PTSD)

- The diagnosis of PTSD is based on identifying exposure to a specific fear-evoking, and usually life-threatening, event (e.g. being involved in a natural disaster or serious physical assault).

- The main symptoms of PTSD include increased arousal, numbing of emotions, flashbacks and the re-experiencing of the trauma.

- The lifetime prevalence rate for PTSD is between 1 and 3 per cent (even though around 50 per cent of adults experience at least one event in their lifetime that might qualify as a PTSD-causing event).

- **Vulnerability factors** for PTSD include a tendency to take personal responsibility for the event, developmental factors such as an unstable early family life, a family history of PTSD and existing high levels of anxiety or a pre-existing psychological disorder.

- There is no consensus on a specific psychological model of PTSD, and current explanations include: (1) the **theory of shattered assumptions**, (2) **classical conditioning**, (3) **emotional processing theory**, (4) **'mental defeat'** and (5) **dual representation theory**.

- Attempting to prevent the development of PTSD through the rapid and immediate debriefing of trauma victims (**critical incident stress debriefing**) is now generally acknowledged to be ineffective and even counterproductive.

- The most effective forms of treatment for PTSD are **exposure therapies**, where sufferers are helped by the therapist to confront and experience events and stimuli relevant to their trauma. These may include **imaginal flooding** or **eye-movement desensitization and reprocessing** (EMDR). Graduated exposure treatment can be supplemented with **cognitive restructuring** designed to evaluate and change dysfunctional beliefs about the world.

5.7 ANXIETY-BASED PROBLEMS REVIEWED

In this chapter we have reviewed six of the main anxiety-based problems – specific phobia, social phobia, panic disorder, generalized anxiety disorder (GAD), obsessive-compulsive disorder (OCD) and post-traumatic stress disorder (PTSD). Common to all of these disorders is the intense experience of anxiety that the individual finds distressing and which causes significant impairment in social, occupational or other important areas of functioning. At this point it is worth referring back to Table 5.1, where we began by summarizing some of the important features of these problems. This table shows that anxiety manifests itself in many different ways in these different disorders – as pathological worrying in GAD, as compulsive ritualized thoughts and actions in OCD, as physical panic attacks in panic disorder and as the re-experiencing of trauma in PTSD. Many of these anxiety problems are precipitated by periods of stress in a person's life (e.g. panic disorder, GAD, OCD), yet we do not yet know why an individual who has experienced a period of life stress will develop one particular disorder (e.g. OCD) rather than another (e.g. panic disorder). This will be an important issue for future clinical research.

Just as the symptoms of these anxiety-based problems are often quite different, so are the theories that try to explain them, and there is certainly no single, unified theory that can convincingly account for the development of anxiety-based problems generally. However, there are some features that are common to these different problems and this may provide some insight into how different anxiety-based problems develop. These features include the information processing and interpretational biases that accompany most anxiety disorders (see section 5.4.1.1), and also the dysfunctional beliefs that anxiety sufferers seem to form which maintain their symptoms (e.g. the spider phobic's beliefs that spiders are threatening and harmful, and the GAD sufferer's belief that worrying is an important and necessary activity to engage in). These phenomena may eventually form the basis of a unified theory of anxiety-based problems.

Finally, now that you have reached the end of this chapter, you can test out your knowledge of the symptoms of anxiety-based disorders by completing the diagnostic tree shown in Figure 5.9.

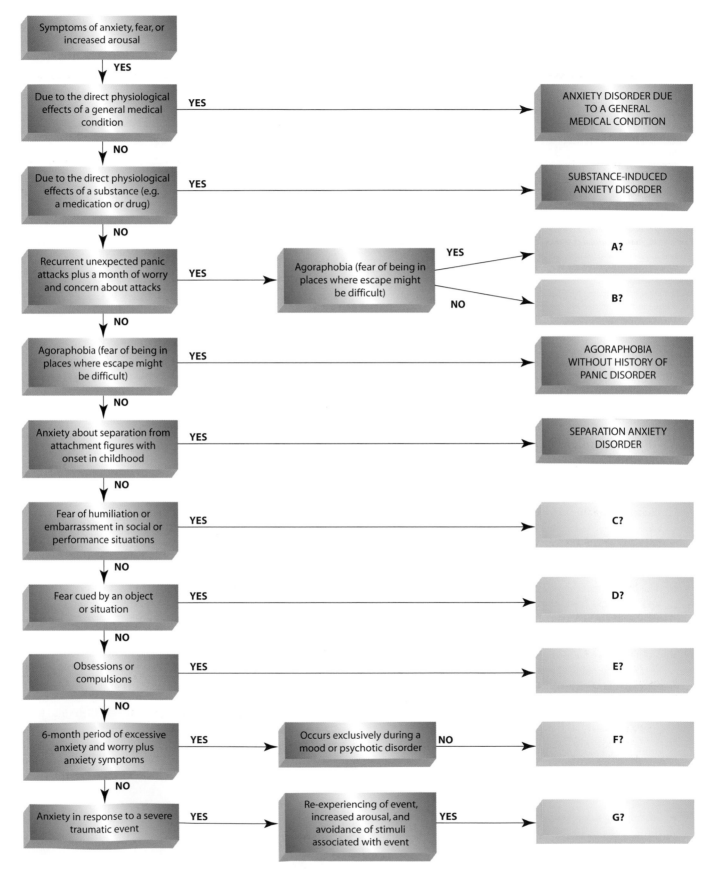

Figure 5.9
Source: adapted from DSM-IV-TR.

LEARNING OUTCOMES

When you have completed this chapter, you should be able to:

1 Describe the kinds of presenting symptoms that are associated with individual anxiety-based problems.

2 Describe the characteristics and diagnostic criteria of six of the important anxiety disorders.

3 Describe, compare and contrast at least two contemporary theories of the aetiology of each disorder.

4 Distinguish between biological and psychological explanations of anxiety-based problems.

5 Describe the relevance of research methodologies that have contributed to the understanding of the acquisition of anxiety.

6 Describe, compare and contrast at least two therapeutic procedures used for each individual anxiety disorder.

KEY TERMS

Adaptive fallacy (SP) *126*
Anxiety disorder *118*
Anxiety sensitivity (PD) *137*
Anxiety Sensitivity Index (PD) *137*
Behavioural rehearsal (SOC, PD, OCD) *145*
Biological challenge tests (PD) *135*
Biological preparedness (SP) *125*
Catastrophic misinterpretation of bodily sensations (PD) *137*
Catastrophizing (GAD) *141*
Cingulatomy (OCD) *154*
Cognitive restructuring (SP, SOC, PD, GAD, OCD, PTSD) *145*
Comorbidity *118*
Compulsions (OCD) *146*
Disease-avoidance model (SP) *126*
Disgust (SP) *126*
Dual representation theory (PTSD) *159*
Emotional processing theory (PTSD) *158*
Exposure and ritual prevention treatments (OCD) *152*
Eye-movement desensitization and reprocessing (EMDR) (PTSD) *160*
Generalized anxiety disorder *139*
Hyperventilation (PD) *135*
Imaginal flooding (SP, PTSD) *160*

Incubation (SP) *124*
Inflated responsibility (OCD) *149*
Information processing biases in anxiety (GAD) *142*
'Mental defeat' (PTSD) *158*
Mood-as-input hypothesis (OCD) *151*
Non-associative fear acquisition (SP) *125*
Obsessions (OCD) *146*
Obsessive-compulsive disorder (OCD) *146*
Panic (PD) *126*
Panic disorder *133*
Phobic beliefs (SP) *121*
Post-traumatic stress disorder *154*
Psychological debriefing (PTSD) *159*
Relaxation training (SP, GAD) *145*
Self-focused attention (SOC) *131*
Self-monitoring (GAD) *145*
Social phobia *128*
Specific phobia *121*
Stimulus control treatment (GAD) *145*
Suffocation alarm theories (PD) *135*
Theory of shattered assumptions (PTSD) *157*
Thought suppression (OCD) *151*
Thought-action fusion (OCD) *151*

REVIEWS, THEORIES AND SEMINAL STUDIES

Links to Journal Articles

Anxiety (General)

De Ruiter, C., Rijken, H., Garssen, B., van Schaik, A. & Kraaimaat, F. (1989). Comorbidity among the anxiety disorders. *Anxiety Disorders, 3*, 57–68.

Deacon, B.J. & Abramowitz, J.S. (2004). Cognitive and behavioral treatments for anxiety disorders: A review of meta-analytic findings. *Journal of Clinical Psychology, 60*, 429–441.

Hettema, J.M., Neale, M.C. & Kendler, K.S. (2001). A review and meta-analysis of the genetic epidemiology of anxiety disorders. *American Journal of Psychiatry, 158*, 1568–1578.

Krijn, M., Emmelkamp, P.M.G., Olafsson, R.P. & Biemond, R. (2004). Virtual reality exposure therapy of anxiety disorders: A review. *Clinical Psychology Review, 24*, 259–281.

Lepine, J.P. (2002). The epidemiology of anxiety disorders: Prevalence and societal costs. *Journal of Clinical Psychiatry, 63*, 4–8.

Rodriguez, B.F., Weisberg, R.B., Pagano, M.E., Machan, J.T. et al. (2004). Frequency and patterns of psychiatric comborbidity in a sample of primary care patients with anxiety disorders. *Comprehensive Psychiatry, 45*, 129–137.

5.1 Specific Phobias

Cook, M. & Mineka, S. (1990). Selective associations in the observational learning of fear in rhesus monkeys. *Journal of Experimental Psychology: Animal Behavior Processes, 16*, 372–389.

Davey, G.C.L. (1992b). Classical conditioning and the acquisition of human fears and phobias: A review and synthesis of the literature. *Advances in Behaviour Research and Therapy, 14*, 29–66.

Davey, G.C.L. (1995). Preparedness and phobias: Specific evolved associations or a generalized expectancy bias. *Behavioral and Brain Sciences, 18*, 289–325.

Delprato, D.J. (1980). Hereditary determinants of fears and phobias: A critical review. *Behavior Therapy, 11*, 79–103.

Koch, E.I., Spates, C.R. & Himle, J.A. (2004). Comparison of behavioral and cognitive-behavioral one-session exposure treatments for small animal phobias. *Behaviour Research and Therapy, 42*, 1483–1504.

Merckelbach, H., de Jong, P.J., Muris, P. & van den Hout, M. (1996). The etiology of specific phobias: A review. *Clinical Psychology Review, 16*, 337–361.

Ohman, A. & Mineka, S. (2001). Fears, phobias, and preparedness: Toward an evolved module of fear and fear learning. *Psychological Review, 108*, 483–522.

Poulton, R. & Menzies, R.G. (2002). Non-associative fear acquisition: A review of the evidence from retrospective and longitudinal research. *Behaviour Research and Therapy, 40*(2), 127–149.

Seligman, M.E.P. (1971). Phobias and preparedness. *Behavior Therapy, 2*, 307–320.

Watson, J.B. & Rayner, R. (1920). Conditioned emotional reactions. *Journal of Experimental Psychology, 3*, 1–14.

5.2 Social Phobia

Bogels, S.M. & Mansell, W. (2004). Attention processes in the maintenance and treatment of social phobia: Hypervigilance, avoidance and self-focused attention. *Clinical Psychology Review, 24*, 827–856.

Davidson, J.R.T. (2003). Pharmacotherapy of social phobia. *Acta Psychiatrica Scandinavica, 108*, 65–71.

Heinrichs, N. & Hofmann, S.G. (2001). Information processing in social phobia: A critical review. *Clinical Psychology Review, 21*, 751–770.

Hirsch, C.R. & Clark, D.M. (2004). Information-processing bias in social phobia. *Clinical Psychology Review, 24*, 799–825.

Neal, J.A. & Edelmann, R.J. (2003). The etiology of social phobia: Toward a developmental profile. *Clinical Psychology Review, 23*, 761–786.

Rapee, R.M. & Spence, S.H. (2004). The etiology of social phobia: Empirical evidence and an initial model. *Clinical Psychology Review, 24*, 737–767.

Rodebaugh, T.L. & Chambless, D.L. (2004). Cognitive therapy for performance anxiety. *Journal of Clinical Psychology, 60*, 809–820.

Rodebaugh, T.L., Holaway, R.M. & Heimberg, R.G. (2004). The treatment of social anxiety disorder. *Clinical Psychology Review, 24*, 883–908.

Spurr, J.M. & Stopa, L. (2002). Self-focused attention in social phobia and social anxiety. *Clinical Psychology Review, 22*, 947–975.

Stravynski, A., Bond, S. & Amado, D. (2004). Cognitive causes of social phobia: A critical appraisal. *Clinical Psychology Review, 24*, 421–440.

5.3 Panic Disorder

Austin, D.W. & Richards, J.C. (2001). The catastrophic misinterpretation model of panic disorder. *Behaviour Research and Therapy, 39*, 1277–1291.

Bouton, M.E., Mineka, S. & Barlow, D.H. (2001). A modern learning theory perspective on the etiology of panic disorder. *Psychological Review, 108*, 4–32.

Clark, D.M. (1986). A cognitive approach to panic. *Behaviour Research and Therapy, 24*, 348–351.

Clark, D.M., Salkovskis, P.M., Ost, L.-G., Breitholtz, E. et al. (1997). Misinterpretation of body sensations in panic disorder. *Journal of Consulting and Clinical Psychology, 65*, 203–213.

Klein, D.F. (1993). False suffocation alarms, spontaneous panics, and related conditions: An integrative hypothesis. *Archives of General Psychiatry, 50*, 306–317.

Luermans, J.R.L.M., De Cort, K., Scruers, K. & Griez, E. (2004). New insights in cognitive behavioural therapy as treatment of panic disorder: A brief overview. *Acta Neuropsychiatrica, 16*, 110–112.

McNally, R.J. (1990). Psychological approaches to panic disorder: A review. *Psychological Bulletin, 108*, 403–419.

McNally, R.J. (2002). Anxiety sensitivity and panic disorder. *Biological Psychiatry, 52*, 938–946.

Zvolensky, M.J. & Eifert, G.H. (2001). A review of psychological factors/processes affecting anxious responding during voluntary hyperventilation and inhalations of carbon dioxide-enriched air. *Clinical Psychology Review, 21*, 375–400.

5.4 Generalized Anxiety Disorder (GAD)

Durham, R.C., Chambers, J.A., MacDonald, R.R., Power, K.G. & Major, K. (2003). Does cognitive-behavioral therapy influence the long-term outcome of generalized anxiety disorder? An 8–14-year follow-up of two clinical trials. *Psychological Medicine, 33*, 499–509.

Kessler, R.C., Keller, M.B. & Wittchen, H.U. (2001). The epidemiology of generalized anxiety disorder. *Psychiatric Clinics of North America, 24*, 19.

Lang, A.J. (2004). Testing generalized anxiety disorder with cognitive-behavioral therapy. *Journal of Clinical Psychiatry, 65*, 14–19.

Mogg, K. & Bradley, B.P. (1998). A cognitive-motivational analysis of anxiety. *Behaviour Research and Therapy, 36*, 809–848.

Mogg, K., Bradley, B.P., Williams, R. & Mathews, A. (1993). Subliminal processing of emotional information in anxiety and depression. *Journal of Abnormal Psychology, 102*(2), 304–311.

Wells, A. (1999). A metacognitive model and therapy for generalized anxiety disorder. *Clinical Psychology and Psychotherapy, 6*, 86–95.

5.5 Obsessive-Compulsive Disorder (OCD)

Abramowitz, J.S., Brigidi, B.D. & Roche, K.R. (2001). Cognitive-behavioral therapy for obsessive-compulsive disorder: A review of the treatment literature. *Research On Social Work Practice, 11*, 357–372.

Rachman, S. (1998). A cognitive theory of obsessions: Elaborations. *Behaviour Research and Therapy, 36*, 385–401.

Rachman, S. (2002). A cognitive theory of compulsive checking. *Behaviour Research and Therapy, 40*, 625–639.

Salkovskis, P.M. (1985). Obsessional-compulsive problems: A cognitive-behavioural analysis. *Behaviour Research and Therapy, 25*, 571–583.

Salkovskis, P.M., Shafran, R., Rachman, S. & Freeston, M.H. (1999). Multiple pathways to inflated responsibility beliefs in obsessional problems: Possible origins and implications for therapy and research. *Behaviour Research and Therapy, 37*, 1055–1072.

Salkovskis, P.M., Wroe, A.L., Gledhill, A., Morrison, N., Forrester, E., Richards, C., Reynolds, M. & Thorpe, S. (2000). Responsibility attitudes and interpretations are characteristic of obsessive compulsive disorder. *Behaviour Research and Therapy, 38*, 347–372.

Shafran, R. & Rachman, S. (2004). Thought–action fusion: A review. *Journal of Behavior Therapy and Experimental Psychiatry, 35*, 87–107.

Wenzlaff, R.M. & Wegner, D.M. (2000). Thought suppression. *Annual Review of Psychology, 51*, 59–91.

5.6 Post-Traumatic Stress Disorder (PTSD)

Bisson, J.I. (2003). Single-session early psychological interventions following traumatic events. *Clinical Psychology Review, 23*, 481–499.

Brewin, C.R. (2001). Memory processes in post-traumatic stress disorder. *International Review of Psychiatry, 13*, 159–163.

Brewin, C.R. & Holmes, E.A. (2003). Psychological theories of posttraumatic stress disorder. *Clinical Psychology Review, 23*, 339–376.

Candel, I. & Merckelbach, H. (2004). Peritraumatic dissociation as a predictor of post-traumatic stress disorder: A critical review. *Comprehensive Psychiatry, 45*, 44–50.

Ehlers, A. & Clark, D.M. (2000). A cognitive model of posttraumatic stress disorder. *Behaviour Research and Therapy, 38*, 319–345.

Harvey, A.G., Bryant, R.A. & Tarrier, N. (2003). Cognitive behaviour therapy for posttraumatic stress disorder. *Clinical Psychology Review, 23*, 501–522.

McNally, R.J. (2003a). Progress and controversy in the study of posttraumatic stress disorder. *Annual Review of Psychology, 54*, 229–252.

McNally, R.J. (2003b). Psychological mechanisms in acute response to trauma. *Biological Psychiatry, 53*, 779–788.

McNally, R.J., Bryant, R.A. & Ehlers, A. (2003). Does early psychological intervention promote recovery from posttraumatic stress? *Psychological Science, Supplement*, 45–79.

Ozer, R.J. & Weiss, D.S. (2004). Who develops posttraumatic stress disorder? *Current Directions in Psychological Science, 13*, 169–172.

Texts for Further Reading

Barlow, D.H. (2004). *Anxiety and its disorders*, 2nd ed. New York: Guilford Press.

Davey, G.C.L. (Ed.) (1997). *Phobias: A handbook of theory, research and treatment*. Chichester: Wiley.

Davey, G.C.L. & Tallis, F. (Eds.) (1994). *Worrying: Perspectives on theory, assessment and treatment*. Chichester: Wiley.

Davey, G.C.L. & Wells, A. (Eds.) (2005). *Worry and its psychological disorders: Theory, assessment and treatment*. Chichester: Wiley.

Frost, R.O. & Steketee, G. (Eds.) (2002). *Cognitive approaches to obsessions and compulsions: Theory, assessment and treatment*. New York: Pergamon.

Heimberg, R., Liebowitz, M., Hope, D.A. & Schneier, F.R. (Eds.) (1995). *Social phobia: Diagnosis, assessment and treatment*. New York: Guilford Press.

Heimberg, R., Turk, C. & Mennin, D.S. (2004). *Generalized anxiety disorder: Advances in research and practice*. New York: Guilford Press.

Menzies, R.G. & de Silva, P. (Eds.) (2003). *Obsessive-compulsive disorder: Theory, research and treatment*. Chichester: Wiley.

Resick, P.A. (2001). *Stress and trauma*. Hove: Psychology Press.

Taylor, S. (2000). *Understanding and treating panic disorder: Cognitive behavioural approaches*. Chichester: Wiley.

Yule, W. (Ed.) (1999). *Post-traumatic stress disorders: Concepts and therapy*. Chichester: Wiley.

RESEARCH QUESTIONS

- Classical conditioning accounts of phobias would suggest that anyone who has a traumatic experience with a stimulus or situation should develop a phobia of it. However, this is certainly not the case. Why is it that some people acquire phobias after traumatic experiences and others do not?

- Why is it that clinical phobias usually cluster around only a small sub-set of stimuli and situations?

- Are the inherited components found in social phobia specific to this disorder, or is the genetic component a more general one that is shared with other disorders (e.g. a vulnerability to anxiety disorders generally rather than social phobia specifically)?

- Noradrenergic overactivity appears to be a characteristic of panic disorder, but is it a cause of the disorder or just a factor that mediates the symptoms of panic when an attack is triggered?

- People who suffer from panic disorder have a tendency to catastrophically misinterpret bodily sensations as threatening, but how do they acquire this interpretation bias?

- Why do individuals with GAD worry chronically and pathologically when many others – often with more stressful lifestyles – worry significantly less?

- People who are chronic worriers have a tendency to claim that they are 'born worriers' – but is there any evidence for this?

- Neuropsychological studies suggest individuals with OCD possess a number of executive functioning deficits – but do these deficits contribute to the symptoms of OCD or to the sufferer's 'doubting' that things have been done properly?

- A number of anxiety disorders are characterized by the dysfunctional perseveration of certain thoughts, behaviours or activities (e.g. pathological worrying in GAD, compulsive checking in OCD). Is pathological perseveration caused by a single process that is common to these different disorders?

- Around 50 per cent of adults will experience a severe traumatic experience during their lives, but why do only a proportion of those people develop symptoms of PTSD?

- IQ is one of the best predictors of resistance to the development of PTSD. What role does this factor play in preventing PTSD?

CLINICAL ISSUES

- Dysfunctional beliefs about the threats posed by a phobic stimulus or situation are a central feature of specific phobias.

These beliefs will probably need to be challenged and changed to ensure successful treatment.

- High levels of disgust sensitivity are a feature of a number of phobias. Successful treatment may rely not only on reducing fear in these cases, but also on reducing levels of disgust sensitivity.

- Fear of social situations is so pervasive that it has been more generally labelled as 'social anxiety disorder'.

- Cognitive behaviour therapy and pharmacological treatments can often be used together with complementary benefits. In the case of social phobia, drug therapy offers an immediate benefit and CBT helps to maintain therapeutic gains over time.

- Panic disorder appears to manifest itself in different symptoms across different cultures. What implications might this have for the diagnosis and assessment of panic disorder?

- Information processing biases appear to have a causal effect on the experience of anxiety. If so, it may be possible to develop training procedures to rectify these biases and so alleviate the experience of anxiety.

- OCD sufferers often feel unable to expose themselves to their fear triggers and prevent themselves acting out their rituals. How might these problems be overcome when considering treatment for OCD?

- Neurosurgery is often a treatment of last resort for psychological disorders. Is there any justification for performing cingulatomy to treat OCD?

- 'Severe stress' has been included in DSM-IV-TR as a possible causal factor in PTSD. Does this make the symptoms of PTSD easier to fake in those who might benefit financially from a diagnosis?

- The immediate and rapid debriefing of trauma victims does not seem to reduce the subsequent incidence of PTSD. Should any form of intervention or support be offered to victims immediately following large-scale disasters?

- It is claimed that eye-movement desensitization and reprocessing (EMDR) is not a treatment for PTSD that offers anything new beyond existing therapies (even though it appears to have some therapeutic benefits). If so, should it still be used to treat PTSD sufferers?

6 | Depression and Mood Disorders

ROUTE MAP OF THE CHAPTER

This chapter describes depression and mood disorders, their symptoms, theories of their aetiology, and the main forms of treatment for these problems. The two main mood disorders covered are major depression (sometimes known as unipolar depression) and bipolar disorder (characterized by periods of mania alternating with periods of depression). The chapter considers a range of theories of depression and mood disorders, including biological theories and psychological theories. The section on treatment looks at the way in which antidepressant drugs help to alleviate the symptoms of depression, and how psychological therapies have been developed to address the cognitive biases that characterize major depression. The chapter ends by discussing two important clinical phenomena related to mood disorders and depression in particular: suicide and deliberate self-harm.

The overwhelming sadness. To me – it's my menace. My menace was with me in the shower, on the phone, in class. Everywhere. I would become lost in a thoughtless stretch or blank – where distraction to nothing in particular would take over. Consumed by nothing – thinking of nothing, but my mind was locked down – stuck – paralysed. Studying was difficult if not impossible. I was becoming overwhelmed, and not understanding what I was dealing with – no relatable experience – made things almost intolerable. A good day was sleeping until 10 – getting up – maybe going to a morning lecture. Taking another nap in the afternoon – skipping class – reading books to pass the time that seems inescapable. Your mind gets into internal conflicts. Plenty of time for that. Time seems to always stretch in front of you – you can't bear thinking of doing anything to fill the time, but are beaten up by the fact the routine will exist the next day, and the next day, and the next, and why at all bother? What is it all for?

JOE'S STORY (THE MENACE OF MY OWN LIFE)

Introduction

In *Joe's Story*, his account of the experience of depression gives considerable insight into the various disabling features of this psychological problem. These include overwhelming feelings of sadness and lethargy. Each day is as miserable as the next in an unrelenting cycle of emptiness, and Joe hardly ever experiences pleasure or any positive emotion. Those suffering depression lack initiative, and often move and speak more slowly than non-sufferers (Sobin & Sackheim, 1997), they spend more time alone and may stay in bed for long periods – especially delaying getting out of bed in the mornings. Beck (1967) described depression as a 'paralysis of will' in which individuals experience only pessimism and hopelessness about their lives. This can often lead to suicidal thinking, and suicide often feels like the only solution for many individuals suffering depression.

We all experience periods of depression in our lives, and we can usually attribute these periods of depression to specific events. Two types of events are particularly important in triggering periods of depression, and these are *losses* and *failures*. Experiences such as losing a job or the death of a loved one are likely to trigger periods of sadness, lethargy and rumination. Similarly, failures – such as failing an exam or failing to persuade someone you like to date you – can also lead to periods of hopelessness and the fostering of negative cognitions associated with pessimism and self-doubt. Nevertheless, most of us can shake off these feelings

FOCUS POINT **6.1**

Mood disorders and creativity

William Blake, poet
Napoleon Bonaparte, general
Jim Carrey, actor
Agatha Christie, mystery writer
Winston Churchill, British prime minister
Francis Ford Coppola, film director
Ray Davies, musician
T.S. Eliot, poet
Carrie Fisher, writer, actor
F. Scott Fitzgerald, author
Sigmund Freud, physician
Cary Grant, actor
Marilyn Monroe, actress
Wolfgang Amadeus Mozart, composer
Isaac Newton, scientist
Edgar Allen Poe, author
Graham Greene, writer
Gordon Sumner (Sting), musician, composer
Robert Louis Stevenson, author
Liz Taylor, actor
Mark Twain, author
Alfred, Lord Tennyson, poet
Jean-Claude Van Damme, athlete, actor
Vincent van Gogh, artist
Brian Wilson, musician (Beach Boys), composer, arranger

This impressive list consists of artists and celebrities who have all suffered from symptoms of bipolar disorder. Indeed, there is an enduring belief that creativity in the arts is associated with psychological disturbance and even 'madness'. Is this just a myth or is there some truth in this belief? Psychiatrist Kay Jamison (1992) spent some years studying the lives of famous contributors to the arts, including poets, artists and musicians. She concluded that there did seem to be a link between mood disorders such as bipolar disorder and creativity and artistic achievement. She found that British poets during the eighteenth century were significantly more likely than members of the general population to have suffered symptoms of bipolar disorder, to have

been committed to a lunatic asylum or to have committed suicide. The notable list of names above seems to reinforce the belief that mood disorder is a significant factor in creativity and artistic achievement. But what exactly might this link be?

The first question to ask is, 'what comes first, the creativity or the psychological disturbance?' There is some evidence that creative individuals do have a family history of psychological problems, suggesting that their psychological difficulties may precede their creativity. For example, creative individuals often had parents who suffered from psychological disorders, and may have suffered the kind of childhood abuse that may give rise to psychological problems later in life. For instance, the author Virginia Woolf was known to have suffered childhood sexual abuse. In addition to this evidence that psychological problems may precede creativity, some studies have found that individuals with bipolar disorder score higher on measures of creativity than do non-clinical control participants (Richards, Kinney, Lunde, Benet et al., 1988).

In contrast to this evidence, it could be argued that artistic communities, where emotional expression is a valued commodity, are welcoming places for individuals with psychological or mood disorders (Ludwig, 1995). We must also remember that psychological disorder is not a prerequisite for creative achievement: (1) many people make significant artistic and creative contributions without exhibiting any signs of mental health problems and (2) those artists suffering psychological problems often continue to make impressive contributions to their art even after successful treatment of their disorders (Jamison, 1995; Ludwig, 1995).

Even so, it is worth considering how psychological problems such as bipolar disorder might contribute to creativity. First, *mania* gives individuals the energy and sharpened thinking that may be required for creative achievement, and it also gives the individual confidence and feelings of inspiration that may not be otherwise experienced. Second, there is evidence that *depressed mood* can also make a contribution to creativity by raising performance standards. For example, Martin and Stoner (1996) found that negative moods lead to lower confidence in the adequacy of creative effort, and this spurs on individuals in negative moods to greater efforts.

---

within a few days or weeks, and get on productively with our lives. For others, however, the symptoms of depression may linger on and spread to all aspects of their lives – emotional, behavioural, cognitive and physical – and this can result in diagnosable bouts of major depression that are debilitating enough to prevent an individual from living a normal day-to-day life. In extreme cases the symptoms of depression can develop even without the occurrence

of a precipitating life event, such as a loss or a failure, and will often persist for much longer than would be expected following a loss such as a bereavement.

Depression is the prominent emotion in mood disorders, but it can often be associated with its opposite –

> **Depression**   A mood disorder involving emotional, motivational, behavioural, physical and cognitive symptoms.

Mania   An emotion characterized by boundless, frenzied energy and feelings of euphoria.

namely, mania. *Mania* is an emotion characterized by boundless, frenzied energy and feelings of euphoria. As we shall see later, individuals who have a bipolar mood disorder frequently oscillate between deep depression and frenetic mania.

Depression involves emotional, motivational, behavioural, physical and cognitive symptoms. The *emotional* experiences of depressed individuals are usually restricted to negative ones and these are often described as 'sad, hopeless, miserable, dejected and discouraged'. Such individuals are often close to tears and have frequent crying episodes. Only very rarely do depressed individuals report experiencing pleasant or positive emotions: they exhibit a complete loss of sense of humour and rarely display positive facial expressions (Sloane, Strauss & Wisner, 2001). Anxiety is also commonly experienced with depression, which suggests that many sufferers may experience simultaneously a range of negative emotions (Bakish, 1999) that may be reflective of a single underlying symptomatology.

Depressed individuals exhibit a range of *motivational* deficits, including a loss of interest in normal daily activities or hobbies. They exhibit a lack of initiative and spontaneity, and frequently report 'not caring anymore' and not getting pleasure from activities that they previously enjoyed. This lack of initiative may manifest itself initially in social withdrawal (depressed individuals regularly report wanting to stay where they are and to be left alone), and appetite and sexual desire can also be significantly reduced.

Depressed individuals exhibit a number of *behavioural* symptoms, including a slowness of speech and behaviour generally

(Joiner, 2002). They become physically inactive, stay in bed for long periods, and reports of decreased energy, tiredness and fatigue are common. Even the smallest of tasks seem to require substantial physical exertion.

Physical symptoms include sleep disturbance such as middle insomnia (waking up during the night and having difficulty getting back to sleep) and terminal insomnia (waking early and being unable to return to sleep). In some cases depression can be associated with oversleeping (hypersomnia), where the individual indulges in increased daytime sleeping. Depressed individuals also complain of regular headaches, indigestion, constipation, dizzy spells and general pain (Fishbain, 2000).

Arguably the most disabling of the symptoms of depression are its *cognitive* features. As we shall see later, many theories of depression view these cognitive symptoms as central and as factors that need to be addressed in order to complete effective treatment. In particular, depressed individuals tend to have developed extremely negative views of themselves, the world around them and their own future (Beck, 1987; Gable & Shean, 2000), and this generates *pessimistic* thinking where sufferers believe nothing can improve their own lot. This in turn leads to a lack of initiative, with individuals reporting impaired ability to think, concentrate or make decisions. This inability to affect the future also generates other problematic beliefs, such as a sense of worthlessness, shame and guilt. Because of this, many depressed individuals develop the dysfunctional belief that others would be better off if they were dead, and this can often lead to transient but recurrent suicidal thoughts.

6.1 THE CHARACTERISTICS OF DEPRESSION AND MOOD DISORDERS

Major depression   A psychological problem characterized by relatively extended periods of clinical depression which cause significant distress to the individual and impairment in social or occupational functioning.

Unipolar depression   A psychological disorder characterized by relatively extended periods of clinical depression that cause significant distress to the individual and impairment in social or occupational functioning (see also major depression).

Bipolar disorder   A psychological disorder characterized by periods of mania that alternate with periods of depression.

There are two main types of clinical depression. The most common is **major** or **unipolar depression**, and the second is **bipolar disorder**. Table 6.1 summarizes the main features of these two types of mood disorder, and readers may want to refer back to this table when they have read and digested the information in this chapter.

Major depression is one of the most common of all the psychological problems. It is characterized by relatively

extended periods of clinical depression which cause significant distress to the individual and impairment in social or occupational functioning. Bipolar disorder is characterized by periods of mania that alternate with periods of depression, which leads individuals with bipolar disorder to describe their lives as an 'emotional roller-coaster'. Sufferers experience the extremes of these emotions in ways that cause emotional discomfort and distress. The personal accounts of experiences of bipolar disorder described in Client's Perspective 6.1 provide some insight into the desperation generated by periods of depression and the frightening confusion that can be experienced during periods of sustained mania.

Someone who suffers bipolar disorder and is in a manic phase can be recognized by many characteristics, including the expression of a constant, sometimes unconnected stream of thoughts and ideas: attention span may be limited and the person shifts rapidly from topic to topic. The person will be loud and often interrupt ongoing conversations to talk about something that has just caught his or her attention. Individuals in a manic phase may spontaneously start conversations with strangers, and indulge in inappropriate or imprudent sexual interactions. These behaviours are usually recognized as excessive by those who know the sufferer, but any attempt to quell these excesses is usually met with anger and annoyance. As a result, irritability and lability of mood are

Table 6.1 *Depression and mood disorders: summary*

DISORDER AND LIFETIME PREVALENCE RATES	DEFINITION	MAIN DSM-IV-TR DIAGNOSTIC FEATURES	KEY FEATURES	THEORIES OF AETIOLOGY	MAIN FORMS OF TREATMENT
MAJOR DEPRESSION (5.2%–17.1%)	Feelings of sadness, hopelessness, being miserable and dejected Motivational deficits including loss of interest in normal daily activities Behavioural symptoms such as physical inactivity, decreased energy Physical symptoms such as insomnia or hypersomnia Cognitive features such as pessimistic thinking, negative beliefs about the world and hopelessness	5 or more from 9 specific symptoms present during the same 2-week period At least one of the symptoms is either depressed mood or loss of interest in pleasure Symptoms cause significant distress or daily impairment Symptoms are not better accounted for by significant losses, such as bereavement Symptoms persist for longer than 2 months	Most prevalent of the main psychological disorders Commonly comorbid with other Axis I and Axis II disorders Twice as common in women than in men Associated with imbalances in brain neurotransmitters such as serotonin and norepinephrine Associated with negative biases in ways of thinking and processing information	Genetic factors Role of neurotransmitters serotonin and norepinephrine Role of specific brain abnormalities Neuroendocrine factors Psychoanalytic accounts Behavioural theories Interpersonal theories Role of negative cognitions and self-schema Learned helplessness Attribution theory Hopelessness theory	Medication (such as tricyclic drugs, MAOIs and SSRIs) Electroconvulsive therapy (ECT) Psychoanalysis Social skills training Behavioural activation therapy Cognitive therapy Mindfulness-based cognitive therapy (MBCT)
BIPOLAR DISORDER (0.4%–1.6%)	Periods of mania that alternate with periods of depression	Presence or history of a manic episode and one or more major depressive episode If currently in a manic episode, there has been a history of at least one major depressive episode	Periods of extreme mania alternate with periods of major depression In Bipolar II disorder, depression alternates with mild manic episodes (hypomania) 10–25% of first-degree relatives of sufferers have also reported significant symptoms of mood disorder	Genetic factors Role of neurotransmitters serotonin and norepinephrine	Medication (lithium carbonate) Electroconvulsive therapy (ECT) Cognitive therapy in conjunction with appropriate medication

often significant features of the manic individual. Periods of mania can last for days or even weeks, and onset can occur rapidly over the course of a single day (see Table 6.2).

6.1.1 Major Depression

The DSM-IV-TR criteria for major depression are described in Table 6.3. Five or more of a range of symptoms have to be present during a 2-week period, and these symptoms must cause significant distress or impairment of normal day-to-day functioning. For a diagnosis of major depression, the severity of symptoms should not be easily explained in terms of a recent loss (such as a bereavement), and should not be associated with a general medical condition (such as heart disease or cancer), and should not be associated with substance abuse. A substance-induced mood disorder is a separate diagnosis given when depression occurs in the context of withdrawal from a drug of abuse (such as cocaine).

CLIENT'S PERSPECTIVE 6.1

The experience of bipolar disorder

Descriptions offered by people with bipolar disorder give valuable insights into the various mood states associated with the disorder.

- **Depression**: 'I doubt completely my ability to do anything well. It seems as though my mind has slowed down and burned out to the point of being virtually useless ... [I am] haunt[ed] ... with the total, the desperate hopelessness of it all ... Others say, "It's only temporary, it will pass, you can get over it," but of course they haven't any idea of how I feel, although they are certain they do. If I can't feel, move, think or care, then what on earth is the point?'

- **Hypomania**: 'At first when I'm high, it's tremendous ... ideas are fast ... like shooting stars you follow until brighter ones appear ... All shyness disappears, the right words and gestures are suddenly there ... uninteresting people, things become intensely interesting. Sensuality is pervasive; the desire to seduce and be seduced is irresistible. Your marrow is infused with unbelievable feelings of ease, power, well-being, omnipotence, euphoria ... you can do anything ... but, somewhere this changes.'

- **Mania**: 'The fast ideas become too fast and there are far too many ... overwhelming confusion replaces clarity ... you stop keeping up with it – memory goes. Infectious humour ceases to amuse. Your friends become frightened ... everything is now against the grain ... you are irritable, angry, frightened, uncontrollable, and trapped.'

Clinical Commentary

These accounts provide an insight into how the different mood states in bipolar disorder are experienced, and how the transition from a depressive episode moves through the mild manic episode called hypomania to full-blown mania. Typical of the transition from depression to full-blown mania are: (1) the overwhelming flow of thoughts and ideas that lead to the sufferer seeming incoherent and interrupting ongoing conversations; (2) the temptation to indulge in inappropriate sexual interactions as everyone around becomes a focus of interest and shyness is lost; and (3) the inevitable drift by the sufferer into irritability, frustration and anger as friends and acquaintances try to quell the excesses of thought and behaviour.

Table 6.2 *DSM-IV-TR criteria for a manic episode*

A A distinct period of abnormality and persistently elevated, expansive, or irritable mood, lasting at least 1 week (or any duration if hospitalization is necessary).

B During the period of mood disturbance, three (or more) of the following symptoms have persisted (four if the mood is only irritable) and have been present to a significant degree:

(1) inflated self-esteem or grandiosity

(2) decreased need for sleep (e.g. feels rested after only 3 hours of sleep)

(3) more talkative than usual or pressure to keep talking

(4) flight of ideas or subjective experience that thoughts are racing

(5) distractibility (i.e. attention too easily drawn to unimportant or irrelevant external stimuli)

(6) increase in goal-directed activity (either socially, at work or school, or sexually) or psychomotor agitation

(7) excessive involvement in pleasurable activities that have a high potential for painful consequences (e.g. engaging in unrestrained buying sprees, sexual indiscretions, or foolish business investments)

C The symptoms do not meet criteria for a mixed episode.

D The mood disturbance is sufficiently severe to cause marked impairments in occupational functioning or in usual social activities or relationships with others, or to necessitate hospitalization to prevent harm to self or others, or there are psychotic features.

E The symptoms are not due to the direct physiological effects of a substance (e.g. a drug of abuse, a medication, or other treatment) or a general medical condition (e.g. hyperthyroidism).

Table 6.3 *DSM-IV-TR criteria for major depressive episode*

A Five (or more) of the following symptoms have been present during the same 2-week period and represent a change from previous functioning; at least one of the symptoms is either (1) depressed mood or (2) loss of interest or pleasure.

Note: Do not include symptoms that are clearly due to a general medical condition, or mood-incongruent delusions or hallucinations.

(1) Depressed mood most of the day, nearly every day, as indicated by either subjective report (e.g. feels sad or empty) or observation made by others (e.g. appears tearful).

(2) Markedly diminished interest or pleasure in all, or almost all, activities most of the day, nearly every day (as indicated by either subjective account or observation made by others).

(3) Significant weight loss when not dieting or weight gain (e.g. a change of more than 5% of body weight in a month), or decrease or increase in appetitie nearly every day.

(4) Insomnia or hypersomnia nearly every day.

(5) Psychomotor agitation or retardation nearly every day (observable by others, not merely subjective feelings of restlessness or being slowed down).

(6) Fatigue or loss of energy nearly every day.

(7) Feelings of worthlessness or excessive or inappropriate guilt (which may be delusional) nearly every day (not merely self-reproach or guilt about being sick).

(8) Diminished ability to think or concentrate, or indecisiveness, nearly every day (either by subjective account or as observed by others).

(9) Recurrent thoughts of death (not just fear of dying), recurrent suicidal ideation without a specific plan, or a suicide attempt or a specific plan for commiting suicide.

B The symptoms do not meet the criteria for a mixed episode.

C The symptoms cause clinically significant distress or impairment in social, occupational, or other important areas of functioning.

D The symptoms are not due to the direct physiological effects of a substance (e.g. a drug of abuse, a medication) or a general medical condition (e.g. hypothyroidism).

E The symptoms are not better accounted for by bereavement, i.e. after the loss of a loved one, the symptoms persist for longer than 2 months or are characterized by marked functional impairment, morbid preoccupation with worthlessness, suicidal ideation, psychotic symptoms, or psychomotor retardation.

Chronic mood disturbances primarily characterized by depressive symptoms can also be diagnosed, although these conditions must have been apparent for at least 2 years, and would normally not be severe enough to disrupt normal social and occupational functioning and warrant a diagnosis of major depression. These are *dysthymic disorder*, in which the sufferer has experienced at least 2 years of depressed mood for more days than not. Individuals diagnosed with this disorder experience many of the behavioural and cognitive characteristics of major depression, but these are less severe (meeting only three or more of the symptom criteria for major depression). *Cyclothymic disorder* is characterized by at least 2 years of hypomania symptoms that do not meet the criteria for a manic episode (see Table 6.2), and the sufferer will experience alternating periods of withdrawal then exuberance, inadequacy then high self-esteem, and so on.

> **Dysthymic disorder** A form of depression in which the sufferer has experienced at least 2 years of depressed mood for more days than not.

> **Cyclothymic disorder** A form of depression characterized by at least 2 years of hypomania symptoms that do not meet the criteria for a manic episode and in which the sufferer experiences alternating periods of withdrawal then exuberance, inadequacy and then high self-esteem.

However, diagnosing depression is a controversial issue for a number of reasons. Firstly, DSM-IV-TR requires the identification of five symptoms for a period of 2 weeks for a diagnosis of major depression. But are such people any different in their experiences and their functioning from someone who exhibits only three symptoms? With only three symptoms, the depression would be labelled as sub-clinical, yet studies have suggested that individuals with three symptoms exhibit similar levels of distress and problems with day-to-day living as individuals with five symptoms (Gotlib, Lewinsohn & Seeley, 1995).

Secondly, depression is one of the most prevalent of all psychological problems and is experienced in some form or other by almost everyone at sometime in their life. Indeed, experiencing depression is the third most common reason for consulting a doctor or GP in the UK (Singleton, Bumpstead, O'Brien et al., 2001). In order for GPs to be able to provide treatment for such individuals, there is a tendency for them to overdiagnose mild or moderate depression (Middleton, Shaw, Hull & Feder, 2005). This raises a number of issues, including the possible stigmatization that such a label might incur for the patient. In addition, lay beliefs about depression suggest that many people already view depression as a 'disease' that is a normal consequence of everyday life stress (Lauber, Falcato, Nordt & Rossler, 2003). If lay people already view depression as a disease or biological illness, and GPs are more than willing to diagnose it, then, as we discussed in Focus Point 1.1, we run the risk of the medicalization of normal everyday negative emotions such as mild distress or even unhappiness (Shaw & Woodward, 2004).

Thirdly, depression occurs in a variety of different guises within psychopathology and is commonly comorbid with other important disorders (Kessler, Nelson, McGonagle, Liu et al., 1996) (see Table 6.4). This has given rise to a range of different diagnosable disorders that have depression as a central feature within them. As a result, major depression is a relatively 'pure' diagnosis where the cause of

Table 6.4 *Comorbidity of major depressive disorder with other DSM disorders*

	Lifetime comorbidity %	12-month comorbidity %
Anxiety Disorders		
Generalized anxiety disorder (GAD)	17.2	15.4
Agoraphobia	16.3	12.6
Specific phobia	24.3	23.7
Social phobia	27.1	20.0
Panic disorder	9.9	8.6
Post-traumatic stress disorder (PTSD)	19.5	15.2
Any anxiety disorder	58.0	51.2
Substance Use Disorders		
Alcohol dependency	23.5	13.0
Drug dependency	13.3	7.5
Alcohol abuse without dependency	4.1	1.4
Drug abuse without dependency	6.5	1.1
Any substance use disorder	38.6	18.5
Other Disorders		
Dysthymia	6.7	4.0
Conduct disorder	16.2	–
Aggregate Number of Disorders		
One	24.7	58.9
>One	74.0	26.9
Two	17.4	15.4
>Three	31.9	16.5

Note that the lifetime comorbidity rate of major depression with another anxiety disorder is 58% and with more than one other DSM disorder is 74%, suggesting that individuals with depression tend to experience a range of negative emotions and comorbid disorders.

Source: Kessler, Nelson, McGonagle, Liu et al. (1996).

Plate 6.1
Seasonal affective disorder is a depression that usually occurs in the winter months in temperate climates. A treatment often recommended by clinicians is to take a winter holiday in a sunny place!

Seasonal affective disorder is a condition of regularly occurring depressions in winter with a remission the following spring or summer. It is a relatively common condition, affecting 1–3 per cent of adults in temperate climates. The main symptoms include depressed mood, lack of energy, hypersomnia, craving for carbohydrates, overeating and weight gain (Rosenthal & Blehar, 1989). There is some evidence that individuals who develop SAD do so because the longer periods of darkness in winter increase their secretion of the hormone *melatonin*, which acts to slow organisms down, making them sleepy and less energetic (Wetterberg, 1999). The answer to this is to provide individuals suffering from SAD with light therapy or photo therapy in which they are exposed to periods of artificial sunlight during the darker winter months (Magnusson & Boivin, 2003; Gitlin, 2002).

> **Melatonin** A hormone which acts to slow organisms down, making them sleepy and less energetic.

Chronic fatigue syndrome is characterized by depression and mood fluctuations together with physical symptoms such as extreme fatigue, muscle pain, chest pain, headaches, and noise and light sensitivity (Bell, 1991; Wessely, 1992). Its causes are unclear at present, and this may be the reason why it is given a variety of names, including 'yuppie flu' because of its tendency to afflict predominantly successful young people – especially women – struggling with stressful work and family responsibilities (Ho-Yen, 1990). About 75 per cent of reported cases are adult white females (Showalter, 1997), but this may simply reflect the reluctance of males to report such symptoms. The causes of CFS have not been clearly identified, although theories have argued for the involvement of viral or immunological factors (Behan, More & Behan, 1991) and environmental stressors such as pollution or organophosphates (Jason, Wagner, Taylor, Ropacki et al., 1995). Other researchers have pointed out that depression can be identified as a risk factor in CFS, with a predisposition among CFS sufferers to develop depression and to exhibit frequency of depression prior to

depression cannot be attributed either to some other Axis I or Axis II disorder (such as the consequences of substance abuse) or to specific biological, environmental factors or other life events (such as postnatal depression).

Two prominent examples of diagnosable problems with depression as a significant element are *seasonal affective disorder (SAD)* and *chronic fatigue syndrome (CFS)* or myalgic encephalomyelitis (ME), and it is worth discussing these in a little more detail.

> **Seasonal affective disorder (SAD)**
> A condition of regularly occurring depressions in winter with a remission the following spring or summer.

> **Chronic fatigue syndrome (CFS)**
> A disorder characterized by depression and mood fluctuations together with physical symptoms such as extreme fatigue, muscle pain, chest pain, headaches and noise and light sensitivity.

Plate 6.2
Famous British experimental psychologist Professor Stuart Sutherland suffered with bipolar disorder for many years. He provided a riveting first-person account of his experiences in the book *Breakdown: A Personal Crisis and a Medical Dilemma* (1998).

CFS onset at twice the level of controls (Straus, Dale, Tobi, Lawley et al., 1988). Interestingly, studies that have provided cognitive behaviour therapy for adolescents with CFS have resulted in significant decreases in fatigue severity and functional impairment, suggesting that addressing psychological factors in CFS may play a significant role in successfully treating the syndrome (Stulemeijer, de Jong, Fiselier, Hoogveld et al., 2005).

6.1.2 Bipolar Disorder

DSM-IV-TR defines two main types of bipolar disorder, namely bipolar I disorder and bipolar II disorder. Table 6.5 illustrates the main diagnostic features of these two definitions. The most common of these two diagnoses is bipolar I disorder, where individuals exhibit full manic and major depressive episodes in alternating sequences. In bipolar II disorder, major depressive episodes alternate with periods of *hypomania* (mild manic episodes). While the symptoms of bipolar II disorder must be sufficiently severe to cause distress or impairment, individuals with this disorder can often be relatively productive during their periods of hypomania (Jamison, 1995).

Hypomania   Mild episodes of mania.

SELF-TEST QUESTIONS

- What are the two main mood disorders?
- Name at least five of the symptoms that must be present during a two-week period for a diagnosis of major depression.
- What are dysthymic disorder and cyclothymic disorder?
- Can you describe some of the problems involved in diagnosing major depression?
- Can you describe some of the main features of seasonal affective disorder (SAD) and chronic fatigue syndrome (CFS)?
- What is the distinction between bipolar I disorder and bipolar II disorder?

Table 6.5 *DSM-IV-TR criteria for bipolar I and bipolar II disorder*

Bipolar I disorder

A   Currently (or most recently) in a manic episode.

B   There has previously been at least one major depressive episode, manic episode, or mixed episode.

C   The mood episodes in Criteria A and B are not better accounted for by schizoaffective disorder and are not superimposed on schizophrenia, schizophreniform disorder, delusional disorder, or psychotic disorder not otherwise specified.

Bipolar II disorder

A   Presence (or history) of one or more major depressive episodes.

B   Presence (or history) of at least one hypomanic episode.

C   There has never been a manic episode or a mixed episode.

D   The mood symptoms in Criteria A and B are not better accounted for by schizoaffective disorder and are not superimposed on schizophrenia, schizophreniform disorder, delusional disorder, or psychotic disorder not otherwise specified.

E   The symptoms cause clinically significant distress or impairment in social, occupational, or other important areas of functioning.

SECTION SUMMARY

6.1 The Characteristics of Depression and Mood Disorders

- **Major depression** (or **unipolar depression**) and **bipolar depression** are the two main types of clinical depression.

- Bipolar disorder is characterized by periods of **mania** that alternate with periods of depression.

- Depression is the third most common reason for consulting a doctor or GP in the UK.

- The lifetime comorbidity rate of major depression with another anxiety disorder is 58 per cent and with more than one other DSM disorder is 74 per cent, suggesting that individuals with depression experience a range of negative emotions.

- **Seasonal affective disorder** (**SAD**) and **chronic fatigue syndrome** (**CFS**) are two prominent disorders with depression as a significant element.

6.2 THE PREVALENCE OF DEPRESSION AND MOOD DISORDERS

Depression is arguably the most prevalent of the psychopathologies that are covered in this book. Estimates of lifetime prevalence rates for major depression in American community samples range from 5.2 per cent to 17.1 per cent (Kessler, McConagle, Zhao, Nelson et al., 1994; Weissman, Bland, Canino, Faravelli et al., 1996), and depression is now so commonly recognized that it contributes 12 per cent to the total burden of non-fatal global disease (Ustun, Ayuso-Mateos, Chatterji, Mathers et al., 2004).

DSM-IV-TR gives the lifetime risk for major depression as between 10 and 25 per cent for women and between 5 and 12 per cent for men, and for bipolar I disorder as 0.4–1.6 per cent across both men and women. However, gauging the prevalence of depressive symptoms has been difficult because (1) prevalence rates appear to differ significantly across different cultures; (2) the incidence of the diagnosis of depression has increased steadily over the last 90 years; and (3) different studies have tended to use different diagnostic tools when assessing prevalence. For example, studies conducted by the Crossnational Collaborative Group reported very large cultural variations in the prevalence of major depression. These ranged from 1.5 per cent in Taiwan to 19.0 per cent in Lebanon. Lifetime prevalence rates for Puerto Rico and Korea were relatively low at 4.3 per cent and 2.9 per cent respectively compared to 10.2 per cent for the US (Weissman, Bland, Canino, Faravelli et al., 1996). There appear to be a number of reasons for these large international variations in lifetime prevalence rates. These include: (1) the stigmatizing of psychopathology in many non-Western societies such as Taiwan, indicating that many individuals in those societies will be unwilling to report symptoms of major depression (Compton, Helzer, Hwu, Yeh et al., 1991); (2) higher levels of somatization (the expression of psychological distress in physical terms) in non-Western countries (Simon, von Korff, Piccinelli, Fullerton et al., 1999); (3) the fact that – unlike many other psychopathologies (such as obesity and hypertension) – depression cannot be observed or measured directly, so there will always be an element of subjectivity in the way the symptoms are measured and recorded (Patten, 2003); and (4) lifetime prevalence rates will always be affected by recall problems, and recall failure with age appears to account for the fact that lifetime prevalence rates decrease with increasing age cohorts (Patten, 2003).

The incidence of major depression has steadily increased since 1915 and median age of onset has decreased to around 27 years in the US (Kessler, 2002). Women are almost twice as vulnerable to periods of major depression as men (Nolen-Hoeksema, 2002), and this is independent of cultural background.

SELF-TEST QUESTIONS

● Why has it been difficult to gauge the prevalence of depressive disorders?
● What are the lifetime prevalence rates of the main mood disorders and are these prevalence rates showing any trends over time?

ACTIVITY BOX 6.1

Why are women twice as likely as men to be diagnosed with major depression?

The prevalence rate for major depression is between 10 and 25 per cent for women and only 5–12 per cent for men, so what accounts for this major sex difference? You might like to begin a group discussion by asking males and females in your group to say how their experiences as a man or woman might influence their susceptibility to developing episodes of depression.

Prior to your group discussion, you might find it useful to read *Journal of Affective Disorders*, 74, 1 (2003), which is a dedicated special issue on women and depression.

Your discussion may want to take into account the following facts:

● There is no sex difference in the rate of experienced depression prior to age 14–15 years (Nolen-Hoeksema, 2001).

● Women are more likely to ruminate about their depressive symptoms, whereas men tend to try to distract themselves or express their depression as anger (Mirowsky & Ross, 1995; Just & Alloy, 1997).

● After puberty, females tend to be less at ease with the physical changes occurring in their body than are males (Harter, 1999).

● After puberty, women experience more life stressors than men (Hankin & Abramson, 2001).

● Being married and having children increases the risk of major depression in women, but not in men (Lucht, Schaub, Meyer, Hapke et al., 2003).

Think about the following possibilities:

● Do women get more depressed than men because they feel they have less control over their lives? Are women more likely to blame themselves for failures than men?

● Do Western societies set higher cultural standards for women than men (e.g. body shape standards are more defined for women than men), and do women get depressed when they fail to meet these relatively high standards?

● Are men simply less likely to admit that they are depressed than women?

Researchers are far from agreed as to the reasons why twice as many women as men suffer from depression, so there are no right or wrong answers and your group discussion will add to this ongoing debate.

SECTION SUMMARY

6.2 The Prevalence of Depression and Mood Disorders

- Estimates of lifetime prevalence rates for major depression range from 5.2 per cent to 17.1 per cent.

- Major depression is almost **twice as common** in women as in men.

- The incidence of major depression has increased since 1915 with a median onset age of around 27 years.

- The lifetime risk for bipolar disorder is 0.4 per cent to 1.6 per cent.

6.3 THE AETIOLOGY OF DEPRESSION AND MOOD DISORDERS

6.3.1 Biological Theories

6.3.1.1 Genetic Factors

There is good evidence that depressive symptoms run in families, and this suggests the possible existence of an inherited or genetic component to major depression and bipolar disorder. For example, family studies have indicated that 10–25 per cent of first-degree relatives of bipolar disorder sufferers have also reported significant symptoms of mood disorder (Gershon, 2000), and it has been estimated that approximately 7 per cent of the first-degree relatives of sufferers also have bipolar disorder (Kelsoe, 2003) – this is compared to a lifetime prevalence rate in the general population of between 0.4 and 1.6 per cent. However, the increased risk of depressive symptoms for relatives of major depression sufferers is significantly less (5–10 per cent) than for bipolar disorder, but still higher than would be expected in the general population (Kendler, Pederson, Johnson, Neale et al., 1993).

Twin studies also suggest a significant inherited component in mood disorders. For example, Table 6.6 shows the concordance rates for mood disorders in sets of monozygotic (MZ) twins and dizygotic (DZ) twins (Kelsoe, 2003). Concordance rates average 69 per cent and 29 per cent for MZ and DZ twins respectively, suggesting that sharing all genes as opposed to half of genes more than doubles the risk for developing a mood disorder. With respect to individual mood disorders, twin studies of major depression have indicated concordance rates of 46 per cent and 20 per cent respectively for MZ and DZ twins (McGuffin, Katz, Watkins & Rutherford, 1996), and 58 per cent and 17 per cent respectively in the case of bipolar disorder (Bertelsen, Harvald & Hauge, 1977). These results

Table 6.6 *Concordance rates in selected twin studies of bipolar disorder (if one twin suffers from bipolar disorder, the percentage probability that the other twin will also suffer from the disorder)*

Study	Monozygotic twins (MZ) %	Dizygotic twins (DZ) %
Rosanoff et al. (1935)	69.6	16.4
Kallman (1954)	92.6	23.6
Bertelsen (1979)	58.3	17.3
Kendler et al. (1993)	60.7	34.9
TOTAL	**69.6**	**29.3**

Source: Kelsoe (2003).

clearly support the case for a genetic component to depression, and recent estimates suggest that around 30 per cent of the variance in depressive symptomatology can be accounted for by inherited factors (Agrawal, Jacobson, Gardner, Prescott et al., 2004).

6.3.1.2 Neurochemical Factors

Depression and mood disorders have been shown to be reliably associated with abnormalities in the levels of certain brain neurotransmitters. Two neurotransmitters are particularly significant: *serotonin* and *norepinephrine* (Delgardo & Moreno, 2000). Depression is regularly associated with low levels of both these neurotransmitters, and the mania found in bipolar disorder is found to be associated specifically with high levels of norepinephrine. A number of factors led to these findings about the importance of serotonin and norepinephrine levels. First, in the 1950s it was noticed that many medications for high blood pressure also caused depression (Ayd, 1956), and this effect was found to be the result of such medications decreasing brain serotonin levels. The 1950s also saw the development of drugs that significantly alleviated the symptoms of depression. The main ones were *tricyclic drugs* (such as imipramine) and *monoamine oxidase (MAO) inhibitors* (such as tranylcypromine). Both of these drugs have their effects by increasing levels of both serotonin and norepinephrine in the brain. These findings led to the development of neurochemical theories of depression, which

> **Serotonin** An important brain neurotransmitter where low levels are ascuated with depression.

> **Norepinephrine** An adrenal hormone which functions as a neurotransmitter and is associated with symptoms of both depression and mania.

> **Tricyclic drugs** A group of drugs which have their effects by increasing levels of both serotonin and norepinephrine in the brain.

> **Monoamine oxidase (MAO) inhibitors** A group of antidepressant drugs which have their effects by increasing levels of both serotonin and norepinephrine in the brain.

argued that depression was caused by either low norepinephrine activity (Bunney & Davis, 1965) or low serotonin activity (Golden & Gilmore, 1990). Because these neurotransmitters are necessary for the successful transmission of impulses between neurons, their abnormally low levels in depressed individuals may account for the cognitive, behavioural and motivational deficits found in major depression and the depressed phases of bipolar disorder.

Tricyclic drugs have their beneficial effects by preventing the reuptake by the presynaptic neuron of serotonin and norepinephrine. This results in higher levels of these neurotransmitters in the synapse, which facilitates the transmission of impulses to the postsynaptic neuron – thus facilitating brain activity. More recently, the development of *selective serotonin reuptake inhibitors (SSRIs)* (such as Prozac) has allowed researchers to assess the specific role of serotonin in depression, and it is now believed that serotonin levels play a central role in major depression. In contrast, norepinephrine levels were thought to be more important in bipolar disorder, where low levels of this neurotransmitter are associated with depression and high levels with mania (Bunney, Goodwin & Murphy, 1972; Altshuler, Curran, Hauser, Mintz et al., 1995).

However, this picture is relatively simplistic, and the most recent neurochemical theories of mood disorders suggest that inter-

> **Selective serotonin reuptake inhibitors (SSRIs)** A recent group of antidepressant drugs that selectively affect the uptake of only one neurotransmitter – usually serotonin.

actions between different neurotransmitters may be important. Some researchers suggest that depression is associated more with an *imbalance* in neurotransmitters than with deficits in specific neurotransmitters (Rampello, Nicoletti & Nicoletti, 2000). Other theorists have suggested that low levels of serotonin interact with levels of norepinephrine in rather complex ways, such that combinations of low levels of both serotonin and norepinephrine produce depression, but low levels of serotonin and high levels of norepinephrine result in mania (Mandell & Knapp, 1979).

6.3.1.3 Brain Abnormalities and Depression

Recent developments in cognitive neuroscience together with the evolution of new technologies for scanning and photographing the brain (e.g. magnetic resonance imaging, MRI; see Chapter 2, section 2.1.3.2) have led to a greater understanding of the brain areas involved in depression and mood disorders (Davidson, Pizzagalli, Nitschke & Putnam, 2002). Studies have identified dysfunction or abnormalities in a number of brain areas that appear to be associated with depression. These areas are the prefrontal cortex, the anterior cingulate cortex, the hippocampus and the amygdala, all of which are illustrated in Figure 6.2. This raises the question of the role that such areas may play in relation to depression, and Davidson et al. (2002) have attempted to address these issues.

First, depression is associated with significantly lower levels of activation in the *prefrontal cortex* (Drevets, 1998).

> **Prefrontal cortex** An area of the brain which is important in maintaining representations of goals and the means to achieve them.

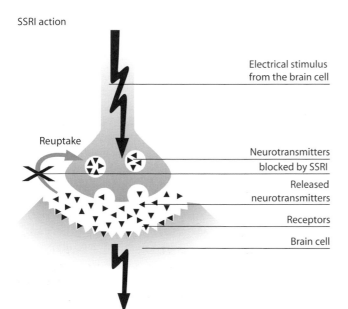

SSRI action

Electrical stimulus from the brain cell

Reuptake

Neurotransmitters blocked by SSRI

Released neurotransmitters

Receptors

Brain cell

Figure 6.1
Neurons release the neurotransmitters serotonin and norepinephrine from their endings when they fire, and these help transmission between brain cells. Some of the neurotransmitter molecules are recaptured by the neuron using a reuptake mechanism. This can occur before they are received by the receptor neuron, thus weakening the transmission between neurons. Both tricyclic drugs and SSRIs have their effect by blocking the reuptake of these neurotransmitters and so ensure that neural transmission is more effective. Tricyclic drugs block the reuptake of both serotonin and norepinephrine, while SSRIs selectively block the reuptake only of serotonin.

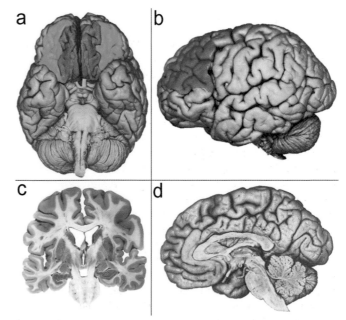

a   b

c   d

Figure 6.2
Key brain regions involved in affect and mood disorders: (a) orbital prefrontal cortex (green) and the ventromedial prefrontal cortex (red); (b) dorsolateral prefrontal cortex (blue); (c) hippocampus (purple) and amygdala (orange); (d) anterior cingulate cortex (yellow).
Source: Davidson, Pizzagalli, Nitschke & Putnam (2002).

This area is important in maintaining representations of goals and the means to achieve them. Decreased activation in this area may result in the failure to anticipate incentives that is a common feature of depression.

Second, decreased *anterior cingulate cortex (ACC)* activation is also reported in major depression (Beauregard, Leroux, Bergman, Arzoumanian et al., 1998). Evidence suggests that ACC activation is present when effortful emotional regulation is required in situations where behaviour is failing to achieve a desired outcome (Ochsner & Barrett, 2001). Davidson et al. (2002) suggest that this may reflect a deficit in the 'will-to-change' that is also characteristic of depressed individuals.

Anterior cingulate cortex (ACC) The frontal part of the cingulate cortex resembling a 'collar' form around the corpus callosum, used for the relay of neural signals between the right and left hemispheres of the brain.

Third, individuals with depression and mood disorders also show signs of dysfunction in the *hippocampus* (Mervaala, Fohr, Kononen, Valkonen-Korhonen et al., 2000). The hippocampus is important in adrenocorticotropic hormone secretion and is also critical in learning about the *context* of affective reactions (Fanselow, 2000). Thus, deficits in hippocampus function in depression may result in the individual dissociating affective responses from their relevant contexts. In depression, this may manifest itself as feelings of sadness occurring independently of contexts in which we would normally expect such emotions (i.e. sadness is experienced in all contexts, not just following relevant life events such as a bereavement).

Hippocampus A part of the brain which is important in adrenocorticotropic hormone secretion and is also critical in learning about the context of affective reactions.

Finally, major depression has also been found to be associated with structural and functional abnormalities in the *amygdala*, and especially with increased amygdala activation (Abercrombie, Schaefer, Larson, Oakes et al., 1998). One role of the amygdala is in directing attention to affectively salient stimuli and prioritizing the processing of such stimuli. The effect of raised levels of activation in the amygdala may therefore result in the depressed individual prioritizing threatening information for processing and interpreting such information negatively.

Amygdala An area of the brain that plays an important role in directing attention to affectively salient stimuli and prioritizing the processing of such stimuli.

These explanations of depressive symptomatology in terms of dysfunction in specific brain areas are not necessarily inconsistent with those theories that attempt to explain depression in terms of neurotransmitter imbalances. It is quite possible that the functional brain deficits reported in depression may indeed result from imbalances in specific neurotransmitters such as serotonin and norepinephrine.

6.3.1.4 Neuroendocrine Factors

We mentioned earlier that the hippocampus is important in adrenocorticotropic hormone secretion, and that depressed individuals frequently exhibit hippocampal abnormalities (Mervaala, Fohr, Kononen, Valkonen-Korhonen et al., 2000). These hippocampal abnormalities are regularly linked with high levels of *cortisol* (an adrenocortical hormone), and patients receiving chronic corticosteroid therapy for endocrine problems have smaller hippocampal volumes and higher depression ratings than non-patient controls (Brown, Woolston, Frol, Bobadilla et al., 2004). Persistent psychological distress is a common feature of patients being treated for endocrine disease, with studies showing that around 26 per cent meet DSM-IV-TR criteria for major depression (Sonino, Navarrini, Ruini, Ottolini et al., 2004). High levels of cortisol may lead to depression by causing enlargement of the adrenal glands and in turn lowering the frequency of serotonin transmitters in the brain (Roy, Virkkunen & Linnoila, 1987). We saw earlier that low levels of the neurotransmitter serotonin in the brain have been established as an important factor in depression. Cortisol is also a hormone that is released by the body during times of stress (Holsboer, 2001), and it is no coincidence that periods of depression are often preceded by stressful life events. So, according to this account, life stressors raise levels of the adrenocortical hormone cortisol, which in turn lowers levels of the brain neurotransmitter serotonin, which results in the cognitive, behavioural and motivational symptoms of depression.

Cortisol An adrenocortical hormone.

SUMMARY

The preceding evidence suggests that biological factors may play an important role in the development and maintenance of mood disorders such as depression. There is clearly an inherited component (which accounts for about a third of the variance in measures of depression), and abnormalities in specific brain neurotransmitters such as serotonin and norepinephrine have been clearly linked to symptoms of depression. Recent developments in brain scanning technology have also allowed researchers to identify abnormalities in specific areas of the human brain that are associated with depression. These are all impressive and important findings, but we must remember that depression and mood disorders almost certainly do not stem solely from biological dysfunction. As we shall see in the next section, psychological and cognitive factors are equally important in the aetiology and maintenance of mood disorders, and supplement our knowledge of biological factors. Biological and psychological explanations are not mutually exclusive and they attempt to explain phenomena at different levels of description. Indeed, it is still not clear whether many of the biological factors we have described in section 6.3.1 are truly *causal* factors in depression, or whether they simply represent biological changes that reflect the *experience* of depression. That is, biological factors may give rise to many of the symptoms of depression, but psychological processes may in turn trigger these biological factors.

6.3.2 *Psychological Theories*

6.3.2.1 **Psychodynamic Explanations**

There are a number of different psychodynamic views of depression (see Blatt & Homann, 1992), but the most well established is the psychoanalytic account pioneered by Freud (1917/1963) and Abraham (1916/1960). This view argues that depression is a response to loss, and, in particular, a response to the loss of a loved one such as a parent. The first stage of response to this loss is called *introjection*, where individuals regress to the oral stage of development, allowing them to integrate the identity of the person they have lost with their own. Introjection also allows individuals to direct all of the feelings they would have for the loved one onto themselves. These feelings include anger if they feel that the loved one has 'deserted' them and guilt if they experience any positive emotions in the wake of the loss. Individuals begin to experience self-hatred, which develops very rapidly into low self-esteem, and this adds to feelings of depression and hopelessness.

> **Introjection**   A response to a loss where individuals regress to the oral stage of development, which allows them to integrate the identity of the person they have lost with their own.

Because such losses return individuals to the oral stage of development, *psychoanalysis* argues that depression has a functional role to play in that it returns individuals to a period in their lives when they were dependent on others (their parents). During their depressed state, this regression to the oral stage allows individuals to become dependent on their relationships with others in order to utilize the support that this will offer. One problem with this psychoanalytic interpretation is that not everyone who experiences depression has lost a loved one. This led Freud to propose the concept of *symbolic loss* in which other kinds of losses in one's life (e.g. losing a job) are viewed as equivalent to losing a loved one. These losses then cause individuals to regress to the oral stage of development and may trigger memories of inadequate parental support during childhood. In addition, parental loss is no longer seen as a necessary condition for the development of depression, and poor parenting is a more significant risk factor (Lara & Klein, 1999). Support for this view comes from studies that have shown a relationship between risk for depression in adulthood and having experienced a particular kind of parenting style known as *affectionless control* (Garber & Flynn, 2001). This type of parenting is characterized by high levels of overprotection combined with a lack of warmth and care.

> **Symbolic loss**   A Freudian concept whereby other kinds of losses within one's life (e.g. losing a job) are viewed as equivalent to losing a loved one.

> **Affectionless control**   A type of parenting characterized by high levels of overprotection combined with a lack of warmth and care.

There is some empirical support for this psychoanalytic view of depression. For example, individuals who report that their childhood needs were not adequately met by their parents are more likely to become depressed after experiencing a loss (Goodman, 2002). Secondly, there is evidence for a link between parental loss and depression. Women whose mothers either died or abandoned them during their childhood are more likely to develop depression than women who have not had these kinds of experiences (Harris, Brown & Bifulco, 1990). Nevertheless, there are a number of difficulties with the psychoanalytic view. First, much of the empirical evidence that is consistent with this view is also consistent with many other theories of depression, so the evidence does not help to differentiate between theoretical approaches. Secondly, many individuals who experience parental loss or poor parenting do not go on to develop depression. Psychoanalytic approaches do not clearly explain why this is the case. Finally, because of the way that psychodynamic theories are formulated, many of the key aspects of the theory are difficult to test. Concepts such as introjection, fixation at the oral stage of development and symbolic loss are all difficult to operationalize and measure, and thus difficult to verify empirically. This difficulty is compounded by the Freudian belief that such processes are thought to operate at the unconscious level.

6.3.2.2 **Behavioural Theories**

The most obvious characteristics of depressed individuals include their lack of motivation and initiative, a considerably diminished behavioural repertoire and a view of the future that lacks positive and fulfilling experiences. Some theorists have suggested that these characteristics provide evidence that depression results from a lack of appropriate reinforcement for positive and constructive behaviours (Lewinsohn, 1974). This leads to the extinction of existing behaviours, and to a 'behavioural vacuum' in which the person becomes inactive and withdrawn. It is certainly the case that periods of depression follow life 'losses' such as bereavement, retirement or redundancy, and each of these events represents the loss of important sources of reward and reinforcement for social and occupational behaviours. In support of this account, it has been shown that depressed individuals report fewer rewards in their life than non-depressed individuals, and introducing rewards into the lives of depressed individuals helps to elevate their mood (Lewinsohn, Youngren & Grosscup, 1979; Jacobson, Martell & Dimidjian, 2001).

The fact that life 'losses' are likely to result in the reduction of reinforcing events for the depressed individual also leads to a vicious cycle that can establish depression as a chronic condition. For example, once the individual becomes depressed, then his or her lack of initiative and withdrawal are unlikely to lead to the development of other alternative sources of reinforcement. Indeed, the demeanour of depressed individuals is likely to be an active contributor to their lack of reinforcement – especially social reinforcement. For example, depressed individuals are significantly more likely than non-depressed individuals to elicit negative reactions in others (Joiner, 2002) – perhaps because they do not enter into the reciprocal reinforcing activities that social interaction requires. Depressed individuals are also less skilled at interacting with others than non-depressed individuals (Joiner, 2001; Segrin, 2000). In particular, they will usually communicate negative attitudes, appear withdrawn and unresponsive and tend to demand reassurance. Indeed, when interacting with depressed individuals, non-depressed control participants exhibit less positive social behaviour, are less verbal and are less positive than when interacting with a non-depressed individual (Gotlib & Robinson, 1982).

"I GUESS RETIREMENT IS OKAY, BUT WHAT I MISS MOST IS GOOFING OFF ON COMPANY TIME."

Plate 6.3
Retirement represents an important loss of sources of rewards for a range of activities, and this may account for the depression that individuals often experience immediately after retiring.

The frequent failure of depressed individuals to elicit reinforcing reactions from individuals with whom they are communicating has led to *interpersonal theories* of depression. These theories argue that depression is maintained by a cycle of reassurance seeking from depressed individuals that is subsequently rejected by family and friends because of the negative way in which depressed individuals talk about their problems (Joiner, 1995). The negative beliefs about themselves, their world and their future lead depressed individuals to doubt any reassurances they are given by friends and family, and this continual doubting may come to annoy friends and family who try to provide reassurance (Joiner & Metalsky, 1995). Interestingly, excessive reassurance seeking in depressed individuals predicts future depressive symptoms (Joiner, Metalsky, Katz et al., 1999), and roommates of depressed college students report greater hostility to them than to non-depressed roommates (Joiner, Alfano & Metalsky, 1992). Evidence such as this appears to support the view that the behaviour and attitudes displayed by depressed individuals elicit negative responses in others, and this in turn can exacerbate the symptoms of depression.

However, we must be cautious about how we interpret this evidence as a causal factor in depression. First, much of the research on the link between lack of reinforcement and depression has been retrospective in nature, and it is quite reasonable to suppose that depressed individuals may underestimate the extent of the actual rewards in their life. Secondly, individuals must first

> **Interpersonal theories** Theories that argue that depression is maintained by a cycle of reassurance-seeking by depressed individuals that is subsequently rejected by family and friends because of the negative way in which depressed individuals talk about their problems.

become depressed before their 'depressed' symptoms can become a source of irritation to others and cause difficulties in social interaction. Although interpersonal theories of depression may explain the maintenance of depression, and even predict relapse, we may need to look elsewhere for the initial causes of depression.

Negative Cognitions and Self-Schemas One of the most influential of all the theories of depression is Beck's cognitive theory (Beck, 1967, 1987). This theory introduced the idea that depression could be caused by biases in ways of thinking and processing information. We know that depressed individuals indulge in a good deal of 'negative thinking', and that they experience more negative intrusive thoughts than non-depressed individuals (Reynolds & Salkovskis, 1992). Facts such as this have led Beck (1987) to claim that depressed individuals have developed a broad-ranging **negative schema** that tends them towards viewing the world and themselves in a negative way. In turn, these negative schemas influence the selection, encoding, categorization and evaluation of stimuli and events in the world in a way that leads to a vicious cycle of depressive affect and symptomatology. Beck argued that these negative schemas are relatively stable characteristics of the depressed individual's personality and develop as a result of early adverse childhood experiences – especially concerning loss (such as the loss of a parent figure). In later life, a stressful experience will reactivate this negative schema and give rise to the biased thinking that generates depressive symptoms such as deficits in motivational, affective, cognitive and behavioural functioning.

> **Negative schema** A set of beliefs that tends individuals towards viewing the world and themselves in a negative way.

Beck argued that the depressed individual's negative schema maintained some interrelated aspects of negative thinking that he called the **negative triad**. In particular, depressed people hold negative views of *themselves* (e.g. 'I am unattractive'), negative views of their *future* (e.g. 'I will never achieve anything') and negative views of the *world* (e.g. 'the world is a dangerous and unsupportive place'). This set of negative beliefs eventually generates self-fulfilling prophecies (see Figure 6.3). That is, the depressed individual interprets events negatively, fails to take the initiative, and then inevitably experiences failure. The negative triad of beliefs leads to a number of systematic biases in thinking, including arbitrary inference, selective abstraction, overgeneralization, magnification and minimization, personalization and all-or-none thinking (see Table 6.7).

> **Negative triad** A theory of depression in which depressed people hold negative views of *themselves* (e.g. 'I am unattractive'), of their *future* (e.g. 'I will never achieve anything') and of the *world* (e.g. 'The world is a dangerous and unsupportive place').

There is considerable evidence that depressed individuals do show the negative cognitive biases that Beck's theory predicts. First, some studies have shown attentional biases to negative information in depressed individuals that results in them prioritizing that negative information. In the Emotional Stroop Procedure (see Chapter 5, Research Methods Box 5.2), depressed individuals are slower at naming the colour of negative words than positive words, suggesting that their attention is drawn towards the meaning of such words (Gotlib & Cane, 1987). Also, in a dichotic

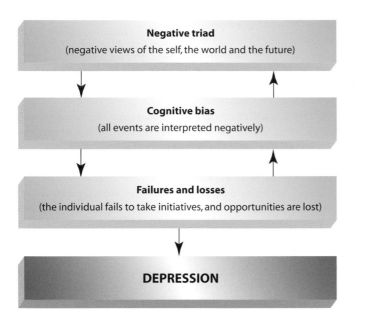

Figure 6.3 *Beck's negative schema in depression.*
This figure shows how the negative biases in the thinking of depressed individuals lead to a vicious cycle in which depression becomes a self-fulfilling prophecy.

Table 6.7 *Thinking biases in Beck's model of depression*

Arbitrary inference	Jumping to a conclusion when evidence is lacking or is actually contrary to the conclusion.
Selective abstraction	Abstracting a detail out of context and missing the significance of the total situation.
Overgeneralization	Unjustified generalization on the basis of a single incident (e.g. making a single mistake and concluding 'I never do anything right').
Magnification and minimization	Perceiving events as either totally bad or neutral or irrelevant. Catastrophizing is an example of magnification, in which the individual takes a single fact to its extreme (e.g. a scratch on a new car means the car is wrecked and needs replacing).
Personalization	The propensity to interpret events in terms of their personal meaning to the individual rather than their objective characteristics (e.g. believing that a frown on another person's face means they are annoyed specifically with you).
All-or-none thinking	Events are labelled as black or white, good or bad, wonderful or horrible (e.g. assuming that everyone will either accept you or reject you).

listening procedure, depressed individuals have greater difficulty ignoring negative words that are presented as distractors than do non-depressed participants (Ingram, Bernet & McLaughlin, 1994). The exact nature of this attentional bias is unclear, and some studies have failed to replicate these experimental effects (e.g. Mogg, Bradley, Williams & Mathews, 1993). Nevertheless, there is sufficient evidence to suggest that there is a bias towards processing negative information in depression – especially if it is information that is specifically relevant to depression (rather than general negative words) (Gotlib, Gilboa & Sommerfeld, 2000).

Second, memory biases are also apparent in depression, with depressed individuals able to recall more negative words than positive words in explicit memory tests (Mathews & MacLeod, 1994), but this again seems to apply predominantly to depression-relevant material rather than to threat-relevant material generally (Watkins, Mathews, Williamson & Fuller, 1992). Furthermore, recent studies have indicated that depressed individuals will remember more negative than positive information about themselves (Alloy, Abramson, Murray, Whitehouse et al., 1997), and of particular interest is the biased recall of autobiographical memories by depressed individuals. Not only do they recall fewer positive autobiographical experiences than non-depressed individuals, but those positive memories that are retrieved are more general and less detailed (Williams & Scott, 1988; Raes, Hermans, Williams & Eelen, 2006). Subsequent studies have suggested that there may be an association between experiencing early life trauma (such as childhood abuse) and reduced autobiographical memory specificity (Raes, Hermans, Williams & Eelen, 2005), and that poorly detailed autobiographical memories may be linked to the deficits in problem-solving ability that are characteristic of depressed individuals (Pollock & Williams, 2001).

Third, there is experimental evidence that depressed individuals exhibit the interpretational bias that would lead them to interpreting ambiguous events negatively or to judge events more negatively. There is considerable evidence, for example, that depressed affect is associated with more critical self-judgement and a raising of personal performance standards (Forgas, Bower & Krantz, 1984; Scott & Cervone, 2002).

In addition to the evidence supporting the existence of negative information processing biases in depression, there is also evidence that supports specific predictions from Beck's theory. For example, studies using the Dysfunctional Attitude Scale (DAS), which measures dysfunctional negative beliefs, have shown that negative thinking in combination with a recent negative life event can trigger depression (Lewinsohn, Rohde, Seeley & Baldwin, 2001). Further research has suggested that depressed individuals may have two different types of negative schema – one related to dependency and the other related to criticism (Nietzel & Harris, 1990). In the case of a dependency self-schema, losses would trigger depression (e.g. bereavement), but in the case of the criticism self-schema, depression would be triggered by failures (e.g. failing an interview) (Coyne & Whiffen, 1995).

Finally, we tend to associate depression, and Beck's cognitive theory of depression in particular, with **pessimistic thinking** caused by negative self-schemas. However, evidence suggests that what depressed individuals may actually lack is the positive interpretation bias possessed by non-depressed individuals. It turns out that depressed individuals are much more accurate in experimental studies at evaluating (1) how much control they may have over a situation (Alloy & Abramson, 1979) and (2) the impression they made on others in a social situation (Lewinsohn, Sullivan & Grosscup, 1980). In contrast, non-depressed individuals are unduly *optimistic* in their estimates. This suggests that depressed individuals may be much more objective about the judgements they make, and it is non-depressed individuals who possess a positive bias that may act to 'make them feel good about themselves' (Lewinsohn, Sullivan & Grosscup, 1980).

> **Pessimistic thinking** A form of dysfunctional thinking where sufferers believe nothing can improve their lot.

In summary, Beck's cognitive theory of depression has been significantly influential in determining the way we conceptualize, research and treat depression. It has generated a range of research on cognitive biases in depression and has contributed substantially to cognitive-based treatments of depression (see section 6.4.2). However, it is still unclear whether the negative cognitive biases defined by Beck's theory actually cause depression, or whether these biases are simply a consequence of experienced depression. Further research will be needed to clarify issues such as these.

Learned Helplessness and Attribution

During a person's lifetime he or she may experience a number of unavoidable and uncontrollable negative life events. These may include the sudden death of a close friend or relative, or being made redundant from a job. Seligman (1975) proposed that depression could be linked specifically to these kinds of experiences, and that they give rise to a 'cognitive set' that makes the individual learn to become 'helpless', lethargic and depressed. It is the perceived uncontrollability of these negative life events that is important, and which leads individuals to the pessimistic belief that negative life events will happen whatever they do. Seligman (1974) first derived this hypothesis from animal learning experiments in which dogs were first given unavoidable electric shocks, and then subsequently taught to learn a simple avoidance response that would avoid the shocks. He found that dogs that were given prior unavoidable electric shocks were subsequently unable to learn the avoidance response and simply lay down in the apparatus and 'quietly whined'. One example of how **learned helplessness** theory has been applied to depression is in the case of battered women. Walker (2000) has suggested that a pattern of repeated partner abuse leads battered women to believe that they are powerless to change their situation. As a result, such women come

> **Learned helplessness** A theory of depression that argues that people become depressed following unavoidable negative life events because these events give rise to a cognitive set that makes individuals learn to become 'helpless', lethargic and depressed.

to exhibit all the symptoms of depression and display the 'passivity' found in **battered woman syndrome**.

> **Battered woman syndrome** The view that a pattern of repeated partner abuse leads battered women to believe that they are powerless to change their situation.

However, while animal experiments on learned helplessness do appear to have a formalistic similarity to human depression, there are a number of reasons for believing that this is not a full or comprehensive account of depression. First, some studies with humans have suggested that prior experience with uncontrollable negative events may actually facilitate subsequent performance (Wortman & Brehm, 1975). Secondly, many depressed individuals see themselves as being responsible for their failures and losses – yet someone who perceives herself as helpless should not blame herself for these events. Thirdly, in the specific case of battered woman syndrome, passivity may not be the result of the woman learning that she is helpless, but it may be a learned adaptive response to abuse. This may take the form of the woman thinking, 'If I do not make requests and acquiesce to his demands, he is less likely to hit me' (Peterson, Maier & Seligman, 1993).

These difficulties and inconsistencies in the original learned helplessness theory led to the development of a revised theory that included the important concept of *attribution* (Abramson, Seligman & Teasdale, 1978). *Attributional theories* of depression argue that people learn to become helpless, or more specifically 'hopeless', because they possess certain attributional styles that generate pessimistic thinking. Attributions are the explanations that individuals have for their behaviour and the events that happen to them. In particular, Abramson, Seligman and Teasdale (1978) argue that people become depressed when they attribute negative life events primarily to factors that either cannot easily be manipulated or are unlikely to change. In particular, people who are likely to become depressed attribute negative life events to (1) *internal* rather than external factors (e.g. to personal traits rather than to outside events), (2) *stable* rather than unstable factors (e.g. things that are unlikely to change in the near future) and (3) *global* rather than specific factors (e.g. causes that have an effect over many areas of their life rather than being specific to one area of functioning).

> **Attribution theories** Theories of depression which suggest that people who are likely to become depressed attribute negative life events to internal, stable and global factors.

Table 6.8 provides an example of the range of attributions that someone might make in relation to failing a maths exam. In this case, the global, stable and internal attribution is 'I lack intelligence', and this attribution is likely to have a number of negative consequences. First, it is the kind of cause that is not easily changed so that future failures might be avoided. Second, it reflects negatively on the individual's self-concept, and so is likely to reduce self-esteem. Third, it is a global attribution, and so the individual is likely to believe that he or she will fail at many other things, not just a maths exam, which is likely to lead to the kinds of pessimistic thinking typical of depression. In contrast, if the student had attributed his or her failure to specific, unstable factors, such as 'I am fed up with maths' or 'My maths test was numbered 13', he or she would have been less likely to experience helplessness (because these are factors that could change quite easily) or reduced self-esteem.

Table 6.8 *Why I failed my GCSE maths exam*

Degree	Internal (Personal)		External (Environmental)	
	Stable	Unstable	Stable	Unstable
Global	I lack intelligence	I am exhausted	These tests are unfair	It's an unlucky day
Specific	I lack mathematical ability	I am fed up with maths	The test is unfair	My maths test was numbered 13

People who become depressed tend to attribute negative life events to internal, stable global causes (in this example, 'I lack intelligence'). In contrast, had the individual attributed his or her failure to specific, unstable factors (such as 'I am fed up with maths' or 'My maths test was numbered 13'), he or she is less likely to experience helplessness.

In order to test the attributional account of depression, Peterson, Semmel, von Baeyer, Abramson et al. (1982) developed the Attributional Style Questionnaire (ASQ), which measures tendencies to make the particular kinds of causal inference that are hypothesized to play a causal role in depression (see Table 6.9 for some sample items). A number of studies have subsequently found that use of the global-stable attributional style is a vulnerability factor for future depression (Butters, McClure, Siegert & Ward, 1997; Chaney, Mullins, Wagner, Hommel et al., 2004) – especially following negative life events (Hankin & Abramson, 2002). A study by Metalsky, Joiner, Hardin and Abramson (1993) gave students the ASQ prior to a mid-term exam and then measured depressive symptoms over the subsequent 5 days. They found that the students' enduring depressive reactions during this period were predicted by a global/stable attributional style together with low self-esteem and exam failure. This suggests that the global/stable attributional style in the context of a negative life event (exam failure) is a good predictor of subsequent depression.

Hopelessness Theory The attributional/helplessness account of depression has been further refined to account for the fact that attributional style appears to interact with a number of other factors to cause depression. Abramson, Metalsky and Alloy (1989) suggested that the tendency to attribute negative events to global/stable causes represents a diathesis which, in the presence of negative life events, increases vulnerability to a group of depressive symptoms, including retarded initiation of voluntary responses, apathy, lack of energy and psychomotor retardation.

Table 6.9 *The Attributional Style Questionnaire (ASQ)*

The ASQ contains a number of hypothetical situations designed to measure the individual's bias towards making certain kinds of attributions for both positive and negative events. Abramson, Seligman and Teasdale (1978) argued that people who attribute negative events to internal, stable and global events are most likely to develop helplessness and depression.

Sample situation and items

You have been looking for a job unsuccessfully for some time.

1   Write down the *one* major cause.

2   Is the unsuccessful job search due to something about you or to something about other people in the circumstances?

TOTALLY DUE TO OTHER PEOPLE OR CIRCUMSTANCES	1	2	3	4	5	6	TOTALLY DUE TO ME

3   In the future when looking for a job, will this cause be present?

WILL NEVER AGAIN BE PRESENT	1	2	3	4	5	6	WILL ALWAYS BE PRESENT

4   Is the cause something that just influences looking for a job or does it also influence other areas of your life?

INFLUENCES JUST THIS PARTICULAR SITUATION	1	2	3	4	5	6	INFLUENCES ALL SITUATIONS IN MY LIFE

5   How important would this situation be if it happened to you?

NOT AT ALL IMPORTANT	1	2	3	4	5	6	EXTREMELY IMPORTANT

Item 2 measures internality, item 3 measures stability and item 4 measures globality.

Hopelessness theory A theory of depression in which individuals exhibit an expectation that positive outcomes will not occur, negative outcomes will occur, and that the individual has no responses available that will change this state of affairs.

This cluster of symptoms is known as *hopelessness*, which is an expectation that positive outcomes will not occur, negative outcomes will occur, and that the individual has no responses available that will change this state of affairs. Hopelessness theory is very similar to attributional/helplessness accounts in that negative life events are viewed as interacting with a global/stable attributional style to generate depressed symp-

tomatology. However, hopelessness theory also predicts that other factors, such as low self-esteem, may also be involved as vulnerability factors (Metalsky, Joiner, Hardin & Abramson, 1993).

Many studies have supported the hopelessness theory by confirming that depression can be predicted by a combination of negative attributional style, negative life events and low self-esteem (Alloy, Lipman & Abramson, 1992; Metalsky & Joiner, 1992; Metalsky, Joiner, Hardin & Abramson, 1993), and that the negative attributional style is significantly more related to hopelessness depression symptoms (e.g. lethargy, hopelessness, difficulty making decisions) than endogenous depression symptoms

RESEARCH METHODS IN CLINICAL PSYCHOLOGY BOX 6.1

Prospective studies

Questionnaire studies are usually designed to see whether there are any relationships (i.e. correlations) between different measures. This is a very useful first step in researching a topic because it tells us what measures or constructs appear to be strongly associated. For example, measures of negative attributional style (attributing negative events to global/stable causes) are found to be highly correlated with measures of depression (Alloy, Lipman & Abramson, 1992).

Theorists who support the hopelessness theory of depression would say that these kinds of correlations provide support for that theory, i.e. support for the view that a negative attributional style is a causal factor in developing depression. However, when two measures are highly correlated, we must be cautious for at least two reasons.

(1) We cannot infer that there is a causal relationship between these measures, because their association might be mediated by some third variable that has not been measured. For example, negative attributional style and depression might be highly correlated because they are both related to the number of negative life events the people have experienced.

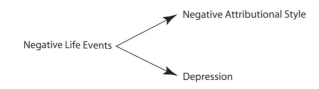

(2) Similarly, if there is a causal relationship between two variables that are highly correlated, we do not know the direction of that causal relationship. While hopelessness theory predicts that negative attributional style should cause depression, a correlation between these two variables is just as likely to imply that depression causes a negative attributional style.

Negative Attributional Style

Depression

One way to overcome some of these difficulties in interpreting results from correlational studies is to conduct what are known as *prospective studies*.

Prospective studies take measures of the relevant variables at a particular point in time (usually called TIME 1), and then go back to the same participants at some future time or times and take the same measures again (usually called TIME 2). Using this method, researchers can see if measures of a variable at TIME 1 (e.g. negative attributional style) predict, or are correlated with, measures of variables taken at TIME 2 (e.g. depression). In addition, because researchers will have taken measures of depression at both TIMES 1 and 2, they can see whether levels of negative attributional style predict *changes* in depression scores between TIMES 1 and 2. This procedure allows researchers to make much stronger statements about the possible temporal relationship between two variables, and whether one variable is a *risk factor* for the other (i.e. whether negative attributional style is a risk factor for increased depression over time).

Such a prospective study was undertaken by Robinson and Alloy (2003). Using undergraduate students as participants, they took measures of negative attributional style (using the Cognitive Style Questionnaire) and depression (using the Beck Depression Inventory) at TIME 1. Regular prospective assessments then took place every 6 months for 2.5 years (TIME 2, TIME 3 . . . etc.). Even when the level of depressive symptoms at TIME 1 was taken into account, they found that measures of variables such as negative attributional style predicted the incidence and number of future depressive episodes. They concluded that negative cognitive style (including negative attributional style) was a risk factor for future depression.

(e.g. loss of interest in sex, loss of appetite, loss of weight) (Joiner, 2001). In addition to predicting many symptoms of depression, hopelessness is also a construct that has been shown to predict suicidal tendencies and, in particular, completed suicide (Conner, Duberstein, Conwell, Seidlitz et al., 2001).

Nevertheless, despite the enhanced ability of the evolved model to predict depressive episodes, there are still a number of limitations to hopelessness theory: (1) many of the studies claiming to support hopelessness theory have been carried out on healthy or only mildly depressed participants who are not representative of individuals who are clinically depressed (Coyne, 1994); (2) a majority of studies testing the model are correlational in nature, and so cannot provide any evidence on the possible causal role of hopelessness cognitions in generating depression (Henkel, Bussfield, Moller & Hegerl, 2002); (3) the model does not explain all of the depressive symptoms required for a DSM-IV-TR diagnosis, only those related to hopelessness; and (4) there is some evidence that the negative attributional style disappears during remission or recovery from depression (Hamilton & Abramson, 1983), which suggests that it may not be a universal or enduring feature of individuals who experience depression. This latter fact raises the question of what comes first, the negative attributional style or symptoms of depression? (See Research Methods Box 6.1.)

SELF-TEST QUESTIONS

- Describe the evidence that suggests there is a genetic component to both major depression and bipolar disorder.
- What role do the neurotransmitters serotonin and norepinephrine play in depression?
- How have abnormalities in certain brain areas been linked to the experience of depression?
- How are cortisol levels supposed to be involved in the development of depression?
- Why is the individual's response to loss so important in psychodynamic theories of depression?
- Can you describe how behavioural theories and interpersonal theories explain the development of depression?
- What is Beck's 'negative triad'?
- What is the evidence that depressed individuals hold negative beliefs about themselves and the world?
- What are the benefits and the limitations of learned helplessness as an explanation of depression?
- What kinds of attributions are likely to lead to depressed thinking?
- What are the important features of hopelessness theory of depression?

- Depressed mood has been shown to be associated with abnormal activity in a number of brain areas, including the **prefrontal cortex**, the **anterior cingulate cortex**, the **hippocampus** and the **amygdala**.

- High levels of **cortisol** may lead to depression by causing enlargement of the adrenal glands and in turn lowering the frequency of serotonin transmitters in the brain.

- **Psychoanalytic theory** argues that depression is a response to loss, and the loss of a loved one such as a parent.

- **Behavioural theories** claim that depression results from a lack of appropriate reinforcement for positive and constructive behaviours, and this is especially the case following a 'loss' such as bereavement or redundancy.

- **Interpersonal theories** of depression claim that depressed individuals alienate family and friends because of their perpetual negative thinking, and this alienation in turn exacerbates the symptoms of depression.

- **Beck's cognitive theory of depression** argues that depression is maintained by a **negative schema** that leads depressed individuals to hold negative views about themselves, their future and the world (the **negative triad**).

- **Learned helplessness theory** argues that people become depressed following unavoidable negative life events because these events give rise to a cognitive set that makes individuals learn to become 'helpless', lethargic and depressed.

- **Attributional** accounts of depression suggest that people who are likely to become depressed attribute negative life events to internal, stable and global factors.

- **Hopelessness** is a cluster of depression symptoms that are characterized by an expectation that positive outcomes will not occur, negative outcomes will occur, and the individual has no responses available that will change this state of affairs.

SECTION SUMMARY

6.3 The Aetiology of Depression and Mood Disorders

- There is good evidence for a **genetic** component to both major depression and bipolar disorder. 10–25 per cent of first-degree relatives of bipolar disorder sufferers also report symptoms of mood disorder, as do 5–10 per cent of first-degree relatives of major depression sufferers.

- Low levels of the brain neurotransmitters **serotonin** and **norepinephrine** are associated with depressed mood.

6.4 THE TREATMENT OF DEPRESSION AND MOOD DISORDERS

The previous sections illustrate the broad range of theories addressing the aetiology of depression, and these theories have each given rise to a variety of different treatments for depression-based mood disorders. These include a number of biologically based treatments such as drug therapy and electroconvulsive therapy (ECT), which address the known neurochemical imbalances in depression, and a wide range of psychological therapies including psychodynamic, behavioural and cognitive behavioural therapies. In 2004, the UK National Institute for Clinical Excellence (NICE) proposed a ***stepped-care model*** for the treatment of depression that emphasized that the type of treatment provided for depressed individuals should be tailored to the severity of their symptoms and their personal and social circumstances.

> **Stepped-care model** A treatment for depression that emphasizes that the type of treatment provided for depressed individuals should be tailored to the severity of their symptoms and their personal and social circumstances.

Figure 6.4 illustrates this stepped-care model. Interesting features of this model for service provision are: (1) GPs are advised to ensure that proper assessment is made of individuals who might present with symptoms of depression, and they should not simply respond by providing medication; (2) medication is not recommended for the initial treatment of depression but should be reserved for the treatment of moderate to severe depression where there is more evidence for its effectiveness; and (3) mild depression should be treated primarily with brief behavioural and cognitive interventions, including structured exercise (3 sessions per week of moderate duration for 10–12 weeks), guided self-help and computerized CBT programmes (an example of which is *Beating the Blues* – see Treatment in Practice Box 6.1, and Chapter 4, section 4.1.2.3). When evaluating the different forms of therapy for depression discussed below, readers should bear in mind the NICE recommendations that certain types of therapy may be more appropriate and more effective for different levels of severity.

6.4.1 Biological Treatments

6.4.1.1 Drug Therapy

We saw earlier that depression is commonly associated with deficits or imbalances in the neurotransmitters serotonin and nore-pinephrine, and over the past 50 years various drugs have been developed that attempt to address these imbalances and deal with the symptoms of depression. The three main types of medication for depression are (1) tricyclic drugs (such as imipramine), (2) monoamine oxidase inhibitors (MAOIs) (such as tranylcypromine) and (3) selective serotonin reuptake inhibitors (SSRIs) (such as Prozac). The first two types of drug have their effect by increasing levels of both serotonin and norepinephrine in the brain, while SSRIs act selectively on serotonin and prevent its reuptake by the presynaptic neuron (see Figure 6.1). All of these drugs act by facilitating the transmission of impulses between neurons.

Treatment outcome studies have generally indicated that depressed individuals given these forms of medication benefit when compared with individuals taking placebos. Around 60–65 per cent of individuals taking tricyclic drugs show improvement (Gitlin, 2002) along with around 50 per cent taking MAOIs (Thase, Trivedi & Rush, 1995). Although these forms of drug treatment are relatively effective, they often have significant physical and psychological side effects (see Table 6.10). The most recently developed of these drugs, SSRIs, do have some benefits over tricyclic drugs and MAOIs in that they produce fewer side effects (Enserink, 1999) and it is harder to overdose on them (Isbister, Bowe, Dawson & Whyte, 2004). However, SSRIs such as fluoxetine (Prozac) take around 2 weeks to begin to have an effect on symptoms (which is roughly the same as tricyclics), and also have their own side effects such as headache, gastric disorders and sexual dysfunction (Rosen, Lane & Menza, 1999). There is also controversy about whether SSRIs such as Prozac increase the risk of suicide. Recent meta-analyses suggest that increased risk of suicide with the use of SSRIs cannot be ruled out, but these risks should be balanced against the effectiveness of SSRIs in treating depression (Gunnell, Saperia & Ashby, 2005).

Nevertheless, despite these cautions, the drugs that have been developed to treat depression do help to alleviate symptoms in a significant number of cases, they provide relatively rapid relief

Step 5: Inpatient care, crisis teams	Risk to life, severe self-neglect	Medication, combined treatments, ECT
Step 4: Mental health specialists including crisis teams	Treatment-resistant, recurrent atypical and psychotic depression, and those at significant risk	Medication, complex psychological interventions, combined treatments
Step 3: Primary care team, primary care mental health worker	Moderate or severe depression	Medication, psychological interventions, social support
Step 2: Primary care team, primary care mental health worker	Mild depression	Watchful waiting, guided self-help, computerized CBT, exercise, brief psychological interventions
Step 1: GP, practice nurse	Recognition	Assessment

Figure 6.4 *The NICE stepped-care model for depression.*
This model provides a framework by which practitioners can identify the most effective interventions for different severities of depression.

CLINICAL PERSPECTIVE: TREATMENT IN PRACTICE BOX 6.1

Beating the Blues using computerized CBT

The UK National Institute for Clinical Excellence (NICE) guidelines for treating depression recommend that computerized CBT (CCBT) is considered for mild depression (see Chapter 4, section 4.1.2.3).

One particular programme that has been developed for this purpose is *Beating the Blues*, which uses interactive multimedia techniques to maximize user-friendliness and patient engagement. It provides role models in the form of case study videos that guide the patient's progress at each stage of therapy.

Patients follow a unique pathway through the programme driven by their current needs, including homework projects to complete between sessions, and clinical outcomes are monitored on a session-by-session basis.

The programme helps the user to identify thinking errors, challenge negative automatic thoughts, modify attributional style and identify core negative beliefs. It also provides guidance on behavioural techniques (such as graded exposure, sleep management, problem solving, task breakdown, activity scheduling) that are designed to promote more helpful thinking styles and behavioural repertoires.

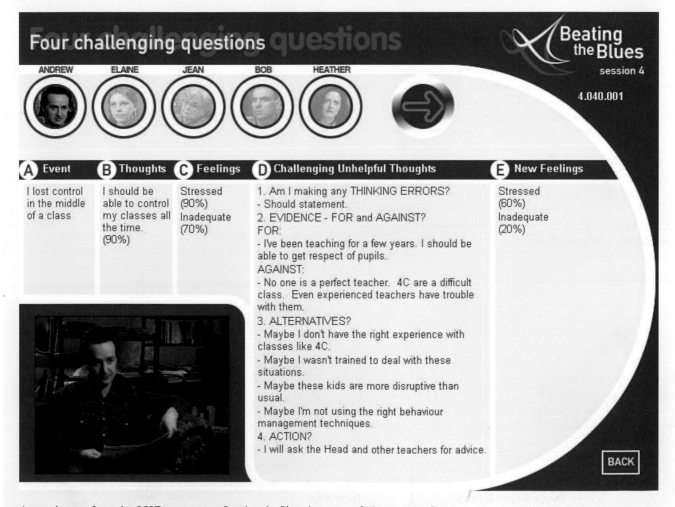

A sample page from the CCBT programme Beating the Blues (courtesy of Ultrasis UK Ltd).

Table 6.10 *Side effects of drugs used to treat major depression and bipolar disorder*

Category	Side effects
Tricyclic drugs	Blurred vision, anxiety, fatigue, dry mouth, increased risk of heart attack and stroke, constipation, gastric disorders, hypotension, sexual dysfunction, weight gain
Monoamine oxidase inhibitors (MAOIs)	Hypertension, dry mouth, dizziness, headaches and nausea
Selective serotonin reuptake inhibitors (SSRIs)	Anxiety, fatigue, gastric disorders, headaches, dizziness, sleeping difficulties
Lithium	Cardiac arrhythmia, fatigue, blurred vision, tremors; on overdose can cause delirium, convulsions and fatalities

from symptoms in around half of those treated, and are effective not only with bouts of major depression, but also with chronic depressive disorders such as dysthymic disorder (Hellerstein, Kocsis, Chapman, Stewart et al., 2000). However, relapse is a common occurrence after drug treatment for depression has been withdrawn (Reimherr, Strong, Marchant, Hedges et al., 2001), and a more effective treatment is to combine drug therapy with psychological therapies such as CBT (Kupfer & Frank, 2001).

In contrast to those drugs prescribed for major or unipolar depression, the drug therapy of choice for bipolar disorder is *lithium carbonate*. Around 80 per cent of bipolar disorder sufferers who take lithium benefit from it, and the drug can provide relief from symptoms of both manic and depressive episodes (Prien & Potter, 1993). There is some debate about how lithium actually moderates the symptoms of bipolar disorder. Early views suggested that lithium stabilizes the activity of sodium and potassium ions in the membranes of neurons, and it is the instability of these ions that gives rise to the symptoms of bipolar disorder (Swonger & Constantine, 1983). Other accounts argue that it changes synaptic activity in neurons in such a way as to help neurotransmitters to bind to a receiving neuron, thus helping to facilitate and stabilize neuronal transmission (Ghaemi, Boiman & Goodwin, 1999). More recently, it has been suggested that lithium modulates neuronal transmission by affecting the expression of genes that govern these activities (Lenox & Hahn, 2000). For most individuals with bipolar disorder, it is recommended that lithium is taken continually because discontinuation increases the risk of relapse (Suppes, Baldessarini, Faedda & Tohen, 1991). In addition, an added disadvantage of lithium treatment is the difficulty in prescribing a suitable dosage on an individual basis. Lithium is a toxic substance, and an effective dose for alleviating symptoms is often close to the toxic level. As a consequence, an overdose can cause delirium, convulsions and, in rare cases, can be fatal.

Lithium carbonate A drug used in the treatment of bipolar disorder.

6.4.1.2 Electroconvulsive Therapy (ECT)

Electroconvulsive therapy was first discovered as a method of treatment in the 1930s (Bini, 1938) and involves passing an electric current of around 70–130 volts through the head of the patient for around half a second. It was first used as an experimental means of inducing brain seizures, but was subsequently found to have beneficial effects on symptoms of severe depression. Today, ECT is used primarily with individuals suffering severe depression who have not responded well to other forms of treatment (Cohen, Taieb, Flament, Benoit et al., 2000). While it can provide effective short-term relief from symptoms of severe depression, it also has a number of controversial features.

Electroconvulsive therapy (ECT) A method of treatment for depression or psychosis, first devised in the 1930s, which involves passing an electric current of around 70–130 volts through the head of the patient for around half a second.

First, it has a number of side effects, the most common of which is memory loss that affects the ability to learn new material (anterograde amnesia) and the ability to recall material learned before the treatment (retrograde amnesia). These effects can last for up to 7 months following ECT (Hay, 1991; Lisanby, Maddox, Prudic, Devanand et al., 2000). Second, many people find the idea of having a strong electric current passed through their brain frightening, and will be resistant to the use of this kind of therapy. Indeed, many view the physical nature of ECT as a form of 'assault' on the patient, and a means of managing unruly inpatients rather than a form of therapy. This was a view that was strikingly portrayed in the 1975 film *One Flew Over The Cuckoo's Nest* starring Jack Nicholson. Third, no one is clear how ECT does work in alleviating the symptoms of severe depression, but it has been suggested that shock affects the levels of serotonin and norepinephrine in the brain (Mann & Kapur, 1994). However, this beneficial effect may be short term and limited to as little as four weeks (Breggin, 1997), and the relapse rate is high (Royal College of Psychiatrists, 2002). Other researchers have argued that the short-term beneficial effects of ECT are nothing more than would be expected follow-

Plate 6.4
Jack Nicholson's character in the famous 1975 film *One Flew Over The Cuckoo's Nest* was subjected to ECT treatment, and this unsympathetic portrayal led many to view ECT as a form of patient management rather than treatment.

ing *any* trauma to the brain – with immediate symptoms being confusion, headache and nausea followed by a period of emotional shallowness, denial and artificial euphoria that may last for a few weeks (Breggin, 1997).

Nevertheless, despite these criticisms, ECT may still have a role to play in the treatment of severe depression. Its almost immediate beneficial effects are particularly helpful with severe depression, when other treatments have failed, and in alleviating depression when suicide is a real possibility.

6.4.2 Psychological Treatments

6.4.2.1 Psychoanalysis

Psychoanalysis An influential psychological model of psychopathology based on the theoretical works of Sigmund Freud.

In section 6.3.2.1 we discussed some of the psychodynamic explanations of depression. Central to these accounts is the view that depression is a response to loss (perhaps of a loved one) and may manifest as *symbolic loss*, in which other kinds of losses (such as losing a job) are seen as equivalent to losing a loved one. Psychodynamic theories (such as those developed by Freud and Abraham) argue that the individual's response to loss is to turn his or her anger at the loss inwards; this, in turn, can develop into self-hate resulting in low self-esteem. The aim of psychodynamic therapy, therefore, is to help the depressed individual achieve insight into this repressed conflict and to help release the inwardly directed anger. Psychodynamic therapy does this by using various techniques to help people explore the long-term sources of their depression (see Chapter 4, section 4.1.1.1). These will involve exploring conflicts and problematic relationships with attachment figures such as parents and discussing long-standing defensive patterns. For example, the psychodynamic therapist may use *free association* or *dream interpretation* to help the individual recall early experiences of loss that may have contributed to repressed conflicts and symptoms of depression. In this way, psychodynamic therapies attempt to bring meaning to the symptoms of depression and help individuals understand how early experiences may have contributed to their symptoms and affected their current interpersonal relationships.

Free association A technique used in psychoanalysis where the client is encouraged to verbalise all thoughts, feelings and images that come to mind.

Dream interpretation The process of assigning meaning to dreams.

Evidence for the therapeutic efficacy of psychodynamic therapies in the treatment of depression is meagre. This is in part because processes within psychodynamic therapies are difficult to objectify and study in a controlled way. Psychodynamic therapists also differ significantly in the way they interpret psychodynamic principles in practice. A controlled study by the American Psychiatric Association (APA, 1993) reported that there was no evidence for the long-term efficacy of psychodynamic treatment of depression, although some more recent studies have indicated that short-term psychodynamic interventions may be as effective as CBT (Leichsenring, 2001).

6.4.2.2 Social Skills Training

It was Lewinsohn and his colleagues (e.g. Lewinsohn & Shaw, 1969) who first drew attention to the fact that depressed individuals (1) have deficits in the general social skills that are required for efficient and effective interactions and (2) possess a demeanour that others (e.g. other family members) find aversive. These two features of the depressed individual will act to accentuate depression by reducing both the frequency of social interactions and the rewards that the individual might obtain from such interactions. The interpersonal social skills deficits possessed by depressed individuals range from negative self-evaluation of their own skills to deficits in behavioural indicators of social skills such as eye contact, relevant facial expressions and speed of response in conversations (Segrin, 2000).

In response to these deficits, *social skills training* therapy for depression was developed (Becker, Heimberg & Bellack, 1987). Social skills training assumes that depression in part results from the individual's inability to communicate and socialize appropriately, and that addressing these skill deficits should help to alleviate many of the symptoms

Social skills training A therapy for depression that assumes that depression in part results from an individual's inability to communicate and socialize appropriately, and that addressing these skill deficits should help to alleviate many of the symptoms of depression.

of depression. This may involve training assertion skills, conversational interaction skills, dating skills and job interview skills and can involve procedures such as modelling, rehearsal, role-playing and homework assignments out of the therapeutic setting (Jackson, Moss & Solinski, 1985; Becker, Heimberg & Bellack, 1987).

An example of one particular social skills training programme for depression is that designed by Herson, Bellack and colleagues (Hersen, Bellack & Himmelhoch, 1980). This involved 1-hour sessions for 12 weeks and began by focusing on skills appropriate for interactions with family, friends, work colleagues and strangers respectively. Particular features of this programme included (1) role-playing tasks, feedback, modelling and positive reinforcement for appropriate behaviours and (2) attention to the specific details of social interactions such as smiles, gestures and use of eye contact. Clients were subsequently given homework tasks requiring them to practise their skills outside of the therapy situation. As a result of this programme, clients showed not only improvements in their social skills but also a decrease in symptoms of depression that was still apparent 6 months after the end of the programme. Studies evaluating the efficacy of social skills training for depression have shown that such programmes result in an improvement in a range of social skills and a decrease in reported symptoms of depression (Zeiss, Lewinsohn & Munoz, 1979). They also suggest that social skills training is equally as effective as other psychological therapies commonly employed for depression (Fine, Forth, Gilbert & Haley, 1991; Miller, Norman, Keitner, Bishop & Dow, 1989).

6.4.2.3 Behavioural Activation Therapy

Behavioural theories of depression emphasize that depression may be triggered by a life-event loss (such as a bereavement), and this event may represent the loss of important sources of reward and reinforcement for the individual. This leads the depressed individual into a vicious cycle where this lack of reward generates depressive symptoms. In turn, the individual's depressive behaviour may ultimately lead to aversive social consequences in the form of negative social reactions from friends and family (Coyne, 1976). This view has led to the development of *behavioural activation therapies* for depression that attempt to increase clients' access to pleasant events and rewards and decrease their experience of aversive events and consequences (Lewinsohn, Sullivan & Grosscup, 1980). Early behavioural activation programmes attempted to achieve these goals through daily monitoring of pleasant/unpleasant events and the use of behavioural interventions that developed activity scheduling (e.g. scheduling reinforcing activities so that they reinforce less attractive activities). They also include social skills and time management training (Lewinsohn & Shaffer, 1971; Zeiss, Lewinsohn & Munoz, 1979). The use of behavioural activation therapy was given a further boost by the fact that a number of studies demonstrated that cognitive change is just as likely to occur following purely behavioural interventions as after cognitive interventions (Jacobson & Gortner, 2000; Simons, Garfield & Murphy, 1984). That is, reductions in negative thinking and negative self-statements in depression can be decreased by behavioural interventions that contain no explicit cognitive change components. Recent developments of behavioural activation therapy include the self-monitoring of pleasant/unpleasant experiences and the identification of behavioural goals within major life areas (e.g. relationships, education) that can be targeted for development and reinforcement. Treatment in Practice Box 6.2 gives an example of how a brief behavioural activation therapy programme is structured and executed (Lejuez, Hopko, LePage, Hopko & McNeil, 2001).

> **Behavioural activation therapy**
> A therapy for depression that attempts to increase clients' access to pleasant events and rewards and decrease their experience of aversive events and consequences.

Outcome studies suggest that behavioural activation therapies are at least as effective as supportive psychotherapy in reducing the symptoms of depression (Hopko, Lejuez, LePage et al., 2003), and equally as effective as CBT in preventing relapse after 24 months (Gortner, Gollan, Dobson & Jacobson, 1998).

6.4.2.4 Cognitive Therapy

As we saw in section 6.3.2, dysfunctional cognitions appear to play an important part in the maintenance of depressive symptoms. Beck's cognitive theory of depression (Beck, 1967, 1987) argues that depression is maintained by a systematic set of dysfunctional negative beliefs that form a negative schema though which depressed individuals view themselves, their world and their future. From this theory Beck developed one of the most successful and widely adopted therapeutic approaches for depression, which has come to be known by various names including *cognitive therapy*, *cognitive retraining* or *cognitive restructuring*. The thrust of this approach is (1) to help depressed individuals identify their negative beliefs and negative thoughts, (2) to challenge these thoughts as dysfunctional and irrational, and (3) to replace these negative beliefs with more adaptive or rational beliefs.

> **Cognitive therapy** A form of psychotherapy based on the belief that psychological problems are the products of faulty ways of thinking about the world.

> **Cognitive retraining** An approach to treating depression developed by Aaron Beck. Also known as **cognitive therapy** or **cognitive restructuring**.

For example, depressed individuals tend to hold beliefs and attributional styles that are *overgeneralized*. They will respond to a specific failure (such as failing their driving test) with statements such as 'Everything I do ends in failure' or 'The world is against me'. The cognitive therapist will attempt to identify these overgeneralized beliefs and challenge them as irrational – using, if at

CLINICAL PERSPECTIVE: TREATMENT IN PRACTICE BOX 6.2

Brief Behavioural Activation Treatment for Depression (BATD)

BATD is conducted over 8–15 sessions. Sessions progress through the following stages:

1 Assessing the function of depressed behaviour; weakening access to positive reinforcement (e.g. sympathy) and negative reinforcement (e.g. escape from responsibilities); establishing rapport with the client and introducing the treatment rationale.

2 Increasing the frequency and subsequent reinforcement of healthy behaviour; clients begin a weekly self-monitoring exercise that serves as a baseline assessment of daily activities and orients clients to the quantity and quality of their

activities, and generates ideas about activities to target during treatment.

3 Emphasis is shifted to identifying behavioural goals within major life areas, such as relationships, education, employment, hobbies and recreational activities, physical/health issues, spirituality.

4 Following goal setting, an activity hierarchy is constructed in which 15 activities are rated ranging from 'easiest' to 'most difficult' to accomplish. With progress being monitored by the therapist, over a period of weeks the client progressively moves through the hierarchy from easiest to most difficult. Clients are urged to identify weekly rewards that can be administered if activity goals are met.

Source: Hopko, Lejuez, Ruggiero & Eifert (2003)

all possible, relevant examples from the client's own experiences. In addition to this, clients will be asked to monitor the **negative automatic thoughts** that give rise to negative beliefs and depressive symptoms, often using a form which allows them to link the automatic thoughts to particular situations and outcomes, and to think through possible rational alternatives to the negative automatic thought. The overall philosophy of cognitive therapy for depression is to correct the negative thinking bias possessed by depressed individuals. In some cases this aim can be supplemented with the use of *reattribution training* (Beck, Rush, Shaw & Emery, 1979). Reattribution training attempts to get clients to interpret their difficulties in more hopeful and constructive ways rather than in the negative, global, stable ways typical of depressed individuals (see Table 6.11).

Outcome studies have shown that cognitive therapy is usually at least as effective as drug therapy in treating the symptoms of depression (Rush, Beck, Kovacs & Hollon, 1977), and some have

Negative automatic thoughts
Negatively valenced thoughts that the individual finds difficult to control or dismiss.

Reattribution training   A technique used in the treatment of depression which attempts to get clients to interpret their difficulties in more hopeful and constructive ways rather than in the negative, global, stable ways typical of depressed individuals.

Table 6.11 *Thought record form for recording negative automatic thoughts*

Below is an example of a thought record form used to record the negative automatic thoughts ('hot thoughts') experienced by depressed individuals. The form relates these thoughts to possible situational triggers and attempts to get the depressed individual to think up evidence that might be contrary to that 'hot thought'.

1 Situation	2 Moods	3 Automatic Thoughts (Images)	4 Evidence that Supports the Hot Thought	5 Evidence that Does Not Support the Hot Thought	6 Alternative/ Balanced Thoughts	7 Rate Moods Now
Who? What? When? Where?	What do you feel? Rate each mood (0–100%)	What was going through your mind just before you started to feel this way? Any other thoughts? Images?			Write an alternative or balanced thought. Rate how much you believe in each alternative or balanced thought (0–100%)	Re-rate moods listed in column 2 as well as any new moods (0–100%)
At home – alone – Saturday 9:30pm	Depressed 100% Disappointed 100% Empty 100% Confused 100% Unreal 100%	I want to go numb so I don't have to feel anymore I'm not making any progress I'm so confused that I can't think clearly The pain is so great that I have to kill myself Nothing helps Life is not worth living I'm such a failure I'm so empty inside	I just have to die The pain is unbearable Killing myself is the only way to get rid of the pain I've tried many types of psychotherapy and many medications which haven't helped	In the past, talking about my feelings sometimes helped me feel better I have felt suicidal and in severe emotional pain before and have got through it I'm learning to think differently which will help Other people think I have positive qualities Some days I do feel better I laugh occasionally		

Source: Greenberger & Padesky (1995).

shown that it is superior to drug therapy at 1-year follow-up (Blackburn & Moorhead, 2000; Hollon, Shelton & Davis, 1993). DeRubeis, Hollon, Amsterdam, Shelton et al. (2005) compared cognitive therapy with drug therapy (paroxetine) and a placebo-control condition. After 8 weeks they found improvement in 43 per cent of the cognitive therapy group and in 50 per cent of the drug treatment group, against only 25 per cent in the placebo group, and these levels of improvement were maintained at 16 weeks. Cognitive therapy also appears to have longer-term beneficial effects by preventing relapse (Hensley, Nadiga & Uhlenhuth, 2004; Jarrett, Kraft, Doyle, Foster et al., 2001), but a combination of cognitive therapy with drug treatment appears to be superior to either treatment alone (Kupfer & Frank, 2001). Cognitive therapy has also been successfully adapted to treat individuals with bipolar disorder in conjunction with appropriate medication (Newman, Leahy, Beck et al., 2002), and this helps the sufferer with medication compliance, mood monitoring, anticipating stressors, interpersonal functioning and problem solving (Scott, Garland & Moorhead, 2001; Danielson, Feeny, Findling & Youngstrom, 2004).

While there is no doubt that cognitive therapy is successful in helping to treat depression, there is still some debate about *how* it achieves these effects. We have seen earlier that cognitive change is just as likely to occur following purely behavioural treatments as it is after cognitive treatments. Cognitive therapy contains both elements of cognitive restructuring, which aims to change cognitions directly, and behavioural exercises designed to establish new cognitions – so is the cognitive restructuring element entirely necessary? In addition, there is evidence that cognitive therapy not only changes negative cognitions, but also results in improvements in abnormal biological processes (Blackburn & Moorhead, 2000). This raises the question of whether cognitive therapy has its effects by changing cognitions or biological processes. Nevertheless, regardless of *how* it works, cognitive therapy certainly *does* work, and recent evidence suggests that it not only reduces the occurrence of negative cognitions in depression, but it also helps to dissociate negative cognitions from the symptoms of depression better than other treatments (Beevers & Miller, 2005).

6.4.2.5 Mindfulness-Based Cognitive Therapy (MBCT)

A critical issue in the treatment of depression is how to predict and eliminate possible relapse after remission or successful treatment. In the case of major depression, it appears that the risk of relapse increases with every consecutive bout of depression, and this increased risk also means that depression can reoccur with less and less external provocation (such as a stressful life event) (Kendler, Thornton & Gardner, 2000). This increased risk of relapse in recovered depressed individuals appears to be caused by periods of negative mood (dysphoria) activating patterns of negative or depressogenic thinking such as self-devaluation and hopelessness (Ingram, Miranda & Segal, 1998; Segal, Gemar & Williams, 1999). That is, as soon as the recovered depressed individual begins to feel depressed again, this reactivates negative thinking that leads to a downward spiral to relapse.

Mindfulness-based cognitive therapy (MBCT) was developed in order to try to combat this linkage between periods of dysphoria and the onset of negative thinking. It aims to get individuals to take a 'decentred' perspective by being aware of negative thinking patterns and viewing them purely as mental events rather than as accurate reflections of reality (Teasdale, 1988; Teasdale, Segal & Williams, 1995). MBCT is based on an integration of aspects of CBT and components of the mindfulness-based stress reduction programme that contains elements of meditation and provides training in the deployment of attention (Kabat-Zinn, 1990). Clients are taught to become more aware of, and relate differently to, their thoughts, feelings and bodily sensations, and to treat thoughts and feelings as passing events in the mind rather than identifying with them. MBCT also teaches skills that allow individuals to disengage from habitual dysfunctional cognitive routines and depression-related patterns of ruminative thought. Studies suggest that MBCT can significantly reduce the probability of future relapse. Ma and Teasdale (2004) found that MBCT reduced relapse from 78 per cent to 36 per cent, and in participants who had experienced four or more bouts of depression only 38 per cent of those receiving MBCT relapsed compared with 100 per cent in the treatment-as-usual control group. These findings suggest that teaching previously depressed individuals to adopt a detached, decentred relationship to their depression-related thoughts and feelings can have significant therapeutic gains.

> **Mindfulness-based cognitive therapy (MBCT)** A treatment which has been developed to prevent relapse in recovered depressed individuals by making them aware of negative thinking patterns that may trigger subsequent bouts of depression.

SELF-TEST QUESTIONS

- Can you describe the NICE stepped-care model for the treatment of depression?
- What drugs are important in controlling brain neurotransmitter levels, and how do they have their effect?
- What are the important components of social skills training for depression?
- What is the rationale behind behavioural activation therapy for depression?
- How does cognitive therapy attempt to eradicate negative thinking?
- What is reattribution training?
- What is mindfulness-based cognitive therapy and what role does it play in the control of depression?

SECTION SUMMARY

6.4 The Treatment of Depression and Mood Disorders

- Drug treatments have been developed that attempt to address the imbalance in neurotransmitters such as serotonin and norepinephrine.

- Three main types of medication for depression are **tricyclic drugs**, **monoamine oxidase inhibitors (MAOIs)** and **selective serotonin reuptake inhibitors (SSRIs)**.

- **Lithium carbonate** is the main drug prescribed for bipolar disorder.

- **Electroconvulsive therapy (ECT)** is sometimes used with individuals suffering severe depression who have not responded well to other forms of treatment.

- **Psychodynamic therapy** uses a range of techniques (e.g. free association, dream analysis) to help individuals to explore the long-term sources of their depression.

- **Social skills training** assumes that depression results from the depressed individual's inability to communicate and socialize appropriately. Social skills training programmes attempt to address this deficit.

- **Behavioural activation therapies** attempt to increase the individual's access to pleasant events and rewards and decrease his or her experience of aversive events.

- **Cognitive therapy** for depression attempts to help the depressed individual identify negative beliefs and thoughts, challenge these beliefs as irrational, and replace them with positive rational beliefs.

- Outcome studies suggest that cognitive therapy is at least as effective as drug therapy.

- **Mindfulness-based cognitive therapy (MBCT)** has been developed to prevent relapse in recovered depressed individuals by making them aware of negative thinking patterns that may be triggered by subsequent bouts of depression.

6.5 SUICIDE AND DELIBERATE SELF-HARM

Suicide attempts usually occur in the context of mental health problems generally, and it has been estimated that 90 per cent

> **Suicide** The action of killing oneself intentionally.

of suicide victims have a diagnosable psychiatric disorder at the time of their death (Isometsa, Henriksson, Marttunen et al., 1995). Over half of those that successfully commit suicide are usually significantly depressed before the fatal attempt (Isaacson & Rich, 1997), and the cognitive construct of 'hopelessness' is probably one of the best single predictors of suicide (Beck, Steer, Kovacs & Garrison, 1985) (see section 6.3.2.2). Thus, there is a very strong link between depression, suicide and parasuicide, and suicidal thoughts form part of the diagnostic criteria for major depression in DSM-IV-TR.

In 2000, the World Health Organization (WHO) predicted that a million people would die worldwide each year as a result of suicide – a global mortality rate of 16 per 100,000. Also, the worldwide rate for suicide has been gradually increasing year by year, with WHO estimating an increase of 60 per cent over the past 45 years. Studies that have investigated the lifetime prevalence rates for suicide suggest that 13.5 per cent of people report lifetime suicidal ideation, 3.9 per cent have planned a suicide and 4.6 per cent have attempted suicide (Kessler, Borges & Walters, 1999). However, suicide rates differ significantly across different countries (some European and Asian countries report over twice the rate of suicide than Central and South American countries – see Figure 6.5). The likelihood of

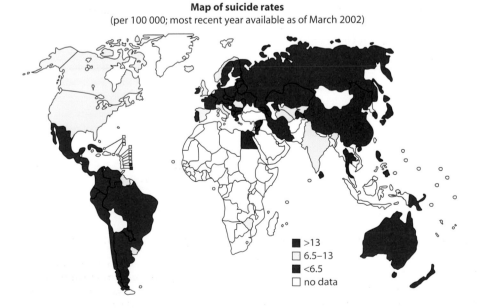

Map of suicide rates
(per 100 000; most recent year available as of March 2002)

- ■ >13
- □ 6.5–13
- ■ <6.5
- □ no data

Figure 6.5 *Map of suicide rates, 2002.*
This map of world suicide rates published in 2002 shows that suicide rates can differ significantly across different countries, with rates in many parts of Europe and Asia at twice the recorded rate found in South and Central America.

Source: www.who.int/mental_health/prevention/suicide/suicideprevent/en/

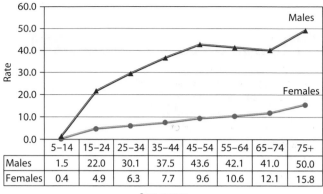

Age group	5–14	15–24	25–34	35–44	45–54	55–64	65–74	75+
Males	1.5	22.0	30.1	37.5	43.6	42.1	41.0	50.0
Females	0.4	4.9	6.3	7.7	9.6	10.6	12.1	15.8

Figure 6.6 *Distribution of suicide rates per 100,000 by gender and age, 2000.*

In 2000 the World Health Organization published figures showing suicide rates per 100,000 of the population by age and gender. These figures show that the incidence of suicide tends to increase with age, and that the rate for males is over twice that for females.

Source: www.who.int/mental_health/prevention/suicide/suicidecharts/en/

Table 6.12 *Characteristics that define suicide attempters and completers*

Characteristics	Attempters	Completers
Gender	Mainly female	Mainly male
Age	Mainly young	Increased risk with age
Method	Pills, cutting	More violent (guns, jumping)
Common diagnoses	Mild depression, borderline personality disorder, schizophrenia	Major depression, alcoholism
Dominant affect	Depression with anger	Depression with hopelessness
Motivation	Change in situation, cry for help	Death, self-annihilation

Source: Fremouw, Callahan & Kashden (1993).

an individual committing suicide tends to increase with age, although there has been an alarming increase in the number of younger people attempting suicide in recent years, with a rise in the US of 200 per cent since 1960 (US National Centre for Health Statistics; see Figure 6.6). Women are around three times more likely to *attempt* suicide than men, but the rate for *successful* suicide is around four times higher in men than women (Peters & Murphy, 1998). This is because men will tend to adopt more lethal methods than women (such as guns and jumping: see Table 6.12).

As we mentioned earlier, suicidal phenomena are becoming more common in teenagers and adolescents, and suicide is reported to be the second or third most frequent cause of death among 15- to 24-year-olds in many countries (Commonwealth Department of Health and Family Services, Australia, 1997). Up to 15 per cent of American high school students have been reported as attempting suicide at least once (King, 1997). Suicidal phenomena in adolescents include suicide attempts, deliberate self-harm, and suicidal plans, threats and thoughts (Hawton, Rodham, Evans & Weatherall, 2002).

Deliberate self-harm A parasuicidal phenomenon that commonly includes cutting or burning oneself, taking overdoses, hitting oneself, pulling hair or picking skin, or self-strangulation.

One particular form of parasuicidal phenomenon in adolescence is **deliberate self-harm** (Gratz, 2003; Fox & Hawton, 2004). This commonly includes cutting or burning, taking overdoses, hitting the self, pulling hair or picking skin, or self-strangulation. Although this kind of self-harm is usually non-fatal and only 13 per cent of attempts require hospital visits (Hawton, Hall, Simkin et al., 2003), non-fatal self-harm often leads to repetition and in some cases to successful suicide (Owens, Horrocks & House, 2002). Focus Point 6.2 looks at some of the features of adolescent self-harm and its relationship to suicide.

The reasons for the increase in adolescent suicide rates are unclear, but a number of factors may be relevant:

1 Modern teenagers are probably exposed to many of the life stressors experienced by adults, yet may lack the coping resources to deal with them effectively (Mazza & Reynolds, 1998).

2 Suicide is a sociological as well as a psychological phenomenon, and media reports of suicide often trigger a significant increase in suicides (Bandura, 1986). This is especially true in the case of adolescents and teenagers, where news of celebrity suicides is often associated with increases in the rate of teenage suicide attempts.

3 There is a strong relationship between depression, substance abuse and suicide, and the increasing use of drugs and alcohol in young teenagers may well provide one of the reasons for increased rates of suicide and parasuicide in this group (Gould & Kramer, 2001).

6.5.1 Risk Factors for Suicide

One of the best predictors of future suicide attempts is a history of at least one previous suicide attempt (Leon, Friedman, Sweeney et al., 1990). However, since only 20–30 per cent of those who attempt suicide have made a previous attempt, it is important to look at other risk factors. Suicide is a complex phenomenon and risk factors encompass a broad range of domains such as psychiatric, psychological, physical, personal, familial and social factors

Self-harm

Comments from an adolescent self-harmer posted on an Internet message board:

"Hello . . . Um where to start. The thing is self-harm is the only way I can deal with things. Ive tried everything in the book and yeah, none of it even comes close to cutting. I tried the rubber-band thing and ended up with huge welts that actually bruised and thats just another form of self-harm. I tried writing, doing other things . . . None of it helps. My scars are another thing about self-harm that I cant draw myself away from. I like them in some odd way . . . I know. Your probably thinking im insane or an attention-getter or something . . . But is there ANY-ONE who feels the same? I mean likes the way it feels and honestly doesnt want to stop even though its bad and all . . . ?"

Self-harm is defined as 'an expression of personal distress, usually made in private, by an individual who hurts him- or herself' (UK NICE, 2004). It is now preferred to the term 'attempted suicide' or 'parasuicide' because the range of motives or reasons for this behaviour includes several non-suicidal intentions and can often be an expression of distress and desire for escape from troubling situations. Rather than employing normal coping strategies, such as talking to a friend or family member about their problem, individuals who self-harm are likely to be withdrawn and depressed, and feel they have no one to turn to. Self-harm is not just a phenomenon that is found with depression, it is also a prominent feature of many other diagnosable disorders, including personality disorders (particularly borderline personality disorder; see Chapter 11) and eating disorders (see Chapter 9). There is currently no accepted overarching theory of why individuals self-harm, although some theorists suggest that self-harm is reinforced because it enables individuals to escape from or avoid unwanted emotional experiences (Chapman, Gratz & Brown, 2006).

The most common forms of deliberate self-harm include (1) cutting or burning, (2) taking overdoses, (3) hitting oneself, walls or hard objects, (4) pulling hair or picking skin and (5) self-strangulation. Surveys of adolescent self-harm suggest that around 7 per cent of 15- to 16-year-olds in the UK had deliberately self-harmed in the previous year, but only 12.6 per cent required hospital treatment. Deliberate self-harm was more common in females (11.2 per cent) than in males (3.2 per cent) (Hawton, Rodham, Evans & Weatherall, 2002).

Factors that predict self-harm in adolescent females include recent self-harm by friends, self-harm by family members, drug misuse, depression, anxiety, impulsivity and low self-esteem. The two most common reasons for self-harming are 'to find relief from a terrible state of mind' and 'because I wanted to die' (Hawton, Rodham, Evans & Weatherall, 2002).

In 2005, Hawton and James published the following facts about deliberate self-harm in young people.

Possible motives or reasons underlying self-harm

- To die
- To escape from unbearable anguish
- To escape the situation
- To show desperation to others
- To change the behaviour of others
- To 'get back at' other people or make them feel guilty
- To gain relief from tension
- To seek help

Common problems preceding self-harm

- Difficulties or disputes with parents
- School or work problems
- Difficulties with boyfriends or girlfriends
- Disputes with siblings
- Physical ill-health
- Difficulties or disputes with peers
- Depression
- Bullying
- Low self-esteem
- Sexual problems
- Alcohol and drug abuse
- Awareness of self-harm by friends or family

Preventing self-harm can be difficult because acts of self-harm are often impulsive and carried out in secret. Denial is a common feature of those who self-harm, especially when the self-harm may have a positive effect by providing temporary relief from individuals' difficulties. However, it may be possible to target vulnerable groups and to ensure that they have access to mental health services and support services. Vulnerable groups that have been identified include (1) depressed adolescents, (2) those with interpersonal crises, such as those who have lost a partner or have run away from home, and (3) those who have previously self-harmed (especially in conjunction with substance misuse and conduct disorder) (Hawton & James, 2005).

The most effective form of treatment for deliberate self-harm appears to be problem-solving therapy. This is often used with adolescents and enables them to bring new coping strategies to the difficulties in their lives. When extended to the individual's family, this type of therapy can facilitate the sharing and expression of feelings. CBT for depression can also be used if depression and low self-esteem are major underlying factors in an individual's self-harm.

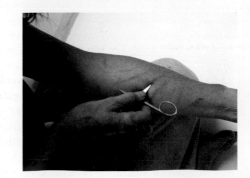

Plate 6.5

Michael Hutchence, formerly lead singer of the Australian rock band INXS, committed suicide in a hotel room in November 1997. Such celebrity suicides are often followed by a brief increase in adolescent suicides, suggesting that suicide has a sociological as well as a psychological aspect to it.

(Evans, Hawton & Rodham, 2004). For example, (1) suicide is related to diagnoses of depression, schizophrenia, borderline personality disorder, panic disorder, alcoholism and substance abuse (e.g. Isometsa, Henriksson, Marttunen et al., 1995); (2) psychological predictors of suicide include the cognitive construct of 'hopelessness' (Alloy, Abramson, Hogan, Whitehouse et al., 2000)

and low self-esteem (Fergusson & Lynskey, 1995); and (3) both poor physical health and physical disability are predictors of suicide (Dubow, Kausch, Blum, Reed et al., 1989). In addition, family difficulties are often associated with adolescent suicide attempts. One particular study found that the families of adolescent suicide attempters exhibited more conflict, more childhood sexual abuse and poorer parental control than the families of adolescents who had not attempted suicide (Gould & Kramer, 2001).

Perhaps not surprisingly, **life stress** is one of the most significant predictors of suicide, and suicide attempts are often preceded by a significant negative life event. The types of life events that may trigger suicide can differ across age groups. For adolescents and teenagers these are more likely to be relationship issues, separations and interpersonal conflicts; in middle age they are more likely to be financial issues; and in later life they tend to be related to disability and physical health (Rich, Warsradt, Nemiroff, Fowler et al., 1991). Table 6.13 shows a list of factors associated with adolescent suicide attempts according to whether they are vulnerability or stress factors. These emphasize the interrelationship between familial factors (such as family discord), cognitive factors (such as low self-esteem), life stressors (such as sexual abuse) and existing psychiatric problems (such as eating disorders or substance abuse) in the aetiology of adolescent suicide.

6.5.2 Identifying and Preventing Suicide

It is notoriously difficult to pick up the signs that an individual is seriously contemplating a suicide attempt. Prior to an attempt, suicidal individuals will often seem calm, rational, and even

Table 6.13 *Risk factors associated with adolescent attempted suicide and self-harm according to vulnerability factors, stress factors or both*

Vulnerability factors	Stress factors	Vulnerability and stress factors
Strong evidence for an association		
Family suicidal behaviour	Depression	Living apart from parents
	Alcohol abuse	Antisocial behaviour (especially in females)
	Use of hard drugs	Sexual abuse
	Mental health problems	Physical abuse
	Suicidal behaviour by friends	Unsupportive parents
	Family discord (especially for females)	
	Poor peer relationships	
Suggestive evidence for an association		
Poor communication with family	Hopelessness	Low self-esteem
	Eating disorders	Poor physical health
	Smoking	Physical disability
	Drug use	Sexual activity
	Sleep difficulties	
	Media exposure to suicide	

Source: Evans, Hawton & Rodham (2004).

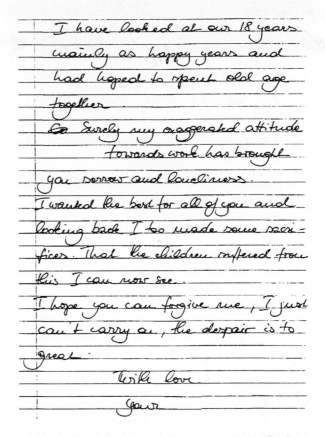

FOCUS POINT 6.3

Suicide notes

- Around one in three people who commit suicide leave a suicide note. Analysis of such notes can provide an insight into the feelings and motives of individuals who are no longer around to explain why they took their own life.

- This suicide note was written by an individual who committed suicide by jumping under a moving train in the UK. It is typical in that it is short, expresses guilt at the action, but also emphasizes the extreme pain and hopelessness that the victim experiences.

- Most suicide notes are addressed to specific individuals, usually in an attempt by the victim to justify his or her actions to family and friends. However, they can often be as confusing as they are enlightening – especially since those taking their own lives may be in such a confused and desperate state that they do not fully understand their own reasons for committing suicide (Shneidman, 1973).

- Research on the content of suicide notes has not particularly enlightened us as to why some people commit suicide, but there are age differences in the content of such notes. Young people usually point to interpersonal relations as the reason for their suicide, middle-aged people tend to report simply being unable to cope with life stressors, and older individuals are more likely to report being driven to suicide by health problems and physical disabilities (Lester, 1998).

show signs of improvement in their psychological condition. This calm and rationality may simply reflect the period of thought and planning that many who decide to attempt suicide go through. Individuals planning suicide will often meticulously dispose of their possessions, plan how their family will be cared for and take time to plan the act itself – often choosing a time and place where they cannot be disturbed. According to Kessler, Borges and Walters (1999), a national survey of suicide in the USA suggested that about 39 per cent of those who attempt suicide are determined to die, while 47 per cent do not wish to die but are communicating a 'cry for help' to friends and relatives in an attempt to convey their pain and hopelessness. The survey also suggested that around 72 per cent of those who had constructed a suicide plan went on to make a suicide attempt. Kessler et al. suggest that prevention is best focused on those who plan suicide attempts and identifying those factors that indicate that a suicidal individual is drawing up a plan.

The fact that around half of those attempting suicide do not want to die but need to convey their pain and despair means that intercepting these individuals before they make a successful suicide attempt is important. The main forms of intervention include 24-hour helplines and telephone support lines such as those provided by the Samaritans in the UK (www.samaritans.org.uk/). School-based educational programmes are also being developed that are aimed at warning teenagers about the early signs of suicidal tendencies in their peers and providing them with appropriate support information. However, while these prevention schemes have some success with some groups of users (e.g. young females), they are less effective in preventing suicide in other groups (e.g. adolescent boys) (Gould & Kramer, 2001).

SELF-TEST QUESTIONS

- Can you name the main risk factors for suicide?
- How is deliberate self-harm defined and what kinds of problems lead adolescents in particular to self-harm?

SECTION SUMMARY

6.5 Suicide and Deliberate Self-Harm

- Over half of those who successfully commit **suicide** are significantly depressed before the fatal attempt.

- 13.5 per cent of people report suicidal ideation during their lifetime.

- Women are three times more likely to attempt suicide than men, but the rate for successful suicide is four times higher in men than women.

- **Deliberate self-harm** is a parasuicidal phenomenon that is common in adolescence. It commonly includes cutting,

burning, overdoses, hitting oneself, pulling hair, picking skin or self-strangulation.

- Risk factors for suicide include an existing psychiatric diagnosis, low self-esteem, poor physical health and physical disability, and experiencing a significant negative life event.

- The main forms of intervening to prevent suicide include 24-hour helplines and telephone support lines (e.g. the Samaritans), and school-based educational programmes warning about the early signs of suicidal tendencies.

6.6 DEPRESSION AND MOOD DISORDERS REVIEWED

Depression is arguably the most prevalent of all the main psychopathology symptoms we cover in this text (lifetime prevalence rates between 5.2 and 17.1 per cent). It afflicts women twice as frequently as men, and it is estimated that it contributes 12 per cent to the total burden of non-fatal global disease (Ustun, Ayuso-Mateos, Chatterji, Mathers et al., 2004). It is an emotion that all of us experience at some point – especially in relation to losses and failures in our lives. However, for some it is a sustained, crippling and distressing problem (look again at the personal account given at the beginning of this chapter), and may even lead to suicidal ideation and suicide attempts (see section 6.5).

The other main mood disorder covered in this chapter is bipolar disorder, characterized by alternating periods of depression and mania (see Client's Perspective 6.1). This is a significantly less prevalent disorder (lifetime prevalence rate is between 0.4 and 1.6 per cent) that appears to have a basis in neurotransmitter imbalances in the brain (section 6.3.1). A look back at Table 6.1 will show the range of different theories that have been developed to try to explain all or parts of the symptoms of depression. These theories range from biological theories covering inherited factors, brain neurochemical imbalances and brain abnormalities, to a full spectrum of psychological theories attempting to explain both the behavioural and cognitive features of depression (section 6.3). Drug treatments, such as tricyclic drugs, monoamine oxidase inhibitors (MAOIs) and, more recently, selective serotonin reuptake inhibitors (SSRIs), have been shown to alleviate many of the symptoms of severe depression (section 6.4.1). However, both behavioural and cognitive therapies appear to show promise as long-term effective treatments for depression (section 6.4.2). Such therapies help sufferers by enabling them to identify and challenge ingrained negative views of themselves and the world.

LEARNING OUTCOMES

When you have completed this chapter, you should be able to:

1 Describe the characteristics and main diagnostic criteria of depression and bipolar disorder.

2 Compare and contrast at least two biological theories of the aetiology of depression and mood disorders.

3 Compare and contrast at least two psychological theories of the aetiology of depression and mood disorders.

4 Distinguish between biological and psychological theories of depression.

5 Describe and evaluate the role of cognitive factors in explaining the development of depression.

6 Compare and contrast biological, behavioural and cognitive therapies for depression.

7 Summarize the main psychological characteristics of suicide and deliberate self-harm.

KEY TERMS

Affectionless control *181*

Amygdala *180*

Anterior cingulate cortex (ACC) *180*

Attribution theories *184*

Battered woman syndrome *184*

Behavioural activation therapy *192*

Bipolar disorder *171*

Chronic fatigue syndrome (CFS) *175*

Cognitive restructuring *192*

Cognitive retraining *192*

Cognitive therapy *192*

Cortisol *180*

Cyclothymic disorder *174*

Deliberate self-harm *196*

Depression *170*

Dream interpretation *191*

Dysthymic disorder *174*

Electroconvulsive therapy (ECT) *190*

Free association *191*

Hippocampus *180*

Hopelessness theory *186*

Hypomania *176*

Interpersonal theories *182*

Introjection *181*

Learned helplessness *184*

Lithium carbonate *190*

Major depression *171*

Mania *171*

Melatonin *175*

Mindfulness-based cognitive therapy (MBCT) *194*

Monoamine oxidase (MAOI) inhibitors *178*

Negative automatic thoughts *193*

Negative schema *182*

Negative triad *182*

Norepinephrine *178*

Pessimistic thinking *184*

Prefrontal cortex *179*

Psychoanalysis *191*

Reattribution training *193*

Seasonal affective disorder (SAD) *175*

Selective serotonin reuptake inhibitors (SSRIs) *179*

Serotonin *178*

Social skills training *191*

Stepped-care model *188*

Suicide *195*

Symbolic loss *181*

Tricyclic drugs *178*

Unipolar depression *171*

REVIEWS, THEORIES AND SEMINAL STUDIES

Links to Journal Articles

6.2 The Prevalence of Depression and Mood Disorders

Cuellar, A.K., Johnson, S.L. & Winters, R. (2005). Distinctions between bipolar and unipolar depression. *Clinical Psychology Review, 25*, 307–339.

Kessler, R.C., Nelson, C.B., McGonagle, K.A., Liu, J., Schwartz, M. & Blazer, D.G. (1996). Comorbidity of DSM-III-R major depressive disorder in the general population: Results from the US national comorbidity survey. *Journal of Psychiatry, 168*, 17–30.

Kessler, R.C., Rubinow, D.R., Holmes, C., Abelson, J.M. & Zhao, S. (1997). The epidemiology of DSM-III-R bipolar disorder in a general population survey. *Psychological Medicine, 27*, 1079–1089.

Nolen-Hoeksema, S. (2001). Gender differences in depression. *Current Directions in Psychological Science, 10*, 173–176.

Patten, S.B. (2003). International differences in major depression prevalence: What do they mean? *Journal of Clinical Epidemiology, 56*, 711–716.

6.3 The Aetiology of Depression and Mood Disorders

Abramson, L.Y., Metalsky, G.I. & Alloy, L.B (1989). Hopelessness depression: A theory-based subtype of depression. *Psychological Review, 96*, 358–372.

Abramson, L.Y., Seligman, M.E.P. & Teasdale, J.D. (1978). Learned helplessness in humans: Critique and reformulation. *Journal of Abnormal Psychology, 87*, 49–74.

Afari, N. & Buchwald, D. (2003). Chronic fatigue syndrome: A review. *American Journal of Psychiatry, 160*, 221–236.

Ax, S., Gregg, V.H. & Jones, D. (2001). Coping and illness cognitions: Chronic fatigue syndrome. *Clinical Psychology Review, 21*, 161–182.

Blatt, S.J. (1998). Contributions of psychoanalysis to the understanding and treatment of depression. *Journal of the American Psychoanalytic Association, 46*, 723–752.

Davidson, R.J., Pizzagalli, D., Nitschke, J.B. & Putnam, K. (2002). Depression: Perspectives from affective neuroscience. *Annual Review of Psychology, 53,* 545–574.

Delgado, P.L. & Moreno, F.A. (2000). Role of norepinephrine in depression. *Journal of Clinical Psychiatry, 61,* 5–12.

Kelsoe, J.R. (2003). Arguments for the genetic basis of the bipolar spectrum. *Journal of Affective Disorders, 73,* 183–197.

Kwon, P. & Laurenceau, J.P. (2002). A longitudinal study of the hopelessness theory of depression: Testing the diathesis-stress model within a differential reactivity and exposure framework. *Journal of Clinical Psychology, 58,* 1305–1321.

Magnusson, A. & Boivin, D. (2003). Seasonal affective disorder: An overview. *Chronobiology International, 20,* 189–207.

Metalsky, G.I., Joiner, T.E., Hardin, T.S. & Abramson, L.Y. (1993). Depressive reactions to failure in a naturalistic setting: A test of the hopelessness and self-esteem theories of depression. *Journal of Abnormal Psychology, 102,* 101–109.

Segrin, C. (2000). Social skills deficits associated with depression. *Clinical Psychology Review, 20,* 379–403.

6.4 The Treatment of Depression and Mood Disorders

DeRubeis, R.J., Hollon, S.D., Amsterdam, J.D., Shelton, R.C., Young, P.R., Salomon, R.M., O'Reardon, J.P., Lovett, M.L., Gladis, M.M., Brown, L.L. & Gallop, R. (2005). Cognitive therapy vs. medications in the treatment of moderate to severe depression. *Archives of General Psychiatry, 62,* 409–416.

Hopko, D.R., Lejuez, C.W., Ruggiero, K.J. & Eifert, G.H. (2003). Contemporary behavioural activation treatments for depression: Procedures, principles, and progress. *Clinical Psychology Review, 23,* 699–717.

Teasdale, J.D., Segal, Z.V., Williams, J.M.G., Ridgeway, V.A., Soulsby, J.M. & Lau, M.A. (2000). Prevention of relapse/recurrence in major depression by mindfulness-based cognitive therapy. *Journal of Consulting and Clinical Psychology, 68,* 615–623.

Thase, M.E. & Kupfer, D.J. (1996). Recent developments in the pharmacotherapy of mood disorders. *Journal of Consulting and Clinical Psychology, 64,* 646–659.

6.5 Suicide and Deliberate Self-Harm

Evans, E., Hawton, K. & Rodham, K. (2004). Factors associated with suicidal phenomena in adolescents: A systematic review of population-based studies. *Clinical Psychology Review, 24*(8), 957–979.

Hawton, K., Rodham, K., Evans, E. & Weatherall, R. (2002). Deliberate self-harm in adolescents: Self-report survey in schools in England. *British Medical Journal, 325*(7374), 1207–1211.

Texts for Further Reading

Donnellan, C. (Ed.) (2003). *Coping with depression.* Cambridge: Independence.

Moore, R.G. & Garland, A. (2003). *Cognitive therapy for chronic and persistent depression.* Chichester: Wiley.

Power, M. (Ed.) (2003). *Mood disorders: A handbook of science and practice.* Chichester: Wiley.

Reynolds, W.M. & Johnston, H.F. (Eds.) (1994). *Handbook of depression in children and adolescents.* New York: Plenum.

Yufit, R.I. & Lester, D. (Eds.) (2004). *Assessment, treatment, and prevention of suicidal behavior.* Chichester: Wiley.

RESEARCH QUESTIONS

- What is the exact role of neurotransmitters such as serotonin in the experience of depression? Is depression associated with an imbalance in neurotransmitters or a deficit in specific neurotransmitters?

- Abnormalities in certain brain areas have been associated with depression. How are these brain abnormalities involved? Do they *cause* depression, or are they simply a *consequence* of experiencing depression?

- Is the association between dysfunction in specific brain areas and depression consistent or inconsistent with evidence of the role of neurotransmitter imbalances in depression?

- In what way can biological (e.g. neurotransmitter imbalances) and psychological processes (e.g. cognitive biases in thinking about the self and the world) be integrated to explain the aetiology of depression?

- Because of the way that psychoanalytic theory is formulated, can its explanation of depression ever be verified?

- Are interpersonal theories of depression merely accounts of how depression is maintained rather than how it is acquired?

- Do depressed individuals have a negative bias when making judgements about themselves and the world, or is it non-depressed individuals who have a positive bias?

- Do the negative thinking biases defined by Beck (e.g. the negative triad) actually *cause* depression, or are they simply a *consequence* of being depressed?

- In battered woman syndrome, have such women learned to be helpless or have they simply learned that acquiescence is an adaptive response to abuse?

- To what extent is hopelessness theory a full explanation of depression? What evidence is there that hopelessness causes depression rather than being just a consequence of being depressed?

- Cognitive change is just as likely to occur after behavioural treatments for depression as after cognitive treatments. So is the cognitive restructuring element really necessary?

- Adolescent suicide rates have increased substantially over the past 40 years. What are the factors that have contributed to this rise?

CLINICAL ISSUES

- DSM-IV-TR requires the identification of five symptoms for a period of 2 weeks for a diagnosis of major depression. But are such people any different in their experience of depression from those who exhibit only three symptoms?

- What are the clinical consequences of lay people viewing depression as a 'disease' or illness?

- How difficult is it to diagnose 'pure' depression when depression is so frequently comorbid with other Axis I and Axis II disorders?

- Prevalence rates for depression appear to vary significantly across different cultures. What implication does this have for diagnosing depression?

- Unlike many other psychological disorders, depression cannot easily be observed or directly measured. What implication does this have for diagnosing depression?

- How important is a GP's assessment of individuals who might present with symptoms of depression for subsequent treatment within the NICE stepped-care model?

- What are the dangers of prescribing SSRIs as a lone treatment for depression?

- Lithium carbonate is the drug of choice for treating bipolar disorder. What are the dangers associated with this form of treatment? Are there any acceptable and effective psychological therapies for bipolar disorder?

- Is there any reason why electroconvulsive therapy (ECT) should be used as a treatment for depression?

- People contemplating suicide are often calm and rational, and appear to show signs of improvement in their condition. Given these misleading outward signs, is there any way to identify individuals who are seriously contemplating a suicide attempt?

- Acts of self-harm are often impulsive, carried out in secret, and denial is a common feature of those who self-harm. Given these characteristics, how can people who regularly self-harm be identified and helped?

7 | Experiencing Psychosis: Schizophrenia and its Symptoms

ROUTE MAP OF THE CHAPTER

This chapter describes the symptoms of psychosis and examines the heterogeneous diagnostic category known as schizophrenia. We begin by describing the main symptoms of psychosis and give an insight into what it is like to experience these symptoms. The chapter then covers the various diagnostic sub-categories of schizophrenia and the stages through which psychotic symptoms develop. We then describe and evaluate a range of explanations of psychosis. These theories often attempt to explain symptoms at a number of different levels, such as biological, psychological and social. Next the chapter considers a range of biological and psychological treatments for psychotic symptoms, closing with an examination of the role of community care as a means of long-term supervision and management for those suffering from psychosis.

Trying to look at the lead up to an illness is difficult. Before I had any symptoms, I was generally feeling like I couldn't cope, but I didn't know how to go about getting any help. I was in a bad relationship and it ended, but I dearly wanted something to take its place.

I moved to Birmingham, to do a Post Graduate Diploma in Housing. I recognized that I wasn't really feeling together, but I just hoped that things would improve. I lived on my own in a bed-sit and generally became antagonistic towards others.

I had passed my first year exams and was working as a student placement for Warwick District Council. By about October of 1992, I believed that DJs on the radio were talking directly to me. When I told other people this they just laughed. But these DJs started to become very important to me, so I continued to believe it was happening, despite what other people were saying. I just kept it as my secret, until eventually when I was not at work I would listen to the radio 24 hours a day.

I believed that a radio DJ wanted a relationship with me, and throughout the course of our courtship (over the airwaves), the DJ and myself would actually discover the meaning of life. Everything had a meaning and eventually I had a sort of vision: God, he spoke to me and said 'No matter what happens, I will always love you'. I felt special and chosen and at the same time I thought that other people were telepathic and could read my mind.

I was still working and started a two-week placement at Newtown neighbourhood office. By now the world looked very different, with people being able to read my mind. Whenever names were said such as Lorraine or Pat, it had something to do with the state of my relationship with the radio DJ. Lorraine meant sorrow or floods of tears like rain, Pat meant that someone was patronizing me, or I them, depending on the context. Jackie meant that I was being chucked or that I was chucking him. I used to ring up the radio station under different names, all of which had a hidden meaning, such as Dawn – meaning that something had just dawned on me. Maureen meant that I was marooned.

Whilst on this placement (I was only there for two days), I began to get physical or tactile hallucinations. I thought that I had been shot in the head to remove a blood clot. Then, as I was working with one of my colleagues, I actually felt my brain crack open, then masses of blood came out of one of my ears, then a small trickle from the other. This for me meant that I was dead or dying in spirit, which I believed in more than the mortal body. At this point I started crying. My colleague went to put his hands on my arm, which he quickly removed as my arms were red hot. I asked to go home early, which was allowed.

That night, I thought that the devil was after me, I saw him come through one of the speakers of my stereo system. I was also probably hearing voices, but they were mixed in with the talk of the radio DJs. Suddenly, I became frustrated and ran out of the house into the middle of the road and started screaming. My neighbour came out and told me to come inside. He told me he had called the police and I started thumping him thinking he was the devil.

The experiences of the illness left me socially inept, mainly because I couldn't think to speak and engage in interpersonal relationships. I tried very hard to overcome the symptoms of the illness, including lack of motivation, but I was also conscious not to do too much. I did voluntary work and finished off my course. But, I was generally feeling different and less capable than everyone else. I tended to sleep an awful lot, but always tried to keep going, although many times I felt like giving up. But, this time I had come so far away from my delusions that there seemed like no going back. Eventually, I found employment and I am currently working part-time.

SOPHIE'S STORY

Introduction

Psychotic symptoms can be crippling and are characterized by disturbances in thought and language, sensory perception, emotion regulation and behaviour. Sufferers may experience sensory hallucinations and also develop thought disorders which may lead to pervasive false beliefs or delusions about themselves and the world around them. Individuals with psychotic symptoms may often withdraw from normal social interaction because of these disturbances of perception and thought, and this can result in poor educational performance, increasing unproductivity, difficulties in interpersonal relationships, neglect of day-to-day activities and a preoccupation with a personal world to the exclusion of others. As a result, many individuals exhibiting psychotic symptoms fall to the bottom of the social ladder or even become homeless because they cannot hold down a job or sustain a relationship – a phenomenon known as *downward drift* (Hollingshead & Redlich, 1958) (see section 7.5.3).

> **Downward drift** A phenomenon in which individuals exhibiting psychotic symptoms fall to the bottom of the social ladder or even become homeless because they cannot hold down a job or sustain a relationship.

Sophie's Story illustrates a number of the defining and common features of psychotic experience. Her story starts with a stressful life – exemplified by being in a difficult relationship – and an overwhelming feeling of being unable to cope. Whilst living alone she finds maintaining relationships with others difficult. The developing symptoms of psychosis include delusions (that the DJ is talking directly to her and that others are developing telepathic powers that enable them to read her mind), and she begins to feel that she possesses special powers. Eventually Sophie begins to experience sensory hallucinations in which she feels that she has been shot in the head and her brain has cracked open. Sophie's story ends with her experiences leaving her feeling socially inept and affecting her longer-term ability to be productive and motivated.

Psychosis is a collection of disparate symptoms that can leave an individual feeling frightened and confused. The presence of a number of these characteristic symptoms may lead to a diagnosis of *schizophrenia* (see Table 7.1). DSM-IV-TR describes the symptoms characteristic of schizophrenia as comprising cognitive and emotional dysfunctions that include dysfunctions of perception, inferential thinking, language and communication, behavioural monitoring, affect, fluency, productivity of thought and speech, and attention. Importantly, no single symptom is indicative of a diagnosis of schizophrenia, and, as we shall see later, the diagnosis involves the identification of a variable set of symptoms indicative of impaired occupational and social functioning. Before you move on to read in detail about the diagnosis of schizophrenia, look at Focus Point 7.1, which guides you through some examples of the main symptoms of psychotic experience. You may also want to read the summary in Table 7.1 to give you an overview of psychosis. You can refer back to this table when you have read the chapter in detail.

> **Schizophrenia** The main diagnostic category for psychotic symptoms. The five central characteristics are (1) delusions, (2) hallucinations, (3) disorganized speech (e.g. incoherence), (4) grossly disorganized or catatonic behaviour and (5) flattened affect, poverty of speech and apathy.

FOCUS POINT 7.1

Commonly experienced psychotic symptoms

This box helps you to familiarize yourself with some of the commonly occurring psychotic symptoms before we proceed to describing and investigating these symptoms in more detail. Remember, individuals diagnosed with schizophrenia do not necessarily show all of these symptoms – only a specified constellation of them (see Table 7.2). The main clinical symptoms include (1) distortions of perception and reality, (2) disorganized speech and thought disorder and (3) disorders of motor behaviour.

Distortions of perception and reality
People with a diagnosis of schizophrenia may have perceptions of reality that are strikingly different from the reality seen and shared by others around them. Living in a world distorted by hallucinations and delusions, sufferers may feel frightened, anxious and confused.

Hallucinations and illusions
Hallucinations and illusions are disturbances of perception that are common in people diagnosed with schizophrenia. Hallucinations are perceptions that occur without an appropriate sensory input. Although hallucinations can occur in any sensory form – auditory (sound), visual (sight), tactile (touch), gustatory (taste) and olfactory (smell) – hearing voices that other people do not hear is the most common type of hallucination. Sufferers may interpret these voices as describing their own activities, directly conversing with them, warning of impending dangers or ordering them to behave in certain ways. Illusions, on the other hand, occur when a sensory stimulus is present but is incorrectly interpreted by the individual. An example of a visual

Figure 1

sensory illusion is shown in Figure 1 above. The driver's eyes reflected in the rear-view mirror of a car seem to suddenly switch to another set of eyes staring back at the driver.

Delusions

Delusions are false personal beliefs and may take on different themes. For example, individuals experiencing paranoid-type symptoms – roughly one-third of people diagnosed with schizophrenia – often have delusions of *persecution*, or false and irrational beliefs that they are being cheated, harassed, poisoned or conspired against. These individuals may believe that they, or a member of their family or someone close to them, are the focus of this persecution. In addition, delusions of *grandeur*, in which a person may believe he or she is a famous or important figure, may occur. Sometimes the delusions experienced by people diagnosed with schizophrenia are quite bizarre: for instance, believing that a neighbour is controlling their behaviour with magnetic waves; that people on television or radio are directing special messages to them (see *Sophie's Story*); or that their thoughts are being broadcast aloud to others. However, such false beliefs are often very difficult to challenge. Sufferers are frequently able to defend their deluded beliefs in a coherent way and unable to understand that other people find their delusional beliefs implausible (McGuire, Junginger, Adams, Burright et al., 2001).

In a famous study reported by Rokeach (1964), the author took three individuals diagnosed with schizophrenia – each of whom believed he was Jesus Christ – and transferred them to the same ward to live together. Presumably all three of them couldn't be Jesus Christ – so would this weaken the delusional beliefs of any of them? It did not – even after 2 years of living together! One claimed that he was the real Jesus Christ because he had created the other two himself; the second claimed that he had evidence that the others were in fact mere mortal 'creatures'; and the third said he knew that the others were impostors, where they came from and what they did for a living.

Disorganized speech and thought disorder

Psychotic symptoms frequently exhibit a range of attributes that indicate disordered thinking and disordered speech. Below are examples of some of the more common of these symptoms.

Word salad

In many cases the language of the person experiencing a psychotic episode appears so disorganized that there seems to be no link between one phrase and the next. This is known as a *word salad*. Some word salads simply do not seem to be attempts to communicate anything structured and appear to drift without substance from one unconnected sentence to the next. For example:

> *'Everything is going around in slow motion. The boxes are clanging and chattering to be let out. Behind my forehead the past is surfacing mixing a bottle of acid solution. A stake jams a door that leads to a mirage of broken appearances. Inside a box, pounding fists try to pull down my imagination. The ground work is split into hundreds of pieces; each fragment is separate as if it had some kind of individual purpose. The truth is locked up in a unit.'*

In other cases word salads appear to be sets of phrases or words linked by association to the previous phrase. For example, in answer to the question 'What colour is your dress?', a sufferer answered: 'red . . . Santa Claus . . . flying through the sky . . . God'. This is known as *loose association* or *derailment* and makes it very difficult to follow the conversation of an individual when a single, often unimportant word from the previous sentence becomes the focus of the next sentence.

Neologisms

Many individuals suffering psychotic symptoms often make up words and use them in their attempts to communicate. These *neologisms* are frequently constructed by condensing or combining several words. Some examples from individual sufferers are given below:

SPECTROAUTOROTATION	Circling in everywhere, as with checkers or a bat in baseball
SNIGGERATION	A giggle or sniggering. I do it sometimes
RELAUDATION	Praising over and over
CIRCLINGOLOGY	Study of a rolling circle; a fruit can in the form of a cylinder rolling

Clanging

People exhibiting psychotic symptoms often try to communicate using words that rhyme. This is known as *clanging*. Go back to *Sophie's Story* at the beginning of this chapter. You will see that she used a series of names to denote the state of her mind or how she was feeling. These names rhymed with words that described her feelings, e.g. Lorraine – tears like rain; Pat – patronizing; Jackie – being chucked; Maureen – marooned. In other cases sufferers only appear able to construct sentences if the words in them rhyme. This communication may begin with a sensible response but then degenerates into nonsense because of the urge to 'clang', as the following transcript shows:

TH: 'What colour is your dress?'
CL: 'Red . . . Like a bed.'
TH: 'Why is it like a bed?'
CL: 'Because it's dead.'
TH: 'Why is a bed like being dead?'
CL: 'I dunno . . . maybe it's a med.'
TH: 'What's a med?'
CL: 'A bled.'

Disorders of motor behaviour

Individuals suffering psychosis can also exhibit a number of problems associated with disorders of motor behaviour, although these types of symptoms are more often found in the more severe and chronic cases of psychosis. The two most common motor symptoms are stereotypy and catatonic stupor.

Stereotypy

One common symptom of chronic psychosis is *stereotypy* of response movement, which indicates reduced purposeful control of behaviour. During stereotypy, individuals repetitively indulge in the same, simple motor behaviour pattern. Examples of repetitive stereotypic behaviours include head rubbing, agitated pacing backwards and forwards, repetitive smacking or patting of parts of the body or repetitive manipulation of an object.

Catatonia

In some very severe cases of psychosis, the individual may lapse into a *catatonic stupor*. Those who lapse into this state become withdrawn and inactive for long periods. In extreme cases this may take the form of catatonic rigidity, in which the individual will adopt a rigid, often awkward posture for many hours. Others exhibit what is know as *waxy flexibility*, and will maintain a posture into which they have been placed by someone else.

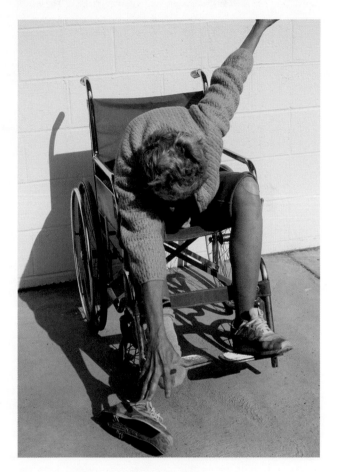

Figure 2

Table 7.1 *Experiencing psychosis: summary*

LIFETIME PREVALENCE RATES	DEFINITION	MAIN DSM-IV-TR DIAGNOSTIC FEATURES	SUB-TYPES OF SCHIZOPHRENIA	KEY FEATURES	THEORIES OF AETIOLOGY	MAIN FORMS OF TREATMENT
0.5–2% *24 million sufferers worldwide* *No difference in prevalence rates between men and women*	Cognitive and emotional dysfunctions that include dysfunctions of perception, inferential thinking, language and communication, behavioural monitoring, affect, fluency, productivity of thought and speech, and attention Main clinical symptoms include delusions, hallucinations, disorganized speech (incoherence), disorganized or catatonic behaviour, flat affect, poverty of speech and apathy	5 important characteristics include (1) delusions, (2) hallucinations, (3) disorganized speech, (4) grossly disorganized behaviour and (5) flat affect and apathy The first 4 of these are known as POSITIVE symptoms, and the final one represents a NEGATIVE symptom 2 or more of the 5 symptoms must be present for a significant proportion of time during a 1-month period These symptoms must also be associated with marked social or occupational dysfunction	PARANOID SCHIZOPHRENIA Delusions or auditory hallucinations associated with persecution or grandeur DISORGANIZED SCHIZOPHRENIA Disorganized speech, behaviour and flat affect CATATONIC SCHIZOPHRENIA Disturbances of motor behaviour (immobility), mutism, etc. RESIDUAL TYPE Lack of prominent positive symptoms but evidence of flat affect and other negative symptoms	A heterogeneous disorder in which no single symptom is a defining feature Consists of positive symptoms (distortions of normal functioning, e.g. hallucinations) and negative symptoms (diminution or loss of normal functions, e.g. flat affect and apathy) Develops through 3 well-defined stages: (1) prodromal stage, (2) active stage and (3) residual stage Caused by a combination of a genetically inherited predisposition and environmental stress (a diathesis-stress perspective) Positive symptoms associated with excess activity of neurotransmitters such as dopamine Antipsychotic drugs can successfully suppress positive symptoms Most sufferers will require lifetime care and supervision ranging from continuous medication and psychological and family-based treatments to longer-term community care and management	An overall diathesis-stress perspective Genetic factors Role of brain neurotransmitters, especially excess activity of the neurotransmitter dopamine Role of specific brain abnormalities Psychodynamic theories The role of operant reinforcement Dysfunctions in normal cognitive processes, such as attention and orienting Abnormal attributional processes and cognitive biases in information processing Theory of mind deficits Social theories such as the sociogenic hypothesis, social selection theory and social labelling Familial factors, such as a stressful family environment and expressed emotion	Hospitalization and custodial care Electroconvulsive therapy (ECT) and psychosurgery Antipsychotic drugs Social skills training Cognitive behaviour therapy (CBT) Family interventions and family therapy Community care

7.1 HISTORY OF SCHIZOPHRENIA AS A DIAGNOSTIC CATEGORY

The symptoms of psychosis have been reported throughout history. However, because the symptoms can be so varied and wide ranging, 'schizophrenia' has only gradually been isolated as a single diagnostic category to cover these heterogeneous characteristics.

In 1896 the European psychiatrist Emil Kraepelin was the first to distinguish schizophrenia from a range of other psychiatric symptoms (such as manic depressive illness). He did this by bringing together a number of contemporary diagnostic concepts including paranoia, catatonia and hebephrenia (symptoms indicative of incoherence and fragmentation of personality) under the general term *dementia praecox*. He assumed that dementia praecox was a single disease that manifested itself in late adolescence or early adulthood and had a deteriorating prognosis from which there was no recovery.

Dementia praecox An early, general term for a number of diagnostic concepts including paranoia, catatonia and hebephrenia (symptoms indicative of incoherence and fragmentation of personality).

In contrast to Kraepelin, the Swiss psychiatrist Eugen Bleuler (1908) did not believe that the onset of dementia praecox was simply restricted to adolescence and early adulthood, nor that it inevitably led to dementia. He preferred to use the term schizophrenia (from the Greek *schiz*, to split, and *phren*, the mind), because he felt that it properly described the splitting of different psychological functions within a single personality. Unfortunately, this term has also had its problems, with the popular belief that the term schizophrenia refers to a split or double personality. In order to try to unify the various symptoms under a single diagnostic category, Bleuler used the concept of the 'breaking of associative threads' as being central to all of the symptoms of schizophrenia. That is, effective thinking, communication and action were not possible if the ability to associate things together was disrupted. In this respect, it is interesting to note that in later sections of this chapter we will see that there is evidence that at least some of the clinical symptoms of schizophrenia may be determined by dysfunctions in associative and attentional processes (see section 7.5.2).

SELF-TEST QUESTIONS

- What were Kraepelin and Bleuler's contributions to the identification and diagnosis of schizophrenia?

SECTION SUMMARY

7.1 History of Schizophrenia as a Diagnostic Category

- The symptoms of schizophrenia were first distinguished by European psychiatrist Emil Kraepelin and called **dementia praecox**.

- The Swiss psychiatrist Eugen Bleuler later coined the term **schizophrenia** (from the Greek *schiz*, to split, and *phren*, the mind).

'THIS IS OUR SCHIZOPHRENIA WING. TWO ROOMS PER PERSON.'

Plate 7.1
When the term schizophrenia was first used, it generated a popular belief that the term referred to a split or double personality, when in fact Bleuler meant it to describe the splitting of different psychological functions within a single personality.

7.2 THE NATURE OF PSYCHOTIC SYMPTOMS

DSM-IV-TR lists five important characteristics for diagnosing schizophrenia, of which two or more must be present for a significant portion of time during a 1-month period. The individual's behaviour must also have been noticeably disturbed for at least 6 months. These five central characteristics are: (1) delusions, (2) hallucinations, (3) disorganized speech (e.g. incoherence), (4) grossly disorganized or catatonic behaviour and (5) negative symptoms such as flattened affect, alogia (poverty of speech) or avolition (apathy). These signs and symptoms must also be associated with marked social or occupational dysfunction (see Table 7.2). The first four of these characteristics are known as *positive symptoms*, because they tend to reflect an excess or distortion of normal functions (e.g. developing inappropriate beliefs or perceiving things that are not there), while the final

Positive symptoms Characteristics of psychotic symptoms which tend to reflect an excess or distortion of normal functions.

Table 7.2 *DSM-IV-TR diagnostic criteria for schizophrenia*

A Characteristic symptoms: two (or more) of the following, each present for a significant portion of the time during a 1-month period:

   (1) delusions

   (2) hallucinations

   (3) disorganized speech (e.g. frequent derailment or incoherence)

   (4) grossly disorganized or catatonic behaviour

   (5) negative symptoms, i.e. affective flattening, alogia or avolition

B Social/occupational dysfunction: For a significant proportion of the time since the onset of the disturbance, one or more of the major areas of functioning such as work, interpersonal relations, or self-care are markedly below the level achieved prior to the onset.

C Duration: Continuous signs of disturbance persist for at least 6 months, including at least 1 month of symptoms that meet Criterion A.

D The disturbances should NOT be due to schizoaffective disorder and mood disorder, the direct physiological effects of a substance (e.g. a drug of abuse or a medication), a medical condition, or a developmental disorder such as autism or pervasive developmental disorder.

Negative symptoms   Symptoms of psychosis which tend to reflect a diminution or loss of normal functions (e.g. withdrawal or lack of emotion).

7.2.1 Clinical Symptoms

7.2.1.1 Delusions

Delusions   Firmly held but erroneous beliefs that usually involve a misinterpretation of perceptions or experiences.

Delusions are firmly held but erroneous beliefs that usually involve a misinterpretation of perceptions or experiences. Such delusions are commonly experienced by around 75 per cent of individuals hospitalized because of their psychotic symptoms (Maher, 2001). While some delusions may be clearly bizarre (e.g. the individual may believe that his or her entire internal organs have been taken out and replaced by those of someone else), others may not (e.g. a paranoid belief that the individual is constantly under surveillance by the police). Regardless of how bizarre a delusion is, sufferers are often

able to bring reason and logic to support their delusion – even though the underlying belief itself is clearly absurd (Maher, 2001). This ability to support absurd beliefs with logical thought has led some clinicians to suggest that delusions may be the result of an inability to integrate perceptual input with prior knowledge even though rational thought processes are still intact (Frith, 1996; Frith & Dolan, 2000). For other clinicians it is suggestive of the development of biased information processing and the development of dysfunctional beliefs about the world (e.g. Freeman, Garety, Kuipers, Fowler et al., 2002; Morrison, 2001b).

The main types of delusion found in those experiencing psychosis are: (1) *delusions of persecution* (paranoia), in which individuals believe they are being persecuted, spied upon or are in danger (usually as the result of a conspiracy of some kind); (2) *delusions of grandeur*, in which individuals believe they are someone with fame or power (e.g. Jesus Christ or a famous music star); (3) *delusions of control*, where individuals believe that their thoughts, feelings or actions are being controlled by external forces (e.g. extraterrestrial or supernatural beings); this is often associated with the belief that control is being exerted through devices (such as the radio) which are sending messages directly to the person's brain; (4) *delusions of reference*, where individuals believe that independent external events are making specific reference to them (e.g. in *Sophie's Story*, she believes that the DJ on the radio is talking directly to her); and (5) *nihilistic delusions*, where individuals believe that some aspect of either the world or themselves has ceased to exist (e.g. the person may believe that he or she is in fact dead).

One common feature of psychotic thought is that sufferers frequently believe that their thoughts are being interfered with or controlled in some way, either by being openly broadcast to others or by having thoughts planted in their mind by external forces (see Focus Point 7.3). This type of delusion is so common that it may offer some insight into the cognitive deficits underlying a majority of psychotic thought. For example, in an experimental study, Blakemore, Oakley and Frith (2003) used hypnosis to generate beliefs in non-clinical participants that their self-generated actions could be attributed to an external source. They found that such erroneous beliefs generated higher than normal levels of activation in the parietal cortex and cerebellum and they suggest that these areas of the brain may be altered during

category represents what are known as *negative symptoms*, which reflect symptoms characteristic of a diminution or loss of normal functions.

Delusions of persecution   Delusions in which the individual believes he or she is being persecuted, spied upon or is in danger (usually as the result of a conspiracy of some kind).

Delusions of grandeur   Delusions in which the individual believes he or she is someone with fame or power (e.g. Jesus Christ, or a famous music star).

Delusions of control   Delusions where the person believes that his or her thoughts, feelings or actions are being controlled by external forces (e.g. extraterrestrial or supernatural beings).

Delusions of reference   Delusions where the individual believes that independent external events are making specific reference to him or her.

Nihilistic delusions   Delusions where individuals believe that some aspect of either the world or themselves has ceased to exist (e.g. the person may believe that they are in fact dead).

FOCUS POINT 7.2

Erotomania and stalking

....

Swedish police have arrested a 34-year-old man accused of stalking Agnetha Faltskog of the 70s Swedish pop phenomenon Abba. According to reports in the Swedish daily Expressen, Ms Faltskog filed an official complaint against the man last week, saying she feared for her life after being stalked for three years.

The man was detained two days later. The man had reportedly become smitten by the singer when he was eight years old and had left his native Netherlands to buy a house near Ms Faltskog's country estate at Ekero near Stockholm.

According to Expressen, she told police that the stalker had sent her some 300 letters between 1997 and 1999, telephoned her up to three times a day and followed her wherever she went.

(BBC News website, 4 April 2000)

One form of psychotic delusion is called erotomania. This is a relatively rare disorder where an individual has a delusional belief that a person of higher social status falls in love and makes

amorous advances towards him or her. As a result of these delusions, individuals suffering erotomanic delusions may often end up stalking their target by regularly visiting their homes in an attempt to meet and talk with the person or by following them as they go about their daily business.

There are two types of erotomanic delusion. The first is where individuals believe their victim loves them. In this case the individual believes he is having a relationship with his victim, and he will make regular attempts to try to contact and meet his victim in order to substantiate the relationship. The American actress Rebecca Schaeffer was tragically shot in 1989 by a stalker who was rebuffed by her when attempting to talk to her about their 'relationship'. The second form of erotomanic delusion is when the individual believes that he is destined to be with his victim, even though he is aware he may never have met that person. So if he pursues the victim long enough, he will eventually come to have a relationship with his victim. An example of this is the case of Agnetha Faltskog from the Swedish pop group Abba (pictured), who was stalked for some years by a Dutch man who believed he was destined to be with her.

Stalking appears to be on the increase in many Western countries (Pathe, 2002), causes substantial distress to its victims, and can be caused by a range of psychopathologies (e.g. erotomanic delusions, severe personality disorder, obsessive-compulsive disorders). Studies of individuals with erotomanic delusions indicate that they are usually isolated loners without a partner or full-time occupation and around half have a first-degree relative with a delusional disorder (Kennedy, McDonough, Kelly & Berrios, 2002). Many also develop fantasies in which they are driven to protect, help or even harm their victims (Menzies, Federoff, Green & Isaacson, 1995). One example is the German stalker who was obsessed with tennis star Steffi Graf. This drove him to attack and stab her tennis rival, Monica Seles, during a tournament in Hamburg in 1993 in a deluded attempt to try to further Graf's career.

psychotic episodes so that self-produced actions and thoughts are experienced as external.

7.2.1.2 Hallucinations

People suffering psychotic symptoms regularly report sensory abnormalities across a broad range of sensory modalities, and this is usually manifested as perceiving things that are not there. *Hallucinations* can occur in any modality (e.g. auditory, olfactory, gustatory

Hallucinations A sensory experience in which a person can see, hear, smell, taste or feel something that isn't there.

and tactile), but the most common are auditory hallucinations, which are reported by around 70 per cent of sufferers (Cleghorn, Franco, Szechtman, Kaplan et al., 1992). Auditory hallucinations are usually manifested as voices, which can be experienced as external voices commanding the individual to act in certain ways, two or more voices conversing with each other, or a voice commentating on the individual's own thoughts. In all cases these voices are perceived as being distinct from the individual's own thoughts. Research of brain areas involved in speech generation and the perception of sounds suggests that when sufferers claim to hear voices, this is associated with neural activation in these areas of the brain (Keefe, Arnold, Bayen, McEvoy et al., 2002;

FOCUS POINT 7.3

Delusions and thought control

One frequent psychotic symptom is that individuals often believe that their thoughts are being interfered with or controlled in some way, either by being openly broadcast to others or by having thoughts planted in their mind by external forces. The following examples are taken from a paper published in the *British Journal of Psychiatry* (Mellor, 1970).

- 'I am thinking about my mother and suddenly my thoughts are sucked out of my mind by a phrenological vacuum extractor, and there is nothing in my mind, it is empty.'

- 'As I think, my thoughts leave my head on a type of ticker tape. Everyone around has only to pass the tape through their mind and they know my thoughts.'

- 'I look out of the window and I think the garden looks nice and the grass looks cool, but the thoughts of Eamon Andrews come into my mind. There are no other thoughts there, only his. He treats my mind like a screen and flashes his thoughts on it like you flash a picture.'

In many of these cases individuals diagnosed with schizophrenia may believe that their thoughts are either open to external scrutiny or are being controlled by external forces because they experience self-produced actions or thoughts as being external (Blakemore, Oakley & Frith, 2003). It is not clear why individuals diagnosed with schizophrenia should make this external attribution, but it may result (1) from a reality-monitoring deficit as a result of being unable to clearly identify the source of a perception or sensation (Brebion, Amador, David, Malaspina et al., 2000) or (2) an attributional bias, in which individuals diagnosed with schizophrenia have developed a bias towards interpreting negative events or thoughts to external causes (Bentall, Kaney & Dewey, 1991).

McGuire, Silbersweig, Wright, Murray et al., 1996), and the sufferer attributes them to external sources.

Visual hallucinations are the second most common type of hallucination. They can take either a diffuse form, as in the perception of colours and shapes that are not present, or they can be very specific, such as perceiving that a particular person (e.g. a partner or parent) is present when they are not. Other hallucinations can be tactile and somatic (e.g. feeling that one's skin is tingling or burning) or olfactory and gustatory (e.g. experiencing smells that are not present or foods that taste unusual).

For those who believe that their hallucinations are real, such experiences can be extremely frightening. However, while some individuals suffering psychosis are convinced their hallucinations are real, many others are aware that their hallucinations may *not* be real. This suggests that psychotic episodes may be associated with a ***reality-monitoring deficit***. That is, individuals suffering psychotic symptoms may have difficulty identifying the source of a perception and difficulty distinguishing whether it is real or imagined. In support of this possibility, Brebion, Amador, David, Malaspina et al. (2000) found that when individuals diagnosed with schizophrenia and non-clinical controls were asked to remember words that had been generated either by themselves or by the experimenter, schizophrenic individuals differed in three important ways from non-clinical controls:

1 They were more likely to identify items as having been in the generated list of words when they were not (false positives).

> **Reality-monitoring deficit** Where an individual has a problem distinguishing between what actually occurred and what did not occur.

2 They were more likely to report that words they had generated themselves were generated by the experimenter.

3 They were more likely to report that spoken items had been presented as pictures.

These results suggest that individuals diagnosed with schizophrenia have both a reality-monitoring deficit (i.e. a problem distinguishing between what actually occurred and what did not occur) and a ***self-monitoring deficit*** (i.e. they cannot distinguish between thoughts and ideas they generated themselves and thoughts or ideas that other people generated).

> **Self-monitoring deficit** Where individuals cannot distinguish between thoughts and ideas they generated themselves and thoughts or ideas that other people generated.

7.2.1.3 Disorganized Speech (Incoherence)

Individuals suffering psychosis can display disorders of speech and communication in a variety of different ways. The most common are ***derailment*** or ***loose associations***, where individuals may drift quickly from one topic to another during a conversation. Their answers to questions may be tangential rather than relevant (***tangentiality***), and in some cases their speech may be so

> **Derailment** A disorder of speech where the individual may drift quickly from one topic to another during a conversation.

> **Loose associations** A disorder of speech where the individual may drift quickly from one topic to another during a conversation.

> **Tangentiality** A disorder of speech in which answers to questions may be tangential rather than relevant.

FOCUS POINT 7.4

Examples of psychotic speech

The following are some examples of psychotic speech which convey (1) the tendency to jump from one topic to the next even within sentences (examples of what are called loose associations), and (2) poverty of content even in speech which appears to be detailed (in terms of number of words) and is grammatically correct.

'Covering up the secret of the lies, hiding in cover, I'm an undercover detective from Bakes-Ville. Using white lies to cover up the black lies things become complicated. When asked questions concerning my family I become tight lipped. Shutting my mouth with invisible tooth picks I pretend to be a rotten piece of meat. Nobody knows me as far as anybody is concerned I could be a Russian Spy. One short answer brief and to the point, hinting for everyone to back off. The fear of closeness stiffens my posture and within minutes I'm quick to get away.'

'The television is speaking in coded messages. The man in the box is telling me to be quiet. Tuning out, I try to pick up any clues that the world is bent on killing me. Lost in the chattering voices above my head I stretch my ear trying to hear the noises that keep on buzzing. The breaking point has come. Running ahead of me, hallucinations embark on a trail of disfigured faces.'

'If anyone tries to detect me I'll hide behind a clown's mask and pretend to be real. The danger of being found persists to scare me. Becoming so absorbed in new disguises I forget to remember I am made of pain. The genesis of mental illness is my middle name and the devil certainly does own my soul. Under the moon personality disorders surface on windmills over a spring of fresh water. The genuine feeling of sadness and fear are there toppled with candy coating and sugar bears.'

Source: www.schizophrenia-help.com/
schizophrenia__tracey.htm

Clanging   A form of speech pattern in schizophrenia where thinking is driven by word sounds. For example, rhyming or alliteration may lead to the appearance of logical connections where none in fact exists.

Neologisms   Made-up words used in an attempt to communicate.

Word salad   Where the language of a person experiencing a psychotic episode is so disorganized that there seems to be no link between one phrase and the next.

disorganized that it is neither structured nor comprehensible. Instances of the latter are *clanging* and the use of *neologisms* and *word salads* (see the examples given in Focus Point 7.1).

Focus Point 7.4 provides an example of the confused speech generated by individuals diagnosed with schizophrenia, showing how their conversation is prone to jump from one topic to the next on the basis of loose or irrelevant associations between words or ideas. These loose associations that appear to govern psychotic speech suggest that sufferers (1) have difficulty inhibiting associations between thoughts (Titone, Holzman & Levy, 2002) and so tend to follow the track of the first association that comes to mind, and (2) have difficulties understanding the full context of a conversation (Cohen, Barch, Carter & Servan-Schreiber, 1999), and so cannot distinguish the full meaning of a conversation or sentence from its detail. The result of these loose associations is that psychotic speech can be very detailed in terms of number of words, breadth of ideas and grammatical correctness, but it will usually convey very little. This *poverty of content* is clearly seen in the example given in Focus Point 7.4.

Poverty of content   A characteristic of the conversation of individuals suffering psychosis in which their conversation has very little substantive content.

7.2.1.4 Grossly Disorganized or Catatonic Behaviour

DSM-IV-TR describes how 'grossly disorganized' behaviour can be indicative of a diagnosis of schizophrenia in a number of ways. Behaviour may be childlike and silly (and inappropriate for the person's chronological age), or inappropriate to the context (e.g. masturbating in public). It may be unpredictable and agitated (e.g. shouting and swearing in the street) and the individual may have difficulty completing any goal-directed activity (e.g. an inability to focus on or complete basic day-to-day tasks such as cooking or maintaining personal hygiene). The person's appearance may be dishevelled and he or she may well dress in an inappropriate manner (e.g. wearing heavy, thick clothing in hot weather or walking around in public in only their underwear).

Catatonic behaviour   Behaviour characterized by a significant decrease in reactivity to the environment (catatonic stupor), maintaining rigid, immobile postures (catatonic rigidity), resisting attempts to be moved (catatonic negativism) or purposeless and excessive motor activity that often consists of simple, stereotyped movements (catatonic excitement or stereotypy).

Catatonic motor behaviours are characterized by a significant decrease in reactivity to the environment (catatonic stupor), maintaining rigid, immobile postures (catatonic rigidity), resisting attempts to be moved (catatonic negativism) or purposeless and excessive motor activity that often consists of simple, stereotyped movements (catatonic excitement or stereotypy; see Focus Point 7.1).

7.2.1.5 Affective Flattening, Alogia (Poverty of Speech) and Avolition (Apathy)

Affective flattening Limited range and intensity of emotional expression; a 'negative' symptom of schizophrenia.

Blunted or *affective flattening* is when the individual shows little or no emotion. This is conveyed in an expressionless and unresponsive facial appearance, lack of eye contact and monotonous voice tone. Flat affect is often accompanied by *anhedonia*, which is an inability to react to enjoyable or pleasurable events (Kring & Neale, 1996). However, it may also simply represent an inability to show emotions to others. *Alogia* is characterized by a lack of verbal fluency in which the individual gives very brief, empty replies to questions. *Avolition* represents an inability to carry out or complete normal day-to-day goal-oriented activities, and this results in the individual showing little interest in social or work activities. These particular clinical symptoms are collectively known as *negative symptoms*, because they represent a loss or diminution of normal functions. However, the clinician has to be very careful when including these negative symptoms in his or her diagnosis of schizophrenia. This is because these symptoms can be viewed as being on a continuum with normality (i.e. some people are naturally less emotionally responsive, less vocal and less motivated than others), and they represent common side effects of other diagnostic categories such as major depression. DSM-IV-TR recommends that these negative symptoms should not be used in the diagnosis of schizophrenia if they can clearly be attributed to other factors such as medication side effects, depression, environmental understimulation or demoralization (see Table 7.2).

Anhedonia Inability to react to enjoyable or pleasurable events.

Alogia A lack of verbal fluency in which the individual gives very brief, empty replies to questions.

Avolition Inability to carry out or complete normal day-to-day goal-oriented activities.

7.2.2 Schizophrenia Sub-Types

Because psychotic symptoms can be so varied, DSM-IV-TR defines a number of categories or sub-types of schizophrenia that are based on the major or most prominent symptoms displayed by the individual. The main sub-types of schizophrenia are (1) paranoid schizophrenia, (2) disorganized schizophrenia, (3) catatonic schizophrenia and (4) residual schizophrenia.

7.2.2.1 Paranoid Schizophrenia

Paranoid schizophrenia A sub-type of schizophrenia characterized by the presence of delusions of persecution.

Paranoid schizophrenia is characterized by the presence of delusions or auditory hallucinations. The delusions are usually persecutory or grandiose and the auditory hallucinations will usually relate to the content of the persecutory theme (such as hearing the voices of people that the individual believes are trying to access his or her thoughts). Individuals diagnosed with paranoid schizophrenia display anxiety, anger and aloofness; they are usually argumentative and their delusional beliefs may tend them to either violence or suicide. They also develop ideas of reference in which they display a bias towards interpreting all events or experiences (whether irrelevant or unimportant) as supporting their persecutory delusions, and they have an attributional style that blames others for negative events (Bentall, Corcoran, Howard, Blackwood et al., 2001). In some cases individuals will develop delusions of grandeur in which they have an exaggerated view of their own importance, or the delusions may focus on the belief that a sexual partner is being unfaithful (delusional jealousy).

A diagnosis of paranoid schizophrenia is one of the most common forms of psychosis, with around 50 per cent of those diagnosed with schizophrenia also being diagnosed as the paranoid sub-type (Guggenheim & Babigian, 1974). It is also one of the less severe sub-types of schizophrenia, in that paranoid schizophrenics are often lucid and rarely exhibit the cognitive and neurological deficits found in other sub-types (Strauss, 1993). Onset tends to be later in life than other sub-types (i.e. usually after 25 years of age) and the prognosis is usually good; with suitable treatment, sufferers are often able to live independently.

7.2.2.2 Disorganized Schizophrenia

The distinguishing features of *disorganized schizophrenia* (also known as hebephrenic schizophrenia) are disorganized speech, disorganized behaviour and flat or inappropriate affect. This diagnostic sub-type represents the classic stereotype of the schizophrenic as someone who is thought disordered and who is unable to respond appropriately to the world. Individuals will show impaired performance on cognitive and neurological tasks, exhibit examples of disordered speech and communication (such as word salads, neologisms and clanging), and also show deficits in goal-oriented behaviour (i.e. will be unable to sustain the behaviours needed for normal daily living and may even become incontinent). The mood disorder in those diagnosed with disorganized schizophrenia may manifest either as flat affect or as inappropriate laughter and silliness. This diagnostic sub-type has a gradual onset, usually from late adolescence, and sufferers tend to become more and more withdrawn and less reactive to events around them.

Disorganized schizophrenia A sub-type of schizophrenia in which disorganized speech, disorganized behaviour and flat or inappropriate affect are distinguishing features.

7.2.2.3 Catatonic Schizophrenia

The *catatonic schizophrenia* diagnostic sub-type is characterized by severe disturbances of motor behaviour, including immobility, excessive motor activity (including violent behaviour), extreme negativism,

Catatonic schizophrenia A sub-type of schizophrenia characterized by severe disturbances of motor behaviour, including immobility, excessive motor activity (including violent behaviour), extreme negativism, mutism, peculiarities of voluntary movement, echolalia (repeating what is said by others) or echopraxia (imitating the behaviour and movements of others).

CASE HISTORY 7.1

Catatonia and disturbances of motor behaviour

'Anna was brought to the psychiatric hospital by the police for an emergency admission after she had attacked a child. She had walked up to a 9-year-old girl at a bus stop and tried to strangle her. Some passers-by fortunately intervened, restraining Anna, and called the police. At first she fought violently and tried to get at the child, but then suddenly she became motionless and rigid as a statue, with one arm stretched out towards the child and a wild stare on her face. When police arrived, it was difficult to get her into the car, because she would not move and resisted attempts to move her. She almost had to be carried to the police car and forced into it. . . .

When she was brought to the ward, she remained standing just inside the entrance and resisted invitations to go further. She refused to have anything to eat and would not go to the examination room. She remained standing rigid, with her right arm stretched out in front of her, staring at her hand. . . . (That night) she lay in bed in the position where she had been placed staring at the ceiling. The next morning Anna was found standing rigid again, this time behind the door. . . .

Anna's sister reported that . . . for the last 2–3 months Anna had seemed reclusive and odd, with recurrent episodes of muteness and staring that lasted for several minutes. Several times she made peculiar statements that "children are trying to destroy mathematics" or "rational figures have a hard time".'

Source: Ustun, Bertelsen, Dilling, van Drimmelen et al. (1996)

Clinical Commentary

Catatonia is a relatively rare condition marked by severe behavioural disturbances. Usually the catatonic individual adopts bizarre and often rigid body postures, such as Anna does once she has been brought into hospital. However, many individuals suffering catatonia will often indulge in frenzied violent behaviour, like Anna, and their behaviour alternates between withdrawn immobility and frantic motor activity. The amount of energy required to adopt a rigid, uncomfortable posture – as many catatonic patients do – must be immense, and although it might seem to be a form of withdrawal, many individuals with catatonia seem to be quite aware of what is going on around them.

mutism, peculiarities of voluntary movement, echolalia (repeating what is said by others) or echopraxia (imitating the behaviour and movements of others). In extreme cases an individual may exhibit catatonic stupor or complete immobility, often associated with maintaining awkward body positions for long periods of time (see Focus Point 7.1 and Case History 7.1).

7.2.2.4 Residual Type

Residual type A category of schizophrenia when the individual has experienced at least one previous psychotic episode and there is currently a lack of prominent positive symptoms (e.g. delusions, hallucinations, disorganised speech), but there is evidence of ongoing negative symptoms (e.g. flat affect, poverty of speech).

The *residual type* category is used when the individual has experienced at least one previous psychotic episode and there is currently a lack of prominent positive symptoms (e.g. delusions, hallucinations, disorganized speech), although there is evidence of ongoing negative symptoms (e.g. flat affect, poverty of speech). Symptoms indicative of the residual sub-type are usually time limited, and this diagnosis often describes the symptoms of an individual who is in transition between a full-blown psychotic episode and remission.

SELF-TEST QUESTIONS

- What are the five important characteristics for diagnosing schizophrenia and how many are required to confirm the diagnosis?
- What is the difference between the positive and negative symptoms of schizophrenia?
- Can you name some of the different types of delusional states found in schizophrenia?
- What are the most common forms of hallucination experienced in schizophrenia and approximately what percentage of sufferers report hallucinations?
- Can you name the different forms of disordered speech and communication exhibited by individuals diagnosed with schizophrenia and provide some examples of each?
- What are the characteristics of catatonia?
- Can you describe some of the specific symptoms that are collectively known as negative symptoms?
- What are the four main sub-types of schizophrenia?

SECTION SUMMARY

7.2 The Nature of Psychotic Symptoms

- The **five central characteristics** of schizophrenia are (1) delusions, (2) hallucinations, (3) disorganized speech (e.g. incoherence), (4) grossly disorganized or catatonic behaviour and (5) flattened affect, poverty of speech and apathy.

- The first four characteristics are known as **positive symptoms**, and the fifth category represents **negative symptoms**.

- 75 per cent of people hospitalized with a diagnosis of schizophrenia experience delusions.

- The main types of **delusions** are (1) delusions of persecution, (2) delusions of grandeur, (3) delusions of control, (4) delusions of reference and (5) nihilistic delusions.

- Around 70 per cent of individuals diagnosed with schizophrenia report auditory hallucinations.

- Individuals suffering hallucinations may have a **reality-monitoring deficit** (an inability to distinguish between what actually occurs and what does not).

- The most common forms of **disorganized speech** are derailment, loose associations, clanging, neologisms and word salads.

- **Grossly disorganized behaviour** is usually behaviour inappropriate to a context (e.g. masturbating in public). Catatonic motor behaviours are characterized by a decrease in reactivity and maintaining rigid, immobile postures.

- Negative symptoms are characterized by flat affect, lack of interest in social or work activities, poverty of speech (**alogia**) and apathy (**avolition**).

- There are **four sub-types** of schizophrenia: (1) paranoid schizophrenia, (2) disorganized schizophrenia, (3) catatonic schizophrenia and (4) residual schizophrenia.

- **Paranoid schizophrenia** is one of the most common forms, with around 50 per cent of sufferers being diagnosed with this form.

7.3 THE PREVALENCE OF SCHIZOPHRENIA

The lifetime prevalence rate for diagnosed schizophrenia is between 0.5 and 2 per cent, and this figure seems to be similar across

a range of different countries and cultures when strict diagnostic criteria are applied (Kendler, Gallagher, Abelson & Kessler, 1996; Jablensky, 2000). Studies by the World Health Organization (WHO) indicate that schizophrenia affects around 24 million people worldwide, and that the clinical syndrome of schizophrenia (i.e. its range of presenting symptoms) is also very similar across countries (Jablensky, Sartorius, Emberg, Anker et al., 1992). Interestingly, the course of schizophrenia tends to be less severe in developing countries than in developed ones (Thara, Henrietta, Joseph, Rajkumar et al., 1994). The reasons for this difference in prognosis are unclear, although the central support role of the family and differences in beliefs about the origins of psychological disorders in developing countries may be important (Lin & Kleinman, 1988).

Some studies have identified some consistent cultural differences in the prevalence of schizophrenia within individual countries. For example, in a UK-based study, King, Nazroo, Weich, McKenzie et al. (2005) found that the reporting of psychotic symptoms was higher in ethnic minority groups than in ethnic white individuals. This increase in the reporting of symptoms was twice as high in people of African-Caribbean origin than in whites. There have been a number of hypotheses that have attempted to explain this apparent cultural difference, and there is at least some evidence that the higher symptom levels in black American men than in white American men may be the result of racial disparities in mental health treatment between blacks and whites in the USA (Whaley, 2004).

In other within-country studies, immigrants have been shown to have significantly higher rates of schizophrenia diagnosis than members of the indigenous population. A personal or family history of migration is an important risk factor, and immigrants from developing countries are at greater risk than those from developed countries (Cantor-Graae & Selten, 2005). At least part of the explanation for the higher incidence in immigrants can be traced to the stress caused by many of the initial consequences of immigration, such as language difficulties, unemployment, poor housing and low socioeconomic status (Hjern, Wicks & Dalman, 2004).

Finally, the incidence of schizophrenia is similar for males and females, although females tend to have a later age of onset and fewer hospital admissions. This may be the result of females attaining higher levels of social role functioning before illness, which confers a better outcome (Hafner, 2000; Murray & van Os, 1998; Angermeyer, Kuhn & Goldstein, 1990). In addition, and for whatever reasons, individuals diagnosed with schizophrenia also tend to have a shorter life span than normal, and die around 10 years earlier than individuals who have never been diagnosed with schizophrenia (Jeste, Gladsjo, Lindamer et al., 1996). At least part of this shorter average life expectancy may be accounted for by the relatively high rate of suicide or attempted suicide in individuals diagnosed with schizophrenia. Studies suggest that between 5 and 15 per cent of those diagnosed with schizophrenia successfully commit suicide – a rate that is at least 8 times higher than the rate of suicide in the general population (Abed, Vaidya & Baker, 2000).

SELF-TEST QUESTIONS

- What is the estimated lifetime prevalence rate for a diagnosis of schizophrenia?
- Some ethnic and cultural differences in the prevalence rates of schizophrenia have been found within individual countries. Can you describe some of these differences?

SECTION SUMMARY

7.3 The Prevalence of Schizophrenia

- The lifetime prevalence rate for a diagnosis of schizophrenia is between 0.5 and 2 per cent, and is similar across different countries and cultures.

- Rates of diagnosis of schizophrenia tend to be higher in some ethnic groups (e.g. people of African-Caribbean origin in the UK), and in immigrant populations generally.

7.4 THE COURSE OF PSYCHOTIC SYMPTOMS

Psychotic symptoms usually develop through a well-defined succession of stages. The three predominant phases are (1) the prodromal stage, (2) the active stage and (3) the residual stage.

7.4.1 The Prodromal Stage

The large majority of those who develop psychotic symptoms show the first signs during late adolescence or early adulthood. A study of nine countries by the WHO found that 51 per cent of individuals diagnosed with schizophrenia were aged between 15 and 25 years of age (Sartorius, Jablensky, Korten, Ernberg et al., 1986), and over 80 per cent are between 15 and 35 years of age. For some individuals, the onset of psychotic symptoms can be rapid and dramatic, but for most it represents a slow deterioration from normal functioning to the delusional and dysfunctional thinking characteristic of many forms of schizophrenia. This deterioration normally takes place over an average of 5 years (Hafner, Maurer, Loffler, van der Heiden et al., 2003). This slow deterioration, known as the *prodromal stage*, is first exhibited as slow withdrawal from normal life and social interaction, shallow and inappropriate emotions, and deterioration in personal care and work or school performance.

> **Prodromal stage**   The slow deterioration from normal functioning to the delusional and dysfunctional thinking characteristic of many forms of schizophrenia, normally taking place over an average of 5 years.

That psychosis initially develops during late adolescence is one of the basic facts of this psychopathology, but why should onset occur during this rather specific point in an individual's life span? The course of psychosis is best understood in terms of a diathesis-stress model, in which psychotic symptoms are caused by an underlying inherited biological vulnerability, but this vulnerability only manifests as specific symptoms if the individual has certain critical and stressful life experiences. There is a good deal of evidence that over 70 per cent of individuals who first show symptoms of psychosis have experienced stressful life events in the previous 3 weeks (Brown & Birley, 1968), and the transition from adolescence to adulthood is arguably one of the most stressful periods of an individual's life. In addition, Harrop and Trower (2001) argue that prodromal-like signs in normal adolescents appear to be linked to normal development, and that psychotic symptoms may emerge from a troubled teenage state that has failed to cope with normal maturation. This leaves the adolescent unable to cope with a majority of the life challenges that he or she will have to deal with at this stage of development; the resulting response is a withdrawal from social interaction and a fall in educational performance. Eventually such tendencies will become noted by family and friends, and the development of disordered thoughts, delusions and erratic and bizarre behaviour mark the onset of the active stage.

CASE HISTORY 7.2

The prodromal stage: Identifying the early signs

'Fifteen-year-old Caitlin was an excellent student with many friends when she entered the ninth grade. One year later, she suddenly became restless in school, stopped paying attention to her teachers, and eventually failed all of her subjects. At home she appeared increasingly withdrawn and isolated, spending hours sleeping or watching television. The previously even-tempered adolescent became angry, anxious, and suspicious of those around her, and was occasionally seen talking to herself while making repetitive, odd hand motions. Several years later, hearing voices and insisting that the CIA was hatching an elaborate plot to murder her and her family, she was diagnosed with schizophrenia.'

Source: www.swedish.org/16945.cfm

Clinical Commentary

This description of the development of Caitlin's symptoms is typical of the prodromal stage of schizophrenia. She became withdrawn, ill-tempered, anxious and suspicious, and showed a marked decline in academic performance. Unfortunately, these signs are often difficult to differentiate from many of the behavioural changes exhibited by normal individuals as they progress through adolescence, so diagnosis at an early stage is often difficult. These difficulties with early diagnosis are unfortunate, because evidence suggests that the earlier treatment begins after the development of actual psychosis, the more rapid the immediate recovery and the better the overall outcome.

Some more specific prodromal features associated with schizophrenia include:

- Peculiar behaviors
- Impairment in personal hygiene and grooming
- Inappropriate affect (e.g. laughing when talking about something sad)
- Vague, overly elaborate or circumstantial speech
- Poverty of speech
- Odd beliefs or magical thinking
- Unusual perceptual experiences

7.4.2 The Active Stage

In the **active stage**, the individual begins to show unambiguous symptoms of psychosis, including delusions, hallucinations, disordered speech and communication, and a range of full-blown symptoms that are outlined in section 7.2.1 of this chapter.

> **Active stage** The stage in which an individual begins to show unambiguous symptoms of psychosis, including delusions, hallucinations, disordered speech and communication, and a range of full-blown symptoms.

7.4.3 The Residual Stage

Recovery from the symptoms of psychosis is usually gradual, but many sufferers may still retain some symptomatology over the longer term. The **residual stage** is reached when individuals cease to show prominent signs of positive symptoms (such as delusions, hallucinations and disordered speech). However, during the residual stage they may well still exhibit negative symptoms, such as blunted affect and withdrawal from social interaction, and find it difficult to cope with normal day-to-day activities such as holding down a job.

> **Residual stage** The stage of psychosis when the individual ceases to show prominent signs of positive symptoms (such as delusions, hallucinations or disordered speech).

Long-term studies have suggested that around 28 per cent of sufferers will remit after one or more active stage, 22 per cent will continue to show positive symptoms over the long term, and around 50 per cent will alternate between active and residual stages (Wiersma, Nienhuis, Slooff & Giel, 1998). These statistics indicate that relapse is relatively common. Relapse can often be traced to either (1) stressful life events or return to a stressful family environment after a period of hospitalization or care (see section 7.5.3), or (2) non-adherence to medication.

It is estimated that around 40–50 per cent of those diagnosed with schizophrenia fail at some point to adhere to their course of medication (Lacro, Dunn, Dolder, Leckband et al., 2002), and partial compliance is likely to result in significantly higher levels of relapse and rehospitalization (Eaddy, Grogg & Locklear, 2005). The factors most associated with non-adherence or non-compliance with medication include poor insight, negative attitudes to medication, a history of non-adherence, substance abuse, inadequate discharge or after-care planning and poorer therapeutic relationships between patient and service providers (Lacro et al., 2002).

SELF-TEST QUESTIONS

- What are the three main stages through which psychotic symptoms normally develop?
- What are the factors that may contribute to relapse following recovery from an acute psychotic episode?

SECTION SUMMARY

7.4 The Course of Psychotic Symptoms

- Schizophrenia develops through three well-defined stages: (1) the **prodromal stage**, (2) the **active stage** and (3) the **residual stage**.

- The large majority of those who develop psychotic symptoms show the first signs during late adolescence or early adulthood.

- Around 70 per cent of those who show first signs of psychotic symptoms have experienced stressful life events in the previous 3 weeks.

- Around 28 per cent of those diagnosed with schizophrenia will remit after one or more active stages, 22 per cent will continue to show positive symptoms over the long term, and 50 per cent will alternate between active and residual stages.

7.5 THE AETIOLOGY OF PSYCHOTIC SYMPTOMS

The evidence we have reviewed so far portrays psychosis as a broad range of loosely associated symptoms. It can manifest as disordered thinking and communication, disordered perceptions, hallucinations and delusions, and as behavioural deficits. In addition, no one single clinical symptom is the cardinal feature by which the DSM-IV-TR diagnostic category of schizophrenia is characterized. This being the case, theories of the aetiology of psychosis are also diverse, including biological, psychological and sociological approaches to understanding this psychopathology.

Diathesis-stress The perspective that psychopathology is caused by a combination of a genetically inherited biological diathesis (a biological predisposition to schizophrenia) and environmental stress.

The overarching approach to understanding psychosis is a *diathesis-stress* perspective. That is, psychosis is thought to be caused by a combination of a genetically inherited biological diathesis (a biological predisposition to schizophrenia) and environmental stress. This means that even if you have a genetically pre-programmed disposition to psychosis, you may well not develop any symptoms unless you experience certain forms of severe life stressors. Such stressors might involve early rearing factors (Schiffman, Abrahamson, Cannon, LaBrie et al., 2001), dysfunctional relationships within the family (Bateson, 1978), or an inability to cope with the stresses of normal adolescent development (Harrop & Trower, 2001) or with educational or work demands.

This diversity of approach has meant that most theories focus on explaining specific features of psychosis rather than attempting to elaborate an all-inclusive explanation. For example, some theories have attempted to identify the inherited component of psychotic symptoms, while others have investigated the abnormalities in brain biochemistry or brain function that accompany psychosis. Still others have tried to understand the cognitive deficits that underlie delusions and disordered thought and communication. Others have attempted to identify the nature of the stressors that might trigger psychotic symptoms in vulnerable individuals. Finally, sociocultural views of psychosis take an entirely different perspective. They claim that the course of psychotic symptoms may be determined by the simple act of diagnosing someone with schizophrenia or by the fact that the individual is born into a disadvantaged socioeconomic group. Factors such as these may be enough to promote the development of psychotic symptoms. We will explore all of these different approaches in the following sections.

7.5.1 Biological Theories

7.5.1.1 Genetic Factors

It has always been known that psychotic symptoms appear to run in families, which suggests that there may well be some form

Table 7.3 *Concordance rates for individuals with a diagnosis of schizophrenia*

Relation to proband	% Diagnosed with schizophrenia
Spouse	1.00
Grandchildren	2.84
Nieces/nephews	2.65
Children	9.35
Siblings	7.30
Dizygotic (fraternal) twins	12.08
Monozygotic (identical) twins	44.30

Source: Gottesman, McGuffin & Farmer (1987).

of inherited predisposition. That psychosis has an inherited component has been supported by the results of *concordance studies*. Table 7.3 shows the probability with which a family member or relative will develop the disorder if an individual in the same family is diagnosed with schizophrenia. This shows that the probability with which the family member or relative will develop schizophrenia is dependent on how closely the individuals are related – or more specifically, how much genetic material the two have in common (Gottesman McGuffin & Farmer, 1987; Cardno, Marshall, Coid, Macdonald et al., 1999). Recent studies have suggested that an individual who has a first-degree relative diagnosed with schizophrenia is 10 times more likely to develop psychotic symptoms than someone who has no first-degree relatives diagnosed with schizophrenia (Schneider & Deldin, 2001).

However, simply because psychotic symptoms tend to run in families does not establish a genetic basis for this psychopathology. For example, some family environments may have dysfunctional elements (e.g. difficulties in communication between family members) which may give rise to the development of psychosis. In order to examine the genetic basis more carefully, many researchers have undertaken *twin studies*, in which they have compared the probability with which monozygotic (MZ) and dizygotic (DZ) twins both develop symptoms indicative of schizophrenia. MZ

Concordance studies Studies designed to investigate the probability with which family members or relatives will develop a psychological disorder depending on how closely they are related – or, more specifically, how much genetic material they have in common.

Twin studies Studies in which researchers have compared the probability with which monozygotic (MZ) and dizygotic (DZ) twins both develop symptoms indicative of a psychopathology in order to assess genetic contributions to that psychopathology.

twins share 100 per cent of their genetic material, whereas DZ twins share only 50 per cent of their genes, so a genetic explanation of psychotic symptoms would predict that there would be greater concordance in the diagnosis of schizophrenia in MZ than in DZ twins. This can clearly be seen in Table 7.3, where the concordance rate for MZ twins is 44 per cent, but falls to only 12 per cent in DZ twins.

As convincing as these data may seem, there are still problems in interpreting twin studies. For example, (1) MZ twins will always be the same sex, whereas DZ twins may not be; (2) MZ twins are usually physically identical, unlike DZ twins, and this may lead to family and friends treating MZ twins more similarly than they would DZ twins (i.e. MZ twins could experience more similar environmental factors than DZ twins); and (3) MZ twins are likely to have shared the same placenta prior to birth whereas DZ twins do not, and this would mean that any interuterine abnormalities would be more likely to affect both MZ twins through the shared placenta (Davis & Phelps, 1995).

However, many of these difficulties of interpretation can be overcome by studying the *offspring* of MZ and DZ twins rather than the twins themselves (Gottesman & Bertelsen, 1989). If one MZ twin develops psychotic symptoms and the other does not, any genetic element in psychosis should still show up in the children of *either* of the two MZ twins. That is, the children of the MZ twins should still exhibit similar rates of risk for schizophrenia (because they have inherited the same predisposition) – even though one of their parents developed schizophrenia and the other did not. This is exactly what Gottesman and Bertelsen (1989) found: 16.8 per cent of the offspring of the MZ twins that were diagnosed with schizophrenia were likely to develop psychotic symptoms themselves, and 17.4 per cent of the offspring of the MZ twins that were *not* diagnosed with schizophrenia were also likely to develop psychotic symptoms. This suggests that a genetic risk factor has been passed on to offspring, even though one set of parents did not develop schizophrenia themselves.

Another way of tackling the problems of separating out the influence of genetic inheritance and environmental experience is to look at the incidence of schizophrenia in children who are biologically similar but have been reared apart (*adoption studies*). If there is an important genetic element to psychosis, then we would expect the children of a mother diagnosed with schizophrenia to have similar probabilities of developing schizophrenia regardless of whether they had been reared with their mother or not. A seminal study by Heston (1966) compared 47 adopted children who were reared apart from their schizophrenic biological mothers with 50 control adopted children whose mothers were not diagnosed with schizophrenia. He found symptoms of psychosis in 16.6 per cent of the adopted children of the schizophrenic mothers, and no symptoms in the adopted children of mothers without schizophrenia. Studies of adopted children conducted in Denmark have shown similar results. Kety (1988) and Kety, Wender, Jacobsen, Ingraham et al. (1994) found that adopted children who develop psychotic symptoms are significantly more likely to have had biological relatives with a diagnosis of schizophrenia (21.4 per cent)

Adoption studies Research conducted on children who are biologically similar but have been reared apart.

than adoptive relatives with a diagnosis of schizophrenia (5.4 per cent).

These types of studies provide strong evidence for a genetic component to schizophrenia and psychosis. However, some more recent adoption studies suggest that genetic liability still interacts with environmental factors to predict the development of psychotic symptoms. Wahlberg, Wynne, Hakko, Laksy et al. (2004) found that in adopted children, inherited genetic factors were an important predictor of a diagnosis of schizophrenia but only in combination with certain environmental factors found in the adopted home environment. In this particular study, an adopted child was more likely to be diagnosed with schizophrenia if he or she had a biologically inherited predisposition *and* was brought up in an adopted home environment where there were dysfunctional communication patterns (see section 7.5.3). While genetic inheritance is an important predictor of psychotic symptoms, this is further evidence that genetic factors interact with environmental factors in a way predicted by diathesis-stress models.

If, as seems likely, there is a genetic component to psychosis, how is it transmitted between related individuals, and how does this inherited component influence the development of psychotic symptoms? In recent years, much effort has been directed at attempting to identify the specific genes through which the risk for psychosis may be transmitted (Harrison & Owen, 2003), the chromosomes on which these genes are located (Kendler, Myers, O'Neill, Martin et al., 2000), and how these genes and their possible defects may give rise to psychotic symptoms (Andreasen, 2001). These endeavours have primarily involved *genetic linkage analyses*, in which blood samples are collected in order to study the inheritance patterns within families that have members diagnosed with schizophrenia. Linkage analyses work by comparing the inheritance of characteristics for which gene location is well known (e.g. eye colour) with the inheritance of psychotic symptoms. If the inheritance of, for example, eye colour follows the same pattern within the family as psychotic symptoms, then it can reasonably be concluded that the gene controlling psychotic symptoms is probably found on the same chromosome as the gene controlling eye colour, and is probably genetically linked to that 'marker' characteristic in some way. Research Methods Box 7.1 illustrates an example of how a particular trait of those diagnosed with schizophrenia, in this case poor eye-tracking of a moving object, can be used as a genetic marker to track other psychotic symptoms that may be linked genetically to this characteristic.

Genetic linkage analyses Analyses involving comparisons of the inheritance of characteristics for which gene location is well known (e.g. eye colour) with the inheritance of symptoms of psychopathology.

Using analyses such as these, genes associated with the development of psychotic symptoms have been identified primarily on chromosomes 8 and 22 (Kendler, Myers, O'Neill, Martin et al., 2000) and also on chromosomes 2, 3, 5, 6, 11, 13 and 20 (Badner & Gershon, 2002; Levinson, Lewis & Wise, 2002). These findings make it clear that if there is a genetic predisposition for psychotic symptoms, it is not transmitted solely through a single gene. This may be because psychosis represents a number of rather different psychopathologies, each of which contributes to the

RESEARCH METHODS IN CLINICAL PSYCHOLOGY BOX 7.1

Smooth-pursuit eye-tracking as a marker for the inheritance of psychosis

Smooth-pursuit eye-tracking is the ability to follow a moving object in a smooth, continuous movement with your eyes while keeping your head still. However, many individuals with a diagnosis of schizophrenia are unable to do this, and can only follow a moving object with jerky movements of the eyes (known as saccadic movements) (Schneider & Deldin, 2001). This may seem like a relatively innocuous symptom, but it is important because it is a characteristic that can be used as a *genetic marker* for schizophrenia. That is, unlike the broader symptoms of schizophrenia (such as thought disorder, delusions and hallucinations), abnormalities in smooth-pursuit eye-tracking are probably related to a rather specific neurological abnormality which may be directly linked to abnormalities in individual genes. If this is so, then the gene responsible for specific eye-tracking deficits may also be associated with many of the more disabling symptoms of schizophrenia. So, by tracing the gene responsible for eye-tracking deficits, we may also locate the gene or genes responsible for other psychotic symptoms.

There is now a large body of evidence indicating that around 30–45 per cent of first-degree relatives of individuals diagnosed with schizophrenia exhibit poor performance in smooth-pursuit eye-tracking tasks – even when those first-degree relatives have not been diagnosed with schizophrenia (Karoumi, Saoud, d'Amato, Rosenfeld et al., 2001; Louchart de la Chapelle, Nkam, Houy, Belmont et al., 2005) – and this suggests that deficits in eye-tracking performance are likely to be an indicator of an inherited predisposition to schizophrenia. In addition, studies of twins in which only one of the pair has developed psychotic symptoms (discordant twins) show that concordance of eye-tracking abnormalities are twice as high in monozygotic twins (MZ) than dizygotic (DZ) twins (Levy & Holzman, 1997) (see section 7.5.1.1 for an explanation of concordance studies in twins), providing more evidence for the involvement of inherited genetic factors. Studies have still been unable to track down the specific gene associated with this eye-tracking abnormality, although there is some evidence that it may be linked with a number of genes that are also responsible for interfering with dopamine metabolism (Trillenberg, Lencer & Heide, 2004), and this may be the important connection between eye-tracking deficits and the broader symptoms of schizophrenia.

---

heterogeneity of schizophrenia as a diagnostic category (Joober, Boksa, Benkelfat & Rouleau, 2002). Even if there is an important inherited component to psychosis, as the data suggest, then what is it that is transmitted genetically that gives rise to psychotic symptoms? We do not yet know enough about the specific genes implicated in psychosis, but if the involvement of individual genes were confirmed, then this may well help us to identify dysfunctions in specific biochemical pathways and molecular mechanisms that are implicated by these genes.

7.5.1.2 Biochemical Factors

Cognition and behaviour are very much dependent on the efficient working of brain neurotransmitters which enable effective communication between brain cells and functionally different parts of the brain itself. It is not surprising, therefore, that many researchers have suspected that the thought disorders, hallucinations and behaviour problems characteristic in the diagnosis of schizophrenia may be caused by malfunctions in these brain neurotransmitters. The biochemical theory of schizophrenia that has been most prominent over the past 50 years is known as the *dopamine hypothesis*. This account argues that the symptoms of schizophrenia are importantly related to

Dopamine hypothesis A theory which argues that the symptoms of schizophrenia are related to excess activity of the neurotransmitter dopamine.

excess activity of the neurotransmitter dopamine. There are a number of factors that have led to the implication of excess dopamine activity.

First, the discovery of antipsychotic drugs that helped to alleviate the symptoms of psychosis (such as the *phenothiazines*) led to the discovery that such drugs acted by blocking the brain's dopamine receptor sites and so reduced dopamine activity (Schneider & Deldin, 2001). Interestingly, while the administration of antipsychotic drugs alleviated many of the positive symptoms of schizophrenia, such as thought disorder and social withdrawal, it also had the side effect of producing muscle tremors very similar to those seen in Parkinson's disease, and it was already known that Parkinson's disease was caused by low levels of dopamine. In contrast, when people suffering Parkinson's disease were given the drug L-dopa to raise brain dopamine levels, they often began to exhibit psychotic symptoms (Grilly, 2002). This evidence strongly suggests that either high levels of brain dopamine or excess dopamine activity are responsible for many of the symptoms of psychosis. Subsequent research has suggested that many antipsychotic drugs have their effect by binding specifically to dopamine receptors and reducing brain dopamine activity (Burt, Creese & Snyder, 1977).

Phenothiazines A group of antipsychotic drugs that help to alleviate the symptoms of psychosis by blocking the brain's dopamine receptor sites and so reduce dopamine activity.

Second, during the 1970s it was noticed that there was a strong link between excessive use of amphetamines and a syndrome known as ***amphetamine psychosis***. When taken in high doses for long periods of time, amphetamines produce behavioural symptoms in humans and animals that closely resemble symptoms of psychosis. These include paranoia and repetitive, stereotyped behaviour patterns (Angrist, Lee & Gershon, 1974). Subsequently we have learned that amphetamines produce these disturbed behaviour patterns by increasing brain dopamine activity, and giving amphetamines to those diagnosed with schizophrenia actually increases the severity of their symptoms (Faustman, 1995).

> **Amphetamine psychosis** A syndrome in which high doses of amphetamines taken for long periods of time produce behavioural symptoms in humans and animals that closely resemble symptoms of psychosis.

Third, brain imaging studies have indicated that individuals diagnosed with schizophrenia show excessive levels of dopamine released from areas of the brain such as the basal ganglia – especially when biochemical precursors to dopamine, such as dopa, are administered to the individual (Carlsson, 2001; Goldsmith, Shapiro & Joyce, 1997).

Finally, post-mortem studies have found increased levels of dopamine and significantly more dopamine receptors in the brains of deceased schizophrenia sufferers, especially in the limbic area of the brain (Seeman & Kapur, 2001).

So, how might excess dopamine activity be involved in the production of psychotic symptoms? First, it may be that dopamine receptors in those diagnosed with schizophrenia are too sensitive, and messages being transmitted by this system are sent too often and too easily. This could give rise to the disorganized thinking and communication styles typical of psychosis, and this is consistent with the fact that dopamine neurons are known to play a critical role in controlling and guiding attention (Cohen, Semple, Gross, Nordahl et al., 1988). In addition, a number of brain imaging studies have confirmed that individuals diagnosed with schizophrenia have more dopamine receptors in the brain, and that these are often more sensitive than those receptors found in non-sufferers (Goldsmith, Shapiro & Joyce, 1997).

However, excess dopamine activity may only be responsible for some of the symptoms of psychosis, and in particular, only those related to positive symptoms. This is supported by the fact that antipsychotic drugs, which attempt to raise dopamine activity, are largely effective only for positive symptoms (hallucinations, thought disorder) but not for negative symptoms (blunted or flat affect, withdrawal). Subsequent developments of the dopamine hypothesis have attempted to explain this discrepancy by suggesting that excess dopamine activity may be limited to certain neural pathways – in particular the mesolimbic pathway (Davis, Kahn, Ko & Davidson, 1991) (see Figure 7.1). This may then result in the reduced activity of dopamine neurons in other areas of the brain such as the prefrontal cortex, which may cause some of the negative symptoms of schizophrenia.

While the dopamine hypothesis has been an influential biochemical theory of schizophrenia for more than 30 years, there is still some evidence that does not fit comfortably within this hypothesis. First, while antipsychotic drugs are usually effective in dealing with many of the symptoms of schizophrenia, they do not start having an effect on symptoms until about 6 weeks after

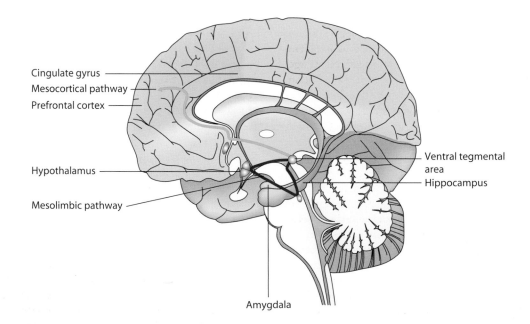

Figure 7.1
Abnormalities in dopamine activity may be linked to the brain's mesocortical pathway and the mesolimbic pathway. Both begin in the ventral tegmental area, but the former projects to the prefrontal cortex and the latter to the hypothalamus, amygdala, hippocampus and nuclear accumbens. The dopamine neurons in the prefrontal cortex may be underactive (leading to the negative symptoms of schizophrenia), and this underactivity may then fail to inhibit dopamine neurons in the mesolimbic pathway causing an excess of dopamine activity in this pathway (resulting in positive symptoms) (e.g. Davis, Kahn, Ko & Davidson, 1991).

treatment has commenced. This is unusual, because antipsychotic drugs are known to start blocking dopamine receptors in the brain within hours of administration, so we would expect improvement to be immediate (Sanislow & Carson, 2001; Davis, 1978). Secondly, many new antipsychotic drugs are effective despite having only a minimal effect on brain dopamine levels (e.g. clozapine), or appear to be effective because they block not only dopamine receptors but also serotonin receptors (Nordstrom, Farde, Nyberg, Karlsson et al., 1995). This has led many researchers to suggest that psychotic symptoms may not be related to excess dopamine activity alone, but to an interaction between dopamine and serotonin activity (Kapur & Remington, 1996). These more recent developments suggest that any biochemical theory of schizophrenia will be a complex one that includes important interactions between different neurotransmitters.

7.5.1.3 Brain Abnormalities

Recent developments in brain imaging (such as MRI, which measures brain structure, and PET, which measures brain functioning; see Chapter 2, section 2.1.3.2) have indicated that there are a number of significant differences between the brains of individuals diagnosed with schizophrenia and non-diagnosed controls (e.g. Shenton, Dickey, Frumin & McCarley, 2001). First, the brains of individuals with schizophrenia tend to be smaller than those of non-diagnosed controls, and this is also the case in first-degree relatives of sufferers who have not developed psychotic symptoms (Ward, Friedman, Wise & Schulz, 1996; Baare, van Oel, Pol, Schnack et al., 2001). This suggests that smaller brain size may be determined by genetic rather than environmental factors. Second, the most frequently confirmed finding is that schizophrenia is associated with enlarged ventricles (the areas in the brain containing cerebrospinal fluid), and this is associated with overall reduction in cortical grey matter (Andreasen, Flashman, Flaum, Arndt et al., 1994). In cases of chronic schizophrenia, the enlargement of the ventricles is a continuous ongoing process (Mathalon, Sullivan, Lim & Pfefferbaum, 2001), which may suggest that enlarged ventricles are a consequence of schizophrenic symptoms rather than a cause of it. However, enlarged ventricles are found even in individuals who have just experienced their first psychotic episode, implying that this may be a feature that is present prior to the development of the first symptoms (Cecil, Lenkinski, Gur & Gur, 1999).

Brain imaging studies have also shown abnormalities in three specific areas of the brain: the *frontal lobes*, the *temporal lobes-limbic structures* and the *basal ganglia* and *cerebellum* (Shenton, Dickey, Frumin & McCarley, 2001; Gur, Cowell, Latshaw,

Frontal lobes   One of four parts of the cerebrum that control voluntary movement, verbal expressions, problem solving, will power and planning.

Temporal lobes-limbic structures The areas of the brain that lie at the side of the head behind the temples and which are involved in hearing, memory, emotion, language, illusions, tastes and smells.

Basal ganglia   A series of structures located deep in the brain responsible for motor movements.

Cerebellum   The part of the brain at the back of the skull that coordinates muscular activity.

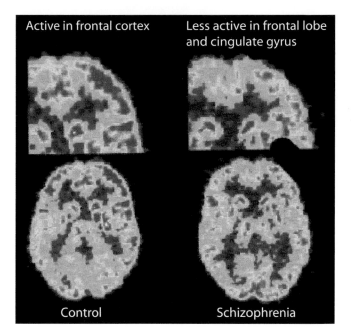

Figure 7.2
This PET scan shows sections of brains from a patient diagnosed with schizophrenia (right) and a healthy control (left). In the top pictures, higher activation is indicated by red areas, which are more widespread in the brain of the healthy control. The bottom pictures show ventricular enlargement in the brain of the individual diagnosed with schizophrenia (indicated by dark blue areas), which is a common feature of the brains of individuals diagnosed with schizophrenia.

Source: reproduced by permission of Monte S. Buchsbaum, Mount Sinai School of Medicine.

Turetsky et al., 2000; Gur, Turetsky, Cowell, Finkelman et al., 2000). Figure 7.2 shows how a PET scan reveals decreased frontal lobe activity in a schizophrenia sufferer compared with a healthy control participant, as well as the enlarged ventricles in the brain of the schizophrenia sufferer. The relative underactivity in the frontal lobes of those diagnosed with schizophrenia has been shown to be associated with poor performance on cognitive tasks associated with speed and accuracy, abstraction/categorization and memory and sustained attention, and it is also associated with negative symptoms of schizophrenia such as blunted affect and social withdrawal (Antonova, Sharma, Morris & Kumari, 2004; Artiges, Martinot, Verdys, Attar-Levy et al., 2000; Pinkham, Penn, Perkins & Lieberman, 2003). In contrast, abnormalities in neural activity in the temporal lobes-limbic system are more associated with the positive symptoms of schizophrenia such as hallucinations and symptoms of thought disorder (McCarley, Salisbury, Hirayasu, Yurgelun-Todd et al., 2002). Consistent with this, auditory hallucinations have been shown to be associated with neural activation in the temporal lobes-limbic system (Shergill, Brammer, Williams, Murray et al., 2000). Poor performance on executive tasks (such as card sorting) and goal-directed activity have been associated with significantly smaller basal ganglia structures in individuals with schizophrenia (Stratta, Mancini, Mattei, Daneluzzo, et al., 1997), and abnormalities in the cerebellum have been associated with deficits in verbal ability and narrative memory, but only in males diagnosed with schizophrenia (Levitt, McCarley, Nestor, Petrescu et al., 1999).

These findings tend to suggest that abnormalities in different areas of the brain may each be associated with different symptoms of psychosis. Some individuals with a diagnosis of schizophrenia show abnormalities in some of these brain areas, but many others show abnormalities in all of them – which explains why many exhibit both positive and negative symptoms (Kubicki, Westin, Maier, Frumin et al., 2002). However, it is important to be clear about whether these brain abnormalities are a *consequence* of developing psychotic symptoms or are actually a *cause* of those symptoms. The latter is probably the case because of two facts: (1) structural brain changes are evident in individuals diagnosed with schizophrenia prior to or just after their first psychotic episode

(McCarley, Salisbury, Hirayasu, Yurgelun-Todd et al., 2002), and (2) these brain abnormalities are also apparent in first-degree relatives of individuals diagnosed with schizophrenia, even though these relatives may not have developed any symptoms of psychosis themselves (McDonald, Grech, Toulopoulou, Schulze et al., 2002).

This evidence supports the view that there is a genetic risk for these brain abnormalities. However, there is further evidence indicating that they may result from abnormal early brain development, and it may be an inherited factor that affects this early neurodevelopment (Allin & Murray, 2002). Many of the neurological defects found in schizophrenia research are ones that could only have occurred during early brain development when the complex structure of the brain is developing, and this suggests that prenatal factors may be important in causing subsequent brain abnormalities (Allin & Murray, 2002). In particular, individuals diagnosed with schizophrenia do not show the normal

FOCUS POINT 7.5

Viral infections and psychotic symptoms

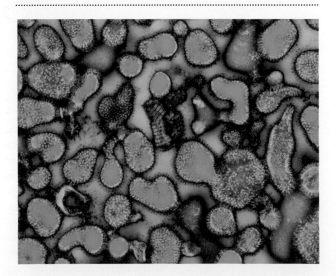

One interesting hypothesis is that psychotic symptoms may be triggered by viral infections experienced either prenatally or postnatally (Torrey, 1991; Mednick, Machon, Huttunen & Bonett, 1988). There is a range of converging, but largely circumstantial, evidence for the involvement of viral infections in the aetiology of psychosis. First, epidemiological studies have shown that people diagnosed with schizophrenia are significantly more likely than others to have been born in the winter, and so were more likely to have been exposed to viruses prenatally or during the first 6 months of their lives (Torrey, Miller, Rawlings & Yolken, 1997). Second, there also appears to be a relationship between

the outbreak of epidemics, such as influenza epidemics, and the development of psychotic symptoms. Individuals who were exposed prenatally to influenza are significantly more likely to develop psychotic symptoms in later life (Mednick, Machon, Huttunen & Bonett, 1988). Third, mothers of individuals diagnosed with schizophrenia are more likely to have been exposed to influenza during pregnancy than the mothers of individuals who are not diagnosed with schizophrenia. In particular, this exposure to the virus appears to be important during the first trimester (Brown, Begg, Gravenstein, Schaefer et al., 2004) and the third trimester (de Messias, Cordeiro, Sampaio, Bartko et al., 2001) – and the latter is a prenatal period which is known to be connected to the possible development of brain abnormalities associated with schizophrenia.

Most viral infections have their effects relatively immediately, so how might viral infections prenatally or in early childhood lead to the development of psychotic symptoms in later adolescence? One possibility is that viral infections – especially prenatally – might disrupt brain development and lead to the kinds of brain abnormalities that are typical in individuals diagnosed with schizophrenia (see section 7.5.1). To this extent, animal research is currently providing some useful information suggesting that rats or mice prenatally infected with viruses such as influenza experience developmental abnormalities that result in permanent changes in brain structure and function (Pearce, 2001; Fatemi, Pearce, Brooks & Sidwell, 2005). However, we must remember that not everyone who is exposed to viruses at a critical age develops psychotic symptoms, and we need to be able to explain this fact. For example, it may be that if viruses do cause developmental abnormalities leading to psychotic symptoms, this may only happen in those who already have an inherited vulnerability to these symptoms.

hemispheric asymmetry in brain development that occurs during the second trimester of pregnancy (4–6 months), and this may give rise to deficits in those areas of the brain concerned with language and associative learning (Sommer, Aleman, Ramsey, Bouma et al., 2001). In addition, brain damage or abnormalities that occur after the third trimester of pregnancy are normally self-repairing through a process known as glial reactions. That such repair is not found in post-mortem studies of the brains of individuals diagnosed with schizophrenia suggests that brain areas must have been damaged or suffered abnormal development prior to the third trimester (Brennan & Walker, 2001). This evidence suggests that abnormal brain development found in individuals diagnosed with schizophrenia may predate birth, and it is quite possible that abnormal neurodevelopment in the second or third trimester of pregnancy may be the way in which genetic factors may influence the development of psychotic symptoms.

7.5.2 Psychological Theories

Over the past 30 years or so most research has been focused on genetic and biological theories of schizophrenia, and psychological models have generally received less attention. However, there is no doubt that psychological processes (and their dysfunction) can be identified in the aetiology of psychotic symptoms. Psychological theories are involved in explaining these symptoms in a number of important ways:

1 They can be used to describe the cognitive and behavioural deficits that may be caused by possible underlying biological dysfunctions; for example, excessive dopamine activity may give rise to attentional deficits that can be described in terms of dysfunctions of normal cognitive processes.

2 Psychosis is considered to be primarily a diathesis-stress disorder in which a biological predisposition is triggered by environmental stress, and psychological models can help to explain how environmental stressors might activate psychotic symptoms. For example, some psychodynamic theories of psychosis suggest that unnurturing parents may cause confusion and stress in their children, which gives rise to psychotic symptoms.

3 Some basic psychological processes may be directly involved in shaping some of the deluded thinking and bizarre behaviour typical of psychosis; for example, a tendency to attribute negative events to external sources may give rise to paranoid beliefs.

7.5.2.1 Psychodynamic Theories

Freud (1915, 1924) hypothesized that psychosis is caused by regression to a previous ego state which gives rise to a preoccupation with the self. This is known in psychoanalytic terminology as regression to a state of *primary narcissism* characteristic of the oral stage of development. This regression

Primary narcissism Regression to a previous ego state which gives rise to a preoccupation with the self.

is thought to be caused by cold and unnurturing parents, and the regression to a state of primary narcissism gives rise to a loss of contact with reality. Freud described the symptoms of thought disorder, communication disorder and withdrawal typical of psychosis as evidence of a self-centred focus. He argued that any attempts to re-establish contact with reality give rise to the hallucinations and delusions characteristic of psychosis.

In the 1950s and 1960s, many psychodynamic explanations of psychosis were related to dysfunctional family dynamics and were championed by such contemporary psychodynamic theorists as Gregory Bateson and R.D. Laing. Prior to this, Fromm-Reichmann (1948) had developed the concept of the *schizophrenogenic mother* – literally, a mother who causes schizophrenia! According to Fromm-Reichmann, schizophrenogenic mothers were cold, rejecting, distant and dominating. Such mothers demanded dependency and emotional expressions from their children, but simultaneously rejected displays of affection and even criticized the dependency that they implicitly attempted to foster in their children. This account suggests that when subjected to such conflicting messages and demands from a dominant close relative, the child withdraws and begins to lose touch with reality – at least in part as a way of avoiding the stresses and conflicts created by the mother.

Schizophrenogenic mother A cold, rejecting, distant and dominating mother who causes schizophrenia according to Fromm-Reichmann.

The empirical evidence supporting these psychodynamic theories of psychosis is meagre. First, genetic accounts of psychosis are now largely accepted as important contributors to psychosis – even by psychodynamic theorists – and have been incorporated in some way into psychodynamic theories. In some cases it is argued that inherited biological predispositions may facilitate regression to earlier psychological states (Willick, Milrod & Karush, 1998), while others suggest biological predispositions may prevent the individual from developing an 'integrated self', which gives rise to the disrupted behaviour patterns exhibited in individuals diagnosed with schizophrenia (Pollack, 1989). Second, there is very little evidence that mothers of individuals displaying psychotic symptoms actually possess the characteristics of the schizophrenogenic mother described by Fromm-Reichmann (Waring & Ricks, 1965).

7.5.2.2 Behavioural Theories

There are a number of views that suggest a role for learning and conditioning in the development of psychotic symptoms – if not as a full theory of psychosis, then as an explanation of why unusual behaviour patterns are typical of many forms of psychosis. Ullman and Krasner (1975) argued that the bizarre behaviours of individuals diagnosed with schizophrenia developed because they are rewarded by a process of operant reinforcement. That is, because of the disturbed family life often experienced by individuals diagnosed with schizophrenia and the attentional difficulties that are a central feature of the psychopathology, such individuals tend to find it difficult to attend to normal social cues and involve themselves in normal social interactions. Instead, their attention becomes attracted to irrelevant cues, such as an insect on the floor, an unimportant word in a conversation or a background

Can perfectly normal processes cause bizarre behaviour?

A revealing study by Ayllon, Haughton and Hughes in 1965 provides insight into some of the processes that might generate the kinds of bizarre and apparently irrational behaviour that make up some forms of psychopathology.

The researchers used operant reinforcement methods (see Chapter 1, section 1.1.3.2) to reward a female patient diagnosed with schizophrenia for carrying a broom. Whenever she was observed holding the broom, a nurse would approach her, offer her a cigarette or give her a token which could be exchanged for a cigarette. After a period of this reinforcement, the patient was carrying the broom around for most of the day, and even took it to bed with her when she slept.

At this point the researchers called in two psychiatrists (who were unaware of the reinforcement schedule) to give their opinions on the nature of the behaviour. One of them gave the following reply:

> Her constant and compulsive pacing, holding a broom in the manner she does, could be seen as a ritualistic procedure, a magical action. . . . Her broom would be then: (1) a child that gives her love and she gives him in return her devotion, (2) a phallic symbol, (3) the scepter of an omnipotent queen . . . this is a magical procedure in which the patient carries out her wishes, expressed in a way that is far beyond our solid, rational and conventional way of thinking and acting.
>
> (Ayllon et al., 1965, p. 3)

First, this psychodynamic explanation given by one of the psychiatrists is a good example of how easy it is to over-speculate about the causes and meaning of a behaviour when the real causes are unknown.

Second, it shows how behaviour that is viewed as representative of psychopathology can be acquired through a perfectly normal learning mechanism (in this case, operant reinforcement).

---

noise. Attention to irrelevant cues such as these makes their behaviour look increasingly bizarre, and as a result it gets more and more attention, which acts as a reinforcer to strengthen such behaviours.

There is some limited evidence to support the view that inappropriate reinforcement may generate some bizarre behaviours, and it may account for the *frequency* of inappropriate behaviour emitted by an individual diagnosed with schizophrenia. For example, Focus Point 7.6 describes a study conducted some years ago by Ayllon, Haughton and Hughes (1965). They reinforced a female resident in a psychiatric hospital for carrying a broom. Whenever she was observed holding the broom, nurses were asked to approach her, offer her a cigarette or give her a token which could be exchanged for a cigarette. Eventually, when this behaviour was established, it was transferred from a continuous to an intermittent reinforcement schedule until the patient was carrying the broom around for a considerable part of the day. This study suggests that what look like quite bizarre and inappropriate behaviours can be developed by simple contingencies of reinforcement.

Further support for a learning view comes from evidence that extinction procedures can be used to eliminate or to significantly reduce the frequency of inappropriate behaviours simply by withdrawing attention or withholding rewards when these inappropriate behaviours are emitted. Ayllon (1963) describes the behaviour of a 47-year-old female diagnosed with schizophrenia who insisted on wearing around 25 pounds of excess clothing, even in hot weather. This individual's bizarre clothing habits were, however, soon returned to normal when a weight limit was set each time she tried to enter the hospital dining room. On each day, she was allowed into the dining room only if she weighed 2 pounds less than the previous day. This could only be achieved by discarding some of the excess clothing, and within 14 weeks she was down to wearing quite normal clothing. The fact that inappropriate behaviours can be eliminated and acceptable social and self-care behaviours developed using operant reinforcement procedures does suggest that at least some of the unusual behaviours emitted by individuals diagnosed with schizophrenia may be under the control of contingencies of reinforcement.

7.5.2.3 Cognitive Theories

Psychological or cognitive processes are undoubtedly involved in generating some of the main symptoms of psychosis. In some cases symptoms may be generated by deficits in some normal cognitive processes (such as attention), while in other cases biases in normal psychological processes may be responsible (e.g. biases in attributional processes). We will discuss the role of three different cognitive factors in this section: (1) attentional processes, (2) attributional and interpretational biases and (3) deficits in theory of mind (TOM).

Attentional Processes One of the most obvious characteristics of psychosis is individuals' seeming inability on some occasions to make simple associations between relevant events (e.g. sticking to the theme of a conversation), while on other occasions they make associations that are irrelevant (e.g. being unable to prevent themselves from 'clanging' or emitting words that rhyme). These opposing tendencies seem to reflect deficits in attentional processes, where the individual seems unable to focus attention on relevant aspects of the environment (underattention), or overattends to irrelevant aspects of the environment (overattention).

Orienting response A physiological reaction consisting of changes in skin conductance, brain activity, heart rate and blood pressure.

One characteristic of normal attentional processes is the *orienting response*, which is a physiological reaction consisting of changes in skin conductance, brain activity, heart rate and blood pressure. These responses naturally occur when the individual is presented with a novel or prominent stimulus, and they indicate that the stimulus is being attended to and processed. However, around 50 per cent of individuals diagnosed with schizophrenia show abnormalities in their orienting reactions, suggesting that they are not attending to or processing important environmental stimuli (Olbrich, Kirsch, Pfeiffer & Mussgay, 2001). While we might expect such difficulties in attentional processing to give rise to disordered thinking and responding to environmental stimuli, deficits in orienting responses have also been found to be correlated with the negative symptoms of schizophrenia such as withdrawal and blunted affect (Slaghuis & Curran, 1999).

In contrast, overattention is when an individual attends to all aspects of his or her environment and is unable to filter out irrelevant stimuli. Studies have shown that individuals with a diagnosis of schizophrenia are highly distractable, and perform poorly at cognitive tasks when they are also presented with irrelevant, distracting stimuli or information (Wielgus & Harvey, 1988). Interestingly, such individuals actually perform *better* than non-diagnosed control participants at tasks where attending to distracting stimuli can improve performance. For example, the *negative priming effect* is when a non-clinical participant shows an increased reaction time when asked to name a target word he or she has previously been asked to ignore. However, participants diagnosed with schizophrenia fail to exhibit this negative priming effect, and perform just as well whether they have been asked to ignore the relevant prime or not (Peters, Pickering, Kent, Glasper et al., 2000). This inability to screen out irrelevant stimuli or to ignore distractions correlates highly with many of the positive symptoms of schizophrenia (Cornblatt, Lenzenweger, Dworkin & Kimling, 1985) and may well be a contributing factor to the disordered thought and communication exhibited by individuals diagnosed with the disorder.

Attributional and Interpretational Biases Of specific interest to cognitive theorists are the delusional beliefs that are regularly developed during psychotic episodes. Over 50 per cent of individuals diagnosed with schizophrenia are diagnosed with paranoid schizophrenia (Guggenheim & Babigian, 1974). This raises the issue of why so many sufferers should develop these particular kinds of delusions. Amongst individuals diagnosed with schizophrenia who are living in the community, Harris (1987) found that they were 20 times more likely than non-sufferers to report intrusive or confrontational experiences, such as threats from landlords, police enquiries, burglaries and unwanted sexual propositions, so there may be some basis in experience to the development of persecutory beliefs. However, some researchers have pointed out that paranoid delusions may also be the result of *abnormal attributional processes*, which suggests that they have a bias towards attributing negative life events to external causes (Bentall, 1994;

Abnormal attribution processes
The view that paranoid delusions may be the result of a bias towards attributing negative life events to external causes.

Bentall & Kinderman, 1998, 1999; Bentall, Corcoran, Howard, Blackwood et al., 2001). For example, using the Attributional Style Questionnaire (see Chapter 6, Table 6.9), Kaney and Bentall (1989) found that patients with paranoid delusions made excessively stable and global attributions for negative events (just like depressed individuals), but also attributed positive events to internal causes and negative events to external causes. A subsequent study by Bentall, Kaney and Dewey (1991) found that this tendency of individuals with paranoid delusions to attribute negative events to external causes was only evidenced when there was a perceived threat to the self – they did not necessarily attribute negative events to external sources when describing the experiences of others.

These preceding studies all suggest that individuals exhibiting paranoid delusions have had significantly more negative, threatening life events than control individuals without a diagnosis, and have also developed a bias towards attributing negative events to external causes. At the very least, this attributional bias will almost certainly act to maintain paranoid beliefs and delusions that someone or something external is threatening them.

Attributional accounts of psychotic delusions have been supplemented by findings that a number of other *information processing biases* may be involved in the development of delusions and, in particular, persecutory delusions. For

Information processing biases
Biases in interpreting, attending to, storing or recalling information which may give rise to dysfunctional thinking and behaving.

example, Morrison (2001b) has argued that many individuals diagnosed with schizophrenia have a bias towards interpreting cognitive intrusions as threatening in some way. In this case, a perfectly normal auditory hallucination may then be interpreted as threatening (e.g. 'I must be mad', 'The devil is talking to me', 'If I do not obey the voices they will hurt me'), and this misinterpretation causes anxiety, negative mood and physiological arousal which produces more hallucinations, which are in turn interpreted negatively, and so on (Baker & Morrison, 1998).

Other factors may also be involved in setting the conditions for an interpretational bias that will generate threatening ideation. Freeman, Garety, Kuipers, Fowler et al. (2002) have argued that four factors are important in contributing to the development of cognitive biases involved in persecutory ideation. These are: (1) anomalous experiences (such as hallucinations) that do not appear to have a simple and obvious explanation (and are therefore open to biased interpretations); (2) anxiety, depression and worry, which would normally cause a bias towards negative thinking and threatening interpretations of events (see Chapter 5, section 5.4.1.1); (3) reasoning biases on the part of individuals which lead them to seek confirmatory evidence for their persecutory interpretations rather than question them; and (4) social factors, such as isolation and trauma, which add to feelings of threat, anxiety and suspicion. This view is supported by evidence suggesting that individuals with persecutory delusions have high levels of negative mood, such as depression (Freeman, Garety & Kuipers, 2001), and rarely consider alternative (non-delusional) explanations of their experiences (Freeman, Garety, Fowler, Kuipers et al., 2004). Interestingly, this cognitive model of persecutory delusions can also be applied to understanding why psychoactive drug use (such as cannabis) can increase the risk of developing schizophrenic symptoms. This is discussed more fully in Focus Point 7.7.

FOCUS POINT **7.7**

Cannabis use and psychotic symptoms

'Brian, my brother, started smoking at a very young age, in his teens. He was a daily smoker and he used to smoke the equivalent of a pack of cigarettes a day. I had a phone call once from the police in High Wycombe saying they had found him. He was talking like a Rastafarian and he believed he was John the Baptist. I had to get him sectioned, which absolutely broke the family up. My father and mother had very old-fashioned ideas about mental illness – you didn't speak about it – and they practically disowned him. He came to live with me. He would be awake all night and sleep all day. One doctor asked me if he was smoking cannabis and I said he was – she believed that was what triggered his downfall. They put him on medication because they believed he was schizophrenic – he was hearing voices, saw messages in the paper and was having delusions of grandeur. I believe the last time anyone saw him was around High Wycombe in 1996 and he was basically living the life of a down- and out. I believe his problems were brought on by the smoking. He had to live 28 days off it while in hospital and he improved. He seemed in better shape to me.'

This BBC news interview describes how one woman believed that smoking cannabis had caused her brother to develop psychotic symptoms. There has long been a view that regular psychotropic drug use may be related to the development of psychotic symptoms. In recent years this has focused on the relationship between cannabis use and subsequent diagnosis of schizophrenia (Arsencault, Cannon, Witton & Murray, 2004). Concern about the possible relationship between cannabis use and schizophrenia has been fuelled by a dramatic increase in cannabis use by adolescents and young adults over the past two decades (Smart & Ogbourne, 2000) and the possible impact this might have on mental health if there is a causal link between cannabis use and psychotic symptoms.

Cross-sectional studies have shown that individuals diagnosed with schizophrenia use cannabis significantly more often than other individuals in the general population (Degenhardt & Hall, 2001). Some have argued that this relationship between cannabis use and schizophrenia reflects a form of 'self-medication', in which individuals may start using cannabis because of a predisposition for schizophrenia (Khantzian, 1985). However, others have argued for a direct causal link between cannabis use and schizophrenia, and case history studies frequently describe psychotic episodes being preceded by the heavy use of cannabis (Wylie, Scott & Burnett, 1995).

Prospective studies that have monitored cannabis use and psychotic symptoms in individuals over a lengthy period of time appear to indicate that there is indeed a causal link between cannabis and the development of psychotic symptoms. First, Andreasson, Allebeck, Engstrom and Rydberg (1987) found a dose-response relationship between cannabis use at 18 years and later increased risk of psychotic symptoms. Subsequent prospective studies have found that 18-year-olds meeting the criteria for cannabis dependency had rates of subsequent psychotic symptoms that were twice the rate of young people not

meeting these criteria (Fergusson, Horwood & Swain-Campbell, 2003). Also, this relationship could not be explained by high cannabis use being associated with any pre-existing psychiatric symptoms (Fergusson, Horwood & Ridder, 2005). Statistical modelling of these longitudinal data show that the direction of causality is from cannabis use to psychotic symptoms and not vice versa (Fergusson et al., 2005). In addition, further studies have demonstrated that cannabis use increases the risk of psychotic symptoms, but has a greater impact on those who already have a vulnerability to schizophrenia (Verdoux, Gindre, Sorbara, Tournier et al., 2003; Henquet, Krabbendam, Spauwen, Kaplan et al., 2005).

So, if there is a causal link between cannabis use and schizophrenia, what is the mechanism that mediates this link? First, there may be a neurological explanation. Recent research suggests that cannabis has an important effect on brain chemistry, and the compound tetrahydrocannabinol (THC) that is found in cannabis can release the neurotransmitter dopamine (Tanda, Pontieri & DiChiara, 1997). Excess dopamine activity has been identified in the aetiology of schizophrenia, and heavy cannabis use may therefore raise brain dopamine activity to levels triggering psychotic episodes. Alternatively, Freeman, Garety, Kuipers, Fowler et al. (2002) have argued that anomalous experiences (which do not have a simple and obvious explanation) are one of the fundamental factors contributing to the development of delusional thinking, and psychoactive street drugs such as cannabis are likely to increase the frequency of such anomalous experiences. If the individual is in an anxious state and already feeling isolated, then these anomalous experiences are likely to be interpreted threateningly and give rise to the persecutory and paranoid ideation often found in schizophrenia.

Deficits in Theory of Mind (TOM) Another cognitive account of psychotic delusions alludes to the possible inability of individuals diagnosed with schizophrenia to understand the mental state and intentions of others. Individuals who cannot infer the beliefs, attitudes and intentions of others are said to lack a ***theory of mind (TOM)***, and this is a deficit that is known to be prominent in autistic individuals (see Chapter 16, section 16.4.2.2). Frith (1992) has argued that TOM deficits may also be an important factor in the development and maintenance of psychotic delusional beliefs. If individuals diagnosed with schizophrenia are unable to infer the intentions or mental states of others, then they may begin to believe that others are either hiding their intentions or their intentions are hostile. In one study, Corcoran, Cahill and Frith (1997) tested the ability of individuals diagnosed with schizophrenia to understand different types of jokes. In one set of jokes, participants needed to infer the mental state of one of the characters in order to understand the joke; in the other set of jokes, only interpretation of the physical events in the cartoon was needed (see Figure 7.3). The researchers found that individuals with persecutory delusions found the first type of joke more difficult to understand. However, individuals without persecutory delusions found both types of jokes equally easy to understand. Furthermore, in tasks designed to test the ability of individuals to understand situations in which individuals hold false beliefs or intend to deceive, individuals with persecutory delusions performed significantly worse than non-clinical control participants (Frith & Corcoran, 1996).

> **Theory of mind (TOM)** The ability to understand one's own and other people's mental states.

Findings such as these suggest that individuals suffering paranoid delusions do indeed show TOM deficits where they have difficulty inferring the intentions and mental states of others. However, whether these TOM deficits are specific to paranoid delusions is unclear. More recent evidence has indicated that TOM deficits can be found in other schizophrenia sub-types, such as those with symptoms of thought disorder (Sarfati, Hardy Bayle, Besche & Widlocher, 1997) and those who exhibit primarily negative symptoms (Sergi, Rassovsy, Widmark et al., 2007). This suggests that while TOM deficits may contribute to paranoid beliefs, they may also be a general feature of psychosis regardless of the sub-type.

7.5.3 Sociocultural Theories

The overarching diathesis-stress model of schizophrenia emphasizes that a biological predisposition interacts with environmental or life stressors to trigger psychotic symptoms. Sociocultural views of schizophrenia attempt to supplement this view by identifying social, cultural or familial factors that generate stressors that could precipitate psychotic symptoms. First, we will look at general social factors that have been implicated in the aetiology of psychosis, then we will examine more closely how the family environment can influence the development of psychotic symptoms.

7.5.3.1 Social Factors

The highest rates of schizophrenia diagnosis are usually found in poorer inner-city areas and in those of low socioeconomic status,

"It's no wonder we're an endangered species, really."

Figure 7.3 *Two typical cartoons taken from the study by Corcoran, Cahill & Frith (1997).*
In type (a) jokes, participants need to infer the mental state of one of the characters to understand the joke. If individuals with persecutory delusions lack a theory of mind, they will find these jokes difficult to understand. The type (b) joke is an example of a physical/behavioural joke, where only interpretation of the physical events in the cartoon is needed to understand the joke. Corcoran et al. found that individuals with persecutory delusions found type (a) jokes more difficult to understand, whereas people without persecutory delusions were equally able to understand both types (a) and (b).

and this has given rise to two rather different sociocultural accounts of schizophrenia. The first is known as the ***sociogenic hypothesis***. This claims that individuals in low socioeconomic classes experience

> **Sociogenic hypothesis** The theory that individuals in low socioeconomic classes experience significantly more life stressors than individuals in higher socioeconomic classes, and these stressors are associated with unemployment, poor educational levels, crime and poverty generally.

significantly more life stressors than individuals in higher socio-economic classes, and these stressors are associated with unemployment, poor educational levels, crime and poverty generally. Having to endure these stressors may trigger psychotic symptoms in vulnerable people. A study conducted in Denmark indicated that factors associated with low socioeconomic status may be risk factors for psychosis. These include unemployment, low educational attainment, lower wealth status, low income, parental unemployment and parental lower income (Byrne, Agerbo, Eaton & Mortensen, 2004). Studies conducted on immigrants have also indicated that such groups have a higher incidence of the diagnosis of schizophrenia. This has been attributed to the stress caused by many of the initial consequences of immigration, such as language difficulties, unemployment, poor housing and low socioeconomic status (Hjern, Wicks & Dalman, 2004).

However, while this evidence provides some support for the sociogenic hypothesis, there is little evidence that socioeconomic class *per se* increases the risk of psychotic symptoms. In particular, parental socioeconomic class is not a significant risk factor for a diagnosis of schizophrenia (Byrne, Agerbo, Eaton & Mortensen, 2004), and studies of individuals with a diagnosis of schizophrenia have indicated that, although they may be of low socioeconomic status, they are as likely to have parents from a higher socioeconomic class as a low one (Turner & Wagonfeld, 1967).

An alternative explanation for the fact that individuals diagnosed with schizophrenia appear to have low socioeconomic status is that the intellectual, behavioural and motivational problems afflicting individuals with psychotic symptoms mean they will suffer a *downward drift* into unemployment, poverty and the

Social-selection theory   The theory that the intellectual, behavioural and motivational problems afflicting individuals with psychotic symptoms mean they will suffer a downward drift into unemployment, poverty and the lower socioeconomic classes as a result of their disorder.

lower socioeconomic classes *as a result of their disorder*. This is known as the *social-selection theory*, and claims that individuals displaying psychotic symptoms will drift into lifestyles where there is less social pressure to achieve, no need for them to hold down a regular job, and where they can cope with their difficulties on a simple day-to-day basis. This hypothesis is supported by the fact that many individuals diagnosed with schizophrenia may have parents with high socioeconomic status, even though they themselves are living in poverty-ridden areas of towns and cities (Turner & Wagonfeld, 1967).

Social labelling   The theory that the development and maintenance of psychotic symptoms are influenced by the diagnosis itself.

One final sociocultural view of schizophrenia is known as *social labelling*, in which it is argued that the development and maintenance of psychotic symptoms are influenced by the diagnosis itself (Modrow, 1992). In particular, if someone is diagnosed as 'schizophrenic', then it is quite possible that (1) others will begin to behave differently towards him or her and define any deviant behaviour as a symptom of schizophrenia, and (2) the person who is diagnosed may assume a 'role' as someone who has a disorder, and play that role to the detriment of other – perhaps more adaptive – roles. At the very least this is likely to generate a self-fulfilling prophecy, in which a diagnosis leads to individuals and their family and friends behaving in ways which are likely to maintain pathological symptoms. Evidence for such an effect can be found in the classic study by Rosenhan (1973), in which eight individuals without any symptoms of psychopathology presented themselves at psychiatric hospitals complaining of various psychotic symptoms. Not only were these 'normal' individuals immediately diagnosed with schizophrenia, they were also subsequently treated in an authoritarian and uncaring manner by hospital staff, began to feel powerless, bored and uninterested, and even had great difficulty being viewed and treated as 'normal' once they had left the hospital!

7.5.3.2 Familial Factors

There is a general belief across most theoretical perspectives on schizophrenia that the characteristics of the family are in some way important in making an individual vulnerable to acquiring psychotic symptoms. As we have already seen, some psychodynamic views believed that certain characteristics possessed by the mother were important in precipitating psychosis (the schizophrenogenic mother: see section 7.5.2.1). However, more recently, attention has turned from the characteristics of individual family members to the patterns of interactions and communications within the family.

Some approaches suggest that the risk factor within families for the development of psychotic symptoms lies in the way that parents and children communicate. In the 1950s, Bateson, Jackson, Haley and Weakland (1956) argued that psychosis may develop in families where communication is ambiguous and acts to double-bind the child. This *double-bind hypothesis* claims that the individual is subjected within the family to contradictory messages from loved ones

Double-bind hypothesis   Theory advocating that psychotic symptoms are the result of an individual being subjected within the family to contradictory messages from loved ones.

(e.g. a mother may both request displays of affection, such as a hug, and then reject them as being a sign of weakness). This leaves the individual in a conflict situation, and he or she may eventually withdraw from all social interaction. Focus Point 7.8 offers some examples of double-bind situations and conversations. It is clear from these examples that, whichever of the themes the child reads into the ambiguous message, he or she is in a no-win situation.

The double-bind hypothesis has subsequently been superseded by more empirical research which has identified a construct called *communication deviance (CD)* in families and which is related to the development of psychotic

Communication deviance (CD)   A general term used to describe communications that would be difficult for ordinary listeners to follow and leave them puzzled and unable to share a focus of attention with the speaker.

symptoms. CD is a general term used to describe communications that would be difficult for ordinary listeners to follow and leave them puzzled and unable to share a focus of attention with the speaker. Such communications would include (1) abandoned or abruptly ceased remarks or sentences, (2) inconsistent references to events or situations, (3) using words or phrases oddly or wrongly or (4) use of peculiar logic. Studies have demonstrated that CD is a stable characteristic of families with offspring who develop psychotic

FOCUS POINT **7.8**

Double-bind and paradoxical communication

Below are some visualizations inspired by double-bind theory where the verbal message may contradict the implied message, thus invalidating both.

Do not
read
this
sign

Paradoxically, you cannot do
what the sign asks and implies
simultaneously.

With paradox there is essentially no choice,
although there is the illusion of choice.

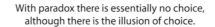

| Be independent | Do something spontaneous |

You can neither obey nor disobey because
whatever you do will be wrong.

YOU KNOW I LOVE YOU   I FEEL REALLY VERY HAPPY   I CAN'T TAKE IT ANYMORE

Source: www.envf.port.ac.uk/illustration/images/vlsh/dbpc.htm

symptoms (Wahlberg, Wynne, Keskitalo, Nieminen et al., 2001). When children with a biological predisposition to schizophrenia have been adopted and brought up in homes with adopted parents who do not have a biological predisposition to schizophrenia, CD has been found to be an independent predictor of the adopted child developing psychotic symptoms (Wahlberg, Wynne, Hakko, Laksy et al., 2004). This suggests that CD is a risk factor for a diagnosis of schizophrenia that is independent of any biological or inherited predisposition, and that CD is not simply the product of a shared genetic defect between parents and offspring.

Another construct that has been closely linked to the appearance and reappearance of psychotic symptoms is known as *expressed emotion (EE)*. The importance of the family environment in contributing to psychotic symptoms was first recognized when it was found that individuals who left hospital following treatment for psychosis were more likely to relapse if they returned to live with parents or spouses than if they went to live in lodgings or to live with siblings (Brown, Carstairs & Topping, 1958). From this research it was discovered that many

Expressed emotion (EE) A qualitative measure of the 'amount' of emotion displayed, typically in the family setting, usually by a family or caretakers.

of the discharged patients were returning to environments where communications were often hostile and critical. This led to the development of the construct of EE, which refers to high levels of criticism, hostility and emotional involvement between key members of a family. See Activity Box 7.1 for some examples of high EE.

Since its development, EE has been shown to be a robust predictor of relapse (Kavanagh, 1992) and, in particular, relapse involving positive psychotic symptoms. Families high in EE tend to be intolerant of the sufferer's problems and have inflexible strategies for dealing with his or her difficulties and symptoms. High EE families also have an attributional style which tends to blame the sufferer for his or her condition and the consequences of his or her symptoms (Weisman, Nuechterlein, Goldstein & Snyder, 2000; Barrowclough, Johnston & Tarrier, 1994). It is not clear how high EE within a family might influence tendency to relapse – if indeed there is a causal relationship between high EE in a family and sufferer relapse. However, some studies have indicated that interventions to moderate high EE levels in a family may actually have a beneficial effect on relapse, suggesting a possible causal link between high EE and relapse (Hogarty, Anderson, Reiss, Kornblith et al., 1986; Tarrier, Barrowclough, Vaughn, Bamrah et al., 1988).

ACTIVITY BOX 7.1

Families with high levels of expressed emotion (EE):

1 exhibit high levels of criticism;

2 show hostility towards the individual diagnosed with schizophrenia;

3 are intolerant of the sufferer's problems;

4 employ inflexible strategies for dealing with the symptoms of schizophrenia;

5 blame the sufferer for his or her symptoms and behaviour;

6 have a tendency to attribute the sufferer's behaviour to global, stable causes, making it difficult to conceive of change and improvement.

Can you identify these characteristics in the fragments of conversation below? These are statements made by members of families with high EE talking about the individual who has been diagnosed with schizophrenia.

'Four days ago he told my wife that he was going to kill the police . . . now whether that's just bravado, that's just childish, the sort of thing a child would do.'

'He has this thing that he is the most important person and they'd have to wait for him, so he'd have to miss appointments.'

'He knows I don't like swearing, so he would continue to swear . . . I think he did it just to be difficult.'

'When he came back with his funny ideas about blacks' persecution and natural health I just thought it was typical Nicholas picking things up en route, he's not too strong a character and tends to absorb other people's views.'

'The other day she threatened to top herself. Now that is not her, that is not an expression that she would use. It's completely out of character with her . . . It's a bit of emotional blackmail; she wants me to take her home.'

'She's a bit on the lazy side, and she's not very logical. If you are cleaning a place out, she'll help, but she won't finish things.'

'He was smoking very heavily, which he hadn't been doing before . . . he really wasn't the smoking type, you know, he got with some friends who smoked and he kept on smoking.'

SUMMARY

The overarching explanation of psychosis is one of *diathesis-stress*. That is, individuals who develop psychotic symptoms have an inherited vulnerability to develop these symptoms (diathesis), which are likely to be triggered by experiencing environmental stressors. We have discussed a mixture of biological, psychological (cognitive) and sociocultural theories of psychosis. These rather different types of explanation are by no means mutually exclusive. They all aim to explain different features of psychosis, often at different levels of description. For example, it is pretty much established that psychosis has an inherited component and that the development of psychotic symptoms is associated with abnormalities in brain neurotransmitter activity (e.g. excess dopamine activity) and abnormalities in specific brain areas (such as the frontal lobes, the temporal lobes-limbic structures and the basal ganglia and cerebellum). These biological abnormalities in turn appear to give rise to deficits in cognitive functioning, such as problems in attention and ability to orient towards and process new stimuli. Other psychological approaches attempt to account for specific aspects of psychosis, such as the development of paranoid delusions (e.g. attributional biases, information processing biases and theory of mind deficits) and explain why psychotic symptoms develop so commonly during adolescence (e.g. as a result of the stressors associated with normal development). Finally, sociocultural theories of psychosis try to explain the uneven distribution of schizophrenia diagnosis across socioeconomic and ethnic groups, and have sought to identify sources of life stressors that may trigger psychotic symptoms. These may include dysfunctional family structures and deviant forms of family communication. All of these views are relevant to a full picture of psychosis.

SELF-TEST QUESTIONS

- What is the diathesis-stress perspective that is used to explain the aetiology of psychotic symptoms?
- Concordance studies, twin studies and adoption studies are used to determine the extent of genetic factors in psychosis. Can you give examples of these types of methods?
- What are genetic linkage analyses and how are they used to identify the specific genes through which the risk for psychosis may be transmitted?
- What is the dopamine hypothesis and how did the role of dopamine in psychosis come to be discovered?
- What abnormalities can be found in the brains of individuals diagnosed with schizophrenia, and which brain areas are most affected by these abnormalities?
- Can you describe the evidence supporting the view that brain abnormalities in individuals diagnosed with schizophrenia may result from abnormal prenatal development?
- What are the main features of psychodynamic explanations of psychosis?

- Can you describe some of the attentional deficits that are characteristic of psychosis and explain how they might contribute to the clinical symptoms?
- A number of cognitive biases have been implicated in the development of some psychotic symptoms. What are these biases and how might they contribute to factors such as delusional thinking?
- What is a sociocultural theory of psychosis? Can you describe and evaluate the significance of two sociocultural accounts of psychosis?
- What is double-bind hypothesis and how does it try to explain the development of psychotic symptoms?
- What are (1) expressed emotion and (2) communication deviance, and what is the evidence that they constitute a risk factor for the development of psychotic symptoms?

SECTION SUMMARY

7.5 The Aetiology of Psychotic Symptoms

- The overarching approach to understanding psychosis is a **diathesis-stress perspective** in which a combination of genetically inherited predisposition (diathesis) and environmental stress is thought to cause psychotic symptoms.

- **Concordance studies** suggest that an individual who has a first-degree relative diagnosed with schizophrenia is 10 times more likely to develop psychotic symptoms than someone who has no first-degree relatives diagnosed with schizophrenia.

- The concordance rate for schizophrenia in MZ twins is 44 per cent but falls to 12 per cent in DZ twins.

- **Adoption studies** show that the probability of an adopted child developing schizophrenia is linked to the probability of the biological mother developing schizophrenia, and not to the probability of the adopted mother developing schizophrenia.

- **Genetic linkage** analyses have helped to identify some of the specific genes through which the risk for psychosis might be transmitted.

- The main biochemical theory of schizophrenia is the **dopamine hypothesis**, which argues that psychotic symptoms are related to excess activity of the neurotransmitter dopamine.

- Psychotic symptoms are associated with **brain abnormalities**, including smaller brain size and enlarged ventricles (the areas in the brain containing cerebrospinal fluid).

- Brain imaging studies of individuals diagnosed with schizophrenia have shown abnormalities in the frontal lobes, the temporal lobes-limbic structures and the basal ganglia and cerebellum.

- Evidence suggests that schizophrenia may also be associated with abnormal prenatal brain development.

- **Psychodynamic theories** of psychosis have claimed that it is (1) due to regression to a state of **primary narcissism** or (2) develops because of a **schizophrenogenic mother** who fosters psychotic symptoms in her offspring.

- At least some inappropriate behaviour patterns exhibited by individuals diagnosed with schizophrenia may be developed and maintained through processes of operant reinforcement (**behavioural theories**).

- Around 50 per cent of individuals diagnosed with schizophrenia show abnormalities in their orienting reactions, suggesting an inability to attend to and process relevant stimuli.

- Individuals with paranoid delusions tend to exhibit abnormal attributional processes, which leads them to attribute all negative events to external sources.

- **Information processing biases** may also be involved in the development of delusions because such individuals have a tendency to interpret cognitive intrusions as threatening or negative.

- There is evidence that individuals diagnosed with schizophrenia may not be able to understand the mental states of others (a **theory of mind deficit**), and this may be a factor in the development of delusions – especially delusions of persecution.

- The **sociogenic hypothesis** claims that individuals in low socioeconomic classes experience significantly more life stressors than those in higher socioeconomic classes, and this is more likely to contribute to the increased prevalence of the diagnosis of schizophrenia in low socioeconomic groups.

- **Social-selection theory** argues that there are more individuals diagnosed with schizophrenia in low socio-economic groups because after they have developed psychotic symptoms they will drift downwards into unemployment and low-achieving lifestyles.

- **Social labelling theory** claims that once an individual has been diagnosed with schizophrenia, such labelling is likely to give rise to circumstances that will tend to maintain psychotic symptoms.

- High levels of **expressed emotion** (high levels of criticism, hostility and emotional involvement between family members) and **communication deviance** (poorly structured means of communication between family members) within the families of individuals diagnosed with schizophrenia have been shown to be associated with relapse and the development of positive symptoms.

7.6 THE TREATMENT OF PSYCHOSIS

With appropriate medication, care and supervision, most people who have suffered psychotic symptoms can eventually cope with many aspects of day-to-day living, although others may still find it difficult to hold down a job or make lasting relationships. Supervision and care are often necessary because relapse is a common feature of psychosis. After recovery from a first episode, studies have shown that around 81 per cent will relapse within the following 5 years, and 78 per cent will also have a second relapse within that time. Discontinuing antipsychotic drug therapy increases the risk of relapse by almost 5 times (Robinson, Woerner, Alvir, Geisler et al., 1999).

These are important problems for the control and treatment of psychosis. In addition, individuals diagnosed with schizophrenia often lack insight into their disorder, deny they are ill, or are too distracted and disabled to respond either to reflective therapies or to the requirements of care programmes. As a result, rates of medication non-adherence among outpatients diagnosed with schizophrenia have been found to approach 50 per cent during the first year after hospital discharge (Weiden & Olfson, 1995). Factors such as these often impose intolerable burdens on the families and carers of those diagnosed with schizophrenia. The sufferer's frequently disturbed and disruptive behaviour and denial of illness often leave families with little alternative than to seek involuntary hospitalization for the individual and the prescription of antipsychotic drugs at the earliest opportunity. The kinds of difficulties and confrontations involved in dealing with psychosis in the family are described in Client's Perspective Box 7.1.

We will begin our discussion of the treatment of psychotic symptoms by describing the various hospitalization regimes that have been associated with the care and treatment of psychosis. We will then discuss the various specific forms of treatment, including biological interventions (psychosurgery and drug therapy) and psychological interventions (social skills training, cognitive behaviour therapy and family therapy interventions). Finally, we will discuss the role of community care (e.g. assertive community treatment and assertive outreach programmes) in addressing the longer-term needs of those with a diagnosis of schizophrenia.

7.6.1 Hospitalization and Custodial Care

Traditionally, the disrupted and disruptive behaviour of individuals displaying psychotic symptoms meant that the first forms of intervention were likely to involve restraint and *custodial care*. Even up until the 1970s in both the UK and the USA, *hospitalization* was usually the norm, and lifelong hospitalization was not uncommon for individuals with chronic symptoms. However, it became clear that custodial care of this kind was neither economically viable nor conducive to providing an environment in which patients had an opportunity to improve. Because of the growing numbers of inpatients diagnosed with schizophrenia, the burden of care came to rest more and more on nurses and attendants who, because of insufficient training and experience, would resort simply to restraint as the main form of intervention. This would often lead to deterioration in symptoms, with patients developing what was called *social breakdown syndrome*, consisting of confrontational and challenging behaviour, physical aggressiveness and a lack of interest in personal welfare and hygiene (Gruenberg, 1980).

Between 1950 and 1970, the limitations of hospitalization were being recognized and there was some attempt to structure the hospital environment for patients. The first attempts were known as *milieu therapies*, which aimed to create a

> **Custodial care** A form of hospitalization or restraint for individuals with psychopathologies whose behaviour is thought of as disruptive.

> **Hospitalization** The placement of an individual in hospital for medical care.

> **Social breakdown syndrome** A deterioration in the symptoms of psychosis consisting of confrontational and challenging behaviour, physical aggressiveness and a lack of interest in personal welfare and hygiene.

> **Milieu therapies** An early type of therapeutic community on a psychiatric ward designed to develop productivity, independence, responsibility and feelings of self-respect.

CLIENT'S PERSPECTIVE 7.1

A family perspective

People involved with schizophrenia note that the family, most often the primary caregiver, is under a great deal of stress every day. This personal stress is something that often goes unacknowledged. The family member diagnosed with schizophrenia becomes a priority, and other family members forget their own needs. The day-to-day tasks involved in caring for a dependent – sudden crises, worry, financial problems, searching for community services, coping with bureaucracy, becoming an advocate, squeezing out precious moments for other family members – are all energy sapping. Eventually families end up with stress exhaustion, and this can lead to depression, anxiety, burnout and psychosomatic illnesses.

The strain of having a relative exhibiting psychotic symptoms can begin in the very early days, when that person first behaves unusually. Normally, when we see someone who is visibly handicapped – for example, using a wheelchair or white cane – we are inclined to offer that person our support. With psychosis, however, often the only way one realizes that something is wrong is to actually see someone exhibit 'weird' or inappropriate behaviour. It is common that people will be disturbed by such behaviour, and they tend to withdraw from interactions. When 'weird' and inappropriate behaviour occurs within a family, the reaction is not much different, and may even be hostile. In the early days, family members may be bewildered and resentful, and often blame and criticize the individual exhibiting the symptoms. Family members may blame other members of the family as their fear and frustration grow.

The following is a list of negative responses that families found very common, both in the early days and in reaction to a diagnosis of schizophrenia:

- denial of the illness entirely: 'This can't happen in our family.'
- denial of the severity of the illness: 'She's just going through a phase.'
- refusal to discuss one's fears
- withdrawal from usual social functions
- shame and guilt: 'Where did we go wrong?'
- feelings of isolation: 'Nobody knows what I'm going through.'
- bitterness: 'It isn't fair. Why us?'
- blame: 'You should have stayed home with the kids.'
- preoccupation with moving away: 'Maybe if we left the city, lived in the country.'
- excessive searching for possible explanations: 'Maybe we punished her too much.'
- inability to think or talk about anything but the illness
- extreme ambivalence towards the sufferer
- marital dissension; eventual divorce
- sibling rivalry and refusal to talk to or be with the afflicted sibling
- increased drinking or dependence upon tranquillizers
- depression
- insomnia, weight loss, anxiety

Because the different relationships within a family can show signs of strain during the very early days, families of individuals diagnosed with schizophrenia stress the importance of joining a support group as soon as the diagnosis has been determined. Listening to others who have been through the experience helps the family to acknowledge their feelings of anger, confusion, guilt, shame and so on, and to realize that these feelings are all normal.

The other reason for joining a support group early is to find ways of avoiding the burnout that so often comes with the burden of caring for someone diagnosed with schizophrenia. Feelings of chronic fatigue and utter exhaustion, a lack of interest in life, a lack of self-esteem and a loss of empathy for the person diagnosed with schizophrenia are common to people who have been coping alone for a number of years. These people are the 'walking wounded', and may suffer from headaches, insomnia, drug and alcohol abuse, depression and stress-related illnesses.

Families offer the following ideas for avoiding burnout:

1 Be aware of your health on a day-to-day basis. Eat nutritiously. Join an exercise club. Go for walks as often as possible. Get enough sleep. Visit your own doctor for regular check-ups. Let him or her know that you are the caregiver of a relative with schizophrenia.

2 Learn about relaxation techniques.

3 Schedule a break for yourself every day.

4 Take regular holidays if you can afford to. Try to get a day or a night to yourself every now and then: will a friend stay overnight while you go to a hotel? (Some families, who are able to be flexible about vacations, go on holiday when a bed is available at a local group home. This sort of respite care is becoming more readily available.)

5 Avoid self-blame and destructive self-criticism.

6 Take a school course – give yourself a few hours when you have to concentrate on something else.

7 If your relative lives away from home, don't visit more than three times a week after the initial transition. Limit phone calls.

8 Try not to neglect the other relationships in your family.

9 Share your grief and problems with supportive people. Be careful from whom you seek advice. (For example, misinformed people may suggest that schizophrenia is something you caused.)

10 Aim for teamwork in your family.

11 Recognize that successful treatment and workable aftercare programmes require the coordinated and shared efforts of several groups of caregivers.

12 Realize that life must go on for you and for others in the family. This attitude may benefit your relative. He or she may be strengthened by the realization that life goes on.

13 Keep on top of developments in your relative's illness that may indicate that a change of lifestyle is necessary. For example, many families have found that although their relative lived at home successfully for a number of years, at some point a change occurred that lowered the quality of life for everyone. Do not insist on keeping your relative at home if different housing is now indicated.

14 Keep your religious beliefs. This may be important to your relative.

15 Keep a sense of humour.

16 Never lose hope.

Source: adapted from www.mentalhealth.com

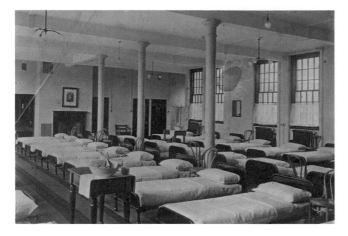

Plate 7.2
This photograph shows a ward in Cardiff City Mental Hospital, Whitchurch, UK, in the early twentieth century. Beds are crowded close together, allowing little personal space for patients, who were often hospitalized for much of their life.

therapeutic community on the ward that would develop productivity, independence, responsibility and feelings of self-respect. This included mutual respect between staff and patients, and the opportunity for patients to become involved in vocational and recreational activities. Patients exposed to milieu therapy were more likely to be discharged from hospital sooner and were less likely to relapse than patients who had undergone traditional custodial care (Paul & Lentz, 1977; Cumming & Cumming, 1962).

A further therapeutic refinement of the hospital environment came with the development of **token economy** programmes (Ayllon & Azrin, 1968). These were programmes based on operant reinforcement, where patients would receive tokens (rewards) for emitting desired behaviours. These desired behaviours would usually include social and self-help behaviours (e.g. communicating coherently to a nurse or other patient, or washing or combing hair), and tokens could subsequently be exchanged for a variety of rewards such as chocolate, cigarettes and hospital privileges. A number of studies have demonstrated

> **Token economy** A reward system which involves participants receiving tokens for engaging in certain behaviours which at a later time can be exchanged for a variety of reinforcing or desired items.

FOCUS POINT 7.9

The decline of the token economy

Despite their apparent therapeutic advantages, recent surveys indicate that the use of token economies in clinical settings is in serious decline (Corrigan, 1995; Hall & Baker, 1973; Boudewyns, Fry & Nightengale, 1986; Dickerson, Tenhula & Green-Paden, 2005). A number of reasons have been put forward for this decline.

- There are legal and ethical issues that need to be considered. This is especially so when decisions have to be made about who will participate in token economies, for how long, and what will be made available as positive reinforcers. Legislation over the past 25 years has sought to protect patients' rights, and treatment staff are severely constrained with regard to the use of more basic items as reinforcers (Glynn, 1990) – especially when patients now have a legal right to their own personal property and humane treatment including such things as a comfortable bed, chair, bedside table, nutritious meals and cheerful furnishings.

- One of the major challenges for token economies has been the maintenance and generalization of therapeutic effects.

To the extent that patients can obtain reinforcers outside the programme and avoid punishment by exiting from the programme, the therapeutic benefit of token economies becomes less useful (Glynn, 1990). It is true that some studies have shown that behaviours targeted for improvement in a token economy scheme return to low baseline levels outside of the programme (e.g. Ayllon & Azrin, 1968; Walker & Buckley, 1968). However, other studies have shown positive effects of maintenance and generalization (Banzett, Liberman & Moore, 1984). Nevertheless, it should be pointed out that generalization is not a passive process, and clinicians must actively build into the programme strategies that transfer positive effects to settings outside the treatment scheme (Stokes & Baer, 1977; Stokes & Osnes, 1988).

- Some other proponents of token economy schemes have argued that their decline has been the result of misconceptions about the nature and efficacy of such programmes, which claim that they are not therapeutically effective, their benefits do not generalize, they fail to provide individualized treatment, they are abusive and cohersive, and they are not practical to implement in the context of present-day attempts to treat patients in the community. Corrigan (1995) argues that these objections are all unfounded, and that the token economy remains an important and valuable tool for the management of patients and staff in treatment settings.

Source: Davey (1998)

that token economies can have significant therapeutic gains. For example, Gripp and Magaro (1971) showed that patients in a token economy ward improved significantly more than patients in a traditional ward, while Gershone, Errickson, Mitchell and Paulson (1977) found that patients in a token economy scheme were better groomed, spent more time in activities and less time in bed, and made fewer disturbing comments than patients on a traditional ward. Patients on token economy schemes also earn discharge significantly sooner than patients who are not on such schemes or have been involved in a milieu therapy programme (Hofmeister, Scheckenbach & Clayton, 1979; Paul & Lentz, 1977). However, despite the apparent success of token economies, their use in the hospital setting has been in serious decline since the early 1980s (Dickerson, Tenhula & Green-Paden, 2005). Some of the reasons for this decline are discussed in Focus Point 7.9.

Since the 1970s treatment and care of individuals diagnosed with schizophrenia has moved away from long-term hospitalization to various forms of community care (see section 7.6.5). However, the psychiatric hospital is still an important part of the treatment picture for those displaying psychotic symptoms – especially since it will often be the environment in which treatment takes place for an individual's first acute psychotic episode, and approximately 50 per cent of all sufferers will return to hospital after at least one relapse (Lien, 2002). However, length of stay in hospital for individuals diagnosed with schizophrenia has been significantly reduced as a result of the development of more effective antipsychotic drugs and extensive and supportive community care and outreach programmes.

7.6.2 Biological Treatments

7.6.2.1 Electroconvulsive Therapy (ECT) and Psychosurgery

Electroconvulsive therapy (ECT)
A method of treatment for depression or psychosis, first devised in the 1930s, which involves passing an electric current of around 70–130 volts through the head of the patient for around half a second.

Psychosurgery   Brain surgery used to treat symptoms of psychopathology.

Prefrontal lobotomy   A surgical procedure that involves severing the pathways between the frontal lobes and lower brain areas.

Early forms of intervention for psychosis seem particularly barbaric in retrospect. Between the 1930s and 1950s, invasive interventions such as ECT (Bini, 1938) and prefrontal lobotomy (Moniz, 1936) were used on thousands of schizophrenia sufferers. *Electroconvulsive therapy (ECT)* involves inducing brain seizures by passing an electric current through the head of the patient for around half a second (see Chapter 6, section 6.4.1.2). Today it tends to be used to treat psychotic symptoms when they are comorbid with depression that has failed to respond to other forms of treatment. *Prefrontal lobotomy* is a surgical procedure that involves severing the pathways between the frontal lobes and lower brain areas and was used frequently for patients who were disruptive or violent. The procedure did appear to have the effect of making such individuals more passive, and many were able to be discharged from

hospital. However, during the 1950s, the wisdom of the procedure came to be questioned. Fatality rates from the procedure were unacceptably high (between 1.5 and 6 per cent) and lobotomies significantly affected the patient's intellectual capacities and emotional responsiveness (Tierney, 2000). While lobotomies had seemed to be a good way of reducing overcrowding in hospitals in the 1930s, the development of effective antipsychotic drugs in the 1950s provided a more acceptable and less invasive means of controlling psychotic symptoms.

7.6.2.2 Antipsychotic Drugs

Specially developed antipsychotic drugs and medications are the first line of intervention for psychotic symptoms, and arguably the most effective treatment for the positive clinical symptoms. The main classes of drugs used for the treatment of psychotic symptoms are known as *antipsychotics* or *neuroleptics* (because some of these drugs produce undesired motor behaviour effects similar to the symptoms of neurological diseases such as Parkinson's disease). Nowadays, antipsychotic drugs can be divided into three broad categories: (1) typical or conventional antipsychotics; (2) less typical anti-psychotics; and (3) atypical antipsychotics. Table 7.4 shows the main types of antipsychotic drugs used, their generic name, their usual trade name, and examples of recommended maintenance doses.

Antipsychotic drugs   Drug treatments intended to treat symptoms of psychosis and schizophrenia

Neuroleptics   A class of drugs used for the treatment of psychotic symptoms.

Typical antipsychotics consist of the traditional drugs that have been developed over the past 50 years (such as chlorpromazine and haloperidol). Less typical antipsychotics refer to those that are used in more specific circumstances and may have more specific effects on brain neurotransmitters (such as loxapine). Atypical antipsychotics are those that have been developed in recent years and have been shown to be more effective over a broader range of symptoms (Citrome, Bilder & Volavka, 2002). They are associated with less risk of relapse (Leucht, Barnes, Kissling, Engel et al., 2003) and with less risk of involuntary motor behaviour side effects (Csernansky & Schuchart, 2002).

The first antipsychotic drugs were developed in the 1940s and 1950s, when a number of researchers discovered that antihistamine drugs used to combat allergies – such as phenothiazines and chlorpromazines – also helped to calm patients before surgery. This led to these drugs being used with individuals, such as those with psychotic symptoms, who showed signs of extreme psychological disorder (Delay & Deniker, 1952). They found a marked and consistent drop in psychotic symptoms in such patients with the use of these drugs, and by the late 1950s such drugs had been widely adopted for use with individuals diagnosed with schizophrenia. These drugs were revolutionary in their effects, and were the first form of treatment that appeared to successfully and reliably reduce the positive symptoms of schizophrenia (such as hallucinations and disordered thought and communication). These traditional antipsychotic drugs appear to have their therapeutic effects by blocking excessive dopamine activity in the brain (Grilly, 2002).

However, there are a number of problems with the use of antipsychotic drugs. First, they are not a 'cure' for psychosis, and

CLIENT'S PERSPECTIVE 7.2

The experience of hospitalization

Janey describes her first experience of a psychiatric ward after exhibiting psychotic symptoms in 1985. She then describes her experiences on being readmitted to the same ward after relapse in 2000.

1985

'The ward was supposed to be for twenty-four people but it was my bad luck that they were decorating one of the other wards and we had four extra beds squashed into various corners. The whole area smelled of smoke, floor cleaner and urine – in that order. I was given a bed – one of five in a four-person room – and introduced to my two neighbours. A nurse went through my things, listing my valuables and in the end confiscating my birth control pills. I argued about that too because I didn't see how oestrogen and progesterone could be seen as dangerous.

The other patients terrified me; some seemed to have strange glassy-eyed expressions or shambling walks. There were people pacing the ward in silence, someone smashed a guitar against the wall, another person wet the floor. One of my room-mates, an oldish, sleepy-looking woman called Amy, told me that she had entered "The Brain of Britain" programme in the past, but frankly I didn't believe her. And there was a young man in a wheelchair, who, I was informed, had jumped off a building. Most people were smoking heavily.

I ate someone else's dinner (they were on leave) because food was ordered two days ahead and I had yet to fill in menus. Then I retreated onto my bed to hide and to try to read – desperately attempting to act normal so I could go home as soon as possible. Fortunately, my husband came to visit me and I felt happier for a while.

I heard a weird conversation between two women in my room who were to have a treatment in the morning. Both were scared because they didn't know what to expect and I couldn't imagine what was going to happen to them.

That night I had to queue at the drug trolley for my birth control pill. The quantity of medication some of the patients were getting surprised and shocked me. The only drug whose name I recognized was chlorpromazine because I had been given it when I was fifteen. Some people received a bright orange sticky liquid that had to be measured out carefully, others a large amount of a brown liquid.

Afterwards there was hot milk to make a bedtime drink of chocolate or Ovaltine but I was not quick enough so I didn't get any. I spent the night getting up to switch the night light off because it was too bright to sleep, only to have the staff switch it back on again. The bed was not very comfortable and creaked with every breath. It took a long time for morning to come.

I spent the next few days feeling bored and frustrated because I was not allowed off the ward on my own and there was not a lot to do. The two women went for their treatment. One came back with a headache and one felt sick and was told to go and lay on her bed. There was intense drama for a while when a man abruptly kicked at one of the doors and tore it off its hinges. Someone seeing it set an alarm off and suddenly there were nurses everywhere. The man (who never spoke the whole time I was there) was given some medication and order was resumed. The Christmas decorations were put up – paper chains and plastic baubles only. Later another man in black leather silently and inexplicably held my hand while we were watching TV.'

2000

'Of course the building hasn't changed and although there have obviously been several facelifts within the ward, it still has that lived-in look, with splodges of something-or-other on the floor and walls. The internal structure of the place has changed a little, so the nurses have a big room, as compared with a little one (six years ago) and a nursing station (fifteen years ago). I didn't walk into a sea of smoke this time, all smoking has been confined to one room. We have carpet in the corridor and there are more single rooms too. But other than that, the basic cubicle with bed, wardrobe and locker are the same. Drug times, ward rounds and that sort of thing seem immutable, set in stone. Unfortunately even some of the patients have stayed the same – though I suppose they can say that of me.

The rules of the ward are stricter, with notices pinned up to remind us of them. "No visitors until four o'clock", "no mobile phones", "no smoking except in the smoking room", "drug and alcohol use will result in the police being called", etc. And good behaviour is enforced with a "sin bin", the seclusion room (I was threatened with seclusion for kicking the door in a moment's temper). Surprisingly, all of this makes for a more relaxed, less dog-eat-dog atmosphere.

There is a mission statement on the wall by the new and bigger nurses' room now. It contains lots of long words like "integrity", "confidentiality" and "valuing individuals" – the shortest is "caring". I guess this is a response to hospital trusts and "the Patients' Charter" though I'm not sure that practically it makes any difference at all. Observation levels are more relaxed, the hell of having a nurse with one all the time (even in the loo) seems to have disappeared. The food is still bad, with little green vegetables. The queue for medication still takes time to get through, and ECT is still done on Tuesday and Friday. Sadly, the suicide of those with a mental health problem has not changed at all. During my three weeks in the ward, one of my fellow patients found a way to kill himself.

Once more I'm back out in the community, trying to sort my life and planning not to have to go into hospital again.'

Source: adapted from www.schizophrenia.co.uk/ treatment/treatment_articles/treatment

Table 7.4 *Antipsychotic drugs used to treat psychotic symptoms*

Typical antipsychotics are the traditional drugs that have been developed over the past 50 years; less typical antipsychotics are those that are used less frequently but may have some specific benefits in individual cases (e.g. lozapine is more tranquillizing and may be used in an emergency); atypical antipsychotics are those that have been developed in more recent years, appear to have fewer disturbing side effects, and are more effective over a broader range of symptoms.

Classification	Generic name	Trade name	Recommended dose/dose range/day[a]
Typical antipsychotics	Chlorpromazine	Thorazine	75–300 mg
	Trifluoperazine	Vesprin	10 mg
	Fluphenazine	Prolixin, Permitil	2.5–20 mg
	Haloperidol	Haldol	5–100 mg
	Perphenazine	Trilafon	12–24 mg
Less typical antipsychotics	Thioridazine	Mellaril	150–600 mg
	Pimozide	Orap	2–20 mg
	Loxapine	Loxitane	20–100 mg
Atypical antipsychotics	Olanzapine	Zyprexa	5–20 mg
	Rispiridone	Risperdal	4–6 mg
	Clozapine	Clozaril	150–300 mg
	Quetiapine	Seroquel	300–450 mg

[a] *Effective Health Care*, Vol. 5, No. 6 (1999).

tend to act to suppress rather than eliminate symptoms. As a result, sufferers usually need lifelong medication to control their symptoms. Second, these types of drugs have a number of undesirable side effects. These include tiredness, lack of motivation, dry mouth, blurred vision, constipation, impotence and dizziness resulting from lowered blood pressure. Most importantly, between 20 and 25 per cent of people who take typical antipsychotic drugs for any period of time will develop disorders of motor movement such as **tardive dyskinesia** (Grilly, 2002). Typical symptoms include movement disorders that resemble symptoms of Parkinson's disease, including limb tremors, involuntary tics, lip-smacking and chin-wagging, shuffling gait and emotionless expressions. These symptoms appear to result from the lowering of brain dopamine activity that is a consequence of typical antipsychotic drug use. Such problematic side effects cause around 50 per cent of those treated with typical antipsychotic drugs to quit medication after less than a year (Harvard Mental Health Letter, 1995), with a resulting significant increase in the probability of relapse.

The more recently developed atypical antipsychotic drugs (such as clozapine, rispiridone and olanzapine) have a number of benefits over traditional antipsychotics: (1) their neurological effects selectively target certain types of dopamine receptors and also influence serotonin receptors in ways which make their therapeutic effects more specific (Worrell, Marken, Beckman & Ruehter, 2000); (2) they are associated with significantly less risk of relapse than traditional antipsychotics (Leucht, Barnes, Kissling, Engel et al., 2003); (3) they produce significantly fewer major side effects, such

Tardive dyskinesia A disorder of motor movement.

as involuntary motor behaviour disturbances (Csernansky & Schuchart, 2002); (4) sufferers taking the atypical antipsychotics are more likely to comply with and persevere with their medication regimes than those taking traditional antipsychotics (possibly because of fewer disturbing side effects) (Dolder, Lacro, Dunn & Jeste, 2002); and (5) while being highly effective for positive symptoms, atypical antipsychotics also help to reduce the frequency and magnitude of negative symptoms (Grilly, 2002).

The development of new drug treatments for psychosis is an important ongoing process, and it is still unclear what biochemical mechanisms many of these drugs influence to have their successful therapeutic effects. However, antipsychotic drugs have become a central feature of treatment for psychotic symptoms.

7.6.3 *Psychological Therapies*

7.6.3.1 Social Skills Training

So far in this chapter we have seen ample evidence that there are deficits in the behavioural, cognitive and emotional responses of individuals diagnosed with schizophrenia. This may lead their friends and family to view their behaviour as inappropriate, their thoughts as confused, and their emotional responses as erratic. An obvious consequence of these characteristics is that it will make it difficult for sufferers to interact socially with others, to live normal lives in which they can readily negotiate normal day-to-day activities, and to develop close relationships with others. In fact, the inappropriate responses of individuals displaying psychotic symptoms may generate a vicious cycle in which inappropriate behaviour causes others to back off from contact with the sufferer, which in turn is likely to exacerbate symptoms and generate feelings of alienation and worthlessness.

One obvious way to intervene in this cycle is to provide sufferers with training in the appropriate social skills they will need to deal with basic everyday interactions. Social skills training consists of a combination of role-playing, modelling and positive reinforcement, and individuals are taught how to react appropriately in a range of useful social situations. Such training will provide clients with a range of transferable social skills, such as conversational skills, appropriate physical gestures, eye contact and positive and appropriate facial expressions (Smith, Bellack & Liberman, 1996). In addition, clients will be asked to role-play in certain specific scenarios (e.g. how to respond to someone who has just done them a favour). They are also positively rewarded for appropriate reactions. Such training may have other tangential benefits in helping clients to maintain contact with outreach or community supervisors, and help them to find work (e.g. how to behave in job interviews) and find accommodation (Pratt & Mueser, 2002).

There is some evidence that social skills training has a number of beneficial effects on symptoms. In comparison with either no structured treatment or occupational therapy, social skills training appears to promote better social skills and independent living skills and to result in lower rates of rehospitalization (Liberman, Wallace, Blackwell et al., 1998; Hogarty, 2002). However, when only randomized control trials involving social skills training are analysed, there appears to be no clear evidence for the benefits of social skills training on relapse rate, global adjustment, social functioning, quality of life or treatment compliance (Pilling, Bebbington, Kuipers, Garety et al., 2002). Such negative findings suggest that the generalization of social skills training may be more difficult than was initially thought, and such therapies may need to be redeveloped in order to ensure that a broader range of skills are learned (Huxley, Rendall & Sederer, 2000).

7.6.3.2 Cognitive Behaviour Therapy (CBT)

Because of their confused thinking, frequent lack of insight into their disorder and the potential difficulties in communicating with individuals exhibiting psychotic symptoms, cognitive therapies were previously thought to be an inappropriate and ineffective form of treatment. This view was strengthened by the belief that most of the disordered thinking in schizophrenia was the result of dysfunctional brain neurotransmitter mechanisms rather than psychological factors. However, as we have seen in section 7.5 on aetiology, there is a developing body of evidence to suggest that some psychological processes may be involved in generating and maintaining psychotic thought, particularly delusions and paranoid views of the world (Bentall, Corcoran, Howard, Blackwood et al., 2001; Morrison, 2001b), and it is becoming clear that CBT can be adapted to effectively target and challenge these dysfunctional thoughts (Kingdon & Turkington, 2004; Haddock & Slade, 1995; Morrison, Renton, Dunn, Williams et al., 2003; Fowler, Garety & Kuipers, 1995).

Cognitive therapy methods have also been found to be effective in other areas of treatment, including (1) helping sufferers to adjust to the realities of the outside world after dehospitalization (known as personal therapy), (2) helping with medication compliance, (3) providing training for deficits in basic cognitive skills, such as memory and attention (known as cognitive rehabilitation), and (4) helping individuals with paranoid symptoms to reattribute their paranoid delusions to normal daily events rather than the threatening, confrontational causes they believe underlie them (known as reattribution therapy). We will discuss each of these cognitive interventions in turn.

When individuals diagnosed with schizophrenia are discharged from hospital after an acute episode, they usually find themselves in a challenging environment in which their cognitive skills and their ability to cope leave a lot to be desired. As a consequence, relapse rates are usually high. *Personal therapy* is a broad-based cognitive behaviour programme that is designed to help such individuals with the skills needed to adapt to day-to-day living after discharge. Clients are taught a range of skills in either a group setting or on an individual basis, including:

> **Personal therapy** A broad-based cognitive behaviour programme that is designed to help individuals with the skills needed to adapt to day-to-day living after discharge from hospital.

1 learning to identify signs of relapse (e.g. social withdrawal) and what to do in such circumstances;

2 acquiring relaxation techniques designed to help them deal with the anxiety and stress caused by challenging events (e.g. to reduce levels of anger that might give rise to unnecessary aggression);

3 identifying inappropriate emotional and behavioural responses to events, and learning new and adaptive responses (e.g. to help with gaining and maintaining employment and accommodation);

4 identifying inappropriate cognitions and dysfunctional thinking biases that might foster catastrophic and deluded thinking (and so help clients to prevent intrusive catastrophic thinking);

5 learning to deal with negative feedback from others and to resolve interpersonal conflicts (known as criticism management and conflict resolution); and

6 learning how to comply with medication regimes (Hogarty, Greenwald, Ulrich, Kornblith et al., 1997; Hogarty, Kornblith, Greenwald, DiBarry et al., 1997).

More recently, this form of intervention has been broadened to address deficits in both social cognition (the ability to act wisely in social situations) and neurocognition (basic abilities in cognitive functioning, such as memory and attention). This is known as *cognitive enhancement therapy* (Hogarty & Flesher, 1999) (see Treatment in Practice Box 7.1). Treatment methods address the impairments, disabilities and handicaps associated with the cognitive styles

> **Cognitive enhancement therapy** A form of intervention which addresses deficits in both social cognition (the ability to act wisely in social situations) and neurocognition (basic abilities in cognitive functioning, such as memory and attention).

CLINICAL PERSPECTIVE: TREATMENT IN PRACTICE BOX 7.1

Cognitive enhancement therapy

Cognitive enhancement therapy is an approach that provides individuals diagnosed with schizophrenia with cognitive exercises that will help them develop cognitive functions that have been impaired by their disorder. These include such skills as attention, memory and problem solving. The following 'categorization exercise' is designed to help develop working memory and abstraction skills.

Patients are asked to group the following words into four coherent categories:

love	iron	air	home
nylon	human	spider	sand
stone	food	clay	wood
steel	water	pig	paper
virus	flower	ink	glass

The categories of 'living things' and 'things one needs to live' are fairly obvious, but the last two are sufficiently ambiguous to require abstraction. Many clients will initially group items such as iron, wood, glass and steel into a category of 'building materials', and ink, paper, clay, sand and nylon into 'art supplies'. However, with some subtle coaching, clients are encouraged to seek a more abstract basis for sorting (e.g. 'Does nylon really have anything in common with sand?'). Success can be achieved when patients reason that ink, paper, glass, steel and nylon are all 'fabricated materials'. The skills that clients require to complete this task successfully include remembering previous failed attempts, remembering the words that require further categorization, and remembering individual words within the context of categories that have already been established. As such, the task provides clients with training in memory and abstraction skills that they can take to other problem-solving situations.

Source: Hogarty & Flesher (1999)

---

apparent in the positive, negative and disorganized symptoms of schizophrenia. The approach integrates computer-assisted training in neurocognition with social cognitive group exercises to develop social skills and coping strategies. Studies suggest that this general form of skills training enables clients to cope well with life outside of the hospital (Hogarty, Greenwald, Ulrich, Kornblith et al., 1997; Hogarty, Kornblith, Greenwald, DiBarry et al., 1997) and to show improvement in social and cognitive skills up to 24 months after entering such therapy programmes (Hogarty, Flesher, Ulrich, Carter et al., 2004).

Individuals diagnosed with schizophrenia often exhibit a range of deficits in basic cognitive functioning. These include deficits in perceptual skills, memory, verbal and full-scale IQ, verbal fluency and serial learning (Nathaniel-James, Brown & Ron, 1996; Purcell, Lewine, Caudle & Price, 1998; Riley, McGovern, Mockler, Doku et al., 2000). In addition, deficits in these basic skills are also good predictors of poor social outcomes and poor problem-solving performance (Green, Kern, Braff & Mintz, 2000), so attempting to develop and improve these basic cognitive processes may well have a broader impact by improving social functioning generally (Wykes & van der Gaag, 2001). This type of approach is known as cognitive rehabilitation (because the training methods are very similar to those used to rehabilitate individuals with neurological brain injury such as stroke patients) or as *cognitive remediation therapy (CRT)*.

Finally, CBT has been applied to the treatment of psychotic symptoms in ways that attempt to challenge and replace any dysfunctional beliefs or interpretation biases that generate and maintain psychotic thinking. This approach is more reminiscent of the way CBT is used in the treatment of anxiety disorders and major depression (see Chapter 5, Treatment in Practice Box 5.3). For example, Morrison (2001b) has argued that many individuals diagnosed with schizophrenia have a bias towards interpreting cognitive intrusions as threatening in some way (e.g. 'If I do not obey the voices they will hurt me'). This misinterpretation causes a vicious cycle that produces more hallucinations, which are in turn interpreted negatively, and so on. Having interpreted a hallucination as threatening, many individuals may then indulge in what are known as 'safety behaviours' which effectively prevent them from *disconfirming* their belief that the hallucination is threatening. Safety behaviours include things like lying down, drinking alcohol or shouting at the voices to go away (Frederick & Cotanch, 1995), and they may actually have the effect of increasing the frequency of hallucinations (Nayani & David, 1996).

Cognitive behaviour therapy (CBT) for schizophrenia attempts to tackle these problems by challenging clients' interpretation of their hallucinations, generating alternative acceptable explanations for them, and helping clients to understand how their hallucinations might have developed through normal experience. A number of outcome studies have indicated that CBT is a useful adjunctive treatment for the positive symptoms of schizophrenia, and is better at reducing symptoms than standard psychiatric care or no treatment (Tarrier & Wykes, 2004; Zimmerman, Favrod, Trieu & Pomini, 2005). Some studies suggest the therapeutic effects of CBT for positive symptoms are relatively long lasting (up to 12 months – Zimmerman et al., 2005).

Cognitive remediation therapy (CRT)
A treatment programme for clients designed to develop and improve basic cognitive skills and social functioning generally.

Cognitive behaviour therapy (CBT)
A form of counselling and psychological therapy with a focus on understanding how our thoughts affect our behaviour.

CBT has also been successfully used in a preventative programme designed to reduce future symptoms in individuals at risk for developing psychotic symptoms (Morrison, Bentall, French, Walford et al., 2002). However, further detailed research is necessary to determine if CBT is an equivalent or more effective treatment than other programmes.

CBT can also be extended to psychotic symptoms in the form of *reattribution therapy*. We have already noted that paranoid individuals make more attributions for negative events that are of an external rather than internal nature, and this appears to maintain their delusions that someone or something external is threatening them (Lee, Randall, Beattie & Bentall, 2004). Reattribution therapy can be used to challenge these dysfunctional attributions, and clients are encouraged to consider more normal causes for their hallucinations than the dysfunctional or delusional ones they may hold. Treatment will usually involve monitoring the frequency of delusional beliefs, attempting to generate alternative explanations for delusional beliefs, and then providing behavioural experiments that will enable clients to test out the reality of their beliefs (Alford & Beck, 1994; Chadwick & Lowe, 1994). Frequently, a verbal challenge will be enough to get clients to reject their dysfunctional belief (e.g. the therapist may simply ask whether it makes sense for things to be the way the client says they are, and a logical discussion of evidence may be sufficient); in other cases a 'reality test' in the form of a behavioural experiment may be necessary. For example, in the case of a client who maintained he could tell what was going to be said on television before it was actually said, a video recording was put on pause at prearranged times and the client was asked to say what was coming up (Chadwick & Lowe, 1990).

In summary, CBT had originally looked like an unlikely source of effective treatment for psychotic symptoms, but research in recent years has indicated that cognitive factors may play a significant role in developing and maintaining pathological thought processes in schizophrenia. Dysfunctional beliefs, information processing and reasoning biases and rigid attributional styles may all contribute to delusional ideation in particular, and CBT methods are ideally suited to correcting these factors. CBT methods can also be incorporated successfully into programmes designed to raise the cognitive and social functioning of those diagnosed with schizophrenia, and this can be found in cognitive enhancement therapy and cognitive rehabilitation.

> **Reattribution therapy** A treatment used in helping individuals with paranoid symptoms to reattribute their paranoid delusions to normal daily events rather than the threatening, confrontational causes they believe underlie them.

7.6.4 Family Interventions

In section 7.5.3 of this chapter we discovered that the family environment for someone diagnosed with schizophrenia may contribute to both the development of symptoms and the risk of relapse. In particular, expressed emotion (EE) and communication deviance (CD) within families are factors that have been shown to be associated with relapse and the development of positive symptoms. Families with high levels of EE and CD have difficulty with effective communication between family members, high levels of criticism, a tendency to blame the sufferer for his or her symptoms and the family consequences of those symptoms, and possess inflexible strategies for dealing with difficulties. Clearly, if these characteristics can be addressed and modified, then this should be reflected in lower risk for positive symptoms and relapse.

Family interventions can take many forms. The main features of a majority of these types of intervention are that they are designed to educate the family about the nature and symptoms of psychosis and how to cope with the difficulties that arise from living with someone with a diagnosis of schizophrenia. More specifically:

1 families learn about the diagnosis, prevalence and aetiology of psychotic symptoms;

2 they learn about the nature of antipsychotic medication and how to help the sufferer to comply with his or her medication regime;

3 they are taught how to recognize the signs of relapse and to identify and deal with stressors that could cause relapse;

4 through social skills training, they learn how to identify and solve problems and to achieve family goals;

5 families will also learn how to share experiences and avoid blaming either themselves or the sufferer for his or her symptoms and the consequences of those symptoms.

These educational targets are achieved in a variety of ways. For example, high EE families may be asked to watch videos of how low EE families interact (modelling) (Penn & Mueser, 1996). Counselling can be provided to help family members interact in less emotional ways, and group discussions where families share their experiences can help to provide reassurance and a network of social support (known as *supportive family management*). A more intensive form of family intervention is known as *applied family management*, which goes beyond education and support to include active behavioural training elements. Communication and coping skills can be taught with the active involvement of members of the family by using modelling, role-playing, providing positive and corrective feedback and through homework assignments. For example, families may be taught to have one member chair a problem-solving meeting (leading the family through the steps) and another as secretary (recording information on a problem-solving form). As homework, families may be asked to meet weekly to practise problem solving without the presence of a therapist or facilitator (Mueser, Sengupta, Schooler, Bellack et al., 2001).

Outcome studies have indicated that family interventions significantly reduce the risk of relapse, reduce symptoms and improve the sufferer's social and vocational functioning for periods up to 2 years (Huxley, Rendall & Sederer, 2000). Family interventions that are conducted for longer than 9 months appear to be particularly effective (Kopelowicz & Liberman, 1995). Recent

> **Supportive family management**
> A method of counselling in which group discussions are held where families share their experiences and which can help to provide reassurance and a network of social support.

> **Applied family management**
> An intensive form of family intervention which goes beyond education and support to include active behavioural training elements.

Working with Psychosis: A Clinical Psychologist's Experience

'I have worked with people with psychosis for the last five years. Most of the work that I have done has involved either cognitive behavioural therapy (CBT) or family intervention (FI) and has been provided through the NHS. When I started this work I was anxious about trying out these therapies with people with psychosis. I had experience of CBT working well in trauma, anxiety and depression but was unsure how the therapy would translate into psychosis.

A typical week would include a whole variety of very different tasks. The main focus of the work is the therapy itself, but there is a lot that goes on alongside that. Usually I attend the Community Mental Health Team meeting where clinical cases are discussed and the team decides on who in the team is best for an individual to see. The team is made up of nurses, social workers, occupational therapists, psychiatrists and psychologists and each professional group takes a slightly different perspective on the case in hand.

In addition there are assessments to conduct. I will usually see three or four people a week for an initial assessment and then write up this information and take it back to the team meeting for allocation. Some more time is spent writing letters to clients or to GPs and also in speaking on the telephone to those people.

The bread and butter of the job is the clinical work itself. Psychosis is often confusing and terrifying for those who experience it. This may seem like a self-evident and simplistic statement. However, keeping a focus on the distress that people experience helps me a great deal in my work. It is easy to be blinded by the delusions and hallucinations and to fail to consider the confusion, distress and fear that so often go with them.

So, as a start point when working in psychosis, I tend to try to consider what people with psychosis have in common with other people rather than what sets them apart. In this way I can draw on my experiences of working in anxiety, depression and trauma when I meet, and try to help, someone with psychosis.

In my experience cognitive behavioural therapy can help someone make sense of psychotic experiences by helping them make links between emotional states, thoughts, beliefs, traumatic life events and psychotic symptoms. Helping people to make sense of psychotic and emotional experiences by discussing psychological formulations can help them make connections between seemingly unconnected events or beliefs and disabling and distressing psychotic symptoms. In order to succeed in this work it is first essential to engage well with a client. Engagement in CBT for psychosis is a big challenge to therapists. For some people having the time and space to talk through their experiences in detail is very liberating and although it is hard work (for all parties) can be very rewarding too.

Family interventions (FI) make up another large part of my clinical work. They have been designed to minimize the negative impact of a client's symptoms on carers and to reduce the risk of client relapse. Central importance is given to the task of defusing the large range of difficult emotions that psychosis can often engender in families, for example, anger and fear. The intervention is based upon a positive view of individuals with psychosis and their caregivers; the strengths of the family unit are explicitly recognized and family members are mobilized as supportive therapeutic allies. I conduct the FI work with my colleague (who is also a clinical psychologist) and usually we try to see families in their own homes.

There is still a lot to learn about how psychology can help people with psychosis and that is what makes this area of work so challenging and rewarding.'

studies have suggested that no one form of family intervention is necessarily more effective than others (Huxley, Rendall & Sederer, 2000), but educational interventions without accompanying behavioural training components may be less effective at achieving some goals, such as medication adherence (Zygmunt, Olfson, Boyer & Mechanic, 2002).

7.6.5 Community Care

Community care Care that is provided outside a hospital setting.

With the development of relatively effective antipsychotic drugs in the 1950s and 1960s, it became clear that most people diagnosed with schizophrenia could be treated to a point where they were capable of living at least some kind of life back in the community. This helped relieve the economic burden of lifelong hospitalization and custodial care. However, even when living back in their communities, it was clear that individuals diagnosed with schizophrenia would often need support and supervision. They would need help maintaining their necessary medication regime, finding and keeping a job or applying for and securing welfare benefits. They might also need help with many aspects of normal daily living that others would take for granted, such as personal hygiene, shopping, feeding themselves, managing their money and coping with social interactions and life stressors.

In 1963, the US Congress passed a Community Mental Health Act which specified that, rather than be detained and treated in hospitals, people with mental health problems had the right to receive a broad range of services in their communities. These services included outpatient therapy, emergency care, preventative care and aftercare. Growing concerns about the rights of mental

Plate 7.3
Assertive outreach staff try to meet their clients in their own environments. For many homeless individuals suffering psychotic symptoms, this may mean parks, streets or cafés. The aim of such programmes is to help individuals with their medication regimes, provide assistance in dealing with everyday life and its stressors, and help with securing welfare benefits. These programmes also aim to help build a long-term relationship between the individual and local mental health services.

Table 7.5 *The aims and characteristics of assertive outreach programmes*

AIMS:
Assertive outreach services aim to help clients to:

- Reduce their number of hospital admissions, in terms of both frequency and duration
- Find and keep suitable accommodation
- Sustain family relationships
- Increase social network and relationships
- Improve their money management
- Increase medication adherence
- Improve their daily living skills
- Undertake satisfying daily activities (including employment)
- Improve their general health
- Improve their general quality of life
- Stabilize symptoms
- Prevent relapse
- Receive help at an early stage

CORE CHARACTERISTICS:
Assertive outreach involves targeting clients with severe and enduring mental health problems who have difficulty engaging with services:

- It is multidisciplinary, comprising a range of professional disciplines (nurses, psychiatrists and social workers at a minimum; also, depending on user needs, support workers, workers who have also been service users, psychologists, occupational therapists, housing workers, substance misuse specialists and vocational specialists)
- There is a low ratio of service users to workers, usually 10 clients per caseload
- There is intensive frequency of client contact compared to that of standard community mental health teams (ideally an average of four or more contacts per week with each client)
- An emphasis on engaging with clients and developing a therapeutic relationship
- Offers or links to specific evidence-based interventions
- Time-unlimited services with a no drop-out policy
- Work with people in their own environment, often their own home; engages with the user's support system of family, friends and others
- A team approach that provides flexible and creative support to the individual case coordinators

health patients and a change in social attitudes away from the stigma associated with mental health problems meant that other countries around the world swiftly followed suit in making mental health treatment and aftercare available in the community (Hafner & van der Heiden, 1988). These events led to the development of a combination of services usually termed assertive community treatment or assertive outreach. In the USA alone, this has led to around a tenfold decrease in the number of people being treated in hospital for mental health problems (Torrey, 2001).

Assertive community treatment
Programmes to help people recovering from psychotic episodes with their medication regimes, offering psychotherapy, assistance in dealing with everyday life and its stressors, guidance on making decisions, residential supervision and vocational training.

Assertive outreach A way of working with groups of individuals with severe mental health problems who do not effectively engage with mental health services.

Assertive community treatment programmes help people recovering from psychotic episodes with their medication regimes, psychotherapy, assistance in dealing with everyday life and its stressors, guidance on making decisions, residential supervision and vocational training (Bebbington, Johnson & Thornicroft, 2002). In the UK, *assertive outreach* is a way of working with groups of individuals with severe mental health problems who do not effectively engage with mental health services. Assertive outreach staff would expect to meet clients in their own environments, whether at home or in a café, park or street, with the aim of building a long-term relationship between the client and mental health services. Table 7.5 provides a list of some of the main aims and characteristics of assertive outreach programmes in the UK, all of which emphasize teaching basic living skills, providing support and guidance, and preventing relapse and hospitalization.

There is good evidence that community care programmes help to stabilize the condition of individuals diagnosed with schizophrenia, ensure that they integrate more effectively into their local communities, comply with their medication regimes and stay out of hospital longer than sufferers who are not part of a community care programme (Madianos & Madianou, 1992; Hansson, Middelboe, Sorgaard, Bengtsson-Tops et al., 2002; Bebbington, Johnson & Thornicroft, 2002). However, community care services are often difficult to resource and to coordinate, and it has been estimated that in any one year in the USA, between 40 and 60 per cent of all people experiencing symptoms of psychosis receive no treatment at all (Wang, Demler & Kessler, 2002). In addition, long-term studies of community care in the UK suggest that it helps to maintain clinical and social functioning at a stable level, but does not necessarily help to *improve* these aspects of the sufferer's life (Reid, Johnson, Bebbington, Kuipers et al., 2001).

The community care approach has also given rise to concerns for the physical safety of individuals with mental health problems who are exposed to the stresses and rigours of everyday life, and for the safety of others in the communities in which they live. For example, studies in the UK have suggested that 41 per cent of people with mental health problems living in the community suffer physical and verbal harassment, compared with 15 per cent in the general population, and this abuse is usually carried out by teenagers and neighbours (Berzins, Petch & Atkinson, 2003). There is also concern about the role of individuals diagnosed with schizophrenia as victims or perpetrators of violent crime such as homicide. A Danish study discovered that the risk of being a victim of homicide was increased sixfold for people diagnosed with a mental illness such as schizophrenia compared with individuals without a psychiatric diagnosis (Hiroeh, Appleby, Mortensen & Dunn, 2001). The study argued that individuals diagnosed with schizophrenia may be at such increased risk of a violent death because of a number of factors:

1 they are likely to live in places such as inner cities where crime is more prevalent;

2 they may have behavioural characteristics such as alcohol or drug abuse that increases the risk;

3 they might provoke the hostility of others because of their psychotic symptoms (such as paranoia);

4 because of their symptoms, they may be less aware of their own safety needs;

5 they may be killed by others with mental health problems with whom they are in contact;

6 they may be more likely to be victims of motiveless killings because of their appearance, which may be unkempt and dirty.

In contrast, tragic and high-profile murders carried out by people with mental health problems have often been used to imply that the community care approach to mental health care is dangerous and has failed (see Focus Point 7.10). However, there is little evidence to support this view. First, studies of murders committed by individuals with mental health problems in the UK

FOCUS POINT 7.10

Do violent acts by individuals diagnosed with schizophrenia imply that care in the community has failed?

Violent or homicidal acts in the community by people with mental health problems tend to receive high-profile treatment in the media. But is there any evidence that the risk of violence by individuals with a diagnosis of schizophrenia has increased with the introduction of care in the community?

The following is an example of how the media portray such incidents.

The failure of care in the community?

Schizophrenic Christopher Clunis knifed musician Jonathan Zito, 27, to death at a London Underground station in 1992. Mr Zito's wife Jayne set up the Zito Trust to campaign on the issue of the release of mentally ill patients.

The Trust says that over 100 people have been killed by care in the community patients in the last five years. It claims that approximately two people every month are murdered because of the country's failure to provide adequate care services.

Failures of the mental health system?

- Jason Mitchell, 25, beheaded his father Robert and strangled pensioners Arthur and Shirley Williams in Bramford in Suffolk in 1994. After being arrested, Mitchell was alleged to have sung 'It's a Wonderful Life' in his police cell.

- John Rous, 47, stabbed unqualified care worker Jonathan Newby to death at a residential care home in Oxford in 1995. Less than an hour earlier he had called the police to warn them he would 'tear out his victim's liver'.

- In 1996 Darren Carr, 26, was jailed for the manslaughter of Susan Hearmon and her daughters Kylie, six, and Anne, four, after he set fire to their house in Abingdon in Oxfordshire. Carr had been detained in a psychiatric hospital before the killing but doctors decided he could be discharged.

● Stephen Laudat, 26, stabbed grandfather Bryan Bennett more than 80 times at a day centre in Stratford in east London in 1994 because he thought his victim was the gang leader Ronnie Kray. The killing came eight months after Laudat had been released from a hospital back into the community. An inquiry found he had not been taking medication to control his actions.

● Anthony Smith, a 24-year-old paranoid schizophrenic, stabbed his mother Gwendoline and 11-year-old half-brother with a Bowie knife at their home in Sandiacre in Derbyshire in 1995. The double killing came one month after Smith had discharged himself from hospital.

The Health Secretary, Frank Dobson, says there will not be a return to the old-style asylums, but mental health campaigners believe there needs to be a massive capital investment into mental health provision to protect the public and the mentally ill.

(BBC News website, 17 January 1998)

Despite the horror depicted in these individual cases, such incidents are still relatively rare given the number of patients diagnosed with schizophrenia who are treated in managed regimes within the community. People diagnosed with schizophrenia are not especially prone to violence and often prefer to be left alone. If people have no record of criminal violence *before* they develop psychotic symptoms and are not substance abusers, they are unlikely to commit crimes *after* they develop psychotic symptoms. Most violent crimes are not committed by people diagnosed with schizophrenia, and most people diagnosed with schizophrenia do not commit violent crimes. However, substance abuse often increases violent behavior,

whether or not the person exhibits psychotic symptoms (see below). If someone with paranoid schizophrenia becomes violent, his or her violence is most often directed at family members and takes place at home. Have a look at the following facts, which are important in assessing the risk to the public posed by individuals diagnosed with schizophrenia who are being treated in the community.

● The number of murders committed by individuals with mental health problems in the UK between 1957 and 1995 has remained at more or less the same level (Taylor & Gunn, 1999).

● Rates of increase in violent crime in Australia between 1975 and 1995 increased at identical rates in both the general population and individuals diagnosed with schizophrenia (Wallace, Mullen & Burgess, 2004).

● In New Zealand between 1970 and 2000, 8.7 per cent of homicides were committed by individuals who were subsequently found unfit to stand trial because of mental health problems. The percentage of homicides committed by individuals with mental health problems fell from 19.5 per cent in 1970 to 5.0 per cent in 2000 (Simpson, McKenna, Moskowitz, Skipworth et al., 2004).

● In an Austrian study between 1975 and 1999, major mental disorders (such as schizophrenia) were found to be associated with an increased likelihood of committing homicide (twofold in males and sixfold in women) (Schanda, Knecht, Schreinzer, Stompe et al., 2004).

● A UK study has indicated that when individuals with mental health problems do commit a homicide, (1) they are likely to be male, (2) they are likely to have a diagnosis of schizophrenia, (3) they are most likely to kill a family member or close friend and (4) they are likely to be indulging in either alcohol or substance misuse at the time of the homicide (McGrath & Oyebode, 2005).

between 1957 and 1995 have remained at more or less the same level (Taylor & Gunn, 1999). Secondly, an analysis of Australian statistics between 1975 and 1995 showed that 21.6 per cent of individuals diagnosed with schizophrenia living in the community were likely to have committed a criminal offence over this period, compared with 7.8 per cent of the general population. In addition 8.2 per cent of individuals diagnosed with schizophrenia were likely to have been convicted of an offence involving violence compared with 1.8 per cent of the general population. However, the rate of increase in convictions over this time was not significantly different between individuals diagnosed with schizophrenia and the general population, suggesting that the introduction of community care had not disproportionately increased the incidence of violent behaviour by individuals with schizophrenia (Wallace, Mullen & Burgess, 2004).

What is of some concern, however, is the apparent prevalence of substance and chemical abuse by individuals suffering psychosis and

living in the community. The lifetime prevalence rate for substance abuse among people diagnosed with schizophrenia is around 50 per cent, and may be significantly higher in those who are homeless (Kosten & Ziedonis, 1997). In their Australian study, Wallace, Mullen and Burgess (2004) found that between 1975 and 1995, substance abuse problems for individuals diagnosed with schizophrenia increased from 8.3 per cent to 26.1 per cent, and significantly higher rates of criminal conviction were found for those with substance abuse problems (68.1 per cent compared to 11.7 per cent). We know that regular use of some substances (such as cannabis: see Focus Point 7.7) can directly increase the risk of developing positive symptoms, and that the use of others (such as cocaine and amphetamines) can exacerbate these symptoms (Laruelle & Abi-Dargham, 1999). The challenge for community care programmes is to tackle what appear to be increasing levels of substance abuse in individuals with psychotic symptoms living in the community, and, in so doing, to decrease the risk of relapse and hospitalization.

SUMMARY

Treating psychotic symptoms is a relatively long-term process. This may require immediate and urgent treatment with antipsychotic drugs to deal with the positive symptoms found during early psychotic episodes, psychological therapies to deal with the longer-term cognitive and behavioural deficits that may restrict full social and occupational functioning, family-based therapies to help maintain a stable, stress-free environment in which the risk of relapse is minimized, and long-term community care to help recovering sufferers with their medication regimes, residential supervision, vocational training and regular access to mental health services. Figure 7.4 provides an example of how the UK National Institute for Clinical Excellence (NICE) recommends different interventions to be considered in planning for recovery from an acute episode of schizophrenia. This demonstrates that long-term treatment has a range of components, including psychological treatments (e.g. CBT and family therapy), plans for supervising the medication regime, and assessing occupational and social functioning. However, there are a range of differing views across the medical, psychological and social spectrum about what is the best approach to take for the long-term treatment of individuals with schizophrenia. Some of these views are controversial, but are worth discussing. Activity Box 7.2 provides an opportunity for you to consider some of these alternative views.

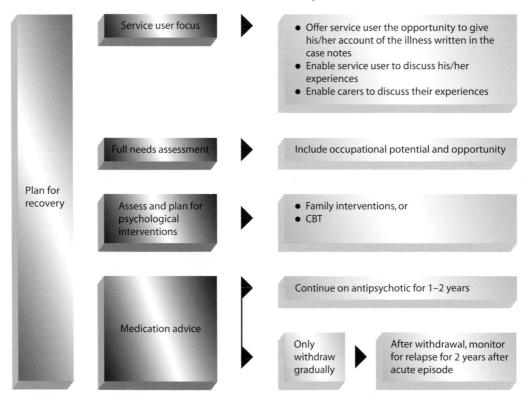

Towards end of acute episode

Plan for recovery

- **Service user focus**
  - Offer service user the opportunity to give his/her account of the illness written in the case notes
  - Enable service user to discuss his/her experiences
  - Enable carers to discuss their experiences

- **Full needs assessment**
  - Include occupational potential and opportunity

- **Assess and plan for psychological interventions**
  - Family interventions, or
  - CBT

- **Medication advice**
  - Continue on antipsychotic for 1–2 years
  - Only withdraw gradually
  - After withdrawal, monitor for relapse for 2 years after acute episode

Figure 7.4
An example of how the UK National Institute for Clinical Excellence (NICE) recommends that acute psychotic episodes should be managed and treated. This shows that longer-term planned treatment can include psychological treatments (CBT, family therapy), long-term medication with support and guidance for this regime, and assessment of occupational potential.
Source: NICE, *Clinical algorithms and pathways to care* (December 2002).

ACTIVITY BOX 7.2

Below is an extract from an article by British psychologist Oliver James that was published in *The Guardian* newspaper in October 2005. You may like to read this with your fellow students and then discuss the issues he raises in relation to the material you have read in sections 7.5 and 7.6 of this chapter.

New research on schizophrenia suggests that the drugs won't always work

Oliver James

Rates of schizophrenia vary as much as 16-fold around the world, as does its course. It is less common in developing nations and tends to last much longer and be more severe in rich, industrialized nations compared with poor, developing ones (even so, about 20% of schizophrenics in developed nations recover completely without taking anti-psychotic drugs). In fact, if you become ill in a developing nation where hardly anyone is treated with drugs, you are 10 times less likely to have any recurrence of the illness – a huge difference, also nothing to do with genes.

What it may have a lot to do with is the administration of drugs (see British psychologist Richard Bentall's book, *Madness Explained*). They have been shown to impede traumatized people from understanding their voices or visions and recovering from them. There is a close relationship between the drug companies and the psychiatric establishment. While it may not be the intention, the establishment explanation of the causes of and solutions to schizophrenia are crucial components in the process of selling drugs. If patients can be persuaded their illness is an unchangeable genetic destiny and that it is a physical problem requiring a physical solution, drug companies' profits will grow. An analysis in *Acta Psychiatrica Scandinavica* by New Zealand psychologist John Read shows those who buy this genetic fairytale are less likely to recover, and that parents who do so are less supportive of their offspring.

The huge importance to drug company profits of the bio-genetic refrain becomes apparent when you learn that most people do not hum along with it. Surveys find that the majority of people mention such environmental factors as trauma, stress and economic hardship as the commonest causes of schizophrenia. It may be seen that the drug companies have an uphill struggle to persuade them otherwise, for which they badly need the help of the psychiatric establishment's towrope. In Read's analysis, letting go of that rope will prevent it strangling the many schizophrenics whose illness has been caused by abuse. Genes may still emerge as a major cause of vulnerability to schizophrenia, as may problems during pregnancy. There is already no question that illicit hallucinogenic drugs are a major reason some vulnerable people become ill. But even if this is true, following Read's important work, it will be hard to ignore its implications.

The Guardian, Saturday 22 October, 2005

Bentall, R.P. (2005). *Madness explained: Psychosis and human nature*. Harmondsworth: Penguin.

Read, J., van Os, J., Morrison, A.P. & Ross, C.A. (2005). Childhood trauma, psychosis and schizophrenia: A literature review with theoretical and clinical implications. *Acta Psychiatrica Scandinavica, 112*, 330–350.

- Given the evidence provided in sections 7.5 and 7.6, how would you evaluate Oliver James's views?
- Is the role of genetic inheritance overemphasized in the explanation and treatment of psychotic symptoms?
- Does the policy of long-term treatment with antipsychotic drugs prevent individuals 'coming to terms' with their delusions and hallucinations as suggested by James?
- Are the symptoms that constitute schizophrenia an 'unchangeable genetic destiny that requires a physical solution' such as drugs?

Remember to make your arguments objective and evidence-based. Support your arguments with facts from empirical studies that are described in Sections 7.5 and 7.6 or are taken from the additional reading material highlighted in those sections.

SELF-TEST QUESTIONS

- Can you describe two types of structured therapeutic environments that were developed for individuals with psychotic symptoms who had been hospitalized?
- What are antipsychotic drugs, how are they thought to deal with psychotic symptoms, and how are they categorized?
- What problematic side effects do antipsychotic drugs have?
- What are the important characteristics of social skills training for individuals diagnosed with schizophrenia?
- What are the different forms of CBT used to treat individuals diagnosed with schizophrenia, and with what particular types of symptoms are they most effective?
- Can you describe a typical family-based intervention for psychosis and the factors that such interventions are designed to address?
- What are the different types of community care programmes provided for individuals diagnosed with schizophrenia, and is there any evidence for their effectiveness in controlling psychotic symptoms?

SECTION SUMMARY

7.6 The Treatment of Psychosis

- Around 81 per cent of those who have had a first psychotic episode will relapse within the following 5 years.

- Hospitalization for schizophrenia in the 1960s–1970s led to the development of structured therapeutic environments for patients such as **milieu therapies** and **token economies**.

- **Electroconvulsive therapy (ECT)** and **psychosurgery** were common forms of treatment for psychosis prior to the development of antipsychotic drugs.

- **Antipsychotic drugs** are relatively successful for treating the positive symptoms of schizophrenia. They are thought to be effective because they reduce excessive levels of dopamine activity in the brain.

- **Social skills training** can be used to help psychosis sufferers to react appropriately in a range of useful social situations.

- **Personal therapy** is a broad-based cognitive behaviour programme designed to help individuals diagnosed with schizophrenia to acquire the skills required to adapt to day-to-day living after discharge from hospital.

- **Cognitive enhancement therapies** are designed to help individuals diagnosed with schizophrenia to address deficits in social cognition (the ability to act wisely in social situations) and neurocognition (memory and attention).

- **Cognitive behaviour therapy (CBT)** for psychotic symptoms helps to address any abnormal attributional processes and information processing and reasoning biases that may give rise to delusional thinking.

- **Family interventions** are designed to educate the family about the nature of psychotic symptoms and how to cope with difficulties that arise from living with someone with a diagnosis of schizophrenia.

- **Assertive community treatment** and **assertive outreach** are forms of community care that help individuals recovering from psychotic symptoms with their medication regimes, psychotherapy, decision-making, residential supervision and vocational training.

7.7 EXPERIENCING PSYCHOSIS REVIEWED

Psychosis is a collection of disparate symptoms that can leave an individual feeling frightened and confused, and specific combinations of symptoms may lead to a diagnosis of schizophrenia. Positive symptoms include major disturbances in thought and language, delusional thinking and sensory hallucinations. The negative symptoms include withdrawal, flat affect, poverty of speech and apathy. These combinations of symptoms also frequently result in a marked inability to undertake normal social and occupational functioning.

The prominent approach to explaining the development of psychotic symptoms is a diathesis-stress one. That is, there is clear evidence for a genetic predisposition to psychotic symptoms, but the symptoms appear to be triggered by experiencing environmental stress. The genetic predisposition does not appear to be a specific one, and is not transmitted through a single gene (Kendler et al., 2000). Nor is the nature of the environmental stressors that may trigger psychotic symptoms fully understood. These may range from stressful life experiences (such as unemployment) (Brown & Birley, 1968), to dysfunctional family environments (where intrafamily communication may be problematic) (Goldstein, 1987), to the hassles and challenges encountered in normal adolescent development (Harrop & Trower, 2001). There is, however, good evidence that many of the symptoms of psychosis are associated with excess brain neurotransmitter activity – especially the neurotransmitter dopamine (Seeman & Kapur, 2001). In this respect, the development of increasingly effective antipsychotic drugs over the past 50 years has meant than many sufferers can lead relatively normal lives without experiencing the disabling positive symptoms that appear to be linked to excess dopamine activity (e.g. disordered speech and thought, hallucinations).

However, after an initial psychotic episode, relapse is the norm rather than the exception and around 50 per cent of sufferers will rarely fully recover from the effects of their symptoms (Wiersma, Nienhuis, Slooff & Giel, 1998). Because of this, long-term care and supervision are required. This means that individuals diagnosed with schizophrenia will often need (1) lifelong medication, (2) individual therapies to deal with their specific cognitive and behavioural deficits (e.g. social skills training, CBT), (3) family interventions designed to ensure a family environment that minimizes stressors, maintains a medication regime and can recognize early signs of relapse, and (4) longer-term community care to provide guidance on decision-making, residential supervision and vocational training and to ensure that a long-term relationship between the individual and mental health services is maintained.

LEARNING OUTCOMES

When you have completed this chapter, you should be able to:

1 Describe the main clinical symptoms of psychosis, its sub-types, the stages through which psychosis develops, and the key features of DSM-IV-TR diagnosis of schizophrenia.

2 Describe and evaluate the main biological theories of the aetiology of psychosis – especially the role of brain neurotransmitters and brain abnormalities.

3 Describe, evaluate and compare the main psychological and sociocultural theories of the aetiology of psychosis.

4 Describe and evaluate the role of familial and psychological factors in relapse following remission.

5 Describe a range of treatments for psychotic symptoms, including biological, psychological, familial and community care interventions.

6 Compare and contrast the different roles played by different interventions in treating symptoms, preventing relapse and providing longer-term care and support.

KEY TERMS

REVIEWS, THEORIES AND SEMINAL STUDIES

Links to Journal Articles

Psychotic Symptoms, Prevalence, Stages and Diagnosis of Schizophrenia

Cantor-Graae, E. & Selten, J.P. (2005). Schizophrenia and migration: A meta-analysis and review. *American Journal of Psychiatry, 162*, 12–24.

Harrop, C. & Trower, P. (2001). Why does schizophrenia develop at late adolescence? *Clinical Psychology Review, 21*, 241–266.

King, M., Nazroo, J., Weich, S., McKenzie, K., Bhui, K. et al. (2005). Psychotic symptoms in the general population of England: A comparison of ethnic groups (The EMPIRIC study). *Social Psychiatry and Psychiatric Epidemiology, 40*, 375–381.

Mueser, K.T. & McGurk, S.R. (2004). Schizophrenia. *Lancet, 363*, 2063–2072.

The Aetiology of Psychosis: Biological Theories

Antonova, E., Sharma, T., Morris, R. & Kumari, V. (2004). The relationship between brain structure and neurocognition in schizophrenia: A selective review. *Schizophrenia Research, 70*, 117–145.

Fergusson, D.M., Horwood, L.J. & Ridder, E.M. (2005). Tests of causal linkages between cannabis use and psychotic symptoms. *Addiction, 100*, 354–366.

Harrison, P.J. & Owen, M.J. (2003). Genes for schizophrenia? Recent findings and their pathophysiological implications. *Lancet, 361*, 417–419.

Niznikiewicz, M.A., Kubicki, M. & Shenton, M.E. (2003). Recent structural and functional imaging findings in schizophrenia. *Current Opinions in Psychiatry, 16*, 123–147.

The Aetiology of Psychosis: Psychological and Sociocultural Theories

Bentall, R.P., Corcoran, R., Howard, R., Blackwood, N. & Kinderman, P. (2001). Persecutory delusions: A review and theoretical integration. *Clinical Psychology Review, 21*, 1143–1192.

Bentall R.P., Kinderman P. & Kaney S. (1994). The self, attributional processes and abnormal beliefs: Towards a model of persecutory delusions. *Behaviour Research and Therapy, 32*, 331–342.

Freeman, D. & Garety, P.A. (2004). Bats amongst the birds (the psychology of paranoia). *Psychologist, 17*, 642–645.

Morrison, A.P. (2001b). The interpretation of intrusions in psychosis: An integrative cognitive approach to hallucinations and delusions. *Behavioural and Cognitive Psychotherapy, 29*, 257–276.

Wahlberg, K.E., Wynne, L.C., Keskitalo, P., Nieminen, P. et al. (2001). Long-term stability of communication deviance. *Journal of Abnormal Psychology, 110*, 443–448.

Wearden, A.J., Tarrier, N. & Barrowclough, C. (2000). A review of expressed emotion research in health care. *Clinical Psychology Review, 20*, 633–666.

The Treatment of Psychosis: Biological Treatments

Goldman-Rakic, P.S., Castner, S.A., Svensson, T.H., Siever, L.J. & Williams, G.V. (2004). Targeting the dopamine D-1 receptor in schizophrenia: Insights for cognitive dysfunction. *Psychopharmacology, 174*, 3–16.

Leucht, S., Barnes, T.R.E., Kissling, W., Engel, R.R., Correll, C. & Kane, J.M. (2003). Relapse prevention in schizophrenia with new-generation antipsychotics: A systematic review and exploratory meta-analysis of randomized controlled trials. *American Journal of Psychiatry, 160*, 1209–1222.

Miyamoto, S., Duncan, G.E., Marx, C.E. & Lieberman, J.A. (2005). Treatments for schizophrenia: A critical review of pharmacology and mechanisms of action of antipsychotic drugs. *Molecular Psychiatry, 10*, 79–104.

The Treatment of Psychosis: Psychological and Family Interventions

Chadwick, P.D.J. & Lowe, C.F. (1990). Measurement and modification of delusional beliefs. *Journal of Consulting and Clinical Psychology, 58*, 225–232.

Dickerson, F.B., Tenhula, W.N. & Green-Paden, L.D. (2005). The token economy for schizophrenia: A review of the literature and recommendations for future research. *Schizophrenia Research, 75*, 405–416.

Hogarty, G.E. & Flesher, S. (1999). Practice principles of cognitive enhancement therapy for schizophrenia. *Schizophrenia Bulletin, 25*, 693–708.

Mueser, K.T., Sengupta, A., Schooler, N.R., Bellack, A.S., Xei, H.Y. et al. (2001). Family treatments and medication dosage reduction in schizophrenia: Effects on patient social functioning, family attitudes, and burden. *Journal of Consulting and Clinical Psychology, 69*, 3–12.

Pilling, S., Bebbington, P., Kuipers, E., Garety, P. et al. (2002). Psychological treatments in schizophrenia: I. Meta-analysis of family intervention and cognitive behaviour therapy. *Psychological Medicine, 2002*, 763–782.

Tarrier, N. & Wykes, T. (2004). Is there evidence that cognitive behaviour therapy is an effective treatment for schizophrenia? A cautious or cautionary tale? *Behaviour Research and Therapy, 42*, 1377–1401.

Wykes, T. & van der Gaag, M. (2001). Is it time to develop a new cognitive therapy for psychosis – Cognitive remediation therapy (CRT)? *Clinical Psychology Review, 21*, 1227–1256.

Community Care

Berzins, K.M., Petch, A. & Atkinson, J.M. (2003). Prevalence and experience of harassment of people with mental health problems living in the community. *British Journal of Psychiatry, 183*, 526–533.

Hiroeh, U., Appleby, L., Mortensen, P.B. & Dunn, G. (2001). Death by homicide, suicide, and other unnatural causes in people with mental illness: A population-based study. *Lancet, 358*, 2110–2112.

Reid, Y., Johnson, S., Bebbington, P.E., Kuipers, E., Scott, H. & Thornicroft, G. (2001). The longer-term outcomes of community care: A 12-year follow-up of the Camberwell High Contact Survey. *Psychological Medicine, 31*, 351–359.

Texts for Further Reading

Bentall, R.P. (Ed.) (2004). *Models of madness: Psychological, social and biological approaches to schizophrenia.* London: Brunner-Routledge.

Bentall, R.P. (2005). *Madness explained: Psychosis and human nature.* Harmondsworth: Penguin.

Green, M.F. (2001). *Schizophrenia revealed: From neurons to social interactions.* New York: W.W. Norton.

Hirsch, S.R. & Weinberger, D.R. (2003). *Schizophrenia.* Oxford: Blackwell Science.

Torrey, F.E. (2001). *Surviving schizophrenia: A family manual.* London: HarperCollins.

RESEARCH QUESTIONS

- The course of schizophrenia appears to be less severe in developing countries than in developed ones. Are the reasons for this related to cultural differences in (1) the support role of the family, (2) beliefs about the origins of psychological disorders or (3) the stigma associated with psychological disorder?

- Why is the reporting of psychotic symptoms almost twice as high in people of African-Caribbean origin in the UK than in whites?

- Studies across a range of countries have shown that immigrant populations have been shown to exhibit significantly higher rates of schizophrenia diagnosis than members of the indigenous population. Why is this?

- Why do individuals diagnosed with schizophrenia have a significantly shorter life span than normal, and tend to die around 10 years earlier than individuals who have never been diagnosed with schizophrenia?

- Why do the large majority of individuals who develop psychotic symptoms show the first signs of symptoms during late adolescence? What is important about this period of life that triggers these symptoms?

- Evidence suggests that there is an important inherited component to psychosis, but what is it that is transmitted genetically that gives rise to psychotic symptoms?

- How is excess dopamine activity involved in the production of psychotic symptoms?

- If antipsychotic drugs have their effect by reducing levels of dopamine activity in the brain, why do these drugs take up to 6 weeks to have an effect on symptoms when we know that such drugs start blocking dopamine receptors almost immediately?

- A diagnosis of schizophrenia is associated with enlarged ventricles in the brain, but is this enlargement a cause of symptoms or simply a consequence of the symptoms?

- A diagnosis of schizophrenia is associated with brain abnormalities in the frontal lobes, the temporal lobes-limbic system and the basal ganglia and cerebellum. However, are the abnormalities a cause of psychotic symptoms or simply a consequence of the disorder?

- Are the brain abnormalities found in individuals diagnosed with schizophrenia a result of *prenatal* abnormal brain development?

- Regular cannabis use has been associated with higher risk for developing psychotic symptoms. Does this reflect a form of 'self-medication', in which individuals may start using cannabis because of a predisposition for psychotic symptoms, or is there a direct causal link between regular cannabis use and the development of psychotic symptoms?

- Are theory of mind (TOM) deficits a contributing factor to the development of paranoid delusions, or do TOM deficits have some broader role to play in generating a range of different symptoms (e.g. thought disorder, negative symptoms)?

- How do high levels of expressed emotion (EE) in the families of individuals diagnosed with schizophrenia contribute to an increased risk of relapse?

CLINICAL ISSUES

- DSM-IV-TR requires the identification of two or more symptoms from a list of five for the diagnosis of schizophrenia. What implications does this have for a conception of schizophrenia as a homogeneous condition?

- The negative symptoms of schizophrenia are often taken as the first signs of relapse, but how cautious should the clinician be in using these symptoms as indicators of schizophrenia when they can be viewed as being on a continuum with normality (e.g. some people are naturally less emotionally responsive, less vocal and less motivated than others)?

- What can be done to ensure that individuals diagnosed with schizophrenia adhere to their long-term medication regimes?

- What are the implications of diagnosing someone with schizophrenia? Is this likely to have a negative effect on their longer-term improvement?

- Token economies on psychiatric wards have been shown to be an effective way of improving psychotic symptoms, alleviating negative symptoms and speeding discharge from hospital. So why has their use in therapeutic setting been in serious decline over the past 20 years?

- Should electroconvulsive therapy (ECT) and psychosurgery still be used in extreme cases, even though the mechanisms by which they may alleviate psychotic symptoms are still relatively unclear?

- Antipsychotic drugs are very effective at alleviating the positive symptoms of schizophrenia, but they also have a number of serious side effects. How should a decision be made to continue or discontinue medication when side effects are apparent, and what alternatives does the clinician have to antipsychotic drugs when treating positive symptoms?

- Is social skills training an effective way to treat individuals diagnosed with schizophrenia? Do social skills, if learned, generalize easily to everyday situations?

- Cognitive behaviour therapy (CBT) for psychotic symptoms appears to be a useful way of treating these symptoms, but is it more or less effective than other forms of treatment?

- Should all family interventions in schizophrenia treatment programmes include behavioural training programmes, or is the communication of information about how families should deal with the disorder sufficient?

- What are the practical problems associated with setting up and managing a community care service for individuals with a diagnosis of schizophrenia? Are such programmes capable of reaching all sufferers within a community?

- Is there any evidence that community care services help to improve the social and occupational functioning of individuals diagnosed with schizophrenia?

- What are the disadvantages of treating individuals diagnosed with schizophrenia in the community?

- Over the past 20–30 years, substance abuse among people diagnosed with schizophrenia has increased significantly. What has contributed to this increase and what can be done to address it?

8 Substance Abuse and Dependency

ROUTE MAP OF THE CHAPTER

This chapter begins by discussing substance abuse and dependency generally, including general diagnostic criteria and prevalence rates. We then look at the specific characteristics of a number of drugs whose use regularly gives rise to abuse and dependency. We examine alcohol and nicotine use in detail, then discuss a range of stimulant, sedative and hallucinogenic drugs. In particular, we review the physical and psychological effects of these drugs, their prevalence of use, the nature of abuse of and dependency on these substances, and the costs of dependency in psychological, physical health and economic terms. The chapter then reviews a developmental model of substance dependency in which the risk factors that contribute to experimentation, regular use and abuse and dependency are considered. Finally, we cover the various types of treatment for substance use disorders and evaluate their success.

My name is Tim and I am from Yorkshire. I had a normal life until I was 12 years old, and then my mother and father started to fight. The fights were very violent and quite frightening; I have since learnt that this was mostly my mother's fault. It became apparent that we were left outside pubs a lot but it seemed normal. My two brothers and I suffered a terrible few years; the scars are still with us.

Our house was sold and we ended up on a bad council estate in Sheffield which has since been knocked down. The violent drinking bouts got worse and I left home although I was 15. I still found a job but suffered terribly over leaving my younger brothers. I found a bedsit and a job and the peace was heavenly. I then moved to Derby to live with my uncle's family and eventually got married to a lovely lady and had two daughters.

My drinking started in Derby. No one thing made me drink but I gradually drank more and more over the years. I started my own catering business and was extremely successful. I employed 65 staff and enjoyed all the benefits of being my own boss. I had money, cars and plenty of time to drink!! I did not know then what would happen because of my drinking. My wife told me about my behaviour but I ignored her and her advice. I would not listen to anyone. Worst of all, I was out on the road driving to my catering sites and drinking all day. I still functioned but I do not know how to this day nor do I know how I kept my licence.

I sold my company and borrowed £100,000 from the bank to buy – yes, you guessed – a pub/restaurant. What a nightmare – my own 'booze' on tap!! Needless to say, the venture was doomed from the start. I drank morning, noon and night and had plenty of friends, or so I thought. Eventually my wife left me and went back to her parents, and I do not blame her.

I went bankrupt and moved to a bedsit once again. I then went on cider and anything else I could get. I had defrauded the Customs and Excise while I was drinking so I ended up in prison for 12 months, which was a disaster. They put me in charge of the officers' mess and bar!!!! Needless to say, I was in seventh heaven and came out a complete wreck and moved from city to city for ten years. I was sacked from numerous chefs' jobs and was in and out of several mental hospitals all over the country. I did stay dry for a while but when my father died I started to drink again and went back to prison as I wanted the peace and friendship I found the first time; however, this was not meant to be and I found it very hard to cope without the booze second time around.

I was begging in Soho when I decided to try and turn my life around. I moved to Leicester where – through Alcoholics Anonymous – I stopped drinking. I did have relapses but following hepatitis, jaundice and a bleeding throat I stopped four and a half years ago. I could not suffer those terrible withdrawals again and I still have the scars of drinking – epilepsy and digestive problems. But I am dry.

TIM'S STORY

Introduction

The term drug can be very loosely defined as any substance, other than food, that affects either our bodies or our minds in some way. Such substances may give us energy, relax us when nervous, change our ways of thinking, distort our perceptions or change our moods. They can, of course, have these effects either for better or for worse, and the short-term benefit of a substance may lead to longer-term physical and mental costs (as the experience of Tim, above, clearly demonstrates). Nevertheless, in most Westernized cultures, drugs are almost a normal part of daily life. We use drugs to wake up in the morning (caffeine in tea and coffee), to stay alert during the day (nicotine in cigarettes), to reduce pain (aspirin and paracetamol), to control our physical shape (dieting pills) and to relax (alcohol, sleeping pills). While the use of drugs in this way may seem to provide benefits to daily living, there are a number of problems that arise out of this culture:

1 While many of these substances have short-term benefits, they may have longer-term negative physical and psychological effects with persistent use (e.g. alcohol).

2 Many people become either psychologically or physically addicted to a drug and continue to use it when it no longer has the original benefits (e.g. sleeping pills and dieting pills).

3 Many people move on from legal drugs to taking illegal substances, many of which are physically damaging and highly addictive, and frequently blight social, educational and occupational performance (e.g. cocaine, heroin, solvents and hallucinogens such as LSD).

The abuse and misuse of drugs has become one of society's biggest problems. Substance abusers often pay a high personal cost for their dependency in terms of failed relationships, ruined careers, poor health and premature death. Society also pays a high cost in terms of lost productivity and the strain such abuse puts on national health resources. The World Health Organization (WHO) estimated that in 2005: (1) there were 76.3 million people worldwide with alcohol use disorders; (2) at least 15.3 million people have drug use disorders; (3) there were 1.1 thousand million smokers in the world, with smoking estimated to cause 90 per cent of all instances of lung cancer in men, and 70 per cent in women; and (4) 3.1 per cent of the global population were consuming drugs in the late 1990s, 147 million using cannabis, 33 million using amphetamine-type stimulants (including 7 million using the stimulant Ecstasy, MDMA), 13 million taking cocaine and 13 million abusing opiates, including heroin. Globally, 0.4 per cent of deaths can be attributed to illicit drug use, and 4 per cent of the burden of disease and 3.2 per cent of all deaths globally can be attributed to alcohol alone (World Health Report, 2002).

Equally alarming is the frequency of drug use in adolescents and schoolchildren. Usage and dependency at such an early age may well lead to lifelong dependency and health problems. In the USA, over 50 per cent of adolescents have tried illegal drugs at least once (Johnston, O'Malley & Bachman, 2001). In the UK, surveys indicate that 38 per cent of 15-year-olds have used an illegal drug in the year prior to the survey, and 23 per cent in the previous month (Department of Health, National Report, 2004). In addition, once someone has used one illegal drug, a majority will go on to abuse more than one (e.g. cocaine, cannabis, crack cocaine) (Tsuang, Lyons, Meyer, Doyle et al., 1998), and multiple drug abuse significantly increases other risks to well-being such as being in a car crash, mental health problems, violent behaviour and promiscuous sexual behaviour (Greenwood, White, Page-Shafer, Bein et al., 2001).

The significant risk to physical health, mental health, social integration and productivity posed by substance abuse and dependency makes it quite a suitable subject for prevention and treatment. If we look at *Tim's Story* at the beginning of this chapter, we can see that his alcohol abuse and dependency resulted in failed relationships, a ruined career and business, criminality, physical health problems such as hepatitis, jaundice and epilepsy, and mental health problems requiring hospitalization. The remainder of this chapter will look at some of the physical and psychological factors that lead to dependency on, and abuse of, a range of substances, and how these problematic behaviour patterns can be treated. These factors are summarized at the outset in Table 8.1. First, however, it is necessary to describe some of the terminology commonly used in this area of psychopathology and to look at the more general criteria for diagnosing and describing substance abuse and dependency.

Plate 8.1
Ex-Manchester United and Northern Ireland footballer George Best had a lifelong struggle with alcohol dependency. He suffered many of the problems associated with alcohol abuse, including relationship problems, poor physical health including a liver transplant, a stunted professional career (he ended his playing career for Manchester United at age 26 years), and a premature death aged 59 because of his alcohol-related health problems. Like most people with a substance use disorder, his life centred entirely around his substance dependency. He is famously remembered for saying, 'I spent a lot of money on booze, birds and fast cars – the rest I just squandered!'

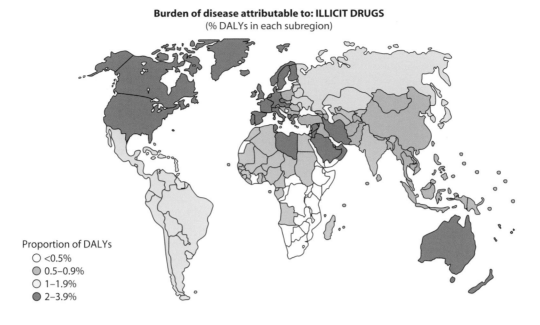

Burden of disease attributable to: ILLICIT DRUGS
(% DALYs in each subregion)

Proportion of DALYs
○ <0.5%
◉ 0.5–0.9%
○ 1–1.9%
● 2–3.9%

Figure 8.1
This World Health Organization (WHO) map shows the percentage of people in different areas of the world who die prematurely or who become disabled prematurely because of illicit drug use (DALY = Disability Adjusted Life Years)

Source: World Health Organization (2006).

Table 8.1 *Substance abuse and dependency: summary*

DISORDER AND LIFETIME PREVALENCE RATES	DEFINITION	MAIN DSM-IV-TR DIAGNOSTIC FEATURES	KEY FEATURES	THEORIES OF AETIOLOGY (BOTH ABUSE AND DEPENDENCY)	MAIN FORMS OF TREATMENT (BOTH ABUSE AND DEPENDENCY)
SUBSTANCE ABUSE **Lifetime prevalence rates:** No systematic data – see sections on individual substances for prevalence of use data	A pattern of drug or substance use that occurs despite knowledge of the negative effects of the drug, but has not progressed to full-blown dependency	Recurrent substance use resulting in impaired social and occupational functioning Using substance in physically hazardous circumstances (e.g. driving) Recurrent substance-related legal problems Continued substance use despite personal problems	Failure to meet many normal daily obligations because of the drug Using the substance in ways that may be physically hazardous Legal problems resulting from behaviour caused directly or indirectly by the drug Continuing to use the drug even though it causes personal and social problems	Availability of and easy access to the drug Familial factors (use by other family members and parental neglect or abuse) Peer group influences Effects of media and advertising Mood alteration effects Self-medication	Self-help groups Drug-prevention schemes Residential rehabilitation Aversion therapy Behavioural self-control training (BSCT) Controlled drinking Cognitive behaviour therapy (CBT)

Table 8.1 *(Cont'd)*

DISORDER AND LIFETIME PREVALENCE RATES	DEFINITION	MAIN DSM-IV-TR DIAGNOSTIC FEATURES	KEY FEATURES	THEORIES OF AETIOLOGY (BOTH ABUSE AND DEPENDENCY)	MAIN FORMS OF TREATMENT (BOTH ABUSE AND DEPENDENCY)
SUBSTANCE DEPENDENCY **Lifetime prevalence rate 5.1%**	A cluster of cognitive, behavioural and physiological symptoms indicating that the individual continues use of the substance despite significant substance-related problems	Evidence for tolerance and withdrawal effects Unsuccessful effects to quit or cut down Significant time spent obtaining and using the substance Social and occupational impairment Continued substance use despite knowledge of its negative physical and psychological effects	Characterized by drug tolerance effects (need for increased amounts to achieve the same effects) Withdrawal symptoms indicate that the body requires the drug in order to maintain physical stability Lack of the drug causes a range of negative and aversive physical effects Preoccupation with attempts to obtain the drug Frequent unsuccessful attempts to cut down or quit the drug Frequent unintentional overuse Abandoning or neglecting important life activities because of the drug (e.g. neglecting family, work, education) Highly comorbid with other psychiatric disorders	Expectations and beliefs about the drug Cultural factors Genetic predispositions Effect of cognitive deficits on judgement and decision-making Effects of comorbid psychiatric diagnoses Poverty	Family and couple therapy Detoxification Drug maintenance therapy

8.1 DEFINING AND DIAGNOSING SUBSTANCE ABUSE AND DEPENDENCY

Traditionally, pathology associated with substance and drug use falls into two categories: substance abuse and substance dependency. These categories are still not unambiguously defined. However, Table 8.2 indicates that substance abuse can be loosely defined as the use of a substance despite its negative or adverse consequences, and substance dependency as the continued use of the substance *despite* its problematic consequences. When the person's 'normal' body state is the drugged state (so that the body requires the substance to feel normal), this is known as **addiction**,

> **Addiction** When a person's 'normal' body state is the drugged state (so that the body requires the substance to feel normal).

Table 8.2 *Basic terminology in the study and treatment of substance abuse and dependency*

Terminology	Definition
Addiction	Drug use to the point where the body's 'normal' state is the drugged state (so the body requires the drug to feel normal). *Addiction is a term that is rarely used nowadays because it implies that drug dependency is primarily a physical one, whereas in reality it is a complex mix of physical and psychological dependency*
Substance dependency	A cluster of cognitive, behavioural and physiological symptoms indicating that the individual continues use of the substance despite significant substance-related problems (DSM-IV-TR, p. 192)
Psychological dependency	The user's tendency to alter his or her life because of the drug, and to centre his or her activities around the drug
Craving	A strong subjective drive to use the substance
Tolerance	The need for greater amounts of the drug or substance to achieve intoxification (or the desired effect) or a markedly diminished effect with continued use of the same amount of the drug or substance (DSM-IV-TR, p. 192)
Withdrawal	A maladaptive behavioural change, with physiological and cognitive concomitants, that occurs when blood or tissue concentrations of a substance or drug decline in an individual who has previously maintained prolonged heavy use of the substance or drug (DSM-IV-TR, p. 194)
Substance	A drug of abuse, a medication, or a toxin
Substance abuse	A maladaptive pattern of substance use manifested by recurrent and significant adverse consequences related to the repeated use of substances (but not applicable to nicotine and caffeine use – see diagnostic criteria for substance abuse)

Craving The strong subjective drive that addicts have to use a particular substance.

and *craving* is the term used for the strong subjective drive that addicts have to use the substance. Substance dependency has not been easy to define, and there are still many arguments about what constitutes dependency on a drug or substance.

The term *psychological dependency* is used when it is clear that individuals have changed their lives to ensure continued use of the drug, that all their activities are centred on the drug and its use, and that this leads to neglect of other important activities such as work, social and family commitments. While the physical consequences of substance abuse and dependency can be devastating (in terms of their negative effects on physical health and longevity), the challenges for psychopathology are arguably to prevent substance abuse, to develop interventions to help alleviate abuse and dependency, and to understand the conditions under which some individuals develop substance abuse and dependency. DSM-IV-TR has defined both substance abuse and dependency in behavioural terms rather than physical terms. That is, the problem lies not in the drug itself but in how individuals use the drug and its negative effects on their daily lives.

Table 8.3 shows the DSM-IV-TR criteria for *substance dependence*. Dependency is characterized by both tolerance and withdrawal effects. *Tolerance* refers to the need for increased amounts of the substance in order to achieve similar effects across time. *Withdrawal* indicates that the body requires the drug in order to maintain physical stability, and lack of the drug causes a range of negative and aversive physical consequences (e.g. anxiety, tremors and, in extreme cases, death). Behavioural features of dependency include: (1) unsuccessful attempts to cut down on use of the drug; (2) a preoccupation with attempts to obtain the drug (e.g. theft of money to buy illegal drugs, driving long distances late at night to buy alcohol, multiple visits to doctors to obtain prescription drugs); (3) unintentional overuse, where people find they have consumed more of the substance than they originally intended (e.g. ending up regularly drunk after only going out for a quick drink after work); and (4) abandoning or neglecting important life activities because of the drug (e.g. failing to go to work because of persistent hangovers, neglecting friendships, relationships, child care and educational activities). It is also important to emphasize at this early stage that substance dependency is a *chronic relapsing condition*, in which substance users find their habits hard to eliminate, and it is almost normal following treatment for substance dependency to be associated with multiple relapses. We will discuss the conditions that lead to this syndrome in more detail in section 8.5.

Substance abuse can be considered as a pattern of drug or substance use that occurs despite knowledge of the negative effects of the drug,

Psychological dependence When individuals have changed their life to ensure continued use of a particular drug such that all their activities are centred on the drug and its use.

Substance dependence A maladaptive pattern of substance use, leading to clinically significant impairment or distress.

Tolerance The need for increased amounts of a substance in order to achieve similar effects across time.

Withdrawal Where the body requires the drug in order to maintain physical stability, and lack of the drug causes a range of negative and aversive physical consequences (e.g. anxiety, tremors and, in extreme cases, death).

Substance abuse A pattern of drug or substance use that occurs despite knowledge of the negative effects of the drug, but where use has not progressed to full-blown dependency.

Table 8.3 *DSM-IV-TR diagnostic criteria for substance dependency*

A maladaptive pattern of substance use, leading to clinically significant impairment or distress, as manifested by three (or more) of the following, occurring at any time in the same 12-month period:

(1) tolerance, as defined by either of the following:

   (a) a need for markedly increased amounts of the substance to achieve intoxication or desired effect

   (b) markedly diminished effect with continued use of the same amount of the substance

(2) withdrawal, as manifested by either of the following:

   (a) the characteristic withdrawal syndrome for the substance

   (b) the same (or closely related) substance is taken to relieve or avoid withdrawal symptoms

(3) the substance is often taken in larger amounts or over a longer period than was intended

(4) there is a persistent desire or unsuccessful efforts to cut down or control substance use

(5) a great deal of time is spent in activities necessary to obtain the substance (e.g. visiting multiple doctors or driving long distances), use the substance (e.g. chain smoking), or recover from its effects

(6) important social, occupational, or recreational activities are given up or reduced because of substance use

(7) the substance use is continued despite knowledge of having a persistent or recurrent physical or psychological problem that is likely to have been caused or exacerbated by the substance (e.g. current cocaine use despite recognition of cocaine-induced depression, or continued drinking despite recognition that an ulcer was made worse by alcohol consumption).

but where use has not progressed to full-blown dependency (see Table 8.4). Characteristic of substance abuse is: (1) failure to meet many normal daily obligations because of the drug (e.g. repeated absences from work); (2) using the substance in ways which may be physically hazardous (e.g. drinking and driving); (3) legal problems resulting from behaviour caused directly or indirectly by the drug (e.g. being arrested for being drunk and disorderly); and (4) continuing to use the drug even though it causes a range of personal and social problems and difficulties (e.g. quarrels with spouse or physical or verbal fights). Definitions of dependency and abuse differ primarily in terms of severity, with substance dependency being more severe than substance abuse – particularly in terms of tolerance and withdrawal effects and in the degree of disruption caused by the substance to daily living.

Apart from these general criteria for substance dependency and abuse, DSM-IV-TR provides diagnostic criteria for a list of more specific substance use disorders. A summary of these is given in Table 8.5, together with some examples of the drugs that are abused. Finally, the term *substance use disorder (SUD)* is often used in the literature to indicate that an individual has at least one substance disorder diagnosis, whether it is a general diagnosis of substance dependency or abuse, or a more specific substance category disorder.

Substance use disorder (SUD) Where an individual has at least one substance disorder diagnosis, whether it is a general diagnosis of substance dependency or abuse, or a more specific substance category disorder.

SELF-TEST QUESTIONS

- Can you define the terms craving, tolerance and withdrawal?
- What are the main diagnostic criteria for substance abuse and substance dependency?

Table 8.4 *DSM-IV-TR diagnostic criteria for substance abuse*

A   A maladaptive pattern of substance use leading to clinically significant impairment or distress, as manifested by one (or more) of the following, occurring within a 12-month period:

   (1) recurrent substance use resulting in a failure to fulfill major role obligations at work, school, or home (e.g. repeated absence or poor work performance related to substance use; substance-related absences, suspensions, or expulsions from school; neglect of children or household)

   (2) recurrent substance use in situations in which it is physically hazardous (e.g. driving a car or operating a machine when impaired by substance use)

   (3) recurrent substance-related legal problems (e.g. arrests for substance-related disorderly conduct)

   (4) continued substance use despite having persistent or recurrent social or interpersonal problems caused or exacerbated by the effects of the substance (e.g. arguments with spouse about consequences of intoxication, physical fights)

B   The symptoms have never met the criteria for substance dependency for this class of substance.

Table 8.5 *Specific substance abuse disorders*

Diagnostic category	Examples of abused substances
Alcohol-related disorders	Alcohol
Amphetamine (or amphetamine-like) related disorders	Amphetamine, dextroamphetamine, metamphetamine ('speed'), appetite suppressants ('diet pills')
Caffeine-related disorders	Coffee, tea, caffeinated soda, over-the-counter analgesics, cold remedies, weight loss aids
Cannabis-use disorders	Cannabis, hashish, 'grass'
Cocaine-related disorders	Cocaine, 'crack cocaine'
Hallucinogen-related disorders	Lysergic acid diethylamide (LSD), morning glory seeds, mescaline, MDMA 'Ecstasy'
Inhalant-related disorders	Aliphatic and aromatic hydrocarbons found in substances such as petrol, glue, paint thinners, butane gas lighter refills, disposable cigarette lighters and aerosol sprays generally
Nicotine-related disorders	Cigarettes, chewing tobacco, snuff, pipes and cigars
Opiod-related disorders	Morphine, heroin, codeine, hydromorphine, methadone, oxycodone, meperidine, fentanyl
Phencyclidine (or phencyclidine-like) related disorders	Phencyclidine, ketamine, cyclohexamine, dizocilpine
Sedative-, hypnotic-, or anxiolytic-related disorders	Benzodiazepines, carbamates, barbiturates (sleeping medications) and anti-anxiety medications generally

SECTION SUMMARY

8.1 Defining and Diagnosing Substance Abuse and Dependency

- **Substance dependency** is characterized by both tolerance and withdrawal effects.

- **Substance abuse** is a pattern of substance use that occurs despite knowledge of the negative effects of the substance, but where it has not yet progressed to full-blown dependency.

- **Substance use disorder** (**SUD**) is used to indicate that an individual has at least one substance diagnosis disorder.

8.2 THE PREVALENCE AND COMORBIDITY OF SUBSTANCE USE DISORDERS

Drug use and dependency is highly prevalent in the general populations of many countries, although rates of substance use disorders will vary markedly across countries depending on the legal, moral and religious attitudes to drugs in those countries. The lifetime prevalence rate for substance dependency has been calculated at 5.1 per cent in the US Epidemiologic Catchment Area Study. Warner, Kessler, Hughes, Anthony et al. (1995) reported that amongst

Table 8.6 *Comorbidity of substance use disorders with other psychiatric disorders*[a]

Psychiatric disorder	% of individuals also diagnosed with a substance use disorder (SUD)
Bipolar disorder	60.7
Major depression	18
Obsessive-compulsive disorder (OCD)	32.8
Panic disorder	35.8
Schizophrenia	47
Bulimia nervosa	28
Personality disorders	42

[a] Rate of substance use disorders in the general population is around 5%.

Source: data taken from Brooner, King, Kidorf, Schmidt et al. (1997); Fischer, Owen & Cuffel (1996); Regier, Farmer, Rae, Locke et al. (1990); Zanarini, Frankenburg, Dubo, Sickel et al. (1998); Lacey (1993).

individuals in the USA aged between 15 and 54 years, 51 per cent had used illegal drugs, non-medical prescription drugs (e.g. sedatives, tranquillizers) or inhalants at some point in their lives, and 15.4 per cent had done so in the previous 12 months.

A particularly important aspect of substance use disorders is that they are highly comorbid with a range of other Axis I and Axis II disorders. There is an especially strong association of lifetime mood and anxiety disorders with substance use disorders (Merikangas, Mehta, Molnar, Walters et al., 1998). Studies suggest significantly higher levels of substance use disorders in individuals with bipolar disorder, major depression, anxiety disorders such as obsessive-compulsive disorder and panic disorder, schizophrenia, bulimia nervosa and personality disorders than in the general population (see Table 8.6). The high level of comorbidity between substance use disorders and other Axis I and II psychological disorders has generated a number of hypotheses about why substance use disorders occur so regularly in the context of other psychological disorders. One view is that substance abuse and dependency may be a risk factor for the later development of a psychiatric illness (e.g. Wylie, Scott & Burnett, 1995). However, the majority of current evidence is consistent with the view that psychiatric and psychological disorders usually predate substance abuse and dependency (Merikangas, Mehta, Molnar, Walters et al., 1998; Abraham & Fava, 1999). A recent UK study indicated that the risk for substance abuse attributable to prior psychiatric illness was 14.2 per cent, compared to a risk for psychiatric illness attributable to substance abuse of only 0.2 per cent (Frisher, Crome, MacLeod, Millson et al., 2005). This suggests a 'self-medication' effect, in which individuals with an established psychiatric disorder start using substances to alleviate the negative emotional and behavioural effects of the disorder (Mueser, Drake, & Wallach, 1998; but see Chapter 7, Focus Point 7.7 for an account of a causal relationship between cannabis use and psychotic symptoms).

SELF-TEST QUESTIONS

- How are substance use disorders and other psychiatric disorders related? Is one a risk factor for the other?

SECTION SUMMARY

8.2 The Prevalence and Comorbidity of Substance Use Disorders

- The lifetime prevalence rate for substance dependency is around 5 per cent.

- Substance use disorders are **highly comorbid** with a range of other Axis I and Axis II disorders.

8.3 CHARACTERISTICS OF SPECIFIC SUBSTANCE ABUSE DISORDERS

In this chapter we need to look closely at the nature of different substance abuse disorders. We will be discussing in some detail both alcohol abuse and dependency and nicotine abuse and dependency because of the close links that use of these substances have with normal everyday life. We will then turn to look at the characteristics of three specific groups of substances: *stimulants* (e.g. cocaine, amphetamines and caffeine), *sedatives* (e.g. opiates, such as heroin, and barbiturates) and *hallucinogens* (e.g. LSD and other hallucinogenics, cannabis and MDMA, better known as Ecstasy). In each case, we will discuss the characteristics of the substance, how it has its physical and psychological effects, its prevalence of use, the nature of abuse of and dependency on the substance, and finally, the costs of dependency in psychological, physical health and economic terms.

Stimulants Substances that increase central nervous system activity and increase blood pressure and heart rate.

Sedatives Central nervous system depressants which slow the activity of the body, reduce its responsiveness, and reduce pain tension and anxiety. This group of substances includes alcohol, the opiates and their derivatives (heroin, morphine, methadone and codeine), and synthesized tranquillizers such as barbiturates.

Hallucinogens Psychoactive drugs which affect the user's perceptions. They may either sharpen the individual's sensory abilities or create sensory illusions or hallucinations.

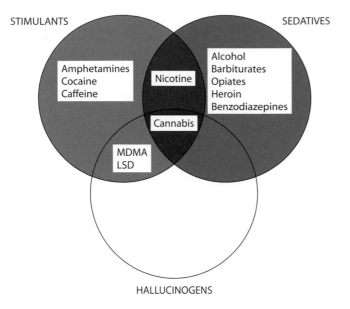

STIMULANTS

SEDATIVES

Amphetamines
Cocaine
Caffeine

Nicotine

Alcohol
Barbiturates
Opiates
Heroin
Benzodiazepines

Cannabis

MDMA
LSD

HALLUCINOGENS

Figure 8.2
A drug chart showing how the different substances described in this chapter overlap across categories.

It is important to be aware that relatively few of the drugs under discussion fit simply and easily into any one of these drug categories: many have multiple effects, and some overlap between categories. That is why each textbook you read on this topic appears to have a different form of categorization! However, Figure 8.2 provides a drug chart which maps how the different substances described in this chapter overlap across categories. This shows that nicotine can act as both a stimulant and a depressant, hallucinogenic drugs such as LSD and MDMA have both hallucinogenic and stimulant properties, and cannabis is probably the most difficult to categorize because it can have a variety of psychological and physical effects.

SELF-TEST QUESTIONS

● Can you name the main groupings into which drugs of abuse are categorized?

8.3.1 Alcohol

Alcohol is one of the most commonly used drugs in a very large number of countries worldwide (see Focus Point 8.1). In most countries it is also legal and can be easily purchased and consumed. In the USA, over 65 per cent of people will at some time consume a drink that contains alcohol (Centers for Disease Control and Prevention, 2002); in the UK this figure rises to 92 per cent of males and 86 per cent of females (WHO, 2004). However, patterns of alcohol consumption appear to have become ever more problematic, with surveys in 2000 suggesting that 26 per cent of the UK population could be labelled as *hazardous drinkers* – that is, they have 5 or more standard drinks (males) or 3 or more standard drinks (females) on a typical drinking day (WHO, 2004). In many countries, there has

Alcohol A colourless volatile liquid compound which is the intoxicating ingredient in drinks such as wine, beer and spirits.

Hazardous drinkers Individuals who have 5 or more standard drinks (males) or 3 or more standard drinks (females) on a typical drinking day.

FOCUS POINT **8.1**

Alcohol (depressant)

Also known as: Booze.

What it looks like and how it's taken: Drunk as 'alcopops', spirits, beers and wines.

Immediate effects: Enters the bloodstream within 30 minutes and then travels straight to the brain. Reduces inhibitions and increases sense of relaxation. Each unit takes an hour for the body to process.

Short-term risks: Hangover including dehydration, headache, nausea and depression. Intoxication can lead to aggressive/irrational behaviour and accidents.

Long-term risks: Regular heavy drinking can cause stomach disorders, cancer of mouth, throat and gullet, liver cirrhosis, brain damage, high blood pressure, problems with the nervous system, sexual and mental health problems, and family and work problems.

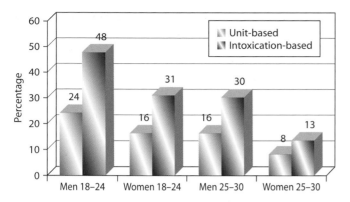

Figure 8.3 *Binge drinking in the UK.*
Percentage of men and women in the UK who reported drinking more than 8 units of alcohol (men) and 6 units of alcohol (women) on an average drinking day in the previous week (unit-based). The intoxication-based definition is based on self-reported frequency of having felt 'very drunk' a minimum of once or twice a month in the last 12 months.
Source: data produced by the Institute of Alcohol Studies, 2005.

also been an alarming increase in the number of younger people regularly drinking alcohol. In 2002, 61 per cent of English schoolchildren below the age of 11 years reported having consumed alcohol (WHO, 2004). What is known as 'heavy episodic' drinking or **binge drinking** has also reached epidemic levels in many European countries. Binge drinking refers to a high intake of alcohol in a single drinking occasion. There is no single definition of binge drinking, but in the UK it is normally defined as taking at least 8 units (males) or 6 units (females) of alcohol in a single day. In the UK, 58 per cent of men and 34 per cent of women report binge drinking at least once a month (WHO, 2004), and binge drinking is particularly problematic in teenagers and younger adults. Figure 8.3 shows that almost half of males between the ages of 18 and 24 surveyed in the UK reported binge drinking in the previous week.

Binge drinking   A high intake of alcohol in a single drinking occasion.

Alcohol has its physical and psychological effects when its main constituent, **ethyl alcohol**, is absorbed into the bloodstream through the lining of the stomach and intestine. Alcohol then reaches the brain and central nervous system via the bloodstream. At first, alcohol acts to relax the individual by influencing the receptors associated with the neurotransmitter GABA. This facilitates this neurotransmitter's inhibitory function by preventing neurons firing and making the drinker feel more relaxed (Harvey, Foster, MacKay, Carroll et al., 2002). Initially this makes the drinker more talkative, friendly, confident and happy. As more alcohol is absorbed into the central nervous system, the second stage of intoxication makes the drinker become less able to make judgements; talk is less coherent, memory is affected, and behaviour may switch from being relaxed and happy to emotional and aggressive. Finally, the physical effects of alcohol intoxication

Ethyl alcohol   The main constituent of alcohol.

include motor coordination difficulties (in balance and walking), slowed reaction times and blurred vision. This course of the effect of alcohol is known as **biphasic drug effect**, because the initial effects act as a stimulant (making the drinker reactive and happy), but the later effects act as a depressant (making the drinker sluggish and experience negative emotions).

Biphasic drug effect   Where the initial effects of a drug may act as a stimulant (e.g. alcohol making the drinker reactive and happy), but the later effects act as a depressant (making the drinker sluggish and experience negative emotions).

We can see how drinking alcohol can be appealing to many people because of its initial effects (i.e. it helps alleviate stress after a busy day at work, increases sociability, reduces inhibitions, etc.). However, many of the so-called effects of alcohol are actually mythical and result from a drinker's *expectations* about alcohol's effects rather than its real effects. For example, in a couple of classic studies, Lang, Goeckner, Adessor and Marlatt (1975) and Wilson and Lawson (1976) gave participants a disguised non-alcoholic beverage when they were expecting alcohol. They subsequently reported increases in sexual arousal and aggression, even though they had become less physiologically aroused. Expectations about the effects of alcohol appear to play an important role in drinking behaviour, with positive expectancies about the effects of alcohol being a significant predictor of its use (Sher, Wood, Wood et al., 1996).

Plate 8.2
Although alcohol initially makes the drinker more talkative, friendly and confident, continued consumption acts as a depressant which makes the drinker sluggish and causes motor coordination problems including problems in balance, blurred vision, slowed reaction times and uncoordinated speech.

ACTIVITY BOX 8.1

How many units of alcohol do you consume in a week?

What is a unit of alcohol?

One unit of alcohol is 10 ml (1 cl) by volume, or 8 g by weight, of pure alcohol. For example:

- One unit of alcohol is about equal to:
  - half a pint of ordinary strength beer, lager or cider (3–4 per cent alcohol by volume), or
  - a small pub measure (25 ml) of spirits (40 per cent alcohol by volume), or
  - a standard pub measure (50 ml) of fortified wine such as sherry or port (20 per cent alcohol by volume).
- There are one and a half units of alcohol in:
  - a small glass (125 ml) of ordinary strength wine (12 per cent alcohol by volume), or
  - a standard pub measure (35 ml) of spirits (40 per cent alcohol by volume).

A more accurate way of calculating units is as follows. The percentage alcohol by volume (% abv) of any drink equals the number of units in one litre of that drink. For example:

- Strong beer at 6% abv has 6 units in one litre. If you drink half a litre (500 ml) – just under a pint – then you have had three units.
- Wine at 12% abv has 12 units in one litre. If you drink a quarter of a litre (250 ml) – two small glasses – then you have had three units.

Check your weekly alcohol levels

Unless you're teetotal, you probably drink more than you think. The medically recommended units of alcohol per week are 14 for women and 21 for men. How do you compare? Take a minute to try this test. Enter the number of units you consume each day for a week. The chart will then tell you whether the number of units you have consumed in a week is above or below the recommended level.

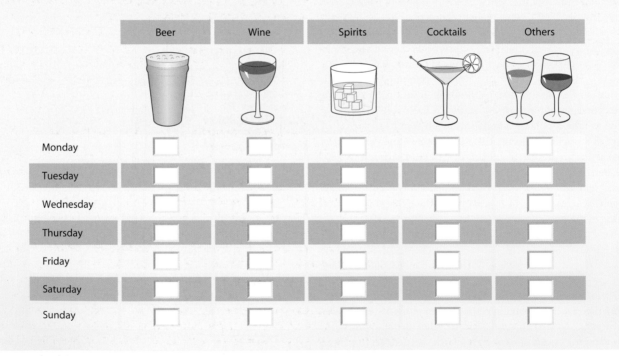

8.3.1.1 Alcohol Abuse and Dependency

Because of its short-term positive psychological and physical effects, and probably equally as much because of the positive cognitive expectations that have built up around the consumption of alcohol in a number of societies, it has come to be seen by many as a way of enduring life's problems and relieving tension. However, because of its availability, many come to use alcohol to the point where it begins to have significant negative effects on both physical and psychological health. With increased use, the body begins to show tolerance to alcohol and the drinker has to consume ever larger amounts to achieve the same effects. The long-term physical effects of heavy alcohol consumption include withdrawal symptoms when the body is deprived of alcohol. These include restlessness, inability to sleep, anxiety and depression, muscle tremors and rises in blood pressure and temperature. Following withdrawal after extended heavy drinking over a number of years, the drinker may experience *delirium tremens (DTs)*, where he or she becomes delirious, experiences unpleasant hallucinations and exhibits shaking and muscle tremors. Longer-term negative physical effects of heavy alcohol consumption include hypertension, heart failure, stomach ulcers, cancer, cirrhosis of the liver, brain damage (including shrinkage of the frontal lobes) and early dementia.

> **Delirium tremens (DTs)**   The effects of withdrawal after extended heavy drinking over a number of years where the drinker may become delirious, experiences unpleasant hallucinations, and exhibits shaking and muscle tremors.

Furthermore, many of the effects of long-term alcohol dependency are similar to malnutrition. This is because alcohol contains calories but is entirely devoid of any required nutrients. This leads drinkers to feel full but take in little or no nutrition. As a consequence, vitamin and mineral deficiencies can lead to dementia and memory disorders, such as *Korsakoff's syndrome*. One indirect physiological risk associated with heavy drinking in women is *foetal alcohol syndrome*, in which heavy drinking by mothers during pregnancy can cause a whole range of physical and psychological abnormalities in the child, including physical deformities, heart problems, stunted growth, hyperactivity and intellectual disability (Hankin, 2002). Finally, the important physical effects of alcohol abuse and dependency discussed in this section substantially reduce longevity in drinkers. The number of alcohol-related deaths in the UK has more than doubled between 1979 and 2000 (Baker & Rooney, 2003), suggesting that long-term drink-related disorders are a significant cause for concern.

> **Korsakoff's syndrome**   A syndrome involving dementia and memory disorders which is caused by long-term alcohol abuse and dependency.

> **Foetal alcohol syndrome**   Where heavy drinking by a mother during pregnancy can cause a whole range of physical and psychological abnormalities in the child, including physical deformities, heart problems, stunted growth, hyperactivity and intellectual disability.

The diagnostic criteria for alcohol dependency and abuse are based on the criteria for substance dependency and abuse given in Tables 8.3 and 8.4. *Alcohol dependency* is supported specifically by evidence of tolerance effects and withdrawal symptoms that develop within 4–12 hours of restricted consumption. However, many individuals with alcohol dependency may never experience withdrawal once a pattern of compulsive drinking develops in which their whole life centres around obtaining and consuming alcohol. *Alcohol abuse* has fewer symptoms than dependency and is usually less severe, but work performance and child care or household responsibilities may be significantly affected either by the after-effects of drinking (e.g. hangovers) or by being intoxicated while trying to perform these functions. Interestingly, a US national survey indicated that workplace alcohol use and impairment directly affected an estimated 15 per cent of the US workforce, with 1.6 per cent working under the influence of alcohol and 9.2 per cent working with a hangover (Frone, 2006). Alcohol abuse is also characterized by drinkers putting themselves at physical risk while intoxicated, including drink driving and becoming engaged in violent arguments (see section 8.3.1.4 below). Such individuals will also continue to drink when they know that their drinking is a cause of significant social or interpersonal problems (such as their physical abuse of family members, or problems in their relationship with a partner).

8.3.1.2 Prevalence of Use

The lifetime prevalence rate for alcohol dependency and abuse is around 15 per cent, with almost twice as many men as women being diagnosed (Kessler & Zhao, 1999; Kessler, McGonagle, Zhao, Nelson et al., 1994). The rate of alcohol dependency in the general population at any one time is around 5 per cent (DSM-IV-TR). There are some ethnic differences in prevalence rates, with white Americans being more likely to be diagnosed than black Americans, and rates of diagnosis are also inversely related to educational level. Alcohol dependency and abuse are frequently associated with abuse of other drugs and are highly comorbid with other psychiatric disorders. For example, heavy alcohol use is often part of *polydrug abuse*, or abuse of more than one drug at a time, and over 80 per cent of alcohol abusers are smokers (Shiffman, Fischer, Paty, Gnys et al., 1994). Finally, alcohol dependency and abuse are frequently comorbid with a range of other psychological disorders, including personality disorders, mood disorders, anxiety disorders and schizophrenia (Kessler, Crum, Warner, Nelson et al., 1997). Alcohol appears to play an important role in around 25 per cent of all suicides, and is associated with suicide completion and use of more lethal weapons during suicide attempts (Sher, 2006).

> **Polydrug abuse**   Abuse of more than one drug at a time.

8.3.1.3 The Course of Alcohol Use Disorders

Alcohol use disorders often pass through stages of heavy and regular drinking, then on to alcohol abuse, and finally end up in many cases as alcohol dependency disorder (Jellinek, 1952). These stages can be fairly clearly defined in *Tim's Story* given at the beginning of this chapter. However, patterns of alcohol use do vary considerably, and a systematic decline into alcohol dependency is not the only outcome of heavy drinking. For example, around 50 per cent of people who are diagnosed with alcohol abuse do *not* go on to show any signs of alcohol dependency five years later (Hasin, van Rossem, McCloud & Endicott, 1997), and alcohol abuse is only diagnosed in around 67 per cent of individuals diagnosed with alcohol dependency (Hasin & Grant, 2004). Also, as we have seen earlier, many people exhibit highly fluctuating drinking patterns by binge drinking on some days of the week, but abstaining on others.

There are also some important gender differences in the course of alcohol use disorders. There is usually a shorter period between onset of heavy drinking and a diagnosis of alcohol abuse in women than in men (Mezzich, Moss, Tarter, Wolfenstein et al., 1994), and women tend to begin drinking later in life than men, develop dependency at a later age, and are more likely to have a stressful life event precipitating heavy drinking than men (Gomberg, 1997). Women are more likely than men to combine alcohol with other

FOCUS POINT 8.2

Treating alcohol dependency

Like most of the substance use disorders, alcohol dependency is difficult to treat successfully. This is because of a number of factors:

1 Many people dependent on alcohol use it as a way of coping with life stresses and difficulties, and this can easily lead to relapse when stress is experienced during or after treatment.

2 Alcohol dependency is often comorbid with other psychological disorders, which makes treatment of the dependency more problematic.

3 Alcohol is often part of *polydrug abuse*, where those dependent on alcohol also abuse other drugs as well, and the use of one drug (e.g. nicotine) is likely to trigger the use of another (e.g. drinking alcohol).

Treatments for alcohol dependency take a variety of different forms, and some of them are described here. The most successful forms of treatment, however, are usually *multifaceted approaches* that combine a number of individual therapies into a single coherent programme for the client.

Self-help groups
The most commonly sought sources of help for alcohol-related problems are community self-help groups such as Alcoholics Anonymous (AA) (www.alcoholics-anonymous.org.uk/). AA describes what it calls 12 steps that alcoholics should achieve during the recovery process (www.alcoholics-anonymous.org.uk/geninfo/05steps.shtml). Its *12-step programme* has been shown to achieve long-term abstinence in around 25 per cent of participants and a significant decrease in alcohol consumption in 78 per cent (Ouimette, Finney & Moos, 1997). Many of the beneficial effects of self-help groups such as AA may be attributable to clients replacing social networks of drinking friends with other AA members.

Motivational enhancement therapy (MET)
This form of cognitive behaviour therapy places the responsibility for change on clients and attempts to provide them with a range of skills to deal with their drinking (Miller & Rollnick, 2002). The therapist provides individual feedback to clients on the effects of their drinking (such as the effects on other family members), explores the benefits of abstinence, and then designs a treatment programme specifically tailored to the individual's own needs. MET is one of the most successful and cost-effective therapeutic approaches for alcohol dependency. Studies suggest that around 50 per cent of clients report that both levels of drinking and alcohol-related problems decreased significantly in the 12 months following treatment (UKATT Research Team, 2005).

Social behaviour and network therapy (SBNT)
This is a treatment aimed at mobilizing and developing a positive social network for the client that will facilitate a change in drinking behaviour (Copello, Orford, Hodgson, Tober et al., 2002). The therapist works with both the client and those in the client's social network who are willing to support the client's efforts to change (such as family, friends or work colleagues). The aim is to create a supportive social network that will sustain abstinence beyond the therapy period. Controlled outcome studies suggest that SBNT also has similar success rates to MET (UKATT Research Team, 2005).

Pharmacotherapy
Drugs have been developed that attempt to block alcohol–brain interactions that might promote alcohol dependency. One of these is the drug *naltrexone*, which helps prevent relapse in those recovering from alcohol dependency. *Acamprosate* has also been shown to be successful as a treatment, with outcome studies suggesting that it enabled twice as many clients to remain abstinent 1 year later than did psychosocial therapy alone (Swift, 1999). In addition, some drugs, such as *ondansetron*, have been shown to be effective with early-onset alcoholics who began drinking heavily before 25 years of age (Johnson, Roache, Javors, DiClemente et al., 2000).

Brief interventions
Many people with alcohol-related problems frequently receive brief periods of treatment, such as counselling (five or fewer sessions). Such treatments are usually conducted by GPs, nursing staff or trained counsellors and consist mainly of communicating alcohol-relevant health advice, providing information on the negative consequences of drinking, and offering practical advice on community resources that might help achieve moderation or abstinence. Controlled trials in the USA and Canada have demonstrated that this approach significantly reduced alcohol-related problems and increased use of health care services (Fleming, Barry, Manwell, Johnson et al., 1997; Israel, Hollander, Sanchez-Craig, Booker et al., 1996). Brief interventions are particularly valuable for helping those in the early stages of alcohol use who are at risk of developing full-blown alcohol use disorders.

substances – particularly tranquillizers and barbiturates – to drink alone, and to seek treatment for their dependency earlier. At present there is very little evidence to determine how these gender differences are caused, but they could easily result from differences in social role or from biological factors to do with the lower physiological tolerance rates of females to alcohol.

Finally, there are a number of risk factors for alcohol use disorders that might give us some insight into why some individuals develop such problematic dependencies. Alcohol use disorders are predicted by a number of factors, including:

1 a family history of alcoholism, suggesting that there may be a genetic component to the disorder (see section 8.4.3.1), or that the offspring model their drinking behaviour on that of their parents, or that parental drinking gives rise to stressful childhood experiences that precipitate drinking in the offspring (Sher, 1991; Windle & Searles, 1992);

2 long-term negative affect, including neuroticism and depression (Sher, Trull, Bartholow & Vieth, 1999);

3 a diagnosis of childhood conduct disorder (Johnson, Arria, Borges, Ialongo et al., 1995; Rohde, Lewinsohn & Seeley, 1995);

4 experiencing life stress and particularly childhood life stressors (Wilsnack, Vogeltanz, Klassen & Harris, 1997);

5 holding beliefs that drinking alcohol will have a favourable outcome (e.g. that it reduces tension or makes social interactions easier) (Greenbaum, Brown & Friedman, 1995).

While there is no indication that these risk factors act *causally* to precipitate alcohol use disorders, they do suggest a syndrome that consists of alcohol use in the context of negative affect (including depression) and negative and stressful life experiences. This pattern is consistent with the fact that over 30 per cent of individuals diagnosed as alcohol dependent have other comorbid psychiatric disorders (Farrell, Howes, Bebbington, Brugha et al., 2003).

8.3.1.4 The Costs of Alcohol Use Disorders

Apart from the obvious personal and physical costs attributable to alcohol use disorders, there is also a range of broader social costs. In economic terms, alcohol-related problems cost the US economy around $185 billion in 1998 in terms of lost productivity, health care and other costs (National Institute of Alcohol Abuse and Alcoholism, 2001). Annual alcohol-related costs of crime and public disorder in the UK in 2003 were estimated at £7.3 billion and workplace costs at £6.4 billion. Costs to the UK National Health Service alone are £1.7 billion per annum, including 1 in 26 NHS bed days for alcohol-related health problems and up to 35 per cent of all accident and emergency attendance costs (WHO, 2004). Accidents and crime are two of the biggest social problems associated with alcohol misuse. Drink driving accounts for 20 per cent of all driver road deaths in the UK, and a significantly higher percentage in the US (Kennedy, Isaac & Graham, 1996), and level of alcohol use is one of the best predictors of an individual being involved in recurrent motor vehicle crashes (Fabbri, Marchesini, Dente, Iervese et al.,

2005). Alcohol also increases the risk of death from boating accidents (Smith, Keyl, Hadley, Bartley et al., 2001) and drownings (Bell, Amoroso, Yore, Senier et al., 2001). In a review of the relationship between drinking and health in a range of countries worldwide, Norstrom and Ramstedt (2005) found that per capita alcohol consumption in a country significantly predicted (1) mortality from liver cirrhosis and other alcohol-related diseases, (2) mortality from accidents and homicide and (3) death from suicide.

Finally, alcohol use has come to be closely associated with criminal and illegal activities, and with violence and abuse. Alcohol consumption has been found to be significantly related to violent crime (Friedman, Glassman & Terras, 2001), rape and sexual assault (Merrill, Thomsen, Gold & Milner, 2001) and child molestation (Aromacki & Lindman, 2001). Table 8.7 lists some of the statistics relating to the social costs of alcohol use in the UK. Many of these are concerned with criminal behaviour including illegal drink driving.

Table 8.7 *The social costs of alcohol in the United Kingdom*

- 38.5% of individuals attending a hospital Accident & Emergency department are misusers of alcohol.

- 6% of road traffic accidents involve illegal alcohol levels.

- 15% of road deaths occur when someone driving was over the legal limit.

- 20% of drivers killed on the roads have illegal blood alcohol levels.

- 30% of pedestrians killed on the road are over the legal driving limit (and this figure rises to 75% between the hours of 10 p.m. and 4 a.m.).

- 6% of all deaths in the UK in 2001 were alcohol-related deaths.

- 60% of binge drinkers admit to criminal and/or disorderly behaviour during or after drinking alcohol.

- 39% of binge drinkers aged 18–24 had committed a criminal offence in the previous 12 months.

- 43% of individuals who committed suicide in Northern Ireland in 1997 were diagnosable with alcohol use disorders.

- 47% of offenders in 2001 were perceived to be under the influence of alcohol by their victims in violent incidents.

- 30–60% of child protection cases involve alcohol.

Source: WHO Global Status Report on Alcohol (2004).

SUMMARY

Alcohol use disorders cause significant short-term and long-term impairment, including impairment to occupational, educational and social functioning, and they have important detrimental long-term effects on health. Alcohol use disorders are also closely associated with a range of social problems, such as drink driving, violent crime and criminal activities generally. It is still unclear why some people acquire an alcohol dependency, although alcohol use disorders are highly co-morbid with other psychiatric disorders – including other substance abuse disorders. This suggests that, for many people, alcohol use may become a means of coping with adverse or challenging life experiences because most alcohol users have an expectancy that drinking alcohol will have beneficial effects (e.g. reduce tension or make social interactions easier).

SELF-TEST QUESTIONS

- How is binge drinking defined, and how prevalent is it amongst young people?
- How does alcohol make the drinker feel relaxed and less stressed?
- What are the main symptoms of withdrawal from alcohol in heavy drinkers?
- Can you name the main criteria for alcohol abuse and alcohol dependency?
- What are the important gender differences in the course of alcohol use disorders?
- What are the main risk factors for alcohol use disorders, and can any of them be identified as causal factors?
- Can you list the economic and health costs of alcohol use disorders?

8.3.2 Nicotine

Nicotine is the addictive agent found in tobacco and is normally taken as cigarettes, chewing tobacco, snuff, and in pipes and cigars. Smoking tobacco actually delivers nicotine to the brain faster than if it were intravenously injected, so it is a highly efficient and effective way of experiencing the drug. Nicotine has a number of physical effects. First, it acts as a stimulant by increasing blood pressure and heart rate. Paradoxically, it also has a calming effect by lowering self-reported stress levels and reducing the smoker's feelings of anxiety and anger (Warburton, 1992). In survey studies, smokers usually endorse statements such as 'Smoking relaxes me when I am upset or nervous' and 'Smoking calms me down' (Ikard, Green & Horn, 1969). However, nicotine does have a number of important negative effects. Smokers regularly report adverse moods when they have not smoked recently, and feelings of stress and irritability are commonly experienced in the periods between cigarettes or when attempting to quit smoking (Hughes, Higgins & Hatsukami, 1990).

These characteristics suggest that nicotine is an addictive drug that develops physical and psychological dependency. First, there is growing evidence to suggest that nicotine has its effects by releasing dopamine in the mesolimbic system of the brain (Stahl, 1996). The effects of dopamine release in this brain region are to elevate mood, decrease appetite and enhance cognitive functioning generally, and these are consequences that are similar to the effects of other addictive drugs such as cocaine (Stein, Pankiewicz, Hanch, Clo et al., 1998). Second, the reported calming effect of nicotine may simply represent the reversal of the unpleasant abstinence or withdrawal effects experienced if the smoker has not taken nicotine in the recent past (Parrott, 1999). Interestingly,

> **Nicotine**   The addictive agent found in tobacco; it acts as a stimulant by increasing blood pressure and heart rate.

FOCUS POINT **8.3**

Nicotine (stimulant/depressant)

Also known as: (Contained in tobacco) fags, ciggies.

What it looks like and how it's taken: Cigarettes, pipes, cigars, loose tobacco, chewing tobacco. Is smoked or chewed.

Immediate effects: Acts fast, first increasing alertness then producing a sense of relaxation.

Short-term risks: Nicotine dependency can develop quite rapidly and regular smokers often feel anxious and irritable if unable to smoke. Smoking can restrict growth in young people.

Long-term risks: Other chemicals in tobacco cause lung cancer and stomach diseases, heart disease, circulation problems, wrinkled skin and premature ageing.

when asked to report their moods over a normal day, smokers report significant fluctuations in moods, with reports of normal moods during smoking and increased stressful and irritable periods between cigarettes (Parrott, 1994). Smokers' stress levels appear to be similar to those of non-smokers only just after they have smoked, and become worse than those of non-smokers during periods of abstinence or between cigarettes (Parrott & Garnham, 1998). This suggests that smokers need to smoke simply to experience positive mood levels similar to those of non-smokers, and that the stress and irritability they experience between cigarettes are withdrawal symptoms caused by their dependency on nicotine (Schachter, 1978). We will return to some of these issues later.

8.3.2.1 Prevalence of Use

After alcohol, nicotine is the second most widely used drug worldwide. About one-third of the adult global population smokes; among teenagers aged 13–15 years, about 1 in 5 smokes worldwide. While the rate of smoking is gradually falling in developed nations, it is rising by 3.4 per cent per year in the developing world (WHO, 2004). Evidence suggests that around 50 per cent of those who start smoking in their adolescent years will go on to smoke for at least a further 15–20 years. Figure 8.4 shows that in the UK the number of smokers has decreased steadily since the 1970s, although around 25 per cent of adults aged 16 or over still reported smoking regularly in 2005. Surveys in the USA also report a gradual decrease in tobacco use since the 1970s, with a similar figure of 25 per cent of the population still smoking regularly (Schmitz, Schneider & Jarvik, 1997). The level of use in smokers is also still unacceptably high, with male smokers reporting an average of 15 cigarettes a day, compared to 13 a day for women (UK Government Statistics, 2005). These figures are worrying when we come to look at the adverse long-term health consequences of smoking (see section 8.3.2.4). It is worth noting that 68 per cent of smokers in the UK

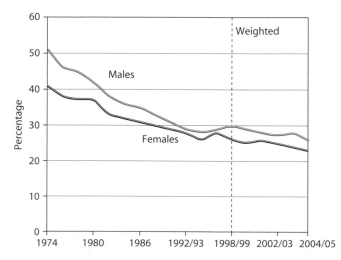

Figure 8.4 *Smoking prevalence in the UK.*
Percentage of adults who smoked cigarettes in the UK between 1974 and 2005.
Source: UK Government Statistics (2005).

said they wanted to give up, but 55 per cent said it would be difficult to go without a cigarette for a day. One of the main DSM criteria for substance dependency is repeated unsuccessful attempts to control use of the substance.

8.3.2.2 Nicotine Abuse and Dependency

The diagnostic criteria for nicotine abuse and dependency are based primarily on those for substance abuse and dependency given in Tables 8.3 and 8.4. When taken for the first time, nicotine may cause nausea and dizziness, and it may have a more intense effect when taken first thing in the morning. However, with repeated use, these effects become significantly weaker as a tolerance to the drug builds up. Abstinence or restricted access to nicotine produces a well-defined withdrawal syndrome. This consists of dysphoric or depressed mood, insomnia, irritability, frustration, anger, anxiety, difficulty concentrating, restlessness and impatience, decreased heart rate, and increased appetite or weight gain. A heavy smoker can exhibit these symptoms after only a few hours' voluntary or enforced abstinence (such as on an airplane journey).

It is estimated that around 80–90 per cent of regular smokers meet the diagnostic criteria for nicotine dependency. This is associated with a number of additional characteristics, such as (1) a greater level of difficulty in quitting, (2) smoking soon after waking, (3) smoking when ill, (4) difficulty refraining from smoking and (5) smoking more in the morning than the afternoon (DSM-IV-TR, p. 266). Nicotine dependency is also found to be comorbid with a range of other psychiatric disorders, with estimates of between 55 and 90 per cent of individuals with other psychiatric disorders smoking, compared to around 25–30 per cent of the general population (DSM-IV-TR).

8.3.2.3 Why Do People Smoke?

So why do so many people become addicted to a drug as potentially dangerous as nicotine? Any answer to this question has to consider why people *start* smoking, why they *continue* to smoke – even when they are aware of the health risks – and why they find it so *difficult to quit*.

First, most smokers start smoking during childhood and early adolescence, and the age at which smoking begins is decreasing – especially among young women (Youth Risk Behavior Survey, 1997). There is clear evidence that young people are socially motivated to take up smoking (Allbutt, Amos & Cunningham-Burley, 1995), but this only rarely takes the form of deliberate 'pressure' or 'persuasion' by others (Lucas & Lloyd, 1999; Schofield, Pattison, Hill & Borland, 2001). In most cases young people appear to take up smoking in order to conform with group norms – that is, they can make themselves appear more like others in the group by conforming to behaviours that are typical in the group, such as smoking (Schmitt, Branscombe & Kappen, 2003). This being the case, smoking will be facilitated in groups that have smoking as a central feature of their identity, and new members of that group will start smoking in order to *self-categorize* themselves as members of the group. Schofield, Pattison, Hill and Borland (2001) found that particular group labels (such as 'rebels', 'illegal drug users', 'motorbike riders') were associated with extensive

FOCUS POINT **8.4**

Quitting smoking

As we have already noted, smokers find it extremely hard to quit the habit – even though they may be fully aware of the health implications of their habit, and even when they themselves are already suffering from smoking-related diseases. Since around 80–90 per cent of all smokers would meet DSM-IV-TR criteria for substance dependency, successfully treating nicotine dependency is likely to need a range of approaches, including psychological and pharmaceutical.

Smoking is difficult to treat because

1 smokers are constantly suffering nicotine withdrawal symptoms when not smoking, and this drives the craving for further cigarettes;

2 smokers come to use cigarettes as a way of dealing with any negative mood (not just those associated with withdrawal), so any life problems that cause negative affect will also trigger the desire to smoke.

For these reasons, treatment programmes for smokers tend to have poor success rates and high relapse rates, and only around 10–20 per cent of those who try to quit on their own are still abstinent a year later (Lichtenstein & Glasgow, 1992). There are some important predictors of whether an attempt to quit will fail; these include: (1) a diagnosis of major depression (Glassman, 1993) – 50 per cent of smokers who make repeated unsuccessful attempts to quit can be diagnosed with major depression; (2) regular bouts of negative mood which increase cigarette cravings; and (3) whether the person has to spend periods of time in environments where smoking is common and cigarettes are readily available (e.g. pubs and bars).

Some of the main forms of intervention for smoking are described below.

Nicotine replacement therapy (NRT)

This type of therapy aims to replace the nicotine from cigarettes by means of skin patches, chewing gum, lozenges, inhalators or nasal sprays. Preliminary studies suggest that NRT is significantly more effective than a placebo, and around 17 per cent of people using NRT have fully abstained for 12 months following the treatment (National Institute for Clinical Excellence, 2002).

Bupropion

This mild antidepressant drug acts as a selective inhibitor of dopamine and noradrenaline reuptake and is thought to act directly on the brain pathways involved in dependency and withdrawal. Bupropion is significantly more effective than a placebo control, and 19 per cent of those taking the drug had not smoked in the 12 months following the treatment (National Institute for Clinical Excellence, 2002).

Aversion therapy

This treatment attempts to replace the pleasant feelings associated with smoking a cigarette with negative consequences such as feeling ill or nauseous. One form of aversion therapy is known as *rapid smoking*, where smokers puff on a cigarette roughly every 4–5 seconds until they feel ill and cannot take anther puff (Spiegler & Guevremont, 2003). This type of treatment is known to reduce craving but has had limited success at controlling actual smoking behaviour (Houtsmuller & Stitzer, 1999).

Cognitive behaviour therapy (CBT)

Because depression and negative mood appear to be factors that are regularly associated with failure to quit smoking, recent treatments have adapted CBT for depression for use in smoking cessation programmes. In this case, CBT is used to help smokers develop alternative strategies for dealing with depression and negative mood that do not involve a return to smoking. Such interventions have been shown to produce higher rates of abstinence than standard health education interventions (Hall, Reus, Munoz, Sees et al., 1998).

Complementary therapies

Two forms of complementary therapy frequently used by smokers in order to try to quit are *hypnotherapy* and *acupuncture*. There is some evidence that hypnotic and suggestion-based approaches do yield higher rates of abstinence relative to waiting-list and no treatment controls, but there is little systematic evidence to suggest that hypnotherapy is more effective than equivalent placebos (Green & Lynn, 2000; Villano & White, 2004) – so those 'Stop smoking in one session' signs outside your local holistic health centre might be somewhat misleading! There is some evidence that compared with control participants, acupuncture can help smokers to reduce their levels of smoking over a number of years (He, Medbo & Hostmark, 2001). However, there is little more than anecdotal evidence that acupuncture is an effective means of quitting smoking (Villano & White, 2004).

smoking, and the degree of smoking determined how strongly an individual identified with that group. In such groups, in-group favouritism is also expressed by the sharing of cigarettes, and smoking is used to cement friendships and to indicate commitment to the group (Stewart-Knox, Sittlington, Rugkasa, Harrisson et al., 2005).

These findings suggest that smoking is not just a simple dependency used to change a physical and psychological state but has a complex social function – especially during early social development. Another important factor that influences young people to start smoking is *advertising*. Many countries have now banned explicit advertising of cigarettes. However, tobacco companies are still able to advertise implicitly through sponsorship of major public events, and are able to advertise their products explicitly in many developing countries. Studies suggest that advertising increases children's awareness of smoking and encourages them to take up the behaviour (While, Kelly, Huang & Charlton, 1996). Even in countries where there is a partial ban on tobacco advertising, adolescents' smoking behaviour is linked to market exposure (Braverman & Aaro, 2004) and to smoking images found in fashion, entertainment and gossip magazines (Carson, Rodriguez & Audrain-McGovern, 2005).

Secondly, when people have started smoking, what makes them continue to smoke, even though they may be well aware of the negative health implications of smoking? A number of theorists have argued that persistent smoking is a learned habit that is maintained by a number of rewarding or reinforcing consequences. O'Leary and Wilson (1975) argued that the central nervous system (CNS) stimulant properties of nicotine mean that smokers feel the post-cigarette benefits of increased concentration and better cognitive performance (Wesnes & Warburton, 1983), and these consequences of smoking reinforce the act of smoking. However, these seem rather weak rewards for maintaining a life-threatening activity.

More recently, theories of the maintenance of smoking have looked towards the stress-reducing effects of smoking as a possible reinforcer (Schachter, 1982; Parrott, 1998, 1999). However, nicotine is not a natural stress reliever – it is, as we have already noted, a CNS stimulant. So why do smokers report feeling more relaxed after smoking? Parrott (1998, 1999) has argued that as time since the last cigarette increases, nicotine withdrawal symptoms start to take hold, and the smoker becomes increasingly nervous, irritable and lacking in concentration. Smoking a cigarette then generates feelings of relaxation, pleasure and improved concentration as nicotine levels increase and normal psychological functioning is restored.

This suggests that mood modulation is an important part of nicotine dependency, and cigarette smoking may become a conditioned response to *any form of stress*, not just stress caused by nicotine withdrawal. This model explains not only why smoking becomes an addictive activity, but also why relief from stress and negative mood plays such an important role in maintaining smoking. For example, (1) relapse during attempts to quit smoking frequently occurs under conditions of high stress (Shiffman, 1982); (2) nicotine dependency is related to the number of adverse childhood experiences and the incidence of depression in young adults (Anda, Croft, Felitti, Nordenberg et al., 1999); and (3) individuals with depression or anxiety develop nicotine dependency more rapidly than others (Kinnunen, Doherty, Militello & Garvey, 1996). However, we must be clear that these so-called stress-relieving benefits of smoking experienced by smokers may be deceptive. As we mentioned earlier, smokers' stress levels appear to be similar to those of non-smokers only just after having smoked (Parrott & Garnham, 1998), so smokers need to smoke simply to experience positive mood levels similar to non-smokers. In addition, prospective studies have shown that smoking at age 18 years increases the risk of an anxiety- or depression-based disorder later in life, suggesting that the effects of smoking are far from simply palliative (McGee, Williams, Poulton & Moffitt, 2000).

8.3.2.4 The Costs of Nicotine Use

Like many addictive drugs, arguably the main costs of nicotine dependency are those to physical health. Smoking is the single largest preventable cause of disease and premature death in the world (WHO, 2004), and it is a significant factor in heart disease, stroke, chronic lung cancer, and cancer of the larynx, oesophagus, mouth, bladder, cervix, pancreas and kidneys. It is estimated that between 1950 and 2000, 60 million people worldwide have died from nicotine-related diseases (Peto, 1994). In the UK, over 300,000 patients are admitted to NHS hospitals every year due to smoking-related diseases (Royal College of Physicians, 2002). It is also estimated that half of all teenagers who are currently smoking will die from diseases caused by tobacco if they continue to smoke. One quarter will die before they reach 70 years of age and will lose, on average, 21 years of life (Peto, 1994).

The economic cost of tobacco-related health problems is staggering, with the US public health service estimating a cost of $50 billion a year for the treatment of smoking-related diseases and $47 billion a year in lost earnings and productivity. In the UK, the treatment of smoking-related disorders costs the NHS around

Plate 8.3
Young people are rarely pressurized into using drugs by their peers. They will usually start using a drug in order to self-categorize themselves as a member of a particular group.

£1.4–1.5 billion a year, including £127 million to treat lung cancer alone (Parrott, Godfrey, Heather, Clark et al., 2006).

Finally, the health hazards associated with smoking extend beyond those who smoke. Cigarettes give off smoke that contains a complex mix of thousands of chemicals, many of which can have toxic effects if inhaled. Such *passive smoking* from *second-hand smoke*, of course, represents a health risk to those non-smokers who share environments with smokers. Just 30 minutes of exposure to secondhand smoke is enough to reduce blood flow to the heart, and non-smokers who are exposed to secondhand smoke in the home have a 25 per cent increased risk of heart disease. In particular, passive smoking is a substantial danger to health in the case of babies and young children, causing increases in respiratory infections and asthma attacks (Cowley, 1992; Skorge, Eagen, Eide, Gulsvik et al., 2005). Across the UK as a whole, it is estimated that passive smoking at work is likely to be responsible for the deaths of 2 employed people each working day (617 deaths a year). Passive smoking at home accounts for another 2,700 deaths in persons aged 20–64 years and 8,000 deaths among people over 65 years (Jamrozik, 2005).

> **Passive smoking**   The breathing in of air that contains other people's smoke.

> **Second-hand smoke**   Environmental tobacco smoke that is inhaled involuntarily or passively by someone who is not smoking.

SUMMARY

....

It is estimated that 80–90 per cent of regular smokers meet the diagnostic criteria for nicotine dependency. Smoking appears to be maintained by the smoker's need to reverse the unpleasant nicotine withdrawal effects that are experienced between cigarettes or during abstinence. Eventually, many smokers come to use cigarettes as a response to any form of stress or negative affect (such as depression). Nicotine dependency does not have many of the short-term costs associated with alcohol dependency (such as impairment of occupational and social functioning), but it does have significant medium- to long-term health costs, and is the single largest cause of premature death worldwide.

SELF-TEST QUESTIONS

- What are the main physical effects of nicotine?
- Can you describe the main features of the nicotine withdrawal syndrome?
- Can you explain why people start and continue to smoke even though smoking has important negative health consequences?
- What are the main risks of smoking to physical health?

8.3.3 Stimulants

Stimulants are substances that increase central nervous system activity and increase blood pressure and heart rate. As a result, they facilitate alertness, provide feelings of energy and confidence, and speed up thinking and behaviour. One of the drugs we have already discussed – nicotine – has stimulant effects. In this section, we will discuss three more stimulant drugs, namely, cocaine, amphetamine and caffeine. The popular recreational drug MDMA (3, 4-methylenedioxymethamphetamine) – better known as Ecstasy – is also a stimulant similar to amphetamine, but it has hallucinogenic effects and will be discussed later in this chapter (see Focus Point 8.8).

8.3.3.1 Cocaine

Cocaine is a natural stimulant derived from the coca plant of South America. After it has been processed, cocaine is an odourless white powder that can be injected, snorted or, in some forms (e.g. crack cocaine), smoked. When used for recreational purposes it is usually snorted and absorbed into the bloodstream through the mucus membrane of the nose. The 'rush' caused by a standard dose of cocaine takes approximately 8 minutes to take effect and lasts for about 20 minutes. The rush often brings feelings of euphoria and has its initial effects on the brain to make users feel excited and energized. After these initial effects, the drug then affects other parts of the central nervous system to produce increased alertness, arousal and wakefulness. The main effects of cocaine are caused by the drug blocking the reuptake of dopamine in the brain (see Figure 8.5). This facilitates neural activity and results in feelings of pleasure and confidence (Volkow, Wang, Fischman, Foltin et al., 1997).

> **Cocaine**   A natural stimulant derived from the coca plant of South America which, after processing, is an odourless, white powder that can be injected, snorted or, in some forms (e.g. crack cocaine), smoked.

In the early years of the twentieth century, many people viewed cocaine as a drug with a number of positive attributes. The fictional character Sherlock Holmes used it to relieve pain, Sigmund Freud began using it to reduce depression, and it was even used in the original Coca-Cola recipe until 1903 – so it was assumed that its benefits outweighed its costs. However, during the 1970s and 1980s, use of cocaine as a recreational drug became widespread. During this time, it became clear that cocaine had many negative effects, including tolerance, and was associated with severe withdrawal symptoms. High doses of the drug cause *cocaine intoxication*, where the individual begins to feel anxious, tense or angry, has impaired judgement, and may have psychotic and hallucinogenic episodes. The physical effects of intoxication may include radical changes in blood pressure, perspiration or chills, nausea or vomiting, cardiac irregularities, confusion, and even seizures or coma (DSM-IV-TR, p. 245). Chronic use results in tolerance, with the user taking larger and larger doses to achieve the same effects. Such chronic use may cause changes in personality, long-term irritability, paranoid thinking, disturbances in eating and sleeping, memory deficits and significantly increased risk of strokes (Satel & Edell, 1991; Lundqvist, 2005).

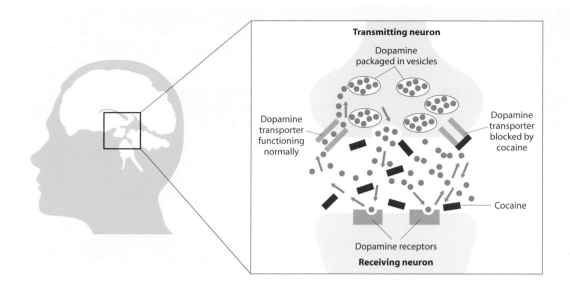

Figure 8.5 *The neural effects of cocaine.*
Cocaine appears to have its effects on a neural system in a region of the brain called the *ventral tegmental area (VTA)*. Nerve cells originating in the VTA extend to the region of the brain known as the *nucleus accumbens*, one of the areas of the brain which mediates feelings of pleasure. In normal circumstances dopamine is released by a neuron into the synapse where it can bind with dopamine receptors on neighbouring neurons. Normally dopamine is then recycled back into the transmitting neuron by a specialized protein called the *dopamine transporter*. If cocaine is present, it attaches to the dopamine transporter and blocks the normal recycling process. This results in a buildup of dopamine in the synapse which contributes to the pleasurable effects of cocaine.

Cocaine can also be taken in two other forms. In the 1970s, cocaine was relatively expensive and was known as the 'celebrity drug'. However, the synthesizing of cocaine into other forms led to a huge increase in use during the 1970s. First, cocaine can be ingested by *free-basing*. This is where a purer cocaine alkaloid is separated by heating the processed cocaine and inhaled by smoking. This is rapidly absorbed and reaches the brain in just a few seconds. It produces an intense but brief 'high', followed by restlessness and discomfort. Currently, many people use a form of free-base cocaine known as *crack cocaine*, which is free-based cocaine boiled down into crystalline balls. Because of its relative cheapness, and its rapid but intense effects, crack cocaine has made the drug accessible to many who could not afford it before (such as those in poor urban areas and schoolchildren). This led to dramatic increases in cocaine use in the 1990s – especially amongst school and college students (Johnston, O'Malley & Bachman, 2001).

> **Free-basing**   A purer cocaine alkaloid which is separated by heating processed cocaine and inhaled by smoking.

> **Crack cocaine**   Free-based cocaine boiled down into crystalline balls.

Plate 8.4 (*left*)
Many substances that are currently drugs of abuse were originally used because it was thought they had positive or medicinal effects. Cocaine was used in the original Coca-Cola recipe until 1903 because it was presumed to act as a tonic and stimulant.

FOCUS POINT 8.5

Cocaine and crack (stimulant)

Also known as: Cocaine: coke, charlie, snow, crack, rocks.

What it looks like and how it's taken: Cocaine is a white powder that is snorted or dissolved and injected. Crack, a stronger version, comes as rocks or stones and is smoked or injected.

Immediate effects: Cocaine acts fast and the effects last about 20–30 minutes. Users feel confident, strong and alert, and may be left craving more. Crack acts faster. More intense effects last about 10 minutes.

Short-term risks: Some users may feel tense and anxious while using and afterwards many feel very tired and depressed. It can also cause convulsions, chest pain and sudden death from heart attack or stroke. Sniffing can damage the inside of the nose. Smoking crack can cause breathing problems and lung damage.

Long-term risks: Frequent use can lead to paranoia, hallucinations, aggression and weight loss. Cocaine and especially crack cocaine are highly addictive. Chronic use also causes severe damage to heart and circulation, brain damage and severe mental health problems.

Prevalence of Use The lifetime prevalence rate of cocaine use in developed countries is between 1 and 3 per cent (WHO, 2006). In European countries this varies between 0.5 and 6 per cent, with Spain and the UK being at the upper end of this range (European Monitoring Centre for Drugs and Drug Addiction, 2004). This figure rises to 14.4 per cent in the USA (National Household Survey on Drug Abuse, 2002). Use by young adults aged 15–34 is around 4 per cent in the UK, with users either discontinuing use after a brief period of experimentation or continuing to use it at weekends and in recreational settings (such as bars and clubs).

Cocaine Abuse and Dependency Because the effects of cocaine last only for around 30 minutes, there is a need for frequent doses to maintain the rush caused by the drug. This means that the user may spend large sums of money on the drug in relatively short periods of time, and may even resort to theft and fraud to obtain funds to buy the drug. Cocaine dependency occurs when the individual finds it difficult to resist using the drug whenever it is available (see also the criteria for substance dependency in Table 8.3). This in turn leads to neglect of important responsibilities such as those associated with work or child care. There is even some evidence from animal studies that a single exposure to cocaine induces long-term changes in dopamine neurons in the brain, leaving the casual user vulnerable to longer-term drug dependency (Ungless, Whistler, Malenka & Bonci, 2001). Tolerance occurs with repeated use, requiring larger doses and greater expense for similar effects. When users are not taking cocaine, severe with-

drawal symptoms can occur, particularly hypersomnia, increased appetite, and negative and depressed mood, and these increase the craving for further use or relapse during abstinence. Erratic behaviour, social isolation and sexual dysfunction are regular characteristics of long-term cocaine dependency, and the long-term user may well develop symptoms of other psychological disorders such as major depression, social phobia, panic disorder, generalized anxiety disorder and eating disorders (DSM-IV-TR, p. 247).

Cocaine abuse is characterized by episodic, problematic use of the drug over a brief period of a few hours or a few days. These episodes may well occur around paydays or special occasions such as parties, holidays or at weekends. Acute intoxication is often associated with cocaine abuse, and this is characterized by rambling speech, headaches, tinnitus, paranoid ideation, auditory and tactile hallucinations, anger and emotional instability generally.

The Costs of Cocaine Dependency Apart from the negative effects of regular use on occupational, social and educational functioning, cocaine also has a number of adverse cognitive and health effects. For example, cocaine abusers regularly show evidence of deficits in decision-making, judgement and working memory (Simon, Domier, Sim, Richardson et al., 2002; Pace-Schott, Stickgold, Muzur, Wigren et al., 2005), and there is evidence from animal studies that regular cocaine use also disrupts learning – although it is still unclear whether these effects are permanent deficits caused by cocaine use (Kantak, Udo, Ugalde, Luzzo et al., 2005).

CLIENT'S PERSPECTIVE 8.1

Cocaine dependency

It all began in 1983 when I first starting doing cocaine. At first it was something that I did about once a week. Usually on a Friday night and into Saturday. I would use it to go out to the bars and go drinking. I would buy a gram, and usually there would be a little left over for Saturday morning. This went on for several months and as I came in contact with more people who liked coke, I would start to split grams with people during the week. This increased till I was doing that every day; this took about a year to develop. I was fixing business machines and would collect a little money every day; by the second year I would buy coke at least once a day. I thought that I would try selling it, to help with the costs that were starting to add up. But the coke I would buy would always end up being snorted by myself and a couple close friends. By the third year nearly all of my money was going for coke. Food became secondary to me and I would skip days eating to be able to afford coke. I started to hang out with a guy who shot his coke up with needles. We became best friends, I would fix a machine and he would be waiting for me in my car, we would instantly go and buy coke with the money that I had just made, occasionally stopping somewhere for a sandwich, which was all that I would eat any more.

This went on till I was made homeless but we managed to get a cheap flat to share. I started to get concerned that I had a habit that I could not kick. I saw many people wreck their lives during this period. In fact my business was in serious trouble as I never paid my bills. Part of the problem was that coke was really 'the'

thing to do in this town at the time. Seemed everyone I knew was into it. It was a real social drug. I stopped doing it at bars, and would go back to the flat and just lay around doing coke all the time. My friend shot his, I snorted mine. In desperation to make more money I expanded the territory that I was working and would drive 80 miles to do service calls. I was doing about a gram a day, my friend doing the same in his veins. My attitude in life became one of giving up and thinking that I would die eventually, but that was OK, as long as I could do coke till I did.

Alan's Story

Clinical Commentary

Like many people, Alan began using cocaine as a recreational drug, taking it mainly at weekends and when socializing in bars. Because the drug has a relatively brief 'high' (around 30 minutes), users require more and more regular doses in order to maintain the euphoria generated by cocaine. The cost of this leads to significant financial problems. As is typical of individuals with cocaine dependency, Alan began to neglect his responsibilities, including failing to pay bills and losing his home. Eventually, psychological dependency was complete when his life revolved entirely around acquiring and taking the drug.

There is also accumulating evidence that cocaine use by pregnant mothers can cause significant developmental deficits in their newborn offspring, and this is manifested as retarded development in the first 2 years of life (Singer, Arendt, Minnes et al., 2002), a higher incidence of attention deficit hyperactivity disorder (ADHD) at age 6 (Linares, Singer, Kirchner, Short et al., 2006), and deficits in visual motor development (Arendt, Short, Singer, Minnes et al., 2004). At least a partial cause of these effects may be the role of cocaine in causing irregularities in placental blood-flow during pregnancy.

Finally, because of its effects on blood pressure and cardiovascular functioning, high doses of cocaine can cause heart problems and brain seizures, although it is unusual for death to be solely attributed to cocaine abuse. However, cocaine may be an important contributor to death by aggravating existing cardiovascular problems (e.g. arrhythmias, heart attacks, cerebral haemorrhages) (see Focus Point 8.6). In a UK study, 30.4 per cent of 112 regular male cocaine users with an average age of 44 years showed evidence of coronary artery aneurysms, compared with only 7.6 per cent of non-cocaine users (Satran, Bart, Henry, Murad et al., 2005), indicating an important and significant increase in cardiovascular disease in regular cocaine users.

8.3.3.2 Amphetamines

Amphetamines are a group of synthetic drugs used primarily as a central nervous system stimulant. Common forms are amphetamine itself (benzedrine), dextroamphetamine (dexedrine) and *methamphetamine* (methedrine). These are highly addictive drugs that are used primarily to generate feelings of energy and confidence, and to reduce feelings of weariness and boredom. They were originally synthesized in the 1920s as an inhalant to aid breathing, but came to be used later as a means of appetite control and to combat feelings of lethargy and depression. When used in small doses, amphetamines enable individuals to feel alert, confident and energized. They also help motor coordination but, contrary to popular belief, do not help intellectual skills (Tinklenberg, 1971). They also have a number of physical effects, such as increasing blood pressure and heart rate, but can cause headaches, fevers, tremors and nausea.

> **Amphetamines** A group of synthetic drugs used primarily as a central nervous system stimulant. Common forms are amphetamine itself (Benzedrine), dextroamphetamine (Dexedrine) and methamphetamine (Methedrine).

> **Methamphetamine** A synthetic drug related to amphetamine, used illegally as a stimulant.

FOCUS POINT 8.6

Cocaine stopped Entwistle's heart

On 11 December 2002, the BBC News website reported:

The Who bassist John Entwistle died after taking cocaine that caused his already diseased heart to fail, a coroner has ruled. The 57-year-old was found dead in a hotel room in Las Vegas in June as the band were about to embark on a US tour. A report from consultant Dr Jeremy Uff of Gloucestershire Royal Hospital said there was evidence of high blood pressure and high cholesterol, which had been compounded by smoking.

Coroner Lester Maddrell said he could not reduce the verdict to a simple phrase, but added that the cocaine in his body had compounded heart disease that was already present. 'He died from the effects of a single moderate usage of cocaine superimposed upon ischaemic heart disease caused by a naturally occurring coronary,' he said. An inquest held in the US had already ruled that Entwistle died after using a 'significant amount of cocaine' which brought on heart failure.

Clinical Commentary

There are few deaths that are directly attributable to cocaine use, but cocaine is known to exacerbate already existing cardiovascular problems because of its effect on blood pressure levels and heart rate.

Amphetamines have their effects by causing the release of neurotransmitters norepinephrine and dopamine, and simultaneously blocking their reuptake. They are normally taken in a pill or capsule form, but methamphetamine can be taken intravenously or by 'snorting'. In its clear, crystal form, the latter is known as 'ice', 'crank' or 'crystal meth', and dependency on methamphetamine can be particularly rapid. With the use of higher doses, and during withdrawal, users experience a range of negative symptoms, including anxiety, paranoia, irritability, confusion and restlessness (Kaplan & Sadock, 1991).

Prevalence of Use In a 1996 US survey, around 1 per cent of adults acknowledged using amphetamines in the previous year, with a peak of usage in 26- to 34-year-olds (6 per cent). The lifetime prevalence of amphetamine use disorders is around 1.5 per cent (DSM-IV-TR). The World Health Organization estimates that around 33 million people worldwide use amphetamine-type stimulants, and this accounts for around 16 per cent of worldwide illicit drug abuse.

Amphetamine Abuse and Dependency Although the effects of amphetamine are longer lasting than other stimulants, such as cocaine, tolerance to amphetamine occurs rapidly and higher and higher doses are needed to achieve similar stimulant effects (Comer, Hart, Ward, Haney et al., 2001). Once high dose usage is achieved, the stimulant effects of amphetamine also become associated with intense but temporary psychological symptoms such as anxiety, paranoia and psychotic episodes resembling schizophrenia (see below). Those who are dependent on methamphetamine (so-called 'speed freaks') will often use the drug continuously for a number of days, experiencing a continuous 'high' without eating or sleeping. This will be followed by a few days feeling depressed and exhausted, but then the cycle starts again. Speed freaks who behave in this way become unpredictable, anxious, paranoid and aggressive, and may be a danger to themselves and others. Dependency is indicated by regular use of the drug whenever it is available, neglect of normal responsibilities associated with work or family, and continuing use when the individual is aware that using the drug is causing family or employment problems. *Amphetamine intoxication* normally begins with a 'high' followed by feelings of euphoria, energy, talkativeness and alertness, but is equally likely to be followed by stereotyped, repetitive behaviour, anger, physically aggressive behaviour and impaired judgement. Physical symptoms of intoxication include pupillary dilation, perspiration or chills, nausea or vomiting, chest pains and, in extreme cases, seizures or coma. Withdrawal symptoms can appear within a few hours or a few days of ceasing use of amphetamine, and are associated with depression, fatigue, vivid and unpleasant dreams, insomnia and increased feelings of agitation.

The Costs of Amphetamine Dependency   A number of studies using both human and non-human participants have suggested that regular use of amphetamines (especially methamphetamine) may cause long-term central nervous system damage (Frost & Cadet, 2000; Volkow, Chang, Wang, Fowler et al., 2001). Volkow et al. (2001) found that chronic methamphetamine use inhibited the production of the neurotransmitter dopamine in the orbitofrontal cortex, and this may play a significant role in maintaining addictive behaviours. For example, the orbitofrontal cortex is associated with compulsive behaviour and with resistance to extinction of a behaviour even when rewards are withdrawn. These effects are very similar to those reported by drug addicts who claim that once they start using a drug such as methamphetamine, they cannot stop – even when the drug is no longer pleasurable.

Finally, we noted in Chapter 7 that many of the symptoms of amphetamine abuse and intoxication are similar to the symptoms of schizophrenia – especially paranoid schizophrenia (Snyder, 1986). There is some evidence that methamphetamine psychosis resulting from long-term methamphetamine abuse may cause permanent changes in brain dopamine metabolism similar to the brain dopamine abnormalities found in schizophrenia (Yui, Ikemoto, Ishiguro & Goto, 2000).

8.3.3.3 Caffeine

Caffeine   A central nervous system stimulant that increases alertness and motor activity and combats fatigue; found in a number of different products, including coffee, tea, chocolate and some over-the-counter cold remedies and weight-loss aids.

We are probably all familiar with taking *caffeine* in one form or another – as are around 85 per cent of the world's population. Caffeine can be found in a number of different products, including coffee, tea, chocolate and some over-the-counter cold remedies and weight-loss aids. Caffeine is a central nervous system stimulant that increases alertness and motor activity and combats fatigue. However, it can also reduce fine motor coordination and cause insomnia, headaches, anxiety and dizziness (Paton & Beer, 2001). Caffeine enters the bloodstream through the stomach and increases brain dopamine levels in a similar way to amphetamine and cocaine. Caffeine in the body reaches its peak concentration within an hour, and has a half-life of 6 hours, which implies that if you have a cup of coffee at 4 p.m. that contains 200 mg of caffeine, you will still have around 100 mg of caffeine in your body 6 hours later at 10 p.m. So while caffeine may have beneficial short-term effects on alertness, it may have detrimental longer-term effects which may prevent you from sleeping. The average caffeine intake per day in most of the developing world is less than 50 mg, compared with highs of 400 mg in the UK and other European countries (DSM-IV-TR). It is taken more by men than women, and caffeine intake usually decreases with age, with older people showing more intense reactions and reporting greater interference with sleep.

Although caffeine consumption is almost a daily occurrence for most people, it can still lead to both *caffeine intoxication* and *caffeine*

withdrawal. Table 8.8 shows the DSM-IV-TR criteria for caffeine intoxication, which includes a range of physical and psychological effects. More importantly, experiencing caffeine intoxication on a regular basis can disrupt social and occupational areas of functioning. Even individuals whose caffeine consumption is relatively low can experience withdrawal symptoms if they go without caffeine for as little as 2 days. These symptoms include headaches, depression, anxiety and fatigue (Silverman, Evans, Strain & Griffiths, 1992).

SELF-TEST QUESTIONS

- What are the main stimulant drugs of abuse?
- Can you describe the main effects of a standard dose of cocaine?
- What are the different forms of cocaine, how are they administered and what different effects do they have?
- How does cocaine cause feelings of euphoria and ecstasy?
- What are the main cognitive and health effects of regular cocaine use?
- What are the main symptoms of amphetamine intoxication?
- Can you describe the main features of caffeine intoxication and caffeine withdrawal?

Table 8.8   *Do you drink too much coffee? The criteria for caffeine intoxification*

A   Recent consumption of caffeine, usually in excess of 250 mg (more than 2–3 cups of brewed coffee).

B   Five (or more) of the following signs, developing during, or shortly after, caffeine use:

(1)   restlessness
(2)   nervousness
(3)   excitement
(4)   insomnia
(5)   flushed face
(6)   diuresis
(7)   gastrointestinal disturbance
(8)   muscle twitching
(9)   rambling flow of thought and speech
(10)   tachycardia or cardiac arrhythmia
(11)   periods of inexhaustibility
(12)   psychomotor agitation

C   The symptoms in Criterion B cause clinically significant distress or impairment in social, occupational, or other important areas of functioning.

D   The symptoms are not due to a medical condition and are not better accounted for by another mental disorder (e.g. an anxiety disorder)

Source: DSM-IV-TR, p. 232.

8.3.4 Sedatives

Sedatives are a central nervous system depressant that slows the activity of the body, decreases its responsiveness and reduces pain tension and anxiety. This group of substances includes alcohol (see section 8.3.1), the opiates and their derivatives (heroin, morphine, methadone and codeine), and synthesized tranquillizers such as barbiturates. This group of drugs has a number of detrimental effects on regular users, including rapid tolerance effects and severe withdrawal symptoms, and high doses can cause disruption to vital bodily functions.

8.3.4.1 Opiates

Opiates   Opium, taken from the sap of the opium poppy. Its derivatives include morphine, heroin, codeine and methadone.

The **opiates** consist of opium – taken from the sap of the opium poppy – and its derivatives, which include morphine, heroin, codeine and methadone. In the 1800s, opium was used mainly to treat medical disorders because of its ability to relax the patient and reduce both physical and emotional pain. Both morphine and heroin were new drugs derived from opium during the late nineteenth and early twentieth centuries. Both were used as analgesics, but over time it became apparent that both were highly addictive, since even after having been successfully treated with morphine or heroin, patients were unable to give up using them. Finally, a synthetic form of opium, called **methadone**, was developed by the Germans during World War II. Unlike the other opiates, methadone can be taken orally (rather than injected) and is longer lasting. **Heroin** is currently the most widely abused of the opiates. It is purchased in a powder form and is normally taken by injection usually directly into a vein (known as 'mainlining'). In contrast, methadone is frequently used as a replacement drug for heroin abusers because of its slow onset and weaker effects.

In the 1990s, heroin became the recreational drug of choice for many in Europe and the USA. Most opiates and their derivatives cause drowsiness and euphoria. In addition, heroin gives a feeling of ecstasy immediately after injection (known as a 'rush', which lasts for 5–15 minutes). For about 5–6 hours after this rush, users forget all worries and stresses; they experience feelings of euphoria and well-being and lose all negative feelings. However, as with many other drugs, individuals who regularly use heroin rapidly develop tolerance effects and experience severe withdrawal symptoms that begin about 6 hours after they have injected the dose.

Opiates have their effects by depressing the central nervous system. The drug attaches to brain receptor sites that normally receive **endorphins** and stimulates these receptors to

Methadone   A synthetic form of opium.

Heroin   A highly addictive drug derived from morphine, often used illicitly as a narcotic.

Endorphins   The body's natural opioids. The release of these neurotransmitters acts to relieve pain, reduce stress and create pleasurable sensations.

FOCUS POINT 8.7

Heroin (depressant)

Also known as: Smack, scag, H, junk, gear.

What it looks like and how it's taken: Brownish-white powder. Some heroin comes in a brown/black form that looks like hard toffee. Smoked, dissolved or injected.

Immediate effects: Slows the brain, heart rate and breathing. Small doses bring a sense of warmth and well-being; larger doses make users drowsy and relaxed, and free from worry and pain.

Short-term risks: There is a real risk of drug overdose, possibly leading to coma or death, particularly when mixed with other drugs.

Long-term risks: Heroin is highly addictive and larger and more frequent doses may be needed to feel 'normal'. Injecting can damage veins; sharing needles can spread hepatitis and HIV.

produce more endorphins (Gerrits, Wiegant & van Ree, 1999). Endorphins are the body's natural opioids, and release of these neurotransmitters acts to relieve pain, reduce stress and create pleasurable sensations.

Prevalence of Use It is estimated that 13.5 million people worldwide take opiates, including 9.2 million who use heroin (WHO, 2006). The lifetime prevalence rate for heroin use in the USA was around 1 per cent in 1996. A 1997 survey in the USA suggested that 2 per cent of high school seniors admitted taking heroin, and 10 per cent admitted inappropriate use of analgesics generally (DSM-TR-IV). In 2000, 1 per cent of 16- to 29-year-olds in the UK reported using heroin in the previous year (Home Affairs Committee, 2002). During the 1990s, the number of heroin users in the UK doubled every four years.

Opiate Abuse and Dependency Most opiate users build up a tolerance to the drug quickly and have to use larger and larger doses to experience equivalent physical and psychological effects. Also associated with repeated use are severe withdrawal effects. In the case of heroin, withdrawal symptoms will begin around 6 hours after injection. Without further doses the user will experience a range of aversive withdrawal symptoms, beginning with feelings of anxiety, restlessness, muscle aches, increased sensitivity to pain and a renewed craving for the drug. More severe withdrawal is associated with muscle aches, insomnia and fever. Acute withdrawal symptoms for heroin usually peak within 1–3 days and will subside over a period of 5–7 days.

Opiate dependency is indicated by compulsive, prolonged administration of amounts in excess of those needed for pain relief and is associated with disruption of normal social, occupational and recreational activities. However, *opiate abuse* is associated with less frequent use than is found in dependency, and many users seem able to use opiates such as heroin as a periodic recreational drug while continuing to lead reasonably functioning lives in the interim. For example, a Scottish study of long-term heroin users who had never been in specialized treatment revealed that they had levels of occupational status and educational achievement similar to the general UK population (Shewan & Delgarno, 2005).

Shewan and Delgarno found that use of heroin in this sub-group had relatively few health risks. They suggested the terms *controlled drug user* or *unobtrusive heroin user* to describe them. There is other evidence that opiate use need not necessarily lead to long-term dependency. Some theorists believe that opiate drug use is linked to life stressors, and if these stressors are temporary, then so will be the drug use (Alexander & Hadaway, 1982). In support of this view, many US soldiers became regular heroin abusers during the Vietnam War, but relatively few continued to use the drug once they had returned home (Bourne, 1974a).

Controlled drug user A long-term drug user who has never been in specialized treatment and who displays levels of occupational status and educational achievement similar to the general population.

Unobtrusive heroin user A long-term heroin user who has never been in specialized treatment and who displays levels of occupational status and educational achievement similar to the general population.

The Costs of Opiate Dependency Apart from the severe withdrawal symptoms experienced after drug use, there are a number of risks that regular opiate users face. These include (1) the risk of accidental overdose if inexperienced users fail to properly dilute pure forms of heroin for use (Corwin, 1996), (2) being sold street heroin that contains potentially lethal additives, such as cyanide or battery acid, and (3) the risk of contracting the human immunodeficiency virus (HIV) or hepatitis from sharing unsterilized needles. The number of deaths from opiate overdoses in the UK has more than doubled between 1993 and 2000, and in a long-term US study of heroin addicts, 28 per cent had died before the age of 40. Interestingly, only one-third of these deaths were from overdose, and over half were from homicide, suicide or accident (Hser, Anglin & Powers, 1993). The high cost of opiate drugs such as heroin also leads regular users into illegal activities to raise money for their dependency, the most common being theft, fraud and prostitution. Heroin use is also highly associated with crime generally, and in the mid-1990s, according to UK Home Office estimates, around 20 per cent of all people arrested in the UK were taking heroin. So while we reported earlier that it is possible for some heroin users to live reasonably normal lives, there are still significant risks to the life and health of many heroin users.

8.3.4.2 Barbiturates and Benzodiazepines

Barbiturates and benzodiazepines are synthesized drugs that were first developed in the early 1900s as sedatives, sleeping aids and anti-anxiety drugs. They are usually taken in pill or capsule form and have similar effects to alcohol in that they make the individual relaxed and reduce anxiety. Because their effects are similar to those of alcohol, barbiturates are often sold illegally as an alternative to alcohol. In these circumstances, barbiturates have been given the nicknames 'barbs' or 'downers' by abusers, or are given other names often based on the colour of the capsule, such as 'reds' or 'yellows'. Barbiturates that used to be very commonly abused included amobarbital (amytal), pentobarbital (nembutal) and secobarbital (seconal). Because they are not prescribed much these days, these drugs have only a limited presence in the illicit drug market, where they may be available as capsules and tablets or sometimes in a liquid form or as suppositories. Their use has been superseded by benzodiazepines such as xanax and valium.

Both barbiturates and benzodiazepines are thought to have their relaxing effect by facilitating the action of the inhibitory brain neurotransmitter GABA (Mazarakis & Nestoros, 2001; Nutt & Malizia, 2001). Just like alcohol, higher doses of barbiturates make the individual sleepy, and speech may become slurred and motor coordination is affected. At very high doses, barbiturates can have lethal effects by affecting breathing (by relaxing the diaphragm muscles), reducing blood pressure and causing coma. In contrast, benzodiazepines do not affect breathing as radically as barbiturates, and are therefore less likely to have lethal effects when overdosed. Tolerance to barbiturates builds up very rapidly, and in some cases users may be taking many times the dose that would kill a non-user.

Barbiturates A class of sedative drugs related to a synthetic compound (barbituric acid) derived from uric acid.

Withdrawal symptoms with barbiturates are also severe – especially after abrupt termination of use – and can be associated with convulsions and delirium (Schuckit, 1995). Because barbiturates and alcohol have similar effects on the central nervous system, use of both simultaneously can have additive and often lethal effects. Many accidental deaths resulting from barbiturate use are because they have been combined with alcohol. More recently, the problems associated with use of many of the original barbiturates have meant that they have been superseded for medicinal purposes by benzodiazepines, and non-barbiturate sedatives are now regularly used as sleeping aids and as anxiolytics to treat anxiety. Even though benzodiazepines are probably one of the most widely prescribed groups of drugs in the UK and are usually prescribed in mild doses, they can still cause some patients to become dependent in the same way as barbiturates.

Barbiturate and Benzodiazepine Abuse and Dependency

Regular patterns of barbiturate and benzodiazepine use can result in abuse and dependency, whether they have been legitimately acquired on prescription or illegally acquired on the street. Tolerance

Plate 8.5
Film star Marilyn Monroe was found dead on 5 August 1962 with fatal levels of barbiturates in her bloodstream. Up until the 1970s, barbiturates were a regularly prescribed drug, but became the drug of choice for suicides because of their lethal effects when taken in overdose. After the 1970s barbiturates were gradually replaced by less toxic drugs, and this significantly reduced successful suicide attempts using barbiturates.

effects and withdrawal symptoms are usually taken as evidence of dependency, and dependency may be confirmed when an individual gives up important activities (such as work, education or child care) to obtain the drug. Sedative intoxication generally is associated with a number of signs, including slurred speech, uncoordinated motor movements, impairment in attention and memory and, in extreme cases, stupor or coma (DSM-IV-TR, p. 87). Abuse of sedatives, including barbiturates, can also give rise to risky or aggressive behaviours, such as driving under the influence of the drug (remember, barbiturates have similar effects to alcohol), and regularly getting into arguments with friends and relatives.

The Costs of Barbiturate and Benzodiazepine Dependency

Overdoses of barbiturates can be lethal – as we discussed earlier. An overdose induces sleep and then prevents respiration by affecting the diaphragm muscles. Because of this, barbiturate overdoses have over the years become a popular method of suicide – especially when combined with alcohol. Barbiturates and alcohol together have almost four times the effect of either taken alone (Combs, Hales & Williams, 1980), and barbiturate overdoses taken with alcohol may well cause many deaths that are not necessarily intentional suicide attempts. Because of their lethal effects at overdose, studies have demonstrated that suicide attempts are significantly more likely to be successful using barbiturates than other prescription drugs such as benzodiazepines and tricyclic antidepressants (Michel, Waeber, Valach, Arestegui et al., 1994). However, since the 1970s, barbiturate prescribing has decreased significantly as medical practitioners use the less potent benzodiazepines. The decline in sales and prescription of barbiturates has been closely associated with a decline in suicides using barbiturates (Oliver & Hetzel, 1973; Carlsten, Allebeck & Brandt, 1996). This decline has been most marked in women, who tend to use less violent suicide methods than men, and some studies suggest that the gradual withdrawal of barbiturates from the market has caused a significant and lasting decrease in female suicide rates (Schapira, Linsley, Linsley, Kelly et al., 2001).

SELF-TEST QUESTIONS

- Can you name the different types of opiates that are the main drugs of abuse?
- What are the health risks faced by individuals with opiate dependency?
- What are barbiturates and what effect do they have on the central nervous system?
- Why can regular barbiturate use be lethal?

8.3.5 Hallucinogenic Drugs

Psychoactive drugs, or hallucinogens, have their effects by changing the user's perceptions. They may either sharpen the individual's sensory abilities or create sensory illusions or hallucinations. Unlike stimulants and sedatives, they have less significant effects on arousal levels and are less addictive than these other two classes of substances. In this section we will discuss two hallucinogenic drugs, cannabis and lysergic acid diethylamide (LSD). Focus Point 8.8 describes some of the features of the combined hallucinogen and stimulant **MDMA**, known as

FOCUS POINT 8.8

Ecstasy: The dance drug

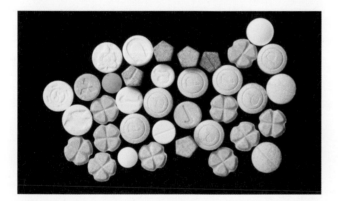

Most readers will by now be aware of the drug MDMA (3,4-methylenedioxymethamphetamine) – better known as the 'clubbing drug' Ecstasy. Over the past decade, Ecstasy has become the drug of choice for those regularly attending techno-dance parties, raves or nightclubs. It is usually taken in pill form and acts as both a stimulant and hallucinogen. It gives users added energy to continue partying and elevates mood. In the UK, about 10 per cent of young adults between 15 and 29 years have used Ecstasy (Ramsay, Partridge & Byron, 1999), and this figure increases to around 90 per cent of those who regularly attend raves and nightclubs (Bean, Stratford, White, Goodman et al., 1997).

Ecstasy has its effects by releasing the neurotransmitters serotonin and dopamine (Malberg & Bronson, 2001). Elevated levels of serotonin generate feelings of euphoria, well-being and sociability, and sounds and colours are experienced more intensely (high levels of brain serotonin are also found in individuals with bipolar disorder experiencing a manic phase). Effects can be experienced within around 20 minutes of taking the dose and will last for around 6 hours. However, high levels of brain dopamine can cause psychotic symptoms, such as paranoid thinking and confusion, and these are symptoms often experienced by regular Ecstasy users.

There are also a number of dangers associated with regular Ecstasy use:

- The drug causes severe dehydration by significantly reducing sweat production. This can cause heat stroke in hot environments such as raves or nightclubs. Even trying to counteract these effects by increasing fluid intake can cause hyponatremia or water intoxication (Braback & Humble, 2001).

- As a stimulant, Ecstasy increases heart rate and blood pressure, and this can be potentially dangerous for users with existing cardiovascular problems.

- Ecstasy is known to be a selective neurotoxin that destroys the axons to which serotonin would normally bind (Ricaurte, Yuan & McCann, 2000). Because of this, Ecstasy is thought to cause a range of long-term problems including memory deficits, verbal-learning deficits, sleep problems, lack of concentration and increased depression and anxiety (Reneman, Booij, Schmand, Brink et al., 2000; Jansen, 2001).

There is some debate amongst researchers about whether these longer-term consequences of regular Ecstasy use are permanent or not, and what kind of evidence might indicate that they are. For example:

1 It is much easier to get positive findings published in scientific journals than negative findings, so many studies that find no long-term effects of Ecstasy may go unreported (Cole, Sumnall & Grob, 2002a).

2 Ecstasy users and non-users are self-selected groups that may differ on many other characteristics (such as IQ, intelligence, sleep loss and other drug use; Curran, 2000). Thus, any differences in cognitive or psychological functioning between users and non-users could be due to these other between-group differences rather than to Ecstasy use *per se*.

A more in-depth discussion can be found in a special issue of the *Psychologist* dedicated to these issues (Vol. 15, No. 9, 2002).

Ecstasy   An illegal amphetamine-based synthetic drug with euphoric effects. Also known as MDMA (3,4-methylenedioxymethamphetaime).

8.3.5.1 Cannabis

Cannabis   A natural drug derived from the hemp plant, *cannabis sativa*.

Hashish   The most powerful of the cannabis group of drugs.

Marijuana   A derivative of cannabis consisting of dried and crushed cannabis leaves.

Ecstasy – a substance that has become an important recreational drug over the past two decades.

The drug *cannabis* is derived from the hemp plant, *cannabis sativa*. The most powerful of the cannabis group of drugs is *hashish*, and a weaker derivative – known as *marijuana* – consists of dried and crushed cannabis leaves. Cannabis is normally smoked after being rolled into a cigarette known as a 'joint'. However, it can also be eaten. The effects of cannabis are to produce feelings of relaxation (at low doses), euphoria, sociability and sharpened perceptions that sometimes result in mild sensory hallucinations (known as being 'spaced out'), but it can also cause difficulties in concentration and impairment of memory. Although it is primarily classified as a sedative/depressant because of its relaxing effects, it can sometimes also have stimulant effects and make some individuals agitated and paranoid. For example, when larger doses are taken, cannabis may exacerbate an already frightened, stressed or paranoid state, causing anxiety and distress. Sensory distortions may also give the user feelings of depersonalization similar to those experienced during panic attacks (see Chapter 5,

section 5.3), and some cannabis users become gripped by feelings of panic and anxiety.

The main active ingredient in cannabis is THC (Δ^9-tetrahydro-cannabinol), and the amount of THC in cannabis will determine the strength of its psychoactive effects. THC is generally believed to have low addictive properties, although it is still possible for regular cannabis users to become dependent on the drug (see below). THC has a mild stimulant effect by increasing heart rate, and has its psychoactive effects by influencing cannabinoid brain receptors CB1 and CB2 found in the hippocampus, cerebellum and striatum (Ameri, 1999). These receptors appear to influence levels of dopamine in those brain areas known to play a role in mediating reward and pleasure experiences, and this seems to be the route by which cannabis has its most important positive psychoactive effects.

Cannabis was used in the mid-twentieth century for its supposed medicinal properties, which included its analgesic effects (see Focus Point 8.9), but it was smoked mainly for pleasure. It is now an illegal drug in most countries even though its effects on behaviour and health are less severe than many other illicit drugs. There is some concern, however, that regular cannabis use may have permanent effects on cognitive functioning and psychological and physical health (Kalant, 2004; Iversen, 2005; Johns, 2001). We will discuss the relevant evidence on these issues later in this section.

Prevalence of Use   Cannabis is undoubtedly the most widely cultivated, trafficked and used illicit drug in the world. It is estimated that around 2.5 per cent of the world's population use cannabis at least once a year (WHO, 2006), and the use of cannabis has increased significantly since the 1960s – especially in developed

FOCUS POINT 8.9

The medical applications of cannabis

Long before it became an illegal drug, cannabis was used primarily for medicinal purposes. It was known to have relaxing and analgesic effects, and was used in the 1970s to reduce the nausea and lack of appetite caused by chemotherapy in cancer patients (Sallan, Zinberg & Frei, 1975). Neurophysiological studies have shown that cannabis has moderate analgesic effects, which are caused by the active ingredient in cannabis, THC, helping to block pain signals reaching the brain (Richardson, Kilo & Hargreaves, 1998). These analgesic effects are more powerful than codeine and of longer duration.

Because of the potential medical applications of cannabis as a powerful analgesic, there have been significant lobbies in many countries to legalize the drug for medical use. In a UK survey, individuals reported the medicinal use of cannabis with chronic pain, multiple sclerosis, depression, arthritis and neuropathy (Ware, Adams & Guy, 2005). Cannabis has also been involved in the treatment of patients with seizures, glaucoma,

asthma and anxiety (Mather, 2001). Recent outcome studies that have employed double-blind randomized controlled trials and placebo controls in patients with neuropathic pain or multiple sclerosis have demonstrated that cannabis reduced the severity of reported pain significantly more in the cannabis-treated than in the placebo group (Berman, Symonds & Birch, 2004; Zajicek, Fox, Sanders, Wright et al., 2003).

Problems with the medical application of cannabis are that (1) it is still an illegal drug in most developed countries and (2) smoking cannabis may not be the healthiest way to take the drug given the potential health risks associated with smoking (Mather, 2001). However, many governments are now licensing the use of cannabis-based drugs for use with specific patient groups. For example, in 2005, the UK Home Office licensed the drug Sativex for individual patient use (such as those with multiple sclerosis where cannabis has been shown to ease stiffness, muscle spasms and pain). Sativex avoids the problems of smoking by providing the active ingredients THC and cannabidol in a mouth spray.

countries in North America, Western Europe and Australia. In 2000 the lifetime prevalence rate for cannabis use in the UK was around 27 per cent, with 9 per cent having used it in the last 12 months (Ramsay, Baker, Goulden, Sharpe et al., 2001). While rates of use in the UK had remained relatively stable between 1994 and 2000, there was a significant increase in use by young people aged 20–24 years (from 23 per cent to 27 per cent). In the USA, approximately 50 per cent of individuals between 18 and 25 years of age report having tried cannabis (National Institute on Drug Abuse, 1988), and about 6 per cent of US high school seniors reported smoking cannabis in the year 2000 (Johnston, O'Malley & Bachman, 2001). In the USA and Europe, cannabis use increased dramatically in the 1970s and early 1980s and rose again during the 1990s, but has remained fairly stable since then (Johnston, O'Malley & Bachman, 2001). Recent population surveys indicate that a significant proportion of the European adult population (aged 15–64 years) have tried the substance at least once, ranging from 5–10 per cent in Belgium, Estonia, Hungary and Portugal to 24–31 per cent in Denmark, Spain, France and the United Kingdom. However, cannabis use is concentrated mainly among young adults (aged 15–34 years), with 20 per cent of this age range in the UK admitting to cannabis use in the previous 12 months (European Monitoring Centre for Drugs and Drug Addiction, 2004).

Cannabis Abuse and Dependency Over the past few decades, the cannabis available on the street has become stronger and in many cases THC content has risen from 1–5 per cent to 10–15 per cent (DSM-IV-TR). As a result, there is increasing evidence for a cannabis abuse and dependency syndrome in many users. For example, tolerance and withdrawal effects have been reported in some individuals who use cannabis regularly. Objective studies have indicated that cannabis can cause tolerance effects, and individuals who use cannabis daily over months or years may develop a need for more potent forms of cannabis that would be toxic to most non-users (Nowlan & Cohen, 1977). In heavy users, dependency is indicated by withdrawal during periods of abstention, and these include flu-like symptoms, restlessness and irritability (Kouri & Pope, 2000). Symptoms usually begin within 1–3 days after cessation of use, peak between days 2 and 6, and usually last a maximum of 14 days (Budney, Moore, Vandrey & Hughes, 2003).

Cannabis dependency is observed when an individual spends much of his or her time daily acquiring and smoking the drug, and this may severely interfere with family, school, work or recreational activities. Cannabis abuse is characterized by signs of cannabis intoxication. The symptoms of intoxication after recent use of cannabis include impaired motor coordination, euphoria, anxiety, sensations of slowed time, impaired judgement generally, and physical signs such as increased appetite, dry mouth and tachycardia (DSM-IV-TR, p. 238). Abuse and dependency usually develop over a period of time that is characterized by continuing increased use and reduction in pleasurable effects. Estimates of the number of users who meet DSM-IV-TR criteria for cannabis dependency vary considerably between studies and countries. Australian studies have suggested that the level of dependency in the general population is 2 per cent, but as high as 32 per cent amongst cannabis users (Swift, Hall & Teesson, 2001a,b). A study of teenagers and young adults in New Zealand and Germany found rates of cannabis dependency of 8 per cent and 10 per cent

respectively (Poulton, Moffitt, Harrington, Milne et al., 2001; von Sydow, Lieb, Pfister, Hofler et al., 2001). These studies suggest that cannabis dependency may be a characteristic of at least 1 in 3 regular cannabis users, and can be diagnosed in around 1 in 10 teenagers and young adults.

Studies have identified a number of risk factors for developing cannabis dependency, including:

1 age of onset – the earlier first use is recorded, the higher the likelihood of cannabis dependency (Taylor, Malone, Iacono & McGue, 2002);

2 tobacco smoking and regularity of cannabis use are both independent predictors of cannabis dependency (Coffey, Carlin, Lynskey, Li et al., 2003);

3 impulsiveness and unpredictability of moods (Simons & Carey, 2002);

4 a diagnosis of conduct disorder and emotional disorders during childhood (Meltzer, Gatwood, Goodman & Ford, 2003);

5 dependency on alcohol and other drugs (Degenhardt, Hall & Lynskey, 2001).

Like many substance use disorders, cannabis dependency is a risk factor for a number of other psychiatric diagnoses. These include anxiety and panic disorder (Thomas, 1996), major depression (Chen, Wagner & Anthony, 2002), increased tendency for suicide (Beautrais, Joyce & Mulder, 1999) and schizophrenia (Degenhardt & Hall, 2001). This once again begs the question of whether individuals suffering psychological problems are likely to resort to cannabis use as a form of self-medication, or whether cannabis use is linked to a future increase in psychiatric diagnoses. The evidence on this is far from clear, although prospective studies indicate that (1) there is a causal link between regular cannabis use and the development of psychotic symptoms typical of schizophrenia (Fergusson, Horwood & Ridder, 2005; see also Chapter 7, Focus Point 7.7), and (2) daily cannabis users may double their risk of subsequently developing symptoms of anxiety and depression (Patton, Coffey, Carlin, Degenhardt et al., 2002). Also, in a longitudinal New Zealand study, McGee, Williams, Poulton and Moffitt (2000) found that mental health problems at age 15 years were a predictor of cannabis use at age 18 years, but that cannabis use at age 18 predicted increased risk of mental health problems at age 21 years. While these studies tend to suggest that regular cannabis use indeed predicts increased risk for subsequent mental health problems, the causal relationship may not be direct. For example, both heavy cannabis use and mental health problems are also associated with factors like low socioeconomic status, childhood behavioural problems and parental neglect, and it may be these factors that act as causes of both cannabis use and subsequent mental health problems.

The Costs of Cannabis Dependency We have just discussed the possibility that regular heavy cannabis use may be associated with increased risk for a number of mental health problems such as anxiety, depression and schizophrenia. Such use is also associated with a range of cognitive deficits and with health problems.

Regular cannabis use is associated with a range of cognitive deficits while individuals are under the influence of the drug. These include deficits in reaction time, decreased attention span, deficits in verbal ability, slower problem solving and loss of short-term memory (Lundqvist, 2005; Kalant, 2004). This has important implications for cannabis users when complex psychomotor skills are required while engaging in potentially dangerous activities. One such activity is driving, and there is evidence that cannabis use does affect both driving skills and driving safety (Smiley, 1999). Laboratory studies have demonstrated that perceptual and motor speed and accuracy are significantly affected after smoking cannabis (Kurzthaler, Hummer, Miller, Sperner-Unterweger et al., 1999). Other studies have looked at the role of cannabis use in drivers involved in accidents. For example, the active ingredient in cannabis, THC, is found in the blood of impaired or accident-involved drivers with a frequency that significantly exceeds that in the general population (Kalant, 2004). Scandinavian studies have indicated that 1 in 10 of drivers arrested for impaired driving tested positive for cannabis (Christophersen, Ceder, Kristinsson, Lillsunde et al., 1999; Steentoft, Muller, Worm & Toft, 2000). However, we must remain cautious about what we conclude from these findings. Many of those involved in car accidents are young, risk-taking males who are more likely to be using cannabis and other substances (such as alcohol), so cannabis use may not necessarily be the main cause of accidents in these groups.

We know that cannabis causes cognitive deficits while the individual is under the influence of the drug, but does regular cannabis use cause long-term, permanent damage to cognitive skills and achievement generally? First, cannabis use is associated with a syndrome of underachievement, in which regular users exhibit lower IQ (Fried, Watkinson, James & Gray, 2002), lower educational achievement (Gruber, Pope, Hudson & Yurgelun-Todd, 2003) and motivational deficits (Lane, Cherek, Pietras & Steinberg, 2005). However, there is very little evidence for permanent neuropsychological deficits in cannabis users (Gonzalez, Carey & Grant, 2002), and any cognitive deficits found during cannabis use do not appear to persist after the individual stops using the drug (Iversen, 2005). Nevertheless, regular heavy users are likely to have lower educational achievement and lower income than non-users, which may be due to a number of factors:

1 educational performance and subsequent career prospects being impaired by use of cannabis during school and college years;

2 heavy cannabis use being associated with deprivation and poor educational opportunities;

> **Amotivational syndrome**   A syndrome in which those who take up regular cannabis use are more likely to be those who exhibit apathy, loss of ambition and difficulty concentrating.

3 an *amotivational syndrome* in cannabis users, in which people who take up regular cannabis use are more likely to be those who exhibit apathy, loss of ambition and difficulty concentrating (Maugh, 1982).

There is also some debate about whether regular cannabis use has long-term physical health consequences. First, cannabis generally contains more tar than normal cigarettes, and so presents a significant risk for smoking-related diseases such as cancer. Studies have suggested that cannabis smoke can cause mutations and cancerous changes (Marselos & Karamanakos, 1999), but there is only modest epidemiological evidence suggesting that cannabis users are more prone to cancer than non-users (Sidney, Quesenberry, Friedman et al., 1997; Zhang, Morgenstern, Spitz et al., 1999). Second, regular cannabis use does appear to be associated with a reduction in the male hormone testosterone (Grinspoon, Bakalar, Zimmer et al., 1997), and there is a possibility that this could cause impaired sexual functioning in the young males who are the main users of cannabis. Third, chronic cannabis use does appear to impair the efficiency of the body's immune system (Nahas, Paton & Harvey, 1999), although as yet there has been no obvious effect of this found on the rate of physical illnesses in cannabis users. This suggests that, while some negative health consequences of cannabis use have been mooted, there is very little in the way of conclusive and unambiguous evidence that any long-term physical health threats are significant (Iversen, 2005).

8.3.5.2 Lysergic Acid Diethylamide (LSD)

LSD is a hallucinogenic drug that was first synthesized by the Swiss chemist Albert Hoffman in 1938. It was probably the first of the widely used *psychodelic drugs* and came to be fashionable as a 'mind-expanding' drug associated with the social changes and experimentation that took place during the 1960s and 1970s. LSD, commonly referred to as 'acid', is sold on the street in tablets, capsules and, occasionally, liquid form. It is odourless, colourless, has a slightly bitter taste and is usually taken by mouth. Often LSD is added to absorbent paper, such as blotting paper, or to sugar cubes. The drug starts to take effect around 30 to 90 minutes after being taken. Physical effects include dilated pupils, raised body temperature, increased heart rate and blood pressure, sweating, sleeplessness, dry mouth and tremors.

> **Lysergic acid diethylamide (LSD)**
> A hallucinogenic drug which produces physical effects including dilated pupils, raised body temperature, increased heart rate and blood pressure, sweating, sleeplessness, dry mouth and tremors.
>
> **Psychodelic drugs**   Consciousness-expanding or mind-manifesting drugs.

LSD produces sharpened perceptions across a variety of senses. Colours can be enhanced and users come to focus their attention on very small details in their environment. Advocates of the drug claim that this heightened perception can open up new states of awareness and allow users to become more enlightened about the world and themselves. However, because of its sensory-enhancing properties, LSD can also cause hallucinations, including distorted perceptions of space and time (Kaplan & Sadock, 1991), perceiving people and objects that are not present, and enabling users to believe they have attributes that they in fact do not possess. On a number of occasions this latter effect can have dangerous consequences, when users who believe they have the power of flight have thrown themselves out of upper-storey windows.

The awareness-enhancing properties of LSD can also have negative consequences. If the user is feeling anxious or stressed after having taken LSD, these feelings can be exaggerated to the point where the individual can experience extreme terror or panic. Such experiences are known as 'bad trips', and feelings subside as the dose wears off. However, regular users can come to experience what are known as 'flashbacks'. These involve a vivid re-experiencing of a trip that can occur days, months or even years

FOCUS POINT 8.10

LSD (hallucinogen)

....

Also known as: Acid.

What it looks like and how it's taken: Comes in small squares of paper, often printed with designs, or as tiny tablets called microdots and dots. Tablets are swallowed. It is a myth that LSD can be absorbed through the skin from transfers.

Immediate effects: Hallucination – the 'trip'. Starts within an hour and can last 8–12 hours. Surroundings seem different: colours are brighter, sounds new, movement and time may seem to speed up or slow down.

Short-term risks: Trips cannot be controlled, changed or stopped. A bad trip can be terrifying, and requires help and reassurance from others. Mental health problems can be triggered and existing conditions made worse.

Long-term risks: Users may have 'flashbacks' in which they relive a trip without taking the drug again.

CLIENT'S PERSPECTIVE 8.2

The LSD trip

....

And so the tale begins. At around eight in the morning, I unwrapped the cubes, gave two to Peter, and popped five in my mouth. I then sat and tried to control my slight anxiety. After a little while I began experiencing a slight sense of euphoria, and oddly shaped dark blobs began to skitter across the white ceiling in my living room. Obviously the trip had begun.

For a time I wasn't seeing anything particularly cosmic; however, the euphoria continued to build. And build. It was becoming almost painfully intense. For a little while I tried hugging a small end table to my chest in an attempt to find some solidity. We decided to head outside. For a time we sat on the hill that descended from my home and looked about. I remember glancing at the sky and seeing the clouds boiling and twisting intensely. My sense of time was becoming increasingly unreliable. One moment we were sitting at the top of the hill, the next we were sitting halfway down another hill, the next near some trees several hundred meters away. I knew I had walked those distances, and could even remember doing so, but I felt almost as if I had teleported about. My euphoria had

Psychedelic trance party wall paintings.

steadied off just short of unbearable, and for a time I rolled around in the grass giggling like mad, looking at the turbulent skies.

My eyes were now watering quite a bit, and I was beginning to have trouble seeing anything clearly. It seemed as if I was peering though a heat mirage, and my peripheral vision almost totally consumed by twisting smoke. I happened to glance up, and see a blurry figure standing by our pool.

It was nothing, but I had been frightened. My euphoria was rapidly replaced by entirely less pleasant emotions. Going back inside and sitting in the back porch, I became consumed by paranoia.

Befuddled by wildly swinging emotions, an absent sense of time, and the inability to sense anything clearly, my short-term memory took a long walk off a short plank, and I began reacting to everything I perceived as if it were real. I came to the logical conclusion that time had ended, and my soul was all that existed. Everything I saw was wreathed by burning light and my vision was frequently fading to white.

We went back inside, and Peter went off on his own for a while. I began attempting to adjust myself to my new, godlike powers. I attempted to teleport into the kitchen. I succeeded. I then commanded a glass of water to be instantly filled. Again success. Deciding to step up, I decided that I must be infinitely wise, and attempted to expand my mind to contain all the secrets of mathematics. Failure! I became terribly nervous. If I were equal to God, shouldn't I be able to comprehend something puny like the sum of mathematical knowledge? I tried again, and failed. I tried something simple, like recalling the entire contents of a book to my head. Failure! I sat down on a couch in the living room and began to panic again. I tried to conjure a glass of water. Failure! I immediately realized that I was going to be trapped in the ending of time in the universe Peter had created, powerless.

I now felt physically paralyzed. I slouched on the couch, consumed by despair. Events seemed to catch and repeat, clear indications to me that time was 'winding down'. I lapsed into a catatonic state for hours, convinced that I was experiencing the same moment endlessly.

Well, that's my LSD overdose story. If you choose to use LSD or similar drugs, be careful that you don't forget that their mind-altering properties are far more significant and powerful than their ability to alter your vision. Be careful and stay safe. If I had believed I was still mortal during the worst parts of my experience, I would not have hesitated to kill myself to escape what I thought my fate would be: an eternal prison in the dying universe of my own living room.

Source: www.everything2.com/index.pl?node_id=1376897

after the actual LSD trip (Abraham & Wolf, 1988). Client's Perspective Box 8.2 describes the experiences of an LSD user and how her experiences while under the influence of the drug affect her perceptions and emotions.

LSD appears to have its effects by influencing neurons in the brain that normally control visual information and emotion, and it does this by affecting the levels of the neurotransmitter serotonin in these brain areas (Goodman, 2002).

Prevalence of Use In the USA and Europe, use of LSD peaked during the 1960s and 1970s and has been gradually declining ever since as stimulant drugs such as cocaine and amphetamines became the recreational drug of choice. In 2003, 10.3 per cent of Americans aged 12 years and over reported using LSD at least once in their lifetime, and 0.2 per cent had used it in the last year (Farrell, Howes, Bebbington, Brugha et al., 2003). In the UK, around 3 per cent of young people aged 16–24 years reported using LSD in 2001, and this figure has declined regularly since 1996 (UK Home Office, 2004).

Hallucinogen Abuse and Dependency While LSD is not generally considered to be a physically addictive drug, its regular use can still foster dependency. Hallucinogen use (such as LSD or MDMA) is normally restricted to just 2–3 times per week in regular users, but cravings for these drugs have been reported after individuals have stopped using them (DSM-IV-TR). Because most hallucinogens have an extended duration of action and a long half-life, individuals with hallucinogen dependency can spend many hours and even days recovering from the effects of the drug. Some hallucinogens – such as MDMA – are often associated with physical 'hangover' symptoms that occur the day after use.

Symptoms of MDMA hangovers include insomnia, fatigue, drowsiness, headaches and sore jaw muscles from teeth clenching. Such symptoms will inevitably interfere with normal occupational and social functioning for some time after drug use. Reported levels of hallucinogen dependency and abuse are quite low, with a 1992 US study reporting lifetime rates at 0.6 per cent and a 12-month prevalence rate of 0.1 per cent (DSM-IV-TR).

The Costs of LSD Use The effects of LSD are generally unpredictable, and prior to use individuals will not be sure whether they will experience a bad trip or not. If a large dose is taken, this can cause hallucinations and sensory changes that can make users frightened, cause panic, and make users think they are going crazy. Although LSD is not considered an addictive drug, it can have tolerance effects where regular users have to take larger and larger doses to achieve similar effects. In a small number of individuals, regular use can be associated with psychiatric disorders such as psychotic symptoms or chronic depression. However, it is unclear whether such individuals already had underlying psychiatric problems prior to their regular use of the drug. As we have described elsewhere, regular drug use can tend to become heavy and regular in individuals with pre-existing psychiatric problems.

SELF-TEST QUESTIONS

- What are the physical and cognitive effects of cannabis?
- What are the main features of cannabis dependency, cannabis abuse and cannabis intoxication?
- What are the main risk factors for cannabis dependency?
- What are the cognitive deficits that some clinicians argue are associated with regular cannabis use?
- What are the main cognitive and behavioural effects of lysergic acid diethylamide (LSD), and how does it have these effects?

SECTION SUMMARY

8.3 Characteristics of Specific Substance Use Disorders

- Substances of abuse can be categorized in three broad groups, namely **stimulants** (e.g. cocaine), **sedatives** (e.g. heroin) and **hallucinogenic drugs** (e.g. LSD).

8.3.1 Alcohol

- Alcohol has its effects by binding to the neurotransmitter **GABA**, preventing neurons firing and making drinkers feel more relaxed.
- Many of the so-called 'positive' effects of alcohol are mythical and result from drinkers' **expectations** about alcohol's effects.
- **Longer-term negative physical effects** of alcohol include hypertension, heart failure, stomach ulcers, cancer, cirrhosis of the liver, brain damage and early dementia.
- **Korsakoff's syndrome** and **foetal alcohol syndrome** are physiological risks associated with heavy drinking.
- The lifetime prevalence rate for alcohol dependency is around 15 per cent.

8.3.2 Nicotine

- Nicotine has its effects by releasing **dopamine** in the brain, which acts to elevate mood.
- Regular smokers need to smoke simply to experience positive mood levels similar to non-smokers.
- Young people are socially motivated to take up smoking, but rarely as a result of direct pressure and more as a means of **self-categorizing** themselves as members of a particular group.
- **Mood manipulation** is an important part of nicotine dependency, and smoking a cigarette may eventually become a conditioned response to any form of stress.
- There are substantial health risks to smoking. **Passive smoking** or **secondhand smoke** is also an important health risk for non-smokers.

8.3.3 Stimulants

- Stimulant drugs include **cocaine**, **amphetamine** and **caffeine**.
- **Cocaine** causes feelings of **euphoria** by blocking the reuptake of dopamine in the mesolimbic areas of the brain.
- Cocaine is usually snorted, but can also be inhaled by smoking, which is known as **free-basing**.
- The lifetime prevalence rate of cocaine use in developed countries is between 1 and 3 per cent.
- Cocaine can be an important contributor to death by aggravating existing cardiovascular problems.
- **Amphetamines** are a group of synthetic drugs used primarily as a **central nervous system stimulant**.
- Amphetamines have their effects by causing the release of the neurotransmitters **norepinephrine** and **dopamine**, and simultaneously blocking their reuptake.
- In 1996 around 1 per cent of US adults acknowledged using amphetamines in the previous year.

- **Caffeine** enters the bloodstream through the stomach and increases brain dopamine levels in a similar way to amphetamine and cocaine.

8.3.4 Sedatives

- Sedatives are a central nervous system depressant that slows the activity of the body and reduces pain, tension and anxiety. They include **opiates** and **barbiturates**.
- Opiates (such as **heroin**) attach to brain receptor sites that normally receive **endorphins**, and encourage the receptors to produce more endorphins, which relieve pain, reduce stress and create pleasurable sensations.
- It is estimated that 13.5 million people worldwide take opiates, including 9.2 million who use heroin.
- Some heroin users, known as **controlled drug users** or **unobtrusive heroin users**, seem able to use the drug without it affecting their social and occupational functioning.
- **Barbiturates** are synthesized drugs developed as sedatives and sleeping aids.
- Barbiturates are thought to have their relaxing effects by facilitating the action of the inhibitory brain neurotransmitter **GABA** (in a similar way to alcohol).

8.3.5 Hallucinogenic Drugs

- Hallucinogenic drugs have their effects by changing the user's perceptions. They include **cannabis**, **lysergic acid diethylamide (LSD)** and **MDMA** (better known as **Ecstasy**).
- The drug cannabis is derived from the hemp plant *cannabis sativa*, and is also known as **hashish** and **marijuana**.
- The main active ingredient in cannabis is **THC** (Δ^9-**tetrahydrocannabinol**), the amount of which determines the strength of it psychoactive effects.
- It is estimated that 2.5 per cent of the world's population use cannabis at least once a year.
- **Risk factors** for developing cannabis dependency include early age of first use, tobacco smoking, impulsiveness and unpredictability of moods, diagnosis of childhood conduct disorder, and dependency on alcohol and other drugs.
- Cannabis dependency is a risk factor for a number of psychiatric diagnoses including **anxiety**, **panic disorder**, **major depression** and **schizophrenia**.
- Regular cannabis use predicts lower educational achievement and lower income than non-use.
- **Lysergic acid diethylamide (LSD)** is a hallucinogenic drug first synthesized in 1938.
- LSD has both **awareness-enhancing properties** and occasional negative consequences known as '**bad trips**'.
- LSD appears to have its effects by influencing neurons in the brain that normally control emotion and visual information, and it does this by affecting levels of the neurotransmitter **serotonin**.
- 0.2 per cent of Americans claim to have used LSD in the previous 12 months.

8.4 THE AETIOLOGY OF SUBSTANCE ABUSE AND DEPENDENCY

We have so far described the characteristics of some of the main substances of abuse, and in some cases have discussed factors that lead to abuse of and dependency on that substance. In this section we will look in more general terms at processes that lead some individuals to become substance dependent. We will also examine why it is that these individuals differ from people who may simply experiment with drugs without it significantly interfering with their daily lives (e.g. Shewan & Delgarno, 2005).

The aetiology of substance dependency has to be viewed in developmental terms because most individuals who become dependent will go through a series of stages that lead to their dependency. At each stage there may be quite different risk factors that influence transition to the next stage. Figure 8.6 represents three important stages that individuals go through towards substance abuse and dependency, together with the risk factors that can influence this transition at each stage. Individuals do not necessarily progress to the next stage unless the factors that mediate that transition are present. For example, many substance users experience only stages 1 and 2 (experimentation and regular use), and do not necessarily go on to become dependent on the drug in a way that significantly affects their occupational, social and family functioning. There may be some overlap between mediating factors and stages (e.g. believing that smoking won't harm you may not only lead to regular use but can also be a factor leading to nicotine dependency). However, Figure 8.6 provides a reasonable overview of how risk factors may influence substance use at different stages of development. We will now continue to look at the risk factors that influence substance use at these different stages.

FOCUS POINT 8.11

Does taking 'soft' drugs lead to using 'harder' drugs?

Because cannabis use is prevalent amongst teenagers and young adults, there has long been concern that early cannabis use may be the first step that leads young people to experiment with 'harder', more addictive drugs, such as cocaine and heroin. This supposed progression from less addictive drugs, such as cannabis, to more addictive drugs may then trap the individual into a cycle of substance dependency.

Is there any truth to this theory? Certainly there is evidence that regular users of addictive drugs such as cocaine and heroin did start out by using cannabis, and cocaine use, for example, is significantly predicted by earlier cannabis use (Kandel, Murphy & Karus, 1985). Another relevant fact is that cannabis users are more likely than non-users to go on to try cocaine or heroin (Miller & Volk, 1996). However, these findings do not imply in any way that cannabis users will always go on to use more addictive drugs, and 40 per cent of regular cannabis users do not go on to experiment with cocaine or heroin (Stephens, Roffman & Simpson, 1993).

We tend to assume that because much drug use is associated with dependency, individual users will automatically be dragged along a path of ever-worsening abuse, and that cannabis use will inevitably lead down a slippery slope to dependency. However, we must remember that many regular substance users – even those who use potentially highly addictive drugs such as cocaine, heroin and amphetamines – manage successfully to confine their use to recreational purposes only, using the drug only when socializing or at weekends. This controlled use does not appear to interfere substantially with occupational, social or educational functioning (e.g. Shewan & Delgarno, 2005).

So why do some people appear to progress from softer drugs during adolescence to substance dependency during adulthood? One theory is that progression to long-term dependency is found primarily in those who have either psychological problems at the outset of their drug use or are suffering life stress (Alexander & Hadaway, 1982). Indirect support for this theory comes from studies showing that drug abuse often stops when life stressors disappear (Bourne, 1974a), and that many users of addictive drugs such as cocaine and heroin are capable of kicking their habit and turning to softer drugs, such as cannabis, as a safer option.

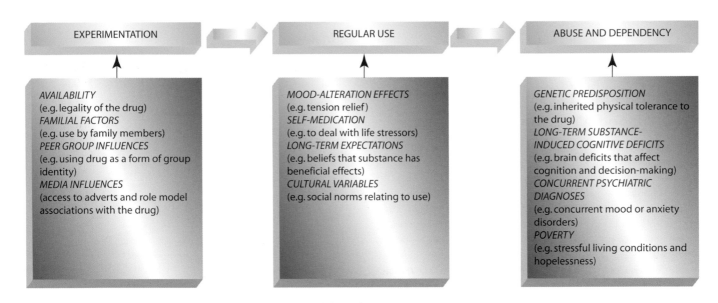

Figure 8.6 *The developmental model of substance abuse and dependency.*

8.4.1 Experimentation

8.4.1.1 Availability

> **Experimentation** A period when an individual may try out different drugs. In some cases this period of experimentation may lead to regular drug use.

Whether an individual can readily get access to the substance is an important factor in the early stages of substance use. Factors such as whether the drug is legally available (e.g. alcohol and cigarettes) and cost are also important determinants of initially experimenting with the drug. For example, there is evidence for an inverse relationship between the use of a drug and its cost – especially amongst young adolescents. This is true for alcohol and for cigarettes (Stead & Lancaster, 2005; Room, Babor & Rehm, 2005) and suggests that strategies such as enforcing the minimum age for purchase of tobacco and alcohol and increasing their price may be effective means of controlling early use (Ogilvie, Gruer & Haw, 2006).

8.4.1.2 Familial Factors

Two important factors that can influence early substance use are (1) whether the substances are regularly used by other family members and (2) whether the family environment is problematic. For example, if a child's parents both smoke, then the child is significantly more likely to smoke at an early age, and if both parents regularly drink alcohol, then the child is also more likely to drink at an early age (Hawkins, Graham, Maguin, Abbott et al., 1998). Neglectful parenting also increases the use of alcohol, cigarettes and cannabis by the child (Cadoret, Yates, Troughton, Woodworth et al., 1995). The negative background factors that predict longer-term substance use include (1) substance use in the childhood home, (2) extreme poverty in the childhood home, (3) marital or legal problems in the household, (4) childhood neglect and abuse and (5) serious psychiatric illness in the household (Alverson, Alverson & Drake, 2000; Wills, DuHamel & Vaccaro, 1995).

8.4.1.3 Peer Group Influences

As we saw in the case of nicotine use, adolescents can begin smoking because of peer group influences. These influences are not necessarily direct pressure to use the substance but take the form of conforming to group norms, so adolescents will start using a substance in order to *self-categorize* themselves as a member of a particular group (Schofield, Pattison, Hill & Borland, 2001). This suggests that social networks can have a strong influence on an individual's initial substance use. Identifying as part of a group that uses legal drugs, such as cigarettes and alcohol, also predicts increased use of other drugs in late adolescence (Chassin, Curran, Hussong & Colder, 1996). Apart from the importance of social groups determining substance use, it is also the case that substance use will determine the kinds of social groups with which an individual will mix. For example, once an individual becomes a regular drinker, he or she begins to choose social groups with similar drinking patterns, and drinking in a social group environment that supports alcohol consumption can act to consolidate regular use (Bullers, Cooper & Russell, 2001).

8.4.1.4 Media Influences

Substance use in young adolescents is significantly influenced by advertising and exposure to the product in media contexts such as television programmes and magazines. Exposure to advertising has been shown to be an important factor in encouraging children to take up smoking (While, Kelly, Huang & Charlton, 1996), and a US study found that exposure to in-store beer displays, magazines with alcohol advertisements and television beer advertising predicted drinking in school-age children (Ellickson, Collins, Hambarsoomians & McCaffrey, 2005). While banning direct advertising of a product has been shown to produce a significant fall in adolescent use of that product (Saffer, 1991), substance use (such as smoking) is still linked to indirect exposure to images found in fashion, entertainment and gossip magazines (Carson, Rodriguez & Audrain-McGovern, 2005).

8.4.2 Regular Use

8.4.2.1 Mood-Alteration Effects

One of the main reasons for using drugs is that they have important mood-altering effects. Alcohol makes the drinker friendly, confident and relaxed (Harvey, Foster, MacKay, Carroll et al., 2002); smokers claim that smoking cigarettes has a relaxing and calming effect (Ikard, Green & Horn, 1969); stimulants such as cocaine and amphetamines affect the CNS and brain neurotransmitters to cause feelings of euphoria, energy and confidence (Volkow, Wang, Fischman, Foltin et al., 1997); opiates such as heroin generate immediate feelings of ecstasy and feelings of well-being and loss of negative emotions; and hallucinogens such as cannabis produce feelings of relaxation, euphoria, sociability and sharpened perceptions. It makes sense, therefore, to hypothesize that regular use of these substances is reinforced by their general mood-enhancing effects – especially in individuals who may normally experience negative affect (e.g. depression, life stress).

A good deal of research has been carried out on the putative tension or stress-reducing effects of smoking and drinking. There is some evidence that alcohol may reduce tension, even in individuals who are not alcohol dependent (Sher & Levenson, 1982), and this is consistent with the drinker's everyday belief that drinking is a good way to unwind, such as after a demanding day at work. However, the picture is not quite that simple. Alcohol appears to reduce responding in the presence of both negative and positive affect, and so may simply have an *arousal-dampening* effect regardless of the valency of the drinker's emotional state (Stritzke, Patrick & Lang, 1995).

Subsequent studies have indicated that alcohol has its apparent arousal-dampening effects by altering perception and attention. The alcohol-intoxicated individual has less cognitive capacity available to process all ongoing information, thus alcohol acts to narrow attention, which means that the drinker processes fewer cues less well. This is known as *alcohol myopia* (Steele & Josephs, 1990), and means that the drinker's behaviour is likely to be under the influence of the most salient cues in the situation. In lively, friendly environments this will result in the drinker processing only these types of cues. As a consequence, he or she will feel happy and sociable, and will not have the capacity to simultaneously process worries or negative emotions. However, in drinking situations where there are no happy, lively cues (such as in the case of the unhappy lone drinker), the reduced cognitive processing can result in attentional focusing on negative thoughts, experiences and emotions, which means that the drinker experiences more negative affect than if he or she had abstained.

In the case of nicotine, we saw in section 8.3.2 that there is evidence that regular smokers use nicotine as a means of coping

Alcohol myopia The situation where an alcohol-intoxicated individual has less cognitive capacity available to process all ongoing information, and so alcohol acts to narrow attention and means that the drinker processes fewer cues less well.

© Mike Baldwin / Cornered

"So she left you. Maybe it wasn't your fault. Sometimes circumstances are beyond your lack of self-control."

Plate 8.6
Alcohol has an attention-narrowing effect known as alcohol myopia, which means that the drinker's behaviour comes under the control of the most salient cues in the environment. If these are 'happy' cues, the drinker will feel happy and sociable. However, if the person is drinking alone and ruminating over personal problems, this can lead him or her to focus exclusively on negative thoughts and emotions.

with stress (Schachter, 1982; Parrott, 1998, 1999). This begins when the smoker lights a cigarette in order to alleviate nicotine withdrawal symptoms. After regular use, however, many smokers come to associate smoking with tension relief generally, and so become conditioned to having a cigarette during or after *any* stressful experience (Kassel, 2000). This gives feelings of relaxation and improved concentration as nicotine levels increase, and functions to reinforce the act of smoking. Consistent with this view is the longitudinal finding that increases in negative affect and stressful life events are associated with increases in smoking (Wills, Sandy & Yaeger, 2002).

In summary, there is clear evidence that many substances appear to have mood-altering effects, and so substance use may be maintained by these effects. However, in many cases, these affects are more complicated than they appear to the user. For example, alcohol appears not to have a simple mood-enhancing effect but has an attention-focusing effect, which makes drinkers feel relaxed and happy only when there are happy cues for them to focus on. In addition, the tension relief that smokers report after having a cigarette may only be relieving the negative effects of nicotine withdrawal and bringing smokers up to the positive mood levels normally experienced by non-smokers.

8.4.2.2 Self-Medication

Rather than simply being used as a means of reducing the effects of everyday tensions and stressors, substance use can become regular as a means of *self-medication* when individuals are suffering more severe adjustment difficulties such as those caused by diagnosable psychiatric disorders.

Self-medication Self-administration of often illicit drugs by an individual to alleviate perceived or real problems, usually of a psychological nature.

This view is supported by the fact that substance use disorders are highly comorbid with a range of other psychiatric disorders, including bipolar disorder, depression, eating disorders, schizophrenia, personality disorders and anxiety disorders such as obsessive-compulsive disorder, post-traumatic stress disorder and panic disorder (Regier, Farmer, Rae, Locke et al., 1990; Brooner, King, Kidorf, Schmidt et al., 1997) (see Table 8.6), and self-medication is frequently reported by substance users as a motive for using the substance (Sbrana, Bizzarri, Rucci, Gonnelli et al., 2005). There is evidence that anxiety disorders and depression predate the onset of substance use disorders such as alcohol dependency (Merikangas, Mehta, Molnar, Walters et al., 1998; Liraud & Verdoux, 2000), which is again consistent with the view that drugs are used for medication purposes after a psychiatric disorder has already developed. However, if individuals who use drugs for self-medication purposes are aware of the longer-term negative effects of these drugs, why do they continue to use them? Drake, Wallach, Alverson and Mueser (2002) suggest a number of reasons for continued use:

1 the drug has intrinsic rewarding effects and leads to physical dependency;

2 the lives of individuals with psychiatric disorders are so miserable that the medicinal effects of the drug offset its negative effects;

3 the drug may not only reduce tension and negative affect, it may also have other positive consequences such as helping the individual to cope in social situations.

8.4.2.3 Long-Term Expectations and Beliefs

Substance users can also become regular users because they develop expectations that the substance will have positive effects. For example, young adolescents who believe that alcohol affects behaviour in positive ways (e.g. by increasing physical pleasure, enhancing sexual performance, facilitating socially assertive behaviour) are significantly more likely to begin drinking than adolescents who do not hold these beliefs, and are also more likely to become problem drinkers (Goldman, Brown & Christiansen, 1987; Christiansen, Roehling, Smith & Goldman, 1989). In many cases these beliefs appear to be culturally generated, because empirical studies suggest that alcohol does not increase levels of sexual arousal or aggression, but in fact reduces physiological arousal (Lang, Goeckner, Adessor & Marlatt, 1975; Wilson & Lawson, 1976). Many regular substance users also develop erroneous beliefs that the substance they use is harmless, and these beliefs help to maintain regular use. For example, the increase in cannabis use during the 1990s was mainly confined to those individuals who considered cannabis to be harmless (US Department of Health and Human Sciences, 1994), and many regular smokers believe that smoking may cause cancer and illness in other smokers, but not in themselves (Ayanian & Cleary, 1999).

8.4.2.4 Cultural Variables

There are some cultural factors that will influence the transition from first use to regular use. For example, alcohol consumption differs significantly across different countries and is most prevalent in wine-drinking societies (such as France, Italy and Spain) where drinking alcohol is widely accepted as a social and recreational activity (deLint, 1978). Increased use in these countries may be caused by the regular availability of alcohol in certain situations, such as drinking wine with meals, and the availability of wine and alcohol in a broad range of social settings. There are also some culturally determined differences in beliefs about the effects of drugs that appear to affect the frequency of use. For instance, Ma and Shive (2000) found that white Americans reported significantly less risk associated with a range of drugs (alcohol, cigarettes, cocaine and cannabis) than African or Hispanic Americans. The former group was found to use all of these drugs significantly more than the latter groups.

8.4.3 Abuse and Dependency

8.4.3.1 Genetic Predisposition

Selective breeding studies with animals suggest that there may be a number of genetically inherited factors that make individuals prone to substance abuse and dependency. For example, mice have been bred to exhibit a preference for and dependency on drugs such as alcohol (Melo, Shendure, Pociask & Silver, 1996).

The study of inherited factors in humans has been confined mostly to the study of alcohol abuse and dependency. Twin studies have indicated that the concordance rates for alcohol abuse in MZ and DZ twins respectively are 54 per cent and 28 per cent (Kaji, 1960), indicating a strong genetic component in alcohol abuse. A similar genetic predisposition has been found in twin studies of cannabis abuse (Kendler & Prescott, 1998), nicotine dependency (True, Xian, Scherrer, Madden et al., 1999) and drug abuse generally (Tsuang, Lyons, Meyer, Doyle et al., 1998). Adoption studies also support a role for genetic inheritance in alcohol use disorders. Cadoret, Troughton, O'Gorman and Heywood (1986) found that adopted children were more likely to develop an alcohol use disorder if their biological parents also had a substance disorder rather than if their adopted parents had a disorder. This suggests that factors related to genetic inheritance are more important in determining alcohol abuse than exposure to drinking in the adopted home environment.

So how might genetic factors put some individuals more at risk for substance abuse and dependency than others? There are a number of different possibilities. First, a genetic predisposition for alcohol dependency may interact with environmental factors such as stress (a diathesis-stress model). Cloninger (1987) has argued that a genetic predisposition for alcohol dependency will be activated only by experiencing environmental stress (e.g. low socioeconomic status). However, other studies have indicated that there may be a more general genes–environment interaction, where a genetic predisposition for alcohol dependency will only cause alcohol abuse if other environmental factors are present. These environmental factors are not necessarily stressors, but include factors which might facilitate alcohol use, such as living in places where there are large numbers of young people (Dick, Rose, Viken, Kaprio et al., 2001) or peer pressure or parental modelling (Rose, 1998). These environmental factors seem to be important because they are likely to initiate drinking. Once drinking has started, genetic factors then appear to play a significant role in determining regular use, abuse and dependency (Heath, 1995).

Secondly, genetic factors may influence tolerance levels to drugs such as alcohol, or affect central nervous system responses to the drug (Schuckit, 1983). Alcohol dependency requires users to drink a lot and to do this regularly, and many individuals who develop alcohol use disorders appear to have inherited a strong tolerance for alcohol. That is, they report low levels of intoxication after a drinking bout and show fewer signs of physical intoxication (such as body sway) (Schuckit, 1994; Schuckit & Smith, 1996), and these higher thresholds for intoxication may permit heavier and heavier bouts of drinking that are typical of alcohol use disorders.

Thirdly, there is considerable evidence that certain genes influence sensitivity to alcohol, and it is the inheritance of these genes that determines whether a drinker will become dependent. The main candidate is a gene known as ALDH2 (Wall, Shea, Chan & Carr, 2001). Alcohol metabolism in the liver goes through two main stages. These are the conversion of alcohol into a toxic substance called acetaldehyde, followed by conversion of acetaldehyde into non-toxic acetic acids. ALDH2 is thought to affect the rate at which acetaldehyde is metabolized. If it is metabolized more slowly, individuals will begin to feel the negative effects of its toxicity, such as nausea, headaches, stomach pains and physical signs of intoxication. Interestingly, many Asians are known to have a mutant allele for ALDH2 which slows acetaldehyde metabolism and allows it to build up after a drinking bout. This makes drinking large amounts of alcohol aversive and appears to be an important factor in explaining why Asians develop alcohol use disorders at only about half the rate of non-Asians (Tu & Israel, 1995). Other mutant forms of this gene which allow rapid metabolism of acetaldehyde may be the inherited factor that causes tolerance effects in some individuals and leads to regular alcohol use and dependency. That such a tolerance is inherited is supported by the fact that sons of heavy alcohol users report being less intoxicated than others after a standard amount of alcohol and show fewer physical signs of intoxication (Schuckit, Tsuang, Anthenelli, Tipp et al., 1996). Recent studies have identified a form of the ALDH2 allele in white American college students that is associated with lower rates of alcohol use disorder, lower levels of drinking and with alcohol-induced headaches (Wall, Shea, Luczak, Cook et al., 2005). This suggests that variations in the form of this gene can have an important influence on alcohol consumption and alcohol use disorders.

8.4.3.2 Long-Term Substance-Induced Cognitive Deficits

As you have read earlier in this chapter, there is much speculation about whether regular substance use causes long-term brain damage and permanent deficits in cognitive processes. Evidence for most of these claims is still fairly equivocal – especially in the case of substances such as cannabis or MDMA (Iversen, 2005; Cole, Sumnall & Grob, 2002a,b). However, most substance use disorders tend to be associated with a syndrome of underachievement, and abusers often exhibit lower IQ, lower educational achievement and motivational deficits compared with non-users. This may be a consequence of individuals who have intellectual and motivational deficits prior to drug use lacking the necessary coping skills to pull themselves out of the vicious downward spiral of abuse and dependency. However, an alternative explanation is that regular substance use may *cause* these intellectual and motivational deficits, resulting in poorer judgement and decision-making skills, and making such individuals more prone to falling into a pattern of long-term abuse. For example, there is growing evidence that regular substance abuse can have long-term effects on the balance and availability of important brain neurotransmitters such as dopamine and serotonin (Nestler, 2001; Heinz, Mann, Weinberger & Goldman, 2001). In post-mortem studies of the brains of regular cocaine users, Little, Krolewski, Zhang and Cassin (2003) found damage to striatal dopamine fibres resulting in neuronal changes causing disordered mood and disruption to motivational processes. This illustrates one possible route through which regular use could develop into long-term dependency, as changes in brain structures caused by the drug affect mood and motivation to such an extent that the user has significantly fewer cognitive resources available to fight dependency.

8.4.3.3 Concurrent Psychiatric Diagnoses

We have already discussed the role that comorbid psychiatric disorders can play in turning first-time users into regular users because of the medicating properties the drug has on psychiatric symptoms. However, comorbid psychiatric problems appear to play an important role throughout the developmental process to full abuse and dependency. For instance, once users have entered treatment for their dependency, treatment outcomes are significantly poorer for users with comorbid psychiatric disorders, and this is usually due to increased tendency to relapse after treatment (Grella, Hser, Joshi & Rounds-Bryant, 2001). There are at least two factors that contribute to this poor treatment outcome:

1 Individuals with comorbid psychiatric disorders are likely to face more life stressors after treatment (e.g. negative emotional states) and are less likely to have the coping resources required to deal with these stressors than those without psychiatric comorbidity (Ramo, Anderson, Tate & Brown, 2005). This returns them to drug self-medication as a way of coping.

2 Users with a psychiatric comorbidity are less likely to consider that drugs are problematic compared to their peers and tend to relapse very soon after treatment (Ramo,

Anderson, Tate & Brown, 2005). This suggests that they lack the motivation to abstain, even though their difficulties are compounded by psychiatric comorbidity.

In summary, psychiatric comorbidity is a real risk factor for transition both from first use to regular use, and from regular use to abuse and dependency, and is an important factor in determining relapse from treatment.

8.4.3.4 Poverty

Without doubt there are important socioeconomic factors at work in determining whether individuals will use drugs and develop from being regular users into being drug dependent. One such factor is poverty. There is evidence that an individual's first experience with an illicit drug increases in probability if he or she lives in or near an economically poor neighbourhood (Petronis & Anthony, 2003). This is perhaps not surprising given that such individuals may well be unemployed, have no other forms of recreation available to them, have little hope of occupational or educational fulfillment, and already live in sub-cultures that revere drug dealing as a high-status profession. Such conditions are perfect for the downward spiral into drug abuse and dependency, and are likely to represent circumstances in which individuals will have poor access to treatment services and long-term psychiatric support. Endemic drug use in poor communities fosters other problems, including infections such as HIV and hepatitis C contracted through injecting drugs intravenously (Rosenberg, Drake, Brunette, Wolford et al., 2005). Finally, substance dependency in poor areas also fosters crime in the form of robbery, fraud and prostitution (as the only means for users to secure money to buy drugs) and violent crime and racketeering as dealers battle to sell their illicit products.

SUMMARY

The acquisition of substance abuse and dependency has to be viewed as a developmental process that progresses through a number of well-defined stages, with different factors being involved in establishing substance use at these different stages. The main stages of development that we have highlighted are experimentation (the factors that influence first use of a substance), regular use (the factors that influence the move from experimentation to regular use) and abuse and dependency (the factors that make some people continue to use drugs even though this activity has significant negative effects on their lives and health). It is important to understand that use may be confined to any one of these stages, and many regular users can often function relatively successfully in their social, work and family environments. However, in terms of understanding psychopathology, it is the development from regular use to abuse and dependency that is of most interest to us as practitioners and clinical psychologists.

SELF-TEST QUESTIONS

● Is there any evidence that using 'soft' drugs leads to the use of 'hard' drugs?
● What factors lead young people to experiment with drugs?
● How do peer group influences affect whether a young person will try a new drug?
● What factors lead individuals to become regular users of a substance?
● In what ways do different drugs such as alcohol, nicotine, cocaine, heroin and cannabis alter the user's mood?
● What is the evidence that regular drug use can become a form of self-medication when the user has severe adjustment difficulties?
● What are the main factors that maintain substance abuse and dependency?
● How have twin and adoption studies shown that there is an inherited component to alcohol abuse and dependency?
● How does the gene ALDH2 influence whether a drinker is likely to become alcohol dependent?
● What kinds of long-term cognitive deficits can regular substance use cause, and how might they be implicated in maintaining substance use disorders?
● What is the link between poverty and substance use disorders?

SECTION SUMMARY

8.4 The Aetiology of Substance Abuse and Dependency

● The aetiology of substance dependency has to be viewed in developmental terms as individuals go through stages of **experimentation**, **regular use** and then **substance abuse and dependency**.

8.4.1 Experimentation

● Early use is influenced by the **availability** of the drug and its **economic cost**.

● Whether substances are regularly used by **family members** and whether the **family environment** is problematic can also hasten experimentation with drugs.

● **Peer groups** influence first substance use as individuals start using a substance in order to self-categorize themselves as members of a particular group.

● Substance use in young adolescents is significantly influenced by **advertising** and exposure to substances (such as cigarettes and alcohol) in the media.

8.4.2 Regular Use

● Almost all substances of dependency have **mood-altering effects** by either creating states of euphoria or ecstasy or reducing tension or stress. These factors may contribute to regular use.

● Substance use can become regular as a means of **self-medication** when the individual is suffering severe adjustment difficulties such as those caused by psychiatric disorders.

- Substance users can become regular users because they develop **expectations** that the substance will have positive effects.

8.4.3 Abuse and Dependency

- **Twin** and **adoption studies** suggest that alcohol abuse and dependency have important **inherited** characteristics.

- A gene known as **ALDH2** affects the rate at which alcohol is metabolized and will influence the individual's tolerance of alcohol.

- Regular users may become drug dependent because they lack the **motivation** and the **coping skills** to pull themselves out of a downward spiral into abuse and dependency.

- **Psychiatric comorbidity** is a risk factor for transition both from first use to regular use and from regular use to abuse and dependency.

- Endemic drug use is associated with **poverty** and poor communities, which also fosters health problems such as **HIV**, and **crime** and **prostitution**.

8.5 THE TREATMENT OF SUBSTANCE ABUSE AND DEPENDENCY

Treating individuals with substance use disorders is not a simple or easy process. At the point where users reach the stage of abuse and dependency, they are usually physically and psychologically addicted to the drug, suffer severe withdrawal symptoms when abstaining from the drug, and probably mix in social circles that will provide regular temptations to use the drug. In addition, substance dependency is often associated with other comorbid psychiatric disorders that will need to be addressed in a full intervention plan. Many younger individuals with substance dependency also do not see their drug taking as dangerous or problematic (Ramo, Anderson, Tate & Brown, 2005), and so have a high risk of relapse after treatment. It is often the case that those with most severe dependencies live miserable and unfulfilled lives. They may be homeless or living in poverty, and the relief from these conditions provided by the drug may be the individual's only solace.

Because of these difficulties, treatment interventions with clients suffering substance use disorders are usually multifaceted and address the individual's problems at a range of different levels. Table 8.9 provides an example of the stepped-care approach to treating drug misuse developed in the UK (UK National Treatment

Table 8.9 *A four-tier stepped-care framework for drug and alcohol treatment services in the UK*

In 2002 the UK Department of Health published a four-tier framework for the treatment of drug and substance abuse in the UK. These four tiers recommend the types of intervention required for clients with different needs and different severity of abuse and dependency, and all local regions are required to provide services at all four levels. Examples of some of the services provided by each tier are given below. The various treatment approaches provided by tiers 3 and 4 are discussed in section 8.5. Tiers 1 and 2 attempt to provide more general support for substance abusers in terms of assessment, community support (e.g. advice on health, housing and employment) and open-access facilities that clients can use for advice and support.

Tier 1 Assessment, Community Support and Referral

- Drug and alcohol screening and assessment
- Health promotion advice and information
- Support and advice on health care, social care, housing and employment

Tier 2 Open-Access Treatment Services

- Risk-reduction services (such as needle exchange facilities)
- Services that reduce risk of overdose and other drug-related harm
- Outreach services targeting high-risk groups
- Motivational and brief interventions for service users

Tier 3 Community-Based Treatment Services

- Comprehensive assessment and development of an agreed care plan with the client
- Structured programmes of care, including psychiatric interventions, structured counselling, CBT, motivational interventions and community detoxification programmes
- Community-based aftercare for clients leaving residential rehabilitation
- Provision of a community-based detoxification service

Tier 4 Residential Services

- Specialist drug and alcohol residential rehabilitation programmes
- Residential care
- Inpatient drug dependency treatment

Source: UK National Treatment Agency (2002).

Agency for Substance Abuse, 2002). This model provides health care advice, general community support, easy-access drop-in facilities for drug abusers and structured treatment programmes – both community-based and residential, depending on the severity of the dependency. Treatment programmes are usually multi-faceted in that they combine a range of specific intervention procedures designed to make clients aware of the circumstances and environmental stimuli that trigger substance use, deal with any comorbid disorders, develop motivation to change, and teach the social and coping skills needed to deal with life without drugs. These may also be combined with detoxification procedures designed to address the physical dependency that drug use has developed. In the following sections, we will begin by looking briefly at some community care practices, and then turn to specific psychological and detoxification approaches.

8.5.1 Community-Based Programmes

Self-help groups   Group therapy which brings together people who share a common problem in an attempt to share information and help and support one another.

Alcoholics Anonymous (AA)   A support group for alcoholics who are trying to abstain.

Community-based services come in a number of forms. They can be *self-help groups*, such as *Alcoholics Anonymous (AA)* (see Focus Point 8.2), which tries to help alcoholics replace networks of drinking friends with other AA members. Controlled outcome studies that have looked at the effectiveness of self-help groups such as AA suggest that participation can be an effective form of long-term abstinence up to 8 years after joining the self-help group (Timko, Moos, Finney & Lesar, 2000).

Drug-prevention schemes   Community-based services whose purpose is to try to prevent first use of a drug or to prevent experimentation with a drug developing into regular use – usually through information about the effects of drugs and through developing communication and peer-education skills.

Drug-prevention schemes are now widespread and take many forms. Their purpose is to try to prevent first use of a drug or to prevent experimentation with a drug developing into regular use, usually through providing information about the effects of drugs and advice to develop communication and peer-education skills. In the UK, government-sponsored schemes have four elements, which focus respectively on young people (especially in schools), communities (targeting young people and their parents who may be specifically at risk), treatment and availability. Constant advice and information are also provided through 24-hour telephone helplines and internet websites (e.g. www.talk-tofrank.com/). Prevention schemes are often local and tailored to the specific needs of the community. They aim to educate schoolteachers and parents on how to deal with specific drug-related incidents and how to provide drug advice to young people.

More recent schemes train young people themselves to deliver drug education information to their peers. Treatment in Practice Box 8.1 provides examples of two local community drug-prevention schemes that have used these approaches. Particular strategies that drug prevention schemes use are:

1 *Peer-pressure resistance training*, where students learn assertive refusal skills when confronted with drugs.

Peer-pressure resistance training
A strategy used by drug prevention schemes where students learn assertive refusal skills when confronted with drugs.

2 Campaigns to counter the known effects of the media and advertising (e.g. by combating tobacco advertising with anti-smoking messages).

3 *Peer leadership*, where young people are trained to provide anti-drugs messages to their peers (see Treatment in Practice Box 8.1).

Peer leadership   A strategy used by drug prevention schemes where young people are trained to provide anti-drugs messages to their peers.

4 Changing erroneous beliefs about drugs (e.g. that use is more prevalent than it is, or that a drug's effects are relatively harmless).

The evidence on the effectiveness of these types of schemes is difficult to gauge because they take place across different types of communities characterized by different risk factors and employ a range of different strategies over different timescales. However, some studies have indicated that, at the very least, such schemes do appear to *delay* the onset of drug use – even if longer-term effects are difficult to evaluate (Sussman, Dent, Simon, Stacy et al., 1995).

Residential rehabilitation centres are also important in the treatment and longer-term support of individuals with substance use disorders. Such centres allow people to live, work and socialize with others undergoing treatment in an environment that offers advice, immediate support, and group and individual treatment programmes. They provide clients with an opportunity to learn the social and coping skills necessary for the transition back to a normal life. In such centres, detoxification programmes can be monitored and supported with the help of peripatetic key workers. Residential rehabilitation programmes usually combine a mixture of group work, psychological interventions, social skills training and practical and vocational activities. In the UK, clients would normally begin residential rehabilitation after completing inpatient detoxification. There are very few studies that have objectively examined the contribution of residential rehabilitation centres to recovery from drug abuse and dependency. Despite the support offered by residential rehabilitation centres, the percentage of clients in such centres who do not complete their treatment programme is still unacceptably high (Westreich, Heitner, Cooper, Galanter et al., 1997). Perhaps not surprisingly, non-completers fare significantly less well than completers (Aron & Daily, 1976; Berger & Smith, 1978).

Residential rehabilitation centres
Centres which allow people to live, work and socialize with others undergoing treatment in an environment that offers advice, immediate support, and group and individual treatment programmes enabling clients to learn the social and coping skills necessary for the transition back to a normal life.

CLINICAL PERSPECTIVE: TREATMENT IN PRACTICE BOX 8.1

Drug prevention schemes

Prevention schemes are often local and tailored to the specific needs of the community. They aim to educate schoolteachers and parents on how to deal with specific drug-related incidents and how to provide drug advice to young people. They also involve young people as facilitators of drug prevention information. Two recent schemes in the UK, described below, provide an illustration of the methods used.

CASCADE, Birmingham

CASCADE helps young people to make an informed choice about drugs and their drug use. It trains and supports local young people as peer educators. Research suggests that many young people reject health messages regarding the risks associated with drugs. One of the problems is seen to be that adult professionals often deliver drug education to young people as passive recipients rather than as stakeholders in the learning process. The young peer educators work mainly in Solihull's secondary schools, youth clubs, colleges and hostels. The volunteers are aged up to and including 25. All young people are welcome to become involved on the CASCADE programme, and training and support are free and ongoing. The project aims

to ensure that those using drugs can get help if they have a problem and that everyone has access to accurate information about drugs. Evaluations conducted by the Home Office and others suggest that the use of credible young people as drug educators is a positive way forward.

Supporting Teachers, Parents and Schools, Teeside

The team consists of staff from education, health promotion and the police (an officer is seconded from the Cleveland force), offering a multi-agency approach to drugs education. The team works with schools to train teachers, school governors, parents and ancillary staff such as caretakers on drugs education issues. The team supports schools to develop drugs policies and education programmes which can be adapted to suit the particular circumstances of individual schools (e.g. faith schools) but which are based on a coherent and consistent approach. The project is linked with the Healthy Schools programme and coordinated by local school drugs coordinators. The team works with parents via schools, providing drugs awareness sessions and implementing the PRIDE model (Parents' Role in Drug Education), which engages parents both in the classroom and through homework. The team uses creative techniques such as puppetry to help teachers deliver the PHSE curriculum on drugs awareness.

8.5.2 Behavioural Therapies

There is a tradition of using behavioural therapies with many substance use disorders. These therapies are mainly adaptations of conditioning principles to the practical difficulties involved in controlling and preventing substance abuse and dependency. Behavioural therapies have a number of aims:

1   to change substance use from a positive or pleasurable experience to a negative or aversive one (e.g. aversion therapy) (Wiens, Montague, Manaugh & English, 1976);

2   to help the individual identify environmental stimuli and situations that have come to control substance use (e.g. behavioural self-control training, BSCT) (Miller, Leckman, Delaney & Tinkcom, 1992);

3   to reinforce abstinence by rewarding users when they provide drug-free urine specimens (e.g. contingency management) (Petry, 2000);

4   to teach users alternative behaviours that are likely to compete with substance use behaviours (e.g. relaxation,

meditation, social skills and anger management) (Azrin, Acierno, Kogan, Donohue et al., 1996).

8.5.2.1 Aversion Therapy

Aversion therapy has been regularly used in the context of a number of substance disorders, most notably with alcohol dependency. Using a classical conditioning paradigm, clients are given their drug (the conditioned stimulus) followed immediately by another drug (the aversive unconditioned stimulus) that causes unpleasant physiological reactions such as nausea and sickness (Lemere & Voegtlin, 1950). The assumption here is that pairing the favoured drug with unpleasant reactions will make that drug less attractive. In addition, rather than physically administering these drugs in order to form an aversive conditioned response, the whole process can be carried out covertly by asking clients to imagine taking their drug followed by imagining some upsetting or repulsive consequence. This

> **Aversion therapy** An aversive form of classical conditioning. For example, in treatment for substance dependency, clients are given their drug (the conditioned stimulus) followed immediately by another drug (the aversive unconditioned stimulus) that causes unpleasant physiological reactions such as nausea and sickness.

Covert sensitization A variant on aversion therapy for substance abuse where clients are asked to imagine taking their drug followed by imagining some upsetting or repulsive consequence.

variant on aversion therapy is known as *covert sensitization* (Cautela, 1966). However, there is limited evidence that aversion therapy has anything but short-lived effects (Wilson, 1978), and outcomes are significantly less favourable when clients with long-standing substance dependency are treated in this way (Howard, 2001). Nevertheless, aversion therapy can be used as part of a broader treatment package involving community support, detoxification and social skills training.

8.5.2.2 Behavioural Self-Control Training (BSCT)

Behavioural self-control training (BSCT) A treatment procedure for substance dependency that teaches clients how to restructure and control their behaviour and environment in order to prevent substance use.

Behavioural self-control training (BSCT) is a treatment procedure that teaches clients how to restructure and control their behaviour and environment in order to prevent drug use. This approach is also based on conditioning principles, including (1) stimulus control, where clients learn to identify environmental situations that trigger drug use and avoid or minimize them (e.g. identifying a stressful day at work as a trigger for drinking, and so avoiding pubs or bars); (2) using rewards to reinforce abstinence (e.g. a trip to the cinema or the theatre as a reward for not drinking for a specified period of time); (3) learning to be aware of when and how frequently drug taking occurs (e.g. by keeping a diary noting all times that drinking occurs); and (4) setting attainable goals in a structured, step-by-step approach to treatment (e.g. by setting *non-abstinence* goals that are achievable) (Hester, 1995). BSCT continues to be a valuable tool for therapists in this area, and a number of new variations on this methodology have been developed over the years (e.g. moderation-oriented cue exposure) (Saladin & Santa Ana, 2004).

Controlled drinking A variant of BSCT in which emphasis is put on controlled use rather than complete abstinence.

A particularly important variant of BSCT is known as *controlled drinking*. Traditionally it has been assumed that a 'cure' for a substance use disorder entails complete abstinence, but programmes have been developed more recently that put the emphasis on controlled use rather than complete abstinence. This approach, pioneered by Sobell and Sobell (1993), has been particularly useful for treating alcohol dependency. The assumptions here are that: (1) in modern-day Western societies it is difficult to avoid alcohol altogether, so it is better to have the aim of controlling drinking rather than avoiding alcohol completely; and (2) teaching clients to have control over their drinking behaviour has other benefits, such as improved self-esteem, a sense of responsibility and feelings of control over particular domains in their life. Absence of these latter characteristics often drives individuals to alcohol dependency in the first place. Clients undergo social skills training in order to negotiate situations in which they would otherwise drink excessively, relaxation training to prevent stressors that might trigger drinking, and are encouraged to think positively about other domains in their life (e.g. to eat healthily). Clients are also taught to believe that they have real control over their drinking, and the BSCT methods outlined above are regularly used to provide clients with adaptive strategies for control. Finally, controlled drinking also teaches clients to be aware that a lapse is not catastrophic but is often inevitable and natural, and that they can use the self-control and social skills they have learned to overcome lapses. Outcome studies suggest that controlled drinking is achievable, can be as effective over the longer term as treatments that require total abstinence (Foy, Nunn & Rychtarik, 1994), and can help individuals to moderate their intake and to live more fulfilled and healthier lives (Sobell & Sobell, 1995). Controlled drinking is also an accepted treatment strategy for a majority of substance abuse services in the UK (Rosenberg & Melville, 2005).

8.5.3 Cognitive Behavioural Therapies (CBT)

As we mentioned earlier, substance abuse disorders are notoriously difficult to treat over the longer term. Individuals can usually quit the substance in the short term, but relapse is common in up to 90 per cent of those receiving treatment for substance dependency (Brownell, 1986). As a result, a successful treatment programme has to deal as effectively with relapses as it does in getting clients to quit in the first place. Two factors appear to be important in determining whether a relapse will lead to regular use again. These are: (1) the client's beliefs about relapse; and (2) experiencing stressful emotional states, such as anxiety, depression, anger and frustration, which are responsible for around 30 per cent of all relapses after treatment (Cummings, Gordon & Marlatt, 1980). In order to counter these relapse factors, therapists have developed variants of CBT that address dysfunctional beliefs about relapse and can also provide help in coping with stressful emotions. In the first case, individuals will often hold dysfunctional beliefs about relapse that facilitate further regular use. These may include beliefs such as 'If I lapse, then my treatment has failed', 'If I lapse, then I am a worthless individual who doesn't deserve to get better', or 'I've had one drink, so I may as well get drunk' (Marlatt & Gordon, 1985). These are what are known as *abstinence violation* beliefs, which contribute to the transition from relapse 'slips' to full relapse. CBT attempts to identify such dysfunctional beliefs, to challenge them (e.g. relapse doesn't inevitably mean total loss of control), and to provide clients with the skills required to negotiate a relapse successfully.

Abstinence violation Dysfunctional beliefs about relapse following treatment for substance dependency that facilitate further regular substance use.

In order to deal with the second factor, CBT programmes have been developed that help clients to deal effectively with negative emotions, stress and the factors that might give rise to stress. This is also known as *motivational-enhancement training (MET)* and provides training in communication,

Motivational-enhancement training (MET) An intervention for substance abuse and dependency involving communication training, work- and school-related skills, problem-solving skills, peer-refusal skills, negative mood management, social support and general relapse prevention.

work- and school-related skills, problem-solving skills, peer-refusal skills, negative mood management, social support and general relapse prevention methods (Miller & Rollnick, 1991). Both forms of CBT have been shown to be more effective in establishing long-term abstinence and effective drug avoidance behaviours than traditional aftercare or control conditions (McAuliffe, 1990; Farabee, Rawson & McCann, 2002), and are particularly effective if combined with family therapy (Waldron, Slesnick, Brody, Turner et al., 2001).

8.5.4 Family and Couples Therapy

Many regular drug abusers are young people who often live with their families, and because of this family members can often provide support during treatment on a day-by-day basis. However, family therapy is important for a number of other reasons. First, many of the parents of substance abusers are also abusers themselves, and as such may constitute part of the problem that needs to be addressed. Secondly, individuals with substance abuse problems (such as problem drinkers) will often physically and sexually abuse members of their family, and so therapy may often need to involve those who have regular close contact with the abuser. Family therapy is an effective way of identifying and altering dysfunctional family patterns that may contribute to adolescent substance abuse (Alexander & Parsons, 1973). Family therapists will attempt to engage members of the family in the treatment process and to reduce blaming behaviour. Subsequently, the therapist will use contingency management and behavioural contracting procedures, and teach communication and problem-solving skills in order to facilitate more adaptive patterns of interaction within the family. This approach has been shown to be particularly successful in dealing with adolescent substance use problems, and is generally as effective in the long term as individual psychotherapies such as CBT (Waldron, Slesnick, Brody, Turner et al., 2001). Specifically involving a client's spouse or partner in therapy also has important beneficial effects, not only for the support that the partner can offer when required, but also for identifying specific problems in a relationship that may be contributing to substance abuse. Outcome studies have indicated that, when compared with no treatment, couples therapy produces longer periods of abstinence and improvements in the quality of the couple's relationship (Fals-Stewart, Birchler & O'Farrell, 1996).

8.5.5 Biological Treatments

Drugs are used to treat substance use disorders in a variety of ways. Collectively, these treatments are known as **detoxification** and are often used in conjunction with psychological treatments or as a precursor to psychological treatments (to wean heavy users off regular substance use and make them amenable to other forms of therapy). Detoxification is a process of systematic and supervised withdrawal from substance use that is managed either in a residential setting or on an outpatient basis. Drug use during

Detoxification   A process of systematic and supervised withdrawal from substance use that is either managed in a residential setting or on an outpatient basis.

detoxification can take a number of forms: (1) to help reduce withdrawal symptoms (e.g. anxiolytic drugs); (2) to prevent relapse by using antagonistic drugs to make subsequent substance use aversive (e.g. Antabuse, a drug that causes vomiting if alcohol is consumed); (3) to block the pleasurable CNS effects of a substance (e.g. naxolone, used with individuals who are opiate dependent in order to prevent opiates having their usual effects on brain neurotransmitter receptor sites); and (4) to wean users onto a weaker substance (e.g. **methadone maintenance programmes**, where users take a less virulent opiate in order to wean themselves off heroin).

Methadone maintenance programmes   A detoxification programme where users take a less virulent opiate in order to wean themselves off heroin.

Drugs that help reduce withdrawal symptoms include clonidine, which reduces noradrenergic activity in the brain (Baumgartner & Rowan, 1987), and acamprosate, a drug that helps to reduce the cravings associated with withdrawal (Mason, 2001). Basic anxiolytic and antidepressant drugs can also be used to improve mood and alleviate negative emotions experienced during withdrawal (Cornelius, Salloum, Mezzich, Cornelius et al., 1995).

Antabuse (disulfiram) has been used for over 60 years in the detoxification of individuals with alcohol dependency. It affects the metabolism

Antabuse (disulfiram)   A drug used in the detoxification of individuals with alcohol dependency.

of alcohol so that the normal process of converting toxic alcohol products into non-toxic acetic acids is slowed, which causes individuals to feel nauseous or vomit whenever they take alcohol. However, the use of Antabuse does have some problems. It is rarely effective when patients are given the drug to take unsupervised, and noncompliance and drop-out rates from such programmes are high (Fuller, Branchley, Brightwell, Derman et al., 1986). Secondly, it does have a number of side effects, and in some rare cases causes liver disease and hepatitis (Mohanty, LaBrecque, Mitros & Layden, 2004). However, when taken in properly supervised programmes, Antabuse has been shown to be more effective at reducing drinking behaviour than placebo controls (Chick, Gough, Falkowski, Kershaw et al., 1992; Fuller & Gordis, 2004). Indeed, some long-term studies of alcohol treatment have suggested that abstinence rates of 50 per cent are achievable up to 9 years after initial treatment with the supervised and guided use of alcohol deterrents such as Antabuse (Krampe, Stawicki, Wagner, Bartels et al., 2006).

A further set of drugs used to treat substance use disorders includes those that influence brain neurotransmitter receptor sites and prevent the neuropsychological effects of stimulants, opiates and hallucinogens. For example, drugs such as **naltrexone**, **naxolone** and the more recently developed **buprenorfine** attach to endorphin receptor sites in the brain. This prevents

Naltrexone   One of a set of drugs used to treat substance use disorders which influence brain neurotransmitter receptor sites and prevent the neuropsychological effects of stimulants, opiates and hallucinogens.

Naxolone   One of a set of drugs used to treat substance use disorders which influence brain neurotransmitter receptor sites and prevent the neuropsychological effects of stimulants, opiates and hallucinogens.

Buprenorfine   An opioid drug used in the treatment of opioid addiction.

opioids such as heroin from having their normal effect of stimulating these sites to produce more endorphins that create the feeling of euphoria. Such drugs do appear to reduce craving for opiates and help the therapeutic process when combined with other forms of psychological therapy (Streeton & Whelan, 2001). However, such drugs do come with a cost. Dosage has to be properly regulated, otherwise clients may be thrown rapidly into an aversive withdrawal (Roozen, de Kan, van den Brink, Kerkhof et al., 2002), and narcotic antagonists such as naltrexone and naxolone are only effective for as long as clients are taking them. However, because these drugs affect the release of endorphins, they have been used to help treat a number of substance use disorders, including alcohol (O'Malley, Krishnan-Sarin, Farren & O'Connor, 2000), cocaine and opiate dependency (O'Brien, 2005). The reason why such drugs may be effective over a range of substances that have their psychoactive effects across different brain neurotransmitter pathways is because they suppress the release of endorphins, and endorphin receptors are closely associated with the brain's reward centres (Leri & Burns, 2005).

Drug maintenance therapy   A drug treatment programme in which severe cases of substance abuse and dependency are treated by substituting a drug that has lesser damaging effects.

Hair sample analysis   A method of collecting data about previous drug use by analysing the small amounts of the drug that accumulate in the hair.

Finally, *drug maintenance therapy* involves treating severe cases of substance abuse and dependency by substituting a drug that has lesser damaging effects. For example, many heroin users put themselves at risk from overdoses, contaminated street heroin and using unsterilized needles. To try to address these issues as rapidly as possible, users can be switched from heroin to the less virulent opium derivative methadone. Methadone has a slower onset and weaker effects, and can be taken orally rather than injected. Initial outcome studies suggested that methadone treatment is helpful in enabling heroin addicts to withdraw from the drug. However, we must remember that methadone is itself an addictive drug that can be difficult to withdraw from (Kleber, 1981), and because of this methadone maintenance therapy can last for many years (Smyth, Barry, Lane, Cotter et al., 2005). Most recent outcome studies suggest that methadone maintenance therapy is most effective when part of a multifaceted structured therapy programme that includes psychotherapy, drug education and skills training (O'Brien & McKay, 2002), and when non-drug-using family members and friends are included in the treatment (Kidorf, King, Neufeld, Stoller et al., 2005). As well as contributing to the success of treatment in a multifaceted approach, methadone maintenance therapy has the added benefits of increasing the likelihood of entering into longer-term comprehensive treatment, reducing heroin use and criminal behaviour, and reducing health risks such as the number of HIV cases (Schwartz, Highfield, Jaffe, Brady et al., 2006; Farrell, Gowing, Marsden, Ling et al., 2005). While drug maintenance therapies have been largely confined to treating opiate dependency, there have been recent attempts to develop substitute drugs for other dependencies. One such example is Sativex, an aerosol that combines THC and non-psychoactive cannabis ingredients for the treatment of cannabis dependency. Sativex has the benefit of having weaker effects than cannabis and is taken orally rather than smoked (Kleber, 2005) (see also Focus Point 8.9).

RESEARCH METHODS IN CLINICAL PSYCHOLOGY BOX 8.1

Hair sample analysis

Many methods of collecting data about substance abuse are relatively unreliable. Self-report is obviously problematic, because users will often have reasons to lie about their drug use (if it involves legal issues such as child custody), or their recall of drug use may be affected by the changed states of consciousness caused by regular use of certain substances. Even blood and urine samples can be very variable in the data they provide (Spiehler & Brown, 1987), and are certainly not suitable for estimating longer-term drug use.

However, one relatively reliable method of collecting data about drug use is through *hair sample analysis* (e.g. Uhl & Sachs, 2004). Small amounts of the drug accumulate in hair after use. Because head hair grows at approximately 0.8–1.3 cm per month, a record of drug use is available over a period of weeks or months after intake. A hair sample of only 3–5 cm in length is required to provide a record of drug use over the previous 3–4 months. High-performance chromatography is used to identify the concentrations of any drugs taken up into the hair sample.

Hair sample analysis is used not only as a more reliable way of collecting research data about previous drug use, but also for medico-legal purposes where users need to prove long-term abstinence (especially in cases related to rehabilitation and legal custody). It is also used to provide a longer-term record of drug use in the case of individuals who may have died from overdose (Tagliaro, Battisti, Smith & Marigo, 1998), and has been used to detect the use of opiates, cocaine, cannabis and amphetamines (Jurado & Sachs, 2003).

Nevertheless, hair sample analysis is not a foolproof way of estimating drug use, and it does have its own drawbacks as a methodology. For instance, it is not suitable as a measure of current drug use, only as a method of estimating previous medium-term use. It also cannot be used on those who present with very short hair or no head hair!

SUMMARY

The treatment of substance use disorders is inevitably a multi-faceted one, with most mental health services providing a range of treatments (detoxification, skills training, behavioural and cognitive therapies, and family and couple therapies) in a variety of settings (e.g. individual, community-based or residential). Treatments usually involve a combination of drug-based detoxification, psychological therapy and skills training, and will usually attempt to involve the client's family and friends in the therapeutic process. Substance use disorders are difficult to treat and we described some of the difficulties at the outset of this section. Nevertheless, outcomes are often good,

and total abstinence is an achievable goal – even with severely addictive substances such as opiates and stimulants. For example, a long-term study of heroin dependency in a small town in the south-east of England 33 years after initial treatment found that 42 per cent of those treated had been abstinent for 10 years (Rathod, Addenbroke & Rosenbach, 2005). This suggests that long-term dependency is not inevitable after exposure to addictive drugs, and individuals can often control their use as well as receive effective treatment for their dependency when required.

SELF-TEST QUESTIONS

- Why are substance use disorders not particularly easy to treat?
- Can you describe the different kinds of community-based programmes that help to prevent or treat substance use disorders?
- How have the principles of behaviour therapy been adapted to treat substance use disorders?
- Can you name the main features of aversion therapy, behavioural self-control training (BSCT) and controlled drinking?

- What are some of the benefits of using controlled drinking goals rather than complete abstinence?
- What are abstinence violation beliefs and how do cognitive behaviour therapies (CBT) attempt to treat them?
- What is meant by the term detoxification, and how are drugs used in detoxification programmes?
- How have drugs such as naltrexone, naxolone and buprenorfine proved to be useful in the treatment of substance use disorders?

SECTION SUMMARY

8.5 The Treatment of Substance Abuse and Dependency

- Treatment of substance use disorders is difficult because of the **physical effects** of dependency, the probability of **comorbid psychiatric disorders** and high rates of **relapse**.
- Treatment interventions are usually **multifaceted** and address the individual client's problems at a range of different levels.
- One form of community-based service is **self-help groups** such as Alcoholics Anonymous (AA).
- **Drug prevention schemes** are used with young people to try to prevent first drug use.
- **Residential rehabilitation centres** provide a controlled environment for detoxification and longer-term support for individuals with substance use disorders.
- **Behaviour therapies** adapted to treat substance use disorders include aversion therapy, behavioural self-control training (BSCT) and controlled drinking.
- **Controlled drinking** can be used as a non-abstinence approach to treating alcohol abuse and dependency.
- **Cognitive behavioural therapies (CBT)** are used primarily to change individuals' beliefs about their substance use.

- CBT is particularly useful for challenging and changing **abstinence violation** beliefs, where individuals believe that a single lapse means they will relapse totally back into dependency.
- **Motivational-enhancement training (MET)** provides communication training, work- and school-related skills, problem-solving skills, peer-refusal skills, relapse prevention methods and negative mood management.
- **Family and couple therapy** is useful for ensuring that family members understand the reasons for the substance use and can provide help and support during and after treatment.
- **Detoxification** is a process of systematic and supervised withdrawal from substance use that often employs the controlled use of drugs to combat the physical problems of withdrawal and dependency.
- **Antabuse (disulfiram)** causes alcohol to produce toxins which make the individual feel unwell and has been used for over 60 years as a means of controlling alcohol dependency.
- **Drug maintenance therapy** involves treating severe cases of substance use (e.g. heroin dependency) by substituting a drug that has a lesser effect (e.g. methadone).

8.6 SUBSTANCE ABUSE AND DEPENDENCY REVIEWED

As well as being important social and health problems, substance abuse and dependency raise many mental health issues. Substance use disorders are associated with criminal behaviour (often violent crime), short- and long-term health problems, disruption to social and occupational functioning, and increased risk of psychiatric comorbidity. The main substances of abuse can be grouped into stimulants (e.g. cocaine, amphetamine), sedatives (e.g. opiates, barbiturates) and hallucinogenic drugs (e.g. LSD). Legal drugs such as alcohol and nicotine can also foster dependency and can cause significant long-term health problems.

Most of the drugs associated with abuse and dependency have important mood-altering effects that make users feel confident, relaxed (alcohol, cannabis), euphoric (heroin, cocaine) or energized (amphetamines, MDMA). More significantly, these effects also alleviate any negative or stressful mood users may be feeling prior to use. Most of these substances also have addictive properties as users quickly develop a tolerance to the drug and experience worsening withdrawal symptoms during abstinence.

Substance use disorders can be seen as developing through a number of different stages, with different factors affecting transition from one stage to the next (see Figure 8.6). The three stages highlighted here are experimentation (what determines first use), regular use, and abuse and dependency (what makes some people use drugs regularly even though this activity has significant negative effects on their health and social and occupational functioning).

Some people do seem to move down a slippery slope from experimentation to abuse and dependency, but we have to be clear that many other people do not, and people can be regular substance users without this affecting their family, social or occupational functioning. However, when the stage of substance abuse and dependency is reached, this is often associated with comorbid psychiatric problems or simply with poverty. In the former case, many who are substance dependent use their drug to self-medicate against the negative effects of their comorbid psychopathy (e.g. depression, eating disorders, anxiety disorders). In the case of poverty, the mood-altering effects of the drug may provide relief from miserable and unfulfilled lives.

Treatment of substance use disorders is usually multifaceted, and many health services provide a tiered approach by offering a range of treatments, advice and training facilities in a variety of settings (e.g. individual, community-based or residential). Substance use disorders can be difficult to treat because of the difficulties of dealing with withdrawal symptoms, the fact that the drug has probably been the user's main method of coping with emotional and life stressors, frequent comorbidity of other mental health problems, and temptation to relapse after treatment. However, outcome studies suggest that with appropriate support and aftercare, treatment can result in long-term abstinence in a significant proportion of clients.

LEARNING OUTCOMES

When you have completed this chapter, you should be able to:

1 Describe the main diagnostic criteria for substance use and dependency and be able to define key terms such as craving, tolerance and withdrawal.

2 Describe the specific characteristics of a range of substances that give rise to dependency and abuse, including specific stimulants, sedatives and hallucinogenic drugs.

3 Describe and evaluate the psychological, physical health and economic costs of specific substance use disorders.

4 Describe a developmental model of substance dependency and evaluate the risk factors that contribute to the different stages in this model.

5 Describe a tiered approach to treating substance use disorders, and evaluate the efficacy of a range of psychological and biological treatment methods.

KEY TERMS

Abstinence violation *301*
Addiction *261*
Alcohol *266*
Alcohol myopia *294*
Alcoholics Anonymous (AA) *299*
Amotivational syndrome *288*
Amphetamines *279*
Antabuse (disulfiram) *302*
Aversion therapy *300*
Barbiturates *283*
Behavioural self-control training (BSCT) *301*
Binge drinking *267*
Biphasic drug effect *267*
Buprenorfine *302*
Caffeine *281*
Cannabis *286*
Cocaine *276*
Controlled drinking *301*
Controlled drug user *283*
Covert sensitization *301*
Crack cocaine *277*
Craving *262*
Delirium tremens (DTs) *269*
Detoxification *302*
Drug maintenance therapy *303*

REVIEWS, THEORIES AND SEMINAL STUDIES

Links to Journal Articles

Diagnosis and Prevalence of Substance Use Disorders

Sbrana, A., Bizzarri, J.V., Rucci, P., Gonnelli, C. et al. (2005). The spectrum of substance use in mood and anxiety disorders. *Comprehensive Psychiatry, 46*, 6–13.

Warner, L.A., Kessler, R.C., Hughes, M., Anthony, J.C. & Nelson, C.B. (1995). Prevalence and correlates of drug use and dependence in the United States: Results from the National Comorbidity Study. *Archives of General Psychology, 52*, 219–229.

8.3 Specific Substance Use Disorders

Garbutt, J.C., West, S.L., Carey, T.S., Lohr, L.N. & Crews, F.T. (1999). Pharmacological treatment of alcohol dependence: A review of the evidence. *JAMA: Journal of the American Medical Association, 281*, 1318–1325.

Iversen, L. (2005). Long-term effects of exposure to cannabis. *Current Opinion in Pharmacology, 5*, 69–72.

Jovanovski, D., Erb, S. & Zakzanis, K.K. (2005). Neurocognitive deficits in cocaine users: A quantitative review of the evidence. *Journal of Clinical and Experimental Neuropsychology, 27*, 189–204.

Kalant, H. (2004). Adverse effects of cannabis on health: An update of the literature since 1996. *Progress in Neuro-Psychopharmacology and Biological Psychiatry, 28*, 849–863.

Kiefer, F. & Mann, K. (2005). New achievements and pharmacotherapeutic approaches in the treatment of alcohol dependence. *European Journal of Pharmacology, 526*, 163–171.

Lundqvist, T. (2005). Cognitive consequences of cannabis use: Comparison with abuse of stimulants and heroin with regard to attention, memory and executive functions. *Pharmacology, Biochemistry and Behavior, 81*, 319–330.

Parrott, A.C. (1999). Does cigarette smoking cause stress? *American Psychologist, 54*, 817–820.

Shewan, D. & Delgarno, P. (2005). Evidence for controlled heroin use? Low levels of negative health and social outcomes among non-treatment heroin users in Glasgow (Scotland). *British Journal of Health Psychology, 10*, 33–48.

UKATT Research Team (2005). Effectiveness of treatment for alcohol problems: Findings of the randomized UK alcohol treatment trial (UKATT). *British Medical Journal, 331*, 541.

8.4 The Aetiology of Substance Abuse and Dependency

Alverson, H., Alverson, M. & Drake, R.E. (2000). An ethnographic study of the longitudinal course of substance abuse among people with severe mental illness. *Community Mental Health Journal, 36*, 557–569.

Crome, I. & Bloor, R. (2005). Substance misuse and psychiatric comorbidity. *Current Opinion in Psychiatry, 18*, 435–439.

Drake, R.E., Wallach, M.A., Alverson, H.S. & Mueser, K.T. (2002). Psychosocial aspects of substance abuse by clients with severe mental illness. *Journal of Nervous and Mental Disease, 190*, 100–106.

Ogilvie, D., Gruer, L. & Haw, S. (2006). Young people's access to tobacco, alcohol and other drugs. *British Medical Journal, 331*, 393–396.

Ridenour, T.A., Maldonado-Molina, M., Compton, W.M., Spitznagel, E.L. & Cottler, L.B. (2005). Factors associated with the transition from abuse to dependency among substance abusers: Implications for a measure of additive liability. *Drug and Alcohol Dependence, 80*, 1–14.

Steele, C.M. & Josephs, R.A. (1990). Alcohol myopia: Its prized and dangerous effects. *American Psychologist, 45*, 921–933.

Tsuang, M.T., Bar, J.L., Harley, R.M. & Lyons, M.J. (2001). The Harvard Twin Study of Substance Abuse: What we have learned. *Harvard Review of Psychiatry, 9,* 267–279.

Wall, T.L., Shea, S.H., Chan, K.K. & Carr, L.G. (2001). A genetic association with the development of alcohol and other substance use behaviour in Asian Americans. *Journal of Abnormal Psychology, 110,* 173–178.

8.5 The Treatment of Substance Abuse and Dependency

Fuller, R.K. & Gordis, E. (2004). Does disulfiram have a role in alcoholism treatment today? *Addiction, 99,* 21–24.

Kleber, H.D. (2005). Future advances in addiction treatment. *Clinical Neuroscience Research, 5,* 201–205.

Saladin, M.E. & Santa Ana, E.J. (2004). Controlled drinking: More than just a controversy. *Current Opinion in Psychiatry, 17,* 175–187.

Sobell, M.B. & Sobell, L.C. (1995). Controlled drinking after 25 years: How important was the great debate? *Addiction, 90,* 1149–1153.

Swearington, C.E., Moyer, A. & Finney, J.W. (2003). Alcoholism treatment outcome studies, 1970–1998: An expanded look at the nature of the research. *Addictive Behaviors, 28,* 415–436.

Texts for Further Reading

Galizio, M. & Maisto, S.A. (2002). *Determinants of substance abuse: Biological, psychological and environmental factors.* New York: Kluwer Academic.

Petersen, M., Petersen, T. & McBride, A. (Eds.) (2008). *Working with substance misusers: A guide to theory and practice.* London: Routledge.

Rotgers, F., Morgenstern, J. & Walters, S.T. (2006). *Treating substance abuse.* New York: Guilford Press.

Thombs, D.L. (2006). *Introduction to addictive behaviors.* New York: Guilford Press.

RESEARCH QUESTIONS

- There is a high level of comorbidity between substance use disorders and other psychiatric disorders. Is this because substance use is a risk factor for subsequent mental health problems, or because individuals with prior psychiatric disorders turn to drugs as a form of self-medication?

- Why do around half of those diagnosed with alcohol abuse go on to develop dependency, while the other half do not?

- There are important gender differences in the course of alcohol use disorders. What factors are important in determining these differences?

- A number of risk factors have been identified for alcohol use disorders. Are any of these factors direct causes of alcohol use disorders?

- Do cigarette smokers smoke in order to reverse aversive nicotine withdrawal effects and bring their mood levels up to those of non-smokers?

- Why do smokers continue to smoke, even though they are aware of the negative health implications of smoking?

- Nicotine is a CNS stimulant – so why do smokers report feeling more relaxed after smoking?

- Can a single exposure to some highly addictive drugs (such as cocaine) induce long-term changes in dopamine neurons?

- Are the cognitive deficits found in cocaine users permanent?

- Does regular use of amphetamines cause long-term CNS damage?

- Why is it that some people can use heroin as a periodic recreational drug without disruption to occupational and social functioning, while others fall into a cycle of abuse and dependency?

- What is the evidence that regular cannabis use has permanent effects on cognitive functioning?

- Is there a direct causal link between regular cannabis use and the development of psychotic symptoms typical of schizophrenia?

- There is a link between regular cannabis use and mental health problems, but are both these factors caused by a third variable such as low socioeconomic status, childhood behavioural problems or parental neglect?

- Regular, heavy cannabis users are more likely to have lower educational achievement and lower income than non-users. Is this because those who take up cannabis are more likely to exhibit apathy and lack of ambition?

- Do regular drinkers maintain their alcohol dependency by choosing to mix in social groups with similar drinking patterns?

- Does alcohol have a simple arousal-dampening effect, or are its effects cause by attentional narrowing?

- If individuals who use drugs for self-medication purposes are aware of the long-term negative effects of the drug, why do they continue to use them?

- How do genetic factors put some people more at risk for substance use disorders than others?

- Is long-term drug dependency caused by drug-induced changes in mood, motivation and cognitive functioning which provide the user with fewer resources to fight dependency?

- Do drug prevention schemes simply delay the onset of drug use in young people?

- Why are narcotic antagonists such as naxolone, naltrexone and buprenorfine effective over a range of substances, each of which have their psychoactive effects by influencing different brain neurotransmitter pathways?

CLINICAL ISSUES

- Substance use disorders are characterized by physical as well as psychological dependency. How can clinicians develop effective psychological treatments that will also deal with physical dependency?

- Relapse after treatment for substance use disorders frequently occurs under conditions of stress. How can clinicians deal with this problem?

- Many individuals suffering substance use disorders develop erroneous beliefs that the substance they use is harmless. How can clinicians challenge these beliefs?

- Substance use disorders are frequently comorbid with other psychiatric disorders and treatment outcomes are significantly poorer in such cases.

- Many individuals with long-term substance use problems may be homeless, unemployed and living in poverty. How much is this a problem in the successful treatment of such disorders?

- Residential rehabilitation centres are an important element of the service provision for the treatment of substance use disorders, but drop-out rates from such schemes are still unacceptably high. What can be done to deal with this problem?

- The effects of aversion therapy are often short-lived. Does such a therapy have a role to play in treating substance use disorders?

- Some drugs, such as alcohol and nicotine, are freely and legally available in many societies, so is total abstinence a realistic aim of treatment for abuse of and dependency on these substances?

- Many members of the families of substance abusers are substance dependent themselves. How can this be addressed in treatment?

- Detoxification schemes that require a client to self-administer detoxification drugs have high non-compliance and drop-out rates. Have treatment programmes developed ways of dealing with this problem?

- Are drug maintenance therapies helpful, especially when they may simply substitute one substance dependency for another?

9 Eating Disorders

ROUTE MAP OF THE CHAPTER

This chapter covers the description, aetiology and treatment of the three main eating disorders, namely anorexia nervosa, bulimia nervosa and binge-eating disorder. The chapter begins by describing the main symptoms and diagnostic features of these disorders, then explores their historical, cultural and demographic distribution. Eating disorders have their origins in a range of psychological, sociological and biological processes, all of which are explored in the section on aetiology. Eating disorders are complex and difficult to treat. The final section discusses those treatments that have so far proved most effective, namely pharmacological treatments, family therapy and cognitive behaviour therapy (CBT).

Introduction

For as long as I can remember, I've wanted to do everything under the sun – and be the best at it. If I got a C I'd be really hard on myself, and my parents made it pretty clear they wanted me to get a scholarship, since paying for college would be a challenge.

Plus, things weren't so great at home. I'd always had a terrible relationship with my dad. I felt like he ignored me most of the time. He could be pretty scary. Like screaming at me for little things – like leaving crumbs on the kitchen table after making a snack. I'd tell him when he hurt my feelings, but he'd just walk away and slam the door. On top of it all, he and my mum were fighting a lot, too.

It was hard to be at school and even harder to be at home. As a result, I began eating less. Starving myself wasn't my actual goal at first – just more of a response to everything going on in my life. But I started to lose weight.

Soon, my clothes got looser. Then I became a vegetarian, also cutting out all foods with chemicals and preservatives. I lost even more. I felt I had finally found something I could completely control – my weight. Even though my life felt crazy, I could do this one thing very well and, initially, I got a high from this accomplishment. Gaining or losing a single pound determined my mood for the whole day.

I remember watching a film in health class about the dangers of anorexia. I even hung warning posters around school during Eating Disorders Awareness Week. But I never connected my own weight loss to anorexia. Denial, of course, is a symptom of the disease. A voice in my head kept telling me the less food I let touch my lips, the more stable and safe I would be. My friends and family kept telling me I was too skinny, but no one could force me to eat. And, to be honest, it made me feel powerful that I could ignore pleas and starve myself. Even as my bones poked out from under my skin, I could not admit to anyone – including myself – how incredibly sick I was.

AMY'S STORY (GIRL'S LIFE, FEB–MARCH, 2002)

Introduction

Amy's Story illustrates what a slippery slope the descent into an eating disorder can be. The story starts with someone who is troubled in various spheres of her life, including school life and home life. In Amy's case, this leads more by accident than design to a reduction in eating. Eventually, controlling eating becomes a goal in itself and a source of satisfaction when even the smallest of dietary goals are met. The obvious physical consequences of lack of nutrition are exhaustion and lack of concentration, menstrual irregularities, proneness to infections, insomnia, dizzy spells and sensitivity to cold. *Amy's Story* also highlights some of the risk factors that have been found to predict the development of an eating disorder such as anorexia, including high levels of perfectionism and parents who exhibit coercive control or who are hostile and unresponsive to the individual's needs. Also characteristic of the disorder, and featured in *Amy's Story*, are the need to control eating as a central feature of eating disorders generally, the development of very durable and resistant beliefs about the need to diet and control eating, and the use of denial as a means of avoiding confronting the disorder and challenging dysfunctional beliefs about eating. Focus Point 9.1 summarizes some of the warning signs of anorexia nervosa, many of which will have been apparent as Amy developed her own eating disorder.

Disorders of eating are complex and have their roots in psychological, sociological and cultural phenomena. In many of today's cultures, individuals are torn between advertising that implores them to eat a range of foods high in calories, and campaigns designed to promote selective and healthy eating, because being overweight is closely associated with increase of certain illnesses and higher death rates. Eating behaviour is also influenced by media representations of ideal body shapes. These prompt appearance-conscious individuals to control and restrict their eating in order to achieve these media-portrayed ideals of a slim body. Given these pressures, and the psychological factors that accompany them, it is not surprising that eating patterns can become pathological and result in disorders of both undereating (anorexia nervosa) and overeating (bulimia nervosa and binge-eating disorder). Recent figures suggest that obesity is increasing significantly in Western cultures. In the UK, obesity has trebled over the last 20 years, with

Plate 9.1
In Western societies, people are regularly torn between advertisements that implore them to eat a range of different foods (above) and campaigns designed to develop healthy eating (right). Perhaps as a result of these conflicting messages, the incidence of both disorders of undereating (anorexia nervosa) and obesity is on the rise.

24 million overweight adults in England alone (of these, 1 in 5 are clinically obese).

At the other end of the eating spectrum, between 25 and 30 per cent of females claim to be dieting or actively attempting to

FOCUS POINT 9.1

Warning signs of anorexia nervosa

- Is the individual losing a lot of weight? Has she fallen 7 pounds below the normal weight range for someone of her height?
- Is she becoming an obsessive calories-counter? Does she eat only very low-calorie foods, like salad and fruit?

- Is she becoming secretive or evasive about her eating habits? Does she eat out of sight or in private?
- Has she started to become obsessive about exercise, or any other daily routine (e.g. homework)?
- Is she suffering unusually from infections, constipation, dizzy spells, insomnia, or does she complain of the cold?

Source: www.annecollins.com/eating-disorders/anorexia.htm

Plate 9.1 *(cont'd)*

What's your body mass index (BMI)?

A healthy weight range is based on a measurement known as the ***body mass index (BMI)***. You can calculate this if you know your weight and your height.

To calculate your BMI, divide your weight (in kilograms) by the square of your height (in metres):

weight (in kilograms) / height (in metres)^2

- A BMI of 25 to 29.9 is considered overweight, and one of 30 or above is considered obese.

- People with BMIs between 19 and 22 live longest. Death rates are significantly higher for people with indices 25 and above.

- If your BMI is below 18.5, then you would normally be considered to be underweight.

- A BMI of less than 15, with rapid weight loss and medical complications, is sometimes used as a criterion for hospitalization in the case of anorexia nervosa.

- However, two people can have the same BMI but a different percentage of body fat. A bodybuilder with a large muscle mass and a low percentage of body fat may have the same BMI as a person who has more body fat because BMI is calculated using weight and height only.

- Remember, BMI alone is not diagnostic. It is one of many risk factors for disease and death. As a person's BMI increases, the risk for many diseases increases as well. It is important to talk with your doctor about other measures and risk factors (e.g., waist circumference, smoking, physical activity level, diet.)

When you have calculated your BMI, think about how this makes you feel. Are you dissatisfied with your weight even though your BMI may be within an acceptably normal range?

---

lose weight (McVey, Tweed & Blackmore, 2004; Wardle & Johnson, 2002). Such is the contemporary drift towards extreme eating patterns that 13.4 per cent of girls and 7.1 per cent of boys have been found to engage in disordered eating patterns, including excessive fasting or dieting, overeating or binge eating (Neumark-Sztainer & Hannan, 2000). Apart from the cultural pressures that can trigger overeating and undereating, psychological factors also represent both risk factors and outcomes of disordered eating. As we shall see later in this chapter, developmental and psychological processes appear to act as vulnerability factors in the development of eating disorders, and eating disorders themselves can result in psychological symptoms such as low self-esteem, substance misuse and suicidal ideation (Neumark-Sztainer & Hannan, 2000).

This chapter covers the three main eating disorders, namely anorexia nervosa, bulimia nervosa and binge-eating disorder, and for each one discusses diagnosis and prevalence, the role of socio-cultural factors, aetiology and treatment. Table 9.1 provides details of the eating disorders to be covered in this chapter, and readers may wish to refer back to this summary as they read through the chapter.

Body mass index (BMI)   A way of measuring a healthy weight range, derived by using both height and weight measurements.

Table 9.1 *Eating disorders: summary*

DISORDER AND LIFETIME PREVALENCE RATES	DEFINITION	MAIN DSM-IV-TR DIAGNOSTIC FEATURES	KEY FEATURES	THEORIES OF AETIOLOGY	MAIN FORMS OF TREATMENT
ANOREXIA NERVOSA (0.5%)	Self-starvation and a refusal to maintain a minimally normal body weight	Refusal to maintain body weight above a minimally normal weight for age and height Intense fear of gaining weight Disturbance in the way in which individuals perceive their body shape	Afflicts mainly adolescent women with onset in early to middle teens Characterized by a pathological fear of weight gain and distortions of body image Highly comorbid with major depression and OCD Mortality rates are still unacceptably high (5–8%)	Genetic factors Role of brain deficits (e.g. lateral hypothalamus) Neuroendocrine dysfunction Sociocultural influences (e.g. media influences) Peer influences Familial factors (e.g. dysfunctional family systems) Experiential factors (e.g. childhood sexual abuse) Dispositional factors (e.g. low self-esteem)	Antidepressant drug treatment (e.g. SSRIs) Interpersonal psychotherapy Family therapy
BULIMIA NERVOSA (1%–3%)	Recurrent episodes of binge eating followed by periods of purging or fasting	Recurrent episodes of binge eating Recurrent inappropriate compensatory behaviour to prevent weight gain Binge eating and compensatory behaviours occur at least twice a week for 3 months Self-evaluation is unduly influenced by body shape and weight	Recurrent episodes of binge eating followed by periods of purging or fasting Typical onset in late adolescence or early adulthood 90% of sufferers are female Characterized by a loss of control over eating patterns Associated with guilt, shame and high levels of self-disgust, low self-esteem and feelings of inadequacy A disorder closely linked to Western cultural ideals of body weight and eating behaviour Often comorbid with major depression and borderline personality disorder (BPD)	Genetic factors Role of brain serotonin levels Sociocultural influences (e.g. media influences) Peer influences Familial factors (e.g. dysfunctional family systems) Experiential factors (e.g. childhood sexual abuse) Dispositional factors (e.g. low self-esteem)	Antidepressant drug treatment (e.g. SSRIs) CBT
BINGE-EATING DISORDER (BED) (1%–3%)	Recurrent episodes of binge eating without associated purging or fasting	Recurrent episodes of binge eating Marked distress regarding binge eating is present Binge eating occurs, on average, at least 2 days a week for 6 months Binge eating is NOT associated with regular use of compensatory behaviours	Characterized by recurrent episodes of binge eating Sufferers usually overweight or obese Associated with high levels of depression, impaired work and social functioning, low self-esteem and dissatisfaction with body shape Incidence in women is 1.5 times higher than in men	Dispositional factors (e.g. low self-esteem) (Included in DSM-IV-TR for further study)	Antidepressant drug treatment (e.g. SSRIs) CBT

9.1 DIAGNOSIS AND PREVALENCE

9.1.1 *Anorexia Nervosa*

The main symptoms of ***anorexia nervosa*** are self-starvation and a refusal to maintain a minimally normal body weight. Examples resembling anorexia have been reported throughout history (see section 9.2, below). It is a disorder that afflicts mainly adolescent women and tends to have an onset in early to middle teens following either a period of life stress or an intense period of dieting. Ten times more females than males are afflicted by the disorder (Walters & Kendler, 1995). In recent years there appears to be an increasing trend towards early-onset anorexia in girls between 8 and 13 years of age (Lask & Bryant-Waugh, 2000). Important features of anorexia nervosa include:

(1) a refusal to maintain a minimal body weight;

(2) a pathological fear of gaining weight;

(3) a distorted body image in which, even when clearly emaciated, sufferers continue to insist they are overweight.

Weight loss is often viewed as an important achievement (see the example of Amy at the beginning of this chapter), and weight gain as a significant loss of self-control. Even when individuals suffering anorexia do admit they may be underweight, they often deny the important medical implications of this and will continue to focus on reducing fat in areas of their body that they believe are too 'fat'. Table 9.2 sets out the DSM-IV-TR diagnostic criteria for anorexia nervosa, which stress objective levels for judging whether an individual is underweight (body weight less than 85 per cent of that expected). The criteria also emphasize the pathological fear of weight gain in sufferers and the distortions in self-perception that accompany anorexia. DSM-IV-TR also distinguishes two types of anorexia nervosa. These are the ***restricted type anorexia nervosa***, in which self-starvation is not associated with concurrent purging (e.g. self-inducing vomiting or use of laxatives), and the ***binge-eating/purging type anorexia nervosa***, where the sufferer regularly engages in purging activities to help control weight gain.

Because of the severe physical effect of this disorder on the body, anorexia nervosa is usually associated with a number of biological symptoms that are

Anorexia nervosa (AN)   An eating disorder, the main features of which include a refusal to maintain a minimal body weight, a pathological fear of gaining weight and a distorted body image in which sufferers continue to insist they are overweight.

Restricted type AN   A type of anorexia nervosa in which self-starvation is not associated with concurrent purging (e.g. self-inducing vomiting or use of laxatives).

Binge-eating/purging type AN   A type of eating disorder in which the sufferer regularly engages in purging activities to help control weight gain.

Table 9.2 *DSM-IV-TR diagnostic criteria for anorexia nervosa*

A Refusal to maintain body weight at or above a minimally normal weight for age and height (e.g. weight loss leading to maintenance of body weight less than 85% of that expected; or failure to make expected weight gain during period of growth.

B Intense fear of gaining weight or becoming fat, even though underweight.

C Disturbance in the way in which one's body weight or shape is experienced, undue influence of body weight or shape on self-evaluation, or denial of the seriousness of the current low body weight.

D In postmenarcheal females, amenorrhea, i.e. the absence of at least three consecutive menstrual cycles.

effects of the self-imposed starvation regime. These include (1) tiredness, cardiac arrhythmias, low blood pressure and slow heartbeats resulting from altered levels of body electrolytes such as sodium and potassium; (2) dry skin and brittle hair; (3) kidney and gastrointestinal problems; (4) the development of lanugo (a soft, downy hair) on the body; (5) the absence of menstrual cycles (***amenorrhea***); and (6) hypothermia, often resulting in feeling cold even in hot environments. In many cases, starvation has the effect of severely weakening the heart muscles as the body uses these muscles as a source of protein. As a result, mortality rates (including suicides) in anorexia nervosa and bulimia nervosa are still unacceptably high, ranging from 5 to 8 per cent (Herzog et al., 2000; Steinhausen, Seidel & Metzke, 2000).

Amenorrhea   The abnormal failure to menstruate.

DSM-IV-TR cites the lifetime prevalence rate for females at around 0.5 per cent, with the incidence of the disorder increasing over the past century until the 1970s (Hoek & van Hoeken, 2003). There is some evidence that cultural and societal factors can affect the frequency of anorexia, so that prevalence rates may differ across cultures and across time (see section 9.3.2 below) (Miller & Pumariega, 2001). However, recent analysis suggests that anorexia may represent a similar proportion of the general psychiatric population in several Western and non-Western nations (examples of the latter include Korea, Iran, Hong Kong, Japan, Malaysia and Egypt), and there is growing evidence that it is not just a disorder of affluent Western cultures (Keel & Klump, 2003).

High rates of comorbidity exist between anorexia and other Axis I and Axis II disorders. For example, studies suggest that between 50 and 68 per cent of anorexia sufferers also have a life-long diagnosis of major depression (Halmi, Eckert, Marchi, Sampugnaro et al., 1991), and between 15 and 69 per cent of anorexia sufferers also meet diagnostic criteria for OCD or obsessive-compulsive personality disorder (OCPD) at some time during their life (Hudson, Pope, Jonas & Yurgelson-Todd, 1983;

Wonderlich, Swift, Slotnick & Goodman, 1993). However, comorbidity between eating disorders, substance abuse and borderline personality disorder appears to be restricted primarily to those eating disorders that involve self-purging of some kind (e.g. bulimia nervosa, binge-eating disorder and binge-eating/purging type AN) (O'Brien & Vincent, 2003). The fact that anorexia nervosa is highly comorbid with OCD and OCPD, and that obsessive-compulsive personality traits may be common factors in the development of both anorexia and OCDP, has led some to suggest that obsessive and perfectionist traits such as those observed in OCD and OCPD may be a vulnerability factor in the development of anorexia (O'Brien & Vincent, 2003; Serpell, Livingstone, Neiderman & Lask, 2002).

9.1.2 Bulimia Nervosa

Bulimia nervosa (BN) An eating disorder, the main features of which are recurrent episodes of binge eating followed by periods of purging or fasting.

Like anorexia nervosa, *bulimia nervosa* is also a disorder that is characterized by fear of weight gain and a distorted perception of body shape. The main feature of bulimia is recurrent episodes of binge eating (often eating more than a normal person's full daily intake of food in one episode), followed by periods of purging or fasting. In the *purging sub-type*, the individual regularly engages in self-induced vomiting or the misuse of laxatives, diuretics or enemas (vomiting is the most common form of purging and occurs in 80–90 per cent of those who present for treatment). In the *nonpurging sub-type*, the individual attempts to compensate for binge eating by indulging in excessive fasting or exercise. Most bulimia sufferers are not usually overweight compared to the norm for their height (Gordon, 2001), and they do not usually become underweight as a result of their purging; this distinguishes them from those suffering from the binge-eating/purging anorexia nervosa sub-type.

Purging sub-type BN A type of bulimia nervosa in which the individual regularly engages in self-induced vomiting or the misuse of laxatives, diuretics or enemas.

Nonpurging sub-type BN A type of bulimia nervosa in which the individual attempts to compensate for bingeing by indulging in excessive fasting or exercise.

Bulimia nervosa has a typical onset in late adolescence or early adulthood, and about 90 per cent of those suffering bulimia are female (Gotestam & Agras, 1995). Bulimia is frequently triggered by concerns about weight and body shape, and may have its origins in a period of dieting. What is perplexing about bulimia is that individuals with strong concerns about their weight and body shape should indulge in such regular bouts of excessive overeating (between 2 and 12 bouts per week; Garfinkel, Kennedy & Kaplan, 1995); this suggests that they have lost control over their eating patterns. Because of this lack of control over an area of their life that is important to them, sufferers usually become ashamed of their binges and try to conceal them. Consequently, binges tend to occur in secret, taking in foods that are normally quick and easy to consume, such as sweets, ice cream, cakes, bread and toast. Binge episodes are often well planned in advance, and can be triggered by periods of dysphoric or depressed mood, interpersonal stressors

Table 9.3 *DSM-IV-TR diagnostic criteria for bulimia nervosa*

A   Recurrent episodes of binge eating. An episode of binge eating is characterized by both of the following:

   (1)   eating, in a discrete period of time (e.g. within any 2-hour period), an amount of food that is definitely larger than most people would eat during a similar period of time and under similar circumstances;

   (2)   a sense of lack of control over eating during the episode (e.g. a feeling that one cannot stop eating or control what or how much one is eating).

B   Recurrent, inappropriate compensatory behaviour in order to prevent weight gain, such as self-induced vomiting; misuse of laxatives, diuretics, enemas or other medications; fasting; or excessive exercise.

C   The binge eating and inappropriate compensatory behaviours both occur, on average, at least twice a week for 3 months.

D   Self-evaluation is unduly influenced by body shape and weight.

E   The disturbance does not occur exclusively during episodes of anorexia nervosa.

or intense hunger following an extended period of dietary restraint. Perhaps, at least in part, as a result of this perceived lack of control over their eating behaviour, individuals with bulimia report high levels of self-disgust, low self-esteem, feelings of inadequacy and high levels of depression (Shisslak, Pazda & Crago, 1990; Carroll, Touyz & Beumont, 1996).

Bulimia displays significantly fewer physical symptoms than anorexia, but the most common physical sign is permanent loss of dental enamel as a result of regular induced vomiting. In some cases swollen parotid glands can produce a typical puffy face appearance. Extreme eating patterns caused by regular bingeing and purging can produce menstrual irregularity.

Bulimia is significantly more common than anorexia. The lifetime prevalence rate among women is between 1 and 3 per cent (Gordon, 2001; Hoek & van Hoeken, 2003). In men, the prevalence rate is approximately ten times lower. The incidence of bulimia in women in Western cultures appears to be increasing, but few, if any, cases of bulimia have been reported in women who have not been exposed to some extent to Western ideals and influences (Keel & Klump, 2003; see below). This suggests that bulimia may be a disorder very closely linked to Western cultural ideals surrounding body shape and eating behaviours, and so prevalence is likely to be influenced by changes in social conditions. Interestingly, in a study of bulimia nervosa incidence in the UK from 1988 to 2000, Currin, Schmidt, Treasure and Jick (2005) found that rates of bulimia rose to a peak in 1996 but then subsequently declined (see Figure 9.1). They relate these fluctuations in incidence

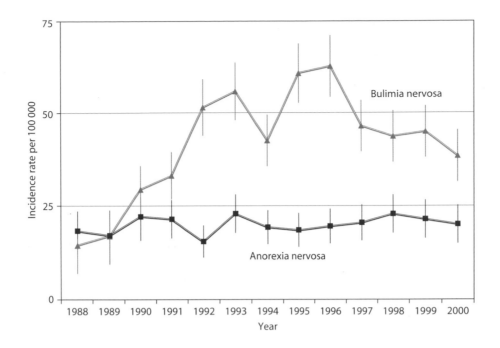

Figure 9.1
In the UK between 1988 and 2000, the incidence of anorexia nervosa remained relatively stable, but incidence of bulimia nervosa increased from 1988 to 1996 and then subsequently decreased.

Source: after Currin, Schmidt, Treasure & Jick (2005).

Plate 9.2
The increase in rates of bulimia nervosa in the UK up to 1996 has been attributed to the publication of Princess Diana's battle with bulimia during the early 1990s. A decline in the incidence of bulimia after 1996 also appears to coincide with her death in 1997.

to the press coverage given to Princess Diana's battle with bulimia during the early 1990s, and note that the decline in bulimia incidence in the UK appears to coincide with her death in 1997.

Bulimia nervosa is often found to be comorbid with other Axis I and Axis II disorders. Major depression is the most commonly diagnosed comorbid disorder, with between 36 and 63 per cent of bulimia sufferers being diagnosed with depression (Brewerton, Lydiard, Herzog, Brotman et al., 1995). Increases in bulimia during winter months also appear to be linked to symptoms of seasonal affective disorder (SAD) (Lam, Lee, Tam, Grewal & Yatham, 2001), suggesting that dysphoric mood disorder is a common concurrent symptom of bulimia. There has also been evidence for a strong link between bulimia and Axis II borderline personality disorders (BPD). Studies have suggested that between 33 and 61 per cent of women with bulimia meet the criteria for a personality disorder (Schmidt & Telch, 1990; Carroll, Touyz & Beumont, 1996). There is also strong evidence for a link between the bulimic behaviours of bingeing and purging and substance abuse. This includes heavy alcohol use (Lacey, 1993), increased incidence of the use of soft and hard drugs when compared with anorexia sufferers and non-clinical controls (Corbridge & Bell, 1996), and abuse of laxatives, diet pills, diuretics and emetics (Bulik, Sullivan, Epstein, McKee et al., 1992). The frequent comorbidity of bulimia with both personality disorders and substance abuse has led to the proposal that bulimia is a part manifestation of a broader 'multi-impulsive' syndrome in which individuals find it difficult to control many aspects of their behaviour, including eating and the use of alcohol and drugs (Lacey, 1993).

A detailed case history of the development of bulimia is described in Case History 9.1.

CASE HISTORY 9.1

Bulimia nervosa

Susan was the elder child and only daughter of a policeman and a nurse. When she was 11 her father left home and went to live with another woman. Susan was very angry, and had almost no contact with her father for the next eight years. She tried to be supportive to her mother. They became very close. Her mother tended to confide in her to an unusual degree and together they looked after Susan's brother, Sean, who had been only 6 when his father left.

Susan had no major regrets when her parents were finally divorced two years later. However, she was not sure how she felt when her mother started going out with John, a colleague from work, and within six months announced that they were to marry.

Susan felt uncomfortable with John. He tried hard to be friendly but tended to tease her about the way she was always going on diets that lasted just a day or two.

Over the next year Susan felt more and more isolated and unhappy at home. She tried to spend as little time there as possible. She went out almost every evening, often ending up drinking a lot. This added to her difficulties. She greatly resented it when John started to behave like a strict father. There were lots of rows between them. Later that year, she took her GCSE exams but the results were disappointing.

When Susan was 17 she met a professional footballer called Mark, who was seven years her senior. It was a difficult relationship, because although Mark was lively and glamorous, he also seemed to be rather unreliable. Just before Christmas, as she was wondering whether to finish with him, she found that she was pregnant. To her surprise, Mark seemed pleased at the prospect of being a father, and they decided to live together. Her mother and stepfather protested but Susan suspected that they were relieved that she was leaving home.

Susan dropped out of her course at Easter and gave birth to a baby boy, Rory, in July. She had put on a lot of weight during her pregnancy and afterwards felt fat and unattractive. She wanted to lose weight but found it difficult. Sometimes she was uninterested in food, while at other times she ate far more than she intended. She became mildly depressed and miserable.

She loved Rory but found motherhood overwhelming. With the start of the football season, Mark was often away and seemed less interested in the baby now. As the months went by, the couple fought more and more. Susan worried that Mark would meet other women on his trips away from home. And he became possessive, hating her to go out even with her old girlfriends. She felt increasingly unhappy and isolated, much as she had done a year or so before.

This time, however, she felt that there was no obvious escape route. She certainly did not want to go back to her mother's house. She also regretted giving up her education, but when she talked to Mark about going back to college he accused her of

wanting to meet other men. In the midst of a row, he called her fat, ugly and boring. He said that she had 'let herself go'. Susan was angry and upset, but secretly these were the very things she had been thinking about herself.

She made another resolution to lose weight. She started by going on a crash diet. She was pleased to lose some weight quickly but felt unhappy, hungry, preoccupied with food and irritable. One evening Mark telephoned yet again to say that he would not be home. She felt angry, upset and out of control. She stuffed herself with food until she could physically eat no more. Then she felt panicky and guilty. She made herself vomit. The next day she resolved to eat even less, but a week later she binged again. Much as she tried to stop, she felt caught in a pattern and soon was bingeing several times a week. Although her eating was now wildly erratic, her weight stayed much the same.

Susan left Mark shortly after Rory's first birthday. The final straw came when Mark hit her in an outburst of jealousy. She had recently re-established contact with her father and he threatened to 'sort out' Mark if she stayed. At first she went home to her mother. After a few weeks she moved to a flat on her own and started to build a new life.

In some ways, things began to look up. However, she still felt lonely and unsure of herself. At times she would feel quite desperate and even thought of trying to kill herself. She resumed some contact with Mark, but just as friends. She went out occasionally with her old friends and attended a regular aerobics class. She started a course at the local college and talked of eventually going on to university. To other people it looked as if all was well, but secretly her life revolved around a battle with bingeing and vomiting. She had become stuck within bulimia nervosa.

Source: www.familydoctor.co.uk/htdocs/EATING/
EATING_specimen.html

Clinical Commentary

Susan's case contains a number of elements that are typical of individuals who develop bulimia. She had a difficult home environment and needed to adjust to significant changes in parental relationships. She experienced teasing about her weight and appearance at home, and underachieved at school. Her subsequent marriage was a difficult one in which she probably experienced little control over her life, and she had no obvious means of escape from her situation. Arguments with her husband reinforced her belief that she had 'let herself go', and she resolved to diet to lose weight. Dieting then triggered feelings of extreme hunger, which led to binge eating following anger at her husband's failure to come home one night. Following the binge, feelings of self-disgust and shame led to purging. This starts a vicious cycle in which, after each binge, Susan resolves to eat less but inevitably ends up bingeing again.

9.1.3 Binge-Eating Disorder

Binge-eating disorder (BED) An eating disorder characterized by recurrent episodes of binge eating without the purging or fasting that is associated with bulimia nervosa.

Binge-eating disorder is characterized by recurrent episodes of binge eating, but without the associated purging or fasting associated with bulimia. Those suffering binge-eating disorder tend to be overweight, and usually have a long history of failed attempts to diet and lose weight. As a result, individuals with binge-eating disorder feel a lack of control over their eating behaviours and this causes them significant distress. Differentiating between a diagnosis of binge-eating disorder and bulimia nervosa is often difficult and depends on how frequently the individual indulges in compensatory behaviours such as purging. Because of this uncertainty about the distinctiveness of the two syndromes, binge-eating disorder has been included in DSM-IV-TR as a diagnostic category so that its distinctiveness can be clarified by 'further study'. Indeed, because of the overlap in symptoms, some view binge-eating disorder only as a less severe form of bulimia (Hay & Fairburn, 1998; Striegel-Moore, Cachelin, Dohm, Pike et al., 2001).

Binge-eating disorder typically develops during late adolescence or early adulthood. To be diagnosed with binge-eating disorder, an individual must exhibit binge eating at least twice a week for 6 months (Table 9.4). Binge-eating disorder is associated with high levels of major depression, impaired work and social functioning, low self-esteem and dissatisfaction with body shape (Striegel-Moore et al., 2001). The prevalence of binge-eating disorder in the general population is between 1 and 3 per cent, but is as high as 30 per cent among individuals seeking weight loss treatment (Dingemans, Bruna & van Furth, 2002). While the majority of sufferers are women, the incidence of binge-eating disorder in women is only one and a half times higher than in men (Stice, Telch & Rizvi, 2000; Striegel-

Table 9.4 *DSM-IV-TR research criteria for binge-eating disorder*

A Recurrent episodes of binge eating. An episode of binge eating is characterized by both of the following:

(1) eating, in a discrete period of time (e.g. within any 2-hour period), an amount of food that is definitely larger than most people would eat during a similar period of time and under similar circumstances;

(2) a sense of lack of control over eating during the episode (e.g. a feeling that one cannot stop eating or control what or how much one is eating).

B The binge-eating episodes are associated with three (or more) of the following:

(1) Eating much more rapidly than normal.

(2) Eating until feeling uncomfortably ill.

(3) Eating large amounts of food when not feeling physically hungry.

(4) Eating alone because of being embarrassed by how much one is eating.

(5) Feeling disgusted with oneself, depressed or very guilty after overeating.

C Marked distress regarding bingeing is present.

D The binge eating occurs, on average, at least 2 days a week for 6 months.

E The binge eating is not associated with the regular use of inappropriate compensatory behaviours (e.g. purging, fasting, excessive exercise) and does not occur exclusively during the course of anorexia nervosa or bulimia nervosa.

CASE HISTORY 9.2

Binge-eating disorder

Nancy had not had a food binge for over 2 years when she flew from Miami to Chicago to attend the wedding of her friend's daughter. Single, independent and devoted to her work, Nancy had just sold her first screenplay. She was pleased but she was also experiencing the 'postpartum' letdown that always occurred when she finished a major project.

Despite knowing, from 2 years in Overeaters Anonymous (OA), that she needed to keep a safe distance from food, especially in emotionally hard times, Nancy spent the entire day of the wedding rehearsal party in the company of food.

When night and the guests came, the flurry of activity made it easy for Nancy to disappear – physically and emotionally – into a binge. She started with a plate of what would have been an 'abstinent' meal (an OA concept for whatever is included on one's meal plan): pasta salad, green salad, cold cuts and a roll. Although the portions were generous, Nancy wanted more. She spent the next 5 hours eating, at first trying to graze among the guests, but then when shame set in, retreating to dark corners of the room to take frantic, stolen bites.

Nancy stuffed herself with crackers, cheeses, bread, chicken, turkey, pasta and salads, but all that was a prelude to what she really wanted: sugar. She'd been waiting for the guests to leave the dining room, where the desserts were. When they finally did, she cut herself two pieces of cake, then two more, then ate directly from the serving tray, shoving the food into her mouth. She reached for cookies, more cake and cookies again. Heart racing, terrified of being discovered, Nancy finally tore herself away and slipped out onto the terrace.

By now, in what she thought of as a 'food trance', Nancy piled her plate with bread, onto which she smeared some unidentifiable spread. Though the food tasted like mud, Nancy kept eating. Soon, other guests came out to the terrace, leaving Nancy feeling she had to move again, which she did, stepping into the kitchen – and the light. When Nancy glanced down at her plate, she was horrified: ants were crawling all over it. Instead of reflexively spitting out the food, Nancy, overcome by shame, could only swallow. Then her eyes began to search the debris on her plate for uncontaminated morsels. Witnessing her own

madness, Nancy began to cry. She flung the plate into the trash and ran to her room.

That event marked the beginning of a 6-month relapse into binge eating since the problem began 15 years earlier. During the relapse, she binged on foods and refined carbohydrates, returned to cigarette smoking to control the bingeing, and once again was driven to 'get rid' of the calories by incessant exercise after each binge, walking 4 or 5 hours at a time, dragging her bicycle up and down six flights of stairs, and biking miles after dark in a dangerous city park.

Throughout the relapse, Nancy went to therapy and to OA. But the bingeing worsened, as did the accompanying isolation and depression, which kept her awake, often crying uncontrollably, until the early morning hours. Finally, her therapist, a social worker, referred her to a psychiatrist, who put her on an antidepressant that has been used to control binge eating and on a structured food plan that excluded refined sugars, breads, crackers and similar carbohydrates. Within a few weeks, Nancy was able to stop bingeing, come out of the depression and resume her life. After 2 years on the medication, and the gradual reintroduction of breads and related carbohydrates into her diet, Nancy was able to stop taking the antidepressant without depression or return to binge eating. She continues to be active in OA.

Source: www.twilightbridge.com/truestories/bulimianervosa.htm

Clinical Commentary

Nancy's case history is a good example of how a person can lose control of her own eating patterns and eating behaviour. Features that are typical of binge-eating disorder include: (1) eating significantly more than a normal meal portion in one session; (2) an uncontrollable urge to continue eating despite the situation and surroundings; (3) forcing oneself to eat food that is unpalatable or contaminated; (4) a desire to conceal one's overeating from others; and (5) subsequent shame, self-disgust and depression when the binge episode is over.

FOCUS POINT 9.2

Eating disorder symptoms

Anorexia nervosa

- Rapid weight loss
- Excessive concern with body shape and weight
- Preoccupation with food and calories
- Decrease in variety of foods eaten
- Skipping meals
- Ritualized eating and food preparation
- Menstrual irregularities
- Excessive exercise

Bulimia nervosa

- Fear of loss of control over eating
- Excessive concern with body shape and weight
- Feelings of shame and secrecy concerning bulimic behaviours
- Consuming large amounts of food at one time (bingeing)
- Self-induced vomiting
- Abuse of laxatives, diuretics or diet pills

Binge-eating disorder

- Fear of loss of control over eating
- Bingeing
- Feelings of disgust
- Poor self-esteem

Source: www.hopkinsmedicine.org/jhhpsychiatry/ed1.htm

Moore & Franko, 2003). A cross-cultural study by Pike, Dohn, Streigel-Moore, Wilfley and Fairburn (2001) found that the incidences of the disorder in white and black American women were very similar, although black American women appeared to show less concern about the disorder than white American women. The case of Nancy is portrayed in Case History 9.2. This example illustrates many of the behavioural and cognitive traits exhibited by individuals suffering from binge-eating disorder.

SELF-TEST QUESTIONS

- What are the three main eating disorders defined by DSM-IV-TR?
- Can you describe the main diagnostic criteria for anorexia nervosa, bulimia nervosa and binge-eating disorder?
- What are the prevalence rates for the main eating disorders, and how do incidence rates compare between males and females?
- Both anorexia nervosa and bulimia nervosa are highly comorbid with other Axis I and Axis II disorders – which ones?

SECTION SUMMARY

9.1 Diagnosis and Prevalence

- There are three important eating disorders defined by DSM-IV-TR. These are **anorexia nervosa**, **bulimia nervosa** and **binge-eating disorder**.

- The important features of anorexia nervosa are a refusal to maintain a minimal body weight, a pathological fear of gaining weight and a distorted body image in which sufferers continue to insist they are overweight.

- Lifetime prevalence rates for anorexia nervosa are around 0.5 per cent.

- There are high rates of comorbidity between anorexia nervosa and other Axis I and Axis II disorders such as major depression and OCD.

- The main features of bulimia nervosa are recurrent episodes of binge eating followed by periods of purging or fasting.

- Bulimia nervosa is characterized by high levels of self-disgust, low self-esteem, feelings of inadequacy and high levels of depression.

- The lifetime prevalence rate for bulimia nervosa amongst women is 1–3 per cent.

- Bulimia nervosa is often comorbid with major depression, borderline personality disorders and substance abuse.

- Binge-eating disorder is characterized by recurrent episodes of binge eating without the purging or fasting that is associated with bulimia nervosa.

- Binge-eating disorder is associated with high levels of major depression, impaired work and social functioning, low self-esteem and dissatisfaction with body shape.

9.2 HISTORICAL AND CULTURAL ISSUES

There is considerable evidence that the prevalence of eating disorders differs both between and within cultures as a function of historical changes in cultural trends and social norms. This provides strong support for the view that some of the origins of eating disorders lie in the values and ideals defined by cultures. If so, examining historical and culture-bound examples of eating disorders should help us to identify some of the factors that make individuals vulnerable to eating disorders.

9.2.1 Historical Examples of Eating Disorders

Examples of disordered eating behaviour can be found throughout history, and many bear a resemblance to the eating disorders we find today (Keel & Klump, 2003). Cases of self-starvation have been reported in classical and medieval times, often as a means of achieving heightened spirituality amongst religious devotees. Bell (1985) called this **holy anorexia**, citing the example of St Catherine of Siena who began self-starvation at the age of 16 and continued until her death in 1380 (at the age of 32). Like modern-day anorexics, St Catherine portrayed herself as being afflicted by an inability to eat, and all attempts by peers and superiors to induce eating in such fasting saints usually failed. From the sixteenth to eighteenth centuries, reports of self-starvation were relatively common (McSherry, 1985), with the case of Mary, Queen of Scots (1542– 87) being a prominent one. During the nineteenth century, study of self-starvation became more systematic within the medical profession, with Marce (1860) describing a form of hypochondria in which 'young girls, who at the period of puberty and after a precocious physical development, become subject to inappetency carried to the utmost limits' (1860, p. 264). Probably the first use of the term anorexia nervosa was by Imbert (1840), who characterized *anoréxie nerveuse* by loss of appetite, refusal to eat and emaciation (Vandereycken & Van Deth, 1994).

However, while these historical examples have a formalistic similarity to modern-day eating disorders, the issue of the motivation behind self-starvation in these historical examples is important. At least some of the earliest examples of self-starvation appear to be motivated by religious and spiritual factors, while examples from the eighteenth and nineteenth centuries were justified as either forms of convalescence or hysterical paralysis (Habermas, 1996). However, Habermas (1989) quite rightly points out that individuals with eating disorders tend to hide their goal of losing weight and give other explanations for their refusal to eat. This may also be true of the historical examples we have reviewed here.

Historical examples resembling bulimia nervosa are much rarer than those resembling anorexia nervosa. Most examples taken

Holy anorexia   Self-starvation reported in classical and medieval times, often as a means of achieving heightened spirituality amongst religious devotees.

Plate 9.3
Mary, Queen of Scots, is just one historical figure who appeared to suffer from symptoms very similar to anorexia nervosa.

from classical times through to the nineteenth century report individuals exhibiting periods of fasting followed by a binge–purge cycle, which suggests that bingeing and purging were rarely found outside of the context of fasting or self-starvation (Keel & Klump, 2003). However, in the seventeenth century, Silverman (1987) reports a description of *fames canina*, a disorder characterized by large food intake followed by vomiting (Stein & Laakso, 1988). Interestingly, however, when symptoms similar to bulimia are reported in historical writings, most cases involve adult men. This is quite unlike the current-day disorder of bulimia, which is primarily an affliction of females.

Fames canina   An eating disorder characterized by large food intake followed by vomiting reported in the seventeenth century.

This brief review suggests that disordered eating (especially self-starvation) has been around as long as people have been able to write about it and report it. In different periods of history, the motivations for self-starvation appear to be different, although the symptoms remain remarkably similar. One implication of this is that disordered eating symptoms similar to modern-day disorders have been around for a considerable period of history. However, changes in contemporary sociocultural factors may influence the frequency and prevalence of such disorders by providing a motivation for disordered eating (e.g. religious fasting would have provided a suitable trigger for self-starvation in vulnerable individuals in classical and medieval times). In addition, sociocultural factors can also provide socially acceptable means of hiding the psychological reasons for self-starvation and loss of appetite. For example, when fasting became an acceptable form of convalescence from illness in the eighteenth and nineteenth centuries, this may have provided a suitable means of hiding the anorexic individual's simple desire to restrict and control his or her eating (just as the trend to diet to achieve a media-driven thin ideal serves the same purpose today).

9.2.2 Cultural Differences in Eating Disorders

A number of studies have suggested that cultural differences and cultural change may be associated with differences in vulnerability to eating disorders, and indeed may represent direct risk factors for eating disorders (Miller & Pumariega, 2001). The cultural differences in eating disorders are most striking in relation to bulimia. In an exhaustive study of the literature available at the time, Keel and Klump (2003) found no studies reporting the presence of bulimia in individuals who had not been exposed to Western ideals, and concluded that there does not appear to be a form of bulimia that is not related to weight concerns which are generated by exposure to Western cultural ideals. That is, when individuals from non-Western countries such as Iran, Pakistan, Egypt and Malaysia have exhibited symptoms of bulimia, they have usually been exposed to Western standards through learning English, being of high socioeconomic status or being educated beyond secondary level.

The role of culture in the development of anorexia nervosa is rather more complicated. Even within individual Western societies (such as the USA), individual cultural groups show differences in the prevalence of eating disorders, which can often be traced to differences in cultural ideals and practices. For example, African American women are less likely than white women to have eating disorders (Lovejoy, 2001), but both African American women and children have larger ideal physiques than their white counterparts and are more satisfied with their own body shapes (Powell & Kahn, 1995; Thompson, Corwin & Sargent, 1997; Neumark-Sztainer & Hannan, 2000). As a result, African American women are more likely to develop an eating disorder that does not involve a drive towards thinness, and so tend to develop bulimia rather than anorexia (Striegel-Moore & Smolak, 1996). However, exposure of ethnic minorities to the dominant thin ideal of American culture seems to be leading to increases in eating-disorder prevalence in these minorities. In the USA, rates of eating disorders in immigrant Asian females and Hispanic American women are significantly on the increase (Chamorro & Flores-Ortiz, 2000).

Despite these within-culture ethnic differences in vulnerability to eating disorders, symptoms indicative of anorexia nervosa have been reported in every non-Western region of the world and epidemiological studies suggest that its prevalence may be very similar to that in Western nations (Keel & Klump, 2003). This may well be because most countries in the world are nowadays subject to at least some Western influence. However, anorexia symptoms have still been reported in individuals who could not have been exposed to Western cultural influence. For instance, Abou-Saleh, Younis and Karim (1998) report a case of anorexia nervosa in an 18-year-old nomadic woman from the Empty Quarter in the United Arab Emirates. The fact that cases of anorexia are reliably reported in areas of the world where Western influences and ideals are almost nonexistent has led Keel and Klump (2003) to suggest that contemporary Western ideals may determine some aspects of anorexia (e.g. weight concern and body dissatisfaction), but are not necessary for producing the self-starving syndrome typical of anorexia. In effect, the presence of weight concerns or body dissatisfaction does not appear to be a universal motivating factor for food refusal in anorexia.

This summary suggests that cultural factors do appear to influence the prevalence of eating disorders, and the emphasis placed on weight concern and body shape in Western cultures is a potentially important contributor to the development of an eating disorder. As both non-Western countries and ethnic minorities within Western countries become more and more influenced by Western ideals, rates of eating disorder appear to rise in these communities. However, such Western ideals do not appear to be a *necessary* condition for anorexia.

9.2.3 Demographic Factors Within Cultures

Females are ten times more likely to develop an eating disorder than males (Striegel-Moore, 1997), and the reason for this sex-linked effect appears to be the idealization of female weight, size and body shape by the Western media (Harrison, 2001). This results in female thinness becoming an important social value that is associated with social acceptance and social rewards (Spitzer, Henderson & Zivian, 1999).

Plate 9.4
Western media regularly portray female role models as either naturally thin (and therefore representative of only a minority of the female population) or unnaturally thin. Young adolescent females then strive to achieve these relatively unattainable, or simply unhealthy, ideals.

Interestingly, at a time when the population of the USA is becoming heavier (James, Leach, Kalamara & Shayeghi, 2001), and obesity is set to become the number one cause of death in the UK, studies have suggested that men would prefer their body shape to be around 30 pounds heavier than their current weight (McCreary & Sadava, 1999) – presumably because they believe their body is not muscular enough. In contrast, females identify their ideal body weight as an average of around 40 pounds less than their weight (Irving, 2001). These differences in culturally determined ideal weight expectations appear to be largely responsible for the sex-related difference in prevalence rates for eating disorders. A fact that reflects the importance of shape ideals is that eating disorders in males are significantly higher in groups of males whose body weight and shape are of more significance and importance to them. For example, compared to the adult male population, the prevalence rates for eating disorders are significantly higher in male bodybuilders, athletes (Byrne & McLean, 2002) and ballet dancers (Ravaldia, Vannacci, Zucchi,

Mannucci et al., 2003). Also, the instance of eating disorders is significantly higher amongst gay men than amongst heterosexual men (Strong, Williamson, Netemeyer & Geer, 2000), reflecting the relatively greater importance placed on male physical appearance and attractiveness by gay subculture. Thus, even within cultures, whenever emphasis and importance are placed on body shape, size and weight, the rate of eating-disordered behaviour is likely to rise within that sub-group. The fact that the media often create body shape, size and weight *ideals* that are rather extreme from the average or norm – even within these sub-groups – is simply more grist to this mill.

SELF-TEST QUESTIONS

- Can you describe some examples of eating-disordered behaviour that have been reported throughout history? How do these reports resemble the modern-day symptoms of anorexia and bulimia?
- How do historical and cultural aspects of eating disorders help us to understand these disorders?
- How do the symptoms and incidences of eating disorders differ across cultures and ethnic groups?

SECTION SUMMARY

9.2 Historical and Cultural Issues

- Some of the origins of eating disorders lie in the **values** and **ideals defined by cultures**.

- Examples of disordered eating can be found throughout history, but examples of bulimia are much rarer than the self-starvation typical of anorexia.

- Changes in **sociocultural factors** may influence the frequency and prevalence of eating disorders.

- There is little evidence for examples of bulimia in individuals who have not had exposure to Western ideals.

- Eating disorders are less prevalent in ethnic minorities in the USA, but their incidence is increasing as these

minorities are exposed to the dominant thin ideal espoused by American culture.

- Examples of the self-starvation typical of anorexia nervosa can be found in cultures where Western ideals are nonexistent, which suggests than anorexia may not simply be a disorder caused by exposure to Western body image ideals.

- Females are 10 times more likely to develop an eating disorder than males.

- The importance of body shape ideals as a risk factor for eating disorders is reflected in the fact that eating disorders in males are significantly higher in groups of males whose body weight and shape are of more significance to them (e.g. bodybuilders, athletes, ballet dancers).

9.3 THE AETIOLOGY OF EATING DISORDERS

Like so many other psychological disorders, eating disorders do not appear to be caused by one single factor but have their origins in a range of psychological, sociological and biological processes, all of which appear to converge to generate the different eating disorder profiles. So broad is the range of influences that has been identified in this aetiology that many researchers have limited themselves simply to defining the risk factors that underlie eating disorders (e.g. Polivy & Herman, 2002; Jacobi, Hayward, de Zwaan, Kraemer et al., 2004; Ghaderi & Scott, 2001). Because of this complexity, theories of the aetiology of eating disorders based on the description of either psychological or biological processes are relatively under-

developed. We tend to have a good idea of *what* factors are involved in eating disorders (i.e. what represent risk factors), but relatively little insight into *how* they are involved. Figure 9.2 illustrates a recent attempt to classify the risk factors for anorexia and bulimia across a developmental timeframe, showing how important risk factors are at a number of different levels of description. These include 'pre-natal' risk factors such as gender and ethnicity, early developmental influences that generate eating difficulties such as infant sleeping and eating patterns, early experiences such as sexual abuse and physical neglect, dispositional factors such as low self-esteem, perfectionism and negative self-evaluation affect, familial factors such as parental obesity and parental attitudes to weight, adolescent attitudes to dieting and exercise, and comorbid psychological disorders such as OCD and social phobia (see also Lindberg & Hjern, 2003). What you will also see from Figure 9.2 is that different eating disorders such as anorexia and bulimia often have identical risk factors, and it is not clear why an individual may

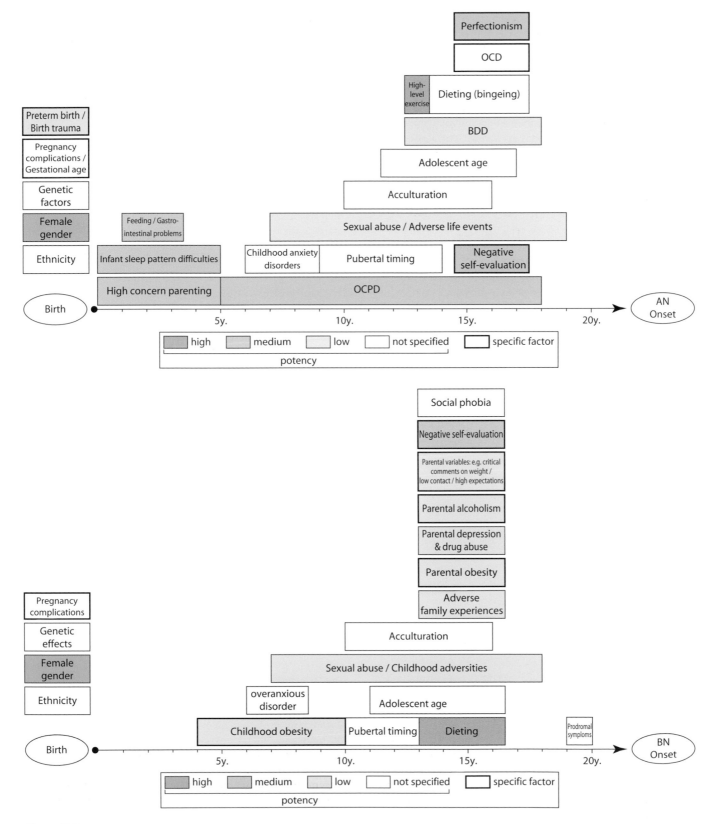

Figure 9.2
Classification of the known risk factors for anorexia and bulimia across a developmental timeframe. This illustration shows how important risk factors are at a number of different levels of description.

Source: after Jacobi, Hayward, de Zwaan, Kraemer et al. (2004).

develop one of these disorders rather than the other. As a consequence, it is often difficult to separate out theories of the aetiology of anorexia and bulimia. Many of the following theories are thus addressed at understanding eating disorders generally rather than individual eating disorders specifically.

We have already described how the occurrence of eating disorders appears to be linked to culture and ethnicity, and this alone should give us some insight into the sociological influences linked to eating disorders. In the following section we look at risk factors in more detail, and try to elaborate how these risk factors might have their effects on the development of eating disorders.

9.3.1 Biological Factors

While many of the symptoms of eating disorders are physical in nature, the only biological factor that has so far been clearly identified in the aetiology of eating disorders is a genetic one. As we shall see, research on the role of brain neurotransmitters, and the role of the brain and hormonal systems in regulating appetite, does not have such strong supporting evidence. Research in these areas is made more difficult by the fact that changes in brain neurotransmitters and endocrine functioning may be consequences of eating disorders rather than the causes of them.

There is clear evidence that eating disorders do run in families, and this is consistent with there being a *genetic component* to these disorders. First-degree relatives of females with both anorexia and bulimia are significantly more likely to develop these disorders than relatives of a group of females who have never been diagnosed with an eating disorder (Strober, Freeman, Lampert, Diamond et al., 2000; Kassett, Gershon, Maxwell et al., 1989). Community-based twin studies have also contributed to the view that there is an inherited component. Such studies indicate that the heritability component of eating disorders may be greater than 50 per cent (Klump, Miller, Keel, McGue et al., 2001; Kortegaard, Hoerder, Joergensen, Gillberg et al., 2001). In addition, more recent evidence has emerged that identifies the genetic loci for susceptibility to eating disorders on specific chromosomes (e.g. Grice, Halmi, Fichter, Strober et al., 2001). There may also be a shared familial factor across eating disorders, suggesting that if an individual has bulimia, this may raise the chances of a related individual developing not just bulimia, but also either anorexia or bulimia (Kendler, MacLean, Neale, Kessler et al., 1991; Wade, Bulik, Sullivan, Neale et al., 2000). However, Keel and Klump (2003) have argued that the genes contributing to anorexia may well differ from those contributing to bulimia. This is because bulimia appears to be a culture-bound syndrome, whereas anorexia is not (see section 9.2 above), and the universal nature of anorexia suggests that there may be an important genetic component to the self-starvation which is the central feature of anorexia. Nevertheless, while there appears to be a significant inherited component, this research has yet to determine exactly how inherited dispositions increase the likelihood of developing an eating disorder. For example, does the genetic component to anorexia simply increase the tendency to self-starve, or does it increase the vulnerability to other risk factors (such as depression or low self-esteem)?

Because eating disorders involve appetite, a number of theories of both anorexia and bulimia allude to the role of those brain areas involved in regulating appetite (namely, the hypothalamus) and to the neurotransmitters associated with changes in appetite. Animal research has shown that lesions to the *lateral hypothalamus* cause appetite loss resulting in a self-starvation syndrome which is behaviourally similar to that found in anorexia (Hoebel & Teitelbaum, 1966). However, there is good reason to believe that lateral hypothalamus deficits are not a central causal factor in anorexia. First, animal studies show that lateral hypothalamus lesions result in a lack of hunger – but anorexia sufferers usually experience intense hunger even though they are starving themselves. Secondly, while there are hormonal imbalances found in anorexia that are similar to those in animal studies of lateral hypothalamus lesions, these imbalances appear to be the *result* of the disorder rather than a cause of it (Stoving, Hangaard, Hansen-Nord et al., 1999).

> **Lateral hypothalamus** A part of the hypothalamus. Lesions to the lateral hypothalamus cause appetite loss resulting in a self-starvation syndrome which is behaviourally similar to that found in anorexia.

An alternative biological account of both anorexia and bulimia suggests that self-starvation and maintaining a low body weight may be reinforced by the *endogenous opioids* that the body releases during starvation to reduce pain sensation (Hardy & Waller, 1988). In anorexia, starvation may directly increase the levels of opioids, thus producing a state of euphoria; however, because bulimia sufferers are not necessarily overweight, this disorder may be accompanied by *low* levels of opioids, and this is known to promote craving. In support of this latter hypothesis, Brewerton, Lydiard, Laraia, Shook et al. (1992) found low levels of the opioid beta-endorphin in bulimia sufferers. Nevertheless, it is still difficult to interpret the significance of this finding because low opioid levels may be a *consequence* of the cravings that accompany bulimia rather than a cause of them.

> **Endogenous opioids** A compound that the body releases to reduce pain sensation.

Some attempts to explain eating disorders consider *neuroendocrine dysfunction* (e.g. hormonal dysfunction or life stressors causing hormonal dysfunction). Such accounts allude to the fact that appetite is very sensitive to changes in hormonal levels. The evidence for such causes is weak. First, as we have already noted, there is no real evidence for disturbances in the hypothalamus – the brain area responsible for influencing appetite – in individuals with eating disorders (Study Group on Anorexia Nervosa, 1995). Second, it has been suggested that anorexia and bulimia may be affected by brain serotonin levels. The argument here is that anorexia and bulimia sufferers have behavioural and cognitive traits which are very similar to obsessive-compulsive disorder (OCD) (Pryor, Martin & Roach, 1995), and it is known that serotonin levels influence OCD symptoms. However, individuals who have recovered from anorexia do not show persistent anomalies in serotonin regulation (O'Dwyer, Lucey & Russell, 1996), suggesting that fluctuations in serotonin levels in anorexia may, once again, be an effect of the disorder rather than a cause of it.

> **Neuroendocrine dysfunction** Hormonal dysfunction or life stressors causing hormonal dysfunction.

9.3.2 Sociocultural Influences

In section 9.2 above we described how the incidence of eating disorders appears to be importantly affected by factors associated with culture and ethnicity. Rates of both anorexia and bulimia are higher in cultures that have experienced exposure to contemporary Western ideals and standards; indeed, it is arguably the case that bulimia is *only* found in societies that have been exposed to Western cultural influences (Keel & Klump, 2003). This suggests that Western cultural factors are a risk factor for eating disorders. It is important to identify specifically what these factors are and how they might trigger an eating disorder.

9.3.2.1 Media Influences, Body Dissatisfaction and Dieting

As we have pointed out, both anorexia and bulimia are disorders that are largely restricted to females (Streigel-Moore, 1997), and there is growing acknowledgement that the increase in the incidence of eating disorders over the past 20 to 30 years is associated with changes in the ideal female body shape that is communicated to the female populations of Westernized societies. First, the *media* are regularly accused of distorting reality by portraying female body images that are either naturally thin (and therefore representative of only a minority percentage of the female population) or are unnaturally thin (Polivy & Herman, 2002). This is supported by studies which show that the BMI (see Activity Box 9.1) of *Playboy* centrefolds between 1985 and 1997 has continued to fall to a point where almost 50 per cent of the centrefolds had a BMI of less than 18, which is considered to be severely underweight (Owen & Laurel-Seller, 2000). This has resulted in young women adopting ideal body shape goals that are achievable for only around 5 per cent of the female population (Irving, 2001). There is some evidence that exposure to these media-portrayed extreme ideals is related to a drive for thinness in young adolescent girls. For example, Tiggemann and Pickering (1996) found that body shape dissatisfaction and a drive for thinness were significantly associated with watching certain types of television show that portrayed idealized female images. Further studies have shown that body dissatisfaction is directly correlated with the amount of time young female undergraduates spend reading magazines that expose them to idealized female body shapes (Tiggemann, 2003), and also with the amount of time young women spend watching music television channels such as MTV (Tiggemann & Slater, 2004). The more young adolescents (between the ages of 14 and 16 years) indulge in 'celebrity worship' of a media personality and perceive that personality as having a 'good' body shape, the more they view their own body image as poor (Maltby, Giles, Barber & McCutcheon, 2005).

As well as exalting thinness, Western cultures disparage obesity and both implicitly and explicitly associate it with negative characteristics – even though obesity is significantly on the increase in most Western societies. Jokes and cartoons that ridicule obesity

> **Media influence**   A term describing a person's changes in or temptations to change attitude, behaviour and morals as directly influenced by the media.

Plate 9.5
Researchers have discovered that body dissatisfaction in young adolescent females is a function of the amount of time they spend reading celebrity magazines and watching music television channels such as MTV.

are commonplace, and this prejudice appears to be deep-rooted and more acceptable than jokes about race and disability. Research indicates that when parents who were expecting a new baby were shown photographs of an overweight baby, a medium-weight baby and a thin baby, they quite readily rated the overweight baby as less desirable, intelligent, energetic and friendly than either the medium-weight or thin baby. These deep-rooted prejudicial views about the negative characteristics associated with being overweight will also tend individuals towards achieving thin ideal body shapes.

While the preceding evidence suggests that media images of idealized thin body shapes are indeed important in determining attitudes towards body shape, the question we need to ask is *how* this media-based pressure is converted into the eating problems that meet DSM-IV-TR criteria for a psychological disorder. The most obvious route is that idealized media images generate dissatisfaction with the individual's own body shape (especially

Plate 9.6
Jokes and cartoons that ridicule obesity are commonplace in most Western societies and appear to be more acceptable than jokes about race or disability. This helps to associate weight with negative characteristics, which may lead to overweight individuals developing low self-esteem and indulging in inappropriate weight loss behaviours (such as purging or excessive dieting) that precipitate eating disorders.

in comparison with extreme ideals). *Body dissatisfaction* is usually defined as the gap between one's actual and ideal weight and shape (Polivy & Herman, 2002), and most theories of eating disorders implicate body dissatisfaction as an important component of the aetiology (e.g. Stice, 2001; Vohs, Bardone, Joiner, Abramson et al., 1999; Polivy & Herman, 1985). Body dissatisfaction is likely to trigger bouts of *dieting* in order to move towards the ideal body shape, and regular or excessive dieting is also a common precursor to eating disorders (Polivy & Herman, 1985; Stice, 2001). There is no doubt that body dissatisfaction and dieting are important predictors of all eating disorders (Joiner, Heatherton, Rudd & Schmidt, 1997; Steiger, Stotland, Trottier & Ghadirian, 1996; Stice, Shaw & Nemeroff, 1998), but it is important to note that they are not *sufficient* conditions for an individual to develop an eating disorder. For example, (1) many individuals may believe that their actual body shape is quite disparate from their ideal yet be quite happy with that fact (Polivy & Herman, 2002), and (2) many individuals who express real body dissatisfaction do not necessarily go on to develop an eating disorder. Similarly, while dieting is

> **Body dissatisfaction**   The gap between one's actual and ideal weight and shape.

> **Dieting**   A restricted regime of eating, followed in order to lose weight or for medical reasons.

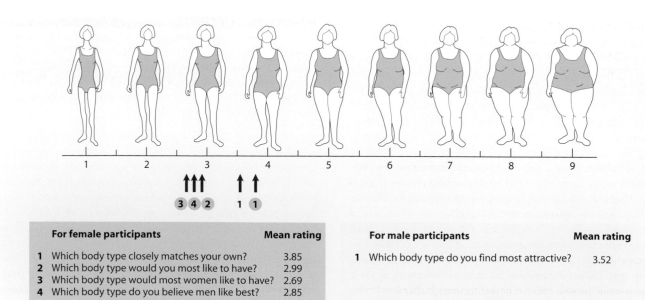

For female participants	Mean rating
1 Which body type closely matches your own?	3.85
2 Which body type would you most like to have?	2.99
3 Which body type would most women like to have?	2.69
4 Which body type do you believe men like best?	2.85

For male participants	Mean rating
1 Which body type do you find most attractive?	3.52

Figure 9.3
Research on female body shape dissatisfaction has demonstrated that females consistently overestimate their own body size compared to (1) the body size they thought men would like most and (2) the body size they think most women would like to have. Interestingly, women rated the body size they thought men would like most as significantly slimmer than the body size men themselves rated as most attractive.

Source: Forbes, Adams-Curtis, Rade et al. (2001).

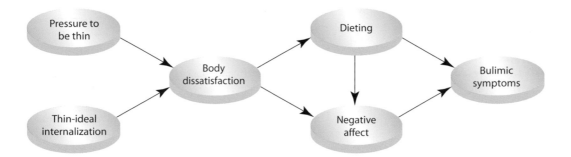

Figure 9.4
Stice's (2001) model of bulimic pathology in which body dissatisfaction plays a central role in mediating bulimic symptoms through its effect on dieting behaviour and the development of negative affect.

FOCUS POINT 9.3

What is the role of body dissatisfaction in eating disorders?

'In our view, while body dissatisfaction is probably a necessary factor in the emergence of eating disorders, it is not sufficient. After all, it is possible to be dissatisfied with one's body and yet not do anything about it. Why is it that of two dissatisfied people, one throws herself into (usually futile) attempts to achieve a satisfactory body, whereas the other remains dissatisfied but does not diet/starve, binge, or purge? The determining factor, we suggest, is whether or not the individual seizes upon weight and shape as the answer to the problems of identity and control. Some young women become invested in achieving a

'perfect' body as an existential project (i.e. as a way of giving their lives meaning, coherence, and emotional fulfillment that are otherwise lacking). Some become invested in achieving complete control over their eating, weight and shape, believing that control in these domains is possible even though such control is not possible elsewhere in their lives. For many with eating disorders, these two goals overlap. In the final analysis, body dissatisfaction may contribute to eating disorders primarily by conferring purpose: The narrow ambitions of the eating disorder patient – in particular, the focus on weight – may make her life simpler, more certain, and more efficacious.'

Source: Polivy & Herman (2002, p. 199)

usually an activity that precedes an eating disorder, many individuals who diet regularly do not go on to develop an eating disorder. This suggests that additional psychological factors are necessary for body dissatisfaction and dieting to develop into an eating disorder. We will discuss some of these factors in section 9.3.4. Nevertheless, body dissatisfaction and dieting are *vulnerability* factors, and this is demonstrated in part by the fact that occupations that require individuals to control and monitor their weight (usually through exercise or dieting) have higher incidences of eating disorders. These occupations include fashion models (Santonastaso, Mondini & Favaro, 2002), actors, athletes (Sudi, Ottl, Payerl, Baumgartl et al., 2004), figure skaters (Monsma & Malina, 2004) and ballet dancers (Ravaldia, Vannacci, Zucchi, Mannucci et al., 2003). Thus, body dissatisfaction and dieting are an important part of the story surrounding the aetiology of eating disorders and are recognized as such in recent models of these disorders (see Figure 9.4) – but they are not the whole story.

9.3.2.2 Peer Influences

Just like the media, *peer influences* can seriously influence an adolescent's view of her body, weight and eating and dieting activities, and adolescent girls tend to learn their attitudes to slimness and dieting through close contact with their peers (Levine, Smolak, Moodey, Shuman et al., 1994). Peer pressure can influence attitudes to body shape and eating in a variety of ways. In some cases, attitudes to eating and body shape within a peer group converge towards those that are socially valued (such as dieting or restricted eating) (Meyer & Waller, 2001), and this convergence also results in the group adopting psychological characteristics that may facilitate pathological eating behaviours, such as perfectionism. A study of adolescent schoolgirls by Eisenberg, Neumark-Sztainer, Story and

> **Peer influences** A term describing a person's changes in or temptations to change attitude, behaviour and morals as directly influenced by his or her peer group.

Perry (2005) found that the use of unhealthy weight-control behaviours (e.g. self-induced vomiting, laxatives, diet pills or fasting) was significantly influenced by the dieting behaviour of close friends, and this influence was effective in generating unhealthy weight-control behaviours regardless of whether the individual was overweight, normal weight or underweight. Despite these findings, it is difficult to determine whether peer influence (1) determines attitudes towards eating and body shape (it is possible that peer groups recruit members on the basis of shared concerns rather than directly changing the attitudes of their members) or (2) has a significant role in the development of eating disorders (while peer pressure can increase the tendency to diet or to be dissatisfied with one's body shape, these factors do not automatically lead to the development of eating disorders).

9.3.2.3 Familial Factors

Familial factors The idea that certain disorders may be the result of the direct influence of family attitudes and dynamics on the behaviour of those in the family.

We have noted earlier that eating disorders have a tendency to run in families, and while this may in part be due to inherited characteristics, it may also be a result of the direct influence of family attitudes and dynamics on the behaviour of those in the family. In particular, Minuchin (Minuchin, Baker, Rosman, Lieberman et al., 1975; Minuchin, Rosman & Baker, 1978) has argued that eating disorders are best understood by considering the family structure of which the sufferer is a part. This *family systems theory* view argues that the sufferer may be embedded in a dysfunctional family structure that actively

Family systems theory A theory which argues that the sufferer may be embedded in a dysfunctional family structure that actively promotes psychopathology.

promotes the development of eating disorders. The family structure may inadvertently, but actively, reinforce a child's disordered eating, and this can function to distract from dealing with other conflicts within the family (such as a deteriorating relationship between the child's mother and father). In Minuchin's view, the families of individuals with eating disorders tend to show at least one of the following characteristics: (1) *enmeshment*, in which parents are intrusive, overinvolved in their children's affairs, and dismissive of their children's emotions and emotional needs (Minuchin et al., 1978); (2) *overprotection*, where members of the family are overly concerned with parenting and with others' welfare, which can often be viewed by the child as coercive parental control (Shoebridge & Gowers, 2000; Haworth-Hoeppner, 2000); (3) *rigidity*, where there is a tendency to maintain the

Enmeshment A characteristic of family systems theory in which parents are intrusive, overinvolved in their children's affairs, and dismissive of their children's emotions and emotional needs.

Overprotection A characteristic of family systems theory where members of the family are overconcerned with parenting and with one another's welfare, and this can often be viewed by the child as coercive parental control.

Rigidity A characteristic of family systems theory where there is a tendency to maintain the status quo within the family.

status quo within the family; and (4) *lack of conflict resolution*, where families avoid conflict or are in a continual state of conflict.

Lack of conflict resolution A characteristic of family systems theory where families avoid conflict or are in a continual state of conflict.

How these characteristics of the sufferer's family influence the development of an eating disorder is unclear, although the family may focus on the disorder once it has developed in order to avoid dealing with other difficult and important problems within the family. The disorder may serve a functional purpose for both the parents (by distracting attention away from other family difficulties such as a problematic relationship between mother and father) and the eating-disordered child (as a tool for manipulating the family) (Minuchin et al., 1978). As we shall see later, the issue of how a dysfunctional family environment may engender an eating disorder is still unclear, but it may do so by generating specific psychological characteristics in the child that play an active role in the acquisition and maintenance of the disorder (Polivy & Herman, 2002).

As an important part of the family, mothers may have a specific influence on the development of eating disorders in their children. Mothers of individuals with an eating disorder are themselves more likely to have dysfunctional eating patterns and psychiatric disorders (Hill & Franklin, 1998; Hodes, Timimi & Robinson, 1997), and these problematic maternal eating patterns appear to produce feeding problems in their offspring at an early age (Whelan & Cooper, 2000). Mothers of sufferers also tend to excessively criticize their daughters' appearance, weight and attractiveness when compared with mothers of non-sufferers (Hill & Franklin, 1998; Pike & Rodin, 1991), and there is a significant inverse relationship between a mother's critical comments and her daughter's chances of successful recovery following treatment (Van Furth, Van Strien, Martina, Vanson et al., 1996).

While this research strongly implicates the involvement of familial factors in the aetiology of eating disorders, Polivy and Herman (2002) quite rightly point out that most of the studies are retrospective and correlational in nature, and so do not imply causation. There may indeed be some form of intrafamilial transmission of disordered eating patterns within families, but it is quite likely that some other factor (biological, psychological or experiential) may be necessary to trigger the severe symptoms typical of a clinically diagnosable disorder (Steiger, Stotland, Trottier & Ghadirian, 1996).

9.3.3 Experiential Factors

There is some evidence that adverse life experiences may act as a vulnerability factor for eating disorders and as a precipitating factor for the onset of an eating disorder. For example, Rastam and Gillberg (1991) found that 14 per cent of anorexia sufferers (compared with 0 per cent of healthy controls) had experienced a negative life experience (e.g. the loss of a first-degree relative) within 3 months prior to the onset of the disorder. Similarly, individuals with bulimia report significantly more adverse life events in the year before onset than age-matched healthy controls (Welch, Doll & Fairburn, 1997).

Individuals with eating disorders report significantly more pre-morbid life stresses and difficulties than do healthy controls (Raffi, Rondini, Grandi & Fava, 2000), and the number of adverse life events has been shown to differentiate between individuals with anorexia and healthy controls (Horesh, Apter, Ishai, Danziger et al., 1996). Like the research on the role of familial factors, such studies are difficult to interpret because they are both retrospective and correlational in nature.

However, one particular form of adverse life experience that has been implicated as a risk factor in eating disorders is ***childhood sexual abuse***. There is consistent evidence for higher levels of childhood sexual abuse in the history of bulimia sufferers than in healthy controls (Steiger, Leonard, Kin et al., 2000; Garfinkel, Lin, Goering, Spegg et al., 1995; Welch & Fairburn, 1994) and in anorexia sufferers than in healthy controls (Brown, Russell, Thornton & Dunn, 1997), but not in binge-eating disorder sufferers (Dansky, Brewerton, Kilpatrick & O'Neal, 1997). One longitudinal study of a large community-based sample of mothers and offspring has indicated that children who had experienced sexual abuse or physical neglect during childhood were also at elevated risk for eating disorders (Johnson, Cohen, Kasen, Smailes et al., 2002).

Childhood sexual abuse The sexual maltreatment of a child.

Given that childhood sexual abuse is now largely accepted as a risk factor for eating disorders (Polivy & Herman, 2002), it is difficult to determine how such early experiences facilitate the risk of developing an eating disorder. One possibility is that adverse early experiences generate other forms of psychopathology that mediate the development of eating disorders (Casper & Lyubomirsky, 1997). For example, Steiger et al. (2000) found that childhood sexual abuse only facilitated bulimia in the presence of borderline personality disorder. Other researchers have argued that eating disorders are a means of coping with the more generalized psychopathology (such as major depression) that results from sexual abuse (Rorty & Yager, 1996). This latter view sees the development of an eating disorder as a way of helping the individual to cope with emotional and identity problems (which may have been caused by earlier adverse life experiences). For example, anorexia enables the individual to exert some control over at least one aspect of her life (i.e. her eating), in circumstances where she may have experienced very little control over many other aspects of her life (Troop, 1998). Similarly, bulimia may also serve as a way of coping with the negative affect caused by earlier life difficulties. Bulimia sufferers gain emotional relief, which is otherwise elusive, by bingeing (and then purging). Eating disorders also allow individuals to construct a coherent sense of self by focusing attention on one limited aspect of their lives. This in turn provides them with rewards that may otherwise have been missing from their lives (by attaining self-determined weight control goals), and also offers a very narrow life focus that may help them to avoid dealing with more deep-seated psychological issues (Polivy & Herman, 2002). Therefore, this rather interesting view of eating disorders views them as a means of coping with other, more global psychopathology. More research is needed to verify this view.

9.3.4 Psychological and Dispositional Factors

Individuals who develop eating disorders do appear to have particular personality and dispositional characteristics that have been variously implicated in the aetiology of those disorders. We have so far identified a number of risk factors for eating disorders, but none of these risk factors appears to be a *sufficient* condition for developing anorexia, bulimia or binge-eating disorder. It may therefore be the case that specific risk factors interact with personality traits to generate an eating disorder.

Various studies have identified personality traits that are characteristic of individuals with diagnosed eating disorders. These traits include:

- perfectionism
- shyness
- neuroticism
- low self-esteem
- high introspective awareness (awareness of bodily sensations)
- negative or depressed affect
- dependence and non-assertiveness (Vitousek & Manke, 1994; Leon, Fulkerson, Perry & Early-Zald, 1995).

It is worth looking in more detail at some of the more important of these characteristics.

Eating disorders are very much associated with negative affect (usually depressed mood), and mood disorders are often comorbid with both anorexia and bulimia (Braun, Sunday & Halmi et al., 1994; Brewerton et al., 1995). While negative mood and stress are commonly reported antecedents of eating disorders (Ball & Lee, 2000), there is some disagreement about whether negative affect is a cause or just a consequence of the disorder. Nevertheless, negative affect has been proposed to play a number of discrete roles in the aetiology of eating disorders. Experimental studies have indicated that induced negative mood does increase body dissatisfaction and body size perception in bulimia sufferers (Carter, Bulik, Lawson, Sullivan et al., 1996), and it may contribute in part to eating disorders through this route. Negative mood states have also been shown to increase food consumption in individuals who are dieting or who have distorted attitudes about eating, and this may represent a role for negative mood in generating the bingeing and purging patterns typical of bulimia sufferers (Herman, Polivy, Lank & Heatherton, 1987). For example, individuals with bulimia try to alleviate their negative mood by eating, and purging allows them to use eating as a mood regulation process without gaining weight. However, when the bulimia sufferer begins to realize that her eating is out of control, this activity no longer provides relief from negative mood and purging may take over as a means of relieving guilt, self-disgust and tension (Johnson & Larson, 1982). This is consistent with laboratory-based studies that reveal that bulimia sufferers show reduced anxiety, tension and guilt following a binge–purge episode (Sanftner & Crowther, 1998). Studies such as these suggest that

RESEARCH METHODS IN CLINICAL PSYCHOLOGY BOX 9.1

Food preload tests

Laboratory procedures have been developed that provide an objective behavioural measure of the tendency to 'binge' eat. One of these is the **food preload test** (see Polivy, Heatherton & Herman, 1988).

This test begins by asking participants to eat a filling preload (e.g. a 15 oz chocolate milkshake or a large bowl of ice cream) under the pretence of rating its palatability.

After eating the preload and making their ratings, participants are then told they can eat as much of the remaining milkshake (or ice cream) as they wish.

The real measure of interest is the amount of milkshake or ice cream that the participant eats at the end of the study: this is a measure of how willing the individual is to continue eating after having already had a full, filling portion of food.

This experimental procedure has shown that willingness to continue eating is a function of a number of factors, including whether the individual (1) is a restrained eater (has a tendency to dieting or has distorted attitudes about eating), (2) has low self-esteem and (3) is in a negative mood. Restrained eaters will eat more food than non-dieters even if they rate the food as relatively unpalatable.

Food preload tests   Laboratory procedures developed to provide an objective behavioural measure of the tendency to binge eat.

the negative mood possessed by individuals with eating disorders may not simply be a consequence of the disorder, but may play an active role in generating symptoms by increasing body dissatisfaction and being involved in processes of mood regulation which act to reinforce disordered eating behaviours.

A second prominent characteristic of individuals with eating disorders is *low self-esteem*. This low self-esteem may simply be a derivative of the specific negative views that those with eating disorders have of themselves (such as being 'fat', having an unattractive body or, in bulimia, having a lack of control over their eating behaviour). However, there is some evidence to suggest that low self-esteem may have a role to play in the development of eating disorders. First, it is a significant prospective predictor of eating disorders in females (suggesting that it is not just a consequence of eating disorders) (Button, Sonugabarke, Davies & Thompson, 1996). Secondly, eating disorders such as anorexia are viewed by some researchers as a means of combating low self-esteem by demonstrating control over one specific aspect of the sufferer's own life – i.e. her eating (Troop, 1998). In this sense, self-esteem may be implicated in the development of eating disorders because controlled eating is the individual's way of combating her feelings of low self-esteem.

Individuals diagnosed with anorexia and, to a lesser extent, those diagnosed with bulimia both score high on measures of *perfectionism*, a personality characteristic which has regularly been implicated in the aetiology of eating disorders (Garner, Olmsted & Polivy, 1983; Bastiani, Rao, Weltzin & Kaye, 1995). Perfectionism is multifaceted and can be either self-oriented (setting high standards for

Low self-esteem   A person's negative, subjective appraisal of himself or herself.

Perfectionism   The setting of excessively high standards for performance accompanied by overly critical self-evaluation.

oneself) or other-oriented (trying to conform to the high standards set by others). It can also be adaptive (in the sense of trying to achieve the best possible outcome) or maladaptive (in terms of striving to attain what may well be unachievable goals) (Bieling, Israeli & Antony, 2004). Perfectionism is a predictor of bulimic symptoms in women who perceive themselves as overweight (Joiner, Heatherton, Rudd & Schmidt, 1997), and both self-oriented and other-oriented perfectionism have been found to be higher in anorexia sufferers than in healthy controls (Cockell, Hewitt, Seal et al., 2002).

Other research has suggested that the perfectionist characteristics displayed by individuals with eating disorders may actively contribute to their disordered eating. For example, Strober (1991) has argued that self-doubting perfectionism predisposes individuals to eating disorders. Perfectionism is highly associated with measures of body dissatisfaction and drive for thinness (Ruggiero, Levi, Ciuna & Sassaroli, 2003), and so it is not difficult to see how perfectionism may be a causal factor in the aetiology of eating disorders as the dieter strives to achieve the perfect body shape or the stringent dieting goals she sets herself. Interestingly, perfectionism is a characteristic of many psychological disorders (Shafran & Mansell, 2001), and is the best predictor of comorbidity across the anxiety disorders (Bieling, Summerfeldt, Israeli & Antony, 2004). So, if perfectionism does play a causal role in eating disorders, we need to ask why it was an eating disorder that developed and not any one of a number of other disorders that have perfectionism as a prominent feature.

SELF-TEST QUESTIONS

- Can you name some of the important risk factors for anorexia and bulimia?
- Can you describe some of the biological factors that might be involved in the development of an eating disorder?
- Can you name some of the important sociocultural factors that influence the development of eating disorders? What evidence is there that these factors influence body dissatisfaction and attitudes to dieting?
- What are the important dispositional factors associated with eating disorders? Do they have a causal role to play in the development of an eating disorder?

SECTION SUMMARY

9.3 The Aetiology of Eating Disorders

- There is evidence of an **inherited** component to eating disorders which may account for up to 50 per cent of the variance in factors causing these disorders.

- Maintaining a low body weight may be reinforced by the **endogenous opioids** that the body releases during starvation to reduce pain sensation.

- Exposure to media-portrayed extreme body shape ideals has been shown to increase body dissatisfaction in young adolescent females, and to increase their tendency to either diet or purge after overeating.

- Body dissatisfaction and dieting are important vulnerability factors for eating disorders.

- **Peer attitudes and views** are an important factor in determining an adolescent girl's attitudes to slimness and dieting.

- Eating disorders have a tendency to run in families, and **family systems** views of eating disorders suggest that a dysfunctional family structure may reinforce a child's disordered eating.

- Mothers may have a specific influence on the development of an eating disorder by producing eating problems in their offspring and criticizing their child's appearance.

- **Adverse life experiences** (such as childhood sexual abuse) may act as a vulnerability factor for eating disorders.

- **Negative affect**, **low self-esteem** and **perfectionism** are all dispositional factors that have been shown to exert a possible causal influence on the development of an eating disorder.

9.4 THE TREATMENT OF EATING DISORDERS

Eating disorders are complex and difficult to treat, and there is – as yet – no reliable treatment programme for any of the disorders. A number of difficulties are encountered when treating eating disorders:

(1) Individuals with eating disorders regularly deny they are ill or have a disorder. Indeed, many individuals with bulimia see their binge-eating and purging patterns as a positive way of controlling weight, and there has been a recent burgeoning of websites extolling the virtues of bingeing and purging as a way of life (see Table 9.5).

Table 9.5

Below are some examples that illustrate how bulimia sufferers use websites to actively swap experiences and information about the best ways of purging, and how best to conceal their activities.

- ok so last night i was purging ya know and i kinda came out with more force than i was expecting well anyway i leaned closer and actually only go half in the toilet. The other half down the side and on my sock and the floor. i spent forever cleaning up but my mum found the left overs and asked if i was sick i said no i think she bought it but she'll be on the look out so how can i hide it better? Seriously i need help!

- i really don't want you to become bulimic because it makes you feel awful, you get headaches, light-headedness, irregular heartbeats and you can rip your throat and you burst blood vessels and all this bad stuff. However, if you do start, to save you a lot of pain, make sure you drink lots of water with everything, and diet coke is good too. Don't try and purge orange juice because it hurts like hell. Make sure you chew everything thoroughly too, otherwise it can get stuck in your throat. And if you see blood when you purge, it is not a good sign and you should stop for a while.

- ok im so sure someone would have to have an answer for me . . . ok so i'm really good at making myself sick . . . but 4 the last 2 days i cant get anything up . . . its nasty tho bc i definatly get dry heaves and i gag for about 10 minutes at a time . . . and the last time i tried it i was choking . . . i could still breath but i was gasping . . . i freaked myself out . . . and i know to chew really well and all that, so i know thats the problem . . . u think its because my esophagus is irritated or something like that?? please give me a bit of advice . . . thanks

- Why is it that I can go without food for most of the day and then when it comes to the evening I go totally crazy and binge, then afterwards I feel really bad and hate myself and vow never to eat that much again, but I always do. Can somebody please give me some ideas on how to stop binging? I'd really appreciate it.

- after you eat would you go to the bathroom? I am relatively new at it but have had some luck but just not as much coming up as I thought. How soon after and how long would you do it for?

Similarly, individuals with anorexia regularly deny they are pathologically underweight, and the fact that they may view their controlled eating as a way of coping with more general psychopathology means that it is often viewed as an activity that has benefits rather than costs (Rorty & Yager, 1996). Because of these factors, as many as 90 per cent of individuals with diagnosable eating disorders are not in treatment (Fairburn, Welch, Norman, O'Connor et al., 1996).

(2) Individuals with severe eating disorders usually need medical as well as psychological treatment, and in the case of anorexia, hospitalization and a period of remedial medical treatment are often necessary to increase weight, rectify body electrolyte imbalances and, in many cases, prevent death by self-starvation.

(3) Eating disorders are often highly comorbid with other psychological disorders, which may make treatment difficult and complex. For example, anorexia and bulimia are often comorbid with major depression and OCD, and some psychological treatments for anorexia have included components used to treat obsessions and compulsions (such as response prevention and exposure methods; see section 9.4.3) (e.g. Wilson, Eldredge, Smith & Niles, 1991). Similarly, treatments for eating disorders often work better with a concurrent antidepressant drug (Agras, Rossiter, Arnow, Schneider et al., 1992). In addition, there is growing evidence that anorexia and bulimia may be comorbid with personality disorders such as OCPD and BPD (Schmidt & Telch, 1990; Carroll, Touyz & Beaumont, 1996; O'Brien & Vincent, 2003), and personality disorders of this kind are themselves quite resistant to treatment (see Chapter 11).

In January 2004, the UK's National Institute for Clinical Excellence (NICE) issued clinical guidelines for the treatment of eating disorders and rated these interventions according to the evidence that supported their effectiveness (Wilson & Shafran, 2005). Table 9.6 shows a summary of these recommendations for both the physical management of patients with anorexia and the psychological and pharmacological treatment of all eating disorders. No specific recommendations were made for anorexia, but the report found good evidence for the effectiveness of cognitive behavioural therapy for both bulimia and binge-eating disorder.

In the following sections, we describe and discuss the main forms of treatment that have been used for eating disorders. These are pharmacological treatments, family therapy and cognitive behavioural therapy (CBT). In addition to these treatments, clinicians have advocated the use of self-help and alternative delivery systems. As you can see from Table 9.6, self-help programmes are an important component of the treatment provision for both bulimia and binge-eating disorder. Bulimia *self-help groups* that use structured manuals and require minimum practitioner management can show significant treatment gains, especially when they help the patient to identify triggers for bingeing and develop preventative behaviours for purging (Cooper, Coker & Fleming, 1994). *Alternative*

Self-help groups Group therapy which brings together people who share a common problem in an attempt to share information and help and support one another.

delivery systems allow access to services for sufferers who, for whatever reason, might not receive other forms of treatment. These include treatment and support via telephone therapy, e-mail, the internet, computer software CD-ROMs and virtual reality techniques (see Chapter 4, section 4.1.2), and an initial assessment of the effectiveness of these methods is encouraging (Myers, Swan-Kremeier, Wonderlich, Lancaster et al., 2004). Finally, clinicians are aware of the importance of *prevention programmes* that put eating disorders into a social context. School-based prevention programmes emphasize:

Alternative delivery systems Treatment methods that allow access to services for sufferers who might not receive other forms of treatment. These include treatment and support via telephone therapy, email, the internet, computer-software CD-ROMs and virtual reality techniques.

Prevention programmes Intervention programmes that attempt to prevent the onset of a psychopathology before the first symptoms are detected.

1 the role played by the media in developing extreme body shape ideals;

2 the need for individuals to develop positive rather than negative attitudes to their bodies;

3 the need for healthy, balanced eating;

4 the development of skills associated with expressing feelings and combating helplessness and submissiveness.

9.4.1 Pharmacological Treatments

Because both anorexia and bulimia are frequently comorbid with major depression, eating disorders have tended to be treated pharmacologically with antidepressants such as *fluoxetine (Prozac)* (Kruger & Kennedy, 2000). There is some evidence that such treatment can be effective with bulimia when compared with placebo conditions. Studies suggest a reduction in the frequency of bingeing and purging with such antidepressants (e.g. Wilson & Pike, 1993; Bellini & Merli, 2004), but more significant treatment gains are reported if antidepressant medication is combined with psychological treatments such as CBT (Pederson, Roerig & Mitchell, 2003). The benefits here appear to be reciprocal in that CBT helps to address the core dysfunctional beliefs in bulimia (see below), and anti-depressant drug treatment appears to reduce the tendency to relapse following cognitive behavioural treatment (Agras, Rossiter, Arnow, Schneider et al., 1992).

Fluoxetine (Prozac) A selective serotonin reuptake inhibitor (SSRI) which reduces the uptake of serotonin in the brain and is taken to treat depression.

Pharmacological treatments with anorexia have tended to be significantly less successful than with bulimia, although the number of studies assessing drug treatment with anorexia has been relatively limited (Pederson, Roerig & Mitchell, 2003). Nevertheless, outcome studies so far have found very little effect of antidepressants on either weight gain in anorexia or significant changes in other core features of the disorder, such as depression, eating attitudes or body shape perceptions (Attia, Haiman, Walsh & Flater, 1998; Biederman, Herzog, Rivinus, Harper et al., 1985). Pharmacological treatments of eating disorders also have the added disadvantage of higher dropout rates from treatment than psychological therapies (Fairburn, Agras & Wilson, 1992), and also have a number of physical side effects.

Table 9.6 *National Institue for Clinical Excellence (NICE) guidelines for the treatment of eating disorders (2004)*

PHYSICAL MANAGEMENT OF WEIGHT GAIN IN ANOREXIA NERVOSA

Managing weight gain

- In most patients, aim should be average weekly weight gain of 0.5–1 kg as inpatient and 0.5 kg as outpatient.
- Regular physical monitoring, and oral multivitamin/multimineral supplement in some cases, is recommended for inpatients and outpatients.
- Total parenteral nutrition should not be used, unless there is significant gastrointestinal dysfunction.

Managing risk

- Health-care professionals should monitor physical risk. If risk increases, frequency of monitoring and nature of investigations should be adjusted accordingly.
- Pregnant women with current or remitted anorexia should be considered for more intensive care to ensure adequate pre-natal nutrition and foetal development.
- Oestrogen should not be given for bone-density problems in children and adolescents, because such treatment may lead to premature fusion of epiphyses.

Feeding against will of patient

- This should be an intervention of last resort.

RECOMMENDED TREATMENT FOR EATING DISORDERS

Anorexia nervosa

Pharmacological
- Drugs should not be used as sole or primary treatment for anorexia.
- All patients with anorexia should have alert placed in their prescribing record about risk of side effects.

Psychological
- Consider cognitive analytic or cognitive behavioural therapies, interpersonal psychotherapy, focal dynamic therapy or family interventions focused on eating disorders.
- Family interventions that directly address the eating disorder should be offered to children and adolescents.

Bulimia nervosa

Pharmacological
- To be offered trial of an antidepressant as alternative to, or in addition to, self-help programme.
- Patients should be informed that antidepressant drugs can reduce frequency of binge eating and purging, but long-term effects are unknown.
- Selective serotonin reuptake inhibitors (specifically fluoxetine) are drugs of first choice for bulimia in terms of acceptability, tolerability and reduction of symptoms. No drugs other than antidepressants are recommended.

Psychological
- Dietary counselling should not be provided as sole treatment.
- As a possible first step, patients with bulimia should be encouraged to follow evidence-based self-help programme.
- Consider direct encouragement and support to patients undertaking evidence-based self-help programme, which may improve outcomes and be sufficient for limited subset of patients.
- Specifically adapted CBT should be offered to adults with bulimia; 16–20 sessions over 4–5 months; interpersonal psychotherapy should be considered as alternative to CBT, but patients should be informed it takes 8–12 months to achieve similar results.

Binge-eating disorder

Pharmacological
- Patients should be informed that selective serotonin reuptake inhibitors can reduce binge eating, but long-term effects are unknown; antidepressants may be sufficient for some patients.

Psychological
- Specifically adapted CBT should be offered to adults with binge-eating disorder.

Source: Wilson & Shafran (2005).

9.4.2 Family Therapy

Family therapy A form of intervention involving family members that is helpful as a means of dealing with psychopathology that may result from the relationship dynamics within the family.

One of the most common therapies used with eating disorder sufferers – and particularly anorexia sufferers – is *family therapy*. This stems mainly from the theories of Minuchin (Minuchin, Baker, Rosman, Lieberman et al., 1975; Minuchin, Rosman & Baker, 1978), whose family systems theory view argues that the sufferer may be embedded in a dysfunctional family structure that actively promotes the development of eating disorders (see section 9.3.2.3). In particular, this view argues that the eating disorder may be hiding important conflicts within the family (such as a difficult relationship between the sufferer's

parents), and the family may be implicitly reinforcing the eating disorder in order to avoid confronting these other conflicts. As we noted in section 9.3.2.3, families of individuals with eating disorders exhibit the characteristics of enmeshment, overprotectiveness, rigidity and lack of conflict resolution, and family therapy can be used to unpack and address these dysfunctional family characteristics.

Treatment in Practice Box 9.1 describes an example of how family therapy is applied in the context of an adolescent family member with anorexia. This example shows how family therapy can be used to explore concerns about relationships and emotional expression within the family, as well as individual feelings of failure, shame and guilt. Exploring these issues throws up other conflicts and difficulties within the family, and how the anorexia sufferer may see herself as trapped within these existing relationships and conflicts (Dallos, 2004).

CLINICAL PERSPECTIVE: TREATMENT IN PRACTICE BOX 9.1

Family therapy for eating disorders

Sandy is 17 and for two years had been suffering with anorexia of such severity as to require two brief stays in hospital. She was living with her parents and older brother. Two older brothers had left home.

Though all were invited, only Sandy and her parents attended for family therapy sessions, which took place at intervals of 3 to 4 weeks over 18 months. The sessions, with the full permission of all of the family, were of 1 hour in length. The therapist remained in the room with them and a team observed from behind a one-way mirror. The team usually joined the family and the therapist after 40–50 minutes and held a reflective discussion with one another in front of the family in which they shared their observations on the family's problems, ideas, understandings and feelings. The family was then invited to comment and held a closing discussion with the therapist after the team had left the room.

The core idea of family therapy is that problems such as anorexia are not simply, or predominantly, individual but are related to wider stresses and distress the family is experiencing. In addition, it is recognized that the sense of failure and blame associated with conditions such as anorexia can paralyse family members' abilities to help one another.

Initially, each member of the family was asked to describe what they saw as the main problems and invited to offer their explanations of the causes. This was followed by a focus on two broad areas:

(a) the impact of the problems on each family member and their relationships with each other;

(b) the influence each family member could exert on the nature of the problems.

At first Sandy's parents indicated that the distress caused by their daughter's anorexia was the main problem for all of them.

However, it quickly emerged that the parents had very different ideas about what caused the problems and what to do to help. Mr Sinclair had a medical and practical view, while Mrs Sinclair had a more relational and emotional one. Through the use of a genogram (family tree), it was revealed that both parents had themselves had very negative experiences of being parented that made it hard for them to know how to comfort and help their children. It also transpired that their marriage was in serious difficulty. Sandy commented that her parents' conflicts upset her and she felt caught in the middle, trying to meet the emotional needs of both of her lonely parents. In effect, she felt like she was a therapist for her own family. (Interestingly, she has gone on to study psychology at university.)

The therapist and the reflecting team discussed the possible impacts that the parents' own experiences may have had on the way they acted towards Sandy. Along with this were discussions of related issues, such as the pressure on young women to conform to stereotypes of thinness and the use of starving as an attempt to exert control in one's life. Some marital work was done separately with the parents to examine their childhoods, their marriage, their own needs and how these impacted on Sandy. Mrs Sinclair in particular felt she had failed as a mother but was relieved to hear that the team did not see it in this way. Sandy gained considerable insight into how the family dynamics across the generations had impacted on her and her parents. She became independent enough to go to university but initially struggled, as did her parents to separate. Some struggle with her weight continues, but she is confident that she will cope in the long term.

Case history provided by Professor Rudi Dallos, Consultant Clinical Psychologist (Somerset Partnership Trust) and Director of Research, Clinical Psychology Teaching Unit, University of Plymouth.

Source: Davey (2004)

However, while there is significant support for the use of family therapy in eating-disordered individuals (e.g. Rosman, Minuchin & Liebman, 1975), well-controlled treatment outcome research remains somewhat limited (Cottrell, 2003).

9.4.3 Cognitive Behaviour Therapy (CBT)

Cognitive behaviour therapy (CBT)
A psychotherapy based on modifying cognitions, assumptions, beliefs and behaviours, with the aim of influencing disturbed emotions.

The treatment of choice for bulimia is generally considered to be *cognitive behaviour therapy (CBT)*. The UK NICE guidelines for the treatment of eating disorders make their strongest recommendation for the use of CBT with bulimia, usually for 16–20 sessions over a period of 4–5 months (Wilson & Shafran, 2005; see Table 9.6). CBT for bulimia is based on the cognitive model developed by Fairburn and colleagues (Fairburn, Shafran & Cooper, 1999). According to this model, individuals with bulimia have a long-standing pattern of negative self-evaluation that interacts with concerns about weight, shape and attractiveness. Such individuals come to evaluate their worth solely in terms of their weight and shape – largely because this is often the only area of their lives that they can control. They develop idealized views of thinness that are often unachievable, and as a result end up in a constant state of dissatisfaction with their body shape and weight. This leads to excessive dieting, and as a result of this dietary restriction they lapse into episodes of bingeing. This in turn invites the use of weight compensation methods such as vomiting and laxative abuse. Each episode of bingeing and purging is followed

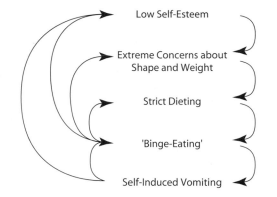

Figure 9.5
Fairburn's (1997b) cognitive model of the maintenance of bulimia, on which contemporary CBT for bulimia is based. Low self-esteem leads to concerns about weight, followed by dietary restriction, which – when dieting fails – leads to binge eating and subsequent purging. Following purging, individuals become more determined to restrict eating, and a vicious cycle is established that maintains the bingeing–purging pattern.

by a more determined effort to restrict eating, which leads to a vicious cycle of bingeing and purging (see Figure 9.5). Treatment in Practice Box 9.2 shows the three stages of CBT that are required to deal with both the symptoms of bulimia and the dysfunctional cognitions that underlie these symptoms. These cover:

(1) meal planning and stimulus control;

(2) cognitive restructuring to address dysfunctional beliefs about shape and weight;

(3) developing relapse prevention methods.

CLINICAL PERSPECTIVE: TREATMENT IN PRACTICE BOX 9.2

The three stages of CBT for bulimia nervosa

Stage 1 (3–9 weeks)

- The cognitive model is explained to clients, and they learn to control eating and reduce dietary restraint.

- Clients learn to control eating by discovering what factors trigger bingeing (e.g. periods of stress or arguments with partners or parents). This is achieved with the use of a diary that allows clients to discover consistencies between life events and bingeing.

- Clients are taught techniques such as stimulus control and meal planning.

- *Stimulus control* is where the client is allowed to eat, but only in certain specified environments (such as the kitchen) or at specific times (e.g. after work). Eventually, eating behaviour is controlled only by these stimuli, and is not triggered at all times in all places.

- *Meal planning* involves ensuring that small, acceptable meals are planned and eaten every day. Reductions in binge eating and purging usually follow the regularization of eating patterns.

Stage 2 (about 8 weeks)

- Clients are taught to identify their thoughts and beliefs about eating and their weight, and to challenge dysfunctional and inappropriate beliefs and thinking patterns.

- The therapist will help to foster healthy ways of thinking about eating and will also address issues about low self-esteem, and how dysfunctional attitudes that might link weight and self-worth are irrational (e.g. 'no one will love me if I am a single pound heavier').

Stage 3 (about 4 weeks)

- Clients are taught various techniques to help prevent relapse.

In stage 1, individuals are taught to identify the stimuli or events that may trigger a binge episode (such as a period of stress or after an argument with a boyfriend or parent). They are also taught not to indulge in extremes of eating behaviour (e.g. dieting and bingeing), and that normal body weight can be maintained simply by planned eating. In stage 2, dysfunctional beliefs about weight, body shape and eating are identified, challenged and replaced with more adaptive cognitions. For example, beliefs that relate eating and weight to self-worth, such as 'no one will love me if I am a single pound heavier', are challenged. In stage 3 relapse prevention is often encouraged with the use of behavioural self-control procedures that enable individuals to structure their daily activities to prevent bingeing and purging, and to reward themselves for 'good' behaviours (e.g. sticking to a planned eating programme) (see Chapter 4, section 4.1.1.2).

Outcome studies indicate that CBT of bulimia is successful for between 40 and 50 per cent of patients treated in this way (Agras, 1997; Fairburn, 1997b; Keel & Mitchell, 1997), which means that it is still far from comprehensive as a treatment method. Follow-up studies suggest that therapeutic gains can be maintained for up to 5 years following treatment (Fairburn, Norman, Welch, O'Connor et al., 1995). Importantly, when CBT is effective, it has been found not only to significantly reduce the behavioural aspects of bulimia such as bingeing and purging (Agras, 1997; Wilson, Fairburn & Agras, 1997), but also to have beneficial effects on core 'cognitive' aspects of bulimia such as beliefs about dietary restraint and low self-esteem (Anderson & Maloney, 2001). CBT has also been shown to be a more comprehensive treatment of bulimia than either antidepressant drugs (Whittal, Agras & Gold, 1999) or other psychotherapeutic interventions such as psychodynamically oriented therapy (Walsh, Wilson, Loeb, Devlin et al., 1997) and interpersonal psychotherapy (Wilson, Fairburn, Agras, Walsh & Kraemer, 2002). When effective, CBT also reports immediate improvement, including 76 per cent of clients showing an improvement in the frequency of binge eating and 69 per cent showing improvement in the frequency of purging within 3 weeks of the start of treatment (Wilson, Loeb, Walsh, Labouvie et al., 1999). Much of this rapid improvement can be put down to the behavioural homework assignments that are a unique feature of CBT and which appear to help alleviate depression and enhance self-efficacy (Burns & Spangler, 2000; Fennell & Teasdale, 1987).

Despite the relative success of CBT with bulimia, and to some extent with binge-eating disorder (Carter & Fairburn, 1998; Ricca, Mannucci, Zucchi, Rotella et al., 2000), it is still far from a complete cure and only effective for around half of those treated. We still await the development of effective CBT interventions for anorexia (but see Bowers, 2001).

SELF-TEST QUESTIONS

● Can you name the three main forms of treatment for eating disorders? Which ones are more suited to bulimia or to anorexia, and why?
● What is the rationale for adopting a CBT approach to the treatment of bulimia nervosa, and what are the important stages of this treatment?

SECTION SUMMARY

9.4 The Treatment of Eating Disorders

● Eating disorders are particularly difficult to treat because of the **denial by sufferers** that they have a disorder, the **medical implications** of the symptoms and **comorbidity** with other psychological disorders.

● There is evidence that **self-help groups**, **alternative delivery systems** and school-based **prevention programmes** may be helpful in lowering the prevalence of eating disorders.

● The major depression that is often comorbid with eating disorders can be treated pharmacologically with antidepressants such as **fluoxetine (Prozac)**.

● One of the most common treatments for eating disorders is **family therapy**, in which the family's role in developing and maintaining an eating-disordered individual is explored.

● The current treatment of choice for bulimia nervosa is considered to be **cognitive behaviour therapy (CBT)**, which attempts to deal with the symptoms of bulimia and the dysfunctional cognitions associated with disordered eating, and provide prevention against relapse.

9.5 EATING DISORDERS REVIEWED

This chapter has reviewed the three main eating disorders – anorexia nervosa, bulimia nervosa and binge-eating disorder. All of these disorders are characterized by dysfunctional eating patterns. Anorexia represents an extreme form of self-starvation while bulimia and binge-eating disorder are characterized by individuals' loss of control over their own eating patterns. In the case of bulimia, individuals attempt to compensate for frequent binge eating by purging and fasting. The individual with binge-eating disorder binges without compensatory behaviour and so frequently ends up overweight or obese. A look back at Table 9.1 shows that these different eating disorders have a number of factors in common, including a predominance of female rather than male sufferers, fear of weight gain, individuals' dissatisfaction with their own body shape and other comorbid psychopathology symptoms such as major depression. The section on aetiology (section 9.3) shows that these three eating disorders often share similar risk factors (see Figure 9.2), and that sociocultural values relating to body shape ideals may play an important role in initiating weight-regulating behaviours in vulnerable individuals. However, we still know very little about why one vulnerable individual becomes anorexic and another bulimic. Treatments for eating disorders are also still at an early stage of development and refinement. Some forms of CBT have been adapted to treating bulimia with some moderate success, and family therapy has been shown to help individuals with anorexia. But success rates are still far from acceptable. In the meantime, antidepressants such as selective serotonin reuptake inhibitors (SSRIs) may provide some short-term relief for the depression that is often comorbid with eating disorders.

LEARNING OUTCOMES

When you have completed this chapter, you should be able to:

1 Describe the characteristics and principal diagnostic criteria of the three main eating disorders.

2 Describe the historical, cultural and demographic distribution of eating disorders, and describe why this information is important in understanding such disorders.

3 Describe a range of risk factors for eating disorders, covering risk factors at different levels of explanation (such as genetic, developmental, cultural and psychological).

4 Describe, compare and contrast at least two therapies commonly used in the treatment of eating disorders.

5 Describe the kinds of presenting symptoms that are associated with anorexia nervosa and bulimia nervosa.

KEY TERMS

Alternative delivery systems *334*
Amenorrhea *315*
Anorexia nervosa (AN) *315*
Binge-eating disorder (BED) *319*
Binge-eating/purging type AN *315*
Body dissatisfaction *328*
Body mass index (BMI) *313*
Bulimia nervosa (BN) *316*
Childhood sexual abuse *331*
Cognitive behaviour therapy (CBT) *337*
Dieting *328*
Endogenous opioids *326*
Enmeshment *330*
Fames canina *322*
Familial factors *330*
Family systems theory *330*
Family therapy *336*
Fluoxetine (Prozac) *334*

Food preload test *332*
Holy anorexia *322*
Lack of conflict resolution *330*
Lateral hypothalamus *326*
Low self-esteem *332*
Media influence *327*
Neuroendocrine dysfunction *326*
Nonpurging sub-type BN *316*
Overprotection *330*
Peer influences *329*
Perfectionism *332*
Pharmacological treatments *334*
Prevention programmes *334*
Purging sub-type BN *316*
Restricted type AN *315*
Rigidity *330*
Self-help groups *334*

REVIEWS, THEORIES AND SEMINAL STUDIES

Links to Journal Articles

Classification and Aetiology of Eating Disorders

Dingemans, A.E., Bruna, M.J. & van Furth, E.F. (2002). Binge-eating disorder: A review. *International Journal of Obesity, 26,* 299–307.

Fairburn, C.G., Shafran, R. & Cooper, Z. (1999). A cognitive behavioural theory of anorexia nervosa. *Behaviour Research and Therapy, 37,* 1–13.

Ghaderi, A. & Scott, B. (2001). Prevalence, incidence and prospective risk factors for eating disorders. *Acta Psychiatrica Scandanavica, 104,* 122–130.

Hoek, H.W. & van Hoeken, D. (2003). Review of the prevalence and incidence of eating disorders. *International Journal of Eating Disorders, 34,* 383–396.

Jacobi, C., Hayward, C., de Zwaan, M., Kraemer, H.C. & Agras, W.S. (2004). Coming to terms with risk factors for eating disorders: Application of risk terminology and suggestions for a general taxonomy. *Psychological Bulletin, 130,* 19–65.

Keel, P.K. & Klump, K.L. (2003). Are eating disorders culture-bound syndromes? Implications for conceptualizing their etiology. *Psychological Bulletin, 129,* 747–769.

Lindberg, L. & Hjern, A. (2003). Risk factors for anorexia nervosa: A national cohort study. *International Journal of Eating Disorders, 34,* 397–408.

Miller, M.N. & Pumariega, A.J. (2001). Culture and eating disorders: A historical and cross-cultural review. *Psychiatry: Interpersonal and Biological Processes, 64,* 93–110.

O'Brien, K.M. & Vincent, N.K. (2003). Psychiatric comorbidity in anorexia and bulimia nervosa: Nature, prevalence, and causal relationships. *Clinical Psychology Review, 23,* 57–74.

Polivy, J. & Herman, C.P. (2002). Causes of eating disorders. *Annual Review of Psychology, 53,* 187–213.

Stice, E. (2001). A prospective test of the dual-pathway model of bulimic pathology: Mediating effects of dieting and negative affect. *Journal of Abnormal Psychology, 110,* 124–135.

Striegel-Moore, R.H. & Franko, D.L. (2003). Epidemiology of binge-eating disorder. *International Journal of Eating Disorders, 34,* 19–29.

Vohs, K.D., Bardone, A.M., Joiner, T.E., Abramson, L.Y. & Heatherton, T.F. (1999). Perfectionism, perceived weight status, and self-esteem interact to predict bulimic symptoms: A model of bulimic symptom development. *Journal of Abnormal Psychology, 108,* 695–700.

The Treatment of Eating Disorders

Anderson, D.A. & Maloney, K.C. (2001). The efficacy of cognitive-behavioral therapy on the core symptoms of bulimia nervosa. *Clinical Psychology Review, 21,* 971–988.

Bellini, M. & Merli, M. (2004). Current drug treatment of patients with bulimia nervosa and binge-eating disorder: Selective serotonin reuptake inhibitors versus mood stabilizers. *International Journal of Psychiatry in Clinical Practice, 8,* 235–243.

Bowers, W.A. (2001). Basic principles for applying cognitive-behavioral therapy to anorexia nervosa. *Psychiatric Clinics of North America, 24,* 293.

Dallos, R. (2004). Attachment narrative therapy: Integrating ideas from narrative and attachment theory in systemic family therapy with eating disorders. *Journal of Family Therapy, 26,* 40–65.

Kruger, S. & Kennedy, S.H. (2000). Psychopharmacotherapy of anorexia nervosa, bulimia nervosa and binge-eating disorder. *Journal of Psychiatry and Neuroscience, 25,* 497–508.

Myers, T.C., Swan-Kremeier, L., Wonderlich, S., Lancaster, K. & Mitchell, J.E. (2004). The use of alternative delivery systems and new technologies in the treatment of patients with eating disorders. *International Journal of Eating Disorders, 36,* 123–143.

Wilson, G.T., Fairburn, C.C., Agras, W.S., Walsh, B.T. & Kraemer, H. (2002). Cognitive-behavioral therapy for bulimia nervosa: Time course and mechanisms of change. *Journal of Clinical and Counselling Psychology, 70,* 267–274.

Wilson, G.T. & Shafran, R. (2005). Eating disorders guidelines from NICE. *Lancet, 365,* 79–81.

Texts for Further Reading

Fairburn, C.G. & Wilson, G.T. (1993). *Binge eating: Nature, assessment and treatment.* New York: Guilford Press.

Levine, M.P., Smolak, L.L. & Striegel-Moore, R. (1996). *The developmental psychopathology of eating disorders: Implications for research, prevention and treatment.* Hillsdale, NJ: Erlbaum.

Treasure, J., Schmidt, U. & van Furth, E. (2003). *Handbook of eating disorders,* 2nd ed. Chichester: Wiley.

Treasure, J., Schmidt, U. & van Furth, E. (2005). *The essential handbook of eating disorders.* Chichester: Wiley.

Werne, J. (1996). *Treating eating disorders.* Chichester: Wiley.

RESEARCH QUESTIONS

- To what extent is exposure to Westernized body shape ideals a *necessary* factor in developing anorexia nervosa and bulimia nervosa? Can this question be answered by examining cultural differences in the prevalence of eating disorders?

- Defining the risk factors involved in eating disorders provides us with a good idea of *what* factors are involved, but not *how* they are involved. What kinds of studies are required to determine whether a risk factor has a *causal* influence on the development of an eating disorder?

- Eating disorders are accompanied by changes in hormonal balance, levels of endogenous opioids and neuroendocrine function. But to what extent are these *causes* of eating disorders as opposed to *effects* of the disorder?

- We know that exposure to media images of ideal body shapes influences attitudes to eating and body shape, but how is this converted into the development of an eating disorder?

- Body dissatisfaction and dieting are central features of a number of models of eating disorders, but why is it that some people who diet and have high body dissatisfaction develop an eating disorder and others do not?

- A dysfunctional family environment is often associated with adolescent eating disorders, but how does that dysfunctional environment help to develop and maintain such disorders?

- Adverse life experiences are a risk factor for eating disorders, but is their role to generate other forms of psychopathology (e.g. depression) that facilitate the development of an eating disorder?

- Negative affect is often viewed as an *outcome* of having a particular psychopathology, but does negative affect have a *causal* effect on the development of eating disorders?

- Perfectionism is a prominent feature of individuals with eating disorders, but it is also a significant feature of many other psychopathologies. So what makes someone with perfectionist characteristics develop an eating disorder rather than some other psychopathology (such as OCD or GAD)?

CLINICAL ISSUES

- Are the high levels of comorbidity between anorexia, OCD and major depression indicative of a broader coherent 'obsession'-based disorder?

- Many individuals with eating disorders try to conceal their symptoms and deny they have a disorder. What problem does this raise for the diagnosis and treatment of eating disorders?

- Are the high levels of comorbidity between bulimia nervosa, borderline personality disorder and substance abuse evidence for viewing bulimia as part of a broader 'multi-impulsive' syndrome?

- Some views of eating disorders see the development of anorexia nervosa as a coping process by which the individual feels able to cope with other emotional and identity problems. Should this be taken into account when attempting to treat the symptoms of anorexia?

- Negative mood states have been shown to play a causal role in eating disorders by raising body dissatisfaction and increasing food intake in individuals who are dieting. Treatments that can help alleviate negative mood (such as antidepressant medications, relaxation training) should therefore have a beneficial effect on eating disorder symptoms.

- While CBT is considered to be the current treatment of choice for bulimia nervosa, it is successful for only 40–50 per cent of patients treated in that way.

10 Sexual and Gender Identity Problems

ROUTE MAP OF THE CHAPTER

This chapter covers the topics of sexual dysfunction, paraphilias and gender identity problems. It begins by looking at the definition of pathological sexual behaviour and the way in which cultural and social factors may determine how sexual dysfunction is identified and diagnosed. The section on sexual dysfunctions describes the various disorders of the sexual cycle, and considers aetiology and a range of treatment options. Paraphilia is largely a male disorder and contains categories associated with sexual offending. The various paraphilias are described and evidence for theories of aetiology is assessed. Finally, we cover some of the aspects of treating paraphilias, including the treatment of sexual offenders. The final section on gender identity disorder discusses its characteristics and what evidence there is for aetiology. The section ends by assessing gender reassignment treatments for gender identity disorder.

I am sure I am not the first cross-dresser to feel this way but when I get the chance to dress at first I am excited, I can hardly wait to put on the stockings, skirt and get all dolled up, and once I am fully dressed I feel so good! Almost like this is the way I am supposed to be but that feeling does not last . . .

Sometimes it will last an hour to hours but I have actually had it diminish within 15 minutes before I feel guilty and then undress and go back to my guy clothes. For some reason a light goes on in my head that tells me, I am a guy . . . why am I wearing a skirt?!? and then I quickly undress.

But then when I am dressed as a guy I will admire women in skirts and dresses and wish that could be me and all I want to do is rush home and dress (when my wife is not home). I would love to tell my wife about my CD'ing but I need to come to terms with it first.

CHRIS'S STORY

So, I have kind of a weird problem here. Normally, getting an erection is no problem for me. I wake up with one every morning, masturbate all the time, sometimes pop them up at inopportune moments, etc. I'm 21, by the way. Also in most sexual encounters there's no problem. I'd say 90% of the time. However, the problem arises (or fails to arise!) when I'm in bed with someone I'm extremely attracted to and very interested in. To date this has only happened with two men, but it is happening with the second of those two people right now and it's driving me crazy. Things will start out fine (i.e. erect) and I can be rolling around in bed with an erection for an hour, but it seems that as soon as it's time for my penis to do its duty (that is when foreplay ends and penetration commences), it deflates and vehemently refuses to be resuscitated. I don't know what to do! It's unendingly embarrassing, but the worst is that it only occurs with people I really like.

JAMES'S STORY

Introduction

Sexual behaviour plays a central role in most of our lives. It is a very personal and individual topic that we very rarely discuss openly with others. Sexual development is also an important part of our lives, where we learn about the nature of sexual behaviour and develop our own personal likes and dislikes about sexual activities. Furthermore, during adolescence and early adulthood, sexual performance is often related to self-esteem, and so becomes an important contributor to psychological development. The importance of sexual behaviour and the critical role it may play in many of our relationships means that it can regularly affect psychological functioning and quality of life generally. There is no definition of what is sexually 'normal', but clinical psychologists may become involved when an individual becomes *distressed* by his or her sexuality or sexual activities or when these cause interpersonal difficulties.

We began this chapter with two quite distinct personal accounts, each of which illustrates in different ways how an individual's sexual performance or sexual activities may cause conflict or distress. *Chris's* cross-dressing provides excitement which quickly gives way to guilt. It is also something he feels he needs to communicate to his wife, but at present cannot. *James's* story is one of problematic sexual performance, where his normally active libido fails him just prior to intercourse with men he particularly likes. Both provide examples of the kinds of cases that clinical psychologists are likely to encounter when sexual activities and sexual performance have an impact on psychological well-being, causing anxiety and distress as well as feelings of guilt, shame and depression.

10.1 DEFINING PATHOLOGICAL SEXUAL BEHAVIOUR

As you can imagine, what constitutes a sexual dysfunction is not a simple matter. Opinions about what is morally and socially acceptable and unacceptable change within societies over time, and there are significant differences between cultures in the implicit rules that constitute acceptable public behaviour (see Chapter 1 and Activity Box 10.1). For example, until 1973 the DSM listed homosexuality as a sexual disorder, along with paedophilia and sadism, but it is now considered a perfectly normal form of sexual activity in most Western societies, and is even considered a proper form of sexual activity for adolescent boys in some societies (Herdt & Stoller, 1990). Studies have indicated that homosexuals do not differ from heterosexuals in terms of their vulnerability to psychopathology generally (Paul, Gonsiorek & Hotvedt, 1982; Saghir, Robins & Walbran, 1969) or the personality dimensions that characterize them (Wilson, 1984). Examples such as this suggest that the actual nature of the sexual activity *per se* does not constitute grounds for labelling it as pathological, and people differ significantly in the range of stimuli that trigger sexual urges or fantasies. However, two factors are important when attempting to identify psychopathology in sexual behaviour.

First, a sexual activity or a sexual problem may be considered a suitable case for psychological treatment if it is frequent, chronic, causes the individual significant distress, and affects interpersonal relationships and other areas of functioning. Such examples include the personal distress and strain on interpersonal relationships caused by problems associated with completion of the normal sexual cycle (see sexual dysfunctions, below). Similarly, the cross-dressing behaviour of Chris in our earlier example caused him to experience guilt and anxiety. Individuals with gender identity problems also experience considerable distress, anxiety and depression at being 'trapped' in what they consider to be a body of the wrong biological sex. Clearly, such distress is the subject matter of psychopathology.

Secondly, some individuals persistently direct their sexual activity at individuals who do not consent to the activity or who cannot legally give consent (e.g. children). Such activities include exhibitionism (exposing of the genitalia to a stranger), paedophilia and rape. DSM-IV-TR includes some of these activities (exhibitionism, paedophilia) even though the diagnostic criteria do not require that the individual committing these acts experience distress. Whether such categories of activity should be labelled as psychopathologies is a debatable point, and in many cases they may be more suitably characterized as illegal criminal activities outlawed by particular societies. These definitions, and the issues that surround them, are certainly not set in stone, and we can expect to see changes in the sexual and gender identity disorders contained in future editions of the DSM and other diagnostic handbooks as cultural and public opinions on the acceptability of sexual activities change over time.

The disorders of sexuality and sexual functioning that we will cover in this chapter fit into three broad categories: (1) *sexual dysfunctions*, which represent problems with the normal sexual response cycle (e.g. lack of sexual desire or pain during intercourse); (2) *paraphilias*, which represent sexual urges or fantasies involving unusual sources of gratification (e.g. non-human objects or non-consenting individuals); and (3) *gender identity disorders*, where the individual is dissatisfied with his or her own biological sex and have a strong desire to be a member of the opposite sex. For each of these categories of disorders we discuss the nature of the disorder, diagnostic criteria, prevalence, aetiology and treatment. For a summary of sexual and gender identity disorders, see Table 10.1.

SELF-TEST QUESTIONS

- What are the sociocultural problems involved in defining pathological sexual behaviour?
- What are the three main groups of sexual and gender identity disorders?

ACTIVITY BOX 10.1

Cultural differences in sexual expression

Dutch Immigrants Must Watch Racy Film

The camera focuses on two gay men kissing in a park. Later, a topless woman emerges from the sea and walks onto a crowded beach. For would-be immigrants to the Netherlands, this film is a test of their readiness to participate in the liberal Dutch culture. If they can't stomach it, no need to apply.

Despite whether they find the film offensive, applicants must buy a copy and watch it if they hope to pass the Netherlands' new entrance examination.

The test, the first of its kind in the world, became compulsory Wednesday, and was made available at 138 Dutch embassies.

'As of today, immigrants wishing to settle in the Netherlands for, in particular, the purposes of marrying or forming a relationship will be required to take the civic integration examination abroad,' the Immigration Ministry said in a statement.

Not everyone is happy with the new test.

Dutch theologian Karel Steenbrink criticized the 105-minute movie, saying it would be offensive to some Muslims.

'It is not a prudent way of welcoming people to the Netherlands,' said Steenbrink, a professor at the University of Utrecht. 'Minister Verdonk has radical ideas.'

But Mohammed Sini, the chairman of Islam and Citizenship, a national Muslim organization, defended the film, saying that homosexuality is 'a reality'. Sini urged all immigrants 'to embrace modernity'.

A censored version with no homosexual and nude material had been prepared because it is illegal to show such images in Iran and some other countries, filmmaker Walter Goverde said.

Source: CBS News, 15 March 2006

This news item provides a good example of the differences in sexual expression found in different societies, and the tensions that these differing views may generate. Whether a sexual behaviour is acceptable or not is certainly not just a matter of psychology – it is determined by cultural or religious norms and the legal restrictions imposed in a particular society. You and your fellow students may wish to discuss some of the issues raised in this news story that relate to how sexual disorders might be defined and categorized. In particular:

- Could a universal set of diagnostic criteria for sexual and gender identity disorders be applied across different cultures?
- Will cultural norms affect how diagnostic criteria for sexual and gender identity disorders are defined?
- If a sexual activity is illegal in a country (e.g. homosexuality in Iran), does this also imply that individuals in that country who indulge in that activity require psychological treatment?
- Do cultural norms about sexual expression influence the kinds of sexual behaviours that are considered pathological?

SECTION SUMMARY

10.1 Defining Pathological Sexual Behaviour

- A sexual activity or a sexual problem can be considered a suitable case for treatment if it is frequent, chronic, causes the individual significant distress, and affects interpersonal relationships and other areas of functioning.

- Some individuals direct their sexual activities at non-consenting others. These include some **paraphilias** and illegal **sexual offences** (e.g. paedophilia).

Table 10.1 *Sexual and gender identity disorders: summary*

DISORDER AND LIFETIME PREVALENCE RATES	DEFINITION	MAIN DSM-IV-TR DIAGNOSTIC FEATURES	KEY FEATURES	THEORIES OF AETIOLOGY	MAIN FORMS OF TREATMENT
SEXUAL DYSFUNCTIONS Lifetime prevalence rates: See Table 10.5 for an estimated list of prevalence rates for specific sexual dysfunctions	A disturbance in the processes that characterize the sexual response cycle or by pain associated with sexual intercourse	See specific diagnostic details in text	Specific sexual dysfunction disorders include: *Disorders of desire*: Hypoactive sexual desire disorder Sexual aversion disorder *Disorders of sexual arousal*: Female sexual arousal disorder Male erectile disorder *Disorders of orgasm*: Female orgasmic disorder Male orgasmic disorder Premature ejaculation *Sexual pain disorders*: Dyspareunia Vaginismus	Psychoanalytic theory Masters & Johnson's two-factor theory Role of interpersonal problems Role of negative emotions and comorbid psychopathology Remote vs immediate causes Biological causes: • Underlying medical conditions • Hormonal abnormalities • Ageing Sociocultural causes	Direct treatments: • 'stop-start' technique • 'squeeze' technique • tease technique • directed masturbation training Couples therapy Sexual skills and communication training Self-instructional training Biological treatments: • Drug treatments • Hormone treatments • Mechanical devices
PARAPHILIAS Life time prevalence rates: (No prevalence rates available)	Recurrent, intense sexually arousing fantasies, sexual urges, or behaviours generally involving (1) non-human objects (e.g. fetishes), (2) the suffering or humiliation of oneself or one's partner (e.g. sexual masochism or sexual sadism) or (3) children or other non-consenting persons (e.g. paedophilia)	See specific diagnostic details in text	Specific paraphilias include: Fetishism Transvestic fetishism Sexual masochism and sexual sadism Exhibitionism Voyeurism Frotteurism Paedophilia The vast majority of the DSM-IV-TR diagnosable paraphilias are mainly male activities Some paraphilias are victimless (e.g. fetishes and transvestic fetishism) while others are defined in law as sexual offences (e.g. exhibitionism, voyeurism, frotteurism, paedophilia)	Hypersexuality as a risk factor for paraphilias Psychodynamic theories (including castration anxiety) Classical conditioning of inappropriate sexual responses Childhood abuse and neglect Cognitive distortions and dysfunctional beliefs, attitudes and schemata Biological theories: • Abnormalities in male sex hormones • Abnormalities in specific brain areas	Behavioural techniques: • Aversion therapy • Covert conditioning • Masturbatory satiation • Orgasmic reorientation CBT Relapse-prevention training Hormonal and drug treatments

Table 10.1 *(Cont'd)*

DISORDER AND LIFETIME PREVALENCE RATES	DEFINITION	MAIN DSM-IV-TR DIAGNOSTIC FEATURES	KEY FEATURES	THEORIES OF AETIOLOGY	MAIN FORMS OF TREATMENT
GENDER IDENTITY DISORDER (GID) **Life time prevalence rates:** Estimated 0.003% in males and 0.001% in females	A sense of gender dysphoria in which the individual has a gender identity that is opposite to his or her biological sex	The individual exhibits a strong and persistent cross-gender identification There must be clear evidence of persistent discomfort with existing biological sex, and strong feelings of the current gender role being inappropriate There must be evidence of significant distress or impairment in social, occupational or other important areas of functioning as a result of these feelings	Also diagnosed in children Most individuals with GID want to change their biological sex and not their gender identity	Only modest evidence that GID results from hormonal imbalances In males, GID has been associated with abnormalities in the brain area controlling sexual behaviour	Gender reassignment surgery Psychological treatments designed to change gender identity beliefs

10.2 SEXUAL DYSFUNCTIONS

Sex is mainly a private subject, and many people rarely talk with anyone other than their partner about intimate sexual matters. During the 1960s and 1970s a greater openness about sex and sexual activities developed as part of the liberalizing climate of the time. Changes in longevity, available leisure time, employment, childrearing practices and media coverage of leisure activities led to increased interest in sexual practices. Similarly, effective oral contraceptives and treatments for venereal disease helped to remove sexual inhibitions. Finally, changes in obscenity laws permitted sexual explicitness in the mass media in a way never previously broadcast. All this led to increased interest in sexual activity generally and sexual satisfaction in particular (Tiefer, 2006). At around this time, Masters and Johnson (1966) were beginning to publish their pioneering research on what they called the 'human sexual response', and the Kinsey reports (Kinsey, Pomeroy, Martin & Gebhard, 1953) provided hitherto unavailable statistical information on the frequency with which Americans engaged in various sexual activities. To most people's surprise, these reports revealed that sexual activities were significantly more widespread than most people were willing to believe at that time. They showed that 90 per cent of males had masturbated, and that oral sex was a common sexual activity. In addition, the studies revealed that around 80 per cent of men and 50 per cent of women had indulged in premarital sex.

More recent data from the UK National Survey of Sexual Attitudes and Lifestyles suggests that sexual activity in both males and females in the UK has increased over the period 1990 to 2000 (see Table 10.2). In 2000, men and women between the ages of 16 and 44 years reported having had an average of 12.7 and 6.5 sexual partners respectively in their lifetime, and 2.6 per cent of men and women reported having had a homosexual relationship. Frequency of sexual activity was also significantly higher in 2000 than in 1990, with 72 per cent of men and 76 per cent of women reporting having had vaginal intercourse in the previous month; 78 per cent of men and 76 per cent of women also reported having had oral sex in the previous year. These increases in sexual activity are also accompanied by significant rises in sexually transmitted infections – a 20 per cent rise in men and 56 per cent rise in women between 1990 and 1999 (Johnson, Mercer, Erens, Copas et al., 2001).

Plate 10.1
Masters and Johnson were the first to publish statistical information on the human sexual response and to develop integrated psychological theories of sexual dysfunction.

Table 10.2 *Changing sexual behaviour in the UK, 1990 to 2000*

Data from the National Survey of Sexual Attitudes and Lifestyles reports significant changes in sexual behaviour between 1990 to 2000. These include:

- A reduction in the age at which sexual intercourse first occurs. By the mid-1990s the average age was 16 years for both sexes.

- The proportion of young people who are sexually active before the age of 16 has increased.

- Women are twice as likely as men to regret their first experience of intercourse and three times as likely to report being the unwilling partner.

- By the 1990s, fewer than 1% of men and women had their first sexual experience with someone they were married or engaged to.

- The proportion of women who had only one sexual partner for life halved between 1990 and 2000.

- Attitudes towards homosexual behaviour, non-exclusive sexual relationships and sex outside of marriage relaxed significantly over the decades leading up to 2000.

- However, the UK public is firmly in favour of monogamy, with 80% of people strongly disapproving of sexual infidelity.

These figures suggest there has been a significant change in behaviour and attitudes towards sex in Western societies over recent decades. There has been an increase in the rate at which both men and women take sexual partners and a drop in the age at which adolescents report having their first sexual experience. This is accompanied by a relaxation of attitudes to homosexual behaviour, non-exclusive sexual relationships and sex outside of marriage. Although sexual activity appears to have increased over the past 20 years, it is difficult to estimate whether this increase has also given rise to increased sexual performance problems. However, the fact that research on sexual activity can nowadays proceed openly and without stigma has meant that significant developments have been made in how we conceptualize sexual activity and categorize potential dysfunctions. For example, the normal sexual cycle has been divided into four distinct stages (see below), and ***sexual dysfunctions*** can occur at any one of them. Table 10.3 lists the specific diagnosable disorders that have been identified with each stage.

> **Sexual dysfunction**   A disturbance in the processes that characterize the sexual response cycle or pain associated with intercourse.

The four stages of the sexual response cycle are: (1) *desire*, relating to the desire to have sex, (2) *arousal*, a subjective sense of sexual pleasure and accompanying physical changes in the genitalia (penile erection in the male, vaginal swelling and lubrication in the female), (3) *orgasm*, the peaking of sexual pleasure, and (4) *resolution*, a post-coital sense of muscular relaxation and well-being. There are no DSM-IV-TR disorders specifically associated with the resolution stage, but there is an additional set of disorders known as sexual pain disorders which can occur at different stages during the sexual cycle and significantly affect the normal sense of well-being experienced during the resolution stage. We will discuss the disorders relating to each stage in more detail later, after we have considered general diagnostic and prevalence issues.

SELF-TEST QUESTION

- Can you describe the four stages of the normal sexual response cycle?

10.2.1 Diagnosis of Sexual Dysfunction

In general terms, a sexual dysfunction is characterized by 'a disturbance in the processes that characterize the sexual response cycle or by pain associated with sexual intercourse' (APA, 2000, p. 535), and specific diagnostic criteria are set out for each of the disorders occurring at these different stages (see Table 10.4 and below). The specific dysfunction must also cause the individual subjective distress, affect areas of functioning such as relationships, and be persistent or recurrent. In each case, the clinician needs to exercise considerable judgement about what might or might not constitute a diagnosable problem in this area. The age and experience of the client need to be considered. For example, sexual activity and performance usually decline with age, and in females may do so after the menopause (Dennerstein & Hayes, 2005) – and often this is a perfectly normal developmental process rather than

Table 10.3 *Stages of the sexual cycle and their associated disorders*

STAGE OF THE SEXUAL CYCLE	DESCRIPTION	DISORDERS	MAIN DIAGNOSTIC SYMPTOM
DESIRE	Sexual thoughts and fantasies and the desire to have sex	HYPOACTIVE SEXUAL DESIRE DISORDER	A deficiency or absence of sexual fantasies and desire for sexual activity
		SEXUAL AVERSION DISORDER	Aversion to and active avoidance of genital sexual contact with a sexual partner
AROUSAL	Subjective sense of sexual pleasure and accompanying physical changes in the genitalia (e.g. penile erection in the male, vaginal swelling and lubrication in the female)	FEMALE SEXUAL AROUSAL DISORDER	A persistent inability to attain or maintain an adequate lubrication–swelling response of sexual excitement
		MALE ERECTILE DISORDER	A persistent inability to attain or maintain an adequate erection
ORGASM	Peaking of sexual pleasure (including ejaculation in the male and vaginal contractions in the female)	FEMALE ORGASMIC DISORDER	In females, a persistent or recurrent delay in, or absence of, orgasm following a normal sexual excitement stage
		MALE ORGASMIC DISORDER	In males, a persistent or recurrent delay in, or absence of, orgasm following a normal sexual excitement stage
		PREMATURE EJACULATION	A persistent onset of orgasm and ejaculation with minimal sexual stimulation and before the individual wishes it
SEXUAL PAIN DISORDERS		DYSPAREUNIA*	Genital pain experienced during or after coitus
		VAGINISMUS*	Persistent involuntary contraction of the perineal muscles of the vagina when vaginal penetration occurs

* Pain can occur both during and after intercourse and affects the normal post-coital sense of well-being.

Table 10.4 *DSM-IV-TR general diagnostic criteria for a sexual dysfunction*

A Persistence of a specific physical or psychological problem (e.g. lack of orgasm, lack of erection, pain during intercourse, lack of sexual desire or interest, etc.).

B The disturbance causes marked distress or interpersonal difficulty.

C The dysfunction is not better accounted for by another Axis I disorder and is not due to the physiological effects of a substance or general medical condition.

a dysfunction. The clinician also needs to take into account the client's ethnic, cultural, religious and social background – factors that may influence desire, expectations and attitudes about performance. Finally, a diagnosis of *sexual dysfunction due to a general medical condition* is given if the dysfunction is known to be caused exclusively by the physiological effects of a general medical condition.

As we mentioned earlier, diagnosis of a dysfunction is given only when the symptoms are persistent, cause the individual significant psychological distress, impair general day-to-day functioning and cause interpersonal distress. In many cases, distress occurs in cases of sexual dysfunction because it is associated with diagnosable mood disorders or anxiety disorders (especially obsessive-compulsive disorder, panic disorder, social phobia and specific phobia), and sexual dysfunction can often be a frequent complication of these latter disorders (Figueira, Possidente, Marques & Hayes, 2001). However, it is important to be aware that a specific sexual dysfunction diagnosis cannot be made if the symptoms can be better accounted for by another Axis I disorder (such as social phobia or panic disorder). Thus, the clinician has to be aware that *symptoms* of sexual dysfunction can occur in the context of other Axis I disorders and need not necessarily represent a diagnosis of sexual dysfunction *per se*.

SELF-TEST QUESTION

● Can you list the DSM-IV-TR general diagnostic criteria for a sexual dysfunction?

10.2.2 Specific Sexual Dysfunction Disorders

Sexual dysfunction disorders have been categorized around the four stages of the sexual cycle, namely desire, arousal, orgasm and resolution (see above, p. 349), and also include a category relating to pain experienced during the sexual cycle.

10.2.2.1 Disorders of Desire

The first phase of the sexual response cycle is the desire stage, which consists of the urge and desire to have sex, to indulge in sexual thoughts and fantasies and to experience sexual attraction to others. DSM-IV-TR identifies two specific disorders of this stage: *hypoactive sexual desire disorder* and *sexual aversion disorder*.

Hypoactive sexual desire disorder A sexual disorder which is characterized by a low level of sexual desire.

Sexual aversion disorder A sexual disorder in which there is an active avoidance of genital sexual contact with a sexual partner.

Hypoactive Sexual Desire Disorder This disorder is characterized by a persistent and recurrent deficiency or absence of desire for sexual activity and absence of sexual fantasies that cause the individual marked distress or interpersonal difficulty. Low sexual desire may be general or it may be focused on sexual activity with one individual (such as the client's partner) or on a particular sexual activity itself (such as oral sex). It is important to recognize that there are many people who experience normal sexual desires, but who – for their own reasons – decide not to engage in sexual activities. Such individuals should not be diagnosed with hypoactive sexual desire disorder. This category is a difficult one for the clinician to diagnose because it does not specify what constitutes a 'deficiency' of sexual desire. Sexual desire will be affected by a broad range of factors, including age, religious views, cultural norms, ethnicity and upbringing, and clinicians need to use their judgement to decide whether what is presented is a problem in need of psychological treatment. In addition, lack of desire is not unusual and often not a problem for many individuals. Surveys suggest that as many as 1 in 3 women and 1 in 6 men report a lack of desire for sex in the previous 12 months

(Laumann, Gagnon, Michael & Michael, 1994). Problems with sexual desire may also stem directly from problems elsewhere, either in the sexual cycle or in personal relationships. For example, lack of sexual desire is often associated with erectile problems in men (Bach, Wincze & Barlow, 2001), poor communication between women and their partners (Stuart, Hammond & Pett, 1987) and fear of loss of control or fear of pregnancy (LoPiccolo & Friedman, 1988). Sexual desire can also be significantly affected by prior physical and sexual trauma such as rape and childhood sexual abuse (Stuart & Greer, 1984).

Sexual Aversion Disorder This is the aversion to and active avoidance of genital sexual contact with a sexual partner in circumstances where this aversion gives rise to marked distress and interpersonal difficulty. The aversion is usually closely associated with feelings of anxiety, fear or disgust, and is often linked to very specific aspects of the sexual act such as fear of vaginal penetration or disgust at genital secretions. This diagnosis is significantly more common in women than in men (Heiman, 2002), and may often result from adverse sexual experiences such as rape or childhood sexual abuse (Berman, Berman, Werbin, Flaherty et al., 1999).

10.2.2.2 Disorders of Sexual Arousal

The second stage of the sexual cycle is arousal, which is characterized by a subjective sense of sexual pleasure and accompanying physical changes in the genitalia. DSM-IV-TR-defined disorders of sexual arousal are *female sexual arousal disorder* and *male erectile disorder*.

Female sexual arousal disorder A sexual disorder in which there is an inability to attain an adequate lubrication–swelling response of sexual excitement and to maintain this state until completion of sexual activity.

Male erectile disorder A sexual disorder in which there is an inability to maintain an adequate erection during sexual activity. Around 10 per cent of males report erection problems, increasing to 20 per cent in the over-50s.

Female Sexual Arousal Disorder This is a persistent or recurrent inability to attain an adequate lubrication–swelling response of sexual excitement, or to maintain this state until the completion of sexual activity. The disturbance must cause the individual marked distress or interpersonal difficulty for diagnosis to be made. It is important to note that this disorder is defined primarily in terms of a deficiency in a physical or physiological response, and as a result may be caused by a range of physical or physiological factors including hormone imbalances, diabetes, medications being taken for other disorders, and a range of other medical problems. Indeed, surveys suggest that as many as 1 in 5 women report problems with vaginal lubrication on a regular basis (Laumann, Gagnon, Michael & Michael, 1994). Female sexual arousal problems rarely occur in isolation. They are regularly associated with orgasmic disorders and may often be accompanied by erectile dysfunctions in the woman's male partner. Indeed, many of the disorders at specific stages in the sexual cycle can have accompanying effects elsewhere, with disorders of sexual desire affecting arousal, and failure of arousal influencing sexual desire during future sexual encounters.

Male Erectile Disorder This is a persistent or recurrent inability to attain an adequate erection or to maintain the erection until completion of sexual activity. This must cause marked distress or interpersonal difficulty for a diagnosis to be made. This can manifest itself in a number of different ways: as a failure to attain an erection from the outset of sexual activity, first experiencing an erection but then losing tumescence prior to penetration, or losing tumescence during penetration but prior to orgasm. Male erectile disorder is one of the most common of the sexual dysfunctions in men, is usually the disorder that is most commonly referred for treatment, and is likely to have a significant impact on the sexual satisfaction of both the sufferer and his partner. The disorder becomes significantly more prevalent with age. Around 10 per cent of males report erection problems, but this figure doubles to 20 per cent in the over-50s (Laumann, Gagnon, Michael & Michael, 1994). The causes of male erectile disorder are complex and appear to range across physical, psychological and sociocultural factors. Hormonal and vascular problems such as high blood pressure, diabetes and heart disease are associated with erectile disorders (Berman, Berman, Werbin, Flaherty et al., 1999), as are activities such as smoking and excessive alcohol consumption (Westheimer & Lopater, 2002). Psychological factors that may affect the ability to achieve and maintain erection include severe depression (Seidman, 2002) and marital, financial and occupational stress (Morokoff & Gilliland, 1993). Also, since achieving an erection is an essential part of the sexual act, many males may acquire what is known as ***performance anxiety***, where fear of failing to achieve a sustained erection causes them to become distanced from the sexual act and fail to become aroused (Masters & Johnson, 1970).

Performance anxiety The fear of failing to achieve an acceptable level of sexual performance, causing an individual to become distanced from the sexual act and fail to become aroused.

10.2.2.3 Disorders of Orgasm

Female orgasmic disorder A sexual disorder characterized by a delay or absence of orgasm during sexual activity; around 10 per cent of adult women may never have experienced an orgasm.

Male orgasmic disorder A sexual disorder in which there is a delay in or absence of orgasm following sexual activity. Around 8 per cent of men report symptoms typical of this disorder.

Premature ejaculation The persistent or recurrent onset of orgasm and ejaculation with minimal sexual stimulation before, on or shortly after penetration, and before the person wishes it to happen.

Orgasm is the third stage of the sexual cycle when sexual stimulation has been sufficient to enable the individual's sexual pleasure to peak. In both males and females this involves a rhythmic muscular contraction of the genitals which results in a release of sexual tension, and in the male is accompanied by ejaculation of semen. There are three DSM-IV-TR-defined disorders of this stage: ***female orgasmic disorder***, ***male orgasmic disorder*** and ***premature ejaculation***.

Female Orgasmic Disorder This is a persistent or recurrent delay in or absence of orgasm following normal sexual excitement which causes the individual marked distress or interpersonal difficulty. Once again, the clinician has to exercise judgement about whether a diagnosis is relevant in individual cases. Women exhibit significant differences in the type and intensity of stimulation that triggers orgasm, and as many as 10 per cent of adult women may never have experienced an orgasm (Andersen, 1983). In addition, whether a woman achieves orgasm or not may be a significant factor in her partner's attitude to sex. During heterosexual sex, a man may believe his partner is not enjoying sex or may feel that he is an inexperienced lover if his partner does not achieve an orgasm. This can often lead to the woman faking orgasm, which around 60 per cent of women claim to have done at some point, and which may have a significant role to play in her failing to achieve full orgasm (McConaghy, 1993). Female orgasmic disorder is one of the most frequent female sexual disorders referred for treatment. It is experienced by around 1 in 4 women at some point in their lives, and more significantly in the postmenopausal period (Heiman, 2002). However, women who are assertive and who have experienced masturbatory orgasm prior to becoming sexually active are significantly less likely to be diagnosed with female orgasmic disorder (Hite, 1976). Early sexual experiences may be important in determining whether a woman develops female orgasmic disorder. For example, positive early sexual encounters fostering emotional involvement are directly related to the probability of reaching orgasm in later sexual encounters (Heiman, Gladue, Roberts & LoPiccolo, 1986). In contrast, an upbringing that implies that the woman should deny her sexuality is more likely to lead to orgasmic dysfunction, as are the experiences of being punished for childhood masturbation and receiving little or no advice or information about menstruation (LoPiccolo, 1997).

Male Orgasmic Disorder This is a persistent or recurrent delay in, or absence of, orgasm following a normal sexual excitement phase which causes the individual marked distress and interpersonal difficulty. The clinician must make judgements about whether orgasm is problematically delayed by taking into account the client's age and the degree of sexual stimulation. Around 8 per cent of men report symptoms typical of male orgasmic disorder (Laumann, Gagnon, Michael & Michael, 1994), and in many cases the problems can be caused by physical factors such as low testosterone levels (Stahl, 2001), alcohol consumption or prescription drugs such as antidepressants and anxiolytic drugs, all of which can affect the response of the sympathetic nervous system (Seagraves, 1995; Altman, 2001). In other cases the individual may feel sexually aroused at the outset of coitus, but over time thrusting becomes a chore rather than a pleasure. This can also be the case when individuals may have been pressurized into having sex with their partners rather than experiencing full desire for it.

Premature Ejaculation This is the persistent or recurrent onset of orgasm and ejaculation with minimal sexual stimulation before, on or shortly after penetration, and before the person wishes it to happen. Premature ejaculation is not unusual when aspects of the sexual activity are novel (e.g. the person is indulging in novel sex acts, with new partners, or has sex only rarely), and this must be taken into account by the clinician when making a diagnosis. Most young males learn to delay orgasm with continued sexual experience and age, although some continue to have premature ejaculation problems – typically men under the age of 30 – and so may seek treatment for the disorder (Bancroft, 1989). Premature ejaculation is a complaint reported by 1 in 3 men at some time in their lives (Laumann, Gagnon, Michael & Michael, 1994), and has been linked to infrequent climactic sex (Spiess, Geer & O'Donohue, 1984), over-responsiveness to tactile stimulation (Rowland, Cooper & Slob, 1996), anxiety caused by hurried sexual experiences in early adulthood (Dunn, Croft & Hackett, 1999) and, in some cases, to physical or biological causes (Metz, Pryor, Nesvacil, Abuzzhab et al., 1997).

10.2.2.4 Sexual Pain Disorders

Dyspareunia A genital pain that can occur during, before or after sexual intercourse. Some clinicians believe this is a pain disorder rather than a sexual dysfunction.

Vaginismus The involuntary contraction of the muscles surrounding the vagina when vaginal penetration is attempted. Of all women who seek treatment for sexual dysfunctions, around 15–17 per cent are suffering from vaginismus.

Pain can become a common experience that is associated with sexual activity. It can occur prior to, during or after sexual intercourse, and significantly affects the feeling of well-being that is an important feature of the resolution stage of the sexual cycle. The two sexual pain disorders are *dyspareunia* and *vaginismus*.

Dyspareunia This is genital pain that can occur before, during or after sexual intercourse, in both males and females. The type of pain experienced may be mild discomfort or sharp pain, but is diagnosed if it causes marked distress and interpersonal difficulty. Those who suffer dyspareunia appear to show normal levels of sexual arousal and also report enjoying sex, but find that their sexual activities are severely limited by their experienced pain. In American surveys, 14 per cent of women and 3 per cent of men have reported pain during sexual activity (Laumann, Gagnon, Michael & Michael, 1994). Very often the causes are physical, and may relate to gynaecological or urological problems in women, or to allergic reactions to substances in contraceptive creams, condoms or diaphragms (e.g. Brown & Ceniceros, 2001). Some psychological factors have also been identified as possible causes of dyspareunia, including a conditioned pain response that has been acquired following a sexual assault (Binik, Bergeron & Khalife, 2000). There is currently some debate about whether dyspareunia is a genuine sexual dysfunction or whether it more properly meets the criteria for a pain disorder, and focusing on a therapeutic approach which tackles the perceived pain element of dyspareunia is often successful (Binik, 2005).

Vaginismus This is the persistent or recurrent involuntary contraction of the perineal muscles surrounding the outer third of the vagina when vaginal penetration is attempted. In some cases even the anticipation of vaginal insertion may result in spasms, and

in severe cases this can physically prevent penetration. The disorder is found more often in younger than in older females, and in those who have either a negative attitude towards sex or a history of being sexually abused. Because the condition can physically prevent coitus, it can be a problem that can prevent sexual enjoyment for both the woman and her partner, and as a result cause problems in existing relationships. Because of its physical nature, vaginismus is a disorder that may often be referred directly to gynaecologists rather than psychologists, but of all women who seek psychological therapy for sexual dysfunctions, around 15–17 per cent are suffering from vaginismus (Rosen & Leiblum, 1995). Both physical and psychological causes for vaginismus have been proposed. It can be associated with medical problems such as infections of the vagina, bladder or uterus, the physical effects of menopause or gynaecological diseases such as herpes simplex (McCormick, 1999). However, poor sex education and knowledge about the sexual act can lead to anxiety about sex that triggers a reflexive contraction of the perineal muscles, and sexual abuse or assault during either childhood or adulthood can cause the muscular contractions to occur as part of a conditioned fear response (Westheimer & Lopater, 2002; Reissing, Binik, Khalife, Cohen et al., 2003).

SUMMARY

The specific disorders that we have discussed can be associated with individual stages of the sexual cycle. However, there is clearly a good deal of overlap between these different disorders, and a disorder in one particular stage of the sexual cycle may well affect performance in other stages (e.g. disorders of arousal and orgasm may subsequently affect sexual urges and desires). Diagnosing a sexual dysfunction is not as simple as referring to a list of criteria symptoms because the clinician has to make judgements about what is dysfunctional in the light of the client's sexual experience, age, religious views, cultural norms, ethnicity and upbringing. The clinician also has to decide whether the sexual problems that are referred are caused primarily by physical or medical conditions, and if so, whether the client might be better referred for medical treatment, perhaps to a pain specialist or a gynaecologist. Finally, it is important to remember that many people may not be particularly satisfied with their own sexual performance or that of their partner, but manage to live their daily lives quite happily. A sexual dysfunction is diagnosed only when the condition is persistent and causes the client considerable distress and significant interpersonal difficulty. Some consequences of this are discussed in Focus Point 10.1.

FOCUS POINT 10.1

Constructing female sexual dysfunction

Sexual dysfunction is not diagnosed simply on the basis of problems in sexual desire and performance but is dependent on the condition causing marked distress and interpersonal difficulty. Clearly, many people may only rarely experience sexual desire and very rarely indulge in sexual activity – but a sizeable proportion of those people are quite happy with this state of affairs, and indeed may even advocate and seek sexual abstinence. But what happens if attempts are made to make such people feel inadequate or in some way 'abnormal'?

In 1966, New York gynaecologist Robert A. Wilson published a best-selling book, *Feminine Forever*, in which he argued that the menopause robbed women of their femininity and sexuality and ruined the quality of their lives. He labelled post-menopausal women as 'castrates' and described the menopause as a 'deficiency disease' that should be treated pharmacologically with hormone replacement therapy. The book and its ensuing publicity had two effects: it made some post-menopausal women begin to believe they were inadequate and had a disorder that needed treatment, while it made many others – especially those in the newly developing feminist movement – believe that menopausal symptoms as described by Wilson were not a medical deficiency but the creation of a sexist society (Houck, 2003).

More recently, other writers have argued that the pharmaceutical industry has attempted to manipulate women's beliefs about their sexuality in order to sell their products (Moynihan,

2006). Some drug companies claim that sexual desire problems affect up to 43 per cent of American women (Moynihan, 2003) and can be successfully treated with, for example, hormone patches. However, others claim that this figure is highly improbable and includes women who are quite happy with their reduced level of sexual interest (Bancroft, Loftus & Long, 2003).

Tiefer (2006) lists a number of processes that have been used in the past, either wittingly or unwittingly, to 'medicalize' what many see as normal sexual functioning. These include:

- Taking a normal function and implying that there is something wrong with it and it should be treated.
- Imputing suffering that is not necessarily there.
- Defining as large a proportion of the population as possible as suffering from the disease.
- Defining a condition as a 'deficiency', disease or disease of hormonal imbalance.
- Taking a common symptom that could mean anything and making it sound as if it is a sign of a serious disease.

While sexual dysfunctions are sometimes caused by medical conditions (see section 10.2.4.2), lack of sexual desire and interest is itself often portrayed as a medical condition in need of treatment. Yet a reduction in sexual interest and desire can be a healthy and adaptive response to normal changes in body chemistry or as a normal reaction to adverse life stressors or relationship changes.

ACTIVITY BOX 10.2

Below are listed a number of very brief case histories. After reading section 10.2.2 of this chapter, examine these descriptions and try to answer the following questions for each case:

(a) Would this case be diagnosable as a sexual dysfunction?

(b) If so, what is the precise disorder?

(c) What factors might have contributed to the disorder?

1 A frustrated and distressed man confides that every time he and his new wife attempt lovemaking, she becomes hysterical and writhes in pain when he attempts vaginal penetration. They have successfully satisfied each other through other means, such as mutual masturbation, but he believes something is wrong or that he is doing something wrong.

2 A 36-year-old man seeks advice because over the last 6 months he has been experiencing the occasional inability to become erect. His relationship is satisfying and he usually enjoys the sexual aspects of his life. However, the man is concerned that the situation may worsen.

3 A 26-year-old woman in a sexually exclusive relationship that has lasted for 1 year wants to know if she is normal because she does not always experience an orgasm, although she enjoys sex with her partner. Her friend told her that something may be wrong if she does not experience orgasm every time she has sex.

4 A 58-year-old woman wants to know why her partner, who is 10 years older than her, has lost his desire for sex. He is not always aroused like he used to be. Her partner enjoys sex but states that it just takes him longer to 'get going'.

5 A 49-year-old woman is concerned that her partner of the same age no longer initiates sexual activity. Her partner has been experiencing irregular menses and low energy for the past year. Nothing seems to stimulate her partner as it used to. When the woman extends foreplay to give her partner more time to respond, she does not respond as before, and this is beginning to affect their relationship in that they do not communicate like they used to.

6 An 18-year-old man has sought advice on two occasions complaining of penile discharge. Both times the findings were negative for any infection, and he seems evasive about the nature of the discharge. It emerges that he has only recently had sex for the first time, and during that encounter he ejaculated almost immediately after vaginal penetration. His girlfriend asked him if 'that was it?'. He believes there is something wrong with him.

Answers

1 **(a)** Yes.

(b) Sexual pain disorder such as dyspareunia or vaginismus.

(c) Physical causes such as allergic reactions; gynaecological diseases or infections of the vagina, bladder or uterus; conditioned fear responses to prior traumatic experiences, such as sexual assault.

2 **(a)** No, because the person's inability to become erect is not persistent and does not diminish sexual satisfaction.

3 **(a)** No, because the woman experiences sexual satisfaction and orgasm at a frequency that is acceptable to her.

4 **(a)** No, because the partner is probably experiencing changes in sexual function that are a normal part of the ageing process.

5 **(a)** Yes.

(b) This could be diagnosable as hypoactive sexual desire disorder because the partner's lack of desire is beginning to significantly affect the couple's relationship.

(c) Poor communication between the couple could be a cause of the problem rather than simply an outcome; changes in hormone levels in the partner as part of the ageing process could also contribute to increased lack of desire.

6 **(a)** Yes.

(b) Premature ejaculation.

(c) This could be caused by lack of sexual experience, over-responsiveness to tactile or other stimulation, or anxiety caused by sexual inexperience or lack of technique.

Source: adapted from www.engenderhealth.org

SELF-TEST QUESTIONS

● Can you name the disorders of desire and their main diagnostic characteristics?
● What are the main disorders of sexual arousal and how are they defined?
● Roughly what percentage of men report erection problems, and how does this change with age?
● What are the main disorders of orgasm and how are they defined in DSM-IV-TR?
● What are the sexual pain disorders and how are they defined?
● What kinds of decisions does a clinician have to make when diagnosing a sexual dysfunction?

10.2.3 Prevalence of Sexual Dysfunctions

In the previous section on specific sexual dysfunctions we gave an indication of the reported prevalence of these sexual problems in the general population. However, these figures differ from those for the number of individuals successfully diagnosed with a disorder according to, for example, the strict diagnostic criteria set out by DSM-IV-TR. This distinction is important because, while some individuals report that they have a particular symptom (e.g. erectile problems), many do not perceive this as problematic or distressing, and so do not meet the DSM-IV-TR criteria for a sexual dysfunction. A study by Wagner, Fugl-Meyer and Fugl-Meyer (2000) found that 69 per cent of men reporting erectile disorder found it problematic, while only 45 per cent of women reporting orgasmic disorders labelled them as problematic. Prevalence rates for a range of sexual dysfunctions that meet DSM-IV-TR diagnostic criteria were reported by Simons and Carey (2001). The pooled findings from over 10 years of prevalence research are given in Table 10.5. These figures suggest that sexual

dysfunctions are amongst some of the more prevalent psychopathologies in the general population (Spector & Carey, 1990), with female hypoactive sexual desire disorder, female orgasmic disorder and sexual pain disorders such as dyspareunia being particularly prevalent in community samples.

SELF-TEST QUESTIONS

● What are the problems involved in trying to assess the prevalence rates of sexual dysfunctions?

10.2.4 The Aetiology of Sexual Dysfunctions

In describing the various sexual disorders in section 10.2.2.1, we hinted in some cases at factors that might cause these specific disorders to develop. This section provides a more thorough review of the aetiology of sexual dysfunction by looking first at the kinds of risk factors that are associated with the development of specific disorders, then examining theories that attempt to explain in more general terms how people might acquire sexual dysfunctions.

10.2.4.1 Risk Factors for Sexual Dysfunctions

Risk factors for individual sexual dysfunctions will usually be gender related to some extent, because many of the disorders apply only to a specific gender (e.g. female sexual arousal disorder, female orgasmic disorder and vaginismus are relevant to women, while male erectile disorder, male orgasmic disorder and premature ejaculation are relevant to men). So, for example, experiencing the menopause is an important risk factor for hypoactive sexual desire disorder in women, and surgically menopausal women (who have undergone hysterectomy) are at significantly greater risk

Table 10.5 *The prevalence of DSM-IV-TR-diagnosed sexual dysfunctions*

DISORDER	PREVALENCE RATE
Hypoactive sexual desire disorder	0–3% (males) 10–46% (females)
Sexual aversion disorder	?
Female sexual arousal disorder	?
Male erectile disorder	0–5%
Female orgasmic disorder	7–10%
Male orgasmic disorder	0–3%
Premature ejaculation	4–5%
Dyspareunia	9–21%
Vaginismus	0.5–1%

Figures represent current prevalence estimates from community samples collated by Simons & Carey (2001) using studies that had defined dysfunction using DSM criteria.

(Dennerstein, Koochaki, Barton & Graziottin, 2006). For specific male dysfunctions such as male erectile disorder, risk factors include ageing, a diagnosis of depression, cigarette smoking and medical conditions such as diabetes and cardiovascular or urogenital disease (Korenman, 2004; Droupy, 2005). For premature ejaculation, risk factors include being young, having experienced divorce and being more educated (Fasolo, Mirone, Gentile, Parazzini et al., 2005). Educational level in men has a complex relationship to sexual dysfunction: men who are more educated are more likely to report premature ejaculation than less educated men (Fasolo, Mirone, Gentile, Parazzini et al., 2005), but less educated men are more likely to report erectile disorder than better educated men (Lyngdorf & Hemmingsen, 2004).

Childhood sexual abuse is also a significant risk factor for sexual dysfunction in later life. In a large-scale Australian study, more than 1 in 3 women and 1 in 6 men reported a history of childhood sexual abuse, and there was a significant association between childhood abuse and symptoms of sexual dysfunction (Najman, Dunne, Purdie, Boyle et al., 2005). Sexual trauma and childhood sexual abuse have been found to be a significant risk factor in specific disorders such as hypoactive sexual desire disorder (Stuart & Greer, 1984), sexual aversion disorder (Berman, Berman, Werbin, Flaherty et al., 1999), dyspareunia (Binik, Bergeron & Khalife, 2000) and vaginismus (Westheimer & Lopater, 2002).

Finally, sexual dysfunction is more prevalent in women than in men (43 per cent and 31 per cent respectively), and is more likely amongst those experiencing poor physical and emotional health generally (Laumann, Paik & Rosen, 1999). However, we must remember that this gender difference may be due at least in part to men being more embarrassed by sexual dysfunction than women, and so reporting disorders significantly less often. For example, a study of male erectile disorder found that 2 out of 3 men suffering erectile dysfunction were embarrassed when discussing this problem with a doctor, and only 25 per cent subsequently sought medical advice (Droupy, 2005).

10.2.4.2 Theories of the Aetiology of Sexual Dysfunction

Psychoanalytic Theory Much of the psychoanalytic approach to understanding behaviour revolves around repressed emotions and desires, and specifically around repressed sexual desires, so it is not unusual that psychodynamic theorists have had something to say about the factors underlying sexual dysfunction. Thus, vaginismus may be seen as a woman expressing hostility towards men, premature ejaculation as a man expressing repressed hostility towards women, and female orgasmic disorder as a function of enduring penis envy. Because sexual activity is usually pleasurable – yet often frowned upon by society – many psychodynamic views see sexual dysfunction as resulting from this conflicting state of affairs. Still others view male sexual dysfunctions such as male erectile disorder as a result of an unresolved Oedipus complex based on a continued sexual attachment of the male to his mother (Fenichel, 1945). Regardless of the theoretical validity of such analyses, these views gave psychoanalysis an important therapeutic function prior to the development of therapies based on more objective and more detailed knowledge of sexual dysfunctions such as those pioneered by Masters and Johnson in the 1970s.

The Two-Factor Model of Masters and Johnson Masters and Johnson were the first researchers to collect detailed information about sexual dysfunctions and to develop a model of sexual dysfunction based on this empirical evidence. Their model had two important components, both of which contributed to sexual dysfunction. The first component consisted of a learned or conditioned factor where adverse early sexual experiences gave rise to a learned fear or anxiety response whenever the individual was engaged in sexual activity. Adverse experiences include (1) psychosexual trauma such as rape or childhood sexual abuse, (2) religious and social taboos giving rise to feelings of shame and guilt about sex, (3) embarrassing or belittling early experiences with sex (e.g. appearing unknowledgeable or inexperienced to a sexual partner) or (4) excessive alcohol use in men, which can affect the ability to achieve and maintain erection.

Once these factors have begun to generate anxiety about sexual performance, the second component of this model is the *spectator role* that individuals adopt in response to their fears and anxieties. Instead of taking a relaxed attitude to sex, the fearful individual constantly monitors his or her own sexual performance and the responses of his or her partner. The individual's focus of attention is thus directed away from the stimuli that provide sexual arousal and sexual pleasure and onto factors that provide feedback about how well he or she is performing. There are some important similarities between this theory of sexual dysfunction and self-focused attention accounts of social phobia (see Chapter 5, section 5.2), where self-focused attention prevents objective processing of the social situation, leading the social phobic to engage in critical self-evaluation, and may well adversely affect his or her actual performance in the social situation. Because of these similarities, many of the processes involved in self-focused attention may also apply to sexual dysfunction.

Although Masters and Johnson's theory was the first attempt to develop an empirical model of sexual dysfunction based on objectively collected data about sexual performance, we must still be cautious about how the two components of their model interact. For example, while it is clear that many people suffering sexual dysfunction experience performance anxiety, it is still not clear whether this anxiety is a *cause* or a *consequence* of the dysfunction. We have already noted that many specific sexual disorders can be caused by physical or medical conditions, and it may be that anxiety about sexual performance is a consequence of sexual performance being impaired by these conditions rather than a cause of the condition *per se*.

Sexual Dysfunction and Interpersonal Problems Interpersonal difficulty is one of the main diagnostic criteria for all of the sexual dysfunctions. That is, the client must report that his or her sexual difficulties are associated with significant problems in relationships. However, sex is usually an interpersonal activity, and it may be that interpersonal problems may be a *cause* rather than simply an *outcome* of the sexual dysfunction. Many clinicians believe that individuals with sexual dysfunctions have both sexual and interpersonal problems, and that the latter may be an important cause of the former (e.g. Rosen & Leiblum, 1995). For example, a couple may develop repressed anger or bitterness towards each other or may develop problems in communication – especially if one of the couple has taken control of the relationship or behaves in ways resented by the other (such as staying out on a regular basis, failing to take equal responsibility for childcare or failing to make an equal contribution to household tasks) (Bach, Wincze & Barlow, 2001). If negative emotion is a central feature of the relationship, then emotions such as resentment, disgust, anxiety, anger, distrust and depression are likely to significantly interfere with the development of positive feelings required in the desire and arousal stages of the sexual cycle. If general communication is poor within a couple, then this is likely to impact importantly on talk about intimate activities such as sex.

Studies have indicated that interpersonal difficulties are apparent in sexual dysfunctions diagnosed in both men and women. They are associated with premature ejaculation and erectile disorders in men (Patrick, Althof, Pryor, Rosen et al., 2005; Swindle, Cameron, Lockhart & Rosen, 2004) and sexual dysfunctions generally in women (Clayton, 2003). Men are also significantly more likely to seek help for their sexual dysfunction if it is associated with interpersonal difficulties (Papaharitou, Athanasiadis, Nakopoulou, Kirana et al., 2006). However, we must still be cautious about how to interpret these findings. They only indicate that there is an association between sexual dysfunction and interpersonal difficulties, and we do not know the direction of any causal relationship.

Apart from general difficulties that may have arisen in a relationship, sexual dysfunction may result from specific deficiencies in sexual knowledge or sexual expertise in one or both of the couple. For example, women who suffer female orgasmic disorder often have partners who are awkward or inexperienced lovers (Kaplan, 1974), and individuals who develop sexual dysfunctions often lack the knowledge and skills required to fully stimulate their partner or satisfy themselves (LoPiccolo & Hogan, 1979). Sexual problems can also develop if one member of a couple is overanxious about pleasing the other, giving rise to performance anxiety that may inhibit sexual feelings and responsiveness to sexual stimuli (Kaplan, 1974).

Finally, untangling the role that interpersonal difficulties may play in *causing* sexual dysfunction is problematic. This is because interpersonal difficulties are very often a central outcome of sexual dysfunction anyway, and a necessary criterion for DSM-IV-TR diagnosis of a disorder. However, therapies for sexual dysfunction that focus on the relationship between couples are often successful, which suggests that at least some of the causes of some sexual dysfunctions lie in the details of individual relationships.

The Role of Negative Emotion and Psychopathology

Satisfying sexual experiences are usually dependent on individuals being open to positive pleasurable emotions and attentive to those stimuli during sexual activity that are likely to provide sexual stimulation and pleasure. Because of this, chronic negative emotions such as depression or anxiety are likely to interfere significantly with sexual performance. Studies suggest that 62 per cent of people with depression are also likely to have a sexual dysfunction, compared with only 26 per cent of people without depression (Angst, 1998). In women, depressive symptoms have been shown to be associated with deficits in sexual desire, sexual fantasy, sexual arousal and orgasmic function (Cyranowski, Frank, Cherry, Houck et al., 2004). Men with depression are almost twice as likely to experience erectile dysfunction as non-depressed men, and the degree of erectile dysfunction increases with increasing degree of depression (Araujo, Durante, Feldman, Goldstein et al., 1998). In addition, women seeking help for sexual dysfunction exhibit characteristics related to depression, such as mood instability and low and fragile self-esteem (Hartmann, Heiser, Ruffer-Hesse & Kloth, 2002). These findings again beg the question of whether depression is a cause or an outcome of sexual dysfunction. Studies that have directly attempted to treat sexual dysfunctions such as erectile disorder using drugs such as vardenafil show a significant remission in depressive symptoms that are directly predicted by improvement in erectile function, which suggests that depression may at least in part be an outcome of sexual dysfunction (Rosen, Shabsigh, Berber, Assalian et al., 2006; see Figure 10.1). However, trying to identify whether depression causes sexual dysfunction by observing improvement in sexual functioning following treatment of the depressive symptoms is problematic. This is because many antidepressant drugs (such as SSRIs) themselves have direct detrimental effects on sexual performance (Rosen, Lane & Menza, 1999).

Anxiety is another negative emotion that can potentially have a significant effect on sexual functioning. We have already discussed the role that performance anxiety may play in causing sexual dysfunction, and anxiety disorders such as panic disorder, social phobia, specific phobia and obsessive-compulsive disorder themselves are associated with sexual dysfunction (Figueira, Possidente,

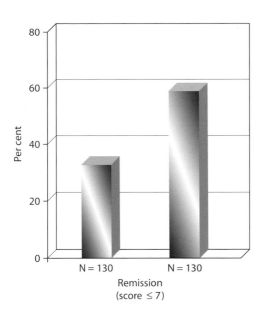

"My foreplay isn't working anymore is it, Angela?"

Plate 10.2

Figure 10.1

The percentage of participants with erectile dysfunction who show remission of depression symptoms following treatment with vardenafil (a drug used for treating erectile dysfunction) (red bar), and a placebo control (blue bar).

Source: Rosen, Shabsigh, Berber, Assalian et al. (2006).

Marques & Hayes, 2001). For example, anxiety disorders can be diagnosed in almost 20 per cent of men suffering from erectile disorder (Mallis, Moysidis, Nakopoulou, Papaharitou et al., 2005). High levels of anxiety may lead to sexual dysfunction simply because it is a negative emotion that may inhibit the development of pleasurable emotions associated with sexual pleasure. It may also prevent allocation of attention to stimuli likely to provide sexual stimulation and pleasure. Specific anxiety disorders may influence sexual performance in quite explicit ways. For example, panic disorder is associated with a fear of bodily sensations, so the increases in heart rate and perspiration caused by sexual activity may be interpreted negatively by someone with panic disorder (Sbrocco, Weisberg, Barlow & Carter, 1997). Similarly, fear of contamination associated with some forms of OCD may make the individual fearful of bodily contact and sexual secretions. Finally, social phobia is known to be associated with a self-critical attitude, which may well give rise to performance anxiety during sexual activity.

Remote vs. Immediate Causes One view of the causes of sexual dysfunction is that chronic sexual dysfunction is caused by a combination of immediate causes and remote causes (Kaplan, 1974). *Immediate causes* are factors that may directly influence sexual performance, such as performance anxiety, communication problems between partners, lack of sexual knowledge or clumsy technique. Many of these are factors that may influence the sexual performance of many people at one time or another, and are not necessarily chronic features of a person's lovemaking. However, these immediate performance problems may arise because of longer-term remote causes of sexual dysfunction, which refer to

more deep-rooted psychological and psychodynamic factors that incline someone to be anxious about their sexual performance. *Remote causes* include feelings of shame and guilt about sexual activity, general feelings of inadequacy or feelings of conflict brought about by long-term life stress (Kaplan, 1979). This view suggests that successful therapy must address not only the immediate performance problems in sexual dysfunction, but also those remote causes that may persist in maintaining factors such as performance anxiety.

Biological Causes There is considerable debate about whether sexual dysfunctions are the result of psychological or organic (biological) causes. In the period following the pioneering work of Masters and Johnson, researchers began to focus on the importance of psychological factors in the aetiology of sexual dysfunction. However, nowadays there is a belief that organic or biological factors may be an underlying factor in many cases, and that these may combine with psychological factors to generate a chronic disorder. Biological causes can be classified into three broad categories: (1) dysfunction caused by an underlying medical condition, (2) dysfunction caused by hormonal abnormalities and (3) changes in sexual responsiveness caused by ageing.

A whole range of medical conditions can give rise to sexual desire and performance problems. For example, male erectile and orgasmic disorders are associated with high blood pressure, diabetes, heart disease, cigarette smoking and alcoholism. Dysfunctions are also associated with a variety of medications such as antidepressant and anxiolytic drugs, and with treatments for hypertension and renal problems (Berman, Berman, Werbin, Flaherty et al., 1999; Altman, 2001). Medical conditions that reduce blood flow to the penis (such as blocked arteries or heart disease) will influence the ability to reach and maintain an erection (Stahl, 2001). Other medical conditions, such as diabetes, multiple sclerosis and renal problems, may cause central nervous system damage which affects sexual performance and desire (Frohman, 2002).

Female arousal and orgasm are also affected by medical conditions in much the same way that these conditions influence erection and ejaculation in men. Female arousal and orgasmic disorder has been linked to multiple sclerosis and diabetes, and both antidepressant (e.g. SSRIs such as Prozac) and anxiolytic medications can affect sexual desire in women as they do in men (Hensley & Nurnberg, 2002). Similarly, sexual pain disorders may have an organic or medical origin, ranging from painful allergic reactions to contraceptive creams, condoms or diaphragms (e.g. in the case of female dyspareunia) to gynaecological diseases and infections of the vagina, bladder or uterus (which may cause symptoms of vaginismus) (Brown & Ceniceros, 2001; McCormick, 1999). Nevertheless, although these forms of organic disorder may be an underlying cause of sexual desire and performance problems, it is quite likely that they will often generate associated psychological problems that give rise to a diagnosable sexual dysfunction. For example, sexual pain or disability caused by disease or medical conditions can give rise to anxiety about sexual performance or to relationship difficulties.

Testosterone   A steroid hormone stimulating development of male secondary sexual characteristics.

Oestrogen   Any of a group of steroid hormones which promote the development and maintenance of female characteristics of the body.

Prolactin   A hormone from the pituitary gland stimulating milk production after childbirth.

Sexual desire and subsequent arousal and orgasm are dependent on levels of the sex hormones **testosterone**, **oestrogen** and **prolactin**, and imbalances in these hormones can cause sexual desire problems in both men and women. In women, either high or low levels of oestrogen can cause sexual desire problems. Oestrogen levels can be affected if a woman is taking the birth pill, which will artificially raise her oestrogen levels, or is being given anti- oestrogen therapy for breast cancer, which will lower oestrogen levels (Amsterdam, Wheler, Hudis & Krychman, 2005). High prolactin levels have the effect of suppressing the hormones responsible for the normal functioning of the ovaries and testes, and in women can therefore lead to menstrual irregularity and/or fertility problems. In men, erectile dysfunction is associated with high levels of prolactin. Erectile problems can be eased with the use of drugs that lower prolactin levels (Spollen, Wooten, Cargile & Bartztokis, 2004).

Finally, one of the important variables that affect sexual functioning is age. The prevalence of sexual dysfunction in both males and females increases with age; for example, reports of erectile problems in men increase significantly after 50 years of age (Laumann, Gagnon, Michael & Michael, 1994). A study of Australian men over the age of 40 indicated that 34 per cent of those men surveyed reported one or more reproductive health disorder, including erectile dysfunction (21 per cent), lower urinary tract symptoms (16 per cent) and prostate disease (14 per cent) (Holden, McLachlan, Pitts, Cumming et al., 2005). Such findings may indicate that levels of male hormones generally decrease with age, or that reproductive health disorders may significantly affect sexual functioning.

Sexual desire and performance also decrease with increased age in women. The menopause has a significant influence here. Menopause is associated with decreases in oestrogen and testosterone levels that can exacerbate female sexual dysfunction (Graziottin & Leiblum, 2005). Studies suggest that around 1 in 4 women report a loss of sexual desire after the menopause, and this is associated with fluctuations in levels of oestrogen and testosterone. However, menopause is associated not only with physical changes but also with psychological changes. Loss of sexual desire in post-menopausal women has been shown to be associated with physical factors such as lower hormonal levels and vaginal dryness and psychological factors such as depression and living with children (Gracia, Sammel, Freeman, Liu et al., 2004).

Sociocultural Causes   The level of sexual dysfunction within a society can change depending on a range of cultural and economic factors within that society. For example, the stress caused by poverty, financial problems or unemployment have all been linked to erectile dysfunctions in men (Morokoff & Gilliland, 1993), and these may be factors that are closely linked to the wealth of a society and the effectiveness of its social services. Many cultures also specify implicit rules about sexual behaviour, and in many cases these rules can cause conflict and sexual dysfunction. For example, the religious and cultural views of many societies require that women should repress or deny their sexuality, so any expression of sexual desire or indulgence in sexual activity is likely to cause personal conflict and feelings of shame and guilt. This view is supported by the fact that many women who have received a strict religious upbringing are more likely to suffer from arousal and orgasmic dysfunction, and may have been punished for any sexual activity during childhood and adolescence (Masters & Johnson, 1970).

SUMMARY

We can see from this section that theories of sexual dysfunction are quite wide-ranging and encompass both psychological and biological explanations. There is no doubt that many cases of sexual dysfunction have an organic or biological basis, including dysfunctions caused by medical conditions, hormone imbalances and changes in biology with age. However, since the pioneering work of Masters and Johnson, psychological factors have also been identified in the aetiology of sexual dysfunction, including performance anxiety, underlying interpersonal problems, existing psychopathology such as depression and anxiety, and a variety of life experiences such as childhood abuse, psychosexual trauma and exposure to religious and social taboos.

SELF-TEST QUESTIONS

- Can you list some of the risk factors that have been associated with sexual dysfunctions?
- How have repressed emotions and desires been used by psychoanalytic theorists to explain sexual dysfunctions?
- What are the two factors in Masters & Johnson's theory of sexual dysfunction?
- How is performance anxiety important in explaining some forms of sexual dysfunction?
- In what ways might interpersonal difficulties be associated with sexual dysfunctions?

- Is there evidence to suggest that negative emotions such as depression and anxiety are outcomes or causes of sexual dysfunctions?
- What is the difference between remote and immediate causes of sexual dysfunctions? Can you give some examples of both?
- Can you name the three broad categories into which the biological causes of sexual dysfunctions can be classified?
- What kinds of medical conditions are associated with sexual dysfunction in men and women?
- In what ways does age affect sexual functioning?

10.2.5 The Treatment of Sexual Dysfunctions

Over the past 60–70 years the treatment of sexual dysfunctions has developed through a number of distinct stages. Prior to the 1950s, psychodynamic therapy was probably the only structured form of treatment available to those courageous enough in the existing social climate to admit sexual problems. With its emphasis on underlying conflicts and tensions tied to repressed sexual desires, psychoanalytic theory seemed ideally suited to treat sexual dysfunctions. However, the liberating social climate of the 1960s and 1970s allowed freer discussion of sexual problems. With this came the pioneering early work of Masters and Johnson, published in their 1970 book, *Human Sexual Inadequacy*. This led to the development of what are now

> **Direct treatments** Behaviourally based treatments for specific symptoms of sexual dysfunctions.

known as ***direct treatments*** for sexual dysfunction, which are often behaviourally based treatments for the specific symptoms of the disorder. So, rather than considering erectile dysfunction to be a manifestation of underlying psychological problems, therapists would provide clients with specific training on how to achieve and maintain an erection (e.g. the 'tease' technique; see below). Most modern-day treatment programmes now include some components designed to directly address the main symptom of the disorder (such as lack of desire, erectile problems or premature ejaculation) as well as components designed to deal with accompanying psychological problems (such as performance anxiety, related depression or relationship problems).

As well as these developments in psychological treatment, there have been significant advances in biological treatments for sexual dysfunctions. Treatments available today include drug and hormone treatments for problems of desire, arousal and orgasm, and mechanical devices for aiding penile erection in men. In the following sections we cover some of these treatments in more detail, beginning with Treatment in Practice Box 10.1, which contains an overview of the general structure of sex therapy. Subsequent sections cover a range of psychological and behavioural therapies in more detail, ending with a description and evaluation of biologically based treatments.

10.2.5.1 Psychological and Behavioural Treatments

Direct Treatment of Symptoms Direct treatments are techniques targeting the specific sexual performance deficit. There are two specific techniques used to help clients with premature ejaculation: the ***stop-start technique*** and the ***squeeze technique***. In the former, the client's partner stimulates the penis until close to ejaculation, at which point the partner is signalled to stop by the client (Semans, 1956). This process continues once the desire to ejaculate subsides. This technique acts to increase the

> **Stop-start technique** A technique used to help clients with premature ejaculation where the client's partner stimulates the penis until close to ejaculation, at which point the partner is signalled to stop by the client.

> **Squeeze technique** A technique used to help clients with premature ejaculation where the client's partner firmly squeezes below the head of the penis just prior to ejaculation.

amount of stimulation required to achieve ejaculation. The squeeze technique is very similar, involving the client's partner firmly squeezing below the head of the penis just prior to ejaculation. This has the effect of reducing the erection and can be repeated several times in order to help the client control ejaculation (St Lawrence & Madakasira, 1992). The 'squeeze' technique has been shown to significantly increase ejaculation latency, and is comparable to the therapeutic effects of a number of drugs used to treat premature ejaculation (Abdel-Hamid, El Naggar & El Gilany, 2001).

A direct treatment method designed to deal with symptoms of erectile dysfunction or male and female orgasmic disorder is the ***tease technique***, which involves the client's partner caressing the client's genitals but stopping when the client becomes aroused

> **Tease technique** A direct treatment method designed to deal with symptoms of erectile dysfunction or male and female orgasmic disorder. It involves the partner caressing the client's genitals, but stopping when the client becomes aroused (e.g. achieves an erection) or approaches orgasm.

(e.g. achieves an erection) or approaches orgasm. This enables couples to experience sexual pleasure without the need to achieve orgasm, and as a result may reduce any performance anxiety that may have been contributing to erectile problems or arousal and orgasmic problems (LoPiccolo, 1997). For individuals with arousal or orgasmic problems, ***directed masturbation training*** is often helpful (Heiman, 2002). With the use of educational material, videos, diagrams and – in some cases – erotic materials,

> **Directed masturbation training** A treatment for individuals with arousal or orgasmic problems using educational material, videos, diagrams and – in some cases – erotic materials.

women can be taught step-by-step to achieve orgasm, even in cases where she has never previously experienced one. This method has been shown to be highly effective, and over 90 per cent of women treated with this method learn how to achieve orgasm during masturbation (Heiman & LoPiccolo, 1988).

Couples Therapy As we have mentioned several times in this chapter, sexual dysfunction may be closely associated with

CLINICAL PERSPECTIVE: TREATMENT IN PRACTICE BOX 10.1

What is sex therapy?

Current forms of sex therapy involve a number of different components designed to identify specific sexual problems, address these specific problems through direct treatment, deal with associated psychological and relationship issues, and provide clients with sexual knowledge and sexual skills. Sex therapy usually treats the couple rather than the individual who manifests the dysfunction, and couples are urged to share the responsibility for the sexual problem. Below are some of these separate components that form the important core stages of sex therapy.

Assessment

Through interview, the therapist collects information about specific sexual problems (e.g. lack of desire in one partner, erectile problems in a male partner) and discusses current life issues and past life events that may be contributing to the problem. This stage is usually accompanied by a medical examination to determine whether there are organic factors contributing to the problem.

Dealing with organic dysfunction

If there are clearly organic or medical factors contributing to the dysfunction (such as low hormone levels, medical conditions such as diabetes or high blood pressure, or other medications such as antidepressants or anxiolytics), then these may be addressed early in the programme (e.g. by reducing levels of antidepressant drugs).

Sexual skills training

Many types of sexual problem arise through lack of knowledge about the physiology of sex and a lack of basic technique during lovemaking. The therapist can address these factors by providing clients with educational materials such as booklets and videos.

Changing dysfunctional beliefs

Sex is associated with a whole range of myths and false beliefs (e.g. 'too much masturbation is bad for you', 'nice women aren't aroused by erotic books or films') (Bach, Wincze & Barlow, 2001). If clients hold these false beliefs, this may prevent them from experiencing full sexual arousal and satisfaction. Using a range of methods, such as those used in CBT (see Chapter 4, section 4.1.1.3), the therapist attempts to identify and challenge any dysfunctional beliefs and replace them with more functional ones.

Direct intervention and behavioural training

Depending on the specific sexual dysfunction that has been referred for treatment, the therapist advises clients on the use of a range of behavioural techniques designed to help their specific problem. These techniques, which are discussed more fully in section 10.2.5.1, include the tease technique for erectile dysfunction, the stop-start technique and squeeze technique for premature ejaculation (Semans, 1956; LoPiccolo, 1997), and directed masturbation training for arousal and orgasmic disorders (Heiman, 2002). The therapist may also teach clients a technique known as *non-demand pleasuring*, which involves a couple exploring and caressing each other's body to discover sexual pleasure rather than achieving orgasm. This allows couples to learn how to give and receive sexual pleasure without the pressure of needing to achieve orgasm.

Dealing with relationship and lifestyle issues

Sexual dysfunction is often related to conflict within the relationship and to stressful lifestyles (e.g. one partner may be dominating and controlling, or the demands of factors such as family and work may be causing unnecessary stress). The therapist usually attempts to identify any factors that may be contributing to the disorder and advises clients on how to improve them.

---

relationship problems. If sexual dysfunctions are a manifestation of broader problems within a relationship, then the latter need to be effectively addressed through *couples therapy*. For example, lack of sexual desire in one partner may be a way for him or her to exert some control within the relationship, especially if there are conflicts over power and control. In such cases underlying sexual dysfunction may entail an implicit reward for both partners, one partner gaining reward through the ability to control sex, and the other gaining reward by viewing his or her partner's lack of desire as a weakness which reinforces the view of himself or herself as controlling. Therapists will explore these issues with couples and try to iden-

Couples therapy A treatment intervention for sexual dysfunction that involves both partners in the relationship.

tify whether there are any implicit payoffs within the relationship for maintaining the sexual dysfunction.

Sexual Skills and Communication Training

For many couples sexual dysfunction is simply another manifestation of the couple's inability to communicate effectively with each other. They may be unable to tell each other what stimulates and pleasures them, or they may be nervous, shy or unknowledgeable about sexual matters. With the use of educational materials and videos, therapists can help

Sexual skills and communication training A treatment method in which a therapist can help clients to acquire a more knowledgeable perspective on sexual activity, communicate to partners effectively about sex, and reduce any anxiety about indulging in sexual activity.

clients to acquire a more knowledgeable perspective on sexual activity, begin to communicate with each other effectively about sex, and reduce any anxiety about indulging in sexual activity (McMullen & Rosen, 1979).

Self-Instructional Training This is a technique that has been used across a range of psychopathologies in order to establish adaptive behaviour patterns. In the context of sexual dysfunctions, *self-instructional training* is used to teach clients to use positive self-instructions at various points during sexual activity in order to guide their behaviour and to reduce anxiety. In particular, negative statements (such as 'I am never going to maintain an erection') can be replaced with positive statements (such as 'I can allow myself to enjoy sex, even if my performance is not perfect'), and this helps to distract clients from anxiety-provoking ideation.

> **Self-instructional training** A technique that has been used across a range of psychopathologies in order to establish adaptive behaviour patterns where the client is taught to provide appropriate self-instructions for behaviour.

Dealing with Remote Causes Many cases of sexual dysfunction have their origins in earlier life experiences. These experiences may simply be embarrassing ones, where individuals have been severely embarrassed by their lack of sexual knowledge or technique during an early sexual encounter, or they may be more severe and traumatic experiences, such as sexual abuse or assault (see section 10.2.4.2). Appropriate counselling, where clients are encouraged to recall these experiences and talk about them, can help to alleviate the associated sexual problems. This approach acts in a similar way to exposure and imaginal flooding therapies for PTSD (see Chapter 5, section 5.6.2.2) by extinguishing the fear that has become associated with these memories.

10.2.5.2 Biological Treatments

Many cases of sexual dysfunction may have biological or organic causes such as medical conditions, hormone imbalances or changes in biology with age, or are a reaction to other medications being taken by the client. This indicates that a biological or medical treatment may be appropriate for the disorder. Biological treatments fall into three broad categories: (1) drug treatments, including medications that directly influence the organic nature of the disorder, (2) hormone treatments designed to correct any hormonal imbalances caused by age or illness, and (3) mechanical devices designed to aid mechanical functioning during sex (such as achieving erection).

Drug Treatments Perhaps the most well-known drug treatment for sexual dysfunction is *Viagra (sildenafil citrate)*, which is used primarily to treat erectile dysfunction in men. Viagra acts directly on the tissue of the penis itself, causing relaxation of the smooth muscle of the penis which increases blood flow and encourages erection. Studies suggest that 75 per cent of men taking Viagra can

> **Viagra (sildenafil citrate)** A drug treatment for sexual dysfunction which is used primarily to treat erectile dysfunction in men.

achieve erection within 60 minutes of administration (Goldstein, Lue, Padma-Nathan, Rosen et al., 1998). In clinical trials, Viagra results in significantly more erections and successful intercourse attempts than a placebo control (Moore, Edwards & McQuay, 2002) (see Figure 10.2). Viagra has also proved to be an effective treatment for male erectile disorder, with over 95 per cent of clients treated with Viagra over a period of 1–3 years expressing satisfaction with their erections and their ability to effectively engage in sex (Carson, Burnett, Levine & Nehra, 2002). In addition, Viagra has been considered to be an effective treatment for male erectile disorder in cases where this is due to a medical condition (such as diabetes or cardiovascular disorder) or as a result of ageing (Salonia, Rigatti & Montorsi, 2003). However, Viagra may not be the treatment of choice for many clients because it also has a number of side effects, such as headaches, dizziness and facial flushing, and may interact badly with some medications for cardiovascular disease (Bach, Wincze & Barlow, 2001).

Other drugs that have proved useful in treating erectile dysfunctions include *yohimbine*, which facilitates norepinephrine excretion in the brain. This appears to have the effect of correcting any brain neurotransmitter problems that are causing the erectile dysfunction (Mann, Klingler, Noe, Roschke et al., 1996). Interestingly, both Viagra and yohimbine have been shown to be effective in treating female sexual desire problems (Hernandez-Serrano, 2001).

> **Yohimbine** A drug treatment for sexual dysfunction which is used primarily to treat erectile dysfunction in men by facilitating norepinephrine excretion in the brain.

Finally, antidepressant SSRIs such as Prozac are also an effective treatment for premature ejaculation. Delayed orgasm is a known side effect of SSRIs in depressed individuals who are taking these medications (Assalian & Margolese, 1996).

Hormone Treatments At least some sexual dysfunctions may result from imbalances in hormone levels. Disorders can result from either high or low levels of oestrogen in women, and from low levels of testosterone or high levels of prolactin in men. These hormonal imbalances can be caused by medical conditions or ageing. Hormone replacement therapy can be used to treat disorders of sexual desire, especially in older women or women who have undergone hysterectomy. The sexual pain disorder dyspareunia can also be alleviated with oestrogen treatment, which can help to improve vaginal lubrication in post-menopausal women (Walling, Andersen & Johnson, 1990).

Mechanical Devices Because an erect penis is such an important contributor to successful sexual penetration, a number of mechanical devices have been developed that can help men with an erectile dysfunction to achieve erection.

The first of these is known as a *penile prosthesis*, an example of which is shown in Figure 10.3. Use of these devices is normally reserved for non-reversible, organic-based erectile problems. The prosthesis consists of a fluid pump located in the scrotum and a semi-rigid rod that is surgically inserted in the penis. A discrete squeeze

> **Penile prosthesis** A mechanical device normally reserved for non-reversible organic-based erectile problems.

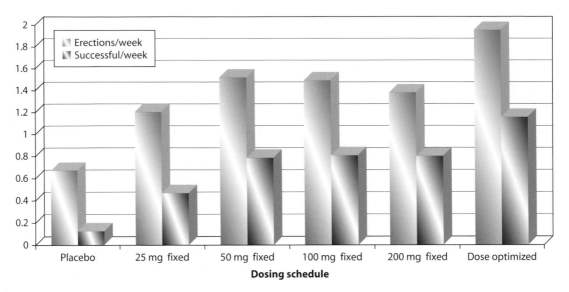

Figure 10.2
Mean number of erections per week (blue) and erections resulting in successful intercourse (red) with placebo and different doses of Viagra (sildenafil citrate).

Source: Moore, Edwards & McQuay (2002).

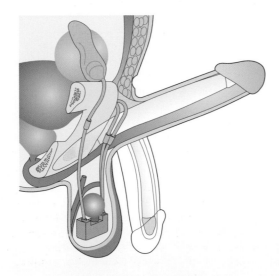

Figure 10.3
The penile prosthesis consists of a fluid pump located in the scrotum and a semi-rigid rod surgically inserted in the penis. Squeezing the pump releases fluid into the rod, making the penis erect.

of the pump releases fluid into the rod, which causes the penis to become erect. Studies suggest that the penile prosthesis is a safe and effective means of dealing with erectile dysfunction caused by organic or medical conditions. Over a period of 7 years since the implant, it was found that the penile prosthesis was still successfully dealing with erectile dysfunction in 82 per cent of patients (Zermann, Kutzenburger, Sauerwein, Schubert et al., 2006).

An alternative to the penile prosthesis is the ***vacuum erection device (VED)***, a hollow cylinder that is placed over the penis. The client draws air out of the cylinder using a hand pump, which has the effect of drawing blood into the penis and causing an erection. As cumbersome as this may seem, many clients prefer the VED to other more conventional treatments for erectile dysfunction such as Viagra. Of those given a choice between equally effective VED or Viagra treatments, 33 per cent preferred the VED, largely because they disliked the adverse side effects of Viagra (Chen, Mabjeesh & Greenstein, 2001).

Vacuum erection device (VED)
A mechanical device normally reserved for non-reversible organic-based erectile problems.

10.2.5.3 Summary of Treatments of Sexual Dysfunction

This section has discussed the range of treatments available for sexual dysfunctions. Multifaceted psychological and behaviourally based treatments are now used to deal with the specific symptoms of sexual disorders as well as any underlying psychological, behavioural and relationship issues. These are supplemented by a variety of drug and biologically based treatments that help to address any physiological, organic or hormonal deficits.

CASE HISTORY 10.1

Erectile dysfunction

R.K., 47, a senior corporate executive, had been happily married for 20 years and had three children, but complained of declining erections. Over the preceding 6 months his erections had become so weak that he could not penetrate. He stopped trying 3 months ago.

He thought that this was due to his highly stressful lifestyle and pressures at the workplace. He took a vacation with his wife, hoping that this would improve matters, but it only made them worse. His wife, at first very cooperative, eventually began to feel rejected and there was a palpable friction in their marriage.

When first seen at the clinic, R.K. was defensive. 'How can this happen to someone like me? I could do it all night, several times a night, night after night. My family doctor says that this kind of thing is quite common these days and it's probably the stress.'

It turned out that R.K. was a diabetic of 8 years' standing. He also had high blood pressure, for which he was on beta blockers. He was obese (209 lbs, 175 cm) and smoked 40 cigarettes a day. He partied 7 days a week and drank quite heavily. He had never exercised in his life. Sadly, his family doctor had never connected any of these to his sexual problem.

Tests revealed that his overall rigidity levels were well below normal and that he had problems with both his arteries and veins. He was eventually cured with an inflatable penile prosthesis.

Source: adapted from www.testosterones.com/

Clinical Commentary

R.K. was quick to link his erectile problems with a stressful lifestyle, and his defensive reaction is typical of a man who values his sexual performance as an indicator of his worth. However, once R.K.'s medical history was investigated, it became clear that there were a variety of organic and lifestyle factors that were contributing to his erectile dysfunction, including a history of diabetes, high blood pressure, medications that can interfere with sexual arousal, and heavy smoking and drinking. Because many of the important causes were organic (e.g. diabetes and cardiovascular problems), the best long-term solution in this case was to implant a mechanical device such as a penile prosthesis to aid erection.

SUMMARY

Sexual dysfunction has an unusual history in the context of psychopathology. In the first half of the twentieth century, sexual problems were rarely admitted and discussed, let alone treated. With the liberating social climate of the 1960s and 1970s this attitude changed, and the pioneering research work of a few dedicated clinicians (such as Masters and Johnson) provided a database of evidence on these kinds of disorders, as well as the first integrated sex therapies for sexual dysfunctions. The causes of sexual dysfunctions range across biological and organic, psychological factors such as performance anxiety and negative cognitions about sex to interpersonal problems. An equally broad range of treatments has been developed to address this array of possible causes. Given all this, it is important to remember that not everyone with less than adequate sexual performance is suffering a sexual dysfunction. The DSM-IV-TR criteria clearly state that any performance deficits must be accompanied by distress and interpersonal difficulties, and it is these latter two factors that define sexual dysfunction disorders (see again Table 10.4).

SELF-TEST QUESTIONS

- What are direct treatments for sexual dysfunctions?
- Can you name and describe at least three direct treatments for sexual dysfunctions?
- Why is couples therapy an important form of treatment for sexual dysfunction?

- What are the main drug treatments for sexual dysfunctions, and what is the evidence that they are successful?
- What are the main mechanical devices used to treat male sexual dysfunctions?

SECTION SUMMARY

10.2 Sexual Dysfunctions

- The four stages of the sexual response cycle are **desire**, **arousal**, **orgasm** and **resolution**, and sexual dysfunctions can be diagnosed in any of these individual stages.

10.2.1 Diagnosis of Sexual Dysfunction

- **Sexual dysfunction** is characterized as 'a disturbance in the processes that characterize the sexual response cycle or by pain associated with intercourse'.

10.2.2 Specific Sexual Dysfunction Disorders

- **Hypoactive sexual desire disorder** is characterized by a low level of sexual desire.

- **Sexual aversion disorder** is an active avoidance of genital sexual contact with a sexual partner.

- **Female sexual arousal disorder** is an inability to attain an adequate lubrication–swelling response of sexual excitement and to maintain this state until completion of sexual activity.

- **Male erectile disorder** is the inability to maintain an adequate erection during sexual activity. Around 10 per cent of males report erection problems, but this increases to 20 per cent in the over-50s.

- **Female orgasmic disorder** is characterized by a delay or absence of orgasm during sexual activity, and around 10 per cent of adult women may never have experienced an orgasm.

- **Male orgasmic disorder** is a delay in or absence of orgasm following sexual activity. Around 8 per cent of men report symptoms typical of this disorder.

- **Premature ejaculation** is the onset of orgasm with minimal sexual stimulation. Treatment for this disorder is typically sought by men under the age of 30 years.

- **Dyspareunia** is genital pain that can occur during, before or after sexual intercourse. Some clinicians believe this is a pain disorder rather than a sexual dysfunction.

- **Vaginismus** is the involuntary contraction of the muscles surrounding the vagina when vaginal penetration is attempted. Of all women that seek treatment for sexual dysfunctions, around 15–17 per cent are suffering from vaginismus.

10.2.3 Prevalence of Sexual Dysfunctions

- Sexual dysfunctions are amongst some of the more prevalent psychopathologies in the general population (see Table 10.5).

10.2.4 The Aetiology of Sexual Dysfunctions

- Sexual dysfunction is more prevalent in women than in men (43 per cent and 31 per cent respectively), and is more likely amongst those experiencing poor physical and emotional health.

- **Psychoanalytic theory** attempts to account for sexual dysfunctions in terms of repressed sexual desires or hostility to the opposite sex.

- **Masters & Johnson** developed a **two-factor model** of sexual dysfunction where (1) early sexual experiences give rise to anxiety during sex, and (2) this anxiety leads the individual to adopt a **spectator role** during sexual activity which directs attention away from stimuli providing sexual arousal.

- **Interpersonal difficulties** may be both a cause and an outcome of sexual dysfunctions.

- **Anxiety** and **depression** are closely associated with sexual dysfunctions, and these negative emotions may interfere with sexual performance.

- The causes of sexual dysfunctions can sometimes be defined in terms of **immediate causes** (e.g. lack of sexual knowledge) and **remote causes** (e.g. feelings of shame and guilt that are a result of a specific upbringing).

- **Biological causes** of sexual dysfunctions can be classified as (1) dysfunctions caused by an underlying medical disorder, (2) dysfunctions caused by hormonal abnormalities and (3) changes in sexual responsiveness with age.

10.2.5 The Treatment of Sexual Dysfunctions

- **Direct treatments** attempt to deal with the specific symptoms of the disorder (e.g. the squeeze technique for premature ejaculation).

- The **stop-start technique**, **squeeze technique** and **tease technique** are all specific behavioural treatments designed to treat premature ejaculation and orgasmic disorders.

- If sexual dysfunctions are a manifestation of broader problems, then **couples therapy** can be adopted.

- **Biological treatments** can be categorized into (1) drug treatments, including medications that directly influence the organic nature of the disorder, (2) hormone treatment designed to correct hormone imbalances caused by age or sickness and (3) mechanical devices, designed to aid mechanical functioning during sex.

- 75 per cent of men who take **Viagra** can achieve erection within 60 minutes of administration. Over 95 per cent of clients treated with Viagra over a 1- to 3-year period express satisfaction with their ability to effectively engage in sex.

- Mechanical devices to aid penile erection and penetration include the **penile prosthesis** and the **vacuum erection device (VED)**.

10.3 PARAPHILIAS

Sexual dysfunctions are one side of the sexual disorders coin, where individuals complain of deficiencies or inadequacies in their sexual desire and performance. On the other side of the coin are those psychopathologies that are associated with high frequencies of sexual activity or unusual sexual activities that are often directed at inappropriate targets. Sexual experience is normally highly valued in Western cultures, but there is now a good deal of evidence that high rates of sexual behaviour can be problematic, interfere with personal happiness and social adjustment, and be channelled into unusual sexual activities (Kafka, 1997, 2003). When high rates of sexual behaviour are channelled into unusual or very specific sexual activities, these are known collectively as *paraphilias*.

Paraphilias   Problematic, high-frequency sexual behaviours or unusual sexual urges and activities that are often directed at inappropriate targets.

DSM-IV-TR defines paraphilias as recurrent, intense sexually arousing fantasies, sexual urges or behaviours generally involving (1) non-human objects (e.g. fetishes), (2) the suffering or humiliation of oneself or one's partner (e.g. sexual masochism or sexual sadism) or (3) children or other non-consenting persons (e.g. paedophilia). A list of the paraphilias included in DSM-IV-TR is provided in Table 10.6.

We have listed these paraphilias in three groups. The first group includes fetishism and transvestic fetishism, where individuals experience sexual desire towards inanimate objects or from cross-dressing. However, to be diagnosed with either of these disorders, these tendencies must cause the individual significant distress or social and/or occupational impairment. The second group consists of sexual sadism and sexual masochism, where individuals experience sexual arousal from the desire either to inflict physical suffering on others (sadism) or to be humiliated or made to physically suffer (masochism). Most often sadomasochistic acts are performed with a consenting partner, but even in such circumstances the individual may be bothered or distressed by these tendencies and acts, and personal distress is an important contributor to diagnosis of these disorders.

The final group consists of exhibitionism, voyeurism, frotteurism and paedophilia. These disorders have been grouped together because they usually involve sexual fantasies, urges and activities directed at non-consenting persons. The exhibitionist exposes himself to unsuspecting victims; the voyeur takes sexual pleasure from watching unsuspecting others, either naked or in the process of undressing; the frotteurist is sexually aroused by rubbing himself against a non-consenting person; and the paedophile has sexual urges towards and indulges in sexual acts with prepubescent children, who – by their very age – are unable to legally consent to these activities. This last group of paraphilias is defined by the fact that the individual does *not* have to experience distress or social or occupational impairment to be diagnosed with the disorder, but merely has to have acted on these urges with non-consenting persons (Hilliard & Spitzer, 2002).

From these categorizations it is clear that some paraphilias are *victimless* (e.g. fetishism and transvestic fetishism), while others will be defined in law as *sexual offences* (e.g. exhibitionism, voyeurism, frotteurism, paedophilia and those acts of sexual sadism where harm is inflicted on others without consent). Some require these activities to cause personal distress to be diagnosed, while others do not. This leads to the question of where the line is drawn between acceptable sexual activity and psychopathology. Clearly, many of

Table 10.6 *Paraphilias*

FETISHISM	Sexual urges that are not directed at another person	Recurrent sexual experiences involving inanimate objects
TRANSVESTIC FETISHISM		A heterosexual male experiences recurrent sexual arousal from cross-dressing
SEXUAL MASOCHISM	Sexual arousal from inflicting or experiencing suffering	Sexual arousal from being humiliated or otherwise forced to suffer
SEXUAL SADISM		Sexual arousal from the psychological or physical suffering of others
EXHIBITIONISM	Sexual urges directed at non-consenting other persons (in many societies these activities represent sexual offences)	Sexual fantasies about exposing the genitals to an unsuspecting stranger
VOYEURISM		Recurrent sexual arousal fantasies involving acts of observing an unsuspecting person who is naked
FROTTEURISM		Recurrent sexual urges to touch and rub against non-consenting people
PAEDOPHILIA		Sexual attraction towards prepubescent children normally of 13 years or younger

the urges and fantasies defined in the diagnostic criteria for paraphilias are experienced by many people, and there is a growing industry willing to cater for these urges in films, magazines and internet sites. However, (1) most people are unwilling to act on their fantasies and are quite happy to restrict their sexual interest in paraphilic activities to viewing erotic or pornographic material; and (2) it is only when a person's sexual urges become linked to just one specific type of stimulus or act that society begins to deem the behaviour as 'abnormal'. We must bear these issues in mind when discussing the individual paraphilias.

ACTIVITY BOX 10.3

Some paraphilias become sexual offences when individuals act on their sexual urges with non-consenting people. This is the case for exhibitionism, voyeurism, frotteurism, paedophilia and, under circumstances where a partner is not consenting, sexual sadism. In 2006, the UK government sought consultation with a view to making it a criminal offence to download sexually violent pornography. This prompted a letter to the *Psychologist* in May 2006, an extract of which is reproduced below:

> The government is considering making it a crime to download sexually violent pornography. This will extend the legislation on child pornography to adult material that is defined as the realistic depicting or acting of a scene that would, if acted out, cause grievous bodily harm. This would include a variety of bondage and masochistic scenes acted out by consenting enthusiasts . . . Simply viewing the material will now constitute a serious criminal offence. And anyone looking at bondage scenes where somebody is wearing a mask and might suffocate (if this scene were acted out 'in reality') must be prepared to defend themselves in court.
>
> The 'evidence' focuses on the effects of pornography on either children or disturbed offenders. We do not dispute that psychopaths may be kick-started into action by all manner of things, including pornography. But there is no evidence at all that those not already predisposed to such action will be similarly affected. The reason the government is concerned about sexually violent pornography is that atrocious crimes may be committed in the making of the material. But of course, this is already a crime, and rightly so. The government's aim here is to punish consumers, not perpetrators.

You might like to consider the issues raised by this debate. In particular:

- Are there grounds for considering downloading sexually violent pornography either a sexual offence or a psychopathology?
- If a behaviour is a sexual offence in law, should it also be considered a psychopathology?
- Could being a 'consumer' of internet pornography contribute to paraphilic behaviour?

The following section describes the diagnostic criteria and main characteristics of each of the paraphilias. We then discuss some of the theories of the aetiology of paraphilias before describing and evaluating forms of treatment.

10.3.1 The Diagnosis and Description of Paraphilias

10.3.1.1 Fetishism

A diagnosis of *fetishism* is given when a person experiences recurrent, intense sexually arousing fantasies and urges involving inanimate objects, and this causes the individual personal distress or affects social and occupational functioning (see Table 10.7). Often fetishes are restricted to articles associated with sex, such as women's clothing or undergarments (bras, stockings, shoes, boots, etc.). Individuals with fetishism may experience strong desires to obtain or touch these items (e.g. by stealing them from washing lines), may ask a sexual partner to wear them during sex, or may masturbate while holding, rubbing or smelling these articles. A fetish will usually have developed by adolescence, and may have done so as a result of specific experiences during childhood or early adolescence. Some individuals exhibit a phenomenon known as *partialism*, which is fascination with an individual object to the point where normal sexual activity no longer occurs. Note that fetishism is not diagnosed if the object concerned is for the purpose of tactile genital stimulation. Focus Point 10.2 provides some case reports of penile injuries published in the *British Medical Journal*, illustrating the lengths some individuals will go to gain sexual excitement. While the injuries incurred were obviously unpleasant for the victims, readers may be amused by the reasons given for the injuries!

> **Fetishism** A paraphilia which involves sexually arousing fantasies and urges directed at inanimate objects.

> **Partialism** A phenomenon in which there is a fascination with an individual object to the point where normal sexual activity no longer occurs.

Table 10.7 *DSM-IV-TR diagnostic criteria for fetishism*

A	Over a period of at least 6 months, recurrent, intense sexually arousing fantasies, sexual urges or behaviours involving the use of non-living objects (e.g. female undergarments).
B	The fantasies, sexual urges or behaviours cause clinically significant distress or impairment in social, occupational or other important areas of functioning.
C	The fetish objects are not limited to articles of female clothing used in cross-dressing (as in transvestic fetishism) or devices designed for the purpose of tactile genital stimulation (e.g. a vibrator).

FOCUS POINT 10.2

Penile injuries resulting from a vacuum cleaner

The following four cases of penile injury were incurred while using a vacuum cleaner in search of sexual excitement. At least two of these injuries were caused by a Hoover Dustette, which has fan blades only 15 cm from the inlet.

Case 1. A 60-year-old man said that he was changing the plug of his Hoover Dustette vacuum cleaner in the nude when his wife was out shopping. It 'turned itself on' and caught his penis, causing tears around the external meatus and deeply lacerating the side of the glans.

Case 2. A 65-year-old railway signalman was in his signal box when he bent down to pick up his tools and 'caught his penis in a Hoover Dustette which happened to be switched on'. He suffered extensive lacerations to the glans, which were repaired with cat gut with a good result.

Case 3. A 49-year-old man was vacuuming his friend's staircase in a loose-fitting dressing gown when, intending to switch the machine off, he leaned across to reach the plug: 'At that moment his dressing gown became undone and his penis was sucked into the vacuum cleaner.' He suffered multiple lacerations to the foreskin as well as lacerations to the distal part of the shaft of the penis.

Case 4. This patient was aged 68, and no history is available except that the injury was caused by a vacuum cleaner. The injury extended through the corpora cavernosa and the corpus spongiosum and caused complete division of the urethra proximal to the corona.

Source: Citron & Wade (1980)

10.3.1.2 Transvestic Fetishism

Transvestic fetishism A paraphilia in which a heterosexual male experiences sexual arousal from cross-dressing in women's clothing.

A diagnosis of *transvestic fetishism* is given when a heterosexual male experiences recurrent, intense sexual arousal from cross-dressing in women's attire, and this causes significant distress or impairment in social or occupational functioning (see Table 10.8). A Swedish study has indicated that 2.8 per cent of men and 0.4 per cent of women report at least one episode of transvestic fetishism during

their life. Risk factors for this disorder include same-sex sexual experiences, being easily sexually aroused, pornography use and relatively high masturbation frequency (Langstrom & Zucker, 2005). In this particular disorder, sexual excitement is achieved primarily because female clothes are a symbol of the individual's femininity rather than because the garments trigger sexual arousal *per se* (as would be the case with a simple fetish). In addition, this diagnosis should not be given if the individual is in the throes of a gender identity disorder (see section 10.4 below). The individual with transvestic fetishism will often keep a collection of women's clothes. Sexual arousal is normally caused by the man having thoughts or images of himself as a female.

Chris's Story at the beginning of this chapter is a typical example of transvestic fetishism. Like Chris, most individuals diagnosed with transvestic fetishism are relatively happily married men, but they are worried about what others (including their wives) might think of their behaviour. As a result, over half of those who admit cross-dressing usually seek counselling at some stage because of its effects on their intimate relationships (Doctor & Prince, 1997). Most men with transvestic fetishism have been cross-dressing for many years, usually since childhood or early adolescence (Doctor & Fleming, 2001), and many women are happy to tolerate their husbands' cross-dressing or even incorporate it into their own sexual activities.

Table 10.8 *DSM-IV-TR diagnostic criteria for transvestic fetishism*

A	Over a period of at least 6 months, in a heterosexual male, recurrent, intense sexually arousing fantasies, sexual urges or behaviours involving cross-dressing.
B	The fantasies, sexual urges or behaviours cause clinically significant distress or impairment in social, occupational or other important areas of functioning.

10.3.1.3 Sexual Masochism and Sexual Sadism

Sexual masochism   A paraphilia in which an individual gains sexual arousal and satisfaction from being humiliated.

Sexual sadism   A paraphilia in which a person gains sexual arousal and satisfaction from the psychological or physical suffering of others.

A diagnosis of *sexual masochism* is given if the individual gains sexual arousal and satisfaction from being humiliated, beaten, bound or otherwise made to suffer, and these urges cause significant distress or social and occupational impairment. In contrast, *sexual sadism* is when the person gains sexual arousal and satisfaction from the psychological or physical suffering of others. A diagnosis of sexual sadism is given if these symptoms cause distress or significant social or occupational impairment to the individual, or if the individual acts on these urges with a non-consenting person (see Tables 10.9 and 10.10).

Sadomasochistic acts are often performed between consenting mutual partners, one who gains satisfaction from sadistic acts and the other who enjoys being humiliated. Sadistic or masochistic activities include acts that emphasize the dominance and control of one person over the other. These may include restraint, blindfolding, spanking, whipping, pinching, beating, burning, rape, cutting, stabbing, strangulation, torture and mutilation. Acts of dominance (or submission) may include forcing the submissive partner to crawl on the floor, or keeping them restrained in a cage. Sexual masochists can often cause their own suffering. One prominent example is known as *hypoxyphilia*, which involves the individual using a noose or plastic bag to induce oxygen deprivation during masturbation. In contrast, when they are unable to obtain consenting partners, sexual sadists may resort to rape, mutilation and murder to satisfy their sexual desires (Dietz, Hazelwood & Warren, 1990). There is a high rate of comorbidity between sexual sadism and impulse disorders. For example, in individuals with a diagnosis of sexual sadism, 31 per cent were also diagnosed with borderline personality disorder, and 42 per cent with antisocial personality disorder (Berger, Berner, Bolterauer, Gutierrez et al., 1999). It is estimated that around 5–10 per cent of the population indulge in some kind of sadomasochistic activity at some time in their life (Baumeister & Butler, 1997). Most are heterosexual, reasonably affluent, well-educated, indulge in these activities with a consenting partner, and are not unduly distressed or disturbed by their sexual predilections (Moser & Levitt, 1987). If this is so, then most sadomasochistic activity does not involve either psychological distress or imposition of a sexual urge on non-consenting persons, and so would not meet the DSM-IV-TR criteria for a disorder. Because sadomasochism is enjoyed by many individuals who incorporate these activities into their normal sexual relationships, there is a growing market for such activities that is catered for by sex shops, underground newspapers and internet websites. Indeed, over the years, sadomasochism (known as S&M) has become a significantly accepted subculture within homosexual circles.

Hypoxyphilia   An act performed by sexual masochists which involves the individual using a noose or plastic bag to induce oxygen deprivation during masturbation.

Table 10.9   *DSM-IV-TR diagnostic criteria for sexual masochism*

A   Over a period of at least 6 months, recurrent, intense sexually arousing fantasies, sexual urges or behaviours involving the act (real, not simulated) of being humiliated, beaten, bound or otherwise made to suffer.

B   The fantasies, sexual urges or behaviours cause clinically significant distress or impairment in social, occupational or other important areas of functioning.

Table 10.10   *DSM-IV-TR diagnostic criteria for sexual sadism*

A   Over a period of at least 6 months, recurrent, intense sexually arousing fantasies, sexual urges or behaviours involving acts (real, not simulated) in which the psychological or physical suffering (including humiliation) of the victim is sexually exciting to the person.

B   The person has acted on these sexual urges with a non-consenting person, or the sexual urges or fantasies cause marked distress or interpersonal difficulty.

10.3.1.4 Exhibitionism

Exhibitionism involves sexual fantasies about exposing the penis to a stranger. These fantasies are usually strong and recurrent to the point where the individual feels a compulsion to expose himself, and this compulsion often makes the individual oblivious of the social and legal consequences of what he is doing (Stevenson & Jones, 1972). The onset of exhibitionism usually occurs before 18 years of age. It is often found in individuals who are immature in their relationships with the opposite sex, and many have problems with interpersonal relationships generally (Mohr, Turner & Jerry, 1964). The exhibitionist will experience strong sexual urges to expose himself to the point where he is unable to control this behaviour. This urge leads him to find a victim in a public place, often a park or a side street, where he exposes himself, usually to a single victim. The victim's response of shock, fear or revulsion often forms part of the gratification that reinforces this behaviour, and the exhibitionist may sometimes masturbate while exposing himself (especially if he finds the victim's reaction to his behaviour sexually arousing), or he may return home to masturbate while fantasizing about the encounter. Exhibitionists will usually expose themselves to women or children. While no physical harm is usually involved, the experience for the victim is often traumatic and may have lasting psychological consequences. (See Table 10.11.)

Exhibitionism   A paraphilia which involves sexual fantasies about exposing the penis to a stranger, usually either a woman or a child.

Table 10.11 *DSM-IV-TR diagnostic criteria for exhibitionism*

A   Over a period of at least 6 months, recurrent, intense sexually arousing fantasies, sexual urges or behaviours involving the exposure of one's genitals to an unsuspecting stranger.

B   The person has acted on these sexual urges, or the sexual urges or fantasies cause marked distress or interpersonal difficulty.

Table 10.12 *DSM-IV-TR diagnostic criteria for voyeurism*

A   Over a period of at least 6 months, recurrent, intense sexually arousing fantasies, sexual urges or behaviours involving the act of observing an unsuspecting person who is naked, in the process of disrobing or engaging in sexual activity.

B   The person has acted on these sexual urges, or the sexual urges or fantasies cause marked distress or interpersonal difficulty.

10.3.1.5 Voyeurism

Voyeurism   A paraphilia which involves experiencing intense sexually arousing fantasies or urges to watch an unsuspecting person who is naked, in the process of undressing or engaging in sexual activity.

A diagnosis of **voyeurism** is given when an individual experiences recurrent, intense sexually arousing fantasies or urges involving the act of observing an unsuspecting person who is naked, in the process of undressing or engaging in a sexual activity (see Table 10.12). Sexual arousal normally comes from the act of looking ('peeping'), and the individual may masturbate while in the act of observing others. However, the individual rarely seeks sexual activity with those being observed. Voyeurism usually begins in early adolescence, and may often constitute the individual's sole sexual activity in adulthood (Kaplan & Krueger, 1997). The risk of being discovered while indulging in voyeurism may also add to the excitement that this behaviour engenders. Voyeurism can be a perfectly acceptable sexual activity when practised between consenting individuals, but it is clearly problematic when the voyeur begins seeking non-consenting victims and violates their privacy.

10.3.1.6 Frotteurism

Frotteurism   A paraphilia which involves recurrent sexual urges to touch and rub up against other non-consenting people – usually in crowded places.

Frotteurism involves intense, recurrent sexual urges to touch and rub up against non-consenting people, usually in crowded places such as underground trains, buses, cinemas or supermarket queues (see Table 10.13). This is usually a male activity, which manifests as a sexual urge to rub the genitalia against

Table 10.13 *DSM-IV-TR diagnostic criteria for frotteurism*

A   Over a period of at least 6 months, recurrent, intense sexually arousing fantasies, sexual urges or behaviours involving touching and rubbing against a non-consenting person.

B   The person has acted on these sexual urges, or the sexual urges or fantasies cause marked distress or interpersonal difficulty.

the victim's thighs and buttocks or to fondle the victim's genitalia or breasts with his hands. This behaviour is usually undertaken in a surreptitious way in order to try to make it appear unintentional or as if someone else in the crowded environment is the culprit. Like exhibitionism and voyeurism, this activity usually begins in adolescence, although it may subside in frequency by the time the individual is in his late 20s. Frotteurism is considered by many to be a form of sexual assault, and at least part of the excitement for frotteurs is the feeling of power it gives them over their victim – a feeling that is relatively common in those who indulge in sexual assault generally.

10.3.1.7 Paedophilia

Paedophilia is defined as sexual attraction towards prepubescent children, normally of 13 years or younger. To be diagnosed with paedophilia, the individual must be at least 16 years of age and at least 5 years older than the victim (see Table 10.14). The central feature of the psychopathology is sexual attraction to children. This is *not* equivalent to 'child sexual abuse', 'incest' or 'child molestation', because the latter represent criminal acts. It is important to make this distinction because not all who sexually abuse children are diagnosable as

Paedophilia   A paraphilia which is defined as sexual attraction towards prepubescent children, normally 13 years or younger.

Table 10.14 *DSM-IV-TR diagnostic criteria for paedophilia*

A   Over a period of at least 6 months, recurrent, intense sexually arousing fantasies, sexual urges or behaviours involving sexual activity with a prepubescent child or children (generally aged 13 or younger).

B   The person has acted on these sexual urges, or the sexual urges or fantasies cause marked distress or interpersonal difficulty.

C   The person is at least 16 years and at least 5 years older than the child or children in Criterion A.

(Diagnosis should not include an individual in late adolescence involved in an ongoing sexual relationship with a 12- or 13-year-old).

paedophiles; for example, many who sexually abuse children may opportunistically select children simply because they are available, and such people do not necessarily have specific fantasies about having sex with children (Fagan, Wise, Schmidt & Berlin, 2002). Those who report paedophilic sexual urges usually report a preference for males or females, or sometimes for both. Those attracted to females usually prefer 8- to 10-year-olds, whereas those attracted to males usually prefer older children (DSM-IV-TR, p. 571). Girls are 3 times more likely than boys to be sexually abused, and children from low-income families are 18 times more likely to be sexually abused (Sedlak & Broadhurst, 1996).

The paedophile's sexual activity with children is usually limited to acts such as undressing the child, exposing himself, masturbating in the presence of the child, or gently touching or fondling the child and his or her genitalia. However, in more severe cases, this activity can extend to performing oral sex acts with the child, or penetrating the child's vagina, mouth or anus with fingers, foreign objects or penis. In general, paedophiles rarely believe that what they are doing is wrong, and often use egocentric forms of rationalization to justify their acts (e.g. the acts had 'educational value' or the child was consenting or gained pleasure from the activity). Because of this, they rarely experience distress or remorse. Thus, unlike many of the other paraphilias, experiencing distress or psychological impairment is not a part of the diagnostic criteria for paedophilia.

There are a number of unofficial sub-types of paedophilia. First, some paedophiles limit their activities to their immediate family (e.g. children, stepchildren, nieces and nephews), and *incest* is listed as a specific sub-type of paedophilia in

Incest   Sexual intercourse or any form of sexual activity between closely related persons.

DSM-IV-TR. Men who indulge in incest tend to differ from other paedophiles (1) by indulging in sexual activity with children of a slightly older age (e.g. an incestuous father may show sexual interest in a daughter only when the daughter begins to become sexually mature), and (2) by having a relatively normal heterosexual sex life outside of the incestuous relationship. In contrast, non-incestuous paedophiles will normally only become sexually aroused by sexually immature children and are sometimes known as *preference molesters* (Marshall, Barbaree & Christophe, 1986). Second, most paedophiles rarely intend to physically harm their victims (even though they may threaten their victims in order to prevent disclosure), but some may only get full sexual gratification from harming and even murdering their victims. This latter group are probably best described as *child rapists*, and appear to be fundamentally psychologically different to other paedophiles in that they often have comorbid diagnoses of personality disorder or sexual sadism (Groth, Hobson & Guy, 1982).

Preference molesters   Non-incestuous paedophiles who normally only become sexually aroused by sexually immature children.

Child rapists   Paedophiles who only get full sexual gratification from harming and even murdering their victims.

Because their behaviour is illegal and socially outlawed, and because they need to gain the trust of their child victims in order to indulge in their sexual activities, most paedophiles develop elaborate ways of gaining access to children. This can involve taking jobs in environments where children are frequently found (e.g. schools, residential children's homes), gaining the confidence of the parents or family of a child, or more recently by 'grooming'

FOCUS POINT 10.3

Paedophile 'grooming' over the internet

A sex offender who was caught through an anti-paedophile website has been warned by a judge he faces a lengthy jail sentence. Lee Costi, 21, appeared at Nottingham Crown Court where he admitted grooming schoolgirls for sex.

Costi, from Haslemere in Surrey, was caught when a Nottingham girl told her mother about his chatroom messages. She contacted a police website known as the Virtual Global Taskforce who then tracked down his other victims. The judge warned Costi he is facing a significant jail term after he pleaded guilty to charges. Costi admitted meeting three girls, aged 13 and 14, following sexual grooming. He also admitted three counts of sexual activity with a child, two counts of making indecent images and the possession of 41 indecent images of children. The judge adjourned Costi's sentencing for psychiatric reports.

BBC News website, 6 April 2006

How do online predators work?

Predators establish contact with kids through conversations in chat rooms, instant messaging, e-mail or discussion boards. Many teens use 'peer support' online forums to deal with their problems. Predators, however, often go to these online areas to look for vulnerable victims.

Online predators try to gradually seduce their targets through attention, affection, kindness and even gifts, and often devote considerable time, money and energy to this effort. They are aware of the latest music and hobbies likely to interest kids. They listen to and sympathize with kids' problems. They also try to ease young people's inhibitions by gradually introducing sexual content into their conversations or by showing them sexually explicit material.

Some predators work faster than others, engaging in sexually explicit conversations immediately. This more direct approach may include harassment or stalking. Predators may also evaluate the kids they meet online for future face-to-face contact.

Source: www.bewebaware.ca/

children in internet chat rooms by pretending to be someone of a similar age to the victim. Focus Point 10.3 provides an example of how paedophiles may 'groom' and 'lure' children for sexual purposes on the internet.

In a qualitative study of the modus operandi of male paedophiles, Conte, Wolf and Smith (1989) were able to describe a standard process through which many paedophiles operated to attract and isolate their victims and desensitize them to their sexual advances. This process included: (1) choosing an open, vulnerable child who would be easily persuaded and would remain silent after the abuse; (2) using non-sexual enticements such as purchases or flattery on early encounters with the child; (3) introducing sexual topics into the conversation; and (4) progressing from non-sexual touching to sexual touching as a means of desensitizing the child to the purpose of the touching. After the abuse, the paedophile would use his adult authority to isolate the child and their 'shared behaviour' from family and peers.

Paedophilia most often begins to manifest during adolescence, but some paedophiles report that their sexual interest in children did not develop until much later in life. In most other ways, paedophiles resemble law-abiding citizens and may be married or recently divorced. They often have steady, respectable jobs. In most cases the victims are well acquainted with the offender (and may often be members of the same close family), and offending may consist of repeated incidents with the same child over many years (Conte & Berliner, 1981; Finkelhor, 1980).

Finally, it is important to remember that by their very age, the victims of paedophilia are non-consenting, and that sexual activity with prepubescent children is illegal in most societies. In a general population study in the USA, 12 per cent of men and 17 per cent of women reported being sexually touched by an older person when they were children (Laumann, Gagnon, Michael & Michael, 1994).

Furthermore, it is important to note that the victims of paedophilia can suffer long-term psychological problems as a result of their experiences. These can manifest as eating disorders, sleep disorders, depression, anxiety disorders such as panic attacks and phobias, self-harm and dissociative disorders, all persevering well into adulthood. These psychological problems are more intense and more enduring if the abuse occurred at an early age and the victim knew his or her abuser well (Kendall-Tuckett, Williams & Finkelhor, 1993).

SELF-TEST QUESTIONS

- What are the three main characteristics used by DSM-IV-TR to define the paraphilias?
- What are the main categories of paraphilia described by DSM-IV-TR?
- Can you differentiate between those paraphilias that can be labelled 'victimless' and those that in many societies would be labelled 'sexual offences'?
- Can you list the main diagnostic criteria for fetishism, transvestic fetishism, sexual masochism and sadism, exhibitionism, voyeurism, frotteurism and paedophilia?
- Can you name some of the unofficial sub-types of paedophilia and describe the differences between them?

10.3.2 The Aetiology of Paraphilias

To date there is relatively little research on the causes of paraphilias, and what research is available has mainly been confined to the study of those paraphilias that involve sexual offending (e.g. paedophilia,

exhibitionism). Traditionally, psychodynamic explanations were popular but they now tend to be superseded by cognitive and, to a lesser degree, biological explanations. We begin this section by looking at some of the risk factors associated with the development of paraphilias to give you an indication of some of the experiential and psychological factors associated with paraphilias.

10.3.2.1 Risk Factors for Paraphilias

It may not have escaped readers' notice that most of the DSM-IV-TR diagnosable paraphilias are predominantly male activities, so being male is in itself a risk factor for paraphilias. For example, surveys have suggested that 89 per cent of acts of child sexual abuse are perpetrated by men, and only 11 per cent by women (Sedlak & Broadhurst, 1996), and male masochists outnumber females by 20 to 1. It is by no means clear why paraphilias should be such a male preserve, but it may in part be due to female sexuality being repressed more than male sexually, especially during socialization. There is some evidence of a link between high rates of sexual activity generally (known as *hypersexuality*), anxiety and depression, and paraphilias (Kafka, 1997: Raymond, Coleman & Miner, 2003). One implication of this is that high rates of sexual activity may lead individuals to evolve specific sexual inclinations and urges that are characteristic of paraphilia. Hypersexuality is found more often in men who are young, have experienced separation from parents during childhood, live in major urban areas, have had sexual experiences at an early age, frequently experience same-sex sexual behaviour, pay for sex, and are relatively more dissatisfied with sexual life than non-hypersexual men (Langstrom & Hanson, 2006). The study by Langstrom and Hanson also identified a strong association between hypersexuality and exhibitionism, voyeurism, and sexual masochism and sexual sadism. Hypersexual men were also characterized by their willingness to indulge in a range of risky behaviours, including tobacco smoking, heavy drinking, using illegal drugs and gambling. These initial studies suggest some kind of important link between hypersexuality and paraphilia, and further research in this area may help to clarify the risk factors and causes of individual paraphilias. Given that we now know some of the factors that predict hypersexuality, these might also play a significant role in predicting the development of paraphilias.

A number of studies have identified some of the risk factors involved in paedophilia. These can be categorized as either remote factors (i.e. factors from the individual's developmental history) or precipitant factors (i.e. factors that lead directly to the expression of paedophile behaviour). Remote risk factors for paedophilia include being a victim of childhood sexual abuse (Freund & Kuban, 1994) or possessing an inadequate attachment style that results from being brought up in a dysfunctional family (Hanson & Slater, 1988). Precipitating risk factors include depression, psychosocial stress (e.g., as a result of losing a relationship or a job) and alcohol abuse (Fagan, Wise, Schmidt & Berlin, 2002). Psychiatric comorbidity is also highly associated with paedophilia, with 93 per cent of paedophiles being diagnosed with at least one other psychopathology during their lifetime, such as major depression or anxiety disorders. In addition, 60 per cent of paedophiles are diagnosed with

Hypersexuality The occurrence of high rates of sexual activity.

a substance abuse disorder, and 60 per cent meet the diagnostic criteria for a personality disorder (Raymond, Coleman, Ohlerking, Christensen et al., 1999). The statistics support the view that psychopathology may be a precipitating factor in triggering paedophile behaviour.

10.3.2.2 The Psychodynamic Perspective

Psychodynamic theorists take a range of views about the causes of paraphilias. They can be viewed either (1) as defensive reactions that are attempting to defend the ego from repressed fears or (2) as representing fixation at a pre-genital stage of development (usually the Oedipal stage). For example, fetishism and paedophilia can be viewed as the behaviour of individuals who find normal heterosexual sex with women too threatening, perhaps because of a *castration anxiety*, and voyeurism is a behaviour that protects the individual from having to deal with the relationships that are often an inherent part of sexual life. In this respect psychodynamic approaches view those with paraphilias as individuals whose sexual development is immature or who are unable to deal with the complexity of relationships that usually surround normal heterosexual behaviour (Lanyon, 1986). Alternatively, paraphilias may be associated with a fixation at the Oedipal stage of development, which is itself associated with castration anxiety. For example, transvestic fetishism is seen as a denial of the mother's castration. Dressing in a woman's clothes but still having a penis underneath the clothing is seen as reassuring the transvestite that his mother has not been castrated and he should not therefore worry about himself being castrated (Nielson, 1960). Castration anxiety again crops up in psychodynamic interpretations of other paraphilias such as sexual sadism, where the sadist is seen as feeling relief from castration anxiety by taking on the role of castrator rather than the castrated.

Because of the way in which psychodynamic theory is couched, it is difficult to find objective evidence to support these explanations of paraphilias. If such factors do underlie paraphilic behaviour, then exploring them in psychoanalysis should help to alleviate these diverse sexual activities. However, there is only modest evidence that psychoanalysis is successful in the treatment of paraphilias (Cohen & Seghorn, 1969), and it is usually entirely ineffective in treating sexual offenders (Knopp, 1976).

Castration anxiety A psychoanalytic term referring to a psychological complex in males with a fear of being castrated.

10.3.2.3 Classical Conditioning

One very simple explanation for the paraphilias is that unusual sexual urges are the result of early sexual experiences (such as masturbation) being associated with an unusual stimulus or behaviour through associative learning (classical conditioning). For example, an adolescent boy's first sexual experiences may be masturbating to pictures of women dressed in fur or leather (resulting in a fur or leather fetish), or masturbating after accidentally seeing a neighbour undressing (resulting in voyeurism). Such early experiences may determine the route an adolescent's sexual development will take. This conditioning account is consistent with the fact that many of the paraphilias first manifest in early adolescence. Support

for the classical conditioning account also comes from an early experiment that attempted to develop a fetish for women's knee-length leather boots in a group of male volunteers. Rachman (1966) showed participants slides of a pair of black, knee-length women's leather boots (the conditioned stimulus, CS) followed immediately by a slide of an attractive female nude (the unconditioned stimulus, UCS). After a number of pairings of the CS with the UCS, participants showed an increase in penis volume (as measured by a phallo-plethysmograph) whenever the CS slide was shown. One participant even generalized this sexual response to pictures of other forms of female footwear! Nevertheless, while the conditioning of a sexual fetish can be experimentally demonstrated under controlled conditions, it is unlikely that conditioning is the cause of all paraphilias. It may account for the initial development of some fetishes, and may also account for why sexual urges initially become associated with specific activities such as voyeurism and frotteurism. However, as normal sexual activities become experienced during adolescence and early adulthood, conditioning theory would predict sexual urges to become associated with these normal sexual activities and links between sexual urges and early, learned paraphilic behaviour should extinguish. Nevertheless, paraphilias frequently persist – even when the sufferer finds them distressing and even when he is also concurrently indulging in normal sexual behaviour.

10.3.2.4 Childhood Abuse and Neglect

As we have seen many times in this book, childhood abuse and neglect is an important predictor of psychological problems later in life, and this is no less true for the development of paraphilias. However, the way in which negative early experiences may facilitate the development of paraphilias is probably complex. First, physical and sexual abuse is a feature of the history of many individuals with paraphilias, as is a history of disturbed and neglectful parenting (Mason, 1997; Murphy, 1997). However, childhood abuse and neglect is not a prerequisite for developing a paraphilia or becoming a sexual offender, and fewer than 30 per cent of sexual offenders have a history of childhood sexual abuse (Maletzky, 1993). Nevertheless, the level of childhood abuse experienced by sexual offenders is almost double the level found in the general population (Laumann, Gagnon, Michael & Michael, 1994), so childhood abuse may presumably contribute to paraphilia in some as yet unspecified way.

Problematic parent–child relationships may also play a significant role in the development of specific paraphilias. For example, neglectful or abusive parenting can leave the child with low self-esteem, poor social skills, a lack of effective coping strategies and an inability to form lasting relationships (Marshall & Serran, 2000). These psychological and behavioural deficits may lead individuals to find sexual satisfaction in ways that do not require them to deal with the consensual relationships required by normal sexual activity (e.g. transvestism, voyeurism, exhibitionism, frotteurism), or may lead them to seek sexual satisfaction with others, such as children, with whom their underdeveloped social and emotional skills do not put them at a disadvantage.

In conclusion, childhood abuse and neglect is certainly a factor that can be found in the history of some individuals who develop

Table 10.15 *Cognitive distortions found in the post-offending statements of paedophiles and exhibitionists*

Function of Statement	Paedophilia	Exhibitionism
Misattributing blame	'She would always run around half-dressed'	'The way she was dressed, she was asking for it'
Denying sexual intent	'I was just teaching her about sex'	'I was just looking for a place to pee'
Debasing the victim	'She always lies'	'She was just a slut anyway'
Minimizing consequences	'She's always been really friendly to me – even afterwards'	'I never touched her – so I couldn't have hurt her'
Deflecting criticism	'This happened years ago, why can't everyone forget about it?'	'It's not like I raped anyone'
Justifying the cause	'If I wasn't molested as a kid, I'd never have done this'	'If I knew how to get dates, I wouldn't have to expose myself'

Source: adapted from Maletzky (2002).

paraphilias, but it is as yet unclear how these experiences might lead to the development of problematic sexual urges.

10.3.2.5 Dysfunctional Beliefs, Attitudes and Schemata

Many problematic behaviours that are central to psychopathology are often maintained by dysfunctional beliefs or biases in information processing that lead individuals to think and behave in the way they do (see Chapters 5 and 6 for examples). This also appears to be true of some of the paraphilias, especially those that are either illegal or involve behaviours towards a non-consenting victim (e.g. paedophilia, exhibitionism, voyeurism). A considerable body of research suggests that cognitive distortions, dysfunctional beliefs and information processing biases play an important role in facilitating paraphilias that involve sexual offending (Abel, Gore, Holland, Camp et al., 1989; Ward, Hudson, Johnston & Marshall, 1997). For example, incest offenders hold beliefs that children are both sexually attractive and sexually motivated (Hanson, Lipovsky & Saunders, 1994), while paedophiles believe that children want sex with adults, and see contact as being socially acceptable and not harmful to the child (Stermac & Segal, 1989). Abel, Gore, Holland, Camp et al. (1989) labelled these beliefs *cognitive distortions* and argued that, for paedophiles, they serve to legitimize or justify sexual involvement with children and function to maintain the behaviour. These beliefs not only act as reasons why the paedophile should sexually offend, they also function as excuses for the behaviour and a means of diffusing responsibility for the behaviour after the act. They also appear to be a means by which paedophiles can maintain their self-esteem after offending (Pollock & Hashmall,

Cognitive distortions   Beliefs held by sexual offenders that enable them to justify their sexual offending.

1991; Ward, Hudson, Johnston & Marshall, 1997). Table 10.15 provides examples of the cognitive distortions found in the post-offending statements of paedophiles and exhibitionists, together with the putative functions that these cognitive distortions serve.

However, there is still some debate about whether sexual offenders such as paedophiles genuinely hold these beliefs or whether they are faked in order to diffuse responsibility after the offence. Using a procedure in which child molesters believed their responses were being monitored by a lie detector, Gannon (2006) found that participants endorsed fewer cognitive distortions than when they believed their responses were unmonitored. This suggests that at least some cognitive distortions may be faked in order to provide post-offence excuses for the paedophile's behaviour (see Research Methods Box 10.1).

The cognitive distortions that many sex offenders hold are often the products of more dynamic cognitive processes. For example, Stermac and Segal (1989) found that sexual offenders interpret sexual information in a biased way, usually in a manner consistent with their underlying beliefs about the acceptability of their behaviour. The researchers found that child molesters differed from other respondent groups by having a predisposition to interpret information as implying that benefits could be gained from sexual contact with children, and that there was greater complicity on the child's part and less responsibility on the adult's part. Finally, more recent research has suggested that sex offenders – and rapists in particular – may have developed integrated cognitive schemata that guide the offender's interactions with their victims and justify their behaviour. Polaschek and Ward (2002) called these *implicit theories*. Offenders use these schemata as causal theories about themselves, their victims and broader categories

Implicit theories   In sexual offending, integrated cognitive schemas that guide sexual offenders' interactions with their victims and justify their behaviour.

RESEARCH METHODS IN CLINICAL PSYCHOLOGY BOX 10.1

Using the bogus pipeline procedure to increase honest responding in paedophiles

Sexual offenders such as paedophiles appear to possess a set of cognitive distortions that serve to legitimize or justify sexual involvement with children and function to maintain the behaviour (Abel, Gore, Holland, Camp et al., 1989) (see Table 10.15). These beliefs may well act as reasons why paedophiles should sexually offend, but there is still some debate about whether sexual offenders genuinely hold these beliefs or whether they are faked in order to diffuse responsibility after the offence. So how might psychologists find out whether these beliefs are real or faked? A study by Gannon (2006) used what is known as a *bogus pipeline* procedure with child molesters. In this procedure, participants are wired up to apparatus that measures skin conductance through electrodes attached to the fingers. Some participants are then told to refrain from answering dishonestly because skin conductance may be related to dishonest responses (as if they were wired up to a 'lie detector', but in fact the evidence that skin conductance can reliably indicate lying is modest).

The study has three stages.

Stage 1

Convicted paedophiles are asked to say whether they agree or disagree with statements related to cognitive distortions in sexual offenders. Example items are the following:

Some children know more about sex than adults	AGREE/DISAGREE
An 8-year-old can enjoy a good sex joke	AGREE/DISAGREE
Children are not as innocent as most people think	AGREE/DISAGREE

Stage 2

One week later the same participants had to respond to the same statements (but they were not told it was the same questionnaire). Half were simply asked to fill out the questionnaire for a second time. The other half were connected to the bogus pipeline and given instructions that skin conductance could detect dishonest responses.

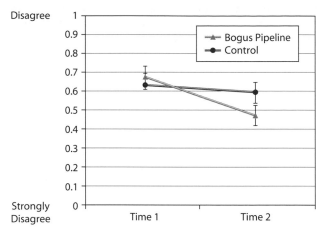

Figure 1

Mean cognitive distortion endorsement ($\pm SE$) for the bogus pipeline and control groups.

Results

The results show that, compared with control participants, those attached to the bogus pipeline showed a significant reduction in agreeing with the cognitive distortion statements between time 1 (when they were not connected to the bogus pipeline) and time 2 (when they were connected to the bogus pipeline).

Conclusions

This imaginative empirical approach to the problem indicates that sexual offenders may to some extent be faking the cognitive distortions they hold in order to justify their sexual offending. However, we must also note that (1) this study does involve some deception, so it is important to ensure that such studies comply with normally accepted ethical guidelines (such as the BPS guidelines on ethical principles for conducting research with human participants, www.bps.org.uk/), and (2) in order to ensure a proper balanced design, at time 2 both experimental and control participants should have been connected to the bogus pipeline, but only the experimental group should be told that it may detect dishonesty – for instance, simply being connected to the bogus pipeline may itself influence responding.

---

of people (such as women or children). Polaschek and Gannon (2004) identified five types of implicit theory held by rapists. These included the beliefs that:

1. women are unknowable (i.e. 'sexual encounters will end up being adversarial because a woman's intentions are unknowable');

2. women are sex objects (i.e. 'women are constantly sexually receptive, and so will enjoy sex even when it is forced on them');

3. the male sex drive is uncontrollable (i.e. 'a man's sex levels will build up to a dangerous level if women do not provide them with reasonable sexual access');

4 men are naturally dominant over women (i.e. 'men are more important in society than women, and a woman should meet a man's needs on demand');

5 the world is a dangerous place (i.e. 'it is a dog-eat-dog world and a man needs to take what he can from it').

Implicit cognitive theories such as these can provide sex offenders with a justification for both impulsive and premeditated sexual offences. They can also be used as a way of denying both the significance of the offence and the offender's responsibility for it.

10.3.2.6 Biological Theories

As we mentioned earlier, the vast majority of those diagnosed with a paraphilia are male. Thus, it has been hypothesized that paraphilia is caused by abnormalities in male sex hormones or by imbalances in those brain neurotransmitters that control male sexual behaviour. *Androgens* are the most important of the male hormones, and it is possible that unusual sexual behaviour,

> **Androgens** The most important of the male hormones. Unusual sexual behaviour, such as impulsive sexual offending involving non-consenting others, may be due to imbalances in these hormones.

such as impulsive sexual offending involving non-consenting others, may be due to imbalances in these hormones. However, there is relatively little convincing evidence that abnormal androgen levels play a significant role in the development of paraphilic behaviour. Nevertheless, androgen levels may help to maintain paraphilic behaviour once it has been acquired (Buvat, Lemaire & Ratajczyk, 1996), and anti-androgen drugs that reduce testosterone levels are regularly used to reduce the sexual urges of those with paraphilia disorders (Bradford & Pawlak, 1993). Abnormalities in brain neurotransmitter metabolism – such as serotonin – have also been associated with paraphilia (Maes, De Vos, van Hunsel, van West et al., 2001), although it is unclear whether such abnormalities are a cause of paraphilia or whether they are a consequence of the anxiety and depression that are frequently comorbid with paraphilic behaviour.

Finally, a small number of studies have identified abnormalities or deficits in brain functioning with paraphilias. First, abnormalities in the brain's temporal lobe have been associated with a number of paraphilias, including sadism, exhibitionism and paedophilia (Mason, 1997; Murphy, 1997; Mendez, Chow, Ringman, Twitchell et al., 2000). However, these abnormalities account for a minority of cases and appear to be related to dysfunction in the temporal lobes leading to sexual disinhibition of previously controlled behaviour. More recent studies (albeit based on a small sample of participants) have identified deficits in cognitive abilities in paedophiles that are mediated by striato-thalamically controlled areas of the frontal cortex (Tost, Vollmert, Brassen, Scmitt et al., 2004). These areas are associated with neuropsychological functions that include response inhibition, working memory and cognitive flexibility, and deficits in these domains are consistent with the finding that paedophiles frequently have lower than expected IQ scores – often as much as two-thirds of a standard deviation below the population mean (Cantor, Blanchard, Robichaud & Christensen, 2005).

SUMMARY

Research on the aetiology of paraphilias has largely been restricted to understanding the causes of those paraphilias that involve sexual offending (e.g. paedophilia) – mainly because of the desire to understand and prevent criminal activity. However, the research that is available has identified some risk factors for paraphilia (e.g. hypersexuality, childhood abuse and neglect), and has also indicated that some paraphilias are associated with cognitive biases and dysfunctional beliefs that act to maintain sexual offending and serve to legitimize or justify sexual activities.

SELF-TEST QUESTIONS

- Can you list some of the main risk factors for paraphilias?
- Paraphilias are highly comorbid with which other psychopathologies?
- What is castration anxiety and how is it used by psychoanalytic theorists to explain paraphilias?
- How is associative learning thought to be involved in the acquisition of some paraphilias?
- Is childhood abuse and neglect an important factor in the development of paraphilias?
- What are cognitive distortions and how are they used by sexual offenders to justify their actions?
- Is there any substantial evidence that sex hormone imbalances are involved in the development of paraphilias?
- What brain area abnormalities have been associated with paraphilia, and how might they cause paraphilic behaviour?

10.3.3 The Treatment of Paraphilias

Attempts to treat paraphilias have a long and complex history, dating back to the first half of the twentieth century when castration was a popular method of treating paraphilias such as paedophilia. However, castration was often reserved for repeated paraphilic behaviour that represented a criminal act and involved non-consenting victims (such as paedophilia and, in earlier times, homosexual behaviour when this was illegal). In many of these cases castration was seen more as a criminal punishment than as a method of treatment, and its effectiveness was often doubted because up to 30 per cent of men treated in this way were still capable of erections and ejaculation up to 10 years after surgery (Grubin & Mason, 1997).

Treatment of paraphilias is further complicated by a number of factors that make successful treatment difficult to achieve:

1 Many paraphilias involve criminal behaviour (e.g. paedophilia, exhibitionism and voyeurism), and this will often mean that sufferers are reluctant to be wholly truthful about their activities or to disclose their sexual activities honestly.

2 For many people with paraphilias, their sexual inclinations involve doing things they particularly enjoy and that

provide sexual satisfaction. If they have been indulging in these activities since early adolescence, then their behaviours may seem to them as normal as conventional sexual behaviour is to non-sufferers (Laws & O'Donohue, 1997).

3 With many of the paraphilias that involve a non-consenting victim, sufferers will often develop a rigid set of beliefs about their activities that enable them to diffuse responsibility for their behaviour and to blame others (e.g. the victim) (Abel, Gore, Holland, Camp et al., 1989; Ward, Hudson, Johnston & Marshall, 1997). Because of this, individuals with paraphilia often deny there is a problem with their behaviour, lack motivation to change, and may even fake compliance with therapy simply because it may allow them to continue their paraphilic activities subsequently (e.g. if treatment is a requirement for release from prison for sexual offences).

4 As we mentioned earlier, paraphilia is highly comorbid with a number of other psychopathologies, including substance abuse, anxiety, depression and personality disorders, and these comorbid disorders may have to be tackled before treatment for the paraphilia itself can be attempted.

We continue this section by describing some of the main treatment methods for paraphilias. Many therapists currently use multifaceted approaches to treatment, and you should bear this in mind when reviewing specific treatment methods. A multifaceted approach might involve, for example, (1) treating the individual behavioural problem (e.g. shifting sexual arousal and satisfaction away from specific or inappropriate stimuli and associating it with more acceptable stimuli); (2) dealing with any dysfunctional beliefs or attitudes that are maintaining the paraphilic behaviour (look back at Table 10.15); and, since many paraphilias are associated with social skills deficits, (3) providing social skills training that will help individuals function more appropriately with consenting partners.

10.3.3.1 Behavioural Techniques

In section 10.3.2 we discussed a number of early theories of paraphilia that viewed these problems as resulting from classical conditioning processes. In these accounts, unconventional stimuli or events (such as specific stimuli in fetishes, watching others naked in voyeurism) have become associated with sexual experiences, such as masturbation, during early adolescence. The assumption of behaviour therapy is that if these behaviours are learned through conditioning, then they can also be 'unlearned' through the use of basic conditioning procedures. Three types of technique are described below: aversion therapy, masturbatory satiation and orgasmic reorientation.

Aversion therapy is based on the assumption that inappropriate stimuli have become positively associated with sexual arousal and sexual satisfaction. In order to break this association, those stimuli must now be paired with negative or aversive experiences. For example, treatment of a fur fetish may involve pairing pictures of fur or women wearing fur clothing with aversive experiences such

as an electric shock or drug-induced nausea. Alternatively, a paedophile may be given electric shocks when shown pictures of naked children. An avoidance component can be added to this treatment in which clients can avoid the negative outcome by pressing a button which changes the picture from their preferred sexual stimulus (e.g. fur, naked child) to an acceptable one (e.g. an attractive adult female).

Aversion therapy can also be used in a *covert conditioning* form, where clients do not actually experience the pairing

> **Covert conditioning** Using the client's ability to imagine events to condition acceptable associations between events.

of sexual stimuli with aversive outcomes but imagine these associations during controlled treatment sessions. For example, a client may be asked to imagine one of his sexual fantasies and then to vividly imagine a highly aversive or negative outcome, such as being found by his wife indulging in the paraphilic sexual activity or being arrested (Barlow, 1993). Aversion therapy has been used to treat fetishes, transvestism, exhibitionism and paedophilia, and there is some evidence that it may have some treatment benefit when combined with other approaches such as social skills training (Marks, Gelder & Bancroft, 1970). However, as we have reported elsewhere in this book, aversion therapy rarely achieves long-term success when used alone – and high rates of relapse are associated with the sole use of aversion therapy (Wilson, 1978).

Satiation is an important conditioning principle in which the unconditioned stimulus (in this case sexual satisfaction) comes to be ineffective because it is experienced in excess, which leads to extinction of the sexual urges that had been conditioned to stimuli or events associated with that unconditioned stimulus (e.g. fetishes). This has led to the development of *masturbatory satiation* as a treatment for paraphilias, in which the

> **Masturbatory satiation** A treatment for paraphilias in which the client is asked to masturbate in the presence of arousing stimuli.

client is asked to masturbate in the presence of arousing stimuli (e.g. women's underwear if the client has an underwear fetish) and to simultaneously verbalize his fantasies on a tape recorder. Immediately after he has ejaculated, the client is instructed to masturbate again no matter how unaroused or uninterested he feels, and to continue for at least an hour (Marshall & Barbaree, 1978). After a number of these sessions, the client often reports that the stimuli that previously sexually aroused him have become boring or even aversive (LoPiccolo, 1985). Latency to ejaculation increases, and the number of sexual fantasies elicited by the paraphilic stimulus significantly decreases (Marshall & Lippens, 1977).

An important task for anyone treating paraphilias is not only to suppress inappropriate or distressing sexual activities (perhaps using the methods described above), but also to replace them with acceptable sexual practices. *Orgasmic reorientation* is a treatment method that aims to make the client sexually aroused by more con-

> **Orgasmic reorientation** A treatment method to replace inappropriate or distressing sexual activities which aims to make the client sexually aroused by more conventional or acceptable stimuli.

ventional or acceptable stimuli. This is a more explicit attempt to recondition sexual urges to more conventional stimuli, and can be used as an extension of the masturbatory satiation technique. The client is first asked to masturbate while attending to conventionally arousing stimuli (such as pictures of nude females), but if he begins to feel bored or lose his erection, he is asked to switch to attending to pictures associated with his paraphilia. As soon as he feels sexually aroused again, he must switch back to attending to the conventional stimulus, and so on. Although there are a number of individual case studies suggesting that some variations of orgasmic reorientation may be successful in helping clients to control their paraphilic behaviour, there are no controlled outcome studies available to evaluate the success of this method over the longer term (Laws & Marshall, 1991).

10.3.3.2 Cognitive Treatment

We saw in the section on aetiology that dysfunctional beliefs play a central role in developing and maintaining a number of paraphilias – especially those paraphilias that involve sexual offending with non-consenting victims. **Cognitive treatment** for these paraphilias often involves cognitive behaviour therapy (CBT) that is adapted to help clients to identify dysfunctional beliefs, to challenge these beliefs, and to replace them with functional and adaptive beliefs about sexual behaviour and sexual partners. Table 10.15 above shows a list of the kinds of dysfunctional beliefs held by paedophiles and exhibitionists. These beliefs act as justifications for sexual offending and are part of a belief system that effectively 'gives permission' to carry out offences.

Challenging dysfunctional beliefs includes:

1   demonstrating to clients that their dysfunctional beliefs are based on their deviant sexual behaviour rather than being justifiable reasons for the behaviour;

2   helping clients to see how they might misinterpret the behaviour of their victims to be consistent with their dysfunctional beliefs;

3   discussing dysfunctional beliefs within existing individual and broader social norms in order to demonstrate that the client's beliefs are not shared by most other members of society (e.g. that women are *not* merely objects for sexual gratification).

The UK Home Office has developed an integrated treatment for sexual offenders called the *Sex Offender Treatment Programme (SOTP)*, which extensively adopts CBT methods for treating imprisoned sex offenders (Beech, Fisher & Beckett, 1999) and has been shown to reduce reconvictions for sexual and violent offences (Friendship, Mann & Beech, 2003). Treatment in Practice Box 10.2 provides an overview of the main features of SOTP that are addressed by cognitive behavioural approaches.

> **Sex Offender Treatment Programme (SOTP)**   An integrated treatment for sexual offenders developed by the UK Home Office.

CLINICAL PERSPECTIVE: TREATMENT IN PRACTICE BOX 10.2

Cognitive behavioural treatment of sexual offenders using the Sex Offender Treatment Programme (SOTP)

SOTP was introduced in 1991 as part of a new strategy for treating sex offenders in the UK. The aim of the programme is to increase the offender's motivation to avoid reoffending and to develop the self-management skills necessary to achieve this. There are six programmes within the SOTP which can be combined in various ways according to the risk and needs of each offender. The overall programme is extensive and may involve up to 300 hours of treatment covering the following topics.

Denial and minimization
Sex offenders typically deny both the full extent of their sexually deviant behaviour and the risk they pose of reoffending. Denial can obstruct full recognition of the risk factors that could lead to future offending. Consequently, the SOTP aims to reduce denial and minimization where it is an obstacle to working towards change of relevant problems.

Damage to victims
Sex offenders often do not recognize or understand the damage they do to their victims. Rather, they believe, for example, that children are unharmed by sexual contact with adults. Using techniques such as discussion, exposure to the accounts of victims' experiences and perspective-taking role plays, sex offenders are educated about the harmful effects of their abuse in an attempt to enable them to see their offences from the point of view of their victims.

Justifications and distorted thinking about offending
Sex offenders typically develop a belief system that 'gives them permission' to carry out their offences. Where such thinking appears related to risk of future offending, these beliefs are challenged using standard CBT methods.

Dysfunctional cognitive schemas
Sex offenders often have hostile orientations towards other people, believing, for example, that women are deceitful, or they are preoccupied with suspicions about others and thoughts of

revenge. These schemas can gradually be modified using standard cognitive therapy techniques and behavioural experiments.

Deviant sexual fantasies

Offenders are taught to modify and control deviant arousal (e.g. sexual urges and fantasies elicited by thoughts of children), and to develop satisfying non-deviant alternative fantasies.

Relapse prevention/good life planning

Offenders are helped to recognize circumstances, situations, moods and types of thought that put them at risk of reoffending. They are given training in self-management skills that may help them to manage triggers for sexual offending and will also help them to avoid situations where triggers for sexual offend-

ing are common. Instead, they are encouraged to focus on new prosocial accomplishments that will lead to a more satisfying and rewarding life so that the need for offending is diminished.

Social and emotional functioning

Low self-esteem and failure to develop a capacity for intimacy in adult relationships are common characteristics of sex offenders. They are taught social and interpersonal skills that will enable them to overcome these lifestyle and personality difficulties. They are also helped to adopt more constructive coping skills to deal with life's daily problems, and are taught emotional management skills. All skills training involves role play and coaching followed by in vivo practice of new behaviours.

Source: after Beech, Fisher & Beckett (1999)

10.3.3.3 Hormonal and Drug Treatments

As we mentioned earlier, castration was the radical form of treatment for dangerous sex offenders during periods of the twentieth century, especially in parts of Europe, and was often offered as an alternative to imprisonment (Abel, Osborn, Anthony & Gardos, 1992). The aim here was to curb the sexual appetite of persistent offenders who were unable to respond to any other form of treatment. An arguably more acceptable way of curbing sexual appetite in those paraphilics who persistently offend is to use

Anti-androgen drugs A group of drugs that significantly decrease the levels of male hormones such as testosterone.

Medroxyprogesterone acetate (MPA) An anti-androgen, testosterone-lowering drug.

Cyproterone acetate (CPA) An anti-androgen, testosterone-lowering drug.

anti-androgen drugs that significantly decrease the levels of male hormones such as testosterone. Currently used testosterone-lowering drugs include *medroxyprogesterone acetate (MPA)* and *cyproterone acetate (CPA)*, both of which have been shown to reduce the frequency of erection and ejaculation, inhibit sexual arousal and reduce the rate of reoffending in sexual

offenders (Hall, 1995; Bradford & Pawlak, 1993; Maletzky & Field, 2003). However, this kind of treatment depends very much on the compliance of the client or offender in taking such drugs regularly. This is particularly important because evidence suggests that offenders will often revert to paraphilic behaviour when they cease taking the drug, even after many years of medication (Berlin & Meinecke, 1981).

An alternative to anti-androgens is the use of antidepressant drugs such as SSRIs (e.g. fluoxetine). There is some modest evidence that such drugs help individuals to control sexual urges, especially if depression is a trigger for indulging in paraphilic behaviour (Kafka & Hennen, 2000). However, despite encouraging short-term effects of treatment with SSRIs, there are as yet no long-term follow-up studies (Maletzky & Field, 2003).

10.3.3.4 Relapse-Prevention Training

Rather than focus on an all-embracing 'cure' for paraphilias, many forms of treatment focus specifically on *relapse prevention*, which is especially relevant in the case of sexual offenders. Relapse prevention

Relapse-prevention training
In paraphilias, a treatment which consists primarily of helping clients to identify circumstances, situations, moods and types of thoughts that might trigger paraphilic behaviour.

Plate 10.3
Ian Huntley was a school caretaker who was given two life sentences in August 2002 for the murders of schoolgirls Holly Wells and Jessica Chapman. Huntley already had nine sex allegations against him in the 1990s, many against young girls. However, by using an alias, he was able to get a job as the caretaker at Soham Village College in Cambridgeshire which Holly and Jessica attended. Sexual offenders regularly take the kinds of jobs that put them in close contact with their victims (e.g. children). Part of current relapse-prevention programmes for sexual offenders is to help them develop skills that will avoid situations that put them at risk of subsequent offending.

consists primarily of helping clients to identify circumstances, situations, moods and types of thoughts that might trigger paraphilic behaviour. For example, a mood trigger might be a period of stress or anxiety or alcohol abuse that precipitates sexual offending, or close contact with children might activate paedophile behaviours. Sexual offenders are also taught to identify the distorted cognitions that might lead to offending (e.g. 'that child is running around half-dressed, so she must be interested in sex') and are taught self-management skills that will enable them to interrupt sequences of thoughts that lead to offending or to avoid situations that place them at risk (e.g. in the case of paedophilia, to avoid taking jobs that involve working with or near children, or living near a school). Relapse-prevention programmes have been shown to be successful in reducing subsequent offending (Marshall & Pithers, 1994), and are important components of many national treatment programmes for sexual offenders (see Treatment in Practice Box 10.2).

10.3.3.5 Summary of the Treatment of Paraphilias

The treatment of paraphilias is generally a difficult process, not least because many diagnosed with paraphilia are also sexual offenders (e.g. paedophiles, exhibitionists, voyeurs). This can lead clients to be less than truthful about their sexual activities and to approach treatment with a relatively ingrained set of beliefs about their activities. Paraphilias are also highly comorbid with other psychopathologies such as substance abuse, anxiety, depression and personality disorders, which makes treatment additionally complex. Most programmes of treatment adopt a multifaceted approach involving behaviour therapy techniques to address the specific sexual behaviour problem (e.g. aversion therapy, masturbatory satiation, orgasmic reorientation) and CBT to deal with the dysfunctional beliefs that underlie many paraphilias and sexual offending in particular. Finally, social skills training and relapse-prevention procedures can be used in an attempt to ensure that individuals are able to cope with the demands of normal sexual relationships and to identify situations and circumstances that might trigger relapse.

SUMMARY

When high rates of sexual behaviour are channelled into unusual or very specific sexual activities, these are known as paraphilias. They range from sexual activities that are victimless (e.g. fetishes and transvestic fetishism) to others that are defined in law as sexual offences (e.g. paedophilia, exhibitionism, voyeurism). Many paraphilias are diagnosed on the basis of unusual, recurrent sexual urges that cause personal distress or affect social and occupational functioning (e.g. fetishism, transvestic fetishism), but others do not require individuals to experience distress, merely that they have acted on their urges with non-consenting victims (e.g. paedophilia, exhibitionism, voyeurism). Research on the aetiology of paraphilias has identified some risk factors (e.g. hypersexuality, childhood abuse and neglect) and has also indicated that dysfunctional beliefs may play an important role in maintaining those paraphilias that are linked to sexual offending (e.g. paedophilia, exhibitionism). Finally, treatments for paraphilias are still relatively underdeveloped and adopt behaviour therapy or CBT techniques to change dysfunctional behaviour and cognitions. Relapse prevention is an important component of treatment for many paraphilias, especially those related to sexual offending.

SELF-TEST QUESTIONS

- Why are paraphilias so difficult to treat?
- How have aversion therapy and covert conditioning been utilized to treat paraphilias?
- What are masturbatory satiation and orgasmic reorientation techniques, and is there any evidence that they can be successfully used to treat paraphilias?
- How has CBT been adapted to help treat paraphilias?
- Can you name the basic principles and stages of the UK SOTP programme used to treat sexual offenders?
- What are the main drug treatments that have been used to treat paraphilias, and what is the evidence that such treatments prevent relapse?
- What are the main principles of relapse-prevention treatments for paraphilias?

SECTION SUMMARY

10.3 Paraphilias

- Paraphilias tend to be problematic, high-frequency sexual behaviours or unusual sexual urges and activities that are often directed at inappropriate targets.

- Some paraphilias are victimless (e.g. fetishes, transvestic fetishism), while others are defined in law as sexual offences (e.g. exhibitionism, voyeurism, frotteurism, paedophilia).

10.3.1 The Diagnosis and Description of Paraphilias

- **Fetishism** involves sexually arousing fantasies and urges directed at inanimate objects.

- **Transvestic fetishism** is when a heterosexual male experiences sexual arousal from cross-dressing in women's clothing.

- **Sexual masochism** is when an individual gains sexual arousal and satisfaction from being humiliated.

- **Sexual sadism** is when a person gains sexual arousal and satisfaction from the psychological or physical suffering of others.

- **Exhibitionism** involves sexual fantasies about exposing the penis to a stranger, usually a women or a child.

- **Voyeurism** involves experiencing intense sexually arousing fantasies or urges to watch an unsuspecting person who is naked, in the process of undressing or engaging in sexual activity.

- **Frotteurism** involves recurrent sexual urges to touch and rub up against other non-consenting people, usually in crowded places.

- **Paedophilia** is defined as sexual attraction towards prepubescent children, normally 13 years or younger.

- Some paedophiles limit their activities to their immediate family (e.g. children, stepchildren, nieces) and **incest** is listed as a specific sub-type of paedophilia in DSM-IV-TR.

- Non-incestuous paedophiles normally only become sexually aroused by sexually immature children, and often develop elaborate ways of gaining access to children through 'grooming' activities.

10.3.2 The Aetiology of Paraphilias

- Most of the DSM-IV-TR diagnosable paraphilias are male activities, and many are also sexual offences (e.g. paedophilia, exhibitionism).

- Both **hypersexuality** and **childhood abuse and neglect** are risk factors for paraphilias.

- **Psychodynamic theory** views paraphilias either (1) as defensive reactions that are attempting to defend the ego from repressed fears, or (2) as representing fixation at a pre-genital stage of development (e.g. the Oedipal stage).

- Many paraphilias develop during early adolescence, and inappropriate sexual urges may have been developed through the association of sexual activities such as masturbation with inappropriate stimuli or activities (the process of **classical conditioning**).

- The level of childhood abuse experienced by sexual offenders is almost double the level found in the general population. However, childhood abuse and neglect is not a sufficient condition for committing a sexual offence, because it is reported by only 30 per cent of sexual offenders.

- Sexual offenders, including paedophiles, develop a set of beliefs or **cognitive distortions** that serve to legitimize or justify their sexual activities.

- Even though **anti-androgen drugs** are regularly used to treat some paraphilias, there is little convincing evidence that abnormal androgen levels play a significant role in the development of paraphilic behaviour.

10.3.3 The Treatment of Paraphilias

- Many paraphilias are difficult to treat because (1) they involve criminal behaviour that makes individuals reluctant to be truthful about their activities, and (2) paraphilias are highly comorbid with other Axis I disorders, which significantly complicates treatment.

- Behavioural treatments for paraphilias include **aversion therapy**, **covert conditioning**, **masturbatory satiation** and **orgasmic reorientation**.

- **CBT** has been adapted to treat paraphilias (especially those involving sexual offending) by addressing the dysfunctional beliefs or cognitive distortions that many sexual offenders develop to legitimize their behaviour.

- Anti-androgen drug treatments for paraphilias include **medroxyprogesterone acetate** (**MPA**) and **cyproterone acetate** (**CPA**), which reduce the frequency of erection and inhibit sexual arousal.

- Because many paraphilias are also sexual offences, **relapse-prevention training** helps clients to identify circumstances that may trigger paraphilic behaviour.

10.4 GENDER IDENTITY DISORDERS

Most of us take our sexual identity for granted. We do not question the sex we were born as, and we find that behaving as either a male or a female is natural and effortless. Our *gender identity* seems to have been determined for as long as we have lived, and we think, act and dress accordingly. However, some individuals develop a sense of *gender dysphoria* (unhappiness with their own gender) and feel that they have a sense of gender that is opposite to the biological sex they were born with. In such circumstances, individuals may see themselves biologically developing as a man or a woman (e.g. growing a beard or developing breasts), but cannot shake off the belief that underneath the physical appearance they are of the opposite gender. This may lead them to cross-dress in clothes of the opposite sex or even seek surgery or take hormones to develop physical features indicative of the opposite sex. When this kind of

Gender identity The internal sense of being either male or female. Usually congruent with biological gender, but not always, as in gender identity disorder.

Gender dysphoria A gender identity disorder in which an individual has a sense of gender that is opposite to his or her biological sex.

gender dysphoria becomes problematic and causes significant personal distress and social and occupational impairment, it may be diagnosed as *gender identity disorder (GID)*.

Forms of GID can also be found in childhood and are associated with cross-gender behaviour that can be easily recognized by parents and carers (Green & Blanchard, 1995). These include playing with toys typical of the opposite sex (e.g. boys playing with dolls), dressing in clothes of the opposite sex, and preferring friends and playmates of the opposite sex. However, most children who adopt this cross-gender behaviour do not go on to develop GID in adulthood (Zucker, Finegan, Deering & Bradley, 1984), so we must be cautious in interpreting such childhood behaviour as a precursor to adult GID.

> **Gender identity disorder**   A sexual disorder where an individual is dissatisfied with his or her biological sex and has a strong desire to be a member of the opposite sex.

10.4.1 Diagnosis and Description of Gender Identity Disorder (GID)

Table 10.16 gives the DSM-IV-TR diagnostic criteria for GID. The main components of the diagnosis are that (1) the individual exhibits a strong and persistent cross-gender identification, and that this is not simply because of the cultural advantages that might be associated with being the opposite sex; (2) there must be clear evidence of persistent discomfort with his or her existing biological sex, and strong feelings of his or her current gender role being inappropriate; and (3) there must be evidence of significant distress or impairment in social, occupational or other important areas of functioning as a result of these feelings.

Individuals with GID usually exhibit a strong preoccupation with their wish to live as a member of the opposite sex, which may lead them to acquire the physical appearance of a member of the opposite sex (by cross-dressing or adopting mannerisms typical of the opposite sex). For example, men may undergo electrolysis to remove body hair or submit themselves to hormone treatments to develop female physical characteristics such as breasts. Those who have strong feelings of gender dysphoria may have problematic sex lives. For example, men with GID who are married may frequently fantasize about being a lesbian lover when they have sex with their wives. Those with same-sex partners often prevent their partner from seeing or touching their genitals. Client's Perspective Box 10.1 provides a personal account given by one man who had felt gender dysphoria from a very early age. Despite having what appeared to others to be a successful business, marriage and family, these feelings were persistent enough to encourage him to seek treatment. In many cases of GID, the feelings of gender dysphoria are so strong that they drive the individual to seek *gender reassignment surgery*, which culminates in changing the individual physically into his or her preferred gender (see section 10.4.3.1).

> **Gender reassignment surgery**   The process of changing biological sex which ends in changing the person's basic biological features to be congruent with his or her gender identity.

A diagnosis of GID can also be given in children. In boys, this may manifest by adopting female roles during play (such as playing

Table 10.16 *DSM-IV-TR diagnostic criteria for gender identity disorder*

A   A strong and persistent cross-gender identification (not merely a desire for any perceived cultural advantages of being the other sex).

    In children, the disturbance is manifested by four (or more) of the following:

(1)   Repeatedly stated desire to be, or insistence that he or she is, the other sex.

(2)   In boys, preference for cross-dressing or simulating female attire; in girls, insistence on wearing only stereotypical masculine clothing.

(3)   Strong and persistent preferences for cross-sex roles in make-believe play or persistent fantasies of being the other sex.

(4)   Intense desire to participate in the stereotypical games and pastimes of the other sex.

(5)   Strong preference for playmates of the other sex.

In adolescents and adults, the disturbance is manifested by symptoms such as a stated desire to be the other sex, frequent passing as the other sex, desire to live or be treated as the other sex, or the conviction that he or she has the typical feelings and reactions of the other sex.

B   Persistent discomfort with his or her sex or sense of inappropriateness in the gender role of that sex.

    In children, the disturbance is manifested by any of the following: in boys, assertion that his penis or testes are disgusting or will disappear or assertion that it would be better not to have a penis, or aversion toward rough-and-tumble play and rejection of male stereotypical toys, games and activities; in girls, rejection of urinating in a sitting position, assertion that she has or will grow a penis, or assertion that she does not want to grow breast or menstruate, or marked aversion towards normative feminine clothing.

    In adolescents and adults, the disturbance is manifested by symptoms such as preoccupation with getting rid of primary and secondary sex characteristics (e.g. request for hormone, surgery or other procedures to physically alter sexual characteristics to simulate the other sex) or belief that he or she was born the wrong sex.

C   The disturbance is not concurrent with a physical intersex condition.

D   The disturbance causes clinically significant distress or impairment in social, occupational or other important areas of functioning.

CLIENT'S PERSPECTIVE 10.1

Gender identity disorder

'On June 1, 1994, when this journal began, I was living entirely as Dan – father, husband and small businessman. I had been married for thirteen years to Alice, with a ten-year-old son and a six-year-old daughter. My family life was good, my business growing, my future bright, but still something was missing.

I had first felt "different" in infant school, where all the other boys seemed to know instinctively how to act, but I had to struggle to learn the male role by rote: it did not come naturally. I never considered the possibility I had the instincts of a female; I simply thought I had none at all.

By age seven, I was regularly sneaking off to dress in the girls' clothes my mother brought in as part of her short-lived ironing business. This was well before puberty and was not an erotic experience, but rather a feeling of completeness and contentment.

Throughout my teenage years, the need to dress as a female came and went in waves, sometimes intense, sometimes absent for years at a time.

I was nonagressive in school, both in sports and dating, and excelled at neither. My only erotic interests were not in what I could do to or with a woman, but what it would be like to be one.

I married as a virgin in 1981, and the longings to be female vanished more than they were there. But, gradually, as I progressed through adult life, the waves became stronger and more frequent. Only twice in my life (both times in my early teen years) had I ventured out as a female, both with such tension from fear of discovery that I did not attempt this again until three years before this journal began.

Suddenly, the need to move in society as a woman became overwhelming, and within two months I had made nearly a dozen outings, tentative at first, then growing bolder as I gained confidence in my ability to "pass" without being "read".

Throughout this period, I was constantly "purging" myself of this "awful" desire. Full of guilt I would throw away all my pills, wigs, clothes, and any other accumulations, only to be driven to rebuild my accoutrements scant days later.

Finally, I came to the decision that this secret side, if not dealt with openly, would lead to self-destruction and the loss of not only my self-respect, but the love of those I loved. So, at the end of July 1994, I mustered the courage to call a gender "hotline" and get a referral to a doctor who provided hormone therapy to transsexuals.'

Clinical Commentary

Dan's case is typical of a majority of men who suffer gender identity disorder. Even though his family life is settled and happy, and his financial situation is secure and promising, he is still unable to reconcile his gender identity with his biological sex, and the urge to act and dress as a woman becomes overwhelming in adult life. His feelings of gender dysphoria began in childhood when playing the male role did not come naturally. However, it is unusual for someone with childhood gender dysphoria to carry those feelings into full adulthood as Dan did. His attempts to cross-dress and take on female gender identity at first made him feel guilty, until he finally took the decision to make a full transition to becoming a woman.

---

with dolls, taking 'mother' roles, avoiding rough-and-tumble play), by exhibiting disgust at their penis, or adopting female activities such as always insisting on sitting on the toilet when urinating. Girls may exhibit strong aversion to their parents' gender role expectations of them, avoid wearing dresses, insist on having short hair, and may also prefer male playmates and contact sports such as football and rugby. In childhood, about 3 per cent of girls and 1 per cent of boys explicitly express a desire to be of the opposite gender (Zucker & Bradley, 1995), but we must remember that the significant majority of them do not grow up to be adults with diagnosable GID. However, a diagnosis of childhood GID does appear to have implications for sexuality generally, because many of those diagnosed with GID in childhood develop homosexual orientations. Green (1987) found that 75 per cent of boys who met the criteria for GID reported homosexual or bisexual fantasies by 19 years of age, and in a review of long-term follow-up studies, Di Ceglie (2000) found that between 50 and 75 per cent of children with GID were homosexual or bisexual as adolescents or adults. Thus, while childhood GID may not be a good predictor of adult GID, it is a better predictor of adult male homosexuality (Menvielle, 1998).

There is very little epidemiological evidence available on which to base the prevalence rates of GID. However, DSM-IV-TR estimates that some European studies suggest that roughly 1 per 30,000 adult males (0.003 per cent) and 1 per 100,000 adult females (0.001 per cent) seek gender reassignment surgery. GID can also be comorbid with a number of Axis I disorders. Many experience high levels of anxiety and depression, and studies suggest that 71 per cent of a sample with GID fulfilled the criteria for a comorbid current and/or lifetime Axis I diagnosis (Hepp, Kraemer, Schnyder, Miller et al., 2005).

SELF-TEST QUESTIONS

● What is gender dysphoria?
● What are the main DSM-VI-TR diagnostic criteria for gender identity disorder?
● What is the evidence that gender identity disorder exhibits in children?

10.4.2 The Aetiology of Gender Identity Disorder

Gender dysphoria is a problem that persists for many individuals over a substantial period of their lives, suggesting the causes of these problems are not trivial. However, there is relatively little research on the aetiology of GID. Some risk factors have been identified, with males with GID reporting distant relationships with their fathers, and females often reporting a history of childhood abuse (Bradley & Zucker, 1997). However, such childhood experiences are by no means universal across individuals with GID. Neither can we assume that GID results from parents and family reinforcing children during childhood for behaving in cross-gender ways. For example, when children dress up in clothes of the opposite sex, they may be rewarded by the attention they receive, but it is relatively rare for children treated in this way to grow into adults with GID (Zucker, Finegan, Deering & Bradley, 1984). Similarly, the prenatal hopes and expectations of parents do not appear to influence the development of GID. Zucker, Wild, Bradleyand Lowry (1993) found that mothers of boys with feminine characteristics were just as likely to have wanted a boy as a girl. These findings suggest that evidence that social development may play a role in the development of GID is equivocal. Let us now turn our attention to biological factors.

10.4.2.1 Biological Factors

One view is that gender identity may be influenced by hormonal factors. In particular, when mothers have taken sex hormones during pregnancy (e.g. to prevent uterine bleeding), the behaviour of their offspring has subsequently been affected in ways consistent with the type of hormone used. When pregnant mothers have taken medications related to male sex hormones, the early behaviour of girls is often more tomboyish than in mothers who had not taken such drugs (Ehrhardt & Money, 1967). Similarly, the male offspring of mothers who took female hormones during pregnancy often display less athletic behaviour than boys whose mothers did not take such hormones (Yalom, Green & Fisk, 1973). Nevertheless, these studies do not imply that such children grow up to develop GID, and the evidence of hormonal abnormalities in adults with GID is modest at best (Carroll, 2000).

Given that there is little or no evidence to relate GID to imbalances in sex hormones, is it possible to identify other biological factors that may play a role in GID? One study has suggested that GID may be associated with abnormalities in those areas of the brain that regulate sexual behaviour. The **bed nucleus of the stria terminalis (BSTc)** is a brain area that is essential for sexual behaviour and is normally larger in males than in females. However, in autopsies carried out on six men who had undergone gender reassignment surgery to become women, Zhou, Hofman, Gooren and Swaab (1995) found a female-sized BSTc in all cases. They concluded that males with GID appear to possess female brain structures that may either have a genetic origin or have been influenced by abnormalities in early brain development.

There have been relatively few studies of the heritability of GID, but a well-controlled child and adolescent twin sample study by Coolidge, Thede and Young (2000) suggested that GID is highly heritable. While this implies a genetic component to GID, it is not clear from these studies how that genetic component is transmitted or through what aspect of GID or its related psychopathology it is manifested.

SELF-TEST QUESTIONS

- Is there any evidence that hormonal imbalances might play a role in the development of gender identity disorder?
- What is the evidence that abnormalities in certain brain areas may be associated with gender identity disorder?
- What is the evidence that there is an inherited component to gender identity disorder?

10.4.3 The Treatment of Gender Identity Disorder

Individuals diagnosed with GID feel that they have a sense of gender that is opposite to the biological sex they were born with, and gender dysphoria involves profound feelings of conflict between gender identity and biological sex. There are two important ways in which this imbalance can be corrected: (1) by attempting to change an individual's biological sex to be congruent with his or her feelings of gender identity, or (2) by using psychological methods to change the individual's gender identity to be congruent with his or her biological sex. Most individuals with GID are usually adamant that their biological sex is 'wrong' and opt for a process that ends in gender reassignment surgery, a process that involves progressive hormone treatment and eventually surgery to change their basic biological features to be congruent with their gender identity. We will discuss this radical treatment option first, then look at more psychologically oriented attempts to modify gender identity itself.

10.4.3.1 Gender Reassignment Surgery

This involves a relatively irreversible process of changing the body's physical characteristics to be consistent with the individual's feelings of gender. Because this involves major changes to the person's anatomy, it is a treatment option that is approached in a graduated way in order to ensure that the client is fully aware of the long-term implications of the treatment and is psychologically adjusted to becoming someone of the opposite biological sex. The progressive stages of gender reassignment surgery are: (1) at least 3 months of counselling or psychotherapy to ensure that the client fully understands the process of treatment and that he or she is fully committed to it; (2) hormone treatment to initiate physical changes such as reducing body hair and developing breasts in men seeking to become biological women, and beard growth and muscle development in women seeking to become men; (3) a crucial real-life test, in which clients must live as their preferred gender for at least 1 year, dressing and presenting themselves as the preferred sex in a way that will lead them to understand what this means over the longer term; and (4) if the first three stages are completed successfully, clients may then proceed to surgery, in which their genitalia are surgically altered to resemble those of their preferred biological sex. A fuller description of these stages in gender reassignment surgery is given in Treatment in Practice Box 10.3.

CLINICAL PERSPECTIVE: TREATMENT IN PRACTICE BOX 10.3

Gender reassignment surgery

What does male to female gender reassignment involve?

For a man wishing to become a woman, treatment would mean taking female hormones for at least 1 year before any irreversible surgery takes place. The hormones reduce body hair, cause breast development and generally make the body shape and skin texture more feminine.

The person would also have to live as a woman, full-time, for a minimum of 1 year before any surgery can be authorized. During this period, some transsexuals may choose to have facial hair removed by electrolysis, undergo cosmetic surgery to make their face more feminine or learn to raise the pitch of their voice. When patients feel ready, they may apply for medical approval of reassignment surgery. The clinical team will review individual patients' progress to see how well they have adapted to their new role, and depending on the results of this evaluation, surgery may then be approved.

Gender reassignment involves major surgery. Under general anaesthetic, the testicles and erectile tissue of the penis are removed. An artificial vagina is then created and lined with the skin of the penis, where the nerves and blood vessels remain largely intact. Tissue from the scrotum is then used to create the labia, and the urethra is shortened and repositioned appropriately.

What does female to male gender reassignment involve?

For a woman wanting to become a man, taking the male hormone testosterone leads to beard growth and muscle development. On the whole, these changes can't be reversed later. As early as 6 months into this programme, it may be possible to have a mastectomy (breast removal). This makes it much easier for the person to appear as a man in public. After at least a year of hormone treatment, the ovaries and uterus are removed.

For many female to male transsexuals, this is as far as they will go with surgery. Going further is more complex, costly and difficult to achieve. For those who do continue, phalloplasty (penis construction) and testicle implants are available. It's also possible to create a male urethra and to move the clitoris to the head of the penis.

Source: www.mind.org.uk/

Despite the radical nature of gender reassignment therapy, outcome studies indicate that a large majority of clients who undergo the full treatment are generally satisfied with the outcome and express no regrets about their decision (Smith, van Goozen & Cohen-Kettenis, 2001). In a Dutch study of 188 GID sufferers who completed gender reassignment surgery, only 2 expressed any regret at their decision. More importantly, the study found that such procedures tended to significantly reduce gender dysphoria and enabled clients to function well psychologically, socially and sexually (Smith, van Goozen, Kuiper & Cohen-Kettenis, 2005). Nevertheless, while such studies seem to indicate that gender reassignment surgery has a largely positive outcome, we must still be cautious about it as a treatment that solves all the problems associated with GID. First, while many suffering GID do go through all four stages of the treatment, a substantial minority drop out of gender reassignment schemes at an early stage. Smith, van Goozen, Kuiper and Cohen-Kettenis (2005) report that of 325 individuals who applied for gender reassignment surgery, 103 dropped out before starting hormone treatment, and a further 34 dropped out before surgery (a dropout rate of 42 per cent). Indeed, many decide not to continue with the treatment during the real-life test, when they discover that the realities of living as someone of the opposite biological sex are not what they imagined. The longer the client is kept in the real-life test phase of the process, the greater the likelihood of a successful outcome (Botzer & Vehrs, 1997). But if the individual with GID already has significant comorbid psychological problems, then these are unlikely to be alleviated by gender reassignment surgery (Botzer & Vers, 1997).

10.4.3.2 Psychological Treatments

An alternative approach to the treatment of GID is to try to modify the client's gender identity to be consistent with his or her biological sex. For example, if an individual feels he is basically female but is biologically male, one approach is to use behavioural and cognitive techniques to try to change the female thoughts and cognitions to male ones. However, a vast majority of those with GID approach treatment adamant that it is their biological sex that is wrong, not their gender identity beliefs, so gender identity change procedures tend to be used relatively infrequently. In one early study, Barlow, Reynolds and Agras (1993) report using behaviour therapy techniques with a 17-year-old gender-dysphoric male who wanted to change his gender identity rather than his biological sex. They used operant reinforcement methods to shape up male-related mannerisms and behaviours, and also used classical conditioning techniques such as aversion therapy to

Ladyboys

In a number of Asian countries, gender reassignment surgery has almost become an art form in itself, and this is especially so in Thailand. Many men in Thailand have dealt with their gender dysphoria and their desire to become women by constructing for themselves a special place in their country's culture. These transsexual individuals are known as *Katoey* or *Ladyboys* and they play a central role in the country's sex industry (as prostitutes) and as popular stage performers. Such individuals see their gender reassignment not just as a means of relieving psychological problems associated with gender dysphoria, but also as an opportunity to become an object of desire and earn a substantial living in a relatively poor economy. Such individuals do not simply replace their male attributes with female ones, they attempt to reconstruct their physical body in the most attractive way. This can involve using hormones to keep their body frames as petite and soft as possible, having silicon implants to enhance breasts, and even having cartilage shaved from their Adam's apple to reduce its prominence. Ladyboys play such an important part in Thailand's current economy that they have almost become accepted as a third gender.

reduce the sexual attractiveness of men. Even though these techniques were primarily behaviour-oriented (rather than using methods aimed at directly changing cognitions and beliefs), they did appear to have some success, and at a 5-year follow-up the client had acquired a male identity and sexually preferred women to men (Barlow, Abel & Blanchard, 1979).

Studies such as this suggest that a gender identity that is inconsistent with biological sex can be successfully changed.

Supplementing behaviour therapy methods with CBT approaches designed to directly challenge and change dysphoric gender identity beliefs may make such treatments even more effective. However, as we outlined at the beginning of this section, the vast majority of individuals with GID are adamant that it is their biological sex that they want to change and not their gender identity, so opportunities to develop more integrated therapies for gender identity may be limited.

SUMMARY

Many individuals have a sense of gender dysphoria, in which they feel they have a gender identity that is incompatible with their biological sex. When this gender dysphoria causes significant distress and affects social, occupational and other important areas of functioning, it may be diagnosed as gender identity disorder (GID). Only a modest amount of research is available on the aetiology of GID, but there is a known inherited element to the disorder, and some as yet unsubstantiated

evidence that abnormalities in brain areas associated with sexual behaviour can be found in sufferers. Treatment for GID is largely through a structured procedure ending in gender reassignment surgery, which attempts to alter the individual's biological sex. There are a few successful attempts in the literature to change gender identity beliefs, but GID sufferers usually prefer to change their biological sex rather than their gender identity beliefs.

SECTION SUMMARY

10.4 Gender Identity Disorders

● Some people develop a sense of **gender dysphoria**, in which they have a sense of gender that is opposite to their biological sex.

● **Gender identity disorder** (**GID**) is found in both adults and children, but childhood GID is only rarely a precursor of adult (GID).

10.4.1 Diagnosis and Description of Gender Identity Disorder (GID)

● Individuals with GID exhibit a strong desire to live as a member of the opposite biological sex, and this may lead them to acquire the physical appearance and mannerisms of the opposite sex.

● Lifetime prevalence rates for GID are very low, and are estimated to be 0.003 per cent in males and 0.001 per cent in females.

10.4.2 The Aetiology of Gender Identity Disorder

● There is relatively little evidence to suggest that GID is caused by imbalances in sex hormones.

● GID does appear to be highly heritable, but it not clear yet how the genetic component is either transmitted or manifested.

10.4.3 The Treatment of Gender Identity Disorder

● The vast majority of individuals with GID want to resolve their conflict between gender identity and biological sex by changing their biological sex rather than their gender identity.

● Changing biological sex is usually undertaken through a process of **gender reassignment surgery**, which ends in changing the person's basic biological features to be congruent with their gender identity.

● While the vast majority of those who complete gender reassignment surgery are satisfied with the outcome, up to 42 per cent of those who apply for gender reassignment surgery drop out before completing the treatment.

10.5 SEXUAL AND GENDER IDENTITY DISORDERS REVIEWED

Sexual behaviour is usually a central feature of our psychology. A satisfying sex life is an important contributor to quality of life, and our sexual urges and attractions can determine how we view ourselves and construct our self-identity. This being the case, it is not surprising that when we encounter problems related to sexual activity, it can be an important source of psychological distress.

Sexual dysfunctions represent a set of diagnosable disorders of the normal sexual cycle, and can be identified as problematic at various points in this cycle (namely, disorders of desire, arousal, orgasm and resolution). The causes of sexual dysfunctions are diverse and include biological and organic factors, psychological factors and interpersonal problems. At one time, open discussion and treatment of sexual problems was considered taboo; however, over the past 50 years, the liberalization of attitudes towards sex has encouraged the development of a range of treatments for such disorders.

In contrast to those who report problems with normal sexual performance, there are individuals who exhibit high frequencies of sexual activity that is triggered by or directed at inappropriate targets. These disorders are collectively known as the paraphilias. Some reflect sexual behaviour that becomes centred on unusual objects or stimuli (e.g. fetishes, transvestic fetishism), while others may involve non-consenting persons (e.g. paedophilia, exhibitionism, voyeurism). Some of these activities acquire their status as psychopathologies because they are associated with personal distress or impairment of normal daily activities (e.g. fetishes). Others are not necessarily associated with personal distress but are diagnosed as disorders because they are activities directed at non-consenting others. As such, these latter examples tend to represent criminal behaviours as well as diagnosable psychopathologies (e.g. paedophilia, exhibitionism). Much of the research on the aetiology of paraphilias has centred on those disorders that represent criminal activities or sexual offences, largely because of the need to help identify and treat such offenders. Treatments for paraphilia are also relatively underdeveloped, principally because of the problems involved in treating people whose behaviour represents sexual offending. Because a number of the paraphilias are sexual offences, much effort has been channelled into developing relapse-prevention procedures designed to reduce the probability of reoffending.

Finally, many individuals feel they have a gender identity that is incompatible with their biological sex, and this is known as gender identity disorder (GID). Both in childhood and in adulthood, such individuals experience gender dysphoria and will regularly refer themselves for psychological counselling. Because a large majority of those with GID are adamant that it is their biological sex they want to change (and not their incompatible gender identity), most opt for gender reassignment surgery in a radical attempt to make their biology compatible with their gender identity.

LEARNING OUTCOMES

When you have completed this chapter, you should be able to:

1 List the various types of sexual dysfunction, their place in the sexual cycle, and describe their diagnostic criteria.

2 Compare and contrast various theories of the aetiology of sexual dysfunctions.

3 Describe and evaluate both psychological and biological treatments for sexual dysfunctions.

4 Describe the basic characteristics of paraphilias and their diagnostic criteria.

5 Describe and evaluate both psychological and biological explanations for the aetiology of paraphilias.

6 Describe and evaluate behavioural, cognitive and biological treatments for paraphilias.

7 Describe the basic features of gender identity disorder and list the diagnostic criteria.

8 Describe and evaluate treatments for gender identity disorder.

9 Discuss some of the conceptual and ethical issues involved in defining and diagnosing sexual and gender identity disorders.

KEY TERMS

Androgens *375*
Anti-androgen drugs *378*
Castration anxiety *372*
Child rapists *370*
Cognitive distortions *373*
Couples therapy *360*
Covert conditioning *376*
Cyproterone acetate (CPA) *378*
Direct treatments *359*
Directed masturbation training *359*
Dyspareunia *352*
Exhibitionism *368*
Female orgasmic disorder *351*
Female sexual arousal disorder *350*
Fetishism *366*
Frotteurism *369*
Gender dysphoria *380*
Gender identity *380*
Gender identity disorder *381*
Gender reassignment surgery *381*
Hypersexuality *371*
Hypoactive sexual desire disorder *350*
Hypoxyphilia *368*
Implicit theories *373*
Incest *370*
Male erectile disorder *350*
Male orgasmic disorder *351*
Masturbatory satiation *376*
Medroxyprogesterone acetate (MPA) *378*

Oestrogen *358*
Orgasmic reorientation *376*
Paraphilias *365*
Partialism *366*
Paedophilia *369*
Penile prosthesis *361*
Performance anxiety *351*
Preference molesters *370*
Premature ejaculation *351*
Prolactin *358*
Relapse-prevention training *378*
Self-instructional training *361*
Sex Offender Treatment Programme (SOTP) *377*
Sexual aversion disorder *350*
Sexual dysfunctions *348*
Sexual masochism *368*
Sexual sadism *368*
Sexual skills and communication training *360*
Squeeze technique *359*
Stop-start technique *359*
Tease technique *359*
Testoterone *358*
Transvestic fetishism *367*
Vacuum erection device (VED) *362*
Vaginismus *352*
Viagra (sildenafil citrate) *361*
Voyeurism *369*
Yohimbine *361*

REVIEWS, THEORIES AND SEMINAL STUDIES

Links to Journal Articles

10.2 Sexual Dysfunctions

Binik, Y.M. (2005). Should dyspareunia be retained as a sexual dysfunction in DSM-V? A painful classification decision. *Archives of Sexual Behavior, 34,* 11–21.

Droupy, S. (2005). Epidemiology and physiopathology of erectile dysfunction. *Annales d'Urologie, 39,* 71–84.

Garber, B. (2005). Inflatable penile prostheses for the treatment of erectile dysfunction. *Expert Review of Medical Devices, 2,* 341–350.

Hartmann, U., Heiser, K., Ruffer-Hesse, C. & Kloth, G. (2002). Female sexual desire disorders: Subtypes, classification, personality factors and new directions for treatment. *World Journal of Urology, 20,* 79–88.

Hayes, R. & Dennerstein, L. (2005). The impact of aging on sexual function and sexual dysfunction in women: A review of population-based studies. *Journal of Sexual Medicine, 2,* 317–330.

Korenman, S.G. (2004). Epidemiology of erectile dysfunction. *Endocrine, 23,* 87–91.

Mercer, C.H., Fenton, K.A., Johnson, A.M., Copas, A.J., MacDowall, W., Erens, B. & Wellings, K. (2005). Who reports sexual function problems? Empirical evidence from Britain's 2000 National Survey of Sexual Attitudes and Lifestyles. *Sexually Transmitted Infections, 81,* 394–399.

Moynihan, R. (2006). The marketing of a disease: Female sexual dysfunction. *British Medical Journal, 330,* 192–194.

Najman, J.M., Dunne, M.P., Purdie, D.M., Boyle, F.M. & Coxeter, P.D. (2005). Sexual abuse in childhood and sexual dysfunction in adulthood: An Australian population-based study. *Archives of Sexual Behavior, 34,* 517–526.

O'Donohue, W.T., Dopke, C.A. & Swingen, D.N. (1997). Psychotherapy for female sexual dysfunction: A review. *Clinical Psychology Review, 17,* 537–556.

O'Donohue, W.T., Swingen, D.N., Dopke, C.A. & Regev, L.G. (1999). Psychotherapy for male sexual dysfunction: A review. *Clinical Psychology Review, 19,* 591–630.

Simons, J.S. & Carey, M.P. (2001). Prevalence of sexual dysfunctions: Results from a decade of research. *Archives of Sexual Behavior, 30,* 177–219.

Waldinger, M.D. & Schweitzer, D.H. (2005). Retarded ejaculation in men: An overview of psychological and neurobiological insights. *World Journal of Urology, 23,* 76–81.

10.3 Paraphilias

Abel, G.G., Gore, D.K., Holland, C.L., Camp, N., Becker, J. & Rather, J. (1989). The measurement of the cognitive distortions of child molesters. *Annals of Sex Research, 2,* 135–153.

Fagan, P.J., Wise, T.N., Schmidt, C.W. & Berlin, F.S. (2002). Pedophilia. *JAMA: Journal of the American Medical Association, 288,* 2458–2465.

Friendship, C., Mann, R. & Beech, A. (2003). *The prison-based Sex Offender Treatment Programme: An evaluation.* Home Office document 205. ISSN 1473-8406.

Kafka, M.P. (1997). Hypersexual desire in males: An operational definition and clinical implications for males with paraphilias and paraphilia-related disorders. *Archives of Sexual Behavior, 26,* 505–526.

Langstrom, N. & Hanson, R.K. (2006). High rates of sexual behavior in the general population: Correlates and predictors. *Archives of Sexual Behavior, 35,* 37–52.

Langstrom, N. & Zucker, K.J. (2005). Transvestic fetishism in the general population. *Journal of Sex and Marital Therapy, 31,* 87–95.

Laws, D.R. & Marshall, W.L. (2003). Masturbatory reconditioning with sexual deviates: An evaluative review. *Advances in Behaviour Research and Therapy, 13*(1), 13–25.

Ward, T., Hudson, S.M., Johnston, L. & Marshall, W.L. (1997). Cognitive distortions in sex offenders: An integrative review. *Clinical Psychology Review, 17,* 479–507.

10.4 Gender Identity Disorders

Coolidge, F.L., Thede, L.L. & Young, S.E. (2002). The heritability of gender identity disorder in a child and adolescent population. *Behavior Genetics, 32,* 251–257.

Hepp, U., Kraemer, B., Schnyder, U., Miller, N. & Delsignore, A. (2005). Psychiatric comorbidity in gender identity disorder. *Journal of Psychosomatic Research, 58*(3), 259–261.

Smith, Y.L.S., van Goozen, S.H.M., Kuiper, A.J. & Cohen-Kettenis, P.T. (2005). Sex reassignment: Outcomes and predictors of treatment for adolescent and adult transsexuals. *Psychological Medicine, 35*(1), 89–99.

Texts for Further Reading

Balon, R. & Taylor, S. (Eds.) (2005). *Handbook of sexual dysfunction.* New York: Marcel Dekker.

Bancroft, J. (Ed.) (1997). *Researching sexual behaviour: Methodological issues.* Indiana: Indiana University Press.

Eldridge, H. (1997). *Therapist guide for maintaining change: Relapse prevention for adult male perpetrators of child sexual abuse.* London: Sage.

Goldstein, I., Traish, A., Davis, S. & Meston, C. (Eds.) (2005). *Women's sexual function and dysfunction.* London: Taylor & Francis.

Seftel, A.D., Padma-Nathan, H., McMahon, G.F. & Althof, S.E. (2004). *Male and female sexual dysfunction.* New York: Mosby.

Ward, T., Polaschek, D. & Beech, A. (2005). *Theories of sexual offending.* Chichester: Wiley.

Wincze, J.P. & Carey, M.P. (2001). *Sexual dysfunction: A guide for assessment and treatment.* New York: Guilford Press.

RESEARCH QUESTIONS

10.2 Sexual Dysfunctions

- Sexual dysfunction is more prevalent in women than in men, but is this at least in part because men are more embarrassed by sexual dysfunction than women, and so report disorders less frequently?

- Is performance anxiety a cause or an effect of specific sexual dysfunctions?

- Are interpersonal problems a cause or an effect of specific sexual dysfunctions?

- Is depression an outcome or a cause of sexual dysfunction?

- SSRIs often help to alleviate sexual dysfunction – is this because SSRIs alleviate depression, which may be a cause of sexual dysfunction?

- Does anxiety contribute to sexual dysfunction by preventing allocation of attention to stimuli likely to provide sexual stimulation and pleasure?

10.3 Paraphilias

- Why are paraphilias overwhelmingly diagnosed mainly in men?

- Is hypersexuality a causal factor in the development of paraphilias?

- Are classical conditioning processes involved in the acquisition of paraphilias during early adolescence?

- Childhood abuse and neglect in sexual offenders is almost twice the level found in the general population. What role does childhood abuse and neglect play in the development of paraphilias that lead to sexual offending?

- Sexual offenders hold distorted beliefs that are consistent with their offending. Do these beliefs play a causal role in their offending or are they faked in order to diffuse responsibililty after the offence?

- What role do abnormalities in brain neurotransmitters – such as serotonin – play in paraphilias?

10.4 Gender Identity Disorders

- Do dysfunctional relationships with parents play any significant role in the development of gender identity disorders?

- Studies suggest that gender identity disorder is highly heritable. If so, how is it genetically transmitted and through what aspect of gender identity disorder is it manifested?

CLINICAL ISSUES

10.2 Sexual Dysfunctions

- Ethnic, cultural, religious and social background will affect beliefs about sexual activity, and clinicians must take this into account when considering a diagnosis of sexual dysfunction.

- Symptoms of sexual dysfunction can occur in the context of other Axis I disorders, and therefore need not necessarily represent a diagnosis of sexual dysfunction.

- Hypoactive sexual desire disorder represents a 'deficiency' of desire – and it is often difficult for a clinician to judge what constitutes a 'deficiency'.

- Dysfunction at specific stages in the sexual cycle can often have accompanying problems elsewhere in the cycle, with disorders of sexual desire affecting arousal, and failure of arousal also influencing sexual desire in future sexual encounters.

- Orgasmic disorders need to be diagnosed by also considering the client's age, and whether age has affected this aspect of sexual performance.

- Premature ejaculation is not unusual when aspects of the sexual activity are novel, and this must be taken into account by the clinician when making a diagnosis.

- There is currently debate about whether dyspareunia is a genuine sexual dysfunction or whether it more properly meets the criteria for a pain disorder.

- When making a diagnosis and selecting a treatment plan, the clinician needs to consider whether the sexual dysfunction is caused primarily by physical or medical conditions, or by psychosocial factors.

- Even when a sexual dysfunction is caused primarily by biological factors, it is likely that the disorder will generate associated psychological problems that require attention.

- A significant minority of men treated for erectile dysfunction with drugs (e.g. Viagra) dislike the side effects of the drug (headaches, dizziness) and prefer alternative mechanical solutions such as a vacuum erection device (VED).

10.3 Paraphilias

- Many of the urges and fantasies defined in the diagnostic criteria for paraphilias are experienced by many people. The clinician must decide when these urges and fantasies are recurrent enough to warrant a diagnosis of paraphilia.

- Many individuals with some paraphilias do not experience distress or remorse at their sexual activities, and so experiencing distress or psychosocial impairment is not a necessary condition for diagnosing paraphilias such as paedophilia, voyeurism and exhibitionism.

- Paraphilias are difficult to treat because many involve criminal activities that lead clients to be untruthful about their feelings and behaviours. They are also often comorbid with other psychopathologies, which further complicates treatment.

- Although aversion therapy is often used for the treatment of certain paraphilias, relapse rates are high if it is the sole form of treatment.

10.4 Gender Identity Disorders

- A diagnosis of gender identity disorder in childhood only rarely leads to this diagnosis in adulthood.

- It is unclear whether gender reassignment surgery solves all the problems associated with gender identity disorders because a substantial proportion of those who apply for gender reassignment surgery drop out of treatment before it is fully completed.

- The opportunity to develop integrated therapies for changing gender identity beliefs is limited by the fact that most individuals with gender identity disorder are adamant that it is their biological sex they want to change, not their gender identity beliefs.

11 | Personality Disorders

ROUTE MAP OF THE CHAPTER

This chapter begins by describing the 10 diagnostically independent personality disorders listed by DSM-IV-TR and considers whether they represent discrete psychopathologies or dimensional extremes of normal behaviour. It then discusses the diagnostic criteria for these disorders and describes studies that have provided data on their prevalence. The section on aetiology reviews the available evidence on how the different personality disorders are thought to develop, examining the childhood and adolescent predictors and risk factors that might help us to forecast personality disorders in adulthood. The chapter concludes with a description and review of the methods of treating people with a diagnosis of personality disorder, considering in particular the difficulties involved in such treatments.

My name is Claire, and I am a 28-year-old female. I have always known that something wasn't right with me, but over time I learned another survival technique called denial. I had my first suicide attempt at age 16 years old and was quickly yanked out of the hospital by a mother who undoubtedly knew that I was just 'putting on an act'. I had explosive rages at friends, family and even strangers. My first 'tantrums' as my mother called them began at age 1. I was never happy, never satisfied, always looking for that adrenaline rush to try and fill the void in my life. There was always, and to a certain degree still is, that missing piece of me. My pattern of unstable relationships was unbearable, love/hate, attracted/disgusted, happy/miserable . . . all or nothing. For a long time, I blamed my problems on other people. I would have times where I would dissociate during a rage when I was of school age only to be told in the office that I hit my best friend for no reason. After time my rages were only directed at strangers and my family. I only have two basic emotions – mad and madder. The consequences of anyone knowing that the pretty, talented, rich girl wasn't perfect were too steep. My mother made sure of that. I have had a few major depressive episodes and I have had only one more suicide attempt in adulthood. I have been on antidepressants for 5 years for help with depression but it has not helped with my intense mood swings in my interpersonal relationships. I consider myself now a low-functioning Borderline because I have not worked a steady job in about 4 years and I began to self-mutilate last year. I really didn't think that picking at my skin with pins and tweezers until I had gaping holes all over my body including my face was anything but a nervous habit.

CLAIRE'S STORY

(CLAIRE IS DIAGNOSED WITH BORDERLINE PERSONALITY
DISORDER AND BIPOLAR DISORDER)

Introduction

We all have personalities. Personalities may be described as enduring features of individuals that determine how we respond to life events and experiences; they also provide a convenient means by which others can label and react to us. To this extent, a personality is a global term that describes how we cope with and adapt and respond to a range of life events, including challenges, frustrations, opportunities, successes and failures. A personality is something that we inwardly experience ourselves and outwardly project to others. While personalities tend to be relatively enduring in their main features, most people evolve through their experiences and learn new and effective ways of behaving that enable them to adapt with increasing success to life's demands. In contrast, some people possess an ingrained and unchanging way of dealing with life's challenges. They rarely learn to adapt their responses or learn new ones. They develop a form of dealing with life events that is fixed and unchanging – despite the fact that they may have maladaptive consequences. They can also introduce disruption and hardship into the lives of others, and frequently cause emotional distress to themselves and those they interact with. Such characteristics are typical of individuals who are diagnosed with *personality disorders*.

> **Personality disorders**   A group of disorders marked by persistent, inflexible, maladaptive patterns of thought and behaviour that develop in adolescence or early adulthood and significantly impair an individual's ability to function.

Personality disorders consist of a loosely bound cluster of sub-types which have the following common features:

1 they are characterized by an enduring pattern of behaviour that deviates markedly from expectations within the culture;

2 they are associated with unusual ways of interpreting events, unpredictable mood swings or impulsive behaviour;

3 they result in impairments in social and occupational functioning;

4 they represent stable patterns of behaving that can be traced back to adolescence or early childhood.

Two of the most well-known of these disorders are borderline personality disorder (BDP), characterized by major and regular shifts in mood, impulsivity and temper tantrums and an unstable self-image, and antisocial personality disorder (APD), which is characterized by a chronic indifference to the feelings and rights of others, lack of remorse, impulsivity and pursuit of the individual's own goals at any cost. Individuals with APD are often labelled *sociopaths* or *psychopaths*.

In DSM-IV-TR, personality disorders are categorized as Axis II disorders because they represent long-standing, pervasive and inflexible patterns of behaviour. Individuals diagnosed with a personality disorder frequently deny their psychopathology, are often unable to comprehend that their behaviour is contrary to conventional and acceptable ways of behaving, and do not associate their psychological difficulties with their own inflexible ways of thinking and behaving. As a consequence, such disorders are very difficult to treat because they represent ingrained ways of thinking and acting.

Claire's Story at the beginning of this chapter describes the experiences and feelings of an individual with borderline personality

Plate 11.1

Two of the most common and severe of the personality disorders are antisocial personality disorder and borderline personality disorder. Behaviour patterns typical of these disorders have been prominently displayed by film characters.

The character played by Glenn Close in the film *Fatal Attraction* exhibited all of the main features of borderline personality disorder (BPD). After having a one-night stand with the character played by Michael Douglas, she is unable to let go of the relationship for fear of rejection, and her attempts to cling on to him become ever more extreme, impulsive and aggressive. Her character shows many symptoms of BPD, including (1) frantic efforts to avoid real or imagined abandonment, (2) unstable and intense personal relationships, (3) impulsivity and difficulty controlling anger and (4) depression and manipulative threats of suicide.

Antisocial personality disorder (APD) is a disorder closely associated with criminal activity, and many films have portrayed characters with the behavioural patterns typical of APD. The main characters in films such as *The Godfather* and *Reservoir Dogs* (especially the character Mr. Blonde, played by Michael Madsen) all show behaviour patterns typified by (1) failure to conform to social norms, (2) deceitfulness and lying, (3) impulsivity and rapid mood changes, (4) lack of remorse, (5) failure to empathize with the feelings of others and (6) remorseless manipulation and exploitation of others to achieve their own goals.

disorder. This account displays features that are common to a number of personality disorders. Claire exhibits frequent mood changes (mood lability), impulsive and aggressive reactions to situations, chronic depression, self-harm and suicide attempts, impaired occupational and social functioning, and an enduring disruptive pattern of behaviour that has been apparent from childhood into adulthood. As we will see later, many personality disorders are also associated with poor or unstable self-image and are frequently comorbid with acute Axis I disorders, particularly depression (both major and bipolar depression) and many of the anxiety disorders (Ehrt, Brieger & Marneros, 2003; Johnson, Cohen, Skodol, Oldham et al., 1999). In addition, the comorbidity of an Axis I disorder with a personality disorder makes the Axis I disorder significantly harder to treat.

Odd/eccentric personality disorders
Personality disorders grouped in Cluster A, the three sub-types of which are (1) paranoid personality disorder, (2) schizotypal personality disorder and (3) schizoid personality disorder.

Dramatic/emotional personality disorders Personality disorders grouped in Cluster B, including (1) antisocial personality disorder (APD), (2) borderline personality disorder (BPD), (3) narcissistic personality disorder and (4) histrionic personality disorder.

Anxious/fearful personality disorders
Personality disorders grouped in Cluster C which exhibit mainly anxious and fearful symptoms and are frequently linked to comorbid Axis I anxiety disorders.

DSM-IV-TR lists 10 diagnostically independent personality disorders, organized into three primary clusters: (1) *odd/eccentric personality disorders*, (2) *dramatic/emotional personality disorders* and (3) *anxious/fearful personality disorders*. These, together with their main features, are summarized in Table 11.1, and you should refer back to this table to check your knowledge when you have read this chapter.

Unlike many other psychopathologies we cover in this book, where a person is initially psychologically healthy and then develops an acute psychopathology

that can be successfully treated, personality disorders normally appear to endure from childhood and resist treatment. This has led some theorists to argue that personality disorders are not discrete disorders in the traditional sense but represent dimensional extremes of normal personality (Costa & MacRae, 1990). There is some evidence for this in that extreme scores on conventional measures of personality (such as the '5-factor' model; Costa & MacRae, 1990) are highly associated with personality disorders (Trull, Widiger, Useda, Holcomb et al., 1998). This finding probably resonates with our own intuitive view that we ourselves and many of the people we know exhibit to some extent and in some circumstances the traits that we might associate with personality disorders (e.g. mood swings, impulsive behaviour, paranoia, lack of social conscience). This suggests that personality disorders may not be *disorders* as such, but simply represent extreme cases on conventional personality dimensions.

Another conceptual difficulty with personality disorders is that many of them contain characteristics that overlap (e.g. impulsivity, poor self-image), and so there is a real temptation for clinicians to diagnose more than one personality disorder in a single individual (Grilo, Sanislow & McGlashan, 2002). Indeed, DSM-IV-TR often defines personality disorders in ways which allow a very heterogeneous group of individuals to be diagnosed under a single diagnostic label; for borderline personality disorder (BPD) in particular, there are almost 100 different permutations of symptoms that would result in a diagnosis. Nevertheless, while these issues are part of the ongoing debate about the validity of personality disorders as a diagnostic category (O'Connor & Dyce, 1998), there is no doubt that many individuals currently diagnosed with personality disorders experience extremes of distress (to the point of self-harm and suicide), suffer impairments in occupational and social functioning, and emit behaviour that can cause significant distress and inconvenience to themselves and others. As such, these seem reasonable grounds for clinical intervention.

Table 11.1 *Personality disorders: summary*

DISORDER AND PREVALENCE RATE IN GENERAL POPULATION	DEFINITION	MAIN DSM-IV-TR DIAGNOSTIC FEATURES	KEY FEATURES	THEORIES OF AETIOLOGY	MAIN FORMS OF TREATMENT
CLUSTER A (Odd/eccentric disorders)					
Paranoid personality disorder (2.5%–4.4%)	An enduring pattern of distrust and suspiciousness of others	Suspects others are harming/deceiving him or her Reads hidden threatening meaning into benign remarks Persistently bears grudges	External attributional style that blames others Higher prevalence rate in females than males	Psychodynamic approaches Schizophrenia spectrum disorder	Medication (e.g. antipsychotic drugs) Psychodynamic therapies
Schizoid personality disorder (1.7%–3.1%)	'Loners' who have very few close relationships and fail to express a normal range of emotions	Neither desires nor enjoys relationships Chooses solitary activities Shows emotional coldness and detachment	May be linked to autism in childhood	Psychodynamic approaches Schizophrenia spectrum disorder	Medication (e.g. antipsychotic drugs) Psychodynamic therapies

Table 11.1 *(Cont'd)*

DISORDER AND PREVALENCE RATE IN GENERAL POPULATION	DEFINITION	MAIN DSM-IV-TR DIAGNOSTIC FEATURES	KEY FEATURES	THEORIES OF AETIOLOGY	MAIN FORMS OF TREATMENT
Schizotypal personality disorder (0.6%–3%)	'Eccentric' behaviour marked by odd patterns of thinking and communication	Has odd beliefs or magical thinking that influences behaviour Unusual perceptual experiences Odd thinking and speech Excessive social anxiety that does not diminish with familiarity	Females tend to show positive symptoms while males show negative symptoms Highly comorbid with other PDs (particularly paranoid and avoidant) Has genetic and behavioural links to schizophrenia Exhibits attentional and memory deficits similar to those in schizophrenia Show abnormalities in frontal and temporal lobes and enlarged ventricles similar to those found in schizophrenia	Schizophrenia spectrum disorder	Medication (e.g. antipsychotic drugs)

CLUSTER B
(Dramatic/emotional disorders)

DISORDER AND PREVALENCE RATE IN GENERAL POPULATION	DEFINITION	MAIN DSM-IV-TR DIAGNOSTIC FEATURES	KEY FEATURES	THEORIES OF AETIOLOGY	MAIN FORMS OF TREATMENT
Antisocial personality disorder (APD) (0.7%–3.6%)	A pervasive pattern of disregard for and violation of the rights of others. Impulsive, irresponsible and dishonest behaviour	Failure to conform to social norms Deceitfulness and lying Reckless disregard for the safety of themselves and others Lack of remorse	Between 50 and 70% of males in prisons meet APD diagnostic criteria The best predictor of APD is a diagnosis of childhood conduct disorder There is a high incidence of APD in the parents of individuals with APD There is a higher concordance rate for APD in MZ than in DZ twins, suggesting a genetic component Individuals with APD show low anxiety levels, failure to learn from negative consequences and neurological impairments indicative of impulsivity	Antisocial behaviour and conduct disorder in childhood Familial factors Childhood abuse, conflict and neglect Genetic factors Dysfunctional cognitive schemas Physiological and neurological factors	Medication (e.g. atypical antipsychotic drugs) CBT Schema therapy Psychodynamic therapies Reasoning and rehabilitation treatment (R&R)
Borderline personality disorder (BPD) (0.7%–2%)	A pervasive pattern of instability of interpersonal relationships, self image and affects, and marked impulsivity	Frantic efforts to avoid real or imagined abandonment Unstable and intense interpersonal relationships Unstable self-image Recurrent suicidal behaviour, gestures or threats, or self-mutilating behaviour	Associated with depression, deliberate self-harm, suicidal ideation and impulsive behaviour such as drug abuse, physical violence and promiscuity Highly comorbid with Axis I mood disorders and anxiety disorders 75% of those diagnosed are female Between 60 and 90% of individuals diagnosed report childhood neglect and physical, sexual and verbal abuse Around 44% of individuals with BPD are also diagnosed with bipolar disorder BPD is also highly comorbid with major depression, panic disorder, social phobia, substance abuse disorder, eating disorders and PTSD May be a sub-type of APD	Childhood abuse, conflict and neglect Genetic factors Bipolar disorder spectrum Object-relations theory	Medication (e.g. antidepressants) Object-relations psychotherapy Dialectical behaviour therapy Psychodynamic therapies CBT Schema therapy

Table 11.1 *(Cont'd)*

DISORDER AND PREVALENCE RATE IN GENERAL POPULATION	DEFINITION	MAIN DSM-IV-TR DIAGNOSTIC FEATURES	KEY FEATURES	THEORIES OF AETIOLOGY	MAIN FORMS OF TREATMENT
Narcissistic personality disorder (0.8%–1%)	A pervasive pattern of grandiosity, need for admiration and lack of empathy	Exaggerated sense of self-importance Requires excessive admiration Is interpersonally exploitative Lacks empathy		Psychodynamic approaches Abnormal parenting styles	Psychodynamic therapies CBT
Histrionic personality disorder (1.8%–3%)	A pervasive pattern of excessive emotionality and attention-seeking. Behaviour is often dramatic	Uncomfortable in situations where he or she is not centre of attention Rapidly shifting and shallow expressions of emotion Shows self-dramatization and exaggerated expressions of emotion	Equally prevalent in males and females	Psychodynamic approaches	Psychodynamic therapies CBT
CLUSTER C *(Anxious/fearful disorders)*					
Avoidant personality disorder (1%–5%)	A pervasive pattern of social inhibition, feelings of inadequacy and hypersensitivity to negative evaluation	Avoids occupational activities that involve interpersonal contact Has fear of being shamed or ridiculed Views self as inadequate and socially inept	Highly comorbid with social phobia, and may be part of a broader social anxiety spectrum Having a family member diagnosed with either social phobia or avoidant PD increases the risk for both disorders two- to threefold Associated with avoidance behaviour generally Higher prevalence rate in females than males	Social anxiety spectrum Psychodynamic approaches	Psychodynamic therapies CBT
Dependent personality disorder (0.4%–1.5%)	Pervasive and excessive need to be taken care of. Submissive and clinging behaviour and great difficulty making everyday decisions	Has difficulty making everyday decisions Needs others to take responsibility for major areas of his or her life Feels uncomfortable or helpless when alone Has difficulty initiating projects because of lack of self-confidence	Characteristics fall into categories of (1) abandonment fears and (2) feelings of dependency and incompetence Higher prevalence rate in females than males Regularly comorbid with mood disorders, social phobia, obsessive-compulsive disorder and panic disorder	Object-relations theory	Object-relations psychotherapy CBT
Obsessive–compulsive personality disorder (OCPD) (1%–7.7%)	Exceptional perfectionist tendencies including preoccupation with orderliness and control at the expense of flexibility, efficiency and productivity	Preoccupied with details, rules, lists, order to the extent that the major point of an activity is lost Shows perfectionism that interferes with task completion Is reluctant to delegate tasks Shows rigidity and stubbornness	Only 22% of individuals with OCD are also diagnosed with OCPD	Abnormal parenting styles Obsessive-compulsive spectrum disorder	CBT

11.1 THE DIAGNOSIS OF PERSONALITY DISORDERS

The three primary personality disorder clusters described by DSM-IV-TR are (1) odd/eccentric personality disorders, (2) dramatic/emotional personality disorders and (3) anxious/fearful personality disorders (see Table 11.1).

11.1.1 Odd/Eccentric Personality Disorders (Cluster A)

The personality disorders grouped in Cluster A all have characteristics that resemble many of the symptoms of schizophrenia (see Chapter 7), but unlike schizophrenia sufferers there is no apparent loss of touch with reality and no experiencing of sensory hallucinations. However, people with Cluster A disorders may behave in ways that are indicative of delusional thinking (e.g. paranoid personality disorder) or exhibit rambling or poorly organized speech (e.g. schizotypal personality disorder). The three sub-types of Cluster A are (1) paranoid personality disorder, (2) schizotypical personality disorder and (3) schizoid personality disorder.

11.1.1.1 Paranoid Personality Disorder

Paranoid personality disorder
A personality disorder characterized by an enduring pattern of distrust and suspiciousness of others.

Those with *paranoid personality disorder* exhibit an enduring pattern of distrust and suspiciousness of others (see Table 11.2). They interpret innocent remarks as threatening and others' intentions as malevolent. They find 'threatening' hidden meaning in everything, and their distrust of others is pervasive and unchanging. If someone points out that their paranoid interpretation of events may be wrong, they will inevitably begin to distrust the person who brought this to their attention. As a result, individuals with paranoid personality disorder avoid close relationships, are often spontaneously aggressive to others, become preoccupied with their mistrust of others to the point of its severely disrupting their work performance, and often feel that they have been deeply and irreversibly betrayed by others, even when there is no objective evidence for this. Individuals with paranoid personality disorder even misinterpret well-intentioned and complimentary statements as criticism, such as interpreting an offer of help as implying that they are not doing a job or task well enough.

Because such individuals are hypervigilant for the potential malevolent intentions of others, they bear grudges, are quick to attack others for what are seen as critical comments, and gather trivial and often circumstantial evidence to support 'jealous' beliefs, especially about partners and colleagues. Because of their perceived need to defend themselves constantly against malevolent others, individuals with paranoid personality disorder need to have a high degree of control over those around them and are

Table 11.2 *DSM-IV-TR criteria for paranoid personality disorder*

A   A pervasive distrust and suspiciousness of others such that their motives are interpreted as malevolent, beginning by early adulthood and present in a variety of contexts, as indicated by four (or more) of the following:

(1)   suspects that others are exploiting, harming, or deceiving him/her;

(2)   is preoccupied with unjustified doubts about the loyalty and trustworthiness of friends etc.;

(3)   is reluctant to confide in others because of unwarranted fear that the information will be used maliciously against him/her;

(4)   reads hidden demeaning or threatening meanings into benign remarks or events;

(5)   persistently bears grudges;

(6)   perceives attacks on his/her character or reputation that are not apparent to others and is quick to react angrily;

(7)   has recurrent suspicions, without justification, regarding fidelity of spouse or sexual partner.

B   Does not occur exclusively during the course of schizophrenia, mood disorder with psychotic features or any other psychotic disorder.

"IT'S A CONSPIRACY. MY FAX, E-MAIL AND VOICE MAIL ARE PLOTTING AGAINST ME!"

Plate 11.2

frequently involved in litigious disputes. They also appear to deploy an attributional style that blames others for everything that goes wrong in their life (Fenigstein, 1996), and this external locus of control is very similar to the attributional style found in schizophrenics with paranoid delusions (Bentall, 1994).

11.1.1.2 Schizoid Personality Disorder

Schizoid personality disorder
A personality disorder in which individuals are often described as 'loners' who fail to express a normal range of emotions and appear to get little reward from any activities.

Individuals with *schizoid personality disorder* are often described as 'loners' who have very few, if any, close relationships with others (except perhaps a single first-degree relative) (see Table 11.3). They fail to express a normal range of emotions and appear to get little sensory or intellectual reward from any activities. They prefer to spend most of their time with themselves and choose jobs and pastimes that do not involve them in interactions with others (e.g. road sweeper or night watchman), although they can be quite successful and efficient at their jobs if they involve relatively little social contact with others. However, they seem to be largely unaffected by both praise and criticism, and prefer mechanical abstract activities – such as computer or mathematical games – to real-life experiences. It has been suggested that there may be some link between the symptoms of autism and a diagnosis of schizoid personality disorder. For example, the lack of emotional responsiveness and the tendency to be withdrawn and uncommunicative resemble the symptoms of autism, and there is some evidence that there may be a modest genetic link between autism and schizoid personality disorder (Wolf, 2000).

11.1.1.3 Schizotypal Personality Disorder

Individuals with *schizotypal personality disorder* usually exhibit 'eccentric' behaviour marked by odd patterns of thinking and communication,

Schizotypal personality disorder
A personality disorder characterized by 'eccentric' behaviour marked by odd patterns of thinking and communication.

and discomfort with close personal relationships (see Table 11.4). In particular, they often exhibit unusual ideas of reference, where they believe that unrelated events pertain to them, that they have extrasensory abilities or that they can influence events external to them in a 'magical' way. For example, they may believe that their partner taking the dog for a walk was a result of them thinking earlier that this needed to be done, or they may indulge in ritualized, superstitious behaviour such as walking back and forth past a lampost five times in an attempt to prevent harm from occurring to a friend or relative. Because of these magical beliefs, they will often become involved with unconventional groups interested in such topics as astrology, extraterrestrial phenomena such as alien abduction, and fringe religious groups. Their speech may have eccentric characteristics, be excessively rambling, and they may use words in unusual ways, although they are able to communicate information and do not exhibit the incomprehensible 'word salads' and derailment typical of schizophrenia (see Chapter 7, section 7.2.1.3).

Table 11.3 *DSM-IV-TR criteria for schizoid personality disorder*

A   A pervasive pattern of detachment from social relationships and a restricted range of expression of emotions in interpersonal settings, beginning by early adulthood and present in a variety of contexts, as indicated by four (or more) of the following:

(1) neither desires nor enjoys close relationships, including being part of a family;

(2) almost always chooses solitary activities;

(3) has little, if any, interest in having sexual experiences with another person;

(4) takes pleasure in few, if any, activities;

(5) lacks close friends or confidants other than first-degree relatives;

(6) appears indifferent to the praise or criticism of others;

(7) shows emotional coldness, detachment or flattened affectivity.

B   Does not occur excessively during the course of schizophrenia, mood disorder with psychotic features or other psychotic disorders.

Table 11.4 *DSM-IV-TR criteria for schizotypal personality disorder*

A   A pervasive pattern of social and interpersonal deficits marked by acute discomfort with, and reduced capacity for, close relationships as well as by cognitive or perceptual distortions and eccentricities of behaviour, beginning by early adulthood and present in a variety of contexts, as indicated by five (or more) of the following:

(1) ideas of reference (excluding delusions of reference);

(2) odd beliefs or magical thinking that influences behaviour and is inconsistent with subcultural norms;

(3) unusual perceptual experiences, including bodily illusions;

(4) odd thinking and speech (e.g. vague, circumstantial);

(5) suspiciousness or paranoid ideation;

(6) inappropriate or constricted affect;

(7) behaviour or appearance that is odd, eccentric or peculiar;

(8) lack of close friends or confidants other than first-degree relatives;

(9) excessive social anxiety that does not diminish with familiarity.

B   Does not occur exclusively during the course of schizophrenia, a mood disorder with psychotic features or another psychotic disorder.

CASE HISTORY 11.1

Schizotypal personality disorder

Ian is 23 and lives at home with his parents. He is unemployed. He spends most of his time watching TV, and often simply sits and stares into space. He says he just feels 'out of it' a lot of the time. He reports that he seems to see himself from outside, as if watching himself in a film and reading from a script. He has tried a few jobs, but never manages to persist at one for very long. At his last job, which was in a DIY store, several customers complained to the manager about Ian talking to them in a rambling and vague way – often about irrelevant things. This led to Ian being sacked from this job. Ian doesn't understand why people don't seem to like him and get along with him. He notices that people move away from him on public transport or avoid talking to him in queues, but nothing he seems to do or say changes this and he now tries to avoid interactions with others because they make him anxious. He has no close relationships and complains of feeling lonely and isolated.

Clinical Commentary

Ian shows many of the diagnosable symptoms of schizotypal personality disorder including unusual ideas of reference (feeling he is in a film), vague and circumstantial speech in conversations, suspiciousness and paranoia about others, a lack of close relationships, and feelings of anxiety in interactions with others. Currently, these characteristics have led to Ians being unemployed and leading the life of a relatively uncommunicative 'loner' who shows little emotion.

Individuals with schizotypal personality disorder find it very difficult to interact in normal social situations: they become anxious and may even develop paranoid symptoms. As a result they often have few, if any, close friends, they are often viewed by others as 'loners', and they tend to drift aimlessly and lead unproductive lives (Skodol, Gunderson, McGlashan, Dyck et al., 2002). Like all of the personality disorders, these characteristics appear to develop in early adulthood and persist over much of the individual's lifetime (see Case History 11.1).

There is a tendency for schizotypal personality disorder to manifest differently in males and females, with females tending to exhibit the positive symptoms typical of magical thinking and ideas of reference, while males tend to show more negative symptoms such as emotional withdrawal. Finally, one persistent problem with the diagnosis of schizotypal personality disorder is that it tends to be highly comorbid with the other personality disorders, in particular paranoid personality disorder and avoidant personality disorder (Morey, 1988), which suggests that there may be some common aetiological factors across these different disorders.

There is some evidence that the schizotypal disorder may be very closely related to schizophrenia. First, schizotypal personality disorder is found to be significantly more common in individuals who have biological relatives with schizophrenia than those who do not (Nicolson & Rapoport, 1999), suggesting a possible inherited link between the two. Secondly, schizotypal personality disorder is significantly more likely to be found in the offspring of individuals with schizophrenia than in the offspring of individuals diagnosed with anxiety disorders or no mental disorder (Hans, Auerbach, Styr & Marcus, 2004). Thirdly, some of the symptoms of schizotypal personality disorder can be successfully treated with antipsychotic drugs also used to treat schizophrenia (Schulz, Schulz & Wilson, 1988). And fourthly, cognitive studies have shown that many of the attentional and working memory deficits found in schizophrenia are also apparent in individuals diagnosed with schizotypal personality disorder (Barch, Mitropoulou, Harvey, New et al., 2004). This kind of evidence suggests that schizotypal personality disorder is closely related in many ways to schizophrenia, and may even represent a risk factor for schizophrenia (Nigg & Goldsmith, 1994) (see section 11.3.1.2)

11.1.2 Dramatic/Emotional Personality Disorders (Cluster B)

People diagnosed with dramatic/emotional personality disorders tend to be erratic in their behaviour, self-interested to the detriment of others, emotionally labile and attention-seeking. These are arguably the most problematic of the personality disorders in terms of the extremes of behaviour they generate and the emotional and personal distress they inflict on others. In this category we describe the symptoms of (1) antisocial personality disorder, (2) borderline personality disorder, (3) narcissistic personality disorder and (4) histrionic personality disorder.

11.1.2.1 Antisocial Personality Disorder (APD)

The fundamental feature of *antisocial personality disorder (APD)* is an enduring disregard for, and violation of, the rights of others. This begins in childhood (with a history of

> **Antisocial personality disorder (APD)**
> A personality disorder, the main features of which are an enduring disregard for, and violation of, the rights of others. It is characterized by impulsive behaviour and lack of remorse, and is closely linked with adult criminal behaviour.

symptoms of conduct disorder; see Chapter 15) and continues into adulthood. The behaviour of individuals with APD deviates substantially from what we would consider to be normal standards of social behaviour, morality and remorse, and is very closely linked with adult criminal behaviour. For example, a survey of prison populations in 12 Western countries found that 47 per cent of male inmates and 21 per cent of female inmates met the diagnostic criteria for APD; this is around 10 times the prevalence rate found in the general population (Fazel & Danesh, 2002). To be diagnosed with APD, an individual must be at least 18 years of age and display some of the following characteristics: (1) failure to conform to social and legal norms, (2) deceitfulness and impulsivity, (3) irritability and aggressiveness, (4) consistent irresponsibility (e.g. repeated failure to honour obligations) and (5) lack of remorse (see Table 11.5).

Sociopath   A person with a personality disorder manifesting itself in extreme antisocial attitudes and behaviour.

Psychopath   A term often used to describe individuals diagnosed with antisocial personality disorder.

The term *sociopath* or *psychopath* is sometimes used to describe this type of personality disorder. Such people are compulsive and persistent liars (Seto, Maric & Barbaree, 2001) who are self-centred to the point of happily gaining profit at the expense of others.

Table 11.5 *DSM-IV-TR criteria for antisocial personality disorder (APD)*

A   There is a pervasive pattern of disregard for and violation of the rights of others occurring since age 15 years, as indicated by three (or more) of the following:

(1) failure to conform to social norms with respect to lawful behaviours as indicated by repeatedly performing acts that are grounds for arrest;

(2) deceitfulness, as indicated by repeated lying, use of aliases or conning others for personal profit or pleasure;

(3) impulsivity or failure to plan ahead;

(4) irritability and aggressiveness, as indicated by repeated physical fights or assaults;

(5) reckless disregard for safety of self and others;

(6) consistent irresponsibility, as indicated by repeated failure to sustain consistent work behaviour or honour financial obligations;

(7) lack of remorse, as indicated by being indifferent to or rationalizing having hurt, mistreated or stolen from another.

B   The individual is at least 18 years of age.

C   There is evidence of conduct disorder with onset before age 15 years.

D   The occurrence of antisocial behaviour is not exclusively during the course of schizophrenia or a manic episode.

Some researchers have distinguished two types of trait in APD. The first is emotional detachment and selfishness in which the individual is remorseless and finds it impossible to empathize with the feelings of others. The second represents an antisocial lifestyle resulting from impulsivity and irresponsibility (Hare, Harpur, Hakistan, Forth et al., 1990). Individuals with APD show a disregard for the safety of themselves and others, and this is evidenced by their impulsive, often aggressive, behaviour and failure to plan ahead. Such individuals are frequently involved in motor accidents as a result of reckless driving (McDonald & Davey, 1996) or commit physical and sexual assaults (including spouse beating or child beating). Impulsivity and irresponsibility can be identified in the daily lives of individuals with APD, who may frequently quit a job without a realistic plan for getting another one, default on debts, or fail to provide child support or support other dependents on a regular basis.

Prior to 1980, APD or psychopathy was defined primarily by personality traits such as egocentricity, deceit, shallow affect, manipulativeness, selfishness and lack of empathy. However, with the introduction of DSM-IV, APD has been defined more in terms of violations of social norms. The reason given for this shift in emphasis is that personality traits are difficult to measure, and it is easier to agree a diagnosis on the basis of well-defined behaviours (such as aggressive behaviours or law-breaking) (Widiger & Corbitt, 1993). These well-defined antisocial behaviours are well represented in the DSM-IV-TR diagnostic criteria for APD (see Table 11.5). This shift in the diagnostic criteria has meant that APD has become very closely associated with criminal activity rather than being purely a psychopathology requiring treatment. Studies that have surveyed prison populations have indicated that the number of males in prisons who meet DSM-III-R or DSM-IV-TR criteria for APD range between 50 and 70 per cent (Fazel & Danesh, 2002; Widiger, Cadoret, Hare, Robins et al., 1996). This indicates that the changes to the diagnostic criteria for APD in DSM-IV-TR have moved this category more towards identifying criminals and criminal behaviour and away from identifying psychological factors that might give rise to such behaviour (such as lack of empathy, superficial interpersonal style, inflated sense of self-importance). There is a real possibility that this move towards defining APD in terms of antisocial activities could fudge the distinction between psychopathology in need of treatment and criminal behaviour in need of restraint. For example, in 1999, the UK Home Office and the Department of Health published a report that introduced a new term – *dangerous people with severe personality disorders (DSPD)*. The report recommended that individuals diagnosed with APD who have a diagnosis of at least one other type of personality disorder should not be released from prison or hospital if they represent a threat to the public, and they may be required to be detained indefinitely. This raises a number of difficult issues for clinical psychologists and others wishing to define the line between psychopathology and social deviance. These issues are discussed more fully in Focus Point 11.1.

Dangerous people with severe personality disorders (DSPD)   A term introduced in 1999 in a report by the UK Home Office and the Department of Health to describe individuals who are diagnosed with antisocial personality disorder and who have, in addition, a diagnosis of at least one other type of personality disorder.

Can we identify people who will behave violently in the future?

In July 1999, the UK Home Office and the Department of Health published a paper called 'Managing Dangerous People With Severe Personality Disorder', which described proposals that the government hoped would be effective in reducing the risk posed by people with dangerous personality disorders.

The report coined the term 'dangerous severe personality disorder (DSPD)', which has no medical, psychological or psychiatric definition and which many regard as a political intervention designed to address public concerns about crime and violence. However, DSPD seems to cover individuals with a diagnosis of antisocial personality disorder (APD) who may present a further risk to the public following release from secure hospitals or prison.

The government white paper recommended that individuals with severe personality disorders should not be released from prison or hospital if they are considered a risk to the public, and that powers should be provided for the indefinite detention of

people with DSPD. This has led to intense debate about the morality of detaining people who have not been convicted of an offence, purely on the basis of a psychological diagnosis.

It also raises questions about whether it is possible to identify individuals who will commit an offence or behave violently in the future, and whether it is possible to treat people with DSPD successfully. A study by Buchanan and Leese (2001) suggested that DSPD was loosely defined and that six people would have to be detained for a minimum of a year in order to prevent one of them from acting violently during that year. This raises two issues: (1) whether it is moral to detain individuals against their will who will not commit an offence and have not been convicted of an offence in the past; and (2) whether individuals should be detained purely on the basis of a psychological diagnosis.

After considerable pressure from mental health organizations, the UK government dropped the proposed bill in March 2006, but the questions surrounding it are ones that you might find useful to discuss with fellow students in seminars or discussion groups.

Source: Davey (2004)

11.1.2.2 Borderline Personality Disorder (BPD)

Borderline personality disorder (BPD)
A personality disorder, the main features of which are instability in personal relationships, a lack of well-defined and stable self-image, regular and unpredictable changes in moods and impulsive behaviour.

The cardinal features of *borderline personality disorder (BPD)* are an enduring pattern of instability in personal relationships, lack of a well-defined and stable self-image, regular and unpredictable changes in moods and impulsive behaviour. These characteristics are pervasive and will have endured from childhood into adulthood (see Table 11.6). All can be seen in the personal account given by Claire at the beginning of this chapter. In particular, individuals with BPD appear to have a significant fear of abandonment and rejection. This leads them to fall into close and conflict-ridden relationships after as little as a single meeting with someone; but they are just as likely to fall out with that person if they interpret the person's behaviour as uncaring or not attentive enough – and this may often be the case, because the feelings of the individual with BPD may not be shared by the other person (Modestin & Villiger, 1989).

Although their behaviour becomes unpredictable and emotional when their expectations for a relationship are not met, individuals with BPD are also riddled with fear about being rejected and losing that relationship. This leads to rapid, ill-tempered mood changes if individuals feel that things 'are not going their way'. The results of this emotional roller-coaster and fear of abandonment and rejection are: (1) regular and unpredictable shifts in

self-image characterized by changing personal goals, values and career aspirations; (2) prolonged bouts of depression (Lewinsohn, Rohde, Seeley, Klein et al., 2000), deliberate self-harm (Sansone, Wiederman & Sansone, 2000), suicidal ideation and actual suicide attempts (Davis, Gunderson & Myers, 1999); and (3) impulsive behaviour such as drug abuse (Trull, Sher, Minks-Brown, Durbin et al., 2000), physical violence and inappropriate promiscuity. Because of its close association with mood disorders, depression and suicide, some researchers have argued that BPD may well be a form of depression (Gunderson & Elliott, 1985), but in fact it is just as likely to be comorbid with Axis I anxiety disorders. Zanarini, Frankenburg, Dubo, Sickel et al. (1998) found that 96.3 per cent of individuals diagnosed with BPD met the criteria for a mood disorder (major depression, dysthymia, bipolar II disorder), but 88.4 per cent also met the criteria for an anxiety disorder, with panic disorder (47.8 per cent) and social phobia (45.9 per cent) being the most prevalent. Interestingly, 64.1 per cent met the criteria for substance abuse disorders, reaffirming the link between BPD and impulsive behaviour, whereas 53 per cent met the criteria for eating disorders. Another important finding was that BPD was comorbid with post-traumatic stress disorder (PTSD) in 55.9 per cent of cases, a finding that is consistent with the view of some clinicians that BPD may be a form of PTSD – especially since many individuals with BPD report a history of traumatic experience related to physical and sexual child abuse (Heffernan & Cloitre, 2000). At the very least, these data suggest that BPD represents a behavioural style that may put an individual at severe risk for a wide range of other psychopathologies.

Table 11.6 *DSM-IV-TR criteria for borderline personality disorder (BPD)*

A pervasive pattern of instability of interpersonal relationships, self-image and affects, and marked impulsivity beginning by early adulthood and present in a variety of contexts, as indicated by five (or more) of the following:

(1) frantic efforts to avoid real or imagined abandonment;

(2) a pattern of unstable and intense interpersonal relationships characterized by alternation between extremes of idealization and devaluation;

(3) identity disturbance: markedly and persistently unstable self-image or sense of self;

(4) impulsivity in at least two areas that are potentially self-damaging (e.g. spending, sex, substance abuse, reckless driving, binge eating);

(5) recurrent suicidal behaviour, gestures or threats, or self-mutilation;

(6) affective instability due to a marked reactivity of mood (e.g. intense episodes of depression, irritability or anxiety that lasts only for a few hours or a few days);

(7) chronic feelings of emptiness;

(8) inappropriate, intense anger or difficulty controlling anger (e.g. fraudulent displays of anger, constant anger, recurrent physical fights);

(9) transient, stress-related paranoid ideation or severe dissociative symptoms.

Table 11.7 *DSM-IV-TR criteria for narcissistic personality disorder*

A pervasive pattern of grandiosity (in fantasy or behaviour), need for admiration and lack of empathy, beginning by early adulthood and present in a variety of contexts, as indicated by five (or more) of the following:

(1) has a grandiose sense of self-importance (e.g. exaggerates achievements and talents, expects to be recognized as superior without commensurate achievements);

(2) is preoccupied with fantasies of unlimited success, power, brilliance, beauty or ideal love;

(3) believes that he/she is 'special' and unique and can only be understood by, or should associate with, other special or high-status people;

(4) requires excessive admiration;

(5) has a sense of entitlement (e.g. unreasonable expectations of favourable treatment);

(6) is interpersonally exploitative (e.g. takes advantage of others to achieve own ends);

(7) lacks empathy: is unwilling to recognize or identify with the feelings and needs of others;

(8) is often envious of others or believes that others are envious of him/her;

(9) shows arrogant, haughty behaviour or attitudes.

11.1.2.3 Narcissistic Personality Disorder

Narcissistic personality disorder
A personality disorder in which individuals overestimate their abilities, inflate their accomplishments, have a pervasive need for admiration and show a lack of empathy with the feelings of others.

Individuals with *narcissistic personality disorder* routinely overestimate their abilities and inflate their accomplishments, and are characterized by a pervasive need for admiration and a lack of empathy with others (see Table 11.7). Such people believe they are superior to others, and expect others to recognize this. They will constantly fish for compliments, and are likely to become angry when compliments are not forthcoming (Gramzow & Tangney, 1992). In their relationships they expect great dedication from others, and may often exploit others for their own gain. They have a lack of empathy for others and either cannot recognize or simply ignore other people's desires and feelings. Because of this, they tend to have a history of problematic relationships. Campbell (1999) found that individuals with narcissistic personality disorder tend to prefer partners who are openly admiring rather than openly loving. However, beneath the façade of bragging about their achievements and talents is a very fragile self-esteem: individuals with narcissistic personality disorder constantly need reassurance. When this does not materialize, they become angry and aggressive.

Because of the apparent lack of empathy and the tendency to exploit others for self-benefit, narcissistic personality disorder has been compared with antisocial personality disorder; indeed, it may be a sub-type of APD in that some features of the disorder (such as a grandiose self-image) predict future criminal or delinquent behaviour (Calhoun, Glaser, Stefurak & Bradshaw, 2001).

11.1.2.4 Histrionic Personality Disorder

Individuals with *histrionic personality disorder* are attention-seeking and uncomfortable or unhappy when they are not the centre of attention. Their

Histrionic personality disorder
A personality disorder in which an individual is attention-seeking and uncomfortable or unhappy when not the centre of attention.

behaviour is often dramatic and their language theatrical and exaggerated (see Table 11.8). For example, they may always seek to be the centre of attention at a party; if they are not, they may suddenly do something dramatic to gain attention (such as make up an intriguing story about themselves or someone else, or create a scene). Similarly, they will make extravagant expressions of emotion towards friends and colleagues and have a style of speech that is excessively impressionistic but lacking in detail. For example, they may describe someone as a 'wonderful person' but then be unable to describe any features that contribute to this assessment. As a result, such individuals are often viewed as shallow, self-dramatizing and easily influenced. They will draw attention to

Table 11.8 *DSM-IV-TR criteria for histrionic personality disorder*

A pervasive pattern of excessive emotionality and attention-seeking, beginning by early adulthood and present in a variety of contexts, as indicated by five (or more) of the following:

(1) is uncomfortable in situations in which he/she is not the centre of attention;

(2) interaction with others is often characterized by inappropriate sexually seductive or provocative behaviour;

(3) displays rapidly shifting and shallow expression of emotions;

(4) consistently uses physical appearance to draw attention to self;

(5) has a style of speech that is excessively impressionistic and lacking in detail;

(6) shows self-dramatization, theatricality and exaggerated expressions of emotion;

(7) is suggestible (i.e. easily influenced by others);

(8) considers relationships to be more intimate than they actually are.

themselves by exaggerating their illnesses (Morrison, 1989) or dressing provocatively or seductively. Because of their shallow and flirtatious nature, individuals with histrionic personality disorder often find it difficult to make lasting relationships, and this is frequently the main reason individuals seek therapy. Although there was traditionally a bias towards diagnosing this disorder more often in women than in men (Anderson, Sankis & Widiger, 2001), most recent surveys suggest that it is equally distributed across men and women (Mattia & Zimmerman, 2001). For example, the expression of histrionic personality disorder may be influenced by sex role stereotypes in which men with the disorder 'may dress and behave in a manner often identified as "macho" and may seek to be the center of attention by bragging about athletic skills, whereas a woman, for example, may choose very feminine clothes and talk about how much she impressed her dance instructor' (APA, 2000, p. 712).

11.1.3 Anxious/Fearful Personality Disorders (Cluster C)

As the name suggests, people with a personality disorder in this cluster exhibit anxious and fearful behaviour. However, unlike the Axis I anxiety disorders, the anxious and fearful behaviour exhibited will have been a stable feature of individuals' behaviour from late childhood into adulthood, and it is usually not possible to identify a specific experience or life event that might have triggered this fear and anxiety. Anxious/fearful personality disorders may be comorbid with some Axis I anxiety disorders (e.g. social

phobia, panic disorder), where triggers for the latter can be identified. But the pattern of behaviour exhibited by individuals with anxious/fearful personality disorders generally tends to represent ingrained ways of dealing and coping with many of life's perceived threats. The three disorders to be described in Cluster C are (1) avoidant personality disorder, (2) dependent personality disorder and (3) obsessive-compulsive personality disorder.

11.1.3.1 Avoidant Personality Disorder

The main features of ***avoidant personality disorder*** are persistent social inhibition (characterized by avoidance of a wide range of social situations), feelings of inadequacy and hypersensitivity to negat-

> **Avoidant personality disorder**
> A personality disorder the features of which are avoidance of a wide range of social situations, feelings of inadequacy, and hypersensitivity to negative evaluation and criticism.

ive evaluation and criticism (see Table 11.9 and Client's Perspective 11.1). These tendencies appear in late childhood or early adolescence and are exhibited across a range of different contexts, including occupational and social contexts and in interpersonal interactions generally. Individuals with avoidant personality disorder are fearful of criticism, disapproval and rejection, and they automatically assume that others will be critical and disapproving. They will avoid school, work and all group activities because of these fears, and are unable to form close relationships unless there is an assurance of uncritical acceptance. They are generally shy, and cannot easily talk about themselves for fear of being ridiculed or shamed. They also have a clear bias for interpreting ambiguous information and comments in a negative way (e.g. someone saying 'I was surprised by the quality of your work' would be

Table 11.9 *DSM-IV-TR criteria for avoidant personality disorder*

A pervasive pattern of social inhibition, feelings of inadequacy and hypersensitivity to negative evaluation, beginning by early adulthood and present in a variety of contexts, as indicated by four (or more) of the following:

(1) avoids occupational activities that involve significant interpersonal contact, because of fears of criticism, disapproval or rejection;

(2) is unwilling to get involved with people unless certain of being liked;

(3) shows restraint within intimate relationships because of fear of being shamed or ridiculed;

(4) is preoccupied with being criticized or rejected in social situations;

(5) is inhibited in new interpersonal situations because of feelings of inadequacy;

(6) views self as socially inept, personally unappealing or inferior to others;

(7) is unusually reluctant to take personal risks or to engage in any new activities because it may prove embarrassing.

CLIENT'S PERSPECTIVE 11.1

Thoughts about avoidant personality disorder

'The way I see it, people like us (with avoidant personality disorder) were born with brains that were very sensitive to social situations. As a child I used to get so frightened and scared that I probably unconsciously decided to build up a defence system against terrible feelings in order to protect myself. I just instinctively knew I had to do something, so my personality was formed in a way designed to avoid the harm. I hated the fact that other kids would be out to criticize me, so I adopted avoidance as a defence system. I had very low self-esteem, so I didn't think anyone liked me anyway. So I tried to stay away from potentially harmful situations, and lived in a world of my own. When I was younger, my classmates used to tell me that at parties they would turn the lights down and dance, but I would sit in the corner playing with my bike-lights. I would often stay off school and read books all day – that would comfort me because I liked the stories. My real life became less important to me, and I didn't participate in social events apart from just trying to be pleasant when needed. As I grew older, I should have developed a different defence system, but I couldn't because I had become pretty much a social outcast, and the fear of being criticized and

rejected had got stronger. It was like I was in a vicious circle that I couldn't get out of.'

Clinical Commentary

In this personal account of avoidant personality disorder, the individual describes how her desire to avoid social encounters developed during childhood from a fear of being criticized (and possibly bullied) by her peers. When avoiding social encounters (e.g. by staying off school), she would reward these avoidance responses by indulging in enjoyable activities, such as reading stories she liked. At adolescence she discovers she has become something of a social outcast, and this maintains her low self-esteem and feelings of not being liked, which further maintains social avoidance. She shows a number of the symptoms of avoidant personality disorder, including avoiding activities that involve significant interpersonal contact because of fears of criticism, disapproval or rejection, a preoccupation with being criticized or rejected in social situations, and a view of herself as socially inept and personally unappealing to others.

interpreted as being critical or disapproving, even though the comments could equally be interpreted as praise). Individuals with avoidant personality disorder are particularly ill at ease with strangers, and will usually avoid interactions with strangers at all costs. As a result they are reluctant to take risks, engage in new activities or even accept job promotions that might involve greater responsibility and interaction with others.

People with avoidant personality disorder generally have low self-esteem, and will frequently feel angry at themselves for being withdrawn and not enjoying the apparent social rewards and intimate relationships experienced by others. As you can imagine, avoidant personality disorder has many features in common with social phobia (Chapter 5, section 5.2), and many individuals diagnosed with avoidant personality disorder also receive a diagnosis of social phobia (Widiger, 2001). However, individuals with social phobia tend to be made anxious by social situations where particular levels of performance might be required (e.g. making a work presentation or having a job interview), whereas the personality disorder is more associated with fear of personal interactions and social relationships generally, as well as the criticism and rejection that individuals believe will be associated with these types of experiences (Turner, Beidel, Dancu & Keys, 1986). In addition, there is some evidence that avoidant personality disorder is associated with avoidance behaviour generally: individuals diagnosed with the disorder show greater avoidance of emotion, novelty and other non-social events than non-sufferers (Taylor, Laposa & Alden, 2004).

However, some clinicians believe that antisocial personality disorder and social phobia are both components of a broader *social anxiety spectrum* (Schneier, Blanco, Antia & Liebowitz, 2002). There is evidence to suggest that: (1) the severity of the symptoms of antisocial personality disorder is significantly increased if it is comorbid with social phobia (Ralevski, Sanislow, Grilo, Skodol et al., 2005); and (2) there is a genetic link between the two disorders, demonstrated by the fact that if an individual is diagnosed with one of the disorders, first-degree relatives of that individual are 2–3 times more likely to be diagnosed with *either* of them (Tillfors, Furmark, Ekselius & Fredrikson, 2001).

> **Social anxiety spectrum** A spectrum of disorder proposed to include both avoidant personality disorder and social phobia.

11.1.3.2 Dependent Personality Disorder

Dependent personality disorder is characterized by a pervasive and excessive need to be taken care of that extends significantly beyond the caring relationships that most individuals have with one another (see Table 11.10). Individuals with dependent personality disorder exhibit submissive and clinging behaviour and have great difficulty

> **Dependent personality disorder** A personality disorder characterized by a pervasive and excessive need to be taken care of, submissive and clinging behaviour, and difficulty making everyday decisions without advice from others.

Table 11.10 *DSM-IV-TR criteria for dependent personality disorder*

A pervasive and excessive need to be taken care of that leads to submissive and clinging behaviour and fears of separation, beginning by early adulthood and present in a variety of contexts, as indicated by five (or more) of the following:

(1) has difficulty making everyday decisions without an excessive amount of advice and reassurance from others;

(2) needs others to assume responsibility for most major areas of his/her life;

(3) has difficulty expressing disagreement with others because of fear of loss of support or approval;

(4) has difficulty initiating projects or doing things on his/her own (because of lack of self-confidence rather than lack of motivation);

(5) goes to excessive lengths to obtain nurturance and support from others, to the point of volunteering to do things that are unpleasant;

(6) feels uncomfortable or helpless when alone because of exaggerated fears of being unable to care for himself/herself;

(7) urgently seeks another relationship as a source of care and support when a close relationship ends;

(8) is unrealistically preoccupied with fears of being left to take care of himself/herself.

Plate 11.3
From letters and biographies of Wolfgang Amadeus Mozart, it was assumed that he may have suffered from bipolar disorder because of periods of depression followed by bouts of mania. However, more recent analyses suggest he may have been suffering from dependent personality disorder because of his mood lability, impulsiveness and negative reactions to his wife's absences (Huguelet & Perroud, 2005).

making everyday decisions (e.g. what clothes to wear) without receiving advice from significant others. They are usually passive and allow others to make all important decisions for them, including where they should live, what job they should choose and how they should spend their free time. They have difficulty expressing disagreement with others and will often agree with things that they know to be wrong or inappropriate rather than risk losing the support and help of those they look to for guidance. They also go to excessive lengths to secure support and guidance from others, even to the point of taking on jobs and tasks that they find unpleasant. They will make regular self-sacrifices and tolerate verbal, physical and even sexual abuse in order to retain their relationship with those they are dependent on (such as the wife who tolerates her husband's infidelities, drunkenness and physical abuse because of fear of losing the support she needs or of being left to care for herself). Such individuals tend to be pessimistic and self-doubting, and belittle their own achievements. They will regularly 'tag along' with significant others in order not to be alone, and usually rebound from one relationship to another in order to ensure the continual care and attention they require.

The characteristics of dependent personality disorder appear to fall into two distinctive categories: (1) attachment/abandonment, in which the individual fears abandonment and constantly seeks attachment with significant others, and (2) dependency/ incompetence, in which the individual has constant feelings of incompetence which drives him or her to rely on others (Gude,

Hoffart, Hedley & Ro, 2004). Because of their self-doubting and over-dependence, individuals with dependent personality disorder often dislike themselves (Overholser, 1996), which may lead to depression, anxiety, eating disorders and suicidal ideation (e.g. Godt, 2002).

11.1.3.3 Obsessive-Compulsive Personality Disorder (OCPD)

Individuals with *obsessive-compulsive personality disorder (OCPD)* show exceptionally perfectionist tendencies including a preoccupation with orderliness and control at the expense of flexibility, efficiency and productivity (see Table 11.11). They stick to rules, work schedules and prearranged procedures to such a degree that the overall purpose of the activity is lost. Diverging from a pre-set schedule causes them significant distress, as does failing to achieve the highest of standards in the things they do, and their attention to detail and inflexibility will often annoy other people because of the delays and inconvenience this may cause. For example, they may hold up a work project by insisting that their component of the project has to be completed

> **Obsessive-compulsive personality disorder (OCPD)** A personality disorder in which individuals show exceptionally perfectionist tendencies including a preoccupation with orderliness and control at the expense of flexibility, efficiency and productivity.

Table 11.11 *DSM-IV-TR criteria for obsessive-compulsive personality disorder (OCPD)*

A pervasive pattern of preoccupation with orderliness, perfectionism and mental and interpersonal control, at the expense of flexibility, openness and efficiency, beginning by early adulthood and present in a variety of contexts, as indicated by four (or more) of the following:

(1)   is preoccupied with details, rules, lists, order, organization or schedules to the extent that the major point of the activity is lost;

(2)   shows perfectionism that interferes with task completion (e.g. is unable to complete a project because his/her own strict standards have not been met;

(3)   is excessively devoted to work and productivity to the exclusion of leisure activities and friendships (not accounted for by economic necessity);

(4)   is overconscientious, scrupulous and inflexible about matters of morality, ethics or values (not accounted for by religious or cultural identification);

(5)   is unable to discard worn-out or worthless objects even when they have no sentimental value;

(6)   is reluctant to delegate tasks or to work with others unless they submit to exactly his/her way of doing things;

(7)   adopts a miserly spending style towards both self and others; money is viewed as being something to be hoarded for future catastrophes;

(8)   shows rigidity and stubbornness.

CASE HISTORY 11.2

Obsessive-compulsive personality disorder (OCPD)

Jane likes to describe herself as a perfect mother. She takes pride in keeping an orderly household and attending all of her daughters' horse-riding events, while being office manager in an insurance company. She knows the schedules of each family member and follows rigid routines to make sure everyone gets to work or school on time. Jane gets very upset when her teenage daughters want to go out with friends at weekends or in the evenings. She says it takes away from their family time and all of her efforts and planning are wasted. She refuses to go out for the evening if this interferes with her planned weekly activities in the house. Her husband doesn't mind Jane planning his schedule but he does protest when he helps out with the household chores because she consistently complains that he hasn't followed her instructions properly. For example, if he does the shopping but does not get the right discounted items, Jane gets upset and accuses him of being careless and extravagant. Jane continually tells everyone that if she wants something doing properly, she has to do it herself, and she will religiously clean the house in exactly the same way every week – whether things are dirty and untidy or not.

Clinical Commentary

Jane exhibits many of the symptoms of OCPD and probably has the minimum four symptoms required for a DSM-IV-TR diagnosis, including: a preoccupation with details, rules, lists, order, organization or schedules to the extent that the major point of the activity is lost (e.g. she does the housework each week in exactly the same way regardless of whether this is necessary); she is excessively devoted to work and productivity to the exclusion of leisure activities; she is reluctant to delegate tasks or to work with others unless they submit to exactly her way of doing things; she shows rigidity and stubbornness; and she adopts a miserly spending style. From this brief case description you can see that Jane frequently gets upset and anxious about family life because of her rigid perfectionism (this may well lead to a comorbid diagnosis of generalized anxiety disorder; see Chapter 5, section 5.4). Her rigid and inflexible behaviour also puts severe strains on family relationships.

meticulously and in the way in which it was originally specified. Individuals with obsessive-compulsive personality disorder nearly always plan ahead meticulously and are unwilling to contemplate changes to their plan. This means that even hobbies and recreational activities are approached as serious tasks requiring organization and scheduling. For example, they will need to plan a visit to a restaurant well in advance, the menu needs to be checked to ensure that everyone will be happy with what is on offer, and the quality of the restaurant's service must be checked with friends who have been there or by consulting dining reviews. If this planning is disrupted (e.g. if the restaurant is closed when the party arrives), this will cause the individual considerable distress and a spontaneous alternative will be difficult for him or her to consider. If things are not done 'their way', this also causes distress. This may be taken to unnecessary extremes (such as asking a child to ride her bike in a straight line or telling people that there is only one way to wash dishes), and they will become upset or angry if people do not comply, although the anger is rarely expressed directly. Because of this they rarely delegate tasks, insisting on doing things themselves, and they often become viewed as 'workaholics'. Their perfectionist tendencies also mean that they often end up hoarding things rather than throwing them away, and they will adopt a miserly attitude to spending, believing that money should not be wasted. As a consequence, they often end up living at a standard well below what they can afford.

While these characteristics may seem very similar to the symptoms of obsessive-compulsive disorder (OCD) (see Chapter 5, section 5.5), there is very little overlap between the two, with obsessive-compulsive personality disorder having a prevalence of only 22 per cent in individuals diagnosed with OCD (Albert, Maina, Forner & Bogetto, 2004). OCD is distinguished by the presence of true obsessions and compulsions which are clearly extreme, ritualistic and maladaptive (e.g. hoarding things until it is impossible to walk through the house, or ritualistically checking that the house is secure to a point where this severely impairs normal daily functioning).

SUMMARY

While the different personality disorders we have discussed may seem to take quite contrasting forms (e.g. some represent withdrawn and avoidant forms of behaviour, some are characterized by behavioural and emotional lability and impulsivity, and others are characterized by intense fears of criticism, rejection and abandonment), they all represent enduring patterns of behaviour that we would consider to be close to the borderline of what is adaptive / maladaptive, normal / abnormal or culturally acceptable / unacceptable. Because the behavioural styles of individuals with personality disorders can be conceptualized as being on normal personality dimensions – albeit at the extremes of these dimensions (Costa & MacRae, 1990) – there is an issue about what it is that is 'disordered' or 'abnormal' about personality disorders. These issues are discussed more fully in Focus Point 11.2. A case can be put that it is not the behavioural styles of individuals with personality disorders *per se* that are pathological, but the behavioural and psychological *consequences* of these behavioural styles that put an individual at risk for more traditional psychological symptoms. Consistent with this view is the fact that most personality disorders are highly comorbid with Axis I disorders such as anxiety and mood disorders (Zanarini, Frankenburg, Dubo, Sickel et al., 1998; Marinangeli, Butti, Scinto, Di Cicco et al., 2000), and it is for these comorbid symptoms that the individual with a personality disorder first seeks or is referred for treatment. Now read Focus Point 11.2 before attempting the activity in Activity Box 11.1.

Plate 11.4
Individuals with obsessive-compulsive personality disorder (OCPD) often persist in an activity until its overall purpose is lost. They attempt to achieve the highest standards in everything they do, and their attention to detail and inflexibility often annoy other people because of the delays this may cause in finishing an activity or project.

SELF-TEST QUESTIONS

● Personality disorders generally consist of a loosely bound cluster of sub-types. What are the four common features of all personality disorders?
● What are (a) the three clusters of personality disorders listed in DSM-IV-TR; (b) the disorders listed in each cluster; and (c) their main defining features?
● Can you list the diagnostic criteria for: (a) antisocial personality disorder; (b) borderline personality disorder?
● Schizophrenia spectrum disorder, bipolar disorder spectrum and social anxiety spectrum are broader disorder categories associated respectively with which individual personality disorders?

What is 'disordered' about personality disorders?

We have already noted earlier in this chapter that there is some conceptual debate about the status of personality disorders. Are they simply extremes of quite normal personality dimensions, or do they represent categories where normal behaviour has become dysfunctional? We do know that behaviours typical of personality disorders tend to be enduring and unchanging over long periods of time from childhood and adolescence into adulthood. In this respect they are different to many other psychopathologies in that we are not easily able to identify points at which the personality style develops, nor can we identify events that might have precipitated these styles. This is quite unlike the discrete developmental stages that can be discerned for many of the Axis I disorders covered in this book. In addition, many of the individuals with patterns of behaviour that are diagnosable as personality disorders are reluctant to admit that their behaviour is problematic (e.g. borderline personality disorder, antisocial personality disorder, narcissistic personality disorder, OCPD). We shall see later that this is behaviour that often resists any form of treatment.

So why are personality disorders included in a book about psychopathology? The answer probably lies in an analysis of the consequences of the behaviour patterns in personality disorders. Many individuals with personality disorders refer themselves for psychological treatment because of factors that are a *consequence* of their behaviour patterns rather than because of the behaviour patterns themselves. Let's look at some of these reasons.

First, some individuals with personality disorders either find themselves unable to form any kind of lasting close relationship (e.g. schizoid personality disorder, avoidant personality disorder, BPD) or find that their close relationships are turbulent and problematic (e.g. paranoid personality disorder, APD, BPD,

narcissistic, histrionic and dependent personality disorders). These are the reasons that many of these individuals first seek therapy. An examination of their individual behavioural styles immediately shows why such individuals have difficulty forming lasting relationships, although this is far from immediately apparent to the individuals themselves.

Secondly, individuals with personality disorders often develop comorbid Axis I disorders associated with anxiety and depression, and it is for these comorbid disorders that such individuals first get referred for treatment. The rates of comorbidity in personality disorders are shown in Table 11.12. Anxiety disorders are common in schizotypal, borderline, avoidant and dependent personality disorders, while depression is common in borderline and dependent disorders. Once again, it is not difficult to see why these Axis I disorders develop in individuals with these particular types of behavioural styles. In many cases anxiety disorders develop because of intense fears of abandonment, criticism or rejection (borderline, avoidant, dependent and histrionic personality disorders) and depressive symptoms develop because of consistently experiencing loss or failure – usually in the context of relationships (e.g. borderline, dependent personality disorders).

Thirdly, individuals with a personality disorder may be referred for treatment because their behavioural style incurs significant risk of harm to either themselves or others. This is fairly self-evident in the case of antisocial personality disorder, where the individual's impulsive behavioural tendencies and willingness to remorselessly violate the rights of others often lead to a disregard for the safety of self and others and to the direct pursuit of physical violence as a means of achieving personal goals. In the case of borderline personality disorder, individuals' behavioural style can often lead to circumstances culminating in self-harm, drug abuse, suicidal ideation and suicide attempts, and it is for these factors that individuals seek or are referred for treatment.

Fourthly, the behavioural styles in a number of personality disorders significantly interfere with individuals' ability to achieve in the occupational and educational spheres of their lives. This is the case to varying degrees with most of the personality disorders, but specifically with antisocial, borderline and avoidant disorders. The failure to hold down a steady job or underachievement in academic performance is another reason why many individuals with personality disorders are initially referred for treatment.

It can be argued, therefore, that it is not the behavioural styles characteristic of personality disorders *per se* that are the subject matter of psychopathology, but the psychological and physical *consequences* that these behavioural styles frequently entail. A summary of the kinds of consequences of personality disorders that are relevant to psychopathology is given in Activity Box 11.1. When viewed in this way, the behavioural styles characteristic of personality disorders represent *risk factors* for more traditional psychological symptoms.

Table 11.12 *Comorbidity of borderline personality disorder and other personality disorders with Axis I disorders*

Axis I category	Axis I disorder	% Borderline personality disorder patients with other Axis I diagnosis	% Other personality disorder patients with other Axis I diagnosis
Mood disorders	Major depression	83%	67%
	Dysthymia	39%	25%
	Bipolar II disorder	10%	1%
Substance abuse disorders	Alcohol abuse/dependency	52%	45%
	Drug abuse/dependency	46%	42%
Anxiety disorders	Panic disorder	48%	20%
	Agoraphobia	12%	3%
	Social phobia	46%	19%
	Specific phobia	32%	15%
	OCD	15%	6%
	PTSD	56%	21%
	Generalized anxiety disorder	13%	3%
Somatization disorders	Somatization disorder	4%	0%
	Hypochondriasis	5%	2%
	Somatoform pain disorder	4%	2%
Eating disorders	Anorexia nervosa	21%	13%
	Bulimia nervosa	26%	17%

Source: Data taken from Zanarini, Frankenburg, Dubo, Sickel et al. (1998). Diagnoses were determined using DSM-III-R criteria, which may give rise to some inconsistencies in comorbidity rates when compared with the current DSM-IV-TR criteria.

ACTIVITY BOX 11.1

The pathological consequences of personality disorders

First, read Focus Point 11.2, which describes one particular view of how patterns of behaviour relevant to personality disorders can have specific psychopathological outcomes. These outcomes may give rise to specific Axis I symptoms, such as anxiety and depression, or to life stressors, such as failed relationships and poor educational or occupational achievements, that prompt the individual with a personality disorder to seek treatment. After reading the various diagnostic characteristics of the main personality disorders in section 11.1, see if you can fill in the specific personality disorders that may have the problematic behavioural styles and pathological outcomes listed below.

PERSONALITY DISORDERS	EXAMPLES OF PROBLEMATIC BEHAVIOURAL STYLE	PATHOLOGICAL CONSEQUENCE OF THE BEHAVIOURAL STYLE
	Behaviour that avoids potential relationships (e.g. withdrawal) or that disrupts relationships (e.g. confrontational, self-oriented behaviour)	Relationship problems: inability to form lasting relationships or turbulent or problematic relationships
	Behaviours associated with fear of rejection, criticism and abandonment	Development of Axis I anxiety disorders
	Behaviours associated with fear of rejection, criticism and abandonment	Development of comorbid major depression, self-harm, suicidal ideation
	Impulsive behaviour; aggressive, angry reactions; behaviours aimed at remorseless short-term self-gain	Behaviour incurs risk of harm to self or others
	Avoidance of interaction with others; emotional lability; consistent failure to honour obligations (irresponsibility)	Behaviour causes impairment in occupational functioning and educational underachievement

Answers

PERSONALITY DISORDERS	EXAMPLES OF PROBLEMATIC BEHAVIOURAL STYLE	PATHOLOGICAL CONSEQUENCE OF THE BEHAVIOURAL STYLE
Schizoid, avoidant, paranoid, antisocial, borderline, narcissistic, histrionic, dependent	Behaviour that avoids potential relationships (e.g. withdrawal) or that disrupts relationships (e.g. confrontational, self-oriented behaviour)	Relationship problems: inability to form lasting relationships or turbulent or problematic relationships
Schizotypal, borderline, avoidant, dependent	Behaviours associated with fear of rejection, criticism and abandonment	Development of Axis I anxiety disorders
Borderline, dependent, avoidant	Behaviours associated with fear of rejection, criticism and abandonment	Development of comorbid major depression, self-harm, suicidal ideation
Antisocial, borderline	Impulsive behaviour; aggressive, angry reactions; behaviours aimed at remorseless short-term self-gain	Behaviour incurs risk of harm to self or others
Most personality disorders, particularly antisocial, borderline, avoidant	Avoidance of interaction with others; emotional lability; consistent failure to honour obligations (irresponsibility)	Behaviour causes impairment in occupational functioning and educational underachievement

SECTION SUMMARY

11.1 The Diagnosis of Personality Disorders

- DSM-IV-TR lists 10 diagnostically independent personality disorders that are organized into 3 primary clusters (1) **odd/eccentric**, containing paranoid, schizoid and schizotypal personality disorders; (2) **dramatic/emotional**, containing antisocial, borderline, narcissistic and histrionic personality disorders; and (3) **anxious/fearful**, containing avoidant, dependent and obsessive-compulsive personality disorders.

- **Paranoid personality disorder** is characterized by an enduring pattern of distrust and suspiciousness of others.

- Individuals with **schizoid personality disorder** are often described as 'loners' who fail to express a normal range of emotions and appear to get little reward from any activities.

- **Schizotypal personality disorder** is characterized by 'eccentric' behaviour marked by odd patterns of thinking and communication.

- The main features of **antisocial personality disorder (APD)** are an enduring disregard for, and violation of, the rights of others. It is characterized by impulsive behaviour and lack of remorse, and is closely linked with adult criminal behaviour.

- The defining characteristics of **borderline personality disorder (BPD)** are instability in personal relationships, a lack of well-defined and stable self-image, regular and unpredictable changes in moods, and impulsive behaviour.

- Individuals with **narcissistic personality disorder** overestimate their abilities, inflate their accomplishments, have a pervasive need for admiration and show a lack of empathy with the feelings of others.

- Individuals with **histrionic personality disorder** are attention-seeking and are uncomfortable or unhappy when they are not the centre of attention.

- The main features of **avoidant personality disorder** are avoidance of a wide range of social situations, feelings of inadequacy and hypersensitivity to negative evaluation and criticism.

- **Dependent personality disorder** is characterized by a pervasive and excessive need to be taken care of, submissive and clinging behaviour and difficulty making everyday decisions without advice from others.

- Individuals with **obsessive-compulsive personality disorder (OCPD)** show exceptionally perfectionist tendencies, including a preoccupation with orderliness and control at the expense of flexibility, efficiency and productivity.

- Many personality disorders are highly **comorbid** with Axis I disorders such as anxiety and mood disorders (including bipolar disorder, major depression, social phobia, panic disorder and PTSD).

11.2 THE PREVALENCE OF PERSONALITY DISORDERS

There has generally been some uncertainty about the actual prevalence rates of personality disorders within the general population, stemming from issues to do with (1) reliability in the diagnosis of personality disorders (McGlashan, Grilo, Sanislow, Ralevski et al., 2005) and (2) potential gender bias in diagnosis of some of the disorders – particularly histrionic, borderline and dependent personality disorders (Widiger & Trull, 1993; Hartung & Widiger, 1998). Table 11.13 shows data from a selection of sources providing prevalence rates from both American and European studies. These data suggest that the prevalence rate for personality disorders in the general population is around 13–14 per cent, which make personality disorders one of the most common of the psychopathologies. From these figures, obsessive-compulsive, avoidant and paranoid personality disorders are the most common, with prevalence rates ranging between 2 and 7 per cent.

There are some significant gender differences in these prevalence rates: 75 per cent of individuals diagnosed with borderline personality disorder are female (Widiger & Trull, 1993), and risk of avoidant, dependent and paranoid personality disorders is also significantly greater amongst women than men (Grant, Hasin, Stinson, Dawson et al., 2004). There was also thought to be a significant gender bias in histrionic personality disorder, with women accounting for around 65 per cent of those diagnosed (Corbitt & Widiger, 1995). However, a change in the diagnostic criteria with the publication of DSM-IV from 'overly concerned with physical attractiveness' to 'consistently uses physical appearance to draw attention to self' appears to have rectified this imbalance to a point where epidemiological studies report no significant difference in rates between genders (e.g. Grant, Hasin, Stinson, Dawson et al., 2004).

There are also a number of risk factors for personality disorders, including (1) low socioeconomic class, (2) living in inner cities, (3) being a young adult and (4) being divorced, separated, widowed or never married (Torgersen, Kringlen & Cramer, 2001; Grant, Hasin, Stinson, Dawson et al., 2004). Childhood physical, verbal and sexual abuse is also a significant risk factor for developing a personality disorder (Johnson, Cohen, Brown, Smailes et al., 1999) – especially borderline personality disorder (Heffernan & Cloitre, 2000) – and significant levels of childhood verbal abuse increase the risk of a number of personality disorders, including paranoid, borderline, narcissistic and obsessive-compulsive (Johnson, Cohen, Smailes, Skodol et al., 2001). These findings suggest that childhood abuse may well be an important factor in the development of a personality disorder in some individuals. However, it is unclear whether other types of risk factors – e.g. low socioeconomic status, living in inner cities, being divorced, separated or never married – are causal factors in developing personality disorders or are simply outcomes of having a personality disorder.

Studies of individuals suffering from psychopathology suggest that individuals with personality disorders are amongst the most frequently treated by mental health professionals. In a study of psychiatric outpatients, Zimmerman, Rothschild and Chelminski (2005) found that slightly less than one-third of all psychiatric outpatients in their sample were diagnosed with at least one DSM-IV personality disorder. This is consistent with the fact that personality disorders are highly comorbid with other psychopathologies,

Table 11.13 *Personality disorders prevalence rates*

CLUSTER	PERSONALITY DISORDER	PREVALENCE RATE IN GENERAL POPULATION (DSM-IV-TR ESTIMATE)	PREVALENCE RATE IN GENERAL POPULATION (USA) (Grant et al., 2004)	PREVALENCE RATE IN GENERAL POPULATION (NORWAY) (Torgersen et al., 2001)
	ALL PERSONALITY DISORDERS		14.7%	13.4%
CLUSTER A (ODD/ECCENTRIC PERSONALITY DISORDERS)	PARANOID	0.5–2.5%	4.4%	2.4%
	SCHIZOID	'uncommon'	3.1%	1.7%
	SCHIZOTYPAL	3%		0.6%
CLUSTER B (DRAMATIC/EMOTIONAL PERSONALITY DISORDERS)	ANTISOCIAL	3% in males 1% in females	3.6%	0.7%
	BORDERLINE	2%		0.7%
	HISTRIONIC	2–3%	1.8%	2.0%
	NARCISSISTIC	<1%		0.8%
CLUSTER C (ANXIOUS/FEARFUL PERSONALITY DISORDERS)	AVOIDANT	0.5–1%	2.3%	5.0%
	DEPENDENT	?	0.4%	1.5%
	OBSESSIVE-COMPULSIVE PERSONALITY DISORDER	1%	7.8%	2.0%

particularly Axis I anxiety and mood disorders (Zanarini, Frankenburg, Dubo, Sickel et al., 1998; see Table 11.12), and it is usually the comorbid and more specific disorder that has brought the individual into treatment. This reflects the view that individuals with a personality disorder often see their behaviour as quite normal (because they have 'always' behaved like that), but what brings them to therapy are the more specific and distressing consequences of their behaviour such as unstable or turbulent relationships, sexual dysfunction, substance abuse, eating disorders, anxiety disorders such as panic disorder or social phobia, mood disorders, deliberate self-harm and suicide attempts.

Finally, because DSM-IV-TR defines personality disorders in terms of behaviour that 'deviates markedly from the expectations of the individual's culture' (APA, 2000, p. 685), we might expect some cultural differences in the rates at which different personality disorders are diagnosed. For example, in some countries it is seen as more acceptable for men to be domineering, demanding and competitive, while women might adopt more submissive and dependent behaviours (see Alarcon, 1996). In these countries we might expect behaviour patterns typical of antisocial or narcissistic personality disorder to be less prevalent in men, and histrionic, avoidant and dependent personality disorders less prevalent in women – because these behaviour patterns are considered to be relatively more acceptable. However, at present there is very little evidence to suggest that the prevalence rates of personality disorders do exhibit cultural differences, as might be predicted if the DSM-IV diagnostic criteria are strictly applied. More cross-cultural studies are required in this respect.

Some recent studies have identified ethnicity as a factor affecting rates of diagnosis of personality disorder. For example, Chavira, Grilo, Shea, Yen et al. (2003) identified significantly higher rates of borderline personality disorder in Hispanic than in Caucasian and African Americans, and higher rates of schizotypal personality disorder in African Americans compared to Caucasians. Grant, Hasin, Stinson, Dawson et al. (2004) also found ethnicity (being a native or black American) to be a risk factor for personality disorders. Once again, research on the issue of ethnicity and personality disorders is at an early stage, and the way ethnicity might influence the development of a personality disorder is still far from clear.

SELF-TEST QUESTIONS

- What is the estimated prevalence rate for personality disorders in the general population?
- Which of the personality disorders are more commonly diagnosed in females than in males?

11.3 THE AETIOLOGY OF PERSONALITY DISORDERS

Explaining the development of the extreme and enduring behavioural styles characteristic of personality disorders is still very much in its infancy. There will almost certainly be no overarching or all-inclusive theory of the aetiology of personality disorders because the different clusters represent quite different patterns of behaviour (eccentric behaviours, dramatic and impulsive behaviours, dependent and avoidant behaviours), so we might expect that different clusters, and indeed, different personality disorders, may be acquired in quite different ways. One characteristic is common to all personality disorders, however, and this is that the respective behaviour patterns are enduring and can be traced back to childhood and early adolescence. This suggests that either inherited or developmental factors may be quite important across all of the personality disorders. While there is some modest evidence for inherited factors in some disorders (e.g. Cluster A disorders, antisocial personality disorder, borderline personality disorder), many of the theories of aetiology focus on early development, and particularly on the role of childhood experiences and parenting styles on the development of personality disorders.

11.3.1 Odd/Eccentric Personality Disorders (Cluster A)

As we mentioned earlier, individuals diagnosed with Cluster A personality disorders have characteristics that resemble many of the symptoms of schizophrenia: they may have paranoid beliefs (paranoid personality disorder), be socially withdrawn with flat affect (schizoid personality disorder), or exhibit rambling or disorganized thoughts and speech (schizotypal personality disorder). As we shall see, these formalistic similarities between Cluster A disorders and schizophrenia have led researchers to argue that they are part of a broader *schizophrenia spectrum disorder*, and so have causes that are closely linked to the aetiology of schizophrenia itself

Schizophrenia spectrum disorder The combination of Cluster A-type personality disorders and schizophrenia.

SECTION SUMMARY

11.2 The Prevalence of Personality Disorders

- The prevalence rate for personality disorders in the general population is around 13–14 per cent, which makes them among the most common of the psychopathologies.

- Borderline, avoidant, dependent and paranoid personality disorders are more prevalent in **females** than in males.

- **Risk factors** for developing a personality disorder include (1) low socioeconomic status, (2) living in inner cities, (3) being a young adult, (4) being divorced, separated, widowed or never married, and (5) childhood neglect and childhood physical, verbal and sexual abuse.

(Siever & Davis, 2004; Bergman, Harvey, Mitropoulou, Aronson et al., 1996). Before we discuss the schizophrenia spectrum approach, let us briefly mention some other approaches to explaining Cluster A disorders.

11.3.1.1 Psychodynamic Approaches

For both paranoid and schizoid personality disorders, psychodynamic theorists have argued that the causes of these disorders lie in the relationships that sufferers had with their parents. In the case of paranoid personality disorder, parents may have been demanding, distant, over-rigid and rejecting (Manschreck, 1996), and the lack of love provided by parents makes the individual suspicious and distrustful of others (Cameron, 1974). In contrast, parents of individuals with schizoid personality disorder may have rejected or even abused their children, resulting in the child being unable to give or receive love (Carstairs, 1992). As we shall see later, there is certainly some evidence that individuals with personality disorders may have suffered childhood abuse and neglect (Johnson, Cohen, Brown, Smailes et al., 1999), so there is some support for this view.

11.3.1.2 The Schizoid Spectrum Disorder

There are four lines of evidence suggesting that Cluster A-type personality disorders are closely related to schizophrenia and make up a schizophrenia spectrum disorder. First, there is considerable evidence suggesting a genetic link between Cluster A disorders and schizophrenia. Studies have indicated that risk for all three types of Cluster A disorder is increased in relatives of individuals diagnosed with schizophrenia (Bernstein, Useda & Siever, 1993; Battaglia, Bernardeschi, Franchini, Bellodi et al., 1995; Nigg & Goldsmith, 1994). Even in adopted children whose biological mothers have been diagnosed with schizophrenia, there is a significantly higher risk of developing schizotypal personality disorder than if the biological mother was not diagnosed with schizophrenia (Tienari, Wynne, Laksy, Moring et al., 2003). All of these studies suggest a genetic link between Cluster A personality disorders and schizophrenia.

Secondly, individuals with Cluster A disorders have been shown to possess brain abnormalities that closely resemble those found in schizophrenia. For example, individuals with schizotypal personality disorder show abnormalities in frontal lobe and temporal lobe activation that are very similar to those found in individuals with schizophrenia (Siever & Davis, 2004). In addition, they exhibit the enlarged ventricles frequently found in the brains of schizophrenics (Buchsbaum, Yang, Hazlett, Siegel et al., 1997) (see Chapter 7, section 7.5.1.3), suggesting similarities in abnormal brain development across schizophrenia and schizotypal personality disorder.

Thirdly, individuals with Cluster A disorders (particularly schizotypal personality disorder) also exhibit some of the physiological abnormalities possessed by individuals with schizophrenia, including impairment of smooth-pursuit eye movements (see Chapter 7, section 7.5.1 and Research Methods Box 7.1) and inability to inhibit the startle response to weak stimuli (Siever, Haier, Coursey, Sostek et al., 1982; Cadenhead, Swerdlow, Shafer, Diaz et al., 2000). Fourthly, individuals with Cluster A disorders also show many of the deficits in cognitive and executive functioning exhibited by individuals with schizophrenia, including impaired working memory, episodic memory, spatial attention and reduced verbal IQ (Dickey, McCarley, Niznikiewicz, Voglmaier et al., 2005; Mitropoulou, Harvey, Zegarelli, New et al., 2005).

Taking all of these factors into account, there is strong evidence linking schizotypal personality disorder to the aetiological factors implicated in schizophrenia generally, and genetic evidence linking paranoid and schizoid personality disorders to the inherited risk component found in schizophrenia. All of this provides support for a schizophrenia spectrum disorder in which Cluster A disorders share aetiologies in common with schizophrenia.

11.3.2 Dramatic/Emotional Personality Disorders (Cluster B)

Some of the Cluster B disorders share a number of characteristics in common, such as impulsivity (antisocial and borderline disorders), lack of empathy (antisocial and narcissistic disorders), and emotional outbursts and aggressiveness (histrionic and borderline disorders), which suggests that there may be some common elements in the aetiology of these disorders. Indeed, certain theorists argue that some of the different Cluster B disorders may be different manifestations of a single underlying disorder with a common aetiology. For example, some researchers consider that antisocial personality disorder and borderline personality disorder are the same underlying disorder which manifests as APD in men and as BPD in women (Widiger & Corbitt, 1997), and that narcissistic personality disorder shares antisocial behaviour, deceitfulness and lack of empathy and remorse with APD. However, as we shall see, most of the research on the aetiology of Cluster B disorders has been directed at attempting to explain the development of the behaviour patterns in individual disorders.

11.3.2.1 Antisocial Personality Disorder

The main behavioural characteristics of antisocial personality disorder are impulsivity, aggressiveness, deceitfulness, lying, irritability, repeated irresponsibility and lack of remorse, and a history of criminal activity and childhood conduct disorder. As with all personality disorders, the theoretical challenge with APD is to explain why certain individuals develop these behavioural styles and why these behaviours are so enduring and resistant to change. Because APD is closely associated with criminal and antisocial behaviour, considerable effort has been invested in attempting to (1) identify childhood and adolescent behaviours that may help to predict later adolescent and adult APD (e.g. patterns of childhood antisocial behaviour or childhood abuse); (2) identify the developmental factors that may give rise to APD (e.g. factors associated with family and early environment); (3) ascertain whether there is an inherited or genetic component to APD; and (4) identify any biological or psychological processes that may be involved in APD (e.g. brain abnormalities or dysfunctional cognitive processes such as faulty beliefs). We will look separately at these approaches to understanding APD.

FOCUS POINT 11.3

Impulse-control disorders

Many of the personality disorders – especially Cluster B disorders – are characterized by impulsivity, including unpredictability in behaviour and aggressive outbursts. However, DSM-IV-TR classifies a number of impulse-based problems separately. These are known as *impulse-control disorders* and are characterized by the failure to resist an impulse, drive or temptation to perform an act that is harmful to the person or to others. There are five main impulse-control disorders:

- **Intermittent explosive disorder**: Discrete episodes of failure to resist aggressive impulses that frequently result in criminal assaults or destruction of property.
- **Kleptomania**: Recurrent failure to resist impulses to steal objects that either have little or no monetary or personal value (e.g. impulsive shoplifting).
- **Pyromania**: Recurrent patterns of fire-setting for pleasure, gratification or relief of tension.
- **Pathological gambling**: Recurrent and persistent maladaptive gambling behaviour that disrupts personal, family or vocational pursuits.
- **Trichotillomania**: Recurrent pulling out of one's hair for pleasure, gratification or relief of tension that results in noticeable hair loss.

In most of these disorders, individuals feel an increasing sense of tension or arousal before committing the impulsive act, then experience pleasure, gratification or relief when the act is committed. Following the act, individuals will often suffer regret or guilt, suggesting that they are aware that their behaviour is wrong but are unable to control it (known as *ego dystonia*).

Many of the impulse-control disorders are frequently comorbid with personality disorders. For example, in one study, 42 per cent of those diagnosed with kleptomania also met the criteria for a personality disorder (the most common were paranoid, schizoid and borderline) (Grant, 2004). However, impulse disorders are classified separately from personality disorders because they are also highly comorbid with a number of other Axis I disorders. Kleptomania and pathological gambling, for example, frequently co-occur with substance abuse disorders, and sufferers of both often have first-degree relatives who are themselves suffering from a substance abuse disorder (Grant, 2006; Dannon, Lowengrub, Aizer & Kotler, 2006). High rates of manic and depressive disorders have also been recorded amongst those with impulse-control disorders (Kim, Grant, Eckert, Faris et al., 2006), but it is not clear whether these mood problems are causes or effects of the impulsive behaviour. For example, pathological gamblers often begin to feel depressed as their financial losses mount and their personal relationships are disrupted. Alternatively, some individuals who are initially depressed may find compulsive gambling gives them an exhilarating 'buzz' that distracts briefly from the pain of depression.

A large-scale survey in the US estimated that the lifetime prevalence rate for impulse-control disorders was 24.8 per cent, with a median age of onset as early as 11 years of age (Kessler, Berglund, Demler, Jin et al., 2005). Given the growing importance of impulse-control disorders as a significant form of mental health problem, we will discuss two of these disorders in a little more detail.

Kleptomania

Those diagnosed with kleptomania steal regularly, impulsively, and will usually take items that have no financial or personal worth. Sufferers experience an often intense period of tension building up before the theft, then relief and gratification afterwards. Thefts are usually undertaken alone, they are not pre-planned, and stolen goods may often be returned after the event. Individuals with kleptomania are usually aware that the act of stealing is wrong and senseless, and feel guilty and depressed about their actions. Opportunistic shoplifting is one common form of kleptomania, but studies suggest that only around 5 per cent of those convicted of shoplifting meet DSM criteria for kleptomania (APA, 2000, p. 668). Kleptomaniacs have been shown to rate their feelings of inner tension before stealing as significantly higher than undiagnosed shoplifters, and they also exhibit significantly greater feelings of relief after the crime (Sarasalo, Bergman & Toth, 1997).

Pathological gambling

Pathological gambling appears to be a growing problem as the opportunities for regular gambling increase. A US study has estimated that around 3.4 per cent of adults can be diagnosed as pathological gamblers (Buckley, 1995), but the problem appears to be significantly greater among adolescents: UK, Canadian and US studies have revealed a prevalence rate that is 2–3 times higher in those under 18 years of age (Shaffer, LaBrie, Scanlon & Cummings, 1993). In the UK, 5 per cent of adolescent fruit machine gamblers meet diagnosable levels of pathological gambling (Griffiths, 2001).

Pathological gambling is persistent and usually disrupts personal, family or vocational pursuits. Sufferers often report seeking the excitement or state of euphoria associated with gambling rather than any financial reward, and will take increasingly greater risks and place significantly larger bets in order to maintain the excitement. Gambling is often reported as a way of avoiding dysphoric or depressed mood: individuals report restlessness and irritability when they are prevented from gambling. There are clear stages to the development of pathological gambling. The first stage often involves some moderate winnings that trigger the compulsion and fuel the excitement. The second stage is losing, where gamblers begin to 'chase' their losses by placing bigger and bigger bets. The final stage is debt, where gamblers begin to lie to family members about their activities, resort to criminal or antisocial behaviour in order to fund their impulsive behaviour (e.g. forging cheques, embezzling money from friends, family or work), and their family and occupational activities become disrupted by the pressing need to indulge in gambling activities. Pathological gambling must be distinguished from social and professional gambling, the former being defined not by the amount of money spent or lost but by the impulsiveness and uncontrollability of the behaviour.

Significant correlations have been found between the ease of access to or number of legal gambling opportunities and recorded cases of pathological gambling (Lester, 1994), which has caused concern over the introduction of new 'supercasinos' in the UK licensed by the Gambling Act passed by Parliament in 2005. Nevertheless, the growing awareness of pathological gambling as a significant mental health problem has led to the development of self-help support groups and prevention programmes – especially for adolescents. Gamblers Anonymous (GA) (www.gamblersanonymous.org.uk) is one form of self-help group that boasts some success in rehabilitating pathological gamblers. However, those who attend GA programmes have usually admitted their addiction and tend to be older, have larger debts, and have been gambling for many years (Petry, 2003).

Community-based prevention schemes for adolescents are also important. Their goals are to: (1) prevent gambling-related problems (e.g. reverting to crime to obtain money to gamble), (2) promote informed, balanced attitudes about gambling and (3) protect vulnerable groups (Shaffer & Korn, 2002). Clinicians have also developed a range of multifaceted therapeutic approaches to deal with gambling, combining CBT, social skills training and coping skills training (Echeburua, Baez & Fernandez-Montalvo, 1996). Recent outcome studies suggest that combining CBT with GA attendance has significantly better outcomes than GA attendance alone (Petry, Ammerman, Bohl, Doersch et al., 2006).

Childhood and Adolescent Behavioural Precursors of APD

Because APD is closely associated with criminal behaviour, and on many occasions with violent or homicidal criminal behaviour, there has been a keen interest in attempting to identify risk factors for APD. Identifying potential risk factors might allow clinicians to predict the development of APD from childhood behaviour patterns or childhood experiences. As we saw earlier, there have been some attempts at legislation to define ways of identifying, restraining and treating potentially violent criminals, even before they may have committed any crime. However, regardless of whether one believes this to be an appropriate approach to the problem (see Focus Box 11.1), identifying childhood antecedents to APD might identify individuals who may respond to early clinical intervention.

Because personality disorders are enduring patterns of behaviour that persist from childhood into adulthood, one of the best predictors of APD in adulthood is a diagnosis of **conduct disorder (CD)** during childhood in which the child exhibits a range of behavioural problems that include fighting, lying, running away from home, vandalism and truancy (Farrington, Loeber & van Kammen, 1990) (see Chapter 15, section 15.2.2).

Conduct disorder (CD) A pattern of behaviour during childhood in which the child exhibits a range of behavioural problems, including fighting, lying, running away from home, vandalism and truancy.

This, however, begs the question of how such antisocial behaviours developed in childhood, and we may have to refer back to ineffective parenting practices, discordant and unstable family life, poor peer relationships and educational failure to trace the origins of these behaviours (Hill, 2003). Persistent and aggressive behaviour before the age of 11 years is also a good predictor of APD in adulthood (Robins, 1966), as are early fighting and hyperactivity (Loeber, Green, Lahey & Kalb, 2000), and low IQ and low self-esteem (Fergusson, Lynskey & Horwood, 1996). In particular, Loeber, Wung, Keenan, Giroux et al. (1993) have argued that there are three pathways that predict APD in adulthood:

1 an 'overt' aggressive pathway that progresses from bullying to fighting to serious violence;

2 a 'covert' aggressive pathway that progresses from lying and stealing to more serious damage to property; and

3 an 'authority conflict' pathway that progresses through various degrees of oppositional and defiant behaviour.

Behaviours in the early stages of each of these pathways predict more serious specific antisocial behaviours later in life.

Some researchers have suggested that conduct disorder in childhood is not the only psychological diagnosis that predicts APD

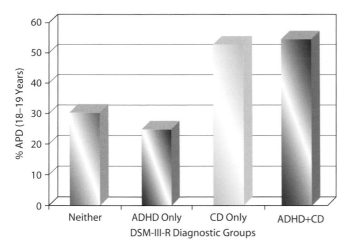

Figure 11.1
Lahey, Loeber, Burke and Applegate (2005) investigated whether a childhood diagnosis of conduct disorder (CD) or attention deficit/hyperactivity disorder (ADHD) predicted a diagnosis of antisocial personality disorder (APD) at 18–19 years of age. The results show that while around 50 per cent of those diagnosed with either CD or CD and ADHD went on to develop APD, ADHD did not predict subsequent APD any better than if a child had neither disorder.

in later life. Lynam (1998) has argued that children with hyperactivity/attention deficits (such as attention-deficit/hyperactivity disorder, ADHD) are 'fledgling psychopaths' who, because of their impulsivity and attentional problems, are likely to develop into long-term psychopaths – not least because their underlying

problems are of a neuropsychological nature and are likely to be resistant to behavioural treatments.

However, more recent studies based on structured diagnostic interviews do not necessarily support this view. Lahey, Loeber, Burke and Applegate (2005) investigated whether a diagnosis of CD or ADHD in males between 7 and 12 years of age predicted a diagnosis of APD at 18–19 years. While conduct disorder predicted subsequent APD in around 50 per cent of the participants, ADHD predicted APD at rates no better than if the child had neither ADHD or CD at ages 7–12 years (see Figure 11.1), suggesting that ADHD during childhood is not a significant differential predictor of APD in later life.

Other studies have emphasized that adolescent problem behaviours are strong predictors of adult APD. McGue and Iacono (2005) found that adolescent smoking, alcohol use, illicit drug use, police trouble and sexual intercourse (all before 15 years of age) each significantly predicted APD symptoms in later life. In fact, for those who exhibited four or more of these problem behaviours prior to age 15, there was a 90 per cent likelihood of subsequent APD diagnosis in males, and a 35 per cent probability in females.

Perhaps disappointingly, most of these studies merely indicate that adult antisocial behaviour defined by APD is predicted by adolescent and childhood antisocial behaviour. However, such studies do demonstrate that the behaviour patterns are enduring and that these behaviours during childhood and early adolescence should be taken as indicators of the possible need for intervention. For factors involved in causing APD we need to explore developmental, psychological and biological factors.

Developmental Factors There are a range of views about how familial factors might influence the development of APD. Because APD is an antisocial disorder, there has been much

FOCUS POINT 11.4

Predictors of antisocial behaviour and violent crime

As antisocial personality disorder is closely associated with criminal and antisocial behaviour, several efforts have been focused on attempting to identify childhood predictors of these behaviours. The hope is that being able to identify such individuals at an early stage may prevent crime, and enable either treatment or re-education programmes to be directed towards individuals at risk of developing APD.

Some childhood and early adolescent predictors of APD that have been identified include:

- a diagnosis of conduct disorder in childhood
- persistent and aggressive behaviour before age 11 years

- fighting and hyperactivity
- low IQ and low self-esteem
- persistent lying
- running away from home
- vandalism
- truancy
- discordant and unstable family life
- educational failure
- adolescent smoking, alcohol use, illicit drug use, police trouble and sexual intercourse before age 15 years
- having at least one parent diagnosed with APD
- coming from a background of family violence, poverty and conflict

speculation about how maladaptive socialization might have contributed to this pattern of behaviour. One important fact is the high incidence of APD in the parents of individuals with APD (Paris, 2001), suggesting that a significant developmental factor may be the learning of antisocial behaviours through modelling and imitation (although this may also indicate a genetic or inherited component – see below). For example, the children of parents with APD may often see aggressive and deceitful behaviour rewarded, especially if a parent has had a relatively successful criminal career. Alternatively, parents may have patterns of parenting which inadvertently reward their children for aggression, impulsivity and deceitfulness (Capaldi & Patterson, 1994). For instance, parents may try to calm down an aggressive or impulsive child by giving him or her toys or sweets – a reaction which is likely to increase the frequency of such behaviours rather than suppress them.

Parents may play a more discrete role in developing APD tendencies through the emotional relationship they have with their children. Psychodynamic explanations of APD argue that a lack of parental love and affection during childhood is likely to lead to the child failing to learn trust (Gabbard, 1990). This lack of love and affection can take a number of forms. There is evidence that individuals with APD come from backgrounds of family violence, poverty and conflict – including separation and divorce (Farrington, 1991; Paris, 2001). In such circumstances, the child is likely to have had little experience of positive emotional relationships and is more likely to have experienced conflict and aggression as a normal way of life. Finally, some studies have identified inconsistent parenting as being important in developing antisocial behaviours. Parents of individuals with APD frequently fail to be consistent in disciplining their children and also fail to teach them empathy and responsibility (Marshall & Cooke, 1999). At least one reason for this lack of consistency in parenting is that many of the fathers of individuals with APD also exhibit the disorder.

However, we must be cautious about how we interpret these developmental factors. They may not represent so much *causal* factors in the development of APD as failures and inconsistencies in parenting that are a *consequence* of having a child with severely disruptive and impulsive behaviour. We must also remember that because an individual with APD may have a parent with the disorder does not mean that he or she has learned such behaviours from the parent: the disorder may involve psychological and biological dysfunctions that may be inherited rather than learned (such as maladaptive physiological reactions that give rise to impulsivity and risk seeking; see below).

Genetic Factors There is clear evidence that APD appears to run in families. Apart from the developmental factors that may contribute to this effect, there is also the possibility that there is a genetic or inherited component to APD. Twin studies have demonstrated significantly higher concordance rates for APD in MZ twins than in DZ twins (Lyons, True, Eisen, Goldberg et al., 1995), and adoption studies have shown that incidence of APD in the adopted child is better predicted by APD in the biological than in the adopted mother (Ge, Conger, Cadoret, Neiderhiser et al., 1996). However, twin and adoption studies have also indicated that there are important environmental factors involved in the development of childhood antisocial behaviour and APD. The home environment and parenting behaviour of adoptive parents have a significant role to play in the development of antisocial behaviours in the adopted child, with conflict and violence in the adopted home contributing significantly to the development of antisocial behaviours in the adopted child (Reiss, Heatherington, Plomin, Howe et al., 1995). Adopted parents may also react to any inherited antisocial characteristics exhibited by the adopted child in ways which may compound their problems, for example by responding to antisocial behaviour in the child with harsh discipline, hostility and lack of warmth (Ge, Conger, Cadoret, Neiderhiser et al., 1996).

Cognitive Models Some recent models have argued that individuals with APD have developed dysfunctional cognitive schemas that cause their responses to various situations to be extreme, impulsive and changeable. For example, Young, Klosko and Weishaar (2003) have suggested that individuals with APD possess five important and relatively independent *dysfunctional schemas* that determine their responses and reactions. When responding to important events, they are assumed to switch quickly and unpredictably between schemas in a way that makes their behaviour appear impulsive and erratic. Young et al. proposed five important *schema modes* which, it is claimed, are developed as a result of abuse and neglect experienced during childhood (Horowitz, Widom, McLaughlin & White, 2001; Marshall & Cooke, 1999). The five dysfunctional schemas are:

> **Dysfunctional schemas** In personality disorders, a set of dysfunctional beliefs that are hypothesized to maintain problematic behaviour characteristic of a number of personality disorders (e.g. antisocial personality disorder and borderline personality disorder).

1 the Abandoned and Abused Child mode (generating feelings of pain, fear of abandonment and inferiority);

2 the Angry and Impulsive Child mode (where bottled-up aggression is discharged as anger);

3 the Punitive Parent mode (where individuals view themselves as having done something wrong, evil and worthless);

4 the Detached Protector mode (a state where individuals endeavour not to feel the pain and emotion caused by the first three modes); and

5 the Bully and Attack mode (where individuals hurt other people to overcompensate for, or to cope with, mistrust, abuse, deprivation and defectiveness) (Lobbestael, Arntz & Sieswerda, 2005).

The development of instruments to measure these various schema modes has shown that individuals diagnosed with APD do indeed score higher on measures of these five dysfunctional modes than non-clinical participants (Lobbestael, Arntz & Sieswerda, 2005). Individuals with APD are assumed to switch rapidly and unpredictably from a 'Healthy Adult' mode – where their behaviour appears normal – to pathological modes, particularly Angry and Impulsive Child mode and Bully and Attack mode. Because schemas such as these form part of the individual's normal way of thinking, the person with APD does not recognize them as faulty. If such dysfunctional schemas do represent important causal factors in the antisocial behaviour exhibited by individuals with

APD, then challenging and replacing these dysfunctional schemas may represent a useful starting point for treating the disorder (Beck & Freeman, 1990).

Physiological and Neurological Factors Individuals with APD show some interesting physiological characteristics that may help to explain aspects of their behaviour, such as their failure to learn from experience and their inability to empathize with the feelings of others. Firstly, they exhibit significantly lower levels of anxiety than normal control participants. This is exhibited as a relative inability to learn to avoid physically aversive stimuli such as electric shock (Lykken, 1957), lower reactivity and baseline levels of physiological indicators of anxiety such as skin conductance (Herperts, Werth, Lukas, Qunaibi et al., 2001; Hare, 1978) and a failure to exhibit increased startle reactions when being shown stimuli designed to elicit negative emotions (Levenston, Patrick, Bradley & Lang, 2000).

Secondly, individuals with APD regularly respond to emotional or distressing stimuli with slow autonomic arousal and appear to possess low levels of electroencephalographic (EEG) activity (Dinn & Harris, 2000; Lindberg, Tani, Virkkunen, Porkka-Heiskanen et al., 2005). This suggests that they may have difficulty maintaining normal daytime arousal and may also be able to ignore threatening or distressing stimuli more easily than most people. This in turn may explain why individuals with APD are unable to identify with the distress of others (see Figure 11.2; Blair, Jones, Clark & Smith, 1997), and may also be more risk-seeking than normal because of the need to experience higher levels of stimulation before they feel aroused (Hesselbrock & Hesselbrock, 1992).

Thirdly, individuals with APD frequently fail to show any signs of fear learning in aversive conditioning procedures (where, for example, a conditioned stimulus predicts the presentation of an aversive unconditioned stimulus such as an electric shock)

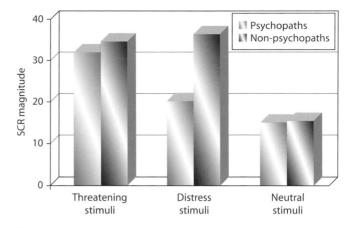

Figure 11.2
This study shows that psychopaths respond with lower magnitude arousal and anxiety responses to distressing stimuli than non-psychopaths (as measured by the magnitude of their skin conductance responses, SCR). This may help to explain why psychopaths and individuals with APD may not react emotionally to the distress of others.

Source: data taken from Blair, Jones, Clark & Smith (1997).

(Lykken, 1995). Functional brain imaging studies have shown that this failure to learn is accompanied by inactivity in the brain circuits believed to mediate fear learning (the limbic-prefrontal circuit) (Birbaumer, Viet, Lotze, Erb et al., 2005). These findings are consistent with the fact that individuals with APD usually fail to learn from experience about events that have negative outcomes, and they will continue to persevere with their ingrained set of responses in such circumstances.

RESEARCH METHODS IN CLINICAL PSYCHOLOGY BOX 11.1

Deficits in fear conditioning in antisocial personality disorder (APD)

A seminal study by Lykken (1957) suggested that individuals with what was then labelled as a sociopathic personality were unable to learn to avoid psychically aversive stimuli. This learning deficit may explain why individuals with APD are able to ignore threatening signals and also appear to lack the ability to learn from experience about events that have negative outcomes.

This learning deficit can be demonstrated in a simple laboratory-based conditioning experiment. Laboratory studies such as this often serve as good analogues of real-life learning situations.

A study by Birbaumer, Viet, Lotze, Erb et al. (2005) replicated Lykken's original study. The researchers used a differential aversive conditioning procedure in which male faces acted as the conditioned stimuli (CSs). For some participants, faces with a moustache were followed by an aversive unconditioned stimulus (US) (in this case a painful pressure applied to the hand or arm) (CS+), while faces without a moustache were followed by nothing (CS−). For other participants the painful US followed the faces without moustaches, and the faces with moustaches were followed by nothing (a counterbalanced procedure so that conditioning could not be affected by the specific features of the CS). See Figure 1.

Normally, participants would show signs of anxiety during the CS+ (as recorded by physiological measures such as skin

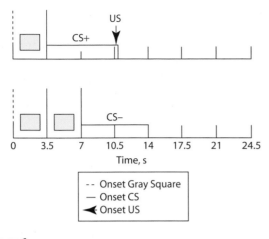

Figure 1

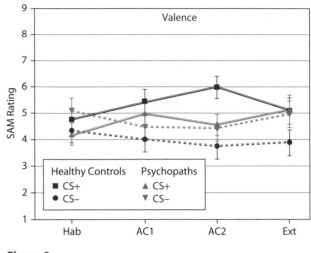

Figure 2

conductance levels), and would also rate the CS+ face as less pleasant than the CS– face. Birbaumer et al. compared the performance of 10 psychopaths (six of whom met DSM-IV criteria for APD) with 10 healthy control participants. Figure 2 shows the pleasantness ratings for CS+ and CS– for both groups. While the normal, healthy participants rated the CS+ as signi-

ficantly less pleasant than the CS–, the psychopaths showed no difference in pleasantness ratings even after 16 pairings of CS+ with the US (AC1 and AC2 in Figure 2), suggesting that they had failed to learn the significance of the aversive-signalling CS+.

A number of recent studies have also indicated that individuals with APD have impaired performance on neuropsychological tests of prefrontal cortex functioning (Dinn & Harris, 2000), areas of the brain that play an important role in inhibiting impulsivity. This

may represent a brain abnormality that contributes to the impulsive behaviour exhibited by such individuals. It may also help to explain some aspects of their antisocial behaviour by their apparent inability to inhibit inappropriate behaviours in social contexts.

SUMMARY

Predictive theories of the aetiology of APD are still very much in their infancy, but we have already learned some interesting facts about the kinds of factors that put an individual at risk for developing APD. APD appears to run in families, with a genetic element being involved and the family environment playing a significant role. Children raised in families low on parental love, with inconsistent or violent parenting or with parental conflict, are more likely to develop APD, as are individuals who have suffered childhood abuse or neglect. Individuals with APD also appear to have dysfunctional cognitive schemas that lead them to behave either aggressively or impulsively. However, we still need to discover whether there is a link between the development of these dysfunctional schemas and their early

experiences. Finally, individuals with APD show a number of physiological and neurological characteristics, such as physiological indicators of low anxiety, low levels of baseline arousal and reactivity, lack of learning in simple aversive conditioning procedures, and neurological impairments indicative of impulsivity. These characteristics all appear to be consistent with the behavioural characteristics of APD (such as aggressive and impulsive behaviour, lack of empathy and failure to learn acceptable adaptive responses), but we are still unclear about whether these physiological and neurological indicators are true *causes* of APD or whether they are simply *correlates* of behaviour patterns that have been acquired in other ways (such as through childhood experiences).

11.3.2.2 Borderline Personality Disorder

Individuals with BPD exhibit a wide range of behavioural and psychological problems including fear of abandonment and rejection, unpredictable mood swings, impulsivity, and frequent and prolonged bouts of depression often associated with suicidal ideation, self-harm and suicide attempts. This is a diverse range of characteristics for a single theory to encompass, without even considering the fact that BPD is commonly comorbid with at least one or more Axis I disorder (see section 11.1.2.2). As we shall see below, theories developed to address the aetiology of BPD often try to explain the development of one aspect of the disorder, such as fear of abandonment, mood lability or impulsivity. However, it is worth starting this section with an overview of some of the risk factors that predict the development of BPD before moving on to more specific biological and psychological theories.

Risk Factors for Borderline Personality Disorder Many studies have reported that individuals with BPD report a history of difficulties in childhood, many associated with problematic parenting. These include childhood physical, verbal and sexual abuse (Herman, Perry & van der Kolk, 1989; Zanarini, Williams, Lewis, Reich et al., 1997), childhood neglect or rejection (Zanarini, Frankenburg, Reich et al., 2000; Guttman, 2002), inconsistent or loveless parenting (Kernberg, 1985), and inappropriate parental behaviour such as persistent substance and alcohol abuse or promiscuity (Graybar & Boutilier, 2002). Individuals with BPD report rates of childhood physical, sexual and verbal abuse and neglect ranging from 60 to 90 per cent (Gabbard, 1990), including 67–87 per cent for sexual abuse (Bryer, Nelson, Miller & Krol, 1987). Herman, Perry and van der Kolk (1989) found rates of 71 per cent for physical abuse amongst people diagnosed with BPD compared to only 38 per cent amongst psychiatric patients who had not been diagnosed with BPD.

Other studies have identified a number of developmental antecedents of BPD, including abuse, neglect, environmental instability, paternal psychopathology and academic underachievement and low intelligence and artistic skills (Helgeland & Torgersen, 2004). However, despite these developmental risk factors being significant predictors of BPD, we must remember that around 20 per cent of individuals who develop BPD have never reported experiencing childhood abuse or neglect (Graybar & Boutilier, 2002), so such experiences are not a *necessary* condition for developing BPD.

Biological Theories of Borderline Personality Disorder Biological theories cover genetic factors, brain and neurological abnormalities, and biological contributions to impulsivity. First, there is some modest evidence for a genetic component to BPD. The disorder does appear to run in families (Baron, Risch, Levitt & Gruen, 1985), and twin studies have indicated concordance rates of 35 per cent and 7 per cent for MZ and DZ twins respectively (Torgersen, Lygren, Oien, Skre et al., 2000). Genetic analyses have also indicated that traits common in BPD, such as neuroticism and emotional dysregulation (labile moods and unpredictable rapid mood changes), have a strong inherited component (Nigg &

Goldsmith, 1994; Livesley, Jang & Vernon, 1998). More recent research has linked BPD with bipolar disorder, and the two are often comorbid (Smith, Muir & Blackwood, 2004). Deltito, Martin, Riefkohl, Austria et al. (2001) have estimated that around 44 per cent of individuals with BPD belong to a broader ***bipolar disorder spectrum***, which may help to account for their regular and unpredictable mood changes. Because we already know that there is a significant genetic component to bipolar disorder (see Chapter 6, section 6.3.1.1), this provides circumstantial evidence for a genetic component to at least some of the symptoms characteristic of BPD.

> **Bipolar disorder spectrum** A proposed spectrum of disorder encompassing both bipolar disorder and borderline personality disorder.

Secondly, evidence suggests that individuals with BPD have a number of brain abnormalities that may give rise to impulsive behaviour. They tend to possess relatively low levels of the brain neurotransmitter serotonin, which is associated with impulsivity (Norra, Mrazek, Tuchtenhagen, Gobbele et al., 2003), and this may account for their regular bouts of depression (see Chapter 6, section 6.3.1.3). There is also some evidence for dysfunction in brain ***dopamine*** activity in BPD: dopamine activity is known to play an important role in emotion information processing, impulse control and cognition (Friedel, 2004). However, much of this evidence is currently circumstantial and derives mainly from the fact that administration of drugs that influence serotonin and dopamine activity also appear to influence BPD symptoms.

> **Dopamine** A compound that exists in the body as a neurotransmitter and as a precursor of other substances including adrenalin.

Thirdly, neuroimaging techniques used with individuals with BPD have revealed abnormalities in a number of brain areas, primarily in frontal lobe functioning and in the limbic system, including the hippocampus and amygdala (Juengling, Schmahl, Hesslinger, Ebert et al., 2003; Soloff, Meltzer, Becker, Greer et al., 2003). The frontal lobes are thought to play a significant role in impulsive behaviour, while the amygdala is an important part of the brain system controlling and regulating emotion, and these abnormalities may contribute to some of the defining behavioural features of BPD. Nevertheless, while these abnormalities are important correlates of BPD symptoms, it is still far from clear whether they represent a *consequence* of the disorder or a genetically or developmentally determined *cause* of the disorder (Lieb, Zanarini, Schmahl, Linehan et al., 2004).

Psychological Theories of Borderline Personality Disorder We have seen that a majority of individuals with BPD report experiencing relatively high levels of childhood abuse and difficult or neglectful parenting. A number of psychological theories of BPD thus attempt to explain how these experiences cause the behavioural and emotional problems characteristic of the disorder.

Some forms of psychodynamic theory, such as ***object relations theory***, argue that

> **Object relations theory** A theory which argues that individuals with borderline personality disorder have received inadequate support and love from important others (such as parents), resulting in an insecure ego which is likely to lead to lack of self-esteem and fear of rejection.

people are motivated to respond to the world through the perspectives they have learned from important other people in their developmental past. However, if these significant others have offered only inadequate support and love, or have in fact been actively abusive, then this is likely to cause the child to develop an insecure ego, which is likely to lead to lack of self-esteem, increased dependence and a fear of separation and rejection – all central features of BPD (Bartholomew, Kwong & Hart, 2001; Kernberg, 1985). Object relations theory also argues that individuals with weak egos engage in a defence mechanism called *splitting*, which means that they evaluate people, events or things in a completely black or white way, often judging people as either good or bad with no shades of grey. This may give rise to their difficulties with relationships, where their all-or-none assessments mean that someone they evaluate as 'good' can just as quickly become 'bad' on the basis of a single act or statement (e.g. if a partner does not return from a work social event at exactly the time he said he would, the individual with BDP is likely to respond with anger and threaten to withdraw from the relationship). While object relations theory is consistent with the fact that a majority of individuals with BPD have experienced childhood abuse, conflict and neglect, one problem is that such experiences are common features of many of the personality disorders (including antisocial, paranoid, narcissistic and obsessive-compulsive personality disorders) (Klonsky, Oltmanns, Turkheimer & Fiedler, 2000). This being the case, an account such as object relations theory does not easily explain how such negative early experiences get translated into BPD rather than other disorders that also have such experiences as part of their history.

> **Splitting** An element of object relations theory which argues that individuals with weak egos engage in a defence mechanism by which they evaluate people, events or things in a completely black or white way, often judging people as either good or bad with no shades of grey.

We have already noted the high levels of comorbidity between the different personality disorders (Marinangeli, Butti, Scinto, Di Cicco et al., 2000). In particular, between 10 and 47 per cent of individuals with BPD also display antisocial behaviour and meet the diagnostic criteria for antisocial personality disorder (APD) (Zanarini, Frankenburg, Dubo, Sickel et al., 1998). This suggests that there may be some commonality of aetiology between the two disorders, and indeed we have already noted that significant childhood abuse and neglect is apparent in both groups. This has led Young, Klosko and Weishaar (2003) to suggest that individuals with BPD may develop a similar set of dysfunctional schema modes to those acquired by individuals with APD, which we have described above (section 11.3.2.1). Young et al. have argued that these dysfunctional schemas also determine reactions to events in individuals with BDP. Subsequent studies have confirmed that individuals with APD and BPD do score higher than non-patients on measures of these dysfunctional schemas. They also report levels of childhood abuse that were higher than non-patients (Lobbestael, Arntz & Siewerda, 2005). This suggests a significant amount of similarity in both the developmental history of BPD and APD and the dysfunctional cognitive schemas that characterize these disorders. This has led some researchers to argue that APD and BPD may be different manifestations of one single underlying disorder which may express itself as BPD in women and APD in men (Paris, 1997; Widiger & Corbitt, 1997).

11.3.2.3 Narcissistic Personality Disorder

As we described earlier, individuals suffering narcissistic personality disorder overestimate their abilities and inflate their accomplishments, and have a complete lack of empathy with the desires and feelings of others. However, underneath this grandiose exterior is a very frail self-esteem, which means that they constantly need to check for reassurance.

Psychodynamic theories of narcissistic PD have argued that the traits associated with this disorder result from childhood experiences with cold, rejecting parents who rarely respond with praise to their children's achievements or displays of competence (Kohut & Wolf, 1978). Indeed, such parents may often dismiss their children's successes in order to talk about their own achievements. Because of these experiences, these children try to find ways of defending against feelings of worthlessness, dissatisfaction and rejection by convincing themselves that they are worthy and talented (Wink, 1996; Kernberg, 1985). The end product is someone with a vulnerable self-esteem who seeks reassurance about his talents and achievements from himself and others, and who has developed a lack of empathy with others because of the cold and uncaring parenting he has experienced. In support of this view, there is some evidence that individuals with narcissistic PD are more likely to come from backgrounds involving child abuse, conflict and neglect (Kernberg, 1985). However, evidence of childhood abuse and neglect is not a sufficient condition for a child to develop narcissistic PD, and some other theorists have argued that the disorder results from 'doting' parents who treat their children too positively in a way that fosters unrealistic grandiose self-perceptions (Millon, 1990). Interestingly, there is some circumstantial evidence to support this view, in that measures of narcissism show that scores are often higher in firstborns or only children, where parents may have been able to devote more time and attention to their children (Curtis & Cowell, 1993).

Narcissistic personality disorder is also closely associated with antisocial personality disorder (APD), and narcissistic individuals regularly act in self-motivated, deceitful and aggressive ways very reminiscent of APD. However, individuals with narcissistic PD can reliably be differentiated from individuals with APD by their tendency to exaggerate their talents and to regard themselves as unique and superior to others (Gunderson & Ronningstam, 2001), so we may need to look closely at factors that determine this difference. Case History 11.3 describes the story of Brian Blackwell, an A-level student from Liverpool diagnosed with narcissistic personality disorder who murdered both his parents. His behaviour is suggestive of APD in that he is deceitful, a pathological liar and apparently remorseless in killing his parents. However, he had a grandiose view of himself as brilliant and untouchable, and regularly bragged about fantasy achievements and talents. Far from coming from a background of childhood abuse and neglect, he was an only child whose parents doted on their son and told friends of their great aspirations for him. You might like to consider how these facts fit in with the theoretical accounts of narcissistic PD that we have described in this section.

CASE HISTORY 11.3

Narcissistic personality disorder

Brian Blackwell used his parents' credit cards for a spending spree

A public schoolboy who admitted killing his parents before using their credit cards to fund a £30,000 spending spree has been jailed for life. Brian Blackwell, 19, stabbed his father Sydney, 72, and mother Jacqueline, 61, at their home in Melling, Merseyside, Liverpool Crown Court was told. Blackwell admitted manslaughter with diminished responsibility. He suffers 'narcissistic personality disorder'. Blackwell was arrested at the home of his girlfriend in Childwall, Liverpool, in September 2004. An only child described as an 'exemplary student', he had studied A-levels at the £7,000-a-year Liverpool College and was weeks away from starting a degree in medicine at Nottingham University. Blackwell's personality disorder meant he fantasized about unlimited success, power and brilliance. He falsely claimed he was a professional tennis player and applied for 13 credit cards in his father's name to fund his fantasies.

After battering and stabbing his parents, he went on holiday to the US with his girlfriend Amal Saba, where his excesses included spending £2,200 on a three-night stay in the Presidential Suite of the Plaza Hotel in New York. His parents' neighbours were originally not suspicious about their disappearance as the couple frequently went to Spain on holiday.

But their decomposed bodies were discovered after a neighbour called at their three-bedroomed bungalow and noticed an unusual smell. Their extensive injuries led police to believe at first that they may have been shot. The couple had high expectations for their son, telling people he was destined to become 'not just a doctor – a surgeon'. David Steer QC, prosecuting, said there was nothing to indicate that he had premeditated the killings. He told the court that sufferers of narcissistic personality disorder typically flew into a rage if their fantasy world was challenged or threatened.

Speaking outside the court, Det. Chf. Insp. Mike Keogh, of Merseyside Police, said officers could 'not begin to imagine the distress and pain that these terrible deaths have caused'. 'This has been a very tragic case involving the death of a mother and father, leaving the remaining family shattered,' he said. 'Throughout this investigation we have found almost overwhelming evidence of two caring parents who doted on their son Brian and had ambitions only for him to fulfil his undoubted potential.'

BBC News, 29 July 2005

Clinical Commentary

Many researchers believe that narcissistic personality disorder is closely associated with antisocial personality disorder. Individuals with the disorder usually show clear signs of deceitfulness, lying, lack of empathy with the feelings of others, acting impulsively and aggressively, showing no remorse for acts of harm or violence, and going to any lengths to achieve their own personal goals. Narcissistic personality disorder is differentiated from APD by individuals' grandiose view of themselves and their need to brag about fantasized achievements. The parents of some individuals with narcissistic personality disorder undoubtedly dote on them, and may treat them too positively in a way that fosters unrealistic and extravagant self-perceptions (Millon, 1996).

11.3.2.4 Histrionic Personality Disorder

There has been relatively little research into the aetiology of histrionic personality disorder, and theories that are currently available tend to have developed from psychodynamic accounts originally designed to understand hysteria generally. These types of accounts argue that the dramatic displays of emotion and attention-seeking behaviour characteristic of individuals with histrionic PD are manifestations of underlying conflict – especially conflicts related to acceptance by and relationships with members of the opposite sex. Psychodynamic theories often differ as to the causes of the conflicts that underlie attention-seeking and dramatic behaviour. Some suggest that the disorder is fostered by inconsistencies in parental attitudes towards sex, where parents convey the view that sex is both dirty and exciting (Apt & Hurlburt, 1994). Others suggest that the disorder arises from a childhood experience of parenting that is cold and controlling, leaving the child searching desperately for love and assurance (Bender, Farber & Geller, 2001). Finally, other psychodynamic views focus specifically on the relationship between father and daughter. Because of a lack of maternal attention, some daughters may actively seek the attention and approval of their fathers, which leads to a flirtatious relationship between father and daughter that the daughter carries on to other relationships later in life (Phillips & Gunderson, 1994).

There is little objective evidence at present to differentiate between any of these particular psychodynamic accounts, which appear to be focused more on explaining the disorder in females than in males. As such, they may all be relatively inadequate accounts of histrionic PD, especially since more recent surveys have indicated that it is a disorder that is relatively equally distributed across men and women (Mattia & Zimmerman, 2001).

11.3.3 Anxious/Fearful Personality Disorders (Cluster C)

Personality disorders in Cluster C exhibit mainly anxious and fearful symptoms and are frequently linked to comorbid Axis I anxiety disorders. Very little research has been carried out on the aetiology of disorders in this cluster, although there have been attempts to view them as part of larger anxiety-based spectra of disorders (such as avoidant personality disorder within a social anxiety spectrum, and obsessive-compulsive personality disorder within an obsessive-compulsive spectrum) (e.g. Schneier, Blanco, Antia & Liebowitz, 2002). As such, it would then be assumed that the personality disorders share some of the aetiological features of their corresponding anxiety disorders, although this has yet to be confirmed empirically.

11.3.3.1 Avoidant Personality Disorder

Avoidant personality disorder is characterized by feelings of inadequacy, fear of criticism, disapproval and rejection, and avoidance of most personal interactions with others. It is also associated with avoidance behaviour generally and may be part of a broader social anxiety spectrum (Schneier, Blanco, Antia & Liebowitz, 2002). Like many of the personality disorders, the aetiology of avoidant personality disorder has not been extensively researched. However, there have been a few studies investigating the correlates and risk factors associated with avoidant PD. For example, avoidant PD has been shown to be closely associated with scores on a variety of personality dimensions, including introversion, neuroticism, low self-esteem and pessimism, and to self-reports of elevated emotional responsiveness to threat and reduced emotional responsiveness to incentives (Meyer, 2002). Family studies have also found that having a family member diagnosed with either social phobia or avoidant PD increases the risk for both these disorders 2–3 fold (Tillfors, Furmark, Ekselius & Frederickson, 2001), suggesting a close relationship between the development of social phobia and avoidant PD. Finally, when compared with individuals with either major depression or other personality disorders, individuals with avoidant PD report poorer child and adolescent athletic performance, less involvement in hobbies during adolescence and less adolescent popularity (Rettew, Zanarini, Yen, Grilo et al., 2003). This study also demonstrated higher levels of childhood physical and emotional abuse in the avoidant PD group than in the depressed group, although this factor did not differentiate individuals with avoidant PD from individuals with other forms of PD. What such studies do suggest is that (1) avoidant PD is closely associated with social phobia, and both may be part of a broader social anxiety spectrum; and (2) there are some important childhood precursors which suggest that underperformance across a variety of childhood social domains may be predictive of later avoidant PD.

Finally, avoidant PD is closely associated with low self-esteem and feelings of shame and guilt. Psychodynamic accounts suggest that negative childhood experiences and childhood underachievement may contribute to a negative self-image (Gabbard, 1990). We have seen that there is some evidence for childhood negative experiences and underachievement being precursors to later avoidant PD, but it is still far from clear whether these experiences are *consequences* of the developing disorder or whether they are *causal* factors, nor is it evident how such experiences might lead to the development of low self-esteem, shame and guilt.

11.3.3.2 Dependent Personality Disorder

Some clinicians have highlighted what appear to be many formalistic similarities between dependent personality disorder and depression. These similarities include indecisiveness and passiveness, pessimism and self-doubting, and low self-esteem. We have already seen in Chapter 6 that individuals suffering depressed mood continually seek reassurance from family and friends, just as individuals with dependent personality disorder continually seek support and guidance (Joiner, Metalsky, Katz et al., 1999). A possible link between dependent personality disorder and depression is also supported by the fact that drugs used to treat depression significantly decrease symptoms of dependent personality disorder as well (Ekselius & von Knorring, 1998). This has led psychodynamic theorists to develop models of the aetiology of dependent personality disorder that closely resemble those for depression (see Chapter 6). For example, object relations theorists claim that dependence and fear of rejection are fostered by childhood neglect or loss of a parent during childhood. Alternatively, other psychodynamic theorists claim that overprotective parenting may cause subsequent separation anxiety, depression and the development of dependent personality disorder (Bornstein, 1996). Clearly, these very different accounts require some further evidence to differentiate them. Unfortunately, there are currently no systematic data on the childhood experiences of individuals who subsequently develop dependent personality disorder that might help to shed light on these different accounts.

Apart from formalistic similarities with depression, dependent personality disorder has been found to be regularly comorbid with a number of Axis I anxiety disorders, particularly social phobia, obsessive-compulsive disorder and panic disorder (McLaughlin & Mennin, 2005). But once again, it is unclear whether dependent personality disorder is associated with an increased risk for developing an anxiety disorder (and what the mechanism for this increased risk might be), or whether anxiety disorders increase the risk for dependent personality disorder. Further research is needed to clarify these relationships and to help understand aetiological factors important to the development of dependent personality disorder.

11.3.3.3 Obsessive-Compulsive Personality Disorder

A first place to look for evidence relating to the aetiology of obsessive-compulsive personality disorder would be its apparently related Axis I disorder, obsessive-compulsive disorder. However, a review of the facts does not indicate a particularly close link between the two disorders. While the symptoms of OCPD are very similar to those of OCD, the reported comorbidity of OCPD in individuals with OCD is relatively low at 22 per cent (Albert, Maina, Forner & Bogetto, 2004). In fact, this study found that comorbidity of OCPD in individuals with panic disorder was 17 per cent, suggesting that OCPD is found at approximately the same level in individuals with panic disorder as it is in individuals with OCD. In addition, family studies have indicated that individuals with OCPD are no more likely than chance to have close relatives with OCD, which does not suggest a genetic link between OCPD and OCD (Nestadt, Samuels, Riddle, Bienvenu et al., 2000).

At present there is very little evidence available that enables us to identify important factors in the aetiology of OCPD, and significantly less that enables us to predict those individuals who will develop OCPD as opposed to OCD. Some studies of nonclinical populations indicate that there may be a single underlying vulnerability factor for both OCPD and OCD, which may be related to a parenting style that includes psychological manipulation and guilt induction (Aycicegi, Harris & Dinn, 2002). Yet this still begs the questions of (1) why OCPD and OCD are not highly comorbid if they share similar vulnerability factors and (2) why some people develop OCPD and not OCD.

SUMMARY

This section has illustrated that the aetiology of personality disorders – compared with many other psychopathologies – is relatively underresearched. APD and BPD have received the most attention, while research on the aetiology of other personality disorders is still at a very early stage (e.g. the Cluster C disorders). Because personality disorders tend to be an enduring feature of an individual's behaviour from childhood into adulthood, researchers have tended to look for factors in childhood that might either put an individual at risk for developing a personality disorder or be a direct causal factor in determining the behavioural styles characteristic of the different disorders. For example, a diagnosis of conduct disorder in childhood appears to be a predictor of APD in later life, as does childhood neglect and abuse in BPD. Some studies have looked at whether there is a genetic component to personality disorders, but apart from the Cluster A disorders (paranoid, schizoid and schizotypal personality disorders), the evidence for an inherited factor in the other personality disorders is modest.

SELF-TEST QUESTIONS

- Can you describe the evidence suggesting that Cluster A disorders are genetically linked with schizophrenia?
- What are the risk factors and childhood precursors predictive of adult antisocial personality disorder?
- What is the evidence for a genetic element to antisocial personality disorder?
- Some theories argue that dysfunctional cognitive schemas underlie antisocial personality disorder. Can you name the important schema modes described by these theories?
- What are the physiological and neurological factors associated with antisocial personality disorder, and how might they contribute to typical APD behaviour patterns?
- Can you describe the evidence suggesting that negative childhood experiences might be important in the aetiology of borderline personality disorder?
- What is the evidence for a link between borderline personality disorder and bipolar disorder?
- How do psychodynamic theories attempt to explain the development of borderline personality disorder?
- What might be the role of abnormal parenting in the development of narcissistic and histrionic personality disorders?
- What is the evidence for a genetic link between avoidant personality disorder and social phobia?
- What is the evidence for a link between dependent personality disorder and mood disorders?
- Is there any evidence for a link between obsessive-compulsive personality disorder and its Axis I counterpart, obsessive-compulsive disorder?

SECTION SUMMARY

11.3 The Aetiology of Personality Disorders

11.3.1 Cluster A Disorders

- Behavioural and genetic links between Cluster A disorders (paranoid, schizoid and schizotypal personality disorders) and schizophrenia suggest that they may be part of a broader **schizophrenia spectrum disorder**.

- **Psychodynamic** approaches to paranoid personality disorder suggest that parents may have been demanding, distant, over-rigid and rejecting, giving rise to a lack of trust in others.

- The risk of all three types of Cluster A disorder is increased in relatives of individuals diagnosed with schizophrenia, suggesting a **genetic link** between schizophrenia and the Cluster A personality disorders.

11.3.2.1 Antisocial Personality Disorder

- One of the best predictors of antisocial personality disorder in adulthood is **conduct disorder** in childhood.

- Adolescent smoking, alcohol use, illicit drug use, police trouble and sexual intercourse before the age of 15 years **significantly predict** antisocial personality disorder in later life.

- Antisocial personality disorder appears to run in families, suggesting that APD may be acquired through **social learning** and **imitation**.

- **Psychodynamic** approaches to antisocial personality disorder suggest that lack of parental love and affection during childhood and inconsistent parenting are likely to lead to the child failing to learn trust.

- Twin studies have demonstrated significantly higher concordance rates for antisocial personality disorder in MZ than in DZ twins, suggesting a **genetic** element to the disorder.

- Individuals with both antisocial personality disorder and borderline personality disorder appear to possess a set of **dysfunctional cognitive schemas** that give rise to their unpredictable mood swings and impulsive behaviour.

- Individuals with antisocial personality disorder show a number of **physiological** and **neurological characteristics**, such as physiological indicators of low anxiety, low levels of baseline arousal and reactivity, lack of learning in simple aversive conditioning procedures and neurological impairments indicative of impulsivity.

11.3.2.2 Borderline Personality Disorder

- Individuals with borderline personality disorder report rates of **childhood physical, sexual and verbal abuse** and **neglect** ranging from 60 to 90 per cent, suggesting that these experiences may be important in the development of BPD.

- Twin studies of borderline personality disorder have indicated concordance rates of 35 per cent and 7 per cent for MZ and DZ twins respectively, suggesting a **genetic** element to BPD.

- Recent research has linked borderline personality disorder with mood disorders. Around 44 per cent of individuals with BPD belong to a broader **bipolar disorder spectrum**, which may account for the regular and unpredictable mood swings in BPD.

- Neuroimaging studies of borderline personality disorder have identified **brain abnormalities** in the limbic system, including the hippocampus and amygdala.

- **Object relations theory** argues that individuals with borderline personality disorder have received inadequate support and love from important others (such as parents), and that this results in an insecure ego which is likely to lead to lack of self-esteem and fear of rejection.

- Between 10 and 47 per cent of individuals with borderline personality disorder also meet the diagnostic criteria for antisocial personality disorder, suggesting a **link** between the two disorders.

11.3.2.3 Narcissistic Personality Disorder

- **Psychodynamic** theories of narcissistic personality disorder argue that the traits associated with this disorder result from childhood experiences with cold, rejecting parents who rarely praised their children's achievements.

- Narcissistic personality disorder is also closely associated with **antisocial personality disorder**: narcissistic individuals will regularly act in self-motivated, deceitful and aggressive ways reminiscent of APD.

11.3.2.4 Histrionic Personality Disorder

- There is relatively little research on the aetiology of histrionic personality disorder, and theories that are currently available tend to have developed from **psychodynamic** accounts.

11.3.3 Cluster C Disorders

- Having a family member diagnosed with either social phobia or avoidant personality disorder increases the risk for both disorders two- to threefold, suggesting that both social phobia and avoidant personality disorder may be part of a broader **social anxiety spectrum** that has a **genetic** element.

- Dependent personality disorder has many features similar to **depression**, including indecisiveness, passiveness, pessimism, self-doubting and low self-esteem. Drugs used to treat depression are also successful at alleviating the symptoms of dependent personality disorder.

- Dependent personality disorder is regularly **comorbid** with a number of Axis I disorders, particularly social phobia, panic disorder and obsessive-compulsive disorder.

- The reported comorbidity of obsessive-compulsive personality disorder (OCPD) in individuals with obsessive-compulsive disorder (OCD) is as low as 22 per cent, suggesting that the two disorders are **not** closely related.

11.4 TREATING PEOPLE WITH A DIAGNOSIS OF PERSONALITY DISORDER

A number of important factors make treating personality disorders problematic, requiring an approach rather different from those employed for most Axis I disorders. Firstly, as we have mentioned throughout this chapter, personality disorders are enduring patterns of behaviour that individuals have usually deployed from childhood into adulthood. As a consequence, individuals usually cannot see their behaviour as problematic and are unlikely to believe they need to change their behaviour, let alone seek treatment for it. Secondly, individuals with personality disorders possess patterns of behaviour that are likely to make them susceptible to a range of other Axis I disorders (such as anxiety disorders or depression); we discussed the extent of this comorbidity earlier. Individuals with personality disorders are usually first referred for treatment in connection with these comorbid Axis I problems (e.g. depression and suicidal ideation in borderline personality disorder; social phobia in avoidant personality disorder; panic disorder or social phobia in dependent personality disorder; see again Table 11.12). To add to these problems, Axis I disorders that are comorbid with a personality disorder are difficult to treat successfully (Crits-Christoph & Barber, 2002). There may be many reasons for these difficulties, for example:

1 Such individuals are significantly more disturbed and may require more intensive treatment than individuals with an Axis I disorder alone.

2 Many personality disorders consist of ingrained behavioural styles that are likely to continue to cause future life difficulties that may trigger symptoms of Axis I disorders (e.g. the individual with borderline personality disorder is likely to continue to have turbulent and unstable relationships that may cause future bouts of depression and suicidal ideation).

3 Many of the personality disorders have features which make such individuals manipulative and unable to form trusting relationships (e.g. antisocial personality disorder, borderline personality disorder, narcissistic personality disorder). This makes the development of a working, trusting relationship between therapist and client very difficult, even when it comes to treating just the comorbid Axis I disorder.

Thirdly, it is worth referring back to Focus Point 11.2 and asking what it is about personality disorders that is disordered and requires treatment – especially if the behavioural styles typical of the personality disorders are really only extremes of what otherwise might be considered to be normal personality dimensions (Costa & MacRae, 1990). Because individuals with personality disorders exhibit extremes of behaviour on normal personality dimensions (such as extraversion/introversion, conscientiousness, agreeableness/antagonism), it may be more realistic to try to moderate the existing behaviours of such individuals rather than attempt to change them completely. For example, the behaviours of individuals with obsessive-compulsive personality disorder may be quite adaptive in some circumstances and situations (e.g. when dealing with an important work project), but inappropriate and maladaptive in others (e.g. when obsessively organizing family and friends on a holiday). Taking this into account, the therapist may be more successful in trying to 'normalize' the extreme behavioural styles of the individual with a personality disorder, rather than trying to change his or her ingrained behaviour patterns completely (Millon, 1996). These are all factors to bear in mind when reviewing the treatments that have been applied to personality disorders.

Finally, the scope of the personality disorders and their varied behavioural characteristics mean that treatments are very often geared towards the requirements of individual disorders. This being so, therapists have utilized a broad range of differing therapeutic procedures with varying degrees of success. Below, we discuss these differing approaches in turn. In general, individuals with personality disorders need to (1) acquire a range of life skills, (2) learn emotional control strategies and (3) acquire the skill of **mentalization**, which is the ability to reflect on their experiences, feelings and thoughts and to assess their meaning and importance. These are all goals of therapy that can be identified across a range of conceptually different treatments for the personality disorders.

> **Mentalization** The ability to reflect on experiences, feelings and thoughts, and to assess their meaning and importance.

11.4.1 Drug Treatments

Drugs are frequently used in an attempt to treat individuals with personality disorders, but they tend to be used to tackle symptoms of any comorbid Axis I disorder rather than the symptoms of the personality disorder itself (but see Newton-Howes & Tyrer, 2003). Individuals with comorbid anxiety disorders, such as social phobia or panic disorder, can be prescribed tranquillizers such as benzodiazepine, while those with comorbid major depression may receive antidepressants such as the selective serotonin reuptake inhibitor fluoxetine (Prozac) (Rinne, van den Brink, Wouters & van Dyck, 2002). Lithium chloride can also be administered to individuals who have comorbid bipolar disorder (sometimes diagnosed with borderline personality disorder and antisocial personality disorder) in order to stabilize their moods and reduce antisocial behaviour. Antipsychotic drugs (such as risperidone) can also be effective in reducing the symptoms of Cluster A personality disorders, which are known to have some relationship with the symptoms of schizophrenia (Koenigsberg, Goodman, Reynolds, Mitropoulou et al., 2001). More recently, atypical antipsychotic drugs (such as quetiapine) have been shown to reduce impulsivity, hostility, aggressiveness, irritability and rage outbursts in individuals with antisocial personality disorder (Walker, Thomas & Allen, 2003).

11.4.2 Psychodynamic and Insight Approaches

As we saw in section 11.3, psychodynamic approaches have a long history of attempting to explain the development of personality disorders, so it is not surprising that psychodynamic and insight therapies generally should also be prominently involved in treatments for these disorders. Problematic relationships with parents and childhood neglect and abuse are factors that are prominent in attempts to explain many of the personality disorders, and exploring and resolving these developmental experiences is seen as an important role for psychodynamic therapies.

Psychodynamic therapists view *insight* as the crucial mechanism of change in personality disorders, not least because most individuals with personality disorders do not initially view their behaviour as problematic. This approach is particularly important when treating individuals with BPD, who represent a serious challenge to therapists of any theoretical orientation. Individuals with BPD are manipulative and frequently game-play with the therapist in order to ascertain how special they are (e.g. by phoning the therapist regularly at inconvenient times), or they make dramatic gestures to seek attention (e.g. by threatening suicide attempts). They also lack trust, making it difficult to develop a working relationship between therapist and client whatever the therapeutic approach being used. Finally, BPD is typical of most of the Cluster B personality disorders in that individuals view the causes of their problems as external (i.e. the fault of other people), which makes any form of insight therapy difficult.

However, psychodynamic therapists have taken a more active approach to treating personality disorders, attempting to identify and block manipulative behaviours at an early stage, exposing the 'weak egos' and fragile self-image that usually underlie many of the personality disorders. As a particular example of psychodynamic treatment, *object relations psychotherapy* attempts to strengthen an individual's weak ego so that he or she is able to address issues without constantly flipping from one extreme view to another (Kernberg, 1985). In the case of BPD, for example, object relations psychotherapy attempts to show clients how their normal way of behaving is defensive (e.g. when they blame others for problems in their life) and that their judgements are often simplistic, falling into simple dichotomous categories (such as either 'good' or 'bad') which cause them to swing regularly from positive to negative ways of thinking. It then offers clients more adaptive ways of dealing with important life issues by, for example, teaching them that other people may possess *both* good and bad characteristics, rather than being all 'good' or all 'bad'.

Object relations psychotherapy A treatment developed specifically to deal with the difficulties posed by the treatment of individuals with personality disorders such as borderline personality disorder.

While it is difficult to assess the effectiveness of psychodynamic approaches to treatment objectively, there is some evidence that psychodynamic psychotherapies do have a beneficial effect on the symptoms of personality disorders. Some studies have suggested that clients do show significant improvements in symptoms during treatment (Svartberg, Stiles & Seltzer, 2004), and that short-term psychodynamic therapy is at least as effective as CBT (Leichsenring & Leibing, 2003) and a range of other treatments-as-usual, including general community-based psychiatric treatment (Fonagy, Roth & Higgitt, 2005).

11.4.3 Dialectical Behaviour Therapy

One particular form of therapy that has been successfully used to treat individuals with personality disorders is *dialectical behaviour therapy* (Linehan, 1987). This approach takes the client-centred view of accepting clients for what they are, but attempts to provide them with insight into their dysfunctional ways of thinking about and categorizing the world. This therapy is designed to provide clients with the necessary skills to overcome their problematic ways of thinking and behaving – not an easy thing to do with a group of people who are usually very sensitive to criticism and emotionally unstable, and who will probably react to any challenge to their current ways of thinking in extreme ways (even threatening suicide). As a result, the dialectical behaviour therapist has to convey complete acceptance of what the client does to enable a successful dialogue to ensue about the client's problems and difficulties.

Dialectical behaviour therapy A client-centred therapy for personality disorder that attempts to provide clients with insight into their dysfunctional ways of thinking about the world.

Dialectical behaviour therapy subsequently includes skills training designed to teach individuals to be mindful of their maladaptive ways of thinking about the world (e.g. that others are not always to blame for the bad things that happen), to learn to solve problems effectively, to control their emotions (such as their anger outbursts) and to develop more socially acceptable ways of dealing with their life problems.

This approach has been particularly successful with individuals with BPD (Robins & Chapman, 2004), and has been shown to be more effective than treatment-as-usual in reducing self-harm, suicide attempts and hospitalization (Linehan, Heard & Armstrong, 1993), and it is particularly effective as a treatment for BPD over the longer term when combined with appropriate medication (Soler, Pascual, Campins, Barrachina et al., 2005).

11.4.4 Cognitive Behaviour Therapy

Because of the resistance of many personality disorders to 'insight' therapies, it was originally felt inappropriate to try to apply cognitive behaviour therapy to this category of psychopathologies. However, over the past 10 years, there has been significant progress in developing CBT in ways which are directly relevant to the behavioural, emotional and cognitive problems found in personality disorders. Applying CBT to the treatment of people with a diagnosis of personality disorder was arguably first pioneered by Aaron Beck and colleagues, who attempted to apply CBT methods first developed to treat depression (see Chapter 6) (Beck & Freeman, 1990). This meant exploring the range of

CLINICAL PERSPECTIVE: TREATMENT IN PRACTICE BOX 11.1

CBT for personality disorders

The normal stages through which CBT progresses in the treatment of a personality disorder are described below.

(1) During the initial sessions the therapist deals with any coexisting Axis I problems (usually specific anxiety disorders such as panic disorder or social phobia or major depression; see Table 11.12).

(2) The therapist then teaches the client to identify and evaluate key negative automatic thoughts (e.g. 'nobody likes me' or 'I am worthless' in avoidant or dependent personality disorders).

(3) The therapist then structures the sessions carefully to build a collaborative and trusting relationship with the client, especially in the case of those disorders where clients are distrusting or manipulative (e.g. borderline personality disorder).

(4) The therapist may then employ guided imagery to unravel the meaning of new and earlier experiences that may have contributed to the dysfunctional behaviour patterns (such as problematic early childhood and parenting experiences).

(5) In collaboration with the client, the therapist prepares homework assignments tailored to the client's specific issues.

(6) Finally, the therapist applies specific cognitive, behavioural and emotion-focused schema-restructuring techniques to dispute core beliefs and to develop new and more adaptive beliefs and behaviour (see also schema therapy).

Two main treatment objectives are: (1) to help the client develop new and more adaptive core beliefs and (2) to help the client develop more adaptive problem-solving interpersonal behaviours.

---

logical errors and dysfunctional schemas that might underlie problematic behaviour within individual personality disorders. For instance, an example of a logical error would be an individual with obsessive-compulsive personality disorder believing that she is incompetent if she does just one thing wrong. Such individuals may also have developed dysfunctional schemas that generate problematic behaviour and cause emotional distress. In the case of OCPD, the individual may have developed beliefs that everything has to be done correctly (perhaps because of parental pressure to be perfectionist), and when one thing is not done properly this causes emotional distress and anxiety. In most cases, the way in which CBT is constructed depends very much on the individual personality disorder diagnosed and on the cognitive factors relevant to the individual client (see Beck & Freeman, 1990). Treatment in Practice Box 11.1 provides a brief summary of the stages through which conventional CBT for personality disorders would normally proceed.

As a specific example, the way in which dysfunctional schemas may develop in borderline personality disorder is outlined in Figure 11.3. Childhood abuse is assumed to contribute to the development of a number of schemas typical of BPD. This leads to the self being viewed as bad, vulnerable and helpless, others as malevolent, abusing and rejecting, and experienced emotion as dangerous; 'clinging' then becomes a strategy designed to get support from others, but is alternated with 'keeping distance' because of distrust. These negative, dysfunctional schemas give rise to

hypervigilance and the constant expectation of threat and danger (Arntz, 1999). In addition, because childhood traumas have never been fully emotionally processed, this has resulted in stunted emotional-cognitive development, so that individuals with BPD show dichotomous thinking (black/white, good/bad thinking with no shades of grey).

CBT can be used in its traditional way to challenge the status of these dysfunctional schemas and to attempt to replace them with more functional schemas and views of the world. However, when treating individuals with BPD in particular, the therapist must avoid direct challenges with clients about their beliefs because of their intense sensitivity to criticism, and so usually has to approach this stage of therapy empathetically (McGinn & Young, 1996). The therapist may attempt to approach the process of changing dysfunctional schemas by *reparenting* the client, allowing him or her to form an emotional attachment to the client in order to challenge dysfunctional schemas (Young, Klosko & Weishaar, 2003).

A more recent development of CBT for personality disorders is known as *schema-focused cognitive therapy* or *schema therapy*. Central to this approach is the concept of

> **Reparenting** A therapy process in which clients allow the therapist to form an emotional attachment to them in order to challenge dysfunctional schemas.

> **Schema therapy** An integrative approach to the treatment of personality disorders based on the principles of cognitive behaviour therapy.

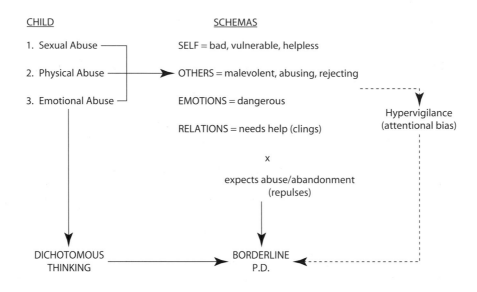

Figure 11.3
A schematic representation of the way that dysfunctional schemas are thought to develop in borderline personality disorder. See text for further elaboration.

Source: Arntz (1999).

early maladaptive schemas (EMSs), which are thought to develop during childhood and result in dysfunctional beliefs and behaviours during adulthood (Young, Klosko & Weishaar, 2003). We touched on these maladaptive schemas and their putative role in determining the unpredictable, antisocial and impulsive behaviours typical of the more severe personality disorders earlier in this chapter (section 11.3.2.1). For example, if a child is continually criticized by parents, she may develop the schema 'I am defective'. In order to cope with this schema, the child will develop strategies that in the longer term are maladaptive and act to reinforce the schema. For example, she may develop a variety of strategies that enable her to avoid thinking about this schema, such as storming off at the slightest hint of criticism, summarily breaking off relationships if there is an indication that her partner is not being affectionate, or inflicting self-harm as a means of distracting from the schema.

Schema therapy outlines three specific stages for therapy in these circumstances. First, clients need to be convinced that their problems and symptoms are not *evidence for* their maladaptive schemas but that, in contrast, their maladaptive schemas are actually a *cause* of their symptoms. Developing self-knowledge is important in understanding that maladaptive schemas are related to unfortunate childhood circumstances rather than representing truths about the way that person is. The second stage is to attempt to identify and prevent schema avoidance responses, so that clients can experience, accept and tolerate the negative and

painful emotional states that ensue when schema avoidance is prevented. Thirdly, through the therapist's questioning and comments, clients are helped to examine the life experiences that have given rise to the maladaptive schemas. This final stage of therapy is intended to reduce the belief in maladaptive schemas and to develop adaptive alternative perspectives on their problematic life experiences.

These brief examples indicate that the development of specific CBT procedures for personality disorders is still an active process. Procedures have been developed that are specific to the cognitive and behavioural requirements of individual disorders (Beck & Freeman, 1990), and current attempts are being made to identify maladaptive schemas that are important determinants of the behavioural styles typical of disorders such as BPD and APD (Young, Klosko & Weishaar, 2003). It is still very early to be able to say with any confidence that CBT offers an important and effective method of treatment for personality disorders. However, a number of controlled studies have shown that CBT for personality disorders is superior to non-therapy control conditions in reducing symptoms (Linehan, Tutek, Heard & Armstrong, 1994; Linehan, Schmidt, Dimeff, Craft et al., 1999) and are equally as effective as psychodynamic therapy (Leichsenring & Leibing, 2003). Preliminary studies also indicate that, after being treated with CBT, between 40 and 50 per cent of clients will have recovered after 1.3–2 years (Perry, Banon & Ianni, 1999; Svartberg, Stiles & Seltzer, 2004).

Treating antisocial personality disorder: Can personality disorders be treated in prison populations?

We noted earlier in this chapter that the diagnosis of antisocial personality disorder is closely linked with adult criminal behaviour. Surveys of prison populations have indicated that between 50 and 70 per cent of males in prisons meet the diagnostic criteria for APD (Fazel & Danesh, 2002; Widiger, Cadoret, Hare, Robins et al., 1996), and many of these men have been imprisoned for violence, sexual offences and homicide. Between 56 and 72 per cent of men convicted of serious sexual offences have been shown to be diagnosed with APD (Dunsieth, Nelson, Brusman-Lovins, Holcomb et al., 2004; McElroy, Soutullo, Taylor, Nelson et al., 1999), and in a Finnish study, a diagnosis of APD increased the likelihood of an individual being convicted of homicide tenfold (Eronen, Hakola & Tihonen, 1996). In addition, the UK Home Office recognized the important link between violent criminal behaviour and APD by coining the term 'dangerous people with severe personality disorders (DSPD)' to describe individuals who have APD plus at least one other personality disorder. The Home Office report also recognized the difficulty in successfully treating such individuals and recommended that people diagnosed with DSPD might be required to be detained indefinitely (see Focus Point 11.1).

This raises the issue of whether the symptoms of individuals with APD who have committed serious criminal acts can be successfully treated. We have discussed the general difficulties of treating individuals with Cluster B personality disorders. They are manipulative, suspicious, hostile to criticism, lack trust in others and are constantly prone to lying in order to achieve their aims. This makes it difficult to form any kind of meaningful therapist–client relationship regardless of the theoretical orientation of the therapy. Finally, individuals with APD do not usually believe there is anything wrong with their behaviour: it has often enabled them to achieve their goals, so why should they change? This does not bode well for successful treatment of APD in criminal populations.

If an individual with APD is incarcerated in prison, this makes treating the disorder even more difficult because of the unusual cultural requirements of prisons. DSM-IV-TR defines a personality disorder as 'an enduring pattern of behaviour that deviates markedly from expectations within that culture', but as Rotter, Way, Steinbacher, Sawyer et al. (2002) point out, jails and prisons have their own cultural norms that require behaviours such as suspiciousness, hostility, social withdrawal and self-centredness. These are all behaviours that could be construed as adaptive in institutions such as prisons, where individuals have to look out for themselves and distrust others in order to survive (Rotter & Steinbacher, 2001). For example, an 'inmate code of conduct' might include:

- Do your own time (mind your own business, look out for yourself, keep to yourself).
- Don't snitch (don't report other inmates, don't trust staff).
- Don't show weakness (look tough, appear dangerous, act violently if necessary).

In the film Dead Man Walking, *Sean Penn plays Matthew Poncelet, a man convicted of the cold-blooded murder of a young couple. Like many murderers with antisocial personality disorder, Poncelet denies the crime, claiming that he is the patsy. But his true nature is out there for all to see. He is cold, calculating and without remorse. In a news clip of his court conviction, Poncelet draws his manacled hand across his throat in a chilling and remorseless threat to his jury.*

Such behaviours look exactly like the main symptoms of APD! So, in effect, attempting to treat APD in prisons is equivalent to trying to persuade incarcerated prisoners to behave maladaptively, and perhaps to leave themselves open to abuse and manipulation by other prisoners.

Nevertheless, there have been many attempts, in both Europe and the USA, to develop prison therapeutic communities that may help to reduce reoffending – although it is important to note that these aims are not the same as attempting to reduce symptoms of APD. Such therapeutic communities have been based on behavioural or cognitive behavioural principles in an attempt to target cognitive deficits that relate to offending behaviour. This scheme is known as Reasoning and Rehabilitation (R&R) (Robinson & Porporino, 2001). The treatment targets are self-control (thinking before acting), interpersonal problem-solving skills, social perspective taking, critical reasoning skills, cognitive style and understanding the values that govern behaviour. It is worth noting that many of these goals would address behaviours typical of individuals with APD (e.g. impulsiveness, lack of empathy). The programme has been used in prisons in the USA, Spain, UK, Canada and New Zealand, and outcome studies have suggested that they result in a modest but significant reduction in reoffending, normally between 5 and 15 per cent (Robinson, 1995; Friendship, Blud, Erikson, Travers & Thornton, 2003; Raynor & Vanstone, 1996).

SUMMARY

We have reviewed a range of difficulties involved in the treatment of individuals with personality disorders which make successful treatment hard to achieve. These difficulties include: (1) denial of any psychopathology; (2) personality characteristics that make it difficult to form a trusting relationship with a therapist; (3) persistent behavioural patterns that are likely to continue to cause future life difficulties; and (4) comorbid Axis I disorders that usually need to be addressed and treated before tackling any underlying personality disorder. Despite these difficulties, therapists have been imaginative in developing a range of psychological treatments designed to tackle the important features of personality disorders. First, drugs may be used to reduce the symptoms of any comorbid Axis I disorder such as major depression, bipolar disorder or anxious psychopathologies generally. Subsequently, a range of insight-based therapies (such as dialectical behaviour therapy) or specially developed cognitive therapies (such as schema-focused cognitive therapy) can be used to address dysfunctional ways of thinking and maladaptive cognitive schemas. In general, individuals with a personality disorder need to: (1) acquire a range of adaptive life skills (allowing them to interact and socialize successfully); (2) learn emotional control strategies (to control anger outbursts and acute periods of depression); and (3) acquire skills which enable them to reflect objectively on their experiences, feelings and thoughts, rather than reacting impulsively and emotionally to challenging events.

SELF-TEST QUESTIONS

- Can you name the factors that make personality disorders so difficult to treat?
- What is the evidence in favour of a role for drug treatment in the management of personality disorders?
- What are the difficulties involved in adapting cognitive behaviour therapies to the treatment of personality disorders such as antisocial and borderline personality disorders?
- What are the main features of object relations psychotherapy and dialectical behaviour therapy as applied to the treatment of personality disorders?

SECTION SUMMARY

11.4 Treating People with a Diagnosis of Personality Disorder

- Personality disorders are particularly difficult to treat successfully because: (1) individuals with personality disorders regularly **deny** they have problems that require treatment; and (2) they are also highly **comorbid** with Axis I disorders, which makes the individual significantly more disturbed.

- **Drug treatments** can be used to tackle symptoms of any comorbid Axis I disorder, which in turn makes the personality disorder itself more accessible to treatment.

- Individuals with **borderline personality disorder** represent a challenge to therapists of any theoretical persuasion because they are manipulative, frequently game-play with the therapist, and make dramatic gestures to seek attention (such as threatening suicide).

- **Object relations psychotherapy** and **dialectic behaviour therapy** are both treatments that have been developed specifically to deal with the difficulties posed by the treatment of individuals with personality disorders such as BPD.

- More recently, cognitive therapies have been developed which attempt to identify and change any logical errors, dysfunctional beliefs and maladaptive schemas possessed by the individual with personality disorders (e.g. **schema-focused cognitive therapy** or **schema therapy**).

11.5 PERSONALITY DISORDERS REVIEWED

Personality disorders represent longstanding, pervasive and inflexible patterns of behaviour that deviate from acceptable norms within individual cultures. They are associated with unusual ways of interpreting events (e.g. paranoid and schizotypal personality disorders), unpredictable mood swings (e.g. borderline personality disorder) or impulsive behaviour (e.g. antisocial personality disorder). These patterns of behaviour can be traced back to childhood and early adolescence and represent ways of behaving that are likely to have consequences that put the individual at risk for a range of other Axis I disorders (such as major depression or anxiety disorders). While DSM-IV-TR lists 10 diagnostically independent personality disorders organized into three primary clusters (odd/

eccentric, dramatic/emotional and anxious/fearful), some theorists have argued that personality disorders are not discrete disorders but represent dimensional extremes of normal personality (e.g. Costa & MacRae, 1990; Widiger & Simonsen, 2005).

Lifetime prevalence rates for personality disorders are around 14–15 per cent (see Table 11.13), which suggests that they are among the most common psychopathologies and among the most frequent classes of disorder treated by mental health professionals (Zimmerman, Rothschild & Chelminski, 2005). However, personality disorders are particularly difficult to treat for a number of reasons. They are frequently comorbid with Axis I disorders (which complicates treatment), individuals with personality disorders frequently deny their behaviour is problematic, and they can be distrusting and manipulative in therapy. However, a number of recently developed insight and cognitive therapies do appear to have some success in treating some of the more problematic personality disorders (such as borderline personality disorder). These include object relations psychotherapy (Kernberg, 1985), dialectical behaviour therapy (Linehan, 1987), cognitive therapy (Beck & Freeman, 1990) and schema-focused cognitive therapy (Young, Klosko & Weishaar, 2003).

Explaining the aetiology and development of personality disorders is still largely in its infancy. However, because personality disorders are enduring and can be traced back to childhood as persistent patterns of behaviour, many theories of personality disorders look to childhood experiences and developmental factors for the causes of these extreme behaviour patterns. It is certainly the case that childhood abuse, neglect and conflict can be found in the history of many personality disorders such as borderline personality disorder and antisocial personality disorder (Paris, 2001). Nevertheless, some other theorists note that individual personality disorders appear to have close links with individual Axis I disorders and may form part of broader spectrums of disorder. For example:

1 Cluster A disorders (paranoid, schizoid and schizotypal personality disorders) have strong behavioural and genetic links with schizophrenia and may form part of a broader schizophrenia spectrum disorder (Siever & Davis, 2004).

2 Borderline personality disorder is frequently comorbid with bipolar depression and may belong to a broader bipolar disorder spectrum that may explain the regular mood swings in BPD (Deltito, Martin, Riefkohl, Austria et al., 2001).

3 Avoidant personality is closely associated with social phobia and may form part of a broader social anxiety spectrum (Schneier, Blanco, Antia & Liebowitz, 2002).

All of these factors indicate that personality disorders are challenging to the researcher and therapist in many respects: they are difficult to categorize as discrete disorders, they are difficult to treat successfully, and theories of their aetiology are still only at the speculative and early stages of development.

LEARNING OUTCOMES

When you have completed this chapter, you should be able to:

1 Describe the main diagnostic criteria for the DSM-IV-TR-listed personality disorders and evaluate some of the controversial issues concerning both diagnosis and comorbidity.

2 Describe and evaluate the main theories of the aetiology of a number of personality disorders, particularly Cluster A disorders, antisocial personality disorder, borderline personality disorder and Cluster C disorders.

3 Describe and evaluate the factors that make the treatment of people with a diagnosis of personality disorder so problematic.

4 Describe and evaluate 3 or 4 psychological therapies that have been developed to treat people with a diagnosis of personality disorder.

KEY TERMS

REVIEWS, THEORIES AND SEMINAL STUDIES

Links to Journal Articles

11.1 The Diagnosis of Personality Disorders

Costa, P.T. & MacRae, R.R. (1990). Personality disorders and the five-factor model of personality. *Journal of Personality Disorders, 4*, 362–371.

Gunderson, J.G. & Ronningstam, E. (2001). Differentiating narcissistic and antisocial personality disorders. *Journal of Personality Disorders, 15*, 103–109.

Hartung, C.M. & Widiger, T.A. (1998). Gender differences in the diagnosis of mental disorders: Conclusions and controversies of the DSM-IV. *Psychological Bulletin, 123*, 260–278.

Looper, K.J. & Paris, J. (2000). What dimensions underlie cluster B personality disorders? *Comprehensive Psychiatry, 41*, 432–437.

Parker, G., Both, L., Olley, A., Hadzi-Pavlovic, D. et al. (2002). Defining disordered personality functioning. *Journal of Personality Disorders, 16*, 503–522.

Rotter, M.R., Way, B., Steinbacher, M., Sawyer, D. & Smith, H. (2002). Personality disorders in prison: Aren't they all antisocial? *Psychiatric Quarterly, 73*, 337–349.

Smith, D.J., Muir, W.J. & Blackwood, D.H.R. (2004). Is borderline personality disorder part of the bipolar spectrum? *Harvard Review of Psychiatry, 12*, 133–139.

Widiger, T.A. & Simonsen, M.D. (2005). Alternative dimensional models of personality disorder: Finding a common ground. *Journal of Personality Disorders, 19*, 110–130.

11.2 The Prevalence of Personality Disorders

Cale, E.M. & Lilienfeld, S.O. (2002). Sex differences in psychopathology and antisocial personality disorder: A review and integration. *Clinical Psychology Review, 22*, 1179–1207.

Fazel, S. & Danesh, J. (2002). Serious mental disorder in 23,000 prisoners: A systematic review of 62 surveys. *Lancet, 359*, 545–550.

Grant, B.F., Hasin, D.S., Stinson, F.S., Dawson, D.A. et al. (2004). Prevalence, correlates, and disability of personality disorders in the United States: Results from the National Epidemiologic Survey on alcohol and related conditions. *Journal of Clinical Psychiatry, 65*, 948–958.

Marinangeli, M.G., Butti, G., Scinto, A., Di Cicco, L. et al. (2000). Patterns of comorbidity among DSM-III-R personality disorders. *Psychopathology, 33*(2), 69–74.

Torgersen, S., Kringlen, E. & Cramer, V. (2001). The prevalence of personality disorders in a community sample. *Archives of General Psychiatry, 58*, 590–596.

Zimmerman, M., Rothschild, L. & Chelminski, I. (2005). The prevalence of DSM-IV personality disorders in psychiatric outpatients. *American Journal of Psychiatry, 162*, 1911–1918.

11.3 The Aetiology of Personality Disorders

Bandelow, B., Krause, J., Wedekind, D. et al. (2005). Early traumatic life events, parental attitudes, family history, and birth risk factors in patients with borderline personality disorder and healthy controls. *Psychiatry Research, 134*, 169–179.

Friedel, R.O. (2004). Dopamine dysfunction in borderline personality disorder: A hypothesis. *Neuropsychopharmacology, 29*, 1029–1039.

Ge, X., Conger, R.D., Cadoret, R.J., Neiderhiser, J.M. et al. (1996). The developmental interface between nature and nurture: A mutual influence model of child antisocial behaviour and parent behaviours. *Developmental Psychology, 32*, 574–589.

Helgeland, M.I. & Torgersen, S. (2004). Developmental antecedents of borderline personality disorder. *Comprehensive Psychiatry, 45*, 138–147.

Hill, J. (2003). Early identification of individuals at risk for antisocial personality disorder. *British Journal of Psychiatry, 182*, S11–S14.

Holmes, S.E., Slaughter, J.R. & Kashani, J. (2001). Risk factors in childhood that lead to the development of conduct disorder and antisocial personality disorder. *Child Psychiatry and Human Development, 31*, 183–192.

Lahey, B.B., Loeber, R., Burke, J.D. & Applegate, B. (2005). Predicting future antisocial personality disorder in males from a clinical assessment in childhood. *Journal of Consulting and Clinical Psychology, 73*, 389–399.

Lieb, K., Zanarini, M.C., Schmahl, C., Linehan, M.M. & Bohus, M. (2004). Borderline personality disorder. *Lancet, 364*, 453–461.

Lobbestael, J., Arntz, A. & Sieswerda, S. (2005). Schema modes and childhood abuse in borderline and antisocial personality disorders. *Journal of Behavior Therapy and Experimental Psychiatry, 36*, 240–253.

Lykken, D.T. (1957). A study of anxiety in the sociopathic personality. *Journal of Abnormal and Social Psychology, 55*(1), 6–10.

McGue, M. & Iacono, W.G. (2005). The association of early adolescent problem behaviour with adult psychopathology. *American Journal of Psychiatry, 162*, 1118–1124.

Monarch, E.S., Saykin, A.J. & Flashman, L.A. (2004). Neuropsychological impairment in borderline personality disorder. *Psychiatric Clinics of North America, 27*, 67.

Nigg, J.T. & Goldsmith, H.H. (1994). Genetics of personality disorders: Perspectives from personality and psychopathology research. *Psychological Bulletin, 115*, 346–380.

Ravelski, E., Sanislow, C.A., Grilo, C.M., Skodol, A.E. et al. (2005). Avoidant personality disorder and social phobia: Distinct enough to be separate disorders? *Acta Psychiatrica Scandinavica, 113*, 208–214.

Siever, L.J. & Davis, K.L. (2004). The pathophysiology of schizophrenia disorders: Perspectives from the spectrum. *American Journal of Psychiatry, 161*, 398–413.

Tienari, P., Wynne, L.C., Laksy, K., Moring, J. et al. (2003). Genetic boundaries of the schizophrenia spectrum: Evidence from the Finnish adoptive family study of schizophrenia. *American Journal of Psychiatry, 160*, 1587–1594.

11.4 Treating People with a Diagnosis of Personality Disorder

Arntz, A. (1999). Do personality disorders exist? On the validity of the concept and its cognitive-behavioral formulation and treatment. *Behaviour Research and Therapy, 37*, S97–S134.

Friendship, C., Blud, L., Erikson, M., Travers, R. & Thornton, D. (2003). Cognitive-behavioural treatment for imprisoned offenders: An evaluation of HM Prison Service's cognitive skills programmes. *Legal and Criminological Psychology, 8*, 103–114.

Leichsenring, F. & Leibing, E. (2003). The effectiveness of psychodynamic therapy and cognitive behaviour therapy in the treatment of personality disorders: A meta-analysis. *American Journal of Psychiatry, 160*, 1223–1232.

Linehan, M.M. (1987). Dialectical behaviour therapy for borderline personality disorder. *Bulletin of the Menninger Clinic, 51*, 261–276.

McQuillan, A., Nicastro, R., Guenot, F., Girard, M. et al. (2005). Intensive dialectical behaviour therapy for outpatients with borderline personality disorder who are in crisis. *Psychiatric Services, 56*, 193–197.

Newton-Howes, G. & Tyrer, P. (2003). Pharmacotherapy for personality disorders. *Expert Opinion on Pharmacotherapy, 4*, 1643–1649.

Texts for Further Reading

Alwin, N., Blackburn, R., Davidson, K., Hilton, M., Logan, C. & Shine, J. (2006). *Understanding personality disorder: A report of the British Psychological Society*. Leicester: BPS.

Bateman, A. & Fonagy, P. (2004). *Psychotherapy for borderline personality disorder: Mentalization-based treatment*. Oxford: Oxford University Press.

Beck, A.T., Freeman, A. & Davis, D. (Eds.) (2003). *Cognitive therapy of personality disorders*. New York: Guilford Press.

Benjamin, L.S. (2002). *Interpersonal diagnosis and treatment of personality disorders*. New York: Guilford Press.

Lenzenweger, M.F. & Clarkin, J.F. (Eds.) (2005). *Major theories of personality disorder* (2nd ed.). New York: Guilford Press.

Livesley, W.J. (Ed.) (2001). *Handbook of personality disorders: Theory, research and treatment*. New York: Guilford Press.

Magnavita, J.J. (Ed.) (2004). *Handbook of personality disorders: Theory and practice*. Chichester: Wiley.

Millon, T. (2004). *Personality disorders in modern life*. Chichester: Wiley.

Oldham, J.M., Skodol, A.E. & Bender, D.S. (Eds.) (2005). *The American Psychiatric Publishing textbook of personality disorders*. Washington, DC: American Psychiatric Publishing.

Patri, C.J. (2005). *Handbook of psychopathy*. New York: Guilford Press.

Young, J., Klosko, J. & Weishaar, M.E. (2003). *Schema therapy: A practitioner's guide*. New York: Guilford Press.

RESEARCH QUESTIONS

- It has been suggested that there is a link between adult schizoid personality disorder and childhood symptoms of autism. What is the evidence for this link?

- Why are prevalence rates for some personality disorders, such as borderline, avoidant, dependent and paranoid personality disorders, significantly higher in females than in males?

- Risk factors for personality disorders include low socioeconomic status, living in inner cities, and being divorced, separated or never married. Are these *causal* factors in developing personality disorders or simply *outcomes* of having a personality disorder?

- Recent studies have identified ethnicity as a factor affecting rates of diagnosis of personality disorders. How might ethnicity influence the development or diagnosis of a personality disorder?

- Can an overarching theory of the aetiology of all personality disorders ever be achieved? If so, what would such a theory look like?

- There are genetic and behavioural links between Cluster A disorders and schizophrenia. Does this make the Cluster A disorders (paranoid, schizoid and schizotypal personality disorders) part of a broader schizophrenia spectrum disorder?

- Are antisocial personality disorder and borderline personality disorder the same underlying disorder that manifests differently in men as APD and in women as BPD?

- Why do individuals diagnosed with personality disorders develop such enduring patterns of maladaptive behaviour that are so resistant to change?

- Conduct disorder is a significant predictor of antisocial personality disorder in later life, but does this beg the question of how conduct disorders developed in the first place?

- What is the evidence that children with hyperactivity/attention deficits (ADHD) are significantly likely to develop antisocial personality disorder in adulthood?

- The fathers of individuals with antisocial personality disorder are significantly more likely to have a diagnosis of APD themselves. Is this evidence for genetic or social learning processes in the aetiology of APD?

- There is evidence that individuals diagnosed with antisocial personality disorder have experienced inconsistent or neglectful parenting. However, is this a *cause* of APD or is inconsistent or neglectful parenting a *consequence* of having a child with APD?

- Individuals diagnosed with antisocial personality disorder appear to have dysfunctional cognitive schemas that lead them to behave either aggressively or impulsively. Is there a link between the development of these dysfunctional schemas and early experience?

- Are the physiological and neurological factors that accompany antisocial personality disorder (such as low anxiety levels, low levels of baseline arousal, neurological impairments) causes of APD or simply correlates of the behaviour patterns associated with APD?

- Childhood abuse and neglect appears to be a risk factor in around 80 per cent of those who develop borderline personality disorder. What are the important risk factors in the remaining 20 per cent who do not experience childhood abuse and neglect?

- Individuals with borderline personality disorder appear to possess relatively low levels of the brain neurotransmitter serotonin and dysfunctions in brain dopamine activity. Are these important causal factors in the behaviour patterns associated with BPD?

- Childhood abuse, conflict and neglect are experiences common to many of the personality disorders. How do such experiences get translated into the development of one particular personality disorder rather than another?

- Conflicting theories suggest that narcissistic personality disorder is caused either by childhood neglect or by 'doting' parents who treat their children too positively. Which theory is correct?

- Psychodynamic accounts suggest that negative childhood experiences and childhood underachievement may contribute to avoidant personality disorder. But are these experiences a *cause* of the disorder or simply *consequences* of the disorder?

- Different forms of psychodynamic theory argue that dependent personality disorder is fostered by childhood neglect or, alternatively, by overprotective parenting. Which is correct?

- Obsessive-compulsive personality disorder and obsessive-compulsive disorder have a relatively low comorbidity rate of 22 per cent. Why do some people go on to develop OCPD and others develop OCD?

CLINICAL ISSUES

- Comorbidity of an Axis I disorder with a personality disorder makes the Axis I disorder harder to treat.

- Are personality disorders discrete disorders or simply representative of extremes on conventional personality dimensions?

- Many of the personality disorders contain characteristics that overlap (e.g. impulsivity, poor self-image) and this often leads to the diagnosis of more than one personality disorder in the same individual.

- Schizotypal personality disorder has a number of behavioural and genetic links with schizophrenia, which suggests it may not be a discrete and independent disorder but part of a broader schizophrenia spectrum disorder.

- Recent changes in the diagnosis of antisocial personality disorder have moved towards defining it in terms of antisocial activities. This could blur the distinction between psychopathology in need of treatment and criminal behaviour in need of restraint.

- Borderline personality disorder is so closely associated with mood disorders, depression and suicide that it may well be a form of depression rather than a discrete and independent disorder.

- Borderline personality disorder is comorbid with post-traumatic stress disorder in 56 per cent of cases, which has led some theorists to suggest that it may be a form of PTSD rather than a discrete and independent disorder.

- Because of lack of empathy and the tendency to exploit others for personal benefit, narcissistic personality disorder may be a sub-type of antisocial personality disorder.

- Histrionic personality disorder may manifest differently in females and males, making it difficult to diagnose reliably across gender.

- Avoidant personality disorder is commonly comorbid with social phobia, which suggests it may be part of a broader social anxiety spectrum disorder rather than a discrete independent disorder.

- Because the patterns of behaviour exhibited by individuals with personality disorders can be considered to be on dimensions of normal behaviour (albeit at the extremes of these dimensions), the behavioural styles of these individuals *per se* may not be pathological but their behavioural styles may make them vulnerable to developing more traditional psychological symptoms (such as anxiety and depression).

- Individuals with personality disorders rarely believe they have a disorder that requires treatment, and this makes successful therapy difficult to achieve.

- Borderline personality disorder is regularly comorbid with bipolar disorder. BPD may therefore be part of a broader bipolar disorder spectrum rather than a discrete and independent disorder.

- Dependent personality disorder shares a number of characteristics with depression (e.g. indecisiveness, passiveness, pessimism, self-doubting, low self-esteem), which suggests that it may be a disorder that is not independent of mood disorders generally.

- Many of the personality disorders (e.g. antisocial, borderline, narcissistic personality disorders) have features that make the individual manipulative and unable to form trusting relationships. This means that it is very difficult to develop a working, trusting relationship between therapist and client.

- Some therapeutic approaches to personality disorders (e.g. dialectical behaviour therapy) emphasize that the therapist needs to convey complete acceptance of what the client does to enable a successful dialogue to ensue about the client's problems and difficulties.

- Cognitive therapies for personality disorders aim to challenge the client's dysfunctional belief systems. However, the therapist must avoid direct challenges because such individuals are often highly sensitive to criticism, hostile to views other than their own, and exhibit extreme mood swings which mean they may summarily leave therapy if directly challenged.

12 | Somatoform Disorders

ROUTE MAP OF THE CHAPTER

This chapter begins by describing some of the features
of those disorders collectively known in DSM-IV-TR as
somatoform disorders. These are conversion disorder,
somatization disorder, body dysmorphic disorder, hypochondriasis and pain disorder. Next it describes the diagnostic criteria, characteristics and prevalence rates of the
five main disorders. This is followed by a discussion of
some of the main theories of their aetiology, including
the benefits and limitations of such theories. Finally, the
chapter describes the range of treatments that have been
used with somatoform disorders and assesses their modes
of operation and efficacy.

Sometimes I don't know why I bother trying to look nice. I used to be able to pull it off. When I was younger I guess. I feel like my skin has changed, I can see more wrinkles, and it's dryer. I don't know how to describe my skin. It's never been normal, always had some sort of problem with oil and blemishes, but now it seems dry and old, still with the blemishes. The dark circles under my eyes are always visible no matter how much I try to cover them up with concealer. I just look old. I'm 27 years old and I look like I'm 58. I have the skin of a 58-year-old with blemishes. I also have the most horrific bump on my nose, in certain lights it shows up worse than others. I want to get a nose job. I don't know what I'm going to do about my skin, I hide behind my baseball cap all the time. My boyfriend hates it. But he doesn't understand how scary it is to let my face be shown in daylight – to let the world see the horrible bags under my eyes and my deformed nose and my wrinkles and my blemished skin. I know I need help, because it deeply affects my life. I don't enjoy life the way normal people do.

JANE'S STORY

Introduction

How many of us hate a particular feature of our physical appearance, yet manage to get on with our lives nonetheless? How often do we have physical symptoms such as aches and pains that trigger worries about contracting cancer or heart disease? For some people these everyday experiences are enough to cause significant distress and to interfere with their normal day-to-day living. When such concerns and worries become obsessive or a source of chronic anxiety or depression, they may be diagnosed as symptoms of a somatoform disorder. Somatoform disorders are characterized by the presence of physical symptoms suggestive of a medical or neurological condition, but full medical examination and tests provide no diagnosable evidence for an underlying medical problem. In order to be defined as a psychopathology, the symptoms must cause significant distress or impairment in social, occupational or other areas of functioning.

In the example we used to begin this chapter, *Jane* is suffering from *body dysmorphic disorder*. She has become obsessionally concerned about imagined or minor physical defects in her appearance (she perceives these to be blemished skin, a bump on her nose and dark circles under her eyes), and is even thinking of surgery to get these features changed. This preoccupation causes her significant distress and impairs her social, and probably her occupational, activities. In all probability, her friends and family do not

FOCUS POINT 12.1

Munchausen's syndrome by proxy

Beverley Allitt was a nurse who was convicted in 1993 of killing four children and injuring nine others at Grantham Hospital, Lincolnshire. While working on a children's ward in the hospital, she was found to be secretly injecting infants with insulin, a drug that induces cardiac arrest, causing brain damage and death. During the time she was involved in these killings, she was also befriending the parents of her victims and displaying what appeared to be a caring and sympathetic manner. She received 13 life sentences for her crimes, yet her motives for the killings have never been fully explained. One theory is that she was suffering from **Munchausen's syndrome by proxy**, a controversial diagnosis in which sufferers are prompted to deliberately falsify illnesses in others in order to attract attention to themselves.

What motivates some carers and parents to deliberately inflict illness, pain and even death knowingly on young children? Most mothers diagnosed with Munchausen's syndrome by proxy are emotionally needy and require attention and praise, which they receive when appearing caring and loving towards their ill child. They often have poor relationships with their partners, receive little in the way of support outside of the medical environment, and regularly exhibit low self-esteem. Many have a good knowledge of medicine and medical procedures, which allows them to cause their child's illness with a minimum of suspicion (Bluglass, 2001; Adshead & Brooke, 2001).

The syndrome is sometimes known as *factitious illness by proxy* or *abnormal illness behaviour by proxy* and is notoriously difficult to diagnose. This is because most victims are very young children, many of whom may have genuinely experienced acute life-threatening events whose causes are difficult to detect (such as sudden infant death syndrome, SIDS) (Galvin, Newton & Vandeven, 2005). In such circumstances, carers who present the problems of their children in unusual ways are often treated with suspicion – especially if their own emotional needs are consistent with those often found in Munchausen's syndrome by proxy (Pankratz, 2006).

see her in the way she sees herself and have never commented on these supposed defects.

Many individuals with somatoform disorders believe that their problems are genuinely medical and are often disbelieving when told there is no diagnosable evidence for a medical problem. In addition, those with symptoms that mimic neurological disorders, such as full or partial blindness or loss of feeling (anaesthesia), genuinely believe they have a disability, although their normal functioning can often be demonstrated in situations where drugs or hypnosis are used to alter levels of consciousness, or where elegant experimental methods are employed to infer ability (e.g. Grosz & Zimmerman, 1970).

It is also important when diagnosing some somatoform disorders (such as conversion disorder, somatization disorder, hypochondriasis and pain disorder) to differentiate true disorders from malingering. Claiming to have a physical illness when there isn't one is not just a ploy to avoid work or other situations that an individual may not enjoy: it can also be an actively deployed coping strategy in times of stress. The difference is that malingerers are fully aware that they are exaggerating or inventing their symptoms, while individuals with somatoform disorders are not. This is not an easy distinction to make. However, malingerers tend to be defensive when interviewed about their symptoms, whereas many with somatoform disorders often display a surprising indifference about their symptoms (e.g. those with conversion disorder), especially when the symptoms would be disturbing to most people (e.g. blindness, paralysis). This is sometimes known as *la belle indifférence*, or 'beautiful indifference'.

La belle indifférence An indifference about real symptoms (especially when the symptoms would be disturbing to most people) sometimes displayed by individuals with somatoform disorders.

Factitious disorders A set of physical or psychological symptoms that are intentionally produced in order to assume the sick role.

DSM-IV-TR does include a specific set of diagnostic criteria for physical or psychological symptoms that are *intentionally* produced in order to assume the sick role. Known as *factitious disorders*, these are seen as being quite different from malingering. In the case of malingering, individuals may intentionally produce symptoms for a specific reason (e.g. to avoid jury service or working in a stressful environment). In contrast, in factitious disorders the individual's motivation is to adopt the sick role – perhaps for the attention that this role will bestow. Individuals diagnosed with factitious disorders are usually pathological liars who have developed an extensive knowledge of medicine and medical terminology. An extreme form of factitious disorder is known as *Munchausen's syndrome*. A related disorder is *Munchausen's syndrome by proxy*, discussed in more detail in Focus Point 12.1, in which parents or carers make up or induce physical illnesses in others (such as their children). The reasons that drive individuals to deliberately make others ill are unclear, although such people often crave the attention and praise they receive in caring for someone who is ill (Abdulhamid, 2002).

Munchausen's syndrome An extreme form of factitious disorder in which individuals make up or induce physical illnesses.

Munchausen's syndrome by proxy An extreme form of factitious disorder in which parents or carers make up or induce physical illnesses in others (such as their children).

Finally, it is important to be able to differentiate between individuals with symptoms of somatoform disorders and those with genuine neurological and medical problems. Usually a thorough medical or neurological examination will fail to reveal any underlying medical condition. However, there is evidence that many symptoms diagnosed as a somatoform disorder (such as conversion disorder) may be neurological disorders in the early stages of development. In the 1980s as many as 80 per cent of a sample of individuals diagnosed with conversion disorder went on to develop a *bona fide* neurological problem (Gould, Miller, Goldberg & Benson, 1986). However, more recent studies suggest that misdiagnosis may have fallen to as little as 13 per cent – presumably as a result of more stringent and accurate neurological testing (Kent, Tomasson & Coryell, 1995).

This introduction to somatoform disorders indicates that:

1 Somatoform disorders are defined by the presence of physical symptoms suggestive of a medical or neurological problem.

2 The symptoms usually cannot be attributed to any underlying medical or neurological condition.

3 Individuals genuinely believe that they have a medical condition or a physical disability.

4 Symptoms cause significant distress or impairment of social or occupational functioning.

The specific somatoform disorders we discuss in the next section are (1) conversion disorder, (2) somatization disorder, (3) body dysmorphic disorder, (4) hypochondriasis and (5) pain disorder. After describing the main characteristics of these disorders we then discuss aetiology and treatment. Table 12.1 provides an overview of the important features of somatoform disorders which you may like to consult again once you have finished reading this chapter.

Table 12.1 *Somatoform disorders: summary*

DISORDER AND PREVALENCE RATES	DEFINITION	MAIN DSM-IV-TR DIAGNOSTIC FEATURES	KEY FEATURES	THEORIES OF AETIOLOGY (all somatoform disorders)	MAIN FORMS OF TREATMENT (all somatoform disorders)
Conversion disorder **Lifetime prevalence rate <1%**	The presence of symptoms or deficits affecting voluntary motor or sensory function	Symptoms affecting voluntary motor or sensory function Symptom is not feigned Symptom cannot be explained by a general medical condition Symptom causes distress and impairment	Common symptoms are paralysis, impaired balance, localized motor function weakness Neurological examination fails to reveal any underlying medical cause Usually develops in adolescence or early adulthood Symptoms may differ across cultures	Psychodynamic interpretations (particularly of conversion disorder and somatization disorder) The relationship between consciousness and behaviour (e.g. in conversion disorder and some forms of somatization disorder) The role of life stress, childhood abuse and anxiety Learning to play a 'sick role'	Psychodynamic therapy Behaviour therapy • Changing reinforcement contingencies • Behavioural stress management • Exposure and response prevention CBT Drug treatments
Somatization disorder **Lifetime prevalence rates: 0.2–2% in women; <0.2% in men**	Recurring multiple, clinically significant somatic symptoms that require medical treatment	A history of many physical complaints beginning before age 30 years Must have (1) four pain symptoms from different sites, (2) two gastrointestinal symptoms, (3) one sexual symptom and (4) one pseudoneurological symptom Symptoms cannot be explained by a known medical condition Symptom causes distress and impairment	Anxiety and depression are caused by the symptoms themselves Often comorbid with other Axis I disorders	Cognitive factors (such as information processing biases and dysfunctional beliefs) Sociocultural factors Biological factors	

Table 12.1 *(Cont'd)*

DISORDER AND PREVALENCE RATES	DEFINITION	MAIN DSM-IV-TR DIAGNOSTIC FEATURES	KEY FEATURES	THEORIES OF AETIOLOGY (all somatoform disorders)	MAIN FORMS OF TREATMENT (all somatoform disorders)
Body dysmorphic disorder Community prevalence rate 7%	Preoccupation with assumed defects in physical appearance	Preoccupation with imagined defect in appearance Symptom causes distress and impairment	Complaints include flaws in facial features, hair thinning, acne, wrinkles, scars, vascular markings, facial hair and body shape generally Associated with compulsive checking of physical features and avoidance of social situations Many seek cosmetic surgery in order to correct 'deficits' Often associated with depression and suicidal ideation		
Hypochondriasis Community prevalence rate 1–5%	Unfounded preoccupation with fears of having or contracting a serious disease or illness based on misinterpreting bodily symptoms	Preoccupation with fears of having a serious disease Preoccupation persists despite medical reassurances Duration of the disturbance is at least 6 months Symptom causes distress and impairment	Preoccupation with bodily functions (e.g. heart rate, coughs and ambiguous bodily sensations) Associated with intrusive thoughts about death and illness Sufferers readily seek medical opinion and medical knowledge but are unwilling to deny they have an illness		
Pain disorder 12-month prevalence rate 8.1%	A preoccupation with, and fear of, pain itself	Pain in one or more anatomical sites Psychological factors are judged to have an important role The symptom or deficit is not intentionally feigned Symptom causes distress and impairment	Pain is viewed as disabling, often non-localizable and described in negative emotional terms rather than sensory terms (e.g. 'pain is frightening' rather than 'pain is like a stabbing sensation') Associated with anxiety and depression		

12.1 THE DIAGNOSIS AND CHARACTERISTICS OF INDIVIDUAL SOMATOFORM DISORDERS

12.1.1 Conversion Disorder

Conversion disorder The presence of symptoms or deficits affecting voluntary motor or sensory function.

The basic feature of *conversion disorder* is the presence of symptoms or deficits affecting voluntary motor or sensory function suggestive of an underlying medical or neurological condition. For a diagnosis of conversion disorder, symptoms must cause significant distress or impair social, occupational or other functioning. Common motor symptoms are paralysis, impaired balance, localized motor function weaknesses, atonia (lack of normal muscle tone), difficulty swallowing and urinary retention. Common sensory symptoms include loss of touch or pain sensation, double vision, blindness, deafness, hallucinations and, on some occasions, seizures or convulsions. However, in conversion disorder, thorough medical and neurological examination may fail to reveal any underlying medical cause for these deficits. The symptoms are also often preceded by conflicts or other life stressors (Roelofs, Spinhoven, Sandijck et al., 2005), suggesting a psychological rather than a medical cause (see Table 12.2).

Sufferers do not appear to intentionally produce these symptoms, but more educated individuals may display more subtle symptoms and deficits that closely resemble known neurological deficits. However, conversion symptoms often fail to behave in ways expected by the known neurology. For example, in the conversion symptom known as *glove anaesthesia*, numbness begins at the wrist and is experienced evenly across the hand and all fingers (Figure 12.1). Yet, if a specific nerve to the hand, such as the ulnar nerve, is damaged, numbness should extend only to the ring finger and little finger. Similarly, damage to the radial nerve should affect only the thumb, index finger, middle finger and part of the ring finger.

Glove anaesthesia A conversion disorder symptom in which numbness begins at the wrist and is experienced evenly across the hand and all fingers.

Conversion symptoms are frequently inconsistent. Sufferers may often use a 'paralyzed' limb when dressing or may reflexively catch a ball unexpectedly thrown to them with their 'paralyzed' hand. Individuals with conversion disorder also tend to exhibit what is known as *la belle indifférence* ('beautiful indifference') towards their disability. Whereas most people who experience a sudden loss of physical ability would be frightened and distraught, individuals with conversion disorder tend to be largely philosophical and willing to talk at length about their symptoms. Some psychodynamic approaches to the explanation of conversion disorder suggest that this

Table 12.2 *DSM-IV-TR diagnostic criteria for conversion disorder*

A   One or more symptoms or deficits affecting voluntary motor or sensory function that suggest a neurological or other general medical condition.

B   Psychological factors are judged to be associated with the symptom or deficit because the initiation or exacerbation of the symptom or deficit is preceded by conflicts or other stressors.

C   The symptom or deficit is not intentionally produced or feigned (as in factitious disorder or malingering).

D   The symptom of deficit cannot, after appropriate investigation, be fully explained by a general medical condition, or by the direct effects of a substance, or as a culturally sanctioned behaviour or experience.

E   The symptom or deficit causes clinically significant distress or impairment in social, occupational or other important areas of functioning or warrants medical evaluation.

F   The symptom or deficit is not limited to pain or sexual dysfunction, does not occur exclusively during the course of somatization disorder and is not better accounted for by another mental disorder.

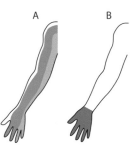

Figure 12.1
Glove anaesthesia. (A) Areas of the arm's skin that send sensory information to the brain by way of different nerves. (B) A typical region of anaesthesia in a patient with conversion disorder. If there were a nerve injury (in the spinal cord), the anaesthesia would extend over the length of the arm, following the nerve distribution shown in (A).

indifference appears to reflect a form of 'relief' that their symptoms may prevent individuals from having to deal with current conflicts and stress (Kuechenoff, 2002; Temple, 2002). Prior to its inclusion in the DSM, conversion disorder was popularly known as *hysteria* in psychodynamic circles.

Hysteria A common term used in psychodynamic circles to describe conversion disorder (prior to the latter's inclusion in the DSM).

Some vigilance must be exercised to ensure that conversion symptoms are not the result of developing neurological problems: it is estimated that between 13 and 30 per cent of individuals diagnosed with conversion disorder have later been found to develop some relevant neurological deficit (Maldonado & Spiegel, 2003; Kent, Tomasson & Coryell, 1995). In a majority of cases, however, symptoms may represent a 'symbolic resolution of an unconscious psychological conflict, reducing anxiety and serving to keep the conflict out of awareness' (APA, 2000, p. 494).

Conversion symptoms usually develop in adolescence or early adulthood, and usually after some stressful life event. Severity of the symptoms can be linked to the severity of the life stressor. Important stressful life events that can contribute to conversion disorder include work experiences and relationship difficulties (Roelofs, Spinhoven, Sandijck et al., 2005). However, symptoms can often spontaneously remit, only to return at a later time, and there is some evidence to suggest that a history of trauma and childhood abuse may be a vulnerability factor (Bowman & Markland, 1996).

The lifetime prevalence rate of conversion disorder is thought to be less than 1 per cent, and it is significantly more common in women than in men (Maldonado & Spiegel, 2003). There are also important cultural differences in the way that conversion disorder manifests itself. For example, Janca, Isaac, Bennett and Tacchini (1995) found that sexual and menstrual symptoms were prominent in Western cultures, complaints of body temperature irregularities are only found in Nigeria, kidney problems only in China, and body odour complaints only in Japan. In addition, the *lower* the economic or educational standards in a culture or community, the *higher* the prevalence of conversion disorder (Maldonado & Spiegel, 2003). Similarly, the *higher* the educational standards in a community, the *more likely* it is that the symptoms will resemble a known medical or neurological disorder (Tezzi, Duckworth & Adams, 2001).

Conversion disorder is also highly comorbid with many Axis I disorders, suggesting that it is only one symptom of broader-ranging psychological problems. A study by Sar, Akyuz, Kundakci, Kiziltyan et al. (2004) found at least one other psychiatric diagnosis in 89.5 per cent of a group of individuals with a diagnosis of conversion disorder. Comorbid diagnoses included generalized anxiety disorder, major depression, specific phobia, obsessive-compulsive disorder and dissociative disorders. Other common comorbid diagnoses include substance abuse and personality disorders such as borderline personality disorder and histrionic personality disorder (Binzer, Anderson & Kullgren, 1997; Rechlin, Loew & Joraschky, 1997).

12.1.2 Somatization Disorder

Somatization disorder A pattern of recurring, multiple, clinically significant somatic symptoms that require medical treatment and cause significant impairment in social, occupational and other areas of functioning.

The cardinal feature of ***somatization disorder*** is a pattern of recurring, multiple, clinically significant somatic symptoms that require medical treatment and that cause significant impairment in social, occupational and other areas of

functioning. To meet the diagnostic criteria for somatization disorder, an individual must display all of the following: (1) at least four pain symptoms in different bodily locations (e.g. back, head, extremities, rectum), (2) two gastrointestinal symptoms (diarrhoea, nausea), (3) one sexual or reproductive symptom (other than pain) (e.g. irregular periods in women or erectile dysfunction in men) and (4) one neurological symptom for which there is no obvious evidence of a neurological deficit (e.g. similar to the symptoms displayed in conversion disorder). In addition, these multiple complaints cannot be explained by a known general medical condition (see Table 12.3).

Somatization disorder differs from hypochondriasis (see section 12.1.4) because in the former it is the symptoms themselves (e.g. the pain they cause) that troubles the sufferer, whereas in the latter it is the prospect of contracting a disease or illness from the symptoms that is distressing. Individuals diagnosed with somatization disorder report a very wide range of often unconnected physical symptoms, and as a result are major users of health care services (Tezzi, Duckworth & Adams, 2001). While the symptoms they report are not usually indicators of any underlying medical condition, they will often develop medical disorders as a result of exploratory surgery and medication use (Holder-Perkins & Wise, 2001). They often seek treatment from several different doctors simultaneously, which can also lead to combinations of treatments that cause actual medical problems.

The lifetime prevalence rate of somatization disorder is around 0.2–2 per cent in women and less than 0.2 per cent in men (APA, 2000, p. 487). It usually begins in early adulthood but can often spontaneously remit, only to appear again a few years later (Cloninger, Martin, Guze & Clayton, 1986). Prevalence rates tend to be higher in some Latin countries (e.g. South America, Puerto Rico) and amongst African American and Hispanic women (Tomasson, Kent & Coryell, 1991; Escobar, Burnam, Karno, Forsythe et al., 1987). It is unclear why there are cultural differences in prevalence rates. At least one possibility is that different cultures view the expression of distress in different ways, and in many cultures the expression of physical pain is often an acceptable and established way of communicating psychological distress.

Like conversion disorder, somatization disorder is also closely associated with other psychiatric diagnoses and Axis I disorders such as anxiety disorders and major depression (Gureje, Simon, Ustun & Goldberg, 1997). It can be associated with impulsive and antisocial behaviour, suicide threats and deliberate self-harm, making the lives of individual sufferers chaotic and complicated (APA, 2000, p. 487).

12.1.3 Body Dysmorphic Disorder

At the beginning of this chapter we related *Jane's Story*, which described how distressed Jane became by what she felt were major defects in her appearance. The diagnostic category called ***body dysmorphic disorder*** is a preoccupation with such assumed defects in appearance. The defect is usually imagined, but if there is a physical anomaly present, those suffering

Body dysmorphic disorder
Preoccupation with assumed defects in physical appearance.

Table 12.3 *DSM-IV-TR diagnostic criteria for somatization disorder*

A   A history of many physical complaints beginning before age 30 years that occur over a period of several years and result in treatment being sought or significant impairment in social, occupational or other important areas of functioning.

B   Each of the following criteria must have been met, with individual symptoms occurring at any time during the course of the disturbance:

   (1)   Four pain symptoms: A history of pain related to at least four different sites or functions (e.g. head, abdomen, back, joints, extremities, chest, rectum, during menstruation, during sexual intercourse or during urination).

   (2)   Two gastrointestinal symptoms: A history of at least two gastrointestinal symptoms other than pain (e.g. nausea, bloating, vomiting other than during pregnancy, diarrhoea or intolerance of several different foods).

   (3)   One sexual symptom: A history of at least one sexual or reproductive symptom other than pain (e.g. sexual indifference, erectile or ejaculatory dysfunction, irregular menses, excessive menstrual bleeding, vomiting through pregnancy).

   (4)   One pseudoneurological symptom: A history of at least one symptom or deficit suggesting a neurological condition not limited to pain (conversion symptoms such as impaired coordination or balance, paralysis or localized weakness, difficulty swallowing or lump in throat, aphonia, urinary retention, hallucinations, loss of touch or pain sensation, double vision, blindness, deafness, seizures, dissociative symptoms such as amnesia or loss of consciousness other than fainting).

C   Either (1) or (2):

   (1)   After appropriate investigation, each of the symptoms in Criterion B cannot be fully explained by a known medical condition or the direct effects of a substance (e.g. a drug of abuse or medication).

   (2)   When there is a related general medical condition, the physical complaints or resulting social or occupational impairment are in excess of what would be expected from the history, physical examination or laboratory findings.

D   The symptoms are not intentionally produced or feigned.

Table 12.4 *DSM-IV-TR diagnostic criteria for body dysmorphic disorder*

A   Preoccupation with an imagined defect in appearance. If a slight physical anomaly is present, the person's concern is markedly excessive.

B   The preoccupation causes clinically significant distress or impairment in social, occupational or other important areas of functioning.

C   The preoccupation is not better accounted for by another mental disorder (e.g. dissatisfaction with body shape and size in anorexia nervosa).

Common complaints include flaws in facial features or facial asymmetry, hair thinning, acne, wrinkles, scars, vascular markings, irregular complexions or excessive facial hair. Other common preoccupations include body shape generally (e.g. preoccupations with being obese or overweight), and dissatisfaction with specific body parts such as breasts, genitals or buttocks. Sufferers are so embarrassed about their supposed appearance defects that they will often only talk about them in general terms, and may simply refer to themselves as being 'ugly'. Sufferers can also become obsessive about their defects and spend many hours a day viewing themselves in mirrors or attempting to deal with their problems by excessive grooming behaviour (e.g. skin picking, hair combing, applying cosmetics, dieting). Such behaviours usually add to the distress experienced. Individuals with body dysmorphic disorder also develop dysfunctional beliefs about their appearance and are quite convinced that their own perceptions are correct and undistorted. As a result, they may regularly seek cosmetic surgery in order to correct their 'defects'. In a study of individuals seeking cosmetic surgery, Aouizerate, Pujol, Grabot, Faytout et al. (2003) found that 9.1 per cent of applicants were diagnosable with body dysmorphic disorder. In fact, in those applicants who had no defects or only a slight physical defect, 40 per cent were diagnosable with body dysmorphic disorder. Body dysmorphic disorder can also occur in those who are preoccupied with their musculature and is often associated with excessive weight training and the use of body-building anabolic steroids (Olivardia, Pope & Hudson, 2000). Such an obsession with a muscular appearance is often called *muscle dysmorphia*.

A preoccupation with apparent physical defects often leads to the *catastrophizing* of these characteristics, and sufferers will frequently comment on their appearance to others in negative ways (e.g. 'I am ugly', 'I am fat'). Nevertheless, regular reassurance from others fails to change these views, and sufferers can

Muscle dysmorphia An obsession with a muscular appearance, often associated with excessive weight training and the use of body-building anabolic steroids.

Catastrophizing An example of magnification, in which the individual takes a single fact to its extreme.

from body dysmorphic disorder will greatly exaggerate its importance. In diagnosing this disorder, preoccupations with defects in appearance must cause significant distress or impairment in social, occupational or other functioning (see Table 12.4).

slip into a negative decline which incurs further psychopathology such as major depression, anxiety, social phobia, deliberate self-harm and suicide attempts (Phillips, 2001). In addition, adolescents with body dysmorphic disorder experience high levels of impairment in school and work functioning, with studies reporting attempted suicide rates as high as 45 per cent (Phillips, Didie, Menard, Pagano et al., 2006).

The exact prevalence rates of body dysmorphic disorder are unclear, although a nationwide German study suggested a community prevalence rate of around 7 per cent, of which 19 per cent reported suicidal ideation and 7 per cent reported suicide attempts due to appearance concerns (Rief, Buhlmann, Wilhelm, Borkenhagen et al., 2006). The disorder can begin in early adolescence and even childhood – sometimes as a result of teasing about appearance or as a result of parental neglect (Cororve & Gleaves, 2001; Phillips, 2001). Like many other somatoform disorders, it is highly comorbid with other Axis I disorders such as eating disorders (Ruffolo, Phillips, Menard, Fay et al., 2006), obsessive-compulsive disorder, social phobia and impulse control disorders (Frare, Perugi, Ruffalo & Toni, 2004).

12.1.4 Hypochondriasis

Hypochondriasis Unfounded preoccupation with fears of having or contracting a serious disease or illness based on misinterpreting bodily symptoms.

Health anxiety Another term for hypochondriasis.

Hypochondriasis (also often known as *health anxiety*) is a preoccupation with fears of having or contracting a serious disease or illness based on a misinterpretation of bodily signs or symptoms, even though a thorough medical examination fails to identify any underlying medical condition. This unwarranted fear of illness persists despite medical reassurance. Preoccupation with bodily signs of developing a disease or illness must cause significant distress or impairment in social or occupational functioning and must have been present for at least 6 months for a diagnosis to be made (see Table 12.5).

Preoccupation can be with bodily functions (e.g. heart rate, sweating), minor physical abnormalities (e.g. coughs or spots), or with vague and ambiguous bodily sensations (e.g. 'aching veins'). In the case of hypochondriasis, it is not the symptoms that cause immediate distress but the thought of what illness or disease these symptoms may signal (e.g. a heart attack, cancer). Sufferers will regularly read about medical conditions, which will increase their alarm and distress. They will also consult medical opinion on a regular basis, and be entirely unconvinced by reassurances that they do not have an illness. This regularly leads to a breakdown in the doctor–patient relationship and sufferers would rather believe they are not getting proper medical treatment than admit that they have a psychopathology. Fear of ageing and death is also associated with hypochondriasis, and may be associated with strict health regimes and use of alternative medicines (Fallon & Feinstein, 2001). Individuals with hypochondriasis are also prone to intrusive thoughts about illness, death and dying and usually catastrophize their symptoms. For example, they are likely to believe that an ambiguous bodily sensation (e.g. an increase in heart rate) is attributable to an illness rather than a non-threatening consequence (e.g. having just walked up a flight of stairs) (MacLeod, Haynes & Sensky, 1998), and that a blotch on the skin may be the start of a cancer (Rief, Hiller & Margraf, 1998). Such individuals are not necessarily better able to detect bodily sensations than non-sufferers, but they do possess a negatively based reporting style which means they interpret sensations significantly more negatively than non-sufferers (Aronson, Barrett & Quigley, 2006).

The prevalence rate for hypochondriasis in the general population is estimated to be 1–5 per cent (APA, 2000, p. 505) but can be as high as 36 per cent in chronic pain patients (Rode, Salkovskis, Dowd & Hanna, 2006). Hypochondriasis can begin at any age, but onset is most common during early adulthood. It is frequently comorbid with other Axis I disorders, including mood disorders and obsessive-compulsive disorder (Noyes, 1999; Abramowitz & Braddock, 2006). Finally, risk factors for developing hypochondriasis include a history of childhood abuse (Salmon & Calderbank, 1996), having an overprotective mother (Baker & Merskey, 1982) and having had close family members who have suffered a genuine physical illness (Robbins & Kirmayer, 1996).

12.1.5 Pain Disorder

The central feature of *pain disorder* is that the pain itself (and not any other feature of the physical symptoms) is the

Pain disorder A preoccupation with, and fear of, pain itself.

Table 12.5 *DSM-IV-TR diagnostic criteria for hypochondriasis*

A Preoccupation with fears of having, or the idea that one has, a serious disease based on the person's misinterpretation of bodily symptoms.

B The preoccupation persists despite appropriate medical evaluation and reassurance.

C The belief in Criterion A is not of delusional intensity (as in delusional disorder) and is not restricted to a circumscribed concern about appearance (as in body dysmorphic disorder).

D The preoccupation causes clinically significant distress and impairment in social, occupational or other important areas of functioning.

E The duration of the disturbance is at least 6 months.

F The preoccupation is not better accounted for by generalized anxiety disorder, obsessive-compulsive disorder, panic disorder, a major depressive episode, separation anxiety or another somatoform disorder.

HYPOCHONDRIACS ANONYMOUS

.NAF.

"I'll be home early. They all phoned in sick again."

Plate 12.1

Table 12.6 *DSM-IV-TR diagnostic criteria for pain disorder*

A   Pain in one or more anatomical sites is the predominant focus of the clinical presentation and is of sufficient severity to warrant clinical attention.

B   The pain causes clinically significant distress or impairment in social, occupational or other important areas of functioning.

C   Psychological factors are judged to have an important role in the onset, severity, exacerbation or maintenance of the pain.

D   The symptom or deficit is not intentionally produced or feigned.

E   The pain is not better accounted for by a mood disorder or psychotic disorder and does not meet the criteria for dyspareunia.

predominant focus of the individual's complaints. A diagnosis is given only if the pain causes significant distress or impairment in social, occupational or other functioning. The pain should not be produced intentionally or feigned (as in factitious disorder), and may result in major disruption to the individual's day-to-day living, including an inability to work or attend school (see Table 12.6). Sufferers make frequent use of health care services and a range of medications. This will also cause problems in family life (e.g. marital discord).

In most cases of pain disorder, the pain appears to be more severe and persistent than can be explained by any relevant medical causes. Sub-types of pain disorder include: (1) those that are associated with only psychological factors without evidence for a general medical condition; and (2) those whose onset can be attributed to a general medical condition that may play an important role in generating the experience of pain. Pain disorder can become specifically associated with substance abuse – especially if the sufferer is attempting to find medications that may alleviate the pain – as well as with depression. Threatened or attempted suicide is also a significant risk in pain disorder.

Most of us experience pain at some point in our lives, and many do so almost on a daily basis. However, the reported pain associated with pain disorder tends to be more severe than average, is more disabling, less localizable and often described in negative emotional terms rather than in sensory terms (e.g. 'the pain is frightening' rather than 'the pain is like a stabbing sensation') (Streltzer, Eliashopf, Kline & Goebert, 2000). A number of studies have indicated that individuals with pain disorder have a set of

information processing biases that lead them to interpret ambiguous bodily sensations as indicators of pain, which suggests that they are simply fearful of pain and have developed a phobia of pain that makes them hypervigilant for pain cues (McCracken, Zayfert & Gross, 1992). This is consistent with many sufferers also experiencing anxiety and depression, which leads them to catastrophize the pain symptoms and to a heightened experience of pain (Crombez, Eccleston, Baeyens & Eelen, 1998). How individuals interpret the pain experience has an important impact. For example, those who interpret their pain as being indicative of tissue damage or illness tend to be more avoidant and more disabled than those who do not have such an interpretive bias (Vlaeyens, Kole-Snijders, Rottveel, Rusenik et al., 1995), and fear of pain is a better predictor of disability than either pain severity or physical pathology (Crombez, Eccleston, Baeyens & Eelen, 1998).

Pain disorder may be one of the most prevalent psychopathologies, with a 12-month prevalence rate of 8.1 per cent found in a German population. Of those with diagnosed pain disorder, 53 per cent exhibited concurrent anxiety and depression (Frohlich, Jacobi & Wittchen, 2006).

SELF-TEST QUESTIONS

● Can you describe the main diagnostic criteria for conversion disorder together with its main features?
● How do cultural factors affect the prevalence rate and manifestation of conversion disorder symptoms?
● What are the main diagnostic criteria for somatization disorder?
● What are the main Axis I disorders that tend to be comorbid with somatoform disorders?
● What are the main diagnostic criteria for body dysmorphic disorder, and what are the usual types of bodily/facial features that sufferers complain about?
● What kinds of behaviours and thoughts might act to maintain body dysmorphic disorder?
● What is muscle dysmorphia?
● Can you describe the main diagnostic criteria for hypochondriasis? By what other name is this disorder sometimes known?
● What are the main diagnostic criteria for pain disorder, and how do sufferers tend to describe their pain symptoms?

SECTION SUMMARY

12.1 The Diagnosis and Characteristics of Individual Somatoform Disorders

- The basic feature of **conversion disorder** is the presence of symptoms or deficits affecting voluntary motor or sensory function.

- It is estimated that between 13 and 30 per cent of individuals diagnosed with conversion disorder have later been found to have some **neurological deficit**.

- Conversion symptoms usually develop in adolescence and severity of symptoms can be linked to the severity of **life stressors**.

- The lifetime prevalence rate for conversion disorder is less than 1 per cent.

- There are significant **cultural differences** in the way that conversion disorder symptoms manifest themselves.

- Conversion disorder is frequently **comorbid** with anxiety disorders, major depression, dissociative disorders, substance abuse and personality disorders.

- **Somatization disorder** is a pattern of recurring multiple, clinically significant somatic symptoms that require medical treatment.

- Individuals diagnosed with somatization disorder are usually **major users** of health care services.

- The lifetime prevalence rate of somatization disorder is around 0.2–2 per cent in **women** and less than 0.2 per cent in **men**.

- Somatization disorder is closely associated with other Axis I disorders such as **anxiety disorders** and **major depression**.

- **Body dysmorphic disorder** is a preoccupation with assumed defects in appearance. Common complaints include flaws in facial features, facial asymmetry, hair thinning, acne, wrinkles and scars.

- Individuals with body dysmorphic disorder indulge in **compulsive behaviours** such as persistent grooming or looking at themselves in mirrors. They also develop tendencies to avoid showing their 'defective' body part and avoid social situations generally.

- Similar symptoms to body dysmorphic disorder can be found in some weight-trainers who become obsessed with their musculature. This is known as **muscle dysmorphia**.

- Prevalence rates are unclear, but a German study indicated a community prevalence rate of around 7 per cent for body dysmorphic disorder.

- **Hypochondriasis** (also known as **health anxiety**) is a preoccupation with fears of having or contracting a serious illness based on a misinterpretation of bodily signs or symptoms.

- Individuals with hypochondriasis regularly read about medical conditions and consult medical opinion. They are also entirely unconvinced by reassurances that they do not have a medical illness.

- The prevalence rate for hypochondriasis in the general population is estimated to be 1–5 per cent.

- In **pain disorder**, the central feature is that the pain itself (and not other features of the physical symptoms) is the predominant focus of the individual's complaints.

- The pain reported by those with pain disorder tends to be more severe than average, is more disabling, less localizable and is often described in **negative** terms rather than sensory terms.

- Pain disorder may be one of the most prevalent psychiatric conditions with a 12-month prevalence rate of around 8.1 per cent.

12.2 THE AETIOLOGY OF SOMATOFORM DISORDERS

The most traditional explanations of somatoform disorders have been couched in psychodynamic terms – primarily because some of Freud's most influential writings concerned hysteria and the causes of unexplained physical symptoms. However, since then a number of different approaches to explaining somatoform disorders have developed, including learning accounts and cognitive accounts. Nevertheless, regardless of the theoretical approach to the aetiology of somatoform disorders, any explanation must address certain key questions. These include:

1 Are physical symptoms a manifestation of underlying psychological conflict and stress?

2 Are physical symptoms generated in an involuntary fashion?

3 What is the role of life stress and childhood abuse in the development of somatoform disorders?

4 How do sufferers acquire the biased thinking and dysfunctional beliefs about health that help to maintain many of the somatoform disorders?

12.2.1 Psychodynamic Interpretations

Some of Freud's most famous writings were on the subject of hysteria and how inner conflict, repressed emotions and life stress could be manifested in somatic symptoms. The basic psychodynamic view of somatoform disorders is one of *conflict resolution* in which distressing memories, inner conflict, anxiety and unacceptable thoughts are repressed in consciousness but outwardly expressed as somatic symptoms. For example, Freud believed that somatic symptoms such as those found in conversion disorder (then known as hysteria) were associated with distressing memories of childhood seduction. These might be actual experiences of childhood abuse or simply imagined as fantasies during the Oedipal period of development. When these memories are reawakened during puberty, this causes intense anxiety and conflict resulting in somatic symptoms and repression of these memories. The somatic symptoms served the purpose of helping to suppress these memories and to relieve anxiety, and this was consistent with the fact that most individuals with conversion disorder exhibited a calm philosophical attitude to their disability (*la belle indifférence*), suggesting that it was a state in which they experienced some relief from stress and conflict.

> **Conflict resolution** The basic psychodynamic view of somatoform disorders in which distressing memories, inner conflict, anxiety and unacceptable thoughts are repressed in consciousness but outwardly expressed as somatic symptoms.

Underlying sexual conflict was also seen by psychodynamic theorists as being an important contributor to other somatoform disorders such as somatization disorder and hypochondriasis. Freud believed that repressed sexual energy was often turned inward on the self, transforming it into physical symptoms that created physical pain or were interpreted as indicators of illness and disease. Indeed, psychodynamic theorists often view those suffering from somatoform disorders as regressing to the state of a sick child, unconsciously seeking attention and relief from symptoms and responsibilities and thus reducing experienced anxiety (Kuechenoff, 2002; Kellner, 1990; Phillips, 1996).

These psychodynamic accounts appear to make intuitive sense in that those who develop somatoform disorders often appear to have either a history of conflict, stress and abuse or have recently experienced an important life stressor (Bowman & Markland, 1996; Roelofs, Spinhoven, Sandijck et al., 2005). Nevertheless, an important aspect of the psychodynamic conflict-resolution model is that the physical symptoms cause relief either from anxiety or from having to deal with current conflicts and stress (Temple, 2002). In contrast, disorders such as somatization disorder and hypochondriasis appear to involve high levels of anxiety (Noyes, Kathol, Fisher, Phillips et al., 1994), and a sizeable minority of those with conversion disorder also fail to exhibit the calming effects of *la belle indifférence* (Gureje, Simon, Ystun & Goldberg, 1997). This suggests that the supposed psychologically beneficial effects of somatization as proposed by psychodynamic theory are often difficult to find.

12.2.2 Consciousness and Behaviour

One important feature of some somatoform disorders, such as conversion disorder and somatization disorder, is that the sufferer appears able to generate physical symptoms or deficits (e.g. medical symptoms, blindness) in an involuntary fashion. That is, there is a dissociation between the individual's behaviour and his or her awareness of that behaviour. For example, in conversion disorder, sufferers appear genuinely unable to experience certain sensory input (e.g. when exhibiting blindness or loss of feeling). However, studies suggest that such individuals can experience the sensory input at some level of processing, but are consciously unaware of it.

Theodor and Mandelcorn (1973) describe a study undertaken with a 16-year-old girl who complained of a loss of peripheral vision with no underlying neurological explanation for it. In their study they presented a buzzer followed by a bright visual stimulus to the girl's central or peripheral visual field on a percentage of the trials. The girl's task was to report whether a visual stimulus had followed the buzzer or not. They found that the girl always correctly reported when the buzzer was followed by a stimulus to the central visual field. However, she was only 30 per cent correct when reporting a visual stimulus to the peripheral visual field. Theodor and Mandelcorn argued that a person who truly had no peripheral vision would have reported a visual stimulus at chance level, i.e. on 50 per cent of the trials. The girl with a somatoform disorder in fact performed significantly worse than this, suggesting that at some level of consciousness she was aware of the peripheral visual stimulus but was suppressing reporting it.

In a similar study, Zimmerman and Grosz (1966) found that an individual with hysterical blindness performed a visual task at significantly below chance level when a truly blind individual should be performing at chance level. They also found that when visual stimuli were presented in a non-random predictable sequence, their patient still performed at well below chance level: even a truly blind person would have performed above chance on this task. Both these studies indicate that a person with conversion disorder can discriminate relevant incoming sensory information at some level, even if they use that information in a way that results in their performing significantly below what would be expected of someone who was blind! Evidence such as this might initially suggest that sufferers are simply faking symptoms and trying to behave in ways that are consistent with these symptoms. However, if it is faking, then the individual has taken great pains to be consistent in his or her behaviour, often over long periods of time and in difficult situations.

A very early explanation of these types of symptoms was proposed by Janet (1907), who suggested that patients suffering from hysteria experience a spontaneous narrowing of attention after being exposed to trauma. This attentional narrowing limits the number of sensory channels that can be attended to and leads to the loss of voluntary control over neglected channels. This results in the patient being rendered anaesthetic for any information coming in to the unattended modality, even though the information is still processed outside of conscious awareness. As a result, the patient may be unable consciously to access information from these channels and experiences blindness or paralysis, depending on the sensory channel that has been neglected.

A similar explanation of these anomalous findings is provided by Oakley (1999). He draws attention to the many similarities between the behaviour of the individual with conversion disorder

or somatization disorder and the effects of *hypnosis*. First, many of the symptoms of conversion disorder are similar to physical states that can be easily established by hypnosis (e.g. blindness, paralysis), and they also display a degree of involuntariness. That is, both the conversion disorder patient and the person under hypnosis regularly report that they have no voluntary control over a movement or a sensation (e.g. they may be unable to raise their arm). In drawing these two areas together, Oakley (1999) has proposed that similar mechanisms could be responsible for both conversion/somatization symptoms and behaviour under hypnosis. So an action or incoming sensory information may often be processed at a range of different levels of mental functioning, but for some reason may not be selected for conscious processing (presumably one of the last stages of this process). Under hypnosis this last stage of processing can often be prevented by suggestions from an external source (such as the hypnotist), and it will appear to the individual that he or she has no control over his or her actions or perceptions. Oakley proposes a similar effect in conversion disorder in which some presumably internal processes have prevented sensory information from being analysed by conscious awareness. Because the sensory information is processed at lower mental levels, this explains why individuals with hysterical blindness can respond in ways that suggest visual information is being received (e.g. by performing at significantly below chance on a visual recognition task) but are not consciously aware that visual stimuli are being perceived and responded to. As appealing as this explanation is, it still begs the question of how and why sensory information is blocked from conscious awareness in individuals with conversion disorder. This is an aspect that still needs to be fully explored and understood.

> **Hypnosis** A therapeutic technique in which the patient is placed in a trance.

Plate 12.2
There are many similarities between the behaviour of an individual with conversion disorder or somatization disorder and the effects of hypnosis. Many of the symptoms of conversion disorder (e.g. blindness, paralysis) are similar to physical states that can be established by hypnosis, and similar mechanisms affecting the conscious experience of sensory input may be responsible for some somatoform disorders and behaviour under hypnosis.

12.2.3 Life Stress, Childhood Abuse and Anxiety

A significant factor in the history of most somatoform disorders is either a history of trauma or abuse or significant periods of stress and anxiety. Both appear to be important risk factors in developing a somatoform disorder. For example, a history of childhood trauma appears to increase vulnerability to conversion disorder (Bowman & Markland, 1996), and high levels of negative life events in the year prior to onset have been found in individuals with *globus pharyngis* (a form of conversion disorder in which sufferers experience a sensation of a lump in the throat) (Harris, Deary & Wilson, 1996). Individuals with somatization disorder tend to report histories of physical and sexual abuse (Holder-Perkins & Wise, 2001), as do those with hypochondriasis (Salmon & Calderbank, 1996), and parental neglect is a factor often found in the history of body dysmorphic disorder (Phillips, 1991). In addition, many somatoform disorders develop following exposure to acute stressors, such as recent loss (Van Ommeren, Sharma, Komproe, Sharma et al., 2001), relationship difficulties (Craig, 2001) and exposure to dead bodies following military combat (Labbate, Cardena, Dimitreva, Roy et al., 1998).

Nevertheless, we must be cautious about what these findings mean in the aetiology of somatoform disorders. Firstly, not everyone who develops a somatoform disorder reports having had high levels of childhood abuse or neglect or having had a significant number of negative life events generally (e.g. Sar, Akyuz, Kundakci, Kiziltyan et al., 2004), so such experiences are not a *necessary* condition for developing a somatoform disorder. Secondly, the actual levels of stress reported by individuals with somatoform disorders are not necessarily significantly higher than those reported by individuals with other psychopathologies, so stress levels *per se* do not differentially predict the development of a somatoform disorder (Roelofs, Spinhoven, Sandijck et al., 2005). Third, high levels of childhood trauma and negative life events can be found in the histories of a wide range of psychopathologies (e.g. personality disorders, eating disorders, anxiety disorders), so why should someone who has this kind of traumatic history develop a somatoform disorder rather than any of these other disorders (although it must be admitted that somatoform disorders are regularly comorbid with many other Axis I disorders)?

Some theories do specify a central role for stress and early negative experiences in the development of somatoform disorders. One example is the conflict-resolution model adopted by many psychodynamic theorists (see p. 448); another is the attentional-narrowing model of hysteria proposed by Janet (1907) (see pp. 448–449). However, the role of stress and childhood trauma in other theories is often underdeveloped, and this is an aspect of our understanding of the aetiology of somatoform disorders that needs to be explored.

12.2.4 Learning Approaches

A number of theorists have suggested that somatoform disorders may develop because many of the aspects of these disorders are learned through specific types of experiences. For example, Craig, Boardman, Mills, Daly-Jones et al. (1993) have argued that many individuals learn to interpret emotional symptoms as indicative of physical illness. This learning could occur in a number of ways. First, individuals suffering conversion disorder, somatization disorder and hypochondriasis all report having had early childhood experiences where close members of their family experienced physical illness or somatic symptoms (Tezzi, Duckworth & Adams, 2001), so expressing any negative feelings (emotional or physical) may occur through somatization because of exposure to modelling by important family members. In support of this view, Craig, Cox and Klein (2002) compared the childhood histories of three groups of women: those with somatization disorder, those with a long-term illness and healthy controls. They found that women with somatization disorder were 3 times more likely than women in the other groups to have had a parent with a serious physical illness.

A related view is that expressing symptoms of physical illness may be reinforced by parents. For example, some parents may view all underlying problems (including psychological ones) as being physical rather than emotional, and subtly encourage their children to report psychological problems in physical terms (Latimer, 1981). In an insightful study, Craig, Bialas, Hodson et al. (2004) observed mothers playing with their 4- to 8-year-old children. Mothers who exhibited somatization symptoms were less emotionally expressive than control mothers during most play tasks. However, they were significantly *more* responsive to their children when they played with medically related toys (e.g. a medical box). In this way, mothers who already display somatization symptoms may pass this predisposition on to their children through the differential display of attention in medically related contexts.

Finally, early learning of the kind described above means that many individuals may learn to describe emotional symptoms in physical terms and in extreme cases begin to adopt what is known as a *sick role*. Adopting a sick role has a number of disadvantages: it means a loss of power and influence as the individual relinquishes tasks and duties to others; it also involves a loss of pleasure, especially if an individual becomes house-bound or even bedridden because of his or her symptoms. However, Ullman and Krasner (1975) have argued that adopting a sick role can have significant advantages and rewards in terms of the attention sufferers are likely to receive from others, and the absolving of responsibility can be viewed as a way of opting out of dealing directly with life stressors and conflicts. In this case, adopting the sick role becomes a coping style for adult life. While this view is consistent with the fact that somatizing mothers may teach their children similar tendencies, adopting a sick role implies that the individual is unable to cope with the normal rigours and challenges of daily life. Convincing evidence that this is indeed the case still needs to be collected.

> **Sick role** Playing the role of being sick as defined by the society to which the individual belongs.

Nevertheless, there does seem to be some reasonable evidence that children may learn somatizing attitudes from their parents in various ways, and this may provide a basis for the possible development of somatoform disorders in later life.

12.2.5 Cognitive Factors

One important feature of most of the somatoform disorders is that sufferers believe they have physical deficits or symptoms that are significant and threatening, but in most cases there is little or no medical justification for these beliefs. This strongly suggests that sufferers have developed thinking and information processing biases that lead them to believe they have medical symptoms when in fact they do not. Such cognitive biases can take a number of forms. They may involve *interpretation biases*, in which individuals interpret ambiguous bodily sensations as threatening and evidence for a potential serious illness. For example, when someone with hypochondriasis experiences a stomach pain, he or she may interpret this catastrophically as a possible symptom of stomach cancer, rather than, say, the result of eating something that was 'off'. This biased thinking then gives rise to a range of consequences that are likely to reinforce the biased belief, including increased fear and anxiety, preoccupation with similar symptoms and reassurance-seeking (Warwick, 1995) (see Figure 12.2).

> **Interpretation biases** Cognitive biases in which an individual interprets ambiguous events as threatening and evidence for potential negative outcomes.

In a similar vein, Barsky (1992) argued that patients with somatization disorder have a bias towards describing minor automatic

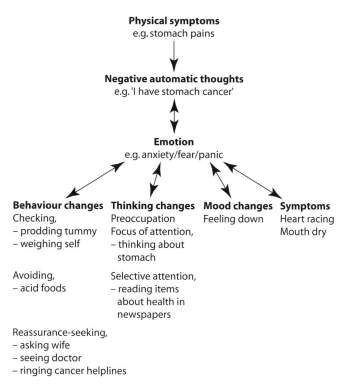

Figure 12.2

This cognitive model of hypochondriasis illustrates how physical symptoms or bodily sensations evoke negative automatic thoughts about illness. These thoughts then trigger feelings of anxiety, which in turn trigger a range of behavioural, cognitive and mood reactions that reinforce biased beliefs and hypochrondriacal symptoms.

Source: Warwick (1995).

bodily sensations in a catastrophic manner, which leads to a significantly higher level of reported symptoms. In support of these views, Lim and Kim (2005) used an Emotional Stroop Procedure (see Chapter 5, Research Methods Box 5.2) to demonstrate that individuals diagnosed with a somatoform disorder showed a significant Stroop interference effect for physical threat words (e.g. injury, seizure, inflammation), suggesting that these individuals consciously and selectively attended to physical symptom-related cues. In addition, Haenen, de Jong, Schmidt, Stevens et al. (2000) found that individuals with hypochondriasis who were given ambiguous health-related vignettes about illness and death were significantly more likely than controls to interpret these vignettes as serious and threatening.

One interesting feature of individuals with hypochondriasis and somatizing disorder is their tendency to reject diagnoses that disagree with their own beliefs about their health and to seek further opinions, presumably in the belief that someone will agree with their own view. Smeets, de Jong and Mayer (2000) found that individuals with hypochondriasis possessed a *reasoning bias* that supported

Reasoning bias   The tendency of individuals with hypochondriasis to reject diagnoses that disagree with their own beliefs about their health and to seek further opinions – presumably in the belief that someone will agree with their view.

this 'doctor shopping'. They actively sought out and accepted information that agreed with their own view of their medical state, but ignored or rejected arguments against their own beliefs. This process inevitably maintains hypochondriacal thinking and generalized anxiety about health issues.

Recent accounts of pain disorder have also taken a cognitive perspective. Sufferers are characterized by the fact that they usually fear pain itself rather than the illness, injury or disease that might give rise to pain, and so when experiencing pain they have a tendency to *catastrophize* it (Crombez, Eccleston, Baeyens & Eelen, 1998). Studies suggest that individuals with pain disorder have a bias towards attending to pain and are unable to distract themselves from pain-related thoughts (Sullivan, Bishop & Pivik, 1995). Also, they are significantly impaired in their ability to use pain distraction coping strategies (Heyneman, Fremouw, Gano, Kirkland et al., 1990). This attentional predisposition to monitor pain also appears to extend to situations that might cause pain or injury. For example, Vlaeyens, Kole-Snijders, Rotteveel, Rusenik et al. (1995) found that individuals with chronic low back pain possessed irrational fears of injury and bodily movements that motivated avoidance behaviours and the monitoring of back sensations – presumably in an attempt to detect potential back pain.

The preceding evidence strongly suggests that many somatoform disorders are maintained by cognitive factors that take the form of (1) attentional biases to physical threats; (2) biases towards interpreting body sensations and symptoms as threatening; (3) reasoning biases that maintain beliefs about illness and being ill; and (4) catastrophizing of symptoms. However, none of these accounts explains how the individual with somatoform disorders *acquires* these thinking and information processing biases. Some insight into how these biases might develop has been provided by Brown (2004). Brown argues that *rogue representations* are developed by a range of experiences, and these representations provide inappropriate templates by which information is selected and interpreted. Rogue representations can be created by experiences that include:

Rogue representations   In somatoform disorders, representations which provide inappropriate templates by which information about body shape and health are selected and interpreted.

1   a history of physical illness that causes a tendency to interpret any sensation as a symptom of illness;

2   a history of experiencing emotional states that have strong physical manifestations (e.g. anxiety is associated with shaking, palpitations, nausea, muscle tension, chest pain, dizziness); such experiences might arise from childhood trauma and abuse and result in a tendency to interpret such symptoms fearfully; and

3   exposure to physical illness in others (e.g. abnormal levels of illness in the family), which creates a memory template by which one's own physical sensations are interpreted.

In support of this account, there is good evidence to suggest that individuals with somatoform disorders do experience these factors with significantly greater frequency than non-sufferers (Schrag, Brown & Trimble, 2004; Tezzi, Duckworth & Adams,

ACTIVITY BOX 12.1

Pain Anxiety Symptoms Scale (PASS)

One theory of pain disorder is that some individuals learn to interpret pain in a threatening way. This leads to avoidance of situations that might cause pain (e.g. heavy physical work) and to hypervigilance to bodily sensations and pain that reinforce the personal experience of pain. In order to measure the degree to which people 'fear' pain symptoms, McCracken, Zayfert and Gross (1992) developed the Pain Anxiety Symptoms Scale (PASS). You might like to complete this questionnaire in order to acquire some experience of the questions that relate to fear of pain. The higher your score on an individual sub-scale, the more you are likely to view pain as threatening.

Individuals who experience pain develop different ways to respond to that pain. We would like to know what you do and what you think about when in pain. Please use the rating scale below to indicate how often you engage in each of the following thoughts or activities. Circle any number from 0 (NEVER) to 5 (ALWAYS) for each item.

		NEVER					ALWAYS
1.	I think that if my pain gets too severe, it will never decrease	0	1	2	3	4	5
2.	When I feel pain I am afraid that something terrible will happen	0	1	2	3	4	5
3.	I go immediately to bed when I feel severe pain	0	1	2	3	4	5
4.	I begin trembling when engaged in activity that increases pain	0	1	2	3	4	5
5.	I can't think straight when I am in pain	0	1	2	3	4	5
6.	I will stop any activity as soon as I sense pain coming on	0	1	2	3	4	5
7.	Pain seems to cause my heart to pound or race	0	1	2	3	4	5
8.	As soon as pain comes on I take medication to reduce it	0	1	2	3	4	5
9.	When I feel pain I think that I may be seriously ill	0	1	2	3	4	5
10.	During painful episodes it is difficult for me to think of anything else besides the pain	0	1	2	3	4	5
11.	I avoid important activities when I hurt	0	1	2	3	4	5
12.	When I sense pain I feel dizzy or faint	0	1	2	3	4	5
13.	Pain sensations are terrifying	0	1	2	3	4	5
14.	When I hurt I think about the pain constantly	0	1	2	3	4	5
15.	Pain makes me nauseous (feel sick)	0	1	2	3	4	5
16.	When pain comes on strong I think I might become paralysed or more disabled	0	1	2	3	4	5
17.	I find it hard to concentrate when I hurt	0	1	2	3	4	5
18.	I find it difficult to calm my body down after periods of pain	0	1	2	3	4	5
19.	I worry when I am in pain	0	1	2	3	4	5
20.	I try to avoid activities that cause pain	0	1	2	3	4	5

© Lance McCracken.

There are 4 sub-scales that measure (1) avoidance of pain (by adding the scores for items 3 + 6 + 8 + 11 + 20); (2) fearful appraisal of pain (by adding the scores for items 1 + 2 + 9 + 13 + 16); (3) cognitive anxiety (by adding the scores for items 5 + 10 + 14 + 17 + 19); and (4) physiological anxiety (by adding the scores for items 4 + 7 + 12 + 15 + 18).

2001; Holder-Perkins & Wise, 2001; Hotopf, Mayou, Wadsworth & Wessely, 1999).

12.2.6 Sociocultural Approaches

There is some evidence that sociocultural factors can influence both the prevalence of somatoform disorders and the nature of the symptoms exhibited in specific disorders. For example, we saw earlier in this chapter that cultural factors can influence prevalence rates in somatization disorder and the types of symptoms experienced in conversion disorder (see section 12.1). Being ill involves playing a social role that is often shaped by the society to which the individual belongs (Fox, 1989). This role is known as the *sick role*, and even across societies it is defined in ways that may help individuals cope with psychological distress and conflict. For example, the sick role in most societies means that the sick person (1) is exempt from his or her normal social roles for the duration of the illness, and (2) is often seen as not responsible for his or her illness (Parsons, 1951). Thus, playing the sick role can provide relief from the stresses and strains of everyday living. However, the likelihood of an individual adopting the sick role as a way of coping with stress and conflict will depend on attitudes towards unexplained somatic symptoms in different cultures. In some cultures, expressing physical pain is an accepted way of communicating psychological distress, and rates of somatoform disorder tend to be higher in such cultures – e.g. in Latin countries and amongst American Hispanic women (Tomasson, Kent & Coryell, 1991; Escobar, Burnam, Karno, Forsythe et al., 1987). In such communities, individuals may be encouraged to somatize psychological distress in a way that allows them to more readily adopt a sick role (Goldberg & Bridges, 1988).

In addition to cultural factors that affect the somatization of psychological distress, socioeconomic standards also influence prevalence rates. Individuals who live in rural areas, are less well educated and have a poorer standard of living are more likely to exhibit somatoform disorders (Maldonado & Spiegel, 2003) – possibly because in such socioeconomic groups the expression of psychological distress is less acceptable and so psychological symptoms are expressed as physical illness.

One final social factor can be identified in the aetiology of conversion disorder. Physical symptoms associated with conversion disorder can often be 'contagious' and affect a number of people within a single social setting or social group. This is similar to the physical symptoms of hysteria that were often reported in young women at pop concerts during the 1960s and 1970s. Examples of contagion appear to occur following an acute period of stress within a closely knit social group, where all those involved display very similar unexplained somatization symptoms. A recent example of this was reported by Cassady, Kirschke, Jones, Craig et al. (2005) within an Amish community in the USA. Four individuals developed motor deficits (inability to hold up their heads) and weight loss symptoms following a period of acute stress within the closely knit community. Examples of 'contagious hysteria' such as this continue to be reported, but as yet there is no convincing explanation for these multiple cases of somatoform symptoms.

12.2.7 Biological Factors

Because somatoform disorders involve what are apparently physical symptoms, it is reasonable to ask whether there are any underlying biological causes for these disorders. We know that (1) a certain percentage of those with conversion disorder and somatization disorder do have medical conditions that could contribute to their psychopathology (Maldonado & Spiegel, 2003; Hilder-Perkins & Wise, 2001) and that (2) many who develop somatoform disorders have a history of physical illness in their family (Hotopf, Mayou, Wadsworth & Wessely, 1999). Both of these factors provide grounds for exploring the role of biological factors.

Torgersen (1986) investigated a possible genetic component to somatoform disorders by investigating the presence of somatoform disorder in MZ and DZ twins. He found that MZ twins had a higher concordance rate for somatoform disorders than DZ twins, which is consistent with there being a genetic component to these disorders, but the sample he used was particularly small. Some studies have investigated inherited aspects of somatoform disorder using adoption studies, but these have only served to further confuse the role of inheritance in somatoform disorders. Bohman, Cloninger, von Knorring and Sigvardsson (1984) and Cloninger, Sigvardsson, von Knorring and Bohman (1984) traced the histories of the biological and adoptive parents of 859 women with somatization disorder. However, rather surprisingly, they found that the biological fathers of these women had significantly higher levels of alcoholism or violent crime than would be expected by chance, suggesting a biological or genetic link between antisocial behaviour and somatization disorder! We await further larger-scale genetic studies of somatoform disorders that may clarify these findings.

Because of the startling symptoms of conversion disorder, such as paralysis and blindness, there have been a number of studies that have investigated the role of the brain in this disorder. Studies that have monitored the brain waves of individuals with conversion disorder suggest that sensory information is reaching the appropriate areas of the brain but is not being registered in consciousness. Marshall, Halligan, Fink et al. (1997) carried out a positron emission tomography (PET scan) study of a conversion disorder patient who had a paralysed left leg. They found increased activation in the right orbitofrontal and anterior cingulated cortices, but an absence of activity in the right primary cortex when the patient attempted to move the leg. This suggests that unexplained paralysis involves some form of inhibition of primary motor activity by brain areas such as the orbitofrontal and anterior cingulated cortices. Interestingly, this same pattern of excitation and inhibition can be found in PET scans of individuals who have leg paralysis induced by hypnosis (Halligan, Athwal, Oakley & Frackowiak, 2000), suggesting that paralysis caused by conversion disorder and hypnosis may reflect very similar underlying brain processes. These findings suggest that brain areas that would normally instigate movement are being activated, but other areas of the brain that would not be involved are being activated in order to inhibit the movement (e.g. orbitofrontal and anterior cingulated cortices; see Research Methods Box 12.1).

RESEARCH METHODS IN CLINICAL PSYCHOLOGY BOX 12.1

Brain imaging using positron emission tomography (PET)

Many psychopathologies are either associated with brain abnormalities or caused by unusual patterns of activation in the brain. Thus, understanding a particular disorder can be helped significantly by procedures that allow researchers to look directly at the structure and functioning of the brain.

Positron emission tomography (commonly known as PET scans) involves injecting radioactive molecules into the bloodstream. These molecules are then tracked by a scanner as they are metabolized in the brain. Differences in metabolism rates in the brain are detected and show up on a screen as different colour contrasts. Lighter and warmer colours denote areas when metabolism (and therefore brain activity) is high. This technique is useful for detecting which areas of the brain are active when the individual engages in a particular behaviour (see Section 2.1.3 in Chapter 2).

A study by Marshall, Halligan, Fink et al. (1997) used PET scanning methods to try to identify the areas of the brain that became active when an individual with conversion disorder attempted to move his paralysed left leg. They found that when the patient tried to move the paralysed leg, areas not normally associated with movement became active (the right cingulated cortex and the right orbitofrontal cortex). They hypothesized that the activation of these areas somehow actively inhibited or prevented leg movement. In a similar study, Halligan, Athwal, Oakley and Frackowiak (2000) used the same PET procedure with a patient whose left leg had been paralysed by hypnosis. The resulting scan showed that exactly the same areas of the brain are activated when the hypnotized individual tries to move his leg – suggesting that paralysis in both conversion disorder and under hypnosis may be a result of movement being inhibited by the activation of certain cortical brain areas.

SUMMARY

Theories of the aetiology of somatoform disorders attempt to explain the development of these disorders at a number of different levels. Common to many of these accounts are (1) the role of anxiety, depression and existing psychological conflict in generating somatoform symptoms; (2) the part that playing the sick role might have in coping with psychological stress, and the way that this role might be reinforced by family, associates and medical practitioners; and (3) the role of biased thinking and dysfunctional beliefs in maintaining beliefs about illness in those with somatoform disorders. The startling and disabling nature of the symptoms in conversion disorder has meant that some theoretical accounts are addressed solely at this unique feature of the disorder. These accounts include those that attempt to explain how sensory information is blocked from consciousness and how an individual may lose voluntary control over his or her movements (e.g. in brain scan studies, comparisons of conversion disorder with hypnosis).

SELF-TEST QUESTIONS

- What are the main features of psychodynamic explanations of somatoform disorders? What is meant by a 'conflict resolution' view of somatoform symptoms?
- Can you describe at least one experimental study showing that those suffering from conversion disorder are aware of sensory stimuli at some level of processing?
- What was Janet's (1907) explanation of the aetiology of conversion disorder?
- Why is it helpful in understanding conversion disorder symptoms to make comparisons between conversion disorder and behaviour under hypnosis?
- What kinds of negative life events and stressors have been noted as risk factors in the development of somatoform disorders?
- What is the evidence that those suffering from somatoform disorders may have learned to adopt a sick role during childhood?
- What is the experimental evidence that individuals with somatoform disorders have information processing biases?
- What are rogue representations, and how might they affect thinking about illness symptoms?
- What is the sick role, and how might it help an individual cope with stress?
- How have brain scanning technologies been used to throw light on the mechanisms underlying conversion disorder symptoms?

SECTION SUMMARY

12.2 The Aetiology of Somatoform Disorders

- The **psychodynamic** interpretation of somatoform disorders is mainly one of **conflict resolution** in which distressing memories, inner conflict, anxiety and unacceptable thoughts are repressed in consciousness but outwardly expressed as somatic symptoms.

- In disorders such as conversion disorder, there appears to be a **dissociation** between the individual's behaviour and his or her awareness of that behaviour.

- Studies suggest that in conversion disorder, **sensory input** is processed at some level, but is unavailable at the level of conscious awareness.

- There are many similarities between the behaviour of individuals with conversion disorder and the effects of **hypnosis**, suggesting that similar mechanisms may be responsible for both.

- A significant factor in the history of most somatoform disorders is either a **history of trauma or abuse**, or **significant periods of stress and anxiety**.

- However, a history of stress and abuse is not a *necessary* condition for developing a somatoform disorder.

- Some **learning accounts** of somatoform disorder suggest that expressing symptoms of physical illness may be reinforced during childhood by parents or carers.

- Many individuals with somatoform disorders may have learned to adopt a **sick role**, which may be a form of coping with life stressors.

- Most of the somatoform disorders are characterized by **cognitive and information processing biases**, including (1) interpretation biases, (2) reasoning biases, (3) catastrophizing of symptoms and (4) the development of inappropriate rogue representations which reinforce the dysfunctional thinking that maintains somatoform symptoms.

- **Sociocultural factors** can influence both the prevalence of somatoform disorders and the nature of the symptoms exhibited.

- Physical symptoms associated with conversion disorder can often be **contagious** and affect a number of people within a single social setting or social group.

- Both **twin** and **adoption studies** have provided only indirect evidence for a genetic component to somatoform disorders.

- **PET scans** suggest that increased activation in some areas of the cortex may inhibit the movement of 'paralysed' limbs in individuals with conversion disorder. A similar effect can be found in individuals whose limbs are paralysed by hypnosis.

12.3 THE TREATMENT OF SOMATOFORM DISORDERS

One of the main problems in treating somatoform disorders is that they manifest as physical or medical symptoms. Thus, sufferers will initially undertake a lengthy period of medical treatment in order to discover whether there are any underlying physical causes for their symptoms. This not only allows symptoms to become entrenched before psychological therapy is attempted, but it may also contribute to sufferers' resistance to psychological therapy. For example, many sufferers of disorders such as conversion disorder, somatizaton disorder and hypochondriasis frequently deny they have a psychological problem and continue to search for a medical 'solution' to their symptoms. This denial of an underlying psychological cause makes treatment problematic.

Secondly, we have already noted that somatoform disorders are highly comorbid with other Axis I disorders, and especially with symptoms of anxiety and depression. This raises a 'chicken and egg' question about which symptoms come first. For instance, many people who are anxious and depressed come to have concerns about their physical health as a result of their anxiety and depression (Noyes, Kathol, Fisher, Phillips et al., 1994), and it is often the case that treating the anxiety or depression will significantly reduce illness symptoms and worries (Smith, 1992). In addition, somatoform disorders such as body dysmorphic disorder and hypochondriasis are often comorbid with obsessive-compulsive disorder (OCD); as we shall see later in this section, treatments for OCD are also successful in treating the symptoms of these two somatoform disorders (Phillips, 1998; Rosen, 1996).

This section now considers the types of treatment that are often used with somatoform disorders.

12.3.1 Psychodynamic Therapy

In the section on aetiology we noted that psychodynamic accounts of somatoform disorders take a 'conflict resolution' view of these disorders in which inner conflict, anxiety and distressing memories are repressed in consciousness and outwardly expressed as somatic symptoms. *Psychodynamic approaches* therefore focus on procedures designed to bring these repressed thoughts and memories into consciousness where they can be effectively dealt with. This will in turn alleviate the somatic symptoms that are a consequence of repression. Nevertheless, somatic symptoms are often quite resistant to a psychodynamic approach, not least because clients may continue to believe that they have a physical and not a psychological problem. In a study following up the progress of individuals with somatoform disorders, Kent, Tomasson and Coryell (1995) found that 63 per cent of conversion patients and 92 per cent of somatization patients still met the diagnostic criteria for these disorders 4 years after initial diagnosis. However, meta-analyses have indicated that psychodynamic therapy for somatoform disorders is (1) more effective than no treatment or treatment as usual, and (2) is likely to be more successful the greater the competence of the therapist and his or her ability to form a therapeutic alliance with the client (Leichsenring, 2005).

> **Psychodynamic approaches** Theories which assume that unconscious conflicts develop early in life. Part of the therapy is designed to identify life events that may have caused these unconscious conflicts.

12.3.2 Behaviour Therapy

Many somatoform disorders involve some learning of behaviourally based components that can be treated by the use of the learning principles implicit in *behaviour therapy*. Two prominent examples of such components include (1) the reinforcing function of attention given to individuals (e.g. by family members or medical professionals) that will maintain their 'illness' behaviours (such as staying away from work or complaining about pain), and (2) continuous checking for physical signs of illness or deformity, which are prominent in hypochondriasis, somatization disorder and body dysmorphic disorder.

> **Behaviour therapy** A form of treatment that aims to change behaviour by means of systematic desensitization, behaviour modification or aversion therapy.

In the case of the former, Liebson (1967) reports an intervention that attempted to change the reinforcement contingencies controlling the illness behaviour of a client who had given up his job because of pain and weakness in his legs. Liebson persuaded the client's family to stop giving him attention for illness-related behaviours such as being idle at home or complaining of pain. In addition, the therapist arranged for him to get a pay rise if he went back to work. This approach makes the reinforcement contingencies more functional by providing motivation to work and removing any incentive to feel ill or incapacitated.

Similar approaches can be used to extinguish reassurance-seeking behaviour in individuals with hypochondriasis. This type of programme attempts to minimize the anxiety relief that clients get from reassurance-seeking from the therapist, friends and family. It can also be supplemented by coping skills training, in which the client receives advice on how to cope with anxiety and training in the skills required in social or work settings. Also useful are relaxation training and behavioural techniques designed to reduce worrying. This form of *behavioural stress management* has been found to be significantly more effective than no treatment control conditions (Clark, Salkovskis, Hackmann et al., 1998), and follow-up studies suggest that clients treated by these procedures were still symptom-free 5 years after treatment (Warwick & Marks, 1988).

> **Behavioural stress management** Behavioural techniques designed to reduce worrying and increase relaxation

Behavioural methods can be used to prevent and extinguish undesirable behaviours associated with somatoform disorders. One particular form of treatment that has been borrowed from obsessive-compulsive disorder treatment programmes is *exposure and response prevention* procedures (see Chapter 5, section 5.5.3.1). For example, individuals with body dysmorphic disorder often avoid either looking at their own bodies or displaying their so-called physical defects in public. These avoidance responses serve to maintain the anxiety associated with the disorder. Avoidance can be addressed by getting clients to construct an exposure hierarchy of avoided situations ranked from least to most distressing. Under controlled conditions, clients can then successively expose themselves to these situations (Phillips, 1998; Rosen, 1996). The response prevention aspect of this form of treatment involves preventing repetitive behaviours that act to maintain body dysmorphic beliefs. These behaviours may include mirror-checking, excessive grooming, reassurance-seeking and comparing oneself with others. This may be achieved by getting clients to remove or cover up mirrors, limit grooming time and so on (see Treatment in Practice Box 12.1). Such methods have been shown to be effective in significantly reducing the symptoms of body dysmorphic disorder (McKay, 1999) and the symptoms associated with hypochondriasis (Visser & Bouman, 2001).

> **Exposure and response prevention** The most common, and arguably the most successful, treatment for OCD.

12.3.3 Cognitive Behaviour Therapy

As we saw in the previous section on aetiology, cognitive factors appear to play an important role in the acquisition and maintenance of somatoform disorders. Sufferers appear to acquire interpretation biases, in which they view ambiguous stimuli as evidence of illness or physical problems. They also possess (1) reasoning biases in which they tend to accept only information that is consistent with their illness beliefs; (2) negative thought patterns that lead to the catastrophizing of physical symptoms into beliefs about full-blown illness; and (3) a set of underlying beliefs about their disorder that help to support their symptoms (e.g. hypochondriasis sufferers may hold dysfunctional beliefs that all physical sensations are indicators of impending illness). Such cognitive factors

CLINICAL PERSPECTIVE: TREATMENT IN PRACTICE BOX 12.1

Common treatments for body dysmorphic disorder

Body dysmorphic disorder is a preoccupation with an imagined defect in appearance. Sufferers become obsessed with their defect and may check their image in mirrors or groom themselves compulsively. They become both anxious and depressed as they acquire avoidance responses to help them cope with their supposed defect. Sufferers often wear clothing that hides their defect or completely avoid any social situation.

Successful treatments for body dysmorphic disorder have included those described below.

Exposure and response prevention

This involves exposing clients gradually to appropriate social situations where they can find out that others do not share their opinion of their appearance. In addition, a programme is drawn up to prevent repetitive checking and grooming behaviours such as looking in mirrors. Exposure and response prevention is a procedure that has been borrowed from the successful treatment of OCD (e.g. Phillips, 1998).

Cognitive restructuring

This helps clients to identify dysfunctional thoughts (e.g. 'I cannot have high self-esteem if I am ugly') and to replace them with functional beliefs (e.g. 'Self-esteem is too complex to be based solely on appearance') (e.g. Veale, Gournay, Dryden, Boocock et al., 1996).

Psychoeducation

This provides clients with basic information about the psychology of physical appearance, the concept of body image, how body dysmorphic disorder develops, how cognitions affect emotion, and how symptoms and avoidance responses can be managed (e.g. Rosen, 1996).

Reverse role-play

This involves a role-play that requires clients to research and debate beliefs contrary to their own ideas and values about body image and physical appearance. This enables clients to express more appropriate functional beliefs and helps reduce avoidance responses (e.g. Newell & Shrubb, 1994).

Antidepressant drugs

Some studies indicate that the symptoms of body dysmorphic disorder can be significantly reduced by administering antidepressant drugs such as SSRIs and tricyclic antidepressants (Hollander, Allen, Kwon, Aronowitz et al., 1999).

---

appear to play an important role in most somatoform disorders, especially somatization disorder, hypochondriasis, body dysmorphic disorder and pain disorder. This being the case, cognitive behaviour therapy (CBT) seems particularly well suited to treating such dysfunctional beliefs and thought patterns.

CBT has proven to be particularly effective with people diagnosed with hypochondriasis. Such sufferers tend to interpret anything to do with bodily symptoms or health issues as threatening (Smeets, de Jong & Mayer, 2000). CBT can be used to challenge these dysfunctional beliefs and replace them with more functional health beliefs. Case History 12.1 relates the symptoms of a hypochondriac patient who was convinced he had leukaemia after

developing a harmless rash (Salkovskis & Warwick, 1986). The treatment for this case involved asking the client to test either of two competing hypothesis: (1) that he was suffering from a life-threatening illness or (2) that he had a problem with anxiety which was maintained by repeated medical consultation and checking of his symptoms. He was also asked to stop indulging in behaviours that might maintain his anxiety such as checking to see if his rash had extended, continually seeking consultations with his doctor and reading medical textbooks. After around 30 days, his symptoms had significantly reduced. He was no longer regularly seeking medical reassurance about his symptoms and his self-rated scores on measures of health anxiety and illness beliefs had also

CASE HISTORY 12.1

Hypochondriasis

A is a 32-year-old married engineer. He developed an acute urticarial rash, consisting of typical eruptions of intensely itchy weals surrounded by red areas. (Urticaria may occur as a sensitivity response to certain foods or as a reaction to drugs such as penicillin: However, in 50 per cent of chronic cases, a cause is never found. It is *not* associated with any malignant condition.) His rash persisted for several months, despite advice and treatment from his family doctor and dermatologist. He had had a previous episode of urticaria, which was salicylate induced, but apart from this has been completely healthy. Physical examination and investigations revealed no significant abnormality, and a diagnosis of idiopathic urticaria was made. Despite this reassurance, he became increasingly anxious that he had a serious underlying condition such as leukaemia, and sought repeated consultations. His belief in the idea that he had leukaemia had arisen in the first instance because a skin specialist had attempted to reassure him by giving him some medical details. Specifically, this doctor had told him that the rash arose because his white blood cells were attacking foreign matter in his blood cells. The patient had interpreted this as meaning that there was something wrong with his white blood cells, signifying that he had leukaemia. He inspected his rash frequently, read textbooks in an effort to discover 'the real cause', and could talk of little

else to his wife, family and friends. Eventually, he became suicidal, unable to work and was admitted psychiatrically.

Source: Salkovskis & Warwick (1986), p. 598

Clinical Commentary

This patient exhibits many of the classic symptoms of an individual with hypochondriasis. He is obsessed with his symptoms, continually checks his rash to see if it has grown, and can talk of nothing else to friends and family. The continual checking of symptoms and reassurance-seeking from friends and family merely act to maintain his anxiety. He also displays a number of cognitive biases typical of hypochondriasis. He interprets his rash and the explanation given to him by a skin specialist in threatening terms – even though there are many other explanations for them. He is also unmoved by reassurances from doctors that his condition is not life-threatening. He has a bias to dismiss evidence that is not consistent with his own view of his symptoms and to accept only evidence that is consistent with his view. Treatment consisted of CBT to deal with these cognitive biases, described more fully in the text.

significantly decreased. Randomized control trials indicate that CBT for hypochondriasis is significantly more effective at treating symptoms than normal medical care, and at 12-month follow-up, clients treated with CBT had significantly lower levels of hypochondriacal symptoms, beliefs and attitudes (Barsky & Ahern, 2004).

CBT is also an important treatment method with pain disorder. As we saw earlier, pain disorder is associated with the tendency to be hypervigilant for pain cues and to view potential pain cues as threatening and fear-evoking (McCracken, Zayfert & Gross, 1992). CBT for pain disorder would normally include: (1) educating clients about factors that can influence the experience of chronic pain; (2) cognitive and behavioural procedures designed to increase physical activity and adaptive responses to pain; and (3) training in skills designed to modify the perception of pain (e.g. relaxation) and related bodily sensations (e.g. challenging beliefs that all bodily sensations are indicators of pain; Dworkin, Turner, Wilson, Massoth et al., 1994). In a randomized controlled trial, Turner, Manci and Aaron (2006) compared the effectiveness of CBT and an education/attention control condition for temporomandibular disorder pain (pain associated with the muscles in the head and neck). Compared to the control con-

dition at 12-month follow-up, the CBT group showed significantly lower levels of dysfunctional pain beliefs and pain catastrophizing, and significantly lower self-report levels of pain.

Finally, CBT has been used successfully in the treatment of body dysmorphic disorder. Such individuals possess a set of dysfunctional beliefs that their body or parts of their body are defective or ugly, and avoidance responses (such as avoiding exposing so-called 'defective' or 'ugly' body parts in public) serve to maintain anxiety about appearance. CBT can be used to identify and challenge these dysfunctional beliefs about appearance. The purpose of this is to help clients develop and accept beliefs that 'beauty is subjective' or that 'self-esteem is too complex to be based solely on physical appearance' (Veale, Gournay, Dryden, Boocock et al., 1996).

Cognitive restructuring also involves encouraging clients to abandon negative self-statements of body dissatisfaction and replace them with more neutral descriptions that are free from emotionally loaded self-criticism (Rosen, 1996; Schmidt & Harrington, 1995; Cororve & Gleaves, 2001). Case History 12.2 describes the story of a body dysmorphic disorder sufferer who believed he had abnormally small hands. As a result he started

CASE HISTORY 12.2

Body dysmorphic disorder

The patient is a 24-year-old Caucasian male in his senior year of college. He presented at intake by stating 'I've got a physical deformity (small hands) and it makes me very uncomfortable, especially around women with hands bigger than mine. I see my deformity as a sign of weakness; it's like I'm a cripple.'

The patient reported that his body dysmorphic disorder (BDD) concerns began when he was 18 years old and was working as a landscaping assistant with a large firm. After receiving instructions to plant some shrubs three handwidths apart, the patient reported that his boss angrily reviewed his work, saying: 'You have the smallest hands I've ever seen! You need to replant the shrubs five handwidths apart!' After this incident, the patient began comparing his hand size with others and also became increasingly anxious when exposing his hands to others. He spent considerable time researching hand sizes for different populations and stated at intake that his middle finger is one and one-fourth inches smaller than the average size for a male in the United States.

The patient reported that he viewed his small hands as a sign of weakness and inferiority. He also reported being concerned that women might believe that small hands are indicative of having a small penis. The patient began worrying about negative evaluation of his hands throughout most of the day. He began avoiding normal social engagements and became

significantly depressed. At intake the patient was avoiding employment interviews due to BDD-related anxiety, as well as avoiding dating and non-dating relationships.

Source: Schmidt & Harrington (1995), pp. 162–163

Clinical Commentary

In this example, the patient has catastrophized what was originally an off-the-cuff remark by an employer to proportions where it affects every sphere of his life. He is constantly obsessed by what he believes to be the small size of his hands, and seeks information to confirm his belief that his hands are unusually small. He has also developed other dysfunctional beliefs about his hands which have a significant effect on his day-to-day living. He believes, for instance, that hand size is indicative of penis size, and that women will think he has a small penis. As a consequence, he has stopped dating women. His negative beliefs about his hand size have eventually led to a range of avoidance behaviours, including quitting work and avoiding relationships generally. These symptoms were tackled using standard CBT techniques.

avoiding social situations and became significantly depressed. Schmidt and Harrington (1995) used CBT to treat this individual by (1) getting him to gather normative information about hand size (e.g. by observing others), which indicated that his hands were not abnormally small; (2) getting him to read a study which suggested that hand size was not one of the physical features most commonly noticed in individuals; and (3) getting other people to notice his hands and seeing if they commented on his hand size (e.g. by regularly having his ring size taken in jewellery stores). After 9 sessions of therapy, the client exhibited significant improvement in anxiety and depression and significant decreases in symptom severity and the strength of dysfunctional beliefs.

12.3.4 Drug Treatments

Throughout this chapter we have continually emphasized the important relationship between somatoform disorders and anxiety and depression. Anxiety and depression are regularly comorbid with conversion disorder (Sar, Akyuz, Kundakci, Kiziltyan et al.,

2004), somatization disorder (Gureje, Simon, Ustun & Goldberg, 1997), body dysmorphic disorder (Frare, Perugi, Ruffalo & Toni, 2004), hypochondriasis (Abramowitz & Braddock, 2006) and pain disorder (Frohlich, Jacobi & Wittchen, 2006). What is not clear is whether heightened anxiety and depression *precede* the somatoform symptoms or whether they are a *consequence* of having a somatoform diagnosis.

At least some studies suggest that depression and anxiety may be a significant factor in maintaining the disorders. For example, when treated with antidepressant drugs such as SSRIs or tricyclic antidepressants (see Chapter 4, section 4.1.1.6), individuals with body dysmorphic disorder often exhibit rapid improvement in symptoms (Hollander, Allen, Kwon, Aronowitz et al., 1999), as do individuals with hypochondriasis (Fallon & Feinstein, 2001), individuals with pain disorder (Wilson & Gil, 1996) and individuals with somatization disorder (Noyes, Happel, Muller, Holt et al., 1998). Nevertheless, none of these studies was undertaken under strictly controlled conditions, with appropriate non-treatment controls and suitable follow-up procedures, so while the findings are encouraging, they do not unequivocally demonstrate that antidepressant drugs alone are an effective treatment for somatoform symptoms.

SUMMARY

A range of different treatments have been utilized with somatoform disorders. Traditionally, psychodynamic therapy has been a significant method of treating hysteria-based disorders such as conversion disorder, although the evidence for the medium-term success of such interventions is meagre. Both behaviour therapy and CBT have become important interventions over the past 10–15 years. Specific techniques include behavioural stress management (for hypochondriasis and somatization disorder) and exposure and response prevention (for hypochondriasis and body dysmorphic disorder). CBT has been successfully used across a range of somatoform disorders to challenge dysfunctional beliefs and to correct interpretational biases (e.g. with hypochondriasis, body dysmorphic disorder and pain disorder).

SELF-TEST QUESTIONS

- What are the two main difficulties encountered when attempting to treat somatoform disorders with psychological therapies?
- Can you describe the main features of behavioural stress management procedures for somatoform disorders?
- What therapeutic methods have been borrowed from the treatment of OCD to deal with somatoform symptoms? Which somatoform disorders are they likely to be successful with, and why?
- Which somatoform disorders have been successfully treated using basic CBT methods?
- Which CBT methods are likely to be successful with many somatoform disorders?
- What is the evidence that drug treatments are effective in treating the symptoms of somatoform disorders?

SECTION SUMMARY

12.3 The Treatment of Somatoform Disorders

- Somatoform disorders can be **difficult to treat** because sufferers (1) believe their problems have medical rather than psychological origins; (2) usually have other comorbid Axis I disorders that complicate treatment.

- **Psychodynamic therapy** attempts to bring repressed thoughts and memories that may cause somatic symptoms into consciousness where they can be effectively dealt with.

- **Behavioural stress management** attempts to deal with somatoform symptoms by eliminating reassurance-seeking in clients and supplementing it with coping skills training, relaxation training and techniques designed to reduce worrying.

- **Exposure and response prevention** procedures have been borrowed from the treatment of OCD. They attempt to prevent both compulsive behaviours associated with somatoform symptoms (e.g. compulsive mirror-checking and grooming in body dysmorphic disorder) and avoidance responses (such as avoiding social situations).

- **CBT** can be used across a range of somatoform disorders (especially hypochondriasis, somatization disorder, body dysmorphic disorder and pain disorder) in order to challenge and replace the dysfunctional beliefs that maintain somatoform symptoms.

- **Antidepressant drugs** such as SSRIs or tricyclic antidepressants have been used to reduce the symptoms of many somatoform disorders, although evidence for the long-term effectiveness of this kind of treatment is still modest.

12.4 SOMATOFORM DISORDERS REVIEWED

Somatoform disorders are a group of loosely associated disorders, all of which can be characterized by psychological problems manifesting as physical symptoms or as psychological distress caused by physical symptoms or physical features. In most cases the physical symptoms have no detectable medical cause, but neither are symptoms being faked by sufferers. The causes of the symptoms appear to lie in psychological factors such as life stress, anxiety and a history of conflict or abuse. In many cases individuals may have learned through experience to adopt a sick role, which allows them to opt out of stressful daily living; in other cases it is clear that sufferers have developed a range of cognitive biases and dysfunctional beliefs that maintain their illness symptoms (e.g. hypochondriasis, body dysmorphic disorder, pain disorder). CBT is becoming increasingly adopted as an effective method for treating many somatoform disorders by challenging and correcting dysfunctional thinking and beliefs. Because of many similarities between OCD and somatoform disorders such as hypochondriasis and body dysmorphic disorder, treatments effective for OCD are also proving useful in treating somatoform symptoms (e.g. exposure and response prevention methods). At this stage you may like to return to Table 12.1 and refamiliarize yourself with the key features of somatoform disorders.

LEARNING OUTCOMES

When you have completed this chapter, you should be able to:

1 Describe the main diagnostic criteria and symptom characteristics for the DSM-IV-TR-listed somatoform disorders, and evaluate some of the issues concerning diagnosis, comorbidity and prevalence.

2 Describe and evaluate the main theories of the aetiology of somatoform disorders, and be able to compare psychological and biological explanations.

3 Describe and evaluate 3 or 4 psychological therapies that have been developed to treat somatoform disorders, and discuss how these therapies address the underlying causes of individual disorders.

KEY TERMS

Behaviour therapy *456*
Behavioural stress management *456*
Body dysmorphic disorder *443*
Catastrophizing *444*
Conflict resolution *448*
Conversion disorder *442*
Exposure and response prevention *456*
Factitious disorders *439*
Glove anaesthesia *442*
Health anxiety *445*
Hypnosis *449*
Hypochondriasis *445*

Hysteria *442*
Interpretation biases *450*
La belle indifférence *439*
Munchausen's syndrome *439*
Munchausen's syndrome by proxy *439*
Muscle dysmorphia *444*
Pain disorder *445*
Psychodynamic approaches *456*
Reasoning bias *451*
Rogue representations *451*
Sick role *450*
Somatization disorder *443*

REVIEWS, THEORIES AND SEMINAL STUDIES

Links to Journal Articles

12.1 The Diagnosis and Characteristics of Individual Somatoform Disorders

Abramowitz, J.S. & Braddock, A.E. (2006). Hypochondriasis: Conceptualization, treatment, and relationship to obsessive-compulsive disorder. *Psychiatric Clinics of North America, 29,* 503.

Aouizerate, B., Pujol, H., Grabot, D., Faytout, M. et al. (2003). Body dysmorphic disorder in a sample of cosmetic surgery applicants. *European Psychiatry, 18,* 365–368.

Castle, D.J. & Rossell, S.L. (2006). An update on body dysmorphic disorder. *Current Opinion in Psychiatry, 19,* 74–78.

Frare, F., Perugi, G., Ruffalo, G. & Toni, C. (2004). Obsessive-compulsive disorder and body dysmorphic disorder: A comparison of clinical features. *European Psychiatry, 19,* 292–298.

Frohlich, C., Jacobi, F. & Wittchen, H.U. (2006). DSM-IV pain disorder in the general population: An exploration of the structure and threshold of medically unexplained pain symptoms. *European Archives of Psychiatry and Clinical Neuroscience, 256,* 187–196.

Mayou, R., Kirmayer, L.J., Simon, G., Kroenke, K. et al. (2005). Somatoform disorders: Time for a new approach in DSM-IV. *American Journal of Psychiatry, 162,* 847–855.

Phillips, K.A., Didie, E.R., Menard, W., Pagano, M.E. et al. (2006). Clinical features of body dysmorphic disorder in adolescents and adults. *Psychiatry Research, 141,* 305–314.

12.2 The Aetiology of Somatoform Disorders

Brown, R.J. (2004). Psychological mechanisms of medically unexplained symptoms: An integrative conceptual model. *Psychological Bulletin, 130,* 793–812.

Craig, T.K.J., Bialas, I., Hodson, S. et al. (2004). Intergenerational transmission of somatization behaviour. 2. Observation of joint attention and bids for attention. *Psychological Medicine, 34,* 199–209.

Crombez, G., Eccleston, C., Baeyens, F. & Eelen, P. (1998). When somatic information threatens, catastrophic thinking enhances attentional interference. *Pain, 75,* 187–198.

Grosz, H.J. & Zimmerman, J. (1970). A second detailed case study of functional blindness: Further demonstration of the contribution of objective psychological laboratory data. *Behavior Therapy, 1,* 115–123.

Kozlowska, K. (2005). Healing the disembodied mind: Contemporary models of conversion disorder. *Harvard Review of Psychiatry, 13,* 1–13.

Lim, S.-L. & Kim, J.-H. (2005). Cognitive processing of emotional information in depression, panic and somatoform disorder. *Journal of Abnormal Psychology, 114,* 50–61.

Marshall, J.C., Halligan, P.W., Fink, G.R. et al. (1997). The functional anatomy of hysterical paralysis. *Cognition, 64,* B1–8.

McCracken, L.M., Zayfert, C. & Gross, R.T. (1992). The Pain Anxiety Symptoms Scale: Development and validation of the scale to measure fear of pain. *Pain, 50,* 67–73.

Roelofs, K., Spinhoven, P., Sandijck, P. et al. (2005). The impact of early trauma and recent life-events on symptom severity in patients with conversion disorder. *Journal of Nervous and Mental Diseases, 193,* 508–514.

Sar, V., Akyuz, G., Kundakci, T., Kiziltyan, E. et al. (2004). Childhood trauma, dissociation, and psychiatric comorbidity in patients with conversion disorder. *American Journal of Psychiatry, 161,* 2271–2276.

Smeets, G., de Jong, P.J. & Mayer, B. (2000). If you suffer from a headache, then you have a brain tumour: Domain-specific reasoning 'bias' and hypochondriasis. *Behaviour Research and Therapy, 38,* 763–776.

Warwick, H.M.C. (1995). Assessment of hypochondriasis. *Behaviour Research and Therapy, 33,* 845–853.

Young, J.T. (2004). Illness behaviour: A selective review and synthesis. *Sociology of Health and Illness, 26,* 1–31.

12.3 The Treatment of Somatoform Disorders

Barsky, A.J. & Ahern, D.K. (2004). Cognitive behaviour therapy for hypochondriasis: A randomized control study. *JAMA: Journal of the American Medical Association, 291,* 1464–1470.

Clark, D.M., Salkovskis, P.M., Hackmann, A. et al. (1998). Two psychological treatments for hypochondriasis: A randomized controlled trial. *British Journal of Psychiatry, 173,* 218–225.

Cororve, M.B. & Gleaves, D.H. (2001). Body dysmorphic disorder: A review of conceptualizations, assessment, and treatment strategies. *Clinical Psychology Review, 21,* 949–970.

Dworkin, S.F., Turner, J.A., Wilson, L., Massoth, D. et al. (1994). Brief group cognitive-behavioral intervention for temporomandibular disorders. *Pain, 59,* 175–187.

Salkovskis, P.M. & Warwick, H.M.C. (1986). Morbid preoccupation, health anxiety and reassurance: A cognitive-behavioural approach to hypochondriasis. *Behaviour Research and Therapy, 24,* 597–602.

Schmidt, N.B. & Harrington, P. (1995). Cognitive-behavioral treatment of body dysmorphic disorder: A case report. *Journal of Behavior Therapy and Experimental Psychiatry, 26,* 161–167.

Tazaki, M. & Landlaw, K. (2006). Behavioural mechanisms and cognitive-behavioural interventions of somatoform disorders. *International Review of Psychiatry, 18,* 67–73.

Turner, J.A., Manci, L. & Aaron, L.A. (2006). Short- and long-term efficacy of brief cognitive behavioural therapy for patients with chronic temporomandibular pain disorder: A randomized, controlled trial. *Pain, 121,* 181–194.

Texts for Further Reading

Akiskal, H.S., Mezzich, J.E. & Okasha, A. (Eds.) (2005). *Somatoform disorders.* Chichester: Wiley.

Asmundson, G.J.G., Taylor, S. & Cox, B. (2001). *Health anxiety: Clinical and research perspectives on hypochondriasis and related conditions.* Chichester: Wiley.

Bouman, T.K. (2006). *Understanding and treating somatoform disorders: A cognitive behavioural perspective.* Chichester: Wiley.

Phillips, K.A. (2005). *The broken mirror: Understanding and treating body dysmorphic disorder.* Oxford: Oxford University Press.

Veale, D. & Neziroglue, F. (2006). *Body dysmorphic disorder: A treatment manual.* Chichester: Wiley.

RESEARCH QUESTIONS

- Is there significant evidence that somatoform symptoms represent a physical manifestation of underlying psychological problems?

- In conversion disorder, conscious control over either sensory input or voluntary movements appears to be blocked. What are the brain processes involved in causing this lack of conscious control?

- Not everyone who develops a somatoform disorder reports having had a significant number of negative life events (such as childhood neglect or abuse), so what triggers the development of somatoform disorders in such individuals?

- Why does an individual develop a somatoform disorder when he or she has a history of risk factors that may indicate the development of some other Axis I disorder (e.g. an eating disorder, depression)?

- What is the role of stress and trauma in the aetiology of somatoform disorders?

- Is there any convincing evidence that adopting a sick role is a means of coping with life stress?

- Information processing biases may well explain how somatoform disorders are maintained, but what factors lead the individual to develop these biases in the first place?

- Physical symptoms associated with conversion disorder can often be contagious and affect a number of people at the same time. What is the mechanism that underlies this group manifestation of symptoms?

- Is there an inherited component to somatoform disorders?

- Are there any convincing controlled studies supporting the view that antidepressants are an effective treatment for somatoform disorders?

CLINICAL ISSUES

- How do you differentiate genuine somatoform disorders from faked responses or malingering?

- Is it possible to differentiate those with genuine somatoform disorders from those with genuine or developing neurological or medical problems?

- Because somatoform disorders are highly comorbid with other Axis I disorders, are somatoform disorders simply one symptom of broader-ranging psychological problems?

- Individuals with somatoform disorders strongly believe that their symptoms are medical in nature. What implications does this have for successful psychological treatment?

- Is comorbid anxiety and depression a cause or a consequence of developing somatoform symptoms? What implications does this question have for successful treatment of somatoform symptoms?

13 | Dissociative Experiences

ROUTE MAP OF THE CHAPTER

This chapter describes the diagnosis and characteristics of four dissociative disorders, namely dissociative amnesia, dissociative fugue, dissociative identity disorder (DID, formally multiple personality disorder) and depersonalization disorder. The aetiology section discusses a range of theories of the development of dissociative experiences, including psychodynamic theory, cognitive models, and the role that therapy may play in constructing dissociative symptoms. Treatments for dissociative experiences are relatively underdeveloped. In the final section, we discuss in particular the use of psychoanalysis and hypnotherapy in treating such disorders.

This is DID . . . dissociative identity disorder . . . multiple personality disorder. We are a freak.

I've started writing this a million times . . . I don't know how to explain this. I know I hide. I don't want you to know me. I feel shame about who I am . . . maybe that word defines me . . . shame. I lived through childhood abuses that one only hears about . . . between the ages of 4 and 20. I think. I am not sure. I don't even know if I remember everything yet. That's a part of the disorder . . . forgetting. The other part of the disorder is having 11 other people living inside of me. Therapy is working. Most of the time I remember when they are out now . . . in the past they used to come out and I wouldn't know about it unless they left a clue behind . . . lots of clues for me to see. Sometimes they would hurt me . . . intentionally. Sometimes I would hear them screaming in my head or saying things to me . . . sometimes derogatory, sometimes soothing . . . sometimes they would only cry. Sometimes I would find things that I couldn't understand. Waking with a teddy bear beside me that I didn't remember. Buying toys and items that I would never buy . . . losing money . . . people saying hello to me in the street who I didn't know. My spouse looks at me and asks me who I am half the time. My spouse no longer knows me but still loves me and I reciprocate. Without the support I couldn't make it.

MICHAEL'S STORY

Introduction

Michael's Story describes the presence of many distinct identities that each periodically take control of his behaviour. These are often known as multiple personalities and identities, and sufferers may often be unaware that they present these different personalities to the world. This disorder, known as *dissociative identity disorder*, represents a failure to integrate various aspects of identity, consciousness and memory. As we shall see, in many cases dissociative disorders develop because individuals are attempting to cope with psychological distress and conflict that may be related to earlier traumatic life experiences. Being able to adopt different personalities and repress specific memories is viewed by many theorists as a way of coping with the anxiety and stress derived from these earlier life experiences (e.g. Gleaves, 1996).

Dissociative disorders generally are characterized by significant changes in an individual's sense of identity, memory, perception or consciousness. These changes can be either gradual or sudden, transient or chronic. Symptoms of these disorders include an inability to recall important personal or life events (e.g. dissociative amnesia, dissociative fugue), a temporary loss or disruption of identity (e.g. dissociative identity disorder), or significant feelings of *depersonalization* in which individuals feel that something about themselves has been altered (depersonalization disorder). To a certain degree we all experience these kinds of feelings during our lifetime: we sometimes have brief periods of memory loss, become confused about our identity, and may feel 'strange' or depersonalized (Kihlstrom, 2001). A community sample study by Seedat, Stein and Forde (2003) found that 6 per cent of respondents endorsed 4–5 lifetime dissociative symptoms, and approximately 1 in 3 endorsed at least one lifetime symptom, suggesting that dissociative symptoms are relatively common in the general population.

Very often such experiences coincide with periods of stress or trauma: for instance, it is common for individuals who have experienced severe trauma – such as combat troops or survivors of natural disasters – to experience these kinds of dissociative symptoms (Kozaric-Kovacic & Borovecki, 2005). However, for some individuals, symptoms either become so severe that they significantly disrupt their day-to-day living, or develop into chronic conditions rather than temporary responses to stress, causing significant distress to the individual. In such circumstances they may become diagnosable as a dissociative disorder. Such disorders are commonly associated with severe psychological stress such as childhood abuse (Tyler, Cauce & Whitbeck, 2004) or life-threatening trauma, and

Plate 13.1
Cases of dissociative disorder increase significantly after war or natural disasters when individuals – such as these refugees fleeing from the conflict in Kosovo in 1999 – often experience life-threatening trauma well beyond that experienced during normal daily living.

are often associated with post-traumatic stress disorder (see Chapter 5, section 5.6) (e.g. Kozaric-Kovacic & Borovecki, 2005).

In this chapter we will discuss four dissociative disorders: (1) dissociative amnesia, (2) dissociative fugue, (3) dissociative identity disorder and (4) depersonalization disorder. Table 13.1

Table 13.1 *Dissociative disorders: summary*

DISORDER AND PREVALENCE RATES	DEFINITION	MAIN DSM-IV-TR DIAGNOSTIC FEATURES	KEY FEATURES	THEORIES OF AETIOLOGY (covering all disorders	MAIN FORMS OF TREATMENT (covering all disorders
Dissociative amnesia **Prevalence rate in a community sample is 1.8%**	An inability to recall important personal information that is usually of a stressful or traumatic nature	Inability to recall important personal information of a stressful nature The disturbance is not the result of another dissociative disorder, the effect of a substance or a neurological condition Causes clinically significant distress or impairment of functioning	Amnesia may extend to a person's own behaviour (e.g. after having committed a violent act) There are 5 different types of memory disturbance in dissociative amnesia	Childhood physical and sexual abuse as an important risk factor Psychodynamic theories The role of fantasy and early childhood dissociative experiences Cognitive approaches: ● State-dependent memory ● Deficits in source-monitoring ability and reality monitoring	Psychodynamic therapy Hypnotherapy Drug treatments

Table 13.1 *(Cont'd)*

DISORDER AND PREVALENCE RATES	DEFINITION	MAIN DSM-IV-TR DIAGNOSTIC FEATURES	KEY FEATURES	THEORIES OF AETIOLOGY *(covering all disorders)*	MAIN FORMS OF TREATMENT *(covering all disorders)*
Dissociative fugue **Prevalence rate is 0.2% in the general population**	The individual suddenly and unexpectedly travels away from home or work, and is unable to recall some or all of his or her past history	Sudden unexpected travel away from home and inability to recall one's past Confusion about personal identity Not due to DID or effects of a substance or a general medical condition Causes clinically significant distress or impairment of functioning	Sufferers often do not have obvious signs of psychopathology In most cases, symptoms are relatively transient (i.e. <24 hours) Disorder becomes more common after traumatic events such as war and natural disasters	Biological explanations Dissociative symptoms as a therapeutic construction	
Dissociative identity disorder (DID) **Prevalence rate in a community sample is 1.5%**	The individual displays two or more distinct identities or personality states that take turns to control behaviour	The presence of two or more distinct identities that take turns to control behaviour Inability to recall important personal information Not due to effects of a substance or a general medical condition	Associated with an inability to recall autobiographical information DID sufferers have an average of around 13 different identities Alter identities usually take on a range of contrasting personalities Usually associated with severe childhood sexual or physical abuse Reported cases of DID have risen dramatically since 1980		
Depersonalization disorder **12-month prevalence rate is 0.8%**	Feelings of detachment or estrangement from the self (such as living in a dream or as standing outside of oneself, watching oneself)	Experiences feelings of detachment from one's mental processes or body Reality testing remains intact Causes clinically significant distress or impairment of functioning Not due to another mental disorder such as schizophrenia, panic disorder etc.	Sufferers often think they are 'going crazy' Many sufferers also report having *déjà vu* experiences Depersonalization experiences can also occur when the individual is in a transitional physiological state		

Table 13.2 *Prevalence and comorbidity of dissociative disorders*

Prevalence of dissociative disorders at mean age 33

Dissociative disorder	Prevalence of disorder in the past year		
	Males (N =309) n (%)	Females (N =349) n (%)	Total sample (N =658) n (%)
Depersonalization disorder	2 (0.6%)	3 (0.9%)	5 (0.8%)
Dissociative amnesia	3 (1.0%)	9 (2.6%)	12 (1.8%)
Dissociative identity disorder (DID)	5 (1.6%)	5 (1.4%)	10 (1.5%)
Dissociative disorder not otherwise specified (DDNOS)	21 (6.8%)	15 (4.3%)	36 (5.5%)
Any dissociative disorder	30 (9.7%)	30 (8.6%)	60 (9.1%)

Prevalence of dissociative disorders among individuals with or without co-occurring psychopathologies in the past year at mean age 33

Psychopathology	Prevalence of dissociative disorder in the past year among individuals	
	Without co-occurring psychopathology % (n/N)	With co-occurring psychopathology % (n/N)
Anxiety disorder	5.6% (30 of 533)	33.3% (25 of 75)
Eating disorder	7.0% (39 of 558)	32.0% (16 of 50)
Mood disorder	5.3% (28 of 527)	33.3% (27 of 81)
Personality disorder	3.9% (20 of 512)	36.5% (35 of 96)
Substance use disorder	7.6% (40 of 526)	18.3% (15 of 82)
Any anxiety, eating, mood, personality or substance use disorder	2.1% (8 of 373)	20.0% (47 of 235)

Source: Johnson, Cohen, Kasen & Brooks (2006).

provides a summary of the important features of dissociative disorders, and you may want to return to this table when you have finished reading the chapter. Table 13.2 shows the prevalence and comorbidity rates for dissociative disorders taken in an American community sample (Johnson, Cohen, Kasen & Brooks, 2006).

These figures suggest a 12-month prevalence rate of 9.1 per cent for dissociative disorders generally in individuals with a mean age of 33 years. Such disorders are also comorbid in around 1 in 3 cases with anxiety disorders, eating disorders, mood disorders or personality disorders.

13.1 THE DIAGNOSIS AND CHARACTERISTICS OF DISSOCIATIVE DISORDERS

13.1.1 *Dissociative Amnesia*

The main feature of **dissociative amnesia** is an inability to recall important personal information that is usually of a stressful or traumatic nature. This memory loss cannot be explained by normal forgetfulness, nor is it the result of any demonstrable damage to the brain (see Table 13.3). Dissociative amnesia normally manifests itself as a retrospectively reported gap or series of gaps in the individual's ability to verbally recall aspects of his or her life history. These gaps are often related to traumatic or stressful experiences such as physical or sexual abuse, involvement in a natural or man-made disaster, being in an accident or experiencing military combat. Periods of amnesia may also extend to aspects of the individual's own behaviour, such as memory loss for violent outbursts, suicide attempts or self-harm. Perpetrators of some violent crimes such as murder have often claimed that they cannot recall anything about the event itself, and may use this in their legal defence (see Focus Point 13.1).

Dissociative amnesia is associated with several types of memory disturbances. *Localized amnesia* is when individuals are unable to recall events that occurred during a specific time period (e.g.

Dissociative amnesia An inability to recall important personal information that is usually of a stressful or traumatic nature.

Localized amnesia A memory disturbance when an individual is unable to recall events that occurred during a specific time period (e.g. memory loss for a period of 2 days following a serious car accident).

Table 13.3 *DSM-IV-TR diagnostic criteria for dissociative amnesia*

A The predominant disturbance is one or more episodes of inability to recall important personal information, usually of a traumatic or stressful nature, that is too extensive to be explained by ordinary forgetfulness.

B The disturbance does not occur exclusively during the course of dissociative identity disorder, dissociative fugue, post-traumatic stress disorder, acute stress disorder or somatization disorder and is not due to the direct physiological effects of a substance (e.g. a drug of abuse, a medication) or a neurological or other general medical condition.

C The symptoms cause clinically significant distress or impairment in social, occupational or other important areas of functioning.

memory loss for a period of 2 days following a serious car accident). *Selective amnesia* is where individuals can recall some, but not all, of the events during a specific time period (e.g. a combat veteran may be able to recall some events during a violent military encounter, but not others). The final three types of dissociative amnesia are the least common, although they represent the most severe types of symptoms. *Generalized amnesia* is a failure of recall that encompasses the person's entire life. Individuals suffering from this type of amnesia may suddenly report to police stations or to hospitals as a result of their disorientation.

Selective amnesia A memory disturbance where an individual can recall some, but not all, of the events during a specific time period (e.g. a combat veteran may be able to recall some events during a violent military encounter, but not others).

Generalized amnesia A memory disturbance where there is a failure of recall that encompasses the person's entire life. Individuals may suddenly report to police stations or hospitals as a result of this disorientation.

FOCUS POINT 13.1

Amnesia and crime

In May 2002, the BBC News website reported how Jan Charlton was convicted of the manslaughter of her boyfriend after hacking him to death with an axe. She claimed in court at Leeds that she did not know she had killed him and 'was in a daze, a total and utter daze'. Professor Michael Kopelman, the psychiatrist who interviewed her, said she claimed she did not remember the killing until the memory came back more than a month after the incident. He told the court that amnesia in homicides was most common in 'crimes of passion'.

Claims of crime-related amnesia such as this are relatively common: between 20 and 30 per cent of individuals who

commit violent crimes report no recollections of the event (Cima, Merckelbach, Hollnack & Knauer, 2003). Although post-crime amnesia is most common for violent crimes, it can also be found in those charged with non-violent crimes such as fraud (Kopelman, Green, Guinan, Lewis et al., 1994). Amnesia may occur when individuals are in a highly altered physiological state, either because of extreme rage or anger or because they are under the influence of alcohol or other substances (Kopelman, 2002).

Nevertheless, there are good incentives for a criminal to fake symptoms of amnesia for a criminal act, and it is estimated that about 20 per cent of criminals who claim amnesia are feigning their memory loss (Hopwood & Snell, 1933). So how can we identify true amnesiacs from those who are faking? One method is to use what is called Symptom Validity Testing (SVT). SVT is a forced-choice questionnaire in which defendants are asked a series of questions about their crime. In each question, defendants must choose between two equally plausible answers, one of which is correct and the other incorrect. Examples include: 'The magazine that was stolen was (1) *Penthouse* or (2) *Playboy*'; 'In the bar there is a huge mirror: (1) yes or (2) no'. If individuals are truly suffering amnesia they should perform at around chance level (i.e. get around 50 per cent correct). However, studies suggest that individuals who are faking amnesia (and so do know the correct answer) perform at levels *significantly below chance* (e.g. get less than 40 per cent correct) (Merckelbach, Hauer & Rassin, 2002; Jelicic, Merckelbach & van Bergen, 2004). This is because they attempt to overcompensate for their knowledge of the crime by tending to choose the wrong answer rather than choosing answers at random.

ACTIVITY BOX 13.1

The Symptom Validity Test

The Symptom Validity Test (SVT) is an instrument that can be used to determine whether an individual who claims he or she has no memory of a crime is faking these symptoms. The SVT consists of forced-choice questions about the crime that the defendant is asked to complete. Individuals who are faking amnesia perform on the SVT at *levels significantly below chance* (i.e. get significantly less than 50 per cent correct). This is because people who attempt to feign no knowledge of a crime they have been involved in overcompensate by selecting the *wrong* answer.

Try this test with a friend. Ask your partner to read the paragraphs in italic below *very carefully*. Tell him or her that you will ask some questions about the text later on (do not let your partner see the questions). Then ask your partner the following 20 questions about the crime, allowing a choice between the two possible answers for each question. If your partner is actively feigning ignorance, he or she will probably score well below 50 per cent correct! (See also Focus Point 13.1.)

From this moment on you are involved in a petty crime. You will steal some money from an envelope. You are on the university campus and you go to the School of Life Sciences. You go into the café in corridor 1C2. There is no one else in the café. You close the door behind you, and notice that the walls have just been freshly painted in a bright yellow colour. You see the white cash till behind the bar. It is closed. You push the 'sale' key and the till opens. There are only coins in the till, but you see a large sealed brown envelope. You take the envelope out of the till and open it. Inside is £200 in ten pound notes. You take the money and put the envelope into the bin beside the water dispenser. At that moment the man working behind the café bar comes into the room. You ask for a cappuccino coffee, drink it very quickly, but to avoid looking suspicious you sit down at a table and stay there reading a newspaper for 15 minutes before leaving.

You are suspected of stealing the money from the till. There are some other suspects and the police are aiming to find the real perpetrator. Under no circumstances do you want to confess to the crime!! Try to convince the police in an intelligent way that you have nothing to do with the crime, so that you will be considered innocent. Act as if you have never been in the café and that you have no knowledge of the theft. The police ask you a series of questions.

1 Was there a water dispenser in the café?
   1) yes   2) no
2 What colour were the café walls?
   1) bright blue   2) bright yellow

3 The café was in:
   1) The School of Life Sciences   2) The Business School
4 When the thief entered the café, the cash till was:
   1) open   2) closed
5 The thief pressed which key to open the till?
   1) the 'Cash' key   2) the 'Sale' key
6 The cash that was stolen was in a:
   1) brown envelope   2) white envelope
7 The cash till was:
   1) brown   2) white
8 The till only contained:
   1) notes   2) coins
9 How much did the thief take from the envelope?
   1) £50   2) £200
10 The stolen money was made up of:
   1) £20 notes   2) £10 notes
11 The suspected thief had what drink before he/she left?
   1) a cappuccino coffee   2) an espresso coffee
12 The person who worked behind the café bar was:
   1) a man   2) a woman
13 What did the thief do with the envelope that contained the money?
   1) put it back in the till after removing the money
   2) put it in the bin in the café
14 How long did the suspected thief remain in the café after stealing the money?
   1) 15 mins   2) 10 mins
15 On which corridor was the café?
   1) 2B4   2) 1C2
16 What was striking about the walls of the café?
   1) they were covered in posters   2) they had been freshly painted
17 The bin in the café was next to
   1) a soft drinks dispenser   2) a water dispenser
18 The envelope in the cash till was
   1) sealed   2) unsealed
19 The suspected thief drank his/her coffee
   1) standing at the bar   2) sitting at a table
20 While drinking his/her coffee, the suspected thief
   1) read a magazine   2) read a newspaper

Source: Jelicic, Merckelbach & van Bergen (2004)

Continuous amnesia A memory disturbance where there is an inability to recall events from a specific time up to and including the present.

Systematic amnesia A memory disturbance where there is a loss of memory that relates to specific categories of information, such as family history.

Continuous amnesia is the inability to recall events from a specific time up to and including the present, while *systematic amnesia* is a loss of memory that relates to specific categories of information, such as family history.

Dissociative amnesia can present in any age group from young children to adults, although it is difficult to diagnose in young children because it can be confused with attentional and educational difficulties. An episode may last for minutes or years, but symptoms can often be alleviated simply by removing the individual from the circumstances or situation that may have caused trauma or stress (e.g. dissociative amnesia may spontaneously remit when a soldier is removed from the locality of the battlefield). Interestingly, individuals with dissociative amnesia are much less disturbed by their symptoms than we might expect, which may imply that the amnesia serves some kind of coping function that enables individuals to deal with stress and trauma (Kihlstrom, 2001).

The prevalence rate for dissociative amnesia in a community sample is around 1.8 per cent, with rates being higher in females than in males (Johnson, Cohen, Kasen & Brooks, 2006; see Table 13.2 above).

13.1.2 Dissociative Fugue

Dissociative fugue The instance of an individual suddenly and unexpectedly travelling away from home or work and being unable to recall some or all of his or her past history.

The basic feature of *dissociative fugue* is that the individual suddenly and unexpectedly travels away from home or from his or her customary place of daily activities and is unable to recall some or all of his or her past history. This is also accompanied by confusion about personal history and identity, and may even involve adopting a new identity. In addition, these symptoms cause the individual significant distress and disruption to daily living (see Table 13.4).

Many individuals with dissociative fugue do not appear to have obvious signs of psychopathology and may only rarely attract attention. Their travelling may extend just to brief trips away or, alternatively, significant wanderings over long periods of time (e.g. covering thousands of miles over many days). When the symptoms remit, individuals often have no memory of their travelling or wandering. Dissociative fugue is therefore more elaborate than basic dissociative amnesia and individuals with the disorder often appear purposeful in their behaviour. In most cases the symptoms are relatively transient: individuals may simply spend the day in the cinema, or go no further than the next town, and recover within 24 hours. Dissociative fugue is associated with periods of stress and trauma, and cases of the disorder become more common after major traumatic events such as war or large-scale natural disasters (Coons, 1999). Dissociative fugue will often remit as suddenly as it began, but usually only when the individual begins to feel 'psychologically safe' (Riether & Stoudemire, 1988).

Table 13.4 *DSM-IV-TR diagnostic criteria for dissociative fugue*

A The predominant disturbance is sudden, unexpected travel away from home or one's customary place of work, with inability to recall one's past.

B Confusion about personal identity or assumption of a new identity (partial or complete).

C The disturbance does not occur exclusively during the course of dissociative identity disorder and is not due to the direct physiological effects of a substance (e.g. drug of abuse, a medication) or a general medical condition (e.g. temporal lobe epilepsy).

D The symptoms cause clinically significant distress or impairment in social, occupational or other important areas of functioning.

A prevalence rate of around 0.2 per cent had been reported in the general population, but this may increase significantly after war and natural disasters (APA, 2000, p. 524).

13.1.3 Dissociative Identity Disorder (DID)

Formerly known as multiple personality disorder, *dissociative identity disorder* is a disorder where the individual displays two or more distinct identities or personality states which take turns to control behaviour. It is also associated with an inability to recall important autobiographical information (see Table 13.5). DID reflects an inability to integrate aspects of identity, memory and consciousness to the extent that each personality state is experienced as if it has its own life history, self-image and identity. Different identities usually have different names and quite often very contrasting personalities (e.g. controlling, destructive, passive). DID is associated with gaps in memory for various life events, and the extent of this amnesia may vary with the nature of the different identities (hostile personalities tend to have more complete memories, whereas passive personalities have fewer). The different identities often deny knowledge of one another, but may battle for control of behaviour. An identity that is not in control may gain access to consciousness by producing auditory hallucinations (e.g. by giving instructions).

Dissociative identity disorder (DID) A dissociative disorder characterized by the individual displaying two or more distinct identities or personality states that take turns to control behaviour (formerly known as multiple personality disorder).

At the beginning of this chapter, *Michael's Story* describes how the sufferer is often unaware that different identities are taking control of his behaviour: he only becomes aware of it after finding certain items around (such as waking up with a teddy bear in his bed). He is also surprised when people he doesn't know say hello

Table 13.5 *DSM-IV-TR diagnostic criteria for dissociative identity disorder (DID)*

A   The presence of two or more distinct identities or personality states (each with its own relatively enduring pattern of perceiving, relating to and thinking about the environment and self).

B   At least two of these identities or personality states recurrently take control of the person's behaviour.

C   Inability to recall important personal information that is too extensive to be explained by ordinary forgetfulness.

D   The disturbance is not due to the direct physiological effects of a substance (e.g. blackouts or chaotic behaviour during alcohol intoxication) or a general medical condition (e.g. complex partial seizures).

Note: In children, the symptoms are not attributable to imaginary playmates or other fantasy play.

to him – people whom one of his other identities has presumably met. The time required to switch from one personality to another is usually very brief, and may be preceded by various physical signs such as rapid blinking, changes in voice or demeanour, an interruption of ongoing speech or thought, and changes in facial expression.

Host identity   The identity that existed before the onset of dissociative identity disorder.

Alter identities   The identities that develop after the onset of dissociative identity disorder.

A distinction can be made between the *host identity* (the one that existed before the onset of the disorder) and *alter identities* (those that develop after the onset). In the simplest form of the disorder, two alternating identities take turns to control behaviour. In many cases the alter may know about the host personality, but not vice versa (Dorahy, 2001). The host may become slowly aware of the existence of the alter identity, as did *Michael*, by encountering evidence that a different personality state has been controlling behaviour. However, many DID sufferers have significantly more than just one alter identity: surveys suggest that the average is around 13 per sufferer (Putnam, 1997). Eighty-five per cent of sufferers also report having at least one alter identity that is a child, and over 50 per cent report having one of the opposite sex (Putnam, Guroff, Silberman, Barban et al., 1986).

In general, alter identities tend to take on a range of contrasting personalities and may individually take charge only of certain areas of the sufferer's life (such as one dealing with sex life, one with work, one with anger, and so on). A significant factor in the history of DID sufferers appears to be childhood trauma: surveys suggest that over 95 per cent of individuals diagnosed with DID report childhood sexual and physical abuse, including incest (Putnam, 1997; Putnam, Guroff, Silberman, Barban et al., 1986).

Many sufferers report their disorder beginning in childhood, often before 12 years of age, and at times of severe trauma (Putnam, 1997). This seems to suggest that DID may be a coping strategy adopted by children and adolescents to distance themselves from experienced trauma (Atchison & McFarlane, 1994). We will discuss this issue more fully in the section on aetiology.

The prevalence rate for DID is around 1.5 per cent in a community sample (Johnson, Cohen, Kasen & Brooks, 2006), but the number of reported cases has risen significantly in recent years. For example, Elzinga, van Dyck and Spinhoven (1998) found that the number of reported cases worldwide rose from 79 in 1980 to 6,000 in 1986, the vast majority of these being reported in the USA. What, then, has caused this significant increase in diagnosed cases of DID? There may be a number of factors, including the following.

1   DID was included for the first time as a diagnostic category in DSM-III, published in 1980.

2   Early cases of DID may simply have been diagnosed as examples of schizophrenia rather than a dissociative disorder (Rosenbaum, 1980).

3   During the 1970s, interest in multiple personality disorder was fuelled by the publication of *Sybil* (Schreiber, 1973), a case history describing an individual with 16 personalities which was later popularized in a Hollywood film.

4   Therapists have increasingly used hypnosis in an attempt to get victims of childhood abuse to reveal details of this abuse or to reveal alter identities. There is some evidence that the power of suggestion under hypnosis may be enough to generate 'multiple personalities' that were not there in the first place (Piper, 1997; Powell & Gee, 1999).

5   Dissociative disorders such as DID are closely associated with trauma and PTSD, syndromes in which interest grew following the experience of veterans of the Vietnam War.

6   Many of the symptoms of DID can be relatively easily faked. Some experts estimate that as many as 25 per cent of DID cases are either faked or induced by therapy (Ross, 1997).

13.1.4   Depersonalization Disorder

The central feature of *depersonalization disorder* is persistent or recurrent episodes of depersonalization. These symptoms are characterized

Depersonalization disorder   Feelings of detachment or estrangement from the self (such as living in a dream or standing outside of oneself, watching oneself).

by feelings of detachment or estrangement from the self. Sufferers may feel that they are living in a dream or in a film, that they are not in control of their behaviour but merely standing outside of themselves and watching themselves. As we mentioned earlier, symptoms of depersonalization are commonly experienced, so depersonalization disorder should only be diagnosed if the symptoms are recurrent, cause severe distress and disrupt day-to-day living (see Table 13.6). Depersonalization symptoms also occur regularly in other disorders, such as panic disorder, schizophrenia and other dissociative disorders, so it is important to determine whether symptoms of these other disorders are present when an individual presents with depersonalization experiences.

CASE HISTORY 13.1

The emergence of 'Evelyn'

Psychiatrist Robert F. Jeans reported the case of a 31-year-old single professional woman called Gina. Her initial symptoms included sleepwalking and screaming in her sleep. Jeans noted that she was uncomfortable about being a woman, and about the thought of having a sexual relationship with her married boyfriend known as T.C. During the course of therapy, he noticed a second personality emerging, who was called Mary Sunshine by Gina and her therapist. Mary was outgoing and more feminine and seductive than Gina. Over time Gina found evidence that Mary had been controlling her behaviour across various aspects of her life: she found hot chocolate drinks in the sink (Gina did not like hot chocolate), large sums of money withdrawn from her bank account, and a sewing machine was delivered that had presumably been ordered by Mary. Mary also seemed to take over Gina's relationship with T.C. and acted as a seductive and warm partner, whereas Gina had often been cynical and cold. Eventually a third personality emerged that appeared to be a synthesis of the features of Gina and Mary. Gina described how this happened:

'I was lying in bed trying to go to sleep. Someone started to cry about T.C. I was sure that it was Mary. I started to talk to her. The person told me that she didn't have a name. Later she said that Mary called her Evelyn but that she didn't like that name. I asked her what she preferred to be called. She replied that she will decide later.

I was suspicious at first that it was Mary pretending to be Evelyn. I changed my mind, however, because the person I talked to had too much sense to be Mary. She said that she realized that T.C. was unreliable but she still loved him and was very lonely. She agreed that it would be best to find a reliable man.

She told me that she comes out once a day for a very short time to get used to the world. She promised that she will come out to see you sometime when she is stronger.

I asked her where Mary was. She said Mary was so exhausted from designing her home that she had fallen asleep.'

(Jeans, 1976, pp. 254–255)

Over time Evelyn appeared more and more and appeared to be an adaptive alter identity that allowed Gina to cope better with the range of issues in her life. Within months she was Evelyn all the time, had no recollection of Mary, and later became successfully married to a physician.

Clinical Commentary

Like many alter identities in DID, Mary evolved primarily to take charge of certain areas of Gina's life – particularly controlling her feminine role and her relationship with T.C. Typically, Gina had no recollection of her behaviour when Mary was in control, and only came to be aware of Mary by encountering evidence that a different personality had been controlling behaviour. In this particular case, Evelyn eventually merged as a synthesis of both Gina and Mary's personalities. This proved to be an adaptive change that enabled Gina to deal with a range of matters across her life.

Table 13.6 *DSM-IV-TR diagnostic criteria for depersonalization disorder*

A   Persistent or recurrent experiences of feeling detached from, and as if one is an outside observer of, one's mental processes or body (e.g. feeling like one is in a dream).

B   During the depersonalization experience, reality testing remains intact.

C   The depersonalization causes clinically significant distress or impairment in social, occupational or other important areas of functioning.

D   The depersonalization experience does not occur exclusively during the course of another mental disorder, such as schizophrenia, panic disorder, acute stress disorder or another dissociative disorder, and is not due to the direct physiological effects of a substance (e.g. a drug of abuse, a medication) or a general medical condition (e.g. temporal lobe epilepsy).

As is the case in panic disorder, sufferers of depersonalization disorder often think they are 'going crazy' – especially if their symptoms are associated with a sense of derealization (a feeling that the world is strange or unreal). Other common symptoms include disturbances in the sense of time, obsessive rumination and somatic concerns. Depersonalization disorder is also highly comorbid with anxiety symptoms and depression, and a past history of anxiety and depression is regularly reported in those suffering depersonalization disorder (Baker, Hunter, Lawrence, Medford et al., 2003).

Depersonalization disorder has been a controversial inclusion in the dissociative disorders category of DSM-IV-TR because it does not obviously involve any disruption of memory. However, many sufferers do report having episodes of *déjà vu*, in which they feel they have been in a situation or done something before when they have not. Some accounts of *déjà vu* suggest that it may well be a failure of recognition memory in which the individual has problems matching current experience with past experience. Failures of recognition memory may underlie many of the symptoms of the disorder (Kihlstrom, 2001).

In everyday life, depersonalization experiences can occur when individuals are in transitional physiological states such as waking up, feeling tired, practising meditation or following an acute stressor or scary experience. Interestingly, depersonalization disorder has been associated with severe life trauma such as childhood physical and emotional abuse (Simeon, Guralnik, Schmeidler, Sirof et al., 2001), and research suggests that depersonalization during periods of stress or trauma may be adaptive in reducing symptoms of anxiety or depression immediately after the event (Shilony & Grossman, 1993). In fact, depersonalization may account for the periods of emotional 'numbing' that individuals feel immediately after a severe traumatic experience, and before developing symptoms of post-traumatic stress disorder (see Chapter 5, section 5.6).

The 12-month prevalence rate for depersonalization disorder is relatively low at 0.8 per cent (Johnson, Cohen, Kasen & Brooks, 2006), but it must be remembered that individual depersonalization experiences are significantly more prevalent than this.

SELF-TEST QUESTIONS

- What are the main diagnostic features of dissociative amnesia?
- Can you name the five types of memory disturbance that occur in dissociative amnesia?
- What are the main diagnostic features of dissociative fugue?
- How does dissociative fugue differ from dissociative amnesia?
- What are the main features of dissociative identity disorder (DID) and what was it previously called?
- Can you describe the difference between host identities and alter identities in DID?
- What is the estimated prevalence rate of DID and what problems are involved in estimating its prevalence?
- What are the main features of depersonalization disorder?

SECTION SUMMARY

13.1 The Diagnosis and Characteristics of Dissociative Disorders

- **Dissociative amnesia** is an inability to recall important personal information that is usually of a stressful or traumatic nature.

- The symptoms of dissociative amnesia can often be alleviated by removing the individual from the situation that may have caused trauma (e.g. removing a soldier from the locality of a battlefield).

- **Dissociative fugue** is where an individual suddenly and unexpectedly travels away from home and is unable to recall some or all of his or her past history.

- **Dissociative identity disorder** (DID) was formerly known as multiple personality disorder and is characterized by the individual displaying two or more distinct identities.

- DID is often associated with childhood abuse. Most sufferers usually exhibit many more than just two distinct alter identities.

- The number of reported cases of DID increased dramatically between 1980 and 1986, although the reasons for this increase are unclear.

- **Depersonalization disorder** is characterized by persistent or recurrent episodes of depersonalization, including feelings of detachment and not being in direct control of one's behaviour.

13.2 THE AETIOLOGY OF DISSOCIATIVE DISORDERS

How and why people develop dissociative disorders are interesting questions. Unlike many other of the Axis I disorders associated with anxiety and depression, the symptoms are often striking and quite frequently found in individuals who have undergone experiences of extreme trauma or stress. There are two important issues that need to be addressed when looking at the causes of dissociative disorders. First, we need to be able to explain how the components of consciousness (e.g. cognition, emotion) become dissociated. Consciousness is normally a fully integrated entity, but in individuals with dissociative disorders some memories can be completely lost or suppressed (as in dissociative amnesia), some aspects of consciousness can be isolated from others (such as the different identities experienced in DID), and individuals can feel that they are dissociated both from themselves and from the outside world (e.g. in depersonalization disorder). Any theory of dissociative disorders needs to explain why some individuals develop these symptoms and how the different components of consciousness become dissociated.

The second issue associated with the aetiology of dissociative disorders is whether the symptoms actually have a functional significance. That is, do the symptoms serve a purpose? In the previous sections of this chapter we alluded to the possibility that dissociative symptoms protect individuals from stressful memories and experiences and help them to cope with day-to-day living, anxiety and depression (e.g. Kihlstrom, 2001; Riether & Stoudemire, 1988; Atchison & McFarlane, 1994). As we consider the various theories of dissociative disorders, it is important to bear these two central issues in mind.

13.2.1 Risk Factors for Dissociative Disorders

Risk factors for dissociative disorders include a history of anxiety and depression that predates the disorder (Putnam, Guroff, Silberman, Barban et al., 1986) and a history of *childhood abuse* (physical and sexual) and childhood neglect: up to

> **Childhood abuse** The physical or psychological maltreatment of a child.

95 per cent of individuals diagnosed with DID report instances of childhood sexual and physical abuse (Putnam, 1997; Putnam, Guroff, Silberman, Barban et al., 1986). Dissociative amnesia and dissociative fugue are both associated with a history of trauma and are more common after major stressful life events such as war or natural disasters (Coons, 1999). What is not clear is whether childhood abuse actively contributes to the development of dissociative disorders in a causal way. However, the strength of dissociative symptoms appears to be directly related to the age of onset of physical and sexual abuse, with higher levels of symptoms reported in those whose abuse began early in life (Chu, Frey, Ganzel & Matthews, 1999). This provides some indirect support for the view

that childhood abuse does play a causal role in the development of dissociative disorders.

The issue of whether being male or female is a risk factor for dissociative disorders is still unclear. Some studies suggest a significantly greater risk of dissociative disorders in women than in men (Putnam & Loewenstein, 2000; Simeon, Gross, Guralnik, Stein et al., 1997), but more recent community-based studies suggest that this may be true only for dissociative amnesia (Johnson, Cohen, Kasen & Brooks, 2006; see Table 13.2 above).

13.2.2 Psychodynamic Theories

The general view of most psychodynamic theories is that dissociative symptoms are caused by *repression*, which is the most basic of the ego defence mechanisms.

Repression A basic psychodynamic defence mechanism that helps to suppress painful memories and prevent stressful thoughts.

In these cases, repression helps to unconsciously suppress painful memories and to prevent stressful thoughts entering consciousness. As a result, repression helps to control conflict, anxiety and depression. According to Freudian views, dissociative amnesia is a simple example of repression, where stressful or traumatic memories are simply suppressed until the individual has the strength to cope with them. These tendencies to repress unwanted or painful memories may be acquired in childhood, when excessively strict parents may instill a strict moral code in their children. When the individual violates this code during adulthood (such as by having an extramarital affair), the expression of these 'unacceptable' id impulses is repressed by unconscious mechanisms that prevent the retrieval of such memories.

DID is viewed as a further form of repression, but one in which repression persists for significantly longer (e.g. throughout a lifetime) in order to repress the memories of very traumatic childhood events (Brenner, 1999; Reis, 1993). In psychodynamic terms, DID sufferers develop alter egos in order to avoid the distressing world they were brought up in, and also to protect themselves from the impulses that they believe may have been the reason for their excessive punishments during childhood. Thus, DID sufferers can disown any 'bad' thoughts or impulses by attributing them to a 'rogue' alter ego.

There is certainly some evidence that individuals with dissociative disorders do experience less conflict and anxiety than individuals with other forms of psychopathology (e.g. substance abuse), and this is evidence that supports the psychodynamic view (Alpher, 1996). However, we must once again return to the problems inherent in testing predictions from psychodynamic accounts because of the difficulties in objectively measuring the concepts and mechanisms described in psychodynamic theory. This is just as much true of psychodynamic accounts of dissociative disorders as it is of any other psychopathology (see Chapter 1, section 1.1.3.1).

13.2.3 The Role of Fantasy and Dissociative Experiences

There is some evidence that dissociative disorders may develop more readily in individuals who have early dissociative or deper-

sonalization experiences. Such individuals may learn to utilize these experiences in order to suppress anxiety and painful memories. For example, in a selection of prison inmates diagnosed with DID, Lewis, Yeager, Swica, Pincus et al. (1997) found that 12 out of 14 cases had longstanding dissociative experiences that predated the full-blown DID symptoms, and 10 of the 14 reported having imaginary companions during childhood. Reporting imaginary companions during childhood is common in individuals with DID (Sanders, 1992), and some theorists have argued that such experiences will predispose an individual to develop DID. For example, Kluft (1992) has argued that a child who constructs imaginary companions may find that she can occasionally use these imaginary personalities to ameliorate periods of stress and conflict. The child may then learn to actively construct these personalities into adaptive alter identities to protect herself from stress. Currently, the only evidence in support of this view is that individuals with dissociative disorders do appear to have a history of dissociative experiences, and they also appear to have strong imaginations and a rich fantasy life, which will contribute to the development of symptoms such as alter identities (Lynn, 1988). We await further evidence on whether an individual actively learns to adapt these experiences to cope with psychological distress.

13.2.4 Cognitive Approaches

A central issue in explaining dissociative disorders is an understanding of how various components of conscious experience come to be detached from each other (e.g. how memory for some events becomes suppressed while memory for others remains intact). Such characteristics suggest that an answer may lie in how normal memory and recall processes are affected in individuals suffering dissociative symptoms. Indeed, many cognitive theorists believe that dissociative disorders represent a disruption of all or part of the sufferer's memory processes (Dorahy, 2001).

For example, do individuals displaying dissociative symptoms show poorer recall for trauma- or abuse-related material in experimental studies? If so, then they may have developed a tendency to avoid encoding traumatic material in memory or they may have developed impaired retrieval processes for such information (McNally, Clancy & Schachter, 2001). Unfortunately, much of the experimental evidence does not support such a simple explanation. In explicit memory tasks – where participants are asked either to remember or to forget words presented in a recall task – individuals with a history of childhood abuse showed no difference in recall of trauma-related words than non-abused control participants (McNally, Metzger, Lasko, Clancy et al., 1998; Cloitre, Cancienne, Brodsky, Dulit et al., 1996). Although these studies did not directly investigate individuals with dissociative symptoms, the findings do suggest that individuals with a history of abuse do not have an automatic tendency to suppress or avoid encoding or recalling traumatic material. However, subsequent studies have suggested that individuals high in dissociative symptoms do have impaired recall for words associated with trauma under conditions of *divided attention* (i.e. when they are asked to perform a concurrent task as well as the memory task) (DePrince & Freyd, 2004) (see Figure 13.1). This suggests that attentional context is important in helping high dissociators to forget trauma-related material.

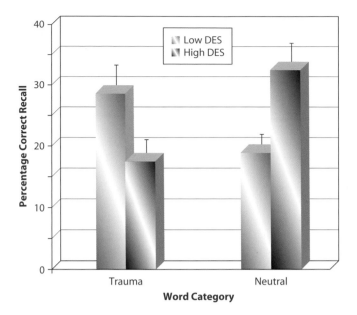

Figure 13.1

Percentage correct recall of to-be-remembered neutral and trauma-related words presented under conditions of divided attention. Red bars represent participants who scored high on dissociative experiences, while blue bars represent those who scored low on dissociative experiences.

Source: DePrince & Freyd (2004).

Dividing their attention across a range of sources may help individuals with dissociative symptoms facilitate forgetting of emotional-relevant or traumatic information.

An alternative explanation of the memory failures experienced by dissociative disorder sufferers is in terms of how changes in their physiological and emotional state can influence recall of memor-

> **State-dependent memory** A well-established cognitive phenomenon in which the individual is more likely to remember an event if he or she is in the same physiological state as when the event occurred.

ies. *State-dependent memory* is a well-established cognitive phenomenon in which individuals are more likely to remember an event if they are in the same physiological state as when the event occurred (Bower, 1981). We have already noted that individuals with dissociative disorders often experience severely traumatic life events that cause significant changes in mood and physiology when such events occur (e.g. being involved in a natural disaster such as an earthquake may be experienced during states of hyperarousal and panic). If the events relating to this experience are encoded in memory during these unusual emotional states, then it may be that individuals will have difficulty recalling them properly in less traumatic emotional states.

State-dependent learning has also been used to explain the between-identity amnesia that is often experienced in DID (Szostak, Lister, Eckhardt & Weingartner, 1995). It has been suggested that most between-identities amnesia will occur between those alter identities that differ most in their normal mood states (e.g. there will be less cross-identity knowledge between identities

that display negative emotions, such as sadness or anger, and those that exhibit mainly positive emotions, such as joy and happiness) (Bower, 1981). Nevertheless, while state-dependent memory may seem like an appealing explanation of dissociative amnesia, there are some difficulties with this explanation. First, dissociative amnesia is usually much more severe than has been reported in basic studies of state-dependent memory. Secondly, individuals with DID have problems with both free-recall memory and recognition memory, although state-dependent memory is usually only found with the former (Peters, Uyterlinde, Consemulder & van der Hart, 1998).

Finally, one other cognitive theory of dissociative symptoms involves the concept of *reconstructive memory*. This view argues that an individual autobiographical memory is stored as a series of discrete elements associated with that experience (e.g. context, emotional state, sensory and perceptual features). These various elements will then be recognized as an autobiographical memory to the extent that the various elements can be retrieved and associated together (the act of reconstruction). In some cases, not all of the elements that go to make up an autobiographical memory may be activated, and this may lead individuals to doubt that the retrieved fragments of memory refer to a memory from their own past. Being unable to recall the relevant elements of an autobiographical experience from memory is known as a deficit in *source-monitoring ability* (Johnson, Hashtroudi & Lindsay, 1993): an example of this is when an individual cannot remember whether she read something in a newspaper or whether it was just a rumour heard from a friend. It has been suggested that dissociative amnesia may result from deficits in both reconstructive memory and source-monitoring abilities. For some reason, individuals with dissociative symptoms may not be able to recover from memory sufficient elements of an autobiographical event to convince them it was an experience that happened to them. In addition, a deficit in *reality monitoring* (a form of source monitoring required to distinguish mental contents arising from experience from those arising from imagination) may lead them to doubt that they have actually had a particular experience (Johnson & Raye, 1981), and both of these processes may contribute to dissociative amnesia. Consistent with this view are findings that women who have experienced childhood sexual abuse and score high on dissociative experiences have greater difficulty than non-abused control participants in distinguishing between words they had seen in a memory test and words they imagined seeing (McNally, Clancy, Barrett & Parker, 2005; Clancy, Schachter, McNally & Pitman, 2000), a finding which suggests that they may well have a deficit in reality monitoring.

However, deficits in reality monitoring can work both ways. They can prevent individuals from identifying an autobiographical

> **Reconstructive memory** A concept of a cognitive theory of dissociative symptoms which argues that an individual autobiographical memory is stored as a series of discrete elements associated with that experience (e.g. context, emotional state, sensory and perceptual features).

> **Source-monitoring ability** The ability to recall the relevant elements of an autobiographical experience from memory.

> **Reality monitoring** A form of source monitoring required to distinguish mental contents arising from experience from those arising from imagination.

memory as one they have actually experienced, but they may also lead to them identifying an *imagined* event as an actual experience. This may be the basis for what have now become known as *false recovered memories of trauma* (Loftus, 1993), in which various therapeutic techniques are used to try to recover repressed childhood memories of trauma but which may actually generate false memories

False recovered memories of trauma
The recovery of repressed childhood memories of trauma that did not actually occur.

of events that did not occur. Such techniques may inadvertently lead clients to falsely recognize imagined experiences as ones that actually happened. This issue is discussed more fully in Focus Point 13.2.

13.2.5 Biological Explanations

Dissociative disorders generate symptoms – such as amnesia – that prima facie look as though they may have been generated by

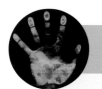

FOCUS POINT 13.2

Repressed memories, recovered memories and false memory syndrome

There has been a belief among many therapists and clinicians that individuals can forget traumatic or stressful events in their life for relatively lengthy periods of time. This view stems from the original works of Freud, who believed that severe trauma was repressed to the unconscious mind because it was too painful to tolerate. Many of the symptoms of dissociative disorders seem to support this belief, especially because many of these disorders are characterized by amnesia and because childhood abuse is a common factor in the history of many with dissociative disorders. However, attempting to confirm that memories have been repressed is a difficult process. For example, it is often difficult to find corroborative evidence even when repressed memories of abuse have been recovered, because many of the recovered memories may be of abuse that the perpetrators are unwilling to substantiate. There are therefore a number of issues to address when considering repressed memories. In particular these are:

● Can memories of early childhood trauma or abuse be repressed?

● If they can be repressed, can they subsequently be recovered?

● If so-called repressed memories are recovered, are they accurate?

Can memories of childhood trauma or abuse be repressed?

Williams (1995) used hospital files to identify 206 women who, as children, had received medical treatment for sexual abuse in the 1970s. Twenty years later, the researcher located these individuals and interviewed them about a range of topics including childhood sexual abuse. Thirty-eight per cent of those interviewed did not report the incident of sexual abuse for which they were hospitalized, but did report other incidents, suggesting that they were not simply holding back sensitive information. Of those who did report the incident of sexual abuse, 16 per cent reported that there were times in their lives

when they had effectively forgotten it. This study suggests that there may be occasions when individuals do fail to recall traumatic events such as childhood abuse. However, this may simply be due to normal processes of forgetting rather than active repression of painful memories.

In contrast, Zola (1998) reports a study investigating the memories of individuals whose childhood traumas were a matter of historical record (e.g. kidnap and Holocaust survivors). In all of these cases there was no evidence of repressed memories for these events in the survivors, and they remembered most of the traumatic events quite vividly. Freyd (1996), however, has argued that childhood sexual abuse is qualitatively different from the traumas experienced by Zola's participants. She suggests that childhood sexual abuse is often perpetrated by a trusted caretaker, such as a parent or close relative, and this gives rise to what is called 'betrayal trauma', which is more likely to be repressed than other forms of trauma. So, studies such as these provide conflicting evidence as to whether trauma memories are repressed or not. If they are subject to periods of amnesia, then it needs to be established whether this is due to normal processes of forgetting or whether it is the result of an active repression process.

If memories of trauma or abuse can be repressed, can they subsequently be recovered?

During the 1980s and 1990s many therapists came to believe that a wide range of psychopathology symptoms were caused by past sexual abuse that was repressed in the memories of the victims. They also believed that a range of therapeutic methods could be used to recover these repressed memories, including hypnotism and directive psychotherapy. These approaches generally came to be known as *recovered memory therapy*, and proponents of this approach had a crusading belief that a wide range of psychopathologies were indicative of childhood sexual abuse (Kaplan & Manicavasagar, 2001).

Much of the impetus for this loose therapeutic movement came from a book called *The Courage to Heal*, written in 1988 by two feminist counsellors, Ellen Bass and Laura Davis. They argued that (1) a large number of people are the victims of

George Franklin (right) spent six years in prison for the murder of an 8-year-old girl based on the memories 'recovered' by his daughter, Eileen (left), under hypnosis 20 years after the event. It turned out that the details Eileen recalled could have come from newspaper reports, and subsequent DNA evidence cleared Franklin of a second murder that his daughter had accused him of.

childhood sexual abuse but do not realize they were abused; and (2) a list of symptoms (e.g. being held in a way that made them feel uneasy) may well be indicative of actual childhood abuse. Their overriding principle was, 'if you feel something abusive happened to you, it probably did!' (1988, p. 21). Therapists who subsequently adopted this approach to treating psychopathology were thus given free rein to indulge in a directive approach attempting to uncover evidence of suppressed memories of childhood abuse, even to the point where clients were told they were 'in denial' if they could not remember instances of abuse! Under such conditions it is almost inevitable that clients will begin to 'recall' instances of abuse that did not actually happen.

If so-called repressed memories are recovered, are they accurate?

There have been a number of high-profile court cases – especially in the USA – where parents or carers have been convicted of childhood abuse on the basis of memories of this abuse recovered by their children while undergoing therapy. In 1990, George Franklin was convicted of murdering a child 20 years earlier on the basis that his daughter suddenly remembered him committing the act while she was undergoing therapy. This conviction was subsequently quashed in 1995 as a result of substantial doubts about the validity of his daughter's memories. This case is an example of what has come to be known as **false memory syndrome**, in which individuals recall memories that subsequently turn out to be false. This does not mean that the individual is actively lying or faking the memory, but a variety of psychological processes might contribute to the individual developing a false memory and believing that it is an accurate record of past events.

Processes that might contribute to false memories are:

- *Over-directive psychotherapy or hypnotherapy*, where clients are encouraged to hold the belief that they have been abused (e.g. Loftus, 1993). Many clients may actively want to believe they have been abused because it would help them to reattribute responsibility or blame for their behaviour or their moods.

- *Poor source-monitoring ability*: when individuals lack the skills to identify the source of a memory, this may lead them to believe that an event that was only imagined actually happened. In support of this view, laboratory-based studies have indicated that women who claim to have recovered memories of childhood abuse are more likely than control participants to recognize material they have actually never seen before (Clancy, Schachter, McNally & Pitman, 2000). They are also less able than control participants to discriminate words they had seen before from words they imagined seeing (McNally, Clancy, Barrett & Parker, 2005).

Conclusions

This debate is complex and ongoing. There is no doubt that *some* people probably do repress memories of childhood abuse, *some* probably recover these memories – either with or without therapy – and *some* probably recall memories of childhood abuse that never actually happened. In a review of the available evidence at the time, Brewin and Andrews (1998) suggested that we should not rule out the possibility that any recovered memories may be genuine, and that each case should be considered on its own merits. In particular, clinicians should be aware that clients are susceptible to suggestion and should avoid discourse that may shape the memories that are eventually reported by their clients.

RESEARCH METHODS IN CLINICAL PSYCHOLOGY BOX 13.1

Measuring proneness to false recognition in recovered memories

Individuals who have suffered amnesia for stressful life events may occasionally recall what have now come to be known as *false recovered memories of trauma*. That is, they may actually recall events that they believed happened, but which objective evidence subsequently suggests did not happen. A classic example of this is described in Focus Point 13.2.

We described in section 13.2 why we think some people might be prone to recalling memories that are false, but how do we go about studying this phenomenon experimentally?

False recognition – the mistaken belief that one has previously encountered a novel item – has been studied extensively in the laboratory. The methods used to investigate this phenomenon have also been applied to the study of false recovered memories in individuals with dissociative disorder symptoms.

In the laboratory procedure, participants are presented with lists of words. Each list is composed of words associated with a single non-presented 'theme word'. For example, a list may consist of words associated with *sweet* (such as *sour, sugar, bitter, candy*). After hearing the lists, participants are then given a recognition test where they are presented with: (1) words that were given in the previous lists; (2) words that were *not* presented before but are related to the theme words (known as *false targets*); and (3) a control set of words that have never been presented before but which are not related to the theme words.

Using college students as participants, many studies have suggested that rates of false recognition of false targets is high – so even non-clinical populations often believe they have seen words in the original lists when in fact they have not (i.e. exhibit false recognition) (Roediger & McDermott, 1995; Schachter, Norman & Koutstaal, 1998).

A number of studies have used this paradigm to test whether individuals with dissociative disorder symptoms have particularly high levels of false recognition. Clancy, Schachter, McNally and Pitman (2000) indeed found that a group of women who reported recovered memories of childhood sexual abuse was more prone to false recognition in this laboratory procedure than other groups (such as women who believed they were sexually abused as children but could not remember it, and women with no history of childhood sexual abuse). Interestingly, people who report having been abducted by space aliens also exhibit proneness to false recognition (Clancy, McNally, Schachter, Lenzenweger et al., 2002).

Experimental studies such as these suggest that false recognition of past experiences is not uncommon. Clinicians need to be aware of this when dealing with the recall of traumatic experiences in clients with dissociative disorders. In addition, this research suggests that some groups of people (i.e. those who claim to have recovered memories of past traumas) are particularly prone to false recognition. It is not at all clear why this is so, but individuals who have undergone severe stress may have deficits in source monitoring – i.e. remembering how, when and why a memory was acquired – and this can be manifested in this simple false recognition laboratory test as well as in real life.

False memory syndrome A syndrome in which individuals recall memories that later turn out to be false.

neurological defects or abnormalities in brain processes. Even so, there is very little evidence that these amnesic symptoms are caused by underlying deficits in brain function. First, memory loss tends to be selective and in many cases it is transitory. This suggests that if there are brain abnormalities causing these symptoms, they too must be selective and transitory. One candidate that has been suggested is undiagnosed *epilepsy* (Sivec & Lynn, 1995). Epileptic seizures are known to be associated with DID and with symptoms of depersonalization disorder such as blackouts and *déjà vu*. Even so, the symptoms of some dissociative disorders – such as DID – are very complex, and it is unlikely that undiagnosed bouts of epilepsy could explain the intricate way in which knowledge about alter identities is suppressed or recovered by the sufferer.

Epilepsy A disorder of the nervous system characterized either by mild, episodic loss of attention or sleepiness or by severe convulsions with loss of consciousness.

An alternative biological explanation alludes to the role of the hippocampus. Recent brain scan studies have suggested that the hippocampus is the area of the brain that brings together the various elements of an autobiographical memory and integrates them to provide individuals with a memory that they recognize as a past personal experience. Given that individuals with dissociative disorders appear to have problems recalling and integrating memories of certain experiences (such as childhood abuse), this may be caused by abnormalities in the hippocampus. Bremner, Krystal, Charney and Southwick (1996) have argued that neurotransmitters released during stress can modulate memory function – particularly at the level of the hippocampus – and this release may interfere with the laying down of memory traces for high-stress incidents such as childhood abuse. In addition, extended periods of stress may instigate long-term, semi-permanent alterations in the release of these neurotransmitters, causing long-term amnesic effects for experiences related to trauma. While these effects of stress on brain function are consistent with many of the symptoms of dissociative disorders, further research on a link between these findings and the development of specific dissociative syndromes is still required.

13.2.6 Dissociative Symptoms as Role-Playing and Therapeutic Constructions

A number of theorists have argued that the more elaborate symptoms of dissociative disorders, such as alter identities in DID, are a form of role-playing by sufferers in order to evoke sympathy and escape responsibility for their actions (Spanos, 1996). Such role-playing is usually reinforced by family, friends and therapists, as it evokes the required attention and allows individuals to absolve themselves of day-to-day responsibilities for their behaviour. In particular, alter identities in DID may be developed in response to particular types of therapeutic intervention. For instance, in Case History 13.1, the therapist's interactions with Gina led to the emergence of an alter identity, which was given the name Mary by both the client and the therapist. In fact, therapists dealing with DID often ask their clients to give a name to an alter identity so that they can talk about this personality more easily. Spanos (1996) suggests that this interactive therapeutic process actually *creates* the client's alter identities. In other words, alter identities may be **constructions** of the therapeutic process itself rather than genuine, full-blown symptoms that precede treatment. Clients then find that these well-defined alter identities serve a useful function in their lives by allowing them to explain away their behaviour and alleviating stress and anxiety.

Therapeutic constructions The view that the multiple personalities found in dissociative identity disorders are merely constructions of the therapeutic process.

What evidence is there that alter identities in DID are a construction of the therapeutic process? Supportive evidence includes the following:

1 Alter identities are significantly less well defined in childhood and appear in adulthood usually after treatment by a therapist has begun (Spanos, 1994; Lilienfeld, Lynn, Kirsch, Chaves et al., 1999).

2 Relatives of individuals with DID rarely report having seen evidence of alter identities before treatment (Piper & Mersky, 2004).

3 Individuals who develop DID usually have strong imaginations and a rich fantasy life that enables them to play different roles with some ease (Lynn, 1988).

4 There is some evidence that many cases of DID are diagnosed by only a relatively small number of clinicians who may have a therapeutic style that allows alter egos to develop; for example, in a Swiss survey, Modestin (1992) found that 66 per cent of the DID diagnoses in the country were made by fewer than 10 per cent of the clinicians in the survey.

5 Individuals diagnosed with dissociative disorders are very susceptible to suggestion and hypnosis (Bliss, 1980), and hypnotherapy is a common form of treatment for DID (see section 13.3.2 below). Spanos (1996) argues that such susceptible individuals may adopt the 'hypnotic role' and simply produce the kind of behaviour that the therapist wants.

6 Spanos (1994) noted that those who support DID as a diagnostic category have described a wide range of symptoms that may be indicative of DID, which justifies constant probing in therapy to confirm a diagnosis. This may occur to the point where therapists *insist* in persuading doubting clients that they have multiple alter egos (Mersky, 1995). Consistent with the desire of many clinicians to diagnose DID is the finding that the prevalence of diagnosed DID has increased dramatically since 1980 (Elzinga, van Dyck & Spinhoven, 1998).

Nevertheless, there is still debate about whether most cases of DID are strategic enactments or not. Gleaves (1996) has provided a vigorous defence of the psychiatric view that DID is a legitimate diagnostic category and not a construction of the therapeutic process. His arguments are as follows.

1 It is not surprising that the rate of DID diagnosis has increased significantly in recent years, since this may be a result of less scepticism about the diagnostic category and a reduction in the misdiagnosis of DID as schizophrenia.

2 There is relatively little evidence that hypnotherapy actively contributes to the development of DID symptoms since the number of clients diagnosed with DID after hypnotherapy is as low as 1 in 4.

3 Core symptoms of DID, such as amnesia, are frequently found in DID sufferers before their first treatment session (Coons, Bowman & Milstein, 1988), so DID cannot be entirely constructed as a result of therapy.

4 Rather than being openly collusive with the therapist about their symptoms, many individuals with DID are highly reluctant to talk about their symptoms and have an avoidant style that is not conducive to revealing a history of abuse or the existence of multiple personalities (Kluft, 1994).

As an epilogue to this debate, it is worth discussing an interesting study conducted by Spanos, Weekes and Bertrand (1985). They designed an experiment based on the famous case of Kenneth Bianchi, who was accused of a series of murders and rapes in Los Angeles in the 1980s. During his psychiatric evaluation under hypnosis, Bianchi revealed evidence of DID symptoms and eventually of an alter identity called Steve whom he claimed committed the rapes and murders. When he came out of the hypnotic state, Bianchi claimed to know nothing about Steve or the murders, or what he had said under hypnosis. Table 13.7 provides a transcript of part of the discussion between the clinician and Bianchi while the latter was under hypnosis. Spanos, Weekes and Bertrand (1985) claim that this is an excellent example of how Bianchi's alter identity was constructed via the therapeutic discussion. Constructing 'Steve' served a useful purpose for Bianchi, because it allowed him to plead not guilty to murder by reason of insanity (i.e. his supposed DID).

In their experimental study, Spanos et al. (1985) asked three groups of students to act out variations of the hypnotherapy procedure undergone by Bianchi. All groups were instructed to play the role of individuals accused of murder. Group 1 was hypnotized

Table 13.7 *Transcript of a discussion between Kenneth Bianchi and a clinician*

The following is a transcript of the discussion that took place between accused murderer Kenneth Bianchi and a clinician while Bianchi was under hypnosis (see text for further elaboration).

Clinician:	I've talked a bit to Ken, but I think that perhaps there might be another part of Ken that I haven't talked to. And I would like to communicate with that other part. And I would like that other part to come to talk to me. . . . And when you're here, lift the left hand off the chair to signal to me that you are here. Would you please come, Part, so I can talk to you . . . ? Part, would you come and lift Ken's hand to indicate to me that you are here . . . ? Would you talk to me, Part, by saying 'I'm here'?
Bianchi:	Yes.
Clinician:	Part, are you the same as Ken or are you different in any way?
Bianchi:	I'm not him.
Clinician:	You're not him. Who are you? Do you have a name?
Bianchi:	I'm not Ken.
Clinician:	You're not him? OK. Who are you? Tell me about yourself. Do you have a name I can call you by?
Bianchi:	Steve. You can call me Steve.

Source: Schwarz (1981), pp. 139–143.

and underwent questioning taken almost verbatim from the Bianchi transcript. Group 2 was also hypnotized and told that under hypnosis many individuals reveal evidence of hidden multiple personalities, but this aspect was not directly addressed in the interview. Group 3 was a control condition that was not hypnotized and was given little or no information about hidden multiple personalities. After the interviews, all participants were questioned about whether they had a hidden personality or second identity.

In Group 1 – which underwent a procedure similar to Bianchi – 81 per cent admitted a second personality. In Group 2 – whose interview did not allude to hidden personalities – only 31 per cent revealed an alter identity. Only 13 per cent of those in Group 3 admitted a hidden personality. Spanos et al. (1985) argued that these results provide evidence that alter identities can be developed as a result of the demand characteristics of the interview style of the therapist, and that such alter identities are strategic enactments that serve the purposes of the client (e.g. by diverting or avoiding blame for his or her behaviour). Nevertheless, while this study provides convincing evidence that *some* alter identities can be developed by the therapist's interviewing style, it is still not evidence that *all* alter identities are strategic enactments.

SUMMARY

We proposed two questions at the outset of this section on aetiology: (1) How do the normally integrated components of consciousness become dissociated in the dissociative disorders? and (2) Do the distinctive symptoms of dissociative disorders (such as amnesia and multiple personalities) have a specific function? We have reviewed a range of theories about how the elements of consciousness become dissociated in these disorders. Cognitive theories try to explain dissociative symptoms primarily by attempting to describe the mechanisms that might mediate effects such as selective amnesia. We reviewed two specific accounts, state-dependent memory and reconstructive memory. The latter additionally argued that individuals with dissociative disorders may suffer deficits in source-monitoring ability and reality monitoring: both may prevent an individual from identifying an autobiographical memory as one he or she has actually experienced. Some relatively undeveloped biological accounts also intimate that selective amnesia may result from abnormal brain processes (such as epilepsy) or deficits in brain function caused by trauma. An alternative view of the striking symptoms of dissociative disorders is that many of them may be a construction of the therapeutic process. In particular, directive therapeutic approaches (including hypnotherapy) may encourage the client to create alter identities that did not exist prior to therapy, or to recall false memories of events that never happened. We concluded that while some symptoms of dissociative disorders may be developed by overly directive therapy techniques, this was unlikely to explain all dissociative symptoms. Finally, in relation to our second question, it is quite likely that the symptoms of dissociative disorders (particularly selective amnesia and alter identities) do serve some kind of palliative role. In the psychodynamic view, they may allow the sufferer to repress traumatic memories that are too painful to tolerate.

SELF-TEST QUESTIONS

- Can you describe some of the main risk factors for dissociative disorders?
- What is the psychodynamic concept of repression, and how does it account for the symptoms of dissociative disorders?
- What is the evidence that fantasy and early dissociative experiences may play a role in the development of dissociative disorders?
- Can you describe the procedure for a laboratory-based experiment designed to investigate deficits in memory processes in individuals with dissociative disorders?
- What is state-dependent memory, and how does it attempt to account for dissociative amnesia?
- Can you explain how deficits in source-monitoring ability or reality monitoring might account for both dissociative amnesia and false recovered memories of trauma?
- What is the evidence that alter identities in DID are a construction of the therapeutic process?

SECTION SUMMARY

13.2 The Aetiology of Dissociative Disorders

- Risk factors for dissociative disorders include physical and sexual **childhood abuse** and a history of trauma generally (e.g. experiencing major stressful life events such as war or natural disasters).

- **Psychodynamic** theorists view dissociative disorders as being caused by **repression**, which is one of the most basic of the ego defence mechanisms.

- Dissociative disorders may develop more readily in those who have experienced dissociative symptoms as a child or who have **strong imaginations** and a **rich fantasy life**.

- **Cognitive** theorists believe that dissociative symptoms are caused by a disruption to the sufferer's memory processes.

- Individuals with dissociative symptoms only appear to have poor memory for trauma information under conditions of **divided attention**.

- Some theorists argue that dissociative amnesia is caused by a deficit in either **source-monitoring ability** or **reality monitoring**.

- Deficits in some memory processes may be the reason why some sufferers are prone to recover **false memories of trauma** that never happened.

- **Biological** accounts suggest that dissociative symptoms may be caused by undiagnosed **epilepsy** or that stress causes permanent changes in the release of neurotransmitters that inhibit the laying down of memory traces.

- Alter identities in DID may be the **construction of the therapeutic process** itself rather than full-blown symptoms that precede treatment.

13.3 THE TREATMENT OF DISSOCIATIVE DISORDERS

The main issues to be addressed in the treatment of dissociative disorders are: (1) helping to alleviate selective amnesia for life events; (2) helping clients to adapt to recovered memories if they are painful or traumatic ones; and (3) helping individuals with DID to identify alter identities and to merge them fully into a single, integrated identity.

Clinicians attempting to treat dissociative disorders face a number of problems:

1 Some of these disorders are rare (e.g. DID), and there have been relatively few cases identified worldwide. This means that therapeutic techniques are relatively underdeveloped and outcome studies designed to assess effectiveness of therapy methods are almost non-existent.

2 Some dissociative disorders such as dissociative amnesia and dissociative fugue often spontaneously remit, so it is difficult in these cases to assess whether the therapeutic methods applied are effective or not.

3 Dealing with recovered memories is often a severely traumatic experience for clients. It may involve the intense re-experiencing of traumatic events (known as *abreaction*: see below) and may continually plunge clients into emotional crisis.

4 Some overly directive therapeutic styles may lead to the recovery of *false memories*, with the potentially broad range of negative consequences that this might have for clients and their family (see again Focus Point 13.2).

5 In DID, integrating alter identities into a single, functional identity is an extremely difficult process. Many clients find that having a series of alter identities is a useful way of explaining their behaviour to others and absolving the 'host' identity from blame and responsibility, so breaking this down is problematic (Hale, 1983). In a survey of 153 clients undergoing therapy for DID, Piper (1994) found that only 38 of 153 (25 per cent) achieved a stable integration of their alter identities. However, more recent longer-term studies have intimated at more optimistic outcomes, with Kluft (2000) finding a successful integration rate of 68 per cent over a period of 3 months after therapy.

6 All dissociative disorders are usually comorbid with a range of other Axis I disorders, particularly with anxiety disorders, depression and PTSD. Dealing with these comorbid problems will thus usually also be a requirement in therapy.

As we mentioned at the beginning of this section, therapies for dissociative disorders are relatively underdeveloped. Below we discuss the most commonly used ones: psychodynamic therapy, hypnotherapy and, to a lesser extent, drug therapy.

13.3.1 *Psychodynamic Therapy*

By far the most common form of treatment for dissociative disorders is psychodynamic therapy – especially psychoanalysis. Freud viewed dissociative symptoms, especially dissociative amnesia, as a form of repression in which memories that were considered too painful to tolerate were repressed to the unconscious mind. Like most approaches to dissociative disorders, psychodynamic therapy requires a measured, step-by-step approach to revealing repressed memories or integrating multiple personalities. The usual process is to begin by establishing a trusting and workable relationship between therapist and client, followed by attempts to deal directly with repressed memories or alter identities. This second stage is clearly the most challenging. Firstly, memory retrieval may be as traumatizing as the original experience. Re-experiencing trauma in this way is known as **abreaction**, which will obviously be distressing to clients and may well initiate further emotional turmoil. In an attempt to avoid full-blown abreaction, some therapists have proposed that repressed memories of abuse should be retrieved only piece by piece, with clients

Abreaction The intense re-experiencing of traumatic events.

learning to adapt emotionally to each memory fragment before moving on to retrieve the next (Kluft, 1999).

Secondly, in the case of clients with DID, this second stage will often be characterized by the client's resistance to integrating multiple identities. For the individual with DID, multiple personalities appear to serve a coping function in allowing them to abdicate responsibility for actions and emotions to individual identities. Successful therapy thus needs to deal with these 'responsibilities'

CLINICAL PERSPECTIVE: TREATMENT IN PRACTICE BOX 13.1

Psychoanalysis: The case of Mary

The following account summarizes the treatment by psychoanalysis of a 25-year-old woman called Mary. She suffers dissociative symptoms and severe depression, probably as the result of a rape experienced when she was a child. Mary was in analysis for 10 years. The excerpts from her therapy described below illustrate some of the clinical issues involved in treating clients with dissociative disorders and the kinds of feelings and emotions they experience when having to come to terms with childhood trauma. Points to look out for are:

- how Mary's alter identity emerges as a result of questioning from her analyst;
- the effect on Mary of recalling memories of the rape;
- how individuals who have suffered early childhood trauma experience shame and feelings of a lack of safety;
- Mary's denial of the rape to the point of amnesia;
- how clients can feel unprotected and vulnerable when they begin to reveal past trauma;
- how Mary eventually comes to terms with her past traumas.

The rape

Mary was raped at age 7 and molested at age 8. She resorted to desperate and extreme defences to protect herself from the impact of the traumas. Mary was acutely depressed when seen by her analyst at age 25. Mary revealed a chronic picture of social isolation since childhood and a chronic depression that began to result in frequent suicide attempts once she reached adolescence. For the first 3 years of treatment she was amnesiac to the molestation and the rape. Mary described her mother as remote emotionally. She saw her father as a stern disciplinarian who always frightened her. Mary gave the appearance of someone very ashamed of herself. She kept her eyes always focused on the ground; she rarely spoke, and when she did speak, she did so in a barely audible whisper. She gave the appearance of a person experiencing shame. She talked about finding her life meaningless. She felt frightened and awkward around people. Her arm displayed a lattice work of scars that were a product of years of self-mutilation.

Mary was seen in analysis 5 times a week for 10 years.

The emergence of an alter identity

Analyst: When I first saw Mary she was struggling to consciously suppress and unconsciously disavow aspects of her personality that upset her to think about. One day a hallucinated 'double' appeared that tormented Mary. The 'double' would sit on the bookshelf during the session and mock Mary. One day I asked to speak to the double. This was a mistake. The 'double' came into Mary's body and informed me that it hated Mary for her cowardice in not facing life, for being frightened by everyone and everything, and for being too 'chicken' to talk to me about things that she needed to talk to me about. However, when I asked the 'double' to leave at the end of the hour, it refused.

It became clear over time that the 'double' represented the return of a dissociated, depressed, angry molested child who wanted help. Now, however, the adult Mary that organized experience and functioned in the world was gone. Her condition worsened. She became increasingly depressed.

Mary functioned on such a concrete level that she was unable to dialogue with the hallucinated 'double'. She asserted she did not know anything about it and could not say very much about anything because the 'double' had all the thoughts.

Clinical Commentary

The return of the memories of the rape was extremely disorganizing. Omnipresent fears of assault coupled with shame over how frightened and defenceless she was came to the fore. The following is typical of the fourth year of psychoanalysis.

Recovering memories of the rape

Mary: I feel as if I'm having a nervous breakdown. I was going to call you last night, but I was afraid it was too late and that wouldn't be fair to you. Someone is going to get me. There are bugs crawling all over me.

Analyst: You're frightened of something, bugged about something specific.

Mary: I'm frightened by being around people because I'm afraid of being raped and beaten. I'm frightened of walking down the street, especially if I see men. I'm afraid of taking a shower at Cynthia's house; frightened I'll be assaulted in the shower. My boss was talking about female parts the other day and I became very frightened. I'm ashamed of how frightened I am and it's difficult to tell you these things.

Analyst: You're ashamed of how frightened you are but you're even more concerned that I will think less of you if you reveal your fear to me.

Clinical Commentary

This intervention and similar ones led to uncovering how much Mary damned herself for being so frightened and not fighting harder during the molestation and rape. She saw her fear as the reason for the rape. She believed that if she had fought harder and not been so frightened, the rape might not have happened.

The sense of safety

Clinical Commentary

Childhood sexual abuse often shatters the individual's sense of safety. Recovery of the memory of the trauma in treatment revives early experiences of being unprotected. Recovery of the trauma for some clients may also bring with it increased dependence on the analyst. They feel unprotected on the inside because they feel unable to repress the memories that come up with increasing force. A client may cling to the analyst because the analyst can provide words for the wordless experience that the client senses will ultimately help her master the trauma.

Mary: What if I really was never molested and I just attached that fear and distress to this imaginary event and it really belongs elsewhere?

Analyst: You are sharing with me that you have not remembered enough to give you a conviction of truth and to be sure that this happened.

Clinical Commentary

It is characteristic of clients in Mary's situation to try to deal with terror by denial. People frequently employ this primitive defence to deal with childhood sexual abuse. Mary was uncertain about what happened to her at this point in the treatment. She often wanted to deny it ever happened. At times, she vacillated between believing that nothing happened to suspecting that her father molested her. It took repeatedly returning to the events for her to get a sense of conviction that it was the son-in-law of the next-door neighbour who raped her. It is also helpful if the analyst can point to other memories that confirm her belief that something really did happen. It helped Mary to remind her of the marked drop in her school grades during this time and the evidence of tissue damage around her traumatically stretched hips.

Withdrawal and detachment as methods of defense

Clinical Commentary

Failure to adequately address the motive for resistance is a frequent cause for clients precipitously leaving treatment. It is necessary to go slowly when uncovering the dissociated trauma and take one's cues from the client in assessing her readiness to go deeper. Adequate analysis of the motives for flight and withdrawal often results in the client spontaneously returning to recollections of the trauma herself.

Mary: I don't know where I am because I retreated from writing this story about being molested and now I feel unreal.

Analyst: When you write about being molested, memories return and you feel it is happening to you again. Therefore you leave your body and feel unreal.

Mary: Just writing about it was enough to do that. I don't want this to happen. I don't want these memories to come back. I want to forget it. All I ever do is think about it. I want to die. I can't see the point of having to live always having to remember the horrible and shameful thing that happened to me.

Analyst: These memories are coming back and wanting to be owned. They want help in being owned and made sense out of so that they could eventually be unremembered. This is difficult to do because you feel so unprotected.

Mary: I'm reliving the most difficult thing in my life, and you're not there! You don't care! If you cared about me, you'd be there for me. You are the only one who understands. I hate how dependent I am on you! I can't see just living to be with you.

Clinical Commentary

Clients often experience themselves as unprotected and in danger as they move towards mastery of the dissociated trauma. They sometimes feel that they have had their defences taken away by the analyst and given nothing in their place.

Reclaiming the body

Mary initially experienced sexual sensations without corresponding fantasies. Mary's initial impulse was to reject the sensations and mutilate her body. She needed help in tolerating the sensations sufficiently so that she could discover what it was that she wanted. This was in the eighth year. This session marked a turning point. Mary increasingly began to acknowledge her fears of being hurt again if she allowed herself to get involved. A need for love and to love emerged as her fears diminished. Her depression lifted, her life began to feel meaningful and she fell in love with a woman. This was the first time in her life that she ever wanted anyone sexually. It was also the first time she ever acknowledged enjoying sex. She moved in with this woman shortly after meeting her. She reported no longer feeling depressed or afraid of involvement.

Source: adapted from Daniel Paul, www.toddlertime.com/

before integration can be achieved. Indeed, in many cases, the sub-personalities view 'fusion' of their identities as a form of death that has to be avoided (Kluft, 2001; Spiegel, 1994).

Finally, if these stages of treatment are progressed successfully, clients will normally need to have training in a range of skills to enable them to cope with day-to-day living, either with their recovered memories or with their newly integrated personality. In particular, training will be needed in how to avoid dissociation when encountering future stressors (Kihlstrom, 2001).

Almost any form of psychotherapy is a lengthy process where dissociative disorders are concerned. Issues have to be approached cautiously, and there may be many occasions when therapy takes steps backwards as well as forwards. In the case of DID, the greater the number of multiple identities that need to be integrated, the longer the therapeutic process will take: an average treatment programme of 500 hours per client over an average of 2 years has been reported (Putnam, Guroff, Silberman, Barban et al., 1986).

13.3.2 Hypnotherapy

Hypnotherapy A form of therapy undertaken while the client is hyprotized.

Hypnotherapy is a method that is used relatively regularly with those who suffer dissociative disorders, because these individuals are unusually susceptible to suggestion and hypnosis (Bliss, 1980). Some clinicians believe that dissociative symptoms such as amnesia or multiple identities are the result of a form of 'self-hypnosis', by which individuals are able to restrict certain thoughts and memories entering consciousness (Frischholz, Lipman, Braun & Sachs, 1992). Using hypnotherapy, the clinician can help guide the client through the recall of repressed memories. Hypnosis is also used to help people to regress to childhood states in an attempt to help them recall significant events that they may have repressed. Drugs such as *sodium amobarbital* and *sodium pentobarbital* can also be used concurrently with hypnotherapy to help clients recall past events (Ruedrich, Chu & Wadle, 1985).

Sodium amobarbital and sodium pentobarbital Drugs which can be used concurrently with hypnotherapy to help clients recall past events.

One assumption in the hypnotherapy approach is that hypnosis will recreate the physical and mental state clients were in prior to experiencing any trauma, which will help them to recall events during earlier stages of their life. This is known as *age regression*. While some clients find this helpful in recalling and dealing with repressed memories, there is no objective evidence that hypnosis does recreate any of the physical or mental states experienced earlier in life. Hypnotherapy is also used in the treatment of DID in order to help bring potential alter identities into consciousness and to facilitate the fusion of identities. However, although hypnotherapy is widely used in the treatment of dissociative disorders, there have been no systematic

Age regression In hypnotherapy, the recreation of the physical and mental state that a client was in prior to experiencing any trauma in order to help the individual recall events during earlier stages of his or her life.

group- or single-case studies of the effectiveness of this technique (Cardena, 2000).

13.3.3 Drug Treatments

Because anxiety and depression are common features of dissociative disorders, and may be diagnosable comorbid conditions, some antidepressant and anxiolytic drugs have been used successfully to treat some of these supplementary symptoms. Antidepressants and tranquillizers have been used to address the depression and anxiety associated with DID, but these drugs tend to have little effect on the main symptoms of DID itself (Simon, 1998). There is, however, some evidence that SSRIs such as Prozac may help to alleviate the symptoms of depersonalization disorder (Simeon, Stein & Hollander, 1995). Because there is some evidence for abnormalities in the endogenous opioid systems in depersonalization disorder, opioid antagonists such as naltrexone have been found to reduce depersonalization symptoms by an average of 30 per cent (Simeon & Knutelska, 2005).

SUMMARY

Treating dissociative disorders can often be a lengthy process, whether through conventional psychotherapy or through hypnotherapy. Treatment in Practice Box 13.1 provides insight into some of the reasons why therapy requires time, especially in allowing clients to adapt to and cope with traumatic memories. As we mentioned earlier, therapies for dissociative disorders are relatively underdeveloped. In part this is because there are relatively few diagnosed cases of some of these disorders (e.g. DID). As a consequence, there are few adequately controlled outcome studies. Apart from the therapies we have discussed in this section, many individuals with dissociative disorders can often be treated with CBT for their depression and anxiety symptoms. Because both dissociative and PTSD symptoms may be an outcome of extreme trauma, those therapies used to treat PTSD also have some success in dealing with dissociative symptoms, for example, therapies such as cognitive restructuring or eye-movement desensitization and reprocessing (see Chapter 5, sections 5.6.2.2 and 5.6.2.3).

SELF-TEST QUESTIONS

- What are the main problems facing clinicians who attempt to treat dissociative disorders?
- Can you describe the main characteristics of psychodynamic therapies for dissociative disorders?
- What is the evidence that hypnotherapy is an effective treatment for dissociative disorders?

SECTION SUMMARY

13.3 The Treatment of Dissociative Disorders

- **Abreaction** and the recovery of **false memories** are important issues to consider in the treatment of dissociative disorders.

- **Psychodynamic therapies** attempt to bring repressed memories back to the conscious mind so that they can be effectively dealt with.

- **Hypnotherapy** is a common form of treatment for dissociative disorders, as sufferers are unusually susceptible to suggestion and hypnosis.

- Some **antidepressant and anxiolytic drugs** have been successful in treating some of the depression- and anxiety-related symptoms of dissociative disorders.

13.4 DISSOCIATIVE DISORDERS REVIEWED

In this chapter we have described the main features of four dissociative disorders – dissociative amnesia, dissociative fugue, dissociative identity disorder (DID) and depersonalization disorder. All represent a failure to integrate various aspects of identity, consciousness and memory, and most involve some form of amnesia for past life events or autobiographical memories. All of these disorders are associated with severe psychological stress. Symptoms may manifest immediately after severe traumatic experiences (such as war or a natural disaster), or they may develop over a number of years. In the latter case, DID is a particular example where selective amnesia and multiple identities may develop many years after severe childhood trauma such as sexual or physical abuse.

There are a number of theories of the aetiology of dissociative symptoms, but most relate in some way to early trauma. Psychodynamic theories claim that dissociative symptoms such as amnesia are ways of coping with severe traumatic experiences by repressing these memories to the unconscious mind. Cognitive accounts are much more interested in the mechanisms by which memories are selectively repressed in dissociative disorders, and laboratory studies have identified deficits in source-monitoring ability and reality monitoring (e.g. not being able to effectively differentiate imagined events from experienced events). In contrast, some theorists believe that many of the symptoms of dissociative disorders (such as the multiple alter identities in DID) are merely constructions of the therapeutic process. That is, therapy that is either too directive or attempts to probe too deeply to confirm a diagnosis of DID actually plays a causal role in the development of alter identities.

Treatments for dissociative disorders are relatively underdeveloped, and the most popular are psychodynamic approaches and hypnotherapy. For many dissociative disorders, therapy can be a lengthy process as the sufferer often has to deal with recovered memories of trauma that may involve intense re-experiencing of these events. The therapeutic process can also be problematic, as we discussed in Focus Point 13.2, where overdirective psychotherapy can often create false recovered memories of trauma and abuse. These false memories can often have catastrophic consequences for both clients and their families.

LEARNING OUTCOMES

When you have completed this chapter, you should be able to:

1 Describe the main diagnostic criteria and symptom characteristics for the DSM-IV-TR-listed dissociative disorders, and evaluate some of the issues concerning diagnosis, comorbidity and prevalence.

2 Describe and evaluate the main theories of the aetiology of dissociative disorders.

3 Evaluate the difficulties associated with treating dissociative experiences, and describe at least 2 therapies that have been used to treat dissociative experiences.

KEY TERMS

REVIEWS, THEORIES AND SEMINAL STUDIES

Links to Journal Articles

13.1 The Diagnosis and Characteristics of Dissociative Disorders

Baker, D., Hunter, E., Lawrence, E., Medford, N., Patel, M. et al. (2003). Depersonalization disorder: Clinical features of 204 cases. *British Journal of Psychiatry*, *182*, 428–433.

Foote, B., Smolin, Y., Kaplan, M., Legatt, M.E. & Lipschitz, D. (2006). Prevalence of dissociative disorders in psychiatric outpatients. *American Journal of Psychiatry*, *163*, 623–629.

Jeans, R.F. (1976). An independently validated case of multiple personality. *Journal of Abnormal Psychology*, *85*, 249–255.

Jelicic, M., Merckelbach, H. & van Bergen, S. (2004). Symptom validity testing of feigned amnesia for a mock crime. *Archives of Clinical Neuropsychology*, *19*, 525–531.

Johnson, J.G., Cohen, P., Kasen, S. & Brooks, J.S. (2006). Dissociative disorders among adults in the community, impaired functioning, and Axis I and II comorbidity. *Journal of Psychiatric Research*, *40*, 131–140.

Seedat, S., Stein, M.B. & Forde, D.R. (2003). Prevalence of dissociative experiences in a community sample: Relationship to gender, ethnicity, and substance use. *Journal of Nervous and Mental Disease*, *191*, 115–120.

13.2 The Aetiology of Dissociative Disorders

Bremner, J.D., Krystal, J.H., Charney, D.S. & Southwick, S.M. (1996). Neural mechanisms in dissociative amnesia for childhood abuse: Relevance to the current controversy surrounding the 'false memory syndrome'. *American Journal of Psychiatry*, *153*, 71–82.

Chu, J.A., Frey, L.M., Ganzel, B.L. & Matthews, J.A. (1999). Memories of childhood abuse: Dissociation, amnesia, and corroboration. *American Journal of Psychiatry*, *156*, 749–755.

Clancy, S.A., Schachter, D.L., McNally, R.J. & Pitman, R.K. (2000). False recognition in women reporting recovered memories of sexual abuse. *Psychological Science*, *11*, 26–31.

DePrince, A.P. & Freyd, J.J. (2004). Forgetting trauma stimuli. *Psychological Science*, *15*, 488–492.

Gleaves, D.H. (1996). The sociogenic model of dissociative identity disorder: A re-examination of the evidence. *Psychological Bulletin*, *120*, 42–59.

Gleaves, D.H., Smith, S.M., Butler, L.D. & Spiegel, D. (2004). False and recovered memories in the laboratory and clinic: A review of experimental and clinical evidence. *Clinical Psychology: Science and Practice*, *11*, 3–28.

Kaplan, R. & Manicavasagar, V. (2001). Is there a false memory syndrome? A review of three cases. *Comprehensive Psychiatry*, *42*, 342–348.

McNally, R.J., Clancy, S.A., Barrett, H.M. & Parker, H.A. (2005). Reality monitoring in adults reporting repressed, recovered, or continuous memories of childhood sexual abuse. *Journal of Abnormal Psychology*, *114*, 147–152.

McNally, R.J., Metzger, L.J., Lasko, N.B., Clancy, S.A. & Pitman, R.K. (1998). Directed forgetting of trauma cues in adult survivors of childhood sexual abuse with and without post-traumatic stress disorder. *Journal of Abnormal Psychology, 107,* 596–601.

Spanos, N.P., Weekes, J.R. & Bertrand, L.D. (1985). Multiple personality: A social psychology perspective. *Journal of Abnormal Psychology, 94,* 362–376.

13.3 The Treatment of Dissociative Disorders

Cardena, E. (2000). Hypnosis in the treatment of trauma: A promising, but not fully supported, efficacious intervention. *International Journal of Clinical and Experimental Hypnosis, 48,* 225–238.

Diseth, T.H. & Christie, H.J. (2005). Trauma-related dissociative (conversion) disorders in children and adolescents: An overview of assessment tools and treatment principles. *Nordic Journal of Psychiatry, 59,* 278–292.

Kluft, R.P. (1999). An overview of the psychotherapy of dissociative identity disorder. *American Journal of Psychotherapy, 53,* 289–319.

Simeon, D. & Knutelska, M. (2005). An open trial of naltrexone in the treatment of depersonalization disorder. *Journal of Clinical Psychopharamacology, 25,* 267–270.

Texts for Further Reading

Chefetz, R.A. (2006). *Dissociative disorders: An issue of psychiatric clinics.* New York: Saunders.

Hunter, M.E. (2004). *Understanding dissociative disorders: A guide for family physicians and health care professionals.* New York: Crown House.

Michelson, L. (1996). *Handbook of dissociation: Theoretical, empirical and clinical perspectives.* New York: Kluwer Academic/Plenum.

Mollon, P. (1996). *Multiple selves, multiple voices: Working with trauma, violation and dissociation.* Chichester: Wiley.

Rieber, R.W. (2006). *The bifurcation of the self: The history and theory of dissociation and its disorders.* New York: Springer.

RESEARCH QUESTIONS

- How do we explain how the components of consciousness become dissociated in dissociative disorders?

- What is the objective evidence that the symptoms of dissociative disorders actually serve a functional purpose (such as alleviating stress and anxiety)?

- Does childhood abuse contribute in a causal way to the development of dissociative disorders?

- Is being female a greater risk factor for the development of dissociative disorders?

- Does a strong imagination and fantasy life in childhood contribute directly to the development of dissociative symptoms (such as alter identities)?

- Can the symptoms of dissociative disorders be explained by the disruption of all or part of the sufferer's memory processes?

- Why do individuals with high levels of dissociative symptoms have impaired recall for trauma words only under conditions of divided attention?

- Can state-dependent memory accounts explain the severe amnesia experienced by individuals with dissociative amnesia?

- What is the evidence that individuals with dissociative symptoms exhibit a deficit in reality monitoring?

- Does stress cause permanent changes in the release of neurotransmitters that inhibit the laying down of memory traces?

- Why are there so few controlled outcome studies of treatments for dissociative identity disorder (DID)?

- Is there any objective evidence that hypnotherapy facilitates recall of early life trauma by recreating the physical or mental states experienced earlier in life?

CLINICAL ISSUES

- How do we determine if the perpetrator of a violent crime who claims amnesia for the event is faking these symptoms or not?

- How do we attempt to diagnose dissociative amnesia in young children, when a diagnosis may be confused with attentional and educational difficulties?

- The number of diagnosed cases of DID has risen significantly in the last 25 years. What problems does this imply for the diagnosis of DID?

- What steps should clinicians take to avoid creating false memories of childhood abuse in their clients suffering dissociative disorders?

- Are multiple personalities simply creations of therapy that has been too directive?

- How do we determine whether the symptoms of DID are faked or not?

- How can a diagnosis of depersonalization disorder be distinguished from panic disorder or PTSD?

- Can constant probing in therapy to confirm a diagnosis actually create multiple alter egos (when attempting to confirm a diagnosis of DID)?

- Cases of DID are relatively rare worldwide, so how does a clinician decide on an appropriate form of treatment for this disorder?

- Is it possible for a clinician to successfully treat a client with a dissociative disorder without the client needing to recover memories of childhood abuse and intensely re-experiencing these traumas during therapy?

- What are the problems involved in treating dissociative disorders when they are often comorbid with other Axis I disorders such as anxiety, depression and PTSD?

- What challenges does the clinician face when attempting to 'fuse' the alter identities of individuals suffering DID?

- Once individuals have suffered dissociative symptoms in the wake of a trauma, how can they be trained to avoid dissociation when encountering future stressors?

14 | Neurological Disorders

ROUTE MAP OF THE CHAPTER

The chapter begins by describing some of the cognitive impairments that characterize neurological disorders and identifying some of the brain areas associated with these deficits. It then discusses various methods used by clinical neuropsychologists to assess cognitive functioning, and considers some of the difficulties associated with diagnosis. The second part of the chapter looks more closely at the various types of neurological disorder and their causes. These can involve cerebral infection, traumatic brain injury, cerebrovascular accidents such as strokes, and degenerative disorders such as Alzheimer's disease. Finally, we cover some of the treatment and rehabilitation programmes that have been developed to tackle neurological disorders, including drug treatments, cognitive rehabilitation procedures and the role of caregiver support programmes.

Within the last 8 months I've been at war with the cooker. I put the oven on at a temperature which I know is right, only to find the meat burnt or not cooked because what I thought was the right temperature was not. It gets me so annoyed. I also forget what time I put things in the oven – even if I repeat it to myself a few times and keep looking at the clock. If I do something else, go upstairs, for example, I cannot remember what time the food went in no matter how I try.

I've had to give up driving. I kept losing concentration and my speed just got faster and faster. I could have caused an accident – especially when feeling disoriented. I still work part-time, but that is slipping something awful. I do things at work alone as much as possible so no one can see the mistakes I'm making. I've had all the tests now, but the neurologist tells me all the findings so far are consistent with AD (Alzheimer's disease). To be honest, trying to get through the day is like knitting with a knotted ball of wool. Every now and again I come to a knot. I try to unravel it but can't, so I knit the knot in. As time goes by, there are more and more knots.

PADDY'S STORY

Introduction

The majority of the disorders we have discussed in this book so far appear to have psychological origins. That is, people have experiences that give rise to problematic ways of thinking and behaving, which in turn may cause distress and form the basis for diagnosable psychopathologies. In contrast, neurological disorders have their origins in damage or abnormalities in the biological substrates that underlie thinking and behaving. This damage or degeneration can be caused by disease, physical trauma (such as brain injury) or genetic predispositions causing irreversible changes in the brain and central nervous system (CNS). By definition, the causes of neurological disorders are biological and can usually be identified as biochemical imbalances in the brain and CNS or direct or indirect damage to brain tissue.

Despite the fact that the causes of neurological disorders are primarily physical, psychology is centrally important in the diagnosis, assessment and rehabilitation of individuals suffering such disorders. For example, some of the first signs of neurological disorders (such as dementia, brain injury or stroke) are deficits in basic cognitive functions such as perception, learning, memory, attention, language and visuospatial skills, as well as deficits in what are known as *executive functions* (i.e. those skills that involve problem-solving, planning and engaging in goal-directed behaviour). Clinical psychologists are therefore actively engaged in assessing these abilities and interpreting whether any deficits are early signs of neurological disorders.

Executive functions   Cognitive skills that involve problem-solving, planning and engaging in goal-directed behaviour.

In addition, neurological disorders not only generate deficits in basic cognitive functioning, they can also affect disposition and personality. An individual diagnosed with a neurological disorder may become both depressed and anxious and require suitable treatment for these conditions. The individual may also display radical changes in personality and behaviour, such as impulsivity or outbursts of aggressive behaviour. These also need to be managed and treated. Finally, clinical psychologists are centrally involved in the development of *rehabilitation programmes* that have a variety of aims, including:

Rehabilitation programmes   Treatment programmes that usually combine a mixture of group work, psychological interventions, social skills training and practical and vocational activities.

1 restoring previously affected cognitive and behavioural functions (often a difficult task);

2 helping clients to develop new skills to replace those that have been lost as a result of tissue damage (e.g. learning to use memory aids);

3 providing therapy for concurrent depression, anxiety or anger problems;

4 providing clients and carers with skills and advice that will help them structure their living environment so as to accommodate changes in cognitive and behavioural abilities.

At the beginning of this chapter, *Paddy's Story* recounts the experiences of someone who is in the early stages of Alzheimer's disease, describing her awareness of memory lapses, mistakes and periodic disorientation that give rise to frustration, anxiety and depression. For many who are in the early stages of a degenerative neurological condition, these experiences can be both frequent and frightening.

We continue this chapter by discussing some of the more general characteristics of neurological disorders and the diagnostic and assessment issues that are relevant to them. Table 14.1 provides a summary of the important features of neurological disorders, which you may want to return to when you have finished reading the chapter.

Table 14.1 *Neurological disorders: summary*

TYPES OF NEUROLOGICAL DISORDER BY CAUSE	EXAMPLES	KEY FEATURES	CAUSES	MAIN FORMS OF TREATMENT AND REHABILITATION (FOR COGNITIVE AND EMOTIONAL DEFICITS)
Cerebral infections	Bacterial meningitis HIV infection Variant Creutzfeldt-Jakob disease (vCJD)	May cause inflammation of the brain or the meninges (the membranous covering of the brain and spinal cord) Cognitive deficits caused by meningitis may be reversible over time Some other cerebral infections (such as vCJD) are currently incurable and cause rapid mental and physical decline	Viruses, bacteria, protozoa or fungal infections	**Drugs** ● Cholinesterase inhibitors (for Alzheimer's) ● Levodopa (for Parkinson's) ● Thrombolytic therapy (for strokes) ● Antiretroviral drugs (for HIV dementia) ● Antidepressants (for disability-related depression)

Table 14.1 *(Cont'd)*

TYPES OF NEUROLOGICAL DISORDER BY CAUSE	EXAMPLES	KEY FEATURES	CAUSES	MAIN FORMS OF TREATMENT AND REHABILITATION (FOR COGNITIVE AND EMOTIONAL DEFICITS)
Traumatic brain injury	Concussion (closed head injury) Contusion Open head injury	Most common cause of neurological impairment Between 70 and 80% of all people who sustain a head injury are male Can cause cognitive impairment and emotional and behavioural changes	Road traffic accidents (40–50% of cases) Domestic and industrial accidents (20–30%) Sports and recreational activities (10–15%) Assaults (10%)	***Cognitive rehabilitation*** For attention deficits: • Attention process training (APT) • Time pressure management (TPM) For visuospaial deficits: • Visual scanning For apraxia: • Gestural training • Virtual reality environments
Cerebrovascular accidents	Stroke	Third most common cause of death in the UK Common long-term symptoms include aphasia, agnosia, apraxia and paralysis Between 14 and 19% of stroke victims meet DSM-IV-TR criteria for major depression	Infarction (blockage of blood flow to the brain) Haemorrhage (rupturing of a blood vessel in the brain) Cerebral embolism (blood clot that lodges in the brain) Cerebral aneurysm (bulging or bursting of the wall of a blood vessel in or near the brain)	For language and communication deficits: • Speech therapy • Constraint-induced movement therapy (CIMT) • Group communication For memory deficits: • Compensatory strategies • Assistive technology • Visual imagery mnemonics • Errorless learning Deficits in executive functioning: • Goal management training • Self-instructional training
Brain tumours	Primary brain tumours	Large tumours lead to swelling in the brain, giving rise to headaches, vomiting, visual problems, tiredness and coma Brain tumours can generate symptoms similar to PTSD, panic disorder and eating disorders Some individuals with brain tumours exhibit acquired sociopathy, which is a reckless disregard for others and a lack of remorse	Tumours can originate in other parts of the body (e.g. lungs, breast) and travel via the bloodstream to the brain Primary brain tumours are those that originate and grow in the brain itself	Holistic rehabilitation methods Caregiver support programmes

Table 14.1 *(Cont'd)*

TYPES OF NEUROLOGICAL DISORDER BY CAUSE	EXAMPLES	KEY FEATURES	CAUSES	MAIN FORMS OF TREATMENT AND REHABILITATION (FOR COGNITIVE AND EMOTIONAL DEFICITS)
Degenerative disorders	Alzheimer's disease Vascular dementia Parkinson's disease Huntington's disease Multiple sclerosis	These are dementias characterized by a slow, general deterioration in cognitive, physical and emotional functioning Most frequently a feature of old age; caused by physical changes in the brain 7% of those over 65 years and 30% of those over 85 years have a degenerative dementia Most common disorders in the UK are Alzheimer's disease (contributing 55%) and vascular dementia (contributing 20%)	Many have a significant inherited component (e.g. Alzheimer's, Huntington's disease) Alzheimer's is caused by abnormal protein synthesis in the brain and faulty production of the brain neurotransmitter acetylcholine Parkinson's disease occurs as a result of degenerative damage to an area of the basal ganglia known as the substantia nigra A number of dementias are associated with the abnormal protein deposits in the brain called Lewy bodies (e.g. Parkinson's disease, Lewy body dementia)	

14.1 THE DIAGNOSIS AND ASSESSMENT OF NEUROLOGICAL DISORDERS

First, let's look at some of the cognitive impairments that are commonly found in neurological disorders. We will then discuss some broader diagnostic and assessment issues.

14.1.1 Cognitive Impairments in Neurological Disorders

14.1.1.1 Learning and Memory Deficits

Amnesia is a common feature of many neurological disorders, including an inability to learn new information, failure to recall past events, and more commonly a failure to recall events in the most recent past. If the neurological condition is caused by a specific traumatic event (such as a head injury), the individual may be unable to recall anything from the moment of the injury or to retain memories of recent events. This is known as *anterograde amnesia* or *anterograde memory dysfunction*. The effects of anterograde amnesia are dramatically displayed in the 2000 film *Memento*, in which the lead character, Leonard, is unable to form new memories as a result of an earlier head injury caused by an assailant. The film graphically describes how Leonard has to develop a series of *ad hoc* ways of coping with his inability to recall recent events. More commonly, in degenerative disorders such as dementia, memory deficits slowly develop from what initially appears like normal forgetfulness to become a more full-blown inability to recall events. In the latter case, sufferers may often seem 'rambling' as they attempt to make up events to fill the gaps in their memory.

> **Anterograde amnesia** Memory loss for information acquired after the onset of amnesia. Also known as **anterograde memory dysfunction**.

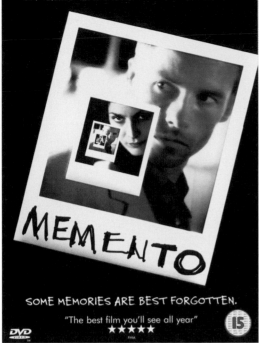

Plate 14.1
The film *Memento* follows Leonard (Guy Pearce), whose head trauma has given him anterograde amnesia, also called anterograde memory dysfunction. While able to remember everything up to the moment of the injury, he is unable to form new long-term memories or retain a memory of recent happenings. He meets people over and over again, unable to determine whether he knows them already or is meeting them for the first time. To remember events and people, Leonard develops and uses a range of memory aids, including polaroid photographs, notes and tattoos.

14.1.1.2 Deficits in Attention and Arousal

Some first indications of neurological problems are when individuals show signs of lack of attention, being easily distracted and performing well-learned activities more slowly than before (such as having difficulty using the controls of a DVD or video machine). They may also have difficulty focusing on or keeping up with a conversation, and need more time to make simple decisions.

14.1.1.3 Language Deficits

Individuals may appear to be rambling during conversations and have difficulty conveying what they have to say in a coherent manner. They may also have difficulty reading and understanding the speech of others. Language deficits are one of the most common features of neurological disorders. Collectively, they are known as *aphasias*. Language impairments can take many forms, including: (1) an inability to comprehend or understand

> **Aphasia** A speech disorder resulting in difficulties producing or comprehending speech.

speech or to repeat speech accurately and correctly; (2) the production of incoherent, jumbled speech (known as *fluent aphasia*); and (3) an inability to initiate speech or respond to speech with anything other than simple words (known as *non-fluent aphasia*).

A distinction can be made between Broca's aphasia and Wernicke's aphasia. Disruption of the ability to speak is known generally as *Broca's aphasia*, which consists of difficulties with word ordering (agrammatism), finding the right word (anomia) and articulation. It is characterized by laborious non-fluent speech involving mispronunciation rather than mis-selection of words. In contrast, *Wernicke's aphasia* is a deficit in the comprehension of speech involving difficulties in recognizing spoken words and converting thoughts into words. Damage to different areas of the left hemisphere (which controls speech) is specific to each of these deficits. Wernicke's aphasia is associated with damage to regions behind the frontal lobes, while Broca's aphasia is more likely to result from damage to the left frontal lobe itself (see Table 14.2 and Figures 14.1 and 14.2).

> **Fluent aphasia** The production of incoherent, jumbled speech.

> **Non-fluent aphasia** An inability to initiate speech or respond to speech with anything other than simple words.

> **Broca's aphasia** Disruption of the ability to speak consisting of difficulties with word ordering, finding the right word and articulation.

> **Wernicke's aphasia** A deficit in the comprehension of speech involving difficulties in recognizing spoken words and converting thoughts into words.

14.1.1.4 Deficits in Visual-Perceptual Functioning

In some cases individuals may be unable to recognize everyday objects and name them correctly. This is known as *agnosia* and can affect a wide

> **Agnosia** The loss of the ability to recognize objects, persons, sounds, shapes or smells while the specific sense is not defective and there is no significant memory loss.

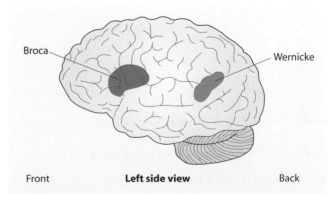

Figure 14.1
Language centres of the left hemisphere (Broca's area and Wernicke's area).

Table 14.2 *Terminology: cognitive impairments in neurological disorders*

TERM	DEFINITION	MAIN BRAIN AREAS AFFECTED
Aphasia	Speech disorder resulting in difficulties producing or comprehending speech	Language centres of the left hemisphere (usually Broca's area or Wernicke's area) (Figure 14.1)
Agnosia	Loss of ability to recognize objects, persons, sounds, shapes or smells while the specific sense is not defective, nor is there any significant memory loss	Occipital or parietal lobes (Figure 14.2)
Apraxia	Loss of the ability to execute or carry out learned (familiar) movements, despite having the desire and the physical ability to perform the movements	Parietal lobes of the left hemisphere (Figure 14.2)
Anterograde amnesia	Memory loss for information acquired after the onset of amnesia	Hippocampus; medial temporal lobes; basal forebrain (Figure 14.2)
Retrograde amnesia	Inability to recall events that occurred before the onset of amnesia	Hippocampus; temporal lobes (Figure 14.2)
Deficits in executive functioning	The inability to effectively problem-solve, plan, initiate, organise, monitor and inhibit complex behaviours	Frontal lobes (especially the prefrontal cortex) (Figure 14.2)

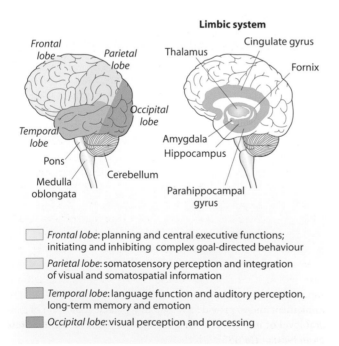

Frontal lobe: planning and central executive functions; initiating and inhibiting complex goal-directed behaviour

Parietal lobe: somatosensory perception and integration of visual and somatospatial information

Temporal lobe: language function and auditory perception, long-term memory and emotion

Occipital lobe: visual perception and processing

Figure 14.2
Anatomy of the brain.

variety of functional skills, such as face perception (prosopagnosia) and musical discrimination (amusia). A famous example of agnosia is recounted in the book *The Man Who Mistook His Wife for a Hat and Other Clinical Tales* by Oliver Sacks. He describes the case of Dr P., a music professor who had developed visual agnosia. He was able to identify and describe complex shapes, but could often not recognize his students' faces and could only identify them when they spoke. The title of the book comes from an occasion when Dr P. was leaving the house and reached for his wife's head, mistaking it for a hat and trying to lift it off. Interestingly, his agnosia only affected his visual perceptions and did not affect his music abilities in any way.

14.1.1.5 Motor Skills Deficits

Some neurological disorders are characterized by impairments in motor performance and coordination. This may involve the inability to move a limb, a tendency to suddenly become paralysed or difficulty in coordinating movements effectively. This is known as *apraxia*. In more complex cases, individuals with apraxia may be able to emit a behaviour under routine conditions (e.g. cleaning their teeth as part of their washing routine first thing in the morning), but are unable to do this on command.

> **Apraxia** Loss of the ability to execute or carry out learned (familiar) movements, despite having the desire and the physical ability to perform the movements.

14.1.1.6 Deficits in Executive Functioning

This reflects an inability to effectively problem-solve, plan, initiate, organize, monitor and inhibit complex behaviours. These functions are normally associated with the *prefrontal cortex*, so damage to this area of the brain is frequently involved when executive function deficits are found. A widely used test of executive functioning is the *Wisconsin card sorting task*, where individuals must sort cards for a number of trials using one rule (e.g. colour), then sort cards using a different rule (e.g. shape). This requires the ability to shift attention and to inhibit an established response pattern. Deficits in executive functioning are revealed in everyday behaviour by examples of poor judgement (e.g. erratic or unsafe driving), inappropriate behaviour (e.g. leaving the house in inappropriate clothing such as pyjamas) and erratic mood swings (e.g. from laughter to hostility).

> **Prefrontal cortex**   The anterior part of the frontal lobes of the brain, lying in front of the motor and premotor areas.

> **Wisconsin card sorting task**   A widely used test of executive functioning where individuals must sort cards for a number of trials using one rule (e.g. colour) and then sort cards using a different rule (e.g. shape).

14.1.1.7 Deficits in Higher-Order Intellectual Functioning

Impairment in more abstract mental tasks is another possible indication of a neurological disorder. Individuals may be unable to make simple mathematical calculations, to reason deductively or to draw on general knowledge when undertaking a task or activity.

14.1.2 Assessment in Clinical Neuropsychology

Identifying that someone has a neurological disorder is a difficult and often lengthy process. Assessment is important for (1) determining the actual nature of deficits and the location of any related tissue damage in the brain; (2) providing information about onset, type, severity and progression of symptoms; (3) helping to discriminate between neurological deficits that have an organic basis and psychiatric symptoms that do not; and (4) helping to identify the focus for rehabilitation programmes and to assess progress on these programmes (Veitch & Oddy 2008). In many cases a diagnosis has to be made on the basis of cognitive and behavioural impairments that are detected by a range of neuropsychological tests. However, in recent times, the results of these tests can be supplemented by findings from EEG analyses, brain scans such as PET scans and fMRI, blood tests and chemical analyses of cerebrospinal fluids. Assessment of cognitive abilities is also supplemented with behavioural observation and information from clients and their families about onset, type, severity and progression of symptoms, together with a detailed history of educational, occupational, psychosocial, demographic, and previous and current medical factors.

Neuropsychological tests themselves can be remarkably accurate in detecting quite specific deficits and also identifying the brain areas where tissue damage may have led to the deficit. Brain scans can then supplement and confirm the results of neuropsychological tests (D'Esposito, 2000). One of the most widely used tests worldwide is the *WAIS-III* (Wechsler Adult Intelligence Scale, third edition) (Wechsler, 2004). This contains scales that measure vocabulary, arithmetic ability, digit span, information comprehension, letter–number sequencing, picture completion ability, reasoning ability, symbol search and object assembly ability. These measures can be aggregated to provide scores on broader indices of ability such as verbal comprehension, perceptual organization (a measure of non-verbal reasoning), working memory and information processing speed. In the UK, the *Adult Memory and Information Processing Battery (AMIPB)* (Coughlan & Hollows, 1985) is in wide use. This comprises two tests of speed of information processing, verbal memory tests (list learning and story recall) and visual memory tests (design learning and figure recall). One of the common neuropsychological tests used in the USA is the *Halstead-Reitan Neuropsychological Test Battery* (Broshek & Barth, 2000), which has been compiled to evaluate brain and nervous system functioning across a fixed set of eight tests. The tests evaluate function across visual, auditory and tactile input, verbal communication, spatial and sequential perception, the ability to analyse information, and the ability to form mental concepts, make judgements, control motor output, and to attend to and memorize stimuli.

Test batteries such as these also provide useful information on the source of any deficits (such as closed head injury, alcohol abuse, Alzheimer's disease and stroke), whether the damage occurred during childhood development, and whether any deficits are progressive. Focus Point 14.1 gives an example of one of the basic tests – the trail-making task – which provides a measure of information processing speed and a range of recognition and visuomotor integration abilities. Many of these tests are so extensive that they may take as long as 6 hours to administer, requiring substantial patience and stamina on the part of both clinician and client. In contrast, some other tests have been developed to be quick and simple to implement and to provide a reasonably reliable indication of general level of impairment. One such test is the *Mini Mental State Examination (MMSE)*, which is a brief 30-item test used to screen for dementia (e.g. in Alzheimer's disease) and which takes about 10 minutes to administer (see Focus Point 14.2).

> **WAIS-III**   The Wechsler Adult Intelligence Scale (third edition), a neuropsychological test that measures vocabulary, arithmetic ability, digit span, information comprehension, letter–number sequencing, picture completion ability, reasoning ability, symbol search and object assembly ability.

> **Adult Memory and Information Processing Battery (AMIPB)**   A neuropsychological test in wide use in the UK, comprising two tests of speed of information processing, verbal memory tests (list learning and story recall) and visual memory tests (design learning and figure recall).

> **Halstead-Reitan Neuropsychological Test Battery**   One of the common neuropsychological tests used in the USA, compiled to evaluate brain and nervous system functioning across a fixed set of eight tests.

> **Mini Mental State Examination (MMSE)**   A structured test that takes 10 minutes to administer and can provide reliable information on a client's overall levels of cognitive and mental functioning.

FOCUS POINT 14.1

The trail-making task

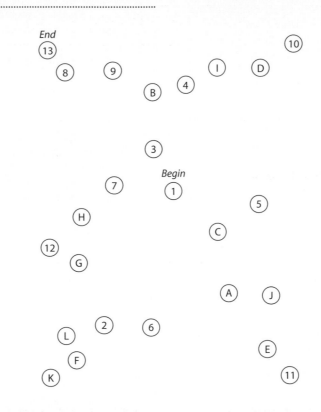

Above is an example of the trail-making task. This consists of a page with circles containing the letters A to L and 13 numbered circles intermixed and randomly arranged. Clients are instructed to connect the circles by drawing lines alternating between numbers and letters in sequential order until they reach the circle labelled 'End'. This test normally takes 5–10 minutes to complete.

The trail-making test helps to evaluate information processing speed, visual scanning ability, integration of visual and motor functions, letter and number recognition and sequencing, and the ability to maintain two different trains of thought.

For adults, scores above 91 seconds have traditionally indicated brain impairment, but completion times may vary significantly with age, education and culture.

14.1.3 The Diagnosis of Neurological Disorders

14.1.3.1 Difficulties of Diagnosis

Diagnosis is made difficult by the fact that the symptoms and deficits found in neurological disorders often closely resemble those of other psychopathologies. For example, cognitive deficits typical of neurological disorders are a regular feature of dissociative disorders (e.g. amnesia) and schizophrenia (e.g. language deficits, information processing deficits, deficits in executive functions). Motor coordination deficits, paralysis and impairments of sensory input are also found in somatoform disorders such as conversion disorder (e.g. hysterical paralysis and blindness; see Chapter 12, section 12.1.1). In addition, in the early stages of a degenerative neurological disorder, people will start to experience cognitive impairments that affect their daily lives, which will often lead to the development of psychological problems (e.g. depression and anxiety) that compound the difficulties of diagnosis (see *Paddy's Story* at the beginning of this chapter). Indeed, prior to the

FOCUS POINT 14.2

Mini Mental State Examination (MMSE)

The MMSE is a good instrument for assessing cognitive function in dementia. It takes about 10 minutes to administer.

Orientation
What is the (year) (season) (date) (day) (month)?

5 ☐

Where are we: (country) (city) (part of city) (number of flat/house) (name of street)?

5 ☐

Registration
Name three objects: 1 second to say each.
Then ask the patient to name all three after you have said them.
Give one point for each correct answer.

3 ☐

Attention and calculation
Serial 7s: Ask the patient to begin with 100 and count backwards by 7. Stop after five subtractions (93, 86, 79, 72, 65). 1 point for each correct.

5 ☐

Recall
Ask for the three objects repeated above (under Registration).
Give 1 point for each correct.

3 ☐

Language
Name a pencil and watch (Show the patient a wristwatch and ask him or her what it is). Repeat for pencil (2 points).

Repeat the following: 'No ifs, ands or buts' (1 point).

Follow a three-stage command: 'Take a paper in your right hand, fold it in half and put it on the floor' (3 points).

Read and obey the following: Close your eyes (1 point).

Write a sentence (1 point).

Copy a design (1 point). On a clean piece of paper, draw intersecting pentagons (as below), each side about 1 inch, and ask him or her to copy it exactly as it is. All 10 angles must be present and two must intersect to score 1 point. Tremor and rotation are ignored.

9 ☐

Total score _____

A score of 20 or less generally suggests dementia but may also be found in acute confusion, schizophrenia or severe depression. Mild Alzheimer's is usually linked to an MMSE score of 21–26, moderate Alzheimer's to scores of 10–20, and severe Alzheimer's to an MMSE score of less than 10.

Variant Creutzfeldt-Jakob disease (vCJD)
A fatal infectious disease that attacks the brain and central nervous system. Commonly known as 'mad cow disease'.

infection and *variant Creutzfeldt-Jakob disease* (or 'mad cow disease' as it is more commonly known).

14.2.1.1 Bacterial Meningitis

Meningitis is still an important cause of death and neurological deficit worldwide, with a mortality rate of between 9 and 33 per cent (van de Beek, de Gans, Spanjaard, Weisfelt et al., 2005). The disease can cause severe physical disability (e.g. hearing loss and loss of vision) and cognitive impairment, such as cognitive slowness, impairment of psychomotor performance, poor visuomotor coordination and psychological symptoms indicating depression. Cognitive slowness may also be a long-term feature of meningitis even when individuals have made a good recovery from the disease itself (van de Beek, Schmand, de Gans, Weisfelt et al., 2002), although recent studies suggest that this effect may be reversible, and impairment may be inversely related to time since the infection (van de Beek, de Gans, Spanjaard, Weisfelt et al., 2005; Bruyn, Kremer, de Marie, Padberg et al., 1989).

14.2.1.2 HIV Infection

Among the viruses that can infect the brain is the human immunodeficiency virus type 1 (HIV-1). The HIV virus tends to enter the central nervous system early in the illness, and neurological difficulties can develop in up to 60 per cent of those infected with the virus (Ghafouri, Amini, Khalili & Sawaya, 2006). On many occasions the impairments caused by infection are usually minor, but over the several years that sufferers may be hosting the virus, it may induce multiple symptoms of motor and cognitive dysfunction and create a syndrome of impairment that is known as *HIV dementia*. This is sometimes known as AIDS dementia complex (ADC) or HIV-1 associated dementia (HAD).

HIV dementia A syndrome of impairment involving multiple symptoms of motor and cognitive dysfunction, sometimes known as AIDS dementia complex (ADC) or HIV-1 associated dementia (HAD).

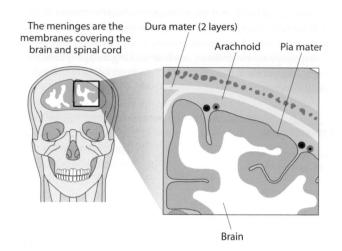

Figure 14.3
The brain is covered by 3 connective tissue layers (the dura mater, arachnoid and pia mater), collectively called the *meninges*, which support blood vessels and contain cerebrospinal fluid. Meningitis is an inflammation of the meninges, which, if severe, may become encephalitis, an inflammation of the brain.

Major clinical symptoms of HIV dementia include impaired short-term memory, lack of concentration, leg weakness, slowness of hand movement and depression (Reger, Welsh, Razani, Martin et al., 2002). A less disabling form of HIV dementia is known as *minor cognitive motor disorder (MCMD)*. This consists of memory loss and reduction of cognitive and computational functions and appears to affect around 30 per cent of those with HIV (Gonzalez-Scarano & Martin-Garcia, 2005).

Minor cognitive motor disorder (MCMD)
A form of HIV dementia consisting of memory loss and the reduction of cognitive and computational functions.

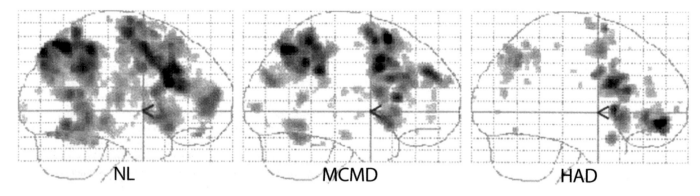

Figure 14.4
Functional MRI (fMRI) scans showing activation during a motor task for HIV patients with normal cognitive (NL), minor cognitive motor disorder (MCMD) and HIV-associated dementia (HAD). Darkened regions indicate areas of activation. Compared with NL, patients with MCMD and HAD have significantly less activation.

Source: Tucker, Robertson, Lin, Smith et al. (2004).

HIV infection appears to cause these cognitive impairments in a variety of ways. Functional MRI scans indicate that HIV infection is associated with progressive cortical atrophy in the grey and white matter in the brain, particularly in the later stages of the disease (Dalpan, McArthur, Aylward, Selnes et al., 1992). However, while the HIV virus can itself attack the central nervous system, neurological deficits are often caused by the body's weakened immune system allowing other infections to attack the brain (Ghafouri, Amini, Khalili & Sawaya, 2006).

14.2.1.3 Variant Creutzfeldt-Jakob Disease (vCJD)

Many readers may recall the high profile given to what was termed 'mad cow disease' in the UK in the 1980s and 1990s. 'Mad cow disease' is a fatal infectious disease known as *spongiform encephalopathy* that attacks the brain and central nervous system. Outbreaks of the disease hit epidemic proportions amongst cattle in the UK during the 1980s, and evidence suggests that the disease was transmitted to humans through contaminated beef. In humans, the disease became known as variant Creutzfeldt-Jakob disease (vCJD). Estimates suggest that over 150 people in the UK have died from the disease between 1995 and 2006 (National Creutzfeld-Jakob Disease Surveillance Unit, 2006).

> **Spongiform encephalopathy**   A fatal infectious disease that attacks the brain and central nervous system. Commonly known as 'mad cow disease' or variant Creutzfeldt-Jakob disease (vCJD).

The disease may have an incubation period of up to 10–15 years, but once symptoms begin to appear, death may occur within 4 months. Early signs of vCJD include changes in mood, temperament and behaviour, followed by impairments in memory and concentration, and confused thinking. Deficits in verbal fluency, numeracy ability, face recognition, memory ability and executive functioning appear rapidly once symptoms have been identified (Kapur, Abbott, Lowman & Will, 2003). The infectious agent in vCJD is thought to be the *prion* (a prion is an abnormal, transmissible agent that is able to induce abnormal folding of normal cellular proteins in the brain, leading to brain damage). Rapid dementia in vCJD appears to result from prions or protein deposits encrusting or replacing neurons in the brain and central nervous system. This occurs at both the cortical and subcortical level, causing deficits in cognitive functioning and basic motor coordination. Case History 14.1 provides a description of how the progressive cognitive impairments caused by vCJD become manifest once symptoms appear.

> **Prion**   An abnormal, transmissible agent that is able to induce abnormal folding of normal cellular proteins in the brain, leading to brain damage. A major contributing factor in variant Creutzfeldt-Jakob disease (vCJD).

14.2.2 Traumatic Brain Injury

One of the most common causes of neurological impairment is traumatic brain injury. This can result from blunt or penetrating

---

CASE HISTORY 14.1

Variant Creutzfeld-Jakob disease (vCJD)

The patient was a right-handed man in his early 20s who presented at the end of July 1998 with a short history of memory difficulties, occasional problems in speech articulation, a change in personality and two episodes of urinary incontinence. His parents thought that the first sign of his illness was evident in May 1998, when he had a slight slurring in his speech during a telephone conversation with them. The first noticeable manifestation of his memory difficulties occurred in early July 1998, when he started a summer work placement and had major limitations in assimilating new information in a computer-based environment where he was taught simple data entry procedures and where, during a previous placement, he had excelled. Although he appeared to have no difficulty using equipment around the home (e.g. the video), he performed such activities much more slowly than before. His mother reported that he was very irritable and argumentative when he came home from university. He later became indifferent and apathetic. She said that he was often stuck for words and that his speech was sometimes incoherent. He had recently written two letters to his girlfriend that did not make any sense. His mother thought that he was nervous about going out on his own. His condition showed a progressive decline and he died in December 1998.

Source: Kapur, Abbott, Lowman & Will (2003)

Clinical Commentary

vCJD may have an incubation period of up to 10–15 years, but the first signs of the illness are emotional changes and confused behaviour. The disease eventually affects every aspect of thinking and behaviour, causing impairments in cognitive functioning, motor coordination and control over bodily functions – each of which is manifested in this case history. Once symptoms have begun to appear, the disease is fatal and death usually occurs within 4–6 months.

trauma to the head as a result of direct injury at the impact site. Indirect injury can also be caused by sudden impacts causing movement of the brain within the skull, leading to injury on the opposite side of the brain to the impact. In 2000/2001 there were over 110,000 admissions to hospitals in England with a primary diagnosis of head injury (Hospital Episode Statistics, 2001). Road traffic accidents accounted for around 40–50 per cent of all head injuries, while domestic and industrial accidents accounted for between 20 and 30 per cent. A majority of the rest were caused by sports and recreational activities (10–15 per cent) and assaults (10 per cent). Interestingly, between 70 and 88 per cent of all people who sustain a head injury are male, and 40–50 per cent are children. While the vast majority of these cases will suffer only a minor head injury, more serious cases will lapse into coma, develop epilepsy or suffer other forms of long-term disability (both physical and intellectual).

Initially assessing whether a head injury is severe and requires immediate medical attention is based on a number of criteria. Referral to an Accident and Emergency (A&E) Department should be made if: (1) a high-energy head injury is involved (e.g. a driving accident); (2) there is a loss of consciousness as a result of the injury; (3) there is amnesia for events before or after the injury; (4) persistent headaches and/or vomiting are experienced; and (5) irritable or altered behaviour is observed following the injury.

Although many victims of head injury will show a slow but gradual improvement over time (e.g. recovery of any memory loss, recovery of motor functions such as balance, dissipation of feelings of confusion and disorientation), severe head injury can be associated with a range of semi-permanent cognitive and neurological deficits, including general deficits in speed of information processing, attention, memory, language skills and executive functioning. If recovery from such deficits occurs, it is likely to happen in the first 6 months following the injury. However, perhaps more dramatic than some of the cognitive deficits resulting from brain injury are the emotional sequelae, which include depression, irritability, fatigue, aggressive behaviour, anxiety, rapid mood shifts and difficulty concentrating (Satz, Forney, Zaucha, Asarnow et al., 1998). These factors can cause a significant decline in the overall quality of life for those with severe brain injury and give rise to intense bouts of depression and suicidal ideation, posing significant challenges for post-injury care and rehabilitation (e.g. Horneman, Folkesson, Sintonen, von Wendt et al., 2005; Baguley, Cooper & Felmingham, 2006; Levin, McCauley, Josic, Boake et al., 2005).

14.2.2.1 Types of Traumatic Brain Injury

There are three basic types of injury that can lead to brain damage. These are concussion, contusion and penetrating head injury.

Concussion An impact to the head which jars the brain and temporarily disrupts its normal functioning.

With *concussion*, the impact to the head jars the brain and temporarily disrupts its normal functioning. Concussion is not a life-threatening injury, but it can cause both short-term and long-term problems. In medical terms, a concussion might be described as

a *closed head injury* or head trauma. The main symptoms are loss of consciousness after the trauma, confusion, headache, nausea or vomiting, blurred vision, loss of short-term memory (individuals may not remember the actual injury as well as what happened immediately before and after the impact) and perseverating (repeating the same thing over and over, despite being told the answer each time, for example, 'Was I in an accident?')

Closed head injury A concussion or head trauma, the symptoms of which include loss of consciousness after the trauma, confusion, headache, nausea or vomiting, blurred vision, loss of short-term memory and perseverating.

Contusion is a more severe trauma in which the brain is not just jarred but the impact also causes bruising to the brain. Contusion is a more

Contusion A severe head trauma in which the brain is not just jarred but the impact also causes bruising to the brain.

serious brain injury than concussion and may result in the patient falling into a coma for hours or days and exhibiting convulsions. On regaining consciousness, victims may often exhibit the symptoms of delirium, including agitated and disoriented behaviour, cognitive impairments and hallucinations. Sportsmen such as boxers may suffer brain injury indicative of contusion, and repeated episodes of contusion can lead to more permanent impairments such as tremors, dizziness, cognitive slowness and memory loss.

Plate 14.2
Ex-world champion heavyweight boxer Muhammad Ali eventually developed Parkinson's disease, believed to have been caused by head injuries sustained while he was active as a boxer. This syndrome, known as dementia pugilistica, can result in structural changes to the brain similar to those found in Parkinson's disease and Alzheimer's disease.

Dementia pugilistica   A syndrome associated with sportsmen, such as boxers, who may suffer brain injury indicative of contusion.

Penetrating head wound   A head injury in which the skull and outer layer of the meninges are breached.

Open head injury   A head injury in which the skull and outer layer of the meninges are breached.

Phineas P. Gage   A victim of a penetrating head injury, one of the first examples to indicate that brain damage could cause radical changes to personality and affect socially appropriate interaction.

This is a syndrome known as *dementia pugilistica*, which can result in structural changes to the brain similar to those found in Alzheimer's disease and Parkinson's disease (Lampert & Hardman, 1984; Davie, Pirtosek, Barker, Kingsley et al., 1995). Indeed, perhaps the best-known example of this syndrome is the ex-world champion heavyweight boxer Muhammad Ali. Ali eventually developed Parkinson's disease, which is believed to have been caused by head injuries sustained while he was active as a boxer.

Finally, a *penetrating head injury* or *open head injury* is one in which the skull and outer layer of the meninges are breached. Penetrating injury can be caused by high-velocity projectiles or objects of lower velocity such as knives or bone fragments from a skull fracture that are driven into the brain. Head injuries caused by penetrating trauma are usually the most serious of the traumatic brain injuries and may cause permanent disability or death.

One famous example of a penetrating head injury is the case of *Phineas P. Gage*, a rail-road construction worker in the USA in the 1840s. He was a foreman who set explosive charges in rock by drilling holes into the rock, then filling them with gunpowder, sand and a fuse with the aid of a large tamping iron. On one unfortunate occasion, the tamping iron caused a spark that ignited the gunpowder and blew the tamping iron clean through Gage's head. Remarkably, he remained conscious after the accident and returned to his boarding house. Although he appeared to make a full physical recovery and returned to work, Gage began to exhibit significant changes in behaviour and personality. Previously Gage had been hard working, responsible and popular, but his physician reported that he had become 'fitful, irreverent, indulging at times in the grossest profanity, manifesting but little deference for his fellows, impatient of restraint or advice when it conflicts with his desires, at times pertinaciously obstinate, yet capricious and vacillating'. The significance of Phineas Gage's story is that it is one of the first examples to indicate that brain damage could cause radical changes to personality and affect socially appropriate interaction. Computer-generated reconstructions of Gage's injury suggest that the tamping iron may have caused significant damage to both frontal lobes, which are areas of the brain that help to integrate emotion and practical decision-making (Damasio, 1994).

14.2.3 Cerebrovascular Accidents

Damage to brain tissue can also occur as a result of a *cerebrovascular accident (CVA)*, otherwise known as a *stroke*. Strokes result from either a blockage or breaking of the blood vessels in the brain and can be defined in two broad ways. An *infarction* is when the blood flow to the brain is impeded in some way, resulting in damage to the brain tissue fed by that blood flow. In contrast, a *haemorrhage* is when a blood vessel in the brain ruptures and affects local brain tissue.

The most common causes of infarction are an embolism or a thrombosis. A *cerebral embolism* is a blood clot that forms somewhere in the body before travelling through the blood vessels and lodging in the brain, causing the brain cells to become damaged as a result of oxygen starvation. *Cerebral thrombosis* occurs when a blood clot (thrombus) forms in an artery (blood vessel) supplying blood to the brain. Furred-up blood vessels with fatty patches of atheroma (an

Cerebrovascular accident (CVA)   Damage to brain tissue caused either by a blockage or breaking of the blood vessels in the brain. Also known as a stroke.

Stroke   A sudden loss of consciousness resulting when the rupture or occlusion of a blood vessel leads to oxygen lack in the brain.

Infarction   The injury caused when the blood flow to the brain is impeded in some way, resulting in damage to the brain tissue fed by that blood flow.

Haemorrhage   The injury caused when a blood vessel in the brain ruptures and affects local brain tissue.

Cerebral embolism   A blood clot that forms somewhere in the body before travelling through the blood vessels and lodging in the brain, causing the brain cells to become damaged as a result of oxygen starvation.

Cerebral thrombosis   An injury caused when a blood clot (thrombus) forms in an artery (blood vessel) supplying blood to the brain. The clot interrupts the blood supply and brain cells are starved of oxygen.

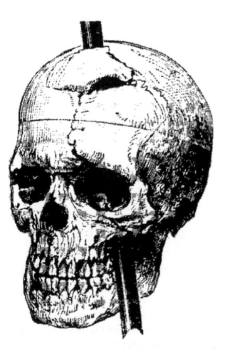

Plate 14.3
This illustration shows how the tamping iron may have penetrated Phineas Gage's skull, crossing the midline and damaging both frontal lobes.

abnormal inflammatory accumulation of macrophage white blood cells within the walls of arteries) may make a thrombosis more likely. The clot interrupts the blood supply and brain cells are starved of oxygen.

Haemorrhaging in the brain is often the result of hypertension or high blood pressure. It is often due to an **aneurysm** or bulging in the wall of the blood vessel, usually an artery at the base of the brain.

> **Aneurysm** A localized bulging in a blood vessel caused by disease or weakening of the vessel wall.

Strokes are remarkably common – especially in individuals over the age of 65 years. In the UK, an estimated 130,000 people a year suffer a stroke, including around 1,000 who are under 30 years of age. Strokes are the third most common cause of death in the UK and the single most common cause of disability: over 250,000 people currently live in the UK with a disability caused by a stroke (Stroke Association, 2006). Symptoms of a stroke often occur very suddenly and unexpectedly. They include numbness, weakness or paralysis on one side of the body (signs of which may be a drooping arm, leg, a lowered eyelid or a dribbling mouth), slurred speech or difficulty finding words or understanding speech, sudden blurred vision or loss of sight, confusion or unsteadiness, and a severe headache. The type and severity of symptoms will depend entirely on the brain area affected by the CVA. Many individuals have what are known as 'silent strokes', which occur in brain areas involved in only minor functions, and exhibit no obvious cognitive or physical impairment. The prevalence of 'silent strokes' in 55- to 64-year-olds has been estimated at 11 per cent, but this rises to 40 per cent in 80- to 85-year-olds (Bryan, Wells, Miller, Elster et al., 1997).

The most common longer-term symptoms of stroke include aphasia, agnosia, apraxia (see Table 14.2) and paralysis. Paralysis often occurs in just one limb or on one side of the body because a CVA usually damages tissue in just one hemisphere of the brain. One of the most common forms of stroke is thrombosis in the left-middle cerebral artery, affecting the left hemisphere. This causes disability to the right-hand side of the body (which is controlled by the left hemisphere) and significant impairment in language ability (e.g. aphasia), since the left hemisphere is critically involved in language generation and comprehension.

As well as physical and cognitive deficits, individuals who have suffered a stroke exhibit emotional disturbance, often manifested as depressed mood or as emotional lability. Depression in particular is a common and significant consequence of strokes: pooled studies suggest that between 14 and 19 per cent of stroke victims meet DSM-IV-TR criteria for major depression (Robinson, 2003), and as many as 40 per cent meet sub-clinical criteria for depression (Fedoroff, Starkstein, Forrester, Geisler et al., 1992). Levels of depression are correlated with the severity of both physical and cognitive deficits (Kauhanen, Korpelainen, Hiltunen, Brusin et al, 1999), suggesting that there may be a link between degree of disability and depression. However, a post-stroke diagnosis of depression also significantly affects rehabilitation and recovery. Recovery from physical and cognitive impairment is significantly retarded in those with depression, and mortality rate 1 year after the stroke is significantly higher in those with depression than without (Robinson, Lipsey, Rao & Price, 1986; Morris, Robinson, Andrezejewski, Samuels et al., 1993) (see Figure 14.5).

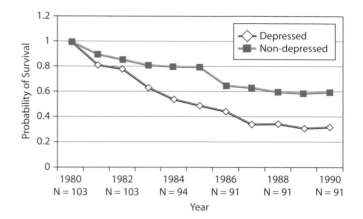

Figure 14.5
Survival curves over 10 years for 37 patients with major or minor depression at the time of in-hospital evaluation compared with 54 patients without depression. By 10-year follow-up, 70 per cent of the patients with major depression and 71 per cent of the patients with minor depression had died compared with 41 per cent of the non-depressed patients.
Source: Morris, Robinson, Andrezejewski, Samuels et al. (1993).

There is a tendency here to conclude that disabilities resulting from a stroke may cause depression, which in turn inhibits recovery. However, the picture is rather more complex than this. Indeed, there seems to be a bidirectional link between stroke and depression. For example, some studies have indicated that depression may even be a risk factor for strokes. In a prospective study, May, McCarron, Stansfield, Ben-Shlomo et al. (2002) found that men with major depressive symptoms were significantly more likely to suffer a stroke within the following 14 years than those without major depressive symptoms. Similarly, treating post-stroke depression with antidepressant medication also has the effect of significantly decreasing mortality rates over a 9-year period (Robinson, Schultz, Castillo, Kopel et al., 2000). All of this suggests that depression is an important feature of disability caused by strokes, and clinical psychologists might be suitably employed to manage depression in attempts to improve recovery rates and reduce mortality rates.

14.2.4 Brain Tumours

A brain tumour is any intracranial tumour created by abnormal and uncontrolled cell division, normally found either in the brain itself, in the cranial nerves, or outside the brain but inside the skull (usually in the meninges). Tumours may originate in a different part of the body as cancer cells in the lungs, breast, kidneys or stomach, and subsequently travel to the brain via the bloodstream. In contrast, *primary brain tumours* are those that originate and grow

> **Primary brain tumour** A brain tumour that originates and grows within the brain itself.

within the brain itself. The kinds of symptoms that a brain tumour will cause depend on both the size and location of the tumour. Many tumours remain benign for many years and generate few, if any, symptoms. However, larger tumours will inevitably lead to swelling, causing intracranial pressure that can give rise to headaches, vomiting, visual problems, tiredness and even coma. As the tumour begins to destroy brain tissue, physical and cognitive impairments become more common; these can include abnormal reflexes, disorientation, memory and attention deficits, and poor motor coordination.

Many individuals with brain tumours also manifest symptoms of other Axis I and II disorders. For example, depression is both a common precursor and a consequence of the diagnosis of a brain tumour (Mainio, Hakko, Niemela, Koivukangas et al., 2005), and brain tumours can often generate symptoms reminiscent of PTSD, panic disorder and eating disorders, amongst others (Moise & Madhusoodanan, 2006). If a tumour goes undetected and continues to grow, it can cause extreme physical and psychological symptoms, including splitting headaches, vomiting and seizures, and sudden and radical changes in personality and behaviour. Some individuals begin to exhibit what is known as *acquired sociopathy*, in which they display a reckless regard for others' personal safety, a lack of remorse and a lack of planning (Damasio, Tranel & Damasio, 1990), as well as overtly psychotic behaviour, such as extreme paranoia and hallucinations.

Acquired sociopathy A reckless regard for others' personal safety, a lack of remorse and a lack of planning, as well as overtly psychotic behaviour such as extreme paranoia and hallucinations, usually caused by an undetected and large brain tumour.

14.2.5 Degenerative Disorders

Degenerative disorders represent those dementias that are characterized by a slow, general deterioration in cognitive, physical and emotional functioning as a result of progressive physical changes in the brain. Deterioration occurs gradually over a number of years. Degenerative disorders are most frequently a feature of older age, where around 7 per cent of individuals over 65 years have diagnosable signs of degenerative dementia, rising to around 30 per cent in those over 85 years of age (Johansson & Zarit, 1995; Kokmen, Beard, Offord & Kurland, 1989). Degenerative disorders can affect both the cerebral cortex and the subcortical regions of the brain. Those that affect cortical areas cause impairments in cognitive abilities such as memory, language, attention and executive functioning (causing amnesia, aphasia, agnosia, slowed thinking and confusion; see Table 14.2). Disorders affecting subcortical regions of the brain may in addition cause emotional disturbances and motor coordination difficulties.

The most common causes of degenerative dementia in the UK are Alzheimer's disease (contributing 55 per cent) and vascular dementia (contributing 20 per cent). Degenerative disorders that in addition significantly affect subcortical areas, and thus emotional behaviour and motor coordination, are Parkinson's disease and Huntington's disease. It is estimated that there are around 18 million people worldwide with degenerative dementia, including

5 million in Europe and 700,000 in the UK; these figures are likely to double by the year 2025 (Alzheimer's Society, 2008).

Diagnosis of degenerative disorders is difficult and complex. Firstly, a degenerative disorder has to be distinguished from the normal process of ageing. Normal ageing naturally results in a moderate deterioration of cognitive abilities (such as forgetting or cognitive slowness) and a deterioration in physical abilities (such as problems with balance and motor coordination). However, degenerative disorders compound this natural process because they represent an active pathological organic deterioration of the brain.

Secondly, it is often difficult to distinguish between the different degenerative disorders that may affect cognitive and physical functioning. Many manifest with very similar cognitive impairments (e.g. amnesia), but there are as yet no definitive medical tests that help to differentiate, say, Alzheimer's disease from other degenerative diseases.

Thirdly, degenerative disorders are most frequently found in the elderly, and this particular population will often present with a wide range of psychological and medical problems that complicate diagnosis. For example, anxiety and depression are common features of old age and may complicate neurological testing. Performance during assessment may also be affected by other physical illnesses or the effects of medications for other ailments.

Finally, how a degenerative disorder manifests on presentation may differ significantly between individuals depending on factors such as their level of education, level of family and social support, and their psychological history. In effect, two individuals with the same disorder may present themselves quite differently and perform quite differently in assessments depending on a range of social and psychological factors. Estimates of the prevalence rates for diagnosed degenerative dementia disorders quite understandably increase with age, ranging from 1.4–1.6 per cent for individuals aged 65–69 years to 16–25 per cent for those over age 85 years (APA, 2000, p. 152).

The following sections continue by describing in detail some of the main degenerative disorders: Alzheimer's disease, vascular dementia, Parkinson's disease, Huntington's disease, and multiple sclerosis.

14.2.5.1 Alzheimer's Disease

Characteristics of Alzheimer's Disease *Alzheimer's disease* is the most common form of dementia. It is a slowly progressive disorder, and neural damage may start 20–30 years before any overt cognitive or behavioural signs of impairment (Davies, Wolska, Hilbich, Multhaup et al., 1988).

Alzheimer's disease A slowly progressive form of dementia involving progressive impairments in short-term memory, with symptoms of aphasia, apraxia and agnosia, together with evidence of impaired judgements, decision-making and orientation.

The disease manifests as progressive impairments in short-term memory, with symptoms of aphasia, apraxia and agnosia, together with evidence of impaired judgements, decision-making and orientation. Early signs of the disease are irritability, lack of concentration and basic failures of short-term memory, such as forgetting that food is cooking or forgetting names. Eventually, individuals become more and more confused and disoriented and may be unable to remember basic general knowledge (e.g. be unable to recite the alphabet), may confuse night and day, and get lost in relatively familiar environments. Many individuals also show personality changes, may exhibit paranoid behaviour, and become generally irritable and difficult to control. Eventually, sufferers become physically weak and bedridden. Their erratic and unpredictable behaviour often becomes problematic for their carers, many of whom are likely to be the elderly spouses of sufferers themselves. The average duration of the disease from onset of symptoms to death is around 8–10 years.

Known risk factors for Alzheimer's disease include the following (Barranco-Quintana, Allam, Del Castillo & Navajas, 2005):

1 age, which is the principle marker for risk of the disease;

2 sex: prevalence is higher in women than in men;

3 genetics: having a first-degree relative with the disease significantly increases risk;

4 family history of dementia: nearly 40 per cent of those with Alzheimer's disease have a family history of dementia;

5 a history of head injury (McDowell, 2001); and

6 low educational status.

Interestingly, some activities appear to have a direct or indirect protective value by predicting lower rates of Alzheimer's disease (even in those with a family history of dementia). These include physical activity, smoking, drinking moderate levels of alcohol and diets high in vitamins B6, B12 and folic acid (Barranco-Quintana, Allam, Del Castillo & Navajas, 2005). However, we must be cautious about how we interpret these factors. For example, smoking may protect against Alzheimer's disease largely because it may prevent smokers from reaching old age, which is when the disease becomes prevalent. In addition, low educational status may be correlated with Alzheimer's disease because it may adversely affect performance on the cognitive tasks used to diagnose the disease.

The DSM-IV-TR diagnostic criteria for dementia of the Alzheimer's type are given in Table 14.4. However, Alzheimer's disease itself is difficult to differentiate from other forms of degenerative dementia and is often easier to identify by successively eliminating other types of disorder that cause dementia symptoms, such as Parkinson's disease, Huntington's disease, hypothyroidism, HIV infection, substance abuse or head trauma. This can be achieved using thyroid function tests, blood tests and a battery of neuropsychological tests of cognitive function. In addition, neuroimaging plays an important part in the diagnosis of Alzheimer's disease, by helping to exclude alternative causes of dementia such as brain tumour, cerebral atrophy and cerebrovascular disease.

Aetiology of Alzheimer's Disease It is only in the past 20–25 years that we have come to understand some of the causes of Alzheimer's disease, and, indeed, to be able to identify it as a specific form of degenerative dementia. The changes that occur to the brain during Alzheimer's disease appear to be structural and involve the development of beta amyloid plaques and neurofibrillary tangles. *Beta amyloid plaques* appear to be caused by abnormal protein synthesis in the brain; they clump together, with the consequence of killing healthy neurons. *Neurofibrillary tangles* consist of abnormal collections of twisted nerve cell threads which result in errors in impulses between nerve

Table 14.4 *DSM-IV-TR diagnostic criteria for dementia of the Alzheimer's type*

A The development of multiple cognitive deficits manifested by both

(1) memory impairment (impaired ability to learn new information or to recall previously learned information)

(2) one (or more) of the following cognitive disturbances:

(a) aphasia (language disturbance)

(b) apraxia (impaired ability to carry out motor activities despite intact motor function)

(c) agnosia (failure to recognize or identify objects despite intact sensory function)

(d) disturbance in executive functioning (i.e. planning, organizing, sequencing, abstracting)

B The cognitive deficits in Criteria A1 and A2 each cause significant impairment in social or occupational functioning and represent a significant decline from a previous level of functioning.

C The course is characterized by gradual onset and continuing cognitive decline.

D The cognitive deficits in Criteria A1 and A2 are not due to any of the following:

(1) other central nervous system conditions that cause progressive deficits in memory and cognition (e.g. cerebrovascular disease, Parkinson's disease)

(2) systemic conditions that are known to cause dementia (e.g. hypothyroidism, vitamin B12 or folic acid deficiency)

(3) substance-induced conditions

E The deficits do not occur excessively during the course of delirium.

F The disturbance is not better accounted for by another Axis I disorder (e.g. major depression, schizophrenia).

Beta amyloid plaques Abnormal cell development, possibly caused by abnormal protein synthesis in the brain which clump together with the consequence of killing healthy neurons.

Neurofibrillary tangles Abnormal collections of twisted nerve cell threads which result in errors in impulses between nerve cells and eventual cell death.

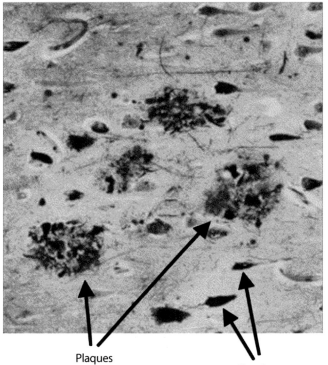

Plaques

Tangles

Figure 14.6
Beta amyloid plaques and neurofibrillary tangles in the cerebral cortex in Alzheimer's disease. Plaques appear to be caused by abnormal protein synthesis in the brain, which clump together and kill healthy neurons. Tangles consist of abnormal collections of twisted nerve cell threads, causing errors in impulses between nerves.

Source: Blennow, de Leon & Zetterberg (2006).

There appears to be a significant inherited component to Alzheimer's disease, with an estimate of up to 50 per cent of first-degree relatives of sufferers also developing the disorder (Korten, Jorm, Henderson, Broe et al., 1993). In addition, twin studies suggest that the heritability of the disease is between 58 and 79 per cent (Gatz, Reynolds, Fratiglioni, Johansson et al., 2006). However, what is inherited in Alzheimer's disease is still not entirely clear: studies have identified a number of chromosomes that appear to carry abnormalities that contribute to Alzheimer's disease in various ways (Pericek-Vance, Bass, Yamaoka, Gaskell et al., 1997; Rocchi, Pellegrini, Siciliano & Murri, 2003). Some of these may increase susceptibility to Alzheimer's disease, while others may have a more direct cause in generating proteins that give rise to the beta amyloid plaques that result in damage to brain tissue. In addition, some genes may play a role in early-onset Alzheimer's disease, while others appear to be linked to late onset (Bertram & Tanzi, 2004). All this suggests that, while there is no doubt about the importance of an inherited component to Alzheimer's disease, it may have multiple causes, and a number of genetic mechanisms may contribute to the factors that lead to degenerative brain damage.

14.2.5.2 Vascular Dementia

Vascular dementia is a degenerative cerebrovascular disease that leads to a progressive decline in memory and cognitive functioning. It occurs when the blood supply carrying oxygen and nutrients to the brain is interrupted by a blocked or diseased vascular system. Vascular dementia can be caused in several different ways. Most commonly, there is a blockage of small blood vessels somewhere in the system of arteries that feeds the brain. Blockages may be caused by plaque build-up on the inside of the artery wall, or by blood clots which have broken loose and block an artery supplying blood to the brain (a cerebral thrombosis). Clots can form as a result of abnormal heart rhythms or other heart abnormalities. Also, a weak patch on an artery wall can balloon outward and form an aneurysm, which can burst and deprive the brain cells of oxygen.

> **Vascular dementia** A degenerative cerebrovascular disease that leads to a progressive decline in memory and cognitive functioning.

Vascular dementia is the second most common cause of dementia after Alzheimer's disease and mainly affects people between the ages of 60 and 75 years. It also affects more men than women. The disorder is associated with medical problems such as blackouts, cardiovascular problems, high blood pressure, kidney failure and retinal sclerosis (scarring of the retina). The main cognitive and behavioural problems associated with vascular dementia are forgetfulness, slurred speech, language problems, lack of concentration, disorientation (getting lost in familiar surroundings), difficulty following instructions, problems handling money, dizziness, leg or arm weakness, moving with rapid shuffling steps, loss of bladder or bowel control, and laughing or crying inappropriately. Onset can be either gradual (if the individual suffers a series of minor strokes over time) or dramatic (if a single stroke is significant enough to cause immediate problems). However, the course of the disorder is nearly always stepwise, with noticeable deterioration in cognitive abilities being followed by periods of stability before another decline takes place.

cells and eventual cell death (Blennow, de Leon & Zetterberg, 2006) (see Figure 14.6). The result of these abnormal cell developments is that there is a gradual shrinkage of healthy brain tissue. The grooves or furrows in the brain, called sulci, are noticeably widened and there is shrinkage of the gyri, the well-developed folds of the brain's outer layer. In addition, the ventricles, or chambers within the brain that contain cerebrospinal fluid, are noticeably enlarged.

Another factor that is thought to be important in Alzheimer's disease is the faulty production of the brain neurotransmitter *acetylcholine*: Alzheimer's disease appears to affect structures involved in the production of acetylcholine. The enzyme acetylcholinesterase normally breaks down acetylcholine after use so it can be recycled, but in Alzheimer's disease acetylcholine levels fall too low and memory and other brain functions are impaired. A number of drug treatments can be utilized to help facilitate acetylcholine production in the brain. We will discuss these in more detail in the section on treatment and rehabilitation.

> **Acetylcholine** A neurotransmitter that appears to be involved in learning and memory.

14.2.5.3 Parkinson's Disease

Parkinson's disease A progressive neurological condition affecting movements such as walking, talking and writing, and causing psychological disturbance in between 40 and 60 per cent of sufferers.

Parkinson's disease is a progressive neurological condition affecting movements such as walking, talking and writing, and it causes psychological disturbance in between 40 and 60 per cent of sufferers. The main symptoms of Parkinson's disease are: (1) tremor, including jerky movements of the arms, hands and head which are also present during resting periods; (2) slowness of movement (bradykinesia): people with Parkinson's may find that they have difficulty initiating movements or find that performing movements takes longer; and (3) stiffness or rigidity of muscles, including problems in standing up from a chair or rolling over in bed. The disease is named after Dr James Parkinson (1755–1824), the London doctor who first identified it as a specific condition.

Parkinson's disease occurs as a result of damage in the basal ganglia, particularly the region of the basal ganglia known as the *substantia nigra*. Cells in this area are responsible for producing the neurotransmitter dopamine, which allows messages to be sent to the parts of the brain that coordinate movement. With the depletion of dopamine-producing cells, these parts of the brain are unable to function normally. It is estimated that over 4 million people worldwide suffer from Parkinson's disease, including 120,000 in the UK (Parkinson's Disease Society, 2008). Symptoms first appear when the individual is over 50 years of age, with men being marginally more likely to develop the disorder than women.

Substantia nigra A region of the basal ganglia.

Sufferers who develop psychological problems experience memory problems and exhibit deficits in learning, judgement and concentration, as well as becoming socially withdrawn and apathetic. It is estimated that up to 75 per cent of individuals with Parkinson's disease may eventually develop dementia, and symptoms can occur as early as 1–2 years after onset of the disease (Williams-Gray, Foltynie, Lewis & Barker, 2006; Ehrt & Aarsland, 2005). As well as signs of cognitive impairment, Parkinson's sufferers also regularly exhibit symptoms of psychosis and depression. Hallucinations occur in between 16 and 40 per cent of sufferers, and this has often been considered as a medication-induced phenomenon. That is, the drugs used to facilitate substantia nigra dopamine production in sufferers are also known to produce psychosis-like symptoms. However, there is reason to believe that psychosis symptoms such as hallucinations may also be intrinsic to the disease and result from progressive dementia or impairments in primary visual processing (Williams-Gray, Foltynie, Lewis & Barker, 2006).

Studies also suggest that depression is a significant feature of Parkinson's disease in between 25 and 40 per cent of sufferers (Leentjens, 2004), which is often considered to be an understandable reaction to having to cope with a chronic and debilitating disease. However, as in the case of Alzheimer's disease, depression is also a significant predictor of subsequent Parkinson's diagnosis, with the incidence of depression increasing significantly in the 3 years prior to diagnosis of Parkinson's (Leentjens, van den Akker, Metsemakers, Lousberg et al., 2003). The fact that depression appears to be a biological risk factor for a number of degenerative dementias has given rise to the view that depression may be accompanied by an *allostatic state* (a biological state of stress) that can accelerate disease processes and cause atrophy of nerve cells in the brain, in turn leading to dementia (McEwen, 2003).

Allostatic state A biological state of stress.

Post-mortem studies of individuals with Parkinson's disease suggest an association between dementia and Lewy body deposition. *Lewy bodies* are abnormal protein deposits that disrupt the brain's normal functioning. These Lewy body proteins are found in an area of the brain stem where they deplete the neurotransmitter dopamine, causing Parkinson's symptoms. These abnormal proteins can also diffuse throughout other areas of the brain, including the cerebral cortex, causing disruption of perception, thinking and behaviour. *Lewy body dementia* also exists in a pure form, accounting for around 15 per cent of dementias, but can be found in conjunction with other brain changes, including those typically seen in Alzheimer's disease and Parkinson's disease (McKeith, Galasko, Kosaka, Perry et al., 1996).

Lewy bodies Abnormal protein deposits that disrupt the brain's normal functioning.

Lewy body dementia A dementing illness associated with protein deposits called Lewy bodies, found in the cortex of the brain.

14.2.5.4 Huntington's Disease

Huntington's disease is an inherited, degenerative disorder of the central nervous system, caused by a dominant gene. This means that anyone who inherits the gene from one of his or her parents will develop the disease with 50 per cent likelihood. Symptoms of the disorder do not normally occur until after the age of 35 years, and can have an even later onset (however, the earlier the onset, the more severe the disease tends to be). It is principally a movement disorder, with the first observable behavioural symptoms manifesting themselves as clumsiness and an involuntary, spasmodic jerking of the limbs. However, many early signs of the disease tend to be radical changes in temperament. The individual may become rude, exhibit unpredictable mood changes, and switch dramatically from depression to euphoria. Cognitive functioning is affected as the disease develops, and this is manifested as impairments in memory, attention and decision-making leading to full dementia. In addition, as the disease progresses, sufferers may also begin to exhibit psychotic symptoms, including hallucinations and delusions.

Huntington's disease An inherited, degenerative disorder of the central nervous system, caused by a dominant gene.

The general psychological syndrome associated with Huntington's disease includes affective symptoms, cognitive deficits, personality disorganization, bloody-mindedness, early loss of common sense, hallucinations, delusional ideation, odd behaviours and obsessions (Wagle, Wagle, Markova & Berrios, 2000). Psychopathological symptoms associated with the disease include depression, mania, schizophrenia, paranoia, anxiety and obsessive-compulsive behaviours (Barquero-Jimenez & Gomez-Tortosa, 2001). About 8 in every 100,000 people in the UK have Huntington's disease – approximately 4,800 people. Because the disease is a genetically inherited one, its prevalence will vary according to the geographical distribution of those with the defective gene. The highest prevalence of this disorder in the world is near Lake Maracaibo in Venezuela, where it affects around 700 per 100,000 of the population.

The genetic abnormality in Huntington's disease is found on the fourth chromosome. This results in the production of a protein, *mutant Huntingtin (mHtt)*, which causes cell death in the basal ganglia – an area of the brain responsible for posture, muscle tone and motor coordination. Pre-symptom testing is possible by means of a blood test which counts the number of mutant repetitions on the relevant gene. A negative blood test means that the individual does not carry the gene, will never develop symptoms and cannot pass it on to children. A positive blood test means that the individual does carry the gene, will develop the disease and has a 50 per cent chance of passing it on to children, assuming he or she lives long enough to do so. Because a positive blood test will have such a dramatic psychological impact, potential sufferers are given intensive counselling and psychological support before undergoing pre-symptom testing.

> **Mutant Huntingtin (mHtt)**   A protein which causes cell death in the basal ganglia and contributes to Huntington's disease.

14.2.5.5 Multiple Sclerosis

> **Multiple sclerosis (MS)**   A degenerative neurological condition which results in the destruction of the myelin sheaths that surround nerve cells and facilitate transmission of nerve impulses in the brain and central nervous system.

Multiple sclerosis (MS) is a degenerative neurological condition which results in the destruction of the myelin sheaths that surround nerve cells and facilitate transmission of nerve impulses in the brain and central nervous system. Because this destruction can occur in any part of the brain or central nervous system, MS can have a broad range of cognitive and behavioural effects that may differ significantly from one sufferer to another. For example, MS can affect motor function, sensory perception (causing blindness), control over bodily functions (e.g. causing incontinence) and cause significant cognitive impairments. Cognitive impairments are reported in up to 70 per cent of MS patients, and the most affected domains are attention, memory and information processing speed. These cognitive deficits are also paralleled by emotional and mood changes demonstrating significant levels of depression and lowered quality of life indicated by negative effects on daily living, employment and relationships (Wallin, Wilken & Kane, 2006). The cognitive deficits in MS are not as pronounced as in many other degenerative diseases, such as Alzheimer's disease, but severity will depend on the individual course of the disease and on progressive damage to the brain and central nervous system. MRI scans have indicated that MS is associated with brain atrophy in a number of areas, including grey matter atrophy in those areas of the brain that control visuospatial ability, problem-solving and memory and learning (Huber, Bornstein, Rammohan, Christy et al., 1992; Sepulcre, Sastre-Garriga, Cercignani, Ingle et al., 2006).

SUMMARY

In this section we have discussed five types of neurological disorder based on the nature of the factor that has precipitated dysfunction. These five factors are cerebral infection, traumatic brain injury, cerebrovascular accidents (strokes), brain tumours and degenerative disorders. All of these can cause cognitive impairment to differing degrees, and the nature of the impairment will depend on the areas of the brain affected by each factor. Cognitive impairments may be relatively specific and result from damage to tissue in areas of the brain dealing with specific functions such as language, memory or visuomotor coordination (see Table 14.2). Such specific disabilities are found most often with traumatic brain injury, cerebrovascular accidents and brain tumours. Other types of disorder are progressive and develop from mild symptoms of cognitive impairment to full-blown dementia; these include some cerebral infections such as HIV or variant CJD, and the degenerative disorders. A common feature of most types of neurological disorder is that they are often associated with other forms of psychopathology, including anxiety, depression and psychosis. Depression is very closely associated with some of the degenerative disorders, such as Alzheimer's and Parkinson's disease, and is not only a frequent consequence of these disorders but also a pre-symptom predictor of the disorder. One feature common to almost all of these types of neurological disorder is that the cognitive, behavioural and emotional deficits that ensue are almost entirely the result of damage to brain tissue caused either through trauma, disease or biochemical abnormalities in the brain. In some cases, the means by which brain tissue is damaged may be common across a number of different types of disorder. For example, there is gathering evidence that the deposition of Lewy bodies in the brain may be one part of the mechanism causing dementia in both Alzheimer's and Parkinson's disease.

SELF-TEST QUESTIONS

- Can you name two or more types of cerebral infection that may cause cognitive deficits?
- What are the different types of traumatic brain injury called, and what are the main causes of traumatic brain injury in the UK?
- What are some of the emotional and psychological consequences of suffering a stroke?
- Can you name the main degenerative disorders?
- Can you describe the main characteristics of Alzheimer's disease?
- What are the main risk factors for Alzheimer's disease, and what changes in the brain are thought to occur during the disorder?
- What areas of the brain are affected by Parkinson's disease, and what are the cognitive and emotional symptoms associated with the disorder?

SECTION SUMMARY

14.2 Types of Neurological Disorder

- There are five main types of neurological disorder, including **cerebral infection**, **traumatic brain injury**, **cerebrovascular accidents** (e.g. strokes), **brain tumours** and **degenerative disorders**.

- Cerebral infections that can give rise to neurological impairments include **bacterial meningitis**, **HIV infection** and **variant Creutzfeldt-Jakob Disease (vCJD)**.

- Traumatic brain injury is one of the most common causes of neurological impairment.

- Types of traumatic brain injury include **concussion**, **contusion** and syndromes such as **dementia pugilistica**.

- Damage to brain tissue can occur as a result of a **cardiovascular accident (CVA)** – otherwise known as a stroke. Strokes are remarkably common in individuals over the age of 65 years.

- Brain tumours can cause neurological damage by growing in the brain (**primary brain tumours**) or by travelling to the brain from other parts of the body.

- Degenerative disorders represent those dementias that are characterized by a slow, general deterioration in cognitive, physical and emotional functioning and affect around 7 per cent of individuals over 65 years of age.

- **Alzheimer's disease** is the most common cause of dementia in the UK (contributing 55 per cent), followed by **vascular dementia** (contributing 20 per cent).

- The changes that occur in the brain during Alzheimer's disease appear to be structural and involve the development of **beta amyloid plaques** and **neurofibrillary tangles**. Alzheimer's is also associated with the faulty production of the brain neurotransmitter **acetylcholine**.

- **Parkinson's disease** causes psychological and cognitive disturbance in between 40 and 60 per cent of sufferers. It appears to be caused as a result of degenerative damage to the region of the **basal ganglia** known as the **substantia nigra**.

14.3 TREATMENT AND REHABILITATION FOR NEUROLOGICAL DISORDERS

Many of the neurological disorders described in this chapter represent irreversible impairment and central nervous system damage. As a consequence, attempts at treatment tend to be oriented towards rehabilitation rather than cure. Nevertheless, impairment in some types of neurological disorder can be reversible: deficits caused by some kinds of cerebral infection are one example (e.g. meningitis and encephalitis). In the case of degenerative disorders such as Alzheimer's disease, recent developments in drug treatments have indicated that progressive impairment can be slowed, affording some respite from the degenerative nature of the disease. However, in many cases, neurological damage is relatively permanent and sufferers must learn to live with the behavioural and cognitive deficits that the disorder brings (e.g. traumatic brain injury, strokes). This has led to the development of a range of rehabilitation procedures designed to provide individual with:

1 exercises that help to improve impaired cognitive functions (e.g. impaired language or memory function);

2 training in the use of cognitive and behavioural aids (e.g. using memory aids or labelling cupboards and drawers in order to remember where things are);

3 assistive technology (e.g. equipment that may aid hearing, speaking or moving about); and

4 basic drug treatment and psychotherapy to help deal with related mood disorders (such as depression).

In some severe cases of neurological disorder, very little in the way of ameliorative therapeutic help can be provided for sufferers. However, there are many national associations (e.g. the UK Alzheimer's Society) that can offer caregivers structured support and advice. We now discuss the various forms of treatment and rehabilitation in more detail.

14.3.1 Biological Treatments

Biological treatments for neurological disorders take a number of forms. The most common are drug treatments that help stabilize or slow degenerative disorders; others include drug treatments to combat cerebral infections, electrical brain stimulation for some forms of dementia, and surgery, chemotherapy or radiation treatment for brain tumours.

14.3.1.1 Drug Treatments

There has been some success in recent years in developing drugs that can help to slow the progress of degenerative disorders such as Alzheimer's disease and Parkinson's disease. In the case of Alzheimer's, we have already noted that the disease is often associated with abnormalities in the production of the brain neurotransmitter acetylcholine. During the course of the disease, an enzyme called acetylcholinesterase breaks down acetylcholine and leads to depletion of the neurotransmitter dopamine. In order to combat this effect, drugs have been developed that prevent acetylcholine breakdown in the synaptic cleft by acetylcholinesterase and increase its uptake in the postsynapyic receptor. The most common of such drugs are donepezil, rivastigmine and galantamine, collectively known as *cholinesterase inhibitors* (Petersen, Thomas, Grundman & Thal, 2005). Randomized, double-blind, placebo-controlled trials suggest that treatment for 6 months with cholinesterase inhibitors produces moderate improvements in cognitive function in those with mild to moderate Alzheimer's disease (Hitzeman, 2006), and prospects are best when treatment begins early in the course of the disease (Seltzer, 2006).

Cholinesterase inhibitors A group of drugs that prevent acetylcholine breakdown in the synaptic cleft by acetylcholinesterase and increase its uptake in the postsynaptic receptor. The most common of these drugs are donepezil, rivastigmine and galantamine.

Although the emphasis has been on identifying early signs of Alzheimer's so that drug treatment can begin as soon as possible, there is some evidence that cholinesterase inhibitors such as donepezil can improve cognition in individuals with severe Alzheimer's (Winblad, Kilander, Eriksson, Minthon et al., 2006), as well as accumulating evidence that donepezil can help to alleviate behavioural symptoms, mood disturbances and delusions associated with Alzheimer's (Cummings, McRae & Zhang, 2006). The UK National Institute for Clinical Excellence (NICE) has recommended to the NHS that donepezil, rivastigmine and galantamine be made available as part of the management of mild and moderate Alzheimer's disease, with those to be targeted scoring 12 points or higher on the Mini Mental State Examination (see Focus Point 14.2).

Parkinson's disease is associated with degeneration in the substantia nigra area of the brain, where the important neurotransmitter dopamine is produced. The main drug that is used to counteract this decline in dopamine is *levodopa*, a natural amino acid that the brain converts into dopamine to replace the depleted neurotransmitter. Although the drug has been relatively successful in helping sufferers to control tremor and other motor symptoms, there is little evidence that levodopa alleviates any of the cognitive impairments associated with Parkinson's dementia (Morrison, Borod, Brin, Halbig et al., 2004). Levadopa administration has to be closely supervised because it also has a number of potential side effcts, including hypertension as well as delusions and hallucinations similar to those found in schizophrenia and amphetamine psychosis.

Levodopa A natural amino acid that is converted by the brain into dopamine and used in the treatment of Parkinson's disease.

Medication can also be successful in reducing disability following cerebrovascular accidents such as strokes. *Thrombolytic therapy* is the use of drugs to break up or dissolve blood clots, one of the main causes of strokes. The most commonly used thrombolytic drug is tissue plasminogen activator (t-PA), which, if administered within the first 3 hours of a stroke, significantly reduces disability (Albers, 1997; Hacke, Donnan, Fieschi, Kaste et al., 2004). Nevertheless, the success of this treatment is critically dependent on individuals being able to identify the early signs of a stroke and seek rapid treatment. Although early administration of thrombolytic therapy can significantly aid survival and physical recovery, there is little evidence that such intervention helps to alleviate the cognitive deficits that may accompany stroke (Nys, van Zandvoort, Algra, Kappelle et al., 2006).

Thrombolytic therapy The use of drugs to break up or dissolve blood clots – one of the main causes of strokes.

Medication is also used in the treatment of brain deficits caused by cerebral infections. Bacterial infections, such as certain types of encephalitis and meningitis, are treatable with antibiotics. However, many viral infections are much more problematic. Steroids can be used to combat viral infections such as herpes encephalitis. In the case of HIV-1-associated dementia, newly developed *antiretroviral drugs* are proving to be effective in reducing the severity of symptoms, although they do not entirely prevent cognitive impairment (Nath & Sacktor, 2006). Usually, up to 3–4 antiretroviral drugs are used that act at different stages of the virus life cycle. This produces a dramatic reduction in viral load (the level of virus in the blood) and prevents further immune damage.

Antiretroviral drugs Chemicals that inhibit the replication of retroviruses, such as HIV.

Finally, mood disorders (such as depression) are a common feature of neurological disorders, including stroke, traumatic brain injury and degenerative disorders. Depression can often adversely affect the course of the disorder, prevent recovery and increase mortality rates (Robinson, Lipsey, Rao & Price, 1986; Leentjens, 2004; Ramasubbu & Patten, 2003). The use of drugs such as SSRIs and tricyclic antidepressants to help alleviate depressed mood has proven to be successful in improving recovery from strokes (Hackett, Anderson & House, 2005), alleviating symptoms of depression in Parkinson's disease (Weintraub, Morales, Moberg, Bilker et al., 2005), and improving mood and cognitive performance following traumatic head injury (Horsfield, Rosse, Tomasino, Schwartz et al., 2002). In at least some of these disorders (e.g. Parkinson's disease), there is a view that depression is an integral symptom of the disorder – especially because depression often precedes and predicts other symptoms of the disease as well as affecting outcome. So tackling depression can be considered a direct treatment of the disorder itself rather than dealing with a side effect of disability (e.g. Leentjens, 2004).

14.3.1.2 Deep Brain Stimulation (DBS)

A recently developed form of treatment for Parkinson's disease involves *deep brain stimulation (DBS)*. This uses a surgically implanted, battery-operated device called a neurostimulator to deliver electrical stimulation to the

Deep brain stimulation (DBS) A form of treatment for Parkinson's disease which uses a surgically implanted, battery-operated device called a neurostimulator to deliver electrical stimulation to the ventral intermediate nucleus of the thalamus or the subthalamic nucleus area in the basal ganglia.

ventral intermediate nucleus of the thalamus or the subthalamic nucleus area in the basal ganglia. These areas of the brain control movement, and through mechanisms that are as yet unclear, electrical stimulation in this area appears to block the abnormal nerve signals that cause tremor and Parkinson's symptoms (Perlmutter & Mink, 2006; Ananthaswamy, 2004). DBS has been shown to result in improvements in physical abilities (e.g. mobility) and global measures of quality of life (Hamani, Neimat & Lozano, 2006), but there is little evidence at present that DBS has any significant effect on cognitive abilities, and it may even be associated with a mild decline in communication skills and language abilities (Castelli, Perozzo, Zibetti, Crivelli et al., 2006; Drapier, Raoul, Drapier, Leray et al., 2005).

14.3.1.3 Surgery, Chemotherapy and Radiation Treatment

As we saw earlier, intracranial brain tumours can be a source of neurological disorder – especially when the tumour leads to intracranial pressure, swelling and damage to brain tissue. An important and obvious way to deal with tumours is to surgically remove them. However, this can be a highly risky strategy if the tumour is located in brain areas which control important cognitive and behavioural functions. An alternative is to use radiation treatment or chemotherapy in an attempt to directly target the tumour and avoid damage to healthy brain tissue. Nevertheless, such procedures are not without their own risks. While successful surgical excision of tumours can often alleviate cognitive dysfunction (such as memory deficits) and increase cerebral blood flow in areas of the brain where the tumour was located (Kupers, Fortin, Astrup, Gjedde et al., 2004), some other studies suggest that postoperative radiation treatments can be associated with long-term risk of cognitive impairment (Surma-aho, Niemela, Vilkki, Kouri et al., 2001).

14.3.2 Cognitive Rehabilitation

The nature and structure of cognitive rehabilitation programmes will inevitably depend on the nature of the cognitive deficits that the individual has suffered, and a number of relatively successful procedures are available that afford some significant gains across a range of functions (Cicerone, Dahlberg, Malec, Langenbahn et al., 2005). Many of these programmes are basic training procedures which give clients structured extensive training in the area of their deficit (e.g. attention, memory, executive functioning). This may be in the form of extended practice at a task (e.g. attention process training), perhaps with the additional use of concurrent feedback on performance so that clients can adjust their functioning, or with the use of assistive technology (e.g. memory aids). In particular, the use of computer-based technology to assist rehabilitation training is a thriving area of development: clinicians may use computers to present specific training programmes such as memory training programmes (Tam & Man, 2004), or to create virtual environments in which clients can learn to coordinate the relevant sequence of actions to complete a task successfully (Zhang, Beatriz, Abreu, Seale et al., 2003). While many rehabilitation programmes

target quite specific impairments, others attempt to address multiple aspects of dysfunction and are known as *holistic rehabilitation* methods. These may address a combination of cognitive, emotional, motivational and interpersonal impairments in the context of an integrated programme of treatment (e.g. Braverman, Spector, Warden, Wilson et al., 1999).

> **Holistic rehabilitation** Treatment methods for neurological disorders which attempt to address multiple aspects of dysfunction.

This section continues by providing some examples of cognitive rehabilitation procedures that have been shown to be effective in the rehabilitation of specific impairments. We then look at an example of the holistic rehabilitation method.

14.3.2.1 Attention Deficits

One form of rehabilitation training for attention deficits is known as *attention process training (APT)*, which uses a number of different strategies to promote and encourage attentional abilities (Park, Proulx & Towers, 1999). Exercises include listening to an auditory tape that contains target words which must be responded to by pressing a buzzer. Learning to shift attention appropriately is also encouraged by learning to attend to a new word following identification of a preceding target word. APT has been shown to be superior to basic therapeutic support in promoting attention and memory functioning (Sohlberg, McLaughlin, Pavese, Heidrich et al., 2000), and has also been shown to provide gains in other everyday skills such as independent living and driving ability (Sohlberg & Mateer, 2001). An alternative approach to dealing with attention deficits is not to try to improve attention itself, but to provide clients with some compensatory skills that allow them to manage their slowed information processing effectively (Fasotti, Kovacs, Eling & Brouwer, 2000). This is known as *time pressure management (TPM)* and is an alternative to 'concentration' training of the kind taught by the APT procedure.

> **Attention process training (APT)** A form of rehabilitation training for attention deficits that uses a number of different strategies to promote and encourage attentional abilities.

> **Time pressure management (TPM)** An approach to dealing with attention deficits which aims not to try to improve attention itself, but to provide clients with some compensatory skills that will allow them to effectively manage their slowed information processing.

14.3.2.2 Visuospatial Deficits

A number of programmes have been developed for the rehabilitation of unilateral visual neglect and to compensate for partial deficits in visual perception caused by neurological disorders. One such example is the computer-assisted training programme designed to aid visual scanning (Webster, McFarland, Rapport, Morrill et al., 2001). This consists of a series of tasks in which clients are asked: (1) to read out coloured numbers projected on to a wall (scanning the full frontal environment); (2) to manually track a red ball projected onto a wall (helping coordination of scanning and physical movement); (3) to react to moving images as they are projected in front of them (facilitating detection of stimuli in space); and (4) to move the projected image of a wheelchair down

CLINICAL PERSPECTIVE: TREATMENT IN PRACTICE BOX 14.1

The virtual reality kitchen

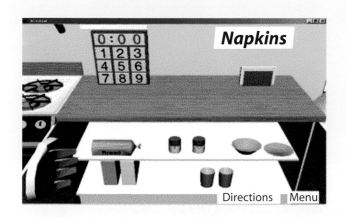

This virtual reality computer programme provides a safe and controlled environment for patients with brain injury to learn and improve basic daily skills such as preparing a meal of a can of soup and a sandwich. All necessary objects are found on the computer screen and can be accessed by using the computer mouse. Prompts appear on the screen initiating actions, sequencing actions and providing reinforcing feedback for correct actions. For example, one of the first steps for preparing a can of soup is to remove the can from the cupboard. If this does not occur within a pre-determined time, the cupboard door is highlighted by a pulsating colour. If the action is still not initiated, a verbal cue tells the patient to 'open the cupboard'. Each action performed by the patient is recorded and his or her performance can be quantitatively assessed over time. Training in virtual environments such as this results in improved performance on the tasks over time and performance on the virtual task correlates well with performance on the tasks in a real kitchen.

Source: Zhang, Beatriz, Abreu, Seale et al. (2003)

a simulated 3-lane road while avoiding obstacles. This procedure has been shown to reduce unilateral visual neglect symptoms and to generalize to improved performance on a real-life wheelchair obstacle course.

14.3.2.3 Apraxia and Deficits in Coordinated Self-Help Behaviours

Apraxia involves an inability to undertake learned and purposeful activities such as dressing or cooking and means that sufferers must rely increasingly on caregivers to help with these activities. For example, limb apraxia is a common symptom of left hemisphere damage and consists of a deficit in performing gestures to verbal command or imitation. Sufferers are particularly impaired when asked to demonstrate how to use an object or carry out actions. They appear to be unable to plan a sequence of actions or may exhibit inappropriate gestures (e.g. they may try to pour water from a bottle into a glass without removing the lid, or to stir the bottle opener in the glass). This is assumed to be an impairment of gesture learning, which is generally considered to be the consequence of a motor memory disorder (Heilman, Schwartz & Geshwind, 1975). One form of rehabilitation training for limb apraxia is *gestural training*, in which clients are taught to recognize gestures and postures that are appropriate and in context. For example,

> **Gestural training** A form of rehabilitation training for limb apraxia in which the client is taught to recognize gestures and postures that are appropriate and in context.

clients may be required to demonstrate the use of a common object (such as a guitar), or be shown a picture of the gesture (e.g. someone playing a guitar) and to replicate that action, or be shown simply a picture of the object and asked to mimic how it is used. Clients may also be shown pictures of people appropriately or inappropriately using objects and asked to identify which of these are correct. Gestural training has been shown to significantly reduce errors in performing everyday actions and to improve recognition of gestures (Smania, Girardi, Domenicali, Lora et al., 2000).

In contrast, computer-based virtual reality environments have been developed to enable disabled individuals with brain injury to learn and improve basic daily living skills in a safe and controlled environment. For example, Zhang, Beatriz, Abreu, Seale et al. (2003) developed a virtual kitchen in which clients can learn the sequence of behaviours required to make a bowl of soup or prepare a sandwich (see Treatment in Practice Box 14.1). Zhang et al. (2003) found that training in virtual environments such as this resulted in improved performance on both tasks, and performance on the virtual task correlated well with performance at the tasks in a real kitchen.

14.3.2.4 Language and Communication Deficits

Impairments in language and communication may manifest in a variety of ways, including deficits in the production of speech (e.g.

CLINICAL PERSPECTIVE: TREATMENT IN PRACTICE BOX 14.2

Gestural training

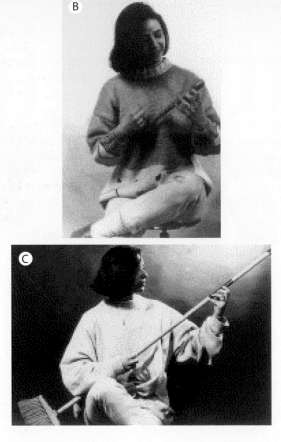

One form of rehabilitation training for limb apraxia is gestural training, in which clients are taught to recognize gestures and postures that are appropriate and in context. This example shows three gestures used in the gesture-recognition test and clients must identify which is an appropriate use of the object. (A) is an appropriate gesture, (B) is a semantically related but inappropriate gesture and (C) is a semantically unrelated and inappropriate gesture.

Source: Smania, Girardi, Domenicali, Lora et al. (2000)

---

fluent aphasia), an inability to comprehend or understand speech, and an inability to initiate speech (e.g. non-fluent aphasia) (see also p. 495 and Table 14.2, p. 496). Many patients undergo standard forms of speech therapy to help promote the production and comprehension of speech. A number of these approaches may combine speech therapy with procedures that permit massed practice of production and comprehension skills, such as the combination of therapist-delivered speech-language training and home-based computer-assisted massed practice (e.g. Wallesch & Johannsen-Horbach, 2004).

There are also a number of specific techniques that are regularly used to treat specific disorders. One common example used with aphasic patients is known as *constraint-induced movement therapy (CIMT)*. This involves the massed practice of verbal responses in which clients may be required to communicate without gesturing or pointing to

> **Constraint-induced movement therapy (CIMT)** A technique used with aphasic patients which involves the mass practice of verbal responses in which the patient may be required to communicate without gesturing or pointing to describe various objects of varying complexity.

describe various objects of varying complexity (Mark & Taub, 2004; Bogey, Geis, Bryant, Moroz et al., 2004)). This constrains clients to the systematic practice of speech acts while avoiding the use of behavioural aids. This form of treatment has been shown to produce improvement on standard clinical scales and self-rated and blind-observer scales of day-to-day communication (Pulvermuller, Neininger, Elbert et al., 2001).

Another specific form of treatment that has been shown to provide significant gains in the production and comprehension of speech is known as *group communication treatment*. This focuses on increasing initiation of conversation and exchanging information using whatever communication means possible, being aware

> **Group communication treatment** A form of treatment used in the production and comprehension of speech, focusing on increasing initiation of conversation and exchanging information using whatever communication means possible.

of personal goals in communication, and gaining confidence in the ability to communicate in personally relevant situations. Elman and Bernstein-Ellis (1999) demonstrated that those patients who received group communication treatment showed significantly greater improvement in functional communication compared with patients not receiving structured treatment.

Finally, a number of specific techniques exist to help individuals with aphasia and traumatic brain injury improve their ability to name objects, improve writing skills and improve sentence production. These may range from the use of cuing techniques to help the patient name specific objects to semantic feature analysis (SFA) designed to improve lexical retrieval by increasing the level of activation within a semantic network (Coelho, McHugh & Boyle, 2000).

14.3.2.5 Memory Deficits

Compensatory strategies Providing patients with memory impairments with specific strategies for remembering material.

Procedures for dealing with memory impairments mainly revolve around what are known as ***compensatory strategies*** – that is, providing patients with specific strategies for remembering material on a daily basis. This may involve assistive technology such as using diaries to aid recall of daily events, labelling cupboards to remember where everyday items are stored or located, or using a pager to remind individuals of important daily events. Wilson, Emslie, Quirk and Evans (1999) report the case study of a young man called George who had severe memory impairments after a head injury sustained in a road traffic accident. Treatment in Practice Box 14.3 shows how the pager could be used to remind George about a range of tasks and activities during the day. Using a pager as a memory prompt has been shown to be effective and easy to implement, and significantly reduces the number of memory and planning problems experienced by people with traumatic brain injury (Wilson, Emslie, Quirk, Evans & Watson, 2005). Pagers are also helpful in establishing daily behavioural patterns, and gains in memory and behaviour can be found even in the weeks after a patient has ceased using the pager.

Computer-based procedures can be used in a variety of ways to aid impaired memory. Computers can function as simple memory aids to enhance prospective memory (e.g. by acting as an electronic diary), by providing memory training exercises, or by instructing the patient in the use of memory strategies (Kapur, Glisky & Wilson, 2004).

Teaching remembering strategies is also beneficial. One technique involves training patients in the use of

Visual imagery mnemonics A technique for teaching remembering strategies in order to help store and retrieve items and events to be remembered.

visual imagery mnemonics in order to help store and retrieve items and events to be remembered. Ten weeks of training in visual imagery techniques has been shown to result in significant improvement in memory functioning 3 months after treatment (Kaschel, Della Sala, Cantagallo, Fahlbock et al., 2002).

CLINICAL PERSPECTIVE: TREATMENT IN PRACTICE BOX 14.3

Using a pager as a memory aid

Below are daily pager messages sent as prompts to George, an individual who had severe memory impairments after a head injury sustained in a road traffic accident.

Time	Message
	MONDAY
7.15am	Time to get up
7.25am	Up yet? Time to wash and shave
7.40am	Take tablets and fill in the time on the checklist
3.00pm	Fold washing and put it away
5.00pm	Prepare the evening meal
6.20pm	Swimming tonight?
8.30pm	Read through today's notes
9.00pm	Take tablets and fill in the time on the checklist

Time	Message
	TUESDAY
7.00am	Time to get up
7.10am	Up yet? Time to wash and shave
7.25am	Take tablets and fill in the time on the checklist
8.30am	Remember keys, wallet and diary
5.00pm	Prepare the evening meal
8.30pm	Read through today's notes
9.00pm	Take tablets and fill in the time on the checklist

Source: after Wilson, Emslie, Quirk & Evans (1999)

Errorless learning A training procedure used in training individuals with amnesia where people are prevented – as far as possible – from making any errors while learning a new skill or new information.

Errorless learning is a technique that has proven to be helpful in training individuals with amnesia. Errorless learning is a training procedure where people are prevented – as far as possible – from making any errors while learning a new skill or new information (Baddeley & Wilson, 1994). In the context of memory impairments, it is useful for teaching new knowledge or training specific skills such as helping patients to find and use the right word to name objects. There is still some debate over whether memory aids (e.g. pagers, diaries, personal organizers) are superior to memory treatments (e.g. attempts to train better memory functioning), but in many cases a combination of both aids and treatments is most effective (e.g. Ownsworth & McFarland, 1999).

14.3.2.6 Deficits in Executive Functioning

As we described earlier, executive functioning involves the integrated use of several cognitive processes by which people problem-solve, plan, initiate, organize and monitor goal-directed activities. Deficits in this collection of integrated skills will obviously require some training in a range of basic abilities, such as attention and memory, as well as more specific training in problem-solving skills and planning and goal management skills. Many effective interventions involve training in problem-solving.

Goal management training (GMT) A procedure that involves training in problem solving to help evaluate a current problem, followed by specification of the relevant goals, and partitioning of the problem-solving process into sub-goals or steps.

One particular procedure is known as *goal management training (GMT)*, which involves training to help evaluate a current problem ('What am I doing?'), followed by specification of the relevant goals, and partitioning of the problem-solving process into sub-goals or steps. Patients are then assisted with the learning and retention of sub-goals ('Do I know the steps?'), followed by self-monitoring of the results of their actions ('Am I doing what I planned to do?') (Levine, Robertson, Clare, Carter et al., 2000).

Other procedures for aiding problem-solving deficits involve cognitive behavioural training in problem-solving skills, exercises for analysing real-life problems, and role-playing of real examples of problem situations. Such training results in significant beneficial effects on measures of executive cognitive functioning up to 6 months after the intervention (e.g. Rath, Simon, Langenbahn, Sherr et al., 2003).

Many types of intervention for executive functioning deficits focus on both behavioural and emotional regulation. Their aim is to train individuals in self-regulation when confronting a problem and to manage their way through the sequence of cognitive and behavioural actions required to solve a problem. One such procedure is known as *self-instructional training (SIT)*, in which individuals learn a set of instructions for talking themselves through particular

Self-instructional training (SIT) A procedure used in the intervention for executive functioning deficits where individuals learn a set of instructions for talking themselves through particular problems.

problems. Such types of intervention have been shown to raise personal self-awareness of deficits and increase use of successful problem-solving strategies. Importantly, these methods have the additional beneficial effects of improving emotional self-regulation and reducing outward expressions of anger and frustration (Medd & Tate, 2000; Ownsworth, McFarland & Young, 2002).

14.3.2.7 Holistic Rehabilitation Methods

Most cognitive rehabilitation techniques have been developed to address individual deficits in cognitive functioning (such as attentional, memory or language deficits). However, there are substantial benefits to adopting a more comprehensive holistic approach to rehabilitation that collectively addresses cognitive, emotional and functional impairments as well as physical disability. For example, Malec and Basford (1996) advocated a comprehensive integrated treatment for individuals with traumatic brain injury that addressed cognitive, interpersonal and emotional concerns, used group interventions that addressed disability awareness and social skills training, and included procedures to enhance vocational functioning (occupational therapy) and independent living skills.

Such approaches are holistic in the sense that they attempt to develop individuals' awareness of their disabilities and to provide them with compensatory skills that enable them to negotiate daily living and regain occupational skills. To this extent, holistic methods differentiate between *restorative* procedures that attempt to provide training to improve cognitive impairments (e.g. intensive training of memory skills) and *compensatory* procedures that enable individuals to achieve daily goals through different means (e.g. using assistive technology such as a pager as a memory aid).

Holistic rehabilitation methods have been shown to promote significant improvement in overall functioning in individuals with traumatic brain injury (Ben-Yishay & Daniels-Zide, 2000), to develop awareness of disabilities and impairments (which is important when attempting to engage patients in rehabilitation programmes) (Fleming & Ownsworth, 2006), and to be superior to standard neurorehabilitation programmes in improving community integration and raising the individual's level of satisfaction with cognitive functioning (Cicerone, Mott, Azulay & Friel, 2004).

14.3.3 Caregiver Support Programmes

Many individuals with neurological disorders are not in primary care but live with their families or with caregivers such as spouses or partners. This puts considerable burden on caregivers generally, usually requiring them to cope with behavioural and cognitive deficits, physical disability, challenging behaviour (such as anger and aggression) and problematic behaviour generally (such as inappropriate social behaviour). In the case of degenerative disorders that do not usually begin to manifest until later life, carers of such individuals will often be elderly spouses or partners (e.g. in the case of Alzheimer's disease). This being so, carers of individuals with neurological disorders need both support and training.

A WEEK IN THE LIFE OF A CLINICAL PSYCHOLOGIST

Working as a Consultant Clinical Neuropsychologist

Monday. 'How do you spell neuropsychologist?' asked the Detective Sergeant on the telephone. He requests a statement relating to whether a client could be a reliable witness in a sexual assault case. I explained to him that since suffering from encephalitis her attention and memory abilities are so poor that it was unlikely she could provide a reasonable account for the police. The call has taken my administration time and once again I begin a new week behind schedule as I rush off to the first meeting of the week.

The community disability team meeting focuses on the most complex cases. A man who has motor neurone disease has now found out his wife has developed multiple sclerosis. Concerns are expressed about a lady with a brain stem stroke. There are concerns her female partner is emotionally abusing her. All agree a vulnerable adults strategy meeting is required. The afternoon is spent supervising colleagues and a new trainee.

Tuesday is spent completing four initial consultations to decide whether psychological intervention can be appropriately offered. A lady with Parkinson's disease who has started having panic attacks. A man who suffered a head injury in a car accident, his parents are struggling to cope with his bad language and temper outbursts. A lady with multiple sclerosis is saddened by having to give up work, and finally a man of 80 who suffered a stroke last summer. His wife feels desperately isolated, as he can no longer drive.

Wednesday. Appropriate psychometric tests are chosen for the man who has come for an outpatient assessment this morning. He has experienced a two-year history of memory problems. Sadly, the man struggles with most tests but particularly those we know are associated with dementia of the Alzheimer's type. A sense of sadness stays with me for the afternoon at the thought of what my feedback has meant to that couple. I resolve to reduce my administration pile by the end of today.

Seven ladies have arrived for my *Thursday* morning relatives group, a meeting for people living with someone who has a neurological diagnosis. The usual issues are discussed, how to cope with the feelings of loss, what to do in response to a partner's temper outbursts and how to minimize cognitive difficulties. Thursday afternoons are usually set aside for outpatient intervention appointments. Today a lady in her forties talks about her sense of isolation since her stroke and requests help to explain the nature of her difficulties to her children. The last appointment of the day brings a feeling of optimism as a young woman who suffered a severe head injury two years ago is pleased to inform me that she is finally living independently and has started a part-time job.

Friday morning is spent making an assessment as to the capacity of a lady with Huntington's disease to manage her finances. Two further outpatient appointments leave just an hour to write up client files and complete an assessment report before meeting the final challenge of the week, Friday evening rush hour!

Caregivers need to give both physical and emotional support to sufferers, and they may also pay a substantial economic cost in terms of loss of income as well as living a restricted social life. It goes without saying that the overall burden on caregivers is proportional to the disabilities experienced by sufferers. Caregivers usually report that their physical and emotional health suffers as a result of caregiving, and many begin to exhibit symptoms of depression. In a study of caregiver burden in Parkinson's disease, perceived burden and quality of life were proportional to disability, range of symptoms and the mental health problems exhibited by the individual with Parkinson's disease (e.g. depression, hallucinations, confusion) (Schrag, Hovris, Morley, Quinn et al., 2006).

Poor quality of life and depression in caregivers can often be traced in part to a lack of skills or strategies for managing sufferers, and many become avoidant copers by avoiding new situations and wishing the problems would simply go away. Avoidant coping such as this is significantly correlated with levels of depression in elderly caregivers or spouses of those with dementia (Mausbach, Aschbacher, Patterson, Ancoli-Israel et al., 2006). To address these problems associated with caregiving, interventions have been designed to provide a range of skills to help day-to-day living with sufferers. These may include advice on how to modify the home environment to support the sufferer (Gitlin, Hauck, Dennis & Winter, 2005), or training in skills to develop self-care behaviours in the sufferer, or to control aggression and wandering (Pinkston, Linsk & Young, 1988). Such programmes have been shown to maintain caregiver positive affect for a period of at least 12 months after the intervention.

Peer support groups are also an important means of maintaining quality of life and positive affect in caregivers. National societies such as the UK Alzheimer's Society (www.alzheimers.org.uk) provide information and advice for caregivers, including advice on how to understand and respect people with neurological disabilities or degenerative disorders, and how to cope with caring for a sufferer. The Alzheimer's Society recommends that caregivers:

1   need to ensure they have sufficient support (either from family or local support groups);

2   should make time each day for themselves;

3   understand their right to local services (such as assessment of needs);

4   should try to involve other family members in caregiving;

5   look after their health (by eating regularly and healthily);

6   check whether they are entitled to any financial benefits;

7   confront and deal with feelings of guilt; and

8   take a regular break or holiday by seeking short-term respite care for the sufferer.

In addition, local groups composed of similar caregivers can provide significant support across a range of needs, including information and education, referral and/or assistance in engaging with local health services, and emotional support (Salfi, Ploeg & Black, 2005). The effects of such support groups can be beneficial,

---

ACTIVITY BOX 14.1

Providing advice and help for caregivers

If you have a friend or relative who cares for someone with a physical or mental disability, you may like to ask them about their experiences as a caregiver. In particular, ask them what practical and emotional problems they encounter caring on a day-by-day basis for a handicapped individual. For example:

● Do they have practical problems around the house (e.g. does the sufferer wander off if doors are left open)?

● Do they understand what support and relief they can get from local services?

● Are they able to look after their own physical and mental health (i.e. do they become depressed and disillusioned)?

● Do they get support and help from friends and family?

Once you have identified some issues that are important for this particular caregiver, you could try to find out:

1   what advice national support groups give in the case of these particular issues, e.g. support groups such as the UK Alzheimer's Society (www.alzheimers.org.uk), the Parkinson's Disease Society (www.parkinsons.org.uk) or the brain injury association Headway (www.headway.org.uk);

2   how carer intervention programmes have been designed to provide caregivers with a range of skills (e.g. how to modify the home environment to support the sufferer or training in skills to develop self-care behaviours by the sufferer) (see Gitlin, Hauck, Dennis & Winter, 2005; Pinkston, Linsk & Young, 1988).

---

even if communication is by telephone or by internet videoconferencing (Marziali, Donahue & Crossin, 2005).

Finally, caregiver interventions not only address the skills and knowledge that will help caregivers to manage a sufferer physically and emotionally. They also help caregivers understand and respect individuals with a neurological or degenerative disorder. Once someone's cognitive and physical abilities begin to decline – especially in old age – it is quite easy to forget that the person is still an individual who should be valued and respected. Advice for caregivers includes taking time to listen to sufferers; taking account of the abilities they do possess and trying to foster these; using respectful forms of address; trying not to talk down to sufferers and respecting their privacy; and always trying to understand how sufferers feel and to make them feel good about themselves (see Table 14.5).

Table 14.5 *Tips for making sufferers of Alzheimer's disease feel good about themselves*

● Avoid situations in which they are bound to fail, as this can be humiliating. Look for tasks they can still manage and activities they enjoy.

● Give plenty of encouragement. Let them do things at their own pace and in their own way.

● Do things with them, rather than for them, to help them retain their independence.

● Break activities down into small steps so that they feel a sense of achievement, even if they can only manage part of a task.

● Our self-respect is often bound up with the way we look. Encourage individuals to take a pride in their appearance, and compliment them on how they look.

Source: Alzheimer's Society Carers' Advice Sheet, June 2005.

SUMMARY

The neurological disorders we have covered in this chapter often represent chronic impairments that are caused by irreversible damage to brain tissue or are the result of progressive degenerative disorders. Because of this, rehabilitation may often be a lengthy process and sufferers are likely to require long-term care of some kind. We noted that there have been important developments in the types of drugs that can slow the progress of degenerative disorders such as

Alzheimer's disease and Parkinson's disease, and antiretroviral drugs have been shown to be effective in reducing the severity of HIV dementia. Medication is also an important treatment for depression, which is a common and significant symptom of neurological disorders. Antidepressants not only help to improve mood, they can also improve cognitive performance.

Cognitive rehabilitation programmes have been developed to help individuals with a range of specific cognitive deficits, including attention deficits, visuospatial deficits, apraxia, language and communication deficits, memory deficits and executive function impairments. These programmes may take a variety of forms, such as (1) massed training to improve cognitive impairments (e.g. memory training); (2) compensatory skills training, which accepts that individuals have particular impairments and helps them to achieve daily goals by other means; (3) computer-assisted training, which can provide the means for remedial cognitive training in both the therapeutic and home environment, or provide virtual environments in which sufferers can learn skills in relative safety; and (4) assistive technology, which is being increasingly utilized as a means of helping disabled individuals to cope with and negotiate daily living (e.g. using a pager to provide reminders for daily activities in individuals with memory deficits).

Finally, because of the nature of neurological disorders and the frequent need for long-term care, programmes of support and training are increasingly becoming available for caregivers. These include programmes to provide emotional support and appropriate management and coping skills for people living with individuals with disabilities, and local or national support groups that provide advice and information.

SELF-TEST QUESTIONS

- What is the difference between a restorative treatment and compensatory skills training?
- How have drugs been used in the treatment of neurological disorders? Do such drugs help in the treatment of the cognitive deficits caused by the disorder?
- Can you describe at least one specific intervention designed to treat each of the following: attention deficits; visuospatial deficits; apraxia; language and communication deficits; memory deficits; deficits in executive functioning?
- What are holistic rehabilitation methods, and how do they differ from specific restorative interventions?
- What are the main problems encountered by those giving care to people suffering from neurological disorders, and what interventions have been developed to help them?

SECTION SUMMARY

14.3 Treatment and Rehabilitation for Neurological Disorders

- Treatment of neurological disorders tends to be based on **restorative treatment** for individual cognitive deficits (e.g. memory training) or **compensatory skills training** based on helping sufferers to deal with the daily living difficulties posed by the deficit.

- Drug treatments include the use of **cholinesterase inhibitors** (Alzheimer's disease), **levodopa** (Parkinson's disease), **thrombolytic therapy** (cerebrovascular accidents and strokes) and **antiretroviral drugs** (HIV dementia).

- **Depression** is also a common feature of many neurological disorders and can be treated with antidepressants and appropriate psychological therapy.

- **Deep brain stimulation** (**DBS**) alleviates symptoms of Parkinson's disease by delivering electrical stimulation to the thalamus and basal ganglia.

- **Cognitive rehabilitation programmes** are usually directed at improving function within specific cognitive deficits (e.g. memory, language).

- Rehabilitation programmes for attention deficits include **attention process training** (**APT**) and **time pressure management** (**TPM**).

- **Gestural training** and the use of **virtual reality environments** can be utilized to treat apraxia and deficits in coordinated self-help behaviours.

- Treatment of language and communication deficits will depend on the specific nature of the problem, but common examples of rehabilitation procedures include **constraint-induced movement therapy** (**CIMT**) and **group communication treatment**.

- Memory deficits can be addressed with the use of **assistive technology** (such as pagers) or specific memory training procedures such as **visual imagery mnemonics** or **errorless learning** procedures.

- Deficits in executive functioning often utilize interventions that involve problem-solving training such as **goal management training** or **self-instructional training** (**SIT**).

- **Holistic rehabilitation** methods collectively attempt to address cognitive, emotional and functional impairments, as well as physical disability.

- Because those suffering neurological disorders live with their families or caregivers, **caregiver interventions** have been developed that help to provide the caregiver with training and support for the task.

14.4 NEUROLOGICAL DISORDERS REVIEWED

Unlike many of the other disorders described in this book, neurological disorders have their origins almost solely in damage or abnormalities in the biological substrates that underlie thinking and behaviour. These disorders give rise to a range of disabilities and impairments, both physical and cognitive, and many are irreversible and permanent deficits. The main causes of neurological disorders are cerebral infections, traumatic brain injuries, cerebrovascular accidents such as strokes, and degenerative disorders such as Alzheimer's disease and Parkinson's disease. Clinical psychologists have a critical interest in neurological disorders because many of the major symptoms are deficits in vital cognitive functions such as learning and memory, attention, language and communication, visual perception, motor skills and executive functions. Because of this, clinicians are involved in the assessment of neurological disorders and the treatment and rehabilitation of these disorders.

Assessment of neurological disorders is often difficult, involving a combination of tests of cognitive functioning (such as the WAIS-III or the Adult Memory and Information Processing Battery), blood tests and analyses of cerebrospinal fluids (to determine the presence of inherited degenerative diseases or infections), and brain scans using EEG, PET or fMRI. While some of the disorders result in immediate impairment (such as traumatic brain injury or stroke), many others are progressive degenerative disorders that develop from mild symptoms of cognitive impairment to full-blown dementia and physical disability (e.g. Alzheimer's disease). While most degenerative disorders afflict the older adult, some can affect younger individuals (e.g. variant CJD and HIV dementia). Many of the neurological disorders are closely associated with other forms of psychopathology, especially depression and psychosis. Depression appears to be both a predictor and a consequence of some neurological disorders (such as stroke or Parkinson's disease) and is considered by some to be an integral feature of those disorders).

Because most of the neurological disorders are caused by irreversible damage to brain tissue, treatment and rehabilitation often take the form of compensatory skills training, which accepts that individuals have a particular impairment and helps them to achieve their daily goals by other means (e.g. by using compensatory strategies, such as memory aids, or assistive technology, such as equipment to aid hearing, speaking or moving about). Nevertheless, there are many specific cognitive rehabilitation procedures that can be used with reasonable success in attempts to restore basic cognitive functions such as memory, attention, language and motor skills. However, because of the long-term nature of many neurological disorders, there is a basic need for long-term care for sufferers, and this is often provided by close family, spouses and partners. This need has given rise to a range of programmes to provide support for caregivers, including basic caregiver skills training (e.g. how to structure the environment for a disabled individual) and emotional support programmes. You may now wish to return to summary Table 14.1 and ensure that you are familiar with the main features of neurological disorders.

LEARNING OUTCOMES

When you have completed this chapter, you should be able to:

1 Describe some of the cognitive impairments that characterize neurological disorders.

2 Describe some of the main methods that clinical neuropsychologists use to assess cognitive functioning in neurological disorders.

3 Describe a range of types of neurological disorders and evaluate their causes.

4 Describe, compare and contrast the various types of treatment and rehabilitation programmes that have been developed to deal with neurological disorders.

KEY TERMS

REVIEWS, THEORIES AND SEMINAL STUDIES

Links to Journal Articles

14.1 The Diagnosis and Assessment of Neurological Disorders

Tagliaferri, F., Compagnone, C., Korsic, M., Servadei, F. et al. (2006). A systematic review of brain injury epidemiology in Europe. *Acta Neurochirurgica, 148,* 255–268.

14.2 Types of Neurological Disorder

Almeida, O.P. & Lautenschlager, N.T. (2005). Dementia associated with infectious diseases. *International Psychogeriatrics, 17,* S65–S77.

Blennow, K., de Leon, M.J. & Zetterberg, H. (2006). Alzheimer's disease. *Lancet, 368,* 387–403.

Damasio, H. (1994). The return of Gage, Phineas: Clues above the brain from the skull of a famous patient. *Science, 265,* 1159.

Ehrt, U. & Aarsland, D. (2005). Psychiatric aspects of Parkinson's disease. *Current Opinion in Psychiatry, 18,* 335–341.

Gatz, M., Reynolds, C.A., Fratiglioni, L., Johansson, B. et al. (2006). Role of genes and environments for explaining Alzheimer's disease. *Archives of General Psychiatry, 63,* 168–174.

Ghafouri, M., Amini, S., Khalili, K. & Sawaya, B.E. (2006). HIV-1 associated dementia: Symptoms and causes. *Retrovirology, 3,* 28–39.

Jarquin-Valdivia, A.A. (2004). Psychiatric symptoms and brain tumors: A brief historical overview. *Archives of Neurology, 61,* 1800–1804.

Kapur, N., Abbott, P., Lowman, A. & Will, R.G. (2003). The neuropsychological profile associated with variant Creutzfeldt-Jakob disease. *Brain, 126,* 2693–2702.

Lauterbach, E.C. (2004). The neuropsychiatry of Parkinson's disease and related disorders. *Psychiatric Clinics of North America, 27,* 801.

Leentjens, A.F.G. (2004). Depression in Parkinson's disease: Conceptual issues and clinical challenges. *Journal of Geriatric Psychiatry and Neurology, 17,* 120–126.

Robinson, R.G. (2003). Poststroke depression: Prevalence, diagnosis, treatment, and disease progression. *Biological Psychiatry, 54,* 376–387.

Wallin, M.T., Wilken, J.A. & Kane, R. (2006). Cognitive dysfunction in multiple sclerosis: Assessment, imaging and risk factors. *Journal of Rehabilitation Research and Development, 43,* 63–71.

14.3 Treatment and Rehabilitation for Neurological Disorders

Cicerone, K.D., Dahlberg, C., Malec, J.F., Langenbahn, D.M. et al. (2005). Evidence-based cognitive rehabilitation: Updated review of the literature from 1998 through 2002. *Archives of Physical Medicine and Rehabilitation, 86,* 1681–1692.

Cicerone, K.D., Levin, H., Malec, J., Stuss, D. & Whyte, J. (2006). Cognitive rehabilitation interventions for executive function: Moving from bench to bedside in patients with traumatic brain injury. *Journal of Cognitive Neuroscience, 18,* 1212–1222.

Cole, K. & Vaughan, F.L. (2005). The feasibility of using cognitive behaviour therapy for depression associated with Parkinson's Disease: A literature review. *Parkinsonism and Related Disorders, 11,* 269–276.

Hackett, M.L., Anderson, C.S. & House, A.O. (2005). Management of depression after stroke: A systematic review of pharmacological studies. *Stroke, 36,* 1092–1097.

Kapur, N., Glisky, E.L. & Wilson, B.A. (2004). Technological memory aids for people with memory deficits. *Neuropsychological Rehabilitation, 14,* 41–60.

LoPresti, E.F., Mihalidis, A. & Kirsch, N. (2004). Assistive technology for cognitive rehabilitation: State of the art. *Neuropsychological Rehabilitation, 14,* 5–39.

Morrison, C.E., Borod, J.C., Brin, M.F., Halbig, T.D. et al. (2004). Effects of levodopa on cognitive functioning in moderate-to-severe Parkinson's disease. *Journal of Neural Transmission, 111,* 1333–1341.

Perlmutter, J.S. & Mink, J.W. (2006). Deep brain stimulation. *Annual Review of Neuroscience, 29,* 229–257.

Seltzer, B. (2006). Cholinesterase inhibitors in the clinical management of Alzheimer's disease: Importance of early and persistent treatment. *Journal of International Medical Research, 34,* 339–347.

Vajda, F.J.E. & Solinas, C. (2005). Current approaches to management of depression in Parkinson's disease. *Journal of Clinical Neuroscience, 12,* 739–743.

Wilson, B.A., Emslie, H., Quirk, K. & Evans, J. (1999). George: Learning to live independently with Neuropage. *Rehabilitation Psychology, 44,* 284–296.

Zhang, L., Beatriz, M.D., Abreu, C., Seale, G.S. et al. (2003). A virtual reality environment for evaluation of a daily living skill in brain injury rehabilitation: Reliability and validity. *Archives of Physical Medicine and Rehabilitation, 84,* 1118–1124.

Texts for Further Reading

Goldstein, L.A. & McNeil, J. (2004). *Clinical neuropsychology: A practical guide to assessment and management for clinicians.* Chichester: Wiley.

Lezak, M.D., Howieson, D.B., Loring, D.W., Hannay, H.J. & Fischer, J.S. (2004). *Neuropsychological assessment.* Oxford: Oxford University Press.

Lichtenberg, P.A., Murman, D.L. & Mellow, A.M. (Eds.) (2003). *Handbook of dementia: Psychological, neurological and psychiatric perspectives.* Chichester: Wiley.

RESEARCH QUESTIONS

- Is the cognitive slowness that is a consequence of viral meningitis reversible?

- Why are between 70 and 88 per cent of all people who sustain a head injury male?

- Depression is a significant predictor of stroke and Parkinson's disease. Is this because depression is an integral component of both disorders?

- Physical activity, smoking, drinking moderate levels of alcohol and diets high in vitamins B6, B12 and folic acid all predict lower levels of Alzheimer's disease. Is this a genuine protective effect, or a statistical artifact?

- Alzheimer's disease has a significant inherited component – but what is it that is inherited in the disorder?

- Are there different genes linked to early- and late-onset Alzheimer's disease?

- Are psychotic symptoms such as hallucinations intrinsic to Parkinson's disease, or are they effects of the medications used to treat the disorder?

- Can depression accelerate disease processes that cause atrophy of nerve cells in the brain (e.g. in disorders such as Alzheimer's and Parkinson's disease)?

- How does deep brain stimulation (DBS) in Parkinson's disease have the effect of alleviating many of the physical symptoms of the disorder?

- What are the more effective means of treating memory deficits – memory aids (e.g. pagers, diaries) or memory treatments (e.g. procedures for training better memory functioning)?

CLINICAL ISSUES

- On what grounds might a clinician decide to provide restorative treatment for a cognitive deficit (e.g. memory training) as opposed to compensatory skills training based on dealing with the daily living difficulties posed by the deficit?

- How might a clinical neuropsychologist differentiate a memory deficit from normal forgetfulness (especially in old age)?

- What are the problems involved in differentiating the symptoms and deficits found in neurological disorders from those found in psychopathologies with predominantly psychological symptoms?

- How might the development of psychological problems (e.g. depression) affect the diagnosis and treatment of a neurological disorder?

- What are the difficulties of diagnosing neurological disorders when the symptoms of a range of different disorders overlap?

- Does treating post-stroke depression (with either drugs or psychological therapy) have a significant effect on the course of the disorder?

- Brain tumours can often generate symptoms reminiscent of PTSD, panic disorder and eating disorders. How does the clinician attempt to clarify diagnosis in such cases?

- What are the problems in distinguishing the symptoms of a degenerative disorder from the normal process of ageing?

- In what ways do anxiety and depression in old age complicate neurological testing?

- How does a clinician take into account individual differences in level of education, level of family and social support, and psychological history when diagnosing neurological disorders?

- Alzheimer's disease is difficult to differentiate from many other forms of degenerative dementia, so how can a relatively reliable diagnosis be made?

- What kinds of support and counselling should be given to individuals who are diagnosed with a potentially untreatable degenerative disorder?

- Drug treatments of degenerative disorders such as Alzheimer's disease tend to be more successful the earlier the disorder is identified. How can clinicians contribute to the early detection of such degenerative disorders?

- The success of thrombolytic therapy for strokes is dependent on the individual being able to identify the early signs of a stroke. How can potential stroke patients be made aware of detecting these early signs and seeking rapid treatment?

- What are the benefits of adopting a holistic approach to neuropsychological rehabilitation?

- Do support programmes for caregivers indirectly provide a better quality of life for those suffering from neurological disorders?

III

Developmental Psychopathology

15 | Childhood Psychological Problems

ROUTE MAP OF THE CHAPTER

This chapter begins by discussing some of the difficulties involved in identifying and diagnosing childhood psychological problems. It goes on to discuss the characteristics, prevalence rates and aetiology of disruptive behaviour problems (examining ADHD and conduct disorder in detail) and of childhood anxiety and depression. The chapter next discusses the main treatment methods used with children and adolescents. It concludes by looking at how coordinated provision of treatment extends across a range of services, including education, health and social services.

My own troubles began when I was 3 years old and my father died abruptly of a brain tumour. A few years later my mother was diagnosed with breast cancer and died when I was 11 years old. Watching so many important people die was frightening and confusing. Even so, the most traumatic event of my childhood was my placement into foster care. Although my aunts and uncles hinted at the possibility, I never believed they would give me away. I threatened to jump off a high building if they went ahead with the plan. I knew they were conspiring to banish me and I didn't trust a single one of them. But they did it anyway. I'd had enough of the cycle of attachment and desertion and decided I wasn't going to become attached to my new foster parents. To the outside world I was withdrawn and detached. Yet towards myself I was overwhelmed by intense feelings of rage and hatred. My foster mother repeatedly spoke of her disappointment in me and angrily talked about sending me away. I knew from my brother that foster children often go from place to place and that being physically or sexually abused was common. During the following 2 years I continued to float through time and space in a state of numb, disorganized misery, going through the emotions but not really alive. I was aware of my impairment, and ashamed of it. I believed I was peculiar. When I was about 16, I became absorbed with the idea that my central problem was a bodily defect, and I focused on one aspect of my anatomy after another, determined to find the specific flaw. At 17 I developed the sensation of a lump in my throat and became convinced I was about to choke to death. I had no labels for any of my experiences, so I didn't realize this latest state was a form of anxiety. Every night I stayed awake to the point of exhaustion.

FRANK'S STORY

Introduction

The study of childhood psychological problems is fraught with a range of difficulties that are not experienced in the study of adult psychopathology. Firstly, any behavioural or psychological problems have to be assessed in the context of the child as a developing organism. For example, bedwetting is quite normal in infancy, but might be a sign of anxiety or adjustment problems after the age of 5 years. Similarly, shyness and withdrawal from social contact are often normal during periods of social development as the child attempts to understand the rules of social interaction and learns how to verbally communicate with others. However, in early adolescence, these phenomena may represent the first signs of psychopathology. In addition, children may often go through brief stages of development when they exhibit behavioural problems or fears and anxieties, but these problems often disappear as rapidly as they appeared. Most parents have experienced a child who refuses to eat, or very suddenly becomes frightened of noises, strangers or certain types of animals, only for this to disappear within a matter of days or weeks. Secondly, because of their immaturity, children will tend to have poor self-knowledge. They may feel that something is wrong, but be unable to label it as anxiety or depression, or convey clearly how they feel to others. In such circumstances, clinicians have to infer psychological states from overt behaviour and decide whether that behaviour is unusual for the developmental stages through which the child is passing.

With these issues in mind, clinicians have tended to organize childhood psychological problems into two broad domains based on the general behavioural characteristics of the child. The first domain covers *externalizing disorders*, which are based on outward-directed behaviour problems such as aggressiveness, hyperactivity, non-compliance or impulsiveness. The second domain covers *internalizing disorders*, which are represented by more inward-looking and withdrawn behaviours, and may represent the experience of depression, anxiety and active attempts to socially withdraw. The former are now more commonly known as *disruptive behaviour disorders* and include DSM-IV-TR diagnosable disorders such as *conduct disorder* and *attention deficit hyperactivity disorder (ADHD)*. As research on internalizing disorders has progressed over recent years, clinicians have been able to develop a clearer understanding of childhood anxiety and depression, how these disorders are manifested and how they can be treated. We will discuss these more fully in section 15.3.

Externalizing disorders Outward-directed behaviour problems such as aggressiveness, hyperactivity, non-compliance or impulsiveness.

Internalizing disorders Inward-looking and withdrawn behaviours, which in children may represent the experience of depression, anxiety and active attempts to socially withdraw.

Frank's Story described at the beginning of this chapter illustrates the kinds of experiences that might give rise to psychological distress in childhood and adolescence and how this distress may be manifested in behaviour. This personal account describes the negative emotional impact on Frank of the death of his mother and father, his feelings of abandonment and powerlessness, and how this affected his ability to form relationships. This in turn gave rise to feelings of guilt, shame and inadequacy, and in adolescence finally manifested as specific psychological problems such as body dysmorphic disorder and somatization disorder. Frank related this story as an adult, and as such was able to look back on his childhood and put his behaviour and emotions into a perspective that enabled him to understand them. But to a child, events often seem confusing and uncontrollable, and clinicians have to interpret what children might be feeling and experiencing from their behaviour alone (for example, much of Frank's behaviour might be seen as internalizing, suggestive of anxiety and depression).

Nevertheless, even during an upbringing that is relatively trauma-free, children will frequently experience childhood as a threatening and frightening time. They will develop anxieties as they experience new people and new situations (Crijnen, Achenbach & Velhulst 1999), will worry about many of their everyday activities such as attending school (Vasey, 1993; Ollendick, King & Muris, 2002), and develop behavioural problems such as temper tantrums, eating irregularities, nightmares and phobias. As the child moves into adolescence even more challenges await as he or she develops sexually, changes physically, encounters educational and occupational challenges, and moves into a new period where feelings of responsibility and self-worth are expected of him or her. It is perhaps not surprising at this stage that many adolescents encounter feelings of confusion, anxiety and depression while attempting to cope with these changes (Lerner, 2002), nor that the initial symptoms of many of the disorders we covered in the section on *Adult Mental Health* first begin to develop during adolescence (e.g. schizophrenia, paraphilias, somatoform disorders).

In the following section of this chapter we look briefly at the difficulties involved in addressing psychological problems of childhood and adolescence, then consider the prevalence rates of specific disorders. The remainder of the chapter examines in detail the diagnosis, aetiology and treatment of the following: (1) attention deficit and disruptive behaviour disorders; (2) childhood anxiety and depression; and (3) symptom-based disorders such as enuresis ('bedwetting'), encopresis (lack of bowel control) and somnambulism (sleepwalking). Table 15.1 provides an overview of the information covered in this chapter – you may want to browse through it before commencing your reading, and refer back to it when you have completed the chapter.

Table 15.1 *Childhood psychological problems: summary*

DISORDER CATEGORY	DISORDER SUB-TYPES AND PREVALENCE RATES	MAIN DSM-IV-TR DIAGNOSTIC FEATURES	KEY FEATURES	THEORIES OF AETIOLOGY	MAIN FORMS OF TREATMENT (ALL DISORDERS)
DISRUPTIVE BEHAVIOUR DISORDERS	*Attention deficit hyperactivity disorder (ADHD)* (3–7% of school-aged children)	Presence of symptoms indicative of either (1) inattention or (2) hyperactivity, or both	Lack of attention in academic, occupational or social situations Hyperactivity manifested as fidgetiness or excessive running or climbing when inappropriate Impulsivity manifested as impatience or difficulty delaying responses	Genetic factors Brain abnormalities Prenatal factors Environmental toxins Parent–child interactions Theory of mind (TOM) deficits Genetic factors	Drug treatments ● SSRIs for depression ● Ritalin and other stimulants for ADHD Behaviour therapy ● Bell-and-battery technique for enuresis ● Systematic desensitization ● Reinforcement techniques ● Behaviour management techniques Family interventions ● Systemic family therapy ● Parent trainng programmes ● Functional family therapy (FFT) CBT for both childhood anxiety and depression Play therapy
	Conduct disorder (Lifetime prevalence rate of 9.5%) *Oppositional defiant disorder (ODD)*	Three or more of the following: (1) aggression to people and animals; (2) destruction of property; (3) deceitfulness or theft; (4) serious violations of rules	Tendency to violent or aggressive behaviour Deliberate cruelty to people or animals Wanton vandalism or damage to property Lying, stealing, cheating and criminal theft Violation of the rights of others Associated with early onset of sexual behaviour, drinking, smoking, substance abuse and general risk-taking behaviour	Neuropsychological deficits Prenatal factors Family environment and parent–child relationships Media and peer influences Cognitive biases Socioeconomic factors	
CHILDHOOD ANXIETY AND DEPRESSION	*Childhood anxiety* ● *Separation anxiety* (2–5% of children and adolescents	Inappropriate and excessive anxiety about separation from home or carers	Develop exaggerated fears that parents will die or become ill Associated with somatic complaints	Genetic factors Trauma and stress experiences	
	● *Obsessive compulsive disorder (OCD)* (prevalence unknown)	See DSM-IV-TR diagnostic criteria for adult OCD (Table 5.1)	Intrusive, repetitive thoughts, obsessions and compulsions Regularly comborbid with tic disorders or Tourette's syndrome	Modelling and exposure to information Parenting style	
	● *Generalized anxiety disorder (GAD)* (<1% of 5- to 10-year-olds)	See DSM-IV-TR diagnostic criteria for adult GAD (Table 5.1)	Associated with increased levels of pathological worrying		

Table 15.1 *(Cont'd)*

DISORDER CATEGORY	DISORDER SUB-TYPES AND PREVALENCE RATES	MAIN DSM-IV-TR DIAGNOSTIC FEATURES	KEY FEATURES	THEORIES OF AETIOLOGY	MAIN FORMS OF TREATMENT (ALL DISORDERS)
	● *Specific phobias* (7% for 8- to 9-year-olds)	See DSM-IV-TR diagnostic criteria for adult specific phobia (Table 5.1)	Important childhood phobias include social phobia and animal phobias		
	Childhood and adolescent depression (2–5% for young children; 4–8% for adolescents, but with up to 25–28% lifetime prevalence rate for adolescents)	See DSM-IV-TR diagnostic criteria for adult major depression (Table 6.1)	In younger children manifests as clingy behaviour, school refusal, somatic complaints and exaggerated fears In adolescence associated with sulkiness, withdrawal from family activities, loss of energy and feelings of guilt and worthlessness	Genetic factors Psychological factors ● The role of depressive parents Pessimistic inferential style	
SYMPTOM-BASED DISORDERS OF CHILDHOOD	*Enuresis* (5–10% for 5-year-olds; 3–5% for 10-year-olds)	Repeated voiding of urine into bed or clothes	Usually occurs as noctural enuresis Can have significant impact on child's general development	Organic factors Childhood stress	
	Encopresis (1% of 5-year-olds)	Repeated passage of faeces into inappropriate places (e.g. clothes or floor)	Often associated with childhood constipation	Childhood constipation Childhood stress	
	Somnambulism (1–5% of children)	Repeated episodes of rising from bed during sleep and walking about	Occurs during slow-wave sleep during the first 3 hours of sleeping	Genetic factors Factors causing sleep fragmentation	

15.1 THE DIAGNOSIS AND PREVALENCE OF CHILDHOOD PSYCHOLOGICAL PROBLEMS: SOME GENERAL ISSUES

15.1.1 Difficulties Associated with Identification and Diagnosis of Childhood Psychological Problems

Having already alluded to some of the difficulties involved in identifying whether a child needs help and treatment for a mental health problem, it is worth considering some of these difficulties before we discuss individual diagnoses. For example:

1   When considering what might be clinically relevant behaviour in children, we first have to consider what is normal for a particular age. Bedwetting is considered relatively normal in children up to the age of 5 years, but it may be a symptom of psychological distress if it occurs after that age.

2   Diagnosing a psychological problem is often dependent on individuals being able to communicate with the practitioner and to articulate how they experience the distress their problems are causing them. However, many children are unable to communicate clearly how they feel (e.g. they may not be able to differentiate feelings of anxiety from feelings of depression). They may also lack self-knowledge and be unable to understand precisely what they are feeling. In extreme cases, some disorders are explicitly associated with an inability to communicate with others (e.g. autistic syndrome disorders), so identification of psychological problems has to take place almost solely on the basis of external observation of the child's behaviour and his or her rate of development.

3   Differences in cultural norms will also affect whether childhood behaviours are seen as problematic or not. Externalizing behaviour problems are most prominent in many Western societies, but some Oriental cultures have relatively low levels of this type of problem (Weisz, Suwanlert, Chaiyasit & Walter, 1987). For example, in those countries that practise Buddhism, externalizing behaviours such as disrespect and aggression are rarely tolerated by parents and teachers and are controlled at an early stage in the child's life.

4   Finally, during childhood and early adolescence, developmental changes occur rapidly, which means that psychological problems can escalate quickly and dramatically. For example, behaviour problems can be generated very rapidly if the development of language skills, self-control skills, social skills and emotional regulation does not proceed normally. This requires that childhood problems be identified early and quickly in order to minimize the psychological damage that prolonged abnormal development could inflict.

15.1.2 Childhood Psychopathology as the Precursor of Adult Psychopathology

The section on *Adult Mental Health* describes how important childhood experiences appear to be in the aetiology of many diagnosable psychological disorders. Childhood trauma and abuse, for example, not only affects childhood behaviour but may also serve as the basis for the development of long-term psychological maladjustment, including major depression, personality disorders such as borderline and antisocial personality disorders, somatoform disorders, dissociative disorders, eating disorders, and sexual and identity disorders. Indeed, prospective studies have indicated that preschool behaviour problems predict psychopathology in later life (Caspi, Newman, Moffit & Silva, 1996). Table 15.2 lists some of the childhood risk factors that have been identified in the aetiology of adult psychopathology, all of which are discussed more fully in the relevant chapters of this book. Childhood risk factors such as these enable researchers and clinicians to identify those groups of children and adolescents who are most likely to be at risk for adult mental health problems. With this in mind, an emerging area of research is ***developmental psychopathology***, which is concerned with mapping how early childhood experiences may act as risk factors for later diagnosable psychological disorders. In doing so, it attempts to describe the pathways by which early experiences may generate adult psychological problems.

> **Developmental psychopathology**   An area of research concerned with mapping how early childhood experiences may act as risk factors for later diagnosable psychological disorders. It also attempts to describe the pathways by which early experiences may generate adult psychological problems.

There are a number of possible ways in which childhood psychopathology may link to adult mental health problems. The simplest relationship is where a childhood disorder merely persists into adulthood in the same form (e.g. where childhood anxiety or depression develops into experienced anxiety and depression in adulthood). One striking example of this was described in Chapter 11, where we noted that childhood conduct disorder and antisocial behaviour often persist into adulthood in the form of antisocial personality disorder (Farrington, Loeber & van Kammen, 1990).

Secondly, a childhood psychopathology may have an adverse affect on subsequent development and indirectly lead to different forms of maladjustment in later life. For example, children who

Table 15.2 *Childhood risk factors for adult mental health problems*

CHILDHOOD EXPERIENCE (RISK FACTOR)	ADULT MENTAL HEALTH PROBLEM	REFERENCE	CHAPTER IN THIS VOLUME
Abnormal parent–child interaction style	Social anxiety	Moore, Whaley & Sigman (2004)	5
	Narcissistic and obsessive-compulsive personality disorder	Johnson, Cohen, Kasen, Smailes et al. (2002)	11
	Antisocial personality disorder	Gabbard (1990)	11
	Borderline personality disorder	Graybar & Boutilier (2002)	11
	Histrionic personality disorder	Bender, Farber & Geller (2001)	11
Childhood abuse (physical and sexual)	Depression (reduced autobiographical specificity)	Raes, Hermans, Williams & Eelen (2005)	6
	Suicide and suicidal ideation	Gould & Kramer (2001)	6
	Eating disorders	Steiger, Leonard, Kin et al. (2000); Brown, Russell, Thornton & Dunn (1997)	9
	Hypoactive sexual desire disorder	Stuart & Greer (1984)	10
	Sexual aversion disorder	Berman, Berman, Werbin, Flaherty et al. (1999)	10
	Vaginismus	DSM-IV-TR	10
	Sexual dysfunction generally	Najman, Dunne, Purdie, Boyle et al. (2005)	10
	Dyspareunia	Binik, Bergerson & Khalife (2000)	10
	Paedophilia	Freund & Kuban (1994)	10
	Paraphilias generally	Mason (1997); Murphy (1997)	10
	Gender identity disorder (GID)	Bradley & Zucker (1997)	10
	Personality disorders generally	Johnson, Cohen, Brown, Smailes et al. (1999)	11
	Borderline personality disorder	Heffernan & Cloitre (2000)	11
	Antisocial personality disorder	Horowitz, Widom, McLaughlin & White (2001)	11
	Narcissistic personality disorder	Kernberg (1985)	11
	Avoidant personality disorder	Rettew, Zanarini, Yen, Grilo et al. (2003)	11
	Conversion disorder	Bowman & Markland (1996)	12
	Hypochondriasis	Salmon & Calderbank (1996)	12
	Somatization disorder	Tezzi, Duckworth & Adams (2001)	12
	Dissociative disorders generally	Tyler, Cauce & Whitbeck (2004)	13
	Dissociative identity disorder (DID)	Putnam (1997)	13
	Depersonalization disorder	Simeon, Guralnik, Schmeidler, Sirof et al. (2001)	13

Table 15.2 *(Cont'd)*

CHILDHOOD EXPERIENCE (RISK FACTOR)	ADULT MENTAL HEALTH PROBLEM	REFERENCE	CHAPTER IN THIS VOLUME
Childhood neglect (e.g. separation, inadequate and ineffectual parenting)	Post-traumatic stress disorder (PTSD)	King, King, Foy & Gudanowski (1996)	5
	Major depression	Lara & Klein (1999); Goodman (2002)	6
	Cannabis, nicotine and alcohol abuse	Cadoret, Yates, Troughton, Woodworth et al. (1995)	8
	Hypersexuality	Langstrom & Hanson (2006)	10
	Paraphilias generally	Mason (1997); Murphy (1997)	10
	Antisocial personality disorder	Hill (2003)	11
	Borderline personality disorder	Guttman (2002)	11
	Dependent personality disorder	Bornstein (1996)	11
	Body dysmorphic disorder	Cororve & Gleaves (2001)	12
Childhood trauma generally	Schizophrenia	Read, van Os, Morrison & Ross (2005)	7
	Alcohol dependency	Sher (1991); Wilsnack, Vogeltanz, Klassen & Harris (1997)	8
	Nicotine dependency	Anda, Croft, Felitti, Nordenberg et al. (1999)	8
	Conversion disorder	Bowman & Markland (1996)	12
	Dissociative identity disorder (DID)	Putnam (1997)	13
Childhood conflict and emotional disturbance	Specific phobias	Freud	5
	Cannabis dependency	Meltzer, Gatwood, Goodman & Ford (2003)	8
Childhood poverty	Schizophrenia	Byrne, Agerbo, Eaton & Mortensen (2004)	7
	Alcohol, nicotine and cannabis abuse	Alverson, Alverson & Drake (2000)	8
	Substance dependency generally	Petronis & Anthony (2003)	8
	Antisocial personality disorder	Paris (2001)	11

fail to form adaptive relationships with their parents early in life exhibit disruptive behaviour in late infancy. Such disruptiveness can result in more general adjustment problems and the development of learning difficulties later in life.

Thirdly, a childhood psychopathology may simply represent the less cognitive precursor of a related adult disorder. For example, adolescent height phobia has been shown to be a risk factor for full-blown panic disorder in adulthood (Starcevic & Bogojevic, 1997). This may result from the fact that the catastrophizing of bodily sensations is a central feature of both disorders and may extend across an increasing number of cognitive and behavioural domains as the individual develops from childhood into adolescence (Davey, Menzies & Gallardo, 1997).

Fourthly, a childhood disorder may not necessarily extend into adulthood but may render the individual vulnerable to later life stressors. For example, if a child loses a parent early in life, this may make him or her vulnerable to depression when experiencing similar types of losses later in life (e.g. following the death of a spouse or close friend).

Fifthly, a childhood disorder may be quite specific to childhood and disappear or change form dramatically once the individual has reached adulthood. One such example is elimination disorders, which we will discuss further in section 15.4.

All of these examples demonstrate that childhood psychopathology has an important influence on adult mental health, but the nature of this influence is not always direct and not always in the same form as the childhood difficulties. You may want to refer back to Table 15.2 and consider what possible developmental processes might link certain childhood experiences with adult psychopathology.

15.1.3 The Prevalence of Childhood Psychological Disorders

Studies of the prevalence of diagnosable childhood psychological disorders estimate that between 10 and 20 per cent of children and adolescents have a diagnosable psychological disorder (e.g. Phares, 2003; McDermott & Weiss, 1995), and boys exhibit higher preval-

ence rates than girls, even though the opposite is the case in adulthood. Figure 15.1 shows the prevalence of psychopathologies found in children and adolescents aged between 5 and 15 years in the UK (Office for National Statistics, 2004). These figures show that boys are more likely to have a disorder than girls, and that the prevalent disorders are conduct disorders in boys and anxiety disorders in girls. Around 7 per cent of 3-year-olds can be expected to show moderate to severe behavioural problems and a further 15 per cent to exhibit more mild difficulties (Richman, Stevenson & Graham, 1982). However, some early developmental problems and specific fears (such as delays in toilet training and 'comfort' habits such as rocking) usually resolve by middle childhood, while others – such as disruptiveness or conduct disorders – seem more persistent. The type of disorder exhibited also changes with age

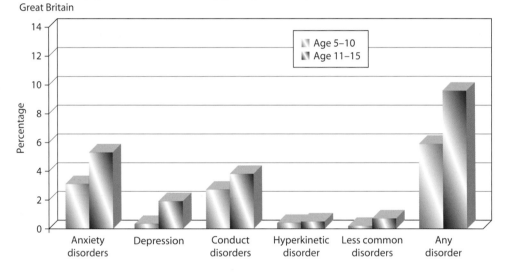

Prevalence of psychiatric disorders among girls aged 5 to 15 years, 1999
Great Britain

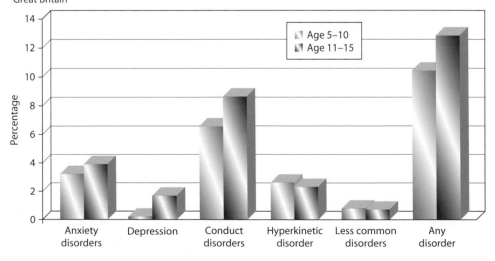

Prevalence of psychiatric disorder among boys aged 5 to 15 years, 1999
Great Britain

Figure 15.1
Prevalence rates of psychopathologies amongst boys and girls aged 5–15 years in the UK, 1999.

Source: Mental Health of Children and Adolescents in Great Britain, 1999 ONS Survey.

and is probably related to the nature of the experiences that children encounter at specific ages. For example, some problems (such as chronic worrying) are rarely found in preschool children, but increase significantly after school entry.

Comorbidity between childhood disorders is also common, particularly between anxiety and depression (Angold, Costello & Erkanli, 1999). In addition, childhood psychopathology is associated with physical health problems and poor educational performance. For example, rates of accidents requiring hospital treatment are more common among children with psychopathology symptoms, as are reports of life-threatening illnesses (Office for National Statistics, 2004). Special educational needs (SEN) are found in a significantly higher percentage of children with psychopathologies than those without. In terms of literacy ability, only 4 per cent of children without a diagnosed psychiatric disorder were classified as showing specific literacy difficulties, compared with 11 per cent for those with emotional problems and 17 per cent for those with hyperkinetic disorders (e.g. attention deficit hyperactivity disorder) (Office for National Statistics, 2004).

Thus, we can see from these facts that childhood psychiatric disorders have implications across a range of developmental domains. Studies of risk factors suggest that children of lone parents are twice as likely to have a mental health problem as those living with married or cohabiting couples (16 per cent compared to 8 per cent). Other known risk factors for childhood psychiatric disorders include parental psychopathology, repeated early separation from parents, harsh or inadequate parenting, exposure to abuse or neglect, and adverse peer group influences (Maugham, 2000) (see also Table 15.2).

SELF-TEST QUESTIONS

- Can you describe four difficulties involved in the detection and diagnosis of childhood psychological disorders?
- What kinds of childhood events act as precursors or risk factors for adult mental health problems?
- How prevalent are childhood psychological disorders?

SECTION SUMMARY

15.1 The Diagnosis and Prevalence of Childhood Psychological Problems: Some General Issues

- There are a number of difficulties associated with recognizing and diagnosing childhood psychological problems, including **communication difficulties** and the child's **underdeveloped self-awareness**.

- Childhood psychopathology is often a **significant precursor** to adult psychopathology.

- Between 10 and 20 per cent of children and adolescents have a diagnosable psychological disorder.

- **Comorbidity** between disorders is common.

15.2 DISRUPTIVE BEHAVIOUR PROBLEMS

This category of childhood disorders covers behavioural problems that are characterized by impulsive, disruptive and poorly controlled behaviour. We all expect children of certain ages to have poor self-control, to throw temper tantrums or to disrupt ongoing activities by failing to show restraint. However, by the time most children enter school, they are expected to be able to restrain their behaviour, attend to tasks when asked, and to attend to and follow appropriate commands. Nevertheless, some individuals find this hard to do – even in late childhood or adolescence. Their inability to restrain themselves and follow instructions leads to the disruption of cooperative and group activities (such as group learning in school), and in extreme cases may represent overtly aggressive behaviour towards peers and adults, including criminal violence and damage to property.

In DSM-IV-TR, disruptive behaviour disorders take two main forms – *attention deficit hyperactivity disorder (ADHD)* and *conduct disorder*. In this section we discuss these two syndromes individually, covering their diagnosis and aetiology.

15.2.1 *Attention Deficit Hyperactivity Disorder (ADHD)*

The main feature of **attention deficit hyperactivity disorder (ADHD)** is a persistent pattern of inattention and/or hyperactivity-impulsivity that is at a significantly higher rate than would be expected for the child at that developmental stage. ADHD can manifest itself behaviourally in many ways, including lack of attention in academic, occupational or social situations; making careless mistakes in school work or other tasks; difficulty maintaining attention until task completion; appearing to have attention elsewhere and a failure to take in or respond to instructions; and a tendency to shift from one task to another without completing any of them.

> **Attention deficit hyperactivity disorder (ADHD)** A persistent pattern of inattention and/or hyperactivity-impulsivity that is at a significantly higher rate than would be expected for a child at his or her developmental stage.

Children with ADHD typically have a strong dislike for tasks that require sustained self-application and mental effort, and are easily distracted by irrelevant stimuli or events. **Hyperactivity** may be manifest as excessive fidgetiness and by not remaining seated when asked. Children with ADHD exhibit excessive running or climbing when inappropriate, or will talk excessively. Infants with the disorder appear to be constantly 'on the go' and jump and climb on furniture. They also have difficulty participating in sedentary activities such as listening to a story. **Impulsivity**

> **Hyperactivity** A higher than normal level of activity.

> **Impulsivity** The act of reacting to a situation without considering the consequences.

manifests as impatience, difficulty in delaying responses appropriately (e.g. attempting to run out of the house before their coat is on), and constantly interrupting others before they have finished speaking. Impulsivity can also result in accidents such as knocking over objects or indulging in dangerous activities (such as riding a bike fast over rough terrain).

15.2.1.1 The Diagnosis of ADHD

The main issue in diagnosing ADHD is to ensure that hyperactivity or inattention is significantly greater than normal for the child's developmental stage, and to ensure that it is a generalized and persistent predisposition rather than one that is confined to a single context. Table 15.3 describes the DSM-IV-TR diagnostic criteria for ADHD, which emphasize that impairment is present before 7 years of age (Criterion B) and is found in two or more contexts (Criterion C).

Most individuals with ADHD present with symptoms of both inattention and hyperactivity, but in some, one or the other pattern may be dominant. This has given rise to diagnostic subtypes such as *attention deficit hyperactivity disorder, predominantly inattentive type* and *attention deficit hyperactivity disorder, predominantly hyperactive-impulsive type*. Each sub-type should be used if six (or more) of the dominant symptoms are present with fewer than six of the less dominant symptoms present. It is often difficult to establish a diagnosis of ADHD in children under the age of 5 years because their behaviour is often more variable and there are often many demands on their developing attentional abilities. However, children younger than 5 years can usually exhibit some form of sustained attention in simple situations such as listening to a story, and a persistent inability to do this in youngsters less than 5 years may indicate the first signs of ADHD.

Around half of those diagnosed with ADHD are also diagnosed with oppositional defiant disorder or conduct disorder (see section 15.2.2). These rates of comorbidity are significantly higher than comorbidity with other psychopathologies (Hinshaw, 1987), which indicates that in many cases ADHD is associated with the violation of social norms and the basic rights of others. It thus raises the question of whether there might be an underlying link between the two disorders (e.g. Quay, 1979). Opinion on this is currently divided, but what is clear is that when a child is diagnosed with both ADHD and an oppositional defiant disorder/conduct disorder, he or she usually exhibits the worst of both disorders (Biederman, Newcorn & Sprich, 1991).

In other cases, children with ADHD can be distinguished from those with oppositional defiant disorder/conduct disorder by the fact that the latter are likely to be more aggressive, live in families with a lower socioeconomic status and have parents who also exhibit antisocial behaviour (Faraone, Biederman, Jetton & Tsuang, 1997; Hinshaw, 1987). In addition, recent studies have suggested that children with a single diagnosis of ADHD are likely to have a better long-term prognosis than those with oppositional defiant disorder/conduct disorder, and childhood ADHD is not a differential predictor of antisocial personality disorder in adulthood (Lahey, Loeber, Burke & Applegate, 2005; see Chapter 11, section 11.3.2.1). However, there is some evidence that in some cases ADHD can lead to earlier onset of conduct disorder. This may be because some children with ADHD become involved in an escalation of symptoms whereby their disruptive behaviour causes aggressive reactions in others, which in turn evokes aggressive and increasingly antisocial reactions in the sufferer (Hinshaw, Lahey & Hart, 1993). Other disorders that are frequently comorbid with ADHD include mood disorders, anxiety disorders, learning disorders and communication disorders (APA, 2000, p. 88), with rates of comorbidity being estimated to range from 12 to 60 per cent (Furman, 2005).

ADHD is usually first recognized by parents when the child is a toddler, although not all hyperactive toddlers go on to develop ADHD. The disorder is usually first diagnosed after the child begins schooling, because learning and adjustment at school are significantly affected by the disorder. As the child develops into adolescence, symptoms usually attenuate and become less pronounced, although about half of sufferers continue to show symptoms well into adulthood, which can detrimentally affect intellectual functioning and IQ (Bridgett & Walker, 2006).

Table 15.3 *DSM-IV-TR diagnostic criteria for attention deficit hyperactivity disorder (ADHD)*

A Either (1) or (2):

(1) Six (or more) of the following symptoms of inattention have persisted for at least 6 months to a degree that is maladaptive and inconsistent with developmental level:

Inattention

(a) Often fails to give close attention to details or makes careless mistakes in schoolwork, work or other activities.

(b) Often has difficulty sustaining attention in tasks or play activities.

(c) Often does not seem to listen when spoken to directly.

(d) Often does not follow through on instructions and fails to finish schoolwork, chores or duties in the workplace (not due to oppositional behaviour or failure to understand instructions).

(e) Often has difficulty organizing tasks and activities.

(f) Often avoids, dislikes or is reluctant to engage in tasks that require sustained mental effort (such as schoolwork).

(g) Often loses things necessary for tasks or activities (e.g. toys, school assignments).

(h) Is often easily distracted by extraneous stimuli.

(i) Is often forgetful in daily activities.

(2) Six (or more) of the following symptoms of hyperactivity-impulsivity have persisted for at least 6 months to a degree that is maladaptive and inconsistent with developmental level:

Hyperactivity

(a) Often fidgets with hands or feet or squirms in seat.

(b) Often leaves seat in classroom or in other situations in which remaining seated is expected.

(c) Often runs about or climbs excessively in situations in which it is inappropriate (in adolescents or adults, may be limited to subjective feelings of restlessness).

(d) Often has difficulty playing or engaging in leisure activities quietly.

(e) Is often 'on the go' or often acts as if 'driven by a motor'.

(f) Often talks excessively.

Impulsivity

(a) Often blurts out answers before questions have been completed.

(b) Often has difficulty awaiting turn.

(c) Often interrupts or intrudes on others (e.g. butts into conversations).

B. Some hyperactive-impulsive or inattentive symptoms that caused impairment were present before age 7 years.

C. Some impairment from the symptoms is present in two or more settings (e.g. at school and at home).

D. There must be clear evidence of clinically significant impairment in social, academic or occupational functioning.

E. The symptoms do not occur exclusively during the course of a pervasive developmental disorder, schizophrenia or any other psychotic disorder.

There is much discussion in the literature about whether ADHD is a culturally constructed disorder – that is, whether rates of diagnosis differ in different cultures because of differing cultural perceptions of children's behaviour. The evidence on this is currently equivocal. Some studies suggest very similar rates of diagnosis across different cultures and ethnic groups (Rohde, Szobot, Polanczyk, Schmitz et al., 2005; Bailey & Owens, 2005), whereas others indicate differing rates of ADHD in different countries (Dwivedi & Banhatti, 2005). Studies indicating different rates of diagnosis may do so because different cultural environments may directly affect a child's behaviour (e.g. Buddhist cultures tend not to tolerate externalizing behaviours) or the attitudes of parents and clinicians towards what is acceptable behaviour. For example, Zwirs, Burger, Buitelaar and Schulpen (2006) found that detection of externalizing disorders was significantly lower in a sample of non-Dutch parents (Moroccan, Turkish and Surinamese) than Dutch parents, and that cultural contexts may have an important influence on whether ADHD symptoms are detected and reported.

15.2.1.2 The Prevalence of ADHD

DSM-IV-TR estimates that around 3–7 per cent of school-age children worldwide are diagnosed with ADHD, although an accurate figure is difficult to establish because of different diagnostic practices over time. Similar rates of diagnosis are found in preschool children (aged 2–5 years) (Egger, Kondo & Angold, 2006). About half those diagnosed with ADHD in childhood will carry that diagnosis into adulthood, where prevalence rates are around 4 per cent (Kessler, Adler, Barkley, Biederman et al., 2006). There is considerable evidence to indicate that ADHD is more common in boys than girls, although reasons for this may include the fact that boys are more likely to be referred for treatment than girls. Recent reviews suggest that although there is a sex difference in rates of diagnosis between boys and girls, ADHD symptoms are not sex-specific (e.g. just as is the case with boys, girls with combined attention deficit and hyperactivity were more likely to be disruptive than those diagnosed with the predominantly single diagnosis); however, identification of girls with ADHD has been hampered by parental and teacher bias (Staller & Faraone, 2006).

15.2.1.3 The Consequences of ADHD

Like most psychopathologies, the symptoms of ADHD have detrimental consequences for sufferers across a range of life domains. Firstly, their attentional deficits and hyperactivity may make them prone to temper outbursts, frustration, bossiness, stubbornness, changeable moods and poor self-esteem. As a result, academic achievement is usually impaired, leading to conflict with teachers and family. Because the disruptive consequences of sufferers' behaviour are pervasive, family members often view the behaviour as intentional, wilful and irresponsible, which can cause resentment within the family (see Activity Box 15.1). Individuals with predominantly inattentive symptoms tend to suffer most in terms of academic achievement, while hyperactivity and impulsivity are associated most with peer rejection and accidental injury. However, in general, children with ADHD have great difficulty making friends and integrating successfully into social groups, usually because their behaviour is aggressive and disruptive (Hinshaw & Melnick, 1995). Indeed, in new social settings, children with ADHD are often singled out and rejected relatively rapidly by their peers (Erhardt & Hinshaw, 1994). In part this is due to their disruptive behavioural symptoms, but in addition children with ADHD frequently fail to understand the intentions of their peers and are unable to translate the correct social response into appropriate behaviour (Whalen & Henker, 1998).

15.2.1.4 The Aetiology of ADHD: Biological Factors

The causes of ADHD can be clustered under two broad headings – *biological* and *psychological*. The current view is that biological factors are particularly important in the aetiology of ADHD, especially inherited factors that may play a strong role in mediating susceptibility to ADHD (Faraone & Khan, 2006).

Genetic Factors   There is now considerable evidence pointing to the involvement of an inherited susceptibility to ADHD. Numerous twin studies have indicated heritability rates ranging between 60 and 90 per cent and environmental influences which, by comparison, are relatively modest (Waldman & Rhee, 2002). In addition, when a parent has ADHD, there is a 50 per cent chance that his or her offspring will also have ADHD (Biederman, Faraone, Mick, Spencer et al., 1995). Adoption studies also suggest that ADHD in the adopted child is more likely to occur if a biological parent has ADHD than if an adopted parent has ADHD (van den Oord, Boomsma & Verhulst, 1994).

However, what is inherited is significantly less easy to determine. At least 7 or 8 genes have been implicated in the disorder (Faraone, 2006), most of which may underlie abnormalities in neurotransmitter systems, particularly the dopamine, norepinephrine and serotonin systems (Waldman & Gizer, 2006). The genes involved are the dopamine transporter gene, the dopamine D4 and D5 receptors and SNAP-25, a gene that controls the way dopamine is released in the brain.

While susceptibility to ADHD appears to have a significant genetic component, additional studies strongly indicate a genes–environment interaction. That is, what is inherited is a vulnerability to ADHD, but ADHD becomes manifest only when certain environmental influences are found. For example, Kahn, Khoury, Nichols and Lanphear (2003) found that children with 2 copies of the 10-repeat allele of a DAT1 gene (a gene related to dopamine regulation in the brain) who were exposed to maternal prenatal smoking exhibited significantly higher levels of hyperactivity, impulsiveness and oppositional behaviours than a control group of children who possessed these genes but whose mothers did not smoke during pregnancy. In addition, children who possessed only one of the risk factors (the high-risk genotype or a mother who smoked during pregnancy) did not show significantly higher levels of ADHD symptoms than children who possessed neither of the risk factors.

Studies such as this indicate that, while inherited factors are critically important in the aetiology of ADHD, they may constitute a vulnerability that converts into ADHD only if certain environmental factors are present. Other environmental risk factors that have been proposed include pre- or perinatal complications and maternal drinking during pregnancy (Mick, Biederman, Faraone, Sayer et al., 2002; Milberger, Biederman, Faraone, Guite et al., 1997; Milberger, Biederman, Faraone & Jones, 1998).

Brain Abnormalities   Magnetic resonance imaging (MRI) studies of the brains of individuals with ADHD have revealed a number of significant differences between ADHD sufferers and non-sufferers (e.g. Krain & Castellanos, 2006; Seidman, Valera & Makris, 2005). First, there is consistent evidence that the brains of children with ADHD are smaller than those of healthy comparison children. Overall brain volume has been shown to be smaller by an average of 3.2 per cent, with the main areas affected being the frontal, parietal, temporal and occipital lobes (Durston, Hulshoff Pol, Schnack, Buitelaar et al., 2004). Other brain areas exhibiting decreased volume in ADHD include the frontal cortex, basal ganglia and cerebellum (Krain & Castellanos, 2006).

ACTIVITY BOX 15.1

ADHD and family dysfunction

Having a child with ADHD is certain to be a challenging experience for parents and other family members. Parents may well suffer burnout in their attempts to control a hyperactive child, deal with the disruption that this can cause in peer and family relationships, and in dealing with the inevitable problems that will arise at school.

In an interesting study published in the *Journal of Attention Disorders*, Kaplan, Crawford, Fisher and Dewey (1998) began with the premise that having any child who is struggling at school (such as one with ADHD) is likely to create stress for parents and detrimentally affect family functioning. However, they wanted to find out whether having a child with ADHD posed additional problems above and beyond the stresses and difficulties resulting from having a child struggling at school.

The researchers obtained information on family functioning from parents whose children were having difficulty at school for various reasons, specifically, from parents who had children with (1) ADHD; (2) a reading disorder; or (3) both ADHD and a reading disorder. They compared this information with that from parents of children who had no disability.

Their survey asked parents to say how much they would endorse statements of the following kind (on a 4-point scale):

- There are lots of bad feelings in the family.
- We don't get along well together.
- We are not able to make decisions on how to solve problems.

Parents endorsing these kinds of statements would be acknowledging high levels of dissatisfaction with how things were going in their family.

The results found that parents of children with ADHD reported significantly higher levels of dissatisfaction with family life than did parents of children with a primary reading disability. This suggests that problems in families with ADHD children are significantly greater than if the child simply has a basic schooling difficulty. Why do you think this might be? Use some of the evidence you've read about in this section to come to a view on this issue. For example, are families with children diagnosed with ADHD more dysfunctional because:

- ADHD disrupts more aspects of family life than those related to learning and education?
- ADHD runs in families, so parents of such children may also be suffering from dysfunctions caused by ADHD?
- having an individual with ADHD in the family disrupts effective communication between members, resulting in disagreements about how to solve problems?
- parents of children with ADHD are less likely than parents of children with a learning disorder to accept that their children have a disorder at all (and thus seek effective help for the problem)?
- ADHD causes frustrations in the family because it is less easy to treat than, say, a reading disability?

Source: adapted from www.focusas.com/ADHD-FamilyLife.html

A range of studies have suggested that brain volume in specific brain areas is inversely correlated with a variety of ADHD symptoms. For example, children with ADHD are known to have deficits in *executive functioning*, and specifically in inhibiting responses, and these functions are normally controlled by the brain's frontal lobes. Studies have found that decreased frontal lobe volume predicts poor performance on tests of attention and on tasks that require behaviour to be inhibited, suggesting that abnormalities in these brain regions may be responsible for some of the symptoms of ADHD (Casey, Castellanos, Giedd, Marsh et al., 1997; Hill, Yeo, Campbell, Hart et al., 2003).

Executive functioning Processes that are involved in planning and attentional control.

Another area of the brain that regularly exhibits abnormalities in association with ADHD symptoms is the cerebellum. In ADHD, abnormalities are usually found in the cerebellum's influence on the cortico-striatal-thalamo-cortical circuits, which are involved in choosing, initiating and carrying out complex motor and cognitive responses (Alexander, DeLong & Strick, 1986; Graybiel, 1998). In this case it is not hard to imagine how dysfunctions in these pathways may result in the disruption of the planning and execution of behaviour.

Prenatal Factors As we have already noted, at least some prenatal experiences appear to interact with a genetic predisposition to cause ADHD. These include maternal smoking and drinking during pregnancy (Mick, Biederman, Faraone, Sayer et al., 2002)

RESEARCH METHODS IN CLINICAL PSYCHOLOGY BOX 15.1

Cognitive tests of ADHD

A variety of tests have been devised that are capable of differentiating between children with ADHD and control participants. The aim of most of these tasks is to test attention or to determine whether the individual is able to successfully inhibit responses when required to do so (see Seidman, 2006).

The continuous performance test (CPT)

The CPT is a computerized visual vigilance/attention task in which the child is seated before a computer monitor and instructed to observe a string of letters presented randomly and at varying speeds. Children are instructed to press the space bar as quickly as possible following all letters except the letter X. Children with ADHD are less able to inhibit responses following the presentation of the target letter X, and also emit longer reaction times following letters that should be responded to (Epstein, Johnson, Varia & Conners, 2001).

The Stroop task

This is generally considered a test of ability to inhibit responses. In the task, a word describing a colour (e.g. RED) is presented in a different colour (e.g. green), and the participant has to respond as quickly as possible by naming the colour ink that the word is written in. Children with ADHD take more time to respond and make more errors than control participants (Shin, 2005). (See also Research Methods Box 5.2.)

The trail-making test

This is a measure involving connecting circles on a page. Children are instructed to connect the circles by drawing lines alternating between circles labelled with numbers and letters in sequential order until they reach the circle labelled 'End' (see Focus Point 14.1). Most studies show that children and adults with ADHD perform significantly worse than control participants (Rapport, van Voorhis, Tzelepis & Friedman, 2001).

The controlled word association test (COWAT)

This test measures verbal fluency in response to single letters, which taps into phonological associations, and category fluency ('name all the animals you can beginning with the letter . . .') (Benton, Hamsher, & Sivan, 1983). This test appears to measure speed of access to words, persistence at a task and processing speed. The majority of studies show impaired performance on this task in children with ADHD compared to controls (Dinn, Robbins & Harris, 2001).

Conners' Parent Rating Scale (CPRS)

The CPRS (Conners, Sitarenios, Parker & Epstein, 1998) is an 80-item scale completed by the child's parent using a 4-point scale. This instrument has well-accepted reliability and validity and is considered to be standard in ADHD diagnosis (Barkley, 1991). Norms by age are available for males and females in 3-year intervals.

---

and general complications associated with childbirth, such as low birthweight (Tannock, 1998). In one study, Schmitz, Denardin, Silva, Pianca et al. (2006) found that pregnant mothers smoking more than 10 cigarettes per day were significantly more likely to give birth to children with ADHD than non-smoking mothers – even when other potential confounding factors such as maternal ADHD, oppositional defiant disorder, birth weight and alcohol use during pregnancy were controlled for. In addition, a study by Milberger, Biederman, Faraone, Guite et al. (1997) found that 22 per cent of mothers of children with ADHD reported smoking a pack of cigarettes a day during pregnancy compared with only 8 per cent of mothers whose children did not develop ADHD. Milberger et al. (1997) hypothesized that prenatal exposure to nicotine caused abnormalities in the dopaminergic neurotransmitter system, resulting in difficulties inhibiting behaviour.

Environmental Toxins Some early accounts of ADHD alluded to the possibility that hyperactivity resulted from various biochemical imbalances caused by such factors as food additives (Feingold, 1973), refined sugar cane (Goyette & Connors, 1977) and lead poisoning (Thompson, Raab, Hepburn, Hunter et al., 1989). However, while there is little evidence to suggest that food

additives generally influence ADHD (Wolraich, Wilson & White, 1995), there is some support for the fact that both levels of lead in the blood and chronic exposure to nicotine increase hyperactivity (e.g. Fung & Lau, 1989).

15.2.1.5 The Aetiology of ADHD: Psychological Factors

Parent–Child Interactions We have already seen that ADHD appears to run in families, which may have implications beyond the fact that there is a genetic component to the disorder. For example, it means that children with ADHD are more likely to be brought up by parents who have the disorder, which may exacerbate any symptoms that are caused by the genetic component alone. Fathers who are diagnosed with ADHD have been found to be less effective parents (in terms of exhibiting ineffective discipline and adopting traditionally conservative father roles) than parents without an ADHD diagnosis (Arnold, O'Leary & Edwards, 1997), which may exacerbate disruptive characteristics the ADHD child exhibits.

Psychodynamic approaches to ADHD have also pointed to the possible role of inconsistent and ineffective parenting of children with ADHD. Bettelheim (1973) proposed that hyperactivity resulted when a predisposition to ADHD is accompanied by authoritarian parenting methods. He argued that such parents are likely to become impatient with a disruptive and hyperactive child, resulting in a vicious cycle whereby constant attempts to discipline the child cause even more defiant reactions on the part of the child, who reacts by defying rules across a range of life contexts (e.g. school, social situations).

Learning theorists have suggested that parents may exacerbate ADHD symptoms in a rather different way. Individuals with ADHD exhibit impulsive and disruptive behaviour, which in many cases will require the need for control by parents. In such circumstances, the attention from parents that these behaviours demand may be rewarding or reinforcing such behaviours, thus increasing their frequency and intensity. While there is no direct evidence to support this view, indirect support comes from studies showing that time-out from positive reinforcement can act as an effective procedure for *reducing* negative and disruptive behaviour in children with ADHD (Fabiano, Pelham, Manos, Gnagy et al., 2004).

Nevertheless, while parent–child interactions of various kinds may exacerbate ADHD symptoms, there is no evidence to suggest that they are the sole cause of these symptoms (Johnston & Mash, 2001).

Theory of Mind (TOM) Deficits We described in section 15.2.1.3 how children with ADHD frequently fail to understand the intentions of their peers in social situations. This has led some theorists to argue that children with ADHD have *theory of mind (TOM)* deficits. Theory of mind is the ability to understand one's own and other people's mental states (Premack & Woodruff, 1978),

> **Theory of mind (TOM)** The ability to understand one's own and other people's mental states.

and it is not difficult to see that if a child has deficits in such abilities, he or she will often react in inappropriate ways to peers and family. However, studies have been inconsistent in showing a relationship between poor performance on TOM tasks and ADHD. For example, Buitelaar, van der Wees, Swaab-Barnveld & van der Gaag (1999) found that children with ADHD diagnoses showed poorer performance on a TOM task than control participants, whereas in a later study, Perner, Kain and Barchfeld (2002) found that children with ADHD showed no impairment at all on an advanced TOM task. However, studies have been consistent in showing that children with ADHD do show impaired performance compared to controls on tasks of executive functioning (Fahie & Symons, 2003; Perner, Kain & Barchfeld, 2002). Executive functioning is the range of skills that require goal-directed behaviour, planning, attentional control and inhibition of inappropriate responses. Such studies have suggested that children with ADHD have specific deficits related to planning and inhibition of behaviour (Papadopoulos, Panayiotou, Spanoudis & Natsopoulos, 2005), and that deficits in these areas of functioning give rise to their behavioural problems. The fact that tests of executive functioning suggest that this is where the cognitive deficits in ADHD lie is consistent with the neurological evidence we reviewed earlier. This evidence indicates strongly that children with ADHD have abnormalities in the frontal lobes of the brain, and it is the frontal lobes that control executive functioning.

SUMMARY

The evidence on the aetiology of ADHD indicates strongly that there is a significant genetic component to the disorder. However, it is not fully clear yet whether this genetic component merely bestows a vulnerability for the disorder or whether it may be a direct cause of abnormalities that underlie ADHD. There are clearly some brain abnormalities that characterize ADHD, including reduced overall brain volume, reduced brain volume particularly in areas such as the frontal cortex, basal ganglia and cerebellum, and abnormalities in the frontal lobes, which may contribute to the deficits in executive functioning that are found in ADHD using cognitive tests. Some pre- and perinatal factors have been identified that may contribute to abnormal development. These include maternal smoking and drinking during pregnancy, and complications at birth, including low birthweight. There is also some evidence that dysfunctional parenting may contribute to the behavioural symptoms of ADHD in children, but there is no evidence that dysfunctional parenting is a sole cause of ADHD.

15.2.2 Conduct Disorder

While ADHD is characterized by behaviour that tends to be disruptive and inappropriate, many children exhibit behaviour that appears almost intentionally vicious, callous and aggressive. It is when such characteristics appear that a diagnosis of *conduct disorder* may be appropriate. Behaviours typical of conduct disorder include violent or aggressive behaviour,

> **Conduct disorder** A repetitive and persistent pattern of behaviour involving the violation of accepted social norms or the basic rights of others.

deliberate cruelty towards people or animals, wanton vandalism or damage to property, lying, stealing and cheating, criminal theft and violation of the rights of others (e.g. trespass, threatening behaviour and verbal abuse). The following sections discuss the diagnosis, prevalence and the known causes of conduct disorder.

15.2.2.1 The Diagnosis of Conduct Disorder

The main feature of conduct disorder is a repetitive and persistent pattern of behaviour involving the violation of accepted social norms or the basic rights of others. There are four main categories of such behaviour: (1) aggressive behaviour that harms or threatens to harm others; (2) behaviour that causes vandalism, property loss or damage; (3) deceitfulness, lying or theft; and (4) the serious violation of accepted rules (such as driving violations). These behaviours must also cause severe impairment in social, academic or occupational functioning, and should be found in a range of different contexts such as home, school or the community (see Table 15.4). For a diagnosis of conduct disorder, characteristic behaviours must have been present for at least 12 months.

Plate 15.1
Behaviours typical of conduct disorder include violent or aggressive behaviour, wanton vandalism or damage to property, and violation of the rights of others.

Children or adolescents with this disorder would normally initiate violence or aggressive behaviour and react violently to others. Their behaviour will frequently include bullying or threatening behaviour, and they often initiate physical fights, carry weapons, are physically cruel to people or animals, and intimidate people into activities by threats of physical force (e.g. force others into sexual activity). Individuals with conduct disorder also have little respect for property and will indulge in acts of vandalism and petty theft. Their lying also extends to breaking promises to obtain goods or benefits, or simply 'conning' others into providing benefits or favours. Finally, children with conduct disorder will usually have a history of breaking rules, including staying out late despite prohibitions, running away from home or staying away from school.

There are two main subtypes of conduct disorder based on the age of onset. *Childhood-onset conduct disorder* is defined by the onset of at least one criterion characteristic of conduct disorder prior to 10 years of age. *Adolescent-onset conduct disorder* is defined by the appearance of conduct disorder symptoms only after the age of 10 years. Such individuals are less likely to be physically aggressive than those with childhood-onset type and usually have better peer relationships.

Childhood-onset conduct disorder
A sub-type of conduct disorder defined by the onset of at least one criterion characteristic of conduct disorder prior to 10 years of age.

Adolescent-onset conduct disorder
A sub-type of conduct disorder defined by the appearance of conduct disorder symptoms only after the age of 10 years.

Like individuals with antisocial personality disorder (see Chapter 11), children and adolescents with conduct disorder display little empathy with the feelings and intentions of others, and usually believe that their aggressive reactions to others are justified. They frequently try to blame others for their misdeeds, and exhibit little or no genuine guilt for their antisocial actions. Risk-taking, frustration, irritability, impulsivity and temper tantrums are regularly associated with conduct disorder and result in higher accident rates for such individuals. Conduct disorder is also associated with early onset of a range of behaviours, including

Table 15.4 *DSM-IV-TR diagnostic criteria for conduct disorder*

A   A repetitive and persistent pattern of behaviour in which the basic rights of others or major age-appropriate societal norms or rules are violated, as manifested by the presence of three (or more) of the following criteria in the past 12 months, with at least one criterion present in the past 6 months:

Aggression to people and animals

(1)   Often bullies, threatens or intimidates others.

(2)   Often initiates physical fights.

(3)   Has used a weapon that can cause serious physical harm to others (e.g. a bat, brick, knife, gun).

(4)   Has been physically cruel to people.

(5)   Has been physically cruel to animals.

(6)   Has stolen while confronting a victim (e.g. mugging).

(7)   Has forced someone into sexual activity.

Destruction of property

(8)   Has deliberately engaged in fire setting with the intention of causing serious damage.

(9)   Has deliberately destroyed others' property (other than by fire setting).

Deceitfulness or theft

(10) Has broken into someone else's house, building, car.

(11) Often lies to obtain goods or favours or to avoid obligations.

(12) Has stolen items of non-trivial value without confronting a victim (e.g. shoplifting).

Serious violations of rules

(13) Often stays out at night despite parental prohibitions, beginning before age 13 years.

(14) Has run away from home overnight at least twice while living in parental or parental surrogate home.

(15) Is often truant from school, beginning before age 13 years.

B   The disturbance in behaviour causes clinically significant impairment in social, academic or occupational functioning.

C   If the individual is 18 years or older, criteria are not met for antisocial personality disorder.

sexual behaviour, drinking, smoking, substance abuse and general risk-taking behaviour (e.g. dangerous and erratic driving). Finally, the disorder is more common in males than in females: males with a diagnosis outnumber females by a ratio of at least 4 to 1, and often higher (Zoccolillo, 1993).

It is important to mention at least three issues related to diagnosis of conduct disorder. Firstly, individuals diagnosed with conduct disorder are usually under 18 years of age, and only diagnosed with the disorder at a later age if the criteria for antisocial personality disorder are not met. Secondly, the clinician will need to take account of the social context in which behaviours characteristic of conduct disorder are found. For example, in certain deprived inner-city areas, behaviours characteristic of conduct disorder may be seen as being protective. That is, they may represent the norm for that environment and may serve an adaptive function in dealing with poverty and the threatening behaviour of others. In addition, immigrants from war-ravaged countries can have a reputation for violence because such behaviour has been necessary for survival in their countries of origin. Clinicians must be sure that a diagnosis of conduct disorder is made only when the characteristic behaviours are symptomatic of dysfunction rather than a reaction to a specific social context.

Oppositional defiant disorder (ODD)
A mild form of disruptive behaviour disorders reserved for children who do not meet the full criteria for conduct disorder.

Finally, a related category of disruptive behaviour disorders in DSM-IV-TR is known as *oppositional defiant disorder (ODD)*. ODD is a diagnosis usually reserved for children who do not meet the full criteria for conduct disorder (e.g. extreme aggression and violence) but who have regular temper tantrums, refuse to comply with requests or instructions, or appear deliberately to indulge in behaviours that annoy others. ODD is common in preschool children, and may even be a precursor to later childhood conduct disorder (Lahey, McBurnett & Loeber, 2000). It is found more often in families where child care has been disrupted (through the child experiencing a number of different caregivers) or in families where at least one parent has a history of mood disorders, antisocial personality disorder, ADHD or substance abuse (APA, 2000, pp. 100–101).

15.2.2.2 The Prevalence and Course of Conduct Disorder

Epidemiological studies indicate that conduct disorder may be relatively common, with prevalence rates ranging from 4 to 16 per cent in boys and from 1.2–9 per cent in girls (Loeber, Burke, Lahey, Winters et al., 2000). A more recent US study estimated the lifetime prevalence rate of conduct disorder at 9.5 per cent (12.0 per cent among males and 7.1 per cent among females), with a median age of onset of 11.6 years (Nock, Kazdin, Hiripi & Kessler, 2006).

The most significant symptoms of conduct disorder begin to appear between middle childhood to middle adolescence, although ODD is a common precursor to conduct disorder in the preschool years. In a majority of individuals the disorder remits by adulthood, but some do go on to meet the criteria for antisocial personality disorder. Indeed, studies suggest that childhood conduct disorder (but not childhood ADHD) predicts antisocial personality disorder in adulthood, but only in lower socioeconomic-status families (Lahey, Loeber, Burke & Applegate, 2005). Children with conduct disorder are also more likely to develop into adulthood with antisocial personality disorder if they have a parent with antisocial personality disorder or have low verbal IQ (Lahey, Loeber, Hart, Frick et al., 1995).

Finally, we have already indicated that conduct disorder prevalence rates for boys are significantly higher than for girls. The disorder also manifests differently in boys and girls. In boys, the main behaviours are aggressive and violent behaviour, fighting, stealing, damage to property and school problems. However, for girls, the most common behaviours are petty theft (such as shoplifting), lying, running away from home, avoiding school and prostitution (Robins, 1991). Indeed, these differential behaviours may have a direct impact on gender differences in prevalence rates since the crimes indulged in by girls (e.g. shoplifting) are often considered less serious than the violent crimes committed by boys, who are usually considered more likely to commit crimes than girls (Zahn-Waxler, 1993).

15.2.2.3 The Aetiology of Conduct Disorder: Biological Factors

Genetic Factors There is now some evidence that conduct disorder and its associated behaviours of aggressiveness and criminality may have a genetic component. Twin studies specifically involving conduct disorders have found a significant genetic influence (Slutske, Heath, Dinwiddie, Madden et al., 1997; Ehringer, Rhee, Young, Corley et al., 2006). Twin studies also suggest that aggressive and violent behaviour (e.g. fighting, cruelty to animals) has a significant inherited component (Edelbrock, Rende, Plomin & Thompson, 1995). Adoption studies have also reported significant genetic and environmental influences on both conduct disorder and criminal behaviour (Simonoff, 2001). Some recent studies have even identified a specific gene, GABRA2, which is associated with childhood conduct disorder (Dick, Bierut, Hinrichs, Fox et al., 2006). Interestingly, this gene is also related to adult alcohol dependency and drug dependency in adolescence. What these studies suggest is that there is probably an inherited component to conduct disorder, perhaps in the form of inherited temperamental characteristics, but that environmental factors also play a major role in determining behaviour patterns typical of conduct disorder.

Neuropsychological Deficits Just as with ADHD, conduct disorder is associated with neuropsychological deficits in cognitive functioning, including deficits in executive functioning (planning and self-control), verbal IQ and memory (Lynam & Henry, 2001). Low IQ is also associated with conduct disorder and is particularly associated with early-age onset conduct disorder independently of related socioeconomic factors such as poverty, race or poor educational attainment (Lynam, Moffitt & Stouthamer-Loeber, 1993). Nevertheless, there is some doubt about whether executive functioning deficits occur in conduct disorder in the absence of ADHD symptoms. For example, Oosterlaan, Scheres and Sergeant (2005) found that while executive functioning deficits were found in children with comorbid conduct disorder and ADHD, no deficits were found in children diagnosed solely with either ODD or conduct disorder.

Prenatal Factors A number of prenatal factors have been identified in the aetiology of conduct disorder. These include maternal smoking and drinking during pregnancy and prenatal and postnatal malnutrition. Maternal smoking has been found to predict the early emergence of conduct problems in the offspring, especially socially resistant and impulsively aggressive behaviour (Wakschlag, Pickett, Kasza & Loeber, 2006), but this may be restricted to mothers and children of low socioeconomic status (Monteaux, Blacker, Biederman, Fitzmaurice et al., 2006). Similarly, delinquent behaviour and poor moral judgement have been found to be higher in children prenatally exposed to alcohol (Schonfeld, Mattson & Riley, 2005). Recent studies also suggest that externalizing behaviours are associated with prenatal malnutrition, especially deficits in proteins, iron and zinc (Liu & Raine, 2006).

However, we must be cautious about how we interpret all of these findings because correlations between prenatal exposure and conduct disorder may be significantly confounded with other risk factors, such as parental depression, family disadvantage and genetic influences (Maugham, Taylor, Caspi & Moffitt, 2004). If so, prenatal exposure may simply be a risk factor for the development of conduct disorder rather than a direct cause of the problem.

15.2.2.4 The Aetiology of Conduct Disorder: Psychological Factors

The Family Environment and Parent–Child Relationships While studies of the heritability of conduct disorder suggest a significant genetic component to the disorder, they also indicate that important and significant environmental factors are involved. Arguably one of the most important of the latter is the family environment and the nature of parent–child interactions during childhood. It is already well documented that risk factors for conduct disorder and ODD include parental unemployment, having a parent with antisocial personality disorder, disrupted child care and childhood abuse or maltreatment (Frick, 1998; Lahey, Loeber, Hart, Frick et al., 1995). For example, inconsistent and harsh parenting is associated with the development of aggressive behaviour and other symptoms of conduct disorder (Coie & Dodge, 1998). This may be because inconsistent discipline may permit the child to get away with behaving antisocially on many occasions, but when disciplining does occur, the child may learn aggressive or violent behaviour from parents who behave aggressively when disciplining their child. Indeed, there is evidence that children who are physically abused by their parents are more likely to be aggressive when they grow up (Crick & Dodge, 1994), and parents who are physically abusive to their children also report more behaviour problems in their children than non-abusive parents (Lau, Valeri, McCarty & Weisz, 2006). However, whatever the mechanism for the relationship, longitudinal studies are generally consistent in indicating that childhood abuse is associated with criminal behaviour, violence and diagnosis of conduct disorder in later childhood and adolescence (Fergusson, Horwood & Lynskey, 1996; Widom & Maxfield, 1996).

In addition to childhood abuse, conduct disorder has been shown to be associated with family environments that are less cohesive, have few intellectual/cultural pursuits, greater levels of family conflict and higher levels of parental stress (Blader, 2006; George, Herman & Ostrander, 2006). Interestingly, many of these familial characteristics associated with conduct disorder are also very closely linked to poverty and social deprivation. We will look at how this socioeconomic factor may influence aetiology on p. 547.

Media and Peer Influences Many children may develop antisocial and aggressive behaviour because they simply mimic the violent activities they see around them in the media or displayed

'ISN'T IT NICE TO SEE THEM USING THEIR KNIFE AND FORK?'

Plate 15.2
Inconsistent and harsh parenting is often associated with the development of symptoms of conduct disorder in children.

by their peers. Statistics from the USA suggest that between 1980 and 1995, violent crime by juveniles increased by over 50 per cent (US Bureau of the Census, 1997), which may be due, at least in part, to the increasing levels of violence viewed by children on TV and in video games. However, while there is some evidence that television violence contributes to children's levels of aggressiveness and subsequent criminality (Hughes & Hasbrouck, 1996), more recent studies tend to suggest that media violence has its effect primarily on children who are already emotionally and psychiatrically disturbed. Studies have demonstrated an effect of violent TV programmes on behavioural and physiological measures of aggression only in children who already have a diagnosis of ADHD, ODD, conduct disorder or disruptive behavioural disorders generally (Grimes, Vernberg & Cathers, 1997; Grimes, Bergen, Nichols, Vernberg et al., 2004).

A more important source of mimicry may be peer behaviour. There is already evidence suggesting that associating with peers who indulge in violent or criminal behaviour is likely to increase one's own delinquent behaviour (Capaldi & Patterson, 1994). In fact, a vicious cycle may develop in which associating with aggressive peers may expose the individual to increasing levels of community violence (e.g. gang fights, violent assaults and robbery). This in turn will facilitate mimicry of violence and increase the perception of violent behaviour being the norm (Lambert, Ialongo, Boyd & Cooley, 2005). However, what is not clear from this research is whether children who already have antisocial and aggressive tendencies choose to mix with similar peers in the first place, so the peer association may merely increase pre-existing tendencies rather than create delinquent behaviour from scratch. There is some evidence that deviant peer affiliation is associated with later antisocial behaviour and substance abuse only in children who already display symptoms of ODD and conduct disorder. Deviant peer affiliation only weakly predicts future anti-social behaviour in individuals without these initial symptoms (Marshal & Molina, 2006).

Another view is that peer factors may facilitate symptoms of conduct disorder in a more indirect way. For example, being rejected by peers has been shown to cause increased aggressiveness, especially in children who have an existing disruptive behaviour disorder such as ADHD (Hinshaw & Melnick, 1995). This may also lead to a vicious cycle, as peers continue to reject adolescents who exhibit increasing levels of antisocial behaviour (Kelly, Jorm & Rodgers, 2006).

In summary, media and peer mimicry effects only appear to facilitate antisocial and aggressive behaviour in those children and adolescents who already display symptoms of conduct disorder. As such, they probably represent mediating variables rather than true causes of the disorder.

Cognitive Factors Conduct disorder is associated with the development of deviant moral awareness. For example, most children grow up learning that certain behaviours are morally acceptable and others are morally and socially unacceptable. However, children with conduct disorder fail to acquire this moral awareness. They are content to achieve their goals using violence and deceit, have little respect for the rights of others, and show little or no remorse for their antisocial acts. Much of this lack of awareness of moral standards may come from the fact that they have developed highly biased ways of interpreting the world. For example, a child with conduct disorder regularly interprets the behaviour of others as hostile or challenging, and this appears to give rise to their aggressive reactions.

Dodge (1991, 1993) has proposed a social-information processing model of antisocial and aggressive behaviour in which a history of trauma, abuse, deprivation and insecure attachment may give rise to specific information processing biases. These biases include hypervigilance for hostile cues and attributing minor provocations to hostile intent, giving rise to unwarranted fear and to aggressive reactions. If children are brought up in a family environment where they learn aggressive behaviour in child–parent interactions (Patterson, Reid & Dishion, 1992), and if they also have their own experiences with successful aggressive tactics, they will evaluate aggression as an adaptive social strategy and use it proactively (see Figure 15.2). In support of this hypothesis, Gouze (1987) found that aggressive children direct their attention selectively towards hostile social cues and have difficulty diverting their attention away from these cues.

Aggressive children also exhibit what is called a **_hostile attributional bias_** (Nasby, Hayden & DePaulo, 1979), in which they will interpret not only ambiguous cues as signalling hostility, but also many cues which are generated by benign intentions (e.g. Dodge, Bates & Pettit, 1990). Once a hostile attribution is made, studies suggest that there is a 70 per cent probability of an aggressive response, compared with only 25 per cent probability following a benign attribution (Dodge, 1991). Because of such information

Hostile attributional bias The tendency of individuals to interpret not only ambiguous cues as signalling hostility, but also many cues that are generated with benign intentions.

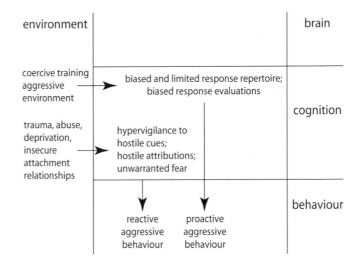

Figure 15.2

Dodge's (1991) social-information processing model of antisocial and aggressive behaviour in which a history of trauma, abuse, deprivation and insecure attachment gives rise to information processing biases, including a tendency to interpret even benign cues as signalling hostility.

Source: Krol, Morton & De Bruyn (2004).

processing and attributional biases, individuals with conduct disorder may be locked into a cycle of hostile interpretations and aggressive responding that becomes difficult to break – especially as continued aggressive behaviour by sufferers is likely to generate genuine hostile intentions from others in the future.

Socioeconomic Factors Delinquent, violent behaviour has been shown to be highly associated with poverty, low socioeconomic class, unemployment, urban living and poor educational achievement. Such factors may be a cause of conduct disorder rather than a consequence of it (Lahey, Miller, Gordon & Riley, 1999). Poverty in turn is likely to give rise to disrupted family life, parental stress, poor educational opportunities and parental neglect – all of which may be contributing factors to the development of conduct disorder.

An instructive study by Costello, Compton, Keeler and Angold (2003) suggests that poverty *per se* does have a direct causal effect on the level of conduct disorder in a local population. They studied conduct disorder in Native American children before and after a casino opened on their reservation which provided income that moved many families out of poverty. This constituted an interesting natural experiment on the role of poverty in childhood disorders. Before the casino opened, children of poor families suffered more symptoms of psychopathology than those of non-poor families. However, after the casino had opened, the children of those families who moved from the poor to non-poor class showed a significant drop in symptoms of conduct disorder and ODD. Levels of these symptoms in families who remained poor after the casino opened did not change. This study provides a striking example of how poverty may represent a genuine causal factor for conduct disorder. However, the exact mechanisms that mediate the relationship between poverty and conduct disorder remain unclear.

SUMMARY

This section has indicated that conduct disorder may have a number of contributing causes. First, there is a significant genetic element that may be related to the inheritance of temperamental factors. However, studies also implicate significant environmental factors in the aetiology of conduct disorder. Certain types of familial environments and parent–child relationships are risk factors for the development of conduct disorder, particularly family environments with disrupted child care, childhood abuse and maltreatment, and inconsistent parenting. Some theories suggest that early experience with maladaptive and abusive parenting may give rise to information processing biases that lead the child to attend to and interpret most social cues as indicative of hostile intent, which generates aggressive responding. There is some modest evidence that media and peer influences may also facilitate aggressive and antisocial behaviour, but only in children who already display symptoms of conduct disorder and ODD. Finally, low socio-economic status and poverty are closely linked with the development of conduct disorder, and at least one study suggests that the link may be causal. However, as yet, the mechanisms by which poverty may cause antisocial and aggressive behaviour in children are unclear.

SELF-TEST QUESTIONS

- Can you name the main symptoms of attention deficit hyperactivity disorder (ADHD)?
- What are the different sub-types of ADHD, and what other disorders is ADHD likely to be comorbid with?
- What is the evidence that ADHD is genetically determined?
- How might deficits in executive functioning cause ADHD symptoms?
- What prenatal factors have been identified as risk factors for ADHD?
- How might parent–child interactional styles exacerbate the symptoms of ADHD?
- Do children diagnosed with ADHD have a theory of mind (TOM) deficit?
- What are the four main categories of symptoms found with conduct disorder?
- What is oppositional defiant disorder (ODD) and how does it differ from conduct disorder?
- Can you summarize the biological factors that may be involved in the aetiology of conduct disorder?
- What is the evidence that children develop symptoms typical of conduct disorder by mimicking the violent activities they see around them in the media or displayed by peers?
- How can interpretation biases account for behaviours typical of conduct disorder?
- What socioeconomic variables act as risk factors for conduct disorder?

SECTION SUMMARY

15.2 Disruptive Behaviour Problems

- **Disruptive behaviour disorders** are characterized by impulsive, disruptive and poorly controlled behaviour.

- The two main disruptive behaviour disorders are **attention deficit hyperactivity disorder (ADHD)** and **conduct disorder**.

- ADHD can manifest itself as **lack of attention**, **hyperactivity** or **impulsivity**.

- Around 3–7 per cent of school-age children worldwide are estimated to be diagnosed with ADHD.

- ADHD significantly affects **educational achievement** and **social integration**.

- ADHD appears to have a significant **inherited** component, ranging between 60 and 90 per cent.

- ADHD is associated with **smaller brain size**, deficits in **executive functioning** and **abnormalities** in the **cerebellum**.

- **Dysfunctional parent–child interactions** may contribute to ADHD, but there is no evidence to suggest these are a sole cause of the disorder.

- **Conduct disorder** is characterized by behaviour that is aggressive, causes vandalism, property loss or damage; by deceitfulness and lying; and by serious violation of accepted rules.

- **Oppositional defiant disorder (ODD)** is a milder form of disruptive behaviour disorders reserved for children who do not meet the full criteria for conduct disorder.

- Prevalence rates for conduct disorder are estimated at 4–16 per cent for boys and 1.2–9 per cent for girls.

- Both **genetic** and **environmental** factors appear to be important in the aetiology of conduct disorder.

- **Psychological factors** influencing conduct disorder symptoms include the nature of the family environment, parent–child relationships and media and peer influences.

- Individuals with conduct disorder appear to develop an **information bias** in which they interpret the benign intentions of others as hostile.

15.3 CHILDHOOD ANXIETY AND DEPRESSION

Frank's Story at the beginning of this chapter graphically illustrates some of the distress experienced by children who are exposed to uncertainty and stress early in their lives. As a result of the loss of his parents and being moved to a foster home, Frank experiences a range of emotions, including rejection, fear, confusion, anger, hatred and misery. By their very nature, children are emotionally naive and will often be unable to label the feelings they experience: they may only know that they feel bad and confused. As was the case with Frank, these feelings often lead the child to become withdrawn and inward-looking (behaviour which the clinician may label as representing an *internalizing disorder*), and may serve as the basis for future disorders in adolescence and early adulthood. All of these factors make it difficult for clinicians to identify childhood anxiety and depression. Children who are anxious and depressed tend to be clinging and demanding of their parents and carers, will go to great lengths to avoid some activities such as school, and express exaggerated fears, especially of events such as separation from, or the death of, a parent or carer. There has been some success recently in identifying specific disorders in childhood, such as separation anxiety disorder, early-onset generalized anxiety disorder (GAD) and obsessive-compulsive disorder (OCD). However, anxiety and depression are frequently comorbid in childhood (Manassis & Monga, 2001), and treatment may need to target both conditions. We now continue by looking separately at the characteristics and known causes of childhood anxiety and childhood depression.

15.3.1 Childhood Anxiety

In childhood, anxiety is primarily manifested as withdrawn behaviour (internalizing). Children avoid activities where they may have to socialize with others (e.g. school), are clinging and demanding of parents and carers (to the point of following a parent from room to room), express a desire to stay at home, and communicate exaggerated fears over such things as the death of carers or of being bullied by peers. Children are less concerned than adults about the specific symptoms of their anxiety, but they do tend to report significantly more somatic complaints than non-anxious children (Hofflich, Hughes & Kendall, 2006). Many childhood anxiety disorders are recognizable as those also found in adulthood (e.g. GAD, OCD, social phobia). However, at least some manifestations of childhood anxiety are confined to childhood, and separation anxiety is one such example.

15.3.1.1 The Features and Characteristics of Childhood Anxiety Problems

Separation Anxiety As the name suggests, *separation anxiety* is an intense fear of being separated from parents or carers. It is commonly found in many children at the end of the first year of life, but in most children this fear gradually

> **Separation anxiety** A childhood anxiety problem involving an intense fear of being separated from parents or carers.

subsides. However, in others it persists well into the school years and may also reappear in later childhood following a period of stress or trauma. Older children with separation disorder become distressed at being away from home and often need to know the whereabouts of parents. They may also develop exaggerated fears that their parents will become ill, die or be unable to look after them (see Table 15.5). Consequences of this anxiety include reluctance to attend school or stay at friends' homes overnight, and many children will require a parent or carer to stay with them at bedtime until they have fallen asleep. As with most childhood anxiety disorders, sufferers also report physical complaints such as stomach aches, headaches, nausea and vomiting. Separation anxiety is often a normal feature of early development, but it can be triggered and exaggerated by specific life stressors, such as the death of a relative or pet, an illness, a change of schools or moving home.

The estimated prevalence rate of diagnosable separation anxiety is between 2 and 5 per cent of all children and adolescents (Silove & Manicavasagar, 2001), although the disorder tends to be relatively unstable over time and has a high incidence of spontaneous remission (Cantwell & Baker, 1989). However, once they have reached the age for school attendance, many children suffering separation disorder go on to exhibit school refusal problems (Egger, Costello & Angold, 2003).

Obsessive-Compulsive Disorder (OCD) *Obsessive-compulsive disorder (OCD)* is now recognized as a relatively common anxiety disorder found in childhood. Its phenomenology is very similar to adult OCD, with the main

> **Obsessive-compulsive disorder (OCD)** A disorder characterized either by obsessions (intrusive and recurring thoughts that the individual finds disturbing and uncontrollable) or by compulsions (ritualized behaviour patterns that the individual feels driven to perform in order to prevent some negative outcome heppening).

features of the disorder in children manifesting as intrusive, repetitive thoughts, obsessions and compulsions (see Chapter 5, section 5.5). The most common obsession themes in children are contamination, aggression (harm or death), symmetry and exactness; in adolescence, religious and sexual obsessions become common (Geller, Biederman, Faraone, Agranat et al., 2001). Common compulsive behaviours in children and adolescents include washing, checking, ordering, touching, repeating and reassurance-seeking, as well as covert behaviours such as reviewing or cancelling thoughts, silent prayers or counting (Franklin, Kozak, Cashman, Coles et al., 1998). In adults, compulsions (e.g. behavioural rituals) are rarely found without accompanying obsessions (e.g. intrusive thoughts), but in children compulsions without obsessions can be quite common. They are frequently tactile (e.g. touching, tapping or rubbing rituals) and may be accompanied by behavioural tics (Leckman, Grice, Barr, de Vries et al., 1995) (see Case History 15.2).

Age of onset for childhood OCD can be as early as 3–4 years of age, but the mean age of onset is more likely to be around 10 years (Swedo, Rapoport, Leonard, Lenane et al., 1989). Childhood OCD is regularly found to be comorbid with a range of other disorders, including *tic disorders*, *Tourette's syndrome* (see Focus Point 15.1), other anxiety disorders and

> **Tic disorders** Uncontrollable physical movements such as facial twitches, rapid blinking or twitches of the mouth.

> **Tourette's syndrome** A disorder in which motor and vocal tics occur frequently throughout the day for at least 1 year.

Table 15.5 *DSM-IV-TR diagnostic criteria for separation anxiety*

A   Developmentally inappropriate and excessive anxiety concerning separation from home of from those to whom the individual is attached, as evidenced by three (or more) of the following:

   (1)   Recurrent excessive distress when separation from home or major attachment figures occurs or is anticipated.

   (2)   Persistent and excessive worry about losing, or about possible harm befalling, major attachment figures.

   (3)   Persistent and excessive worry that an untoward event will lead to separation from a major attachment figure (e.g. getting lost or being kidnapped).

   (4)   Persistent reluctance or refusal to go to school or elsewhere because of fear of separation.

   (5)   Persistently and excessively fearful or reluctant to be alone or without major attachment figures at home or without significant adults in other settings.

   (6)   Persistent reluctance or refusal to go to sleep without being near a major attachment figure or to sleep away from home.

   (7)   Repeated nightmares involving the theme of separation.

   (8)   Repeated complaints of physical symptoms (such as headaches, stomach aches, nausea or vomiting) when separation from major attachment figures occurs or is anticipated.

B   The duration of the disturbance is at least 4 weeks.

C   The onset is before age 18 years.

D   The disturbance causes clinically significant distress or impairment in social, academic (occupational) or other important areas of functioning.

E   The disturbance does not occur exclusively during the course of a pervasive developmental disorder, schizophrenia or other psychotic disorder.

CASE HISTORY 15.2

Childhood and adolescent OCD

Andy was a 13-year-old boy diagnosed with isolated testicular relapse of acute lymphoblastic leukemia 40 days before coming to psychiatric attention. He was first diagnosed with acute lymphoblastic leukemia at age 10. After his initial diagnosis, he experienced remission at the end of chemotherapy induction and finished his treatment for acute lymphoblastic leukemia.

Three years later he began further drug treatment for his leukemia. The psychiatric consultation-liaison service evaluated him after he expressed bothersome obsessive thoughts, compulsive behaviors and insomnia beginning 24–36 hours after completing a 28-day course of steroid drug treatment. Andy had no history of psychiatric illness or treatment.

At his initial interview, Andy described increasingly troublesome obsessions over the previous 2 days. He felt that he was 'going crazy' and feared that he would forget how to talk and lose his cognitive abilities. He repeated mantras, reassuring himself that if he remained calm, these thoughts would pass. He sought reassurance from his mother and the interviewers, and repeated the 'ABCs' to reassure himself that he could think clearly. His mood was dysphoric, which he attributed to both insomnia and worry surrounding his constant bombardment of unwanted thoughts. He reported no depressive symptoms, perceptual disturbances or suicidal thoughts. He displayed no manic symptoms.

Andy's symptoms rapidly worsened within 24 hours. His thoughts became dominated by fears that he would be condemned to hell and that he deserved this fate. He noted images in his mind of self-harm and harming family members. He struggled against these thoughts and images, as well as guilt from having them, by repeatedly telling family members that he loved them. He continued to deteriorate and struck himself in the head with the blunt end of an axe. He stated that he had no desire to die but had become convinced of the validity of the emerging thoughts that he should harm himself. Although he did not sustain serious injury, he was admitted to a child and adolescent psychiatric inpatient unit for safety.

Source: adapted from Morris, Meighen & McDougle (2005)

Clinical Commentary:

Andy's symptoms are typical of many adolescents suffering OCD. In his case, these are obsessive thoughts about going mad and harming himself and others. In an attempt to try to prevent his obsessive thoughts entering consciousness, he indulges in protective behaviours such as repeating mantras, seeking reassurance from adults and reciting the alphabet. The symptoms appear to be precipitated by a stressful illness, and such stressors are common precursors of OCD symptoms in both children and adults. OCD symptoms would normally appear very slowly and have a gradual onset, unlike Andy's, which appeared very rapidly over a period of a few weeks. Such rapid acquisition may have been facilitated by the abrupt cessation of steroid drugs that he was receiving as part of his treatment for leukaemia.

FOCUS POINT 15.1

Childhood OCD, tic disorder and Tourette's syndrome

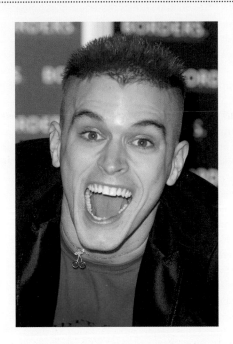

In 2006, 24-year-old Pete Bennett was the winner of Channel 4's seventh *Big Brother* competition. He attracted early attention because he has Tourette's syndrome, which causes him to twitch and swear involuntarily. Tourette's syndrome (also known as Tourette's or TS) is a disorder with onset in childhood, characterized by the presence of multiple physical (motor) tics and at least one vocal (phonic) tic. It is important to understand that

these are chronic and involuntary. Someone with TS may be able to suppress them for a period, but eventually they have to let the tics out. While in the Big Brother house, Pete Bennett frequently found himself swearing involuntarily and shouting 'w*****s' at his startled housemates.

Tics usually start in childhood around the age of 7 and are likely to persist throughout life, though the symptoms often decrease towards the end of adolescence. The first symptoms are usually facial tics such as rapid blinking or twitches of the mouth, but TS may start with sounds such as throat clearing and sniffing, or even with multiple tics of movements and sounds. Tourette's syndrome and behavioural tics are often comorbid with a diagnosis of OCD in childhood. Studies suggest that up to 60 per cent of children seeking treatment for OCD have a life-time history of tics (Leonard, Lenane, Swedo, Rettew et al., 1992), and some theorists believe that OCD is a heterogeneous disorder with an inherited component that can manifest either as OCD obsessions or compulsions or as behavioural or vocal tics (Pauls, Alsobrook, Goodman, Rasmussen et al., 1995).

OCD symptoms and behavioural and vocal tics can cause obvious problems for a child, providing a source of anxiety and fear for the sufferer and provoking ridicule and victimization by peers (Storch, Ledley, Lewin, Murphy et al., 2006). The severity of behavioural and vocal tics is usually directly related to levels of stress, so learning how to control stress can greatly reduce symptoms (e.g. by learning relaxation techniques). In some cases a less socially acceptable tic can be replaced with a more socially acceptable one using behaviour therapy methods, and medication can also be used to help control the condition. Treatments normally used with OCD symptoms (such as exposure and response prevention or CBT: see Chapter 5, sections 5.5.3.1 and 5.5.3.2) can also be effective with behavioural tics (Verdellen, Keijsers, Cath & Hoogduin, 2004; Turner, 2006).

---

eating disorders (Geller, Biederman, Griffin, Jones et al., 1996). Specifically, over 60 per cent of children seeking treatment for OCD symptoms also have a lifetime history of tics or Tourette's syndrome (Leonard, Lenane, Swedo, Rettew et al., 1992), and 50 per cent of children with Tourette's syndrome subsequently develop OCD (Leckman, 1993). This suggests that childhood OCD and tic disorder may be different manifestations of the same underlying disorder (Swedo & Leonard, 1994).

Generalized Anxiety Disorder (GAD)

In children, as in adulthood, *generalized anxiety disorder (GAD)*

> **Generalized anxiety disorder (GAD)**
> A pervasive condition in which the sufferer experiences continual apprehension and anxiety about future events, which leads to chronic and pathological worrying about those events.

usually takes the form of anticipatory anxiety, in which the main feature is chronic worrying about potential problems and threats (see also Chapter 5, section 5.4). Even in childhood, GAD is differentiated from other forms of childhood anxiety by being associated with significantly increased levels of pathological worrying (Tracey, Chorpita, Douban & Barlow, 1997), and what children worry about appears to be determined by their age. For example, Muris, Merckelbach and Luijten (2002) found that 4- to 7-year-olds tended to worry about personal harm, separation from parents and imaginary creatures, whereas 11- to 13-year-olds worried more about social threats and being punished. The number of worries also increases with age: the number of worries reported by 8-year-olds is almost double that reported by 5-year-olds (Muris, Meesters, Merckelbach, Sermon et al., 1998). Epidemiological studies have differed in their estimates of GAD in childhood populations: one UK study has estimated GAD in less than 1 per cent of 5- to 10 year-olds, while an American study reports 11 per cent of 6- to 11-year-olds meeting the criteria for 'overanxious disorder'.

Specific phobia   Excessive, unreasonable, persistent fear triggered by a specific object or situation.

Specific Phobias *Specific phobias* are often common in the normal development of children. For example, fear of heights, water, spiders, strangers and separation often occurs in the absence of individual learning experiences and appear to represent characteristics of normal stages through which the child develops. A fear may appear suddenly and intensely, then disappear almost as quickly (Poulton & Menzies, 2002). However, for some children fears may persist and become problematic, preventing normal daily functioning. One such example in childhood is *social phobia*, which often begins in childhood as a fear of strangers. Most children will grow out of this fear by around 2–3 years of age, but some persist with their fear of social situations and may find it very difficult to speak to or be in the presence of strangers. If pushed into social situations, they will often become mute, blush, withdraw or show extreme emotional responses (e.g. burst into tears) (Vasey, 1995). However, children and adolescents with social phobia are usually well adjusted in all other situations that do not involve significant social interaction, for example, at home. This differs from separation disorder, which is characterized by clinging and demanding behaviour at home.

Social phobia   A severe and persistent fear of social or performance situations.

The prevalence for specific phobias in 8- to 9-year-olds is estimated to be around 7 per cent for boys and 10 per cent for girls (Lichtenstein & Annas, 2000), which is very similar to the lifetime prevalence rates reported in adults (APA, 2000, p. 447).

15.3.1.2 The Aetiology of Childhood Anxiety Problems

Childhood anxiety and its associated disorders appear to result from a combination of inherited factors and childhood experiences. Children inherit a temperament that may make them more or less vulnerable to life stressors such as inadequate parenting or physical trauma. In addition, children seem to be particularly vulnerable to learning fear and anxiety through indirect routes, such as information from adults, peers and television (Field, 2006a). We also need to be aware that the kinds of life events that might mean relatively little to an adult can be viewed as extremely stressful for a child, including such events as the death of a pet, an illness, starting school or moving house.

Genetic Factors Twin and familial studies of childhood anxiety disorders tend to indicate a significant, but modest, inherited component. In a familial study of childhood OCD, Pauls, Alsobrook, Goodman, Rasmussen et al. (1995) found that rates of OCD were significantly greater in the first-degree relatives of children with OCD than in the relatives of control participants without OCD. However, the inherited component appeared to be non-specific, since children with OCD were just as likely to have first-degree relatives with behavioural tics as with specific OCD symptoms. In a study of 8- to 9-year-old twins with specific childhood phobias (animal, situational and mutilation fears), Lichtenstein and Annas (2000) found that both heritable and environmental factors (such as trauma, vicarious learning, negative information) were important in determining differences in fearfulness between children. Studies such as these indicate a role for genetic factors, but inherited factors are most likely to be non-specific and determine overall levels of temperament (e.g. baseline levels of fearfulness) rather than specific symptoms. In support of this view, a study of 1,058 pairs of twins aged 8–16 years by Lau, Eley and Stevenson (2006) concluded that levels of state anxiety (anxiety experienced at the moment) are largely determined by environmental factors, but trait anxiety (representing a longer-term sensitivity to anxiety) showed moderate genetic effects.

Trauma and Stress Experiences Table 15.2 provides striking examples of how childhood trauma and stress represent significant risk factors for a range of later diagnosable adult psychological disorders. It is self-evident that these experiences will inevitably cause significant psychological stress during childhood (see *Frank's Story* at the beginning of this chapter). Many of these experiences (such as childhood physical and sexual abuse) represent extreme experiences for any individual, and there are clear links between such experiences and childhood anxiety generally (e.g. Feerick & Snow, 2005; Whiffen & MacIntosh, 2005). However, during childhood, many experiences that seem relatively unexceptional may seem stressful to a child who is relatively inexperienced in the world and can provide events that trigger bouts of anxiety and distress. For example, living with illnesses such as asthma or eczema has been shown to significantly increase childhood anxiety and reduce quality of life (Lewis-Jones, 2006; Gillaspy, Hoff, Mullins, van Pelt et al., 2002), and the death of a pet – to which a child may become significantly attached – can cause prolonged anxiety and depression (Kaufman & Kaufman, 2006). An event such as a minor road traffic accident may be a new and frightening experience for a child, and a common consequence of such an experience is a mixture of PTSD symptoms, anxiety and depression (Schafer, Barkmann, Riedesser & Schulte-Markworth, 2006).

Modelling and Exposure to Information Whether it is in school, at home or through the media, young children are regularly exposed to information about potential threats and dangers. Children are bombarded with violent and threatening images on television and are constantly warned about the dangers of sexual molestation, abduction or drugs. Experimental evidence suggests that information of this kind may be an important source of childhood fears. Field (2006a) and his colleagues have developed a valuable experimental procedure for studying how information about a stimulus or event might cause subsequent fear and anxiety. Children are shown pictures of animals they are unfamiliar with (e.g. toy monsters or rare Australian marsupials) and then given some information about that animal. Some participants are told the animal is benign and friendly, while others are told it is scary and dangerous. In a study with 7- to 9-year-old children, Field, Argyris and Knowles (2001) found that fear beliefs about an animal increased significantly if children had been given negative information about it – but only if that information had been provided by an adult and not by a peer.

Subsequent studies indicate that the fear generated by negative information can be detected using both explicit and implicit measures of fear, will result in behavioural avoidance of the animal, and can be detected up to 6 months later (Field & Lawson, 2003; Lawson, Banerjee & Field, 2007). In addition, most recent studies indicate that the child's levels of trait anxiety facilitate the learning of fear in such situations by increasing biases to attend to stimuli associated with threat information (Field, 2006b). Studies such as these indicate that negative information about a stimulus or event – especially if it is provided by an authoritative source such as an adult – can cause changes in fear beliefs and behavioural avoidance that are relatively long lasting (up to at least 6 months).

Parenting Style Children are highly dependent on their parents or carers for guidance and emotional support during their development, so it is not surprising that dysfunctional forms of parenting may cause psychological and adjustment problems during childhood. Parents may be detached, rejecting, overcontrolling, overprotective or demanding, and each of these different parenting styles may cause anxiety and maladjustment in the child. Research into how parenting style might influence childhood anxiety is relatively underdeveloped at present. However, some studies suggest links between overprotective and overanxious parenting and a child who is overanxious or suffers anxiety separation (Rapee, 1997; Giotakos & Konstantopoulos, 2002), which appears to result from parents' overprotectiveness generating a lack of confidence and feelings of inadequacy in the child (Woodruff-Borden, Morrow, Bourland & Cambron, 2002). Specifically, Rapee (2001) has argued that there may be a reciprocal relationship between child temperament and parenting whereby parents of children with an anxious temperament are more likely to become overinvolved with the child in an attempt to reduce the child's distress. However, this overinvolvement is likely to increase the child's vulnerability to anxiety by increasing his or her perception of threat, reducing the child's perceived control over threat and increasing avoidance of threat. Hudson and Rapee (2002) provided some experimental support for this view by reporting that mothers of children with an anxiety disorder were more likely to be intrusive while the child was completing a puzzle task than were mothers of non-anxious control children.

If overprotective parents appear to generate anxiety in their children, so do parents who are rejecting and hostile. Children who experience rejecting or detached parents also show increased levels of anxiety and are often overly self-critical and have poor self-esteem (Chartier, Walker & Stein, 2001; Hudson & Rapee, 2001). For example, anxiety sensitivity (concern over the physical symptoms of anxiety, such as trembling or shaking) is known to be a factor that mediates emotional distress in both adulthood and childhood and has been linked to exposure to parental threatening, hostile and rejecting behaviours (Scher & Stein, 2003).

Clearly, parenting style is likely to be an important factor influencing the development of anxiety symptoms in children. Both overprotective and rejecting styles appear to have adverse effects and facilitate anxiety and its cognitive and behavioural

correlates (e.g. hypervigilance for threat, avoidance behaviour). Further research is clearly required in this area to clarify the various mechanisms by which such parenting styles have their effects.

15.3.2 Childhood Depression

Depression in childhood is notoriously difficult to identify, and parents and teachers regularly fail to recognize its symptoms – especially in very young children (Tarullo, Richardson, Radke-Yarrow & Martinez, 1995). In early childhood, depression manifests as clingy behaviour, school refusal and exaggerated fears and is also associated with an increased frequency of somatic complaints, such as stomach aches and headaches. By adolescence, as many as 28 per cent of adolescents aged up to 19 years will have experienced a diagnosable episode of depression (Lewinsohn, Rohde & Seeley, 1998). Depression in adolescence manifests as sulkiness, withdrawing from family activities, weight disturbance, loss of energy, feelings of worthlessness and guilt and – in extreme cases – suicidal ideation (Roberts, Lewinsohn & Seeley, 1995). The following sections cover the diagnosis and prevalence of childhood depression, followed by some of the theories of its aetiology.

15.3.2.1 The Diagnosis and Prevalence of Childhood Depression

With some minor amendments, the diagnostic criteria for depression in childhood are essentially the same as those specified for adult major depression (see Chapter 6, Table 6.3; APA, 2000, p. 356). However, some of the symptoms may change with age. Somatic complaints, irritability and social withdrawal are prominent in younger children, but psychomotor retardation (slowed thinking and movement) and hypersomnia (excessive sleeping) are more common in adolescents.

Rates of depression in children are variable and can depend on age. Studies suggest a prevalence rate of between 2 and 5 per cent for younger children (Cohen, Cohen, Kasen, Velez et al., 1993; Lewinsohn, Hops, Roberts, Seeley et al., 1993), which rises to between 4 and 8 per cent for adolescents (Birmaher, Ryan, Williamson, Brent et al., 1996). As we mentioned earlier, lifetime prevalence rates for depression in adolescents is estimated to be as high as 25–28 per cent (Lewinsohn, Rohde & Seeley, 1998; Kessler, Avenevoli & Merikangas, 2001). There are also some gender differences in adolescence, with depression occurring at almost twice the rate for girls as it does for boys (Hankin, Abramson, Moffit, Silva et al., 1998). In addition, depressed girls more often report weight/appetite disturbances and feelings of worthlessness/guilt than depressed boys (Lewinsohn, Rohde & Seeley, 1998). Lewinsohn, Roberts, Seeley, Rohde et al. (1994) estimated that the mean duration of major depression in adolescence was 26 weeks, with longer durations associated with earlier onset and suicidal ideation. Estimates suggest that around 1–2 per cent of adolescents will have made a suicide attempt between the ages of 14 and 18 years (Lewinsohn, Rohde & Seeley, 1998).

Childhood depression is highly comorbid with other psychopathologies, and around half of adolescents diagnosed with depression experience at least one other disorder during their lifetime: 20 per cent will be diagnosed with another anxiety disorder and between 13 and 30 per cent also exhibit a substance use disorder (e.g. alcohol or drug abuse) (Lewinsohn, Rohde & Seeley, 1998). In addition, preadolescent depression has been found to be a risk factor for earlier onset of alcohol use in adolescence (Wu, Bird, Liu, Fan et al., 2006). Comorbid depression has a number of serious negative consequences for children and adolescents. It has been shown to adversely affect academic performance, impair social functioning generally, be associated with increased conflict with parents and increase the risk of suicide attempts (Lewinsohn, Rohde & Seeley, 1995).

15.3.2.2 The Aetiology of Childhood Depression

Childhood depression appears to have only a modest genetic component, so early experience appears to be a more significant contributor to the disorder. As a result, interest in the aetiology of childhood depression has focused mainly on early experiences, parent–child interactions and cognitive factors. We begin by reviewing the risk factors for childhood depression, then assess the evidence for biological and psychological influences.

Risk Factors for Childhood Depression Table 15.6 provides an overview of the risk factors known to be associated with depression in adolescents. These range across: (1) dispositional factors and existing psychological problems; (2) stress experiences; (3) poor coping skills; (4) poor social support; (5) physical health problems; and (5) poor academic performance. The greater the number of these risk factors experienced by an adolescent, the greater the probability that he or she will become depressed in the future (Lewinsohn, Rohde & Seeley, 1998). Taking the relevant risk factors into account, Lewinsohn, Rohde and Seeley (1998) have drawn up a profile of the 'prototypical adolescent most at risk for depression'. This is described in Focus Point 15.2.

In younger children, childhood abuse or neglect is closely related to the development of depression and appears to generate feelings of worthlessness, betrayal, loneliness and guilt (Dykman, McPherson, Ackerman, Newton et al., 1997; Wolfe & McEachran,

Table 15.6 *Risk factors for adolescent depression*

Domain	Specific risk factor
Cognitive	Depressotypic negative cognitions* Depressotypic attributional style*
Dispositional factors and other psychopathologies	Self-consciousness Low self-esteem Emotional reliance Current depression Internalizing problem behaviours Externalizing problem behaviours Past suicide attempts Past depression Past anxiety
Stress	Daily hassles Major life events
Social and coping skills	Low self-rated social competence Poor coping skills Interpersonal conflict with parents
Social support	Low social support from family Low social support from friends
Physical	Physical illness Poor self-rated health Reduced level of activities Lifetime number of physical symptoms Current rate of tobacco use
Academic	School absenteeism Dissatisfaction with grades

* See p. 555, 'Psychological Factors', for a fuller description.
Source: Lewinsohn, Rohde & Seeley (1998).

FOCUS POINT 15.2

The prototypical adolescent at risk for depression

Lewinsohn, Rohde and Seeley (1998) have provided the following description of the prototypical adolescent most at risk for adolescent depression:

The prototypical adolescent most likely to become depressed is a 16-year-old female who had an early or late puberty. She is experiencing low self-esteem/poor body image, feelings of worthlessness, pessimism, and self-blame. She is self-conscious and overly dependent on others, although she feels that she is receiving little support from her family. She is experiencing both major and minor stressors, such as conflict with parents, physical illness, poor school performance, and relationship breakups; she is coping poorly with the ramifications of these events. Other psychopathologies, including anxiety disorders, smoking, and past suicidality, are probably present.

Lewinsohn, Rohde & Seeley (1998), p. 778

1997). Predictors of depression in children younger than 5 years of age include parental marital partner changes, mother's health problems in pregnancy, child's health over the first 6 months of life, maternal anxiety and marital satisfaction early in the child's development, and the mother's attitude towards caregiving (Najman, Hallam, Bor, Callaghan et al., 2005). Many of these risk factors may affect the quality of mother–child interactions during early development, which may be a significant factor in the development of childhood depression (see below).

Genetic Factors Studies of the heritability of childhood depression have been variable in their findings. Twin studies suggest a significant genetic element in childhood depression, but they also indicate a substantial environmental component (Thapar & Rice, 2006). Familial studies have indicated a strong link between parental depression and childhood depression. For example, offspring of parents with major depression have been found to be more psychologically and socially impaired and to have significantly higher rates of depression than the offspring of non-depressed parents (Kramer, Warner, Olfson, Ebanks et al., 1998; Carter, Garrity-Rokous, Chazan-Cohen, Little et al., 2001). While this evidence is consistent with an inherited view of childhood depression, it could also imply that the behaviour of depressed parents creates adverse early experiences that precipitate depression in the child (see later). Finally, the fact that childhood experiences may be significantly more important than inherited factors in causing childhood depression comes from adoption studies. Such studies have provided little or no evidence for a genetic influence on depressive symptoms in childhood (Rice, Harold & Thapar, 2002).

Psychological Factors Two major areas of research into the aetiology of childhood depression are (1) the role of parent–child interaction and (2) the development of dysfunctional cognitions that shape and support depressive thinking in childhood.

We have already noted that children who have depressed parents are themselves more prone to depression. This relationship could be mediated in a variety of ways. Firstly, parents who are depressed may simply transmit their negative and low mood to their children through their interactions with them, and children may simply model the behavioural symptoms of depression exhibited by their parents (Jackson & Huang, 2000). Alternatively, depressed parents may not be able to respond properly to their children's emotional experiences, and thus may leave the child either feeling helpless or unable to learn the necessary emotional regulation skills required to deal with provocative experiences. In support of this view, a study of mother–child interactions by Shaw, Schonberg, Sherrill, Huffman et al. (2006) found that depressed mothers were significantly less responsive to their children's expressions of distress than non-depressed mothers. This suggests that depressed mothers may be less sensitive or less knowledgeable about their offspring's emotional distress, and this lack of responsiveness may facilitate internalizing symptoms typical of childhood depression.

Unfortunately, many parents exhibit symptoms of depression – especially in the immediate post-partum period – and this factor may be significant in generating internalizing symptoms in their infant offspring. For example, Paulson, Dauber and Leiferman (2006) estimated that 14 per cent of mothers and 10 per cent of fathers exhibited significant levels of depressive symptoms up to 9 months after the birth of a child. In addition, mothers who were post-partum depressed were less likely to engage in healthy feeding and sleeping practices with their infant. Depression in both mothers and fathers was associated with fewer positive enrichment activities with the child (e.g. reading, singing songs and telling stories).

As the child grows older, symptoms of depression often come to be associated with dysfunctional cognitive characteristics that may function to maintain depressed behaviour. For example, attributional models of adult depression suggest that the depressed individual has acquired (1) a *pessimistic inferential style* (attributing negative events to stable, global causes), (2) a tendency to catastrophize the consequences of negative events and (3) a tendency to infer negative self-characteristics (see Chapter 6) (Abramson, Metalsky & Alloy, 1989). Research on cognitive factors in childhood depression has focused mainly on the role of pessimistic inferential styles and how they interact with negative experiences. For example, children with a pessimistic inferential style have been shown to be more likely to experience increases in self-reported depressive symptoms following negative events than children who do not possesses this inferential style (Hilsman & Garber, 1995), and a pessimistic inferential style interacts with daily hassles (daily annoyances like losing a key or missing a bus) to predict increases in depressive symptoms (Brozina & Abela, 2006). Such studies suggest that as the depressed child develops cognitively, he or she may develop negative ways of construing events that, in conjunction with negative experiences, act to maintain depressed symptomatology.

> **Pessimistic inferential style**
> The attribution of negative events to stable, global causes.

SELF-TEST QUESTIONS

- Can you name four different types of diagnosable childhood anxiety disorder?
- How might negative information provide a basis for the learning of anxious responding?
- How might overprotective parents generate anxiety in their children?
- How prevalent is depression in childhood and adolescence?
- Can you name some risk factors that may make individuals vulnerable to adolescent depression?
- What is a pessimistic inferential style and how might it contribute to depression in children and adolescents?

SECTION SUMMARY

15.3 Childhood Anxiety and Depression

- Childhood anxiety and depression are known generally as **internalizing disorders**.

- Diagnosable forms of childhood anxiety include **separation anxiety, obsessive-compulsive disorder**

(OCD), **generalized anxiety disorder (GAD)**, **specific phobias** and **social phobia**.

- **Genetic** factors may play a role in childhood anxiety, but probably only by determining general levels of **temperament**.

- Both **trauma and stress** experiences, as well as **exposure to threat-relevant information**, have been shown to cause increases in anxious responding.

- An **overprotective parenting style** may contribute to, or exacerbate, childhood anxiety.

- As many as 28 per cent of adolescents up to the age of 19 years may have experienced diagnosable episodes of depression.

- Childhood depression is highly **comorbid** with other psychological problems and can have detrimental effects on educational and social functioning.

- Studies suggest a **modest genetic component** to childhood depression and a **substantial environmental component**.

- Being reared by a depressed parent may contribute to childhood depression. As the child grows older, he or she may develop a **pessimistic inferential style**.

15.4 SYMPTOM-BASED PROBLEMS OF CHILDHOOD

There is also a range of other important childhood psychological problems that are labelled primarily on the basis of their main symptom. The problems we discuss in this section are enuresis (repeated involuntary discharge of urine leading to bed or clothes wetting), encopresis (lack of bowel control) and somnambulism (sleepwalking). You may also want to look at Chapter 9 on eating disorders since many of the symptoms of eating disorders also appear during early adolescence.

15.4.1 Enuresis

Most children acquire bladder control between 2 and 3 years of age. However, for some children a lack of control will persist beyond that age and they may continue to wet their bed at night or their clothes during the day.

15.4.1.1 Diagnosis and Prevalence of Enuresis

DSM-IV-TR defines *enuresis* as the repeated voiding of urine during the day or at night into either bed or clothes, usually involuntarily. To qualify for a diagnosis, the voiding of urine must occur at least twice a week for at least 3 months, and the child must be at least 5 years of age (see Table 15.7).

> **Enuresis**   The repeated involuntary voiding of urine during the day or at night into either bed or clothes.

Enuresis can be divided into primary and secondary. *Primary enuresis* is when the child has never experienced a lengthy spell of bladder control, while *secondary enuresis* is when bladder control is still problematic but the child has been dry for a period of up to 6 months. Enuresis can occur during the day, but is significantly more common during the night (*nocturnal enuresis*). Primary nocturnal enuresis is more likely to be associated with maturational delay and low birth weight (Jarvelin, Vikevainen-Tervonen, Moilanen & Huttunen, 1988), while secondary nocturnal enuresis is frequently associated with higher incidence of psychosocial factors such as parental separation or disharmony (von Gontard, Hollmann, Eiberg, Benden et al., 1997).

> **Primary enuresis**   Enuresis when the child has never experienced a lengthy spell of bladder control.

> **Secondary enuresis**   Enuresis when bladder control is still problematic, but the child has been dry for a period of up to 6 months.

> **Nocturnal enuresis**   Enuresis occurring during the night.

While enuresis is not necessarily a symptom of more general psychological problems (Butler, 2001), it can have a significant impact on the child's own development and the attitudes and behaviour of parents. For example, children with nocturnal enuresis may experience humiliation, social isolation, fear of detection and a sense of immaturity (Butler, 1994), while van Tijen, Messer and

Table 15.7 *DSM-IV-TR diagnostic criteria for enuresis*

A   Repeated voiding of urine into bed or clothes (whether involuntary or intentional).

B   The behaviour is clinically significant as manifested by either a frequency of twice a week for at least 3 consecutive months or the presence of clinically significant distress or impairment in social, academic (occupational) or other important areas of functioning.

C   Chronological age is at least 5 years (or equivalent developmental level).

D   The behaviour is not due exclusively to the direct physiological effect of a substance (e.g. a diuretic) or a general medical condition (e.g. diabetes, spina bifida, a seizure disorder).

Namdar (1988) found that bedwetting was the most distressing event reported by children after parental divorce and fights. For parents, enuresis is an obvious source of concern to the point where many parents – especially those already experiencing stress – become intolerant of the behaviour, causing an obvious worsening of child–parent relationships.

The prevalence rates for enuresis are typically between 5 and 10 per cent for 5-year-olds and between 3 and 5 per cent for 10-year-olds (APA, 2000, p. 120). Studies of nocturnal enuresis suggest that 15.5 per cent of children aged 7.5 years wet the bed, but most do so once, or less than once, a week. Of these, only 2.6 per cent met DSM-IV-TR criteria for noctural enuresis (Butler, Golding & Northstone, 2005). Epidemiological studies suggest that at age 7 years, the rate of enuresis for boys is around twice the rate for girls, although these rates become more comparable during adolescence (Verhulst, Vander Lee, Akkerhuis, Sanders-Woudstra et al., 1985). As we might expect, enuresis becomes significantly less prevalent with age, although a small minority (1–2 per cent) continue with nocturnal enuresis into adulthood (Hirasing, van Leerdam, Bolk-Bennink & Janknegt, 1997).

15.4.1.2 The Aetiology of Enuresis

As we mentioned earlier, most children with enuresis do not have other psychological problems, and emotional problems are usually a consequence of enuresis rather than a cause of it. There appears to be a significant genetic component to the disorder, with enuresis occurring frequently within families (a child has a 77 per cent chance of developing enuresis if both parents suffered from the disorder, and a 43 per cent chance if only one parent suffered) (Jarvelin, Vikevainen-Tervonen, Moilanen & Huttunen, 1988). Twin studies suggest a significant inherited component, with concordance rates of 68 per cent for MZ twins compared to 36 per cent for DZ twins (Bakwin, 1971).

Developmental and organic problems may represent the most important causes of enuresis. Enuresis may be a result of delayed maturation of CNS control over bladder contractions and CNS responsiveness to bladder fullness. It has also been found to be associated with other indices of delayed physical development, such as delayed standing, walking, speech and language development, and with poor visuomotor and spatial perception and coordination (Koff, 1995; Butler, 1994; Touchette, Petit, Paquet, Tremblay et al., 2005). In addition, children with enuresis tend to have a smaller functional bladder capacity and weak sphincter control (Dahl, 1992), as well as a greater likelihood of disorders of the genito-urinary tract (Watanabe, Kawauchi, Kitamori & Azuma, 1994).

While most evidence suggests that enuresis has a significant organic or delayed physical development component to it, there are still many psychosocial factors that have been linked to the occurrence of enuresis. These include low socioeconomic status of the family, large or overcrowded families, unemployment in the family and large family size (e.g. Devlin, 1991; Essen & Peckham, 1976). Disruptive childhood experiences are also risk factors for enuresis, including parental divorce or separation (Jarvelin, Moilanen, Kangas, Moring et al., 1991) or the introduction of a new baby into the family (Haug-Schnabel, 1992).

In summary, Butler (2004) has argued that a majority of cases of enuresis can be explained by organic or physical/genetic factors causing delayed physical development. Children with enuresis have uninhibited bladder contractions, smaller functional bladder capacities and an overactive bladder. Such children may need to expel urine more frequently, are less able to control their bladder voluntarily, are less able to distinguish physiological cues for a full bladder, and have a greater inability to arouse from sleep when the bladder reaches maximum capacity. Even so, at least some cases of enuresis may be due to stressful life events given the fact that some disruptive family experiences are significant risk factors for enuresis.

15.4.2 Encopresis

Encopresis is a term that refers to the symptoms exhibited by children aged 4 years or older who have not yet learned appropriate control of bowel movements. DSM-IV-TR describes encopresis as the repeated passing of faeces into inappropriate places (e.g. clothing or the floor). Usually this is involuntary, and must occur at least once a month for at least 3 months in children over the age of 4 years for a diagnosis (see Table 15.8). Many children diagnosed with encopresis also suffer constipation, which may be a significant factor in causing involuntary expulsion of faeces. Alternatively, constipation may be a consequence of the fear of involuntary expulsion of faeces.

> **Encopresis** The repeated passing of faeces into inappropriate places (e.g. clothing or the floor), often associated with childhood constipation.

DSM-IV-TR estimates that approximately 1 per cent of 5-year-olds have encopresis (APA, 2000, p. 117), and it is significantly more prevalent in boys than in girls. It is also highly comorbid with a diagnosis of enuresis, with around half those diagnosed with encopresis also exhibiting enuresis (Unal & Pehlivanturk, 2004). Encopresis can cause significant behavioural and emotional problems for a child. These include feelings of shame and embarrassment (Cox, Morris, Borowitz & Sutphen, 2002) and avoidance of social situations in which they may embarrass themselves (Ross, 1981).

Table 15.8 *DSM-IV-TR diagnostic criteria for encopresis*

A	Repeated passage of faeces into inappropriate places (e.g. clothing or floor), whether involuntary or intentional.
B	At least one such event a month for at least 3 months.
C	Chronological age is at least 4 years (or equivalent developmental level).
D	The behaviour is not due exclusively to the direct physiological effects of a substance (e.g. laxatives) or a general medical condition except through a mechanism involving constipation.

Table 15.9 *DSM-IV-TR diagnostic criteria for sleepwalking disorder*

A   Repeated episodes of rising from bed during sleep and walking about, usually occurring during the first third of the major sleep cycle.

B   While sleepwalking, the person has a blank, staring face, is relatively unresponsive to the efforts of others to communicate with him or her, and can be awakened only with great difficulty.

C   On awakening (either from the sleepwalking episode or the next morning), the person has amnesia for the episode.

D   Within several minutes after awakening from the sleepwalking episode, there is no impairment of mental activity or behaviour (although there may be a short period of confusion or disorientation).

E   The sleepwalking causes clinically significant distress or impairment in social, occupational or other important areas of functioning.

F   The disturbance is not due to the direct physiological effects of a substance (e.g. a drug of abuse or a medication) or a general medical condition.

episode usually lasts only a few minutes, and internal stimuli – such as a full bladder – or sudden arousal from non-rapid eye-movement sleep may trigger an episode (Szelenberger, Niemcewicz & Dabrowska, 2005). DSM-IV-TR reports that between 10 and 30 per cent of children have had at least one sleepwalking episode, and between 1 and 5 per cent may meet the diagnostic criteria for sleepwalking disorder.

The causes of sleepwalking disorder are only poorly understood. It takes place during slow-wave or non-rapid eye-movement sleep, and may be caused by a sudden arousal from this stage of sleep (Szelenberger, Niemcewicz & Dabrowska, 2005). Most children with somnambulism also suffer night terrors and 61 per cent have been found to exhibit additional sleep disorders such as sleep-disordered breathing or restless leg syndrome (Guilleminault, Palombini, Pelayo & Chervin, 2003). Predisposing factors for sleepwalking may be a genetically determined tendency for deep sleep and factors that facilitate slow-wave sleep, combined with environmental factors that increase sleep fragmentation, such as stress or anxiety-provoking life events (Klackenberg, 1982). At least some studies have indicated that specific genes may be responsible for causing disorders of motor control during sleep, including REM sleep disorders and somnambulism (Lecendreux, Bassetti, Dauvilliers, Mayer et al., 2003).

SELF-TEST QUESTIONS

- What is enuresis and how might organic problems contribute to its development?
- Can you describe the main features of somnambulism and some of the factors that may contribute to its development?

15.4.3 Somnambulism

Somnambulism   Repeated episodes of complex motor behaviour initiated during sleep. Also known as **sleepwalking disorder**.

Somnambulism, or *sleepwalking disorder*, is often found in children and adolescents between the ages of 6 and 12 years. However, despite being prevalent during this age range, it is categorized in DSM-IV-TR as a sleep disorder rather than a disorder of childhood. Sleepwalking disorder is defined by DSM-IV-TR as repeated episodes of complex motor behaviour initiated during sleep (see Table 15.9). Such episodes usually occur during slow-wave sleep, and so occur most frequently within the first 3 hours of falling asleep.

Individuals are usually unaware that they are moving around, are unresponsive to communications from others, and may be confused when awoken from a bout of sleepwalking. Most frequently, sleepwalking episodes are mundane and unexceptional, but on some occasions sufferers may leave the bedroom, negotiate stairs and even leave the building in which they are sleeping. Some children who sleepwalk may also indulge in complex behaviours such as eating or using the toilet, and may also exhibit inappropriate behaviours, such as urinating in a wardrobe. A sleepwalking

SECTION SUMMARY

15.4 Symptom-Based Problems of Childhood

- **Enuresis** is the repeated involuntary voiding of urine during the day or at night into either bed or clothes.

- Prevalence rates for enuresis are typically 5–10 per cent for 5-year-olds and 3–5 per cent for 10-year-olds.

- Developmental and organic problems may represent the most important causes of enuresis. Enuresis may be a cause of childhood psychological problems rather than a consequence of them.

- **Encopresis** is the repeated passing of faeces into inappropriate places (e.g. clothing or the floor) and is often associated with childhood constipation.

- **Somnambulism**, or **sleepwalking disorder**, is diagnosable in between 1 and 5 per cent of children between 6 and 12 years of age.

- Somnambulism takes place during slow-wave sleep and may be triggered by stress and anxiety.

15.5 THE TREATMENT OF CHILDHOOD PSYCHOLOGICAL PROBLEMS

Many of the treatment methods used with adults have been successfully adapted to treat childhood psychological problems. Children and adolescents with psychological problems often require a multifaceted approach to treatment, necessitating procedures that address one or more of the following issues: (1) specific symptoms (e.g. enuresis); (2) general emotional states and cognitions (such as anxiety or suicidal ideation); (3) behavioural problems (such as behavioural tics, aggressive and disruptive behaviour); and (4) intrafamily relationships (such as issues relating to effective parenting, parent–child communication, or childhood neglect and abuse).

In addition, treatment has to be provided while the child is still a psychologically and physically developing organism, and in the context of possible ongoing educational, social and familial difficulties. It can be seen that this multi-component approach is most likely to require a coordinated provision of supervision and treatment that extends across a range of services, including education, health and social services. Treatment in Practice Box 15.1 provides

CLINICAL PERSPECTIVE: TREATMENT IN PRACTICE BOX 15.1

Children and Adolescent Mental Health Services (CAMHS)

In the 1990s, the UK NHS Health Advisory Service published a wide-ranging review of children and adolescent mental health services in the UK which proposed a four-tier model for planning and delivering mental health services for children. This four-tier scheme has come to be known as Children and Adolescent Mental Health Services (CAMHS). The scheme acknowledges that supporting children and young people with mental health problems is not the responsibility of individual specialist services but requires the cooperation and coordination of all services working with children, whether they are health, education, social services or other agencies.

Details of the four tiers of provision are given below, which provides a rough guide to the services available and the problems treated at each tier. However, not all individual services or individual mental health problems fall into one particular tier. Most children and adolescents with mental health problems are seen at Tiers 1 and 2.

TIER	SERVICES AND AGENCIES INVOLVED	TYPES OF PROBLEMS ADDRESSED
TIER 1	Mainly practitioners who are not mental health specialists: *GPs, health visitors, school nurses, teachers, social workers, youth justice workers, speech and language therapists, voluntary agencies*	• Mental health problems in the initial stages or in mild forms • Offer general advice • Contribute towards mental health promotion • Refer cases to more specialist services if necessary
TIER 2	Practitioners providing services with some mental health focus: *school and GP counsellors, school nurses, paediatricians, family support services, family mediation services, educational psychologists, voluntary sector mental health organizations (specializing in bereavement, domestic violence, etc.)*	• Address problems such as anxiety, sleep disorders, toileting disorders, behavioural difficulties, low mood, adjustment to adverse life events (e.g. bullying, divorce, illness) • More complex cases may need referral to Tier 3
TIER 3	Multidisciplinary teams working in community mental health clinics or child psychiatry outpatient services, providing specialist services for children and adolescents with more severe and persistent disorders	• Severe and persistent cases referred up from Tier 2 • Some cases might come straight to Tier 3, such as psychosis, bipolar disorder, OCD, anorexia, significant self-harm/suicidal ideation
TIER 4	Inpatient services, day units and highly specialized outpatient teams and inpatient units (e.g. *forensic adolescent units, eating disorder units, specialist neuropsychiatric teams, other specialist teams*).	• Similar mental health problems seen at Tier 3, but at the most severe end of the spectrum

an overview of how these coordinated services for childhood mental health problems are structured in the UK under the ***Childhood and Adolescent Mental Health Services (CAMHS)*** scheme. You should bear this structured service in mind when we discuss individual forms of treatment for childhood disorders, because in many countries treatment occurs within coordinated provision structures of this kind.

> **Childhood and Adolescent Mental Health Services (CAMHS)** A four-tier model for planning and delivering mental health services for children in the UK.

In the remainder of this section we look at individual treatment methods that have been applied to childhood psychological problems. The emphasis here is on specific methodologies and how they have been applied. It is important to note that such procedures may often form part of a broader collection of interventions depending on the needs of the individual child.

15.5.1 Drug Treatments

Drug-based treatments of psychological problems in childhood and adolescence are becoming more widely used as we come to understand the effects that various drugs have on children (Walkup, Labellarte & Ginsburg, 2002). SSRIs have been increasingly used to treat childhood depression – especially in adolescents who might be at risk of suicide – and outcome studies suggest that SSRIs such as fluoxetine (Prozac) are more successful at treating symptoms than placebo controls (DeVane & Sallee, 1996). Fluoxetine has also been used in the treatment of childhood anxiety disorders (excluding the treatment of childhood OCD), and clinical trials have found it to be effective in reducing anxiety symptoms and improving functioning generally (Seidel & Walkup, 2006). Nevertheless, there are a number of reasons why we should be cautious about recommending the use of drug treatments with childhood disorders. For example:

1. Complete remission of symptoms is rarely found, especially in the treatment of childhood depression using SSRIs (Treatment for Adolescents with Depression Study Team, US, 2004).

2. SSRIs (whether used for the treatment of depression or anxiety) have a number of undesirable side effects in children, including nausea, headaches and insomnia.

3. To date, outcome studies vary considerably in their trial methodology to the extent that the safety and efficacy of such drug treatments cannot yet be assured (Cheung, Emslie & Mayes, 2005).

4. Doubts about the safety of many antidepressant drugs when used to treat children have been raised in both the USA and UK, to the extent that official warnings have been released in relation to the use of such drugs (Fegert, Janhsen & Boge, 2006).

Despite the difficulties of using pharmacological treatments with childhood anxiety and depression, much greater use has been made of drug treatments in ADHD. US studies indicate that stimulant medication is the most adopted form of treatment for children diagnosed with ADHD, with 42 per cent being treated in this way (Robison, Sclar, Skaer & Galin, 2004).

The most common form of stimulant medication is ***Ritalin*** (methylphenidate), which has been used to treat hyperactive children since the 1950s. Ritalin is an amphetamine which paradoxically has a quietening effect on overactive children, decreasing distractibility and increasing alertness (Konrad, Gunther, Hanisch & Herpertz-Dahlmann, 2004). We are still unsure about how drugs such as Ritalin have their beneficial effects, but it may be that they act on the neurotransmitters noradrenaline and dopamine in areas of the brain that play a part in controlling attention and behaviour. As we saw in section 15.2.1, children with ADHD appear to have some deficits in attention and executive functioning that may be redressed by the effects that Ritalin has on neurotransmitter production. Studies have suggested that amphetamines such as Ritalin are effective in reducing the amount of aggressive behaviour in children with ADHD (Fava, 1997) and can significantly facilitate educational progress (Charach, Ickowicz & Schachar, 2004).

> **Ritalin** (methylphenidate) A stimulant medication that is used to treat ADHD.

However, despite these positive effects, there are still some drawbacks in the use of Ritalin with ADHD. Firstly, while it is effective in reducing symptoms in the short term, its longer-term effects have not been fully documented (Safer, 1997). Secondly, Ritalin has a number of side effects, including reduced appetite, sleeping difficulties, disruption of growth hormone, memory loss and stomach pains. Thirdly, Ritalin is an amphetamine and, as such, can be used as a drug of abuse. There is evidence of adolescents using Ritalin as a recreational drug to obtain a 'high' (Kapner, 2003).

15.5.2 Behaviour Therapy

Behaviour therapy is a useful means of changing quite specific behaviours and can provide learning-based interventions that allow individuals to change old behaviour patterns or learn new ones. Examples of how behaviour therapy has been used in the treatment of childhood psychological problems include: (1) the treatment of symptom-based disorders (such as enuresis); (2) the adaptation of adult behaviour therapy methods (such as systematic desensitization) to use with childhood anxiety disorders; and (3) the development of behaviour change programmes for children with disruptive behaviour disorders.

A widely used classical conditioning method for treating nocturnal enuresis is known as the ***bell-and-battery technique*** (Mikkelsen, 2001). A sensor is placed in the child's underwear when he or she goes to bed. When a single drop of urine is detected by the sensor, it sets off an auditory alarm that wakes the child (see Figure 15.3). This method allows the child to associate the alarm (the unconditioned stimulus, UCS) with the sensation of a full bladder (the conditioned stimulus, CS), so that the child eventually learns to wake up when he or she experiences a full bladder.

> **Bell-and-battery technique** A widely used classical conditioning method for treating nocturnal enuresis.

A WEEK IN THE LIFE OF A CLINICAL PSYCHOLOGIST

Working with Children: A Typical Week in CAMHS

I work in a community CAMHS team (Child and Adolescent Mental Health Services) with five clinical colleagues, and we work from two clinics in different geographical patches.

First thing *Monday* morning is the one time during the week when the whole team meets together. As well as an opportunity to talk about issues affecting the team, this is our chance to discuss referrals that have come in and consider whether we should offer an assessment, recommend an alternative service, or gather more information before deciding. Over lunch I supervise a clinical psychology trainee who is on placement with me for 6 months. We can discuss any issues they are facing. Perhaps they are unsure about a confidentiality issue; for example, a parent is pushing for information about what their teenager is talking about in therapy sessions. We would think together in supervision about what the parent's concerns are, why they might hold these, whether the teenager has disclosed anything that suggests confidentiality should be broken to ensure their safety, or whether it feels important to involve the parent more in the CAMHS work. In the afternoon I have an assessment clinic, where I'll see two to three children and their families who have been recently referred to us. I will try to establish what the current concerns are, why they have arisen, and what needs to be done to help resolve the problems.

Tuesday morning and it's a chance to meet with my colleagues from the wider CAMH service, including other psychologists, working in different localities. We have a business meeting, and also a chance to discuss tricky cases (perhaps involving very complex or inconsistent family systems, very acrimonious or even violent relationships, high levels of risk with regards to self-harm or child protection, and the involvement of multiple professionals) or issues that are of interest to us all, such as new national guidelines or proposed changes to the service. After this, I have my own supervision with a senior psychologist, where I can bring cases for advice as well as exploring my own development as a clinical psychologist.

Tuesday afternoon is clinic time. I will see two or three children or young people for ongoing therapy. This might take the form of just talking, or might involve some play, drawing and games as a way of engaging a child in thinking about difficult issues. Perhaps I'll see a 10-year-old whose fears of what others think of him are getting in the way of going to school, or a 15-year-old with an early history of abuse and rejection who is cutting her arms as a way of trying to cope with feelings of depression and hopelessness. Or I may meet with parents to think about how they can best support their 7-year-old who refuses to do what he is told and shows extreme anger and aggression.

It's *Wednesday* morning, and I am facilitating a group which aims to support parents who have a child with an autistic spectrum disorder. By introducing parents to one another they do not feel so isolated with the difficulties their child has, and they are able to share ideas about what works, and what doesn't! The group is parent-led, so I get to sit back a little and hear the stories they bring.

Once I get back to the office, there is a short time for admin: catching up with my clinical notes, writing letters and reports, and making phone calls to schools, parents, social services, or paediatrics. Working in CAMHS is very much about liaising with other services, as every child exists within systems which influence them. Then it is another clinic for therapy sessions, or perhaps I'll be carrying out more intensive assessments, including psychometric tests or a school observation, perhaps to try to understand why a child might be failing to achieve their potential, or is finding it hard to concentrate in class.

Thursday morning starts with another assessment clinic, followed by our Family Therapy Clinic in the afternoon. In this clinic I work as part of a team, with three colleagues from different professions, including a systemic therapist. One clinician leads the conversation with the family in the room, and the other three form 'the reflecting team', listening to the conversation from an outside perspective, and then sharing our ideas with the family. It's a good time to work together with colleagues and to really focus on the relationships and communication between family members that may be impacting on a problem. For example, perhaps a child's behavioural problem serves a useful function in a family, focusing everyone's attention, so that any thinking about the couple relationship that is falling apart can be avoided. Families can become quite invested in maintaining a problem because change feels too threatening, but family therapy can be a space to consider alternatives and challenge the status quo.

On *Fridays* I have a full day with appointments for therapy and for psychometric assessment. Sometimes, in addition to appointments in the clinic, I'll have a meeting to go to. Perhaps a multi-agency meeting has been called by social services because there are significant concerns about a child's safety or well-being. Or there may be a meeting at a school with regards to a young person struggling to attend school or failing to achieve academically, which may be influenced by their mental health difficulties. Meetings like this are important to ensure that everyone in the system around a child is aware of the issues and are working together to offer the best support.

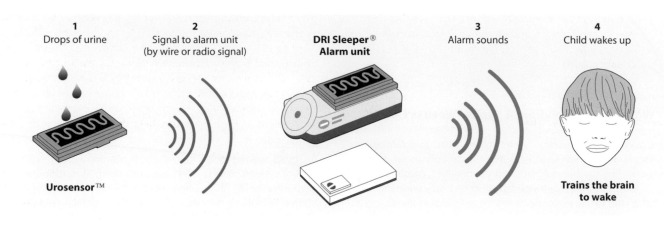

Figure 15.3

The bell-and-battery technique. Drops of urine on the sensor pad set off an alarm that wakes the child; this enables the child with nocturnal enuresis to learn to associate a full bladder with waking up.

> **Systematic desensitization**   An exposure therapy based on the need to expose clients to the events and situations that evoke their distress and anxiety in a graduated and progressive way.

Specific behaviour therapy techniques such as *systematic desensitization* (see Chapter 4, section 4.1.1.2) can also be successfully adapted to treat anxiety-based problems in children (King, Muris, Ollendick & Gullone, 2005), although in vivo methods appear to be significantly more successful than 'imaginal' desensitization, where the child has to imagine being in fearful situations. Sturges and Sturges (1998) report the successful use of systematic desensitization to treat an 11-year-old girl's elevator phobia. Following an injury to her hand in an elevator door, she refused to ride in elevators. The clinicians developed a behavioural hierarchy in which the sequential steps involved the girl approaching and entering an elevator while reciting self-calming statements that she had agreed with the therapists. The child very quickly resumed elevator use with no recurrence of anxiety up to 1 year later.

Selective reinforcement techniques have been used to facilitate academic achievement in children with ADHD and conduct disorder. One view of children with disruptive behaviour disorders is that their disruptive behaviour is positively reinforced by the attention it receives from both peers and adults, and this may especially be the case in the classroom setting. The purpose of introducing a behavioural programme into such settings would be to regularize the reinforcement contingencies in the environment – specifically to ensure that positive behaviours (e.g. attention to the teacher, or thinking through tasks before responding) were rewarded, and disruptive behaviours were not. *Time-out (TO)* from positive reinforcement has been found to be an effective means of reducing disruptive behaviours, including aggressiveness, destruction of property and non-compliance in the classroom (Fabiano, Pelham, Manos, Gnagy et al.,

> **Time-out (TO)**   A means of reducing disruptive behaviours, including aggressiveness, destruction of property and non-compliance in the classroom, by removing the child from the situation and directing him or her, for example, to sit in a specific time-out chair for periods of between 5 and 15 minutes.

2004). In this case, the time-out consisted of the child merely sitting in a specific time-out chair in the classroom for periods of between 5 and 15 minutes. Other studies have established the effectiveness of ignoring non-attention in the classroom (called 'off-task' behaviour) and of rewarding all behaviours that may contribute to the learning task in hand by praising the child. Such behaviours that would be reinforced might include pausing for thought rather than impulsively beginning a task, or communicating appropriately with peers and teachers (Stahr, Cushing, Lane & Fox, 2006).

Finally, *behaviour management techniques* can be used in a range of environments, and can even be taught to parents as an aid to controlling and responding to their children in the home. For example, teaching parents to identify and reward positive behaviour helps to prevent them from focusing on the negative and disruptive behaviours exhibited by children with both ADHD and conduct disorder. This has the effect of facilitating adaptive behaviour in the child and reducing the parents' negative feelings towards the child (Kazdin & Weisz, 2003).

> **Behaviour management techniques**
> Treatment methods that can be used in a range of environments and can even be taught to parents as an aid to controlling and responding to their children in the home.

15.5.3 Family Interventions

Family interventions are popular forms of intervention for many childhood psychological problems, especially since many aetiological models of childhood psychological problems focus on parent–child relationships as a possible cause of the symptoms. Family interventions take a number of forms.

1 *Systemic family therapy* is based on the view that childhood problems result from inappropriate family structure and

> **Systemic family therapy**   A family intervention technique based on the view that childhood problems result from inappropriate family structure and organization. The therapist is concerned with the boundaries between parents and children, and the ways in which they communicate.

organization. The therapist is concerned with the boundaries between parents and children, and the ways in which they communicate (Minuchin, Rosman & Baker, 1978).

Parent training programmes   A family intervention programme which attempts to teach parents a range of techniques for controlling and managing their children's symptoms, used especially with children diagnosed with conduct disorder.

with children diagnosed with conduct disorder (Estrada & Pinsof (1995).

Functional family therapy (FFT)   A form of treatment which incorporates elements of systemic family therapy and CBT, viewing childhood problems as serving a function within the family.

2 *Parent training programmes* attempt to teach parents a range of techniques for controlling and managing their children's symptoms. These are used especially

3 *Functional family therapy (FFT)* incorporates elements of systemic family therapy and cognitive behaviour therapy (CBT). This approach views childhood problems as serving a function within the family, representing maladaptive ways of regulating distance or intimacy between other family members. This type of therapy attempts to change maladaptive interactional patterns and improve communication (Alexander & Parsons, 1982). In this context, you may want to have another look at Treatment in Practice Box 9.1, where Sandy – suffering from anorexia – may be using her eating problems as a means of distancing herself from her parents' conflicts and marriage problems.

These various forms of family therapy have been used with children with conduct disorder, ADHD, childhood depression, anxiety problems and eating disorders. Meta-analyses of systemic and family therapies generally conclude that family interventions have a positive effect when compared with no treatment and some alternative treatments (Hazelrigg, Cooper & Borduin, 1987). However, few studies are yet of sufficient methodological rigour to enable us to make definite statements about the longer-term efficacy of family therapies; sample sizes are small, the age ranges of participants are varied, and there is often a lack of proper randomization in these studies (Cottrell & Boston, 2002).

15.5.4 Cognitive Behavioural Therapy (CBT)

CBT is becoming an increasingly useful treatment method for children and adolescents, especially those suffering from anxiety and depression. CBT is mainly used with adolescents and has been shown to significantly reduce symptoms of both depression (Brent, Holder, Kolko, Birmaher et al., 1997) and anxiety (Manassis, Mendlowitz, Scapillato, Avery et al., 2002). When used to treat adolescent depression, the purpose of CBT is to help depressed individuals become aware of pessimistic and negative thoughts, depressive beliefs and causal attributions in

which they blame themselves for failures but do not take the credit for successes (see section 15.3.2.2). Once these thoughts have been identified, clients are taught how to substitute more realistic and constructive cognitions for the dysfunctional ones. A further goal of the therapy is to increase clients' engagement with behaviours that will elicit positive reinforcement (e.g. Rohde, Feeny & Robins, 2005). Other important components of CBT for adolescent depression that help the efficacy of such treatments include: (1) increasing and improving social interactions; (2) improving problem-solving skills; (3) improving goal-setting and attainment skills; and (4) involving parents closely in the therapy (parents are often the ones who refer their children for treatment, ensure treatment attendance, and may contribute to the child's depression through their own problems and difficulties) (Curry & Wells, 2005).

CBT for anxious children is also constructed to enable children to become aware of problematic thoughts and feelings (Kendall, Kane, Howard & Siqueland, 1990). A typical treatment programme involves: (1) recognition of anxious feelings and somatic reactions; (2) understanding the role of cognitions and self-talk in exacerbating anxious situations; (3) learning the use of problem-solving and coping skills to manage anxiety; (4) using self-evaluation and self-reinforcement strategies to facilitate the maintenance of coping; and (5) implementing a plan of what to do in order to cope when in an anxious situation. CBT has been successfully used to treat a range of childhood anxiety disorders, including OCD, GAD, specific phobias, social phobia and separation anxiety, and has been used with children aged 8–18 years (Chu & Kendall, 2004; O'Kearney, Anstey & von Sanden, 2006). Long-term follow-up studies suggest that treatment gains are maintained over 3 years after treatment (Kendall & Southam-Gerow, 1996).

15.5.5 Play Therapy

Play therapy covers a useful set of techniques that can be used with younger children who are less able to communicate and express their feelings verbally (Carmichael,

Play therapy   A range of play-based therapeutic and assessment techniques that can be used with younger children who are less able to communicate and express their feelings.

2006). Play in itself can have curative properties and can enable children to feel less anxious or depressed. However, it can also be used to help children express their concerns, to control their behaviour (e.g. by learning restraint when a child is impulsive or aggressive), and to learn coping strategies and adaptive responses when experiencing stress (e.g. Pedro-Carroll & Reddy, 2005; Gil, 1991). Through play therapy, children develop a positive relationship with a therapist, learn to communicate with others, express feelings, modify behaviour, develop problem-solving skills and learn a variety of ways of relating to others. As such, play therapy has been used in a range of mental health contexts to control anger and deal with grief and loss, divorce and family problems, crisis and trauma, and has proven useful across a range of childhood psychological problems including anxiety, depression, ADHD, conduct disorder, autism and learning disorders (see Chapter 16) (Landreth, 2002; Bratton, Ray, Rhine & Jones, 2005). Teenagers

Play therapy

Therapist playing with a child using puppets. Child posed by model.

Play therapy is a term used to cover a range of therapies that build on the normal communicative and learning processes of children. Clinicians may use play therapy to help children articulate what is troubling them, to control their behaviour (e.g. impulsive or aggressive behaviour), and to learn adaptive responses when they are experiencing emotional problems or skills deficits. Below are two examples of specific play therapies, one designed to help children practise self-control (the 'Slow Motion Game') and the other to enable children to communicate any distress they are feeling (the 'Puppet Game').

The Slow Motion Game

Therapeutic rationale
It is well known that children learn best by doing. The Slow Motion Game (by Heidi Kaduson; see Kaduson & Schaefer, 2001, pp. 199–202) was designed to have children actively practise self-control over their movements in a playful group context.

Description
Materials needed: Stopwatches for each child, cards (see below), dice, poker chips, paper and colouring materials.

To begin, the therapist introduces the concept of self-control, discussing how it is very difficult to maintain self-control when we are moving too fast. Next, the children are asked to illustrate what fast moving looks like. Once it is clear that the children understand the concept of self-control, each child is given a stopwatch. In the centre of the table are cards created by the therapist with various scenes that the children must act out in slow motion. For example, playing soccer, doing jumping jacks or taking a maths test. The children are instructed to roll the die to see who goes first. The highest number goes first, and that child picks a card and goes to the front of the room with the therapist. The therapist tells the group what that child is going to do in 'very slow motion'. On the count of three, all of the children start their stopwatches. Every 10 seconds, the group

reports to the child performing the task how much time has passed. When the child has reached a full minute, the group yells 'Stop'. Having successfully completed the task, the child receives a poker chip. Then the next child (working in a clockwise direction) picks a card and the game starts again. Once each child has had a turn, the time is increased to 2 minutes, and the second round begins. At the end of the second round, each player will have two chips each, and a snack or treat is provided as a reward. The therapist can also give each child a certificate for 'Achievement in Slow Motion'.

Applications
The Slow Motion Game is successful with any group of children that has difficulty maintaining self-control. Also, common board games can be effectively used to increase children's self-control. For example, Jenga, Operation, Perfection and Don't Break the Ice.

Using a puppet to create a symbolic client

Therapeutic rationale
Puppets serve a crucial role in play therapy. Frequently, children project their thoughts and feelings onto puppets. In this way, puppets allow children the distance needed to communicate their distress. Furthermore, the puppets serve as a medium for the therapist to reflect understanding and provide corrective emotional experiences in the context of the children's play. Most children naturally project their experiences onto the puppets. However, some children are too fearful and withdrawn to become involved in any aspect of therapy. By using the puppet as a symbolic client (a game created by Carolyn J. Narcavage; see Kaduson & Schaefer, 1997, pp. 199–203), the therapist is able to engage these children and overcome resistance. The creation of the symbolic client removes the focus from the child, thereby increasing the child's comfort level and allowing him or her to remain at a safe emotional distance.

Description
Materials needed: Puppets.

Once the therapist recognizes that the child is frightened, the therapist might show the child a puppet, remark that it is frightened, and reassure it of its safety. Next, the therapist should enlist the help of the child in comforting the puppet. By completing these few simple steps, the therapist has achieved three essential goals: the therapist has (a) responded and empathized with the child's feelings in a non-threatening manner, (b) begun the child's participation in therapy and (c) started fostering a positive therapeutic relationship with the child. The puppet often becomes a safety object for the child throughout therapy.

Applications
This technique is particularly effective for any child between 4 and 8 years of age who is anxious or withdrawn in the beginning stages of therapy. A variation of this technique would be to have the puppet present with the same problem as the child and to enlist the child's help in brainstorming solutions to solve the puppet's problem.

Source: Hall, Kaduson & Schaefer (2002)

and adults have also benefited from play therapy methods, and the use of these techniques has increased with these client groups in recent years (Pedro-Carroll & Reddy, 2005). Treatment in Practice Box 15.2 provides a couple of detailed examples of play therapies, while more can be found in Hall, Kaduson and Schaefer (2002).

There has been some criticism of play therapy in the past, with critics suggesting that it lacks an adequate research base to justify its use (Reade, Hunter & McMillan, 1999; Campbell, 1992). However, recent meta-analyses of outcome studies suggest that children treated with play therapy function significantly better after therapy than those who have had no treatment (Bratton, Ray, Rhine & Jones, 2005). Play therapy also appears to be effective across modalities, settings, age and gender, and has positive effects on children's behaviour generally, their social adjustment and their personality.

SUMMARY

This section has described a number of different therapy techniques that are regularly used to treat childhood and adolescent psychological problems. Although drug treatments are becoming more common for a number of disorders, there is still some uncertainty about their effectiveness and their safety. Common treatment methods include behaviour therapy, family therapy, CBT and play therapy. These forms of treatment will be adapted to the specific therapeutic needs of the child and often used in a multi-faceted approach to ensure improvements across emotional, educational and social functioning.

SELF-TEST QUESTIONS

- What is CAMHS, and how does it contribute to the treatment of childhood mental health problems in the UK?
- What drugs are used in the treatment of ADHD and childhood depression? What are the risks of using such drugs?
- How have behaviour therapy techniques been adapted to treat childhood behavioural problems?
- What are the different types of family intervention that might be used in dealing with childhood mental health problems?
- How can CBT be used to treat childhood anxiety and depression?
- What is play therapy and what aspects of childhood psychopathology can it be used to treat?

SECTION SUMMARY

15.5 The Treatment of Childhood Psychological Problems

- Treatment for childhood psychological problems requires a coordinated provision of services that extends across educational, health and social services (e.g. **CAMHS**).

- **Drug treatments** are used for childhood anxiety and depression as well as for ADHD, but there are still significant doubts about the safety of many medications used with children.

- **Ritalin** is a stimulant medication that is used to treat ADHD in around half of those diagnosed with the disorder.

- **Behaviour therapy** techniques can be adapted to treat many childhood behaviour problems. Techniques used include the **bell-and-battery technique** for enuresis, **systematic desensitization** for anxiety problems and **time-out** (**TO**) to reduce disruptive behaviours.

- Important family interventions include **systemic family therapy**, **parent training programmes** and **functional family therapy** (**FFT**).

- **Cognitive behaviour therapy** (**CBT**) has been successfully adapted to treat childhood and adolescent depression and anxiety.

- **Play therapy** covers a range of techniques that can be used with younger children who are less able to communicate and express their feelings.

15.6 CHILDHOOD PSYCHOLOGICAL PROBLEMS REVIEWED

There are a number of difficulties involved in the identification, diagnosis and treatment of childhood psychological problems which are not usually encountered in adult mental health problems. Firstly, children are often unable to communicate any distress they are feeling and may lack the self-awareness to identify individual symptoms of psychopathology, such as anxiety or depression. Secondly, childhood psychopathology is a relatively neglected area of clinical research: much of childhood psychopathology was previously rather simplistically labelled as either internalizing (reminiscent of anxiety or depression) or externalizing (exhibiting signs of disruptive and aggressive behavioural problems). However, research in this area has increased significantly in recent years, and we are now able to identify rather specific childhood disorders such as childhood depression, OCD and generalized anxiety disorder, as well as two important disruptive behaviour disorders – ADHD and conduct disorder.

We are still some way from fully understanding the aetiology of most childhood psychological problems, although some do have significant genetic components (e.g. ADHD, enuresis). Others appear to be related to important developmental factors such as the nature of family environment, parent–child relationships and the socioeconomic climate in which the child is being reared.

Treatment for childhood disorders is usually multifaceted, taking place in the context of coordinated provision of supervision and treatment extending across a range of services, including education, health and social services. While drug treatments for childhood psychological problems are being used more widely than some years ago (e.g. the use of antidepressants such as SSRIs for childhood and adolescent depression), there are still significant doubts about the effectiveness and safety of such treatments. More widely adopted are adaptations of adult psychotherapies, including behaviour therapy, family-based interventions and CBT. Play therapy also offers a useful eclectic intervention that can be used with younger children who are less able to communicate and express their feelings verbally.

LEARNING OUTCOMES

When you have completed this chapter, you should be able to:

1 Describe and evaluate some of the difficulties involved in diagnosing and treating childhood psychological problems.

2 Describe the characteristics of at least 2 disruptive behaviour disorders.

3 Describe the characteristics of childhood anxiety and depression.

4 Compare and contrast theories of the aetiology of disruptive behaviour disorders, childhood anxiety and childhood depression.

5 Describe the characteristics of some of the main therapeutic methods use to treat childhood psychological problems, and evaluate their efficacy.

KEY TERMS

REVIEWS, THEORIES AND SEMINAL STUDIES

Links to Journal Articles

15.1 The Diagnosis and Prevalence of Childhood Psychological Problems: Some General Issues

Lahey, B.B., Loeber, R., Burke, J.D. & Applegate, B. (2005). Predicting future antisocial personality disorder in males from a clinical assessment in childhood. *Journal of Consulting and Clinical Psychology, 73*, 389–399.

Zwirs, B.W.C., Burger, H., Buitelaar, J.K. & Schulpen, T.W.J. (2006). Ethnic differences in parental detection of externalizing disorders. *European Child and Adolescent Psychiatry, 15*, 418–426.

15.2 Disruptive Behaviour Problems

Boonstra, A.M., Osterlaan, J., Sergeant, J.A. & Buitelaar, J.K. (2005). Executive functioning in adult ADHD: A meta-analytic review. *Psychological Medicine, 35*, 1097–1108.

Daley, D. (2006). Attention deficit hyperactivity disorder: A review of the essential facts. *Child Care Health and Development, 32*, 193–204.

Dodge, K.A. (1993). Social-cognitive mechanisms in the development of conduct disorder and depression. *Annual Review of Psychology, 44*, 559–584.

Ehringer, M.A., Rhee, S.H., Young, S., Corley, R. & Hewitt, J.K. (2006). Genetic and environmental contributions to common psychopathologies of childhood and adolescence: A study of twins and their siblings. *Journal of Abnormal Child Psychology, 34*, 1–17.

Furman, L. (2005). What is attention-deficit hyperactivity disorder (ADHD)? *Journal of Child Neurology, 20*, 994–1002.

Hill, D.E., Yeo, R.A., Campbell, R.A., Hart, B., Vigil, J. & Brooks, W. (2003). Magnetic resonance imaging correlates of attention-deficit/hyperactivity disorder in children. *Neuropsychology, 17*, 496–506.

Krain, A.L. & Castellanos, F.X. (2006). Brain development and ADHD. *Clinical Psychology Review, 26*, 433–444.

Krol, N., Morton, J. & De Bruyn, E. (2004). Theories of conduct disorder: A causal modelling analysis. *Journal of Child Psychology and Psychiatry, 45*, 727–742.

Nock, M.K., Kazdin, A.E., Hiripi, E. & Kessler, R.C. (2006). Prevalence, subtypes, and correlates of DSM-IV conduct disorder in the national comorbidity survey replication. *Psychological Medicine, 36*, 699–710.

Seidman, L.J. (2006). Neuropsychological functioning in people with ADHD across the lifespan. *Clinical Psychology Review, 26*, 466–485.

Wladman, I.D. & Gizer, I.R. (2006). The genetics of attention deficit hyperactivity disorder. *Clinical Psychology Review, 26*, 396–432.

15.3 Childhood Anxiety and Depression

Brozina, K. & Abela, J.R.Z. (2006). Symptoms of depression and anxiety in children: Specificity of the Hopelessness Theory. *Journal of Clinical Child and Adolescent Psychology, 35*, 515–527.

Field, A.P. (2006b). Watch out for the beast: Fear information and attentional bias in children. *Journal of Clinical Child and Adolescent Psychology, 35*, 337–345.

Hudson, J.L. & Rapee, R.M. (2002). Parent–child interactions in clinically anxious children and their siblings. *Journal of Clinical Child and Adolescent Psychology, 31*, 548–555.

Lewinsohn, P.M., Rohde, P. & Seeley, J.R. (1998). Major depressive disorder in older adolescents: Prevalence, risk factors, and clinical implications. *Clinical Psychology Review, 18*, 765–794.

Rice, F., Harold, G. & Thapar, A. (2002). The genetic aetiology of childhood depression: A review. *Journal of Child Psychology and Psychiatry and Allied Disciplines, 43*, 65–79.

Shaw, D.S., Schonberg, M., Sherrill, J., Huffman, D., Lukon, J., Obrosky, D. & Kovacs, M. (2006). Responsivity to offspring's expression of emotion among childhood-onset depressed mothers. *Journal of Clinical Child and Adolescent Psychology, 35*, 490–503.

Sheeber, L., Hops, H. & Davis, B. (2001). Family processes in adolescent depression. *Clinical Child and Family Psychology Review, 4*, 19–35.

15.4 Symptom-Based Problems of Childhood

Butler, R.J. (2004). Childhood nocturnal enuresis: Developing a conceptual framework. *Clinical Psychology Review, 24*, 909–931.

Szelenberger, W., Niemcewicz, S. & Dabrowska, A.J. (2005). Sleepwalking and night terrors: Psychopathological and psychophysiological correlates. *International Review of Psychiatry, 17*, 263–270.

Touchette, E., Petit, D., Paquet, J., Tremblay, R.E., Boivin, M. & Montplaisir, J.Y. (2005). Bedwetting and its association with developmental milestones in early childhood. *Archives of Pediatrics and Adolescent Medicine, 159*, 1129–1134.

15.5 The Treatment of Childhood Psychological Problems

Bratton, S.C., Ray, D., Rhine, T. & Jones, L. (2005). The efficacy of play therapy with children: A meta-analytic review of treatment outcomes. *Professional Psychology: Research and Practice, 36*, 376–390.

Brown, R.T., Amler, R.W., Freeman, W.S., Perrin, J.M., Stein, M.T., Feldman, H.M., Pierce, K. & Wolraich, M.L. (2005). Treatment of attention-deficit/hyperactivity disorder: Overview of the evidence. *Pediatrics, 115*, E749–E757.

Cheung, A.H., Emslie, G.J. & Mayes, T.L. (2005). Review of the efficacy and safety of antidepressants in youth depression. *Journal of Child Psychology and Psychiatry, 46*, 735–754.

Cottrell, D. & Boston, P. (2002). Practitioner review: The effectiveness of systemic family therapy for children and adolescents. *Journal of Child Psychology and Psychiatry, 43*, 573–586.

Curry, J.F. & Wells, K.C. (2005). Striving for effectiveness in the treatment of adolescent depression: Cognitive behaviour therapy for mulitisite community intervention. *Cognitive and Behavioural Practice, 12*, 177–185.

Hall, T.M., Kaduson, H.G. & Schaefer, C.E. (2002). Fifteen effective play therapy techniques. *Professional Psychology: Research and Practice, 33*, 515–522.

Kendall, P.C. & Southam-Gerow, M.A. (1996). Long-term follow-up of a cognitive-behavioral therapy for anxiety-disordered youth. *Journal of Consulting and Clinical Psychology, 64,* 724–730.

King, N.J., Muris, P., Ollendick, T.H. & Gullone, E. (2005). Childhood fears and phobias: Advances in assessment and treatment. *Behaviour Change, 22,* 199–211.

Rohde, P., Feeny, N.C. & Robins, M. (2005). Characteristics and components of the TADS CBT approach. *Cognitive and Behavioral Practice, 12,* 186–197.

Turner, C.M. (2006). Cognitive-behavioural theory and therapy for obsessive-compulsive disorder in children and adolescents: Current status and future directions. *Clinical Psychology Review, 26,* 912–938.

Texts for Further Reading

Barkley, R.A. (2006). *Attention-deficit hyperactivity disorder.* New York: Guilford Press.

Chorpita, B.F. (2006). *Modular cognitive-behavioral therapy for childhood anxiety disorders.* New York: Guilford Press.

Fitzgerald, M., Bellgrove, M. & Gill, M. (Eds.) (2007). *Handbook of attention deficit hyperactivity disorder.* Chichester: Wiley.

Herbert, M. (2006). *Clinical child and adolescent psychology: From therapy to practice* (3rd ed.). Chichester: Wiley.

Lahey, B.B., Moffitt, T.E. & Caspi. A. (Eds.) (2003). *Causes of conduct disorder and juvenile delinquency.* New York: Guilford Press.

Lloyd, G., Cohen, D. & Stead, J. (Eds.) (2006). *Critical new perspectives on ADHD.* London: Routledge Falmer.

Nelson, W.M., Finch, A. & Hart, K. (Eds.) (2006). *Conduct disorders: A practitioner's guide to comparative treatments.* New York: Springer.

RESEARCH QUESTIONS

15.2 Disruptive Behaviour Problems

- What is the evidence that ADHD and conduct disorder are part of the same underlying syndrome?

- Why is it that not all hyperactive toddlers go on to develop ADHD?

- Do cultural factors affect the observed prevalence rates of ADHD in different societies?

- There appears to be an important inherited component to ADHD, but what is it that is inherited?

- Do children inherit a genetic vulnerability to ADHD that is converted into full-blown ADHD only if certain environmental factors are present?

- What is the role of prenatal exposure to nicotine in the development of ADHD?

- In what ways might being raised by a parent with ADHD contribute to the child developing ADHD?

- Do children with ADHD have theory of mind (TOM) deficits?

- Do executive functioning deficits occur in conduct disorder in the absence of ADHD symptoms?

- Are socioeconomic factors important in mediating any link between prenatal exposure to alcohol and smoking and the development of conduct disorder?

- Does media violence only increase levels of violent and aggressive behaviour in children who already exhibit symptoms of conduct disorder?

- Are factors such as poverty, low socioeconomic class, unemployment, urban living and poor educational achievement a cause or a consequence of conduct disorder?

15.3 Childhood Anxiety and Depression

- Are childhood OCD and tic disorder different manifestations of the same underlying disorder?

- Risk factors for childhood depression include maternal anxiety and mother's attitude towards caregiving. How might these affect the quality of mother–child interactions and facilitate childhood depression?

- Which is the more important influence on childhood depression, genetics or environment?

- How might having depressed parents cause depression in the child?

15.4 Symptom-Based Problems of Childhood

- Are psychological problems associated with enuresis a cause or consequence of the disorder?

- What is the role of childhood constipation in the aetiology of encopresis?

15.5 The Treatment of Childhood Psychological Problems

- What is the evidence that antidepressants such as SSRIs are effective in treating childhood depression?

- How do stimulant drugs, such as Ritalin, help to control the symptoms of ADHD?

- What do we know about the longer-term effectiveness of family interventions in treating childhood anxiety and depression?

- How can we measure the efficacy of play therapy in the treatment of childhood anxiety and depression?

CLINICAL ISSUES

15.1 The Diagnosis and Prevalence of Childhood Psychological Problems: Some General Issues

- What are the problems involved in attempting to assess a child's psychological problems in the context of the child as a developing organism?

- How do clinicians infer psychopathological internal states in children from overt behaviour?

- How does a clinician decide what behaviour is normal for a particular age?

- How will differences in cultural norms affect whether a child's behaviour is viewed as psychopathological or not?

- How important is it for clinicians to identify and treat a childhood psychological problem as early as possible?

15.2 Disruptive Behaviour Problems

- When diagnosing ADHD, how does a clinician decide whether hyperactivity or inattention is significantly greater than the norm for the child's developmental age?

- How would the clinician establish a diagnosis of ADHD in children under the age of 5 years?

- What are the implications of more boys than girls being referred for the treatment of ADHD?

- How does the clinician establish whether symptoms of conduct disorder are protective rather than symptomatic of dysfunction?

15.3 Childhood Anxiety and Depression

- What are the clinical implications of comorbid childhood anxiety and depression?

- Life events that mean relatively little to an adult may be viewed as extremely stressful by a child. What are the clinical implications of this?

- How might living with illness during childhood affect childhood anxiety?

- How can the identification of childhood depression be improved?

- How do the symptoms of childhood depression change with age, and what implications does this have for diagnosis and treatment?

15.4 Symptom-Based Problems of Childhood

- How can childhood enuresis affect the lives of both children and parents?

15.5 The Treatment of Childhood Psychological Problems

- How is the treatment of childhood psychological problems affected by the fact that the child is a psychologically and physically developing organism and may be experiencing concurrent educational, social and familial difficulties?

- On what basis would the clinician decide to include family interventions in a treatment programme for childhood psychological problems?

16 Learning, Intellectual and Developmental Disabilities

ROUTE MAP OF THE CHAPTER

This chapter begins by describing the way in which learning, intellectual and developmental disabilities are defined and the terminology that is associated with these disabilities. The chapter then proceeds to discuss factors associated with the diagnosis, aetiology and treatment of three groups of disabilities, namely specific learning disabilities (e.g. reading, writing and communications disorders), intellectual disabilities and pervasive developmental disorders (e.g. autistic spectrum disorder).

During childhood, no one knew what I had, I was considered 'crazy' by a doctor at age 1, because I had constant tantrums, which only ended, one day, when my mother took me to the beach during a holiday. My nerves suddenly calmed down, by the sight, and the soothing sounds of the sea. I was beginning to say my first words, and started some progress.

Despite the progress, I still had strange behaviours, like spinning plastic lids, jars and coins. I rejected teddy bears that other toddlers liked, but held on to other objects, like dice (which had a smooth surface and were pleasant to touch). I was terrorized by everyday noises, like planes passing by, thunder, machinery, drills, balloons bursting, and any sudden noise.

Being the firstborn, my mother didn't take notice of behaviours like rocking back and forth, or spending time on a rocking horse in the day care centre as a toddler instead of playing with other kids.

Despite socializing difficulties, my interest for reading and learning the alphabet pleased my mother. Instead of pointing out pictures in a newspaper my mother was reading, I asked her what the letters were, and that prompted her to teach me to read before starting school.

Socially, I had problems that worried people. I was not able to recognize people easily, and was not able to decode non-verbal cues. My mother complained about always having to spell things out to me. While my younger (non-autistic) brother seemed to know instinctively when to bring up a subject, or when to say a joke, I was a nuisance, because I couldn't tell if somebody was angry, sad, tired, etc., just by looking at him/her. I took things literally and was terrorized by my mother's 'threats' which my younger brother did not take seriously. She uttered threats like

'I will send you away' when we behaved badly. My brother was able to understand that she never means it, however I was terrorized by them.

One thing that discouraged socializing was that most others did not like to talk about insects, calculators, or space all the time. Other people liked my subjects 'once in a while' and got angry if I went on and on. My mother constantly reminded me not to talk about the same things over and over. Changing subjects was hard for me. I was fixated on certain subjects like entomology, and arachnology. Nobody cares to hear about the chelate pedipalps of pseudoscorpions.

GEORGE'S STORY

Introduction

Someone suffering from a learning disability may not be able to learn things as quickly as other people. They may have a very specific learning problem: an example of this is a specific reading or writing disorder such as dyslexia. Alternatively, they may suffer wide-ranging impairments in intellectual ability that mean that their contribution to society may be limited and their ability to cope with day-to-day living is impaired. A learning disability is broadly defined as a significant, lifelong condition that is usually present from birth, but it may often not be recognized until the individual fails to reach important milestones in his or her development. Failing to sit up, talk, read or attend to what is going on in the world are all possible signs of a learning disability if these activities do not appear as expected at normal developmental intervals. Most learning disabilities are permanent conditions, but with suitable support and encouragement many people with learning difficulties can acquire practical and social skills even if this may take them longer than normal.

George's Story describes the early life of someone diagnosed with *autistic spectrum disorder*. This involves difficulties in interpreting non-verbal behaviour, impairment in communicating with others, and a repetitive preoccupation with individual objects, activities or topics. This personal account provides a striking insight into how these disabilities can affect normal day-to-day living during childhood. George prefers indulging in stereotyped behaviours, such as rocking, to playing with other children. He is unable to understand both normal verbal innuendo and the non-verbal body language that most of us learn to understand implicitly. This causes him to be seen by others as 'difficult', uncommunicating and 'a nuisance', all of which in turn cause him to feel more anxious and distressed. Most learning disabilities, no matter how specific, cause problems across the whole range of life activities, including educational, social and occupational, but the degree to which sufferers have problems in these areas of functioning will depend on their background and family circumstances as well as on the nature and degree of the disability.

This chapter looks in detail at the various types of learning disability, their aetiology, and the various treatment and caring options that are available for these disabilities. Table 16.1 provides an overall summary of what you will learn about in this chapter. First, however, it is important to understand how learning disabilities are categorized and the terminology that is used to describe these disorders.

Table 16.1 *Learning, intellectual and developmental difficulties: summary*

DISABILITY CATEGORY	DISABILITY SUB-TYPES AND PREVALENCE RATES	MAIN DSM-IV-TR DIAGNOSTIC FEATURES	KEY FEATURES	THEORIES OF AETIOLOGY	MAIN FORMS OF INTERVENTION AND CARE
SPECIFIC LEARNING DISABILITIES	*Reading disorder (dyslexia)* (Prevalence rates range from 3 to 17.5% of school-age children)	Reading achievement significantly below standard for age and IQ Symptoms significantly interfere with academic achievement or other daily activities that require reading skills	Reading achievement significantly below standard for age and IQ Reading characterized by word distortions, substitutions or omissions and is generally slow 60–80% of those diagnosed are boys It is a chronic condition and not a developmental delay	Genetic factors Cognitive factors (Phonological theory) Brain abnormalities (in the temporo-parietal areas)	Reading instruction for at-risk children Inclusion strategies (e.g. providing learning materials in a suitable form)
	Disorder of written expression	Writing skills are significantly below expected for age and IQ Symptoms significantly interfere with academic achievement or daily activities that require the composition of written texts	Writing skills fall short of those expected for age and IQ Characterized by grammatical, punctuation and spelling errors		

Table 16.1 *(Cont'd)*

DISABILITY CATEGORY	DISABILITY SUB-TYPES AND PREVALENCE RATES	MAIN DSM-IV-TR DIAGNOSTIC FEATURES	KEY FEATURES	THEORIES OF AETIOLOGY	MAIN FORMS OF INTERVENTION AND CARE
SPECIFIC LEARNING DISABILITIES (cont'd)	*Mathematics disorder (dyscalculia)* (Prevalence rate of 1% in school-age children)	Mathematics ability below that expected for age and IQ Significantly interferes with academic achievement or daily activities requiring mathematics skills	Mathematical ability falls significantly short of that expected by age and IQ	Genetic factors Perinatal factors (e.g. foetal alcohol syndrome)	
	Expressive language disorder (Prevalence rate of 3–7% in school-age children)	Limited vocabulary, making errors in tense, difficulty recalling words or producing sentences Symptoms significantly interfere with academic or occupational achievement or social communication	Involves levels of expressive language that fall significantly below that expected for age and IQ Characterized by limited amount of speech and difficulty learning new words	Physical problems such as hearing impairment, cleft palate, ear, nose and throat problems Genetic factors Brain abnormalities Emotional factors (e.g. anticipatory anxiety)	Speech therapy Altered auditory feedback (for stuttering) Prolonged speech (for stuttering)
	Phonological disorder (Prevalence rate 2% in 6- to 7-year-olds)	Failure to use developmentally expected speech sounds These difficulties interfere with academic or occupational achievement or social communication	An inability to use developmentally expected speech sounds		
	Stuttering (Community prevalence rate of 0.7% in all individuals)	Disturbance in the normal fluency and timing pattern of speech Symptoms interfere with academic or occupational achievement or social communication	Disturbance in the normal fluency and timing pattern of speech Onset around 2–7 years Good prognosis with around 80% overcoming the disability before adolescence		

Table 16.1 *(Cont'd)*

DISABILITY CATEGORY	DISABILITY SUB-TYPES AND PREVALENCE RATES	MAIN DSM-IV-TR DIAGNOSTIC FEATURES	KEY FEATURES	THEORIES OF AETIOLOGY	MAIN FORMS OF INTERVENTION AND CARE
INTELLECTUAL DISABILITIES	**Prevalence rate of diagnosis of mental retardation (IQ <70) around 1%**	An IQ of <70 Concurrent deficits in adaptive functioning in at least 2 separate areas (e.g. communication, self-care, home living) Onset prior to age 18 years	Traditional criteria for intellectual disabilities based on an individuals' limitations and impairments (e.g. low IQ) Contemporary approaches prefer to evaluate each individual's needs and then suggest strategies for support that will optimize functioning	Chromosomal disorders (e.g. Down syndrome) Metabolic disorders (e.g. phenylketonuria, PKU) Perinatal causes (e.g. congenital rubella syndrome, foetal alcohol syndrome) Childhood environmental causes (e.g. accidents, exposure to toxins, childhood infections, poverty and deprivation)	Prevention strategies (e.g. genetic screening) Behavioural training procedures (e.g. use of applied behaviour analysis) Inclusion strategies (including accessibility strategies, sheltered workshops and supported employment settings)
PERVASIVE DEVELOPMENTAL DISORDERS (PDD)	**AUTISTIC SPECTRUM DISORDER (umbrella term)** *Autistic disorder* **(Prevalence rate 0.05–0.13%)** *Rett's disorder* **(Prevalence rate 0.005–0.01%)** *Childhood disintegrative disorder* **(Prevalence rate 0.002%)** *Asperger's syndrome* **(Prevalence rate 0.03%)**	At least 2 items from: (a) qualitative impairment in social interaction (b) qualitative impairments in communication (c) restricted repetitive and stereotyped patterns of behaviour	Diagnostic criteria known as the 'triad of impairments' Children fail to develop a 'theory of mind' that allows them to understand the emotions and intentions of others 80% of those diagnosed with autistic disorder will have an IQ score <70	Genetic factors Chromosome disorders Brain neurotransmitter imbalances Perinatal factors (e.g. maternal rubella) Brain abnormalities Cognitive factors (including deficits in executive functioning and 'theory of mind')	Drug treatments (e.g. haloperidol, rispiridone, naltrexone) Behavioural training methods (e.g. functional analysis) Inclusion strategies (e.g. supported employment)

16.1 THE CATEGORIZATION AND LABELLING OF LEARNING DISABILITIES

Specific learning disabilities Disorders such as dyslexia and communication disabilities.

Intellectual disabilities A modern term replacing mental retardation to describe the more severe and general learning disabilities.

Pervasive developmental disorders A group of disorders characterized by serious abnormalities in the developmental process, usually associated with impairment in several areas of development. The most commonly diagnosed PDDs are autistic disorder (autism), Rett's disorder, childhood disintegrative disorder and Asperger's syndrome.

Learning disability An umbrella term to cover specific learning disabilities, intellectual disabilities and pervasive developmental disorders.

Mental retardation A DSM-IV-TR-defined disorder in which an individual has significantly below-average intellectual functioning characterized by an IQ of 70 or below.

Developmental disabilities A broad umbrella term used, in the USA, to refer to intellectual disabilities and pervasive developmental disorders such as autism and Asperger's.

In this chapter learning disabilities are divided into three broad categories. These are (1) *specific learning disabilities*, such as dyslexia and communication disabilities; (2) *intellectual disabilities*, covering some of the more severe learning difficulties such as the DSM-IV-TR-defined disorder 'mental retardation'; and (3) *pervasive developmental disorders*, which include autistic spectrum disorders.

There is considerable diversity across different areas of the world about how various learning disabilities should be labelled. In the UK, Europe and much of Australasia, the term *learning disability* is often used as an umbrella term to cover disorders across all three of the main categories described above – and it is especially used in this way by health and social care services. The term *mental retardation* refers to a specific diagnostic category of disorder in DSM-IV-TR, which is defined as significantly below average intellectual functioning characterized by an IQ of 70 or below (APA, 2000, p. 49). However, the term mental retardation is now commonly frowned upon as stigmatizing and demeaning and its use in clinical practice is declining. Nowadays the term is almost never used in the UK and Europe, and in the USA it is being replaced by the term intellectual disabilities to describe the more severe and general learning disabilities. In 2006, even the American Association for Mental Retardation voted to change its name to the American Association on Intellectual and Developmental Disabilities (www.aaidd.org/).

In the USA, the term *developmental disabilities* is coming into common use to cover both intellectual disabilities and pervasive developmental disorders such as autism and Asperger's syndrome. In the UK, many clinicians and health care providers prefer to use the specific terms autism, autistic spectrum disorder and Asperger's rather than a broader umbrella term to refer collectively to these disorders.

If you think this is confusing, that's because it is! There is as yet no international consensus on the use of these categories and labels, and even within countries these terms can change quite frequently to reflect shifts in social attitudes towards individuals with learning disabilities. Nevertheless, no matter how much we may believe that labels for such groups of people may be stigmatizing, it would be difficult to understand the aetiology of these disorders and to organize services and support if there were no way of defining their specific problems. Before continuing, you should remind yourself of the categories of learning disability we will be using in this chapter, and how these may relate to the use of terminologies in different countries.

SELF-TEST QUESTIONS

● How are the terms specific learning disability, intellectual disability and pervasive developmental disorder defined?

SECTION SUMMARY

16.1 The Categorization and Labelling of Learning Disabilities

● The three main categories of learning disabilities are (1) **specific learning disabilities** (e.g. reading disorder), (2) **intellectual disabilities** and (3) **pervasive developmental disorders**.

● **Mental retardation** is a term commonly frowned upon as stigmatizing, but it is still used in DSM-IV-TR as a diagnostic category.

16.2 SPECIFIC LEARNING DISABILITIES

16.2.1 The Description and Diagnosis of Specific Learning Disabilities

In this book, we use the collective term specific learning disabilities to cover a number of disorders that each affects individual performance on standardized tests of academic ability such as reading, mathematics or written expression. Individuals with these disabilities show levels of achievement well below what would be expected for their age, schooling and level of intelligence. As we shall see below, individuals with specific learning disabilities can show

Table 16.2 *Specific learning disabilities*

DISABILITY	DESCRIPTION	EXAMPLE SYMPTOMS
Reading disorder	Reading achievement is substantially below norm for chronological age, intelligence and educational level	• Omits, adds or distorts the sound of words when reading • Reads slowly and with poor comprehension
Disorder of written expression	Writing skills are substantially below those expected for chronological age, intelligence and educational level	• Regular errors in spelling, grammar or punctuation
Mathematics disorder	Mathematics ability is substantially below norm for chronological age, intelligence and educational level	• Difficulty remembering arithmetic facts (e.g. to 'carry' a number) • Failure to understand arithmetic concepts
Expressive language disorder	Scores on tests of expressive language development are substantially below those for chronological age, intelligence and educational level	• Markedly limited vocabulary • Making errors in tense • Difficulty recalling the right word
Phonological disorder	Failure to use developmentally expected speech sounds that are appropriate for age and dialect	• Omitting final consonants from words • Substituting one sound for another (e.g. saying *wabbit* rather than *rabbit*
Stuttering	Disturbance in the normal fluency and time patterning of speech	• Sound and syllable repetitions (e.g. saying *go-go-go-go* instead of *go*) • Pausing within words • Prolonging sounds

deficits in perceptual organization (organizing information), auditory and visual perception, memory and attention. Without special remedial support, individuals with these disabilities normally perform badly at school, are viewed as failures by friends and family, and as a consequence exhibit low self-esteem and motivation (Bjorkland & Green, 1992). Similarly, school dropout rates for children with specific learning disabilities are high, and these individuals will also experience difficulties in occupational and social functioning (APA, 2000, p. 50).

DSM-IV-TR recognizes a number of specific learning disabilities, the main ones being reading disorder, disorder of written expression, mathematics disorder, expressive language disorder, phonological disorder and stuttering. A brief description of each of these is given in Table 16.2. In all cases, DSM-IV-TR diagnosis is given when the symptoms significantly interfere with academic achievement or daily living activities.

Such learning disabilities are also commonly comorbid with other childhood psychological problems. Studies suggest that specific learning disabilities can be diagnosed in 79 per cent of children with bipolar disorder, 71 per cent with ADHD, 67 per cent with autism and slightly lower percentages with anxiety and depression (18–19 per cent) (Mayes & Calhoun, 2006). Literacy problems generally are associated with increased risk for both externalizing and internalizing disorders in childhood, which may be due either to the stressors associated with academic failure (causing anxiety and

depression) or to the fact that certain types of cognitive deficit (such as attention deficits) may be common to a number of different disorders, including specific learning disorders and disruptive behaviour disorders such as ADHD (Maugham & Carroll, 2006).

16.2.1.1 Reading Disorder

Reading disorder is characterized by reading achievement (e.g. accuracy, speed and comprehension) being significantly below standards expected for chronological age, IQ and schooling experience. Reading may be characterized by word distortions, substitutions or omissions, and is generally slow, with the child having difficulty fully comprehending what has been read. Depending on the specific diagnostic criteria used to identify reading disorder, and whether it is classified with disorder of expression to cover broader deficits in general literacy ability, prevalence rates range from 3 to 17.5 per cent of school-age children (DeFries, Fulker & LaBuda, 1987; Shaywitz, Shaywitz, Pugh, Fulbright et al., 1998). Between 60 and 80 per cent of those diagnosed are likely to be boys (APA, 2000, p. 52; Shaywitz, Shaywitz, Fletcher & Escobar, 1990). This gender difference may be due to a number of factors, including:

> **Reading disorder** A specific learning disability characterized by the accuracy, speed and comprehension of reading being significantly below standards expected for chronological age and IQ.

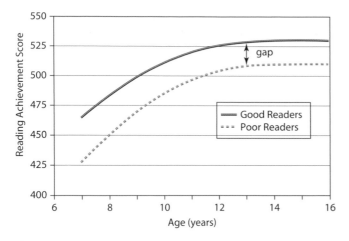

Figure 16.1
Trajectory of reading skills over time in non-impaired and dyslexic readers. Both non-impaired and dyslexic readers improve their reading scores as they get older, but the gap between non-impaired and dyslexic readers remains, suggesting that dyslexia is a deficit and not a developmental lag.
Source: Shaywitz (2003).

1 higher referral rates in males because they may be more disruptive than girls in learning environments;

2 girls may at least partially offset their reading difficulties by enjoying reading more than boys (Chiu & McBride-Chang, 2006);

3 girls may have more effective coping strategies than boys for dealing with reading difficulties (Alexander-Passe, 2006).

Most longitudinal studies suggest that reading disorder is a persistent, chronic condition, which does not simply represent a developmental lag in reading ability (Bruck, 1992; Scarborough, 1990; Francis, Shaywitz, Stuebing, Shaywitz et al., 1996). As can be seen from Figure 16.1, even though children with impaired reading skills show an improvement in reading ability with age, a gap in reading ability remains across time between children with reading impairments and those without.

16.2.1.2 Disorder of Written Expression

Disorder of written expression
A specific learning disability in which writing skills are substantially below those expected for chronological age, intelligence and educational level.

In *disorder of written expression*, writing skills fall significantly below those expected for the child's chronological age, IQ and educational history. The child has difficulty composing written text and exhibits grammatical errors, punctuation errors, poor paragraph organization, spelling errors and poor handwriting. Disorder of written expression is commonly found in combination with reading disorder, and the label *dyslexia* is often used to describe individuals who exhibit both disorders.

Dyslexia A persistent, chronic learning disability in which there are developmental deficits in spelling, reading and writing abilities

Plate 16.1
Reading disorder is most commonly called dyslexia. Dyslexia, however, usually includes deficits in spelling and writing as well as reading. Symptoms of reading disorder include poor comprehension, reversal of words or letters while reading, and difficulty decoding syllables or single words and associating them with specific sounds (phonics). Here, a child with dyslexia attempts to reproduce a teacher's sentence.
Source: Will and Deni McIntyre/Science Source, National Audubon Society Collection/Photo Researchers, Inc. Reproduced with permission.

16.2.1.3 Mathematics Disorder (Dyscalculia)

The main feature of *mathematics disorder (dyscalculia)* is that mathematical or arithmetical ability falls significantly short of that expected for the child's chronological

Mathematics disorder (dyscalculia)
A specific learning disability characterized by mathematical ability being substantially below norm for chronological age, intelligence and educational level.

age, IQ and educational history. Individual skills that may be impaired in mathematical disorder are (1) understanding or naming mathematical terms, (2) decoding problems into mathematical terms, (3) recognizing and reading numerical symbols or arithmetical signs, (4) copying numbers or symbols correctly, (5) remembering to conduct certain mathematical operations (such as 'carrying' figures when making calculations) and (5) following sequences of mathematical steps in the correct order. It is estimated that around 1 per cent of school-age children may be diagnosed with mathematics disorder (APA, 2000, p. 54).

16.2.1.4 Expressive Language Disorder

Expressive language disorder involves levels of expressive language that are significantly below the levels expected for the child's chronological age, IQ and educational history. General features of the disorder include a limited amount of speech, limited vocabulary, difficulty learning new words, difficulty finding the right word (e.g. unable to come up with the word *car*

Expressive language disorder A specific learning disability in which scores on tests of expressive language development are substantially below those for chronological age, intelligence and educational level.

when pointing to a car), shortened sentences, simple grammatical structures (e.g. use of relatively few verb forms), omission of critical parts of sentences, unusual word order and slow language development generally. Expressive language disorder is often comorbid in younger children with phonological disorder, reflecting a general impairment in the fluidity of language and erratic speech rhythms.

Expressive language disorder can be identified as early as age 2–3 years (Eisenwort, Marschik, Fladerer, Motl et al., 2004), but milder forms may not become apparent until early adolescence. Prevalence rates for expressive language disorder are estimated to be between 3 and 7 per cent in school-age children, but may be as common as 10–15 per cent in children under 3 years (APA, 2000, p. 60). However, when diagnosing the disorder, factors such as language deficits caused by brain lesions or head trauma should be taken into account, as should any delay in expressive language development caused by cultural factors such as living in a bilingual community.

16.2.1.5 Phonological Disorder

Phonological disorder   A specific learning disability characterized by the failure to use developmentally expected speech sounds that are appropriate for age and dialect.

Phonological disorder is characterized by an inability to use developmentally expected speech sounds that are appropriate for the individual's age and dialect. This can include errors of sound production (e.g. using a *t* sound to represent the letter *k*) and the omissions of sounds, especially from the ends of words. Sufferers are also unable to categorize speech sounds and to decipher which sounds in the language make a difference in meaning. The most severely misarticulated sounds are those learned later in the developmental process such as *l, r, s, z, th* and *ch*, and lisping is particularly common (e.g. saying *wabbit* instead of *rabbit*). Phonological disorder may often be associated with physical causes, such as a hearing impairment, cleft palate, neurological limitations such as cerebral palsy, and ear, nose and throat problems (Fox, Dodd & Howard, 2002), but at least 3 per cent of preschool children are diagnosed with a phonological disorder of unknown origin. Prevalence rate is around 2 per cent in 6- to 7-year-olds, falling to 0.5 per cent by age 17 years (APA, 2000, p. 66).

16.2.1.6 Stuttering

Stuttering   A disturbance in the normal fluency and time patterning of speech that is inappropriate for the individual's age.

Stuttering is a disturbance in the normal fluency and time patterning of speech that is inappropriate for the individual's age. This disturbance involves (1) frequent repetitions or prolongations of sounds, (2) pauses within words, (3) filled or unfilled pauses in speech, (4) word substitutions to avoid pronouncing problematic words, (5) words produced with an excess of physical tension and (6) monosyllabic word repetitions (e.g. 'go-go-go-go out of the room'). Fearful anticipation of stuttering may develop in many sufferers and may make stuttering worse in stressful situations, such as when giving a speech or at an interview. Stuttering may be accompanied by physical symptoms such as eye

blinks, tics, tremors, jerking of the head or clenching fists. As can be envisaged, stuttering can also have highly detrimental effects on social and occupational functioning. Onset of stuttering typically occurs between 2 and 7 years of age, with a peak onset around 5 years. The onset is usually insidious and initially the child may be unaware of stuttering. However, as awareness increases, the child will develop compensatory strategies for avoiding words and situations that cause stuttering.

Community studies estimate prevalence rates for all individuals at 0.7 per cent, rising to 1.4 per cent in young children and dropping to 0.5 per cent in adolescents (Craig, Hancock, Tran, Craig et al., 2002). However, the prognosis for stuttering is good, with around 40 per cent of sufferers overcoming the problem before they start school, and 80 per cent overcoming it before adolescence (Couture & Guitar, 1993). Stuttering is more common in males than females, with a male-to-female ratio of 4:1 in adolescents and 2.3:1 in both younger children and adults. Of those children diagnosed with stuttering, 12.7 per cent also have phonological disorder, 15.2 per cent have another learning disability and 5.9 per cent have ADHD (Blood, Ridenour, Qualls et al., 2003).

16.2.2 The Aetiology of Specific Learning Disabilities

In the following section, we discuss what is known about the aetiology and causes of some of the more common of the specific learning disabilities described in section 16.2.1.

16.2.2.1 Disorders of Reading and Written Expression (Dyslexia)

As we mentioned earlier, disorders of reading and written expression (dyslexia) are a persistent, chronic condition in which reading ability lags behind that of non-impaired individuals for the course of most of their lifetime. The development of dyslexia can be predicted by a number of risk factors, including difficulty recognizing rhymes at age 4 years (Bradley & Bryant, 1985), difficulty naming everyday objects at age 5 years (Wolf, Bally & Morris, 1986) and difficulty learning syntactic rules at age 2–3 years (Scarborough, 1990). However, the main causes of dyslexia now appear to be identified as abnormalities in specific areas of the brain such as the temporo-parietal region (Shaywitz & Shaywitz, 2005). These abnormalities may be the result of genetic factors and may give rise to the difficulties that sufferers have in decoding and comprehending written material. We review these theories of the aetiology of dyslexia by looking in turn at evidence related to genetic inheritance, cognitive impairments and brain abnormalities.

Genetic Factors   As early as 1950, Hallgren reported that more than 80 per cent of children with dyslexia also had other family members with the disability. More recent studies suggest that between 23 and 65 per cent of children with dyslexia have a parent with the disorder (Scarborough, 1990). In addition, 40 per cent of the siblings of sufferers also exhibit symptoms of dyslexia

(Pennington & Gilger, 1996). This suggests that dyslexia runs in families and so may have an important genetic component. Evidence for this genetic component is supported by studies suggesting that dyslexia concordance rates are significantly higher in MZ than in DZ twins (Stevenson, Graham, Fredman & McLoughlin, 1987). Using genetic markers for dyslexia, linkage studies have implicated genes on a number of chromosomes in the aetiology of dyslexia, including loci on chromosomes 2, 3, 6, 15 and 18 (Fisher & DeFries, 2002). It is assumed that those genes identified participate in brain development and cause the abnormalities in brain development associated with dyslexia (Galaburda, LoTurco, Ramus, Fitch et al., 2006).

Cognitive Factors Research on the aetiology of dyslexia has recently converged on the view that reading disabilities in dyslexia are caused primarily by difficulties in differentiating the elements of speech (phonemes) and associating these sounds with the letters in a written word (Shaywitz, 2003). This is known as the *phonological theory* of dyslexia where, in order to learn to read, the child must learn to recognize that letters and letter strings represent the sounds of spoken language. The deficits in dyslexia impair the child's ability to break up a spoken word into its basic phonological elements and link each letter to its corresponding sound. This deficit is quite independent of other abilities, such as general intelligence, reasoning, vocabulary and use of syntax (Share & Stanovich, 1995; Shankweiler, Crain, Katz, Fowler et al., 1995). Shaywitz and Shaywitz (2005) characterize the experience of the dyslexic in the following way:

> The problem is that the affected reader cannot use his or her higher-order linguistic skills to access the meaning until the printed word has first been decoded and identified. Suppose, for example, an individual knows the precise meaning of the spoken word 'apparition'; however, she will not be able to use her knowledge of the meaning of the word until she can decode and identify the printed word on the page and it will appear that she does not know the word's meaning.
>
> Shaywitz & Shaywitz (2005), p. 1302

Phonological theory The view that reading disabilities in dyslexia are caused primarily by difficulties in differentiating the elements of speech (phonemes) and associating these sounds with the letters in a written word.

Brain Abnormalities Associated with problems in relating written letters to corresponding sounds are deficits in brain functioning in dyslexia – especially in the *temporo-parietal areas* of the brain. Post-mortem studies of the brains of dyslexia sufferers suggest abnormalities in the temporo-parietal brain region (Galaburda, Sherman, Rosen, Aboitiz et al., 1985) and in the number and organization of neurons in the posterior language area of the cortex (Galaburda, 1993). Nevertheless, these abnormalities found in post-mortem studies might simply represent the consequences of a lifetime of poor reading rather than a causal factor in dyslexia.

Functional magnetic resonance imaging (fMRI) studies of the brains of young children with dyslexia indicate that they show significantly less activation in a number of left hemisphere sites when reading than do non-impaired children. These areas include the inferior frontal, superior temporal, parieto-temporal and middle-temporal-middle occipital gyri (Shaywitz, Shaywitz, Pugh, Mencl et al., 2002). This represents a common finding from functional brain imaging studies, suggesting that a failure of proper functioning in left hemisphere posterior brain systems is a cause of impaired reading in children with dyslexia.

Studies of lesions of the temporo-parietal areas of the brain also indicate that this area may be critical for analysing the written word and transforming the symbol into the sounds associated with the linguistic structure of the word (Damasio & Damasio, 1983; McCandliss, Cohen & Dehaene, 2003). Interestingly, brain imaging studies suggest that individuals with dyslexia may attempt to compensate for the lack of function in the temporo-parietal areas of the brain by using other brain areas to help them identify words and associate them with sounds. These compensatory effects involve brain sites required for physically articulating a word, enabling individuals with dyslexia to develop an awareness of the sound structure of a word by forming the word with their lips, tongue and vocal apparatus (Brunswick, McCrory, Price, Frith et al., 1999). Compensatory effects such as this may explain why reading performance in children with dyslexia improves with age, but still fails to reach the standard of non-impaired children (see Figure 16.1).

16.2.2.2 Mathematics Disorder (Dyscalculia)

Mathematics disorder appears to be a specific but chronic condition in which sufferers may perform better than average on measures of IQ, vocabulary and working memory, but still perform significantly poorly on tests of mathematical ability (Landerl, Bevan & Butterworth, 2004). The disorder appears to be the result of specific disabilities in basic number processing and can take three basic forms: (1) a deficit in the memorizing and retrieval of arithmetic facts; (2) developmentally immature strategies for solving arithmetic problems; and (3) impaired visuospatial skills resulting in errors in aligning numbers or placing decimal points (Geary, 1993, 2004).

Dyscalculia appears to have a familial component (Monteaux, Faraone, Herzig, Navsaria et al., 2005), and abnormalities in brain function associated with dyscalculia may be partially transmitted genetically (von Aster, Kucian, Schweiter & Martin, 2005). However, a number of studies have also implicated prenatal factors such as foetal alcohol spectrum disorder (FASD) and low birth weight (O'Malley & Nanson, 2002; Shalev, 2004). Brain functions specializing in number processing are located in various areas of the brain; fMRI studies have implicated abnormalities in the left parieto-temporal and inferior prefrontal cortex areas of the brain and the intraparietal sulcus in mathematics disorder (Dehaene, Molko, Cohen & Wilson, 2004; Molko, Cachia, Riviere, Mangin et al., 2003). Thus, the current evidence suggests a genetic or developmental cause that results in abnormalities of function in those areas of the brain responsible for processing numbers and arithmetic calculations.

16.2.2.3 Communication Disorders

Many communication disorders may be caused by organic problems relating to abnormal development of the physical apparatus required to make and articulate sounds. For example, we have already noted that phonological disorder is often associated with physical causes such as hearing impairment, cleft palate, cerebral palsy, and ear, nose and throat problems. In addition, some theories of stuttering argue that this disorder results from problems with the physical articulation of sounds in the mouth and larynx (Agnello, 1975). However, organic difficulties related to sound production may not represent the whole picture. For example, there is growing evidence of a familial and genetic component to communication disorders such as stuttering (Canhetti-Oliveira & Richieri-Costa, 2006; Andrews, Morris-Yeates, Howie & Martin, 1991), which indicates that the heritability of stuttering may be as high as 71 per cent.

There is also evidence from brain scan studies of abnormalities in certain brain circuits which are related to stuttering. One such circuit is the basal ganglia-thalamocortical motor circuit, which, if impaired, may affect the ability of the basal ganglia to produce timing cues for the initiation of the next motor segment in speech (Alm, 2004). The fact that stuttering may be a problem associated with the sequential production of sounds and words is supported by evidence which suggests that stuttering rarely occurs in one-word utterances and is affected by the length and grammatical complexity of utterances (Bloodstein, 2006).

Finally, there is some evidence that the production of sounds in communication disorders may be affected by emotional factors such as anticipatory anxiety or lack of control over emotional reactions (Karrass, Walden, Conture, Graham et al., 2006). However, some researchers view this association between disorders such as stuttering and anticipatory anxiety as secondary, and as a conditioned consequence of previous stuttering experiences (Alm, 2004).

16.2.3 The Treatment of Specific Learning Disabilities

The inclusion of specific learning and communication difficulties in DSM has been controversial. Many view these problems as developmental ones that require attention in an educational rather than a clinical setting; indeed, many learning disabilities are tackled primarily in the context of the child's educational development (Mishna, 1996). However, specific learning difficulties are frequently associated with clinical problems such as anxiety, depression and disruptive behaviour, and they can create significant problems in social, educational and familial functioning that may require referral to clinical services. Many of the treatments required by individuals with specific learning disorders can be provided by educational psychologists or speech therapists rather than clinical psychologists, and it is not intended to cover these forms of treatment here.

In many cases, such as reading disorders, appropriate reading instruction for at-risk younger children can enable them to become accurate and fluent readers (Alexander & Slinger-Constant, 2004). However, with older individuals suffering from reading disabilities such as dyslexia, a common approach in educational settings is to provide learning materials in a form that allows them to

be most easily negotiated by the dyslexic student. In addition, to compensate for the fact that the dyslexic student's reading is less automatic and more effortful, extra time is given during assessments such as examinations. Focus Point 16.1 illustrates how recent changes in the way that dyslexic students are taught and treated has led to their increasingly successful engagement in education at the highest levels.

Treatment of communication disorders is normally the domain of speech therapists and related disciplines, and there are a number of successful treatment programmes and equipment for disabilities such as phonological disorder and stuttering (Saltuklaroglu & Kalinowski, 2005; Law, Garrett & Nye, 2004). For example, hand-held equipment can provide *altered auditory feedback (AAF)* for stutterers, in terms either of the delay of auditory feedback it gives the sufferer when speaking or through a change in frequency of the voice. Such devices appear to have success in reducing the levels of stuttering, but it is still not clear by what mechanism they have this effect (Lincoln, Packman & Onslow, 2006).

> **Altered auditory feedback (AAF)** A form of treatment for stuttering in which delayed auditory feedback or a change in frequency of the voice is given to clients when they are speaking.

Another successful set of techniques used to address stuttering is known as *prolonged speech*. This teaches sufferers a set of new speech patterns that result in changes in the phrasing and articulation of speech and of the respiratory patterns produced by stutterers while speaking (Packman, Onslow & van Doorn, 1994). The success rates of treatments for stuttering are particularly high and estimated to be around 60–80 per cent. However, this may at least in part be confounded by the fact that much childhood stuttering will usually spontaneously remit after a few years (Saltuklaroglu & Kalinowski, 2005).

> **Prolonged speech** A set of techniques to address stuttering that teach the sufferer new speech patterns, resulting in changes in the phrasing and articulation of speech and of the respiratory patterns produced while speaking.

SUMMARY

In this section we have reviewed the characteristics, aetiology and general treatment of a number of specific learning disabilities. These are largely disabilities associated with reading, writing and communication generally, the most well-known of these disorders being the reading and writing disorder known as dyslexia. While many of these disabilities will require attention in educational rather than clinical settings, they may come to the attention of clinical psychologists because they often become associated with mental health problems and cause significant disruption to social, familial and educational functioning.

FOCUS POINT 16.1

Dyslexia and higher education

Ten to twenty years ago dyslexia sufferers found it very difficult to negotiate any form of higher education successfully, even though they show no impairments in other intellectual abilities such as general intelligence, reasoning, vocabulary and use of syntax. However, in recent times, it has become clear that, with appropriate compensation for their reading disability, dyslexia sufferers can achieve at the highest levels of academia. As Shaywitz and Shaywitz (2005) point out, though dyslexics may have general reading impairments, this does not mean that they cannot become proficient in areas of special interest. For example, the dyslexic child who, in adulthood, becomes interested in molecular biology may learn to decode words that form the mini-vocabulary relevant to molecular biology, even though he or she will show the usual difficulty decoding unfamiliar words. However, problems faced by dyslexics are not confined just to reading speed; they will also have organizational difficulties, spelling problems and difficulty with short-term memory. Because many dyslexics learn to compensate for their impairments, it may not become apparent to many individuals that they have dyslexia until they face the demands of higher education and an undergraduate degree course. Some of the common signs of dyslexic symptoms that may become apparent while studying are listed below.

In 10 years, the number of students known to have dyslexia entering higher education in the UK increased almost eightfold, from 1,679 in 1994 to 13,180 in 2004 – an increase from 0.51 per cent to 3.47 per cent of all students (Higher Education Statistics Agency, 2007). In addition, dyslexic students tend to perform just as well at university as non-impaired students, with no difference between the groups in the final degree classifications obtained (National Working Party on Dyslexia in Higher Education, 1999). Because dyslexia is a chronic condition, it means that dyslexic students will be identical to their non-impaired counterparts except for the fact that their reading is less automatic, more effortful and slow. As a consequence, the provision of extra time when doing assessments is an essential accommodation, and teachers are now routinely asked to take into account the following when teaching dyslexic students:

- Identify key texts on reading lists.
- Be aware that extra time may be needed to complete reading.
- Provide source material in alternative media (tapes, videos, CD-ROMs).
- Avoid asking students to read aloud in class.
- When creating handouts, use appropriately sized and shaped fonts (e.g. Arial size 12); do not use faded, poor originals when making copies.
- Leave points written on the board or OHT as long as possible to allow students extra time to copy down information.

The following are some of the characteristics found amongst students with dyslexia. Dyslexic individuals may not be aware of many of these symptoms until they begin studying in higher education.

Reading	Writing difficulties	Spelling	Oral and written word association
• Slow reader • Can't remember what you just read • Reading out of sequence and omitting words (e.g. 'the student went to the bar' becomes 'the student to the bar') • Often mistaking one word for another (e.g. 'for' and 'from') • Tracking difficulties – skipping over words or lines	• Freezing up when trying to write • Good sentences in your head vanish when you try to write them • Don't spot all errors when proofreading • Teachers say your ideas are good but the structure of your essays is poor • Difficulty using cursive script	• Frequent letter reversals (e.g. 'friend' becomes 'freind') • Usually drop or add letters to words when writing (e.g. 'know' for 'now') • Unable to spell common, everyday words • Letters and words often are out of sequence	• Difficulty translating speech into written words • Problems simultaneously taking notes in lectures and attending to what is going on • Words are heard yet not comprehended

- What are the defining characteristics of reading disorder and why might boys be diagnosed more than girls?
- What are the individual skills that may be impaired in mathematics disorder?
- What are the main characteristics of expressive language disorder, phonological disorder and stuttering?
- What is the evidence that dyslexia is an inherited disorder?

- Can you describe the phonological theory of dyslexia?
- What areas of the brain appear to be most affected in reading disorder and dyslexia?
- What is the evidence that communication disorders might be associated with physical rather than psychological causes?
- Can you describe treatments for stuttering such as altered auditory feedback (AAF) and prolonged speech?

SECTION SUMMARY

16.2 Specific Learning Disabilities

- **Reading disorder** is characterized by the accuracy, speed and comprehension of reading being significantly below standards expected for chronological age and IQ.

- The prevalence rate for reading disorder ranges between 3 and 17.5 per cent; 60–80 per cent of those diagnosed are boys.

- **Disorder of written expression** is commonly found in combination with reading disorder.

- **Expressive language disorder** can be identified as early as 2–3 years and has a prevalence rate of 3–7 per cent in school-age children.

- **Phonological disorder** and **stuttering** are both common forms of communication disorder found in early childhood.

- Disorders of reading, such as **dyslexia**, are known to have an important genetic component and are associated with brain abnormalities in the **temporo-parietal areas**.

- Dyslexia appears to be associated with difficulties differentiating the elements of speech and associating these sounds with the letters in a written word (the **phonological theory**).

- **Treatment** for specific learning disabilities often occurs in an educational rather than a clinical setting.

16.3 INTELLECTUAL DISABILITIES

Intellectual disabilities are defined primarily by three criteria: (1) they are characterized by significantly below-average intellectual functioning – usually based on a suitable measure of IQ; (2) they are characterized by impairments in adaptive functioning generally (e.g. an inability to master social or educational skills that would be expected for the individual's chronological age); and (3) these deficits should be manifest before the age of 18 years and should not be the result of any injury or illness that occurred later in life. As we discussed above, DSM-IV-TR still refers to the major form of intellectual disability as mental retardation, although this term is now considered too stigmatizing and does not convey the fact that individuals with intellectual disabilities can often learn a range of skills and abilities given appropriate education and opportunity. The term *intellectual disability* is becoming increasingly used in Europe and the USA to describe disorders of intellectual functioning, and in the UK the terms *learning disability* and *children with special educational needs* are frequently used to cover both disorders of intellectual ability and more specific learning disabilities (see previous section).

16.3.1 Criteria for Intellectual Disability

We look first at the criteria that have traditionally been used to define intellectual disabilities (e.g. DSM-IV-TR). We then examine some more recent alternative forms of categorization, which focus on the individual's needs and abilities rather than his or her intellectual deficits.

16.3.1.1 Traditional Criteria for Intellectual Disabilities

In DSM-IV-TR, intellectual disabilities are represented by the Axis II disorder mental retardation. The essential diagnostic feature of this disorder is significantly below-average intellectual functioning as measured by an IQ score of less that 70 (two standard deviations below the norm) (Criterion A). The second main criterion is evidence of significant impairments or deficits in adaptive functioning, as evidenced by impaired skills in the following areas: communication, self-care, home living, social/interpersonal skills, use of community resources, self-direction, functional academic skills, work, leisure, health and safety (Criterion B). Finally, Criterion C specifies that the onset of these impairments must have occurred prior to age 18 years (see Table 16.3).

Table 16.3 *DSM-IV-TR diagnostic criteria for mental retardation*

A Significantly sub-average intellectual functioning: an IQ of approximately 70 or below on an individually administered IQ test (for infants, a clinical judgement of significantly sub-average intellectual functioning).

B Concurrent deficits or impairments in present adaptive functioning (i.e. the person's effectiveness in meeting the standards expected for his or her age by his or her cultural group) in at least two of the following areas: communication, self-care, home living, social/interpersonal skills, use of community resources, self-direction, functional academic skills, work, leisure, health and safety.

C The onset is before age 18 years.

IQ tests must be used that are able to take into account the individual's cultural background, native language and any sensory or motor disabilities that the individual exhibits. The adaptive functioning aspect of Criterion B refers generally to how effectively individuals can cope with common modern life demands and how well they are able to meet current standards of personal independence within their culture and social group. Clinicians assessing individuals with intellectual disabilities would also gather information about disabilities from other reliable independent sources, such as teachers and medical doctors.

DSM-IV-TR also divides intellectual disabilities into a number of degrees of severity, depending primarily on the range of IQ score provided by the sufferer. These are:

Mild mental retardation Mental retardation as defined by DSM-IV-TR, represented by an IQ score between 50–55 and 70.

1 *Mild mental retardation*, represented by an IQ score between 50–55 to 70. This category includes around 85 per cent of those diagnosed with an intellectual disability. Individuals in this category usually acquire good social and communication skills, and in adulthood can acquire social and vocational skills adequate for minimum self-support.

Moderate mental retardation Mental retardation as defined by DSM-IV-TR, represented by an IQ score between 35–40 and 50–55.

2 *Moderate mental retardation*, defined as those with an IQ score between 35–40 and 50–55. This category represents about 10 per cent of those categorized with intellectual disabilities. Such individuals can carry on simple conversations, and with support and supervision can profit from vocational training.

Severe mental retardation Mental retardation as defined by DSM-IV-TR, represented by an IQ score between 20–25 and 35–40.

3 *Severe mental retardation*, defined by an IQ score of between 20–25 and 35–40. This group represents around 3–4 per cent of those diagnosed with mental retardation. Individuals in this category are unlikely to acquire much in the way of early communicative speech, but after school age they may be able to acquire some speech and self-care skills. Those diagnosed with severe mental retardation usually require considerable supervision, but can acquire basic vocational skills in sheltered work settings.

4 *Profound mental retardation* is defined by an IQ score below 20–25. This group constitutes around 1–2 per cent of people with intellectual disabilities. Most people in this category usually have an identified neurological condition that is the main cause of the disability, and they will display considerable impairment in sensory-motor functioning. Such individuals may respond to simple commands, but may have little or no other verbal abilities. They are also usually institutionalized because of their severe behaviour problems or concurrent physical handicaps.

Profound mental retardation Mental retardation as defined by DSM-IV-TR, represented by an IQ score below 20–25.

16.3.1.2 Alternative Approaches to Defining Intellectual Disabilities

Rather than simply taking a negative approach to diagnosis and focusing on an individual's limitations, impairments and deficits, more recent views attempt to highlight those factors that might be required to facilitate better intellectual and adaptive functioning in the individual. People with intellectual disabilities differ significantly in the severity of their disabilities, with some able to function almost without notice in everyday life, while others may require constant supervision and sheltered environments in which to live. Similarly, individuals differ significantly in their personalities. Some will be passive, placid and dependent, while others may be aggressive and impulsive. These kinds of issues mean that each individual with an intellectual disability is likely to differ in terms of both level of functioning and what is required to achieve any form of adaptive functioning.

The American Association on Intellectual and Developmental Disabilities (AAIDD) has recently promoted a more individualized assessment of a person's skills and needs rather than an approach based solely on categorizing intellectual and adaptive impairments. This approach emphasizes that individuals have both strengths and limitations, and that an individual's limitations need to be described in a way that enables suitable support to be developed. So, rather than simply forcing individuals into a diagnostic category, this approach evaluates the specific needs of the individual and suggests strategies, services and supports that will optimize individual functioning. Supports are defined as 'the resources and individual strategies necessary to promote the development, education, interests and personal well-being of a person with intellectual disabilities'. Supports can be provided wherever necessary by parents, friends, teachers, psychologists, GPs or any other appropriate person or agency.

People with intellectual disabilities frequently face major stigma and prejudice and are often confronted with significant barriers to realizing their own potential. However, approaches such as that advocated by the AAIDD are designed to enable individuals with intellectual disabilities to achieve their potential. In the UK, the Special Education Needs and Disability Act of 2001 extended the rights of individuals with intellectual disabilities to be educated in mainstream schools. Schools are required to draw up *accessibility strategies* to facilitate the inclusion of pupils with intellectual disabilities and to make reasonable adjustments so that they are not disadvantaged. As a result of such changes in attitude, support and legislation, more than half of those with intellectual disabilities in the UK now live with their parents or carers.

Accessibility strategies Programmes that extend the rights of individuals with intellectual disabilities to be educated according to their needs in mainstream schools.

16.3.2 The Prevalence of Intellectual Disabilities

Estimates of the prevalence levels of intellectual disorders depend very much on how intellectual disabilities are defined. DSM-IV-TR estimates the prevalence rate of a diagnosis of mental retardation at around 1 per cent. However, a UK study looking specifically at the prevalence rate of IQ scores of less than 70 suggests that prevalence of such low IQ scores may be as high as between 5 and 10 per cent in schoolchildren aged 13–15 years. Further analysis suggested that only around 15 per cent of those with IQ scores <70 were already in receipt of a statement of special educational needs (Simonoff, Pickles, Chadwick, Gringas et al., 2006), implying that the majority of the group with low IQ either did not need educational support or were as yet unrecognized as in need of support. Epidemiological studies indicate that there are around 580,000 people in the UK with mild intellectual disabilities (a prevalence rate of around 0.95 per cent), and 217,000 with severe intellectual disabilities (a prevalence rate of 0.35 per cent) (Open Society Institute, 2005). However, the Simonoff, Pickles, Chadwick, Gringas et al. study implies there are likely to be many more people than this suffering some form of intellectual disability which is unrecognized.

16.3.3 The Aetiology of Intellectual Disabilities

First and foremost, the causes of intellectual disability in individual cases are often extremely difficult to isolate and identify. Even when the cause of disability can be identified (such as a chromosomal disorder), two individuals identified with the same cause may exhibit quite different levels of disability. Differential diagnosis is also quite problematic; in many cases it is unclear whether an individual has a specific learning disability, has more general intellectual impairments, is suffering from autistic spectrum disorder (see section 16.4.1), or has psychological or emotional problems. As we shall see in the following sections, the major causes of intellectual disability are biological in nature: over 1,000 forms of impairment based on genetic, chromosomal or metabolic abnormalities have been identified (Dykens & Hodapp, 2001).

However, many researchers believe that an individual's resultant intellectual disability is also influenced considerably by environmental factors. For example, mild or moderate intellectual disability tends to occur more frequently in lower socioeconomic groups, indicating that poverty and associated deprivation may retard intellectual development. One topical example of this is the case of teenage mothers who choose to rear their children. They more often live in poor environments, are more likely to expose their children to alcohol and poor nutrition, and are less likely to provide sensitive parenting (Brooks-Gunn & Chase-Lansdale, 1995; Borkowoski, Whitman, Passino, Rellinger et al., 1992). As a result, mild to moderate intellectual disability is found significantly more frequently in children of teenage mothers than in the children of older mothers (Broman, Nichols, Slaughnessy, Kennedy et al., 1987). (see Focus Point 16.2)

In the following sections, we look first at the known biological causes of intellectual disability, followed by some of the environmental factors thought to be involved. Table 16.4 provides a summary of some of the known causes of intellectual disabilities categorized by the developmental period when they have their effect.

Table 16.4 *Causes of intellectual disability*

Developmental Period	Cause or Risk Factor
Before/during conception	Inherited recessive gene disorders (e.g. phenylketonuria, Tay-Sachs disease)
	Chromosome abnormalities (e.g. Down syndrome, fragile X syndrome)
During pregnancy	Severe maternal malnutrition
	Maternal iodine deficiency
	Maternal infections (e.g. rubella, syphilis, HIV, herpes simplex)
	Maternal drug abuse (e.g. alcoholism, tobacco abuse, illegal drug abuse)
	Maternal medications (e.g. cancer chemotherapy)
During birth	Anoxia and hypoxia (oxygen starvation or insufficient oxygen supply)
	Low birth weight
Early childhood	Brain infections (e.g. encephalitis, meningitis)
	Childhood malnutrition
	Severe head injury (e.g. physical accidents, physical abuse such as shaken baby syndrome)
	Exposure to toxins (e.g. lead, mercury)
	Social deprivation and poverty (e.g. poor parenting, unstimulating infant environment)

16.3.3.1 Biological Causes

Biological factors represent the largest known group of causes of intellectual disabilities. We divide these into three main categories: chromosomal disorders, metabolic causes and perinatal causes.

Chromosomal Disorders For many years now, it has been known that forms of intellectual disability are genetically linked to abnormalities in the X chromosome (the chromosome that also determines biological sex). These abnormalities often manifest as physical weaknesses in the chromosomes or abnormalities resulting from irregular cell division during pregnancy. Chromosomal abnormalities occur in around 5 per cent of all pregnancies, and the majority usually end in spontaneous miscarriages. However, it is estimated that 0.5 per cent of all newborn babies have a chromosomal disorder, although many of these die soon after birth (Smith, Bierman & Robinson, 1978). Chromosomal disorders account for around 25–30 per cent of all diagnosed cases of intellectual disability. The two most prominent forms are Down syndrome and fragile X syndrome.

Down syndrome was first described by British doctor Langdon Down in 1866. However, it was not until 1959 that French geneticist Jerome Lejeune first reported that individuals with Down syndrome almost always possess an extra chromosome in pair 21, which is usually caused by errors in cell division in the mother's womb. Down syndrome occurs in around 1.5 of every 1,000 births (a prevalence rate of 0.15 per cent) (Simonoff, Bolton & Rutter, 1996) and risk is related to the age of the mother. For women aged 20–24 years, the risk is 0.07 per cent. This rises to 1 per cent for women aged 40 years, and up to 4 per cent in women aged over 45 years (Thompson, McInnes & Willard, 1991). Although this link between maternal age and incidence of Down syndrome has been known for some time, it is still unclear how maternal age contributes to the chromosomal abnormalities. The majority of individuals with Down syndrome have moderate to severe intellectual impairment, with a measurable IQ usually between 35 and 55. They also have a distinctive physical appearance, with eyes that slant upward and outward with an extra fold of skin that appears to exaggerate the slant. They are usually shorter and stockier than average, with broad hands and short fingers. They may also have a larger than normal furrowed tongue that makes it difficult for them to pronounce words easily. They suffer physical disability such as heart problems and appear to age rapidly, with mortality high after 40 years of age. Ageing is also closely associated with signs of dementia similar to Alzheimer's disease (see Chapter 14), which may be a result of the causes of both disorders being closely located on chromosome 21 (Zigman, Schupf, Sersen & Silverman, 1995; Selkoe, 1991). Down syndrome can be identified prenatally in high-risk parents by using a procedure known as *amniocentesis*, which involves extracting and analysing the pregnant mother's amniotic

Down syndrome A disorder caused by the presence of an extra chromosome in pair 21 and characterized by intellectual disability and distinguishing physical features.

Amniocentesis A procedure which involves extracting and analysing the pregnant mother's amniotic fluid used prenatally in identifying Down syndrome in high-risk parents.

fluid. This is now a routine procedure for pregnant mothers that is carried out after week 15 of pregnancy, and is recommended in the UK and USA for mothers over the age of 35 years. The results of this process can leave prospective parents with difficult decisions about whether to maintain a pregnancy or not. Even so, amniocentesis will only identify between 15 and 30 per cent of Down syndrome cases in pregnant mothers who are tested.

Another important chromosomal abnormality that causes intellectual disability is known as *fragile X syndrome*. This is where the X chromosome appears to show physical weaknesses and may be bent or broken. Fragile X syndrome occurs in approximately 0.08–0.04 per cent of all births (Hagerman & Lampe, 1999). Individuals with fragile X syndrome possess mild to moderate levels of intellectual disability, and may also exhibit language impairment and behavioural problems such as mood irregularities (Eliez & Feinstein, 2001; Zigler & Hodapp, 1991). Like individuals with Down syndrome, they also have specific physical characteristics, such as elongated faces and large, prominent ears (see Plate 16.2). Recent studies suggest there may be a syndrome of fragile X chromosome in which different individuals manifest rather different symptoms and degrees of disability (Hagerman, 1995). For example, some may have normal IQ levels but suffer specific learning disabilities. Others may exhibit emotional lability and symptoms characteristic of autism such as hand biting, limited speech and poor eye contact (Dykens, Leckman, Paul & Watson, 1988). Intellectual impairment will usually be greatest in males suffering fragile X syndrome because they only have one X chromosome. Because females possess two X chromosomes, the risk of intellectual disability is less (Sherman, 1996).

Fragile X syndrome A chromosomal abnormality that causes intellectual disability where the X chromosome appears to show physical weaknesses and may be bent or broken.

Metabolic Disorders Metabolic disorders occur when the body's ability to produce or break down chemicals is impaired. There are many different types of metabolic disorders, and many can affect intellectual ability. Such disorders are often caused by genetic factors and may be carried by a *recessive gene*. When both parents possess the defective recessive gene, their offspring are in danger of developing the metabolic disturbances linked to that gene. Below we provide examples of two such genetically determined metabolic disorders that affect intellectual ability. These are phenylketonuria (PKU) and Tay-Sachs syndrome.

Recessive gene A gene that must be present on both chromosomes in a pair to show outward signs of a certain characteristic.

Phenylketonuria (PKU) is caused by a deficiency of the liver enzyme phenylalanine 4-hydroxylase, which is necessary for the effective metabolism of the amino acid phenylalanine. As a result of this deficit, phenylalanine and its derivative phenylpyruvic acid build

Phenylketonuria (PKU) A metabolic disorder caused by a deficiency of the liver enzyme phenylalanine 4-hydroxylase, which is necessary for the effective metabolism of the amino acid phenylalanine.

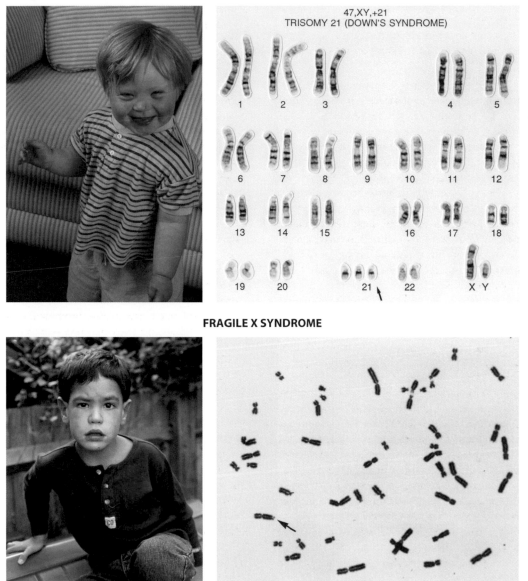

DOWN SYNDROME

47,XY,+21
TRISOMY 21 (DOWN'S SYNDROME)

FRAGILE X SYNDROME

Plate 16.2
The typical facial features of children born with Down syndrome or fragile X syndrome. Individuals with Down syndrome almost always possess an extra chromosome in pair 21. In fragile X syndrome, the X chromosome shows physical weaknesses and may be bent or broken.

up in the body and irreparably damage the brain and central nervous system by preventing effective myelination of neurons (myelination is the development of a protective sheath around the axons of neurons that enables effective transmission between nerve cells). This results in severe intellectual disability and hyperactivity. In the UK, PKU has an incidence of around 1 in 10,000 live births (NSPKU, 2004) and it is estimated that as many as 1 in 70 people may be carriers of the recessive gene responsible for PKU. At-risk parents who may carry the gene are now routinely given blood tests to determine the risk of having a child with PKU. Diet is also an important factor in controlling intellectual deficits in foetuses and offspring at risk of PKU. A special diet low in phenylalanine is recommended for at-risk pregnant mothers. If children with PKU are given diets low in phenylalanine from birth

Table 16.5 *Foods high and low in phenylalanine*

Foods containing high quantities of phenylalanine

MEAT	All kinds – beef, lamb, pork, ham, bacon, chicken, turkey, liver, tongue, kidney, sausages, beefburgers, meat paste, pâté, canned meat (e.g. corned beef)
FISH	All kinds including shellfish, frozen or tinned
EGGS	All kinds
CHEESE	All kinds including cheese spreads
NUTS	
ORDINARY	Bread, flour, cakes and biscuits
SOYA	Foods made from soya such as TVP (meat substitute)
QUORN and TOFU	
SEEDS	

Foods containing low quantities of phenylalanine that can be used in a special diet for those with phenylketonuria (PKU)

FRUIT	Most kinds
VEGETABLES	Most kinds
CEREALS	e.g. cornflour, arrowroot, sago, tapioca
FATS	Butter, margarine, lard, vegetable fats and oils
MISCELLANEOUS	Food essences, salt and pepper, herbs and spices, curry powder, vinegar, mustard

to at least 6 years of age, this can minimize neurological damage and intellectual deficit (Mazzoco, Nord, van Doorninck, Greene et al., 1994) (see Table 16.5).

Tay-Sachs disease   A metabolic disorder caused by a recessive gene which results in an absence of the enzyme hexosominidase A in the brain and central nervous system, eventually causing neurons to die.

Tay-Sachs disease is also a metabolic disorder caused by a recessive gene (often found in children of Eastern European Jewish ancestry). The defective gene results in an absence of the enzyme hexosominidase A in the brain and central nervous system and this eventually causes neurons to die. The disorder is degenerative, with infants of around 5 months showing an exaggerated startle response and poor motor development. Only around 17 per cent of sufferers live beyond 4 years of age (Sloan, 1991), but those who do show rapid decline in cognitive, motor and verbal skills. The disorder is relatively rare, occurring in around 1 in 360,000 live births worldwide, and this rate is being significantly reduced by effective screening.

Perinatal Causes   The period from conception to the early postnatal period is a dangerous one for an organism that is developing as rapidly as a human baby. Because of this, there are considerable prenatal and immediately postnatal factors that put normal development at risk and may cause lifelong intellectual disability. One type of risk involves those factors that can adversely affect the foetus's interuterine environment and its food supply. These include factors such as maternal infections, substance abuse or malnutrition. Disorders acquired during prenatal development are known as *congenital disorders* because they are acquired prior to birth but are not genetically inherited.

Congenital disorders   Disorders acquired during prenatal development prior to birth but which are not genetically inherited.

Maternal diet is one example. For instance, if there is too little iodine in the mother's diet during pregnancy, this can give rise to the condition known as *cretinism*. The mother's iodine deficiency may often be caused by a hormonal imbalance called thyroxine deficiency.

Cretinism   A congenital disorder resulting in slow development, intellectual disabilities and small stature.

Children suffering from this disorder show slow development and intellectual disabilities and often have a small stature. Thankfully, the condition is relatively rare nowadays due to the availability of iodized table salt and the fact that most diets now contain sufficient iodine.

Similarly, mineral and vitamin deficiencies caused by *maternal malnutrition* during pregnancy can result in intellectual disability and significantly affect the child's

Maternal malnutrition   Mineral and vitamin deficiencies during pregnancy can result in intellectual disability and significantly affect the child's physical and behavioural development.

physical and behavioural development (Barrett & Frank, 1987). However, the adverse effects of maternal malnutrition can often be partially rectified by providing newborn infants with intellectually supportive environments and appropriate food supplements (Zeskind & Ramsay, 1981; Super, Herrera & Mora, 1990). In most Westernized societies maternal malnutrition is relatively rare, but when it does occur it probably does so in conjunction with other factors likely to harm the child's intellectual and physical development, such as maternal drug or alcohol addiction, low socioeconomic status and possibly maternal HIV or syphilis infection (see below).

Maternal infectious diseases during pregnancy are another potential cause of intellectual disability in the offspring. Such diseases are most damaging during the first trimester of pregnancy when the foetus has little or no immunological protection. Common maternal diseases that can cause intellectual impairment in the offspring include rubella (German measles), syphilis and HIV, amongst others. If a mother contracts rubella during the first 10 weeks of pregnancy, there is almost a 90 per cent chance that the baby will develop *congenital rubella syndrome (CRS)* resulting in abortion, miscarriage,

Congenital rubella syndrome (CRS)   The constellation of abnormalities caused by infection with the rubella (German measles) virus before birth. The syndrome is characterized by multiple congenital malformations (birth defects) and intellectual disability.

stillbirth or severe birth defects. Up to 20 per cent of babies born live will have CRS, causing heart disease, deafness and intellectual impairment. The incidence of CRS is between 70 and 170 per 100,000 live births, and is still relatively high in developing countries (Cutts & Vynnycky, 1999).

In contrast, *maternal HIV infection* has become an important cause of intellectual disability. If the mother is not being treated for HIV during pregnancy, there is a likelihood that the infection will be passed on to the foetus. The infection can also be passed on through breastfeeding. There is then almost a 50 per cent chance that the newborn child will develop moderate to severe intellectual disabilities. However, in utero transmission of HIV can be reduced from 25 per cent to 8 per cent if the mother is given an antiretroviral drug such as zidovudine during pregnancy and if the newborn child then receives the drug for up to 6 weeks postnatally (Belfer & Munir, 1997).

> **Maternal HIV infection** The incidence of a mother having HIV during pregnancy, leading to a likelihood that the infection will be passed on to the foetus.

A further significant cause of intellectual disability is maternal drug use during pregnancy. In many cases the drugs responsible for offspring intellectual disability may be ones taken for medicinal purposes (such as drugs taken during cancer chemotherapy treatment), but most other cases occur where the mother is a substance abuser. For instance, US studies indicate that 18 per cent of pregnant women smoke tobacco, 9.8 per cent drink alcohol and 4 per cent use illegal drugs (Jones, 2006). *Foetal alcohol syndrome (FAS)* is one such example of maternal drug abuse causing childhood intellectual disabilities. Whenever a pregnant mother drinks alcohol, it will enter the foetus's bloodstream, slowing down its metabolism and affecting development. If this occurs on a regular basis, then development of the foetus will be severely impaired. Children suffering FAS usually have lower birth weight, lower IQ (between 40 and 80) and suffer motor impairments and deficits in attention and working memory (Niccols, 1994; Burden, Jacobson, Sokol & Jacobson, 2005). They also frequently exhibit distinctive facial characteristics, including slit eyes, short noses, drooping eyelids and thin upper lips. In the UK around 20 in every 10,000 babies born have FAS.

> **Foetal alcohol syndrome (FAS)** An example of maternal drug abuse causing childhood intellectual disabilities. Whenever a pregnant mother drinks alcohol, it enters the foetus's bloodstream, slowing down its metabolism and affecting development. If this occurs on a regular basis, then development of the foetus will be severely impaired.

Recently, attention has also been focused on the intellectual and developmental effects on children of illegal drugs use by pregnant mothers. Use of both cocaine and crack cocaine (see Chapter 8) by a pregnant mother can lead to babies being physically addicted to the drug before birth (known as *crack babies*). There is some evidence that this can adversely affect physical development and brain development in particular (Hadeed & Siegel, 1989), resulting in slow language development (van Baar, 1990). However, it is clear that maternal drug-taking while pregnant may often occur

> **Crack baby** A child addicted to cocaine or crack cocaine because of the mother's use of the drug during pregnancy.

in contexts that also contribute to poor intellectual development in the offspring, including the abuse of other drugs, pregnancy deprivations (such as dietary imbalances), and economic and social deprivation (Vidaeff & Mastrobattista, 2003). As such, this makes it difficult to assess the specific affect of maternal cocaine use on offspring intellectual development (Jones, 2006).

One final example of a perinatal cause of intellectual disability is *anoxia*, which is a significant period without oxygen occurring during or immediately after delivery. Lack of oxygen to the brain during the birth process can damage parts of the brain that are yet to develop, and as a result can cause both physical and intellectual impairment (Erickson, 1992). The main neurological birth syndrome caused by anoxia is *cerebral palsy*, which is characterized by motor symptoms that affect the strength and coordination of movement. While the primary disabilities are mainly physical, around one-third of those suffering from cerebral palsy will also suffer some form of intellectual, cognitive or emotional disability as well.

> **Anoxia** A perinatal cause of intellectual disability, being a significant period without oxygen that occurs during or immediately after delivery.

> **Cerebral palsy** The main neurological birth syndrome caused by anoxia which is characterized by motor symptoms that affect the strength and coordination of movement.

Childhood Causes Although a child may be born healthy, there are potentially a number of early childhood factors that might put the child at risk of intellectual disability. Very often these factors operate in conjunction with other causes such as perinatal problems. We look briefly at four groups of potential childhood causes of intellectual disability, namely accidents and injury, exposure to toxins, childhood infections, and poverty and deprivation.

During their early developmental years, young children may be involved in accidents which can often be severe enough to cause irreversible physical damage and intellectual impairment (Ewing-Cobbs, Prasad, Kramer, Cox et al., 2006). Common childhood accidents that may cause permanent intellectual disability include falls, car accidents, near drownings, suffocation and poisoning. However, at least some of the injuries that cause intellectual disability in children may not be genuine accidents but the result of physical abuse by others. A retrospective study of head injuries in children aged between 1 and 6 years of age estimated that 81 per cent of cases could be defined as accidents and 19 per cent as definite cases of abuse (Reece & Sege, 2000).

One form of child abuse that is known to cause intellectual disability is known as *shaken baby syndrome*. This refers to traumatic brain injury that occurs when a baby is violently shaken. In comparison to babies who receive accidental traumatic brain injury, shaken baby injuries have a much worse prognosis, including retinal haemorrhaging that is likely to cause blindness and an increased risk of mental disability such as cerebral palsy or intellectual impairment. Nevertheless, we must remain

> **Shaken baby syndrome** A form of child abuse that is known to cause intellectual disability. It refers to traumatic brain injury that occurs when a baby is violently shaken.

cautious about the degree to which shaken baby syndrome contributes to intellectual disability because of current controversies over how the syndrome should be diagnosed (e.g. Kumar, 2005).

During early development, children may be exposed to toxins which can cause neurological damage resulting in intellectual impairment. One such toxin is lead, which is still frequently found in pollution from vehicles that use leaded petrol. Lead-based paint is also found in older properties, and so may well be a risk factor in children living in deprived, low-socioeconomic areas. Lead causes neurological damage by accumulating in body tissue and interfering with brain and central nervous system metabolism. Children exposed to high levels of lead have been found to exhibit deficits in IQ scores of up to 10 points (Dietrich, Berger, Succop, Hammond et al., 1993). Even in Westernised societies aware of the risks associated with exposure to lead the prevalence of lead poisoning in children aged 1–2 years is still as high as 1 per cent (Ossiander, Mueller & van Enwyk, 2005). Prevalence rates are significantly higher than this in developing countries (Sun, Zhao, Li & Cheng, 2004).

Because a young child's brain is relatively underdeveloped, infectious illnesses such as meningococcal meningitis and encephalitis may cause permanent neurological damage in infancy. While encephalitis causes inflammation of the brain itself, meningitis can cause neurological impairment by inflaming the meninges (the membranous covering of the brain and spinal cord) (see Figure 14.3).

Finally, there is evidence to suggest that social deprivation and poverty can themselves contribute to intellectual disability. Although such factors may not directly cause impairment to the biological substrates underlying intellectual ability, they may contribute a form of intellectual impoverishment that can be measured in terms of lowered IQ scores (Garber & McInerney, 1982). Social deprivation and poverty are also inextricably linked to other risk factors for intellectual disability, including poor infant diet, exposure to toxins (such as lead paint in old or run-down housing), maternal drug-taking and alcoholism, and childhood physical abuse.

Teenage mothers   In relation to intellectual disabilities, young mothers who become pregnant before 18 years of age and who are likely to have lived in deprived areas prior to giving birth, are often unmarried, live in poverty as a result of their premature motherhood, and are likely to have a significantly lower than average IQ.

A cycle of deprivation, poverty and intellectual disability is established when young adolescents in deprived environments themselves give birth to children while still teenagers. Such *teenage mothers* are frequently found to live in deprived areas, are often unmarried, live in poverty as a result of their premature motherhood, and have a significantly lower than average IQ themselves (Carnegie Corporation of New York, 1994; Borkowski, Whitman, Passino, Rellinger et al., 1992). Studies have shown that teenage mothers are significantly more likely to punish their children than praise them, and are significantly less sensitive to their children's needs than older mothers (Borkowski, Whitman, Passino, Rellinger et al., 1992; Brooks-Gunn & Chase-Lansdale, 1995). As a result, children born to teenage mothers are at increased risk of problematic parent–child interactions (Leadbeater, Bishop & Raver, 1996), behavioural difficulties (Fergusson & Lynskey, 1993) and cognitive disadvantage and educational underachievement (Fergusson & Woodward, 1999; Brooks-Gunn, Guo & Fustenberg, 1993). Consequently, mild intellectual disability is reckoned to occur three times more frequently in the children of teenage mothers (Borkowski, Whitman, Passino, Rellinger et al., 1992; Broman, Nichols, Shaughnessy, Kennedy et al., 1987). As we said earlier, it is difficult to estimate how much this is due to the teenage mother's age and her parenting practices, because the child of a teenage mother is significantly more likely to be raised in the kinds of deprived environments that contain many other risk factors for intellectual disability (see Focus Point 16.2).

Finally, one important feature of deprived environments is that they will usually provide significantly decreased levels of stimulation for young children, including lower rates of sensory and educational stimulation, lack of one-to-one child–parent experiences and poverty of verbal communication – all factors that are thought to be associated with poor intellectual development. However, there are some views that claim that lack of stimulation can have a *direct effect* on the early physical development of the brain and so result in permanent impairments to brain functioning. For instance, neural development of the brain occurs most extensively and rapidly in the first year after birth (Kolb, 1989), and a rich, stimulating environment is necessary for full development of the brain's structure (Nelson & Bosquet, 2000). Alternatively, an unstimulating, stressful environment can actually trigger the secretion of hormones that prevent effective brain development (Gunnar, 1998). In a study comparing children brought up in deprived inner-city areas with a group exposed to good nutrition and provided with a stimulating environment, Campbell and Ramsey (1994) found that by 12 years of age, the deprivation experienced by the former group had a significant negative effect on brain functioning.

SUMMARY

From the material covered in this section, you can see that the causes of intellectual disability are diverse. As we mentioned earlier, very often it is impossible to pinpoint the specific cause of an individual's intellectual disability. Intellectual disability caused by chromosomal disorders (such as Down syndrome and fragile X syndrome) and inherited metabolic disorders are some of the more easily identified. Individuals are most at risk of developing permanent intellectual disabilities during early development of their central nervous system, which is why conditions in the uterus and in the immediate postnatal period are critical for normal development. Risk factors that can disrupt normal prenatal development of the brain and central nervous system include maternal infections, alcoholism, drug abuse and malnutrition. Early childhood factors that can affect normal neurological development include accidents, physical abuse, exposure to toxins, infectious illnesses and an early childhood spent in deprivation and poverty. As we have mentioned many times in this section, many of these risk factors may operate concurrently to determine levels of intellectual disability.

Teenage mothers and the cycle of underachievement

Each year in England, 39,000 girls under 18 years of age become pregnant (Department for Education and Skills, 2006). Although around half of these pregnancies lead to an abortion, the remainder become teenage mothers. They are mothers who are likely to have lived in deprived areas prior to giving birth, are often unmarried, live in poverty as a result of their premature motherhood, and are likely to have a significantly lower than average IQ (Borkowski, Whitman, Passino, Rellinger et al., 1992). When teenage girls become mothers in deprived areas, this sets up a cycle of deprivation, poverty and intellectual under-achievement. As a result of their relatively poor parenting skills and the stress that accrues from living in deprived areas, the children of teenage mothers are significantly more likely than the children of older mothers to have behavioural difficulties (Fergusson & Lynskey, 1993) and suffer cognitive impairments and educational underachievement (Fergusson & Woodward, 1999; Brooks-Gunn, Guo & Fustenberg, 1993).

The UK Department for Education and Skills (2006) provided the following stark facts:

- Teenage mothers are less likely to finish their education and are more likely to bring up their children alone in poverty.

- The infant mortality rate for babies born to teenage mothers is 60 per cent higher than for babies born to older mothers.

- Teenage mothers are more likely to smoke during pregnancy and are less likely to breastfeed, both of which have negative consequences for the child.

- Teenage mothers have 3 times the rate of postnatal depression of older mothers and a higher risk of poor mental health for 3 years after the birth.

- Children of teenage mothers are generally at increased risk of poverty, low educational attainment, poor housing and poor health, and have lower rates of economic activity in adult life.

- Rates of teenage pregnancy are highest among deprived communities, so the negative consequences of teenage pregnancy are disproportionately concentrated among those who are already disadvantaged.

As we can see from reading section 16.3.3, many of these conditions represent risk factors for intellectual disability and underachievement for the teenage mother's offspring. These include poor parenting skills, maternal mental health problems, being raised in unstimulating environments abundant in potential stressors, a high likelihood of maternal drug or alcohol abuse during pregnancy, and increased risk of physical abuse or accidents (Moffitt & the E-Risk Study Team, 2002). At age 5, the children of teenage mothers already have a significantly lower IQ than the children of older mothers (Lubinski, 2000).

16.3.4 Interventions for Intellectual Disabilities

Most forms of intellectual disability impose limitations on the sufferer's ability to function fully and actively in society. This means that – depending on the severity of the disability – the individual will need support to cope with many of the rigours of everyday living. As a result of the disability, sufferers are at risk of underachieving in many areas of their life, including educationally, occupationally, economically and socially. In most societies, the days when people with intellectual disabilities were simply institutionalized and provided with little more than custodial care are now gone. Current provision for such people not only attempts to address their needs, but also recognises their fundamental rights as human beings and citizens who have a right to an inclusive lifestyle. Thus, interventions for intellectual disabilities have a number of diverse aims.

At the primary level are those interventions aimed at preventing intellectual disability in the first place by educating potential parents about the risk factors for intellectual disability (e.g. educating parents about the effects of maternal alcohol and drug abuse during pregnancy). A second broad aim of interventions is to make available training programmes that will provide sufferers with enough basic skills to cope with many of the challenges of everyday life (e.g. self-help skills, communication skills). Thirdly, approaches to helping those with intellectual disabilities are based on the principle of *inclusion* in an attempt to help such individuals achieve their potential. In the UK, schools are now required to draw up accessibility strategies to allow pupils with intellectual disabilities to engage in the educational process without being disadvantaged. Similarly, social inclusion is encouraged to provide those with intellectual disabilities the opportunity for personal, social, emotional and sexual development. We now discuss each of these three types of approach to intervention in more detail.

16.3.4.1 Prevention Strategies

In Table 16.4 above we listed many of the causes and risk factors for intellectual disability. As you can probably glean from this list, many of the causes are potentially preventable. This is particularly the case with many perinatal causes, especially those involving maternal factors during pregnancy. For example, foetal alcohol syndrome (FAS) is a significant cause of intellectual disability. Prevention programmes aim to identify those women at risk of alcohol abuse during pregnancy and to provide interventions or alcohol-reduction counselling (Floyd, O'Connor, Sokol, Bertrand et al., 2005). Recognizing those at risk can be achieved by using established diagnostic and screening questionnaires (Mengel, Searight & Cook, 2006). Interventions include providing feedback on rates of drinking behaviour during pregnancy and discussing strategies for avoiding alcohol cravings and binge drinking sessions. Controlled comparison studies suggest that such screening and intervention methods significantly reduce the risk for alcohol-exposed pregnancies compared with non-intervention control participants (Ingersoll, Ceperich, Nettleman, Karanda et al., 2005).

Plate 16.3
Foetal alcohol syndrome (FAS) is a significant cause of intellectual disability. Posters such as this attempt to dissuade women from abusing alcohol during pregnancy.

Prevention can also be achieved in a number of other ways. For example, genetic analysis and counselling enables those parents at risk of abnormal births to be identified, informed of the risk and counselled about how to proceed. Blood tests and tests of amniotic fluid such as amniocentesis enable parents to be informed of risks for a range of disorders, including Down syndrome, Tay-Sachs disease, phenylketonuria and intellectual disability caused by congenital rubella syndrome (CRS). In addition, disabilities related to dietary irregularities can be identified and treated, including providing at-risk pregnant mothers with iodine supplements to prevent cretinism, and suggesting diets low in phenylalanine for pregnant mothers and offspring at risk of phenylketonuria.

Finally, as we saw earlier, conditions associated with poverty and social deprivation also put children at risk of educational underachievement, lower than average IQ and mild intellectual disability. Support programmes in the USA and Europe have been developed to try to counteract this risk factor. For example, family support programmes in the USA have indicated that mothers of low socioeconomic status participating in such schemes are more affectionate and positive with their children and provide more stimulating environments than mothers who are not in such schemes (Johnson, Walker & Rodriquez, 1991). Being a teenage mother is also a risk factor for raising children of lower IQ than average (see Focus Point 16.2). This factor can be tackled in a number of ways, including providing teenage girls with advice on and access to contraception, improving teenage mothers' access to education (Department for Education and Employment, 2001), improving housing quality, and encouraging the presence of a co-residential partner rather than raising a child alone (Berrington, Diamond, Ingham, Stevenson et al., 2004).

16.3.4.2 Training Procedures

The quality of life of people with intellectual disabilities can be improved significantly with the help of basic training procedures that equip them with a range of skills depending on their level of disability. Types of skills include self-help and adaptive skills (such as toileting, feeding and dressing), language and communication skills (including speech, comprehension, sign language), leisure and recreational skills (such as playing games, cooking skills), basic daily living skills (using a telephone, handling money), and controlling anger outbursts and aggressive and challenging behaviour (reducing the tendency to communicate through aggressive or challenging behaviours such as pushing or shouting). Training methods can also be used in more severe cases to control life-threatening behaviours such as self-mutilation or head-banging.

Behavioural techniques that adopt basic principles of operant and classical conditioning are used extensively in these contexts. The application of learning theory to training in these areas is known as *applied behaviour analysis* (Davey, 1998). Basic techniques that are used include operant rein-

> **Applied behaviour analysis**
> Applying the principles of learning theory (particularly operant conditioning) to the assessment and treatment of individuals suffering psychopathology.

forcement (rewarding correct responses, e.g. with attention or praise), response shaping (breaking down complex behaviours into small achievable steps and rewarding each step successively), errorless learning (breaking down a behaviour to be learned into simple components that can be learned without making errors: errorless learning is stronger and more durable than learning with errors), imitation learning (where the trainer demonstrates a response for the client to imitate), chaining (training the individual on the final components of a task first, and then working backwards to learn the earlier steps) and self-instructional training (teaching clients to guide themselves through a task by verbally instructing themselves what to do at each step).

Very often, inappropriate, life-threatening or challenging behaviours may be inadvertently maintained by reinforcement from others in the environment (e.g. self-mutilating behaviour may be maintained by the attention it attracts from family or care staff).

In these cases, a *functional analysis* can be carried out in order to help identify the factors maintaining the behaviour. This is done by keeping a record of the frequency of the behaviours and noting the antecedents and consequences of the behaviour. Once it is known what consequences might be maintaining the behaviour, these can be addressed to prevent the behaviour being reinforced (Mazaleski, Iwata, Vollmer, Zarcone & Smith, 1993; Wacker, Steege, Northrup, Sasso, et al., 1990). See Treatment in Practice Box 16.1.

> **Functional analysis** The use of operant conditioning principles to try to understand what rewarding or reinforcing factors might be maintaining behaviour.

CLINICAL PERSPECTIVE: TREATMENT IN PRACTICE BOX 16.1

A functional analysis of challenging behaviour

Some individuals with intellectual disabilities typically display behaviour that may put them or others at risk, or which may prevent the use of community facilities or prevent them having a normal home life. Challenging behaviours may take the form of aggression, self-injury, stereotyped behaviour or disruptive and destructive behaviour generally. In many cases, a functional analysis may help to identify the factors maintaining challenging behaviour. These may range from social attention, tangible rewards such as a hug, or escape from stressful situations, or they may simply provide sensory stimulation. A functional analysis is undertaken by keeping a record of the frequency of the behaviours and noting the antecedents and consequences of the behaviour. This takes the following form:

A What happens before the challenging behaviour? (*trigger*)

B What does the individual do? (*behaviour*)

C What does the person get as a result of the behaviour? (*consequence*)

A typical ABC chart in which family and carers keep a record of such behaviours often looks like this:

Date	Antecedent (what happened before the behaviour occurred?)	Behaviour (describe exactly what the person did)	Consequence (what happened immediately after the behaviour?)	Signature

A functional analysis case history

Andy is a middle-aged man with severe intellectual disability. He has recently moved into a group home, which he shares with 7 other people. Since he moved in, staff have observed several incidents of self-injury. They report that Andy starts to rock backwards and forwards in his chair; this then escalates into him slapping his face repeatedly. Staff have asked for help.

The staff team working with Andy were asked to complete ABC charts for 4 weeks. These charts were then analysed and it was found that the behaviour tended to occur in the lounge when there were a number of people in the room and the television was on. The consequence of Andy starting to rock and slap himself was that staff would remove him from the room and take him into the kitchen where it was empty and quiet.

It was hypothesized that the function of the behaviour for Andy was to escape from a noisy and crowded situation. Staff decided to respond by watching Andy for early signs that he may be feeling overstimulated and to ask him if he wanted to leave the room.

This led to a reduction of self-injury and later it was noted that Andy would now try to attract staff attention when he wanted to leave.

16.3.4.3 Inclusion Strategies

Policy on the development and education of individuals with intellectual disabilities has changed significantly over the past 20–30 years. Prior to inclusion policies being introduced, even individuals with mild intellectual disabilities were often deprived of any effective participation in the life of the society in which they lived; more often than not, they would be institutionalized or educated separately. However, many countries have introduced accessibility strategies that extend the rights of individuals with intellectual disabilities to be educated according to their needs in mainstream schools. This approach evaluates the individual's specific needs and suggests strategies, services and supports that will optimize the individual's functioning within society. In the UK, the government's strategy for individuals with *special educational needs (SEN)* involves:

> **Special educational needs (SEN)**   A term used in the UK to identify those who require instruction or education tailored to their specific needs.

1   mainstream schools providing the skills and specialist support necessary to meet the needs of all pupils (including many of those with SEN who had previously been excluded);

2   the provision of special schools providing education for children with the most severe and complex needs (see Focus Point 16.3);

3   schools working together with local health services to support the educational inclusion of all children from their local community; and

4   ensuring that parents can be confident that mainstream schools will provide a child with SEN with a good education as a valued member of the community (Department for Education and Skills, 2004).

As a result of this strategy of inclusion, more than half of those individuals with intellectual disabilities in the UK now live with their parents or carers. Social and educational inclusion also has indirect benefits for the individual. Kim, Larson and Lakin (2001) reviewed those studies carried out between 1980 and 1999 that investigated the effects of the shift from institutionalized living to living in the community. Most studies reported an improvement in three areas: (1) overall improvements in coping with day-to-day living and increases in self-esteem; (2) a decrease in the frequency of maladaptive behaviours, such as aggression or anger outbursts; and (3) an improvement in self-care behaviours and social skills. Case History 16.1 recounts the story of Thomas, a Down syndrome sufferer who lives with his family and has benefited in a variety of ways from participating in a range of community activities.

Inclusion policies have resulted in significant improvements in the quality of life experienced by individuals with intellectual disabilities, who now have opportunities to pursue social, educational and occupational goals and explore their own personal development. For example, individuals with intellectual disabilities now have the right to pursue their own sexual and emotional development, usually with the support of their own family. Whereas in the past involuntary sterilization was common for such individuals, appropriate training and counselling now mean that most individuals can be taught about sexual behaviour to a level appropriate for their functioning. This often means that they can learn to use contraceptives, employ responsible family planning, get married and – in many cases – successfully rear a family, either on their own or with the help of local services (Lumley & Scotti, 2001; Levesque, 1996).

Finally, employment opportunities are being made increasingly available to individuals with intellectual disabilities. Many are conscientious and valued workers employed in normal work environments. Others with more specific needs may have to pursue employment within *sheltered workshops* or supported employment settings (see section 16.4.2.4 below),

> **Sheltered workshops**   Settings that provide individuals with intellectual disabilities with employment tailored to their own needs and abilities.

FOCUS POINT 16.3

Key facts on special schools in the UK

- 1.1 per cent of children are educated in special schools. This proportion has fallen from 1.5 per cent in 1983 and varies greatly between local authorities (from 2.4 per cent in Brighton and Hove to 0.1 per cent in Newham).

- Almost 94,000 children attend special schools in the UK, 2,000 of whom are dual registered and spend part of their time in a mainstream school.

- 68 per cent of children in special schools are boys.

- The most common types of special educational needs (SEN) for which special schools are approved are severe learning difficulties, followed by moderate learning difficulties. Over 30 per cent are approved for emotional and behavioural difficulties and autistic spectrum disorder, and 25 per cent for profound and multiple learning difficulties (PMLD).

Source: Pupil Level Annual Schools Census (PLASC) January 2003

CASE HISTORY 16.1

Thomas's story

'Thomas is 23 and lives with his mum and dad. His brother now lives away, but sees him quite regularly.

Thomas has Down syndrome and needs a great deal of support. He goes to college four days a week and, on Fridays, attends a project where he is learning living skills and enjoying cooking. Thomas has a supported work placement for 2 hours a week in a riding stable. He has a hectic social life with weekly activities including riding, sports, going to the gym, trampolining and football. He goes to monthly discos with a group of young people with a learning disability, and is regularly to be found in the local pub playing pool with his friends.

We were transporting him to and from these activities and were concerned that he should be able to mix more with his own age group. We arranged for 15½ hours' worth of direct payments for Thomas to choose someone in his peer group to help him access these activities. There was a great deal of interest in the advert we placed at the local university for a student to help with this and we have had several different students helping over the past year, who have become firm friends. Thomas's current helper, Laura, accompanies him on his outings and Thomas has now become a part of a wider social circle, going to the pub, out for meals and watching videos at Laura's house with her friends, which he greatly enjoys.

Thomas's moods, self-esteem and well-being are greatly improved by the stimulation and social nature of all that he does, as well as the routine and structure it brings to his life.

Thomas and his friends have gained enormous confidence from attending several drama courses and the group has enjoyed the feeling of empowerment and also the opportunity to show their feelings. Last year, a group of 11 young adolescents, including Thomas, attended a week-long outward bound course run by the Calvert Trust without their families. Afterwards, the group made a presentation to about 80 people who had been involved in organizing or fundraising their trip, with a very professional PowerPoint presentation and question and answer session. They were all keen to contribute, wanted to find other groups to make their presentation to and gained lots of confidence from this. It makes a change from the usual painting eggs and bingo offered by local services, just not appropriate for a 22-year-old.'

Source: taken from evidence from a family carer given to the Foundation for People with Learning Disabilities' Inquiry into Meeting the Mental Health Needs of Young People with Learning Disabilities – Count Us In

Clinical Commentary

Thomas is an example of how individuals with intellectual disabilities can benefit significantly from accessibility and inclusion strategies. He has work in a supported employment setting and has a full social life in which he can mix with people of his own age. This approach has the benefit of building confidence and self-esteem, as well as providing the individual with a real sense of empowerment.

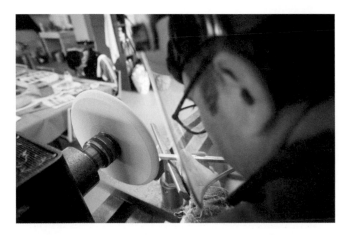

Plate 16.4
Sheltered workshops and supported employment settings provide individuals with intellectual disabilities with employment tailored to their own needs and abilities.

which provide employment tailored to the individual's own needs. The UK government seeks to promote employment as another form of social inclusion for individuals with intellectual disabilities. Those working in a sheltered workshop have been shown to exhibit higher levels of job satisfaction than those who worked outside such a scheme, and those living in a semi-independent home and also worked in a sheltered workshop showed the highest levels of self-esteem (Griffin, Rosenberg & Cheyney, 1996).

16.3.4.4 Summary of Interventions for Intellectual Disabilities

This section has given you a brief insight into some of the interventions deployed in dealing with intellectual disabilities. These include: (1) the use of prevention strategies designed to identify those at risk of having offspring with intellectual disabilities (e.g. those with recessive gene disorders or mothers at risk during pregnancy), providing them with skills to minimize risk and counselling them about the possible outcomes; (2) a range of training programmes and techniques to provide individuals with learning difficulties with a variety of everyday skills; and (3) the adoption of inclusion strategies that provide individuals with educational and occupational environments tailored to meet their needs within mainstream society.

SUMMARY

We began this section by outlining some of the different terminologies now used to describe individuals with intellectual disabilities, including traditional diagnostic categories and more recent alternative approaches that focus on identifying needs and facilitating adaptive functioning. The aetiology of intellectual disorders is a diverse topic, with no identifiable cause being found for a large proportion of intellectual disabilities. Biological causes are primarily responsible for those aetiologies that can be identified. These include chromosomal disorders, recessive gene disorders and perinatal factors. Childhood problems can also contribute to intellectual disability: we discussed the role of accidents, abuse, infectious diseases and the nonspecific detrimental effect that social deprivation and poverty can have on intellectual development. In the final section we covered interventions for the prevention of intellectual disability, and programmes for the care and development of individuals with intellectual disabilities.

SELF-TEST QUESTIONS

- Can you describe both the traditional and more recent alternative approaches to defining intellectual disability?
- What are the different levels of intellectual disability defined in DSM-IV-TR?
- What are the main chromosomal disorders that cause intellectual disability?
- Can you describe at least two metabolic disorders that give rise to intellectual disability?
- What is meant by the term 'congenital disorder' when used in relation to intellectual disability? Can you give some examples of congenital causes of intellectual disability?

- What are the main childhood causes of intellectual disability?
- Can intellectual disability be prevented? Is so, how?
- Can you describe the kinds of training procedures that are used to help individuals with intellectual disabilities acquire self-help and communication skills?
- Can you describe some examples of inclusion strategies that have been used in relation to intellectual disability?

SECTION SUMMARY

16.3 Intellectual Disabilities

- The essential diagnostic feature of intellectual disability is significantly below-average intellectual functioning as measured by an IQ score of <70.

- Modern approaches to defining intellectual disabilities attempt to highlight those factors that might be required to facilitate more adaptive functioning, and to draw up **accessibility strategies** to ensure that such individuals are not excluded or disadvantaged in their education.

- Chromosomal disorders such as **Down syndrome** and **fragile X syndrome** account for around 25–30 per cent of all diagnosed cases of intellectual disability.

- Metabolic disorders that cause intellectual disability are usually carried by a recessive gene and include **phenylketonuria (PKU)** and **Tay-Sachs disease**.

- **Congenital disorders** are those that are acquired prior to birth but are not genetically inherited. Congenital causes of intellectual disability include **maternal malnutrition, congenital rubella syndrome (CRS), maternal HIV infection** and **foetal alcohol syndrome (FAS)**.

- Childhood **environmental causes** of intellectual disability include childhood accidents (including intentional physical abuse by others), exposure to toxins (such as lead), childhood infections and poverty and deprivation.

- **Prevention strategies** for intellectual disability include prevention campaigns and screening for such factors as maternal alcohol abuse and genetic risk factors.

- **Behavioural training procedures** can equip sufferers with a range of self-help and adaptive skills. The application of learning theory in these areas is known as **applied behaviour analysis**.

- **Inclusion strategies** provide those with intellectual disabilities with access to mainstream educational and occupational opportunities.

16.4 PERVASIVE DEVELOPMENTAL DISORDERS

Some disorders are characterized by serious abnormalities in the developmental process. Those that fall under the heading of *pervasive developmental disorders (PDD)* are usually associated with impairment in several areas of development. From early infancy, some children exhibit a spectrum of developmental impairments and delays that include social and emotional disturbances (e.g. poor social interaction with others), intellectual disabilities (e.g. low IQ), language and communication deficits (e.g. failure to learn to speak or develop language skills), and the development of stereotyped or self-injurious behaviour patterns (e.g. hand biting and hair pulling). The most commonly diagnosed PDDs are *autistic disorder* (autism), *Rett's disorder*, *childhood disintegrative disorder* and *Asperger's syndrome*. *Autistic spectrum disorder (ASD)* is an umbrella term that refers to all disorders displaying autistic-style symptoms across a wide range of severity and disability. The disorders described in Table 16.6 are typical examples of sub-groups of autistic spectrum disorder.

Autistic disorder Abnormally impaired development in social interaction and communication and a restricted repertoire of activities and interests.

Rett's disorder A commonly diagnosed pervasive developmental disorder indicative of arrested development across a range of skills.

Childhood disintegrative disorder (CDD) A rare condition characterized by late onset of development and delays in language, social function and motor skills.

Asperger's syndrome Severe and sustained impairment in social interaction, and the development of restricted, repetitive patterns of behaviour, interests and activities.

Autistic spectrum disorder (ASD) An umbrella term that refers to all disorders that display autistic-style symptoms across a wide range of severity and disability.

Table 16.6 *Autistic spectrum disorders*

Disorder	Description	Estimated prevalence rate
Autistic disorder	• Abnormally impaired development in social interaction and communication, and a restricted repertoire of activities and interests • Characterized by stereotyped behaviour patterns in a significant proportion of cases, and intellectual disability in 70% of cases	5–13 per 10,000 births
Rett's disorder	• After a period of normal postnatal development, multiple specific deficits appear after around 5 months of age • Head growth decelerates and previously acquired purposeful hand skills are lost • After 30 months characteristic stereotyped hand wringing and washing gestures develop • There is severe impairment in expression and profound intellectual disability • It is a disorder that is reported almost exclusively in females	0.5–1 per 10,000 births
Childhood disintegrative disorder (CDD)	• Marked regression in multiple areas of functioning following around 2 years of seemingly normal development • Losses in previously acquired language, social skills and adaptive behaviour occur • Most symptoms come to resemble those of autistic disorder, although in the latter there is no loss of previously acquired skills	0.2 per 10,000
Asperger's syndrome	• Severe and sustained impairment in social interaction, and the development of restricted, repetitive patterns of behaviour, interests and activities • Unlike autistic disorder, there are usually no delays in language and communication acquisition, nor any delays in early cognitive development	3 per 10,000

16.4.1 Autistic Disorder

The early development of some children is so profoundly disturbed that from less than 1 year of age it will become apparent to family and friends that the infant's development is not proceeding normally. The child may seem withdrawn, has failed to develop normal means of communication, appears uninterested in his or her surroundings, and has difficulty learning new skills. Case History 16.2 relates some of the behavioural traits of Adam, a 1-year-old child who was later diagnosed with autistic disorder. Typical of autistic spectrum disorders, Adam shows no interest in his surroundings other than an obsessive interest in a small number of toys. He lacks normal communication skills for his age, and appears withdrawn and unable to learn new responses or skills. He also has temper tantrums when he appears unable to express his needs or has his very detailed play routines disrupted.

The two central features of autistic disorder are severe impairments in social interaction and in communication, although the severity of these symptoms depends on the developmental level and age of the individual. Early manifestations of symptoms can be diagnosed as *infantile autism*, but

> **Infantile autism** Early manifestations of the symptoms of autistic disorder.

the disorder is pervasive and is now considered to be a lifelong developmental disorder.

16.4.1.1 Diagnosis and Symptoms of Autistic Disorder

Table 16.7 provides the DSM-IV-TR diagnostic criteria for autistic disorder. There is now general agreement that the autistic spectrum disorder consists of significant and observable impairments in three areas: (1) reciprocal social interactions, (2) communication and (3) imagination and flexibility of thought. These three areas of impairment are known as the *triad of impairments*.

> **Triad of impairments** Impairments in reciprocal social interactions, communication and flexibility of thought that are typical of autistic spectrum disorder.

Impairments of Reciprocal Social Interaction The impairment in reciprocal social interaction is one of the most marked and sustained features of the disorder. Sufferers will exhibit impairment in the use of non-verbal behaviours (e.g. eye contact, appropriate facial expression) and are unable to regulate social interaction and communication. They will rarely approach others, and almost never offer a spontaneous greeting or make eye contact

CASE HISTORY 16.2

Autism

After Adam's first birthday party his mother began to pay attention to some characteristics of her son's personality that didn't seem to match those of the other children. Unlike other toddlers, Adam was not babbling or forming any word sounds, while others his age were saying 'mama' and 'cake'. Adam made no attempt to label people or objects, but would just pronounce a few noises which he would utter randomly through the day.

At the birthday party and in other situations, Adam seemed uninterested in playing with other children or even being around them socially. He seemed to enjoy everyone singing 'Happy Birthday' to him, but made no attempt to blow the candles out on the cake – even after others modelled the behaviour for him.

His parents also noted that Adam had very few interests. He would seek out two or three Disney toys and their corresponding videotapes and that was it. All other games, activities and toy characters were rejected. If pushed to play with something new, he would sometimes throw intense, unconsolable tantrums. Even the toys he did enjoy were typically not played with in an appropriate manner. Often he would line them up in a row, in the same order, and would not allow them to be removed until he decided he was finished with them. If someone else tried to rearrange the toys, he would have a tantrum.

As the months went by and he remained unable to express his wants and needs, Adam's tantrums became more frequent. If his mother did not understand his noises and gestures, he would become angry at not getting what he wanted. He would begin to hit his ears with his hands and cry for longer and longer periods of time.

Source: adapted from Gorenstein & Cromer (2004)

Clinical Commentary

From a very early age, Adam exhibited symptoms of the triad of impairments typical of autistic spectrum disorder. He shows: (1) no sign of engaging in or enjoying reciprocal social interactions (e.g. the lack of interest in socializing with others at his birthday party); (2) a significant delay in the development of spoken speech (illustrated by his failure to form word sounds, label objects or express his wants and needs); and (3) a lack of imagination and flexibility of thought (as demonstrated by his inability to use toys in imaginative play and his inflexibly stereotyped behaviour towards these toys).

Table 16.7 DSM-IV-TR diagnostic criteria for autistic disorder

A   A total of six (or more) items from (1), (2) and (3), with at least two from (1) and one each from (2) and (3):

   (1) Qualitative impairment in social interaction, as manifested by at least two of the following:

      (a) Marked impairment in the use of multiple non-verbal behaviours such as eye-to-eye gaze, facial expression, body postures and gestures to regulate social interaction.

      (b) Failure to develop peer relationships appropriate to the developmental level.

      (c) A lack of spontaneous seeking to share enjoyment, interests or achievements with other people (e.g. by a lack of showing, bringing or pointing out objects of interest).

      (d) Lack of social or emotional reciprocity.

   (2) Qualitative impairments in communication as manifested by at least one of the following:

      (a) Delay in, or total lack of, the development of spoken language (not accompanied by an attempt to compensate through alternative modes of communication such as gesture or mime).

      (b) In individuals with adequate speech, marked impairment in the ability to initiate or sustain a conversation with others.

      (c) Stereotyped and repetitive use of language or idiosyncratic language.

      (d) Lack of varied, spontaneous make-believe play or social imitative play appropriate to developmental level.

   (3) Restricted repetitive and stereotyped patterns of behaviour, interests and activities, as manifested by at least one of the following:

      (a) Encompassing preoccupation with one or more stereotyped and restricted patterns of interest that is abnormal either in intensity or focus.

      (b) Apparently inflexible adherence to specific, non-functional routines or rituals.

      (c) Stereotyped and repetitive motor mannerisms (e.g. hand or finger flapping or twisting, or complex whole-body movements).

      (d) Persistent preoccupation with parts of objects.

B   Delays or abnormal functioning in at least one of the following areas, with onset prior to age 3 years: (1) social interaction, (2) language as used in social communication or (3) symbolic or imaginative play.

C   The disturbance is not better accounted for by Rett's disorder or childhood disintegrative disorder.

---

when meeting or leaving another individual (Hobson & Lee, 1998). In young children, this is often manifested as a clear disinterest in making friends, establishing friendships or any other form of peer communication. Particularly striking is the autistic child's apparent inability to understand the intentions or emotions of others, and his or her universal disinterest in what others are doing. This has led some theorists to suggest that children with autistic disorder fail to develop a theory of mind, that is, they fail to develop an ability to understand the intentions, desires and beliefs of others (see below, section 16.4.1.4). As a result, this makes them unable to understand why other people behave in the way they do. While children with milder forms of the disorder may be able to learn which physical features of a person are associated with the expression of an emotion (e.g. that a frown is associated with anger or disapproval), they are often unable to explain why someone is expressing a particular emotion (Capps, Losh & Thurber, 2000).

Impairments in Communication   There is also a prominent delay in the development of spoken language. In those who do learn to speak, there is an inability to sustain a conversation. When speech does develop, it often fails to follow the normal rules of pitch, intonation or stress, and a child's speech may sound monotonous and disinterested. Grammatical structures are often immature and more than half of those diagnosed with autistic disorder fail to speak at all, but may utter a range of noises and screams which are often unrelated to attempts to communicate. Some individuals exhibit what is known as *echolalia*, which is immediate imitation of words or sounds they have just heard (e.g. if asked 'Do you want a drink?', the child will reply 'Do you want a drink?'). Others who do develop language may only be able to communicate in a limited way and may exhibit oddities in grammar and articulation. For instance, some exhibit *pronoun reversal* in which they refer to themselves as 'he', 'she' or 'you', and this is a feature of speech which is highly resistant to change (Tramonta & Stimbert, 1970). An autistic child's ability to learn language is a good indicator of prognosis. Those who have learned meaningful speech by age

> **Echolalia**   The immediate imitation of words or sounds that have just been heard.

> **Pronoun reversal**   An impairment in communication in which an individual refers to himself or herself as 'he', 'she' or 'you'.

5 years are most likely to benefit from subsequent treatment (Werry, 1996; Kobayashi, Murata & Yoshinaga, 1992).

Impairments in Imagination and Flexibility of Thought

One common feature of individuals with autistic spectrum disorder is that they often display restricted, repetitive and stereotyped patterns of behaviour and interests. This can manifest in childhood as a specific and detailed interest in only a small number of toys. Like Adam in Case History 16.2, they may line up the same set of toys in exactly the same way time after time, and become very distressed if their routine is disrupted or if they are not allowed to complete the routine. There appears to be a need to retain 'sameness' in all their experiences: autistic children may become extremely distressed if the furniture in a room is changed around or they travel on a different route to school one day.

Children with autistic disorder will often form strong attachments to inanimate objects such as keys, rocks, mechanical objects or objects with particular types of tactile characteristics (such as the smooth-surfaced dice described in *George's Story* at the beginning of this chapter). However, when they do play with individual objects, such as a toy car, they rarely indulge in symbolic play (e.g. by moving the car along the floor as if it were travelling somewhere), but instead will usually explore the tactile features of the toy in a stereotyped manner (e.g. by simply rotating the car in their hands for long periods of time). A further common characteristic of autism is the appearance of stereotyped body movements, which can include hand clapping, finger snapping, rocking, dipping and swaying. These patterns of behaviour often appear to be self-stimulatory in nature, and can often become so intense and severe that they may cause physical injury, such as stereotyped hand and finger biting, head banging, hair pulling and scratching.

The primary symptoms we have just reviewed (in social interaction, communication and symbolic or imaginative play) are each central to a diagnosis of autistic disorder, and disturbances in these areas should be apparent before 3 years of age (Criterion B).

In addition to these main symptoms, approximately 80 per cent of those diagnosed with autistic disorder exhibit signs of intellectual disability and will have an IQ score of less than 70 (Gillberg, 1991; Bryson, Clark & Smith, 1988). However, the nature of the intellectual deficits in children with autistic disorder is often different from those with a primary diagnosis of mental retardation (see section 16.3). Individuals suffering autistic disorder usually perform much better on tests of visuospatial ability than tests of social understanding or verbal ability. Thus, they are much better at finding hidden figures in drawings, assembling disassembled objects and matching designs in block-design tests (Rutter, 1983). However, in many cases, individuals with autism may excel at one specific task (such as the ability to calculate dates) or in one particular area (such as mathematics or music). In individuals with multiple cognitive disabilities, extraordinary proficiency in one isolated skill is known as *savant syndrome*, which is a phenomenon that appears to be closely linked to autistic spectrum disorder and is frequently found in Asperger's syndrome (Heaton & Wallace, 2004).

Savant syndrome The phenomenon of extraordinary proficiency in one isolated skill in individuals with multiple cognitive disabilities. It appears to be closely linked to autistic spectrum disorder and is frequently found in Asperger's syndrome.

By definition, the onset of autistic disorder is prior to 3 years of age, but symptoms may be detected by parents much earlier than this. In school-age children and adolescents, sufferers may show some behavioural and developmental gains such as increased social functioning. In adulthood, about 1 in 3 sufferers will be able to live with some degree of partial independence, but only a small minority go on to live and work independently (APA, 2000, p. 73).

Finally, we must conclude by stressing that diagnosing an autistic spectrum disorder is complicated. For example, autistic spectrum disorders can manifest over a range of disabilities, from severe to relatively mild high-functioning autism, and at the high-functioning end of the spectrum, it is often hard to distinguish those symptoms that may be characteristic of autism. Similarly, diagnosis is complicated by the fact that (1) behaviour patterns may change with age, (2) symptoms may be manifested with varying degrees of intellectual disability, and (3) autistic spectrum disorders are often comorbid with other problems such as ADHD and epilepsy.

16.4.1.2 The Prevalence of Autistic Spectrum Disorder

Epidemiological studies estimate the rate of autistic disorder at between 5 and 13 cases per 10,000 (0.05 per cent of births) (APA, 2000, p. 73; Fombonne, 2005). In the UK there are estimated to be around 580,000 people with an autistic spectrum disorder diagnosis. Around 80 per cent of those diagnosed are boys (Volkmar, Szatmari & Sparrow, 1993), and autism appears to occur equally in all socioeconomic classes and racial groups (Fombonne, 2002). Recent epidemiological surveys of autistic spectrum disorder suggest that the prevalence rate of the disorder has been increasing significantly, with recent estimates as high as 1–2 per 1,000 births (between 0.1 and 0.2 per cent) (Chakrabarti & Fombonne, 2005). Asperger's syndrome has been estimated at 3 per 10,000 and childhood disintegrative disorder much less prevalent at about 0.2 per 10,000 (Fombonne, 2005). The causes of this increase in recorded prevalence rates over the last 10 years are unclear, although obvious candidates are improvements in diagnosis and detection and greater public awareness of the disorder (Chakrabarti & Fombonne, 2005; Gernsbacher, Dawson & Goldsmith, 2005). However, other clinicians suspect that this may be a real increase in incidence resulting from an increase in the prevalence of those factors that cause autistic spectrum disorder (e.g. Blaxill, Baskin & Spitzer, 2003) (see Activity Box 16.1).

16.4.1.3 The Aetiology of Autistic Spectrum Disorder: Biological Causes

In the 1960s, it was believed that autistic behaviour was caused by cold or rejecting parenting (e.g. Bettelheim, 1967) – a view that simply added to the distress of parents already having to cope with a child with severe behavioural problems. However, subsequent studies have systematically failed to uphold this view, and have confirmed that the parents of autistic children are no different in their parenting skills from those of non-autistic children (Cox, Rutter, Newman & Bartak, 1975; Cantwell, Baker & Rutter, 1978). Nevertheless, the causes of autistic spectrum disorder are still relatively poorly understood, although it is becoming clear that there is a significant genetic element. However, in individual cases there is likely to be a contribution from environmental factors as well, such as perinatal risk factors (e.g. maternal infections during pregnancy). The various combinations of genetics and environmental risk factors may be the reason why autistic spectrum disorders vary so much in their symptomatology and their severity. As we shall see below, it is now accepted that autistic spectrum disorder is caused primarily by aberrant brain development, which gives rise to the range of impairments in cognitive abilities and social understanding exhibited by sufferers.

Genetic Factors There had been evidence available for some time that the social and language deficits and psychological problems reminiscent of autistic spectrum disorder often had a family history (Folstein & Rutter, 1988; Piven & Palmer, 1999). In particular, there is evidence for a strong familial aggregation of autistic symptoms, as demonstrated in studies of sibling reoccurrence risk (i.e. studies investigating the probability of developing autism given that an individual's sibling is autistic). These studies have estimated that the rate of autism in the sibling of someone with autism ranges between 2 and 14 per cent (Bailey, Phillips & Rutter, 1996; Jorde, Mason-Brothers, Waldmann, Ritvo et al., 1990), which is significantly higher than the 0.05–0.2 per cent prevalence rate found in the general population. Autistic spectrum disorder also appears to co-occur with several known genetic disorders such as phenylketonuria, fragile X syndrome and tuberous sclerosis (Smalley, 1998; Reiss & Freund, 1990), implying a genetic link in its aetiology. There are also familial links between autistic disorder and other psychological problems. For instance, affective disorders are almost three times more common in the parents of autism sufferers than in the parents of children suffering from tuberous sclerosis or epilepsy. While we might expect that having a child with a disability might precipitate such psychological problems, a majority of parents of autistic children developed their affective disorder before the birth of the child (Bailey, Phillips & Rutter, 1996).

Numerous twin studies have confirmed this genetic component to the disorder. In studies comparing concordance rates in MZ and DZ twins, Folstein and Rutter (1977) found concordance in 4 out of 11 MZ twins but none in DZ twins. Subsequent twin studies have found concordance rates of between 60 and 91 per cent for MZ twins and between 0 and 9 per cent for DZ twins (Rutter, MacDonald, Le Couteur, Harrington et al., 1990; Bailey, Le Couteur, Gottesman, Bolton et al., 1995; Steffenberg, Gillberg, Hellgren, Andersson et al., 1989). In addition, more recent twin studies have demonstrated that each of the symptom components of autistic disorder – social impairments, communication impairments and restricted repetitive behaviours – all individually show high levels of heritability (Ronald, Happe, Price, Baron-Cohen et al., 2006).

Despite confirmation from a variety of sources that autistic spectrum disorder has a significant genetic component, it has so far not been possible to clearly identify the genes responsible for transmitting the disorder. This suggests that a single gene is not responsible for the expression of autism, and as many as 15 different genes may be involved (Santangelo & Tsatsanis, 2005).

Even when there is strong evidence to suggest the involvement of a single gene, the significance of the gene in terms of brain development has been difficult to determine (Muhle, Trentacoste & Rapin, 2004). This suggests that autistic spectrum disorder is a complex condition that may involve a range of different genetic influences affecting symptom expression and severity.

Chromosome Disorders Autistic disorder has been found to be associated with a number of chromosomal disorders including fragile X syndrome and tuberous sclerosis (Gillberg & Coleman, 2000). Individual cases of autistic disorder have been linked to aberrations on nearly all chromosomes, including chromosomal duplications, deletions and inversions (Schroer, Phelan, Michaelis, Crawford et al., 1998; Wolpert, Donnelly, Curraro, Hedges et al., 2001). Nevertheless, despite this link to chromosomal problems, this factor probably accounts for fewer than 10 per cent of cases of autistic spectrum disorder (Folstein & Rosen-Sheidley, 2001).

Biochemical Factors One source of the cognitive and behavioural problems exhibited by individuals with autism may be abnormalities in the brain neurotransmitters that regulate and facilitate normal adaptive brain functioning. This has led to a focus of research on the role of specific neurotransmitters in autistic spectrum disorder. Unfortunately, much of the research on the role of brain neurotransmitters in autism has been inconclusive (Lam, Aman & Arnold, 2006). Early studies of children diagnosed with autistic disorder indicated low levels of the neurotransmitters serotonin and dopamine (Chugani, Muzik, Behen, Rothermel et al., 1999; Ernst, Zametkin, Matochik, Pascualvaca et al., 1997), both of which are essential for effective cognitive, behavioural and motor functioning and mood regulation. Research in this area is currently plagued by methodological difficulties, including small sample sizes, contradictory findings using different research methodologies, and failure to use appropriate control conditions (Lam, Aman & Arnold, 2006). However, provided that these issues can be resolved, it appears to be a fruitful area for future research.

Perinatal Factors We noted in our discussion of intellectual disabilities that perinatal factors may play a significant role in determining intellectual impairment, and the same may be true of autistic spectrum disorder. A number of birth complications and prenatal factors have been identified as risk factors in the development of autistic spectrum disorder, including maternal infections such as rubella during pregnancy (Chess, Fernandez & Korn, 1978), intrauterine exposure to drugs such as thalidomide and valproate (Stromland, Nordin, Miller, Akerstrom et al., 1994; Williams, King, Cunningham, Stephan et al., 2001), maternal bleeding after the first trimester of pregnancy (Tsai, 1987) and depressed maternal immune functioning during pregnancy (Tsai & Ghaziuddin, 1997). However, many of these risk factors have been identified only in individual case reports and probably account for a very small percentage of cases of autistic spectrum disorder (Fombonne, 2002; Muhle, Trentacoste & Rapin, 2004). For example, recent studies suggest that congenital rubella infection has been found to be present in less than 0.75 per cent of autistic populations, largely because of the near eradication of the disease in Western countries (Fombonne, 1999).

Some studies also claim to have linked autism to postnatal events such as a link between autistic spectrum disorder, inflammatory bowel disease and administration of the measles, mumps and rubella (MMR) vaccine (Wakefield, Murch, Anthony, Linnell et al., 1998). This claim caused some controversy in the UK at the time because it led to many parents refusing to have their children immunized with the vaccine, thus putting them at significant risk for these infections (see Activity Box 16.1). However, subsequent studies have failed to corroborate an association between administration of MMR and autism (e.g. Madsen, Hviid, Vestergaard, Schendel et al., 2002). In addition, recent studies have failed to find any association between infectious diseases in the first 2 years of life and autism. Rosen, Yoshida and Croen (2007) found that children with subsequent diagnoses of autism had no more overall infections in the first 2 years of life than children without autism.

In conclusion, while a very small minority of cases of autism may be linked to perinatal factors such as those outlined above, congenital and perinatal factors are probably not the primary causes of the disorder.

Brain Abnormalities There is now a good deal of converging evidence from autopsy studies, fMRI studies and studies measuring EEG (electroencephalogram) and ERP (event-related potentials) that autism is associated with aberrant brain development. Autopsy studies of individuals diagnosed with autistic spectrum disorder have revealed abnormalities in a number of brain areas, including the limbic system and the cerebellum. For example, neurons in the limbic system are smaller and more dense than normal, and the dendrites which transmit messages from one neuron to another are shorter and less well developed (Bauman & Kemper, 1994). Abnormalities in the cerebellum appear to correspond to deficits in motor skills such as impaired balance, manual dexterity and grip often found in individuals with autistic spectrum disorder (Gowen & Miall, 2005). Finally, autopsy studies have shown overly large brain size and enlarged ventricles in the brain (Bailey, Luthert, Dean, Harding et al., 1998), and many of these abnormalities are typical of prenatal stages of brain development.

Anatomical and functional imaging studies have supplemented the evidence from autopsy studies and given us an insight into how brain abnormalities in autism progress during different developmental stages. They have confirmed the hypothesis that individuals with autism have abnormalities in a number of brain regions, including the frontal lobes, limbic system, cerebellum and basal ganglia (Sokol & Edwards-Brown, 2004), and they also confirm that autistic individuals have larger brain size and significantly poorer neural connectivity than non-sufferers (McAlonan, Cheung Cheung, Suckling et al., 2005). We have already alluded to the fact that individuals diagnosed with autism lack a theory of mind (the ability to attribute mental states to others or to understand the intentions of others), and fMRI studies indicate that this is associated with decreased activation of the prefrontal cortex and amygdala, areas which form an important component of the brain system underlying the intentions of others (Castelli, Frith, Happe & Frith, 2002).

In addition, 1 in 4 individuals with autistic disorder also exhibit abnormal EEG patterns in the frontal and temporal lobes, and many of them have actual clinical seizures (Dawson, Klinger,

Panagiotides, Lewy et al., 1995; Rossi, Parmeggiani, Bach, Santucci et al., 1995). In contrast, ERP studies provide information from brain activity about how individuals react to external stimuli in the environment. Individuals with autism exhibit ERP patterns that indicate disrupted and abnormal attention to a range of stimuli, including novel stimuli and language stimuli (Courchesne, Townsend, Akshoomoff, Saitoh et al., 1994; Dunn, 1994).

Taken together, these three sources of evidence indicate that individuals with autistic spectrum disorder exhibit abnormalities in a number of different brain areas. These brain areas exhibit both anatomical (i.e. structural) and functional abnormalities (i.e. they do not appear to be able to fulfil the cognitive functions they do in normally developed individuals). These abnormalities appear to be determined by a period of abnormal brain overgrowth in the first 2 years of life (hence studies showing that autistic individuals develop oversize brains), followed by abnormally slow or arrested growth. This deviant brain growth occurs at a time during development when the formation of brain circuitry is at its most vulnerable (Couchesne, 2004).

16.4.1.4 The Aetiology of Autistic Spectrum Disorder: Cognitive Factors

Depending on the severity of their symptoms, individuals with autistic spectrum disorder clearly have problems attending to and understanding the world around them. Most notably, they have difficulty with normal social functioning. In severe cases they may be withdrawn and unresponsive, while less severe cases may exhibit difficulty in reciprocal social interaction, including deficits in communication and in understanding the intentions and emotions of others. Some theorists have argued that these deficits in social skills are a result of deficits in cognitive functioning (Rutter, Bailey, Bolton & Le Couteur, 1994). Firstly, individuals with autistic spectrum disorder appear to exhibit deficits in executive functioning, resulting in poor problem-solving ability and difficulty planning actions, controlling impulses and attention, and inhibiting inappropriate behaviour; these deficits all impact on the ability to act appropriately in social situations. Secondly, some theorists have argued that individuals with autistic spectrum disorder lack a *theory of mind (TOM)*. That is, they fail to comprehend normal mental states

> **Theory of mind (TOM)** The ability to understand one's own and other people's mental states.

and so are unable to understand or predict the intentions of others. We will discuss these two cognitive accounts separately.

Deficits in Executive Functioning Individuals with autistic spectrum disorder generally perform poorly on tests of executive functioning, suggesting that they have difficulty effectively problem-solving, planning, initiating, organizing, monitoring and inhibiting complex behaviours (Ozonoff & McEvoy, 1994; Shu, Lung, Tien & Chen, 2001). Consistent evidence for executive functioning deficits has been found in adults, adolescents and older children with autism (McEvoy, Rogers & Pennington, 1993). However, determining the significance of poor performance on tests of executive functioning is difficult, because executive functioning tasks require the integration of a range of more basic cognitive

ACTIVITY BOX 16.1

Autism and the MMR vaccine

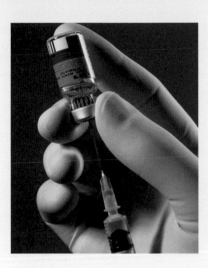

'I have three children. The eldest, who is 15, did not have the MMR injection and is not autistic. The second two, who did have MMR, are both autistic and showed no signs of the condition prior to immunization.'

This was a comment sent to a BBC website by a mother following a TV programme discussing claims that pervasive developmental disorders were associated with the measles, mumps and rubella (MMR) vaccine given to children during infancy. The claim that the MMR vaccine might be a cause of some forms of autism was first made by Wakefield, Murch, Anthony, Linnell et al. (1998). They proposed that the vaccine was linked to a new syndrome consisting of certain gastrointestinal conditions associated with marked regression in multiple areas of functioning after 2 years of age (e.g. childhood disintegrative disorder). This claim caused a significant fall in the number of parents in the UK willing to have their children vaccinated with MMR, resulting in an increase in incidence of mumps, measles and rubella infections.

Evidence for the link between MMR and autism

Wakefield et al. (1998) based their claim of an association between the MMR vaccine and autism on a study of 12 children with inflammatory bowel conditions and regressive developmental symptoms typical of autism. In 8 of the 12 cases, the children's parents suggested that the MMR vaccine might have contributed to the onset of the behavioural problems. We have already noted (p. 00) that epidemiological studies suggest that the prevalence rate of autism has been increasing significantly over the last 10–15 years (Chakrabarti & Frombonne, 2005). Supporters of the link between MMR and autism suggest that the introduction of new 'environmental risk factors', such as new vaccines, may be partly responsible for this increase.

Evidence against the link between MMR and autism

Wakefield et al. (1998) themselves admit that their study did not prove an association between MMR and the development of autistic symptoms. The following factors are important in providing a balanced view of this issue:

- The sample that Wakefield et al. (1998) used to make the claim is very small and very selective (Payne & Mason, 1998), meaning that their findings are neither statistically significant nor generalizable to the population as a whole.

- It is not obvious what the mechanism might be that would link the MMR vaccine with the development of autistic symptoms. Wakefield et al. (1998) attempt to relate their findings to the effect of the vaccine on intestinal disorders, and to the fact that some forms of intestinal disorders can lead to the incomplete breakdown of peptides in the gut, which has been shown to cause autistic-like symptoms (Panksepp, 1979).

- If there is a causal link between MMR and autism, we would expect to find that more children who have been given the MMR vaccine would exhibit autistic symptoms than those who have not received the vaccine. However, numerous studies have indicated that children given MMR are no more likely to develop autistic symptoms than those who have not received the vaccine (DeStefano, Bhasin, Thompson, Yeargin-Allsopp et al., 2004; Farrington, Miller & Taylor, 2001).

- Finally, an interesting experiment to test the hypothesized link between MMR and autism would involve finding out what happens when we stop giving MMR injections. Does the rate of autism go down, as we might predict if the MMR vaccine is the cause of recent rises in the prevalence of autism? Unfortunately, this is not an easy experiment to do! However, Honda, Shimizu and Rutter (2005) report the results of what turned out to be a type of 'natural experiment' in Japan. Japan introduced the MMR vaccine for children in 1977 but terminated the programme in April 1993. Honda et al. found that between 1988 and 1993 (during the time that the vaccine was being administered), the incidence of autistic spectrum disorder (ASD) increased. However, the statistics also show that the incidence of ASD continued to increase in children born after the vaccine had been withdrawn. They conclude that MMR is unlikely to be the main cause of the increase in incidence of ASD in many countries, and that the withdrawal of MMR is unlikely to lead to a reduction in the incidence of ASD.

This issue is still far from resolved, although the weight of evidence is now more consistent with the idea that there is no causal link between the MMR vaccine and autism. *You may want to discuss this evidence with your fellow students, and try to think up some further studies that might contribute to resolving this debate.*

abilities such as shifting attention, memory, sequencing events and inhibiting responses. Nevertheless, even when the basic cognitive processes required for successful executive functioning are analysed separately, individuals with autistic spectrum disorder exhibit deficits in a number of these skills, including categorization and concept formation (Minshew, Meyer & Goldstein, 2002), shifting attention (Akshoomoff, Courchesne & Townsend, 1997; Belmonte, 2000), planning and abstract problem-solving (Hill & Bird, 2006) and short-term and long-term memory (Bachevalier, 1994; Klinger & Dawson, 1996). However, evidence suggests that they fail to exhibit deficits in cognitive inhibition (inhibiting inappropriate responses) (Kleinhans, Akshoomoff & Delis, 2005; Ozonoff & Strayer, 1997) or on tests of semantic fluency (Boucher, 1988; Manjiviona & Prior, 1999). Thus, depending on the degree of severity of the disorder, individuals with autistic spectrum disorder may be deficient only in some of the basic cognitive skills required to complete executive function tasks successfully, and not in others.

Theory of Mind Deficits One influential account of autistic spectrum disorder claims that the fundamental problem for individuals with autism is that they fail to develop a theory of mind (Baron-Cohen, Leslie & Frith, 1985; Baron-Cohen, 2001). That is, individuals with autism fail to develop an awareness that the behaviour of other people is based on mental states that include beliefs and intentions about what they should do; as a result, individuals with autism fail to understand the intentions of others (refer back to *George's Story* at the beginning of this chapter to see how George was unable to comprehend that his mother's threats to send him away were not intentional). There are a number of ways to test whether a child has developed a theory of mind. One traditional method is known as the ***Sally-Anne False Belief Task*** (Baron-Cohen, Leslie & Frith, 1985). This procedure is described more fully in Research Methods Box. 16.1.

Sally-Anne False Belief Task
A method used to test whether a child has developed a 'theory of mind'.

Even adults with high-functioning autism (such as Asperger's syndrome) exhibit theory of mind deficits on some measures. For example, many of the traditional tests of theory of mind are rather static and somewhat removed from the dynamic situations individuals with autism experience in real life. To make such tests more akin to everyday experiences, Heavey, Phillips, Baron-Cohen and Rutter (2000) devised the Awkward Moments Test, in which participants view a series of TV commercials and are then asked questions about the events in each. Individuals with Asperger's syndrome were significantly less able to answer questions about the mental state of the characters in the commercials than an age- and gender-matched control group without autism. However, the two groups did not differ on scores on questions related to recall of events within the TV clips (a memory test), suggesting that the poorer scores on mental state questions by Asperger's syndrome participants were not simply due to a memory deficit. Because of these difficulties in understanding the mental states of others, individuals with autistic spectrum disorder undoubtedly have difficulty indulging in symbolic play with others, actively participating in human interactions and forming lasting relationships.

SUMMARY

As we noted at the outset of this section, autism is a complex disorder which varies considerably in its symptomatology and severity across individuals. Recent research has indicated a significant genetic component to autistic disorder, although it has still not been established how the disorder is inherited, what specific genes are involved, nor how specific genes might influence the expression of autistic symptoms. Autopsy studies, fMRI studies and EEG and ERP studies suggest that individuals with autistic spectrum disorder exhibit deficits in a number of different brain areas, resulting in both structural and functional abnormalities. In cognitive terms, these abnormalities appear to significantly affect executive functioning and prevent autistic individuals from fully developing a theory of mind that will enable them to understand the intentions and emotions of others. Autism may also be a multifaceted syndrome, with a range of different causes, and at least some environmental factors have been implicated in a small proportion of aetiologies. These include maternal rubella during pregnancy, intrauterine exposure to drugs and depressed maternal immune functioning.

16.4.2 The Treatment and Care of Individuals with Autistic Spectrum Disorder

A range of attempts have been made to help individuals with autistic spectrum disorder adapt to day-to-day living and to increase their quality of life. As we described earlier, many individuals with autism have severe communication difficulties and are unable to live a normal life without continuous support and care. Interventions generally take three broad forms: drug treatments to reduce problematic behaviour such as withdrawal, aggression or self-injury; behavioural training to promote basic communication and socializing skills; and inclusion strategies that will support clients attempting to live a relatively normal life within society. Because of the nature of the disorder, there are many problems associated with attempting to treat individuals with autistic spectrum disorder. We will describe these first.

16.4.2.1 Problems in Treating Individuals with Autistic Spectrum Disorder

The very nature of the symptoms of autistic spectrum disorder poses problems for almost any form of intervention designed to improve skills or quality of life. Firstly, one of the main characteristics of autism is that sufferers do not like changes from routine, and any intervention – by its very nature – is designed to implement change.

Secondly, autistic children often appear to be oblivious to the outside world: they respond very poorly to attempts at communication,

RESEARCH METHODS IN CLINICAL PSYCHOLOGY BOX 16.1

The Sally-Anne False Belief Task

How can we measure whether someone can understand the intentions of others? Baron-Cohen, Leslie and Frith (1985) designed an imaginative procedure that has been used many times to assess theory of mind abilities in a range of clinical populations. This is known as the *Sally-Anne false beliefs task*. In this procedure, two dolls are used to act out the story shown above. At the end, children are asked: 'Where will Sally look for her marble?' Children who have developed a theory of mind will say that when Sally comes back from her walk, she will look in the basket for her marble because they will understand that she has not seen Anne move it. Children who are unable to understand that others have different beliefs from themselves will say that Sally will look in the box because that is where they themselves know it is.

Baron-Cohen, Leslie and Frith (1985) conducted this test with three groups of children, all with a mental age of over 3 years. One group was diagnosed with autistic disorder, one with Down syndrome, and the third group consisted of normally developing children. Most of the children with autism answered incorrectly (saying Sally would look in the box), while most of the children in the other two groups gave the right answer (saying Sally would look in the basket). The inclusion in the study of a group of children with Down syndrome showed that the failure on this task of children with autism could not be attributed to their learning difficulties more generally. In addition, all children correctly answered two control questions: 'Where is the marble really?' and 'Where was the marble in the beginning?', demonstrating understanding of the change in the physical location of the marble during the story.

Source: Frith (2003)

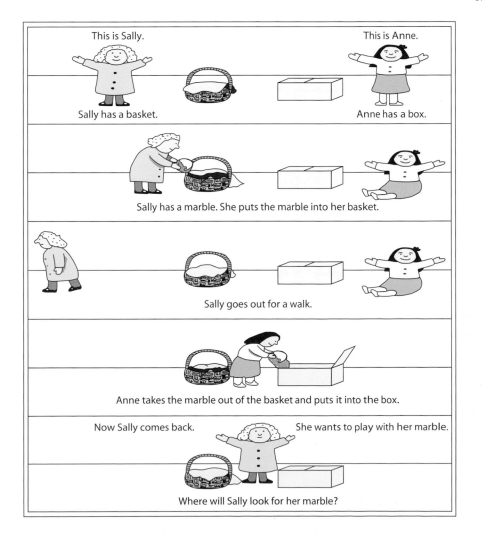

This is Sally.   This is Anne.

Sally has a basket.   Anne has a box.

Sally has a marble. She puts the marble into her basket.

Sally goes out for a walk.

Anne takes the marble out of the basket and puts it into the box.

Now Sally comes back.   She wants to play with her marble.

Where will Sally look for her marble?

and even something as simple as trying to achieve eye contact can be problematic. Because of this, any training programme has to begin at a very basic communication level by, for example, teaching the child to make eye contact (Hwang & Hughes, 2000).

Thirdly, children with autism appear to show interest in only a very limited range of events and objects, and this makes it very difficult to find effective reinforcers that can be used to reward them. Because of their apparent unresponsiveness to communication, praise is often ineffective as a reinforcer and attempts have to be made to find rewards that are highly salient. This may mean having to pair praise with food (so that praise acquires secondary reinforcing properties) (Davison, 1964) or using tactile reinforcers such as a hug or a vibratory stimulus applied to the skin (Johnson & Davey, 1978).

Fourthly, children with autism have over-selective attention that means that if they do attend to the training task, it is likely that anything that is learned may well be situation-specific and will not generalize to other environments or to other similar tasks.

Finally, even in high-functioning sufferers, such as those with Asperger's syndrome, their relatively idiosyncratic social and communicative skills can mean that they are treated with some suspicion and reserve by others in society – even though they are as capable as anyone else at undertaking employment successfully. As we shall see later, this issue means that inclusion strategies require support for both client and employer if high-functioning individuals with autism are to integrate successfully into the working environment.

16.4.2.2 Drug Treatments

A number of drugs are used in the treatment of autism symptoms, mainly to help control problem behaviours. Antipsychotic medications are the most commonly used type of drugs in the treatment of autism, including **haloperidol** and, more recently, **rispiridone**. Antipsychotic drugs such as these have been shown to reduce repetitive and stereotyped behaviours, reduce levels of social withdrawal, and also reduce symptoms associated with aggression and challenging behaviour, such as hyperactivity, temper tantrums, mood changes and self-abusive behaviour (Malone, Gratz, Delaney & Hyman, 2005). However, not all children with autism respond well to this class of drugs, and they can have potentially serious side effects such as sedation, dizziness, increased appetite and weight gain, and result in jerky movement disturbances (dyskinesias) (Campbell, Armenteros, Malone, Adams et al., 1997).

Haloperidol An antipsychotic medication most commonly used in the treatment of autism.

Rispiridone An antipsychotic medication also commonly used in the treatment of autism.

Naltrexone An opioid receptor antagonist which has been found to be beneficial in the control of hyperactivity and self-injurious behaviour.

The opioid receptor antagonist **naltrexone** has also been found to be beneficial in the control of hyperactivity and self-injurious behaviour. A study by Symons, Thompson and Rodriguez (2004) suggested that the drug decreased self-injurious behaviours by over 50 per cent in 47 per cent of the participants in their study. Some studies have even indicated that naltrexone can produce moderate increases in social interaction and communication (Aman & Langworthy, 2000; Kolmen, Feldman, Handen & Janosky, 1995).

16.4.2.3 Behavioural Training Methods

Most training programmes for individuals with autism attempt to develop basic self-help, social and communication skills in individuals who otherwise would be largely uncommunicative and require lifelong care. Most training procedures adopt a conditioning-based approach, in which the clinician attempts to reinforce basic behavioural skills such as attention (eye contact), toileting behaviour, self-help behaviours, initiating interactions with peers and adults, and play behaviour with peers. These methods can also be used to reduce the frequency of disruptive or inappropriate behaviours such as temper tantrums, self-injurious behaviour, repetitive behaviours and aggressive responses (see Treatment in Practice Box 16.1 on functional analysis in individuals with intellectual disorders) (Lovaas, 1987; Davison, 1964).

To supplement basic conditioning principles, therapists also use a range of methods to promote the required behaviours in the first place. These methods include *modelling* (i.e. demonstrating the required behaviour to clients before prompting them to imitate it). This technique is especially helpful when attempting to teach autistic individuals to communicate using sign language. Because many autistic children remain speechless, learning to communicate through sign language has proved a useful way of facilitating interactions with others (Goldstein, 2002). Despite the wide use of these methods to promote basic behaviours, there are very few properly controlled outcome studies that have assessed the relative efficacy of these training procedures (Howlin, 2005). However, in the absence of such studies, the literature does suggest that early intensive behavioural interventions may be the most effective way of promoting the social functioning of autistic individuals over the long term (Howlin, 2005).

Modelling The process of demonstrating a required behaviour to clients before prompting them to imitate it.

Most of these training procedures are time-consuming and repetitive, requiring a significant amount of investment in time and effort by those conducting the training. However, a way of supplementing treatment by professionals is to train parents themselves so that they can apply these behavioural techniques at home (Erba, 2000). This has a number of benefits. It enables the autistic child to learn appropriate behaviours in the environment in which he or she is most likely to be using them (the home); it frees up professional therapists' time; and it offers a tiered structure to treatment that provides a potentially larger number of sufferers with day-to-day treatment. Some studies even suggest that parents may be more effective and efficient trainers than professionals: a study by Koegel, Schreibman, Britten, Burkey et al. (1982) suggested that 25–30 hours of parent training were as effective as 200 hours of similar treatment by professionals in a clinic setting. *Parent-implemented early intervention* has been

Parent-implemented early intervention Using parents as effective trainers to teach children with intellectual disabilities, basic self-help and communication skills.

shown to improve child communication behaviour, increase maternal knowledge of autism, enhance maternal communication style and parent–child interaction, and reduce maternal depression (McConachie & Diggle, 2007). Parents not only learn to use behavioural techniques to train their own children, they can also effectively train others who work with or care for their children to use these techniques (Symon, 2005). This approach effectively expands the group of individuals associated with an autistic child who are skilled in maintaining a consistent training regime for that child.

16.4.2.4 Inclusion Strategies

Many home-based interventions for high-functioning individuals with autistic spectrum disorder teach self-help strategies, social and living skills and self-management designed to help individuals function more effectively in society. However, even when individuals have effectively acquired many of these skills, they may still need to be supported through important life transitions, such as finding and keeping a job. One such support scheme is known as *supported employment*. This provides support to both the employee with autism and the employer, including: (1) training and support for the employer on how to manage the employee with autism; (2) provision of job preparation and interview skills for the employee; (3) support for the employee for as long as it is needed; and (4) regular feedback sessions with both

Supported employment A special programme designed with a built-in support mechanism to help people with physical, mental or developmental disabilities reach and keep their customized vocational goals and objectives

employee and employer. Supported employment schemes have been shown to increase the employee's social integration, increase employee satisfaction and self-esteem (Kilsby & Beyer, 1996; Stevens & Martin, 1999), and promote higher rates of employment compared to a matched control group (Mawhood & Howlin, 1999). Treatment in Practice Box 16.2 provides examples of the types of employment found for individuals under the supported employment scheme.

16.4.2.5 Summary of Interventions for Individuals with Autistic Spectrum Disorder

This section has given a flavour of the broad range of interventions that are available for individuals with autistic spectrum disorder. This client group is particularly problematic because sufferers frequently lack the communicative and attentional skills that are usually an important requirement for behaviour change. However, basic behavioural training methods have proven to be effective at promoting a range of self-help, social and communicative skills in those most severely affected. These methods have been supplemented with the adoption of parent training programmes, which extend the range of individuals with the skills necessary for successful intervention. Drugs are commonly used, primarily to control negative behavioural symptoms such as self-injurious, challenging and hyperactive behaviours, but they may also have some positive impact on communication and social behaviour. High-functioning individuals with autistic spectrum disorder can also receive support in the form of supported employment programmes that help individuals to find and keep a suitable job.

CLINICAL PERSPECTIVE: TREATMENT IN PRACTICE BOX 16.2

Types of jobs found by individuals with autism or Asperger's syndrome using a supported employment scheme

Type of work	% of jobs	Examples of jobs found
Administration/technical	8	Statistician, chemist, research officer, photography
Administration/accounts assistant	22	Archiving, accounts, etc.
Technical assistant	13	Library, finance, technical, BT operator
Data entry	6	Keyboard operator, data input
Data management	3.5	IT analyst, web design
Office work/clerical assistant	19	Offices, banks, etc.
Secretarial	1.5	Hospital and university posts
Shopwork	8	Customer service, travel agents, transport, checkout till, etc.
Stockroom	6	Shelf-stocking, etc.
Postal work	4	Mail delivery/sorting
Other	7	Support worker, nursery, messenger, joiner, gardening, seamstress
Catering	1.5	Chef, kitchen hand
Cleaning	0.5	

Source: Howlin, Alcock & Burkin (2005)

SUMMARY

This final section of the chapter has discussed the group of developmental problems known collectively either as pervasive developmental disorders (PDD) or autistic spectrum disorder (ASD). The specific diagnosable disorders we have mentioned are autistic disorder, Rett's disorder, childhood disintegrative disorder (CDD) and Asperger's syndrome. These disorders are indicative of arrested development across a range of skills. The main characteristics are impairment in reciprocal social interactions, impairments in communication skills, and the presence of stereotyped or repetitive behaviour patterns. Genetic factors have been identified in the aetiology of autistic spectrum disorder, although we have yet to identify the specific genes involved, how these genes might influence the expression of symptoms, and whether genes interact with environment to cause the disorder.

Individuals with autistic disorder also exhibit both functional and structural deficits in a number of brain areas. Cognitive symptoms of autistic spectrum disorder include deficits in some of the skills that contribute to executive functioning, and theory of mind deficits that mean autistic individuals are frequently unable to understand the emotions and intentions of others. Drugs can be used to help control the more disruptive behavioural elements of autistic spectrum disorder (such as self-injurious or aggressive behaviour), but early intensive behavioural interventions appear to be the best way of promoting social functioning over the long term. Finally, high-functioning individuals with autistic spectrum disorder can be helped to establish a successful working career with the help of community inclusion strategies and supported employment schemes.

SELF-TEST QUESTIONS

- What is the triad of impairments that are important in the diagnosis of autistic spectrum disorder?
- What are the current prevalence rates for autistic spectrum disorder, and what factors might be increasing these prevalence rates?
- What is the evidence for autistic spectrum disorder being an inherited disorder?
- What perinatal factors might contribute to autistic symptoms?
- What kinds of studies have contributed to our understanding of brain abnormalities in autistic spectrum disorder?

- What cognitive deficits have individuals with autistic spectrum disorder been shown to have?
- What are the main problems associated with the treatment of individuals with autistic spectrum disorder?
- What drugs are used to treat autistic spectrum disorder, and what symptoms do they attempt to treat?
- What is parent-implemented early intervention, and is it effective?
- What is supported employment when used with higher-functioning individuals with autism? How successful is it?

SECTION SUMMARY

16.4 Pervasive Developmental Disorders

- The **triad of impairments** in autistic spectrum disorder refers to impairments in (1) reciprocal social interaction, (2) communication and (3) imagination and flexibility of thought.

- The prevalence rate of diagnosed autistic spectrum disorders has been increasing over recent years to estimates as high as 1–2 per 1,000 births.

- There is an important **genetic** element to autistic spectrum disorder, although it has not yet been possible to identify the specific genes involved.

- **Perinatal factors** may account for a small percentage of autism cases. Such factors may include maternal rubella during pregnancy, intrauterine exposure to drugs, maternal bleeding after the first trimester and depressed maternal immune functioning during pregnancy.

- There is good evidence from autopsy, fMRI and EEG and ERP studies that autism is associated with **aberrant brain development**.

- Cognitive factors contributing to autistic symptoms include impaired **executive functioning** and **theory of mind** (**TOM**) deficits.

- Drug treatments for children with autism include **haloperidol**, **rispiridone** and **naltrexone**, all of which attempt to treat the negative symptoms of the disorder.

- Behavioural training methods used to teach basic self-help and communication skills include operant conditioning techniques, **modelling** and **parent-implemented early interventions**.

- **Supported employment** has proven successful at helping higher-functioning individuals with autism to find and maintain employment.

16.5 LEARNING, INTELLECTUAL AND DEVELOPMENTAL DISABILITIES REVIEWED

In this chapter we have covered three distinctive types of developmental disorder, namely, specific learning disorders (such as reading disorder and expressive language disorder), intellectual disabilities and pervasive developmental disorders (particularly autism and autistic spectrum disorder). All of these disabilities represent lifelong conditions that are usually present from birth, and characterized by individuals failing to meet important developmental milestones in social behaviour, communication and learning skills.

The range of disability covered by these three areas is broad, with some individuals being so severely affected as to be effectively institutionalized because of their cognitive and behavioural problems or concurrent physical handicaps (e.g. individuals with profound mental retardation). However, many others with these disabilities can function sufficiently well to enjoy relatively normal daily living, and with structured support schemes can succeed in both educational and occupational environments. Recent years have seen rapid developments in inclusion policies designed to extend the rights of individuals with learning and developmental disabilities to be educated and employed in mainstream settings. This has led to a significant improvement in the quality of life and self-esteem experienced by sufferers. You may now like to return to Table 16.1 to familiarize yourself with the main features of these disabilities.

LEARNING OUTCOMES

When you have completed this chapter you should be able to:

1   Discuss the different ways in which learning and developmental disabilities are categorized and labelled.

2   Describe and compare the various types of specific learning disabilities and their aetiology and treatment.

3   Describe the various forms of intellectual disability.

4   Compare and contrast genetic, biological and environmental causes of intellectual disabilities.

5   Describe and evaluate the main forms of intervention, care and support for intellectual disabilities.

6   Describe the diagnostic criteria for the main pervasive developmental disorders.

7   Compare and contrast theories of the aetiology of autistic spectrum disorder.

8   Describe and evaluate the main forms of intervention, care and support for individuals with pervasive developmental disorders.

KEY TERMS

Accessibility strategies *585*
Altered auditory feedback (AAF) *581*
Amniocentesis *586*
Anoxia *589*
Applied behaviour analysis *592*
Asperger's syndrome *597*
Autistic disorder *597*
Autistic spectrum disorder (ASD) *597*
Cerebral palsy *589*
Childhood disintegrative disorder *597*
Congenital disorders *588*
Congenital rubella syndrome (CRS) *588*
Crack baby *589*
Cretinism *588*

Developmental disabilities *576*
Disorder of written expression *578*
Down syndrome *586*
Dyslexia *578*
Echolalia *599*
Expressive language disorder *578*
Foetal alcohol syndrome (FAS) *589*
Fragile X syndrome *586*
Functional analysis *593*
Haloperidol *606*
Infantile autism *598*
Intellectual disabilities *576*
Learning disability *576*
Maternal HIV infection *589*

REVIEWS, THEORIES AND SEMINAL STUDIES

Links to Journal Articles

16.2 Specific Learning Disabilities

Alexander, A.W. & Slinger-Constant, A.M. (2004). Current status of treatments for dyslexia: Critical review. *Journal of Child Neurology, 19*, 744–758.

Bothe, A.K., Davidow, J.H., Bramlett, R.E. & Ingham, R.J. (2006). Stuttering treatment research 1970–2005: I. Systematic review incorporating trial quality assessment of behavioural, cognitive and related approaches. *American Journal of Speech-Language Pathology, 15*, 321–341.

Eckert, M. (2004). Neuroanatomical markers for dyslexia: A review of dyslexia structural imaging studies. *Neuroscientist, 10*, 362–371.

Fox, A.V., Dodd, B. & Howard, D. (2002). Risk factors for speech disorders in children. *International Journal of Language and Communication Disorders, 37*, 117–131.

Galaburda, A.M., LoTurco, J., Ramus, F., Fitch, R.H. & Rosen, G.D. (2006). From genes to behaviour in developmental dyslexia. *Nature Neuroscience, 9*, 1213–1217.

Law, J., Garrett, Z. & Nye, C. (2004). The efficacy of treatment for children with developmental speech and language delay/disorder: A meta-analysis. *Journal of Speech, Language and Hearing Research, 47*, 924–943.

Saviour, P. & Ramachandra, B. (2006). Biological basis of dyslexia: A maturing perspective. *Current Science, 90*, 168–174.

Shalev, R.S. (2004). Developmental dyscalculia. *Journal of Child Neurology, 19*, 765–771.

Shaywitz, S.E. & Shaywitz, B.A. (2005). Dyslexia (specific reading disability). *Biological Psychiatry, 57*, 1301–1309.

16.3 Intellectual Disabilities

Fergusson, D.M. & Woodward, L.J. (1999). Maternal age and educational and psychosocial outcomes in early adulthood. *Journal of Child Psychology and Psychiatry, 43*, 479–489.

Floyd, R.L., O'Connor, M.J., Sokol, R.J., Bertrand, J. & Cordero, J.F. (2005). Recognition and prevention of fetal alcohol syndrome. *Obstetrics and Gynecology, 106*, 1059–1064.

Griffin, D.K., Rosenberg, H. & Cheyney, W. (1996). A comparison of self-esteem and job satisfaction of adults with mild mental retardation in sheltered workshops and supported employment. *Education and Training in Mental Retardation and Developmental Disabilities, 31*, 142–150.

Mengel, M.B., Searight, H.R. & Cook, K. (2006). Preventing alcohol-exposed pregnancies. *Journal of the American Board of Family Medicine, 19*, 494–505.

Moffit, T.E. & the E-Risk Study Team (2002).Teen-aged mothers in contemporary Britain. *Journal of Child Psychology and Psychiatry, 43*, 727–742.

Reece, R.M. & Sege, R. (2000). Childhood head injuries: Accidental or inflicted? *Archives of Pediatrics and Adolescent Medicine, 154*, 11–15.

Simonoff, E., Pickles, A., Chadwick, O., Gringas, P. et al. (2006). The Croydon Assessment of Learning Study: Prevalence and educational identification of mild mental retardation. *Journal of Child Psychology and Psychiatry, 47*, 828–839.

16.4 Pervasive Developmental Disorders

Baron-Cohen, S., Leslie, A. & Frith, U. (1985). Does the autistic child have a theory of mind? *Cognition, 21*, 37–46.

Fombonne, E. (2005). Epidemiology of autistic disorder and other pervasive developmental disorders. *Journal of Clinical Psychiatry, 66*, 3–8.

Honda, H., Shimizu, Y. & Rutter, M. (2005). No effect of MMR withdrawal on the incidence of autism: A total population study. *Journal of Child Psychology and Psychiatry, 46*, 572–579.

Howlin, P. (2005). The effectiveness of interventions for children with autism. *Journal of Neural Transmission: Supplement, 69,* 101–119.

Howlin, P., Alcock, J. & Burkin, C. (2005). An 8-year follow-up of a specialist supported employment service for high-ability adults with autism or Asperger syndrome. *Autism, 9,* 533–549.

Keen, D. & Ward, S. (2004). Autistic spectrum disorder: A child population profile. *Autism, 8,* 39–48.

Kleinhans, N., Akshoomoff, N. & Delis, D.C. (2005). Executive functions in autism and Asperger's disorder: Flexibility, fluency, and inhibition. *Developmental Neuropsychology, 27,* 379–401.

Lam, K.S.L., Aman, M.G. & Arnold, L.E. (2006). Neurochemical correlates of autistic disorder: A review of the literature. *Research in Developmental Disabilities, 27,* 254–289.

McConachie, H. & Diggle, T. (2007). Parent-implemented early intervention for young children with autism spectrum disorder: A systematic review. *Journal of Evaluation in Clinical Practice, 13,* 120–129.

Muhle, R., Trentacoste, S.V. & Rapin, I. (2004). The genetics of autism. *Pediatrics, 113*(5), E472–E486.

Ozonoff, S., Pennington, B.F. & Rogers, S.J. (1991). Executive function deficits in high-functioning autistic individuals: Relationship to theory of mind. *Journal of Child Psychology and Psychiatry, 32,* 1081–1105.

Rosen, N.J., Yoshida, C.K. & Croen, L.A. (2007). Infection in the first two years of life and autism. *Pediatrics, 119,* E61–U18.

Rutter, M. (2005). Aetiology of autism: Findings and questions. *Journal of Intellectual Disability Research, 49,* 231–238.

Santangelo, S.L. & Tsatsanis, K. (2005). What is known about autism: Genes, brain and behaviour. *American Journal of Pharmacogenomics, 5,* 71–92.

Symon, J.B. (2005). Expanding interventions for children with autism. *Journal of Positive Behavior Interventions, 7,* 159–173.

Toal, F., Murphy, D.G.M. & Murphy, K.C. (2005). Autistic-spectrum disorders: Lessons from neuroimaging. *British Journal of Psychiatry, 187,* 395–397.

Tonn, R.T. & Obrzut, J.E. (2005). The neuropsychological perspective on autism. *Journal of Developmental and Physical Disabilities, 17,* 409–419.

Texts for Further Reading

Caine, A. (1998). *Clinical psychology and people with intellectual disabilities.* Chichester: Wiley.

Emerson, E. (2004). *The international handbook of applied research in intellectual disabilities.* Chichester: Wiley.

Emerson, E., Hatton, C., Bromley, J. & Craine, A. (Eds.) (1998). *Clinical psychology and people with intellectual disabilities.* Chichester: Wiley.

Happe, F. (1994). *Autism: An introduction to psychological theory.* London: Routledge.

Harris, C.J. (2005). *Intellectual disability: Understanding its development, causes, evaluation, and treatment.* Oxford: Oxford University Press.

Hayes, C.B. (Ed.) (2006). *Dyslexia in children: New research.* Nova Biomedical.

Jacobson, J.W., Mulick, J.A. & Rojahn, J. (Eds.) (2006). *Handbook of intellectual and developmental disabilities.* New York: Springer.

Ryan, J. & Thomas, F. (1998). *The politics of mental handicap* (rev. ed.). New York: Free Association Books.

Snowling, M.J. & Stackhouse, J. (2005). *Dyslexia, speech and language: A practitioner's handbook* (2nd ed.). Whurr Publishers.

Volkmar, F.R., Paul, R., Klin, A. & Chen, D.J. (Eds.) (2005). *Handbook of autism and pervasive developmental disorders, Vol. 1: Diagnosis, development, neurobiology, and behavior.* Chichester: Wiley.

Volkmar, F.R., Paul, R., Klin, A. & Chen, D.J. (Eds.) (2005). *Handbook of autism and pervasive developmental disorders, Vol. 2: Assessment, interventions, and policy.* Chichester: Wiley.

Wing, L. (2003). *The autistic spectrum: A guide for parents and professionals.* Constable & Robinson.

RESEARCH QUESTIONS

16.2 Specific Learning Disabilities

- Are attentional deficits common to a number of different specific learning disorders?

- Why are 60–80 per cent of those diagnosed with reading disorder boys?

- Why are boys four times more likely than girls to be diagnosed with stuttering?

- How does the expression of certain genes lead to the abnormal brain development associated with dyslexia?

- Are abnormalities found in the temporo-parietal areas of the brain in autopsy studies merely representative of the consequences of a lifetime of poor reading rather than a causal factor in dyslexia?

- To what extent is mathematical disorder (dyscalculia) an inherited disorder?

- Are disorders such as stuttering and phonological disorder merely the result of problems with the physical articulation of sounds?

- Does anxiety cause stuttering, or is it just a consequence of stuttering?

16.3 Intellectual Disabilities

- How does maternal age contribute to chromosomal abnormalities in Down syndrome?

- To what extent is fragile X syndrome a single unitary disorder?

- To what extent is maternal substance abuse a cause of intellectual disabilities independent of the context (e.g. economic and social deprivation) in which the offspring is often raised?

- To what extent does social deprivation and poverty constitute a form of intellectual impoverishment that can cause intellectual disabilities?

- Can lack of stimulation during early childhood directly result in permanent impairments in brain function?

16.4 Pervasive Developmental Disorders

- Why do individuals with autistic disorder usually perform much better on tests of visuospatial ability than tests of social understanding or verbal ability?

- Why has the incidence of autistic spectrum disorder increased significantly over the past 20 years?

- What are the genes responsible for transmitting autistic spectrum disorder, and how does their expression affect the symptoms of autism?

- What role, if any, do brain neurotransmitter abnormalities have in causing the symptoms of autism?

- Does measles-mumps-rubella (MMR) inoculation cause autistic spectrum disorder in vulnerable children?

- Do childhood infections play a role in causing symptoms of autism?

- Do individuals with autistic spectrum disorder have impairments on all the cognitive skills that contribute to executive functioning?

- Are behavioural interventions effective when used with autistic clients?

CLINICAL ISSUES

16.1 The Categorization and Labelling of Learning Disabilities

- Although the phrase mental retardation is usually frowned upon as stigmatizing and demeaning, it is still used as a diagnostic category in DSM-IV-TR.

16.2 Specific Learning Disabilities

- Do specific learning disabilities require attention in an educational rather than a clinical setting?

16.3 Intellectual Disabilities

- Individuals with intellectual disabilities have both strengths and limitations. Limitations need to be described in a way that enables suitable support to be developed and provided.

- Studies suggest that only around 15 per cent of schoolchildren aged 13–15 years with IQ scores <70 are in receipt of a statement of special educational needs.

- What can be done to make the identification of the causes of intellectual disability easier to isolate and identify?

- Differential diagnosis between specific learning disabilities and intellectual disabilities is often problematic.

- Blood tests and procedures such as amniocentesis can leave prospective parents with difficult decisions about whether to maintain a pregnancy if it is likely that their child will be born with intellectual disabilities. How should they be counselled to make this decision?

- What can clinicians do to try to ensure that factors such as social deprivation and poverty do not adversely affect the intellectual and behavioural development of a child?

- How can we improve ways of identifying physical abuse as the cause of developmental and intellectual disabilities in infants?

- Can clinicians do anything to reduce the prevalence of lead poisoning in children?

- How can clinicians contribute to family support programmes that may help mothers of low socioeconomic status to raise their children more effectively?

- How can individuals with moderate to severe levels of intellectual disability be taught to use contraceptives, employ family planning and even rear a family?

16.4 Pervasive Developmental Disorders

- What are the problems inherent in diagnosing autistic spectrum disorder?

- What kinds of problems are involved in interventions for people with autistic spectrum disorder, and how can these problems be overcome?

- To what extent are the idiosyncratic social and communicative skills of individuals with Asperger's syndrome an obstacle to their successfully undertaking employment?

- What are the problems associated with the use of medications in the treatment of autistic spectrum disorder?

- How important is it to train parents of autistic children to apply behavioural interventions at home?

Glossary

ABA design A single-case experiment which involves an initial baseline stage of observation and measurement of behaviour without any intervention (A), followed by a treatment or manipulation stage where the experimental manipulation is introduced and its effect on behaviour observed and measured (B). A final return-to-baseline stage is then introduced (A) in which behaviour is once more observed in the absence of the treatment or manipulation.

ABAB design A single-case experiment, similar to the ABA design, with the addition of a second treatment or manipulation stage, providing extra power in demonstrating that any changes in behaviour are explicitly due to the manipulation or treatment.

ABC chart An observation method that requires the observer to note what happens before the target behaviour occurs (A), what the individual did (B), and what the consequences of the behaviour were (C).

Abnormal attribution processes The view that paranoid delusions may be the result of a bias towards attributing negative life events to external causes.

Abnormal psychology An alternative definition of psychopathology, albeit with negative connotations in regard to being 'not normal'.

Abreaction The intense re-experiencing of traumatic events.

Abstinence violation Dysfunctional beliefs about relapse following treatment for substance dependency that facilitate further regular substance use.

Accessibility strategies Programmes that extend the rights of individuals with intellectual disabilities to be educated according to their needs in mainstream schools.

Acetylcholine A neurotransmitter that appears to be involved in learning and memory.

Acquired sociopathy A reckless regard for others' personal safety, a lack of remorse and a lack of planning, as well as overtly psychotic behaviour such as extreme paranoia and hallucinations, usually caused by an undetected and large brain tumour.

Active stage The stage in which an individual begins to show unambiguous symptoms of psychosis, including delusions, hallucinations, disordered speech and communication, and a range of full-blown symptoms.

Adaptive fallacy The view that it is possible to think up a threatening or dangerous consequence for encountering any stimulus or situation.

Addiction When a person's 'normal' body state is the drugged state (so that the body requires the substance to feel normal).

Adolescent-onset conduct disorder A sub-type of conduct disorder defined by the appearance of conduct disorder symptoms only after the age of 10 years.

Adoption studies Research conducted on children who are biologically similar but have been reared apart.

Adult Memory and Information Processing Battery (AMIPB) A neuropsychological test in wide use in the UK, comprising two tests of speed of information processing, verbal memory tests (list learning and story recall) and visual memory tests (design learning and figure recall).

Aetiology A term widely used in psychopathology to describe the causes or origins of psychological symptoms.

Affectionless control A type of parenting characterized by high levels of overprotection combined with a lack of warmth and care.

Affective flattening Limited range and intensity of emotional expression; a 'negative' symptom of schizophrenia.

Age regression In hypnotherapy, the recreation of the physical and mental state that a client was in prior to experiencing any trauma in order to help the individual recall events during earlier stages of his or her life.

Agnosia The loss of the ability to recognize objects, persons, sounds, shapes or smells while the specific sense is not defective and there is no significant memory loss.

Alcohol A colourless volatile liquid compound which is the intoxicating ingredient in drinks such as wine, beer and spirits.

Alcohol myopia The situation where an alcohol-intoxicated individual has less cognitive capacity available to process all ongoing information, and so alcohol acts to narrow attention and means that the drinker processes fewer cues less well.

Alcoholics Anonymous (AA) A support group for alcoholics who are trying to abstain.

Allostatic state A biological state of stress.

Alogia A lack of verbal fluency in which the individual gives very brief, empty replies to questions.

Alter identities The identities that develop after the onset of dissociative identity disorder.

Altered auditory feedback (AAF) A form of treatment for stuttering in which delayed auditory feedback or a change in frequency of the voice is given to clients when they are speaking.

Alternative delivery systems Treatment methods that allow access to services for sufferers who might not receive other forms of treatment. These include treatment and support via telephone therapy, email, the internet, computer-software CD-ROMs and virtual reality techniques.

Alzheimer's disease A slowly progressive form of dementia involving progressive impairments in short-term memory, with symptoms of aphasia, apraxia and agnosia, together with evidence of impaired judgements, decision-making and orientation.

Amenorrhea The abnormal failure to menstruate.

American Psychiatric Association (APA) A scientific and professional organization that represents psychiatry in the United States.

Amniocentesis A procedure which involves extracting and analysing the pregnant mother's amniotic fluid used prenatally in identifying Down syndrome in high-risk parents.

Amotivational syndrome A syndrome in which those who take up regular cannabis use are more likely to be those who exhibit apathy, loss of ambition and difficulty concentrating.

Amphetamine psychosis A syndrome in which high doses of amphetamines taken for long periods of time produce behavioural symptoms in humans and animals that closely resemble symptoms of psychosis.

Amphetamines A group of synthetic drugs used primarily as a central nervous system stimulant. Common forms are amphetamine itself (Benzedrine), dextroamphetamine (Dexedrine) and methamphetamine (Methedrine).

Amygdala An area of the brain that plays an important role in directing attention to affectively salient stimuli and prioritizing the processing of such stimuli.

Analogue observations Clinical observations carried out in a controlled environment that allows surreptitious observation of the client.

Analogue populations Populations that are usually participants without any mental health problems, which may be human or non-human animals.

Analogue research Research on healthy, non-clinical populations in order to shed light on the aetiology of psychopathology.

Androgens The most important of the male hormones. Unusual sexual behaviour, such as impulsive sexual offending involving non-consenting others, may be due to imbalances in these hormones.

Aneurysm A localized bulging in a blood vessel caused by disease or weakening of the vessel wall.

Anhedonia Inability to react to enjoyable or pleasurable events.

Animal models The use of laboratory animals in research to simulate processes comparable to those occurring in humans.

Anorexia nervosa (AN) An eating disorder, the main features of which include a refusal to maintain a minimal body weight, a pathological fear of gaining weight and a distorted body image in which sufferers continue to insist they are overweight.

Anoxia A perinatal cause of intellectual disability, being a significant period without oxygen that occurs during or immediately after delivery.

Antabuse (disulfiram) A drug used in the detoxification of individuals with alcohol dependency.

Anterior cingulate cortex (ACC) The frontal part of the cingulate cortex resembling a 'collar' form around the corpus callosum, used for the relay of neural signals between the right and left hemispheres of the brain.

Anterograde amnesia Memory loss for information acquired after the onset of amnesia. Also known as **anterograde memory dysfunction**.

Anti-androgen drugs A group of drugs that significantly decrease the levels of male hormones such as testosterone.

Antidepressant drugs Drug treatments intended to treat symptoms of depression and mood disorder.

Antipsychotic drugs Drug treatments intended to treat symptoms of psychosis and schizophrenia.

Antiretroviral drugs Chemicals that inhibit the replication of retroviruses, such as HIV.

Antisocial personality disorder (APD) A personality disorder, the main features of which are an enduring disregard for, and violation of, the rights of others. It is characterized by impulsive behaviour and lack of remorse, and is closely linked with adult criminal behaviour.

Anxiety disorder An excessive or aroused state characterized by feelings of apprehension, uncertainty and fear.

Anxiety sensitivity Fears of anxiety symptoms based on beliefs that such symptoms have harmful consequences (e.g. that a rapid heart beat predicts an impending heart attack).

Anxiety Sensitivity Index A measure, developed by Reiss, Peterson, Gursky & McNally (1986), to measure anxiety sensitivity.

Anxiolytic drugs Drug treatments intended to treat symptoms of anxiety and stress.

Anxious/fearful personality disorders Personality disorders grouped in Cluster C which exhibit mainly anxious and fearful symptoms and are frequently linked to comorbid Axis I anxiety disorders.

Aphasia A speech disorder resulting in difficulties producing or comprehending speech.

Applied behaviour analysis Applying the principles of learning theory (particularly operant conditioning) to the assessment and treatment of individuals suffering psychopathology.

Applied family management An intensive form of family intervention which goes beyond education and support to include active behavioural training elements.

Applied scientist Someone who is competent as both a researcher and a practitioner.

Apraxia Loss of the ability to execute or carry out learned (familiar) movements, despite having the desire and the physical ability to perform the movements.

Asperger's syndrome Severe and sustained impairment in social interaction, and the development of restricted, repetitive patterns of behaviour, interests and activities.

Assertive community treatment Programmes to help people recovering from psychotic episodes with their medication regimes, offering psychotherapy, assistance in dealing with everyday life and its stressors, guidance on making decisions, residential supervision and vocational training.

Assertive outreach A way of working with groups of individuals with severe mental health problems who do not effectively engage with mental health services.

Associated features Features of a disorder that are usually, but not always, present.

Ataque de Nervios A form of panic disorder found in Latinos from the Caribbean.

Attention deficit hyperactivity disorder (ADHD) A persistent pattern of inattention and/or hyperactivity-impulsivity that is at a significantly higher rate than would be expected for a child at his or her developmental stage.

Attention process training (APT) A form of rehabilitation training for attention deficits that uses a number of different strategies to promote and encourage attentional abilities.

Attribution theories Theories of depression which suggest that people who are likely to become depressed attribute negative life events to internal, stable and global factors.

Autistic disorder Abnormally impaired development in social interaction and communication and a restricted repertoire of activities and interests.

Autistic spectrum disorder (ASD) An umbrella term that refers to all disorders that display autistic-style symptoms across a wide range of severity and disability.

Aversion therapy A treatment based on classical conditioning which attempts to condition an aversion to a stimulus or event to which the individual is inappropriately attracted.

Avoidant personality disorder A personality disorder the features of which are avoidance of a wide range of social situations, feelings of inadequacy, and hypersensitivity to negative evaluation and criticism.

Avolition Inability to carry out or complete normal day-to-day goal-oriented activities.

Bacterial meningitis The inflammation (infection) of the meninges, which are the membranes that cover the brain and spine.

Barbiturates A class of sedative drugs related to a synthetic compound (barbituric acid) derived from uric acid.

Basal ganglia A series of structures located deep in the brain responsible for motor movements.

Battered woman syndrome The view that a pattern of repeated partner abuse leads battered women to believe that they are powerless to change their situation.

Beating the Blues A computer-based CBT programme used in the management of mild and moderate depression.

Beck's cognitive therapy Theory that argues that depression is maintained by a 'negative schema' that leads depressed individuals to hold negative views about themselves, their future and the world (the 'negative triad').

Befriending A form of control condition for attention, understanding and caring used in treatment outcome studies.

Behaviour analysis An approach to psychopathology based on the principles of operant conditioning (also known as **behaviour modification**).

Behaviour management techniques Treatment methods that can be used in a range of environments and can even be taught to parents as an aid to controlling and responding to their children in the home.

Behaviour therapy A form of treatment that aims to change behaviour using principles based on conditioning theory.

Behavioural activation therapy A therapy for depression that attempts to increase clients' access to pleasant events and rewards and decrease their experience of aversive events and consequences.

Behavioural model An influential psychological model of psychopathology based on explaining behaviour.

Behavioural rehearsal A coping strategy that involves either the actual or imagined rehearsal of adaptive coping responses that need to be deployed when a worry trigger is encountered.

Behavioural self-control The personal use of operant conditioning principles to change or control one's own behaviour.

Behavioural self-control training (BSCT) A treatment procedure for substance dependency that teaches clients how to restructure and control their behaviour and environment in order to prevent substance use.

Behavioural stress management Behavioural techniques designed to reduce worrying and increase relaxation.

Bell-and-battery technique A widely used classical conditioning method for treating nocturnal enuresis.

Benzodiazepines A group of anxiolytics which have their effect by increasing the level of the neurotransmitter GABA at synapses in the brain.

Beta amyloid plaques Abnormal cell development, possibly caused by abnormal protein synthesis in the brain which clump together with the consequence of killing healthy neurons.

Binge drinking A high intake of alcohol in a single drinking occasion.

Binge-eating disorder (BED) An eating disorder characterized by recurrent episodes of binge eating without the purging or fasting that is associated with bulimia nervosa.

Binge-eating/purging type anorexia nervosa A type of eating disorder in which the sufferer regularly engages in purging activities to help control weight gain.

Biological challenge tests Research in which panic attacks are induced by administering carbon dioxide-enriched air (CO_2) or by encouraging hyperventilation.

Biological preparedness A theory which argues that we have a built-in predisposition to learn to fear things such as snakes, spiders, heights and water because these have been life-threatening to our ancestors.

Biphasic drug effect Where the initial effects of a drug may act as a stimulant (e.g. alcohol making the drinker reactive and happy), but the later effects act as a depressant (making the drinker sluggish and experience negative emotions).

Bipolar disorder A psychological disorder characterized by periods of mania that alternate with periods of depression.

Bipolar disorder spectrum A proposed spectrum of disorder encompassing both bipolar disorder and borderline personality disorder.

Body dissatisfaction The gap between one's actual and ideal weight and shape.

Body dysmorphic disorder Preoccupation with assumed defects in physical appearance.

Body mass index (BMI) A way of measuring a healthy weight range, derived by using both height and weight measurements.

Borderline personality disorder (BPD) A personality disorder, the main features of which are instability in personal relationships, a lack of well-defined and stable self-image, regular and unpredictable changes in moods and impulsive behaviour.

Broca's aphasia Disruption of the ability to speak consisting of difficulties with word ordering, finding the right word and articulation.

Bulimia nervosa (BN) An eating disorder, the main features of which are recurrent episodes of binge eating followed by periods of purging or fasting.

Buprenorphine An opioid drug used in the treatment of opioid addiction.

Caffeine A central nervous system stimulant that increases alertness and motor activity and combats fatigue; found in a number of different products, including coffee, tea, chocolate and some over-the-counter cold remedies and weight-loss aids.

Cannabis A natural drug derived from the hemp plant, *cannabis sativa*.

Case formulation The use of clinical information to draw up a psychological explanation of the client's problems and to develop a plan for therapy.

Case study An in-depth investigation of an individual participant.

Castration anxiety A psychoanalytic term referring to a psychological complex in males with a fear of being castrated.

Catastrophic misinterpretation of bodily sensations A feature of panic disorders where there is a cognitive bias towards accepting the more threatening interpretation of an individual's own sensations.

Catastrophizing An example of magnification, in which the individual takes a single fact to its extreme.

Catatonic behaviour Behaviour characterized by a significant decrease in reactivity to the environment (catatonic stupor), maintaining rigid, immobile postures (catatonic rigidity), resisting attempts to be moved (catatonic negativism) or purposeless and excessive motor activity that often consists of simple, stereotyped movements (catatonic excitement or stereotypy).

Catatonic schizophrenia A sub-type of schizophrenia characterized by severe disturbances of motor behaviour, including immobility, excessive motor activity (including violent behaviour), extreme negativism, mutism, peculiarities of voluntary movement, echolalia (repeating what is said by others) or echopraxia (imitating the behaviour and movements of others).

Cerebellum The part of the brain at the back of the skull that coordinates muscular activity.

Cerebral abscess A localized inflammation of the brain.

Cerebral embolism A blood clot that forms somewhere in the body before travelling through the blood vessels and lodging in the brain, causing the brain cells to become damaged as a result of oxygen starvation.

Cerebral palsy The main neurological birth syndrome caused by anoxia which is characterized by motor symptoms that affect the strength and coordination of movement.

Cerebral thrombosis An injury caused when a blood clot (thrombus) forms in an artery (blood vessel) supplying blood to the brain. The clot interrupts the blood supply and brain cells are starved of oxygen.

Cerebrovascular accident (CVA) Damage to brain tissue caused either by a blockage or breaking of the blood vessels in the brain. Also known as a stroke.

Child rapists Paedophiles who only get full sexual gratification from harming and even murdering their victims.

Childhood abuse The physical or psychological maltreatment of a child.

Childhood and Adolescent Mental Health Services (CAMHS) A four-tier model for planning and delivering mental health services for children in the UK.

Childhood disintegrative disorder (CDD) A rare condition characterized by late onset of development and delays in language, social function and motor skills.

Childhood-onset conduct disorder A sub-type of conduct disorder defined by the onset of at least one criterion characteristic of conduct disorder prior to 10 years of age.

Childhood sexual abuse The sexual maltreatment of a child.

Cholinesterase inhibitors A group of drugs that prevent acetylcholine breakdown in the synaptic cleft by acetylcholinesterase and increase its uptake in the postsynaptic receptor. The most common of these drugs are donepezil, rivastigmine and galantamine.

Chronic fatigue syndrome (CFS) A disorder characterized by depression and mood fluctuations together with physical symptoms such as extreme fatigue, muscle pain, chest pain, headaches and noise and light sensitivity.

Cingulatomy A neurosurgical treatment involving destroying cells in the cingulum, close to the corpus callosum.

Clanging A form of speech pattern in schizophrenia where thinking is driven by word sounds. For example, rhyming or alliteration may lead to the appearance of logical connections where none in fact exists.

Classical conditioning The learning of an association between two stimuli, the first of which (the conditioned stimulus, CS) predicts the occurrence of the second (the unconditioned stimulus, UCS).

Client-centred therapy An approach to psychopathology stressing the goodness of human nature, assuming that if individuals are unrestricted by fears and conflicts, they will develop into well-adjusted, happy individuals.

Clinical audit The use of research methods to determine whether existing clinical knowledge, skills and resources are effective and are being properly used. Also known as **evaluation research**.

Clinical psychology The branch of psychology responsible for understanding and treating psychopathology.

Clinical trials Experimental research studies used to test the effectiveness of treatments for mental health problems.

Closed head injury A concussion or head trauma, the symptoms of which include loss of consciousness after the trauma, confusion, headache, nausea or vomiting, blurred vision, loss of short-term memory and perseverating.

Cocaine A natural stimulant derived from the coca plant of South America which, after processing, is an odourless, white powder that can be injected, snorted or, in some forms (e.g. crack cocaine), smoked.

Cocaine abuse Episodic problematic use of the drug over a brief period of a few hours or a few days.

Cognitive behaviour therapy (CBT) An intervention for changing both thoughts and behaviour. CBT represents an umbrella term for many different therapies that share the common aim of changing both cognitions and behaviour.

Cognitive distortions Beliefs held by sexual offenders that enable them to justify their sexual offending.

Cognitive enhancement therapy A form of intervention which addresses deficits in both social cognition (the ability to act wisely in social situations) and neurocognition (basic abilities in cognitive functioning, such as memory and attention).

Cognitive model An influential psychological model of psychopathology.

Cognitive remediation therapy (CRT) A treatment programme for clients designed to develop and improve basic cognitive skills and social functioning generally.

Cognitive restructuring Methods used to challenge the biases that a client might hold about how frequently bad events might happen and to generate thoughts that are more accurate.

Cognitive retraining An approach to treating depression developed by Aaron Beck. Also known as **cognitive therapy** or **cognitive restructuring**.

Cognitive therapy A form of psychotherapy based on the belief that psychological problems are the products of faulty ways of thinking about the world.

Communication deviance (CD) A general term used to describe communications that would be difficult for ordinary listeners to follow and leave them puzzled and unable to share a focus of attention with the speaker.

Community care Care that is provided outside a hospital setting.

Comorbidity The co-occurrence of two or more distinct disorders.

Compensatory strategies Providing patients with memory impairments with specific strategies for remembering material.

Compulsions Repetitive or ritualized behaviour patterns that an individual feels driven to perform in order to prevent some negative outcome happening.

Computerized axial tomography (CAT) A neuroimaging technique which uses sophisticated versions of X-ray machines and can be used to form a three-dimensional picture of the brain.

Computerized CBT (CCBT) An alternative to therapist-delivered cognitive behaviour therapy which consists of highly developed software packages that can be delivered via an interactive computer interface on a personal computer, over the internet or via the telephone using interactive voice response (IVR) systems.

Concordance studies Studies designed to investigate the probability with which family members or relatives will develop a psychological disorder depending on how closely they are related – or, more specifically, how much genetic material they have in common.

Concurrent validity A measure of how highly correlated scores of one test are with scores from other types of assessment that we know also measure that attribute.

Concussion An impact to the head which jars the brain and temporarily disrupts its normal functioning.

Conditioning A form of learning in which an organism learns to associate events with one another (e.g. classical conditioning or operant conditioning).

Conduct disorder (CD) A pattern of behaviour during childhood in which the child exhibits a range of behavioural problems, including fighting, lying, running away from home, vandalism and truancy.

Confidentiality The right of participants in psychological research to expect that information they provide will be treated in confidence.

Confirmatory bias A clinical bias whereby clinicians ignore information that does not support their initial hypotheses or stereotypes and they interpret ambiguous information as supporting their hypotheses.

Conflict resolution The basic psychodynamic view of somatoform disorders in which distressing memories, inner conflict, anxiety and unacceptable thoughts are repressed in consciousness but outwardly expressed as somatic symptoms.

Congenital disorders Disorders acquired during prenatal development prior to birth but which are not genetically inherited.

Congenital rubella syndrome (CRS) The constellation of abnormalities caused by infection with the rubella (German measles) virus before birth. The syndrome is characterized by multiple congenital malformations (birth defects) and intellectual disability.

Constraint-induced movement therapy (CIMT) A technique used with aphasic patients which involves the mass practice of verbal responses in which the patient may be required to communicate without gesturing or pointing to describe various objects of varying complexity.

Construct validity Independent evidence showing that a measure of a construct is related to other similar measures.

Continuing professional development (CPD) The demonstration by accredited therapists that they regularly update their knowledge of recent developments in treatment techniques.

Continuous amnesia A memory disturbance where there is an inability to recall events from a specific time up to and including the present.

Control Using our knowledge of the causal relationships between events to manipulate behaviour or cognitions.

Control conditions Conditions within an experiment that control for any effects other than that produced by the independent variable.

Control group A group of participants who experience manipulations other than the independent variable being investigated.

Controlled drinking A variant of BSCT in which emphasis is put on controlled use rather than complete abstinence.

Controlled drug user A long-term drug user who has never been in specialized treatment and who displays levels of occupational status and educational achievement similar to the general population.

Contusion A severe head trauma in which the brain is not just jarred but the impact also causes bruising to the brain.

Conversion disorder The presence of symptoms or deficits affecting voluntary motor or sensory function.

Correlational designs Research designs which enable a researcher to determine if there is a relationship between two or more variables.

Cortisol An adrenocortical hormone.

Counselling A profession that aims both to promote personal growth and productivity and to alleviate any personal problems that may reflect underlying psychopathology.

Counterconditioning A behaviour therapy technique designed to use conditioning techniques to establish a response that is antagonistic to the psychopathology.

Couples therapy A treatment intervention for sexual dysfunction that involves both partners in the relationship.

Covert conditioning Using the client's ability to imagine events to condition acceptable associations between events.

Covert sensitization A variant on aversion therapy for substance abuse where clients are asked to imagine taking their drug followed by imagining some upsetting or repulsive consequence.

Crack baby A child addicted to cocaine or crack cocaine because of the mother's use of the drug during pregnancy.

Crack cocaine Free-based cocaine boiled down into crystalline balls.

Craving The strong subjective drive that addicts have to use a particular substance.

Cretinism A congenital disorder resulting in slow development, intellectual disabilities and small stature.

Cronbach's α A statistical test which indicates whether any individual item in an assessment test is significantly reducing the internal consistency of the test.

Cross-sectional design A research design that involves the collection of data from a sample at just one point in time.

Cultural bias The phenomenon of interpreting and judging phenomena in terms particular to one's own culture.

Custodial care A form of hospitalization or restraint for individuals with psychopathologies whose behaviour is thought of as disruptive.

Cyclothymic disorder A form of depression characterized by at least 2 years of hypomania symptoms that do not meet the criteria for a manic episode and in which the sufferer experiences alternating periods of withdrawal then exuberance, inadequacy and then high self-esteem.

Cyproterone acetate (CPA) An anti-androgen, testosterone-lowering drug.

Dangerous people with severe personality disorders (DSPD) A term introduced in 1999 in a report by the UK Home Office and the Department of Health to describe individuals who are diagnosed with antisocial personality disorder and who have, in addition, a diagnosis of at least one other type of personality disorder.

Deception The act of deceiving.

Deep brain stimulation (DBS) A form of treatment for Parkinson's disease which uses a surgically implanted, battery-operated device called a neurostimulator to deliver electrical stimulation to the ventral intermediate nucleus of the thalamus or the subthalamic nucleus area in the basal ganglia.

Defence mechanisms In psychoanalysis, the means by which individuals attempt to control conflict between the id, ego and superego and also reduce stress and conflict from external events.

Defining disorders as discrete entities The tendency to define individuals as either having a particular disorder or not.

Deliberate self-harm A parasuicidal phenomenon that commonly includes cutting or burning oneself, taking overdoses, hitting oneself, pulling hair or picking skin, or self-strangulation.

Delirium A disturbance of consciousness that develops over a short period of time.

Delirium tremens (DTs) The effects of withdrawal after extended heavy drinking over a number of years where the drinker may become delirious, experiences unpleasant hallucinations, and exhibits shaking and muscle tremors.

Delusions Firmly held but erroneous beliefs that usually involve a misinterpretation of perceptions or experiences.

Delusions of control Delusions where the person believes that his or her thoughts, feelings or actions are being controlled by external forces (e.g. extraterrestrial or supernatural beings).

Delusions of grandeur Delusions in which the individual believes he or she is someone with fame or power (e.g. Jesus Christ, or a famous music star).

Delusions of persecution Delusions in which the individual believes he or she is being persecuted, spied upon or is in danger (usually as the result of a conspiracy of some kind).

Delusions of reference Delusions where the individual believes that independent external events are making specific reference to him or her.

Demand characteristics The features of an experiment which are the result of participants acting according to what they believe is expected of them.

Dementia The development of multiple cognitive deficits that include memory impairment and at least one other specific deficit.

Dementia praecox An early, general term for a number of diagnostic concepts including paranoia, catatonia and hebephrenia (symptoms indicative of incoherence and fragmentation of personality).

Dementia pugilistica A syndrome associated with sportsmen, such as boxers, who may suffer brain injury indicative of contusion.

Demonology The belief that those exhibiting symptoms of psychopathology are possessed by bad spirits.

Dependent personality disorder A personality disorder characterized by a pervasive and excessive need to be taken care of, submissive and clinging behaviour, and difficulty making everyday decisions without advice from others.

Dependent variable (DV) The outcome variable that is measured in an experiment.

Depersonalization disorder Feelings of detachment or estrangement from the self (such as living in a dream or standing outside of oneself, watching oneself).

Depression A mood disorder involving emotional, motivational, behavioural, physical and cognitive symptoms.

Derailment A disorder of speech where the individual may drift quickly from one topic to another during a conversation.

Description The defining and categorizing of events and relationships relevant to psychopathology.

Detoxification A process of systematic and supervised withdrawal from substance use that is either managed in a residential setting or on an outpatient basis.

Developmental disabilities A broad umbrella term used, in the USA, to refer to intellectual disabilities and pervasive developmental disorders such as autism and Asperger's.

Developmental psychopathology An area of research concerned with mapping how early childhood experiences may act as risk factors for later diagnosable psychological disorders. It also attempts to describe the pathways by which early experiences may generate adult psychological problems.

Diagnostic criteria A list of symptoms that must be present for the patient to be given a particular diagnostic label.

Diagnostic and Statistical Manual (**DSM**) An American Psychiatric Association handbook for mental health professionals that lists different categories of mental disorders and the criteria for diagnosing them.

Dialectical behaviour therapy A client-centred therapy for personality disorder that attempts to provide clients with insight into their dysfunctional ways of thinking about the world.

Diathesis-stress The perspective that psychopathology is caused by a combination of a genetically inherited biological diathesis (a biological predisposition to schizophrenia) and environmental stress.

Dieting A restricted regime of eating, followed in order to lose weight or for medical reasons.

Differential diagnosis Differentiating a particular disorder from other, similar disorders.

Dimensional approach to classification The idea that symptoms diagnosed as a disorder may just be more extreme versions of everyday behaviour.

Direct treatments Behaviourally based treatments for specific symptoms of sexual dysfunctions.

Directed masturbation training A treatment for individuals with arousal or orgasmic problems using educational material, videos, diagrams and – in some cases – erotic materials.

Disease-avoidance model The view that animal phobias are caused by attempts to avoid disease or illness that might be transmitted by these animals.

Disgust A food-rejection emotion whose purpose is to prevent the transmission of illness and disease through the oral incorporation of contaminated items.

Disorder of written expression A specific learning disability in which writing skills are substantially below those expected for chronological age, intelligence and educational level.

Disorganized schizophrenia A sub-type of schizophrenia in which disorganized speech, disorganized behaviour and flat or inappropriate affect are distinguishing features.

Disorganized speech A common symptom of psychosis that can take a number of forms (e.g. clanging, word salads).

Dissociative amnesia An inability to recall important personal information that is usually of a stressful or traumatic nature.

Dissociative fugue The instance of an individual suddenly and unexpectedly travelling away from home or work and being unable to recall some or all of his or her past history.

Dissociative identity disorder (DID) A dissociative disorder characterized by the individual displaying two or more distinct identities or personality states that take turns to control behaviour (formerly known as multiple personality disorder).

Dopamine A compound that exists in the body as a neurotransmitter and as a precursor of other substances including adrenalin.

Dopamine hypothesis A theory which argues that the symptoms of schizophrenia are related to excess activity of the neurotransmitter dopamine.

Double-bind hypothesis Theory advocating that psychotic symptoms are the result of an individual being subjected within the family to contradictory messages from loved ones.

Double-blind An experimental procedure in which neither the experimenter nor the participant is aware of which experimental condition the participant is in.

Down syndrome A disorder caused by the presence of an extra chromosome in pair 21 and characterized by intellectual disability and distinguishing physical features.

Downward drift A phenomenon in which individuals exhibiting psychotic symptoms fall to the bottom of the social ladder or even become homeless because they cannot hold down a job or sustain a relationship.

Dramatic/emotional personality disorders Personality disorders grouped in Cluster B, including (1) antisocial personality disorder (APD), (2) borderline personality disorder (BPD), (3) narcissistic personality disorder and (4) histrionic personality disorder.

Dream analysis The analysis of dream content as a means of accessing unconscious beliefs and conflicts.

Dream interpretation The process of assigning meaning to dreams.

Drug maintenance therapy A drug treatment programme in which severe cases of substance abuse and dependency are treated by substituting a drug that has lesser damaging effects.

Drug-prevention schemes Community-based services whose purpose is to try to prevent first use of a drug or to prevent experimentation with a drug developing into regular use – usually through information about the effects of drugs and through developing communication and peer-education skills.

Drug treatments The use of pharmacological or drug treatments to alleviate some of the symptoms of psychopathologies.

DSM-IV-TR The most recent version of the *Diagnostic and Statistical Manual*, currently the most widely adopted psychopathology classification system.

Dual representation theory An approach to explaining post-traumatic stress disorder (PTSD) suggesting that it may be a hybrid disorder involving two separate memory systems.

Dysfunctional schemas In personality disorders, a set of dysfunctional beliefs that are hypothesized to maintain problematic behaviour characteristic of a number of personality disorders (e.g. antisocial personality disorder and borderline personality disorder).

Dyslexia A persistent, chronic learning disability in which there are developmental deficits in spelling, reading and writing abilities.

Dyspareunia A genital pain that can occur during, before or after sexual intercourse. Some clinicians believe this is a pain disorder rather than a sexual dysfunction.

Dysthymic disorder A form of depression in which the sufferer has experienced at least 2 years of depressed mood for more days than not.

Echolalia The immediate imitation of words or sounds that have just been heard.

Ecological momentary assessment (EMA) The use of diaries for self-observation or self-monitoring, perhaps by using an electronic diary or a palmtop computer.

Ecological validity The extent to which conditions simulated in the laboratory reflect real-life conditions.

Ecstasy An illegal amphetamine-based synthetic drug with euphoric effects. Also known as MDMA (3,4-methylenedioxymeth-amphetamine).

Effect size An objective and standardized measure of the magnitude of the effect observed in a research study.

Ego In psychoanalysis, a rational part of the psyche that attempts to control the impulses of the id.

Ego defence mechanisms Means by which the ego attempts to control unacceptable id impulses and reduce the anxiety that id impulses may arouse.

Electrocardiogram (ECG) A psychophysiological measurement technique used for measuring heart rate.

Electroconvulsive therapy (ECT) A method of treatment for depression or psychosis, first devised in the 1930s, which involves passing an electric current of around 70–130 volts through the head of the patient for around half a second.

Electrodermal responding A psychophysiological measure which uses electrodes attached to the fingers of participants to test emotional responses such as anxiety, fear or anger by measuring changes in sweat gland activity.

Electroencephalogram (EEG) A psychophysiological assessment measure which involves electrodes being attached to the scalp that record underlying electrical activity and can help to localize unusual brain patterns in different areas of the brain.

Electromyogram (EMG) A psychophysiological measurement technique that measures the electrical activity in muscles.

Emotional processing theory Theory that claims that severe traumatic experiences are of such major significance to an individual that they lead to the formation of representations and associations in memory that are quite different to those formed as a result of everyday experience.

Empathy An ability to understand and experience a client's own feelings and personal meanings, and a willingness to demonstrate unconditional positive regard for the client.

Encephalitis Infections that cause an inflammation of the brain resulting from the direct infection of the brain by a virus.

Encopresis The repeated passing of faeces into inappropriate places (e.g. clothing or the floor), often associated with childhood constipation.

Encounter groups Group therapy which encourages therapy and self-growth through disclosure and interaction.

Endogenous opioids A compound that the body releases to reduce pain sensation.

Endorphins The body's natural opioids. The release of these neurotransmitters acts to relieve pain, reduce stress and create pleasurable sensations.

Enmeshment A characteristic of family systems theory in which parents are intrusive, overinvolved in their children's affairs, and dismissive of their children's emotions and emotional needs.

Enuresis The repeated involuntary voiding of urine during the day or at night into either bed or clothes.

Epidemiological studies Research which takes the form of a large-scale survey used to study the frequency and distribution of disorders within specific populations over a specified period of time.

Epilepsy A disorder of the nervous system characterized either by mild, episodic loss of attention or sleepiness or by severe convulsions with loss of consciousness.

Errorless learning A training procedure used in training individuals with amnesia where people are prevented – as far as possible – from making any errors while learning a new skill or new information.

Essential features Features that 'define' a disorder.

E-therapy A treatment method which involves the use of email and internet technology.

Ethyl alcohol The main constituent of alcohol.

Evaluation research See **clinical audit**.

Evidence-based treatments Treatments whose efficacy has been proven through research using the scientific method.

Executive functioning Processes that are involved in planning and attentional control.

Executive functions Cognitive skills that involve problem-solving, planning and engaging in goal-directed behaviour.

Exhibitionism A paraphilia which involves sexual fantasies about exposing the penis to a stranger, usually either a woman or a child.

Experiential groups Group therapy which encourages therapy and self-growth through disclosure and interaction.

Experiment A design in which the researcher manipulates a particular variable and observes the effect of this manipulation on some outcome, such as the participant's behaviour.

Experimental group A group of participants who experience the independent variable in an experimental study.

Experimental hypothesis A prediction about what the outcome of an experimental manipulation might be (also known as experimental prediction).

Experimentation A period when an individual may try out different drugs. In some cases this period of experimentation may lead to regular drug use.

Exposure and ritual prevention treatments A means of treatment for obsessive-compulsive disorder (OCD) which involves graded exposure to the thoughts that trigger distress, followed by the development of behaviours designed to prevent the individual's compulsive rituals.

Exposure therapy Treatment in which sufferers are helped by the therapist to confront and experience events and stimuli relevant to their trauma and their symptoms.

Expressed emotion (EE) A qualitative measure of the 'amount' of emotion displayed, typically in the family setting, usually by a family or caretakers.

Expressive language disorder A specific learning disability in which scores on tests of expressive language development are substantially below those for chronological age, intelligence and educational level.

External validity The extent to which the results of a study can be extrapolated to other situations.

Externalizing disorders Outward-directed behaviour problems such as aggressiveness, hyperactivity, non-compliance or impulsiveness.

Extinction The classical conditioning principle which assumes emotional problems can be 'unlearned' by disrupting the association between the anxiety-provoking cues or situations and the threat or traumatic outcomes with which they have become associated.

Eye-movement desensitization and reprocessing A form of exposure therapy for PTSD in which clients are required to focus their attention on a traumatic image or memory while simultaneously visually following the therapist's finger moving backwards and forwards before their eyes.

Face validity The idea that a particular assessment method may appear to be valid simply because it has questions which intuitively seem relevant to the trait or characteristic being measured.

Factitious disorders A set of physical or psychological symptoms that are intentionally produced in order to assume the sick role.

False memory syndrome A syndrome in which individuals recall memories that later turn out to be false.

False recovered memories of trauma The recovery of repressed childhood memories of trauma that did not actually occur.

Fames canina An eating disorder characterized by large food intake followed by vomiting reported in the seventeenth century.

Familial factors The idea that certain disorders may be a result of the direct influence of family attitudes and dynamics on the behaviour of those in the family.

Family systems theory A theory which argues that the sufferer may be embedded in a dysfunctional family structure that actively promotes psychopathology.

Family therapy A form of intervention involving family members that is helpful as a means of dealing with psychopathology that may result from the relationship dynamics within the family.

Faulty learning A view that the symptoms of psychological disorders are acquired through the learning of pathological responses.

Fear Fighter A computer-based CBT used in the management of panic and phobia.

Female orgasmic disorder A sexual disorder characterized by a delay or absence of orgasm during sexual activity; around 10 per cent of adult women may never have experienced an orgasm.

Female sexual arousal disorder A sexual disorder in which there is an inability to attain an adequate lubrication–swelling response of sexual excitement and to maintain this state until completion of sexual activity.

Fetishism A paraphilia which involves sexually arousing fantasies and urges directed at inanimate objects.

Flooding A form of desensitization for the treatment of phobias and related disorders in which the patient is repeatedly exposed to highly distressing stimuli.

Fluent aphasia The production of incoherent, jumbled speech.

Fluoxetine (Prozac) A selective serotonin reuptake inhibitor (SSRI) which reduces the uptake of serotonin in the brain and is taken to treat depression.

Foetal alcohol syndrome (FAS) An example of maternal drug abuse causing childhood intellectual disabilities. Whenever a pregnant mother drinks alcohol, it enters the foetus's bloodstream, slowing down its metabolism and affecting development. If this occurs on a regular basis, then development of the foetus will be severely impaired.

Food preload tests Laboratory procedures developed to provide an objective behavioural measure of the tendency to binge eat.

Free association A technique used in psychoanalysis where the client is encouraged to verbalize all thoughts, feelings and images that come to mind.

Free-basing A purer cocaine alkaloid which is separated by heating processed cocaine and inhaled by smoking.

Fragile X syndrome A chromosomal abnormality that causes intellectual disability where the X chromosome appears to show physical weaknesses and may be bent or broken.

Frontal lobes One of four parts of the cerebrum that control voluntary movement, verbal expressions, problem solving, will power and planning.

Frotteurism A paraphilia which involves recurrent sexual urges to touch and rub up against other non-consenting people – usually in crowded places.

Functional analysis The use of operant conditioning principles to try to understand what rewarding or reinforcing factors might be maintaining behaviour.

Functional family therapy (FFT) A form of treatment which incorporates elements of systemic family therapy and CBT, viewing childhood problems as serving a function within the family.

Functional magnetic resonance imaging (fMRI) A development of MRI technology which allows the clinician to take brain images so quickly that tiny changes in brain metabolism can be detected and can provide minute-to-minute information about actual brain activity.

Gender dysphoria A gender identity disorder in which an individual has a sense of gender that is opposite to his or her biological sex.

Gender identity The internal sense of being either male or female. Usually congruent with biological gender, but not always, as in gender identity disorder.

Gender identity disorder A sexual disorder where an individual is dissatisfied with his or her biological sex and has a strong desire to be a member of the opposite sex.

Gender reassignment surgery The process of changing biological sex which ends in changing the person's basic biological features to be congruent with his or her gender identity.

General paresis A brain disease occurring as a late consequence of syphilis, characterized by dementia, progressive muscular weakness and paralysis.

Generalized amnesia A memory disturbance where there is a failure of recall that encompasses the person's entire life. Individuals may suddenly report to police stations or hospitals as a result of this disorientation.

Generalized anxiety disorder (GAD) A pervasive condition in which the sufferer experiences continual apprehension and anxiety about future events, which leads to chronic and pathological worrying about those events.

Genetic linkage analyses Analyses involving comparisons of the inheritance of characteristics for which gene location is well known (e.g. eye colour) with the inheritance of symptoms of psychopathology.

Gestural training A form of rehabilitation training for limb apraxia in which the client is taught to recognize gestures and postures that are appropriate and in context.

Global Assessment of Functioning Scale (GAF) A scale used to assess adaptive functioning which acts as a measure of psychological health that can be contrasted with measures of psychopathology.

Glove anaesthesia A conversion disorder symptom in which numbness begins at the wrist and is experienced evenly across the hand and all fingers.

Goal management training (GMT) A procedure that involves training in problem solving to help evaluate a current problem, followed by specification of the relevant goals, and partitioning of the problem-solving process into sub-goals or steps.

Good psychological health A measure of an individual's current level of adaptive functioning in areas of social relationships, employment and use of leisure time.

Grounded theory An approach to qualitative analysis which involves identifying consistent categories or themes within the data, then building on these to provide more abstract theoretical insights into the phenomenon being studied.

Group communication treatment A form of treatment used in the production and comprehension of speech, focusing on increasing initiation of conversation and exchanging information using whatever communication means possible.

Group therapy Therapy taken in the form of a group, usually when individuals share similar problems or psychopathologies.

Haemorrhage The injury caused when a blood vessel in the brain ruptures and affects local brain tissue.

Hair sample analysis A method of collecting data about previous drug use by analysing the small amounts of the drug that accumulate in the hair.

Hallucinations A sensory experience in which a person can see, hear, smell, taste or feel something that isn't there.

Hallucinogens Psychoactive drugs which affect the user's perceptions. They may either sharpen the individual's sensory abilities or create sensory illusions or hallucinations.

Halperidol An antipsychotic medication most commonly used in the treatment of autism.

Halstead-Reitan Neuropsychological Test Battery A common neuropsychological test used in the USA, compiled to evaluate brain and nervous system functioning across a fixed set of eight tests. The tests evaluate function across visual, auditory and tactile input, verbal communication, spatial and sequential perception, the ability to analyse information, and the ability to form mental concepts, make judgements, control motor output and to attend to and memorize stimuli.

Hashish The most powerful of the cannabis group of drugs.

Hazardous drinkers Individuals who have 5 or more standard drinks (males) or 3 or more standard drinks (females) on a typical drinking day.

Health anxiety Another term for **hypochondriasis**.

Heroin A highly addictive drug derived from morphine, often used illicitly as a narcotic.

Hippocampus A part of the brain which is important in adrenocorticotropic hormone secretion and is also critical in learning about the context of affective reactions.

Histrionic personality disorder A personality disorder in which an individual is attention-seeking and uncomfortable or unhappy when not the centre of attention.

HIV dementia A syndrome of impairment involving multiple symptoms of motor and cognitive dysfunction, sometimes known as AIDS dementia complex (ADC) or HIV-1 associated dementia (HAD).

Holistic rehabilitation Treatment methods for neurological disorders which attempt to address multiple aspects of dysfunction.

Holistic therapies Therapies which emphasize the need to consider the 'whole' person, not just those 'bits' of the person that manifest psychopathology.

Holy anorexia Self-starvation reported in classical and medieval times, often as a means of achieving heightened spirituality amongst religious devotees.

Hopelessness theory A theory of depression in which individuals exhibit an expectation that positive outcomes will not occur, negative outcomes will occur, and that the individual has no responses available that will change this state of affairs.

Hospitalization The placement of an individual in hospital for medical care.

Host identity The identity that existed before the onset of dissociative identity disorder.

Hostile attributional bias The tendency of individuals to interpret not only ambiguous cues as signalling hostility, but also many cues that are generated with benign intentions.

Humanist-existential approach Approach that aims to resolve psychological problems through insight, personal development and self-actualization.

Humanistic therapies Therapies that attempt to consider the 'whole' person and not just the symptoms of psychopathology.

Huntington's disease An inherited, degenerative disorder of the central nervous system, caused by a dominant gene.

Hybrid disorders Disorders that contain elements of a number of different disorders.

Hyperactivity A higher than normal level of activity.

Hypersexuality The occurrence of high rates of sexual activity.

Hyperventilation A rapid form of breathing that results in ventilation exceeding metabolic demand and has an end result of raising blood pH level. A common feature of panic attacks.

Hypnosis A therapeutic technique in which the patient is placed in a trance.

Hypnotherapy A form of therapy undertaken while the client is hyphotized.

Hypoactive sexual desire disorder A sexual disorder which is characterized by a low level of sexual desire.

Hypochondriasis Unfounded preoccupation with fears of having or contracting a serious disease or illness based on misinterpreting bodily symptoms.

Hypomania Mild episodes of mania.

Hypothesis A tentative explanation for a phenomenon used as a basis for further investigation.

Hypothetical constructs Constructs that are not necessarily directly observable but have to be inferred from other data.

Hypoxyphilia An act performed by sexual masochists which involves the individual using a noose or plastic bag to induce oxygen deprivation during masturbation.

Hysteria A common term used in psychodynamic circles to describe conversion disorder (prior to the latter's inclusion in the DSM).

Id In psychoanalysis, the concept used to describe innate instinctual needs – especially sexual needs.

Imaginal exposure A graded exposure to the situations and thoughts that trigger distress using the client's imagination.

Imaginal flooding A technique whereby a client is asked to visualize feared, trauma-related scenes for extended periods of time.

Implicit theories In sexual offending, integrated cognitive schemas that guide sexual offenders' interactions with their victims and justify their behaviour.

Impulsivity The act of reacting to a situation without considering the consequences.

Incest Sexual intercourse or any form of sexual activity between closely related persons.

Incubation A common clinical phenomenon where fear increases in magnitude over successive encounters with the phobic stimulus – even though it is not followed by a traumatic consequence.

Independent variable (IV) The variable that is manipulated in an experiment.

Infantile autism Early manifestations of the symptoms of autistic disorder.

Infarction The injury caused when the blood flow to the brain is impeded in some way, resulting in damage to the brain tissue fed by that blood flow.

Inflated responsibility The belief that one has power to bring about or prevent subjectively crucial negative outcomes. These outcomes are perceived as essential to prevent. They may be actual, that is, having consequences in the real world, and/or at a moral level.

Information processing biases Biases in interpreting, attending to, storing or recalling information which may give rise to dysfunctional thinking and behaving.

Informed consent Detailed information about an experiment given to participants in order to enable them to make an informed decision about participation.

Informed consent form A form giving detailed information about an experiment which participants must sign to acknowledge that they understand what the study involves and that they formally consent to take part in the study.

Intellectual disabilities A modern term replacing mental retardation to describe the more severe and general learning disabilities.

Internal consistency The extent to which all the items in a test consistently relate to one another.

Internal validity Determining whether a treatment works because of the principles it contains.

Internalizing disorders Inward-looking and withdrawn behaviours, which in children may represent the experience of depression, anxiety and active attempts to socially withdraw.

International List of Causes of Death (**ICD**) The international standard diagnostic classification developed by the World Health Organization (WHO).

Interpersonal theories Theories that argue that depression is maintained by a cycle of reassurance-seeking by depressed individuals that is subsequently rejected by family and friends because of the negative way in which depressed individuals talk about their problems.

Interpretation In psychoanalysis, helping the client to identify important underlying conflicts.

Interpretation biases Cognitive biases in which an individual interprets ambiguous events as threatening and evidence for potential negative outcomes.

Inter-rater reliability The degree to which two independent clinicians actually agree when interpreting or scoring a particular test.

Introjection A response to a loss where individuals regress to the oral stage of development, which allows them to integrate the identity of the person they have lost with their own.

IQ (intelligence quotient) tests Intelligence tests used as a means of estimating intellectual ability.

Korsakoff's syndrome A syndrome involving dementia and memory disorders which is caused by long-term alcohol abuse and dependency.

La belle indifférence An indifference about real symptoms (especially when the symptoms would be disturbing to most people) sometimes displayed by individuals with somatoform disorders.

Lack of conflict resolution A characteristic of family systems theory where families avoid conflict or are in a continual state of conflict.

Lateral hypothalamus A part of the hypothalamus. Lesions to the lateral hypothalamus cause appetite loss resulting in a self-starvation syndrome which is behaviourally similar to that found in anorexia.

Learned helplessness A theory of depression that argues that people become depressed following unavoidable negative life events because these events give rise to a cognitive set that makes individuals learn to become 'helpless', lethargic and depressed.

Learning disability An umbrella term to cover specific learning disabilities, intellectual disabilities and pervasive developmental disorders.

Learning theory The body of knowledge encompassing principles of classical and operant conditioning (and which is frequently applied to explaining and treating psychopathology).

Levodopa A natural amino acid that is converted by the brain into dopamine and used in the treatment of Parkinson's disease.

Lewy bodies Abnormal protein deposits that disrupt the brain's normal functioning.

Lewy body dementia A dementing illness associated with protein deposits called Lewy bodies, found in the cortex of the brain.

Lie detector A psychophysiological test which uses changes in autonomic responding in an attempt to identify whether an individual is lying in response to specific preset questions.

Lifetime prevalence The frequency of a disorder within a lifetime.

Line of best fit A straight line used as a best approximation of a summary of all the points in a scattergram.

Lithium carbonate A drug used in the treatment of bipolar disorder.

Localized amnesia A memory disturbance when an individual is unable to recall events that occurred during a specific time period (e.g. memory loss for a period of 2 days following a serious car accident).

Longitudinal studies Research which takes measures from the same participants at two or more different times in order to specify the time relationships between variables. This may extend over many years or over a participant's whole lifetime.

Loose associations A disorder of speech where the individual may drift quickly from one topic to another during a conversation.

Low self-esteem A person's negative, subjective appraisal of himself or herself.

Lysergic acid diethylamide (**LSD**) A hallucinogenic drug which produces physical effects including dilated pupils, raised body temperature, increased heart rate and blood pressure, sweating, sleeplessness, dry mouth and tremors.

Mad Pride A UK organization dedicated to changing the way in which society views people with mental health problems.

Magnetic resonance imaging (**MRI**) A neuroimaging technique which involves the participant being placed inside a large circular magnet that causes the hydrogen atoms in the body to move. This produces an electromagnetic signal that is converted by the scanner's computer into visual pictures of the brain.

Major depression A psychological problem characterized by relatively extended periods of clinical depression which cause significant distress to the individual and impairment in social or occupational functioning.

Male erectile disorder A sexual disorder in which there is an inability to maintain an adequate erection during sexual activity. Around 10 per cent of males report erection problems, increasing to 20 per cent in the over-50s.

Male orgasmic disorder A sexual disorder in which there is a delay in or absence of orgasm following sexual activity. Around 8 per cent of men report symptoms typical of this disorder.

Mania An emotion characterized by boundless, frenzied energy and feelings of euphoria.

Marriage counsellor A counsellor who specializes in marriage problems.

Marijuana A derivative of cannabis consisting of dried and crushed cannabis leaves.

Masturbatory satiation A treatment for paraphilias in which the client is asked to masturbate in the presence of arousing stimuli.

Maternal HIV infection The incidence of a mother having HIV during pregnancy, leading to a likelihood that the infection will be passed on to the foetus.

Maternal malnutrition Mineral and vitamin deficiencies during pregnancy can result in intellectual disability and significantly affect the child's physical and behavioural development.

Mathematics disorder (dyscalculia) A specific learning disability characterized by mathematical ability being substantially below norm for chronological age, intelligence and educational level.

MDMA 3,4-methylenedioxymethamphetamine, the drug Ecstasy.

Media influence A term describing a person's changes in or temptations to change attitude, behaviour and morals as directly influenced by the media.

Medical model An explanation of psychopathology in terms of underlying biological or medical causes.

Medroxyprogesterone acetate (MPA) An anti-androgen, testosterone-lowering drug.

Melatonin A hormone which acts to slow organisms down, making them sleepy and less energetic.

Meningitis The class of infections that cause inflammation of the meninges (the membranous covering of the brain and spinal cord). Symptoms include fever, headache, drowsiness, stiffness in the neck, irritability and cognitive impairments such as memory deficits.

'Mental defeat' A theoretical view of PTSD in which individuals see themselves as victims, process information about the trauma negatively, and view themselves as unable to act effectively.

Mental health counsellor A counsellor who specializes in mental health problems.

Mental retardation A DSM-IV-TR-defined disorder in which an individual has significantly below-average intellectual functioning characterized by an IQ of 70 or below.

Mentalization The ability to reflect on experiences, feelings and thoughts, and to assess their meaning and importance.

Meta-analyses Statistically accepted ways of assessing the strength of a particular finding across a number of different studies.

Methadone A synthetic form of opium.

Methadone maintenance programmes A detoxification programme where users take a less virulent opiate in order to wean themselves off heroin.

Methamphetamine A synthetic drug related to amphetamine, used illegally as a stimulant.

Mild mental retardation Mental retardation as defined by DSM-IV-TR, represented by an IQ score between 50–55 and 70.

Milieu therapy An early type of therapeutic community on a psychiatric ward designed to develop productivity, independence, responsibility and feelings of self-respect.

Mindfulness-based cognitive therapy (MBCT) A treatment which has been developed to prevent relapse in recovered depressed individuals by making them aware of negative thinking patterns that may trigger subsequent bouts of depression.

Mini Mental State Examination (MMSE) A structured test that takes 10 minutes to administer and can provide reliable information on a client's overall levels of cognitive and mental functioning.

Minnesota Multiphasic Personality Inventory (MMPI) The most well-known of the personality inventories used by clinical psychologists and psychiatrists.

Minor cognitive motor disorder (MCMD) A form of HIV dementia consisting of memory loss and the reduction of cognitive and computational functions.

Mixed anxiety-depressive disorder A hybrid disorder exhibiting symptoms of both anxiety and depression.

Mixed designs Research which uses the non-random assignment of participants to groups in an experiment.

MMPI profile A graph providing a distinctive profile indicating the client's general personality features, potential psychopathology and emotional needs taken from the results of the Minnesota Multiphasic Personality Inventory.

Model A hypothetical description of a process or mechanism (such as a process or psychological mechanism involved in psychopathology).

Modelling The process of demonstrating a required behaviour to clients before prompting them to imitate it.

Moderate mental retardation Mental retardation as defined by DSM-IV-TR, represented by an IQ score between 35–40 and 50–55.

Monoamine oxidase inhibitors (MAOIs) A group of antidepressant drugs which have their effects by increasing levels of both serotonin and norepinephrine in the brain.

Mood-as-input hypothesis A hypothesis claiming that people use their concurrent mood as information about whether they have successfully completed a task or not.

Motivational-enhancement intervention (MET) An intervention for substance abuse and dependency involving communication training, work- and school-related skills, problem-solving skills, peer-refusal skills, negative mood management, social support and general relapse prevention.

Multiple-baseline design An experimental design in which the researcher studies several behaviours at a time.

Multiple sclerosis (MS) A degenerative neurological condition which results in the destruction of the myelin sheaths that surround nerve cells and facilitate transmission of nerve impulses in the brain and central nervous system.

Munchausen's syndrome An extreme form of factitious disorder in which individuals make up or induce physical illnesses.

Munchausen's syndrome by proxy An extreme form of factitious disorder in which parents or carers make up or induce physical illnesses in others (such as their children).

Muscle dysmorphia An obsession with a muscular appearance, often associated with excessive weight training and the use of body-building anabolic steroids.

Mutant Huntingtin (mHtt) A protein which causes cell death in the basal ganglia and contributes to Huntington's disease.

Naltrexone An opioid receptor antagonist which has been found to be beneficial in the control of hyperactivity and self-injurious behaviour.

Narcissistic personality disorder A personality disorder in which individuals overestimate their abilities, inflate their accomplishments, have a pervasive need for admiration and show a lack of empathy with the feelings of others.

Narrow inclusion criteria The use in psychopathology research only of individuals with a very specific diagnosis.

National Institute for Health and Clinical Excellence (NICE) An independent UK organization responsible for providing national guidance on promoting good health and preventing and treating ill health.

Natural experiments Research which allows researchers to observe the effects on behaviour of a naturally occurring 'manipulation' (such as an earthquake).

Naxolone One of a set of drugs used to treat substance use disorders which influence brain neurotransmitter receptor sites and prevent the neuropsychological effects of stimulants, opiates and hallucinogens.

Negative automatic thoughts Negatively valenced thoughts that the individual finds difficult to control or dismiss.

Negative correlation A relationship between two variables in which a high score on one measure is accompanied by a low score on the other.

Negative schema A set of beliefs that tends individuals towards viewing the world and themselves in a negative way.

Negative symptoms Symptoms of psychosis which tend to reflect a diminution or loss of normal functions (e.g. withdrawal or lack of emotion).

Negative triad A theory of depression in which depressed people hold negative views of *themselves* (e.g. 'I am unattractive'), of their *future* (e.g. 'I will never achieve anything') and of the *world* (e.g. 'The world is a dangerous and unsupportive place').

Neologisms Made-up words used in an attempt to communicate.

Neuroendocrine dysfunction Hormonal dysfunction or life stressors causing hormonal dysfunction.

Neurofibrillary tangles Abnormal collections of twisted nerve cell threads which result in errors in impulses between nerve cells and eventual cell death.

Neuroleptics A class of drugs used for the treatment of psychotic symptoms.

Nicotine The addictive agent found in tobacco; it acts as a stimulant by increasing blood pressure and heart rate.

Nihilistic delusions Delusions where individuals believe that some aspect of either the world or themselves has ceased to exist (e.g. the person may believe that they are in fact dead).

Nocturnal enuresis Enuresis occurring during the night.

No treatment or a waiting-list control group A group of participants in a randomized controlled trial who control for the effects of spontaneous remission.

Non-associative fear acquisition A model which argues that fear of a set of biologically relevant stimuli develops naturally after very early encounters given normal maturational processes and normal background experiences, and no specific traumatic experiences with these stimuli are necessary to evoke this fear.

Non-fluent aphasia An inability to initiate speech or respond to speech with anything other than simple words.

Non-purging sub-type bulimia nervosa A type of bulimia nervosa in which the individual attempts to compensate for bingeing by indulging in excessive fasting or exercise.

Norepinephrine An adrenal hormone which functions as a neurotransmitter and is associated with symptoms of both depression and mania.

Object relations psychotherapy A treatment developed specifically to deal with the difficulties posed by the treatment of individuals with personality disorders such as borderline personality disorder.

Object relations theory A theory which argues that individuals with borderline personality disorder have received inadequate support and love from important others (such as parents), resulting in an insecure ego which is likely to lead to lack of self-esteem and fear of rejection.

Obsessions Intrusive and recurring thoughts that an individual finds disturbing and uncontrollable.

Obsessive-compulsive disorder (OCD) A disorder characterized either by obsessions (intrusive and recurring thoughts that the individual finds disturbing and uncontrollable) or by compulsions (ritualized behaviour patterns that the individual feels driven to perform in order to prevent some negative outcome happening).

Obsessive-compulsive personality disorder (OCPD) A personality disorder in which individuals show exceptionally perfectionist tendencies including a preoccupation with orderliness and control at the expense of flexibility, efficiency and productivity.

Odd/eccentric personality disorders Personality disorders grouped in Cluster A, the three sub-types of which are (1) paranoid personality disorder, (2) schizotypal personality disorder and (3) schizoid personality disorder.

Oestrogen Any of a group of steroid hormones which promote the development and maintenance of female characteristics of the body.

One-month prevalence The frequency of a disorder within the last month.

Open head injury A head injury in which the skull and outer layer of the meninges are breached.

Operant conditioning The learning of a specific behaviour or response because that behaviour has certain consequences.

Opiates Opium, taken from the sap of the opium poppy. Its derivatives include morphine, heroin, codeine and methadone.

Oppositional defiant disorder (ODD) A mild form of disruptive behaviour disorders reserved for children who do not meet the full criteria for conduct disorder.

Oral stage According to Freud, the first 18 months of life based on the child's need for food from the mother. If the mother fails to satisfy these oral needs, the child may become fixated at this stage and in later life display 'oral stage characteristics' such as extreme dependence on others.

Orgasmic reorientation A treatment method to replace inappropriate or distressing sexual activities which aims to make the client sexually aroused by more conventional or acceptable stimuli.

Orienting response A physiological reaction consisting of changes in skin conductance, brain activity, heart rate and blood pressure.

Overprotection A characteristic of family systems theory where members of the family are overconcerned with parenting and with one another's welfare, and this can often be viewed by the child as coercive parental control.

Paedophilia A paraphilia which is defined as sexual attraction towards prepubescent children, normally 13 years or younger.

Pain disorder A preoccupation with, and fear of, pain itself.

Palliative effect The reduction of the severity of symptoms and alleviation of distress.

Panic A sudden uncontrollable fear or anxiety.

Panic disorder An anxiety disorder characterized by repeated panic or anxiety attacks.

Paranoid personality disorder A personality disorder characterized by an enduring pattern of distrust and suspiciousness of others.

Paranoid schizophrenia A sub-type of schizophrenia characterized by the presence of delusions of persecution.

Paraphilias Problematic, high-frequency sexual behaviours or unusual sexual urges and activities that are often directed at inappropriate targets.

Parent-implemented early intervention Using parents as effective trainers to teach children with intellectual disabilities, basic self-help and communication skills.

Parent training programmes A family intervention programme which attempts to teach parents a range of techniques for controlling and managing their children's symptoms, used especially with children diagnosed with conduct disorder.

Parkinson's disease A progressive neurological condition affecting movements such as walking, talking and writing, and causing psychological disturbance in between 40 and 60 per cent of sufferers.

Partialism A phenomenon in which there is a fascination with an individual object to the point where normal sexual activity no longer occurs.

Passive smoking The breathing in of air that contains other people's smoke.

Peer influences A term describing a person's changes in or temptations to change attitude, behaviour and morals as directly influenced by his or her peer group.

Peer leadership A strategy used by drug prevention schemes where young people are trained to provide anti-drugs messages to their peers.

Peer-pressure resistance training A strategy used by drug prevention schemes where students learn assertive refusal skills when confronted with drugs.

Penetrating head wound A head injury in which the skull and outer layer of the meninges are breached.

Penile prosthesis A mechanical device normally reserved for non-reversible organic-based erectile problems.

Perfectionism The setting of excessively high standards for performance accompanied by overly critical self-evaluation.

Performance anxiety The fear of failing to achieve an acceptable level of sexual performance, causing an individual to become distanced from the sexual act and fail to become aroused.

Personal therapy A broad-based cognitive behaviour programme that is designed to help individuals with the skills needed to adapt to day-to-day living after discharge from hospital.

Personality disorders A group of disorders marked by persistent, inflexible, maladaptive patterns of thought and behaviour that develop in adolescence or early adulthood and significantly impair an individual's ability to function.

Pervasive developmental disorders (PDDs) A group of disorders characterized by serious abnormalities in the developmental process, usually associated with impairment in several areas of development. The most commonly diagnosed PDDs are autistic disorder (autism), Rett's disorder, childhood disintegrative disorder and Asperger's syndrome.

Pessimistic inferential style The attribution of negative events to stable, global causes.

Pessimistic thinking A form of dysfunctional thinking where sufferers believe nothing can improve their lot.

Pharmacological treatments Drug-based treatments for psychopathology.

Phenothiazines A group of antipsychotic drugs that help to alleviate the symptoms of psychosis by blocking the brain's dopamine receptor sites and so reduce dopamine activity.

Phenylketonuria (PKU) A metabolic disorder caused by a deficiency of the liver enzyme phenylalanine 4-hydroxylase, which is necessary for the effective metabolism of the amino acid phenylalanine.

Phineas Gage A victim of a penetrating head injury, one of the first examples to indicate that brain damage could cause radical changes to personality and affect socially appropriate interaction.

Phobic beliefs Beliefs about phobic stimuli that maintain the phobic's fear and avoidance of that stimulus or situation.

Phonological disorder A specific learning disability characterized by the failure to use developmentally expected speech sounds that are appropriate for age and dialect.

Phonological theory The view that reading disabilities in dyslexia are caused primarily by difficulties in differentiating the elements of speech (phonemes) and associating these sounds with the letters in a written word.

Placebo control condition A control group that is included in a clinical trial to assess the effects of participant expectations.

Placebo effect The effect when participants in a clinical trial show improvement even though they are not being given a theoretically structured treatment.

Play therapy A range of play-based therapeutic and assessment techniques that can be used with younger children who are less able to communicate and express their feelings.

Point prevalence The frequency of a disorder in the population at any one point in time.

Polydrug abuse Abuse of more than one drug at a time.

Positive correlation A relationship between two variables in which a high score on one measure is accompanied by a high score on the other.

Positive symptoms Characteristics of psychotic symptoms which tend to reflect an excess or distortion of normal functions.

Positron emission tomography (PET) A neuroimaging technique which scans to allow measurement of both brain structure and function by utilizing radiation emitted from the participant to develop images.

Post-traumatic stress disorder (PTSD) A set of persistent anxiety-based symptoms that occur after experiencing or witnessing an extremely fear-evoking traumatic event.

Poverty of content A characteristic of the conversation of individuals suffering psychosis in which their conversation has very little substantive content.

Prediction A statement (usually quantitative) about what will happen under specific conditions, as a logical consequence of scientific theories.

Predictive validity The degree to which an assessment method is able to help the clinician predict future behaviour and future symptoms.

Preference molesters Non-incestuous paedophiles who normally only become sexually aroused by sexually immature children.

Prefrontal cortex An area of the brain which is important in maintaining representations of goals and the means to achieve them.

Prefrontal lobotomy A surgical procedure that involves severing the pathways between the frontal lobes and lower brain areas.

Premature ejaculation The persistent or recurrent onset of orgasm and ejaculation with minimal sexual stimulation before, on or shortly after penetration, and before the person wishes it to happen.

Prevalence The number of instances of a given disease or psychopathology in a given population at a designated time.

Prevalence rates The representation of incidence by duration of a particular disorder.

Prevention programmes Intervention programmes that attempt to prevent the onset of a psychopathology before the first symptoms are detected.

Primary brain tumour A brain tumour that originates and grows within the brain itself.

Primary enuresis Enuresis when the child has never experienced a lengthy spell of bladder control.

Primary narcissism Regression to a previous ego state which gives rise to a preoccupation with the self.

Prion An abnormal, transmissible agent that is able to induce abnormal folding of normal cellular proteins in the brain, leading to brain damage. A major contributing factor in variant Creutzfeldt-Jakob disease (vCJD).

Privacy The right of participants to decide not to provide some forms of information to the researcher if they so wish (e.g. their age or sexual orientation).

Prodromal stage The slow deterioration from normal functioning to the delusional and dysfunctional thinking characteristic of many forms of schizophrenia, normally taking place over an average of 5 years.

Profound mental retardation Mental retardation as defined by DSM-IV-TR, represented by an IQ score below 20–25.

Projective tests A group of tests usually consisting of a standard fixed set of stimuli that are presented to clients, but which are ambiguous enough for clients to put their own interpretation on what the stimuli represent.

Prolactin A hormone from the pituitary gland stimulating milk production after childbirth.

Prolonged speech A set of techniques to address stuttering that teach the sufferer new speech patterns, resulting in changes in the phrasing and articulation of speech and of the respiratory patterns produced while speaking.

Pronoun reversal An impairment in communication in which an individual refers to himself or herself as 'he', 'she' or 'you'.

Prospective designs Research which takes measures from the same participants at two or more different times in order to specify the time relationships between variables.

Psychiatry A scientific method of treatment that is based on medicine, the primary approach of which is to identify the biological causes of psychopathology and treat them with medication or surgery.

Psychoanalysis An influential psychological model of psychopathology based on the theoretical works of Sigmund Freud.

Psychodelic drugs Consciousness-expanding or mind-manifesting drugs.

Psychodynamic approaches Theories which assume that unconscious conflicts develop early in life. Part of the therapy is designed to identify life events that may have caused these unconscious conflicts.

Psychological debriefing A structured way of trying to intervene immediately after trauma in order to try to prevent the development of PTSD.

Psychological dependence When individuals have changed their life to ensure continued use of a particular drug such that all their activities are centred on the drug and its use.

Psychological models Models which view psychopathology as caused primarily by psychological rather than biological processes.

Psychometric approach The idea that a psychological test assumes that there are stable underlying characteristics or traits (e.g. anxiety, depression, compulsiveness, worry) that exist at different levels in everyone.

Psychopath A term often used to describe individuals diagnosed with antisocial personality disorder.

Psychopathology The study of deviations from normal or everyday psychological functioning.

Psychosurgery Brain surgery used to treat symptoms of psychopathology.

Purging sub-type bulimia nervosa A type of bulimia nervosa in which the individual regularly engages in self-induced vomiting or the misuse of laxatives, diuretics or enemas.

Qualitative methods Research methods that rely on the analysis of verbal reports rather than on statistical analyses of quantifiable data.

Quantitative methods Research methods that place an important emphasis on accurate and valid measurement of behaviour and attempt to draw conclusions from their studies on the basis of statistical inference.

Random assignment Assignment of participants to different treatments, interventions or conditions according to chance.

Randomized controlled trials (RCTs) A procedure for assessing the effectiveness of therapies by comparing the effectiveness of the treatment being assessed (across a range of objective measures) with a variety of control conditions, and with other forms of therapy and treatment (if necessary).

Rational emotive therapy (RET) A cognitive technique developed by Albert Ellis (1962) which addresses how people construe themselves, their life and the world.

Reactivity The effect of increasing the frequency of desirable behaviours and decreasing the frequency of undesirable behaviours as a result of self-monitoring.

Reading disorder A specific learning disability characterized by the accuracy, speed and comprehension of reading being significantly below standards expected for chronological age and IQ.

Reality monitoring A form of source monitoring required to distinguish mental contents arising from experience from those arising from imagination.

Reality-monitoring deficit Where an individual has a problem distinguishing between what actually occurred and what did not occur.

Reasoning bias The tendency of individuals with hypochondriasis to reject diagnoses that disagree with their own beliefs about their health and to seek further opinions – presumably in the belief that someone will agree with their view.

Reattribution therapy A treatment used in helping individuals with paranoid symptoms to reattribute their paranoid delusions to normal daily events rather than the threatening, confrontational causes they believe underlie them.

Reattribution training A technique used in the treatment of depression which attempts to get clients to interpret their difficulties in more hopeful and constructive ways rather than in the negative, global, stable ways typical of depressed individuals.

Recessive gene A gene that must be present on both chromosomes in a pair to show outward signs of a certain characteristic.

Reciprocal inhibition A principle of behaviour therapy in which an emotional response is eliminated not just by extinguishing the relationship between the emotion-inducing cue and the threatening consequence, but also by attaching a response to the emotion-inducing cue which is incompatible with anxiety (e.g. relaxation).

Reconstructive memory A concept of a cognitive theory of dissociative symptoms which argues that an individual autobiographical memory is stored as a series of discrete elements associated with that experience (e.g. context, emotional state, sensory and perceptual features).

Rehabilitation programmes Treatment programmes that usually combine a mixture of group work, psychological interventions, social skills training and practical and vocational activities.

Relapse-prevention training In paraphilias, a treatment which consists primarily of helping clients to identify circumstances, situations, moods and types of thoughts that might trigger paraphilic behaviour.

Relaxation training A method of dealing with the chronic stress experienced by psychopathology sufferers. A specific technique of progressive muscular relaxation is often used, and relaxation is found to be as effective as some forms of cognitive therapy.

Reliability The extent that an assessment method will still provide the same result when used by different clinicians on different occasions.

Reparenting A therapy process in which clients allow the therapist to form an emotional attachment to them in order to challenge dysfunctional schemas.

Replicable Results of research which have been collected under controlled conditions that will allow any other researcher to reproduce those exact same findings.

Repression A basic psychodynamic defence mechanism that helps to suppress painful memories and prevent stressful thoughts.

Residential rehabilitation centres Centres which allow people to live, work and socialize with others undergoing treatment in an environment that offers advice, immediate support, and group and individual treatment programmes enabling clients to learn the social and coping skills necessary for the transition back to a normal life.

Residual stage The stage of psychosis when the individual ceases to show prominent signs of positive symptoms (such as delusions, hallucinations or disordered speech).

Residual type A category of schizophrenia when the individual has experienced at least one previous psychotic episode and there is currently a lack of prominent positive symptoms (e.g. delusions, hallucinations, disorganised speech), but there is evidence of ongoing negative symptoms (e.g. flat affect, poverty of speech).

Response shaping A reinforcement procedure that is used to develop new behaviours.

Restricted type anorexia nervosa A type of anorexia nervosa in which self-starvation is not associated with concurrent purging (e.g. self-inducing vomiting or use of laxatives).

Rett's disorder A commonly diagnosed pervasive developmental disorder indicative of arrested development across a range of skills.

Rigidity A characteristic of family systems theory where there is a tendency to maintain the status quo within the family.

Risk factors Factors which may increase the risk of developing psychopathology later in life.

Rispiridone An antipsychotic medication also commonly used in the treatment of autism.

Ritalin (methylphenidate) A stimulant medication that is used to treat ADHD.

Rogue representations In somatoform disorders, representations which provide inappropriate templates by which information about body shape and health are selected and interpreted.

Rorschach Inkblot Test A projective personality test using inkblots by dropping ink onto paper and then folding the paper in half to create a symmetrical image.

Sally-Anne False Belief Task A method used to test whether a child has developed a 'theory of mind'.

Savant syndrome The phenomenon of extraordinary proficiency in one isolated skill in individuals with multiple cognitive disabilities. It appears to be closely linked to autistic spectrum disorder and is frequently found in Asperger's syndrome.

Scattergram A graphical representation showing the relationship between two variables.

Schema therapy An integrative approach to the treatment of personality disorders based on the principles of cognitive behaviour therapy.

Schizoid personality disorder A personality disorder in which individuals are often described as 'loners' who fail to express a normal range of emotions and appear to get little reward from any activities.

Schizophrenia The main diagnostic category for psychotic symptoms. The five central characteristics are (1) delusions, (2) hallucinations, (3) disorganized speech (e.g. incoherence), (4) grossly disorganized or catatonic behaviour and (5) flattened affect, poverty of speech and apathy.

Schizophrenia spectrum disorder The combination of Cluster A-type personality disorders and schizophrenia.

Schizophrenogenic mother A cold, rejecting, distant and dominating mother who causes schizophrenia according to Fromm-Reichmann.

Schizotypal personality disorder A personality disorder characterized by 'eccentric' behaviour marked by odd patterns of thinking and communication.

Scientific method A research method which espouses the pursuit of knowledge through systematic observation and requires that research findings are replicable and testable.

Scientist-practitioner Someone who is competent as both a researcher and a practitioner.

Seasonal affective disorder (SAD) A condition of regularly occurring depressions in winter with a remission the following spring or summer.

Second-hand smoke Environmental tobacco smoke that is inhaled involuntarily or passively by someone who is not smoking.

Secondary enuresis Enuresis when bladder control is still problematic, but the child has been dry for a period of up to 6 months.

Sedatives Central nervous system depressants which slow the activity of the body, reduce its responsiveness, and reduce pain tension and anxiety. This group of substances includes alcohol, the opiates and their derivatives (heroin, morphine, methadone and codeine), and synthesized tranquillizers such as barbiturates.

Seizisman A state of psychological paralysis found in the Haitian community.

Selective amnesia A memory disturbance where an individual can recall some, but not all, of the events during a specific time period (e.g. a combat veteran may be able to recall some events during a violent military encounter, but not others).

Selective serotonin reuptake inhibitors (SSRIs) A recent group of antidepressant drugs that selectively affect the uptake of only one neurotransmitter – usually serotonin.

Self-focused attention A theory of social phobia arguing that sufferers show a strong tendency to shift their attention inwards onto themselves and their own anxiety responses during social performance – especially when they fear they will be negatively evaluated.

Self-help groups Group therapy which brings together people who share a common problem in an attempt to share information and help and support one another.

Self-instructional training (SIT) A procedure used in the intervention for executive functioning deficits where individuals learn a set of instructions for talking themselves through particular problems.

Self-medication Self-administration of often illicit drugs by an individual to alleviate perceived or real problems, usually of a psychological nature.

Self-monitoring A form of clinical observation which involves asking clients to observe and record their own behaviour, to note when certain behaviours or thoughts occur, and in what contexts they occur.

Self-monitoring deficit Where individuals cannot distinguish between thoughts and ideas they generated themselves and thoughts or ideas that other people generated.

Self-observation A form of clinical observation that involves asking clients to observe and record their own behaviour, perhaps by using a diary or a palmtop computer to note when certain behaviours or thoughts occur and in what contexts they occur.

Sentence completion test An open-ended projective personality test that provides clients with the first part of an uncompleted sentence which they complete with words of their own.

Separation anxiety A childhood anxiety problem involving an intense fear of being separated from parents or carers.

Serotonin An important brain neurotransmitter where low levels are associated with depression.

Service user groups Groups of individuals who are end users of the mental health services provided by, for example, government agencies such as the NHS.

Severe mental retardation Mental retardation as defined by DSM-IV-TR, represented by an IQ score between 20–25 and 35–40.

Sex Offender Treatment Programme (SOTP) An integrated treatment for sexual offenders developed by the UK Home Office.

Sexual aversion disorder A sexual disorder in which there is an active avoidance of genital sexual contact with a sexual partner.

Sexual dysfunction A disturbance in the processes that characterize the sexual response cycle or pain associated with intercourse.

Sexual masochism A paraphilia in which an individual gains sexual arousal and satisfaction from being humiliated.

Sexual sadism A paraphilia in which a person gains sexual arousal and satisfaction from the psychological or physical suffering of others.

Sexual skills and communication training A treatment method in which a therapist can help clients to acquire a more knowledgeable perspective on sexual activity, communicate to partners effectively about sex, and reduce any anxiety about indulging in sexual activity.

Shaken baby syndrome A form of child abuse that is known to cause intellectual disability. It refers to traumatic brain injury that occurs when a baby is violently shaken.

Sheltered workshops Settings that provide individuals with intellectual disabilities with employment tailored to their own needs and abilities.

Sick role Playing the role of being sick as defined by the society to which the individual belongs.

Sigmund Freud An Austrian neurologist and psychiatrist who founded the psychoanalytic school of psychology.

Single-case experiment A single case study in which a participant's behaviour is observed and measured both before and after an experimental manipulation.

Social anxiety spectrum A spectrum of disorder proposed to include both avoidant personality disorder and social phobia.

Social breakdown syndrome A deterioration in the symptoms of psychosis consisting of confrontational and challenging behaviour, physical aggressiveness and a lack of interest in personal welfare and hygiene.

Social constructionism An approach to research in clinical psychology emphasizing that reality is a social construction, and so there are no basic 'truths' of the kind that we seek to discover using the scientific method.

Social labelling The theory that the development and maintenance of psychotic symptoms are influenced by the diagnosis itself.

Social phobia A severe and persistent fear of social or performance situations.

Social selection theory The theory that the intellectual, behavioural and motivational problems afflicting individuals with psychotic symptoms mean they will suffer a downward drift into unemployment, poverty and the lower socioeconomic classes as a result of their disorder.

Social skills training A therapy for depression that assumes that depression in part results from an individual's inability to communicate and socialize appropriately, and that addressing these skill deficits should help to alleviate many of the symptoms of depression.

Sociogenic hypothesis The theory that individuals in low socioeconomic classes experience significantly more life stressors than individuals in higher socioeconomic classes, and these stressors are associated with unemployment, poor educational levels, crime and poverty generally.

Sociopath A person with a personality disorder manifesting itself in extreme antisocial attitudes and behaviour.

Sodium amobarbital A drug which can be used concurrently with hypnotherapy to help clients recall past events.

Sodium pentobarbital A drug which can be used concurrently with hypnotherapy to help clients recall past events.

Somatization disorder A pattern of recurring, multiple, clinically significant somatic symptoms that require medical treatment and cause significant impairment in social, occupational and other areas of functioning.

Somatogenic hypothesis The hypothesis that the causes or explanations of psychological problems can be found in physical or biological impairments.

Somnambulism Repeated episodes of complex motor behaviour initiated during sleep. Also known as sleepwalking disorder.

Source-monitoring ability The ability to recall the relevant elements of an autobiographical experience from memory.

Special educational needs (SEN) A term used in the UK to identify those who require instruction or education tailored to their specific needs.

Specific learning disabilities Disorders such as dyslexia and communication disabilities.

Specific phobia An excessive, unreasonable, persistent fear triggered by a specific object or situation.

Splitting An element of object relations theory which argues that individuals with weak egos engage in a defence mechanism by which they evaluate people, events or things in a completely black or white way, often judging people as either good or bad with no shades of grey.

Spongiform encephalopathy A fatal infectious disease that attacks the brain and central nervous system. Commonly known as 'mad cow disease' or variant Creutzfeldt-Jakob disease (vCJD).

Spontaneous remission The fact that many people who have psychological disorders will simply get better anyway over a period of time, even without therapy.

Squeeze technique A technique used to help clients with premature ejaculation where the client's partner firmly squeezes below the head of the penis just prior to ejaculation.

Stages of development Progressive periods of development from infancy to maturity.

Standardization Statistical norms taken from data that have been collected from large numbers of participants of psychological tests.

State-dependent memory A well-established cognitive phenomenon in which the individual is more likely to remember an event if he or she is in the same physiological state as when the event occurred.

Statistical norm The mean, average or modal example of a behaviour.

Statistical Package for the Social Sciences (SPSS) A computer program specifically developed for statistical analysis for the social sciences.

Statistical significance The degree to which the outcome of a study is greater or smaller than would be expected by chance.

Stepped-care model A treatment for depression that emphasizes that the type of treatment provided for depressed individuals should be tailored to the severity of their symptoms and their personal and social circumstances.

Stimulants Substances that increase central nervous system activity and increase blood pressure and heart rate.

Stimulus control treatment An early behavioural intervention for worry in GAD which adopted the principle of stimulus control. This is based on the conditioning principle that the environments in which behaviours are enacted come to control their future occurrence and can act to elicit those behaviours (the principle of stimulus control).

Stop-start technique A technique used to help clients with premature ejaculation where the client's partner stimulates the penis until close to ejaculation, at which point the partner is signalled to stop by the client.

Stroke A sudden loss of consciousness resulting when the rupture or occlusion of a blood vessel leads to oxygen lack in the brain.

Structured Clinical Interview for DSM-IV-TR (SCID) A branching, structured interview in which the client's response to one question will determine the next question to be asked.

Structured interview An interview in which questions to be asked, their sequence and detailed information to be gathered are all predetermined.

Student counsellor A counsellor who specializes in students' problems.

Stuttering A disturbance in the normal fluency and time patterning of speech that is inappropriate for the individual's age.

Substance abuse A pattern of drug or substance use that occurs despite knowledge of the negative effects of the drug, but where use has not progressed to full-blown dependency.

Substance dependency A maladaptive pattern of substance use, leading to clinically significant impairment or distress.

Substance use disorder (SUD) Where an individual has at least one substance disorder diagnosis, whether it is a general diagnosis of substance dependency or abuse, or a more specific substance category disorder.

Substantia nigra A region of the basal ganglia.

Suffocation alarm theories Models of panic disorder in which a combination of increased CO_2 intake may activate an oversensitive suffocation alarm system and give rise to the intense terror and anxiety experienced during a panic attack.

Suicide The action of killing oneself intentionally.

Superego In psychoanalysis, a development from both the id and ego which represents our attempts to integrate 'values' that we learn from our parents or society.

Supported employment A special programme designed with a built-in support mechanism to help people with physical, mental or developmental disabilities reach and keep their customized vocational goals and objectives.

Supportive family management A method of counselling in which group discussions are held where families share their experiences and which can help to provide reassurance and a network of social support.

Symbolic loss A Freudian concept whereby other kinds of losses within one's life (e.g. losing a job) are viewed as equivalent to losing a loved one.

Syndrome A distinct set of symptoms.

Syndrome (or disorder) spectrum A higher-order categorical class of symptoms.

Syphilis A sexually transmitted disease, the later stages of which are characterized by the inability to coordinate muscle movements, paralysis, numbness, gradual blindness and dementia.

Systematic amnesia A memory disturbance where there is a loss of memory that relates to specific categories of information, such as family history.

Systematic desensitization An exposure therapy based on the need to expose clients to the events and situations that evoke their distress and anxiety in a graduated and progressive way.

Systemic family therapy A family intervention technique based on the view that childhood problems result from inappropriate family structure and organization. The therapist is concerned with the boundaries between parents and children, and the ways in which they communicate.

Systems theory Approach that attempts to understand the family as a social system.

Tangentiality A disorder of speech in which answers to questions may be tangential rather than relevant.

Tardive dyskinesia A disorder of motor movement.

Tay-Sachs disease A metabolic disorder caused by a recessive gene which results in an absence of the enzyme hexosominidase A in the brain and central nervous system, eventually causing neurons to die.

Tease technique A direct treatment method designed to deal with symptoms of erectile dysfunction or male and female orgasmic disorder. It involves the partner caressing the client's genitals, but stopping when the client becomes aroused (e.g. achieves an erection) or approaches orgasm.

Teenage mothers In relation to intellectual disabilities, young mothers who become pregnant before 18 years of age and who are likely to have lived in deprived areas prior to giving birth, are often unmarried, live in poverty as a result of their premature motherhood, and are likely to have a significantly lower than average IQ.

Telephone therapy Treatment and support conducted over the telephone.

Temporal lobes-limbic structures The areas of the brain that lie at the side of the head behind the temples and which are involved in hearing, memory, emotion, language, illusions, tastes and smells.

Test validity The extent that an assessment method actually measures what it claims to be measuring.

Testable A scientific explanation that is couched in such a way that it clearly suggests ways in which it can be tested and potentially falsified.

Testosterone A steroid hormone stimulating development of male secondary sexual characteristics.

Test-retest reliability The extent that a test will produce roughly similar results when the test is given to the same person several weeks or even months apart (as long as no treatments or interventions have occurred in between).

Thematic Apperception Test (TAT) A projective personality test consisting of 30 black and white pictures of people in vague or ambiguous situations.

Theory A set of propositions that usually attempt to explain a phenomenon by describing the cause–effect relationships that contribute to that phenomenon.

Theory of mind (TOM) The ability to understand one's own and other people's mental states.

Theory of shattered assumptions A theory of PTSD that argues that a severe traumatic experience will shatter a person's belief in the world as a safe and benign place, resulting in the symptoms typical of PTSD.

Therapeutic constructions The view that the multiple personalities found in dissociative identity disorders are merely constructions of the therapeutic process.

Thought-action fusion A dysfunctional assumption held by OCD sufferers that having a thought about an action is like performing it.

Thought suppression A defence mechanism used by individuals with obsessive thoughts to actively suppress them (using either thought suppression or distraction techniques).

Thrombolytic therapy The use of drugs to break up or dissolve blood clots – one of the main causes of strokes.

Tic disorders Uncontrollable physical movements such as facial twitches, rapid blinking or twitches of the mouth.

Time-out (TO) A means of reducing disruptive behaviours, including aggressiveness, destruction of property and non-compliance in the classroom, by removing the child from the situation and directing him or her, for example, to sit in a specific time-out chair for periods of between 5 and 15 minutes.

Time pressure management (TPM) An approach to dealing with attention deficits which aims not to try to improve attention itself, but to provide clients with some compensatory skills that will allow them to effectively manage their slowed information processing.

Token economy A reward system which involves participants receiving tokens for engaging in certain behaviours which at a later time can be exchanged for a variety of reinforcing or desired items.

Tolerance The need for increased amounts of a substance in order to achieve similar effects across time.

Tourette's syndrome A disorder in which motor and vocal tics occur frequently throughout the day for at least 1 year.

Transference A technique used in psychoanalysis where the analyst is used as a target for emotional responses: clients behave towards the analyst as they would have behaved towards an important person in their lives.

Transvestic fetishism A paraphilia in which a heterosexual male experiences sexual arousal from cross-dressing in women's clothing.

Triad of impairments Impairments in reciprocal social interactions, communication and flexibility of thought that are typical of autistic spectrum disorder.

Tricyclic antidepressants Antidepressant drugs developed in the 1960s which have their effect by increasing the amount of norepinephrine and serotonin available for synaptic transmission.

Twin studies Studies in which researchers have compared the probability with which monozygotic (MZ) and dizygotic (DZ) twins both develop symptoms indicative of a psychopathology in order to assess genetic contributions to that psychopathology.

Unconditional positive regard Valuing clients for who they are without judging them.

Understanding A full description of how the causal factors affecting psychopathology interact.

Unipolar depression A psychological disorder characterized by relatively extended periods of clinical depression that cause significant distress to the individual and impairment in social or occupational functioning (see also major depression).

Unobtrusive heroin user A long-term heroin user who has never been in specialized treatment and who displays levels of occupational status and educational achievement similar to the general population.

Unstructured interview A free-flowing interview in which questions to be asked, their sequence and detailed information to be gathered are not predetermined.

Vacuum erection device (VED) A mechanical device normally reserved for non-reversible organic-based erectile problems.

Vaginismus The involuntary contraction of the muscles surrounding the vagina when vaginal penetration is attempted. Of all women who seek treatment for sexual dysfunctions, around 15–17 per cent are suffering from vaginismus.

Validity The extent that an assessment method actually does measure what it claims to be measuring.

Variant Creutzfeldt-Jakob disease (vCJD) A fatal infectious disease that attacks the brain and central nervous system. Commonly known as 'mad cow disease'.

Vascular dementia A degenerative cerebrovascular disease that leads to a progressive decline in memory and cognitive functioning.

Viagra (sildenafil citrate) A drug treatment for sexual dysfunction which is used primarily to treat erectile dysfunction in men.

Visual imagery mnemonics A technique for teaching remembering strategies in order to help store and retrieve items and events to be remembered.

Voluntary Of one's own free will or design; not forced or compelled.

Voyeurism A paraphilia which involves experiencing intense sexually arousing fantasies or urges to watch an unsuspecting person who is naked, in the process of undressing or engaging in sexual activity.

WAIS-III The Wechsler Adult Intelligence Scale (third edition). See **Wechsler Adult Intelligence Scale (WAIS)**.

Waiting-list controls The use of patients who are on a waiting list for treatment as a no treatment control condition in treatment outcome studies.

Wechsler Adult Intelligence Scale (WAIS) An intelligence test containing scales that measure vocabulary, arithmetic ability, digit span, information comprehension, letter–number sequencing, picture completion ability, reasoning ability, symbol search and object assembly ability.

Wernicke's aphasia A deficit in the comprehension of speech involving difficulties in recognizing spoken words and converting thoughts into words.

Wisconsin card-sorting task A widely used test of executive functioning where individuals must sort cards for a number of trials using one rule (e.g. colour) and then sort cards using a different rule (e.g. shape).

Withdrawal Where the body requires the drug in order to maintain physical stability, and lack of the drug causes a range of negative and aversive physical consequences (e.g. anxiety, tremors and, in extreme cases, death).

Word salad Where the language of a person experiencing a psychotic episode is so disorganized that there seems to be no link between one phrase and the next.

Yohimbine A drug treatment for sexual dysfunction which is used primarily to treat erectile dysfunction in men by facilitating norepinephrine excretion in the brain.

References

Abbott, M.J. & Rapee, R.M. (2004). Post-event rumination and negative self-appraisal in social phobia before and after treatment. *Journal of Abnormal Psychology, 113*(1), 136–144.

Abdel-Hamid, I.A., El Naggar, E.A. & El Gilany, A.H. (2001). Assessment of as needed use of pharmacotherapy and the pause-squeeze technique in premature ejaculation. *International Journal of Impotence Research, 13*(1), 41–45.

Abdulhamid, I. (2002). Munchausen by proxy. *eMedical Journal, 3*.

Abed, R.T., Vaidya, G. & Baker, I. (2000). Suicide in schizophrenia: A fourteen-year survey in an English health district. *International Journal of Psychiatry in Clinical Practice, 4*(2), 143–146.

Abel, G.G., Gore, D.K., Holland, C.L., Camp, N., Becker, J. & Rather, J. (1989). The measurement of the cognitive distortions of child molesters. *Annals of Sex Research, 2*, 135–153.

Abel, G.G., Osborn, C., Anthony, D. & Gardos, P. (1992). Current treatment of paraphilias. In J. Bancroft, C. Davis & H. Ruppel (Eds.), *Annual Review of Sex Research*, 255–290.

Abercrombie, H.C., Schaefer, S.M., Larson, C.L., Oakes, T.R. et al. (1998). Metabolic rate in the right amygdala predicts negative affect in depressed patients. *Neuroreport, 9*(14), 3301–3307.

Abikoff, H., Gittelman, R. & Klein, D.F. (1980). Classroom observation code for hyperactive children: A replication of validity. *Journal of Consulting and Clinical Psychology, 48*, 555–565.

Abou-Saleh, M.T., Younis, Y. & Karim, L. (1998). Anorexia nervosa in an Arab culture. *International Journal of Eating Disorders, 23*(2), 207–212.

Abraham, H.D. & Fava, M. (1999). Order of onset of substance abuse and depression in a sample of depressed outpatients. *Comprehensive Psychiatry, 40*(1), 44–50.

Abraham, H.D. & Wolf, E. (1988). Visual function in past users of LSD: Psychophysical findings. *Journal of Abnormal Psychology, 97*(4), 443–447.

Abraham, K. (1916/1960). The first pregenital stage of the libido. In *Selected papers in psychoanalysis*. New York: Basic Books.

Abrahamsson, K.H., Hallberg, L.R. & Carlsson, S.G. (2007). Ambivalence in coping with dental fear: A qualitative study. *Journal of Health Psychology, 7*, 653–664.

Abramowitz, J.S. & Braddock, A.E. (2006). Hypochondriasis: Conceptualization, treatment, and relationship to obsessive-compulsive disorder. *Psychiatric Clinics of North America, 29*, 503.

Abramowitz, J.S., Brigidi, B.D. & Roche, K.R. (2001). Cognitive-behavioral therapy for obsessive-compulsive disorder: A review of the treatment literature. *Research On Social Work Practice, 11*, 357–372.

Abramson, L.Y., Metalsky, G.I. & Alloy, L.B (1989). Hopelessness depression: A theory-based subtype of depression. *Psychological Review, 96*, 358–372.

Abramson, L.Y., Seligman, M.E.P. & Teasdale, J.D. (1978). Learned helplessness in humans: Critique and reformulation. *Journal of Abnormal Psychology, 87*, 49–74.

Adebimpe, V.R. (1994). Race, racism, and epidemiological survey. *Hospital and Community Psychiatry, 45*, 27–31.

Adshead, G. & Brooke, D. (Eds.) (2001). *Munchausen's syndrome by proxy: Current issues in assessment, treatment and research*. London: Imperial College Press.

Afari, N. & Buchwald, D. (2003). Chronic fatigue syndrome: A review. *American Journal of Psychiatry, 160*, 221–236.

Agnello, J.G. (1975). Voice onset and voice termination features of stutters. In L.M. Webster & L.C. Furst (Eds.), *Vocal tract dynamics and dysfluency*. New York: Speech and Hearing Institute.

Agras, W.S. (1997). Pharmacotherapy of bulimia nervosa and binge eating disorder: Longer-term outcomes. *Psychopharmacology Bulletin, 33*(3), 433–436.

Agras, W.S., Rossiter, E.M., Arnow, B., Schneider, J.A. et al. (1992). Pharmacological and cognitive-behavioral treatment for bulimia nervosa: A controlled comparison. *American Journal of Psychiatry, 149*(1), 82–87.

Agrawal, A., Jacobson, K.C., Gardner, C.O., Prescott, C.A. & Kendler, K.S. (2004). Population-based twin study of sex differences in depressive symptoms. *Twin Research, 7*(2), 176–181.

Ainsworth, M. (2002). My life as an e-patient. In R.C. Hsiung (Ed.), *E-therapy: Case studies, guiding principles, and the clinical potential of the internet*. New York: W.W. Norton.

Aitken, R.C.B., Lister, J.A. & Main, C.J. (1981). Identification of features associated with flying phobias in aircrew. *British Journal of Psychiatry, 139*, 38–42.

Aklin, W.M. & Turner, S.M. (2006). Toward understanding ethnic and cultural factors in the interviewing process. *Psychotherapy, 43*, 50–64.

Akshoomoff, N.A., Courchesne, E. & Townsend, J. (1997). Attention coordination and anticipatory control. *International Review of Neurobiology, 41*, 575–598.

Alarcon, R.D. (1996). Personality disorders and culture in DSM-IV: A critique. *Journal of Personality Disorders, 10*(3), 260–270.

Albers, G.W. (1997). Rationale for early intervention in acute stroke. *American Journal of Cardiology, 80*(4C), D4–D10.

Albert, U., Maina, G., Forner, F. & Bogetto, F. (2004). DSM-IV obsessive-compulsive personality disorder: Prevalence in patients with anxiety disorders and in healthy comparison subjects. *Comprehensive Psychiatry, 45*(5), 325–332.

Alden, L.E., Mellings, T.M.B. & Laposa, J.M. (2004). Framing social information and generalized social phobia. *Behaviour Research and Therapy, 42*(5), 585–600.

Alden, L.E., Teschuk, M. & Tee, K. (1992). Public self-awareness and withdrawal from social interactions. *Cognitive Therapy and Research, 16*(3), 249–267.

Alexander, A.W. & Slinger-Constant, A.M. (2004). Current status of treatments for dyslexia: Critical review. *Journal of Child Neurology, 19*, 744–758.

Alexander, B.K. & Hadaway, P.F. (1982). Opiate addiction: The case for an adaptive orientation. *Psychological Bulletin, 92*(2), 367–381.

Alexander, G.E., DeLong, M.R. & Strick, P.L. (1986). Parallel organization of functionally segregated circuits linking basal ganglia and cortex. *Annual Review of Neuroscience, 9*, 357–381.

Alexander, J.F. & Parsons, B.V. (1973). Short-term behavioral intervention with delinquent families: Impact on family process and recidivism. *Journal of Abnormal Psychology, 81*, 219–225.

Alexander, J.F. & Parsons, B.V. (1982). *Functional family therapy*. Monterey, CA: Brooks/Cole.

Alexander-Passe, N. (2006). How dyslexic teenagers cope: An investigation of self-esteem, coping and depression. *Dyslexia, 12*(4), 256–275.

Alford, B.A. & Beck, A.T. (1994). Cognitive therapy of delusional beliefs. *Behaviour Research and Therapy, 32*(3), 369–380.

Allbutt, H., Amos, A. & Cunningham-Burley, S. (1995). The social image of smoking among young people in Scotland. *Health Education Research, 10*(4), 443–454.

Allen, C. (1985). *Training for what? Clinical psychologists' perceptions of their roles*. Unpublished MSc dissertation. Department of Psychiatry, University of Newcastle.

Allin, M. & Murray, R. (2002). Schizophrenia: A neurodevelopmental or neurodegenerative disorder? *Current Opinion in Psychiatry, 15*(1), 9–15.

Alloy, L.B. & Abramson, L.Y. (1979). Judgment of contingency in depressed and nondepressed students: Sadder but wiser. *Journal of Experimental Psychology-General, 108*(4), 441–485.

Alloy, L.B., Abramson, L.Y., Hogan, M.E., Whitehouse, W.G. et al. (2000). The Temple-Wisconsin cognitive vulnerability to depression project: Lifetime history of Axis I psychopathology in individuals at high and low cognitive risk for depression. *Journal of Abnormal Psychology, 109*(3), 403–418.

Alloy, L.B., Abramson, L.Y., Murray, L.A., Whitehouse, W.G. & Hogan, M.E. (1997). Self-referent information-processing in individuals at high and low cognitive risk for depression. *Cognition and Emotion, 11*(5–6), 539–568.

Alloy, L.B., Lipman, A.J. & Abramson, L.Y. (1992). Attributional style as a vulnerability factor for depression: Validation by past history of mood disorders. *Cognitive Therapy and Research, 16*(4), 391–407.

Alm, P.A. (2004). Stuttering and the basal ganglia circuits: A critical review of possible relations. *Journal of Communication Disorders, 37*(4), 325–369.

Almeida, O.P. & Lautenschlager, N.T. (2005). Dementia associated with infectious diseases. *International Psychogeriatrics, 17*, S65–S77.

Alpers, G.W., Wilhelm, F.H. & Roth, W.T. (2005). Psychophysiological assessment during exposure in driving phobic patients. *Journal of Abnormal Psychology, 114*, 126–139.

Alpher, V.S. (1996). Identity and introject in dissociative disorders. *Journal of Consulting and Clinical Psychology, 6*, 1238–1244.

Altman, C.A. (2001). Effects of selective serotonin reuptake inhibitors on sexual function. *Journal of Clinical Psychopharmacology, 21*, 241–242.

Altshuler, L.L., Curran, J.G., Hauser, P., Mintz, J. et al. (1995). T-2 hyperintensities in bipolar disorder: Magnetic-resonance-imaging comparison and literature metaanalysis. *American Journal of Psychiatry, 152*(8), 1139–1144.

Alverson, H., Alverson, M. & Drake, R.E. (2000). An ethnographic study of the longitudinal course of substance abuse among people with severe mental illness. *Community Mental Health Journal, 36*, 557–569.

Alzheimer's Society (2008). Retrieved from www.alzheimers.org.uk/site/scripts/documents_info.php?documentID=412&pageNumber=1, February 2008.

Aman, M.G. & Langworthy, K.S. (2000). Pharmacotherapy for hyperactivity in children with autism and other pervasive developmental disorders. *Journal of Autism and Developmental Disorders, 30*(5), 451–459.

Ameri, A. (1999). The effects of cannabinoids on the brain. *Progress in Neurobiology, 58*(4), 315–348.

American Psychiatric Association (1993). Practice guidelines for major depressive disorder in adults. *American Journal of Psychiatry*.

American Psychiatric Association (1994). *Diagnostic and statistical manual of mental disorders* (4th ed.). Washington, DC: American Psychiatric Association.

American Psychiatric Association (2000). *Diagnostic and statistical manual of mental disorders* (4th ed., Text Revision). Washington, DC: American Psychiatric Association.

Amsterdam, A.D., Wheler, J., Hudis, C. & Krychman, M.L. (2005). Female sexual dysfunction and changes in hormonal levels in patients with early breast cancer on anti-estrogen therapy. *Breast Cancer Research and Treatment, 94*, S240–S240.

Ananthaswamy, A. (2004). The Parkinson's fix. *New Scientist, 183*, 40–43.

Anda, R.F., Croft, J.B., Felitti, V.J., Nordenberg, D. et al. (1999). Adverse childhood experiences and smoking during adolescence and adulthood. *JAMA: Journal of the American Medical Association, 282*(17), 1652–1658.

Andersen, B.L. (1983). Primary orgasmic dysfunction: Diagnostic considerations and review of treatment. *Psychological Bulletin, 93*, 105–136.

Anderson, D.A. & Maloney, K.C. (2001). The efficacy of cognitive-behavioral therapy on the core symptoms of bulimia nervosa. *Clinical Psychology Review, 21*, 971–988.

Anderson, K.G., Sankis, L.M. & Widiger, T.A. (2001). Pathology versus statistical infrequency: Potential sources of gender bias in personality disorder criteria. *Journal of Nervous and Mental Disease, 189*(10), 661–668.

Andreasen, N.C. (2001). *Brave new brain: Conquering mental illness in the era of the genome.* New York: Oxford University Press.

Andreasen, N.C., Flashman, L., Flaum, M., Arndt, S. et al. (1994). Regional brain abnormalities in schizophrenia measured with magnetic-resonance-imaging. *JAMA: Journal of the American Medical Association, 272*(22), 1763–1769.

Andreasson, S., Allebeck, P., Engstrom, A. & Ryberg, U. (1987). Cannabis and schizophrenia: A longitudinal study of Swedish conscripts. *Lancet, 2*, 1483–1486.

Andrews, G. & Harvey, R. (1981). Does psychotherapy benefit neurotic patients? A reanalysis of the Smith, Glass and Miller data. *Archives of General Psychiatry, 38*, 1203–1208.

Andrews, G., Morris-Yeates, A., Howie, P. & Martin, N.G. (1991). Genetic factors in stuttering confirmed. *Archives of General Psychiatry, 48*(11), 1034–1035.

Angermeyer, M.C., Kuhn, L. & Goldstein, J.M. (1990). Gender and the course of schizophrenia: Differences in treated outcomes. *Schizophrenia Bulletin, 16*(2), 293–307.

Angold, A., Costello, E.J. & Erkanli, A. (1999). Comorbidity. *Journal of Child Psychology and Psychiatry, 40*, 57–87.

Angrist, B., Lee, H.K. & Gershon, S. (1974). Antagonism of amphetamine-induced symptomatology by a neuroleptic. *American Journal of Psychiatry, 131*(7), 817–819.

Angst, J. (1998). Sexual problems in healthy and depressed persons. *International Clinical Psychopharmacology, 13*, S1–S4.

Antonova, E., Sharma, T., Morris, R. & Kumari, V. (2004). The relationship between brain structure and neurocognition in schizophrenia: A selective review. *Schizophrenia Research, 70*, 117–145.

Antony, M.M., Brown, T.A. & Barlow, D.H. (1997). Heterogeneity among specific phobia types in DSM-IV. *Behaviour Research and Therapy, 35*, 1089–1100.

Aouizerate, B., Pujol, H., Grabot, D., Faytout, M. et al. (2003). Body dysmorphic disorder in a sample of cosmetic surgery applicants. *European Psychiatry, 18*, 365–368.

Apt, C. & Hurlburt, D.H. (1994). The sexual attitudes, behaviour and relationships of women with histrionic personality disorder. *Journal of Sex and Marital Therapy, 20*, 125–133.

Apter, J.T. & Allen, L.A. (1999). Buspirone: Future directions. *Journal of Clinical Psychopharmacology, 19*(1), 86–93.

Araujo, A.B., Durante, R., Feldman, H.A., Goldstein, I. & McKinlay, J.B. (1998). The relationship between depressive symptoms and male erectile dysfunction: Cross-sectional results from the Massachusetts Male Aging Study. *Psychosomatic Medicine, 60*(4), 458–465.

Arendt, R.E., Short, E.J., Singer, L.T., Minnes, S. et al. (2004). Children prenatally exposed to cocaine: Developmental outcomes and environmental risks at seven years of age. *Journal of Developmental and Behavioral Pediatrics, 25*(2), 83–90.

Arnold, E.H., O'Leary, S.G. & Edwards, G.H. (1997). Father involvement and self-reported parenting of children with attention deficit hyperactivity disorder. *Journal of Consulting and Clinical Psychology, 65*, 337–342.

Arntz, A. (1999). Do personality disorders exist? On the validity of the concept and its cognitive-behavioral formulation and treatment. *Behaviour Research and Therapy, 37*, S97–S134.

Arntz, A. (2003). Cognitive therapy versus applied relaxation as treatment of generalized anxiety disorder. *Behaviour Research and Therapy, 41*(6), 633–646.

Arntz, A., Lavy, E., van den Berg, G. & van Rijsoort, S. (1993). Negative beliefs of spider phobics: A psychometric evaluation of the Spider Phobia Beliefs Questionnaire. *Advances in Behaviour Research and Therapy, 15*(4), 257–277.

Aromacki, A.S. & Lindman, R.E. (2001). Alcohol expectancies in convicted rapists and child molesters. *Criminal Behaviour and Mental Health, 11*, 94–101.

Aron, W.S. & Daily, D.W. (1976). Graduates and splitees from therapeutic community drug treatment programs: Comparison. *International Journal of the Addictions, 11*(1), 1–18.

Aronson, K.R., Barrett, L.F. & Quigley, K. (2006). Emotional reactivity and the overreport of somatic symptoms: Somatic sensitivity or negative reporting style? *Journal of Psychosomatic Research*, 60(5), 521–530.

Arsencault, L., Cannon, M., Witton, J. & Murray, R.M. (2004). Causal association between cannabis and psychosis: Examination of the evidence. *British Journal of Psychiatry*, 184, 110–117.

Artiges, E., Martinot, J.L., Verdys, M., Attar-Levy, D. et al. (2000). Altered hemispheric functional dominance during word generation in negative schizophrenia. *Schizophrenia Bulletin*, 26(3), 709–721.

Assalian, P. & Margolese, H.C. (1996). Treatment of antidepressant-induced sexual side effects. *Journal of Sex and Marital Therapy*, 22(3), 218–224.

Atchison, M. & McFarlane, A.C. (1994). A review of dissociation and dissociative disorders. *Australian and New Zealand Journal of Psychiatry*, 28(4), 591–599.

Attia, E., Haiman, C., Walsh, T. & Flater, S.R. (1998). Does fluoxetine augment the inpatient treatment of anorexia nervosa? *American Journal of Psychiatry*, 155(4), 548–551.

Austin, D.W. & Richards, J.C. (2001). The catastrophic misinterpretation model of panic disorder. *Behaviour Research and Therapy*, 39, 1277–1291.

Avina, C. & O'Donohue, W. (2002). Sexual harassment and PTSD: Is sexual harassment diagnosable trauma? *Journal of Traumatic Stress*, 15(1), 69–75.

Ax, S., Gregg, V.H. & Jones, D. (2001). Coping and illness cognitions: Chronic fatigue syndrome. *Clinical Psychology Review*, 21, 161–182.

Ayanian, J.Z. & Cleary, P.D. (1999). Perceived risks of heart disease and cancer among cigarette smokers. *JAMA: Journal of the American Medical Association*, 281(11), 1019–1021.

Aycicegi, A., Harris, C.L. & Dinn, W.M. (2002). Parenting style and obsessive-compulsive symptoms and personality traits in a student sample. *Clinical Psychology and Psychotherapy*, 9(6), 406–417.

Ayd, F.J. (1956). A clinical evaluation of Frenquel. *Journal of Nervous and Mental Disease*, 124, 507–509.

Ayllon, T. (1963). Intensive treatment of psychotic behavior by stimulus satiation and food reinforcement. *Behaviour Research and Therapy*, 1(1), 53–61.

Ayllon, T. & Azrin, N.H. (1968). *The token economy: A motivational system for therapy and rehabilitation*. New York: Appleton-Century-Crofts.

Ayllon, T., Haughton, E. & Hughes, H.B. (1965). Interpretation of symptoms: Fact or fiction. *Behaviour Research and Therapy*, 3(1), 1.

Azrin, N.H. (1976). Improvements in the community-reinforcement approach to alcoholism. *Behaviour Research and Therapy*, 14, 339–348.

Azrin, N.H., Acierno, R., Kogan, E.S., Donohue, B. et al. (1996). Follow-up results of supportive versus behavioral therapy for illicit drug use. *Behaviour Research and Therapy*, 34(1), 41–46.

Baare, W.F.C., van Oel, C.J., Pol, H.E.H., Schnack, H.G. et al. (2001). Volumes of brain structures in twins discordant for schizophrenia. *Archives of General Psychiatry*, 58(1), 33–40.

Bach, A.K., Wincze, J.P. & Barlow, D.H. (2001). Sexual dysfunction. In D.H. Barlow (Ed.), *Clinical handbook of psychological disorders*. New York: Guilford Press.

Bachevalier, J. (1994). Medial temporal lope structures and autism: A review of clinical and experimental findings. *Neuropsychologia*, 32(6), 627–648.

Baddeley, A. & Wilson, B.A. (1994). When implicit learning fails: Amnesia and the problem of error elimination. *Neuropsychologia*, 32(1), 53–68.

Badner, J.A. & Gershon, E.S. (2002). Meta-analysis of whole-genome linkage scans of bipolar disorder and schizophrenia. *Molecular Psychiatry*, 7(4), 405–411.

Bagley, C. & Binitie, A. (1970). Alcoholism and schizophrenia in Irishmen in London. *British Journal of Addiction*, 65, 3–7.

Baguley, I.J., Cooper, J. & Felmingham, K. (2006). Aggressive behavior following traumatic brain injury: How common is common? *Journal of Head Trauma Rehabilitation*, 21(1), 45–56.

Bailey, A., Le Couteur, A., Gottesman, I., Bolton, P. et al. (1995). Autism as a strongly genetic disorder: Evidence from a British twin study. *Psychological Medicine*, 25(1), 63–77.

Bailey, A., Luthert, P., Dean, A., Harding, B. et al. (1998). A clinicopathological study of autism. *Brain*, 121, 889–905.

Bailey, A., Phillips, W. & Rutter, M. (1996). Autism: Towards an integration of clinical, genetic, neuropsychological, and neurobiological perspectives. *Journal of Child Psychology and Psychiatry and Allied Disciplines*, 37(1), 89–126.

Bailey, J.E., Argyropoulos, S.V., Lightman, S.L. & Nutt, D.J. (2003). Does the brain noradrenaline network mediate the effects of the CO_2 challenge? Reply to reviewers' comments. *Journal of Psychopharmacology*, 17(3), 267–268.

Bailey, R.K. & Owens, D.L. (2005). Overcoming challenges in the diagnosis and treatment of attention deficit/hyperactivity disorder in African Americans. *Journal of the National Medical Association*, 97, 5S–10S.

Baker, A. & Rooney, C. (2003). Recent trends in alcohol-related mortality, and the impact of ICD-10 in the monitoring of these deaths in England and Wales. *Health Statistics Quarterly*, 17, 5–14.

Baker, B. & Merskey, H. (1982). Parental representations of hypochondriacal patients from a psychiatric hospital. *British Journal of Psychiatry*, 141, 233–238.

Baker, C.A. & Morrison, A.P. (1998). Cognitive processes in auditory hallucinations: Attributional biases and metacognition. *Psychological Medicine*, 28(5), 1199–1208.

Baker, D., Hunter, E., Lawrence, E., Medford, N., Patel, M. et al. (2003). Depersonalization disorder: Clinical features of 204 cases. *British Journal of Psychiatry*, 182, 428–433.

Bakish, D. (1999). The patient with comorbid depression and anxiety: The unmet need. *Journal of Clinical Psychiatry*, 60, 20–24.

Bakwin, H. (1971). Enuresis in twins. *American Journal of Disease in Childhood*, 121, 222–225.

Ball, K. & Lee, C. (2000). Relationships between psychological stress, coping and disordered eating: A review. *Psychological Health*, 14, 1007–1035.

Bancroft, J. (1989). Sexual desire. *Recherches*, 20(213), 1060.

Bancroft, J., Loftus, J., Long, J.S. (2003). Distress about sex: A national survey of women in heterosexual relationships. *Archives of Sexual Behavior*, 32(3), 193–208.

Bandelow, B., Krause, J., Wedekind, D. et al. (2005). Early traumatic life events, parental attitudes, family history, and birth risk factors in patients with borderline personality disorder and healthy controls. *Psychiatry Research*, 134, 169–179.

Bandura, A. (1986). Fearful expectations and avoidant actions as coeffects of perceived self-inefficacy. *American Psychologist*, 41(12), 1389–1391.

Banzett, L.K., Liberman, R.P. & Moore, J.W. (1984). Long-term follow-up of the effects of behavior therapy. *Hospital and Community Psychiatry*, 35, 277–279.

Barch, D.M., Mitropoulou, V., Harvey, P.D., New, A.S. et al. (2004). Context-processing deficits in schizotypal personality disorder. *Journal of Abnormal Psychology*, 113(4), 556–568.

Barker, C., Pistrang, N. & Elliott, R. (2002). *Research methods in clinical psychology* (2nd ed.). New York: Wiley.

Barkley, R.A. (1991). Attention-deficit hyperactivity disorder. *Psychiatric Annals*, 21(12), 725–733.

Barlow, D.H. (1988). *Anxiety and its disorders: The nature and treatment of anxiety and panic*. New York: Guilford Press.

Barlow, D.H. (1993). Covert sensitization for paraphilia. In J.R. Cautela & A.J. Kearney (Eds.), *Covert conditioning casebook*. Pacific Grove, CA: Brooks/Cole.

Barlow, D.H., Abel, G.G. & Blanchard, E.B. (1979). Gender identity change in transsexuals: Follow-up and replications. *Archives of General Psychiatry*, 36(9), 1001–1007.

Barlow, D.H., Blanchard, E.B., Vermilyea, J.A., Vermilyea, B.B. & DiNardo, P.A. (1986). Generalized anxiety and generalized anxiety disorder: Description and reconceptualization. *American Journal of Psychiatry*, 143(1), 40–44.

Barlow, D.H. & Campbell, L.A. (2000). Mixed anxiety-depression and its implications for models of mood and anxiety disorders. *Comprehensive Psychiatry*, 41(2, Suppl. 1).

Barlow, D.H., Gorman, J.M., Shear, M.K. & Woods, S.W. (2000). Cognitive-behavioral therapy, imipramine, or their combination for panic disorder: A randomized controlled trial. *JAMA: Journal of the American Medical Association, 283*(19), 2529–2536.

Barlow, D.H., Hayes, S.C. & Nelson, R.O. (1984). *The scientist-practitioner: Research and accountability in clinical and educational settings.* Oxford: Pergamon.

Barlow, D.H., Reynolds, E.J. & Agras, W.S. (1993). Gender identity change in a transsexual. *Archives of General Psychiatry, 28*(4), 569–576.

Baron, M., Risch, N., Levitt, M. & Gruen, R. (1985). Genetic analysis of platelet monoamine-oxidase activity in families of schizophrenic patients. *Journal of Psychiatric Research, 19*(1), 9–21.

Baron-Cohen, S. (2001). Theory of mind and autism: A review. In L.M. Gliddon (Ed.), *International review of research in mental retardation* (Vol. 23). San Diego, CA: Academic Press.

Baron-Cohen, S., Leslie, A. & Frith, U. (1985). Does the autistic child have a theory of mind? *Cognition, 21*, 37–46.

Barquero-Jimenez, S. & Gomez-Tortosa, E. (2001). Cognitive disorders in Huntington's disease patients. *Revista de Neurologia, 32*(11), 1067–1071.

Barranco-Quintana, J.L., Allam, M.F., Del Castillo, A. & Navajas, R.F.C. (2005). Alzheimer's disease risk factors. *Revista de Neurologia, 40*(10), 613–618.

Barrett, D.E. & Frank, D.A. (1987). *The effects of undernutrition on children's behaviour.* New York: Gordon & Beach.

Barrowclough, C., Johnston, M. & Tarrier, N. (1994). Attributions, expressed emotion, and patient relapse: An attributional model of relatives' response to schizophrenic illness. *Behavior Therapy, 25*(1), 67–88.

Barsky, A.J. (1992). Amplification, somatization, and the somatoform disorders. *Psychosomatics, 33*, 28–34.

Barsky, A.J. & Ahern, D.K. (2004). Cognitive behaviour therapy for hypochondriasis: A randomized control study. *JAMA: Journal of the American Medical Association, 291*, 1464–1470.

Bartholomew, K., Kwong, M.J. & Hart, S.D. (2001). Attachment. In W.J. Livesley (Ed.), *Handbook of personality disorders: Theory, research and treatment.* New York: Guilford Press.

Basoglu, M., Kilic, C., Salcioglu, E. & Livanou, M. (2004). Prevalence of posttraumatic stress disorder and comorbid depression in earthquake survivors in Turkey: An epidemiological study. *Journal of Traumatic Stress, 17*(2), 133–141.

Bass, C. & Gardner, W. (1985). Emotional influences on breathing and breathlessness. *Journal of Psychosomatic Research, 29*(6), 599–609.

Bastiani, A.M., Rao, R., Weltzin, T. & Kaye, W.H. (1995). Perfectionism in anorexia nervosa. *International Journal of Eating Disorders, 17*(2), 147–152.

Bateson, G. (1978). The double-bind theory: Misunderstood? *Psychiatric News,* April, 40.

Bateson, G., Jackson, D.D., Haley, J. & Weakland, J. (1956). Toward a theory of schizophrenia. *Behavioral Science 1*(4), 251–264.

Battaglia, M., Bernardeschi, L., Franchini, L., Bellodi, L. & Smeraldi, E. (1995). A family study of schizotypal disorder. *Schizophrenia Bulletin, 21*(1), 33–45.

Bauman, M.L. & Kemper, T.L. (1994). Neuroanatomic observations of the brain in autism. In L. Bauman & T.L. Kemper (Eds.), *The neurobiology of autism.* Baltimore: Johns Hopkins University Press.

Baumeister, R.F. & Butler, J.L. (1997). Sexual masochism: Deviance without pathology. In D.R. Laws & W. O'Donohue (Eds.), *Sexual deviance.* New York: Guilford Press.

Baumgartner, G.R. & Rowan, R.C. (1987). Clonidine vs. chlordiazepoxide in the management of acute alcohol withdrawal. *Archives of Internal Medicine, 147*, 1223–1226.

Baxter, L.R., Ackermann, R.F., Swerdlow, N.R., Brody, A., Saxena, S., Schwartz, J.M., Gregortich, J.M., Stoessel, P. & Phelps, M.E. (2000). Specific brain system mediation of obsessive-compulsive disorder responsive to either medication or behaviour therapy. In W.K. Goodman, M.V. Rudorfer & J.D. Maser (Eds.), *Obsessive-compulsive disorder: Contemporary issues in treatment.* Personality and Clinical Psychology Series. Mahwah, NJ: Erlbaum.

Bean, P., Stratford, N., White, C., Goodman, M. et al. (1997). *Release drugs and dance survey: An insight into the culture.* London: Release Publications.

Beatty, M.J., Heisel, A.D., Hall, A.E., Levine, T.R. & La France, B.H. (2002). What can we learn from the study of twins about genetic and environmental influences on interpersonal affiliation, aggressiveness, and social anxiety? A meta-analytic study. *Communication Monographs, 69*(1), 1–18.

Beauregard, M., Leroux, J.M., Bergman, S., Arzoumanian, Y. et al. (1998). The functional neuroanatomy of major depression: An fMRI study using an emotional activation paradigm. *Neuroreport, 9*(14), 3253–3258.

Beautrais, A.L., Joyce, P.R. & Mulder, R.T. (1999). Cannabis abuse and serious suicide attempts. *Addiction, 94*(8), 1155–1164.

Bebbington, P., Johnson, S. & Thornicroft, G. (2002). Community mental health care: Promises and pitfalls. In N. Sartorius & W. Gaebel (Eds.), *Psychiatry in society.* New York: Wiley.

Beck, A.T. (1967). *Depression: Clinical, experimental and theoretical aspects.* New York: Harper & Row.

Beck, A.T. (1987). Cognitive models of depression. *Journal of Cognitive Psychotherapy, 1*, 5–37.

Beck, A.T., Emery, G. & Greenberg, R.L. (1985). *Anxiety disorders and phobias: A cognitive perspective.* New York: Basic Books.

Beck, A.T. & Freeman, A. (1990). *Cognitive therapy for personality disorders.* New York: Guilford Press.

Beck, A.T., Rush, A.J., Shaw, B.F. & Emery, G. (1979). *Cognitive therapy of depression.* New York: Guilford Press.

Beck, A.T., Steer, R.A., Kovacs, M. & Garrison, B. (1985). Hopelessness and eventual suicide: A 10-year prospective study of patients hospitalized with suicidal ideation. *American Journal of Psychiatry, 142*(5), 559–563.

Beck, J.G. & Berisford, M.A. (1992). The effects of caffeine on panic patients: Response components of anxiety. *Behavior Therapy, 23*(3), 405–422.

Becker, R.E., Heimberg, R.G. & Bellack, A.S. (1987). *Social skills training treatment for depression.* New York: Pergamon.

Becker-Blease, K.A. & Freyd, J.J. (2006). Research participants telling the truth about their lives. *American Psychologist, 61*, 218–226.

Beech, A.R., Fisher, D. & Beckett, R.C. (1999). *STEP 3: An evaluation of the prison Sex Offender Treatment Programme.* London: HMSO.

Beevers, C.G. & Miller, I.W. (2005). Unlinking negative cognition and symptoms of depression: Evidence of a specific treatment effect for cognitive therapy. *Journal of Consulting and Clinical Psychology, 73*(1), 68–77.

Behan, W.M.H., More, I.A.R. & Behan, P.O. (1991). Mitochondrial abnormalities in the postviral fatigue syndrome. *Acta Neuropathologica 83*(1), 61–65.

Belar, C.D. & Perry, N.W. (1992). National conference on scientist-practitioner education and training for professional practice of psychology. *American Psychologist, 47*, 71–75.

Belfer, M.L. & Munir, K. (1997). Acquired immune deficiency syndrome. In J.M. Weiner (Ed.), *Textbook of child and adolescent psychiatry.* Washington, DC: American Psychiatric Association.

Bell, D. (1991). *CFIDS: The disease of a thousand names.* New York: Pollard.

Bell, N.S., Amoroso, P.J., Yore, M.M., Senier, L. et al. (2001). Alcohol and other risk factors for drowning among male active duty US army soldiers. *Aviation Space and Environmental Medicine, 72*(12), 1086–1095.

Bell, R.M. (1985). *Holy anorexia.* Chicago: University of Chicago Press.

Bellini, M. & Merli, M. (2004). Current drug treatment of patients with bulimia nervosa and binge-eating disorder: Selective serotonin reuptake inhibitors versus mood stabilizers. *International Journal of Psychiatry in Clinical Practice, 8*, 235–243.

Belmonte, M. (2000). Abnormal attention in autism shown by steady-state visual evoked potentials. *Autism, 4*, 269–285.

Bendall, S., Jackson, H.J., Killackey, E., Allott, K. et al. (2006). The credibility and acceptability of befriending as a control therapy in a randomized controlled trial of a cognitive behaviour therapy for acute first episode psychosis. *Behavioural and Cognitive Psychotherapy, 34*, 277–291.

Bender, D.S., Farber, B.A. & Geller, J.D. (2001). Cluster B personality traits and attachment. *Journal of the American Academy of Psychoanalysis, 29*, 551–563.

Bentacourt, H. & Lopez, S.R. (1993). The study of culture, ethnicity and race in American psychology. *American Psychologist, 48*, 629–637.

Bentall, R.P. (1994). Cognitive biases and abnormal beliefs: Towards a model of persecutory delusions. In A.S. David & J. Cutting (Eds.), *The neuropsychology of schizophrenia*. London: Lawrence Erlbaum.

Bentall, R.P. (2003). *Madness explained: Psychosis and human nature*. London: Penguin.

Bentall, R.P., Corcoran, R., Howard, R., Blackwood, N. & Kinderman, P. (2001). Persecutory delusions: A review and theoretical integration. *Clinical Psychology Review, 21*, 1143–1192.

Bentall, R.P., Kaney, S. & Dewey, M.E. (1991). Paranoia and social reasoning: An attribution theory analysis. *British Journal of Clinical Psychology, 30*, 13–23.

Bentall, R.P. & Kinderman, P. (1998). Psychological processes and delusional beliefs: Implications for the treatment of paranoid states. In S. Lewis, N. Tarrier & T. Wykes (Eds.), *Outcome and innovation in psychological treatment of schizophrenia*. Chichester: Wiley.

Bentall, R.P. & Kinderman, P. (1999). Self-regulation, affect and psychosis: Social cognition in paranoia and mania. In T. Dalgleish & M. Power (Eds.), *Handbook of cognition and emotion*. Chichester: Wiley.

Bentall, R.P., Kinderman, P. & Kaney, S. (1994). The self, attributional processes and abnormal beliefs: Towards a model of persecutory delusions. *Behaviour Research and Therapy, 32*, 331–342.

Benton, A.L., Hamsher, K. & Sivan, A.B. (1983). *Multilingual aphasia examination* (3rd ed.). Iowa City, IA: AJA Associates.

Ben-Yishay, Y. & Daniels-Zide, E. (2000). Examined lives: Outcomes after holistic rehabilitation. *Rehabilitation Psychology, 45*(2), 112–129.

Berger, H. & Smith, M.J. (1978). Voluntary versus prescribed termination of methadone maintenance. *British Journal of Addiction, 73*(2), 178–180.

Berger, P., Berner, W., Bolterauer, J., Gutierrez, K. & Berger, K. (1999). Sadistic personality disorder in sex offenders: Relationship to antisocial personality disorder and sexual sadism. *Journal of Personality Disorders, 13*(2), 175–186.

Bergman, A.J., Harvey, P.D., Mitropoulou, V., Aronson, A. et al. (1996). The factor structure of schizotypal symptoms in a clinical population. *Schizophrenia Bulletin, 22*(3), 501–509.

Berlin, F.S. & Meinecke, C.F. (1981). Treatment of sex offenders with anti-androgenic medication: Conceptualization, review of treatment modalities, and preliminary findings. *American Journal of Psychiatry, 138*(5), 601–607.

Berman, J.R., Berman, L.A., Werbin, T.J., Flaherty, E.E. et al. (1999). Clinical evaluation of female sexual function: Effects of age and estrogen status on subjective and physiologic sexual responses. *International Journal of Impotence Research, 11*, S31–S38.

Berman, J.S., Symonds, C. & Birch, R. (2004). Efficacy of two cannabis-based medicinal extracts for relief of central neuropathic pain from brachial plexus avulsion: Results of a randomized controlled trial. *Pain, 112*(3), 299–306.

Bernstein, D.A., Borkovec, T.D. & Hazlett-Stevens, H. (2000). *New directions in progressive relaxation training: A guidebook for helping professionals*. Westport, CT: Praeger.

Bernstein, D.P., Useda, D. & Siever, L.J. (1993). Paranoid personality disorder: Review of the literature and recommendations for DSM-IV. *Journal of Personality Disorders, 7*(1), 53–62.

Berrington, A., Diamond, I., Ingham, R., Stevenson, J. et al. (2004). *Consequences of teenage parenthood: Pathways which minimize the long-term negative impacts of childbearing*. London: Department of Health.

Bersoff, D.M. & Bersoff, D.N. (1999). Ethical perspectives in clinical research. In P.C. Kendall, J.N. Butcher & G.N. Holmbeck (Eds.), *Handbook of research methods in clinical psychology* (2nd ed.). New York: Wiley.

Bertelsen, A. (1979). A Danish twin study of manic-depressive disorders. In M. Schou & E. Stromgren (Eds.), *Origin, prevention and treatment of affective disorder* (pp. 227–239). London: Academic Press.

Bertelsen, A., Harvald, B. & Hauge, M. (1977). Danish twin study of manic-depressive disorders. *British Journal of Psychiatry, 130* (April), 330–351.

Bertram, L. & Tanzi, R.E. (2004). Alzheimer's disease: One disorder, too many genes? *Human Molecular Genetics, 13*, R135–R141.

Berzins, K.M., Petch, A. & Atkinson, J.M. (2003). Prevalence and experience of harassment of people with mental health problems living in the community. *British Journal of Psychiatry, 183*, 526–533.

Bettelheim, B. (1967). *The empty fortress*. New York: Free Press.

Bettelheim, B. (1973). Bringing up children. *Ladies' Home Journal, 90*, 28.

Biederman, J., Faraone, S., Mick, E., Spencer, T. et al. (1995). High risk for attention deficit hyperactivity disorder among children of parents with childhood onset of the disorder: A pilot study. *American Journal of Psychiatry, 152*, 431–435.

Biederman, J., Herzog, D.B., Rivinus, T.M., Harper, G.P. et al. (1985). Amitriptyline in the treatment of anorexia nervosa: A double-blind, placebo-controlled study. *Journal of Clinical Psychopharmacology, 5*(1), 10–16.

Biederman, J., Newcorn, J. & Sprich, S. (1991). Comorbidity of attention deficit hyperactivity disorder with conduct, depressive, and other disorders. *American Journal of Psychiatry, 148*, 564–577.

Bieling, P.J., Israeli, A.L. & Antony, M.M. (2004). Is perfectionism good, bad, or both? Examining models of the perfectionism construct. *Personality and Individual Differences, 36*(6), 1373–1385.

Bieling, P.J., Summerfeldt, L.J., Israeli, A.L. & Antony, M.M. (2004). Perfectionism as an explanatory construct in comorbidity of Axis I disorders. *Journal of Psychopathology and Behavioral Assessment, 26*(3), 193–201.

Bienvenu, O.J. & Eaton, W.W. (1998). The epidemiology of blood-injection-injury phobia. *Psychological Medicine, 28*(5), 1129–1136.

Bini, L. (1938). Experimental researches of epileptic attacks induced by the electric current. *American Journal of Psychiatry, 94*, 172–183.

Binik, Y.M. (2005). Should dyspareunia be retained as a sexual dysfunction in DSM-V? A painful classification decision. *Archives of Sexual Behavior, 34*, 11–21.

Binik, Y.M., Bergeron, S. & Khalife, S. (2000). Dyspareunia. In S.R. Leiblum & R.C. Rosen (Eds.), *Principles and practice of sex therapy* (3rd ed.). New York: Guilford Press.

Binzer, M., Anderson, P.M. & Kullgren, G. (1997). Clinical characteristics of patients with motor disability due to conversion disorder: A prospective control group study. *Journal of Neurology, Neurosurgery and Psychiatry, 63*, 83–88.

Birbaumer, N., Viet, R., Lotze, M., Erb, M. et al. (2005). Deficient fear conditioning in psychopathy: A functional magnetic resonance imaging study. *Archives of General Psychiatry, 62*(7), 799–805.

Birmaher, B., Ryan, N.D., Williamson, D.E., Brent, D.A. & Kaufman, J. (1996). Childhood and adolescent depression: A review of the past 10 years. *Journal of the American Academy of Child and Adolescent Psychiatry, 35*(12), 1575–1583.

Bisson, J.I. (2003). Single-session early psychological interventions following traumatic events. *Clinical Psychology Review, 23*, 481–499.

Bjorgvinsson, T. & Rosqvist, J. (2008). *Cognitive-behavioral therapy for depression*. London: Routledge.

Bjorkland, D.F. & Green, B.L. (1992). The adaptive nature of cognitive immaturity. *American Psychologist, 47*, 46–54.

Blackburn, I.M., James, I.A. & Flitcroft, A. (2006). Case formulation in depression. In N. Tarrier (Ed.), *Case formulation in cognitive behaviour therapy*. London and New York: Routledge.

Blackburn, I.M. & Moorhead, S. (2000). Update in cognitive therapy for depression. *Journal of Cognitive Psychotherapy: An International Quarterly, 14*, 305–336.

Blader, J.C. (2006). Which family factors predict children's externalizing behaviors following discharge from psychiatric inpatient treatment? *Journal of Child Psychology and Psychiatry, 47*, 1133–1142.

mood disorders in a large clinical sample. *Journal of Abnormal Psychology*, 110, 585–599.

Brown, T.A., O'Leary, T.A. & Barlow, D.H. (2001). Generalized anxiety disorder. In D.H. Barlow (Ed.), *Clinical handbook of psychological disorders*. New York: Guilford Press.

Brownell, K.D. (1986). Public health approaches to obesity and its management. *Annual Review of Public Health*, 7, 521–533.

Brozina, K. & Abela, J.R.Z. (2006). Symptoms of depression and anxiety in children: Specificity of the Hopelessness Theory. *Journal of Clinical Child and Adolescent Psychology*, 35, 515–527.

Bruch, M.A. & Heimberg, R.G. (1994). Differences in perceptions of parental and personal characteristics between generalized and nongeneralized social phobics. *Journal of Anxiety Disorders*, 8(2), 155–168.

Bruck, M. (1992). Persistence of dyslexics' phonological awareness deficits. *Developmental Psychology*, 28, 874–886.

Brunswick, N., McCrory, E., Price, C.J., Frith, C.D. & Frith, U. (1999). Explicit and implicit processing of words and pseudowords by adult developmental dyslexics: A search for Wernicke's Wortschatz? *Brain*, 122, 1901–1917.

Bruyn, G.A.W., Kremer, H.P.H., de Marie, S., Padberg, G.W. et al. (1989). Clinical evaluation of pneumococcal meningitis in adults over a 12-year period. *European Journal of Clinical Microbiology and Infectious Diseases*, 8(8), 695–700.

Bryan, R.N., Wells, S.W., Miller, T.J., Elster, A.D. et al. (1997). Infarctlike lesions in the brain: Prevalence and anatomic characteristics at MR imaging of the elderly: Data from the cardiovascular health study. *Radiology*, 202(1), 47–54.

Bryant, R.A. & Harvey, A.G. (1998). Relationship between acute stress disorder and posttraumatic stress disorder following mild traumatic brain injury. *American Journal of Psychiatry*, 155(5), 625–629.

Bryer, J.B., Nelson, B.A., Miller, J.B. & Krol, P.A. (1987). Childhood sexual and physical abuse as factors in adult psychiatric illness. *American Journal of Psychiatry*, 144(11), 1426–1430.

Bryson, S.E., Clark, B.S. & Smith, I.M. (1988). First report of a Canadian epidemiological study of autistic syndromes. *Journal of Child Psychology and Psychiatry*, 29, 433–445.

Buchanan, A. & Leese, M. (2001). Detention of people with dangerous severe personality disorders: A systematic review. *Lancet*, 358(9297), 1955–1959.

Buchsbaum, M.S., Yang, S., Hazlett, E., Siegel, B.V. et al. (1997). Ventricular volume and asymmetry in schizotypal personality disorder and schizophrenia assessed with magnetic resonance imaging. *Schizophrenia Research*, 27(1), 45–53.

Buckley, J.T. (1995). Nation raising 'a generation of gamblers'. *USA Today*, pp. 1A–2A.

Budney, A.J., Moore, B.A., Vandrey, R.G. & Hughes, J.R. (2003). The time course and significance of cannabis withdrawal. *Journal of Abnormal Psychology*, 112(3), 393–402.

Buitelaar, J.K., van der Wees, M., Swaab-Barneveld, H. & van der Gaag, R. (1999). Theory of mind and emotion-recognition functioning in autistic spectrum disorders in psychiatric control and normal children. *Development and Psychopathology*, 11, 39–58.

Bulik, C.M., Sullivan, P.F., Epstein, L.H., McKee, M. et al. (1992). Drug use in women with anorexia and bulimia nervosa. *International Journal of Eating Disorders*, 11(3), 213–225.

Bullers, S., Cooper, M.L. & Russell, M. (2001). Social network drinking and adult alcohol involvement: A longitudinal exploration of the direction of influence. *Addictive Behaviors*, 26(2), 181–199.

Bunney, W.E. & Davis, J.M. (1965). Norepinephrine in depressive reactions: A review. *Archives of General Psychiatry*, 13(6), 483&.

Bunney, W.E., Goodwin, F.K. & Murphy, D.L. (1972). Switch process in manic-depressive illness. 3. Theoretical implications. *Archives of General Psychiatry*, 27(3), 312&.

Burden, M.J., Jacobson, S.W., Sokol, R.J. & Jacobson, J.L. (2005). Effects of prenatal alcohol exposure on attention and working memory at 7.5 years of age. *Alcoholism: Clinical and Experimental Research*, 29(3), 443–452.

Burkett, B.G. & Whitley, G. (1998). *Stolen valor: How the Vietnam generation was robbed of its heros and its history*. Dallas, TX: Verity.

Burks, H.M. & Stefflre, B. (1979). *Theories of counselling* (3rd ed.). New York: McGraw-Hill.

Burns, D.D. & Spangler, D.L. (2000). Does psychotherapy homework lead to improvements in depression in cognitive-behavioral therapy or does improvement lead to increased homework compliance? *Journal of Consulting and Clinical Psychology*, 68(1), 46–56.

Burr, V. (1995). *An introduction to social constructionism*. London: Routledge.

Burt, D.R., Creese, I. & Snyder, S.H. (1977). Anti-schizophrenic drugs: Chronic treatment elevates dopamine receptor-binding. *Brain Science*, 196(4287), 327–328.

Butcher, J.N., Dahlstrom, W.G., Graham, J.R., Tellegen, A. & Kraemer, B. (1989). *Minnesota Multiphasic Personality Inventory 2: Manual for administration and scoring*. Minneapolis: University of Minnesota Press.

Butler, A.C., Chapman, J.E., Forman, E.M. & Beck, A.T. (2006). The empirical status of cognitive-behavioral therapy: A review of meta-analyses. *Clinical Psychology Review*, 26, 17–31.

Butler, G., Fennell, M., Robson, P. & Gelder, M. (1991). Comparison of behavior therapy and cognitive behavior therapy in the treatment of generalized anxiety disorder. *Journal of Consulting and Clinical Psychology*, 59(1), 167–175.

Butler, R.J. (1994). *Noctural enuresis: The child's experience*. Oxford: Butterworth Heinemann.

Butler, R.J. (2001). Impact of nocturnal enuresis on children and young people. *Scandinavian Journal of Urology and Nephrology*, 35, 169–176.

Butler, R.J. (2004). Childhood nocturnal enuresis: Developing a conceptual framework. *Clinical Psychology Review*, 24, 909–931.

Butler, R.J., Golding, J. & Northstone, K. (2005). Nocturnal enuresis at 7.5 years old: Prevalence and analysis of clinical signs. *BJU International*, 96, 404–410.

Butters, J., McClure, J., Siegert, R. & Ward, T. (1997). Attributions for real and hypothetical events: Do they predict depression? *Australian Journal of Psychology*, 49(1), 42–48.

Button, E.J., Sonugabarke, E.J.S., Davies, J. & Thompson, M. (1996). A prospective study of self-esteem in the prediction of eating problems in adolescent schoolgirls: Questionnaire findings. *British Journal of Clinical Psychology*, 35, 193–203.

Buvat, J., Lemaire, A. & Ratajczyk, J. (1996). Role of hormones in sexual dysfunction, homosexuality, transsexualism, and paraphilia-related disorders: Diagnostic and therapeutic consequences. *Contraception, Fertilité, Sexualité*, 24(11), 834–846.

Byrne, M., Agerbo, E., Eaton, W.W. & Mortensen, P.B. (2004). Parental socio-economic status and risk of first admission with schizophrenia: A Danish national register-based study. *Social Psychiatry and Psychiatric Epidemiology*, 39(2), 87–96.

Byrne, P. (1997). Psychiatric stigma: Past, passing and to come. *Journal of the Royal Society of Medicine*, 90, 618–621.

Byrne, S. & McLean, N. (2002). Elite athletes: Effects of the pressure to be thin. *Journal of Science and Medicine in Sport*, 5(2), 80–94.

Cadenhead, K.S., Swerdlow, N.R., Shafer, K.M., Diaz, M. & Braff, D.L. (2000). Modulation of the startle response and startle laterality in relatives of schizophrenic patients and in subjects with schizotypal personality disorder: Evidence of inhibitory deficits. *American Journal of Psychiatry*, 157(10), 1660–1668.

Cadoret, R.J., Troughton, E., O'Gorman, T.W. & Heywood, E. (1986). An adoption study of genetic and environmental factors in drug abuse. *Archives of General Psychiatry*, 43(12), 1131–1136.

Cadoret, R.J., Yates, W.R., Troughton, E., Woodworth, G. & Stewart, M.A. (1995). Adoption study demonstrating two genetic pathways to drug abuse. *Archives of General Psychiatry*, 52(1), 42–52.

Cahill, S.P., Carrigan, M.H. & Frueh, B.C. (1999). Does EMDR work? And if so, why? A critical review of controlled outcome and dismantling research. *Journal of Anxiety Disorders*, 13, 5–33.

Cale, E.M. & Lilienfeld, S.O. (2002). Sex differences in psychopathology and antisocial personality disorder: A review and integration. *Clinical Psychology Review*, 22, 1179–1207.

Calhoun, G.B., Glaser, B., Stefurak, T. & Bradshaw, C.P. (2001). Preliminary validation of the Narcissistic Personality Inventory – Juvenile Offender. *International Journal of Offender Therapy and Comparative Criminology, 44*, 564–580.

Caliendo, C., Armstrong, M.L. & Roberts, A.E. (2005). Self-reported characteristics of women and men with intimate body piercings. *Journal of Advanced Nursing, 49*, 474–484.

Cameron, N. (1974). Paranoid conditions and paranoia. In S. Arieti & E. Brody (Eds.), *American handbook of psychiatry*. New York: Basic Books.

Campbell, F. & Ramsay, C.T. (1994). Effect of early intervention on intellectual and academic achievement: A follow-up study of children from low-income families. *Child Development, 65*, 684–698.

Campbell, M., Armenteros, J.L., Malone, R.P., Adams, P.B. et al. (1997). Neuroleptic-related dyskinesias in autistic children: A prospective, longitudinal study. *Journal of the American Academy of Child and Adolescent Psychiatry, 36*(6), 835–843.

Campbell, P. (1996). In J. Read & J. Reynolds (Eds.), *Speaking our minds*. Basingstoke: Macmillan.

Campbell, T.W. (1992). Promoting play therapy: Marketing dream or empirical nightmare? *Issues in Child Abuse Accusations, 4*, 111–117.

Campbell, W.K. (1999). Narcissism and romantic attraction. *Journal of Personality and Social Psychology, 77*(6), 1254–1270.

Candel, I. & Merckelbach, H. (2004). Peritraumatic dissociation as a predictor of post-traumatic stress disorder: A critical review. *Comprehensive Psychiatry, 45*, 44–50.

Caneron, N. (1974). Paranoid conditions and paranoia. In S. Arieti & E. Brody (Eds.), *American handbook of psychiatry*. New York: Basic Books.

Canhetti-Oliveira, C.M. & Richieri-Costa, A. (2006). A study of familial stuttering. *American Journal of Medical Genetics Part A, 140a*(19), 2139–2141.

Cantor, J.M., Blanchard, R., Robichaud, L.K. & Christensen, B.K. (2005). Quantitative reanalysis of aggregate data on IQ in sexual offenders. *Psychological Bulletin, 131*(4), 555–568.

Cantor-Graae, E. & Selten, J.P. (2005). Schizophrenia and migration: A meta-analysis and review. *American Journal of Psychiatry, 162*, 12–24.

Cantwell, D. & Baker, L. (1989). Stability and natural history of DSM-III childhood diagnoses. *Journal of the American Academy of Child and Adolescent Psychiatry, 28*(5), 691–700.

Cantwell, D., Baker, L. & Rutter, M. (1978). Comparative study of infantile autism and specific developmental receptive language disorder. 4. Analysis of syntax and language function. *Journal of Child Psychology and Psychiatry and Allied Disciplines, 19*(4), 351–362.

Capaldi, D.M. & Patterson, G.R. (1994). Interrelated influences of contextual factors on antisocial behaviour in childhood and adolescence for males. In D.C. Fowles, P. Sutker & H.S. Goodman (Eds.), *Progress in experimental personality and psychopathology research*. New York: Springer.

Caplan, G. (1964). *Principles of preventative psychiatry*. New York: Basic Books.

Capps, I., Losh, M. & Thurber, C. (2000). 'The frog ate the bug and made his mouth sad': Narrative competence in children with autism. *Journal of Abnormal Child Psychology, 28*(2), 193–204.

Cardena, E. (2000). Hypnosis in the treatment of trauma: A promising, but not fully supported, efficacious intervention. *International Journal of Clinical and Experimental Hypnosis, 48*, 225–238.

Cardno, A.G., Marshall, E.J., Coid, B., Macdonald, A.M. et al. (1999). Heritability estimates for psychotic disorders: The Maudsley Twin psychosis series. *Archives of General Psychiatry, 56*(2), 162–168.

Carlsson, A. (2001). A half-century of neurotransmitter research: Impact on neurology and psychiatry (Nobel Lecture). *Chembiochem, 2*(7–8), 484&.

Carlsten, A., Allebeck, P. & Brandt, L. (1996). Are suicide rates in Sweden associated with changes in the prescribing of medicines? *Acta Psychiatrica Scandinavica, 94*(2), 94–100.

Carmichael, K.D. (2006). *Play therapy: An introduction*. Glenview, IL: Prentice-Hall.

Carnegie Corporation of New York (1994). *Starting points: Meeting the needs of our youngest children*. New York: Carnegie Corporation.

Carroll, J.M., Touyz, S.W. & Beumont, P.J.V. (1996). Specific comorbidity between bulimia nervosa and personality disorders. *International Journal of Eating Disorders, 19*(2), 159–170.

Carroll, R.A. (2000). Assessment and treatment of gender dysphoria. In S.R. Lieblum & R.C. Rosen (Eds.), *Principles and practice of sex therapy*. New York: Guilford Press.

Carroll, S.T., Riffenburgh, R.H., Roberts, T.A. & Myhre, E.B. (2002). Tattoos and body piercings as an indicator of adolescent risk-taking behaviors. *Pediatrics, 109*, 1021–1027.

Carson, C.C., Burnett, A.L., Levine, L.A. & Nehra, A. (2002). The efficacy of sildenafil citrate (Viagra®) in clinical populations: An update. *Urology, 60*(2B), 12–27.

Carson, N.J., Rodriguez, D. & Audrain-McGovern, J. (2005). Investigation of mechanisms linking media exposure to smoking in high school students. *Preventive Medicine, 41*(2), 511–520.

Carson, R.C. (1996). Aristotle, Galileo, and the DSM taxonomy: The case of schizophrenia. *Journal of Consulting and Clinical Psychology, 64*, 1133–1139.

Carstairs, K. (1992). Paranoid-schizoid or symbiotic? *International Journal of Psychoanalysis, 73*, 71–85.

Carter, A.S., Garrity-Rokous, F.E., Chazan-Cohen, R., Little, C. & Briggs-Gowan, M.J. (2001). Maternal depression and comorbidity: Predicting early parenting, attachment security, and toddler social-emotional problems and competencies. *Journal of the American Academy of Child and Adolescent Psychiatry, 40*, 18–26.

Carter, F.A., Bulik, C.M., Lawson, R.H., Sullivan, P.F. & Wilson, J.S. (1996). Effect of mood and food cues on body image in women with bulimia and controls. *International Journal of Eating Disorders, 20*(1), 65–76.

Carter, J.C. & Fairburn, C.G. (1998). Cognitive-behavioral self-help for binge eating disorder: A controlled effectiveness study. *Journal of Consulting and Clinical Psychology, 66*(4), 616–623.

Casey, B.J., Castellanos, F.X., Giedd, J.N., Marsh, W.L. et al. (1997). Implications of right frontostriatal circuitry in response inhibition and attention-deficit/hyperactivity disorder. *Journal of the American Academy of Child and Adolescent Psychiatry, 36*, 374–383.

Casper, R.C. & Lyubomirsky, S. (1997). Individual psychopathology relative to reports of unwanted sexual experiences as predictor of a bulimic eating pattern. *International Journal of Eating Disorders, 21*(3), 229–236.

Caspi, A., Newman, D.L., Moffitt, T.E. & Silva, P.A. (1996). Behavioural observations at age 3 years predict adult psychiatric disorders. *Archives of General Psychiatry, 53*, 1033–1039.

Cassady, J.D., Kirschke, D.L., Jones, T.F., Craig, A.S. et al. (2005). Case series: Outbreak of conversion disorder among Amish adolescent girls. *Journal of the American Academy of Child and Adolescent Psychiatry, 44*(3), 291–297.

Castelli, F., Frith, C., Happe, F. & Frith, U. (2002). Autism, Asperger syndrome and brain mechanisms for the attribution of mental states to animated shapes. *Brain, 125*, 1839–1849.

Castelli, L., Perozzo, P., Zibetti, M., Crivelli, B. et al. (2006). Chronic deep brain stimulation of the subthalamic nucleus for Parkinson's disease: Effects on cognition, mood, anxiety and personality traits. *European Neurology, 55*(3), 136–144.

Castle, D.J. & Rossell, S.L. (2006). An update on body dysmorphic disorder. *Current Opinion in Psychiatry, 19*, 74–78.

Cautela, J.R. (1966). Treatment of compulsive behaviour by covert sensitization. *Psychological Record, 16*, 33–41.

Cave, S. (2002). *Classification and diagnosis of psychological abnormality*. Hove: Psychology Press.

Cecil, K.M., Lenkinski, R.E., Gur, R.E. & Gur, R.C. (1999). Proton magnetic resonance spectroscopy in the frontal and temporal lobes of neuroleptic naive patients with schizophrenia. *Neuropsychopharmacology, 20*(2), 131–140.

Centers for Disease Control and Prevention (CDC) (2002). Alcohol use. NCHS fast stats. www.cdc.gov/nchs/fastats/alcohol.

Chadwick, P.D.J., Birchwood, M. & Trower, P. (1996). *Cognitive therapy for delusions, voices and paranoia*. New York: Wiley.

Chadwick, P.D.J. & Lowe, C.F. (1990). Measurement and modification of delusional beliefs. *Journal of Consulting and Clinical Psychology, 58*, 225–232.

Chadwick, P.D.J. & Lowe, C.F. (1994). A cognitive approach to measuring and modifying delusions. *Behaviour Research and Therapy, 32*(3), 355–367.

Chakrabarti, S. & Fombonne, E. (2005). Pervasive developmental disorders in preschool children: Confirmation of high prevalence. *American Journal of Psychiatry, 162*(6), 1133–1141.

Chambless, D.L. & Ollendick, T.H. (2001). Empirically supported psychological interventions: Controversies and evidence. *Annual Review of Psychology, 52*, 685–716.

Chamorro, R. & Flores-Ortiz, Y. (2000). Acculturation and disordered eating patterns among Mexican American women. *International Journal of Eating Disorders, 28*(1), 125–129.

Chaney, J.M., Mullins, L.L., Wagner, J.L., Hommel, K.A. et al. (2004). A longitudinal examination of causal attributions and depression symptomatology in rheumatoid arthritis. *Rehabilitation Psychology, 49*(2), 126–133.

Chapman, A.L., Gratz, K.L. & Brown, M.Z. (2006). Solving the puzzle of deliberate self-harm: The experiential avoidance model. *Behaviour Research and Therapy, 44*(3), 371–394.

Chapman, T. F. (1997). The epidemiology of fears and phobias. In G.C.L. Davey (Ed.), *Phobias: A handbook of theory, research and treatment.* Chichester: Wiley.

Charach, A., Ickowicz, A. & Schachar, R. (2004). Stimulant treatment over five years: Adherence, effectiveness, and adverse effects. *Journal of the American Academy of Child and Adolescent Psychiatry, 43*(5), 559–567.

Charney, D.S., Heninger, G.R. & Breier, A. (1984). Noradrenergic function in panic anxiety: Effects of yohimbine in healthy subjects and patients with agoraphobia and panic disorder. *Archives of General Psychiatry, 41*(8), 751–763.

Charney, D.S., Heninger, G.R. & Jatlow, P.I. (1985). Increased anxiogenic effects of caffeine in panic disorders. *Archives of General Psychiatry, 42*(3), 233–243.

Charney, D.S., Woods, S.W., Goodman, W.K. et al. (1987). Neurobiological mechanisms of panic anxiety: Biochemical and behavioral correlates of yohimbine-induced panic attacks. *American Journal of Psychiatry, 144*(8), 1030–1036.

Chartier, M.J., Walker, J.R. & Stein, M.B. (2001). Social phobia and potential childhood risk factors in a community sample. *Psychological Medicine, 31*(2), 307–315.

Chassin, L., Curran, P.J., Hussong, A.M. & Colder, C.R. (1996). The relation of parent alcoholism to adolescent substance use: A longitudinal follow-up study. *Journal of Abnormal Psychology, 105*(1), 70–80.

Chavira, D.A., Grilo, C.M., Shea, M.T., Yen, S. et al. (2003). Ethnicity and four personality disorders. *Comprehensive Psychiatry, 44*(6), 483–491.

Chen, C.Y., Wagner, F.A. & Anthony, J.C. (2002). Marijuana use and the risk of major depressive episode: Epidemiological evidence from the United States National Comorbidity Survey. *Social Psychiatry and Psychiatric Epidemiology, 37*(5), 199–206.

Chen, J., Mabjeesh, N.J. & Greenstein, A. (2001). Sildenafil versus the vacuum erection device: Patient preference. *Journal of Urology, 166*(5), 1779–1781.

Chess, S., Fernandez, P. & Korn, S. (1978). Behavioral consequences of congenital rubella. *Journal of Pediatrics, 93*, 699–703.

Cheung, A.H., Emslie, G.J. & Mayes, T.L. (2005). Review of the efficacy and safety of antidepressants in youth depression. *Journal of Child Psychology and Psychiatry, 46*, 735–754.

Chick, J., Gough, K., Falkowski, W., Kershaw, P. et al. (1992). Disulfiram treatment of alcoholism. *British Journal of Psychiatry, 161*, 84–89.

Chiu, M.M. & McBride-Chang, C. (2006). Gender, context and reading: A comparison of students in 43 countries. *Scientific Studies of Reading, 10*, 331–362.

Christiansen, B.A., Roehling, P.V., Smith, G.T. & Goldman, M.S. (1989). Using alcohol expectancies to predict adolescent drinking behavior after one year. *Journal of Consulting and Clinical Psychology, 57*(1), 93–99.

Christophersen, A.S., Ceder, G., Kristinsson, J., Lillsunde, P., Steentoft, A. et al. (1999). Drugged driving in the Nordic countries: A comparative study between five countries. *Forensic Science International, 106*(3), 173–190.

Chu, B.C. & Kendall, P.C. (2004). Positive association of child involvement and treatment outcome within a manual-based cognitive-behavioral treatment for children with anxiety. *Journal of Consulting and Clinical Psychology, 72*(5), 821–829.

Chu, J.A., Frey, L.M., Ganzel, B.L. & Matthews, J.A. (1999). Memories of childhood abuse: Dissociation, amnesia, and corroboration. *American Journal of Psychiatry, 156*, 749–755.

Chugani, D.C., Muzik, O., Behen, M., Rothermel, R. et al. (1999). Developmental changes in brain serotonin synthesis capacity in autistic and nonautistic children. *Annals of Neurology, 45*(3), 287–295.

Cicerone, K.D., Dahlberg, C., Malec, J.F., Langenbahn, D.M. et al. (2005). Evidence-based cognitive rehabilitation: Updated review of the literature from 1998 through 2002. *Archives of Physical Medicine and Rehabilitation, 86*, 1681–1692.

Cicerone, K.D., Levin, H., Malec, J., Stuss, D. & Whyte, J. (2006). Cognitive rehabilitation interventions for executive function: Moving from bench to bedside in patients with traumatic brain injury. *Journal of Cognitive Neuroscience, 18*, 1212–1222.

Cicerone, K.D., Mott, T., Azulay, J. & Friel, J.C. (2004). Community integration and satisfaction with functioning after intensive cognitive rehabilitation for traumatic brain injury. *Archives of Physical Medicine and Rehabilitation, 85*(6), 943–950.

Cima, M., Merckelbach, H., Hollnack, S. & Knauer, E. (2003). Characteristics of psychiatric prison inmates who claim amnesia. *Personality and Individual Differences, 35*, 373–380.

Citrome, L., Bilder, R.M. & Volavka, J. (2002). Managing treatment-resistant schizophrenia: Evidence from randomized clinical trials. *Journal of Psychiatric Practice, 8*, 205–215.

Citron, N.D. & Wade, P.J. (1980). Penile injuries from vacuum cleaners. *British Medical Journal, 281*(6232), 26.

Clancy, S.A., McNally, R.J., Schachter, D.L., Lenzenweger, M.F. & Pitman, R.K. (2002). Memory distortion in people reporting abduction by aliens. *Journal of Abnormal Psychology, 111*(3), 455–461.

Clancy, S.A., Schachter, D.L., McNally, R.J. & Pitman, R.K. (2000). False recognition in women reporting recovered memories of sexual abuse. *Psychological Science, 11*, 26–31.

Clark, D.A. (2006). *Cognitive behavioral therapy for OCD.* New York: Guilford Press.

Clark, D.A. & Beck, A.T. (2003). *Clark-Beck Obsessive-Compulsive Inventory Manual.* San Antonio, TX: San Antonio Psychological Corporation.

Clark, D.M. (1986). A cognitive approach to panic. *Behaviour Research and Therapy, 24*, 348–351.

Clark, D.M. (1988). A cognitive model of panic attacks. In C.G. Last & M. Hersen (Eds.), *Panic: Psychological perspectives.* Hillsdale, NJ: Lawrence Erlbaum.

Clark, D.M., Ball, S. & Pape, D. (1991). An experimental investigation of thought suppression. *Behaviour Research and Therapy, 29*(3), 253–257.

Clark, D.M., Ehlers, A., Hackmann, A., McManus, F. et al. (2006). Cognitive therapy versus exposure and applied relaxation in social phobia: A randomized controlled trial. *Journal of Consulting and Clinical Psychology, 74*, 568–578.

Clark, D.M., Salkovskis, P.M., Hackmann, A. et al. (1998). Two psychological treatments for hypochondriasis: A randomized controlled trial. *British Journal of Psychiatry, 173*, 218–225.

Clark, D.M., Salkovskis, P.M., Hackmann, A., Middleton, H. et al. (1994). A comparison of cognitive therapy, applied relaxation and imipramine in the treatment of panic disorder. *British Journal of Psychiatry, 164*, 759–769.

Clark, D.M., Salkovskis, P.M., Ost, L.-G., Breitholtz, E. et al. (1997). Misinterpretation of body sensations in panic disorder. *Journal of Consulting and Clinical Psychology, 65*, 203–213.

Clark, D.M. & Wells, A. (1995). A cognitive model of social phobia. In M.R. Liebowitz (Ed.), *Social phobia: Diagnosis assessment and treatment.* New York: Guilford Press.

Clayton, A.H. (2003). Sexual function and dysfunction in women. *Psychiatric Clinics of North America*, 26(3), 673&.

Cleghorn, J.M., Franco, S., Szechtman, B., Kaplan, R.D. et al. (1992). Toward a brain map of auditory hallucinations. *American Journal of Psychiatry*, 149(8), 1062–1069.

Clohessy, S. & Ehlers, A. (1999). PTSD symptoms, response to intrusive memories and coping in ambulance service workers. *British Journal of Clinical Psychology*, 38, 251–265.

Cloitre, M., Cancienne, J., Brodsky, B., Dulit, R. & Perry, S.W. (1996). Memory performance among women with parental abuse histories: Enhanced directed forgetting or directed remembering? *Journal of Abnormal Psychology*, 105(2), 204–211.

Cloninger, C.R. (1987). Neurogenetic adaptive mechanisms in alcoholism. *Science*, 236, 410–416.

Cloninger, C.R., Martin, R.L., Guze, S.B. & Clayton, P.J. (1986). A prospective follow-up and family study of somatization in men and women. *American Journal of Psychiatry*, 143(7), 873–878.

Cloninger, C.R., Sigvardsson, S., von Knorring, A.L. & Bohman, M. (1984). An adoption study of somatoform disorders. 2. Identification of two discrete somatoform disorders. *Archives of General Psychiatry*, 41(9), 863–871.

Cochrane, R. (1977). Mental illness in immigrants to England and Wales: An analysis of mental hospital admissions. *Social Psychiatry*, 12, 23–35.

Cockell, S.J., Hewitt, P.L., Seal, B. et al. (2002). Trait and self-presentational dimensions of perfectionism among women with anorexia nervosa. *Cognitive Therapy and Research*, 26(6), 745–758.

Coelho, C.A., McHugh, R.E. & Boyle, M. (2000). Semantic feature analysis as a treatment for aphasic dysnomia: A replication *Aphasiology*, 14(2), 133–142.

Coffey, C., Carlin, J.B., Lynskey, M., Li, N. & Patton, G.C. (2003). Adolescent precursors of cannabis dependence: Findings from the Victorian Adolescent Health Cohort Study. *British Journal of Psychiatry*, 182, 330–336.

Cohen, D., Taieb, O., Flament, M., Benoit, N. et al. (2000). Absence of cognitive impairment at long-term follow-up in adolescents treated with ECT for severe mood disorder. *American Journal of Psychiatry*, 157(3), 460–462.

Cohen, J.D., Barch, D.M., Carter, C. & Servan-Schreiber, D. (1999). Context-processing deficits in schizophrenia: Converging evidence from three theoretically motivated cognitive tasks. *Journal of Abnormal Psychology*, 108(1), 120–133.

Cohen, M. & Seghorn, T. (1969). Sociometric study of the sex offender. *Journal of Abnormal Psychology*, 74, 249–255.

Cohen, P., Cohen, J., Kasen, S., Velez, C.N. et al. (1993). An epidemiologic study of disorders in late childhood and adolescence. 1. Age-specific and gender-specific prevalence. *Journal of Child Psychology and Psychiatry and Allied Disciplines*, 34(6), 851–867.

Cohen, R.M., Semple, W.E., Gross, M., Nordahl, T.E. et al. (1988). The effect of neuroleptics on dysfunction in a prefrontal substrate of sustained attention in schizophrenia. *Life Sciences*, 43(14), 1141–1150.

Coie, J.K. & Dodge, K.A. (1998). Aggression and antisocial behavior. In W. Damon & N. Eisenberg (Eds.), *Handbook of child psychology* (5th ed., Vol. 3). New York: Wiley.

Cole, J., Sumnall, H. & Grob, C. (2002a). Sorted: Ecstasy facts and fiction. *Psychologist*, 15, 464–467.

Cole, J., Sumnall, H. & Grob, C. (2002b). Where are the casualties? Response. *Psychologist*, 15(9), 474.

Cole, K. & Vaughan, F.L. (2005). The feasibility of using cognitive behaviour therapy for depression associated with Parkinson's Disease: A literature review. *Parkinsonism and Related Disorders*, 11, 269–276.

Combs, B.J., Hales, D.R. & Williams, B.K. (1980). *An invitation to health: Your personal responsibility*. Menlo Park, CA: Benjamin/Cummings.

Comer, S.D., Hart, C.L., Ward, A.S., Haney, M. et al. (2001). Effects of repeated oral methamphetamine administration in humans. *Psychopharmacology*, 155(4), 397–404.

Commonwealth Department of Health and Family Services, Australia (1997). *Evaluation of the national mental health strategy*. Canberra: Commonwealth Department of Health and Family Services, Mental Health Branch.

Compton, W.M., Helzer, J.E., Hwu, H.G., Yeh, E.K. et al. (1991). New methods in cross-cultural psychiatry: Psychiatric illness in Taiwan and the United States. *American Journal of Psychiatry*, 148(12), 1697–1704.

Conner, K.R., Duberstein, P.R., Conwell, Y., Seidlitz, L. & Caine, E.D. (2001). Psychological vulnerability to completed suicide: A review of empirical studies. *Suicide and Life-Threatening Behavior*, 31(4), 367–385.

Conners, C.K., Sitarenios, G., Parker, J.D.A. & Epstein, J.N. (1998). The revised Conners' Parent Rating Scale (CPRS-R): Factor structure, reliability, and criterion validity. *Journal of Abnormal Child Psychology*, 26(4), 257–268.

Conte, J.R. & Berliner, L. (1981). Sexual abuse of children: Implications for practice social casework. *Journal of Contemporary Social Work*, 62(10), 601–606.

Conte, J.R., Wolf, S. & Smith, T. (1989). What sexual offenders tell us about prevention strategies. *Child Abuse and Neglect*, 13(2), 293–301.

Cook, M. & Mineka, S. (1990). Selective associations in the observational learning of fear in rhesus monkeys. *Journal of Experimental Psychology: Animal Behavior Processes*, 16, 372–389.

Coolidge, F.L., Thede, L.L. & Young, S.E. (2000). Heritability of the gender identity disorder. *Behavior Genetics*, 30(5), 400.

Coolidge, F.L., Thede, L.L. & Young, S.E. (2002). The heritability of gender identity disorder in a child and adolescent population. *Behavior Genetics*, 32, 251–257.

Coons, P.M. (1999). Psychogenic or dissociative fugue: A clinical investigation of five cases. *Psychological Reports*, 84, 881–886.

Coons, P.M., Bowman, E.S. & Milstein, V. (1988). Multiple personality disorder: A clinical investigation of 50 cases. *Journal of Nervous and Mental Disease*, 176(9), 519–527.

Cooper, J.E. (1994). *Pocket guide to ICD-10 classification of mental and behavioural disorders*. New York: Churchill Livingstone.

Cooper, M. (2003). *Existential therapies*. Thousand Oaks, CA: Sage.

Cooper, M., Turpin, G., Bucks, R. & Kent, G. (2005). *Good practice guidelines for the conduct of psychological research within the NHS*. London: British Psychological Society.

Cooper, P.J., Coker, S. & Fleming, C. (1994). Self-help for bulimia nervosa: A preliminary report. *International Journal of Eating Disorders*, 16(4), 401–404.

Cooper, Z., Fairburn, C.G. & Hawker, D.M. (2004). *Cognitive-behavioral treatment of obesity*. New York: Guilford Press.

Copello, A., Orford, J., Hodgson, R., Tober, G. & Barrett, C. (2002). Social behaviour and network therapy: Basic principles and early experiences. *Addictive Behaviors*, 27(3), 345–366.

Corbitt, E.M. & Widiger, T.A. (1995). Sex differences among the personality disorders: An exploration of the data. *Clinical Psychology: Science and Practice*, 2(3), 225–238.

Corbridge, C. & Bell, L. (1996). An audit of people with eating disorders treated by adult mental health services. *European Eating Disorder Review*, 4(4), 241–248.

Corcoran, R., Cahill, C. & Frith, C.D. (1997). The appreciation of visual jokes in people with schizophrenia: A study of 'mentalizing' ability. *Schizophrenia Research*, 24(3), 319–327.

Cornblatt, B.A., Lenzenweger, M.F., Dworkin, R.H. & Kimling, L.E. (1985). Positive and negative schizophrenic symptoms, attention, and information-processing. *Schizophrenia Bulletin*, 11(3), 397–408.

Cornelius, J.R., Salloum, I.M., Mezzich, J., Cornelius, M.D. et al. (1995). Disproportionate suicidality in patients with comorbid major depression and alcoholism. *American Journal of Psychiatry*, 152(3), 358–364.

Cororve, M.B. & Gleaves, D.H. (2001). Body dysmorphic disorder: A review of conceptualizations, assessment, and treatment strategies. *Clinical Psychology Review*, 21, 949–970.

Corrie, S. & Callahan, M.M. (2000). A review of the scientist-practitioner model: Reflections on its potential contribution to counselling psychology within the context of current health care trends. *British Journal of Medical Psychology, 73*, 413–427.

Corrigan, P.W. (1991). Strategies that overcome barriers to token economies in community programs for severely mentally ill adults. *Community Mental Health Journal, 27*, 7–30.

Corrigan, P.W. (1995). Use of a token economy with seriously mentally ill patients: Criticisms and misconceptions. *Psychiatric Services, 46*, 1258–1263.

Corwin, M. (1996). Heroin's new popularity claims unlikely victims. *Los Angeles Times*.

Costa, P.T. & MacRae, R.R. (1990). Personality disorders and the five-factor model of personality. *Journal of Personality Disorders, 4*, 362–371.

Costantino, G., Flanagan, R. & Malagady, R.G. (2001). Narrative assessments, TAT, CAT and TEMAS. In L.A. Suzuki, J.G. Ponterotto et al. (Eds.), *Handbook of multicultural assessment: Clinical, psychological, and educational applications* (2nd ed.). San Francisco: Jossey-Bass.

Costello, E.J., Compton, S.N., Keeler, G. & Angold, A. (2003). Relationship between poverty and psychopathology: A natural experiment. *JAMA: Journal of the American Medical Association, 290*, 2023–2029.

Cottrell, D. (2003). Outcome studies of family therapy in child and adolescent depression. *Journal of Family Therapy, 25*, 406–416.

Cottrell, D. & Boston, P. (2002). Practitioner review: The effectiveness of systemic family therapy for children and adolescents. *Journal of Child Psychology and Psychiatry, 43*, 573–586.

Coughlan, A.K. & Hollows, S.E. (1985). *The Adult Memory and Information Processing Battery Test Manual*. Psychology Department, University of Leeds, Leeds, UK.

Courchesne, E. (2004). Abnormal brain development in autism spectrum disorder. *Biological Psychiatry, 55*, 47S–47S 163.

Courchesne, E., Townsend, J., Akshoomoff, N.A., Saitoh, O. et al. (1994). Impairment in shifting attention in autistic and cerebellar patients. *Behavioral Neuroscience, 108*(5), 848–865.

Couture, E.G. & Guitar, B.E. (1993). Treatment efficacy research in stuttering. *Journal of Fluency Disorders, 18*, 253–387.

Cowley, G. (1992). A quit-now drive that worked. *Newsweek*, 54.

Cox, A., Rutter, M., Newman, S. & Bartak, L. (1975). Comparative study of infantile autism and specific developmental receptive language disorder. 2. Parental characteristics. *British Journal of Psychiatry, 126*(February), 146–159.

Cox, D.J., Morris, J.B., Borowitz, S.M. & Sutphen, J.L. (2002). Psychological differences between children with and without chronic encopresis. *Journal of Pediatric Psychology, 27*(7), 585–591.

Coyne, J.C. (1976). Depression and response of others. *Journal of Abnormal Psychology, 85*(2), 186–193.

Coyne, J.C. (1994). Self-reported distress: Analog or ersatz depression. *Psychological Bulletin, 116*(1), 29–45.

Coyne, J.C. & Whiffen, V.E. (1995). Issues in personality as diathesis for depression: The case of sociotropy-dependency and autonomy-self-criticism. *Psychological Bulletin, 118*(3), 358–378.

Craig, A., Hancock, K., Tran, Y., Craig, M. & Peters, K. (2002). Epidemiology of stuttering in the community across the entire life span. *Journal of Speech, Language and Hearing Research, 45*(6), 1097–1105.

Craig, T.K.J. (2001). Life events: Meanings and precursors. In P.W. Halligan, C. Bass & J. Marshall (Eds.), *Contemporary approaches to the study of hysteria: Clinical and theoretical perspectives*. Oxford: Oxford University Press.

Craig, T.K.J., Bialas, I., Hodson, S. et al. (2004). Intergenerational transmission of somatization behaviour. 2. Observation of joint attention and bids for attention. *Psychological Medicine, 34*, 199–209.

Craig, T.K.J., Boardman, A.P., Mills, K., Daly-Jones, O. & Drake, H. (1993). The South London somatization study. 1. Longitudinal course and the influence of early-life experiences. *British Journal of Psychiatry, 163*, 579–588.

Craig, T.K.J., Cox, A.D. & Klein, K. (2002). Intergenerational transmission of somatization behaviour: A study of chronic somatizers and their children. *Psychological Medicine, 32*(5), 805–816.

Craske, M.G. & Barlow, D.H. (2001). Panic disorder and agoraphobia. In D.H. Barlow (Ed.), *Clinical handbook of psychological disorders*. New York: Guilford Press.

Craske, M.G., Brown, T.A. & Barlow, D.H. (1991). Behavioral treatment of panic disorder: A 2-year follow-up behavior therapy. *Behavior Therapy, 22*(3), 289–304.

Craske, M.G., Maidenberg, E. & Bystritsky, A. (1995). Brief cognitive-behavioral versus nondirective therapy for panic disorder. *Journal of Behavior Therapy and Experimental Psychiatry, 26*(2), 113–120.

Craske, M.G., Mohlman, J., Yi, J., Glover, D. & Valeri, S. (1995). Treatment of claustrophobias and snake spider phobias: Fear of arousal and fear of context. *Behaviour Research and Therapy, 33*(2), 197–203.

Craske, M.G., Rapee, R.M., Jackel, L. & Barlow, D.H. (1989). Qualitative dimensions of worry in DSM-III-R generalized anxiety disorder subjects and nonanxious controls. *Behaviour Research and Therapy, 27*(4), 397–402.

Craske, M.G. & Sipsas, A. (1992). Animal phobias versus claustrophobias: Exteroceptive versus interoceptive cues. *Behaviour Research and Therapy, 30*(6), 569–581.

Creswell, J.W. (1998). *Qualitative inquiry and research design: Choosing among five traditions*. Thousand Oaks, CA: Sage.

Crick, N.R. & Dodge, K.A. (1994). A review and reformulation of social information-processing mechanisms in children's social adjustment. *Psychological Bulletin, 115*, 74–101.

Crijnen, A.A., Achenbach, T.M. & Velhulst, F.C. (1999). Problems reported by parents of children in multiple cultures: The Child Behavior Checklist syndrome constructs. *American Journal of Psychiatry, 156*, 569–574.

Crisp, A.H., Gelder, M.G., Rix, S., Meltzer, H.I. & Rowlands, O.J. (2000). Stigmatization of people with mental illness. *British Journal of Psychiatry, 177*, 4–7.

Crits-Christoph, P. & Barber, J.P. (2002). Psychological treatments for personality disorders. In P.E. Nathan & J.M. Gorman (Eds.), *A guide to treatments that work* (2nd ed.). Oxford: Oxford University Press.

Crombez, G., Eccleston, C., Baeyens, F. & Eelen, P. (1998). When somatic information threatens, catastrophic thinking enhances attentional interference. *Pain, 75*, 187–198.

Crome, I. & Bloor, R. (2005). Substance misuse and psychiatric comorbidity. *Current Opinion in Psychiatry, 18*, 435–439.

Csernansky, J.G. & Schuchart, E.K. (2002). Relapse and rehospitalization rates in patients with schizophrenia: Effects of second generation antipsychotics. *CNS Drugs, 16*(7), 473–484.

Cuellar, A.K., Johnson, S.L. & Winters, R. (2005). Distinctions between bipolar and unipolar depression. *Clinical Psychology Review, 25*, 307–339.

Cuellar, I. (1998). Cross-cultural clinical psychological assessment of Hispanic Americans. *Journal of Personality Assessment, 70*, 71–86.

Cuijpers, P., van Straten, A. & Smit, F. (2006). Psychological treatment of late-life depression: A meta-analysis of randomized controlled trials. *International Journal of Geriatric Psychiatry, 21*, 1139–1149.

Cuijpers, P., van Straten, A. & Warmerdam, L. (2007). Problem solving therapies for depression: A meta-analysis. *European Psychiatry, 22*, 9–15.

Cumming, J. & Cumming, E. (1962). *Ego and milieu: Theory and practice of environmental therapy*. New York: Atherton.

Cummings, C., Gordon, J.R. & Marlatt, G.A. (1980). Relapse: Prevention and prediction. In W.R. Miller (Ed.), *The addictive disorders: Treatment of alcoholism, drug abuse, smoking and obesity*. New York: Pergamon.

Cummings, J.L., McRae, T. & Zhang, R. (2006). Effects of donepezil on neuropsychiatric symptoms in patients with dementia and severe behavioral disorders. *American Journal of Geriatric Psychiatry, 14*(7), 605–612.

Curran, V. (2000). Is MDMA neurotoxic in humans? An overview of evidence and methodological problems in research. *Neuropsychobiology, 42*, 34–41.

Currin, L., Schmidt, U., Treasure, J. & Jick, H. (2005). Time trends in eating disorder incidence. *British Journal of Psychiatry, 186*, 132–135.

Curry, J.F. & Wells, K.C. (2005). Striving for effectiveness in the treatment of adolescent depression: Cognitive behaviour therapy for mulitisite community intervention. *Cognitive and Behavioural Practice, 12*, 177–185.

Curtis, J.M. & Cowell, D.R. (1993). Relation of birth-order and scores on measures of pathological narcissism. *Psychological Reports, 72*(1), 311–315.

Cuthbert, B.N., Lang, P.J., Strauss, C., Drobes, D. et al. (2003). The psychophysiology of anxiety disorder: Fear memory imagery. *Psychophysiology, 40*, 407–422.

Cuthill, F.M. & Espie, C.A. (2005). Sensitivity and specificity of procedures for the differential diagnosis of epileptic and non-epileptic seizures: A systematic review. *Seizure: European Journal of Epilepsy, 14*, 293–303.

Cutts, F.T. & Vynnycky, E. (1999). Modelling the incidence of congenital rubella syndrome in developing countries. *International Journal of Epidemiology, 28*(6), 1176–1184.

Cyranowski, J.M., Frank, E., Cherry, C., Houck, P. & Kupfer, D.J. (2004). Prospective assessment of sexual function in women treated for recurrent major depression. *Journal of Psychiatric Research, 38*(3), 267–273.

D'Esposito, M. (2000). Functional imaging of neurocognition. *Seminars in Neurology, 20*, 487–498.

Dahl, R.E. (1992). The pharmacological treatment of sleep disorders. *Psychiatric Clinics of North America, 15*(1), 161–178.

Dahlstrom, W.G. & Archer, R.P. (2000). A shortened version of the MMPI-2. *Assessment, 7*, 131.

Daley, D. (2006). Attention deficit hyperactivity disorder: A review of the essential facts. *Child Care Health and Development, 32*, 193–204.

Dallos, R. (2004). Attachment narrative therapy: Integrating ideas from narrative and attachment theory in systemic family therapy with eating disorders. *Journal of Family Therapy, 26*, 40–65.

Dallos, R. & Draper, R. (2005). *Introduction to family therapy: Systemic theory and practice* (2nd ed.). Maidenhead: Open University Press.

Dallos, R. & Stedmon, J. (2006). Systemic formulation: Mapping the family dance. In L. Johnstone & R. Dallos (Eds.), *Formulation in psychology and psychotherapy*. London: Routledge.

Dalpan, G.J., McArthur, J.H., Aylward, E., Selnes, O.A. et al. (1992). Patterns of cerebral atrophy in HIV-1-infected individuals: Results of a quantitative MRI analysis. *Neurology, 42*(11), 2125–2130.

Damasio, A.R. & Damasio, H. (1983). The anatomical basis of pure alexia. *Neurology, 33*, 1573–1583.

Damasio, A.R., Tranel, D. & Damasio, H. (1990). Individuals with sociopathic behavior caused by frontal damage fail to respond autonomically to social stimuli. *Behavioural Brain Research, 41*(2), 81–94.

Damasio, H. (1994). The return of Gage, Phineas: Clues above the brain from the skull of a famous patient. *Science, 265*, 1159.

Daniels, C.W. (2002). Legal aspects of polygraph admissibility in the United States. In M. Kleiner (Ed.), *The handbook of polygraph testing*. San Diego, CA: Academic Press.

Danielson, C.K., Feeny, N.C., Findling, R.L. & Youngstrom, E.A. (2004). Psychosocial treatment of bipolar disorders in adolescents: A proposed cognitive-behavioral intervention. *Cognitive and Behavioral Practice, 11*(3), 283–297.

Dannon, P.N., Lowengrub, K., Aizer, A. & Kotler, M. (2006). Pathological gambling: Comorbid psychiatric diagnoses in patients and their families. *Israel Journal of Psychiatry and Related Sciences, 43*(2), 88–92.

Dansky, B.S., Brewerton, T.D., Kilpatrick, D.G. & O'Neal, P.M. (1997). The National Women's Study: Relationship of victimization and posttraumatic stress disorder to bulimia nervosa. *International Journal of Eating Disorders, 21*(3), 213–228.

Davey, G.C.L. (1988). Dental phobias and anxieties: Evidence for conditioning processes in the acquisition and modulation of a learned fear. *Behaviour Research and Therapy, 27*, 51–58.

Davey, G.C.L. (1989). *Ecological learning theory*. London: Routledge.

Davey, G.C.L. (1992a). Characteristics of individuals with fear of spiders. *Anxiety Research, 4*, 299–314.

Davey, G.C.L. (1992b). Classical conditioning and the acquisition of human fears and phobias: A review and synthesis of the literature. *Advances in Behaviour Research and Therapy, 14*, 29–66.

Davey, G.C.L. (1994a). Self-reported fears to common indigenous animals in an adult UK population: The role of disgust sensitivity. *British Journal of Psychology, 85*, 541–554.

Davey, G.C.L. (1994b). The 'disgusting' spider: The role of disease and illness in the perpetuation of fear of spiders. *Society and Animals, 2*, 17–25.

Davey, G.C.L. (1994c). Worrying as exacerbated problem solving. In G.C.L. Davey & F. Tallis (Eds.), *Worrying: Perspectives on theory, assessment and treatment*. Chichester: Wiley.

Davey, G.C.L. (1994d). Worrying, social problem-solving abilities, and social problem-solving confidence. *Behaviour Research and Therapy, 32*, 327–330.

Davey, G.C.L. (1995). Preparedness and phobias: Specific evolved associations or a generalized expectancy bias. *Behavioral and Brain Sciences, 18*, 289–325.

Davey, G.C.L. (1997). A conditioning model of phobias. In G.C.L. Davey (Ed.), *Phobias: A handbook of theory, research and treatment*. Chichester: Wiley.

Davey, G.C.L. (1998). Learning theory. In C.E. Walker (Ed.), *Comprehensive clinical psychology: Foundations of clinical psychology* (Vol. 1). Oxford: Elsevier.

Davey, G.C.L. (2002). Smoking them out. *Psychologist, 15*, 499.

Davey, G.C.L. (2003). Doing clinical psychology research: What is interesting isn't always useful. *Psychologist, 16*, 412–416.

Davey, G.C.L. (Ed.) (2004). *Complete psychology*. London: Hodder.

Davey, G.C.L. (2006). The catastrophizing interview techniques. In G.C.L. Davey & A. Wells (Eds.), *Worry and its psychological disorders*. Chichester: Wiley.

Davey, G.C.L. (2006b). A mood-as-input account of perseverative worrying. In G.C.L. Davey & A. Wells (Eds.), *Worry and its psychological disorders*. Chichester: Wiley.

Davey, G.C.L. (2006c). Cognitive mechanisms in fear acquisition and maintenance. In M.G. Craske, D. Hermans & D. Vansteenwegen (Eds.), *Fear and learning: Basic science to clinical application*. Washington, DC: American Psychological Association.

Davey, G.C.L. & Levy, S. (1998). Catastrophizing strategies: Internal statements that characterize catastrophic worrying. *Personality and Individual Differences, 26*, 21–32.

Davey, G.C.L., McDonald, A.S., Hirisave, U., Prabhu, G.G., Iwawaki, S., Im Jim, C., Merckelbach, H., de Jong, P.J., Leung, P.W.L. & Reimann, B.C. (1998). A cross-cultural study of animal fears. *Behaviour Research and Therapy, 36*, 735–750.

Davey, G.C.L., Menzies, R.G. & Gallardo, B. (1997). Height phobia and biases in the interpretation of bodily sensations: Some links between acrophobia and agoraphobia. *Behaviour Research and Therapy, 35*, 997–1001.

Davey, G.C.L., Tallis, F. & Capuzzo, N. (1996). Beliefs about the consequences of worrying. *Cognitive Therapy and Research, 20*, 499–518.

Davidson, J.R.T. (2003). Pharmacotherapy of social phobia. *Acta Psychiatrica Scandinavica, 108*, 65–71.

Davidson, K. (2007). *Cognitive therapy for personality disorders*. London: Routledge.

Davidson, R.J., Pizzagalli, D., Nitschke, J.B. & Putnam, K. (2002). Depression: Perspectives from affective neuroscience. *Annual Review of Psychology, 53*, 545–574.

Davie, C.A., Pirtosek, Z., Barker, G.J., Kingsley, D.P.E. et al. (1995). Magnetic-resonance spectroscopic study of Parkinsonism related to boxing. *Journal of Neurology, Neurosurgery and Psychiatry, 58*(6), 688–691.

Davies, L., Wolska, B., Hilbich, C., Multhaup, G. et al. (1988). A4 amyloid protein deposition and the diagnosis of Alzheimer's disease: Prevalence in aged brains determined by immunocytochemistry compared with conventional neuropathologic techniques. *Neurology, 38*(11), 1688–1693.

Davis, J.M. (1978). Dopamine theory of schizophrenia: A two-factor theory. In L.C. Wynne, R.L. Cromwell & S. Matthysse (Eds.), *The nature of schizophrenia*. New York: Wiley.

Davis, K.L., Kahn, R.S., Ko, G. & Davidson, M. (1991). Dopamine in schizophrenia: A review and reconceptualization. *American Journal of Psychiatry, 148*(11), 1474–1486.

Davis, J.O. & Phelps, J.A. (1995). Twins with schizophrenia: Genes or germs. *Schizophrenia Bulletin, 21*(1), 13–18.

Davis, T., Gunderson, J.G. & Myers, M. (1999). Borderline personality disorder. In D.G. Jacobs (Ed.), *The Harvard Medical School guide to suicide assessment and intervention*. San Francisco: Jossey-Bass.

Davison, G.C. (1964). A social learning therapy programme with an autistic child. *Behaviour Research and Therapy, 2*, 146–159.

Davison, G.C. & Lazarus, A.A. (1995). The dialectics of science and practice. In S.C. Hayes, V.M. Follette, T. Risley, R.D. Dawes & K. Grady (Eds.), *Scientific standards of psychological practice: Issues and recommendations*. Reno, NV: Context Press.

Davison, G.C. & Stuart, R.B. (1975). Behavior therapy and civil liberties. *American Psychologist*, 755–763.

Dawes, R.M. (1994). *House of cards: Psychology and psychotherapy built on a myth*. New York: Free Press.

Dawson, G., Klinger, L.G., Panagiotides, H., Lewy, A. & Castelloe, P. (1995). Subgroups of autistic children based on social behavior display distinct patterns of brain activity. *Journal of Abnormal Child Psychology, 23*(5), 569–583.

Deacon, B.J. & Abramowitz, J.S. (2004). Cognitive and behavioral treatments for anxiety disorders: A review of meta-analytic findings. *Journal of Clinical Psychology, 60*, 429–441.

Defries, J.C., Fulker, D.W. & LaBuda, M.C. (1987). Evidence for a genetic etiology in reading disability of twins. *Nature, 329*(6139), 537–539.

Degenhardt, L. & Hall, W. (2001). The association between psychosis and problematic drug use among Australian adults: Findings from the National Survey of Mental Health and Well-Being. *Psychological Medicine, 31*, 659–668.

Degenhardt, L., Hall, W. & Lynskey, M. (2001). The relationship between cannabis use and other substance use in the general population. *Drug and Alcohol Dependence, 64*(3), 319–327.

Dehaene, S., Molko, N., Cohen, L. & Wilson, A.J. (2004). Arithmetic and the brain. *Current Opinion in Neurobiology, 14*(2), 218–224.

De Jong, P.J., Andrea, H. & Muris, P. (1997). Spider phobia in children: Disgust and fear before and after treatment. *Behaviour Research and Therapy, 35*, 559–562.

De Jong, P.J. & Merckelbach, H. (1998). Blood-injection-injury phobia and fear of spiders: Domain-specific individual differences in disgust sensitivity. *Personality and Individual Differences, 24*, 153–158.

Delay, J. & Deniker, P. (1952). Le traitement des psychoses par une méthode neurolytique dérivée d'hibernothérapie: Le 4560 RP utilisé seul en cure prolongée et continue. *Congrès des Médecins Aliénistes et Neurologistes de France et des Pays de Langue Française, 50*, 503–513.

Delgado, P.L. & Moreno, F.A. (1998). Hallucinogens, serotonin and obsessive-compulsive disorder. *Journal of Psychoactive Drugs, 30*(4), 359–366.

Delgado, P.L. & Moreno, F.A. (2000). Role of norepinephrine in depression. *Journal of Clinical Psychiatry, 61*, 5–12.

deLint, J. (1978). Alcohol consumption and alcohol problems from an epidemiological perspective. *British Journal of Alcohol and Alcoholism, 17*, 109–116.

Delprato, D.J. (1980). Hereditary determinants of fears and phobias: A critical review. *Behavior Therapy, 11*, 79–103.

Deltito, J., Martin, L., Riefkohl, J., Austria, B. et al. (2001). Do patients with borderline personality disorder belong to the bipolar spectrum? *Journal of Affective Disorders, 67*(1–3), 221–228.

De Maat, S., Dekker, J., Schoevers, R. & de Jonghe, F. (2006). Relative efficacy of psychotherapy and pharmacotherapy in the treatment of depression: A meta-analysis. *Psychotherapy Research, 16*, 562–572.

De Messias, E.L.M., Cordeiro, N.F., Sampaio, J.J.C., Bartko, J.J. & Kirkpatrick, B. (2001). Schizophrenia and season of birth in a tropical region: Relationship to rainfall. *Schizophrenia Research, 48*(2–3), 227–234.

Dennerstein, L. & Hayes, R.D. (2005). Confronting the challenges: Epidemiological study of female sexual dysfunction and the menopause. *Journal of Sexual Medicine, 2*, 118–132.

Dennerstein, L., Koochaki, P., Barton, I. & Graziottin, A. (2006). Hypoactive sexual desire disorder in menopausal women: A survey of western European women. *Journal of Sexual Medicine, 3*(2), 212–222.

Department for Education and Employment (2001). *Child minders to work for teenage mothers*. London: DfEE.

Department for Education and Skills (2004). *Removing barriers to achievement*. London: DfES Publications.

Department for Education and Skills (2006). *Teenage pregnancy next steps: Guidance for local authorities and primary care trusts on effective delivery of local strategies*. London: DfES Publications.

Department of Health (2004). *United Kingdom drug situation. Annual report to the European Monitoring Centre for Drugs and Drug Addiction*. EMCDDA.

Department of Health (2007). *Improving access to psychological therapies (IAPT) programme*. London: Department of Health.

DePrince, A.P. & Freyd, J.J. (2004). Forgetting trauma stimuli. *Psychological Science, 15*, 488–492.

Derby, K.M., Wacker, D., Sasso, G., Steege, M., Northrup, J., Cigrand, K. & Asmus, J. (1992). Brief functional assessment techniques to evaluate aberrant behavior in an outpatient setting: A summary of 79 cases. *Journal of Applied Behavior Analysis, 25*, 713–721.

DeRubeis, R.J., Hollon, S.D., Amsterdam, J.D., Shelton, R.C., Young, P.R., Salomon, R.M., O'Reardon, J.P., Lovett, M.L., Gladis, M.M., Brown, L.L. & Gallop, R. (2005). Cognitive therapy vs. medications in the treatment of moderate to severe depression. *Archives of General Psychiatry, 62*, 409–416.

De Ruiter, C., Rijken, H., Garssen, B., van Schaik, A. & Kraaimaat, F. (1989). Comorbidity among the anxiety disorders. *Anxiety Disorders, 3*, 57–68.

Desjarlais, R., Eisenberg, L., Good, B. & Kleinman, A. (1996). *World mental health: Problems and priorities in the low-income countries*. Oxford: Oxford University Press.

Desrosiers, A. & Fleurose, S.S. (2002). Treating Haitian patients: Key cultural aspects. *American Journal of Psychotherapy, 56*, 508–521.

DeStefano, F., Bhasin, T.K., Thompson, W.W., Yeargin-Allsopp, M. & Boyle, C. (2004). Age at first measles-mumps-rubella vaccination in children with autism and school-matched control subjects: A population-based study in metropolitan Atlanta. *Pediatrics, 113*(2), 259–266.

DeVane, C.L. & Sallee, F.R. (1996). Serotonin selective reuptake inhibitors in child and adolescent psychopharmacology: A review of published experience. *Journal of Clinical Psychiatry, 57*(2), 55–66.

Devilly, G.J. & Spence, S.H. (1999). The relative efficacy and treatment distress of EMDR and a cognitive-behavior trauma treatment protocol in the amelioration of posttraumatic stress disorder. *Journal of Anxiety Disorders, 13*(1–2), 131–157.

Devlin, J.B. (1991). Prevalence and risk factors for childhood nocturnal enuresis. *Irish Medical Journal, 84*, 118–120.

Di Ceglie, D. (2000). Gender identity disorder in young people. *Advances in Psychiatric Treatment, 6*, 458–466.

Dick, D.M., Bierut, L., Hinrichs, A., Fox, I. et al. (2006). The role of GABRA2 in risk for conduct disorder and alcohol and drug dependence across developmental stages. *Behavior Genetics, 36*, 577–590.

Dick, D.M., Rose, R.J., Viken, R.J., Kaprio, J. & Koskenvuo, M. (2001). Exploring gene–environment interactions: Socioregional moderation of alcohol use. *Journal of Abnormal Psychology, 110*(4), 625–632.

Dickersin, K., Min, Y.-I. & Meinert, C.L. (1992). Factors influencing publication of research results: Follow-up of applications submitted to two institutional review boards. *Journal of American Medical Association, 267*, 374–378.

Dickerson, F.B., Tenhula, W.N. & Green-Paden, L.D. (2005). The token economy for schizophrenia: A review of the literature and recommendations for future research. *Schizophrenia Research, 75*, 405–416.

Dickey, C.C., McCarley, R.W., Niznikiewicz, M.A., Voglmaier, M.M. et al. (2005). Clinical, cognitive, and social characteristics of a sample of neuroleptic-naive persons with schizotypal personality disorder. *Schizophrenia Research, 78*(2–3), 297–308.

Dietrich, K.N., Berger, O.G., Succop, P.A., Hammond, P.B. & Bornschein, R.L. (1993). The developmental consequences of low to moderate prenatal and postnatal lead exposure: Intellectual attainment in the Cincinnati lead study cohort following school entry. *Neurotoxicology and Teratology*, 15(1), 37–44.

Dietz, P.E., Hazelwood, R.R. & Warren, J. (1990). The sexually sadistic criminal and his offenses. *Bulletin of the American Academy of Psychiatry and the Law*, 18, 163–178.

DiNardo, P.A., Guzy, L.T. & Bak, R.M. (1988). Anxiety response patterns and etiological factors in dog-fearful and nonfearful subjects. *Behaviour Research and Therapy*, 26, 245–252.

Dingemans, A.E., Bruna, M.J. & van Furth, E.F. (2002). Binge-eating disorder: A review. *International Journal of Obesity*, 26, 299–307.

Dinn, W.M. & Harris, C.L. (2000). Neurocognitive function in antisocial personality disorder. *Psychiatry Research*, 97(2–3), 173–190.

Dinn, W.M., Robbins, N.C. & Harris, C.L. (2001). Adult attention-deficit/hyperactivity disorder: Neuropsychological correlates and clinical presentation. *Brain and Cognition*, 46(1–2), 114–121.

Diseth, T.H. & Christie, H.J. (2005). Trauma-related dissociative (conversion) disorders in children and adolescents: An overview of assessment tools and treatment principles. *Nordic Journal of Psychiatry*, 59, 278–292.

Doctor, R.F. & Fleming, J.S. (2001). Measures of transgender behaviour. *Archives of Sexual Behavior*, 30, 255–271.

Doctor, R.F. & Prince, V. (1997). Transvestism: A survey of 1032 cross-dressers. *Archives of Sexual Behavior*, 26, 589–605.

Dodge, K.A. (1991). The structure and function of reactive and proactive aggression. In D.J. Pepler & K.H. Rubin (Eds.), *The development and treatment of childhood aggression*. Hillsdale, NJ: Lawrence Erlbaum.

Dodge, K.A. (1993). Social-cognitive mechanisms in the development of conduct disorder and depression. *Annual Review of Psychology*, 44, 559–584.

Dodge, K.A., Bates, J.E. & Pettit, G.S. (1990). Mechanisms of the cycle of violence. *Science*, 250, 1678–1683.

Dolder, C.R., Lacro, J.P., Dunn, L.B. & Jeste, D.V. (2002). Antipsychotic medication adherence: Is there a difference between typical and atypical agents? *American Journal of Psychiatry*, 159(1), 103–108.

Doogan, S. & Thomas, G.V. (1992). Origins of fear of dogs in adults and children: The role of conditioning processes and prior familiarity with dogs. *Behaviour Research and Therapy*, 30, 387–394.

Dorahy, M.J. (2001). Dissociative identity disorder and memory dysfunction: The current state of experimental research and its future directions. *Clinical Psychology Review*, 21, 771–795.

Dosajh, N.L. (1996). Projective techniques with particular reference to ink blot tests. *Journal of Projective Psychology and Mental Health*, 3, 59–68.

Dougherty, D.D., Baer, L., Cosgrove, G.R., Cassem, E.H. et al. (2002). Prospective long-term follow-up of 44 patients who received cingulotomy for treatment-refractory obsessive-compulsive disorder. *American Journal of Psychiatry*, 159(2), 269–275.

Drake, R.E., Wallach, M.A., Alverson, H.S. & Mueser, K.T. (2002). Psychosocial aspects of substance abuse by clients with severe mental illness. *Journal of Nervous and Mental Disease*, 190, 100–106.

Drapier, S., Raoul, S., Drapier, D., Leray, E. et al. (2005). Only physical aspects of quality of life are significantly improved by bilateral subthalamic stimulation in Parkinson's disease. *Journal of Neurology*, 252(5), 583–588.

Drevets, W.C. (1998). Functional neuroimaging studies of depression: The anatomy of melancholia. *Annual Review of Medicine*, 49, 341&.

Droupy, S. (2005). Epidemiology and physiopathology of erectile dysfunction. *Annales d'Urologie*, 39, 71–84.

Dubow, E.F., Kausch, D.F., Blum, M.C., Reed, J. & Bush, E. (1989). Correlates of suicidal ideation and attempts in a community sample of junior-high and high-school students. *Journal of Clinical Child Psychology*, 18(2), 158–166.

Dugas, M.J., Ladouceur, R., Leger, E., Freeston, M.H. et al. (2003). Group cognitive-behavioral therapy for generalized anxiety disorder: Treatment outcome and long-term follow-up. *Journal of Consulting and Clinical Psychology*, 71(4), 821–825.

Dugas, M.J. & Robichaud, M. (2006). *Cognitive-behavioral treatment for generalized anxiety disorder*. London: Routledge.

Dunmore, E., Clark, D.M. & Ehlers, A. (1999). Cognitive factors involved in the onset and maintenance of posttraumatic stress disorder (PTSD) after physical or sexual assault. *Behaviour Research and Therapy*, 37(9), 809–829.

Dunn, K.M., Croft, P.R. & Hackett, G.I. (1999). Association of sexual problems with social, psychological, and physical problems in men and women: A cross-sectional population survey. *Journal of Epidemiology and Community Health*, 53(3), 144–148.

Dunn, M. (1994). Neurophysiologic observations in autism. In M.L. Bauman & T.L. Kempner (Eds.), *The neurobiology of autism*. Baltimore: Johns Hopkins University Press.

Dunsieth, N.W., Nelson, E.B., Brusman-Lovins, L.A., Holcomb, J.L. et al. (2004). Psychiatric and legal features of 113 men convicted of sexual offenses. *Journal of Clinical Psychiatry*, 65(3), 293–300.

Durham, R.C., Chambers, J.A., MacDonald, R.R., Power, K.G. & Major, K. (2003). Does cognitive-behavioral therapy influence the long-term outcome of generalized anxiety disorder? An 8–14-year follow-up of two clinical trials. *Psychological Medicine*, 33, 499–509.

Durston, S., Hulshoff Pol, H.E., Schnack, H.G., Buitelaar, J.K. et al. (2004). Magnetic resonance imaging of boys with attention-deficit/hyperactivity disorder and their unaffected siblings. *Journal of the American Academy of Child and Adolescnt Psychiatry*, 43, 332–340.

Dwivedi, K.N. & Banhatti, R.G. (2005). Attention deficit/hyperactivity disorder and ethnicity. *Archives of Disease in Childhood*, 90, I10–I12.

Dworkin, S.F., Turner, J.A., Wilson, L., Massoth, D. et al. (1994). Brief group cognitive-behavioral intervention for temporomandibular disorders. *Pain*, 59, 175–187.

Dykens, E.M. & Hodapp, R.M. (2001). Research in mental retardation: Toward an etiologic approach. *Journal of Child Psychology and Psychiatry and Allied Disciplines*, 42(1), 49–71.

Dykens, E.M., Leckman, J., Paul, R. & Watson, M. (1988). Cognitive, behavioral, and adaptive functioning in fragile-X and non-fragile-X retarded men. *Journal of Autism and Developmental Disorders*, 18(1), 41–52.

Dykman, R.A., McPherson, B., Ackerman, P.T., Newton, J.E.O. et al. (1997). Internalizing and externalizing characteristics of sexually and/or physically abused children. *Integrative Physiological and Behavioral Science*, 32(1), 62–74.

Eaddy, M., Grogg, A. & Locklear, J. (2005). Assessment of compliance with antipsychotic treatment and resource utilization in a Medicaid population. *Clinical Therapeutics*, 27(2), 263–272.

Echeburua, E., Baez, C. & Fernandez-Montalvo, J. (1996). Comparative effectiveness of three therapeutic modalities in the psychological treatment of pathological gambling: Long-term outcome. *Behavioural and Cognitive Psychotherapy*, 24, 51–72.

Eckert, M. (2004). Neuroanatomical markers for dyslexia: A review of dyslexia structural imaging studies. *Neuroscientist*, 10, 362–371.

Edelbrock, C., Rende, R., Plomin, T. & Thompson, L.A. (1995). A twin study of competence and problem behaviour in childhood and early adolescence. *Journal of Child Psychology and Psychiatry and Allied Disciplines*, 36, 775–789.

Egger, H.L., Costello, E.J. & Angold, A. (2003). School refusal and psychiatric disorders: A community study. *Journal of the American Academy of Child and Adolescent Psychiatry*, 42, 797–807.

Egger, H.L., Kondo, D. & Angold, A. (2006). The epidemiology and diagnostic issues in preschool attention-deficit/hyperactivity disorder: A review. *Infants and Young Children*, 19, 109–122.

Ehlers, A. & Breuer, P. (1992). Increased cardiac awareness in panic disorder. *Journal of Abnormal Psychology*, 101(3), 371–382.

Ehlers, A. & Clark, D.M. (2000). A cognitive model of posttraumatic stress disorder. *Behaviour Research and Therapy*, 38, 319–345.

Ehlers, A., Maercker, A. & Boos, A. (2000). Posttraumatic stress disorder following political imprisonment: The role of mental defeat, alienation, and perceived permanent change. *Journal of Abnormal Psychology*, 109(1), 45–55.

Ehlers, A., Mayou, R.A. & Bryant, B. (1998). Psychological predictors of chronic posttraumatic stress disorder after motor vehicle accidents. *Journal of Abnormal Psychology*, 107(3), 508–519.

Ehrhardt, A.A. & Money, J. (1967). Progestin-induced hermaphroditism. *Journal of Sex Research*, 3(1), 83–100.

Ehringer, M.A., Rhee, S.H., Young, S., Corley, R. & Hewitt, J.K. (2006). Genetic and environmental contributions to common psychopathologies of childhood and adolescence: A study of twins and their siblings. *Journal of Abnormal Child Psychology*, 34, 1–17.

Ehrt, U. & Aarsland, D. (2005). Psychiatric aspects of Parkinson's disease. *Current Opinion in Psychiatry*, 18, 335–341.

Ehrt, U., Brieger, P. & Marneros, A. (2003). Temperament and affective disorders: Historical basis of current discussion. *Fortschritte der Neurologie Psychiatrie*, 71(6), 323–331.

Eisenberg, M.E., Neumark-Sztainer, D., Story, M. & Perry, C. (2005). The role of social norms and friends' influences on unhealthy weight-control behaviors among adolescent girls. *Social Science and Medicine*, 60(6), 1165–1173.

Eisenthal, S., Koopman, C. & Lazare, A. (1983). Process analysis of two dimensions of the negotiated approach in relation to satisfaction in the initial interview. *Journal of Mental and Nervous Diseases*, 171, 49–54.

Eisenwort, B., Marschik, P., Fladerer, A., Motl, S. et al. (2004). Concerning specific language impairment: Intelligibility in expressive language. *Klinische Pädiatrie*, 216(4), 225–229.

Ekselius, L. & von Knorring, L. (1998). Personality disorder comorbidity with major depression and response to treatment with sertraline or citalopram. *International Clinical Psychopharmacology*, 13(5), 205–211.

Eliez, S. & Feinstein, C. (2001). The fragile X syndrome: Bridging the gap from gene to behavior. *Current Opinion in Psychiatry*, 14(5), 443–449.

Ellickson, P.L., Collins, R.L., Hambarsoomians, K. & McCaffrey, D.F. (2005). Does alcohol advertising promote adolescent drinking? Results from a longitudinal assessment. *Addiction*, 100(2), 235–246.

Elliott, R. (1998). Editor's introduction: A guide to the empirically supported treatments controversy. *Psychotherapy Research*, 8, 115–125.

Ellis, A. (1962). *Reason and emotion in psychotherapy*. New York: Lyle Stuart.

Elman, R.J. & Bernstein-Ellis, E. (1999). The efficacy of group communication treatment in adults with chronic aphasia. *Journal of Speech, Language and Hearing Research*, 42, 385–394.

Elzinga, B.M., van Dyck, R. & Spinhoven, P. (1998). Three controversies about dissociative identity disorder. *Clinical Psychology and Psychotherapy*, 5(1), 13–23.

Emmelkamp, P.M.G. (1982). *Phobic and obsessive-compulsive disorders*. New York: Plenum.

Engdahl, B., Dikel, T.N., Eberly, R. & Blank, A. (1997). Posttraumatic stress disorder in a community group of former prisoners of war: A normative response to severe trauma. *American Journal of Psychiatry*, 154(11), 1576–1581.

Enserink, M. (1999). Drug therapies for depression: From MAO inhibitors to substance. *Science*, 284, 239.

Epstein, J.N., Johnson, D.E., Varia, I.M. & Conners, C.K. (2001). Neuropsychological assessment of response inhibition in adults with ADHD. *Journal of Clinical and Experimental Neuropsychology*, 23(3), 362–371.

Erba, H.W. (2000). Early intervention programs for children with autism: Conceptual frameworks for implementation *American Journal of Orthopsychiatry*, 70(1), 82–94.

Erdelyi, M.H. (1992). Psychodynamics and the unconscious. *American Psychologist*, 47, 784–787.

Erhardt, D. & Hinshaw, S.P. (1994). Initial sociometric impressions of attention-deficit hyperactivity disorder and comparison boys: Predictions from social behaviors and from nonbehavioral variables. *Journal of Consulting and Clinical Psychology*, 62(4), 833–842.

Erickson, M.Y. (1992). *Behavior disorders of children and adolescents*. Englewood Cliffs, NJ: Prentice-Hall.

Ernst, M., Zametkin, A.J., Matochik, J.A., Pascualvaca, D. & Cohen, R.M. (1997). Low medial prefrontal dopaminergic activity in autistic children. *Lancet*, 350(9078), 638.

Eronen, M., Hakola, P. & Tihonen, J. (1996). Mental disorders and homicidal behavior in Finland. *Archives of General Psychiatry*, 53(6), 497–501.

Erwin, E. (2000). Is a science of psychotherapy possible? *American Psychologist*, 55, 1133–1138.

Escobar, J.I., Burnam, M.A., Karno, M., Forsythe, A. & Golding, J.M. (1987). Somatization in the community. *Archives of General Psychiatry*, 44(8), 713–718.

Essen, J. & Peckham, C. (1976). Nocturnal enuresis in childhood. *Developmental Medicine and Child Neurology*, 18, 577–589.

Estrada, A.U. & Pinsof, W.M. (1995). The effectiveness of family therapies for selected behavioral disorders of childhood. *Journal of Marital and Family Therapy*, 21, 403–440.

European Monitoring Centre for Drugs and Drug Addiction (2004). *Annual report*.

Evans, E., Hawton, K. & Rodham, K. (2004). Factors associated with suicidal phenomena in adolescents: A systematic review of population-based studies. *Clinical Psychology Review*, 24(8), 957–979.

Everly, G.S., Flannery, R.B. & Mitchell, J.T. (2000). Critical incident stress management (CISM): A review of the literature. *Aggression and Violent Behavior*, 5(1), 23–40.

Ewing-Cobbs, L., Prasad, M.R., Kramer, L., Cox, C.S. et al. (2006). Late intellectual and academic outcomes following traumatic brain injury sustained during early childhood. *Journal of Neurosurgery*, 105(4), 287–296.

Exner, J.E. & Weiner, I.B. (1995). *The Rorschach: A comprehensive system. Vol. 3: Assessment of children and adolescents* (2nd ed.). New York: Wiley.

Eysenck, H.J. (1961). The effects of psychotherapy. In H.J. Eysenck (Ed.), *Handbook of abnormal psychology*. New York: Basic Books.

Eysenck, H.J. (1979). The conditioning model of neurosis. *Behavioral and Brain Sciences*, 2, 155–199.

Eysenck, H.J. (1994). Meta-analysis and its problems. *British Medical Journal*, 309, 789–793.

Fabbri, A., Marchesini, G., Dente, M., Iervese, T. et al. (2005). A positive blood alcohol concentration is the main predictor of recurrent motor vehicle crash. *Annals of Emergency Medicine*, 46(2), 161–167.

Fabiano, G.A., Pelham, W.E., Manos, M.J., Gnagy, E.M. et al. (2004). An evaluation of three time-out procedures for children with attention-deficit/hyperactivity disorder. *Behavior Therapy*, 35(3), 449–469.

Fabiano GA, Pelham WE, Manos MJ, Gnagy EM et al. (2004). An evaluation of three time-out procedures for children with attention deficit/hyperactivity disorder. *Behavior Therapy*, 35, 449–469.

Fagan, P.J., Wise, T.N., Schmidt, C.W. & Berlin, F.S. (2002). Pedophilia. *JAMA: Journal of the American Medical Association*, 288, 2458–2465.

Fahie, C.M. & Symons, D.K. (2003). Executive functioning and theory of mind in children clinically referred for attention and behaviour problems. *Applied Developmental Psychology*, 24, 51–73.

Fairburn, C.G. (1997a). Handbook of eating disorders: Theory, treatment and research: Szmukler, G., Dare, C., Treasure, J. *Psychological Medicine*, 27(1), 245–246.

Fairburn, C.G. (1997b). Eating disorders. In D.M. Clark & C.G. Fairburn (Eds.), *The science and practice of cognitive behaviour therapy*. Oxford: Oxford University Press.

Fairburn, C.G., Agras, W.S. & Wilson, G.T. (1992). The research on the treatment of bulimia nervosa: Practical and theoretical implications. In G.H. Anderson & S.H. Kennedy (Eds.), *The biology of feast and famine: Relevance to eating disorders*. New York: Academic Press.

Fairburn, C.G., Norman, P.A., Welch, S.L., O'Connor, M.E. et al. (1995). A prospective study of outcome in bulimia nervosa and the long-term effects of three psychological treatments. *Archives of General Psychiatry*, 52(4), 304–312.

Fairburn, C.G., Shafran, R. & Cooper, Z. (1999). A cognitive behavioural theory of anorexia nervosa. *Behaviour Research and Therapy, 37,* 1–13.

Fairburn, C.G., Welch, S.L., Norman, P.A., O'Connor, M.E. & Doll, H.A. (1996). Bias and bulimia nervosa: How typical are clinic cases? *American Journal of Psychiatry, 153*(3), 386–391.

Fallon, B.A. & Feinstein, S. (2001). Hypochondriasis. In K.A. Phillips (Ed.), *Somatoform and factitious disorders.* Washington, DC: American Psychiatric Press.

Fals-Stewart, W., Birchler, G.R. & O'Farrell, T.J. (1996). Behavioral couples therapy for male substance-abusing patients: Effects on relationship adjustment and drug-using behaviour. *Journal of Consulting and Clinical Psychology, 64,* 959–972.

Fanselow, M.S. (2000). Contextual fear, gestalt memories, and the hippocampus. *Behavioural Brain Research, 110,* 73–81.

Farabee, D., Rawson, R. & McCann, M. (2002). Adoption of drug avoidance activities among patients in contingency management and cognitive-behavioral treatments. *Journal of Substance Abuse Treatment, 23*(4), 343–350.

Faraone, S.V. (2006). Advances in the genetics and neurobiology of attention deficit hyperactivity disorder. *Biological Psychiatry, 60,* 1025–1027.

Faraone, S.V., Biederman, J., Jetton, J.G. & Tsuang, M.T. (1997). Attention deficit disorder and conduct disorder: Longitudinal evidence for a family subtype. *Psychological Medicine, 27,* 291–300.

Faraone, S.V. & Khan, S.A. (2006). Candidate gene studies of attention-deficit/hyperactivity disorder. *Journal of Clinical Psychiatry, 67,* 13–20.

Farina, A., Gliha, D., Boudreau, L.A., Allen, J.G. & Sherman, M. (1971). Mental illness and the impact of believing others know about it. *Journal of Abnormal Psychology, 77,* 1–5.

Farrell, M., Gowing, L., Marsden, J., Ling, W. & Ali, R. (2005). Effectiveness of drug dependence treatment in HIV prevention. *International Journal of Drug Policy, 16,* S67–S75, Suppl. 1.

Farrell, M., Howes, S., Bebbington, P., Brugha, T., et al. (2003). Nicotine, alcohol and drug dependence, and psychiatric comorbidity: Results of a national household survey. *International Review of Psychiatry, 15*(1–2), 50–56. (Reprinted from *British Journal of Psychiatry, 179* [2001], 432–437.)

Farrington, C.P., Miller, E. & Taylor, B. (2001). MMR and autism: Further evidence against a causal association. *Vaccine, 19*(27), 3632–3635.

Farrington, D.P. (1991). Psychological contributions to the explanations of offending. *Issues in Criminology and Legal Psychology, 1,* 7–19.

Farrington, D.P., Loeber, R. & van Kammen, W.B. (1990). Long-term criminal outcomes of hyperactivity-impulsivity-attention-deficit and conduct problems in childhood. In L.N. Robins & M.R. Rutter (Eds.), *Straight and devious pathways from childhood to adulthood.* New York: Cambridge University Press.

Fasolo, C.B., Mirone, V., Gentile, V., Parazzini, F. & Ricci, E. (2005). Premature ejaculation: Prevalence and associated conditions in a sample of 12,558 men attending the Andrology Prevention Week 2001: A study of the Italian Society of Andrology (SIA). *Journal of Sexual Medicine, 2*(3), 376–382.

Fasotti, L., Kovacs, F., Eling, P.A.T.M. & Brouwer, W.H. (2000). Time pressure management as a compensatory strategy training after closed head injury. *Neuropsychological Rehabilitation, 10*(1), 47–65.

Fatemi, S.H., Pearce, D.A., Brooks, A.I. & Sidwell, R.W. (2005). Prenatal viral infection in mouse causes differential expression of genes in brains of mouse progeny: A potential animal model for schizophrenia and autism. *Synapse, 57*(2), 91–99.

Faustman, W.O. (1995). What causes schizophrenia? In S. Vinogradov (Ed.), *Treating schizophrenia.* San Francisco: Jossey-Bass.

Fava, G.A. (2003). Can long-term treatment with antidepressant drugs worsen the course of depression? *Journal of Clinical Psychiatry, 64,* 123–133.

Fava, M. (1997). Psychopharmacologic treatment of pathologic aggression. *Psychiatric Clinics of North America, 20*(2), 427.

Fazel, S. & Danesh, J. (2002). Serious mental disorder in 23,000 prisoners: A systematic review of 62 surveys. *Lancet, 359,* 545–550.

Fedoroff, J.P., Starkstein, S.E., Forrester, A.W., Geisler, F.H. et al. (1992). Depression in patients with acute traumatic brain injury. *American Journal of Psychiatry, 149*(7), 918–923.

Feerick, M.M. & Snow, K.L. (2005). The relationship between childhood sexual abuse, social anxiety, and symptoms of posttraumatic stress disorder in women. *Journal of Family Violence, 20,* 409–419.

Fegert, J.M., Janhsen, K. & Boge, I. (2006). Drug therapy of depression in childhood and adolescence: What to do in face of multiple warning against SSRI and SNRI? *Psychopharmakotherapie, 13*(3), 84.

Feingold, B.F. (1973). *Introduction to clinical allergy.* Springfield, IL: Charles C Thomas.

Feldman, M.P. & MacCulloch, M.J. (1965). The application of anticipatory avoidance learning to the treatment of homosexuality. I. Theory, technique and preliminary results. *Behaviour Research and Therapy, 2,* 165–183.

Fenichel, O. (1945). *The psychoanalytic theory of neurosis.* New York: W.W. Norton.

Fenigstein, A. (1996). Paranoia. In C.G. Costello (Ed.), *Personality characteristics of the personality disordered.* New York: Wiley.

Fennell, M.J.V. & Teasdale, J.D. (1987). Cognitive therapy for depression: Individual differences and the process of change. *Cognitive Therapy and Research, 11*(2), 253–271.

Fergusson, D.M., Horwood, L.J. & Lynskey, M.T. (1996). Childhood sexual abuse and psychiatric disorder in young adulthood. II. Psychiatric outcomes of childhood sexual abuse. *Journal of the American Academy of Child and Adolescent Psychiatry, 35,* 1365–1374.

Fergusson, D.M., Horwood, L.J. & Ridder, E.M. (2005). Tests of causal linkages between cannabis use and psychotic symptoms. *Addiction, 100,* 354–366.

Fergusson, D.M., Horwood, L.J. & Swain-Campbell, N.R. (2003). Cannabis dependence and psychotic symptoms in young people. *Psychological Medicine, 33*(1), 15–21.

Fergusson, D.M. & Lynskey, M.T. (1993). The effects of maternal depression on child conduct disorder and attention-deficit behaviors. *Social Psychiatry and Psychiatric Epidemiology, 28*(3), 116–123.

Fergusson, D.M. & Lynskey, M.T. (1995). Suicide attempts and suicidal ideation in a birth cohort of 16-year-old New Zealanders. *Journal of the American Academy of Child and Adolescent Psychiatry, 34*(10), 1308–1317.

Fergusson, D.M., Lynskey, M.T. & Horwood, L.J. (1996). Factors associated with continuity and changes in disruptive behavior patterns between childhood and adolescence. *Journal of Abnormal Child Psychology, 24*(5), 533–553.

Fergusson, D.M. & Woodward, L.J. (1999). Maternal age and educational and psychosocial outcomes in early adulthood. *Journal of Child Psychology and Psychiatry, 43,* 479–489.

Ferster, C.B. (1985). Classification of behavioral pathology. In L. Krasner & L.P. Ullman (Eds.), *Research in behavior modification.* New York: Holt Reinhart & Winston.

Feske, U. & Chambless, D.L. (1995). Cognitive-behavioral versus exposure only treatment for social phobia: A meta-analysis. *Behavior Therapy, 26*(4), 695–720.

Field, A.P. (2005a). *Discovering statistics with SPSS* (2nd ed.). Thousand Oaks, CA: Sage.

Field, A.P. (2005b). Meta-analysis. In J. Miles & P. Gilbert (Eds.), *A handbook of research methods for clinical and health psychology.* Oxford: Oxford University Press.

Field, A.P. (2006a). The behavioral inhibition system and the verbal information pathway to children's fears. *Journal of Abnormal Psychology, 115,* 742–752.

Field, A.P. (2006b). Watch out for the beast: Fear information and attentional bias in children. *Journal of Clinical Child and Adolescent Psychology, 35,* 337–345.

Field, A.P. & Davey, G. (2005). Experimental methods in clinical and health research. In J. Miles & P. Gilbert (Eds.), *A handbook of research methods for clinical and health psychology.* Oxford: Oxford University Press.

Field, A.P., Argyris, N.G. & Knowles, K.A. (2001). Who's afraid of the big bad wolf: A prospective paradigm to test Rachman's indirect pathways in children. *Behaviour Research and Therapy*, 39, 1259–1276.

Field, A.P. & Lawson, J. (2003). Fear information and the development of fears during childhood: Effects on implicit fear responses and behavioural avoidance. *Behaviour Research and Therapy*, 41, 1277–1293.

Figueira, I., Possidente, E., Marques, C. & Hayes, K. (2001). Sexual dysfunction: A neglected complication of panic disorder and social phobia. *Archives of Sexual Behavior*, 30(4), 369–377.

Fine, S., Forth, A., Gilbert, M. & Haley, G. (1991). Group therapy for adolescent depressive disorder: A comparison of social skills and therapeutic support. *Journal of the American Academy of Child and Adolescent Psychiatry*, 30(1), 79–85.

Finkelhor, D. (1980). Sex among siblings: A survey on prevalence, variety, and effects. *Archives of Sexual Behavior*, 9(3), 171–194.

Fischer, D.J., Himle, J.A. & Hanna, G.L. (1998). Group behavioral therapy for adolescents with obsessive-compulsive disorder: Preliminary outcomes. *Research on Social Work Practice*, 8(6), 629–636.

Fischer, E.H., Dornelas, E.A. & Goether, J.W. (2001). Characteristics of people lost to attrition in psychiatric follow-up studies. *Journal of Nervous and Mental Disease*, 189, 49–55.

Fischer, E.P., Owen, R.R. & Cuffel, B.J. (1996). Substance abuse, community service use, and symptom severity of urban and rural residents with schizophrenia. *Psychiatric Services*, 47(9), 980–984.

Fishbain, D.A. (2000). Re: The meeting of pain and depression: Comorbidity in women. *Canadian Journal of Psychiatry: Revue Canadienne de Psychiatrie*, 45(1), 88.

Fisher, C.B., Cea, C.D., Davidson, P.W. & Fried, A.L. (2006). Capacity of persons with mental retardation to consent to participate in randomized clinical trials. *American Journal of Psychiatry*, 163, 1813–1820.

Fisher, C.B., Hoagwood, K., Boyce, C., Duster, T. et al. (2002). Research ethics for mental health science involving ethnic minority children and youths. *American Psychologist*, 57, 1024–1040.

Fisher, P. (2008). Anxiety. In G.C.L. Davey (Ed.), *Clinical psychology*. London: Hodder.

Fisher, S. & DeFries, J.C. (2002). Developmental dyslexia: Genetic dissection of a complex cognitive trait. *Nature Reviews of Neuroscience*, 13, 767–780.

Fleming, J.M. & Ownsworth, T. (2006). A review of awareness interventions in brain injury rehabilitation. *Neuropsychological Rehabilitation*, 16(4), 474–500.

Fleming, M.F., Barry, K.L., Manwell, L.B., Johnson, K. & London, R. (1997). Brief physician advice for problem alcohol drinkers: A randomized controlled trial in community-based primary care practices. *JAMA: Journal of the American Medical Association*, 277(13), 1039–1045.

Floyd, R.L., O'Connor, M.J., Sokol, R.J., Bertrand, J. & Cordero, J.F. (2005). Recognition and prevention of fetal alcohol syndrome. *Obstetrics and Gynecology*, 106, 1059–1064.

Foa, E.B. & Cahill, S.P. (2001). Psychological therapies: Emotional processing. In N.J. Smelser & P.B. Bates (Eds.), *International encyclopedia of the social and behavioral sciences*. Oxford: Elsevier.

Foa, E.B., Franklin, M.E., Perry, K.J. & Herbert, J.D. (1996). Cognitive biases in generalized social phobia. *Journal of Abnormal Psychology*, 105(3), 433–439.

Foa, E.B. & Meadows, E.A. (1997). Psychosocial treatments for posttraumatic stress disorder: A critical review. *Annual Review of Psychology*, 48, 449–480.

Foa, E.B. & Rauch, S.A.M. (2004). Cognitive changes during prolonged exposure versus prolonged exposure plus cognitive restructuring in female assault survivors with posttraumatic stress disorder. *Journal of Consulting and Clinical Psychology*, 72(5), 879–884.

Foa, E.B. & Riggs, D.S. (1993). Post-traumatic stress disorder in rape victims. In J. Oldham, M.B. Riba & A. Tasman (Eds.), *American Psychiatric Press review of psychiatry* (Vol. 12). Washington, DC: American Psychiatric Press.

Foa, E.B. & Rothbaum, B.O. (1998). *Treating the trauma of rape*. New York: Guilford Press.

Foa, E.B., Steketee, G. & Rothbaum, B.O. (1989). Behavior/cognitive conceptualization of post-traumatic stress disorder. *Behavior Therapy*, 20, 155–176.

Follette, V.M. & Ruzek, J.I. (2006). *Cognitive behavioral therapies for trauma*. New York: Guilford Press.

Folstein, S.E. & Rosen-Sheidley, B. (2001).Genetics of autism: Complex aetiology for a heterogeneous disorder. *Nature Reviews Genetics*, 2(12), 943–955.

Folstein, S.E. & Rutter, M.L. (1977). Infantile autism: Genetic study of 21 twin pairs. *Journal of Child Psychology and Psychiatry and Allied Disciplines*, 18(4), 297–321.

Folstein, S.E. & Rutter, M.L. (1988). Autism: Familial aggregation and genetic implications. *Journal of Autism and Developmental Disorders*, 18(1), 3–30.

Fombonne, E. (1999). Are measles infections or measles immunizations linked to autism? *Journal of Autism and Developmental Disorders*, 29(4), 349–350.

Fombonne, E. (2002). Epidemiological trends in rates of autism. *Molecular Psychiatry*, 7, S4–S6.

Fombonne, E. (2005). Epidemiology of autistic disorder and other pervasive developmental disorders. *Journal of Clinical Psychiatry*, 66, 3–8.

Fonagy, P., Roth, A. & Higgitt, A. (2005). The outcome of psychodynamic psychotherapy for psychological disorders. *Clinical Neuroscience Research*, 4(5–6), 367–377.

Fontenelle, L.F., Mendlowicz, M.V., Marques, C. & Versiani, M. (2004). Transcultural aspects of obsessive-compulsive disorder: A description of a Brazilian sample and a systematic review of international clinical studies. *Journal of Psychiatric Research*, 38(4), 403–411.

Foote, B., Smolin, Y., Kaplan, M., Legatt, M.E. & Lipschitz, D. (2006). Prevalence of dissociative disorders in psychiatric outpatients. *American Journal of Psychiatry*, 163, 623–629.

Forbes, G.B. (2001). College students with tattoos and piercings: Motives, family experiences, personality factors, and perception by others. *Psychological Reports*, 89, 774–786.

Forbes, G.B., Adams-Curtis, L.E., Rade, B. et al. (2001). Body dissatisfaction in women and men: The role of gender-typing and self-esteem. *Sex Roles*, 44(7–8), 461–484.

Forgas, J.P., Bower, G.H. & Krantz, S.E. (1984). The influence of mood on perceptions of social interactions. *Journal of Experimental Social Psychology*, 20(6), 497–513.

Fowler, D., Garety, P. & Kuipers, E. (1995). *Cognitive therapy for psychosis*. New York: Wiley.

Fox, A.V., Dodd, B. & Howard, D. (2002). Risk factors for speech disorders in children. *International Journal of Language and Communication Disorders*, 37, 117–131.

Fox, C. & Hawton, K. (2004). *Deliberate self-harm in adolescence*. London: Jessica Kingsley.

Fox, R. (1989). *The sociology of medicine: A participant observer's view*. Englewood Cliffs, NJ: Prentice-Hall.

Foy, D.W., Nunn, L.B. & Rychtarik, R.G. (1994). Broad-spectrum behavioral treatment for chronic alcoholics: Effects of training controlled drinking skills. *Journal of Consulting and Clinical Psychology*, 52(2), 218–230.

Foy, D.W., Resnick, H.S., Sipprelle, R.C. & Carroll, E.M. (1987). Premilitary, military, and postmilitary factors in the development of combat-related posttraumatic stress disorder. *Behavior Therapist*, 10, 3–9.

Frampton, I. (2003). Neuropsychological models of OCD. In R.G. Menzies & P. de Silva (Eds.), *Obsessive-compulsive disorder: Theory, research and treatment*. Chichester: Wiley.

Francis, D.J., Shaywitz, S.E., Stuebing, K.K., Shaywitz, B.A. & Fletcher, J.M. (1996). Developmental lag versus deficit models of reading disability: A longitudinal, individual growth curves analysis. *Journal of Educational Psychology*, 88, 3–17.

Franklin, M.E. & Foa, E.B. (1998). Cognitive-behavioral treatments for obsessive-compulsive disorder. In P.E. Nathan & J.M. Gorman (Eds.), *A guide to treatments that work*. New York: Oxford University Press.

Franklin, M.E., Kozak, M.J., Cashman, L., Coles, M. et al. (1998). Cognitive-behavioral treatment of pediatric obsessive-compulsive disorder: An open clinical trial. *Journal of the American Academy of Child and Adolescent Psychiatry, 37,* 412–419.

Frare, F., Perugi, G., Ruffalo, G. & Toni, C. (2004). Obsessive-compulsive disorder and body dysmorphic disorder: A comparison of clinical features. *European Psychiatry, 19,* 292–298.

Frederick, J. & Contanch, P. (1995). Self-help techniques for auditory hallucinations in schizophrenia. *Issues in Mental Health Nursing, 16,* 213–224.

Fredrikson, M., Annas, P., Fischer, H. & Wik, G. (1996). Gender and age differences in the prevalence of specific fears and phobias. *Behaviour Research and Therapy, 34*(1), 33–39.

Freedman, J. & Combs, G. (1996). *Narrative therapy: The social construction of preferred realities.* New York: W.W. Norton.

Freeman, D. & Garety, P.A. (2004). Bats amongst the birds (the psychology of paranoia). *Psychologist, 17,* 642–645.

Freeman, D., Garety, P.A., Fowler, D., Kuipers, E. et al. (2004). Why do people with delusions fail to choose more realistic explanations for their experiences? An empirical investigation. *Journal of Consulting and Clinical Psychology, 72*(4), 671–680.

Freeman, D., Garety, P.A. & Kuipers, E. (2001). Persecutory delusions: Developing the understanding of belief maintenance and emotional distress. *Psychological Medicine, 31*(7), 1293–1306.

Freeman, D., Garety, P.A., Kuipers, E., Fowler, D. & Bebbington, P.E. (2002). A cognitive model of persecutory delusions. *British Journal of Clinical Psychology, 41,* 331–347.

Fremouw, W., Callahan, T. & Kashden, J. (1993). Adolescent suicidal risk: Psychological, problem-solving, and environmental factors. *Suicide and Life-Threatening Behavior, 23*(1), 46–54.

Freud, S. (1915). *Psychopathology of everyday life.* Authorized English edition, with Introduction by A. A. Brill. London: T. Fisher Unwin.

Freud, S. (1917/1963). *A general introduction to psychoanalysis.* New York: Liveright.

Freud, S. (1924). *Neurosis and psychosis.* In the *Standard edition of the complete psychological works of Sigmund Freud,* 24 vols. Ed. and trans. James Strachey. London: Hogarth, 1953–1974; Vol. 19, pp. 149–154.

Freund, K. & Kuban, M. (1994). The basis of the abused abuser theory of pedophilia: A further elaboration on an earlier study. *Archives of Sexual Behavior, 23*(5), 553–563.

Freyd, P. (1996). False memory syndrome. *British Journal of Psychiatry, 169*(6), 794–795.

Frick, P.J. (1998). *Conduct disorders and severe antisocial behaviour.* New York: Plenum.

Fried, P., Watkinson, B., James, D. & Gray, F. (2002). Current and former marijuana use: Preliminary findings of a longitudinal study of effects on IQ in young adults. *Canadian Medical Association Journal, 166*(7), 887–891.

Friedel, R.O. (2004). Dopamine dysfunction in borderline personality disorder: A hypothesis. *Neuropsychopharmacology, 29,* 1029–1039.

Friedman, A.S., Glassman, K. & Terras, A. (2001). Violent behavior as related to use of marijuana and other drugs. *Journal of Addictive Diseases, 20*(1), 49–72.

Friendship, C., Blud, L., Erikson, M., Travers, R. & Thornton, D. (2003). Cognitive-behavioural treatment for imprisoned offenders: An evaluation of HM Prison Service's cognitive skills programmes. *Legal and Criminological Psychology, 8,* 103–114.

Friendship, C., Mann, R. & Beech, A. (2003). *The prison-based Sex Offender Treatment Programme: An evaluation.* Home Office document 205. ISSN 1473-8406.

Frischholz, E.J., Lipman, L.S., Braun, B.G. & Sachs, R.G. (1992). Psychopathology, hypnotizability, and dissociation. *American Journal of Psychiatry, 149*(11), 1521–1525.

Frisher, M., Crome, I., MacLeod, J., Millson, D. & Croft, P. (2005). Substance misuse and psychiatric illness: Prospective observational study using the general practice research database. *Journal of Epidemiology and Community Health, 59*(10), 847–850.

Frith, C.D. (1992). *The cognitive neuropsychology of schizophrenia.* Hillsdale, NJ: Lawrence Erlbaum.

Frith, C.D. (1996). The role of the prefrontal cortex in self-consciousness: The case of auditory hallucinations. *Philosophical Transactions of the Royal Society of London,* 351B.

Frith, C.D. & Corcoran, R. (1996). Exploring 'theory of mind' in people with schizophrenia. *Psychological Medicine, 26*(3), 521–530.

Frith, C.D. & Dolan, R.J. (2000). The role of memory in the delusions associated with schizophrenia. In D.L. Schacter & E. Scarry (Eds.), *Memory, brain, and belief.* Cambridge, MA: Harvard University Press.

Frith, U. (2003). *Autism: Explaining the enigma* (2nd ed.). Oxford: Blackwell.

Frohlich, C., Jacobi, F. & Wittchen, H.U. (2006). DSM-IV pain disorder in the general population: An exploration of the structure and threshold of medically unexplained pain symptoms. *European Archives of Psychiatry and Clinical Neuroscience, 256,* 187–196.

Frohman, E.M. (2002). Sexual dysfunction in neurologic disease. *Clinical Neuropharmacology, 25*(3), 126–132.

Fromm-Reichmann, F. (1948). Notes on the development of treatment of schizophrenia by psychoanalytic psychotherapy. *Psychiatry, 11,* 263–273.

Frone, M.R. (2006). Prevalence and distribution of alcohol use and impairment in the workplace: A US national survey. *Journal of Studies on Alcohol, 67*(1), 147–156.

Frost, D.O. & Cadet, J.L. (2000). Effects of methamphetamine-induced neurotoxicity on the development of neural circuitry: A hypothesis. *Brain Research Reviews, 34*(3), 103–118.

Fuller, R.K., Branchley, L., Brightwell, D.R., Derman, R.M. et al. (1986). Disulfiram treatment of alcoholism: A veterans administration cooperative study. *Journal of the American Medical Association, 256,* 1449–1455.

Fuller, R.K. & Gordis, E. (2004). Does disulfiram have a role in alcoholism treatment today? *Addiction, 99,* 21–24.

Fung, K.P. & Lau, S.P. (1989). Effects of prenatal nicotine exposure on rats' striatal dopaminergic and nicotinic systems. *Pharmacology Biochemistry and Behavior, 33,* 1–6.

Furman, L. (2005). What is attention-deficit hyperactivity disorder (ADHD)? *Journal of Child Neurology, 20,* 994–1002.

Furmark, T. (2002). Social phobia: Overview of community surveys. *Acta Psychiatrica Scandinavica, 105*(2), 84–93.

Gabbard, G.O. (1990). *Psychodynamic psychiatry in clinical practice.* Washington, DC: American Psychiatric Press.

Gable, S.L. & Shean, G.D. (2000). Perceived social competence and depression. *Journal of Social and Personal Relationships, 17*(1), 139–150.

Galaburda, A.M. (1993). Neuroanatomical basis of developmental dyslexia. *Neurologic Clinics, 11,* 161–173.

Galaburda, A.M., LoTurco, J., Ramus, F., Fitch, R.H. & Rosen, G.D. (2006). From genes to behaviour in developmental dyslexia. *Nature Neuroscience, 9,* 1213–1217.

Galaburda, A.M., Sherman, G.F., Rosen, G.D., Aboitiz, F. et al. (1985). Developmental dyslexia: Four consecutive patients with cortical abnormalities. *Annals of Neurology, 18,* 222–233.

Galvin, H.K., Newton, A.W. & Vandeven, A.M. (2005). Update on Munchausen syndrome by proxy. *Current Opinion in Pediatrics, 17*(2), 252–257.

Ganellan, R.J. (1996). Comparing the diagnostic efficiency of the MMPI, MCMI-II, and Rorschach: A review. *Journal of Personality Assessment, 67,* 219–243.

Gannon, T.A. (2006). Increasing honest responding on cognitive distortions in child molesters: The bogus pipeline procedure. *Journal of Interpersonal Violence, 21*(3), 358–375.

Garb, H.N. (1997). Race bias, social class bias, and gender bias in clinical judgment. *Clinical Psychology: Science and Practice, 4,* 99–120.

Garb, H.N. (1998). *Studying the clinician: Judgment research and psychological assessment.* Washington, DC: American Psychological Association.

Garber, B. (2005). Inflatable penile prostheses for the treatment of erectile dysfunction. *Expert Review of Medical Devices, 2,* 341–350.

Garber, H.L. & McInerney, M. (1982). Sociobehavioral factors in mental retardation. In P.T. Legelka & H.G. Prehm (Eds.), *Mental retardation: From categories to people*. Columbus, OH: Charles E. Merrill.

Garber, J. & Flynn, C. (2001). Predictors of depressive cognitions in young adolescents. *Cognitive Therapy and Research, 25*(4), 353–376.

Garbutt, J.C., West, S.L., Carey, T.S., Lohr, L.N. & Crews, F.T. (1999). Pharmacological treatment of alcohol dependence: A review of the evidence. *JAMA: Journal of the American Medical Association, 281*, 1318–1325.

Gardner, H. (1998). Are there additional intelligences? The case for naturalist, spiritual and existential intelligences. In J. Kane (Ed.), *Education, information, and transformation*. Englewood Cliffs, NJ: Prentice-Hall.

Garfinkel, P.E., Kennedy, S.H. & Kaplan, A.S. (1995). Views on classification and diagnosis of eating disorders. *Canadian Journal of Psychiatry: Revue Canadienne de Psychiatrie, 40*(8), 445–456.

Garfinkel, P.E., Lin, E., Goering, P., Spegg, C. et al. (1995). Bulimia nervosa in a Canadian community sample: Prevalence and comparison of subgroups. *American Journal of Psychiatry, 152*(7), 1052–1058.

Garner, D.M., Olmsted, M.P. & Garfinkel, P.E. (1983). Does anorexia nervosa occur on a continuum: Subgroups of weight-preoccupied women and their relationship to anorexia nervosa. *International Journal of Eating Disorders, 2*(4), 11–20.

Garner, D.M., Olmsted, M.P. & Polivy, J. (1983). Development and validation of a multidimensional eating disorder inventory for anorexia nervosa and bulimia. *International Journal of Eating Disorders, 2*, 15–34.

Gatz, M., Reynolds, C.A., Fratiglioni, L., Johansson, B. et al. (2006). Role of genes and environments for explaining Alzheimer's disease. *Archives of General Psychiatry, 63*, 168–174.

Gaus, V.L. (2007). *Cognitive-behavioral therapy for adult Asperger syndrome*. New York: Guilford Press.

Ge, X., Conger, R.D., Cadoret, R.J., Neiderhiser, J.M. et al. (1996). The developmental interface between nature and nurture: A mutual influence model of child antisocial behaviour and parent behaviours. *Developmental Psychology, 32*, 574–589.

Geary, D.C. (1993). Mathematical disabilities: Cognitive, neuropsychological, and genetic components. *Psychological Bulletin, 27*, 398–406.

Geary, D.C. (2004). Mathematics and learning disabilities. *Journal of Learning Disabilities, 37*(1), 4–15.

Geller, D., Biederman, J., Faraone, S., Agranat, A. et al. (2001). Developmental aspects of obsessive-compulsive disorder: Findings in children, adolescents, and adults. *Journal of Nervous and Mental Diseases, 189*, 471–477.

Geller, D., Biederman, J., Griffin, S., Jones, J. & Lefkowitz, T.R. (1996). Comorbidity of juvenile obsessive-compulsive disorder with disruptive behaviour disorders: A review and report. *Journal of the American Academy of Child and Adolescent Psychiatry, 35*, 1637–1646.

General Register Office (1968). *A glossary of mental disorders*. London: General Register Office.

George, C., Herman, K.C. & Ostrander, R. (2006). The family environment and developmental psychopathology: The unique and interactive effects of depression, attention, and conduct problems. *Child Psychiatry and Human Development, 37*, 163–177.

Gernsbacher, M.A., Dawson, M. & Goldsmith, H.H. (2005). Three reasons not to believe in an autism epidemic. *Current Directions in Psychological Science, 14*(2), 55–58.

Gerrits, M.A.F.M., Wiegant, V.M. & van Ree, J.M. (1999). Endogenous opioids implicated in the dynamics of experimental drug addiction: An in vivo autoradiographic analysis. *Neuroscience, 89*(4), 1219–1227.

Gershon, E.S. (2000). Bipolar illness and schizophrenia as oligogenic diseases: Implications for the future. *Biological Psychiatry, 47*(3), 240–244.

Gershone, J.R., Errickson, E.A., Mitchell, J.E. & Paulson, D.A. (1977). Behavioral comparison of a token economy and a standard psychiatric treatment ward. *Journal of Behavior Therapy and Experimental Psychiatry, 8*, 381–385.

Ghaderi, A. & Scott, B. (2001). Prevalence, incidence and prospective risk factors for eating disorders. *Acta Psychiatrica Scandanavica, 104*, 122–130.

Ghaemi, S.N., Boiman, E.E. & Goodwin, F.K. (1999). Kindling and second messengers: An approach to the neurobiology of recurrence in bipolar disorder. *Biological Psychiatry, 45*(2), 137–144.

Ghafouri, M., Amini, S., Khalili, K. & Sawaya, B.E. (2006). HIV-1 associated dementia: Symptoms and causes. *Retrovirology, 3*, 28–39.

Gibbons, R.D., Hedeker, D., Elkin, I., Waternaux, C., Kraemer, H.C., Greenhouse, J.B., Shea, M.T., Imber, S.D., Sotsky, S.M. & Watkins, J.T. (1993). Some conceptual and statistical issues in analysis of longitudinal psychiatric data: Application to the NIMH treatmentof depression Collaborative Research Program dataset. *Archives of General Psychiatry, 50*, 739–750.

Gibson, S.F., Morley, S. & Romeo-Wolff, C.P. (2002). A model community telepsychiatry program in rural Arizona. In R.C. Hsiung (Ed.), *E-therapy: Case studies, guiding principles, and the clinical potential of the internet*. New York: W.W. Norton.

Gil, E. (1991). *Healing power of play: Working with abused children*. New York: Guilford Press.

Gilboa-Schechtman, E., Franklin, M.E. & Foa, E.B. (2000). Anticipated reactions to social events: Differences among individuals with generalized social phobia, obsessive compulsive disorder, and nonanxious controls. *Cognitive Therapy and Research, 24*(6), 731–746.

Gillaspy, S.R., Hoff, A.L., Mullins, L.L., van Pelt, J.C. & Chaney, J.M. (2002). Psychological distress in high-risk youth with asthma. *Journal of Pediatric Psychology, 27*, 363–371.

Gillberg, C. (1991). Outcome in autism and autistic-like conditions. *Journal of the American Academy of Child and Adolescent Psychiatry, 30*, 375–382.

Gillberg, C. & Coleman, M. (2000). *The biology of the autistic syndromes* (3rd ed.). London: Cambridge University Press.

Gillberg, C. & Rastam, M. (1992). Do some cases of anorexia nervosa reflect underlying autistic-like conditions? *Behavioural Neurology, 5*(1), 27–32.

Giorgi, A. (1985). *Phenomenology and psychological research*. Pittsburgh, PA: Duquesne University Press.

Giotakos, O. & Konstantopoulos, G. (2002). Parenting received in childhood and early separation anxiety in male conscripts with adjustment disorder. *Military Medicine, 167*, 28–33.

Gitlin, L.N., Hauck, W.W., Dennis, M.P. & Winter, L. (2005). Maintenance of effects of the home environmental skill-building program for family caregivers and individuals with Alzheimer's disease and related disorders. *Journals of Gerontology Series A: Biological Sciences and Medical Sciences, 60*(3), 368–374.

Gitlin, M.J. (2002). Pharmacological treatment of depression. In I.H. Gotlib & C.L. Hammen (Eds.), *Handbook of depression*. New York: Guilford Press.

Glaser, B. & Strauss, A. (1967). *The discovery of grounded theory: Strategies for qualitative research*. Chicago: Aldine.

Glassman, A.H. (1993). Cigarette smoking: Implications for psychiatric illness. *American Journal of Psychiatry, 150*(4), 546–553.

Gleaves, D.H. (1996). The sociogenic model of dissociative identity disorder: A re-examination of the evidence. *Psychological Bulletin, 120*, 42–59.

Gleaves, D.H., Smith, S.M., Butler, L.D. & Spiegel, D. (2004). False and recovered memories in the laboratory and clinic: A review of experimental and clinical evidence. *Clinical Psychology: Science and Practice, 11*, 3–28.

Glynn, S.M. (1990). Token economy approaches for psychiatric patients: Progress and pitfalls over 25 years. *Behavior Modification, 14*, 383–407.

Godt, K. (2002). Personality disorders and eating disorders: The prevalence of personality disorders in 176 female outpatients with eating disorders. *European Eating Disorder Review, 10*(2), 102–109.

Goldacre, B. (2002). When hospital is a prison. *Guardian*, 16 July.

Goldberg, D.P. & Bridges, K. (1988). Somatic presentations of psychiatric illness in primary care setting. *Journal of Psychosomatic Research, 32*(2), 137–144.

Golden, R.N. & Gilmore, J.H. (1990). Serotonin and mood disorders. *Psychiatric Annals, 20*(10), 580&.

Goldfried, M.R. & Wolfe, B.E. (1996). Psychotherapy practice and research. Repairing a strained alliance. *American Psychologist, 51*, 1007–1016.

Goldman, M.S., Brown, S.A. & Christiansen, B.A. (1987). Expectancy theory: Thinking about drinking. In H.T. Blane & K.E. Leonard (Eds.), *Psychological theories of drinking and alcoholism*. New York: Guilford Press.

Goldman-Rakic, P.S., Castner, S.A., Svensson, T.H., Siever, L.J. & Williams, G.V. (2004). Targeting the dopamine D-1 receptor in schizophrenia: Insights for cognitive dysfunction. *Psychopharmacology, 174*, 3–16.

Goldsmith, S.K., Shapiro, R.M. & Joyce, J.N. (1997). Disrupted pattern of D-2 dopamine receptors in the temporal lobe in schizophrenia: A postmortem study. *Archives of General Psychiatry, 54*(7), 649–658.

Goldstein, A.J. & Chambless, D.L. (1978). Reanalysis of agoraphobia behavior. *Therapy, 9*(1), 47–59.

Goldstein, H. (2002). Communication intervention for children with autism: A review of treatment efficacy. *Journal of Autism and Developmental Disorders, 32*, 373–396.

Goldstein, I., Lue, T.F., Padma-Nathan, H., Rosen, R.C. et al. (1998). Oral sildenafil in the treatment of erectile dysfunction. *New England Journal of Medicine, 338*(20), 1397–1404.

Goldstein, M.J. (1987). Psychosocial issues. *Schizophrenia Bulletin, 13*(1), 157–171.

Gomberg, E.S. (1997). Alcohol abuse: Age and gender differences. In R.W. Wilsnack & S.C. Wilsnack (Eds.), *General and alcohol: Individual and social perspectives*. New Brunswick, NJ: Alcohol Research Dissemination.

Gonzalez, R., Carey, C. & Grant, I. (2002). Nonacute (residual) neuropsychological effects of cannabis use: A qualitative analysis and systematic review. *Journal of Clinical Pharmacology, 42*(11), 48S–57S.

Gonzalez-Scarano, F. & Martin-Garcia, J. (2005). The neuropathogenesis of AIDS. *Nature Reviews Immunology, 5*(1), 69–81.

Goodman, N. (2002). The serotonergic system and mysticism: Could LSD and the nondrug-induced mystical experience share common neural mechanisms? *Journal of Psychoactive Drugs, 34*(3), 263–272.

Goodman, S.H. (2002). Depression and early adverse experiences. In I.H. Gotlib & C.L. Hammen (Eds.), *Handbook of depression*. New York: Guilford Press.

Goorney, A.B. (1970). Treatment of aviation phobias by behaviour therapy. *British Journal of Psychiatry, 117*, 535–544.

Gopaul-McNicol, S. & Armour-Thomas, E. (2002). *Assessment and culture: Psychological tests with minority populations*. San Diego, CA: Academic Press.

Gordon, A. (2001). Eating disorders. 2. Bulimia nervosa. *Hospital Practice, 36*(3), 71–72.

Gorenstein, E.E. & Cromer, R.J. (2004). *Case studies in abnormal psychology* (4th ed.). New York: Worth.

Gorman, J.M., Askanazi, J., Liebowitz, M.R. et al. (1984). Response to hyperventilation in a group of patients with panic disorder. *American Journal of Psychiatry, 141*(7), 857–861.

Gorman, J.M., Kent, J., Martinez, J., Browne, S., Coplan, J. & Papp, L.A. (2001). Physiological changes during carbon dioxide inhalation in patients with panic disorder, major depression, and premenstrual dysphoric disorder: Evidence for a central fear mechanism. *Archives of General Psychiatry, 58*(2), 125–131.

Gortner, E.T., Gollan, J.K., Dobson, K.S. & Jacobson, N.S. (1998). Cognitive-behavioral treatment for depression: Relapse prevention. *Journal of Consulting and Clinical Psychology, 66*, 377–384.

Gotestam, K.G. & Agras, W.S. (1995). General population-based epidemiologic study of eating disorders in Norway. *International Journal of Eating Disorders, 18*(2), 119–126.

Gotlib, I.H. & Cane, D.B. (1987). Construct accessibility and clinical depression: A longitudinal investigation. *Journal of Abnormal Psychology, 96*(3), 199–204.

Gotlib, I.H., Lewinsohn, P.M. & Seeley, J.R. (1995). Symptoms versus a diagnosis of depression: Differences in psychosocial functioning. *Journal of Consulting and Clinical Psychology, 63*(1), 90–100.

Gotlib, I.H., Gilboa, E. & Sommerfeld, B.K. (2000). Cognitive functioning in depression: Nature and origins. In R.J. Davidson (Ed.), *Anxiety, depression and emotion*. Oxford: Oxford University Press.

Gotlib, I.H. & Robinson, L.A. (1982). Responses to depressed individuals: Discrepancies between self-report and observer-rated behavior. *Journal of Abnormal Psychology, 91*(4), 231–240.

Gottesman, I.I. & Bertelsen, A. (1989). Confirming unexpressed genotypes for schizophrenia: Risks in the offspring of Fischer's Danish identical and fraternal discordant twins. *Archives of General Psychiatry, 46*(10), 867–872.

Gottesman, I.I., McGuffin, P. & Farmer, A.E. (1987). Clinical genetics as clues to the real genetics of schizophrenia (a decade of modest gains while playing for time). *Schizophrenia Bulletin, 13*(1), 23–47.

Gould, M.S. & Kramer, R.A. (2001). Youth suicide prevention. *Suicide and Life-Threatening Behavior, 31*(1), 6–31.

Gould, R., Miller, B.L., Goldberg, M.A. & Benson, D.F. (1986). The validity of hysterical signs and symptoms. *Journal of Nervous and Mental Disease, 174*(10), 593–597.

Gould, R.A., Buckminster, S., Pollock, M.H., Otto, M.W. & Yap, L. (1997). Cognitive-behavioral and pharmacological treatment for social phobia: A meta-analysis. *Clinical Psychology: Science and Practice, 4*(4), 291–306.

Gouze, K.R. (1987). Attention and social problem solving as correlates of aggression in preschool males. *Journal of Abnormal Child Psychology, 15*, 181–197.

Gowen, E. & Miall, R.C. (2005). Behavioural aspects of cerebellar function in adults with Asperger syndrome. *Cerebellum, 4*(4), 279–289.

Goyette, C.H. & Connors, C.K. (1977). *Food additives and hyperkinesis*. Paper presented at the 85th Annual Convention of the American Psychological Association.

Gracia, C.R., Sammel, M.D., Freeman, E.W., Liu, L. et al. (2004). Predictors of decreased libido in women during the late reproductive years. *Menopause: The Journal of the North American Menopause Society, 11*(2), 144–150.

Graham, J. & Gaffan, E.A. (1997). Fear of water in children and adults: Etiology and familial effects. *Behaviour Research and Therapy, 35*(2), 91–108.

Graham, J.R. (1990). *MMPI-2: Assessing personality and psychopathology*. New York: Oxford University Press.

Gramzow, R. & Tangney, J.P. (1992). Proneness to shame and the narcissistic personality. *Personality and Social Psychology Bulletin, 18*(3), 369–376.

Grant, B.F., Hasin, D.S., Stinson, F.S., Dawson, D.A. et al. (2004). Prevalence, correlates, and disability of personality disorders in the United States: Results from the National Epidemiologic Survey on alcohol and related conditions. *Journal of Clinical Psychiatry, 65*, 948–958.

Grant, J.E. (2004). Co-occurrence of personality disorders in persons with kleptomania: A preliminary investigation. *Journal of the American Academy of Psychiatry and the Law, 32*(4), 395–398.

Grant, J.E. (2006). Understanding and treating kleptomania: New models and new treatments. *Israel Journal of Psychiatry and Related Sciences, 43*(2), 81–87.

Gratz, K.L. (2003). Risk factors for and functions of deliberate self-harm: An empirical and conceptual review. *Clinical Psychology: Science and Practice, 10*(2), 192–205.

Graybar, S.R. & Boutilier, L.R. (2002). Nontraumatic pathways to borderline personality disorder. *Psychotherapy, 39*(2), 152–162.

Graybiel, A.M. (1998). The basal ganglia and chunking of action repertoires. *Neurobiology of Learning and Memory, 70*, 119–136.

Grayson, J.B. (1999). Goal: A behavioral self-help group for obsessive-compulsive disorder. *Crisis Intervention and Time-Limited Treatment, 5*(1–2), 95–107.

Graziottin, A. & Leiblum, S.R. (2005). Biological and psychosocial pathophysiology of female sexual dysfunction during the menopausal transition. *Journal of Sexual Medicine, 2*, 133–145.

Green, J.P. & Lynn, S.J. (2000). Hypnosis and suggestion-based approaches to smoking cessation: An examination of the evidence. *International Journal of Clinical and Experimental Hypnosis, 48*(2), 195–224.

Green, M.F., Kern, R.S., Braff, D.L. & Mintz, J. (2000). Neurocognitive deficits and functional outcome in schizophrenia: Are we measuring the 'right stuff'? *Schizophrenia Bulletin, 26*(1), 119–136.

Green, R. (1987). *The 'sissy boy syndrome' and the development of homosexuality.* New Haven, CT: Yale University Press.

Green, R. & Blanchard, R. (1995). Gender identity disorders. In H.I. Kaplan & B.J. Sadock (Eds.), *Comprehensive textbook of psychiatry.* Baltimore: Williams & Wilkins.

Greenbaum, P.E., Brown, E.C. & Friedman, R.M. (1995). Alcohol expectancies among adolescents with conduct disorder: Prediction and mediation of drinking. *Addictive Behaviors, 20*(3), 321–333.

Greenberg, D.B., Stern, T.A. & Weilburg, J.B. (1988). The fear of choking: Three successfully treated cases. *Psychosomatics, 29,* 3–17.

Greenberg, L.S., Watson, J.C. & Lietaer, G. (Eds.) (1998). *Handbook of experiential psychotherapy.* New York: Guilford Press.

Greenberger, D. & Padesky, C. (1995). *Clinician's guide to mind over mood.* New York: Guilford Press.

Greenwood, G.L., White, E.W., Page-Shafer, K., Bein, E. et al. (2001). Correlates of heavy substance use among young gay and bisexual men: The San Francisco Young Men's Health Study. *Drug and Alcohol Dependence, 61*(2), 105–112.

Greisberg, S. & McKay, D. (2003). Neuropsychology of obsessive-compulsive disorder: A review and treatment implications. *Clinical Psychology Review, 23*(1), 95–117.

Greist, J.H. (1998). The comparative effectiveness of treatments for obsessive-compulsive disorder. *Bulletin of the Menninger Clinic, 62*(4), A65–A81.

Grella, C.E., Hser, Y.I., Joshi, V. & Rounds-Bryant, J. (2001). Drug treatment outcomes for adolescents with comorbid mental and substance use disorders. *Journal of Nervous and Mental Disease, 189*(6), 384–392.

Grice, D., Halmi, K.A., Fichter, M.M., Strober, M. et al. (2001). Evidence for a susceptibility gene for restricting anorexia nervosa on chromosome 1. *American Journal of Medical Genetics, 105*(7), 585–586.

Griffin, D.K., Rosenberg, H. & Cheyney, W. (1996). A comparison of self-esteem and job satisfaction of adults with mild mental retardation in sheltered workshops and supported employment. *Education and Training in Mental Retardation and Developmental Disabilities, 31,* 142–150.

Griffiths, M. (2001). Gambling: An emerging area of concern for health psychologists. *Journal of Health Psychology, 6*(5), 477–479.

Grigorenko, E.L. & Sternberg, R.J. (1998). Dynamic testing. *Psychological Bulletin, 124,* 75–111.

Grillon, C., Cordova, J., Morgan, C.A., Charney, D.S. & Davis, M. (2004). Effects of the beta-blocker propranolol on cued and contextual fear conditioning in humans. *Psychopharmacology, 175,* 342–352.

Grilly, D.M. (2002). *Drugs and human behaviour* (4th ed.). Boston: Allyn & Bacon.

Grilo, C.M., Sanislow, C.A. & McGlashan, T.H. (2002). Co-occurrence of DSM-IV personality disorders with borderline personality disorder. *Journal of Nervous and Mental Disease, 190*(8), 552–554.

Grimes, T., Bergen, L., Nichols, K., Vernberg, E. & Fonagy, P. (2004). Is psychopathology the key to understanding why some children become aggressive when they are exposed to violent television programming? *Human Communication Research, 30,* 153–181.

Grimes, T., Vernberg, E. & Cathers, T. (1997). Emotionally disturbed children's reactions to violent media segments. *Journal of Health Communication, 2,* 157–168.

Grinspoon, L., Bakalar, J.B., Zimmer, L. et al. (1997). Marijuana addiction. *Science, 277*(5327), 749.

Gripp, R.F. & Magaro, P.A. (1971). A token economy program evaluated with untreated control ward comparisons. *Behaviour Research and Therapy, 9,* 137–149.

Grosz, H.J. & Zimmerman, J. (1970). A second detailed case study of functional blindness: Further demonstration of the contribution of objective psychological laboratory data. *Behavior Therapy, 1,* 115–123.

Groth, N.A., Hobson, W.F. & Guy, T.S. (1982). The child molester: Clinical observations. In J. Conte & D.A. Shore (Eds.), *Social work and child sexual abuse.* New York: Haworth.

Gruber, A.J., Pope, H.G., Hudson, J.I. & Yurgelun-Todd, D. (2003). Attributes of long-term heavy cannabis users: A case-control study. *Psychological Medicine, 33*(8), 1415–1422.

Grubin, D. & Mason, D. (1997). Medical models of sexual deviance. In D.R. Laws & W.T. O'Donohue (Eds.), *Sexual deviance: Theory assessment and treatment.* New York: Guilford Press.

Gruenberg, E.M. (1980). Mental disorders. In J.M. Last (Ed.), *Maxcy-Roseneau public health and preventive medicine* (11th ed.). New York: Appleton-Century-Crofts.

Guarniccia, P.J., De La Cancela, V. & Carrillo, E. (1989). The multiple meanings of *Ataque de Nervios* in the Latino community. *Medical Anthropology, 11,* 47–62.

Gude, T., Hoffart, A., Hedley, L. & Ro, O. (2004). The dimensionality of dependent personality disorder. *Journal of Personality Disorders, 18*(6), 604–610.

Guggenheim, F.G. & Babigian, H.M. (1974). Catatonic schizophrenia: Epidemiology and clinical course: 7-year register study of 798 cases. *Journal of Nervous and Mental Disease, 158*(4), 291–305.

Guilleminault, C., Palombini, L., Pelayo, R. & Chervin, R.D. (2003). Sleepwalking and sleep terrors in prepubertal children. *Pediatrics, 111,* 17.

Gunderson, J.G. & Elliott, G.R. (1985). The interface between borderline personality disorder and affective disorder. *American Journal of Psychiatry, 147,* 277–287.

Gunderson, J.G. & Ronningstam, E. (2001). Differentiating narcissistic and antisocial personality disorders. *Journal of Personality Disorders, 15,* 103–109.

Gunnar, M.R. (1998). Quality of early care and buffering of neuroendocrine stress reactions: Potential effects on the developing human brain. *Preventative Medicine, 27,* 208–211.

Gunnell, D., Saperia, J. & Ashby, D. (2005). Do selective serotonin reuptake inhibitors cause suicide? Reply. *British Medical Journal, 330*(7500), 1148–1149.

Gur, R.E., Cowell, P.E., Latshaw, A., Turetsky, B.I. et al. (2000). Reduced dorsal and orbital prefrontal gray matter volumes in schizophrenia. *Archives of General Psychiatry, 57*(8), 761–768.

Gur, R.E., Turetsky, B.I., Cowell, P.E., Finkelman, C. et al. (2000). Temporolimbic volume reductions in schizophrenia. *Archives of General Psychiatry, 57*(8), 769–775.

Gureje, O., Simon, G.E., Ustun, T.B. & Goldberg, D.P. (1997). Somatization in cross-cultural perspective: A World Health Organization study in primary care. *American Journal of Psychiatry, 154*(7), 989–995.

Guttman, H.A. (2002). The epigenesis of the family system as a context for individual development. *Family Process, 41*(3), 533–545.

Habermas, T. (1989). The psychiatric history of anorexia nervosa and bulimia nervosa: Weight concerns and bulimic symptoms in early case reports. *International Journal of Eating Disorders, 8,* 259–273.

Habermas, T. (1996). In defense of weight phobia as the central organizing motive in anorexia nervosa: Historical and cultural arguments for a culture-sensitive psychological conception. *International Journal of Eating Disorders, 19,* 317–334.

Hacke, W., Donnan, G., Fieschi, C., Kaste, M. et al. (2004). Association of outcome with early stroke treatment: Pooled analysis of ATLANTIS, ECASS, and NINDS rt-PA stroke trials. *Lancet, 363* (9411), 768–774.

Hackett, M.L., Anderson, C.S. & House, A.O. (2005). Management of depression after stroke: A systematic review of pharmacological studies. *Stroke, 36,* 1092–1097.

Haddock, G. & Slade, P.D. (1995). *Cognitive-behavioural interventions for psychotic disorders.* London: Routledge.

Hadeed, A.J. & Siegel, S.R. (1989). Maternal cocaine use during pregnancy: Effect on the newborn infant. *Pediatrics, 84*(2), 205–210.

Haenen, M.A., de Jong, P.J., Schmidt, A.J.M., Stevens, S. & Visser, L. (2000). Hypochondriacs' estimation of negative outcomes: Domain-specificity and responsiveness to reassuring and alarming information. *Behaviour Research and Therapy, 38*(8), 819–833.

Hafner, H. (2000). Onset and early course as determinants of the further course of schizophrenia. *Acta Psychiatrica Scandinavica*, *102*, 44–48.

Hafner, H., Maurer, K., Loffler, W., van der Heiden, W. et al. (2003). Modeling the early course of schizophrenia. *Schizophrenia Bulletin*, *29*(2), 325–340.

Hafner, H. & van der Heiden, W. (1988). The mental health care system in transition: A study in organization, effectiveness, and costs of complementary care for schizophrenic patients. In C.N. Stefanis & D. Rabavillis (Eds.), *Schizophrenia: Recent biosocial developments*. New York: Human Sciences Press.

Hagerman, R.J. (1995). Molecular and clinical correlations in Fragile X syndrome. *Mental Retardation and Developmental Disabilities Research Reviews*, *1*, 276–280.

Hagerman, R.J. & Lampe, M.E. (1999). Fragile X syndrome. In S. Goldstein & C.R. Reynolds (Eds.), *Handbook of neurodevelopmental and genetic disorders in children*. New York: Guilford Press.

Hale, E. (1983). Inside the divided mind. *New York Times Magazine*, 17 April.

Hall, C.C.I. (1997). Cultural malpractice: The growing obsolescence of psychology with the changing US population. *American Psychologist*, *52*, 642–651.

Hall, G.C.N. (1995). Sexual offender recidivism revisited: A meta-analysis of treatment studies. *Journal of Consulting and Clinical Psychology*, *63*, 802–809.

Hall, J. & Baker, R. (1973). Token economy systems: Breakdown and control. *Behaviour Research and Therapy*, *11*, 253–263.

Hall, S.M., Reus, V.I., Munoz, R.F., Sees, K.L. et al. (1998). Nortriptyline and cognitive-behavioral therapy in the treatment of cigarette smoking. *Archives of General Psychiatry*, *55*(8), 683–690.

Hall, T.M., Kaduson, H.G. & Schaefer, C.E. (2002). Fifteen effective play therapy techniques. *Professional Psychology: Research and Practice*, *33*, 515–522.

Halligan, P.W., Athwal, B.S., Oakley, D.A. & Frackowiak, R.S.J. (2000). Imaging hypnotic paralysis: Implications for conversion hysteria. *Lancet*, *355*(9208), 986–987.

Halmi, K.A., Eckert, E., Marchi, P., Sampugnaro, V. et al. (1991). Comorbidity of psychiatric diagnoses in anorexia nervosa. *Archives of General Psychiatry*, *48*(8), 712–718.

Hamani, C., Neimat, J. & Lozano, A.M. (2006). Deep brain stimulation for the treatment of Parkinson's disease. *Journal of Neural Transmission*, Supplement (70), 393–399.

Hamel, M., Schaffer, T.W. & Erdberg, P. (2000). A study of nonpatient preadolescent Rorschach protocols. *Journal of Personality Assessment*, *75*, 280–294.

Hamilton, E.W. & Abramson, L.Y. (1983). Cognitive patterns and major depressive disorder: A longitudinal study in a hospital setting. *Journal of Abnormal Psychology*, *92*(2), 173–184.

Hand, I. (1998). Out-patient, multi-modal behaviour therapy for obsessive-compulsive disorder. *British Journal of Psychiatry*, *173*, 45–52.

Hankin, B.L. & Abramson, L.Y. (2001). Development of gender differences in depression: An elaborated cognitive vulnerability-transactional stress theory. *Psychological Bulletin*, *127*(6), 773–796.

Hankin, B.L. & Abramson, L.Y. (2002). Measuring cognitive vulnerability to depression in adolescence: Reliability, validity, and gender differences. *Journal of Clinical Child and Adolescent Psychology*, *31*(4), 491–504.

Hankin, B.L., Abramson, L.Y., Moffitt, T.E., Silva, P.A., McGee. R. & Angell, K.E. (1998). Development of depression from preadolescence to young adulthood: Emerging gender differences in a 10-year longitudinal study. *Journal of Abnormal Psychology*, *107*(1), 128–140.

Hankin, J.R. (2002). Fetal alcohol syndrome prevention research. *Alcohol Research and Health*, *26*, 58–65.

Hans, S.L., Auerbach, J.G., Styr, B. & Marcus, J. (2004). Offspring of parents with schizophrenia: Mental disorders during childhood and adolescence. *Schizophrenia Bulletin*, *30*(2), 303–315.

Hanson, R.F., Lipovsky, J.A. & Saunders, B.E. (1994). Characteristics of fathers in incest families. *Journal of Interpersonal Violence*, *9*(2), 155–169.

Hanson, R.K. & Slater, S. (1988). Sexual victimization in the history of child sexual abusers: A review. *Annals of Sexual Research*, *1*, 485–499.

Hansson, L., Middelboe, T., Sorgaard, K.W., Bengtsson-Tops, A. et al. (2002). Living situation, subjective quality of life and social network among individuals with schizophrenia living in community settings. *Acta Psychiatrica Scandinavica*, *106*(5), 343–350.

Hardy, B.W. & Waller, D.A. (1988). Bulimia as substance abuse. In W.G. Johnson (Ed.), *Advances in eating disorders*. New York: JAI.

Hare, R.D. (1978). Electrodermal and cardiovascular correlates of sociopathy. In R.D. Hare & D. Schalling (Eds.), *Psychopathic behaviour: Approaches to research*. New York: Wiley.

Hare, R.D., Harpur, T.J., Hakistan, R.A., Forth, A.E. et al. (1990). The revised Psychopathy Checklist: Reliability and factor structure. *Psychological Assessment*, *2*, 338–341.

Harris, B. (1979). Whatever happened to Little Albert? *American Psychologist*, *34*, 151–160.

Harris, M.B., Deary, I.J. & Wilson, J.A. (1996). Life events and difficulties in relation to the onset of globus pharyngis. *Journal of Psychosomatic Research*, *40*(6), 603–615.

Harris, T. (1987). Recent developments in the study of life events in relation to psychiatric and physical disorders. In B. Cooper (Ed.), *Psychiatric epidemiology: Progress and prospects*. London: Croom Helm.

Harris, T.O., Brown, G.W. & Bifulco, A.T. (1990). Depression and situational helplessness mastery in a sample selected to study childhood parental loss. *Journal of Affective Disorders*, *20*(1), 27–41.

Harrison, K. (2001). Ourselves, our bodies: Thin-ideal media, self-discrepancies, and eating disorder symptomatology in adolescents. *Journal of Social and Clinical Psychology*, *20*(3), 289–323.

Harrison, P.J. & Owen, M.J. (2003). Genes for schizophrenia? Recent findings and their pathophysiological implications. *Lancet*, *361*, 417–419.

Harrop, C. & Trower, P. (2001). Why does schizophrenia develop at late adolescence? *Clinical Psychology Review*, *21*, 241–266.

Harter, S. (1999). *The construction of the self: A developmental perspective*. New York: Guilford Press.

Hartmann, U., Heiser, K., Ruffer-Hesse, C. & Kloth, G. (2002). Female sexual desire disorders: Subtypes, classification, personality factors and new directions for treatment. *World Journal of Urology*, *20*, 79–88.

Hartung, C.M. & Widiger, T.A. (1998). Gender differences in the diagnosis of mental disorders: Conclusions and controversies of the DSM-IV. *Psychological Bulletin*, *123*, 260–278.

Harvey, A.G., Bryant, R.A. & Tarrier, N. (2003). Cognitive behaviour therapy for posttraumatic stress disorder. *Clinical Psychology Review*, *23*, 501–522.

Harvey, S.C., Foster, K.L., McKay, P.F., Carroll, M.R. et al. (2002). The GABA(A) receptor alpha(1) subtype in the ventral pallidum regulates alcohol-seeking behaviors. *Journal of Neuroscience*, *22*(9), 3765–3775.

Hasin, D.S. & Grant, B.F. (2004). The co-occurrence of DSM-IV alcohol abuse in DSM-IV alcohol dependence: Results of the national epidemiologic survey on alcohol and related conditions on heterogeneity that differ by population subgroup. *Archives of General Psychiatry*, *61*(9), 891–896.

Hasin, D.S., van Rossem, R., McCloud, S. & Endicott, J. (1997). Differentiating DMS-IV alcohol dependence and abuse by course: Community heavy drinkers. *Journal of Substance Abuse*, *9*, 127–135.

Hathaway, S.R. & McKinley, J.C. (1943). *MMPI manual*. New York: Psychological Corporation.

Haug-Schnabel (1992). Daytime and nighttime enuresis: A functional disorder and its ethological decoding. *Behavior*, *120*, 232–261.

Hawkins, J.D., Graham, J.W., Maguin, E., Abbott, R. et al. (1998). Exploring the effects of age of alcohol use initiation and psychosocial risk factors on subsequent alcohol misuse. *Journal of Studies on Alcohol*, *58*, 280–290.

Haworth-Hoeppner, S. (2000). The critical shapes of body image: The role of culture and family in the production of eating disorders. *Journal of Marriage and the Family*, *62*(1), 212–227.

Hawton, K., Hall, S., Simkin, S. et al. (2003). Deliberate self-harm in adolescents: A study of characteristics and trends in Oxford, 1990–2000. *Journal of Child Psychology and Psychiatry and Allied Disciplines*, 44(8), 1191–1198.

Hawton, K. & James, A. (2005). ABC of adolescence: Suicide and deliberate self-harm in young people. *British Medical Journal*, 330(7496), 891–894.

Hawton, K., Rodham, K., Evans, E. & Weatherall, R. (2002). Deliberate self-harm in adolescents: Self-report survey in schools in England. *British Medical Journal*, 325(7374), 1207–1211.

Hay, D.P. (1991). Electroconvulsive therapy. In J. Sadavoy, L.W. Lazarus & L.F. Jarvik (Eds.), *Comprehensive review of geriatric psychiatry*. Washington, DC: American Psychiatric Press.

Hay, P. & Fairburn, C. (1998). The validity of the DSM-IV scheme for classifying bulimic eating disorders. *International Journal of Eating Disorders*, 23(1), 7–15.

Hayes, R. & Dennerstein, L. (2005). The impact of aging on sexual function and sexual dysfunction in women: A review of population-based studies. *Journal of Sexual Medicine*, 2, 317–330.

Hazelrigg, M.D., Cooper, H.M. & Borduin, C.M. (1987). Evaluating the effectiveness of family therapies: An integrative review and analysis. *Psychological Bulletin*, 101, 428–442.

He, D., Medbo, J.I. & Hostmark, A.T. (2001). Effect of acupuncture on smoking cessation or reduction: An 8-month and 5-year follow-up study. *Preventive Medicine*, 33(5), 364–372.

Head, D. & Harmon, G. (1990). Psychologists and research: Do we practice what we preach? *Clinical Psychology Forum*, 25, 15–16.

Heath, A.C. (1995). Genetic influences on drinking behaviour in humans. In H. Begletter & B. Kissin (Eds.), *The genetics of alcoholism* (Vol. 1). New York: Oxford University Press.

Heaton, P. & Wallace, G.L. (2004). Annotation: The savant syndrome. *Journal of Child Psychology and Psychiatry*, 45(5), 899–911.

Heavey, L., Phillips, W., Baron-Cohen, S. & Rutter, M. (2000). The Awkward Moments Test: A naturalistic measure of social understanding in autism. *Journal of Autism and Developmental Disorders*, 30(3), 225–236.

Heffernan, K. & Cloitre, M. (2000). A comparison of posttraumatic stress disorder with and without borderline personality disorder among women with a history of childhood sexual abuse: Etiology and clinical characteristics. *Journal of Nervous and Mental Disease*, 188, 589–595.

Heginbotham, C. (1998). UK mental health policy can alter the stigma of mental illness. *Lancet*, 352, 1052–1053.

Heilman, D.M., Schwartz, H.D. & Geschwind, N. (1975). Defective motor learning in ideomotor apraxia. *Neurology*, 25, 1018–1020.

Heiman, J.R. (2002). Sexual dysfunction: Overview of prevalence, etiological factors, and treatments. *Journal of Sex Research*, 39(1), 73–78.

Heiman, J.R., Gladue, B.A., Roberts, C.W. & LoPiccolo, J. (1986). Historical and current factors discriminating sexually functional from sexually dysfunctional married couples. *Journal of Marital and Family Therapy*, 12, 163–174.

Heiman, J.R. & LoPiccolo, J. (1988). *Becoming orgasmic: A personal and sexual growth program for women*. New York: Prentice-Hall.

Heimberg, R.G. & Becker, R.E. (2002). *Cognitive behavioural group therapy for social phobia: Basic mechanisms and clinical strategies*. New York: Guilford Press.

Heinrichs, N. & Hofmann, S.G. (2001). Information processing in social phobia: A critical review. *Clinical Psychology Review*, 21, 751–770.

Heinz, A., Mann, K., Weinberger, D.R. & Goldman, D. (2001). Serotonergic dysfunction, negative mood states, and response to alcohol. *Alcoholism: Clinical and Experimental Research*, 25(4), 487–495.

Helgeland, M.I. & Torgersen, S. (2004). Developmental antecedents of borderline personality disorder. *Comprehensive Psychiatry*, 45, 138–147.

Hellawell, S.J. & Brewin, C.R. (2004). A comparison of flashbacks and ordinary autobiographical memories of trauma: Content and language. *Behaviour Research and Therapy*, 42(1), 1–12.

Hellerstein, D.J., Kocsis, J.H., Chapman, D., Stewart, J.W. & Harrison, W. (2000). Double-blind comparison of sertraline, imipramine, and placebo in the treatment of dysthymia: Effects on personality. *American Journal of Psychiatry*, 157(9), 1436–1444.

Helzer, J.E. & Hudziak, J.J. (2002). *Defining psychopathology in the 21st Century: DSM-V and beyond*. Washington, DC: American Psychiatric Press.

Helzer, J.E., Robins, L.N. & McEvoy, L. (1987). Posttraumatic stress disorder in the general population: Findings of the epidemiologic catchment area survey. *New England Journal of Medicine*, 317(26), 1630–1634.

Henkel, V., Bussfeld, P., Moller, H.J. & Hegerl, U. (2002). Cognitive-behavioural theories of helplessness/hopelessness: Valid models of depression? *European Archives of Psychiatry and Clinical Neuroscience*, 252, 240–249.

Henquet, C., Krabbendam, L., Spauwen, J., Kaplan, C. et al. (2005). Prospective cohort study of cannabis use, predisposition for psychosis, and psychotic symptoms in young people. *British Medical Journal*, 330(7481), 11–14.

Hensley, P.L., Nadiga, D. & Uhlenhuth, E.H. (2004). Long-term effectiveness of cognitive therapy in major depressive disorder. *Depression and Anxiety*, 20(1), 1–7.

Hensley, P.L. & Nurnberg, H.G. (2002). SSRI sexual dysfunction: A female perspective. *Journal of Sex and Marital Therapy*, 28, 143–153.

Henwood, K.L. & Pidgeon, N.F. (1992). Qualitative research and psychological theorizing. *British Journal of Psychology*, 83, 97–111.

Hepp, U., Kraemer, B., Schnyder, U., Miller, N. & Delsignore, A. (2005). Psychiatric comorbidity in gender identity disorder. *Journal of Psychosomatic Research*, 58(3), 259–261.

Herdt, G. & Stoller, R.J. (1990). *Intimate communications: Erotics and the study of culture*. New York: Columbia University Press.

Herman, C.P., Polivy, J., Lank, C.N. & Heatherton, T.F. (1987). Anxiety, hunger, and eating behavior. *Journal of Abnormal Psychology*, 96(3), 264–269.

Herman, J.L., Perry, J.C. & van der Kolk, B.A. (1989). Childhood trauma in borderline personality disorder. *American Journal of Psychiatry*, 146(4), 490–495.

Hernandez-Serrano, R. (2001). Advances in the treatment of sexual disorders. *International Medical Journal*, 8, 83–89.

Herperts, S.C., Werth, U., Lukas, G., Qunaibi, M. et al. (2001). Emotion in criminal offenders with psychopathy and borderline personality disorder. *Archives of General Psychiatry*, 58, 737–745.

Hersen, M., Bellack, A.S. & Himmelhoch, J.M. (1980). Treatment of unipolar depression with social skills training. *Behavior Modification*, 4(4), 547–556.

Hertel, P.T., Mathews, A., Peterson, S. & Kintner, K. (2003). Transfer of training emotionally biased interpretations. *Applied Cognitive Psychology*, 17, 775–784.

Herzog, D.B., Greenwood, D.N., Dorer, D.J., Flores, A.T. et al. (2000). Mortality in eating disorders: A descriptive study. *International Journal of Eating Disorders*, 28(1), 20–26.

Hesselbrock, M.N. & Hesselbrock, V.M. (1992). Relationship of family history, antisocial personality disorder and personality traits in young men at risk for alcoholism. *Journal of Studies on Alcohol*, 53(6), 619–625.

Hester, R.K. (1995). Behavioral self-control training. In R.K. Hester & W.R. Miller (Eds.), *Handbook of alcoholism treatment approaches: Effectiveness alternatives* (2nd ed.). Boston: Allyn & Bacon.

Heston, L.L. (1966). Psychiatric disorders in foster home reared children of schizophrenic mothers. *British Journal of Psychiatry*, 112(489), 819&.

Hettema, J.M., Neale, M.C. & Kendler, K.S. (2001). A review and meta-analysis of the genetic epidemiology of anxiety disorders. *American Journal of Psychiatry*, 158, 1568–1578.

Heyneman, N.E., Fremouw, W.J., Gano, D., Kirkland, F. & Heiden, L. (1990). Individual differences and the effectiveness of different coping strategies for pain. *Cognitive Therapy and Research*, 14(1), 63–77.

Hibbert, G.A. (1984). Ideational components of anxiety: Their origin and content. *British Journal of Psychiatry*, 144, 618–624.

Higher Education Statistics Agency (2007). Retrieved from www.hesa.ac.uk/index.php?option=com_datatables&Itemid=121, July 2007.

Hill, A.J. & Franklin, J.A. (1998). Mothers, daughters and dieting: Investigating the transmission of weight control. *British Journal of Clinical Psychology*, *37*, 3–13.

Hill, C.E., Thompson, B.J. & Williams, E.N. (1997). A guide to conducting consensual qualitative research. *Counseling Psychologist*, *25*, 517–572.

Hill, D.E., Yeo, R.A., Campbell, R.A., Hart, B., Vigil, J. & Brooks, W. (2003). Magnetic resonance imaging correlates of attention-deficit/hyperactivity disorder in children. *Neuropsychology*, *17*, 496–506.

Hill, E.L. & Bird, C.A. (2006). Executive processes in Asperger syndrome: Patterns of performance in a multiple case series. *Neuropsychologia*, *44*(14), 2822–2835.

Hill, J. (2003). Early identification of individuals at risk for antisocial personality disorder. *British Journal of Psychiatry*, *182*, S11–S14.

Hilliard, R.B. & Spitzer, R.L. (2002). Change in criterion for paraphilias in DSM-IV-TR. *American Journal of Psychiatry*, *159*(7), 1249.

Hilsman, R. & Garber, J. (1995). A test of the cognitive diathesis-stress model of depression in children: Academic stressors, attributional style, perceived competence, and control. *Journal of Personality and Social Psychology*, *69*, 370–504.

Himle, J.A., Crystal, D., Curtis, G.C. & Fluent, T.E. (1991). Mode of onset of simple phobia subtypes: Further evidence of heterogeneity. *Psychiatry Research*, *36*, 37–43.

Hinshaw, S.P. (1987). On the distinction between attentional deficits/hyperactivity and conduct problems/aggression in child psychopathology. *Psychological Bulletin*, *101*, 443–463.

Hinshaw, S.P., Lahey, B.B. & Hart, E.L. (1993). Issues of taxonomy and comorbidity in the development of conduct disorder. *Development and Psychopathology*, *5*, 31–49.

Hinshaw, S.P. & Melnick, S.M. (1995). Peer relationships in boys with attention deficit hyperactivity disorder with and without comorbid aggression. *Development and Psychopathology*, *7*, 627–647.

Hirasing, R.A., van Leerdam, F.J., Bolk-Bennink, L. & Janknegt, R.A. (1997). Bedwetting in adults. *ICCS Abstracts* (Paris), 84.

Hiroeh, U., Appleby, L., Mortensen, P.B. & Dunn, G. (2001). Death by homicide, suicide, and other unnatural causes in people with mental illness: A population-based study. *Lancet*, *358*, 2110–2112.

Hirsch, C.R. & Clark, D.M. (2004). Information-processing bias in social phobia. *Clinical Psychology Review*, *24*, 799–825.

Hite, S. (1976). *The Hite report: A nationwide study of female sexuality.* New York: Dell.

Hitzeman, N. (2006). Cholinesterase inhibitors for Alzheimer's disease. *American Family Physician*, *74*(5), 747–749.

Hjern, A., Wicks, S. & Dalman, C. (2004). Social adversity contributes to high morbidity in psychoses in immigrants: A national cohort study in two generations of Swedish residents. *Psychological Medicine*, *34*(6), 1025–1033.

Hobfoll, S.E., Spielberger, C.D., Breznitz, S., Figley, C. et al. (1991). War-related stress: Addressing the stress of war and other traumatic events. *American Psychologist*, *46*(8), 848–855.

Hobson, R.P. & Lee, A. (1998). Hello and goodbye: A study of social engagement in autism. *Journal of Autism and Developmental Disorders*, *28*(2), 117–127.

Hodes, M., Timimi, S. & Robinson, P. (1997). Children of mothers with eating disorders: A preliminary study. *European Eating Disorder Review*, *5*(1), 11–24.

Hoebel, B.G. & Teitelbaum, P. (1966). Weight regulation in normal and hypothalamic hyperphagic rats. *Journal of Comparative and Physiological Psychology*, *61*(2), 189.

Hoehn-Saric, R. & McLeod, D.R. (1988). The peripheral sympathetic nervous system: Its role in normal and pathologic anxiety. *Psychiatric Clinics of North America*, *11*, 375–386.

Hoek, H.W. & van Hoeken, D. (2003). Review of the prevalence and incidence of eating disorders. *International Journal of Eating Disorders*, *34*, 383–396.

Hofflich, S.A., Hughes, A.A. & Kendall, P.C. (2006). Somatic complaints and childhood anxiety disorders. *International Journal of Clinical and Health Psychology*, *6*, 229–242.

Hofmann, S.G. & Otto, M.W. (2008). *Cognitive-behavior therapy of social phobia.* London: Routledge.

Hofmeister, J.F., Schneckenbach, A.F. & Clayton, S.H. (1979). A behavioral program or the treatment of chronic patients. *American Journal of Psychiatry*, *136*, 396–400.

Hogarty, G.E. (2002). *Personal therapy for schizophrenia and related disorders: A guide to individualized treatment.* New York: Guilford Press.

Hogarty, G.E., Anderson, C.M., Reiss, D.J., Kornblith, S.J. et al. (1986). Family psychoeducation, social skills training, and maintenance chemotherapy, in the aftercare treatment of schizophrenia. 1. One-year effects of a controlled study on relapse and expressed emotion. *Archives of General Psychiatry*, *43*(7), 633–642.

Hogarty, G.E. & Flesher, S. (1999). Practice principles of cognitive enhancement therapy for schizophrenia. *Schizophrenia Bulletin*, *25*, 693–708.

Hogarty, G.E., Flesher, S., Ulrich, R., Carter, M. et al. (2004). Cognitive enhancement therapy for schizophrenia: Effects of a 2-year randomized trial on cognition and behaviour. *Archives of General Psychiatry*, *61*(9), 866–876.

Hogarty, G.E., Greenwald, D., Ulrich, R.F., Kornblith, S.J. et al. (1997). Three-year trials of personal therapy among schizophrenic patients living with or independent of family. 2. Effects on adjustment of patients. *American Journal of Psychiatry*, *154*(11), 1514–1524.

Hogarty, G.E., Kornblith, S.J., Greenwald, D., DiBarry, A.L. et al. (1997). Three-year trials of personal therapy among schizophrenic patients living with or independent of family. 1. Description of study and effects on relapse rates. *American Journal of Psychiatry*, *154*(11), 1504–1513.

Hohagen, F., Winkelmann, G., Rasche-Rauchle, H., Hand, I. et al. (1998). Combination of behaviour therapy with fluvoxamine in comparison with behaviour therapy and placebo: Results of a multicentre study. *British Journal of Psychiatry*, *173*, 71–78.

Holbrook, T.L., Hoyt, D.B., Stein, M.B. & Sieber, W.J. (2002). Gender differences in long-term posttraumatic stress disorder outcomes after major trauma: Women are at higher risk of adverse outcomes than men. *Journal of Trauma-Injury Infection and Critical Care*, *53*(5), 882–888.

Holden, C.A., McLachlan, R.I., Pitts, M., Cumming, R. et al. (2005). Men in Australia Telephone Survey (MATeS): A national survey of the reproductive health and concerns of middle-aged and older Australian men. *Lancet*, *366*(9481), 218–224.

Holder-Perkins, V. & Wise, T.N. (2001). Somatization disorder. In K.A. Phillips (Ed.), *Somatoform and factitious disorders. Review of psychiatry* (Vol. 20). Washington, DC: American Psychiatric Association.

Hollander, E., Allen, A., Kwon, J., Aronowitz, B. et al. (1999). Clomipramine vs. desipramine crossover trial in body dysmorphic disorder: Selective efficacy of a serotonin reuptake inhibitor in imagined ugliness. *Archives of General Psychiatry*, *56*(11), 1033–1039.

Hollar, M.C. (2001). The impact of racism on the delivery of health care and mental health services. *Psychiatry Quarterly*, *72*, 337–345.

Hollingshead, A.B. & Redlich, F.C. (1958). *Social class and mental illness: A community study.* New York: Wiley.

Hollon, S.D. & Beck, A.T. (1994). Cognitive and cognitive-behavioral therapies. In A.E. Bergin & S.L. Garfield (Eds.), *Handbook of psychotherapy and behaviour change* (4th ed.). New York: Wiley.

Hollon, S.D., Shelton, R.C. & Davis, D.D. (1993). Cognitive therapy for depression: Conceptual issues and clinical efficacy. *Journal of Consulting and Clinical Psychology*, *61*(2), 270–275.

Holmes, S.E., Slaughter, J.R. & Kashani, J. (2001). Risk factors in childhood that lead to the development of conduct disorder and antisocial personality disorder. *Child Psychiatry and Human Development*, *31*, 183–192.

Holsboer, F. (2001). Stress, hypercortisolism and corticosteroid receptors in depression: Implications for therapy. *Journal of Affective Disorders*, *62*, 77–91.

Home Affairs Committee (2002). *The government's drugs policy: Is it working?* www.publications.parliament.uk/pa/cm200102/cmselect/cmhaff/318/31802.htm; retrieved February 2008.

Honda, H., Shimizu, Y. & Rutter, M. (2005). No effect of MMR withdrawal on the incidence of autism: A total population study. *Journal of Child Psychology and Psychiatry*, 46, 572–579.

Hopko, D.R., Lejuez, C.W., LePage, J.P. et al. (2003). A brief behavioral activation treatment for depression: A randomized pilot trial within an inpatient psychiatric hospital. *Behavior Modification*, 27(4), 458–469.

Hopko, D.R., Lejuez, C.W., Ruggiero, K.J. & Eifert, G.H. (2003). Contemporary behavioural activation treatments for depression: Procedures, principles, and progress. *Clinical Psychology Review*, 23, 699–717.

Hopwood, J.S. & Snell, H.K. (1933). Amnesia in relation to crime. *Journal of Mental Science*, 79, 27–41.

Horesh, N., Apter, A., Ishai, J., Danziger, Y. et al. (1996). Abnormal psychosocial situations and eating disorders in adolescence. *Journal of the American Academy of Child and Adolescent Psychiatry*, 35(7), 921–927.

Horneman, G., Folkesson, P., Sintonen, H., von Wendt, L. & Emanuelson, I. (2005). Health-related quality of life of adolescents and young adults 10 years after serious traumatic brain injury. *International Journal of Rehabilitation Research*, 28(3), 245–249.

Horowitz, A.V., Widom, C.S., McLaughlin, J. & White, H.R. (2001). The impact of childhood abuse and neglect on adult mental health: A prospective study. *Journal of Health and Social Behaviour*, 42, 184–201.

Horsfield, S.A., Rosse, R.B., Tomasino, V., Schwartz, B.L. et al. (2002). Fluoxetine's effects on cognitive performance in patients with traumatic brain injury. *International Journal of Psychiatry in Medicine*, 32(4), 337–344.

Hospital Episode Statistics (HES) (2001). Available online at www.nwpho.org.uk/documents.

Hotopf, M., Mayou, R., Wadsworth, M. & Wessely, S. (1999). Psychosocial and developmental antecedents of chest pain in young adults. *Psychosomatic Medicine*, 61(6), 861–867.

Houck, J.A. (2003). 'What do these women want?': Feminist responses to *Feminine Forever*, 1963–1980. *Bulletin of the History of Medicine*, 77(1), 103–132.

Houtsmuller, E.J. & Stitzer, M.L. (1999). Manipulation of cigarette craving through rapid smoking: Efficacy and effects on smoking behavior. *Psychopharmacology*, 142(2), 149–157.

Howard, M.O. (2001). Pharmacological aversion treatment of alcohol dependence: I. Production and prediction of conditioned alcohol aversion. *American Journal of Drug and Alcohol Abuse*, 27, 561–585.

Howlin, P. (2005). The effectiveness of interventions for children with autism. *Journal of Neural Transmission: Supplement*, 69, 101–119.

Howlin, P., Alcock, J. & Burkin, C. (2005). An 8-year follow-up of a specialist supported employment service for high-ability adults with autism or Asperger syndrome. *Autism*, 9, 533–549.

Ho-Yen, D. (1990). Patient management in post-viral fatigue syndrome. *British Journal of General Practice*, 40, 37–39.

Hser, Y.I., Anglin, M.D. & Powers, K. (1993). A 24-year follow-up of California narcotics addicts. *Archives of General Psychiatry*, 50(7), 577–584.

Hsiung, R.C. (Ed.) (2002). *E-therapy: Case studies, guiding principles, and the clinical potential of the internet*. New York: W.W. Norton.

Huber, S.J., Bornstein, R.A., Rammohan, K.W., Christy, J.A. et al. (1992). Magnetic resonance imaging correlates of neuropsychological impairment in multiple sclerosis. *Journal of Neuropsychiatry and Clinical Neurosciences*, 4(2), 152–158.

Hudson, J.I., Pope, H.G., Jonas, J.M. & Yurgelson-Todd, D. (1983). Phenomenologic relationship of eating disorders to major affective disorder. *Psychiatry Research*, 9(4), 345–354.

Hudson, J.L. & Rapee, R.M. (2001). Parent–child interactions and anxiety disorders: An observational study. *Behaviour Research and Therapy*, 39, 1411–1427.

Hudson, J.L. & Rapee, R.M. (2002). Parent–child interactions in clinically anxious children and their siblings. *Journal of Clinical Child and Adolescent Psychology*, 31, 548–555.

Hughes, J.N. & Hasbrouck, J.E. (1996). Television violence: Implications for violence prevention. *School Psychology Review*, 25, 134–151.

Hughes, J.R., Higgins, S.T. & Hatsukami, D. (1990). Effects of abstinence from tobacco: A critical review. *Research Advances in Alcohol and Drug Problems*, 10, 317–398.

Huguelet, P. & Perroud, N. (2005). Wolfgang Amadeus Mozart's psychopathology in light of the current conceptualization of psychiatric disorders. *Psychiatry: Interpersonal and Biological Processes*, 68(2), 130–139.

Huppert, J.D., Schultz, L.T., Foa, E.B. & Barlow, D.H. (2004). Differential response to placebo among patients with social phobia, panic disorder, and obsessive-compulsive disorder. *American Journal of Psychiatry*, 161, 1485–1487.

Huxley, N.A., Rendall, M. & Sederer, L. (2000). Psychosocial treatments in schizophrenia: A review of the past 20 years. *Journal of Nervous and Mental Disease*, 188(4), 187–201.

Hwang, B. & Hughes, C. (2000). The effects of social interactive training on early social communicative skills of children with autism. *Journal of Autism and Developmental Disorders*, 30(4), 331–343.

Ikard, F.F., Green, D.E. & Horn, D. (1969). A scale to differentiate between types of smoking as related to the management of affect. *International Journal of the Addictions*, 4, 649–659.

Ingersoll, K.S., Ceperich, S.D., Nettleman, M.D., Karanda, K. et al. (2005). Reducing alcohol-exposed pregnancy risk in college women: Initial outcomes of a clinical trial of a motivational intervention. *Journal of Substance Abuse Treatment*, 29, 173–180.

Ingram, R.E., Bernet, C.Z. & McLaughlin, S.C. (1994). Attentional allocation processes in individuals at risk for depression. *Cognitive Therapy and Research*, 18(4), 317–332.

Ingram, R.E., Miranda, J. & Segal, Z.V. (1998). *Cognitive vulnerability to depression*. New York: Guilford Press.

Irving, L.M. (2001). Media exposure and disordered eating: Introduction to the special section. *Journal of Social and Clinical Psychology*, 20(3), 259–269.

Isaacs, W., Thomas, J. & Goldiamond, I. (1960). Application of operant conditioning to reinstate verbal behavior in psychotics. *Journal of Speech and Hearing Disorders*, 25, 8–12.

Isaacson, G. & Rich, C.L. (1997). Depression, antidepressants and suicide: Pharmaco-epidemiological evidence. In R.W. Maris, M.M. Silverman & S.S. Canetto (Eds.), *Review of suicidology*. New York: Guilford Press.

Isbister, G.K., Bowe, S.J., Dawson, A. & Whyte, I.M. (2004). Relative toxicity of selective serotonin reuptake inhibitors (SSRIs) in overdose. *Journal of Toxicology: Clinical Toxicology*, 42(3), 277–285.

Isometsa, E., Henriksson, M., Marttunen, M. et al. (1995). Mental disorders in young and middle-aged men who commit suicide. *British Medical Journal*, 310(6991), 1366–1367.

Israel, Y., Hollander, O., Sanchez-Craig, M., Booker, S. et al. (1996). Screening for problem drinking and counseling by the primary care physician–nurse team. *Alcoholism: Clinical and Experimental Research*, 20(8), 1443–1450.

Iversen, L. (2005). Long-term effects of exposure to cannabis. *Current Opinion in Pharmacology*, 5, 69–72.

Iverson, G.L. (2006). Complicated vs. uncomplicated mild traumatic brain injury: Acute neuropsychological outcome. *Brain Injury*, 20(13–14), 1335–1344.

Iwata, B.A., Dorsey, M.F., Slifer, K.J., Bauman, K.E. & Richman, G.S. (1985). Toward a functional analysis of self-injury. In G. Murphy & B. Wilson (Eds.), *Self-injurious behaviour*. Kidderminster: BIHM.

Jablensky, A. (2000). Prevalence and incidence of schizophrenia spectrum disorders: Implications for prevention. *Australian and New Zealand Journal of Psychiatry*, 34, S26–S34.

Jablensky, A., Sartorius, N., Ernberg, G., Anker, M. et al. (1992). Schizophrenia: Manifestations, incidence and course in different cultures: A World Health Organization 10-country study. *Psychological Medicine*, 1–97, Suppl. 20.

Jackson, A.P. & Huang, C.C. (2000). Parenting stress and behavior among single mothers of preschoolers: The mediating role of self-efficacy. *Journal of Social Service Research*, 26(4), 29–42.

Jackson, H.J., Moss, J.D. & Solinski, S. (1985). Social skills training: An effective treatment for unipolar nonpsychotic depression. *Australian and New Zealand Journal of Psychiatry, 19*(4), 342–353.

Jacobi, C., Hayward, C., de Zwaan, M., Kraemer, H.C. & Agras, W.S. (2004). Coming to terms with risk factors for eating disorders: Application of risk terminology and suggestions for a general taxonomy. *Psychological Bulletin, 130*, 19–65.

Jacobsen, L.K., Southwick, S.M. & Kosten, T.R. (2001). Substance use disorders in patients with posttraumatic stress disorder: A review of the literature. *American Journal of Psychiatry, 158*(8), 1184–1190.

Jacobson, N.S. & Christenson, A. (1996). Studying the effectiveness of psychotherapy. *American Psychologist, 51*, 1031–1039.

Jacobson, N.S. & Gortner, E.T. (2000). Can depression be de-medicalized in the 21st century: Scientific revolutions, counter-revolutions and the magnetic field of normal science. *Behaviour Research and Therapy, 38*(2), 103–117.

Jacobson, N.S., Martell, C.R. & Dimidjian, S. (2001). Behavioral activation treatment for depression: Returning to contextual roots. *Clinical Psychology: Science and Practice, 8*(3), 255–270.

Jacobson, N.S. & Weiss, R.L. (1978). Behavioral marriage therapy III. The contents of Gurma et al. may be hazardous to our health. *Family Process, 17*, 149–163.

James, P.T., Leach, R., Kalamara, E. & Shayeghi, M. (2001). The worldwide obesity epidemic. *Obesity Research, 9*, 228S–233S, Suppl. 4.

Jamison, K.R. (1992). *Touched with fire: Manic-depressive illness and the artistic temperament.* New York: Free Press.

Jamison, K.R. (1995). *An unquiet mind.* New York: Vintage.

Jamrozik, K. (2005). Slaying myths about passive smoking. *Tobacco Control, 14*(5), 294–295.

Janca, A., Isaac, M., Bennett, L.A. & Tacchini, G. (1995). Somatoform disorders in different cultures: A mail questionnaire survey. *Social Psychiatry and Psychiatric Epidemiology, 30*(1), 44–48.

Janet, P. (1907). *The major symptoms of hysteria.* London: Macmillan.

Janoff-Bulman, R. (1992). *Shattered assumptions: Towards a new psychology of trauma.* New York: Free Press.

Janov, A. (1973). *Primal scream: Primal therapy – the cure for neurosis.* New York: Abacus.

Jansen, K.L.R. (2001). Mental health problems associated with MDMA use. In J. Holland (Ed.), *Ecstasy: The complete guide: A comprehensive look at the risks and benefits of MDMA.* Rochester, VT: Park Street Press.

Jarquin-Valdivia, A.A. (2004). Psychiatric symptoms and brain tumors: A brief historical overview. *Archives of Neurology, 61*, 1800–1804.

Jarrett, R.B., Kraft, D., Doyle, J., Foster, B.M., Eaves, G.G. & Silver, P.C. (2001). Preventing recurrent depression using cognitive therapy with and without a continuation phase: A randomized clinical trial. *Archives of General Psychiatry, 58*(4), 381–388.

Jarvelin, M.R., Moilanen, I., Kangas, P., Moring, K. et al. (1991). Aetiological and precipitating factors for childhood enuresis. *Acta Pediatrica Scandinavica, 80*, 361–369.

Jarvelin, M.R., Vikevainen-Tervonen, L., Moilanen, I. & Huttunen, N.P. (1988). Enuresis in 7-year-old children. *Acta Pediatrica Scandinavica, 77*(1), 148–153.

Jason, L.A., Wagner, L., Taylor, R., Ropacki, M.T. et al. (1995). Chronic fatigue syndrome: A new challenge for health-care professionals. *Journal of Community Psychology, 23*(2), 143–164.

Jeans, R.F. (1976). An independently validated case of multiple personality. *Journal of Abnormal Psychology, 85*, 249–255.

Jelicic, M., Merckelbach, H. & van Bergen, S. (2004). Symptom validity testing of feigned amnesia for a mock crime. *Archives of Clinical Neuropsychology, 19*, 525–531.

Jellinek, E.M. (1952). Phases of alcohol addiction. *Quarterly Journal of Studies on Alcohol, 13*, 673–684.

Jenike, M.A. (1986). Theories of etiology. In M.A. Jenike, L. Baer & W.E. Minichiello (Eds.), *Obsessive-compulsive disorders.* Littleton, MA: PSG Publishing.

Jeste, D.V., Gladsjo, J.A., Lindamer, L.A. et al. (1996). Medical comorbidity in schizophrenia. *Schizophrenia Bulletin, 22*(3), 413–430.

Johansson, B. & Zarit, S.H. (1995). Prevalence and incidence of dementia in the oldest old: A longitudinal study of a population-based sample of 84–90-year-olds in Sweden. *International Journal of Geriatric Psychology, 10*.

Johns, A. (2001). Psychiatric effects of cannabis. *British Journal of Psychiatry, 178*, 116–122.

Johnson, A.M., Mercer, C.H., Erens, B., Copas, A.J. et al. (2001). Sexual behaviour in Britain: Partnerships, practices, and HIV risk behaviours. *Lancet, 358*(9296), 1835–1842.

Johnson, B.A., Roache, J.D., Javors, M.A., DiClemente, C.C. et al. (2000). Ondansetron for reduction of drinking among biologically predisposed alcoholic patients: A randomized controlled trial. *JAMA: Journal of the American Medical Association, 284*(8), 963–971.

Johnson, C. & Larson, R. (1982). Bulimia: An analysis of moods and behavior. *Psychosomatic Medicine, 44*(4), 341–351.

Johnson, D.L., Walker, T.B. & Rodriquez, G.G. (1991). *Final report of an evaluation of the Avance Parent Education and Family Support Program.* San Antonio, TX: Avance.

Johnson, E.O., Arria, A.M., Borges, G., Ialongo, N. & Anthony, J.C. (1995). The growth of conduct problem behaviors from middle childhood to early adolescence: Sex differences and the suspected influence of early alcohol use. *Journal of Studies on Alcohol, 56*(6), 661–671.

Johnson, J. & Davey, G.C.L. (1978). Vibration and praise as reinforcers for the mentally handicapped. *Mental Retardation, 16*, 339–342.

Johnson, J.G., Cohen, P., Brown, J., Smailes, E.M. & Bernstein, D.P. (1999). Childhood maltreatment increases risk for personality disorders during early adulthood. *Archives of General Psychiatry, 56*(7), 600–606.

Johnson, J.G., Cohen, P., Kasen, S. & Brooks, J.S. (2006). Dissociative disorders among adults in the community, impaired functioning, and Axis I and II comorbidity. *Journal of Psychiatric Research, 40*, 131–140.

Johnson, J.G., Cohen, P., Kasen, S., Smailes, E. & Brook, J.S. (2002). Maladaptive parenting and the association between parental and offspring psychiatric disorders. *Zeitschrift für Psychosomatische Medizin und Psychotherapie, 48*(4), 396–410.

Johnson, J.G., Cohen, P., Skodol, A.E., Oldham, J.M., Kasen, S., Brook, J.S. et al. (1999). Personality disorders in adolescence and risk of major mental disorders and suicidality during adulthood. *Archives of General Psychiatry, 56*(9), 805–811.

Johnson, J.G., Cohen, P., Smailes, E.M., Skodol, A.E. et al. (2001). Childhood verbal abuse and risk for personality disorders during adolescence and early adulthood. *Comprehensive Psychiatry, 42*(1), 16–23.

Johnson, M.K., Hashtroudi, S. & Lindsay, D.S. (1993). Source monitoring. *Psychological Bulletin, 114*(1), 3–28.

Johnson, M.K. & Raye, C.L. (1981). Reality monitoring. *Psychological Review, 88*(1), 67–85.

Johnston, C. & Mash, E.J. (2001). Families of children with attention-deficit/ hyperactivity disorder: Review and recommendations for future research. *Clinical Child and Family Psychology Review, 4*(3), 183–207.

Johnston, L.D., O'Malley, P.M. & Bachman, J.G. (2001). *Monitoring the future: National results on adolescent drug use: Overview of key findings, 2001.* Bethesda, MD: National Institute on Drug Abuse.

Johnston, W.M. & Davey, G.C.L. (1997). The psychological impact of negative TV news bulletins: The catastrophizing of personal worries. *British Journal of Psychology, 88*, 85–91.

Joiner, T.E. (1995). The price of soliciting and receiving negative feedback: Self-verification theory as a vulnerability to depression theory. *Journal of Abnormal Psychology, 104*(2), 364–372.

Joiner, T.E. (2001). Negative attributional style, hopelessness depression and endogenous depression. *Behaviour Research and Therapy, 39*(2), 139–149.

Joiner, T.E. (2002). Depression and its interpersonal context. In I.H. Gotlib & C.L. Hammen (Eds.), *Handbook of depression.* New York: Guilford Press.

Joiner, T.E., Alfano, M.S. & Metalsky, G.I. (1992). When depression breeds contempt: Reassurance seeking, self-esteem, and rejection of depressed college students by their roommates. *Journal of Abnormal Psychology*, 101(1), 165–173.

Joiner, T.E., Heatherton, T.F., Rudd, M.D. & Schmidt, N.B. (1997). Perfectionism, perceived weight status, and bulimic symptoms: Two studies testing a diathesis-stress model. *Journal of Abnormal Psychology*, 106(1), 145–153.

Joiner, T.E. & Metalsky, G.I. (1995). A prospective test of an integrative interpersonal theory of depression: A naturalistic study of college roommates. *Journal of Personality and Social Psychology*, 69(4), 778–788.

Joiner, T.E., Metalsky, G.I., Katz, J. et al. (1999). Depression and excessive reassurance-seeking. *Psychological Inquiry*, 10(4), 269–278.

Jones, H.E. (2006). Drug addiction during pregnancy: Advances in maternal treatment and understanding child outcomes. *Current Directions in Psychological Science*, 15(3), 126–130.

Joober, R., Boksa, P., Benkelfat, C. & Rouleau, G. (2002). Genetics of schizophrenia: From animal models to clinical studies. *Journal of Psychiatry and Neuroscience*, 27(5), 336–347.

Jorde, L.B., Mason-Brothers, A., Waldmann, R., Ritvo, E.R. et al. (1990). The UCLA–University of Utah epidemiologic survey of autism: Genealogical analysis of familial aggregation. *American Journal of Medical Genetics*, 36(1), 85–88.

Jovanovski, D., Erb, S. & Zakzanis, K.K. (2005). Neurocognitive deficits in cocaine users: A quantitative review of the evidence. *Journal of Clinical and Experimental Neuropsychology*, 27, 189–204.

Juengling, F.D., Schmahl, C., Hesslinger, B., Ebert, D. et al. (2003). Positron emission tomography in female patients with borderline personality disorder. *Journal of Psychiatric Research*, 37(2), 109–115.

Jurado, C. & Sachs, H. (2003). Proficiency test for the analysis of hair for drugs of abuse, organized by the Society of Hair Testing. *Forensic Science International*, 133(1–2), 175–178.

Just, N. & Alloy, L.B. (1997). The response styles theory of depression: Tests and an extension of the theory. *Journal of Abnormal Psychology*, 106(2), 221–229.

Kabat-Zinn, J. (1990). *Full catastrophe living: The program of the Stress Reduction Clinic at the University of Massachusetts Medical Center*. New York: Delta.

Kaduson, H.G. & Schaefer, C. (Eds.) (1997). *101 favorite play therapy techniques*. Northville NJ: Jason Aronson.

Kaduson, H.G. & Schaefer, C. (Eds.) (2001). *101 more favorite play therapy techniques*. Northville NJ: Jason Aronson.

Kafka, M.P. (1997). Hypersexual desire in males: An operational definition and clinical implications for males with paraphilias and paraphilia-related disorders. *Archives of Sexual Behavior*, 26, 505–526.

Kafka, M.P. (2003). Sex offending and sexual appetite: The clinical and theoretical relevance of hypersexual desire. *International Journal of Offender Therapy and Comparative Criminology*, 47, 439–451.

Kafka, M.P. & Hennen, J. (2000). Psychostimulant augmentation during treatment with selective serotonin reuptake inhibitors in men with paraphilias and paraphilia-related disorders: A case series. *Journal of Clinical Psychiatry*, 61(9), 664–670.

Kagan, J., Reznick, J.S., Clarke, C., Snidman, N. et al. (1984). Behavioral inhibition to the unfamiliar. *Child Development*, 55, 2212–2225.

Kaji, L. (1960). *Alcoholism in twins: Studies on the etiology and sequels of abuse of alcohol*. Stockholm: Almquist & Wiksell.

Kalant, H. (2004). Adverse effects of cannabis on health: An update of the literature since 1996. *Progress in Neuro-Psychopharmacology and Biological Psychiatry*, 28, 849–863.

Kallman, F. (1954). Genetic principles in manic-depressive psychosis. In P.H. Hoch & J. Zubin (Eds.), *Depression* (pp. 1–24). New York: Grune & Stratton.

Kaltenthaler, E., Parry, G. & Beverley, C. (2004). Computerized cognitive behaviour therapy: A systematic review. *Behavioural and Cognitive Psychotherapy*, 32, 31–55.

Kamphaus, R.W. & Frick, P.J. (2002). *Clinical assessment of child and adolescent personality and behaviour* (2nd ed.). Boston: Allyn & Bacon.

Kandel, D.B., Murphy, D. & Karus, D. (1985). *National Institute of Drug Abuse Research Monograph Series 61*. Washington, DC: NIDA.

Kaney, S. & Bentall, R.P. (1989). Persecutory delusions and attributional style. *British Journal of Medical Psychology*, 62, 191–198.

Kantak, K.M., Udo, T., Ugalde, F., Luzzo, C. et al. (2005). Influence of cocaine self-administration on learning related to prefrontal cortex or hippocampus functioning in rats. *Psychopharmacology*, 181(2), 227–236.

Kaplan, B.J., Crawford, S.G., Fisher, G.C. & Dewey, D.M. (1998). Family dysfunction is more strongly associated with ADHD than with general school problems. *Journal of Attention Disorders*, 2(4), 209–216.

Kaplan, H.I. & Sadock, B.J. (1991). *Synopsis of psychiatry: Behavioral sciences, clinical psychiatry*. Baltimore: Williams & Wilkins.

Kaplan, H.S. (1974). *The new sex therapy: Active treatment of sexual dysfunctions*. New York: Brunner/Mazel.

Kaplan, H.S. (1979). *Disorder of sexual desire*. New York: Brunner/Mazel.

Kaplan, M.S. & Kreuger, R.B. (1997). Voyeurism: Psychopathology and theory. In D.R. Laws & W. O'Donohue (Eds.), *Sexual deviance*. New York: Guilford Press.

Kaplan, R. & Manicavasagar, V. (2001). Is there a false memory syndrome? A review of three cases. *Comprehensive Psychiatry*, 42, 342–348.

Kapner, D.A. (2003). *Fact sheet: Recreational use of Ritalin on college campuses*. Washington, DC: US Department of Education, Higher Education Center for Alcohol and Other Drug Prevention.

Kapur, N., Abbott, P., Lowman, A. & Will, R.G. (2003). The neuropsychological profile associated with variant Creutzfeldt-Jakob disease. *Brain*, 126, 2693–2702.

Kapur, N., Glisky, E.L. & Wilson, B.A. (2004). Technological memory aids for people with memory deficits. *Neuropsychological Rehabilitation*, 14, 41–60.

Kapur, S. & Remington, G. (1996). Serotonin–dopamine interaction and its relevance to schizophrenia. *American Journal of Psychiatry*, 153(4), 466–476.

Karekla, M., Forsyth, J.P. & Kelly, M.M. (2004). Emotional avoidance and panicogenic responding to a biological challenge procedure. *Behavior Therapy*, 35, 725–746.

Karoumi, B., Saoud, M., d'Amato, T., Rosenfeld, F. et al. (2001). Poor performance in smooth pursuit and antisaccadic eye-movement tasks in healthy siblings of patients with schizophrenia. *Psychiatry Research*, 101(3), 209–219.

Karrass, J., Walden, T.A., Conture, E.G., Graham, C.G. et al. (2006). Relation of emotional reactivity and regulation to childhood stuttering. *Journal of Communication Disorders*, 39(6), 402–423.

Kaschel, R., Della Sala, S., Cantagallo, A., Fahlbock, A. et al. (2002). Imagery mnemonics for the rehabilitation of memory: A randomized group controlled trial. *Neuropsychological Rehabilitation*, 12(2), 127–153.

Kassel, J.D. (2000). Smoking and stress: Correlation, causation, and context. *American Psychologist*, 55(10), 1155–1156.

Kassett, J.A., Gershon, E.S., Maxwell, M.E. et al. (1989). Psychiatric disorders in first-degree relatives of probands with bulimia nervosa. *American Journal of Psychiatry*, 146, 1468–1471.

Kaufman, K.R. & Kaufman, N.D. (2006). And then the dog died. *Death Studies*, 30, 61–76.

Kauhanen, M.L., Korpelainen, J.T., Hiltunen, P., Brusin, E. et al. (1999). Poststroke depression correlates with cognitive impairment and neurological deficits. *Stroke*, 30(9), 1875–1880.

Kavanagh, D.J. (1992). Recent developments in expressed emotion and schizophrenia. *British Journal of Psychiatry*, 160, 601–620.

Kazdin, A.E. (1978). Artifact, bias, and complexity of assessment: The ABCs of reliability. *Journal of Applied Behavior Analysis*, 10, 141–150.

Kazdin, A.E. (2001). *Behavior modification in applied settings* (6th ed.). Stanford, CT: Wadsworth.

Kazdin, A.E. & Weisz, J.R. (Eds.) (2003). *Evidence-based psychotherapies for children and adolescents*. New York: Guilford Press.

Keane, T.M., Fairbank, J.A., Caddell, J.M. & Zimering, R.T. (1989). Implosive (flooding) therapy reduces symptoms of PTSD in Vietnam combat veterans. *Behavior Therapy*, 20(2), 245–260.

Keane, T.M., Gerardi, R.J., Quinn, S.J. & Litz, B.T. (1992). Behavioral treatment of post-traumatic stress disorder. In S.M. Turner, K.S. Calhoun

& H.E. Adams (Eds.), *Handbook of clinical behaviour therapy* (2nd ed.). New York: Wiley.

Keane, T.M., Zimering, R.T. & Caddell, J. (1985). A behavioural formulation of posttraumatic stress disorder in Vietnam veterans. *Behavior Therapist*, 8, 9–12.

Keefe, R.S.E., Arnold, M.C., Bayen, U.J., McEvoy, J.P. & Wilson, W.H. (2002). Source-monitoring deficits for self-generated stimuli in schizophrenia: Multinomial modeling of data from three sources. *Schizophrenia Research*, 57(1), 51–67.

Keel, P.K. & Klump, K.L. (2003). Are eating disorders culture-bound syndromes? Implications for conceptualizing their etiology. *Psychological Bulletin*, 129, 747–769.

Keel, P.K. & Mitchell, J.E. (1997). Outcome in bulimia nervosa. *American Journal of Psychiatry*, 154(3), 313–321.

Keen, D. & Ward, S. (2004). Autistic spectrum disorder: A child population profile. *Autism*, 8, 39–48.

Kellner, R. (1990). Somatization. *Journal of Nervous and Mental Disease*, 178, 150–160.

Kelly, C.M., Jorm, A.F. & Rodgers, B. (2006). Adolescents' responses to peers with depression or conduct disorder. *Australian and New Zealand Journal of Psychiatry*, 40, 63–66.

Kelsoe, J.R. (2003). Arguments for the genetic basis of the bipolar spectrum. *Journal of Affective Disorders*, 73, 183–197.

Kenardy, J. & Taylor, C.B. (1999). Expected versus unexpected panic attacks: A naturalistic prospective study. *Journal of Anxiety Disorders*, 13(4), 435–445.

Kendall, P.C., Kane, M., Howard, B. & Siqueland, L. (1990). *Cognitive-behavioral therapy for anxious children: Treatment manual*. Ardmore, PA: Workbook Publishing.

Kendall, P.C. & Southam-Gerow, M.A. (1996). Long-term follow-up of a cognitive-behavioral therapy for anxiety-disordered youth. *Journal of Consulting and Clinical Psychology*, 64, 724–730.

Kendall-Tuckett, K.A., Williams, L.M. & Finkelhor, D. (1993). Impact of sexual abuse on children: A review and synthesis of recent empirical studies. *Psychological Bulletin*, 113(1), 164–180.

Kendler, K.S., Gallagher, T.J., Abelson, J.M. & Kessler, R.C. (1996). Lifetime prevalence, demographic risk factors, and diagnostic validity of nonaffective psychosis as assessed in a US community sample: The National Comorbidity Survey. *Archives of General Psychiatry*, 53(11), 1022–1031.

Kendler, K.S., Maclean, C., Neale, M., Kessler, R., Heath, A. & Eaves, L. (1991). The genetic epidemiology of bulimia nervosa. *American Journal of Psychiatry*, 148(12), 1627–1637.

Kendler, K.S., Myers, J.M., O'Neill, F.A., Martin, R. et al. (2000). Clinical features of schizophrenia and linkage to chromosomes 5q, 6p, 8p, and 10p in the Irish study of high-density schizophrenia families. *American Journal of Psychiatry*, 157(3), 402–408.

Kendler, K.S., Myers, J., Prescott, C.A. & Neale, M.C. (2001). The genetic epidemiology of irrational fears and phobias in men. *Archives of General Psychiatry*, 58(3), 257–265.

Kendler, K.S., Pedersen, N., Johnson, L., Neale, M.C. & Mathe, A.A. (1993). A pilot Swedish twin study of affective illness, including hospital-ascertained and population-ascertained subsamples. *Archives of General Psychiatry*, 50(9), 699–706.

Kendler, K.S. & Prescott, C.A. (1998). Cannabis use, abuse, and dependence in a population-based sample of female twins. *American Journal of Psychiatry*, 155(8), 1016–1022.

Kendler, K.S., Thornton, L.M. & Gardner, C.O. (2000). Stressful life events and previous episodes in the etiology of major depression in women: An evaluation of the 'kindling' hypothesis. *American Journal of Psychiatry*, 157(8), 1243–1251.

Kendler, K.S., Walters, E.E., Neale, M.C., Kessler, R.C., Heath, A.C. & Eaves, L.J. (1995). The structure of the genetic and environmental risk factors for six major psychiatric disorders in women: Phobia, generalized anxiety disorder, panic disorder, bulimia, major depression, and alcoholism. *Archives of General Psychiatry*, 52(5), 374–383.

Kennedy, B.P., Isaac, N.E. & Graham, J.D. (1996). The role of heavy drinking in the risk of traffic fatalities. *Risk Analysis*, 16(4), 565–569.

Kennedy, N., McDonough, M., Kelly, B. & Berrios, G.E. (2002). Erotomania revisited: Clinical course and treatment. *Comprehensive Psychiatry*, 43(1), 1–6.

Kent, D.A., Tomasson, K. & Coryell, W. (1995). Course and outcome of conversion and somatization disorders: A 4-year follow-up. *Psychosomatics*, 36(2), 138–144.

Kent, G. (1997). Dental phobia. In G.C.L. Davey (Ed.), *Phobias: A handbook of theory, research and treatment*. Chichester: Wiley.

Kernberg, O.F. (1985). *Borderline conditions and pathological narcissism*. Northvale, NJ: Jason Aronson.

Kessler, R.C. (2002). Epidemiology of depression. In I.H. Gotlib & C.L. Hammen (Eds.), *Handbook of depression*. New York: Guilford Press.

Kessler, R.C., Adler, L., Barkley, R., Biederman, J. et al. (2006). The prevalence and correlates of adult ADHD in the United States: Results from the National Comorbidity Survey Replication. *American Journal of Psychiatry*, 163, 716–723.

Kessler, R.C., Avenevoli, S. & Merikangas, K.R. (2001). Mood disorders in children and adolescents: An epidemiologic perspective. *Biological Psychiatry*, 49(12), 1002–1014.

Kessler, R.C., Berglund, P., Demler, O., Jin, R., Merikangas, K.R. & Walters, E.E. (2005). Lifetime prevalence and age-of-onset distributions of DSM-IV disorders in the national comorbidity survey replication. *Archives of General Psychiatry*, 62(7), 768.

Kessler, R.C., Borges, G. & Walters, E.E. (1999). Prevalence of and risk factors for lifetime suicide attempts in the national comorbidity survey. *Archives of General Psychiatry*, 56(7), 617–626.

Kessler, R.C., Crum, R.M., Warner, L.A., Nelson, C.B. et al. (1997). Lifetime co-occurrence of DSM-III-R alcohol abuse and dependence with other psychiatric disorders in the national comorbidity survey. *Archives of General Psychiatry*, 54(4), 313–321.

Kessler, R.C., Keller, M.B. & Wittchen, H.U. (2001). The epidemiology of generalized anxiety disorder. *Psychiatric Clinics of North America*, 24, 19.

Kessler, R.C., McGonagle, K.A., Zhao, S., Nelson, C.B. et al. (1994). Lifetime and 12-month prevalence of DSM-III psychiatric disorders in the United States: Results from the national comorbidity study. *Archives of General Psychiatry*, 51, 8–19.

Kessler, R.C., Nelson, C.B., McGonagle, K.A., Liu, J., Schwartz, M. & Blazer, D.G. (1996). Comorbidity of DSM-III-R major depressive disorder in the general population: Results from the US national comorbidity survey. *Journal of Psychiatry*, 168, 17–30.

Kessler, R.C., Rubinow, D.R., Holmes, C., Abelson, J.M. & Zhao, S. (1997). The epidemiology of DSM-III-R bipolar disorder in a general population survey. *Psychological Medicine*, 27, 1079–1089.

Kessler, R.C. & Zhao, S. (1999). The prevalence of mental illness. In A.V. Horowitz & T.L. Scheid (Eds.), *A handbook for the study of mental health: Social contexts, theories, and systems*. Cambridge: Cambridge University Press.

Kety, S.S. (1988). Schizophrenic illness in the families of schizophrenic adoptees: Findings from the Danish national sample. *Schizophrenia Bulletin*, 14(2), 217–222.

Kety, S.S., Wender, P.H., Jacobsen, B., Ingraham, L.J. et al. (1994). Mental illness in the biological and adoptive relatives of schizophrenic adoptees: Replication of the Copenhagen study in the rest of Denmark. *Archives of General Psychiatry*, 51(6), 442–455.

Khan, R.S., Khoury, J., Nichols, W.C. & Lanphear, B.P. (2003). Role of dopamine transporter genotype and maternal prenatal smoking in childhood hyperactive-impulsive, inattentive, and oppositional behaviors. *Journal of Pediatrics*, 143, 104–110.

Khantzian, E.J. (1985). The self-medication hypothesis of addictive disorders: Focus on heroin and cocaine dependence. *American Journal of Psychiatry*, 142(11), 1259–1264.

Kidorf, M., King, V.L., Neufeld, K., Stoller, K.B. et al. (2005). Involving significant others in the care of opioid-dependent patients receiving methadone. *Journal of Substance Abuse Treatment*, 29(1), 19–27.

Kiefer, F. & Mann, K. (2005). New achievements and pharmacotherapeutic approaches in the treatment of alcohol dependence. *European Journal of Pharmacology, 526,* 163–171.

Kihlstrom, J.F. (2001). *Dissociative disorders.* New York: Kluwer Academic/Plenum.

Kilsby, M. & Beyer, S. (1996). Engagement and interaction: A comparison between supported employment and day service provision. *Journal of Intellectual Disability Research, 40,* 348–357.

Kim, M., Cogan, R., Carter, S. & Porcerelli, J.H. (2005). Defense mechanisms and self-reported violence towards strangers. *Bulletin off the Menninger Clinic, 69,* 305–312.

Kim, S., Larson, S.A. & Lakin, K.C. (2001). Behavioural outcomes of deinstitutionalization for people with intellectual disability: A review of US studies conducted between 1980 and 1999. *Journal of Intellectual and Developmental Disability, 26*(1), 35–50.

Kim, S.W., Grant, J.E., Eckert, E.D., Faris, P.L. & Hartman, B.K. (2006). Pathological gambling and mood disorders: Clinical associations and treatment implications. *Journal of Affective Disorders, 92*(1), 109–116.

Kimble, M.O., Kaufman, M.L., Leonard, L.L., Nestor, P.G. et al. (2002). Sentence completion test in combat veterans with and without PTSD: Preliminary findings. *Psychiatry Research, 113,* 303–307.

King, C.A. (1997). Suicidal behaviour in adolescence. In R.W. Maris, M.M. Silverman & S.S. Canetto (Eds.), *Review of suicidology.* New York: Guilford Press.

King, D.W., King, L.A., Foy, D.W. & Gudanowski, D.M. (1996). Prewar factors in combat-related posttraumatic stress disorder: Structural equation modeling with a national sample of female and male Vietnam veterans. *Journal of Consulting and Clinical Psychology, 64*(3), 520–531.

King, M., Nazroo, J., Weich, S., McKenzie, K., Bhui, K. et al. (2005). Psychotic symptoms in the general population of England: A comparison of ethnic groups (The EMPIRIC study). *Social Psychiatry and Psychiatric Epidemiology, 40,* 375–381.

King, N.J., Muris, P., Ollendick, T.H. & Gullone, E. (2005). Childhood fears and phobias: Advances in assessment and treatment. *Behaviour Change, 22,* 199–211.

Kingdon, D.G. & Turkington, D. (2004). *Cognitive therapy of schizophrenia.* New York: Guilford Press.

Kinnunen, T., Doherty, K., Militello, F.S. & Garvey, A.J. (1996). Depression and smoking cessation: Characteristics of depressed smokers and effects of nicotine replacement. *Journal of Consulting and Clinical Psychology, 64*(4), 791–798.

Kinsella, P. (2007). *Cognitive behavioural therapy for chronic fatigue syndrome.* London: Routledge.

Kinsey, A.C., Pomeroy, W.B., Martin, C.E. & Gebhard, P.H. (1953). *Sexual behaviour in the human female.* Philadelphia: Saunders.

Klackenberg, G. (1982). Sleep behaviour studied longitudinally: Data from 4–16 years on duration, night-awakening and bed-sharing. *Acta Pediatrica Scandinavica, 71,* 501–506.

Kleber, H.D. (1981). Detoxification from narcotics. In J.H. Lowinson & P. Ruiz (Eds.), *Substance abuse: Clinical problems and perspectives.* Baltimore: Williams & Wilkins.

Kleber, H.D. (2005). Future advances in addiction treatment. *Clinical Neuroscience Research, 5,* 201–205.

Klein, D.F. (1993). False suffocation alarms, spontaneous panics, and related conditions: An integrative hypothesis. *Archives of General Psychiatry, 50,* 306–317.

Kleinhans, N., Akshoomoff, N. & Delis, D.C. (2005). Executive functions in autism and Asperger's disorder: Flexibility, fluency, and inhibition. *Developmental Neuropsychology, 27,* 379–401.

Kleinknecht, R.A., Kleinknecht, E.E. & Thorndike, R.M. (1997). The role of disgust and fear in blood and injection-related fainting symptoms: A structural equation model. *Behaviour Research and Therapy, 35,* 1075–1087.

Klinger, L.G. & Dawson, G. (1996). Autistic disorder. In E.J. Marsh & R.A. Barkley (Eds.), *Child psychopathology.* New York: Guilford Press.

Klonsky, E.D., Oltmanns, T.F., Turkheimer, E. & Fiedler, E.R. (2000). Recollections of conflict with parents and family support in the personality disorders. *Journal of Personality Disorders, 14*(4), 327–338.

Kluft, R.P. (1992). A specialist's perspective on multiple personality disorder. *Psychoanalytic Enquiry, 12,* 139–171.

Kluft, R.P. (1994). Treatment trajectories in multiple personality disorder. *Dissociation, 7,* 63–75.

Kluft, R.P. (1999). An overview of the psychotherapy of dissociative identity disorder. *American Journal of Psychotherapy, 53,* 289–319.

Kluft, R.P. (2000). The psychoanalytic psychotherapy of dissociative identity disorder in the context of trauma therapy. *Psychanalytic Inquiry, 20,* 259–286.

Kluft, R.P. (2001). Dissociative disorders. In H.S. Friedman (Ed.), *Special articles from the encyclopedia of mental health.* San Diego, CA: Academic Press.

Klump, K.L., Miller, K.B., Keel, P.K., McGue, M. & Iacono, W.G. (2001). Genetic and environmental influences on anorexia nervosa syndromes in a population-based twin sample. *Psychological Medicine, 31*(4), 737–740.

Knopp, F.H. (1976). *Instead of prisons.* Syracuse: Safer Society Press.

Kobayashi, R., Murata, T. & Yoshinaga, K. (1992). A follow-up study of 201 children with autism in Kyushu and Yamaguchi areas, Japan. *Journal of Autism and Developmental Disorders, 22*(3), 395–411.

Koch, E.I., Spates, C.R. & Himle, J.A. (2004). Comparison of behavioral and cognitive-behavioral one-session exposure treatments for small animal phobias. *Behaviour Research and Therapy, 42,* 1483–1504.

Koegel, R.L., Schreibman, L., Britten, K.R., Burkey, J.C. & O'Neill, R.E. (1982). A comparison of parent training to direct child treatment. In R.L. Koegel, A. Rincover & A.L. Egel (Eds.), *Educating and understanding autistic children.* San Diego, CA: College Hill.

Koenigsberg, H.W., Goodman, M., Reynolds, D., Mitropoulou, V. et al. (2001). Risperidone in the treatment of schizotypal personality disorder. *Biological Psychiatry, 49*(8), 119S–120S.

Koff, S.A. (1995). Why is desmopressin sometimes ineffective at curing bedwetting? *Scandinavian Journal of Urology and Nephrology, 173,* 103–108.

Kohut, H. & Wolf, E.S. (1978). Disorders of the self and their treatment: Outline. *International Journal of Psychoanalysis, 59,* 413–425.

Kokmen, E., Beard, C.M., Offord, K.P. & Kurland, L.T. (1989). Prevalence of medically diagnosed dementia in a defined United States population: Rochester, Minnesota, January 1, 1975. *Neurology, 39*(6), 773–776.

Kolb, B. (1989). Brain development, plasticity, and behaviour. *American Psychologist, 44,* 1203–1212.

Kolmen, B.K., Feldman, H.M., Handen, B.L. & Janosky, J.E. (1995). Naltrexone in young autistic children: A double-blind, placebo-controlled crossover study. *Journal of the American Academy of Child and Adolescent Psychiatry, 34*(2), 223–231.

Konrad, K., Gunther, T., Hanisch, C. & Herpertz-Dahlmann, B. (2004). Differential effects of methylphenidate on attentional functions in children with attention-deficit/hyperactivity disorder. *Journal of the American Academy of Child and Adolescent Psychiatry, 43*(2), 191–198.

Kopelman, M.D. (2002). Disorders of memory. *Brain, 125,* 2152–2190.

Kopelman, M.D., Green, R.E.A., Guinan, E.M., Lewis, P.D.R. & Stanhope, N. (1994). The case of the amnesic intelligence officer. *Psychological Medicine, 24*(4), 1037–1045.

Kopelowicz, A. & Liberman, R.P. (1995). Biobehavioral treatment and rehabilitation of schizophrenia. *Harvard Review of Psychiatry, 3*(2), 55–64.

Korchin, S.J. & Sands, S.H. (1983). Principles common to all psychotherapies. In C.E. Walker et al. (Eds.), *The handbook of clinical psychology.* Homewood, IL: Dow Jones-Irwin.

Korenman, S.G. (2004). Epidemiology of erectile dysfunction. *Endocrine, 23,* 87–91.

Kortegaard, L.S., Hoerder, K., Joergensen, J., Gillberg, C. & Kyvik, K.O. (2001). A preliminary population-based twin study of self-reported eating disorder. *Psychological Medicine, 31*(2), 361–365.

Korten, A.E., Jorm, A.F., Henderson, A.S., Broe, G.A. et al. (1993). Assessing the risk of Alzheimer's disease in 1st-degree relatives of Alzheimer's disease cases. *Psychological Medicine, 23*(4), 915–923.

Kosten, T.R. & Ziedonis, D.M. (1997). Substance abuse and schizophrenia: Editors' introduction. *Schizophrenia Bulletin, 23*(2), 181–186.

Koumimtsidis, C., Reynolds, M., Drummond, C., Davis, P., Sell, L. & Tarrier, N. (2007). *Cognitive-behavioural therapy in the treatment of addiction.* New York: Wiley.

Kouri, E.M. & Pope, H.G. (2000). Abstinence symptoms during withdrawal from chronic marijuana use. *Experimental and Clinical Psychopharmacology, 8*(4), 483–492.

Kozaric-Kovacic, D. & Borovecki, A. (2005). Prevalence of psychotic comorbidity in combat-related post-traumatic stress disorder. *Military Medicine, 170*(3), 223–226.

Kozlowska, K. (2005). Healing the disembodied mind: Contemporary models of conversion disorder. *Harvard Review of Psychiatry, 13*, 1–13.

Krain, A.L. & Castellanos, F.X. (2006). Brain development and ADHD. *Clinical Psychology Review, 26*, 433–444.

Kramer, R.A., Warner, V., Olfson, M., Ebanks, C.M., Chaput, F. & Weissman, M.M. (1998). General medical problems among the offspring of depressed parents: A 10-year follow-up. *Journal of the American Academy of Child and Adolescent Psychiatry, 37*, 602–611.

Krampe, H., Stawicki, S., Wagner, T., Bartels, C. et al. (2006). Follow-up of 180 alcoholic patients for up to 7 years after outpatient treatment: Impact of alcohol deterrents on outcome. *Alcoholism: Clinical and Experimental Research, 30*(1), 86–95.

Krapohi, D.J. (2002). The polygraph in personnel screening. In M. Kleiner (Ed.), *The handbook of polygraph testing.* San Diego, CA: Academic Press.

Krijn, M., Emmelkamp, P.M.G., Olafsson, R.P. & Biemond, R. (2004). Virtual reality exposure therapy of anxiety disorders: A review. *Clinical Psychology Review, 24*, 259–281.

Kring, A.M. & Neale, J.M. (1996). Do schizophrenic patients show a disjunctive relationship among expressive, experiential, and psychophysiological components of emotion? *Journal of Abnormal Psychology, 105*(2), 249–257.

Kringlen, E. (1970). Natural history of obsessional neurosis. *Seminars in Psychiatry, 2*(4), 403&.

Kroese, B.S., Dagnan, D. & Loumidis, K. (1997). *Cognitive-behaviour therapy for people with learning difficulties.* London: Routledge.

Krol, N., Morton, J. & De Bruyn, E. (2004). Theories of conduct disorder: A causal modelling analysis. *Journal of Child Psychology and Psychiatry, 45*, 727–742.

Krueger, R.F. & Piasecki, T.M. (2002). Toward a dimensional and psychometrically informed approach to conceptualizing psychopathology. *Behaviour Research and Therapy, 40*, 485–499.

Krueger, R.F., Watson, D. & Barlow, D.H. (2005). Introduction to the special section: Towards a dimensionally based taxonomy of psychopathology. *Journal of Abnormal Psychology, 114*, 491–493.

Kruger, S. & Kennedy, S.H. (2000). Psychopharmacotherapy of anorexia nervosa, bulimia nervosa and binge-eating disorder. *Journal of Psychiatry and Neuroscience, 25*, 497–508.

Krystal, J.H., Deutsch, D.N. & Charney, D.S. (1996). The biological basis of panic disorder. *Journal of Clinical Psychiatry, 57*, 23–33.

Kubicki, M., Westin, C.F., Maier, S.E., Frumin, M. et al. (2002). Uncinate fasciculus findings in schizophrenia: A magnetic resonance diffusion tensor imaging study. *American Journal of Psychiatry, 159*(5), 813–820.

Kuch, K. (1997). Accident phobia. In G.C.L. Davey (Ed.), *Phobias: A handbook of theory, research and treatment.* Chichester: Wiley.

Kuechenoff, J. (2002). Hysterie heute: eine Revision. *Forum Psychoanalysis: Zeitshr. Klin. Theor. Prax., 18*, 224–244.

Kumar, R. (2005). Wrongful diagnosis of child abuse. *Journal of the Royal Society of Medicine, 98*, 386.

Kupers, R.C., Fortin, A., Astrup, J., Gjedde, A. & Ptito, M. (2004). Recovery of anterograde amnesia in a case of craniopharyngioma. *Archives of Neurology, 61*(12), 1948–1952.

Kupfer, D.J. & Frank, E. (2001). The interaction of drug- and psychotherapy in the long-term treatment of depression. *Journal of Affective Disorders, 62*(1–2), 131–137.

Kurzthaler, I., Hummer, M., Miller, C., Sperner-Unterweger, B. et al. (1999). Effect of cannabis use on cognitive functions and driving ability. *Journal of Clinical Psychiatry, 60*(6), 395–399.

Kvale, S. (1996). *Interviews: An introduction to qualitative research interviewing.* Thousand Oaks, CA: Sage.

Kwon, P. & Laurenceau, J.P. (2002). A longitudinal study of the hopelessness theory of depression: Testing the diathesis-stress model within a differential reactivity and exposure framework. *Journal of Clinical Psychology, 58*, 1305–1321.

Kyrios, M. (2003). Exposure and response prevention for OCD. In R.G. Menzies & P. de Silva (Eds.), *Obsessive-compulsive disorder: Theory, research and treatment.* Chichester: Wiley.

Labbate, L.A., Cardena, E., Dimitreva, J., Roy, M. & Engel, C.C. (1998). Psychiatric syndromes in Persian Gulf War veterans: An association of handling dead bodies with somatoform disorders. *Psychotherapy and Psychosomatics, 67*(4–5), 275–279.

Lacey, J.H. (1993). Self-damaging and addictive behaviour in bulimia nervosa: A catchment area study. *British Journal of Psychiatry, 163*, 190–194.

Lacro, J.P., Dunn, L.B., Dolder, C.R., Leckband, S.G. & Jeste, D.V. (2002). Prevalence of and risk factors for medication nonadherence in patients with schizophrenia: A comprehensive review of recent literature. *Journal of Clinical Psychiatry, 63*(10), 892–909.

Ladouceur, R., Talbot, F. & Dugas, M.J. (1997). Behavioral expressions of intolerance of uncertainty in worry: Experimental findings. *Behavior Modification, 21*(3), 355–371.

Laguerre, M.S. (1981). Haitian Americans. In A. Harwood (Ed.), *Ethnicity and medical care.* Cambridge, MA: Harvard University Press.

Lahey, B.B., Loeber, R., Burke, J.D. & Applegate, B. (2005). Predicting future antisocial personality disorder in males from a clinical assessment in childhood. *Journal of Consulting and Clinical Psychology, 73*, 389–399.

Lahey, B.B., Loeber, R., Hart, E.L., Frick, P.J. et al. (1995). Four-year longitudinal study of conduct disorder in boys: Patterns and predictors of persistence. *Journal of Abnormal Psychology, 104*, 83–93.

Lahey, B.B., McBurnett, K. & Loeber, R. (2000). Are attention-deficit/hyperactivity disorder and oppositional defiant disorder developmental precursors to conduct disorder? In A.J. Sameroff & M. Lewis (Eds.), *Handbook of developmental psychopathology* (2nd ed., pp. 431–446). Dordrecht: Kluwer Academic.

Lahey, B.B., Miller, T.L., Gordon, R.A. & Riley, A.W. (1999). Developmental epidemiology of the disruptive behaviour disorders. In H.C. Quay & A. Hogan (Eds.), *Handbook of disruptive behaviour disorders.* New York: Plenum.

Laidlaw, K. (2001). An empirical review of cognitive therapy for late life depression: Does research evidence suggest adaptations are necessary for cognitive therapy with older adults? *Clinical Psychology and Psychotherapy, 8*, 1–14.

Laidlaw, K., Thompson, L.W., Siskin, L.D. & Gallagher-Thompson, D. (2003). *Cognitive behaviour therapy with older people.* Chichester: Wiley.

Lam, D.H., Hayward, P. & Bright, J.A. (1999). *Cognitive therapy for bipolar disorder.* Chichester: Wiley.

Lam, J.N. & Steketee, G.S. (2001). Reducing obsessions and compulsions through behaviour therapy. *Psychoanalytic Inquiry, 21*, 157–182.

Lam, K.S.L., Aman, M.G. & Arnold, L.E. (2006). Neurochemical correlates of autistic disorder: A review of the literature. *Research in Developmental Disabilities, 27*, 254–289.

Lam, R.W., Lee, S.K., Tam, E.M., Grewal, A. & Yatham, L.N. (2001). An open trial of light therapy for women with seasonal affective disorder and comorbid bulimia nervosa. *Journal of Clinical Psychiatry, 62*(3), 164–168.

Lamb, H.R. (1984). Deinstitutionalization and the homeless mentally ill. *Hospital and Community Psychiatry, 35*(9), 899–907.

Lambert, M.J., Shapiro, D.A. & Bergin, A.E. (1986). The effectiveness of psychotherapy. In S.L. Garfield & A.E. Bergin (Eds.), *Handbook of psychotherapy and behavior change* (3rd ed). New York: Wiley.

Lambert, S.F., Ialongo, N.S., Boyd, R.C. & Cooley, M.R. (2005). Risk factors for community violence exposure in adolescence. *American Journal of Community Psychology, 36,* 29–48.

Lampert, P.W. & Hardman, J.M. (1984). Morphological changes in brains of boxers. *Journal of the American Medical Association, 251,* 2676–2679.

Landerl, K., Bevan, A. & Butterworth, B. (2004). Developmental dyscalculia and basic numerical capacities: A study of 8–9-year-old students. *Cognition, 93*(2), 99–125.

Landreth, G.L. (2002). *Play therapy: The art of the relationship.* New York: Brunner-Routledge.

Lane, S.D., Cherek, D.R., Pietras, C.J. & Steinberg, J.L. (2005). Performance of heavy marijuana-smoking adolescents on a laboratory measure of motivation. *Addictive Behaviors, 30*(4), 815–828.

Lang, A.J. (2004). Testing generalized anxiety disorder with cognitive-behavioral therapy. *Journal of Clinical Psychiatry, 65,* 14–19.

Lang, A.R., Goeckner, D.J., Adessor, V.J. & Marlatt, G.A. (1975). Effects of alcohol on aggression in male social drinkers. *Journal of Abnormal Psychology, 84,* 508–518.

Langstrom, N. & Hanson, R.K. (2006). High rates of sexual behavior in the general population: Correlates and predictors. *Archives of Sexual Behavior, 35,* 37–52.

Langstrom, N. & Zucker, K.J. (2005). Transvestic fetishism in the general population. *Journal of Sex and Marital Therapy, 31,* 87–95.

Lanyon, R.I. (1986). Theory and treatment in child molestation. *Journal of Consulting and Clinical Psychology, 54,* 176–182.

Lara, M.E. & Klein, D.N. (1999). Psychosocial processes underlying the maintenance and persistence of depression: Implications for understanding chronic depression. *Clinical Psychology Review, 19*(5), 553–570.

Laruelle, M. & Abi-Dargham, P. (1999). Dopamine as the wind of the psychotic fire: New evidence from brain imaging studies. *Journal of Psychopharmacology, 13*(4), 358–371.

Lask, B. & Bryant-Waugh, R. (Eds.) (2000). *Anorexia nervosa and related eating disorders in childhood and adolescence* (2nd ed.). Hove: Psychology Press.

Latimer, P.R. (1981). Irritable bowel syndrome: A behavioral model. *Behaviour Research and Therapy, 19*(6), 475–483.

Lau, A.S., Valeri, S.M., McCarty, C.A. & Weisz, J.R. (2006). Abusive parents' reports of child behaviour problems: Relationship to observed parent–child interactions. *Child Abuse and Neglect, 30,* 639–655.

Lau, J.Y.F., Eley, T.C. & Stevenson, J. (2006). Examining the state–trait anxiety relationship: A behavioural genetic approach. *Journal of Abnormal Child Psychology, 34,* 19–27.

Lauber, C., Falcato, L., Nordt, C. & Rossler, W. (2003). Lay beliefs about causes of depression. *Acta Psychiatrica Scandinavica, 108,* 96–99.

Laumann, E.O., Gagnon, J.H., Michael, R.T. & Michael, S. (1994). *The social organization of sexuality: Sexual practices in the United States.* Chicago: University of Chicago Press.

Laumann, E.O., Paik, A. & Rosen, R.C. (1999). Lecture 6: The epidemiology of erectile dysfunction: Results from the National Health and Social Life Survey. *International Journal of Impotence Research, 11,* S60–S64.

Lautch, H. (1971). Dental phobia. *British Journal of Psychiatry, 119,* 151–158.

Lauterbach, E.C. (2004). The neuropsychiatry of Parkinson's disease and related disorders. *Psychiatric Clinics of North America, 27,* 801.

Lavender, A. (1996). *A brief history of the development of clinical psychology in the context of developments in the welfare state in general and the NHS in particular.* Unpublished manuscript.

Lavi-Avnon, Y., Yadid, G., Overstreet, D.H. & Weller, A. (2005). Abnormal patterns of maternal behaviour in a genetic animal model of depression. *Physiology and Behavior, 84,* 607–615.

Law, J., Garrett, Z. & Nye, C. (2004). The efficacy of treatment for children with developmental speech and language delay/disorder: A meta-analysis. *Journal of Speech, Language and Hearing Research, 47,* 924–943.

Laws, D.R. & Marshall, W.L. (2003). Masturbatory reconditioning with sexual deviates: An evaluative review. *Advances in Behaviour Research and Therapy, 13*(1), 13–25.

Laws, D.R. & O'Donohue, W.T. (Eds.) (1997). *Sexual deviance: Theory assessment and treatment.* New York: Guilford Press.

Lawson, J., Banerjee, R. & Field, A.P. (2007). The effects of verbal information on children's fear beliefs about social situations. *Behaviour Research and Therapy, 45*(1), 21–37.

Layard, Lord (2007). *The depression report: A new deal for depression and anxiety disorders.* London: Centre for Economic Performances Mental Health Policy Group.

Leach, L.S. & Christensen, H. (2006). A systematic review of telephone-based interventions for mental disorders. *Journal of Telemedicine and Telecare, 12,* 122–129.

Leadbeater, B.J., Bishop, S.J. & Raver, C.C. (1996). Quality of mother–toddler interactions, maternal depressive symptoms, and behavior problems in preschoolers of adolescent mothers. *Developmental Psychology, 32*(2), 280–288.

Lecendreux, M., Bassetti, C., Dauvilliers, Y., Mayer, G., Neidhart, E. & Tafti, M. (2003). HLA and genetic susceptibility to sleepwalking. *Molecular Psychiatry, 8*(1), 114–117.

Leckman, J.F. (1993). Tourette's syndrome. In E. Hollander (Ed.), *Obsessive-compulsive related disorders.* Washington, DC: American Psychiatric Press.

Leckman, J.F., Grice, D.E., Barr, L.C., de Vries, A.L.C. et al. (1995). Tic-related vs. non-tic-related obsessive-compulsive disorder. *Anxiety, 1,* 208–215.

Lee, D.A., Randall, F., Beattie, G. & Bentall, R.P. (2004). Delusional discourse: An investigation comparing the spontaneous causal attributions of paranoid and non-paranoid individuals. *Psychology and Psychotherapy: Theory Research and Practice, 77,* 525–540.

Leentjens, A.F.G. (2004). Depression in Parkinson's disease: Conceptual issues and clinical challenges. *Journal of Geriatric Psychiatry and Neurology, 17,* 120–126.

Leentjens, A.F.G., van den Akker, M., Metsemakers, J.F.M., Lousberg, R. & Verhey, F.R.J. (2003). Higher incidence of depression preceding the onset of Parkinson's disease: A register study. *Movement Disorders, 18*(4), 414–418.

Leff, J., Vearnals, S., Brewin, C.R., Wolff, G. et al. (2000). The London depression intervention trial: Randomized controlled trial of antidepressants vs. couple therapy in the treatment and maintenance of people with depression living with a partner: Clinical outcome and costs. *British Journal of Psychiatry, 177,* 95–100.

Leichsenring, F. (2001). Comparative effects of short-term psychodynamic psychotherapy and cognitive-behavioral therapy in depression. A meta-analytic approach. *Clinical Psychology Review, 21,* 401–419.

Leichsenring, F. (2005). Are psychodynamic and psychoanalytic therapies effective? A review of empirical data. *International Journal of Psychoanalysis, 86,* 841–868.

Leichsenring, F. & Leibing, E. (2003). The effectiveness of psychodynamic therapy and cognitive behaviour therapy in the treatment of personality disorders: A meta-analysis. *American Journal of Psychiatry, 160,* 1223–1232.

Lejuez, C.W., Hopko, D.R., LePage, J.P., Hopko, S.D. & McNeil, D.W. (2001). A brief behavioral activation treatment for depression. *Cognitive and Behavioral Practice, 8*(2), 164–175.

Lemere, F. & Voegtlin, W.L. (1950). An evaluation of aversive treatment of alcoholism. *Quarterly Journal of the Study of Alcoholism, 11,* 199–204.

Lenox, R.H. & Hahn, C.G. (2000). Overview of the mechanism of action of lithium in the brain: Fifty-year update *Journal of Clinical Psychiatry, 61,* 5–15.

Leon, A.C., Friedman, R.A., Sweeney, J.A. et al. (1990). Statistical issues in the identification of risk factors for suicidal behavior: The application of survival analysis. *Psychiatry Research, 31*(1), 99–108.

Leon, A.C., Keller, M.B., Warshaw, M.G., Mueller, T.I. et al. (1999). Prospective study of fluoxetine treatment and suicidal behavior in affectively ill subjects. *American Journal of Psychiatry, 156*(2), 195–201.

Leon, G.R., Fulkerson, J.A., Perry, C.L. & Early-Zald, M.B. (1995). Prospective analysis of personality and behavioral vulnerabilities and gender influences in the later development of disordered eating. *Journal of Abnormal Psychology, 104*(1), 140–149.

Leonard, H.L., Lenane, M.C., Swedo, S.E., Rettew, D. et al. (1992). Tics and Tourette's disorder: A 2- to 7-year follow-up of 54 obsessive-compulsive children. *American Journal of Psychiatry, 149,* 1244–1251.

Lepine, J.P. (2002). The epidemiology of anxiety disorders: Prevalence and societal costs. *Journal of Clinical Psychiatry, 63,* 4–8.

Leri, F. & Burns, L.H. (2005). Ultra-low-dose naltrexone reduces the rewarding potency of oxycodone and relapse vulnerability in rats. *Pharmacology Biochemistry and Behavior, 82*(2), 252–262.

Lerner, R.M. (2002). *Adolescence: Development, diversity, context, and application.* Upper Saddle River, NJ: Pearson Education.

Lester, D. (1994). Access to gambling opportunities and compulsive gambling. *International Journal of the Addictions, 29*(12), 1611–1616.

Lester, D. (1998). Differences in content of suicide notes by age and method. *Perception and Motor Skills, 87,* 530.

Leucht, S., Barnes, T.R.E., Kissling, W., Engel, R.R., Correll, C. & Kane, J.M. (2003). Relapse prevention in schizophrenia with new-generation antipsychotics: A systematic review and exploratory meta-analysis of randomized controlled trials. *American Journal of Psychiatry, 160,* 1209–1222.

Levenston, G.K., Patrick, C.J., Bradley, M.M. & Lang, P.J. (2000). The psychopath as observer: Emotion and attention in picture processing. *Journal of Abnormal Psychology, 109*(3), 373–385.

Levesque, R.J.R. (1996). Regulating the private relations of adults with mental disabilities: Old laws, new politics, hollow hopes. *Behaviour Science and Law, 14,* 83–106.

Levin, H.S., McCauley, S.R., Josic, C.P., Boake, C. et al. (2005). Predicting depression following mild traumatic brain injury. *Archives of General Psychiatry, 62*(5), 523–528.

Levine, B., Robertson, I.H., Clare, L., Carter, G. et al. (2000). Rehabilitation of executive functioning: An experimental-clinical validation of Goal Management Training. *Journal of the International Neuropsychological Society, 6*(3), 299–312.

Levine, M.P., Smolak, L., Moodey, A.F., Shuman, M.D. & Hessen, L.D. (1994). Normative developmental challenges and dieting and eating disturbances in middle school girls. *International Journal of Eating Disorders, 15*(1), 11–20.

Levinson, D.F., Lewis, C.M. & Wise, L.H. (2002). Meta-analysis of genome scans for schizophrenia. *American Journal of Medical Genetics, 114*(7), SL2.

Levitt, J.J., McCarley, R.W., Nestor, P.G., Petrescu, C. et al. (1999). Quantitative volumetric MRI study of the cerebellum and vermis in schizophrenia: Clinical and cognitive correlates. *American Journal of Psychiatry, 156*(7), 1105–1107.

Levy, D.L. & Holzman, P.S. (1997). Eye tracking dysfunction and schizophrenia: An overview with special reference to the genetics of schizophrenia. *International Review of Psychiatry, 9*(4), 365–371.

Lewinsohn, P.M. (1974). Clinical and theoretical aspects of depression. In K.S. Calhoun, H.E. Adams & K.M. Mitchell (Eds.), *Innovative treatment methods of psychopathology.* New York: Wiley.

Lewinsohn, P.M., Hops, H., Roberts, R.E., Seeley, J.R. & Andrews, J.A. (1993). Adolescent psychopathology: I. Prevalence and incidence of depression and other DSM-II-R disorders in high school students. *Journal of Abnormal Psychology, 102,* 133–144.

Lewinsohn, P.M., Roberts, R.E., Seeley, J.R., Rohde, P. et al. (1994). Adolescent psychopathology: II. Psychosocial risk factors for depression. *Journal of Abnormal Psychology, 103,* 302–315.

Lewinsohn, P.M., Rohde, P. & Seeley, J.R. (1995). Adolescent psychopathology: III. The clinical consequences of comorbidity. *Journal of the American Academy of Child and Adolescent Psychiatry, 34,* 510–519.

Lewinsohn, P.M., Rohde, P. & Seeley, J.R. (1998). Major depressive disorder in older adolescents: Prevalence, risk factors, and clinical implications. *Clinical Psychology Review, 18,* 765–794.

Lewinsohn, P.M., Rohde, P., Seeley, J.R. & Baldwin, C.L. (2001). Gender differences in suicide attempts from adolescence to young adulthood. *Journal of the American Academy of Child and Adolescent Psychiatry, 40*(4), 427–434.

Lewinsohn, P.M., Rohde, P., Seeley, J.R., Klein, D.N. & Gotlib, L.H. (2000). Natural course of adolescent major depressive disorder in a community sample: Predictors of recurrence in young adults. *American Journal of Psychiatry, 157*(10), 1584–1591.

Lewinsohn, P.M. & Shaffer, M. (1971). Use of home observations as integral part of treatment of depression: Preliminary report and case studies. *Journal of Consulting and Clinical Psychology, 37*(1), 87&.

Lewinsohn, P.M. & Shaw, D.A. (1969). Feedback about interpersonal behavior as an agent of behavior change: A case study in treatment of depression. *Psychotherapy and Psychosomatics, 17*(2), 82&.

Lewinsohn, P.M., Sullivan, J.M. & Grosscup, S.J. (1980). Changing reinforcing events: An approach to the treatment of depression. *Psychotherapy: Theory Research and Practice, 17*(3), 322–334.

Lewinsohn, P.M., Sullivan, J.M. & Grosscup, S.J. (1982). Behavioral therapy: Clinical applications. In A.T. Rush (Ed.), *Short-term psychotherapy for the depressed patient.* New York: Guilford Press.

Lewinsohn, P.M., Youngren, M.A. & Grosscup, S.J. (1979). Reinforcement and depression. In R.A. Depu (Ed.), *The psychology of the depressive disorders.* New York: Academic Press.

Lewis, D.O., Yeager, C.A., Swica, Y., Pincus, J.H. & Lewis, M. (1997). Objective documentation of child abuse and dissociation in 12 murderers with dissociative identity disorder. *American Journal of Psychiatry, 154*(12), 1703–1710.

Lewis-Jones, S. (2006). Quality of life and childhood atopic dermatitis: The misery of living with childhood eczema. *International Journal of Clinical Practice, 60,* 984–992.

Lewontin, R.C. (1979). Sociobiology as an adaptationist program. *Behavioral Science, 24,* 5–14.

Ley, R. (1987). Panic disorder and agoraphobia: Fear of fear or fear of the symptoms produced by hyperventilation. *Journal of Behavior Therapy and Experimental Psychiatry, 18*(4), 305–316.

Ley, R. & Walker, H. (1973). Effects of carbon dioxide-oxygen inhalation on heart rate, blood pressure, and subjective anxiety. *Journal of Behavior Therapy and Experimental Psychiatry, 4*(3), 223–228.

Liberman, R.P., Wallace, C.J., Blackwell, G., Kopelowicz, A. et al. (1998). Skills training versus psychosocial occupational therapy for persons with persistent schizophrenia. *American Journal of Psychiatry, 155*(8), 1087–1091.

Lichtenstein, E. & Glasgow, R.E. (1992). Smoking cessation: What have we learned over the past decade? *Journal of Consulting and Clinical Psychology, 60*(4), 518–527.

Lichtenstein, P. & Annas, P. (2000). Heritability and prevalence of specific fears and phobias in childhood. *Journal of Child Psychology and Psychiatry and Allied Disciplines, 41,* 927–937.

Liddell, A. & Lyons, M. (1978). Thunderstorm phobias. *Behaviour Research and Therapy, 16,* 306–308.

Lieb, K., Zanarini, M.C., Schmahl, C., Linehan, M.M. & Bohus, M. (2004). Borderline personality disorder. *Lancet, 364,* 453–461.

Lieb, R., Wittchen, H.U., Hoefler, M., Fuetsch, M. et al. (2000). Parental psychopathology, parenting styles, and the risk of social phobia in offspring: A prospective-longitudinal community study. *Archives of General Psychiatry, 57*(9), 859–866.

Liebowitz, M.R., Heimberg, R.G., Fresco, D.M., Travers, J. & Stein, M.B. (2000). Social phobia or social anxiety disorder: What's in a name? *Archives of General Psychiatry, 57*(2), 191–192.

Liebowitz, M.R., Heimberg, R.G., Schneier, F.R., Hope, D.A. et al. (1999). Cognitive-behavioral group therapy versus phenelzine in social phobia: Long-term outcome. *Depression and Anxiety, 10*(3), 89–98.

Liebson, I. (1967). Conversion reaction: A learning theory approach. *Behaviour Research and Therapy, 7,* 217–218.

Lien, L. (2002). Are readmission rates influenced by how psychiatric services are organized? *Nordic Journal of Psychiatry, 56*(1), 23–28.

Lilienfeld, S.O., Lynn, S.J., Kirsch, I., Chaves, J.F. et al. (1999). Dissociative identity disorder and the sociocognitive model: Recalling the lessons of the past. *Psychological Bulletin, 125*(5), 507–523.

Lilienfeld, S.O., Wood, J.M. & Garb, H.N. (2000). The scientific status of projective techniques. *Psychological Science in the Public Interest, 1*, 27–66.

Lim, S.-L. & Kim, J.-H. (2005). Cognitive processing of emotional information in depression, panic and somatoform disorder. *Journal of Abnormal Psychology, 114*, 50–61.

Lin, K.M. & Kleinman, A.M. (1988). Psychopathology and clinical course of schizophrenia: A cross-cultural perspective. *Schizophrenia Bulletin, 14*(4), 555–567.

Linares, T.J., Singer, L.T., Kirchner, H.L., Short, E.J. et al. (2006). Mental health outcomes of cocaine-exposed children at 6 years of age. *Journal of Pediatric Psychology, 31*(1), 85–97.

Lincoln, M., Packman, A. & Onslow, M. (2006). Altered auditory feedback and the treatment of stuttering: A review. *Journal of Fluency Disorders, 31*(2), 71–89.

Lindberg, L. & Hjern, A. (2003). Risk factors for anorexia nervosa: A national cohort study. *International Journal of Eating Disorders, 34*, 397–408.

Lindberg, N., Tani, P., Virkkunen, M., Porkka-Heiskanen, T. et al. (2005). Quantitative electroencephalographic measures in homicidal men with antisocial personality disorder. *Psychiatry Research, 136*(1), 7–15.

Linehan, M.M. (1987). Dialectical behaviour therapy for borderline personality disorder. *Bulletin of the Menninger Clinic, 51*, 261–276.

Linehan, M.M. (1993). *Cognitive-behavioral treatment of borderline personality disorder*. New York: Guilford Press.

Linehan, M.M., Heard, H.L. & Armstrong, H.E. (1993). Naturalistic follow-up of a behavioral treatment for chronically parasuicidal borderline patients. *Archives of General Psychiatry, 50*(12), 971–974.

Linehan, M.M., Schmidt, H., Dimeff, L.A., Craft, J.C. et al. (1999). Dialectical behavior therapy for patients with borderline personality disorder and drug-dependence. *American Journal on Addictions, 8*(4), 279–292.

Linehan, M.M., Tutek, D.A., Heard, H.L. & Armstrong, H.E. (1994). Interpersonal outcome of cognitive-behavioral treatment for chronically suicidal borderline patients. *American Journal of Psychiatry, 151*(12), 1771–1776.

Liraud, F. & Verdoux, H. (2000). Which temperamental characteristics are associated with substance use in subjects with psychotic and mood disorders? *Psychiatry Research, 93*(1), 63–72.

Lisanby, S.H., Maddox, J.H., Prudic, J., Devanand, D.P. & Sackeim, H.A. (2000). The effects of electroconvulsive therapy on memory of autobiographical and public events. *Archives of General Psychiatry, 57*(6), 581–590.

Little, K.Y., Krolewski, D.M., Zhang, L. & Cassin, B.J. (2003). Loss of striatal vesicular monoamine transporter protein (VMAT2) in human cocaine users. *American Journal of Psychiatry, 160*(1), 47–55.

Littlewood, R. (1992). Psychiatric-diagnosis and racial bias: Empirical and interpretative approaches. *Social Science and Medicine, 34*, 141–149.

Liu, J.H. & Raine, A. (2006). The effect of childhood malnutrition on externalizing behaviour. *Current Opinions in Pediatrics, 18*, 565–570.

Livesley, W.J., Jang, K.L. & Vernon, P.A. (1998). Phenotypic and genetic structure of traits delineating personality disorder. *Archives of General Psychiatry, 55*(10), 941–948.

Lobbestael, J., Arntz, A. & Sieswerda, S. (2005). Schema modes and childhood abuse in borderline and antisocial personality disorders. *Journal of Behavior Therapy and Experimental Psychiatry, 36*, 240–253.

Loeber, R., Burke, J.D., Lahey, B.B., Winters, A. & Zera, M. (2000). Oppositional defiant and conduct disorder: A review of the past 10 years. Part I. *Journal of the American Academy of Child and Adolescent Psychiatry, 39*(12), 1468–1484.

Loeber, R., Green, S.M., Lahey, B.B. & Kalb, L. (2000). Physical fighting in childhood as a risk factor for later mental health problems. *Journal of the American Academy of Child and Adolescent Psychiatry, 39*(4), 421–428.

Loeber, R., Wung, P., Keenan, K., Giroux, B. et al. (1993). Developmental pathways in disruptive child behavior. *Development and Psychopathology, 5*(1–2), 103–133.

Loftus, E.F. (1993). The reality of repressed memories. *American Psychologist, 48*(5), 518–537.

Looper, K.J. & Paris, J. (2000). What dimensions underlie cluster B personality disorders? *Comprehensive Psychiatry, 41*, 432–437.

Lopatka, C. & Rachman, S. (1995). Perceived responsibility and compulsive checking: An experimental analysis. *Behaviour Research and Therapy, 33*(6), 673–684.

LoPiccolo, J. (1985). Diagnosis and treatment of male sexual dysfunction. *Journal of Sex and Marital Therapy, 11*, 215–232.

LoPiccolo, J. (1997). Sex therapy: A post-modern model. In R.J. Comer (Ed.), *Abnormal psychology* (2nd ed.). New York: W.H. Freeman.

LoPiccolo, J. & Friedman, J.M. (1988). Broad spectrum treatment of low sexual desire: Integration of cognitive, behavioral and systemic therapy. In S. Leiblum & R.C. Rosen (Eds.), *Sexual desire disorders*. New York: Guilford Press.

LoPiccolo, J. & Hogan, D.R. (1979). Multidimensional treatment of sexual dysfunction. In O.F. Pomerleau & J.P. Brady (Eds.), *Behavioral medicine: Theory and practice*. Baltimore: Williams & Wilkins.

LoPresti, E.F., Mihalidis, A. & Kirsch, N. (2004). Assistive technology for cognitive rehabilitation: State of the art. *Neuropsychological Rehabilitation, 14*, 5–39.

Louchart de la Chapelle, S., Nkam, I., Houy, E., Belmont, A. et al. (2005). A concordance study of three electrophysiological measures in schizophrenia. *American Journal of Psychiatry, 162*(3), 466–474.

Lovaas, O.I. (1987). Behavioral treatment and normal educational and intellectual functioning in young autistic children. *Journal of Consulting and Clinical Psychology, 55*, 3–9.

Lovejoy, M. (2001). Disturbances in the social body: Differences in body image and eating problems among African American and white women. *Gender and Society, 15*(2), 239–261.

Lubinski, D. (2000). Scientific and social significance of assessing individual differences. *Annual Review of Psychology, 51*, 569–578.

Lucas, K. & Lloyd, B. (1999). Starting smoking: Girls' explanations of the influence of peers. *Journal of Adolescence, 22*(5), 647–655.

Lucht, M., Schaub, R.T., Meyer, C., Hapke, U. et al. (2003). Gender differences in unipolar depression: A general population survey of adults between age 18 to 64 of German nationality. *Journal of Affective Disorders, 77*(3), 203–211.

Ludman, E.J., Simon, G.E., Tutty, S. & von Korff, M. (2007). A randomized trial of telephone psychotherapy and pharmacotherapy for depression: Continuation and durability of effects. *Journal of Consulting and Clinical Psychology, 75*, 257–266.

Ludwig, A.M. (1995). *The price of greatness: Resolving the creativity and madness controversy*. New York: Guilford Press.

Luermans, J.R.L.M., De Cort, K., Scruers, K. & Griez, E. (2004). New insights in cognitive behavioural therapy as treatment of panic disorder: A brief overview. *Acta Neuropsychiatrica, 16*, 110–112.

Lumley, V.A. & Scotti, J.R. (2001). Supporting the sexuality of adults with mental retardation: Current status and future direction. *Journal of Positive Behavioral Interventions, 3*, 109–119.

Lundqvist, T. (2005). Cognitive consequences of cannabis use: Comparison with abuse of stimulants and heroin with regard to attention, memory and executive functions. *Pharmacology, Biochemistry and Behavior, 81*, 319–330.

Lutzker, J.R. & Martin, J.A. (1981). *Behavior change*. Monterey, CA: Brooks.

Lykken, D.T. (1957). A study of anxiety in the sociopathic personality. *Journal of Abnormal and Social Psychology, 55*(1), 6–10.

Lykken, D.T. (1995). *The antisocial personalities*. Hillsdale, NJ: Lawrence Erlbaum.

Lynam, D.R. & Henry, V. (2001). The role of neuropsychological deficits in conduct disorders. In J. Hill & B. Maugham (Eds.), *Conduct disorders in childhood and adolescence*. Cambridge: Cambridge University Press.

Lynam, D., Moffitt, T. & Stouthamer-Loeber, M. (1993). Explaining the relationship between IQ and delinquency: Class, race, test motivation, school failure of self-control. *Journal of Abnormal Psychology, 102*, 187–196.

Lynam, D.R. (1998). Early identification of the fledgling psychopath: Locating the psychopathic child in the current nomenclature. *Journal of Abnormal Psychology, 107*, 566–575.

Lynch, D., Tamburrino, M. & Nagel, R. (1997). Telephone counselling for patients with minor depression: Preliminary findings in a family practice setting. *Journal of Family Practice, 44*, 293–295.

Lyngdorf, P. & Hemmingsen, L. (2004). Epidemiology of erectile dysfunction and its risk factors: A practice-based study in Denmark. *International Journal of Impotence Research, 16*(2), 105–111.

Lynn, S.J. (1988). Fantasy proneness: Hypnosis, developmental antecedents, and psychopathology. *American Psychologist, 43*, 35–44.

Lyons, M.J., True, W.R., Eisen, S.A., Goldberg, J. et al. (1995). Differential heritability of adult and juvenile antisocial traits. *Archives of General Psychiatry, 52*(11), 906–915.

Ma, G.X.Q. & Shive, S. (2000). A comparative analysis of perceived rises and substance abuse among ethnic groups. *Addictive Behaviors, 25*(3), 361–371.

Ma, S.H. & Teasdale, J.D. (2004). Mindfulness-based cognitive therapy for depression: Replication and exploration of differential relapse prevention effects. *Journal of Consulting and Clinical Psychology, 72*(1), 31–40.

McAlonan, G.M., Cheung, V., Cheung, C., Suckling, J. et al. (2005). Mapping the brain in autism. A voxel-based MRI study of volumetric differences and intercorrelations in autism. *Brain, 128*, 268–276.

McAuliffe, W.E. (1990). A randomized controlled trial of recovery training and self-help for opioid addicts in New England and Hong Kong. *Journal of Psychoactive Drugs, 22*(2), 197–209.

McCandliss, B.D., Cohen, L. & Dehaene, S. (2003). The visual word form area: Expertise for reading in the fusiform gyrus. *Trends in Cognitive Sciences, 7*(7), 293–299.

McCarley, R.W., Salisbury, D.F., Hirayasu, Y., Yurgelun-Todd, D.A. et al. (2002). Association between smaller left posterior superior temporal gyrus volume on magnetic resonance imaging and smaller left temporal P300 amplitude in first-episode schizophrenia. *Archives of General Psychiatry, 59*(4), 321–331.

McConachie, H. & Diggle, T. (2007). Parent-implemented early intervention for young children with autism spectrum disorder: A systematic review. *Journal of Evaluation in Clinical Practice, 13*, 120–129.

McConaghy, N. (1993). *Sexual behaviour: Problems and management.* New York: Plenum.

McCormick, N.B. (1999). When pleasure causes pain: Living with interstitial cystitis. *Sexuality and Disability, 17*, 7–18.

McCracken, L.M., Zayfert, C. & Gross, R.T. (1992). The Pain Anxiety Symptoms Scale: Development and validation of the scale to measure fear of pain. *Pain, 50*, 67–73.

McCreary, D.R. & Sadava, S.W. (1999). Television viewing and self-perceived health, weight, and physical fitness: Evidence for the cultivation hypothesis. *Journal of Applied Social Psychology, 29*(11), 2342–2361.

McDermott, P.A. & Weiss, R.V. (1995). A normative typology of healthy, subclinical, and clinical behaviour styles among American children and adolescents. *Psychological Assessment, 7*, 162–170.

McDonald, A.S. & Davey, G.C.L. (1996). Psychiatric disorders and accidental injury. *Clinical Psychology Review, 16*, 105–127.

McDonald, C., Grech, A., Toulopoulou, T., Schulze, K. et al. (2002). Brain volumes in familial and non-familial schizophrenic probands and their unaffected relatives. *American Journal of Medical Genetics, 114*(6), 616–625.

MacDonald, C.B. & Davey, G.C.L. (2005a). A mood-as-input account of perseverative checking: The relationship between stop rules, mood and confidence in having checked successfully. *Behaviour Research and Therapy, 43*, 69–91.

MacDonald, C.B. & Davey, G.C.L. (2005b). Inflated responsibility and perseverative checking: The role of negative mood. *Journal of Abnormal Psychology, 114*, 176–182.

McDonough, M. (2003). Pharmacological and neurosurgical treatment of OCD. In R.G. Menzies & P. de Silva (Eds.), *Obsessive-compulsive disorder: Theory, research and treatment.* Chichester: Wiley.

McDowell, I. (2001). Alzheimer's disease: Insights from epidemiology. *Aging Clinical and Experimental Research, 13*(3), 143–162.

McElroy, S.L., Soutullo, C.A., Taylor, P., Nelson, E.B. et al. (1999). Psychiatric features of 36 men convicted of sexual offenses. *Journal of Clinical Psychiatry, 60*(6), 414–420.

McEvoy, R.E., Rogers, S.J. & Pennington, B.F. (1993). Executive function and social communication deficits in young autistic children. *Journal of Child Psychology and Psychiatry and Allied Disciplines, 34*(4), 563–578.

McEwen, B.S. (2003). Mood disorders and allostatic load. *Biological Psychiatry, 54*, 200–207.

McFall, M.E. & Hammen, C.L. (1971). Motivation, structure, and self-monitoring: Role of non-specific factors in smoking reduction. *Journal of Consulting and Clinical Psychology, 37*, 80–86.

McGee, R., Williams, S., Poulton, R. & Moffitt, T. (2000). A longitudinal study of cannabis use and mental health from adolescence to early adulthood. *Addiction, 95*(4), 491–503.

McGinn, L.K. & Young, J.E. (1996). Schema-focused therapy. In P.M. Salkovskis (Ed.), *Frontiers of cognitive therapy.* New York: Guilford Press.

McGlashan, T.H., Grilo, C.M., Sanislow, C.A., Ralevski, E. et al. (2005). Two-year prevalence and stability of individual DSM-IV criteria for schizotypal, borderline, avoidant, and obsessive-compulsive personality disorders: Toward a hybrid model of Axis II disorders. *American Journal of Psychiatry, 162*(5), 883–889.

McGrath, J.M. & Frueh, B.C. (2002). Fraudulent claims of combat status in the VA? *Psychiatric Services, 53*(3), 345.

McGrath, M. & Oyebode, F. (2005). Characteristics of perpetrators of homicide in independent inquiries. *Medicine, Science and the Law, 45*(3), 233–243.

McGue, M. & Iacono, W.G. (2005). The association of early adolescent problem behaviour with adult psychopathology. *American Journal of Psychiatry, 162*, 1118–1124.

McGuffin, P., Katz, R., Watkins, S. & Rutherford, J. (1996). A hospital-based twin register of the heritability of DSM-IV unipolar depression. *Archives of General Psychiatry, 53*(2), 129–136.

McGuire, L., Junginger, J., Adams, S.G., Burright, R. et al. (2001). Delusions and delusional reasoning. *Journal of Abnormal Psychology, 110*, 259–266.

McGuire, P.K., Silbersweig, D.A., Wright, I., Murray, R.M. et al. (1996). The neural correlates of inner speech and auditory verbal imagery in schizophrenia: Relationship to auditory verbal hallucinations. *British Journal of Psychiatry, 169*(2), 148–159.

McIsaac, H. (1995). *Claustrophobia and the MRI procedure.* Unpublished MA thesis, University of British Columbia.

McKay, D. (1999). Two-year follow-up of behavioral treatment and maintenance for body dysmorphic disorder. *Behavior Modification, 23*(4), 620–629.

McKeith, I.G., Galasko, D., Kosaka, K., Perry, E.K. et al. (1996). Consensus guidelines for the clinical and pathologic diagnosis of dementia with Lewy bodies (DLB): Report of the consortium on DLB international workshop. *Neurology, 47*(5), 1113–1124.

McLaughlin, K.A. & Mennin, D.S. (2005). Clarifying the temporal relationship between dependent personality disorder and anxiety disorders. *Clinical Psychology: Science and Practice, 12*(4), 417–420.

MacLeod, A.K., Haynes, C. & Sensky, T. (1998). Attributions about common bodily sensations: Their associations with hypochondriasis and anxiety. *Psychological Medicine, 28*(1), 225–228.

MacLeod, J. (2003). *An introduction to counselling* (3rd ed.). Milton Keynes: Open University Press.

McMullen, S. & Rosen, R.C. (1979). Self-administered masturbation training in the treatment of primary orgasmic dysfunction. *Journal of Consulting and Clinical Psychology, 47*(5), 912–918.

McNally, R.J. (1990). Psychological approaches to panic disorder: A review. *Psychological Bulletin, 108*, 403–419.

McNally, R.J. (1995). Preparedness, phobias, and the Panglossian paradigm. *Behavioral and Brain Sciences, 18*, 303–304.

McNally, R.J. (1997). Atypical phobias. In G.C.L. Davey (Ed.), *Phobias: A handbook of theory, research and treatment.* Chichester: Wiley.

McNally, R.J. (1999). EMDR and mesmerism: A comparative historical analysis. *Journal of Anxiety Disorders*, 13(1–2), 225–236.

McNally, R.J. (2001). On Wakefield's harmful dysfunction analysis of mental disorder. *Behaviour Research and Therapy*, 39, 309–314.

McNally, R.J. (2002). Anxiety sensitivity and panic disorder. *Biological Psychiatry*, 52, 938–946.

McNally, R.J. (2003a). Progress and controversy in the study of posttraumatic stress disorder. *Annual Review of Psychology*, 54, 229–252.

McNally, R.J. (2003b). Psychological mechanisms in acute response to trauma. *Biological Psychiatry*, 53, 779–788.

McNally, R.J., Bryant, R.A. & Ehlers, A. (2003). Does early psychological intervention promote recovery from posttraumatic stress? *Psychological Science, Supplement*, 45–79.

McNally, R.J., Clancy, S.A., Barrett, H.M. & Parker, H.A. (2005). Reality monitoring in adults reporting repressed, recovered, or continuous memories of childhood sexual abuse. *Journal of Abnormal Psychology*, 114, 147–152.

McNally, R.J., Clancy, S.A. & Schachter, D.L. (2001). Directed forgetting of trauma cues in adults reporting repressed or recovered memories of childhood sexual abuse. *Journal of Abnormal Psychology*, 110(1), 151–156.

McNally, R.J. & Louro, C.E. (1992). Fear of flying in agoraphobia and simple phobia: Distinguishing features. *Journal of Anxiety Disorders*, 6, 319–324.

McNally, R.J., Metzger, L.J., Lasko, N.B., Clancy, S.A. & Pitman, R.K. (1998). Directed forgetting of trauma cues in adult survivors of childhood sexual abuse with and without posttraumatic stress disorder. *Journal of Abnormal Psychology*, 107, 596–601.

McNulty, J.L., Graham, J.R., Ben-Porath, Y.S. & Stein, L.A.R. (1997). Comparative validity of MMPI-II scales of African-American and Caucasian mental health center clients. *Psychological Assessment*, 9, 464–470.

McQuillan, A., Nicastro, R., Guenot, F., Girard, M. et al. (2005). Intensive dialectical behaviour therapy for outpatients with borderline personality disorder who are in crisis. *Psychiatric Services*, 56, 193–197.

McRae, A.L., Budney, A.J. & Brady, K.T. (2003). Treatment of marijuana dependence: A review of the literature. *Journal of Substance Abuse Treatment*, 24, 369–376.

McSherry, J.A. (1985). Was Mary Queen of Scots anorexic? *Scottish Medical Journal*, 30, 243–245.

McVey, G., Tweed, S. & Blackmore, E. (2004). Dieting among preadolescent and young adolescent females. *Canadian Medical Association Journal*, 170(10), 1559–1561.

Madianos, M.G. & Madianou, D. (1992). The effects of long-term community care on relapse and adjustment of persons with chronic schizophrenia. *International Journal of Mental Health*, 21(1), 37–49.

Madsen, K.M., Hviid, A., Vestergaard, M., Schendel, D. et al. (2002). A population-based study of measles, mumps and rubella vaccination and autism. *New England Journal of Medicine*, 347, 1477–1482.

Maes, M., De Vos, N., van Hunsel, F., van West, D. et al. (2001). Pedophilia is accompanied by increased plasma concentrations of catecholamines, in particular epinephrine. *Psychiatry Research*, 103(1), 43–49.

Magnusson, A. & Boivin, D. (2003). Seasonal affective disorder: An overview. *Chronobiology International*, 20, 189–207.

Maher, B. (2001). Delusions. In P.B. Sutker & H.E. Adams (Eds.), *Comprehensive handbook of psychopathology* (3rd ed.). New York: Kluwer Academic/Plenum.

Mainio, A., Hakko, H., Niemela, A., Koivukangas, J. & Rasanen, P. (2005). Depression and functional outcome in patients with brain tumors: A population-based 1-year follow-up study. *Journal of Neurosurgery*, 103(5), 841–847.

Malberg, J.E. & Bronson, K.R. (2001). How MDMA works in the brain. In J. Holland (Ed.), *Ecstasy: The complete guide: A comprehensive look at the risks and benefits of MDMA*. Rochester, VT: Park Street Press.

Maldonado, J.R. & Spiegel, D. (2003). Clinical characteristics, pathophysiology and treatment of conversion disorders: A research-based approach. *Psychosomatics*, 44(2), 165.

Malec, J.F. & Basford, J.S. (1996). Postacute brain injury rehabilitation. *Archives of Physical Medicine and Rehabilitation*, 77(2), 198–207.

Maletzky, B.M. (1993). Factors associated with success and failure in the behavioral and cognitive treatment of sex offenders. *Annals of Sex Research*, 6, 241–258.

Maletzky, B.M. (2002). The paraphilias: Research and treatment. In P.E. Nathan & J.M. Gorman (Eds.), *A guide to treatments that work*. New York: Oxford University Press.

Maletzky, B.M. & Field, G. (2003). The biological treatment of dangerous sexual offenders: A review and preliminary report of the Oregon pilot depo-Provera program. *Aggression and Violent Behavior*, 8(4), 391–412.

Malgady, R. & Constantino, G. (1998). Symptoms severity in bilingual Hispanics as a function of clinician ethnicity and language of interview. *Psychological Assessment*, 10, 120–127.

Malizia, A.L., Cunningham, V.J., Bell, C.J., Liddle, P.F. et al. (1998). Decreased brain GABA(A)-benzodiazepine receptor binding in panic disorder: Preliminary results from a quantitative PET study. *Archives of General Psychiatry*, 55(8), 715–720.

Mallis, D., Moysidis, K., Nakopoulou, E., Papaharitou, S. et al. (2005). Psychiatric morbidity is frequently undetected in patients with erectile dysfunction. *Journal of Urology*, 174(5), 1913–1916.

Malone, R.P., Gratz, S.S., Delaney, M.A. & Hyman, S.B. (2005). Advances in drug treatments for children and adolescents with autism and other pervasive developmental disorders. *CNS Drugs*, 19(11), 923–934.

Maltby, J., Giles, D.C., Barber, L. & McCutcheon, L.E. (2005). Intense-personal celebrity worship and body image: Evidence of a link among female adolescents. *British Journal of Health Psychology*, 10, 17–32.

Manassis, K., Mendlowitz, S.L., Scapillato, D., Avery, D. et al. (2002). Group and individual cognitive-behavioral therapy for childhood anxiety disorders: A randomized trial. *Journal of the American Academy of Child and Adolescent Psychiatry*, 41(12), 1423–1430.

Manassis, K. & Monga, S. (2001). A therapeutic approach to children and adolescents with anxiety disorders and comorbid conditions. *Journal of the American Academy of Child and Adolescent Psychiatry*, 40, 115–117.

Mancini, C., van Ameringen, M., Szatmari, P., Fugere, C. & Boyle, M. (1996). A high-risk pilot study of the children of adults with social phobia. *Journal of the American Academy of Child and Adolescent Psychiatry*, 35(11), 1511–1517.

Mandell, A.J. & Knapp, S. (1979). Asymmetry and mood, emergent properties of serotonin regulation: Proposed mechanism of action of lithium. *Archives of General Psychiatry*, 36(8), 909–916.

Manjiviona, J. & Prior, M. (1999). Neuropsychological profiles of children with Asperger's syndrome and autism. *Autism*, 3, 327–356.

Mann, J.J. & Kapur, S. (1994). Elucidation of biochemical basis of the antidepressant action of electroconvulsive therapy by human studies. *Psychopharmacology Bulletin*, 30, 445–453.

Mann, K., Klingler, T., Noe, S., Roschke, J., Muller, S. & Benkert, O. (1996). Effects of yohimbine on sexual experiences and nocturnal penile tumescence and rigidity in erectile dysfunction. *Archives of Sexual Behavior*, 25(1), 1–16.

Manschreck, T.C. (1996). Delusional disorder: The recognition and management of paranoia. *Journal of Clinical Psychiatry*, 57, 32–38.

Marce, L.V. (1860). On a form of hypochondriacal delirium occurring consecutive to dyspepsia and characterized by refusal of food. *Journal of Psychological Medicine and Mental Pathology*, 13, 264–266.

Marcotte, D. (1997). Treating depression in adolescence: A review of the effectiveness of cognitive-behavioral treatments. *Journal of Youth and Adolescence*, 26, 273–283.

Margraf, J., Ehlers, A. & Roth, W.T. (1986). Biological models of panic disorder and agoraphobia: A review. *Behaviour Research and Therapy*, 24(5), 553–567.

Marinangeli, M.G., Butti, G., Scinto, A., Di Cicco, L. et al. (2000). Patterns of comorbidity among DSM-III-R personality disorders. *Psychopathology*, 33(2), 69–74.

Mark, V.W. & Taub, E. (2004). Constraint-induced movement therapy for chronic stroke hemiparesis and other disabilities. *Restorative Neurology and Neuroscience, 22*(3–5), 317–336.

Marks, I.M. (1969). *Fears and phobias.* New York: Academic Press.

Marks, I.M. (1997). Behaviour therapy for obsessive-compulsive disorder: A decade of progress. *Canadian Journal of Psychiatry: Revue Canadienne de Psychiatrie, 42*(10), 1021–1027.

Marks, M. (2003). Cognitive therapy for OCD. In R.G. Menzies & P. de Silva (Eds.), *Obsessive-compulsive disorder: Theory, research and treatment.* Chichester: Wiley.

Marks, I.M., Gelder, M. & Bancroft, J. (1970). Sexual deviants two years after electric aversion. *British Journal of Psychiatry, 117*(537), 173&.

Marks, I.M., Lovell, K., Noshirvani, H. & Livanou, M. (1998). Treatment of posttraumatic stress disorder by exposure and/or cognitive restructuring: A controlled study. *Archives of General Psychiatry, 55*(4), 317–325.

Marlatt, G.A. & Gordon, J.R. (1985). *Relapse prevention: Maintenance strategies in addictive behaviour change.* New York: Guilford Press.

Marselos, M. & Karamanakos, P. (1999). Mutagenicity, developmental toxicity and carcinogenicity of cannabis. *Addiction Biology, 4*(1), 5–12.

Marshall, J.C., Halligan, P.W., Fink, G.R. et al. (1997). The functional anatomy of hysterical paralysis. *Cognition, 64,* B1–8.

Marshall, L.A. & Cooke, D.J. (1999). The childhood experiences of psychopaths: A retrospective study of familial and societal factors. *Journal of Personality Disorders, 13*(3), 211–225.

Marshall, M.P. & Molina, B.S.G. (2006). Antisocial behaviors moderate the deviant peer pathway to substance use in children with ADHD. *Journal of Clinical Child and Adolescent Psychology, 35,* 216–226.

Marshall, W.L. & Barbaree, H.E. (1978). Reduction of deviant arousal: Satiation treatment for sexual aggressors. *Criminal Justice and Behavior, 5*(4), 294–303.

Marshall, W.L., Barbaree, H.E. & Christophe, D. (1986). Sexual offenders against female children: Sexual preferences for age of victims and type of behavior. *Canadian Journal of Behavioural Science: Revue Canadienne des Sciences du Comportement, 18*(4), 424–439.

Marshall, W.L. & Lippens, K. (1977). Clinical value of boredom: Procedure for reducing inappropriate sexual interests. *Journal of Nervous and Mental Disease, 165*(4), 283–287.

Marshall, W.L. & Pithers, W.D. (1994). A reconsideration of treatment outcome with sex offenders. *Criminal Justice and Behavior, 21*(1), 10–27.

Marshall, W.L. & Serran, G.A. (2000). Current issues in the assessment and treatment of sexual offenders. *Clinical Psychology and Psychotherapy, 7*(2), 85–96.

Martin, L.L. & Davies, B. (1998). Beyond hedonism and associationism: A configural view of the role of affect in evaluation, processing, and self-regulation. *Motivation and Emotion, 22*(1), 33–51.

Martin, L.L. & Stoner, P. (1996). Mood as input: What we think about how we feel determines how we think. In L.L. Martin & A. Tesser (Eds.), *Striving and feeling: Interactions among goals, affect, and self-regulation* (pp. 279–301). Mahwah, NJ: Erlbaum.

Marziali, E., Donahue, P. & Crossin, G. (2005). Caring for others: Internet health care support intervention for family caregivers of persons with Alzheimer's, stroke, or Parkinson's disease. *Families in Society: The Journal of Contemporary Social Services, 86*(3), 375–383.

Marzillier, J. (2004). The myth of evidence-based psychotherapy. *Psychologist, 17,* 392–395.

Marzillier, J. & Marzillier, S. (2008). General principles of clinical practice: Assessment, formulation, intervention and evaluation. In G.C.L. Davey (Ed.), *Clinical psychology.* London: Hodder.

Mason, B.J. (2001). Treatment of alcohol-dependent outpatients with acamprosate: A clinical review. *Journal of Clinical Psychiatry, 62* (Suppl. 20), 42–48.

Mason, F.L. (1997). Fetishism: Psychopathology and theory. In D.R. Laws & W. O'Donohue (Eds.), *Sexual deviance.* New York: Guilford Press.

Massion, A.O., Dyck, I.R., Shea, T., Phillips, K.A. et al. (2002). Personality disorders and time to remission in generalized anxiety disorder, social phobia, and panic disorder. *Archives of General Psychiatry, 59*(5), 434–440.

Masters, W.H. & Johnson, V.E. (1966). *Human sexual response.* Boston: Little, Brown.

Masters, W.H. & Johnson, V.E. (1970). *Human sexual inadequacy.* Boston: Little, Brown.

Matchett, G. & Davey, G.C.L. (1991). A test of a disease-avoidance model of animal phobias. *Behaviour Research and Therapy, 29,* 91–94.

Mathalon, D.H., Sullivan, E.V., Lim, K.O. & Pfefferbaum, A. (2001). Progressive brain volume changes and the clinical course of schizophrenia in men: A longitudinal magnetic resonance imaging study. *Archives of General Psychiatry, 58*(2), 148–157.

Mather, L.E. (2001). Medicinal cannabis: Hoax or hope? *Regional Anesthesia and Pain Medicine, 26*(5), 484–487.

Mathews, A. & Mackintosh, B. (2000). Induced emotional interpretation bias and anxiety. *Journal of Abnormal Psychology, 109,* 602–615.

Mathews, A. & MacLeod, C. (1994). Cognitive approaches to emotion and emotional disorders. *Annual Review of Psychology, 45,* 25–50.

Mathews, A. & MacLeod, C. (2002). Induced processing biases have causal effects on anxiety. *Cognition and Emotion, 16,* 331–354.

Mathews, A.M., Bancroft, J., Whitehead, A., Hackmann, A., Julier, D., Bancroft, J., Gath, D. & Shaw, P. (1976). The behavioural treatment of sexual inadequacy: A comparative study. *Behaviour Research and Therapy, 14,* 427–436.

Mattia, J.I. & Zimmerman, M. (2001). Epidemiology. In W.J. Livesley (Ed.), *Handbook of personality disorders: Theory, research and treatment.* New York: Guilford Press.

Maugh, T.H. (1982). Marihuana justifies serious concern. *Science, 215*(4539), 1488–1489.

Maugham, B. (2000). The influence of family, school, and the environment. In M.G. Gelder, J.J. Lopez-Ilbor & N.C. Andreason (Eds.), *New Oxford textbook of psychiatry* (Vol. 2). Oxford: Oxford University Press.

Maugham, B. & Carroll, J. (2006). Literacy and mental disorders. *Current Opinion in Psychiatry, 19*(4), 350–354.

Maugham, B., Taylor, A., Caspi, A. & Moffitt, T.E. (2004). Prenatal smoking and early childhood conduct disorder problems: Testing genetic and environmental explanations of the association. *Archives of General Psychiatry, 61,* 836–843.

Mausbach, B.T., Aschbacher, K., Patterson, T.L., Ancoli-Israel, S. et al. (2006). Avoidant coping partially mediates the relationship between patient problem behaviors and depressive symptoms in spousal Alzheimer caregivers. *American Journal of Geriatric Psychiatry, 14*(4), 299–306.

Mawhood, L. & Howlin, P. (1999). The outcome of a supported employment scheme for high-functioning adults with autism or Asperger syndrome. *Autism: The International Journal of Research and Practice, 3*(3), 229–254.

May, M., McCarron, P., Stansfield, S., Ben-Shlomo, Y. et al. (2002). Does psychological distress predict the risk of ischemic stroke and transient ischemic attack? The Caerphilly study. *Stroke, 33*(1), 7–12.

May, R. (2007). Working outside the diagnostic frame. *Psychologist, 20,* 300–301.

May, R. & Yalom, I. (1995). Existential psychotherapy. In R.J. Corsini & D. Wedding (Eds.), *Current psychotherapies* (5th ed.). Itasca, IL: Peacock.

Mayer, J.D., Salovey, P. & Caruso, D. (2000). Models of emotional intelligence. In R.J. Sternberg (Ed.), *Handbook of intelligence.* Cambridge: Cambridge University Press.

Mayes, S.D. & Calhoun, S.L. (2006). Frequency of reading, math, and writing disabilities in children with clinical disorders. *Learning and Individual Differences, 16*(2), 145–157.

Mayou, R., Bryant, B. & Ehlers, A. (2001). Prediction of psychological outcomes one year after a motor vehicle accident. *American Journal of Psychiatry, 158*(8), 1231–1238.

Mayou, R., Kirmayer, L.J., Simon, G., Kroenke, K. et al. (2005). Somatoform disorders: Time for a new approach in DSM-IV. *American Journal of Psychiatry, 162,* 847–855.

Mazaleski, J.L., Iwata, B.A., Vollmer, T.R., Zarcone, J.R. & Smith, R.G. (1993). Analysis of the reinforcement and extinction components in

DRO contingencies with self-injury. *Journal of Applied Behavior Analysis*, 26, 143–156.

Mazarakis, N.K. & Nestoros, I.N. (2001). The neurophysiological substate of anxiety: The role of the GABAergic system. *Psychology: Journal of Hellenic Psychological Society*, 8, 40–59.

Mazza, J.J. & Reynolds, W.M. (1998). A longitudinal investigation of depression, hopelessness, social support, and major and minor life events and their relation to suicidal ideation in adolescents. *Suicide and Life-Threatening Behavior*, 28(4), 358–374.

Mazzoco, M.M., Nord, A.M., van Doorninck, W., Greene, C.L. et al. (1994). Cognitive development among children with early-treated phenylketonuria. *Developmental Neuropsychology*, 10, 133–151.

Medd, J. & Tate, R.L. (2000). Evaluation of an anger management therapy programme following acquired brain injury: A preliminary study. *Neuropsychological Rehabilitation*, 10(2), 185–201.

Mednick, S.A., Machon, R.A., Huttunen, M.O. & Bonett, D. (1988). Adult schizophrenia following prenatal exposure to an influenza epidemic. *Archives of General Psychiatry*, 45(2), 189–192.

Meehl, P.E. (1996). *Clinical versus statistical prediction: A theoretical analysis and a review of the evidence*. Northvale, NJ: Jason Aronson.

Mellor, C.S. (1970). First rank symptoms of schizophrenia. 1. Frequency in schizophrenics on admission to hospital. 2. Differences between individual first rank symptoms. *British Journal of Psychiatry*, 117(536), 15&.

Melo, J.A., Shendure, J., Pociask, K. & Silver, L.M. (1996). Identification of sex-specific quantitative trait loci controlling alcohol preference in C57BL/6 mice. *Nature Genetics*, 13(2), 147–153.

Meltzer, H., Gatwood, R., Goodman, R. & Ford, T. (2003). Mental health of children and adolescents in Great Britain (Reprinted from 2000). *International Review of Psychiatry*, 15(1–2), 185–187.

Mendez, M.F., Chow, T., Ringman, J., Twitchell, G. & Hinkin, C.H. (2000). Pedophilia and temporal lobe disturbances. *Journal of Neuropsychiatry and Clinical Neurosciences*, 12(1), 71–76.

Mengel, M.B., Searight, H.R. & Cook, K. (2006). Preventing alcohol-exposed pregnancies. *Journal of the American Board of Family Medicine*, 19, 494–505.

Menvielle, E.J. (1998). Gender identity disorder. *Journal of the American Academy of Child and Adolescent Psychiatry*, 37(3), 243–244.

Menzies, R.G. & Clarke, J.C. (1993a). The aetiology of childhood water phobia. *Behaviour Research and Therapy*, 31, 499–501.

Menzies, R.G. & Clarke, J.C. (1993b). The aetiology of fear of heights and its relationship to severity and individual response patterns. *Behaviour Research and Therapy*, 31, 355–365.

Menzies, R.G. & Clarke, J.C. (1995a). The etiology of phobias: A non-associative account. *Clinical Psychology Review*, 15, 23–48.

Menzies, R.G. & Clarke, J.C. (1995b). Danger expectancies and insight in acrophobia. *Behaviour Research and Therapy*, 33, 215–221.

Menzies, R.P.D., Fedoroff, J.P., Green, C.M. & Isaacson, K. (1995). Prediction of dangerous behavior in male erotomania. *British Journal of Psychiatry*, 166, 529–536.

Mercer, C.H., Fenton, K.A., Johnson, A.M., Copas, A.J., MacDowall, W., Erens, B. & Wellings, K. (2005). Who reports sexual function problems? Empirical evidence from Britain's 2000 National Survey of Sexual Attitudes and Lifestyles. *Sexually Transmitted Infections*, 81, 394–399.

Merckelbach, H. & de Jong, P.J. (1997). Evolutionary models of phobias. In G.C.L. Davey (Ed.), *Phobias: A handbook of theory, research and treatment*. Chichester: Wiley.

Merckelbach, H., de Jong, P.J., Muris, P. & van den Hout, M. (1996). The etiology of specific phobias: A review. *Clinical Psychology Review*, 16, 337–361.

Merckelbach, H., Hauer, B. & Rassin, E. (2002). Symptom validity testing of feigned dissociative amnesia: A simulation study. *Psychology, Crime an Law*, 8, 311–318.

Merckelbach, H., Muris, P. & Schouten, E. (1996). Pathways to fear in spider phobic children. *Behaviour Research and Therapy*, 34, 935–938.

Merikangas, K.R., Mehta, R.L., Molnar, B.E., Walters, E.E. et al. (1998). Comorbidity of substance use disorders with mood and anxiety disorders: Results of the International Consortium in Psychiatric Epidemiology. *Addictive Behaviors*, 23(6), 893–907.

Merleau-Ponty, M. (1962). *Phenomenology of perception*. New York: Humanities Press.

Merrill, L.L., Thomsen, C.J., Gold, S.R. & Milner, J.S. (2001). Childhood abuse and premilitary sexual assault in male navy recruits. *Journal of Consulting and Clinical Psychology*, 69(2), 252–261.

Mersky, H. (1995). The manufacture of personalities: The production of multiple personality disorder. In L.M. Cohen, J.N. Berzoff & M.R. Elin (Eds.), *Dissociative identity disorder: Theoretical and treatment controversies*. Northvale, NJ: Aronson.

Mervaala, E., Fohr, J., Kononen, M., Valkonen-Korhonen, M. et al. (2000). Quantitative MRI of the hippocampus and amygdala in severe depression. *Psychological Medicine*, 30, 117–125.

Metalsky, G.I. & Joiner, T.E. (1992). Vulnerability to depressive symptomatology: A prospective test of the diathesis-stress and causal mediation components of the hopelessness theory of depression. *Journal of Personality and Social Psychology*, 63(4), 667–675.

Metalsky, G.I., Joiner, T.E., Hardin, T.S. & Abramson, L.Y. (1993). Depressive reactions to failure in a naturalistic setting: A test of the hopelessness and self-esteem theories of depression. *Journal of Abnormal Psychology*, 102, 101–109.

Metz, M.E., Pryor, J.L., Nesvacil, L.J., Abuzzhab, F. & Koznar, J. (1997). Premature ejaculation: A psychophysiological review. *Journal of Sex and Marital Therapy*, 23(1), 3–23.

Meyer, B. (2002). Personality and mood correlates of avoidant personality disorder. *Journal of Personality Disorders*, 16(2), 174–188.

Meyer, C. & Waller, G. (2001). Social convergence of disturbed eating attitudes in young adult women. *Journal of Nervous and Mental Disease*, 189(2), 114–119.

Meyer, G.J., Finn, S.E., Eyde, L.D., Kay, G.G. et al. (2001). Psychological testing and psychological assessment: A review of evidence and issues. *American Psychologist*, 56, 128–165.

Meyer, T.J., Miller, M.L., Metzger, R.L. & Borkovec, T.D. (1990). Development and validation of the Penn State Worry Questionnaire. *Behaviour Research and Therapy*, 28, 487–495.

Meyer, V. (1966). Modification of expectations in cases with obsessional rituals. *Behaviour Research and Therapy*, 4, 273–280.

Mezzich, A.C., Moss, H., Tarter, R.E., Wolfenstein, M. et al. (1994). Gender differences in the pattern and progression of substance use in conduct-disordered adolescents. *American Journal on Addictions*, 3(4), 289–295.

Michel, K., Waeber, V., Valach, L., Arestegui, G. & Spuhler, T. (1994). A comparison of the drugs taken in fatal and nonfatal self-poisoning. *Acta Psychiatrica Scandinavica*, 90(3), 184–189.

Mick, E., Biederman, J., Faraone, S.V., Sayer, J. et al. (2002). Case-control study of attention-deficit hyperactivity disorder and maternal smoking, alcohol use, and drug use during pregnancy. *Journal of the American Academy of Child and Adolescent Psychiatry*, 41, 378–385.

Middleton, H., Shaw, I., Hull, S. & Feder, G. (2005). NICE guidelines for the management of depression: Are clear for severe depression, but uncertain for mild or moderate depression. *British Medical Journal*, 330(7486), 267–268.

Mikhliner, M. & Solomon, Z. (1988). Attributional style and post-traumatic stress disorder. *Journal of Abnormal Psychology*, 97, 308–313.

Mikkelsen, E.J. (2001). Enuresis and encopresis: Ten years of progress. *Journal of the American Academy of Child and Adolescent Psychiatry*, 40, 1146–1158.

Milberger, S., Biederman, J., Faraone, S.V. & Jones, J. (1998). Further evidence of an association between maternal smoking during pregnancy and attention deficit hyperactivity disorder: Findings from a high-risk sample of siblings. *Journal of Clinical Child Psychology*, 27, 352–358.

Milberger, S., Biederman, J., Faraone, S.V., Guite, J. & Tsuang, M.T. (1997). Pregnancy, delivery and infancy complications: Issues of gene–environment interaction. *Biological Psychiatry*, 41, 65–75.

Miller, I.W., Norman, W.H., Keitner, G.I., Bishop, S.B. & Dow, M.G. (1989). Cognitive-behavioral treatment of depressed inpatients. *Behavior Therapy, 20*(1), 25–47.

Miller, M.N. & Pumariega, A.J. (2001). Culture and eating disorders: A historical and cross-cultural review. *Psychiatry: Interpersonal and Biological Processes, 64*, 93–110.

Miller, P.R., Dasher, R., Collins, R., Griffiths, P. & Brown, F. (2001). Inpatient diagnostic assessments. 1. Accuracy of structured vs. unstructured interviews. *Psychiatry Research, 105*, 255–264.

Miller, T.Q. & Volk, R.J. (1996). Weekly marijuana use as a risk factor for initial cocaine use: Results from a six-wave national survey. *Journal of Child and Adolescent Substance Abuse, 5*(4), 55–78.

Miller, W.L. & Crabtree, B.F. (2000). Clinical research. In N.K. Denzin & Y.S. Lincoln (Eds.), *Handbook of qualitative research*. London: Sage.

Miller, W.R., Leckman, A.L., Delaney, H.D. & Tinkcom, M. (1992). Long-term follow-up of behavioral self-control training. *Journal of Studies on Alcohol, 53*(3), 249–261.

Miller, W.R. & Rollnick, S. (Eds.) (1991). *Motivational interviewing: Preparing people to change addictive behavior*. New York: Guilford Press.

Miller, W.R. & Rollnick, S. (2002). *Motivational interviewing: Preparing people for change* (2nd ed.). New York: Guilford Press.

Millon, T. (1990). The disorders of personality. In L.A. Pervin (Ed.), *Handbook of personality theory and practice*. New York: Guilford Press.

Millon, T. (1996). *Disorders of personality: DSM-IV and beyond* (2nd ed.). New York: Wiley.

Miltenberger, R.G. (1997). *Behavior modification: Principles and procedures*. Pacific Grove, CA: Brooks/Cole.

Mineka, S., Watson, D. & Clark, L.E.A. (1998). Comorbidity of anxiety and unipolar mood disorders. *Annual Review of Psychology, 49*, 377–412.

Minshew, N.J., Meyer, J. & Goldstein, G. (2002). Abstract reasoning in autism: A dissociation between concept formation and concept identification. *Neuropsychology, 16*(3), 327–334.

Minuchin, P. (1985). Families and individual development: Provocations from the field of family therapy. *Child Development, 56*(2), 289–302.

Minuchin, S., Baker, L., Rosman, B.L., Lieberman, R. et al. (1975). Conceptual model of psychosomatic illness in children: Family organization and family therapy. *Archives of General Psychiatry, 32*(8), 1031–1038.

Minuchin, S., Rosman, B.L. & Baker, L. (1978). *Psychosomatic families: Anorexia nervosa in context*. Cambridge, MA: Harvard University Press.

Mirowsky, J. & Ross, C.E. (1995). Sex differences in distress: Real or artifact. *American Sociological Review, 60*(3), 449–468.

Mishna, F. (1996). Clinical report. In their own words: Therapeutic factors for adolescents who have learning difficulties. *International Journal of Group Psychotherapy, 46*, 265–273.

Mitchell, J. & Everly, Jr., G. S. (1993). *Critical incident: stress debriefing. An operations manual for the prevention of traumatic stress among emergency services and disaster workers*. New York: Chevron.

Mitropoulou, V., Harvey, P.D., Zegarelli, G., New, A.S. et al. (2005). Neuropsychological performance in schizotypal personality disorder: Importance of working memory. *American Journal of Psychiatry, 162*(10), 1896–1903.

Miyamoto, S., Duncan, G.E., Marx, C.E. & Lieberman, J.A. (2005). Treatments for schizophrenia: A critical review of pharmacology and mechanisms of action of antipsychotic drugs. *Molecular Psychiatry, 10*, 79–104.

Modestin, J. (1992). Multiple personality disorder in Switzerland. *American Journal of Psychiatry, 149*(1), 88–92.

Modestin, J. & Villiger, C. (1989). Follow-up study on borderline versus nonborderline personality disorders. *Comprehensive Psychiatry, 30*(3), 236–244.

Modrow, J. (1992). *How to become a schizophrenic: The case against biological psychiatry*. Everett, WA: Apollyon Press.

Moffitt, T.E., Caspi, A., Rutter, M. & Silva, P.A. (2001). *Sex differences in antisocial behaviour: Conduct disorder, delinquency, and violence in the Dunedin Longitudinal Study*. Cambridge: Cambridge University Press.

Moffit, T.E. & the E-Risk Study Team (2002).Teen-aged mothers in contemporary Britain. *Journal of Child Psychology and Psychiatry, 43*, 727–742.

Mogg, K. & Bradley, B.P. (1998). A cognitive-motivational analysis of anxiety. *Behaviour Research and Therapy, 36*, 809–848.

Mogg, K., Bradley, B.P. & Halliwell, N. (1994). Attentional bias to threat: Roles of trait anxiety, stressful events, and awareness. *Quarterly Journal of Experimental Psychology, 47A*, 841–864.

Mogg, K., Bradley, B.P., Williams, R. & Mathews, A. (1993). Subliminal processing of emotional information in anxiety and depression. *Journal of Abnormal Psychology, 102*(2), 304–311.

Mogg, K, Millar, N. & Bradley, B.P. (2000). Biases in eye movements to threatening facial expressions in generalized anxiety disorder and depressive disorder. *Journal of Abnormal Psychology, 109*, 695–704.

Mohanty, S.R., LaBrecque, D.R., Mitros, F.A. & Layden, T.J. (2004). Liver transplantation for disulfiram-induced fulminant hepatic failure. *Journal of Clinical Gastroenterology, 38*(3), 292–295.

Mohr, D.C., Hart, S.L., Julian, L., Catledge, C. et al. (2005). Telephone-administered psychotherapy for depression. *Archives of General Psychiatry, 62*, 1007–1014.

Mohr, J.W., Turner, R.E. & Jerry, M.B. (1964). *Pedophilia and exhibitionism*. Toronto: University of Toronto Press.

Moisander, P.A. & Edston, E. (2003). Torture and its sequel: A comparison between victims from six countries. *Forensic Science International, 137*(2–3), 133–140.

Moise, D. & Madhusoodanan, S. (2006). Psychiatric symptoms associated with brain tumors: A clinical enigma. *CNS Spectrums, 11*(1), 28–31.

Molko, N., Cachia, A., Riviere, D., Mangin, J.F. et al. (2003). Functional and structural alterations of the intraparietal sulcus in a developmental dyscalculia of genetic origin. *Neuron, 40*(4), 847–858.

Monarch, E.S., Saykin, A.J. & Flashman, L.A. (2004). Neuropsychological impairment in borderline personality disorder. *Psychiatric Clinics of North America, 27*, 67.

Moniz, E. (1936). *Tentatives opératoires dans le traitement de certaines psychoses*. Paris: Masson.

Monsma, E.V. & Malina, R.M. (2004). Correlates of eating disorders risk among female figure skaters: A profile of adolescent competitors. *Psychology of Sport and Exercise, 5*(4), 447–460.

Monteaux, M.C., Blacker, D., Biederman, J., Fitzmaurice, G. et al. (2006). Maternal smoking during pregnancy and offspring overt and covert conduct problems: A longitudinal study. *Journal of Child Psychology and Psychiatry, 47*, 883–890.

Monteaux, M.C., Faraone, S.V., Herzig, K., Navsaria, N. & Biederman, J. (2005). ADHD and dyscalculia: Evidence for independent familial transmission. *Journal of Learning Disabilities, 38*(1), 86–93.

Montgomery, S.A. (1995). Selective serotonin reuptake inhibitors in the acute treatment of depression. In F.E. Bloom & D. Kupfer (Eds.), *Psychopharmacology: The fourth generation of progress*. New York: Raven.

Moore, P.S., Whaley, S.E. & Sigman, M. (2004). Interactions between mothers and children: Impacts of maternal and child anxiety. *Journal of Abnormal Psychology, 113*(3), 471–476.

Moore, R.A., Edwards, J.E. & McQuay, H.J. (2002). Sildenafil (Viagra) for male erectile dysfunction: A meta-analysis of clinical trial reports. *BMC Urology, 2*.

Morey, L.C. (1988). Personality disorders in DSM-III and DSM-III-R: Convergence, coverage, and internal consistency. *American Journal of Psychiatry, 145*, 573–577.

Morgan, C.D. & Murray, H.A. (1935). A method of investigating fantasies: The Thematic Apperception Test. *Archives of Neurological Psychiatry, 34*, 289–306.

Morokoff, P.J. & Gilliland, R. (1993). Stress, sexual functioning, and marital satisfaction. *Journal of Sex Research, 30*(1), 43–53.

Morris, D.R., Meighen, K.G. & McDougle, C.J. (2005). Acute onset of obsessive-compulsive disorder in an adolescent with acute lymphoblastic leukemia. *Psychosomatics, 46*(5), 458–460.

Morris, P.L.P., Robinson, R.G., Andrezejewski, P., Samuels, J. & Price, T.R. (1993). Association of depression with 10-year poststroke mortality. *American Journal of Psychiatry, 150*(1), 124–129.

Morrison, A., Renton, J., Dunn, H., Williams, S. & Bentall, R. (2003). *Cognitive therapy for psychosis.* London: Routledge.

Morrison, A.P. (2001a). Cognitive therapy for auditory hallucinations as an alternative to antipsychotic medication: A case series. *Clinical Psychology and Psychotherapy, 8*(2), 136–147.

Morrison, A.P. (2001b). The interpretation of intrusions in psychosis: An integrative cognitive approach to hallucinations and delusions. *Behavioural and Cognitive Psychotherapy, 29*, 257–276.

Morrison, A.P., Bentall, R.P., French, P., Walford, L. et al. (2002). Randomized controlled trial of early detection and cognitive therapy for preventing transition to psychosis in high-risk individuals: Study design and interim analysis of transition rate and psychological risk factors. *British Journal of Psychiatry, 181*, S78–S84.

Morrison, C.E., Borod, J.C., Brin, M.F., Halbig, T.D. et al. (2004). Effects of levodopa on cognitive functioning in moderate-to-severe Parkinson's disease. *Journal of Neural Transmission, 111*, 1333–1341.

Morrison, J. (1989). Histrionic personality disorder in women with somatization disorder. *Psychosomatics, 30*(4), 433–437.

Morrow-Bradley, C. & Elliott, R. (1986). Utilization of psychotherapy research by practicing psychotherapists. *American Psychologist, 41*, 188–197.

Moser, C. & Levitt, E.E. (1987). An exploratory-descriptive study of a sado-masochistically oriented sample. *Journal of Sex Research, 23*, 322–337.

Moynihan, R. (2003). The making of a disease: Female sexual dysfunction. *British Medical Journal, 329*, 1363.

Moynihan, R. (2006). The marketing of a disease: Female sexual dysfunction. *British Medical Journal, 330*, 192–194.

Mueser, K.T., Drake, R.E. & Wallach, M.A. (1998). Dual diagnosis: A review of etiological theories. *Addictive Behaviors, 23*(6), 717–734.

Mueser, K.T. & McGurk, S.R. (2004). Schizophrenia. *Lancet, 363*, 2063–2072.

Mueser, K.T., Sengupta, A., Schooler, N.R., Bellack, A.S., Xei, H.Y. et al. (2001). Family treatments and medication dosage reduction in schizophrenia: Effects on patient social functioning, family attitudes, and burden. *Journal of Consulting and Clinical Psychology, 69*, 3–12.

Muhle, R., Trentacoste, S.V. & Rapin, I. (2004). The genetics of autism. *Pediatrics, 113*(5), E472–E486.

Mulkens, S.A.N., de Jong, P.J. & Merckelbach, H. (1996). Disgust and spider phobia. *Journal of Abnormal Psychology, 105*, 464–468.

Muris, P., Meesters, C., Merckelbach, H., Sermon, A. & Zwakhalen, S. (1998). Worry in normal children. *Journal of the American Academy of Child and Adolescent Psychiatry, 37*, 703–710.

Muris, P., Merckelbach, H. & Luijten, M. (2002). The connection between cognitive development and specific fears and worries in normal children and children with below-average intellectual abilities: A preliminary study. *Behaviour Research and Therapy, 40*(1), 37–56.

Murphy, W.D. (1997). Exhibitionism: Psychopathology and theory. In D.R. Laws & W. O'Donohue (Eds.), *Sexual deviance.* New York: Guilford Press.

Murray, E. & Foote, F. (1979). The origins of fear of snakes. *Behaviour Research and Therapy, 17*, 489–493.

Murray, R.M. & van Os, J. (1998). Predictors of outcome in schizophrenia. *Journal of Clinical Psychopharmacology, 18*(2), 2S–4S.

Myers, T.C., Swan-Kremeier, L., Wonderlich, S., Lancaster, K. & Mitchell, J.E. (2004). The use of alternative delivery systems and new technologies in the treatment of patients with eating disorders. *International Journal of Eating Disorders, 36*, 123–143.

Nahas, G.G., Paton, W.D.M. & Harvey, D.J. (1999). The Reims Symposium (1978). Paper given at the Conference on Marihuana and Medicine, 20–21 March, 1998, New York University School of Medicine, New York. *Marihuana and Medicine*, 13–24.

Najman, J.M., Dunne, M.P., Purdie, D.M., Boyle, F.M. & Coxeter, P.D. (2005). Sexual abuse in childhood and sexual dysfunction in adulthood: An Australian population-based study. *Archives of Sexual Behavior, 34*, 517–526.

Najman, J.M., Hallam, D., Bor, W., Callaghan, M., Williams, G.M. & Shuttlewood, G. (2005). Predictors of depression in very young children: A prospective study. *Social Psychiatry and Psychiatric Epidemiology, 40*(5), 367–374.

Nakagawa, A., Marks, I.M., Park, J.M., Bachofen, M. et al. (2000). Self-treatment of obsessive-compulsive disorder guided by manual and computer-conducted telephone interview. *Journal of Telemedicine and Telecare, 6*(1), 22–26.

Narrow, W.E., Rae, D.S., Robins, L.N. & Regier, D.A. (2002). Revised prevalence estimates of mental disorders in the United States: Using a clinical significance criterion to reconcile two survey estimates. *Archives of General Psychiatry, 59*, 115–123.

Nasby, W., Hayden, B. & DePaulo, B.M. (1979). Attributional bias among aggressive boys to interpret unambiguous social stimuli as displays of hostility. *Journal of Abnormal Psychology, 89*, 459–468.

Nath, A. & Sacktor, N. (2006). Influence of highly active antiretroviral therapy on persistence of HIV in the central nervous system. *Current Opinion in Neurology, 19*(4), 358–361.

Nathaniel-James, D.A., Brown, R. & Ron, M.A. (1996). Memory impairment in schizophrenia: Its relationship to executive function. *Schizophrenia Research, 21*(2), 85–96.

National Creutzfeld-Jakob Disease Surveillance Unit (2006). Figures retrieved from www.cjd.ed.ac.uk/figures.htm, November 2006.

National Household Survey on Drug Abuse (2002). Washington, DC: US Department of Health and Human Sciences.

National Institute of Alcohol Abuse and Alcoholism (2001). *Alcohol Alert No. 51: Economic perspectives in alcohol research.* Rockville, MD: Author.

National Institute for Clinical Excellence (2002). *Guidance on the use of nicotine replacement therapy (NRT) and bupropion for smoking cessation.* N0082 1P. London: NICE.

National Institute on Drug Abuse (1988). *National household survey on drug abuse: Main findings 1985.* Washington, DC: Department of Health and Human Sciences.

National Working Party on Dyslexia in Higher Education (1999). *Dyslexia in higher education: Policy, provision and practice.* London: NWPDHE.

Nayani, T.H. & David, A.S. (1996). The auditory hallucination: A phenomenological survey. *Psychological Medicine, 26*(1), 177–189.

Neal, J.A. & Edelmann, R.J. (2003). The etiology of social phobia: Toward a developmental profile. *Clinical Psychology Review, 23*, 761–786.

Neal, J.A., Edelmann, R.J. & Glachan, M. (2002). Behavioural inhibition and symptoms of anxiety and depression: Is there a specific relationship with social phobia? *British Journal of Clinical Psychology, 41*, 361–374.

Nelson, C.A. & Bosquet, M. (2000). Neurobiology of fetal and infant development: Implications for infant mental health. In C.H. Zeanah (Ed.), *Handbook of infant mental health* (2nd ed.). New York: Guilford Press.

Nelson, E.C., Grant, J.D., Bucholz, K.K., Glowinski, A. et al. (2000). Social phobia in a population-based female adolescent twin sample: Co-morbidity and associated suicide-related symptoms. *Psychological Medicine, 30*(4), 797–804.

Nelson, M.L. & Poulin, K. (1997). Methods of constructivist inquiry. In T. Sexton & B. Griffin (Eds.), *Constructivist thinking in counselling practice, research and training.* New York: Teachers College Press.

Nelson, M.L. & Quintana, S.M. (2005). Qualitative clinical research with children and adolescents. *Journal of Clinical Child and Adolescent Psychology, 34*, 344–356.

Nestadt, G., Samuels, J., Riddle, M., Bienvenu, O.J. et al. (2000). A family study of obsessive-compulsive disorder. *Archives of General Psychiatry, 57*(4), 358–363.

Nestler, E.J. (2001). Molecular neurobiology of addiction. *American Journal on Addictions, 10*(3), 201–217.

Neugebauer, R. (1979). Medieval and early modern theories of mental illness. *Archives of General Psychiatry, 36*, 477–483.

Neumark-Sztainer, D. & Hannan, P.J. (2000). Weight-related behaviors among adolescent girls and boys: Results from a national survey. *Archives of Pediatrics and Adolescent Medicine, 154*(6), 569–577.

Newell, R. & Shrubb, S. (1994). Attitude change and behavior therapy in body dysmorphic disorder. 2. Case reports. *Behavioural and Cognitive Psychotherapy, 22*(2), 163–169.

Newman, C.F., Leahy, R.L., Beck, A.T. et al. (2002). *Bipolar disorder: A cognitive therapy approach.* Washington, DC: American Psychological Association.

Newton-Howes, G. & Tyrer, P. (2003). Pharmacotherapy for personality disorders. *Expert Opinion on Pharmacotherapy, 4*, 1643–1649.

Niccols, G.A. (1994). Fetal alcohol syndrome: Implications for psychologists. *Clinical Psychology Review, 14*(2), 91–111.

Nicolas, G., DeSilva, A.M., Grey, K.S. & Gonzalez-Eastep, D. (2006). Using a multicultural lens to understand illness among Haitians living in America. *Professional Psychology: Research and Practice, 37*, 702–707.

Nicolson, R. & Rapoport, J.L. (1999). Childhood-onset schizophrenia: Rare but worth studying. *Biological Psychiatry, 46*(10), 1418–1428.

Nielson, P.E. (1960). A study in transsexualism. *Psychiatric Quarterly, 34*, 203–235.

Nietzel, M.T. & Harris, M.J. (1990). Relationship of dependency and achievement autonomy to depression. *Clinical Psychology Review, 10*(3), 279–297.

Nigg, J.T. & Goldsmith, H.H. (1994). Genetics of personality disorders: Perspectives from personality and psychopathology research. *Psychological Bulletin, 115*, 346–380.

Niznikiewicz, M.A., Kubicki, M. & Shenton, M.E. (2003). Recent structural and functional imaging findings in schizophrenia. *Current Opinions in Psychiatry, 16*, 123–147.

Nock, M.K., Kazdin, A.E., Hiripi, E. & Kessler, R.C. (2006). Prevalence, subtypes, and correlates of DSM-IV conduct disorder in the national comorbidity survey replication. *Psychological Medicine, 36*, 699–710.

Nock, M.K. & Kurtz, S.M.S. (2005). Direct behavioural observation in school settings: Bringing science to practice. *Cognitive and Behavioral Practice, 12*, 359–370.

Nolen-Hoeksema, S. (2001). Gender differences in depression. *Current Directions in Psychological Science, 10*, 173–176.

Nolen-Hoeksema, S. (2002). Gender differences in depression. In I.H. Gotlib & C.L. Hammen (Eds.), *Handbook of depression.* New York: Guilford Press.

Nordstrom, A.L., Farde, L., Nyberg, S., Karlsson, P. et al. (1995). D-1, D-2, and 5-HT2 receptor occupancy in relation to clozapine serum concentration: A pet study of schizophrenic patients. *American Journal of Psychiatry, 152*(10), 1444–1449.

Norra, C., Mrazek, M., Tuchtenhagen, F., Gobbele, R. et al. (2003). Enhanced intensity dependence as a marker of low serotonergic neurotransmission in borderline personality disorder. *Journal of Psychiatric Research, 37*(1), 23–33.

Norris, F.H., Perilla, J.L., Ibanez, G.E. & Murphy, A.D. (2001). Sex differences in symptoms of posttraumatic stress: Does culture play a role? *Journal of Traumatic Stress, 14*(1), 7–28.

Norstrom, T. & Ramstedt, M. (2005). Mortality and population drinking: A review of the literature. *Drug and Alcohol Review, 24*(6), 537–547.

North, C.S., Kawasaki, A., Spitznagel, E.L. & Hong, B.A. (2004). The course of PTSD, major depression, substance abuse, and somatization after a natural disaster. *Journal of Nervous and Mental Disease, 192*(12), 823–829.

Northrup, J., Broussard, C., Jones, K., George, T., Vollmer, T.R. & Herring, M. (1995). The differential effects of teacher and peer attention on the disruptive classroom behavior of three children with a diagnosis of attention deficit hyperactivity disorder. *Journal of Applied Behavior Analysis, 28*, 277–288.

Nowlan, R. & Cohen, S. (1977). Tolerance to marihuana: Heart rate and subjective high. *Clinical Pharmacology and Therapeutics, 22*(5), 550–556.

Noyes, R. (1999). The relationship of hypochondriasis to anxiety disorders. *General Hospital Psychiatry, 21*, 8–17.

Noyes, R., Happel, R.L., Muller, B.A., Holt, C.S. et al. (1998). Fluvoxamine for somatoform disorders: An open trial. *General Hospital Psychiatry, 20*(6), 339–344.

Noyes, R., Kathol, R.G., Fisher, M.M., Phillips, M.M. et al. (1994). Psychiatric comorbidity among patients with hypochondriasis. *General Hospital Psychiatry, 16*, 78–87.

Noyes, R., Woodman, C., Garvey, M.J., Cook, B.L. et al. (1992). Generalized anxiety disorder vs. panic disorder: Distinguishing characteristics and patterns of comorbidity. *Journal of Nervous and Mental Disease, 180*(6), 369–379.

NSPKU (2004). *Management of PKU.* London: National Society for Phenylketonuria.

Nutt, D.J. & Malizia, A.L. (2001). New insights into the role of GABA-sub(A) benzodiazipine receptor in psychiatric disorder. *British Journal of Psychiatry, 179*, 390–396.

Nys, G.M.S., van Zandvoort, M.J.E., Algra, A., Kappelle, L.J. & de Haan, E.H.F. (2006). Cognitive and functional outcome after intravenous recombinant tissue plasminogen activator treatment in patients with a first symptomatic brain infarct. *Journal of Neurology, 253*(2), 237–241.

Oakley, D.A. (1999). Hypnosis and conversion hysteria: A unifying model. *Cognitive Neuropsychiatry, 4*, 243–265.

O'Brien, C.P. (2005). Anticraving medications for relapse prevention: A possible new class of psychoactive medications. *American Journal of Psychiatry, 162*(8), 1423–1431.

O'Brien, C.P. & McKay, J. (2002). Pharmacological treatments for substance use disorders. In P.E. Nathan & J.M. Gorman (Eds.), *A guide to treatments that work* (2nd ed.). London: Oxford University Press.

O'Brien, K.M. & Vincent, N.K. (2003). Psychiatric comorbidity in anorexia and bulimia nervosa: Nature, prevalence, and causal relationships. *Clinical Psychology Review, 23*, 57–74.

Ochsner, K.N. & Barrett, L.F. (2001). A multiprocess perspective on the neuroscience of emotion. In T.J. Mayne & G.A. Bonanno (Eds.), *Emotions: Current issues and future directions.* New York: Guilford Press.

O'Connor, B.P. & Dyce, J.A. (1998). A test of models of personality disorder configuration. *Journal of Abnormal Psychology, 107*(1), 3–16.

O'Donohue, W.T., Dopke, C.A. & Swingen, D.N. (1997). Psychotherapy for female sexual dysfunction: A review. *Clinical Psychology Review, 17*, 537–556.

O'Donohue, W.T., Swingen, D.N., Dopke, C.A. & Regev, L.G. (1999). Psychotherapy for male sexual dysfunction: A review. *Clinical Psychology Review, 19*, 591–630.

O'Dwyer, A.M., Lucey, J.V. & Russell, G.F.M. (1996). Serotonin activity in anorexia nervosa after long-term weight restoration: Response to D-fenfluramine challenge. *Psychological Medicine, 26*(2), 353–359.

Office for National Statistics (2004). *The health of children and young people.* London: Office for National Statistics.

Ogilvie, D., Gruer, L. & Haw, S. (2006). Young people's access to tobacco, alcohol and other drugs. *British Medical Journal, 331*, 393–396.

Ohman, A., Erixon, G. & Lofberg, I. (1975). Phobias and preparedness: Phobic versus neutral pictures as conditioned stimuli for human autonomic responses. *Journal of Abnormal Psychology, 84*(1), 41–45.

Ohman, A. & Mineka, S. (2001). Fears, phobias, and preparedness: Toward an evolved module of fear and fear learning. *Psychological Review, 108*, 483–522.

O'Kearney, R.T., Anstey, K.J. & von Sanden, C. (2006). Behavioural and cognitive behavioural therapy for obsessive compulsive disorder in children and adolescents. *Cochrane Database of Systematic Reviews* (4), Art. No. CD004856 2006.

Olbrich, R., Kirsch, P., Pfeiffer, H. & Mussgay, L. (2001). Patterns of recovery of autonomic dysfunctions and neurocognitive deficits in schizophrenics after acute psychotic episodes. *Journal of Abnormal Psychology, 110*(1), 142–150.

O'Leary, K.D. & Wilson, G.T. (1975). *Behavior therapy: Application and outcome.* Englewood Cliffs, NJ: Prentice-Hall.

Olfson, M. & Klerman, G.L. (1993). Trends in the prescription of antidepressants by office-based psychiatrists. *American Journal of Psychiatry, 150*(4), 571–577.

Olivardia, R., Pope, H.G. & Hudson, J.I. (2000). Muscle dysmorphia in male weightlifters: A case-control study. *American Journal of Psychiatry, 157*(8), 1291–1296.

Oliver, R.G. & Hetzel, B.S. (1973). Analysis of recent trends in suicide rates in Australia. *International Journal of Epidemiology, 2*(1), 91–101.

Ollendick, T.H. & Hirschfeld Becker, D.R. (2002). The developmental and psychopathology of social anxiety disorder. *Biological Psychiatry, 51*, 44–58.

Ollendick, T.H., King, N.J. & Muris, P. (2002). Fears and phobias in children: Phenomenology, epidemiology and aetiology. *Child and Adolescent Mental Health, 7*, 98–106.

O'Malley, K.D. & Nanson, J. (2002). Clinical implications of a link between fetal alcohol spectrum disorder and attention-deficit hyperactivity disorder. *Canadian Journal of Psychiatry: Revue Canadienne de Psychiatrie, 47*(4), 349–354.

O'Malley, S.S., Krishnan-Sarin, S., Farren, C. & O'Connor, P.G. (2000). Naltrexone-induced nausea in patients treated for alcohol dependence: Clinical predictors and evidence for opioid-mediated effects. *Journal of Clinical Psychopharmacology, 20*(1), 69–76.

Oosterlaan, J., Scheres, A. & Sergeant, J.A. (2005). Which executive functioning deficits are associated with AD/HD, ODD/CD and comorbid AD/HD plus ODD/CD? *Journal of Abnormal Child Psychology, 33*, 69–85.

Open Society Institute (2005). *Open Society Mental Health Initiative.*

O'Reilly, M.F. (1995). Functional analysis and treatment of escape-maintained aggression correlated with sleep deprivation. *Journal of Applied Behavior Analysis, 28*, 225–226.

Orr, S.P., Metzger, L.J., Lasko, N.B., Macklin, M.L., Peri, T. & Pitman, R.K. (2000). De novo conditioning in trauma-exposed individuals with and without posttraumatic stress disorder. *Journal of Abnormal Psychology, 109*(2), 290–298.

Ossiander, E.M., Mueller, M.M. & van Enwyk, J. (2005). Childhood lead poisoning in Washington state: A statewide survey. *Archives of Environmental Health, 60*(1), 25–30.

Ost, L.G. (1997). Rapid treatment of specific phobias. In G.C.L. Davey (Ed.), *Phobias: A handbook of theory, research and treatment.* Chichester: Wiley.

Ost, L.G., Alm, T., Brandberg, M. & Breitholtz, E. (2001). One vs. five sessions of exposure and five sessions of cognitive therapy in the treatment of claustrophobia. *Behaviour Research and Therapy, 39*(2), 167–183.

Ottaviani, R. & Beck, A.T. (1987). Cognitive aspects of panic disorder. *Journal of Anxiety Disorders, 1*, 15–28.

Otto, M.W., Pollack, M.H., Maki, K.M., Gould, R.A. et al. (2001). Childhood history of anxiety disorders among adults with social phobia: Rates, correlates, and comparisons with patients with panic disorder. *Depression and Anxiety, 14*(4), 209–213.

Ouimette, P.C., Finney, J.W. & Moos, R.H. (1997). Twelve-step and cognitive-behavioral treatment for substance abuse: A comparison of treatment effectiveness. *Journal of Consulting and Clinical Psychology, 65*(2), 230–240.

Overholser, J.C. (1996). The dependent personality and interpersonal problems. *Journal of Nervous and Mental Disease, 184*(1), 8–16.

Owen, P.R. & Laurel-Seller, E. (2000). Weight and shape ideals: Thin is dangerously in. *Journal of Applied Social Psychology, 30*(5), 979–990.

Owens, D., Horrocks, J. & House, A. (2002). Fatal and non-fatal repetition of self-harm: Systematic review. *British Journal of Psychiatry, 181*, 193–199.

Ownsworth, T.L. & McFarland, K. (1999). Memory remediation in long-term acquired brain injury: Two approaches in diary training. *Brain Injury, 13*(8), 605–626.

Ownsworth, T.L., McFarland, K. & Young, R.M.D. (2002). Self-awareness and psychosocial functioning following acquired brain injury: An evaluation of a group support programme. *Neuropsychological Rehabilitation, 10*(5), 465–484.

Ozer, R.J. & Weiss, D.S. (2004). Who develops posttraumatic stress disorder? *Current Directions in Psychological Science, 13*, 169–172.

Ozonoff, S. & McEvoy, R.E. (1994). A longitudinal study of executive function and theory of mind development in autism. *Development and Psychopathology, 6*(3), 415–431.

Ozonoff, S., Pennington, B.F. & Rogers, S.J. (1991). Executive function deficits in high-functioning autistic individuals: Relationship to theory of mind. *Journal of Child Psychology and Psychiatry, 32*, 1081–1105.

Ozonoff, S. & Strayer, D.L. (1997). Inhibitory function in nonretarded children with autism. *Journal of Autism and Developmental Disorders, 27*(1), 59–77.

Pace-Schott, E.F., Stickgold, R., Muzur, A., Wigren, P.E. et al. (2005). Cognitive performance by humans during a smoked cocaine binge–abstinence cycle. *American Journal of Drug and Alcohol Abuse, 31*(4), 571–591.

Packman, A., Onslow, M. & van Doorn, J. (1994). Prolonged speech and modification of stuttering: Perceptual, acoustic, and electroglottographic data. *Journal of Speech and Hearing Research, 37*(4), 724–737.

Page, A.C. (1994). Blood-injury phobia. *Clinical Psychology Review, 14*, 443–461.

Pankratz, L. (2006). Persistent problems with the Munchausen syndrome by proxy label. *Journal of the American Academy of Psychiatry and the Law, 34*(1), 90–95.

Panksepp, J. (1979). A neurochemical theory of autism. *Trends in Neuroscience, 2*, 174–177.

Papadopoulos, T.C., Panayiotou, G., Spanoudis, G. & Natsopoulos, D. (2005). Evidence of poor planning in children with attention deficits. *Journal of Abnormal Child Psychology, 33*, 611–623.

Papaharitou, S., Athanasiadis, L., Nakopoulou, E., Kirana, P. et al. (2006). Erectile dysfunction and premature ejaculation are the most frequently self-reported sexual concerns: Profiles of 9,536 men calling a helpline. *European Urology, 49*(3), 557–563.

Papp, L.A., Klein, D.F. & Gorman, J.M. (1993). Carbon-dioxide hypersensitivity, hyperventilation, and panic disorder. *American Journal of Psychiatry, 150*(8), 1149–1157.

Paris, J. (1997). Antisocial and borderline personality disorders: Two separate diagnoses or two aspects of the same psychopathology? *Comprehensive Psychiatry, 38*(4), 237–242.

Paris, J. (2001). Psychosocial adversity. In W.J. Livesley (Ed.), *Handbook of personality disorders: Theory, research and treatment.* New York: Guilford Press.

Park, N.W., Proulx, G.B. & Towers, W.M. (1999). Evaluation of the attention process training programme. *Neuropsychological Rehabilitation, 9*(2), 135–154.

Parker, G., Both, L., Olley, A., Hadzi-Pavlovic, D. et al. (2002). Defining disordered personality functioning. *Journal of Personality Disorders, 16*, 503–522.

Parkinson's Disease Society (2008). How many people have Parkinson's? Retrieved from www.parkinsons.org.uk/about-parkinsons/what-is-parkinsons/how-many-people-have-parkinson.aspx, February 2008.

Parrott, A.C. (1994). Individual differences in stress and arousal during cigarette smoking. *Psychopharmacology, 115*, 389–396.

Parrott, A.C. (1998). Nesbitt's paradox resolved? Stress and arousal modulation during cigarette smoking. *Addiction, 93*, 27–39.

Parrott, A.C. (1999). Does cigarette smoking cause stress? *American Psychologist, 54*, 817–820.

Parrott, A.C. & Garnham, N.J. (1998). Comparative mood states and cognitive skills of cigarette smokers, deprived smokers and nonsmokers. *Human Psychopharmacology: Clinical and Experimental, 13*(5), 367–376.

Parrott, S., Godfrey, C., Heather, N., Clark, J. & Ryan, T. (2006). Cost and outcome analysis of two alcohol detoxification services. *Alcohol and Alcoholism, 41*(1), 84–91.

Parsons, T. (1951). *The social system.* New York: Free Press.

Pathe, M. (2002). *Surviving stalking.* New York: Cambridge University Press.

Pato, M.T., Zohar-Kadouch, R., Zohar, J. & Murphy, D.L. (1988). Return of symptoms after discontinuation of clomipramine in patients with obsessive-compulsive disorder. *American Journal of Psychiatry, 145*(12), 1521–1525.

Paton, C. & Beer, D. (2001). Caffeine: The forgotten variable. *International Journal of Psychiatry in Clinical Practice, 5*(4), 231–236.

Patrick, D.L., Althof, S.E., Pryor, J.L., Rosen, R. et al. (2005). Premature ejaculation: An observational study of men and their partners. *Journal of Sexual Medicine, 2*(3), 358–367.

Patten, S.B. (2003). International differences in major depression prevalence: What do they mean? *Journal of Clinical Epidemiology, 56*, 711–716.

Patterson, C.H. (2000). *Person-centered approach and client-centered therapy: Essential readers.* Ross-on-Wye: PCCS Books.

Patterson, G., Reid, J. & Dishion, T. (1992). *Antisocial boys.* Eugene, OR: Castalia.

Patton, G.C., Coffey, C., Carlin, J.B., Degenhardt, L., Lynskey, M. & Hall, W. (2002). Cannabis use and mental health in young people: Cohort study. *British Medical Journal, 325*(7374), 1195–1198.

Patton, R.B. & Shepherd, J.A. (1956). Intercranial tumors found in autopsy in mental patients. *American Journal of Psychiatry, 113*, 319–324.

Paul, G.L. (1966). *Insight vs. desensitization in psychotherapy: An experiment in anxiety reduction.* Stanford, CA: Stanford University Press.

Paul, G.L. & Lentz, R. (1977). *Psychosocial treatment of the chronic mental patient.* Cambridge, MA: Harvard University Press.

Paul, W.M., Gonsiorek, J.C. & Hotvedt, M.E. (Eds.) (1982). *Homosexuality.* Beverly Hills, CA: Sage.

Pauls, D.L., Alsobrook, J.P., Goodman, W., Rasmussen, S. & Leckman, J.F. (1995). A family study of obsessive-compulsive disorder. *American Journal of Psychiatry, 152*, 76–84.

Paulson, J.F., Dauber, S. & Leiferman, J.A. (2006). Individual and combined effects of postpartum depression in mothers and fathers on parenting behaviour. *Pediatrics, 118*, 659–668.

Paurohit, N., Dowd, E.T. & Cottingham, H.F. (1982). The role of verbal and nonverbal cues in the formation of first impressions of black and white counsellors. *Journal of Counselling Psychology, 4*, 371–378.

Pavkov, T.W., Lewis, D.A. & Lyons, J.S. (1989). Psychiatric diagnoses and racial bias: An empirical investigation. *Professional Psychology: Research and Practice, 20*, 364–368.

Payne, C. & Mason, B. (1998). Autism, inflammatory bowel disease, and MMR vaccine. *Lancet, 351*(9106), 907.

Pearce, B.D. (2001). Schizophrenia and viral infection during neurodevelopment: A focus on mechanisms. *Molecular Psychiatry, 6*(6), 634–646.

Pederson, K.J., Roerig, J.L. & Mitchell, J.E. (2003). Towards the pharmacotherapy of eating disorders. *Expert Opinion on Pharmacotherapy, 4*(10), 1659–1678.

Pedro-Carroll, J. & Reddy, L. (2005). A prevention play intervention of foster children's resilience in the aftermath of divorce. In L. Reddy, T. Files-Hall & C. Schaefer (Eds.), *Empirically based play interventions for children.* Washington, DC: American Psychological Association.

Penn, D.L. & Mueser, K.T. (1996). Research update on the psychosocial treatment of schizophrenia. *American Journal of Psychiatry, 153*, 607–617.

Pennington, B.F. & Gilger, J.W. (1996). How is dyslexia transmitted? In C.H. Chase, G.D. Rosen & G.F. Sherman (Eds.), *Developmental dyslexia: Neural, cognitive and genetic mechanisms.* Baltimore: York Press.

Pericek-Vance, M.A., Bass, M.P., Yamaoka, L.H., Gaskell, P.C. et al. (1997). Complete genomic screen in late-onset familial Alzheimer disease: Evidence for a new locus on chromosome 12. *JAMA: Journal of the American Medical Association, 278*(15), 1237–1241.

Perilla, J.L., Norris, F.H. & Lavizzo, E.A. (2002). Ethnicity, culture, and disaster response: Identifying and explaining ethnic differences in PTSD six months after Hurricane Andrew. *Journal of Social and Clinical Psychology, 21*(1), 20–45.

Perlmutter, J.S. & Mink, J.W. (2006). Deep brain stimulation. *Annual Review of Neuroscience, 29*, 229–257.

Perls, F.S. (1969). *Gestalt therapy verbatim.* Moab, UT: Real People Press.

Perna, G., Gabriele, A., Caldirola, D. et al. (1995). Hypersensitivity to inhalation of carbon-dioxide and panic attacks. *Psychiatry Research, 57*(3), 267–273.

Perner, J., Kain, W. & Barchfeld, P. (2002). Executive control and higher-order theory of mind in children at risk of ADHD. *Infant and Child Development, 11*, 141–158.

Perowne, S. & Mansell, W. (2002). Social anxiety, self-focussed attention, and the discrimination of negative, neutral and positive audience members by their non-verbal behaviours. *Behavioural and Cognitive Psychotherapy, 30*, 11–23.

Perry, J.C., Banon, E. & Ianni, F. (1999). Effectiveness of psychotherapy for personality disorders. *American Journal of Psychiatry, 156*(9), 1312–1321.

Persons, J.B. (1989). *Cognitive therapy in practice: A case formulation approach.* New York: W.W. Norton.

Peters, E.R., Pickering, A.D., Kent, A., Glasper, A. et al. (2000). The relationship between cognitive inhibition and psychotic symptoms. *Journal of Abnormal Psychology, 109*(3), 386–395.

Peters, K.D. & Murphy, S.L. (1998). *Deaths: Final data for 1996.* National Vital Statistics Report, 47.

Peters, M.L., Uyterlinde, S.A., Consemulder, J. & van der Hart, O. (1998). Apparent amnesia on experimental memory tests in dissociative identity disorder: An exploratory study. *Consciousness and Cognition, 7*(1), 27–41.

Petersen, R.C., Thomas, R., Grundman, M. & Thal, L. (2005). Treatment of MCI with cholinesterase inhibitors: Current data. *International Psychogeriatrics, 17*, 34.

Peterson, C., Maier, S.F. & Seligman, M.E.P. (1993). *Learned helplessness: A theory for the age of personal control.* New York: Oxford University Press.

Peterson, C., Semmel, A., von Baeyer, C., Abramson, L.Y. et al. (1982). The Attributional Style Questionnaire. *Cognitive Therapy and Research, 6*(3), 287–299.

Peto, R. (1994). Smoking and death: The past 40 years and the next 40. *British Medical Journal, 309*(6959), 937–939.

Petronis, K.R. & Anthony, J.C. (2003). Social epidemiology, intra-neighbourhood correlation, and generalized estimating equations. *Journal of Epidemiology and Community Health, 57*(11), 914.

Petry, N.M. (2000). A comprehensive guide to the application of contingency management procedures in clinical settings. *Drug and Alcohol Dependency, 58*, 9–25.

Petry, N.M. (2003). Patterns and correlates of Gamblers Anonymous attendance in pathological gamblers seeking professional treatment. *Addictive Behaviors, 28*(6), 1049–1062.

Petry, N.M., Ammerman, Y., Bohl, J., Doersch, A. et al. (2006). Cognitive-behavioral therapy for pathological gamblers. *Journal of Consulting and Clinical Psychology, 74*(3), 555–567.

Phares, V. (2003). *Understanding abnormal child psychology.* Hoboken, NJ: Wiley.

Phillips, K.A. (1996). *The broken mirror: Understanding and treating body dysmorphic disorder.* New York: Oxford University Press.

Phillips, K.A. (1998). Body dysmorphic disorder: Clinical aspects and treatment strategies. *Bulletin of the Menninger Clinic, 62*(4), A33–A48.

Phillips, K.A. (2001). *Somatoform and factitious disorders.* Review of Psychiatry (Vol. 20). Washington, DC: American Psychiatric Association.

Phillips, K.A., Didie, E.R., Menard, W., Pagano, M.E. et al. (2006). Clinical features of body dysmorphic disorder in adolescents and adults. *Psychiatry Research, 141*, 305–314.

Phillips, K.A. & Gunderson, J.G. (1994). Personality disorders. In R.E. Hales, S.C. Yudofsky & J.A. Talbott (Eds.), *The American Psychiatric Press textbook of psychiatry* (2nd ed.). Washington, DC: American Psychiatric Press.

Piasecki, T.M., Hufford, M.R., Solham, M. & Trull, T.J. (2007). Assessing clients in their natural environments with electronic diaries: Rationale, benefits, limitations, and barriers. *Psychological Assessment, 19*, 25–43.

Pike, K.M., Dohm, F.A., Striegel-Moore, R.H., Wilfley, D.E. & Fairburn, C.G. (2001). A comparison of black and white women with binge eating disorder. *American Journal of Psychiatry, 158*(9), 1455–1460.

Pike, K.M. & Rodin, J. (1991). Mothers, daughters, and disordered eating. *Journal of Abnormal Psychology, 100*(2), 198–204.

Pilling, S., Bebbington, P., Kuipers, E., Garety, P. et al. (2002). Psychological treatments in schizophrenia: I. Meta-analysis of family intervention and cognitive behaviour therapy. *Psychological Medicine, 2002*, 763–782.

Pinfold, V., Toulmin, H., Thornicroft, G., Huxley, P., Farmer, P. & Graham, T. (2003). Reducing psychiatric stigma and discrimination: Evaluation of educational interventions in UK secondary schools. *British Journal of Psychiatry, 182*, 342–346.

Pinkham, A.E., Penn, D.L., Perkins, D.O. & Lieberman, J. (2003). Implications for the neural basis of social cognition for the study of schizophrenia. *American Journal of Psychiatry, 160*(5), 815–824.

Pinkston, E.M., Linsk, N.L. & Young, R.N. (1988). Home-based behavioral family treatment of the impaired elderly. *Behavior Therapy, 19*(3), 331–344.

Piotrowski, C.S., Belter, R.W. & Keller, J.W. (1998). The impact of 'managed care' on the practice of psychological testing: Preliminary findings. *Journal of Personality Assessment, 70*, 441–447.

Piotrowski, C.S. & Brannen, S.J. (2002). Exposure, threat appraisal, and lost confidence as predictors of PTSD symptoms following September 11, 2001. *American Journal of Orthopsychiatry, 72*(4), 476–485.

Piper, A. (1994). Multiple personality disorder. *British Journal of Psychiatry, 164*, 600–612.

Piper, A. (1997). *Hoax and reality: The bizarre world of multiple personality disorder*. Northvale, NJ: Jason Aronson.

Piper, A. & Mersky, H. (2004). The persistence of folly: A critical examination of dissociative identity disorder. Part I: The excesses of an improbable concept. *Canadian Journal of Psychiatry, 49*, 592–600.

Piven, J. & Palmer, P. (1999). Psychiatric disorder and the broad autism phenotype: Evidence from a family study of multiple-incidence autism families. *American Journal of Psychiatry, 156*(4), 557–563.

Polaschek, D.L.L. & Gannon, T.A. (2004). The implicit theories of rapists: What convicted offenders tell us. *Sexual Abuse: A Journal of Research and Treatment, 16*(4), 299–314.

Polaschek, D.L.L. & Ward, T. (2002). The implicit theories of potential rapists: What our questionnaires tell us. *Aggression and Violent Behavior, 7*(4), 385–406.

Polivy, J. & Herman, C.P. (1985). Dieting and binging: A causal analysis. *American Psychologist, 40*(2), 193–201.

Polivy, J. & Herman, C.P. (2002). Causes of eating disorders. *Annual Review of Psychology, 53*, 187–213.

Polivy, J., Heatherton, T.F. & Herman, C.P. (1988). Self-esteem, restraint, and eating behavior. *Journal of Abnormal Psychology, 97*(3), 354–356.

Polkinghorne, D.E. (1983). Further extensions of methodological diversity for counseling psychology. *Journal of Counseling Psychology, 31*, 416–429.

Pollack, W. (1989). Schizophrenia and the self: Contributions of psychoanalytic self-psychology. *Schizophrenia Bulletin, 15*, 311–322.

Pollard, C.A., Pollard, H.J. & Corn, K.J. (1989). Panic onset and major events in the lives of agoraphobics: A test of contiguity. *Journal of Abnormal Psychology, 98*(3), 318–321.

Pollock, L.R. & Williams, J.M.G. (2001). Effective problem solving in suicide attempters depends on specific autobiographical recall. *Suicide and Life-Threatening Behavior, 31*(4), 386–396.

Pollock, N.L. & Hashmall, J.M. (1991). The excuses of child molesters. *Behavioral Sciences and the Law, 9*(1), 53–59.

Popper, K.R. (1959). *The logic of scientific discovery*. New York: Basic Books.

Porsolt, R.D., Lepichon, M. & Jalfre, M. (1977). Depression: New animal model sensitive to antidepressant treatments. *Nature, 266*, 730–732.

Poulton, R. & Menzies, R.G. (2002). Non-associative fear acquisition: A review of the evidence from retrospective and longitudinal research. *Behaviour Research and Therapy, 40*(2), 127–149.

Poulton, R., Moffitt, T.E., Harrington, H., Milne, B.J. & Caspi, A. (2001). Persistence and perceived consequences of cannabis use and dependence among young adults: Implications for policy. *New Zealand Medical Journal, 114*(1145), 544–547.

Powell, A.D. & Kahn, A.S. (1995). Racial differences in women's desires to be thin. *International Journal of Eating Disorders, 17*(2), 191–195.

Powell, R. & Gee, T.L. (1999). The effects of hypnosis on dissociative identity disorder: A re-examination of the evidence. *Canadian Journal of Psychiatry, 44*, 914–916.

Pratt, P., Tallis, F. & Eysenck, M. (1997). Information-processing, storage characteristics and worry. *Behaviour Research and Therapy, 35*(11), 1015–1023.

Pratt, S. & Mueser, K.T. (2002). Social skills training for schizophrenia. In S.G. Hofmann & M.C. Tompson (Eds.), *Treating chronic and severe mental disorders: A handbook of empirically supported interventions*. New York: Guilford Press.

Premack, D. & Woodruff, G. (1978). Chimpanzee problem-solving: Test for comprehension. *Science, 202*, 532–535.

Prien, R.F. & Potter, W.Z. (1993). Maintenance treatment for mood disorders. In D.L. Dunner (Ed.), *Current psychiatric therapy*. Philadephia: Saunders.

Prince, R. & Tchenglaroche, F. (1987). Culture-bound syndromes and international disease classification. *Culture, Medicine and Psychiatry, 11*, 3–19.

Prochaska, J.O. & Norcross, J.C. (2001). Stages of change. *Psychotherapy, 38*, 443–448.

Prochaska, J.O. & Norcross, J.C. (2003). *Systems of psychotherapy: A transitional analysis* (5th ed.). Pacific Grove, CA: Brookes/Cole.

Proudfoot, J., Ryden, C., Everitt, B., Shapiro, D. et al. (2004). Clinical efficacy of computerized cognitive-behavioural therapy for anxiety and depression in primary care: Randomized controlled trial. *British Journal of Psychiatry, 185*, 46–54.

Pryor, T.L., Martin, R.L. & Roach, N. (1995). Obsessive-compulsive disorder, trichotillomania, and anorexia nervosa: A case report. *International Journal of Eating Disorders, 18*(4), 375–379.

Pulvermuller, F., Neininger, B., Elbert, T. et al. (2001). Constraint-induced therapy of chronic aphasia after stroke. *Stroke, 32*(7), 1621–1626.

Purcell, D.W., Lewine, R.R.J., Caudle, J. & Price, L.R. (1998). Sex differences in verbal IQ performance: IQ discrepancies among patients with schizophrenia and normal volunteers. *Journal of Abnormal Psychology, 107*(1), 161–165.

Putnam, F.W. (1997). *Dissociation in children and adolescents: A developmental perspective*. New York: Guilford Press.

Putnam, F.W., Guroff, J.J., Silberman, E.K., Barban, L. & Post, R.M. (1986). The clinical phenomenology of multiple personality disorder: Review of 100 recent cases. *Journal of Clinical Psychiatry, 47*, 285–293.

Putnam, F.W. & Loewenstein, R.J. (2000). Dissociative identity disorder. In B.J. Sadock & V.A. Sadock (Eds.), *Kaplan and Sadock's comprehensive textbook of psychiatry* (7th ed., Vol. 1). Philadelphia: Lippincott Williams & Wilkins.

Quay, H.C. (1979). Classification. In H.C. Quay & J.S. Werry (Eds.), *Psychological disorders of childhood* (2nd ed.). New York: Wiley.

Rachman, S. (1966). Sexual fetishism: An experimental analogue. *Psychological Record, 16*(3), 293&.

Rachman, S. (1977). Conditioning theory of fear acquisition: Critical examination. *Behaviour Research and Therapy, 15*(5), 375–387.

Rachman, S. (1998). A cognitive theory of obsessions: Elaborations. *Behaviour Research and Therapy, 36*, 385–401.

Rachman, S. (2002). A cognitive theory of compulsive checking. *Behaviour Research and Therapy, 40*, 625–639.

Rachman, S. & DeSilva, P. (1978). Abnormal and normal obsessions. *Behaviour Research and Therapy, 16*(4), 233–248.

Rachman, S., Gruter-Andrew, J. & Shafran, R. (2000). Post-event processing in social anxiety. *Behaviour Research and Therapy, 38*(6), 611–617.

Rachman, S.J. & Levitt, K. (1985). Panics and their consequences. *Behaviour Research and Therapy, 23*, 585–600.

Radomsky, A.S. & Rachman, S. (2004). Symmetry, ordering and arranging compulsive behaviour. *Behaviour Research and Therapy, 42*(8), 893–913.

Raes, F., Hermans, D., Williams, J.M.G. & Eelen, P. (2005). Autobiographical memory specificity and emotional abuse. *British Journal of Clinical Psychology, 44*, 133–138.

Raes, F., Hermans, D., Williams, J.M.G. & Eelen, P. (2006). Reduced autobiographical memory specificity and affect regulation. *Cognition and Emotion, 20*(3–4), 402–429.

Raffi, A.R., Rondini, M., Grandi, S. & Fava, G.A. (2000). Life events and prodromal symptoms in bulimia nervosa. *Psychological Medicine, 30*(3), 727–731.

Ralevski, E., Sanislow, C.A., Grilo, C.M., Skodol, A.E. et al. (2005). Avoidant personality disorder and social phobia: Distinct enough to be separate disorders? *Acta Psychiatrica Scandinavica, 112*(3), 208–214.

Ramasubbu, R. & Patten, S.B. (2003). Effect of depression on stroke morbidity and mortality. *Canadian Journal of Psychiatry: Revue Canadienne de Psychiatrie, 48*(4), 250–255.

Ramo, D.E., Anderson, K.G., Tate, S.R. & Brown, S.A. (2005). Characteristics of relapse to substance use in comorbid adolescents. *Addictive Behaviors, 30*(9), 1811–1823.

Rampello, L., Nicoletti, F. & Nicoletti, F. (2000). Dopamine and depression: Therapeutic implications. *CNS Drugs, 13*(1), 35–45.

Ramsay, J.R. & Rostain, A.L. (2007). *Cognitive behavioral therapy for adult ADHD.* London: Routledge.

Ramsay, M., Baker, P., Goulden, C., Sharpe, C. & Sondhi, A. (2001). *Drug misuse declared in 2000: Results from the British Crime Survey.* Home Office Research Study 224. London: Home Office.

Ramsay, M., Partridge, B. & Byron, C. (1999). Drug misuse declared in 1998: Key results from the British Crime Survey. *Research Findings, 93*, 1–4.

Rao, S.M. (2000). Neuropsychological evaluation. In B.S. Fogel, R.B. Sciffer et al. (Eds.), *Synopsis of neuropsychiatry.* Philadelphia: Lippincott-Raven.

Rapaport, D., Gill, M. & Schaefer, R. (1968). *Diagnostic psychological testing.* New York: International Universities Press.

Rapee, R.M. (1995). Descriptive psychopathology of social phobia. In R.G. Heimberg, M.R. Liebowitz, D.A. Hope & F.R. Schneier (Eds.), *Social phobia: Diagnosis, assessment and treatment.* New York: Guilford Press.

Rapee, R.M. (1997). The potential role of childrearing practices in the development of anxiety and depression. *Clinical Psychology Review, 17*, 47–67.

Rapee, R.M. (2001). The development of generalized anxiety. In M.W. Vasey & M.R. Dadds (Eds.), *The developmental psychopathology of anxiety.* New York: Oxford University Press.

Rapee, R.M., Ancis, J.R. & Barlow, D.H. (1988). Emotional reactions to physiological sensations: Panic disorder patients and non-clinical SS. *Behaviour Research and Therapy, 26*(3), 265–269.

Rapee, R.M., Brown, T.A., Antony, M.M. & Barlow, D.H. (1992). Response to hyperventilation and inhalation of 5.5 percent carbon dioxide-enriched air across the DSM-III-R anxiety disorders. *Journal of Abnormal Psychology, 101*(3), 538–552.

Rapee, R.M. & Heimberg, R.G. (1997). A cognitive-behavioral model of anxiety in social phobia. *Behaviour Research and Therapy, 35*(8), 741–756.

Rapee, R.M. & Lim, L. (1992). Discrepancy between self and observer ratings of performance in social phobics. *Journal of Abnormal Psychology, 101*(4), 728–731.

Rapee, R.M. & Melville, L.F. (1997). Retrospective recall of family factors in social phobia and panic disorder. *Depression and Anxiety, 5*, 7–11.

Rapee, R.M. & Spence, S.H. (2004). The etiology of social phobia: Empirical evidence and an initial model. *Clinical Psychology Review, 24*, 737–767.

Rapoport, J.L. (1989). The biology of obsessions and compulsions. *Scientific American*, 82–89.

Rapport, L.J., van Voorhis, A., Tzelepis, A. & Friedman, S.R. (2001). Executive functioning in adult attention-deficit hyperactivity disorder. *Clinical Neuropsychologist, 15*(4), 479–491.

Raskin, D.C. & Honts, C.R. (2002). The comparison question test. In M. Kleiner (Ed.), *The handbook of polygraph testing.* San Diego, CA: Academic Press.

Rastam, M. & Gillberg, C. (1991). The family background in anorexia nervosa: A population-based study. *Journal of the American Academy of Child and Adolescent Psychiatry, 30*(2), 283–289.

Rath, J.F., Simon, D., Langenbahn, D.M., Sherr, R.L. & Diller, L. (2003). Group treatment of problem-solving deficits in outpatients with traumatic brain injury: A randomized outcome study. *Neuropsychological Rehabilitation, 13*(4), 461–488.

Rathod, N.H., Addenbrooke, W.M. & Rosenbach, A.F. (2005). Heroin dependence in an English town: 33-year follow-up. *British Journal of Psychiatry, 187*, 421–425.

Rauch, S.L., Jenike, M.A., Alpert, N.M., Baer, L. et al. (1994). Regional cerebral blood-flow measured during symptom provocation in obsessive-compulsive disorder using oxygen 15-labeled carbon dioxide and positron emission tomography. *Archives of General Psychiatry, 51*(1), 62–70.

Ravaldia, C., Vannacci, A., Zucchi, T., Mannucci, E. et al. (2003). Eating disorders and body image disturbances among ballet dancers, gymnasium users and body builders. *Psychopathology, 36*(5), 247–254.

Ravelski, E., Sanislow, C.A., Grilo, C.M., Skodol, A.E. et al. (2005). Avoidant personality disorder and social phobia: Distinct enough to be separate disorders? *Acta Psychiatrica Scandinavica, 113*, 208–214.

Raymond, N.C., Coleman, E. & Miner, M.H. (2003). Psychiatric comorbidity and compulsive/impulsive traits in compulsive sexual behavior. *Comprehensive Psychiatry, 44*(5), 370–380.

Raymond, N.C., Coleman, E., Ohlerking, F., Christenson, G.A. & Miner, M. (1999). Psychiatric comorbidity in pedophilic sex offenders. *American Journal of Psychiatry, 156*(5), 786–788.

Raynor, P. & Vanstone, M. (1996). Reasoning and rehabilitation in Britain: The results of the Straight Thinking on Probation (STOP) programme. *International Journal of Offender Therapy and Comparative Criminology, 40*, 272–284.

Read, J., van Os, J., Morrison, A.P. & Ross, C.A. (2005). Childhood trauma, psychosis and schizophrenia: A literature review with theoretical and clinical implications. *Acta Psychiatrica Scandinavica, 112*(5), 330–350.

Reade, S., Hunter, H. & McMillan, I. (1999). Just playing . . . is it time wasted? *British Journal of Occupational Therapy, 62*, 157–162.

Rechlin, T., Loew, T.H. & Joraschky, P. (1997). Pseudoseizure 'status'. *Journal of Psychosomatic Research, 42*(5), 495–498.

Redmond, D.E. (1977). Alterations to the function of the nucleus locus coeruleus: A possible model for studies of anxiety. In I. Hanin & E. Usdin (Eds.), *Animal models in psychiatry and neurology.* New York: Pergamon.

Reece, R.M. & Sege, R. (2000). Childhood head injuries: Accidental or inflicted? *Archives of Pediatrics and Adolescent Medicine, 154*, 11–15.

Reger, M., Welsh, R., Razani, J., Martin, D.J. & Boone, K.B. (2002). A meta-analysis of the neuropsychological sequelae of HIV infection. *Journal of the International Neuropsychological Society, 8*(3), 410–424.

Regier, D.A., Farmer, M.E., Rae, D.S., Locke, B.Z. et al. (1990). Comorbidity of mental disorders with alcohol and other drug abuse: Results from the Epidemiologic Catchment Area (ECA) Study. *JAMA: Journal of the American Medical Association, 264*(19), 2511–2518.

Regier, D.A., Farmer, M.E., Rae, D.S., Myers, J.K. et al. (1993). One-month prevalence of mental disorders in the United States and sociodemographic characteristics: The Epidemiologic Catchment Area Study. *Acta Psychiatrica Scandinavica, 88*, 35–47.

Regier, D.A., Myers, J.K., Kramer, M., Robins, L.N. et al. (1984). The NIMH Epidemiologic Catchment Area Program: Historical context, major objectives, and study population characteristics. *Archives of General Psychiatry, 41*, 934–941.

Reid, Y., Johnson, S., Bebbington, P.E., Kuipers, E., Scott, H. & Thornicroft, G. (2001). The longer-term outcomes of community care: A 12-year follow-up of the Camberwell High Contact Survey. *Psychological Medicine, 31*, 351–359.

Reimherr, F.W., Strong, R.E., Marchant, B.K., Hedges, D.W. & Wender, P.H. (2001). Factors affecting return of symptoms 1 year after treatment in a 62-week controlled study of fluoxetine in major depression. *Journal of Clinical Psychiatry, 62*, 16–23.

Reinecke, M.A., Dattilio, F.M. & Freeman, A. (2006). *Cognitive therapy with children and adolescents*. New York: Guilford Press.

Reis, B.E. (1993). Towards a psychoanalytic understanding of multiple personality disorder. *Bulletin of the Menninger's Clinic, 57*, 309–318.

Reiss, A.L. & Freund, L. (1990). Fragile X syndrome, DSM-III-R, and autism. *Journal of the American Academy of Child and Adolescent Psychiatry, 29*(6), 885–891.

Reiss, D., Hetherington, E.M., Plomin, R., Howe, G.W. et al. (1995). Genetic questions for environmental studies: Differential parenting and psychopathology in adolescence. *Archives of General Psychiatry, 52*(11), 925–936.

Reiss, S. & McNally, R.J. (1985). Expectancy model of fear. In S. Reiss & R.R. Bootzin (Eds.), *Theoretical issues in behaviour therapy*. San Diego, CA: Academic Press.

Reiss, S., Peterson, R.A., Gursky, D.M. & McNally, R.J. (1986). Anxiety sensitivity, anxiety frequency and the prediction of fearfulness. *Behaviour Research and Therapy, 24*(1), 1–8.

Reissing, E.D., Binik, Y.M., Khalife, S., Cohen, D. & Amsel, R. (2003). Etiological correlates of vaginismus: Sexual and physical abuse, sexual knowledge, sexual self-schema, and relationship adjustment. *Journal of Sex and Marital Therapy, 29*(1), 47–59.

Reneman, L., Booij, J., Schmand, B., Brink, W. et al. (2000). Memory disturbances in 'ecstasy' users are correlated with an altered brain serotonin transmission. *Psychopharmacology, 148*, 322–324.

Rennie, D.L., Watson, K.D. & Monteiro, A.M. (2002). The rise of qualitative research in psychology. *Canadian Psychology, 43*, 179–189.

Resick, P.A. (2001). *Stress and trauma*. Hove: Psychology Press.

Resick, P.A. & Schnicke, M.K. (1992). Cognitive processing therapy for sexual assault victims. *Journal of Consulting and Clinical Psychology, 60*(5), 748–756.

Rettew, D.C., Zanarini, M.C., Yen, S., Grilo, C.M. et al. (2003). Childhood antecedents of avoidant personality disorder: A retrospective study. *Journal of the American Academy of Child and Adolescent Psychiatry, 42*(9), 1122–1130.

Reynolds, M. & Salkovskis, P.M. (1992). Comparison of positive and negative intrusive thoughts and experimental investigation of the differential effects of mood. *Behaviour Research and Therapy, 30*(3), 273–281.

Ricaurte, G.A., Yuan, J. & McCann, U.D. (2000). MDMA, 'ecstasy'-induced serotonin neurotoxicity: Studies in animals. *Neuropsychobiology, 42*, 5–10.

Ricca, V., Mannucci, E., Zucchi, T., Rotella, C.M. & Faravelli, C. (2000). Cognitive-behavioural therapy for bulimia nervosa and binge eating disorder: A review. *Psychotherapy and Psychosomatics, 69*(6), 287–295.

Rice, F., Harold, G. & Thapar, A. (2002). The genetic aetiology of childhood depression: A review. *Journal of Child Psychology and Psychiatry and Allied Disciplines, 43*, 65–79.

Rich, C.L., Warsradt, G.M., Nemiroff, R.A., Fowler, R.C. & Young, D. (1991). Suicide, stressors, and the life-cycle. *American Journal of Psychiatry, 148*(4), 524–527.

Richard, D.C.S. & Lauterbach, D.L. (2007). *Handbook of exposure therapies*. New York: Academic Press.

Richards, R., Kinney, D.K., Lunde, I., Benet, M. & Merzel, A.P.C. (1988). Creativity in manic depressives, cyclothymes, their normal relatives, and control subjects. *Journal of Abnormal Psychology, 97*(3), 281–288.

Richardson, J.D., Kilo, S. & Hargreaves, K.M. (1998). Cannabinoids reduce hyperalgesia and inflammation via interaction with peripheral CB1 receptors. *Pain, 75*(1), 111–119.

Richman, N., Stevenson, J. & Graham, P. (1982). *Preschool to school: A behavioural study*. London: Academic Press.

Ridenour, T.A., Maldonado-Molina, M., Compton, W.M., Spitznagel, E.L. & Cottler, L.B. (2005). Factors associated with the transition from abuse to dependency among substance abusers: Implications for a measure of additive liability. *Drug and Alcohol Dependence, 80*, 1–14.

Rief, W., Buhlmann, U., Wilhelm, S., Borkenhagen, A. & Brahler, E. (2006). The prevalence of body dysmorphic disorder: A population-based survey. *Psychological Medicine, 36*(6), 877–885.

Rief, W., Hiller, W. & Margraf, J. (1998). Cognitive aspects of hypochondriasis and the somatization syndrome. *Journal of Abnormal Psychology, 107*(4), 587–595.

Riether, A.M. & Stoudemire, A. (1988). Psychogenic fugue states: A review. *Southern Medical Journal, 81*(5), 568–571.

Riley, E.M., McGovern, D., Mockler, D., Doku, V.C.K. et al. (2000). Neuropsychological functioning in first-episode psychosis: Evidence of specific deficits. *Schizophrenia Research, 43*(1), 47–55.

Rinne, T., van den Brink, W., Wouters, L. & van Dyck, R. (2002). SSRI treatment of borderline personality disorder: A randomized, placebo-controlled clinical trial for female patients with borderline personality disorder. *American Journal of Psychiatry, 159*(12), 2048–2054.

Robbins, J.M. & Kirmayer, L.J. (1996). Transient and persistent hypochondriacal worry in primary care. *Psychological Medicine, 26*(3), 575–589.

Roberts, R.E., Lewinsohn, P.M. & Seeley, J.R. (1995). Symptoms of DSM-III-R major depression in adolescence: Evidence from an epidemiologic survey. *Journal of the American Academy of Child and Adolescent Psychiatry, 34*(12), 1608–1617.

Robins, C.J. & Chapman, A.L. (2004). Dialectical behavior therapy: Current status, recent developments, and future directions. *Journal of Personality Disorders, 18*(1), 73–89.

Robins, L.N. (1966). *Deviant children grown up: A sociological and psychiatric study of sociopathic personalities*. Baltimore: Williams & Wilkins.

Robins, L.N. (1991). Conduct disorder. *Journal of Child Psychology and Psychiatry and Allied Disciplines, 32*, 193–212.

Robins, L.N. & Regier, D.A. (Eds.) (1991). *Psychiatric disorders in America*. New York: Free Press.

Robinson, D. (1995). *The impact of cognitive skills training on post-release recidivism among Canadian federal offenders*. Correctional Service of Canada Research Division.

Robinson, D. & Porporino, F.J. (2001). Programming in cognitive skills: The Reasoning and Rehabilitation programme. In C. Hollin (Ed.), *Handbook of offender assessment and treatment*. Chichester: Wiley.

Robinson, D.G., Woerner, M.G., Alvir, J.M.J., Geisler, S. et al. (1999). Predictors of treatment response from a first episode of schizophrenia or schizoaffective disorder. *American Journal of Psychiatry, 156*(4), 544–549.

Robinson, J.L., Reznick, J.S., Kagan, J. & Corley, R. (1992). The heritability of inhibited and uninhibited behavior: A twin study. *Developmental Psychology, 28*(6), 1030–1037.

Robinson, L.A., Berman, J.S. & Neimeyer, R.A. (1990). Psychotherapy for the treatment of depression: A comprehensive review of controlled outcome research. *Psychological Bulletin, 108*, 30–49.

Robinson, M.S. & Alloy, L.B. (2003). Negative cognitive styles and stress-reactive rumination interact to predict depression: A prospective study. *Cognitive Therapy and Research, 27*(3), 275–291.

Robinson, R.G. (2003). Poststroke depression: Prevalence, diagnosis, treatment, and disease progression. *Biological Psychiatry, 54*, 376–387.

Robinson, R.G., Lipsey, J.R., Rao, K. & Price, T.R. (1986). Two-year longitudinal study of poststroke mood disorders: Comparison of acute-onset with delayed-onset depression. *American Journal of Psychiatry, 143*(10), 1238–1244.

Robinson, R.G., Schultz, S.K., Castillo, C., Kopel, T. et al. (2000). Nortriptyline versus fluoxetine in the treatment of depression and in short-term recovery after stroke: A placebo-controlled, double-blind study. *American Journal of Psychiatry, 157*(3), 351–359.

Robison, L.M., Sclar, D.A., Skaer, T.L. & Galin, R.S. (2004). Treatment modalities among US children diagnosed with attention-deficit hyperactivity disorder: 1995–99. *International Clinical Psychopharmacology, 19*(1), 17–22.

Rocchi, A., Pellegrini, S., Siciliano, G. & Murri, L. (2003). Causative and susceptibility genes for Alzheimer's disease: A review. *Brain Research Bulletin, 61*(1), 1–24.

Rode, S., Salkovskis, P., Dowd, H. & Hanna, M. (2006). Health anxiety levels in chronic pain clinic attenders. *Journal of Psychosomatic Research, 60*(2), 155–161.

Rodebaugh, T.L. & Chambless, D.L. (2004). Cognitive therapy for performance anxiety. *Journal of Clinical Psychology, 60*, 809–820.

Rodebaugh, T.L., Holaway, R.M. & Heimberg, R.G. (2004). The treatment of social anxiety disorder. *Clinical Psychology Review, 24*, 883–908.

Rodriguez, B.F., Weisberg, R.B., Pagano, M.E., Machan, J.T. et al. (2004). Frequency and patterns of psychiatric combordity in a sample of primary care patients with anxiety disorders. *Comprehensive Psychiatry, 45*, 129–137.

Roediger, H.L. & McDermott, K.B. (1995). Creating false memories: Remembering words not presented in lists. *Journal of Experimental Psychology: Learning Memory and Cognition, 21*(4), 803–814.

Roelofs, K., Spinhoven, P., Sandijck, P. et al. (2005). The impact of early trauma and recent life-events on symptom severity in patients with conversion disorder. *Journal of Nervous and Mental Diseases, 193*, 508–514.

Rogers, C.R. (1951). *Client-centered therapy*. Boston: Houghton Mifflin.

Rogers, C.R. (1987). Rogers, Kohut, and Erickson: A personal perspective on some similarities and differences. In J.K. Zeig (Ed.), *The evolution of psychotherapy*. New York: Brunner/Mazel.

Rogers, R., Sewell, K.W., Martin, M.A. & Vitacco, M.J. (2003). Detection of feigned mental disorders: A meta-analysis of the MMPI-2 and malingering. *Assessment, 10*, 160–177.

Rohde, L.A., Szobot, C., Polanczyk, G., Schmitz, M. et al. (2005). Attention-deficit/hyperactivity disorder in a diverse culture: Do research and clinical findings support the notion of a cultural construct for the disorder? *Biological Psychiatry, 57*, 1436–1441.

Rohde, P., Feeny, N.C. & Robins, M. (2005). Characteristics and components of the TADS CBT approach. *Cognitive and Behavioral Practice, 12*, 186–197.

Rohde, P., Lewinsohn, P.M. & Seeley, J.R. (1995). Psychiatric comorbidity with problematic alcohol use in high school students. *Journal of the American Academy of Child and Adolescent Psychiatry, 35*, 101–109.

Rokeach, M. (1964). *The three christs of Ypsilanti*. New York: Random House.

Rollin, B.E. (2006). The regulation of animal research and the emergence of animal ethics: A conceptual history. *Theoretical Medicine and Bioethics, 27*, 285–304.

Ronald, A., Happe, F., Price, T.S., Baron-Cohen, S. & Plomin, R. (2006). Phenotypic and genetic overlap between autistic traits at the extremes of the general population. *Journal of the American Academy of Child and Adolescent Psychiatry, 45*(10), 1206–1214.

Room, R., Babor, T. & Rehm, J. (2005). Alcohol and public health. *Lancet, 365*(9458), 519–530.

Roozen, H.G., de Kan, R., van den Brink, W., Kerkhof, A.J.F.M. & Geerlings, P.J. (2002). Dangers involved in rapid opioid detoxification while using opioid antagonists: Dehydration and renal failure. *Addiction, 97*(8), 1071–1073.

Rorty, M. & Yager, J. (1996). Histories of childhood trauma and complex posttraumatic sequelae in women with eating disorders. *Psychiatric Clinics of North America, 19*(4), 773.

Rosanoff, A.J., Handy, L. & Plesset, I.R. (1935). The etiology of manic-depressive syndromes with special reference to their occurrence in twins. *American Journal of Psychiatry, 91*, 725–762.

Rose, R.J. (1998). A developmental behavioral-genetic perspective on alcoholism risk. *Alcohol Health and Research World, 22*, 131–143.

Rosen, G.M. (2004). Litigation and reported rates of posttraumatic stress disorder. *Personality and Individual Differences, 36*(6), 1291–1294.

Rosen, J.C. (1996). Body image assessment and treatment in controlled studies of eating disorders. *International Journal of Eating Disorders, 20*(4), 331–343.

Rosen, N.J., Yoshida, C.K. & Croen, L.A. (2007). Infection in the first two years of life and autism. *Pediatrics, 119*, E61–U18.

Rosen, R., Shabsigh, R., Berber, M., Assalian, P. et al. (2006). Efficacy and tolerability of vardenafil in men with mild depression and erectile dysfunction: The depression-related improvement with vardenafil for erectile response study. *American Journal of Psychiatry, 163*(1), 79–87.

Rosen, R.C., Lane, R.M. & Menza, M. (1999). Effects of SSRIs on sexual function: A critical review. *Journal of Clinical Psychopharmacology, 19*(1), 67–85.

Rosen, R.C. & Leiblum, S.R. (1995). *Disorders of sexual desire*. New York: Guilford Press.

Rosenbaum, M. (1980). The role of the term schizophrenia in the decline of diagnoses of multiple personality. *Archives of General Psychiatry, 37*, 1383–1385.

Rosenberg, H. & Melville, J. (2005). Controlled drinking and controlled drug use as outcome goals in British treatment services. *Addiction, Research and Theory, 13*(1), 85–92.

Rosenberg, S.D., Drake, R.E., Brunette, M.F., Wolford, G.L. & Marsh, B.J. (2005). Hepatitis C virus and HIV co-infection in people with severe mental illness and substance use disorders. *AIDS, 19*, S26–S33, Suppl. 3.

Rosenhan, D.L. (1973). On being sane in insane places. *Science, 179*, 250–258.

Rosenthal, N. & Blehar, M.C. (Eds.) (1989). *Seasonal affective disorder and phototherapy*. New York: Guilford Press.

Rosenthal, R. & Berven, N.L. (1999). Effects of client race on clinical judgment. *Rehabilitation Counseling Bulletin, 42*, 243–255.

Rosman, B.L., Minuchin, S. & Liebman, R. (1975). Family lunch session: Introduction to family therapy in anorexia nervosa. *American Journal of Orthopsychiatry, 45*(5), 846–853.

Ross, A.O. (1981). *Child behaviour therapy: Principles, procedures and empirical basis*. New York: Wiley.

Ross, C.A. (1997). *Dissociative identity disorder: Diagnosis, clinical features, and treatment of multiple personality* (2nd ed.). New York: Wiley.

Rossi, P.G., Parmeggiani, A., Bach, V., Santucci, M. & Visconti, P. (1995). EEG features and epilepsy in patients with autism. *Brain and Development, 17*(3), 169–174.

Roth, A. & Fonagy, P. (1996). *What works for whom? A critical review of psychotherapy research*. New York: Academic Press.

Roth, W.T., Wilhelm, F.H. & Trabert, W. (1998). Voluntary breath holding in panic and generalized anxiety disorders. *Psychosomatic Medicine, 60*(6), 671–679.

Rothbaum, B.O., Foa, E.B., Riggs, D.S., Murdock, T. & Walsh, W. (1992). Prospective examination of posttraumatic stress disorder in rape victims. *Journal of Traumatic Stress, 5*(3), 455–475.

Rothbaum, B.O., Hodges, L.F., Ready, D., Graap, K. & Alarcon, R.D. (2001). Virtual reality exposure therapy for Vietnam veterans with posttraumatic stress disorder. *Journal of Clinical Psychiatry, 62*(8), 617–622.

Rotter, M.R. & Steinbacher, M. (2001). The clinical impact of doing time: Mental illness and incarceration. In G. Landsburg & G. Smiley (Eds.), *Forensic mental health: Working with offenders with mental illness*. Kingston, NJ: Civic Research Institute.

Rotter, M.R., Way, B., Steinbacher, M., Sawyer, D. & Smith, H. (2002). Personality disorders in prison: Aren't they all antisocial? *Psychiatric Quarterly, 73*, 337–349.

Rovner, S. (1993). Anxiety disorders are real and expensive. *Washington Post*, April.

Rowan, A.N. (1997). The benefits and ethics of animal research. *Scientific American, 276*, 79.

Rowland, D.L., Cooper, S.E. & Slob, A.K. (1996). Genital and psychoaffective responses to erotic stimulation in sexually functional and dysfunctional men. *Journal of Abnormal Psychology, 105*, 194–203.

Roy, A., Virkkunen, M. & Linnoila, M. (1987). Reduced central serotonin turnover in a subgroup of alcoholics. *Progress in Neuropsychopharmacology and Biological Psychiatry, 11*(2–3), 173–177.

Royal College of Physicians (2002). *Nicotine addiction in Britain*. London: RCP Publications.

Royal College of Psychiatrists (2002). Guidelines for ECT anaesthesia. *Psychiatric Bulletin, 26*, 237–238.

Roy-Byrne, P.P. & Cowley, D.S. (1998). Search for pathophysiology of panic disorder. *Lancet, 352*(9141), 1646–1647.

Rozin, P. & Fallon, A.E. (1987). A perspective on disgust. *Psychological Review, 94*, 23–41.

Ruedrich, S.L., Chu, C.C. & Wadle, C.V. (1985). The amytal interview in the treatment of psychogenic amnesia. *Hospital and Community Psychiatry, 36*(10), 1045–1046.

Ruffolo, J.S., Phillips, K.A., Menard, W., Fay, C. & Weisberg, R.B. (2006). Comorbidity of body dysmorphic disorder and eating disorders: Severity of psychopathology and body image disturbance. *International Journal of Eating Disorders, 39*(1), 11–19.

Ruggiero, G.M., Levi, D., Ciuna, A. & Sassaroli, S. (2003). Stress situation reveals an association between perfectionism and drive for thinness. *International Journal of Eating Disorders, 34*(2), 220–226.

Rush, A.J., Beck, A.T., Kovacs, M. & Hollon, S.D. (1977). Comparative efficacy of cognitive therapy and pharmacotherapy in the treatment of depressed outpatients. *Cognitive Therapy and Research, 1*, 17–39.

Rutter, M. (1983). Cognitive deficits in the pathogenesis of autism. *Journal of Child Psychology and Psychiatry, 24*, 513–531.

Rutter, M. (2005). Aetiology of autism: Findings and questions. *Journal of Intellectual Disability Research, 49*, 231–238.

Rutter, M., Bailey, A., Bolton, P. & Le Couteur, A. (1994). Autism and known medical conditions: Myth and substance. *Journal of Child Psychology and Psychiatry and Allied Disciplines, 35*(2), 311–322.

Rutter, M., MacDonald, H., Le Couteur, A., Harrington, R. et al. (1990). Genetic factors in child psychiatric disorders. 2. Empirical findings. *Journal of Child Psychology and Psychiatry and Allied Disciplines, 31*(1), 39–83.

Safer, D.J. (1997). Changing patterns of psychotropic medications prescribed by child psychiatrists in the 1990s. *Journal of Child and Adolescent Psychopharmacology, 7*(4), 267–274.

Saffer, H. (1991). Alcohol advertising bans and alcohol abuse: An international perspective. *Journal of Health Economics, 10*(1), 65–79.

Saghir, M.T., Robins, E. & Walbran, B. (1969). Homosexuality: II. Sexual behaviour of the male homosexual. *Archives of General Psychiatry, 21*, 219–229.

St Lawrence, J.S. & Madakasira, S. (1992). Evaluation and treatment of premature ejaculation: A critical review. *International Journal of Psychiatry in Medicine, 22*(1), 77–97.

Saladin, M.E. & Santa Ana, E.J. (2004). Controlled drinking: More than just a controversy. *Current Opinion in Psychiatry, 17*, 175–187.

Salfi, J., Ploeg, J. & Black, M.E. (2005). Seeking to understand telephone support for dementia caregivers. *Western Journal of Nursing Research, 27*(6), 701–721.

Salkovskis, P.M. (1985). Obsessional-compulsive problems: A cognitive-behavioural analysis. *Behaviour Research and Therapy, 25*, 571–583.

Salkovskis, P.M. (1999). Understanding and treating obsessive-compulsive disorder. *Behaviour Research and Therapy, 37*, S29–S52.

Salkovskis, P.M. & McGuire, J. (2003). Cognitive-behavioural theory of OCD. In R.G. Menzies & P. de Silva (Eds.), *Obsessive-compulsive disorder: Theory, research and treatment*. Chichester: Wiley.

Salkovskis, P.M., Rachman, S., Ladouceur, R., Freeston, M., Taylor, S., Kyrios, M. & Sica, C. (1996). Defining responsibility in obsessional problems. First meeting of Obsessive-Compulsive Cognitions Working Group, Smith College, Boston, USA.

Salkovskis, P.M., Shafran, R., Rachman, S. & Freeston, M.H. (1999). Multiple pathways to inflated responsibility beliefs in obsessional problems: Possible origins and implications for therapy and research. *Behaviour Research and Therapy, 37*, 1055–1072.

Salkovskis, P.M. & Warwick, H.M.C. (1986). Morbid preoccupation, health anxiety and reassurance: A cognitive-behavioural approach to hypochondriasis. *Behaviour Research and Therapy, 24*, 597–602.

Salkovskis, P.M., Wroe, A.L., Gledhill, A., Morrison, N., Forrester, E., Richards, C., Reynolds, M. & Thorpe, S. (2000). Responsibility attitudes and interpretations are characteristic of obsessive compulsive disorder. *Behaviour Research and Therapy, 38*, 347–372.

Sallan, S.E., Zinberg, N.E. & Frei, E. (1975). Antiemetic effect of delta-9-tetrahydrocannabinol in patients receiving cancer chemotherapy. *New England Journal of Medicine, 293*(16), 795–797.

Salman, E., Liebowitz, M., Guarnaccia, P.J., Jusino, C.M., Garfinkel, R. et al. (1998). Subtypes of *Ataques de Nervios*: The influence of coexisting psychiatric diagnosis. *Cult. Med. Psychiatry, 22*, 231–244.

Salmon, P. & Calderbank, S. (1996). The relationship of childhood physical and sexual abuse to adult illness behavior. *Journal of Psychosomatic Research, 40*(3), 329–336.

Salonia, A., Briganti, A., Deho, F. et al. (2003). Pathophysiology of erectile dysfunction. *International Journal of Andrology, 26*(3), 129–136.

Salonia, A., Rigatti, P. & Montorsi, F. (2003). Sildenafil in erectile dysfunction: A critical review. *Current Medical Research and Opinion, 19*(4), 241–262.

Saltuklaroglu, T. & Kalinowski, J. (2005). How effective is therapy for childhood stuttering? Dissecting and reinterpreting the evidence in light of spontaneous recovery rates. *International Journal of Language and Communication Disorders, 40*(3), 359–374.

Sand, P.G., Mori, T., Godau, C., Stober, G. et al. (2002). Norepinephrine transporter gene (NET) variants in patients with panic disorder. *Neuroscience Letters, 333*(1), 41–44.

Sanders, B. (1992). The imaginary companion experience in multiple personality disorder. *Dissociation: Progress in the Dissociative Disorders, 5*, 159–162.

Sanderson, W.C., Rapee, R.M. & Barlow, D.H. (1989). The influence of an illusion of control on panic attacks induced via inhalation of 5.5 percent carbon dioxide-enriched air. *Archives of General Psychiatry, 46*(2), 157–162.

Sanftner, J.L. & Crowther, J.H. (1998). Variability in self-esteem, moods, shame and guilt in women who binge. *International Journal of Eating Disorders, 23*(4), 391–397.

Sanislow, C.A. & Carson, R.C. (2001). Schizophrenia: A critical examination. In P.B. Sutker & H.E. Adams (Eds.), *Comprehensive handbook of psychopathology* (3rd ed.). New York: Kluwer Academic/Plenum.

Sansone, R.A., Wiederman, M.W. & Sansone, L.A. (2000). Medically self-harming behavior and its relationship to borderline personality symptoms and somatic preoccupation among internal medicine patients. *Journal of Nervous and Mental Disease, 188*(1), 45–47.

Santangelo, S.L. & Tsatsanis, K. (2005). What is known about autism: Genes, brain and behaviour. *American Journal of Pharmacogenomics, 5*, 71–92.

Santonastaso, P., Mondini, S. & Favaro, A. (2002). Are fashion models a group at risk for eating disorders and substance abuse? *Psychotherapy and Psychosomatics, 71*(3), 168–172.

Sar, V., Akyuz, G., Kundakci, T., Kiziltyan, E. et al. (2004). Childhood trauma, dissociation, and psychiatric comorbidity in patients with conversion disorder. *American Journal of Psychiatry, 161*, 2271–2276.

Sarasalo, E., Bergman, B. & Toth, J. (1997). Theft behaviour and its consequences among kleptomaniacs and shoplifters: A comparative study. *Forensic Science International, 86*(3), 193–205.

Sarfati, Y., Hardy Bayle, M.C., Besche, C. & Widlocher, D. (1997). Attribution of intentions to others in people with schizophrenia: A non-verbal exploration with comic strips. *Schizophrenia Research, 25*(3), 199–209.

Sartorius, N., Jablensky, A., Korten, A., Ernberg, G. et al. (1986). Early manifestations and first-contact incidence of schizophrenia in different cultures. *Psychological Medicine, 16*(4), 909–928.

Satel, S.L. & Edell, W.S. (1991). Cocaine-induced paranoia and psychosis proneness. *American Journal of Psychiatry, 148*(12), 1708–1711.

Satran, A., Bart, B.A., Henry, C.R., Murad, B. et al. (2005). Increased prevalence of coronary artery aneurysms among cocaine users. *Circulation, 111*(19), 2424–2429.

Satz, P., Forney, D.L., Zaucha, K., Asarnow, R.R. et al. (1998). Depression, cognition, and functional correlates of recovery outcome after traumatic brain injury. *Brain Injury, 12*(7), 537–553.

Saviour, P. & Ramachandra, B. (2006). Biological basis of dyslexia: A maturing perspective. *Current Science, 90*, 168–174.

Saxena, S., Brody, A.L., Schwartz, J.M. et al. (1998). Neuroimaging and frontal-subcortical circuitry in obsessive-compulsive disorder. *British Journal of Psychiatry, 173*, 26–37.

Sbrana, A., Bizzarri, J.V., Rucci, P., Gonnelli, C. et al. (2005). The spectrum of substance use in mood and anxiety disorders. *Comprehensive Psychiatry, 46*, 6–13.

Sbrocco, T., Weisberg, R.B., Barlow, D.H. & Carter, M.M. (1997). The conceptual relationship between panic disorder and male erectile dysfunction. *Journal of Sex and Marital Therapy, 23*(3), 212–220.

Scarborough, H.S. (1990). Very early language deficits in dyslexic children. *Child Development, 61,* 1728–1743.

Schachter, D.L., Norman, K.A. & Koutstaal, W. (1998). The cognitive neuroscience of constructive memory. *Annual Review of Psychology, 49,* 289–318.

Schachter, S. (1978). Pharmacological and psychological determinants of smoking. In R.E. Thornton (Ed.), *Smoking behaviour, physiological and psychological influences.* Edinburgh: Churchill Livingstone.

Schachter, S. (1982). Recidivism and self-cure of smoking and obesity. *American Psychologist, 37,* 436–444.

Schafer, I., Barkmann, C., Riedesser, P. & Schulte-Markworth, M. (2006). Posttraumatic stress syndromes in children and adolescents after road traffic accidents: A prospective cohort study. *Psychopathology, 39,* 159–164.

Schanda, H., Knecht, G., Schreinzer, D., Stompe, T. et al. (2004). Homicide and major mental disorders: A 25-year study. *Acta Psychiatrica Scandinavica, 110*(2), 98–107.

Schapira, K., Linsley, K.R., Linsley, J.A., Kelly, T.P. & Kay, D.W.K. (2001). Relationship of suicide rates to social factors and availability of lethal methods: Comparison of suicide in Newcastle upon Tyne 1961–1965 and 1985–1994. *British Journal of Psychiatry, 178,* 458–464.

Scheff, T.J. (1975). *Labelling madness.* Englewood Cliffs, NJ: Prentice-Hall.

Scher, C.D. & Stein, M.B. (2003). Developmental antecedents of anxiety sensitivity. *Journal of Anxiety Disorders, 17,* 253–269.

Schiffman, J., Abrahamson, A., Cannon, T., LaBrie, J. et al. (2001). Early rearing factors in schizophrenia. *International Journal of Mental Health, 30,* 3–16.

Schmidt, N.B. & Harrington, P. (1995). Cognitive-behavioral treatment of body dysmorphic disorder: A case report. *Journal of Behavior Therapy and Experimental Psychiatry, 26,* 161–167.

Schmidt, N.B., Lerew, D.R. & Jackson, R.J. (1997). The role of anxiety sensitivity in the pathogenesis of panic: Prospective evaluation of spontaneous panic attacks during acute stress. *Journal of Abnormal Psychology, 106*(3), 355–364.

Schmidt, N.B. & Telch, M.J. (1990). Prevalence of personality disorders among bulimics, nonbulimic binge eaters, and normal controls. *Journal of Psychopathology and Behavioral Assessment, 12*(2), 169–185.

Schmitt, M.T., Branscombe, N.R. & Kappen, D.M. (2003). Attitudes toward group-based inequality: Social dominance or social identity? *British Journal of Social Psychology, 42,* 161–186.

Schmitz, J.M., Denardin, D., Silva, T.L., Pianca, T. et al. (2006). Smoking during pregnancy and attention-deficit/hyperactivity disorder, predominantly inattentive type: A case-control study. *Journal of the American Academy of Child and Adolescent Psychiatry, 45,* 1338–1345.

Schmitz, J.M., Schneider, N.G. & Jarvik, M.E. (1997). Nicotine. In J.H. Lowinson, P. Ruiz, R.B. Millman & J.G. Langrod (Eds.), *Substance abuse: A comprehensive textbook.* Baltimore: Williams & Wilkins.

Schneider, F. & Deldin, P.J. (2001). Genetics and schizophrenia. In P.B. Sutker & H.E. Adams (Eds.), *Comprehensive handbook of psychopathology* (3rd ed.). New York: Kluwer Academic/Plenum.

Schneier, F.R., Blanco, C., Antia, S.X. & Liebowitz, M.R. (2002). The social anxiety spectrum. *Psychiatric Clinics of North America, 25*(4), 757&.

Schofield, P.E., Pattison, P.E., Hill, D.J. & Borland, R. (2001). The influence of group identification on the adoption of peer group smoking norms. *Psychology and Health, 16*(1), 1–16.

Schonfeld, A.M., Mattson, S.N. & Riley, E.P. (2005). Moral maturity and delinquency after prenatal alcohol exposure. *Journal of Studies on Alcohol, 66,* 545–554.

Schrag, A., Brown, R.J. & Trimble, M.R. (2004). The validity of self-reported diagnoses in patients with neurologically unexplained symptoms. *Journal of Neurology, Neurosurgery and Psychiatry, 75*(5), 801.

Schrag, A., Hovris, A., Morley, D., Quinn, N. & Jahanshahi, M. (2006). Caregiver-burden in Parkinson's disease is closely associated with psychiatric symptoms, falls, and disability. *Parkinsonism and Related Disorders, 12*(1), 35–41.

Schreiber, F.R. (1973). *Sybil.* Chicago: Regnery.

Schroer, R.J., Phelan, M.C., Michaelis, R.C., Crawford, E.C. et al. (1998). Autism and maternally derived aberrations of chromosome 15q. *American Journal of Medical Genetics, 76*(4), 327–336.

Schuckit, M.A. (1983). The genetics of alcoholism. In B. Tabakoff, P.B. Sulker & C.L. Randall (Eds.), *Medical and social aspects of alcohol use.* New York: Plenum.

Schuckit, M.A. (1994). Low level of response to alcohol as a predictor of future alcoholism. *American Journal of Psychiatry, 151,* 184–189.

Schuckit, M.A. (1995). A long-term study of alcoholics. *Alcohol Health and Research World, 19,* 172–175.

Schuckit, M.A. & Smith, T.L. (1996). An 8-year follow-up of 450 sons of alcoholic and control subjects. *Archives of General Psychiatry, 53*(3), 202–210.

Schuckit, M.A., Tsuang, J.W., Anthenelli, R.M., Tipp, J.E., Nurnberger, J.I. et al. (1996). Alcohol challenges in young men from alcoholic pedigrees and control families: A report from the COGA project. *Journal of Studies on Alcohol, 57*(4), 368–377.

Schulz, S.C., Schulz, P.M. & Wilson, W.H. (1988). Medication treatment of schizotypical personality disorder. *Journal of Personality Disorders, 2,* 1–13.

Schwartz, C.E., Snidman, N. & Kagan, J. (1999). Adolescent social anxiety as an outcome of inhibited temperament in childhood. *Journal of the American Academy of Child and Adolescent Psychiatry, 38*(8), 1008–1015.

Schwartz, R.P., Highfield, D.A., Jaffe, J.H., Brady, J.V. et al. (2006). A randomized controlled trial of interim methadone maintenance. *Archives of General Psychiatry, 63*(1), 102–109.

Schwarz, J.R. (1981). *The Hillside Strangler: A murderer's mind.* New York: American Library.

Scott, J., Garland, A. & Moorhead, S. (2001). A pilot study of cognitive therapy in bipolar disorders. *Psychological Medicine, 31*(3), 459–467.

Scott, W.D. & Cervone, D. (2002). The impact of negative affect on performance standards: Evidence for an affect-as-information mechanism. *Cognitive Therapy and Research, 26*(1), 19–37.

Seagraves, R.T. (1995). Psychopharmacological influences on human sexual behaviour. In J.M. Oldham & M.B. Riba (Eds.), *American Psychiatric Press review of psychiatry* (Vol. 14). Washington, DC: American Psychiatric Press.

Sedlak, A. & Broadhurst, D. (1996). *The Third National Incidence Study of Child Abuse and Neglect: NIS 3.* Washington, DC: US Department of Health and Human Sciences.

Seedat, S., Stein, M.B. & Forde, D.R. (2003). Prevalence of dissociative experiences in a community sample: Relationship to gender, ethnicity, and substance use. *Journal of Nervous and Mental Disease, 191,* 115–120.

Seeman, P. & Kapur, S. (2001). The dopamine receptor basis of psychosis. In A. Brier, P.V. Tran, F. Bymaster & C. Tollefson (Eds.), *Current issues in the psychopharmacology of schizophrenia.* Philadelphia: Lippincott Williams & Wilkins.

Segal, D.L., Hersen, M. & Van Hasselt, V.B. (1994). Reliability of the structured clinical interview for DSM-III-R: An evaluative review. *Comprehensive Psychiatry, 35,* 316–327.

Segal, Z.V., Gemar, M. & Williams, S. (1999). Differential cognitive response to a mood challenge following successful cognitive therapy or pharmacotherapy for unipolar depression. *Journal of Abnormal Psychology, 108*(1), 3–10.

Segrin, C. (2000). Social skills deficits associated with depression. *Clinical Psychology Review, 20,* 379–403.

Seidel, L. & Walkup, J.T. (2006). Selective serotonin reuptake inhibitor use in the treatment of the pediatric non-obsessive-compulsive disorder anxiety disorders. *Journal of Child and Adolescent Psychopharmacology, 16*(1–2), 171–179.

Seidman, L.J. (2006). Neuropsychological functioning in people with ADHD across the lifespan. *Clinical Psychology Review, 26,* 466–485.

Seidman, L.J., Valera, E.M. & Makris, N.M. (2005). Structural brain imaging of attention-deficit/hyperactivity disorder. *Biological Psychiatry, 57,* 1263–1272.

Seidman, S.N. (2002). Exploring the relationship between depression and erectile dysfunction in aging men. *Journal of Clinical Psychiatry, 63,* 5–12.

Seligman, M.E.P. (1971). Phobias and preparedness. *Behavior Therapy, 2,* 307–320.

Seligman, M.E.P. (1974). Depression and learned helplessness. In R.J. Friedman & M.M. Katz (Eds.), *The psychology of depression: Contemporary theory and research.* Washington, DC: Winston-Wiley.

Seligman, M.E.P. (1975). *Helplessness: On depression, development, and death.* San Francisco: Freeman.

Seligman, M.E.P. (1995). The effectiveness of psychotherapy: The Consumer Reports study. *American Psychologist, 50,* 965–974.

Selkoe, D.J. (1991). Amyloid protein and Alzheimer's disease. *Scientific American, 265,* 68–78.

Seltzer, B. (2006). Cholinesterase inhibitors in the clinical management of Alzheimer's disease: Importance of early and persistent treatment. *Journal of International Medical Research, 34,* 339–347.

Semans, J.H. (1956). Premature ejaculation: A new approach. *Southern Medical Journal, 49,* 353–357.

Sensky, T., Turkingon, D., Kingdon, D., Scott, J.L. et al. (2000). A randomized controlled trial of cognitive-behavioral therapy for persistent symptoms in schizophrenia resistant to medication. *Archives of General Psychiatry, 57,* 165–172.

Sepulcre, J., Sastre-Garriga, J., Cercignani, M., Ingle, G.T. et al. (2006). Regional gray matter atrophy in early primary progressive multiple sclerosis: A voxel-based morphometry study. *Archives of Neurology, 63*(8), 1175–1180.

Sergi, M.J., Rassovsky, Y., Widmark, C. et al. (2007). Social cognition in schizophrenia: Relationships with neurocognition and negative symptoms. *Schizophrenia Research, 90*(1–3), 316–324.

Serpell, L., Livingstone, A., Neiderman, M. & Lask, B. (2002). Anorexia nervosa: Obsessive-compulsive disorder, obsessive-compulsive personality disorder, or neither? *Clinical Psychology Review, 22*(5), 647–669.

Seto, M.C., Maric, A. & Barbaree, H.E. (2001). The role of pornography in the etiology of sexual aggression. *Aggression and Violent Behavior, 6*(1), 35–53.

Shaffer, H.J. & Korn, D.A. (2002). Gambling and related mental disorders: A public health analysis. *Annual Review of Public Health, 23,* 171–212.

Shaffer, H.J., LaBrie, R., Scanlon, K.M. & Cummings, T.N. (1993). *At risk, problem and pathological gambling among adolescents: Massachusetts Adolescent Gambling Screen (MAGS).* Cambridge, MA: Harvard Medical School.

Shafran, R. & Mansell, W. (2001). Perfectionism and psychopathology: A review of research and treatment. *Clinical Psychology Review, 21*(6), 879–906.

Shafran, R. & Rachman, S. (2004). Thought–action fusion: A review. *Journal of Behavior Therapy and Experimental Psychiatry, 35,* 87–107.

Shalev, A.Y., Peri, T., Brandes, D., Freedman, S., Orr, S.P. & Pitman, R.K. (2000). Auditory startle response in trauma survivors with posttraumatic stress disorder: A prospective study. *American Journal of Psychiatry, 157*(2), 255–261.

Shalev, R.S. (2004). Developmental dyscalculia. *Journal of Child Neurology, 19,* 765–771.

Shankweiler, D., Crain, S., Katz, L., Fowler, A., Liberman, A., Brady, S., Thornton, R., Lundquist, E., Dreyer, L., Fletcher, J., Stuebing, K., Shaywitz, S. & Shaywitz, B. (1995). Cognitive profiles of reading-disabled children: Comparison of language skills in phonology, morphology and syntax. *Psychological Science, 6,* 149–156.

Shankweiler, D., Liberman, I.Y., Marks, L.S., Fowler, C.A. et al. (1979). The speech code and learning to read. *Journal of Experimental Psychology: Human Learning and Memory, 5,* 531–545.

Shapiro, D.A. (1996). Validated treatments and evidence-based services. *Clinical Psychology: Science and Practice, 3,* 256–259.

Shapiro, D.A., Barkham, M., Rees, A., Hardy, G.E., Reynolds, S. & Startup, M. (1994). Effects of treatment duration and severity of depression on the effectiveness of cognitive-behavioral and psychodynamic-interpersonal psychotherapy. *Journal of Consulting and Clinical Psychology, 62,* 522–534.

Shapiro, F. (1989). Eye-movement desensitization: A new treatment for posttraumatic stress disorder. *Journal of Behavior Therapy and Experimental Psychiatry, 20*(3), 211–217.

Shapiro, F. (1995). *Eye-movement desensitization and reprocessing: Basic principles, protocols, and procedures.* New York: Guilford Press.

Shapiro, F. (1999). Eye-movement desensitization and reprocessing (EMDR): Clinical and research implications of an integrated psychotherapy treatment (Vol. 13, p. 35, 1999). *Journal of Anxiety Disorders, 13*(6), 621.

Shapiro, M.B. (1985). A reassessment of clinical psychology as an applied science. *British Journal of Clinical Psychology, 24,* 1–11.

Share, D.L. & Stanovich, K.E. (1995). Cognitive processes in early reading development: Accommodating individual differences into a model of acquisition. *Issues in Education: Continuing Educational Psychology, 1,* 1–57.

Shaw, D.S., Schonberg, M., Sherrill, J., Huffman, D., Lukon, J., Obrosky, D. & Kovacs, M. (2006). Responsivity to offspring's expression of emotion among childhood-onset depressed mothers. *Journal of Clinical Child and Adolescent Psychology, 35,* 490–503.

Shaw, I. & Woodward, L. (2004). The medicalization of unhappiness? The management of mental distress in primary care. In I. Shaw & K. Kauppinen (Eds.), *Conceptualizing health and illness: European perspectives.* Aldershot: Ashgate.

Shaywitz, B.A., Shaywitz, S.E., Pugh, K.R., Mencl, W.E. et al. (2002). Disruption of posterior brain systems for reading in children with developmental dyslexia. *Biological Psychiatry, 52*(2), 101–110.

Shaywitz, S.E. (2003). *Overcoming dyslexia: A new and complete science-based program for reading problems at any level.* New York: Alfred A. Knopf.

Shaywitz, S.E. & Shaywitz, B.A. (2005). Dyslexia (specific reading disability). *Biological Psychiatry, 57,* 1301–1309.

Shaywitz, S.E., Shaywitz, B.A., Fletcher, J.M. & Escobar, M.D. (1990). Prevalence of reading disability in boys and girls: Results of the Connecticut Longitudinal Study. *JAMA: Journal of the American Medical Association, 264*(8), 998–1002.

Shaywitz, S.E., Shaywitz, B.A., Pugh, K.R., Fulbright, R.K. et al. (1998). Functional disruption in the organization of the brain for reading in dyslexia. *Proceedings of the National Academy of Sciences of the United States of America, 95*(5), 2636–2641.

Sheeber, L., Hops, H. & Davis, B. (2001). Family processes in adolescent depression. *Clinical Child and Family Psychology Review, 4,* 19–35.

Sheffler-Rubenstein, C., Peynircioglu, A.F., Chambless, D.L. & Pigott, T.A. (1993). Memory in sub-clinical obsessive checkers. *Behaviour Research & Therapy, 31,* 759–765.

Shenton, M.E., Dickey, C.C., Frumin, M. & McCarley, R.W. (2001). A review of MRI findings in schizophrenia. *Schizophrenia Research, 49*(1–2), 1–52.

Shepherd, M., Cooper, B., Brown, A. & Kalton, C.W. (1996). *Psychiatric illness in general practice.* London: Oxford University Press.

Sher, K.J. (1991). *Children of alcoholics: A critical appraisal of theory and research.* Chicago: Chicago University Press.

Sher, K.J. & Levenson, R.W. (1982). Risk for alcoholism and individual differences in the stress-response-dampening effect of alcohol. *Journal of Abnormal Psychology, 91*(5), 350–367.

Sher, K.J., Mann, B. & Frost, R.O. (1984). Cognitive dysfunction in compulsive checkers: Further explorations. *Behaviour Research and Therapy, 22*(5), 493–502.

Sher, K.J., Trull, T.J., Bartholomew, B.D. & Vieth, A. (1999). Pesonality and alcoholism: Issues, methods, and etiological processes. In K.E. Leonard & H.T. Blane (Eds.), *Psychological theories of drinking and alcoholism.* New York: Guilford Press.

Sher, K.J., Wood, M.D., Wood, P.K. et al. (1996). Alcohol outcome expectancies and alcohol use: A latent variable cross-lagged panel study. *Journal of Abnormal Psychology, 105*(4), 561–574.

Sher, L. (2006). Alcohol and suicide: Neurobiological and clinical aspects. *Scientific World Journal, 6*, 700–706.

Shergill, S.S., Brammer, M.J., Williams, S.C.R., Murray, R.M. & McGuire, P.K. (2000). Mapping auditory hallucinations in schizophrenia using functional magnetic resonance imaging. *Archives of General Psychiatry, 57*(11), 1033–1038.

Sherman, S. (1996). Epidemiology. In R.J. Hagerman & A.C. Silverman (Eds.), *The fragile X syndrome: Diagnosis, treatment, and research* (2nd ed.). Baltimore: Johns Hopkins University Press.

Shewan, D. & Delgarno, P. (2005). Evidence for controlled heroin use? Low levels of negative health and social outcomes among non-treatment heroin users in Glasgow (Scotland). *British Journal of Health Psychology, 10*, 33–48.

Shiffman, S. (1982). Relapse following smoking cessation: A situational analysis. *Journal of Consulting and Clinical Psychology, 50*, 71–86.

Shiffman, S., Fischer, L.A., Paty, J.A., Gnys, M. et al. (1994). Drinking and smoking: A field study of their association. *Annals of Behavioral Medicine, 16*, 203–209.

Shilony, E. & Grossman, F.K. (1993). Depersonalization as a defense mechanism in survivors of trauma. *Journal of Traumatic Stress, 6*(1), 119–128.

Shin, M. (2005). Interference and cognitive inhibition in children with ADHD using Stroop task. *Psychologia, 48*(3), 171–181.

Shisslak, C.M., Pazda, S.L. & Crago, M. (1990). Body weight and bulimia as discriminators of psychological characteristics among anorexic, bulimic, and obese women. *Journal of Abnormal Psychology, 99*(4), 380–384.

Shneidman, E.S. (1973). Suicide. In *Encyclopedia Britannica*. London: Encyclopaedia Britannica.

Shoebridge, P. & Gowers, S.G. (2000). Parental high concern and adolescent-onset anorexia nervosa: A case-control study to investigate direction of causality. *British Journal of Psychiatry, 176*, 132–137.

Showalter, E. (1997). Chronic fatigue syndrome. In E. Showalter (Ed.), *Hystories: Hysterical epidemics and modern culture*. London: Picador.

Shu, B.C., Lung, F.W., Tien, A.Y. & Chen, B.C. (2001). Executive function deficits in non-retarded autistic children. *Autism, 5*(2), 165–174.

Siddle, D.A.T. (1983). *Orienting and habituation: Perspectives in human research*. Chichester: Wiley.

Sidney, S., Quesenberry, C.P., Friedman, G.D. et al. (1997). Marijuana use and cancer incidence (California, United States). *Cancer Causes and Control, 8*(5), 722–728.

Siever, L.J. & Davis, K.L. (2004). The pathophysiology of schizophrenia disorders: Perspectives from the spectrum. *American Journal of Psychiatry, 161*, 398–413.

Siever, L.J., Haier, R.J., Coursey, R.D., Sostek, A.J. et al. (1982). Smooth pursuit eye tracking impairment: Relation to other markers of schizophrenia and psychologic correlates. *Archives of General Psychiatry, 39*(9), 1001–1005.

Silove, D. & Manicavasagar, V. (2001). Early separation anxiety and its relationship to adult anxiety disorders. In N.W. Vasey & M.R. Dadds (Eds.), *The developmental psychopathology of anxiety*. New York: Oxford University Press.

Silva, R.R., Alpert, M., Munoz, D.M. et al. (2000). Stress and vulnerability to posttraumatic stress disorder in children and adolescents. *American Journal of Psychiatry, 157*(8), 1229–1235.

Silverman, J.A. (1987). Robert Whytt 1714–1766, eighteenth-century limner of anorexia nervosa and bulimia, an essay. *International Journal of Eating Disorders, 6*, 143–146.

Silverman, K., Evans, S.M., Strain, E.C. & Griffiths, R.R. (1992). Withdrawal syndrome after the double-blind cessation of caffeine consumption. *New England Journal of Medicine, 327*(16), 1109–1114.

Simeon, D., Gross, S., Guralnik, O., Stein, D.J., Schmeidler, J. & Hollander, E. (1997). Feeling unreal: 30 cases of DSM-III-R depersonalization disorder. *American Journal of Psychiatry, 154*(8), 1107–1113.

Simeon, D., Guralnik, O., Schmeidler, J., Sirof, B. & Knutelska, M. (2001). The role of childhood interpersonal trauma in depersonalization disorder. *American Journal of Psychiatry, 158*(7), 1027–1033.

Simeon, D. & Knutelska, M. (2005). An open trial of naltrexone in the treatment of depersonalization disorder. *Journal of Clinical Psychopharamacology, 25*, 267–270.

Simeon, D., Stein, D.J. & Hollander, E. (1995). Depersonalization disorder and self-injurious behavior. *Journal of Clinical Psychiatry, 56*, 36–40.

Simon, G.E. (1998). Management of somatoform and factitious disorders. In P.E. Nathan & J.M. Gorman (Eds.), *A guide to treatments that work*. New York: Oxford University Press.

Simon, G.E., von Korff, M., Piccinelli, M., Fullerton, C., Ormel, J. et al. (1999). An international study of the relation between somatic symptoms and depression. *New England Journal of Medicine, 341*(18), 1329–1335.

Simon, S.L., Domier, C.P., Sim, T., Richardson, K. et al. (2002). Cognitive performance of current methamphetamine and cocaine abusers. *Journal of Addictive Diseases, 21*(1), 61–74.

Simonoff, E. (2001). Gene–environment interplay in oppositional defiant and conduct disorder. *Child and Adolescent Psychiatric Clinics of North America, 10*, 351–374.

Simonoff, E., Bolton, P. & Rutter, M. (1996). Mental retardation: Genetic findings, clinical implications and research agenda. *Journal of Child Psychology and Psychiatry and Allied Disciplines, 37*(3), 259–280.

Simonoff, E., Pickles, A., Chadwick, O., Gringas, P. et al. (2006). The Croydon Assessment of Learning Study: Prevalence and educational identification of mild mental retardation. *Journal of Child Psychology and Psychiatry, 47*, 828–839.

Simons, A.D., Garfield, S.L. & Murphy, G.E. (1984). The process of change in cognitive therapy and pharmacotherapy for depression: Changes in mood and cognition. *Archives of General Psychiatry, 41*(1), 45–51.

Simons, J.S. & Carey, M.P. (2001). Prevalence of sexual dysfunctions: Results from a decade of research. *Archives of Sexual Behavior, 30*, 177–219.

Simons, J.S. & Carey, K.B. (2002). Risk and vulnerability for marijuana use problems: The role of affect dysregulation. *Psychology of Addictive Behaviors, 16*(1), 72–75.

Simpson, A.I.F., McKenna, B., Moskowitz, A., Skipworth, J. & Barry-Walsh, J. (2004). Homicide and mental illness in New Zealand, 1970–2000. *British Journal of Psychiatry, 185*, 394–398.

Singer, J.L. (1980). The scientific basis of psychotherapeutic practice: A question of values and ethics. *Psychotherapy Theory, Research and Practice, 17*, 372–383.

Singer, L.T., Arendt, R., Minnes, S. et al. (2002). Cognitive and motor outcomes of cocaine-exposed infants. *JAMA: Journal of the American Medical Association, 287*(15), 1952–1960.

Singleton, N., Bumpstead, R., O'Brien, M., Lee, A. & Meltzer, H. (2001). *Psychiatric morbidity among adults living in private households, 2000*. London: TSO.

Siqueland, L., Kendall, P.C. & Steinberg, L. (1996). Anxiety in children: Perceived family environments and observed family interaction. *Journal of Clinical Child Psychology, 25*(2), 225–237.

Sivec, H.J. & Lynn, S.J. (1995). Dissociative and neuropsychological symptoms: The question of differential diagnosis. *Clinical Psychology Review, 15*, 297–316.

Skegg, K., Nada-Raja, S., Paul, C. & Skegg, D.C.G. (2007). Body piercing, personality, and sexual behaviour. *Archives of Sexual Behavior, 36*, 47–54.

Skinner, C.H., Dittmer, K.I. & Howell, L.A. (2000). Direct observation in school settings: Theoretical isues. In E.S. Shapiro & T.R. Kratochwill (Eds.), *Behavioral assessment in schools: Theory, research and clinical foundations* (2nd ed.). New York: Guilford Press.

Skodol, A.E., Gunderson, J.G., McGlashan, T.H., Dyck, I.R. et al. (2002). Functional impairment in patients with schizotypal, borderline, avoidant, or obsessive-compulsive personality disorder. *American Journal of Psychiatry, 159*(2), 276–283.

Skorge, T.D., Eagan, T.M.L., Eide, G.E., Gulsvik, A. & Bakke, P.S. (2005). The adult incidence of asthma and respiratory symptoms by passive smoking in utero or in childhood. *American Journal of Respiratory and Critical Care Medicine, 172*(1), 61–66.

Slade, P. (1982). Towards a functional analysis of anorexia nervosa and bulimia nervosa. *British Journal of Clinical Psychology, 21*, 167–179.

Slaghuis, W.L. & Curran, C.E. (1999). Spatial frequency masking in positive- and negative-symptom schizophrenia. *Journal of Abnormal Psychology, 108*(1), 42–50.

Sloan, D.M., Strauss, M.E. & Wisner, K.L. (2001). Diminished response to pleasant stimuli by depressed women. *Journal of Abnormal Psychology, 110*(3), 488–493.

Sloan, H.R. (1991). Metabolic screening methods. In J.L. Matson & J.A. Mulick (Eds.), *Handbook of mental retardation* (2nd ed.). New York: Pergamon.

Sloane, R.B., Staples, F.R., Cristol, A.H., Yorkston, N.J. & Whipple, K. (1975). *Psychotherapy versus behaviour therapy*. Cambridge, MA: Harvard University Press.

Slutske, W.S., Heath, A.C., Dinwiddie, S.H., Madden, P.A.F. et al. (1997). Modeling genetic and environmental influences in the etiology of conduct disorder: A study of 2,682 adult twin pairs. *Journal of Abnormal Psychology, 106*, 266–279.

Smalley, S.L. (1998). Autism and tuberous sclerosis. *Journal of Autism and Developmental Disorders, 28*(5), 407–414.

Smania, N., Girardi, F., Domenicali, C., Lora, E. & Aglioti, S. (2000). The rehabilitation of limb apraxia: A study in left-brain-damaged patients. *Archives of Physical Medicine and Rehabilitation, 81*(4), 379–388.

Smart, R. & Ogbourne, A. (2000). Drug use and drinking among students in 36 countries. *Addicitve Behavior, 25*, 455–460.

Smeets, G., de Jong, P.J. & Mayer, B. (2000). If you suffer from a headache, then you have a brain tumour: Domain-specific reasoning 'bias' and hypochondriasis. *Behaviour Research and Therapy, 38*, 763–776.

Smiley, A. (1999). Long-term effects of cannabis on the central nervous system. In H. Kalant, W.A. Corrigall, W. Hall & R.G. Smart (Eds.), *The health effects of cannabis*. Toronto: ARF Books.

Smith, D.J., Muir, W.J. & Blackwood, D.H.R. (2004). Is borderline personality disorder part of the bipolar spectrum? *Harvard Review of Psychiatry, 12*, 133–139.

Smith, D.W., Bierman, E.L. & Robinson, N.M. (1978). *The biologic ages of man: From conception through old age*. Philadelphia: Saunders.

Smith, G. (1992). The epidemiology and treatment of depression when it coincides with somatoform disorders, somatization, or panic. *General Hospital Psychiatry, 14*, 265–272.

Smith, G.S., Keyl, P.M., Hadley, J.A., Bartley, C.L. et al. (2001). Drinking and recreational boating fatalities: A population-based case-control study. *JAMA: Journal of the American Medical Association, 286*(23), 2974–2980.

Smith, M.L. & Glass, G.V. (1977). Meta-analysis of psychotherapy outcome studies. *American Psychologist, 32*, 752–760.

Smith, M.L., Glass, G.V. & Miller, T.I. (1980). *The benefits of psychotherapy*. Baltimore: Johns Hopkins University Press.

Smith, T.E., Bellack, A.S. & Liberman, R.P. (1996). Social skills training for schizophrenia: Review and future directions. *Clinical Psychology Review, 16*(7), 599–617.

Smith, Y.L.S., van Goozen, S.H.M. & Cohen-Kettenis, P.T. (2001). Adolescents with gender identity disorder who were accepted or rejected for sex reassignment surgery: A prospective follow-up study. *Journal of the American Academy of Child and Adolescent Psychiatry, 40*(4), 472–481.

Smith, Y.L.S., van Goozen, S.H.M., Kuiper, A.J. & Cohen-Kettenis, P.T. (2005). Sex reassignment: Outcomes and predictors of treatment for adolescent and adult transsexuals. *Psychological Medicine, 35*(1), 89–99.

Smits, J.A.J., Powers, M.B., Cho, Y.R. & Telch, M.J. (2004). Mechanism of change in cognitive-behavioral treatment of panic disorder: Evidence for the fear of fear mediational hypothesis. *Journal of Consulting and Clinical Psychology, 72*(4), 646–652.

Smyth, B.P., Barry, J., Lane, A., Cotter, M., O'Neill, M. et al. (2005). In-patient treatment of opiate dependence: Medium-term follow-up outcomes. *British Journal of Psychiatry, 187*, 360–365.

Snyder, S. (1986). *Drugs and the brain*. New York: Scientific American Library.

Sobell, M.B. & Sobell, L.C. (1993). *Problem drinkers: Guided self-change treatment*. New York: Guilford Press.

Sobell, M.B. & Sobell, L.C. (1995). Controlled drinking after 25 years: How important was the great debate? *Addiction, 90*, 1149–1153.

Sobin, C. & Sackeim, H.A. (1997). Psychomotor symptoms of depression. *American Journal of Psychiatry, 154*, 4–17.

Sohlberg, M.M. & Mateer, C.A. (2001). Improving attention and managing attentional problems: Adapting rehabilitation techniques to adults with ADD. *Annals of the New York Academy of Sciences, 931*, 359–375.

Sohlberg, M.M., McLaughlin, K.A., Pavese, A., Heidrich, A. & Posner, M.I. (2000). Evaluation of attention process training and brain injury education in persons with acquired brain injury. *Journal of Clinical and Experimental Neuropsychology, 22*(5), 656–676.

Sokol, D.K. & Edwards-Brown, M. (2004). Neuroimaging in autistic spectrum disorder (ASD). *Journal of Neuroimaging, 14*(1), 8–15.

Soler, J., Pascual, J.C., Campins, J., Barrachina, J. et al. (2005). Double-blind, placebo-controlled study of dialectical behavior therapy plus olanzapine for borderline personality disorder. *American Journal of Psychiatry, 162*(6), 1221–1224.

Soloff, P.H., Meltzer, C.C., Becker, C., Greer, P.J. et al. (2003). Impulsivity and prefrontal hypometabolism in borderline personality disorder. *Psychiatry Research: Neuroimaging, 123*(3), 153–163.

Sommer, I., Aleman, A., Ramsey, N., Bouma, A. & Kahn, R. (2001). Handedness, language lateralization and anatomical asymmetry in schizophrenia: Meta-analysis. *British Journal of Psychiatry, 178*, 344–351.

Sonino, N., Navarrini, C., Ruini, C., Ottolini, F. et al. (2004). Persistent psychological distress in patients treated for endocrine disease. *Psychotherapy and Psychosomatics, 73*(2), 78–83.

Spanos, N.P. (1994). Multiple identity enactments and multiple personality disorder: A sociocognitive perspective. *Psychological Bulletin, 116*, 143–165.

Spanos, N.P. (1996). *Multiple identities and false memories: A sociocognitive perspective*. Washington, DC: American Psychological Association.

Spanos, N.P., Weekes, J.R. & Bertrand, L.D. (1985). Multiple personality: A social psychology perspective. *Journal of Abnormal Psychology, 94*, 362–376.

Sparrow, S.S. & Davis, S.M. (2000). Recent advances in the assessment of intelligence and cognition. *Journal of Child Psychology and Psychiatry, 41*, 117–131.

Spector, I.P. & Carey, M.P. (1990). Incidence and prevalence of the sexual dysfunctions: A critical review of the empirical literature. *Archives of Sexual Behavior, 19*(4), 389–408.

Spencer, S.J., Steele, C.M. & Quinn, D.M. (1999). Stereotype threat and women's math performance. *Journal of Experimental Social Psychology, 35*, 4–28.

Spiegel, D. (1994). Dissociative disorders. In R.E. Hales, S.C. Yudofsky & J.A. Talbot (Eds.), *The American Psychiatric Press textbook of psychiatry* (2nd ed.). Washington, DC: American Psychiatric Press.

Spiegler, M.D. & Guevremont, D.C. (2003). *Contemporary behaviour therapy*. Belmont, CA: Thomson/Wadsworth.

Spiehler, V. & Brown, R. (1987). Unconjugated morphine in blood by radioimmunoassay and gas-chromatography mass-spectrometry. *Journal of Forensic Sciences, 32*(4), 906–916.

Spielberger, C.D., Gorsuch, R.L., Lushene, R., Vagg, P.R. & Jacobs, G.A. (1983). *Manual for the Stait-Trait Anxiety Inventory (Form Y)*. Palo Alto: Consulting Psychologists Press.

Spiess, W.F.J., Geer, J.H. & O'Donohue, W.T. (1984). Premature ejaculation: Investigation of factors in ejaculatory latency. *Journal of Abnormal Psychology, 93*(2), 242–245.

Spitzer, B.L., Henderson, K.A. & Zivian, M.T. (1999). Gender differences in population versus media body sizes: A comparison over four decades. *Sex Roles, 40*(7–8), 545–565.

Spitzer, R.L. & Wakefield, J.C. (1999). DSM-IV diagnostic criterion for clinical significance: Does it help solve the false positives problem? *American Journal of Psychiatry*, 1856–1864.

Spitzer, R.M., Gibbon, M. & Williams, J.B.W. (1986). *Structured Clinical Interview for DSM-IV Axis I disorders*. New York: New York State Psychiatric Institute, Biometrics Research Division.

Spollen, J.J., Wooten, R.G., Cargile, C. & Bartztokis, G. (2004). Prolactin levels and erectile function in patients treated with risperidone. *Journal of Clinical Psychopharmacology, 24*(2), 161–166.

Spurr, J.M. & Stopa, L. (2002). Self-focused attention in social phobia and social anxiety. *Clinical Psychology Review, 22,* 947–975.

Stahl, S.M. (1996). *Essential psychopharmacology: Neuroscientific basis and practical applications.* Cambridge: Cambridge University Press.

Stahl, S.M. (2001). The psychopharmacology of sex. Part 2. Effects of drugs and disease on the three phases of human sexual response. *Journal of Clinical Psychiatry, 62,* 147–148.

Stahr, B., Cushing, D., Lane, K. & Fox, J. (2006). Efficacy of a function-based intervention in decreasing off-task behavior exhibited by a student with ADHD. *Journal of Positive Behavior Interventions, 8*(4), 201–211.

Staller, J. & Faraone, S.V. (2006). Attention-deficit hyperactivity disorder in girls: Epidemiology and management. *CNS Drugs, 20,* 107–123.

Stangier, U., Heidenreich, T., Peitz, M., Lauterbach, W. & Clark, D.M. (2003). Cognitive therapy for social phobia: Individual versus group treatment. *Behaviour Research and Therapy, 41*(9), 991–1007.

Starcevic, V. & Bogojevic, G. (1997). Comorbidity of panic disorder with agoraphobia and specific phobia: Relationship with the subtypes of specific phobia. *Comprehensive Psychiatry, 38,* 315–320.

Starcevic, V., Uhlenhuth, E.H., Kellner, R. & Pathak, D. (1992). Patterns of comorbidity in panic disorder and agoraphobia. *Psychiatry Research, 42*(2), 171–183.

Starkman, M.N., Zelnik, T.C., Nesse, R.M. & Cameron, O.G. (1985). Anxiety in patients with pheochromocytomas. *Archives of Internal Medicine, 145*(2), 248–252.

Startup, H.M. & Davey, G.C.L. (2003). Inflated responsibility and the use of stop rules for catastrophic worrying. *Behaviour Research and Therapy, 41,* 495–503.

Stead, L.F. & Lancaster, T. (2005). Interventions for preventing tobacco sales to minors. *Cochrane Database of Systematic Reviews* (1), Art. No. CD001497.pub2.

Steele, C.M. & Josephs, R.A. (1990). Alcohol myopia: Its prized and dangerous effects. *American Psychologist, 45,* 921–933.

Steentoft, A., Muller, M., Worm, K. & Toft, J. (2000). Substances other than alcohol found in the blood among Danish road-users during a week in 1996. *Ugeskr. Laeger, 162,* 5778–5781.

Steffenberg, S., Gillberg, C., Hellgren, L., Andersson, L. et al. (1989). A twin study of autism in Denmark, Finland, Iceland, Norway and Sweden. *Journal of Child Psychology and Psychiatry and Allied Disciplines, 30*(3), 405–416.

Steiger, H., Leonard, S., Kin, N.M.K.N.Y. et al. (2000). Childhood abuse and platelet tritiated-paroxetine binding in bulimia nervosa: Implications of borderline personality disorder. *Journal of Clinical Psychiatry, 61*(6), 428–435.

Steiger, H., Stotland, S., Trottier, J. & Ghadirian, A.M. (1996). Familial eating concerns and psychopathological traits: Causal implications of transgenerational effects. *International Journal of Eating Disorders, 19*(2), 147–157.

Steil, R. & Ehlers, A. (2000). Dysfunctional meaning of posttraumatic intrusions in chronic PTSD. *Behaviour Research and Therapy, 38*(6), 537–558.

Stein, D.M. & Laasko, W. (1988). Bulimia: A historical perspective. *International Journal of Eating Disorders, 7,* 201–210.

Stein, E.A., Pankiewicz, J., Hanch, H.H., Clo, J. et al. (1998). Nicotine-induced limbic cortical activation in the human brain: A functional MRI study. *American Journal of Psychiatry, 155,* 1009–1015.

Stein, M.B., Forde, D.R., Anderson, G. et al. (1997). Obsessive-compulsive disorder in the community: An epidemiologic survey with clinical reappraisal. *American Journal of Psychiatry, 154*(8), 1120–1126.

Steinhausen, H.C., Seidel, R. & Metzke, C.W. (2000). Evaluation of treatment and intermediate and long-term outcome of adolescent eating disorders. *Psychological Medicine, 30*(5), 1089–1098.

Steketee, G. (1993). Social support and treatment outcome of obsessive-compulsive disorder at 9-month follow-up. *Behavioural Psychotherapy, 21*(2), 81–95.

Steketee, G., Frost, R.O., Bhar, S., Bouvard, M. et al. (2005). Psychometric validation of the obsessive belief questionnaire and interpretation of intrusions inventory. Part 2. Factor analyses and testing of a brief version. *Behaviour Research and Therapy, 43,* 1527–1542.

Steketee, G., Frost, R.O. & Kyrios, M. (2003). Cognitive aspects of compulsive hoarding. *Cognitive Therapy and Research, 27*(4), 463–479.

Stephens, R.S., Roffman, R.A. & Simpson, E.E. (1993). Adult marijuana users seeking treatment. *Journal of Consulting and Clinical Psychology, 61*(6), 1100–1104.

Stermac, L.E. & Segal, Z.V. (1989). Adult sexual contact with children: An examination of cognitive factors. *Behavior Therapy, 20*(4), 573–584.

Stevens, P. & Martin, N. (1999). Supporting individuals with intellectual disability and challenging behaviour in integrated work settings: An overview and a model for service provision. *Journal of Intellectual Disability Research, 43,* 19–29.

Stevenson, J., Graham, P., Fredman, G. & McLoughlin, V.A. (1987). Twin study of genetic influences on reading and spelling ability and disability. *Journal of Child Psychology and Psychiatry, 28,* 229–247.

Stevenson, J. & Jones, I.H. (1972). Behavior therapy technique for exhibitionism: Preliminary report. *Archives of General Psychiatry, 27*(6), 839&.

Stewart-Knox, B.J., Sittlington, J., Rugkasa, J., Harrisson, S. et al. (2005). Smoking and peer groups: Results from a longitudinal qualitative study of young people in Northern Ireland. *British Journal of Social Psychology, 44,* 397–414.

Stice, E. (2001). A prospective test of the dual-pathway model of bulimic pathology: Mediating effects of dieting and negative affect. *Journal of Abnormal Psychology, 110,* 124–135.

Stice, E., Shaw, H. & Nemeroff, C. (1998). Dual pathway model of bulimia nervosa: Longitudinal support for dietary restraint and affect-regulation mechanisms. *Journal of Social and Clinical Psychology, 17*(2), 129–149.

Stice, E., Telch, C.F. & Rizvi, S.L. (2000). Development and validation of the eating disorder diagnostic scale: A brief self-report measure of anorexia, bulimia, and binge-eating disorder. *Psychological Assessment, 12*(2), 123–131.

Stokes, T.F. & Baer, D.M. (1977). An implicit technology of generalization. *Journal of Applied Behavior Analysis, 10,* 349–369.

Stokes, T.F. & Osnes, P.G. (1988). The developing applied technology of generalization and maintenance. In R.H. Horner, G. Dunlap & R.L. Koegel (Eds.), *Generalization and maintenance: Life style changes in applied settings.* Baltimore: Brookes.

Stone, A.A. & Shiffman, S. (1994). Ecological momentary assessment (EMA) in behavioral medicine. *Annals of Behavioral Medicine, 16,* 199–202.

Stopa, L. & Clark, D.M. (1993). Cognitive processes in social phobia. *Behaviour Research and Therapy, 31*(3), 255–267.

Storch, E.A., Ledley, D.R., Lewin, A.B., Murphy, T.K. et al. (2006). Peer victimization in children with obsessive-compulsive disorder: Relations with symptoms of psychopathology. *Journal of Clinical Child and Adolescent Psychology, 35*(3), 446–455.

Stoving, R.K., Hangaard, J., Hansen-Nord, M. et al. (1999). A review of endocrine changes in anorexia nervosa. *Journal of Psychiatric Research, 33*(2), 139–152.

Stratta, P., Mancini, F., Mattei, P., Daneluzzo, E. et al. (1997). Association between striatal reduction and poor Wisconsin Card Sorting Test performance in patients with schizophrenia. *Biological Psychiatry, 42*(9), 816–820.

Straus, S.E., Dale, J.K., Tobi, M., Lawley, T. et al. (1988). Acyclovir treatment of the chronic fatigue syndrome: Lack of efficacy in a placebo-controlled trial. *New England Journal of Medicine, 319*(26), 1692–1698.

Strauss, M.E. (1993). Relations of symptoms to cognitive deficits in schizophrenia. *Schizophrenia Bulletin, 19*(2), 215–231.

Stravynski, A., Bond, S. & Amado, D. (2004). Cognitive causes of social phobia: A critical appraisal. *Clinical Psychology Review, 24*, 421–440.

Streeton, C. & Whelan, G. (2001). Naltrexone, a relapse prevention maintenance treatment of alcohol dependence: A meta-analysis of randomized controlled trials. *Alcohol and Alcoholism, 36*(6), 544–552.

Streltzer, J., Eliashopf, B.A., Kline, A.E. & Goebert, D. (2000). Chronic pain disorder following physical injury. *Psychosomatics, 41*(3), 227–234.

Striegel-Moore, R.H. (1997). Risk factors for eating disorders. *Annals of the New York Academy of Sciences, 817*, 98–109.

Striegel-Moore, R.H. & Franko, D.L. (2003). Epidemiology of binge-eating disorder. *International Journal of Eating Disorders, 34*, 19–29.

Striegel-Moore, R.H., Cachelin, F.M., Dohm, F.A., Pike, K.M. et al. (2001). Comparison of binge-eating disorder and bulimia nervosa in a community sample. *International Journal of Eating Disorders, 29*(2), 157–165.

Striegel-Moore, R.H. & Smolak, L. (1996). The role of race in the development of eating disorders. In M.P. Levine, L.L. Smolak & R.H. Striegel-Moore (Eds.), *The developmental psychopathology of eating disorders: Implications for research, prevention and treatment*. Hillsdale, NJ: Lawrence Erlbaum.

Stritzke, W.G.K., Patrick, C.J. & Lang, A.R. (1995). Alcohol and human emotion: A multidimensional analysis incorporating startle-probe methodology. *Journal of Abnormal Psychology, 104*(1), 114–122.

Strober, M. (1991). Disorders of the self in anorexia nervosa: An organismic-developmental paradigm. In C.L. Johnson (Ed.), *Psychodynamic treatments of anorexia nervosa and bulimia*. New York: Guilford Press.

Strober, M., Freeman, R., Lampert, C., Diamond, J. & Kaye, W. (2000). Controlled family study of anorexia nervosa and bulimia nervosa: Evidence of shared liability and transmission of partial syndromes. *American Journal of Psychiatry, 157*(3), 393–401.

Stroh, M. (1999). Doctors make modern house calls over the Internet. *Albuquerque Journal*, pp. C1, C2.

Stroke Association (2006). Retrieved from www.stroke.org.uk/information/index.html, November 2006.

Stromland, K., Nordin, V., Miller, M., Akerstrom, B. & Gillberg, C. (1994). Autism in thalidomide embryopathy: A population study. *Developmental Medicine and Child Neurology, 36*(4), 351–356.

Strong, S.M., Williamson, D.A., Netemeyer, R.G. & Geer, J.H. (2000). Eating disorder symptoms and concerns about body differ as a function of gender and sexual orientation. *Journal of Social and Clinical Psychology, 19*(2), 240–255.

Strongman, K.T. & Russell, P.N. (1986). Salience of emotion in recall. *Bulletin of the Psychonomic Society, 24*, 25–27.

Stuart, F.M., Hammond, D.C. & Pett, M.A. (1987). Inhibited sexual desire in women. *Archives of Sexual Behavior, 16*(2), 91–106.

Stuart, R.B. (1967). Behavioral control of overeating. *Behaviour Research and Therapy, 5*, 357–365.

Stuart, R.B. & Davis, B. (1972). *Slim chance in a fat world: Behavioral control of obesity*. Champaign, IL: Research Press.

Stuart, R.B. & Greer, J.G. (Eds.) (1984). *Victims of sexual aggression: Treatment of children, women and men*. New York: Van Nostrand Reinhold.

Study Group on Anorexia Nervosa (1995). Anorexia nervosa: Directions for future research. *International Journal of Eating Disorders, 17*, 235–242.

Stulemeijer, M., de Jong, L.W.A.M., Fiselier, T.J.W., Hoogveld, S.W.B. & Bleijenberg, G. (2005). Cognitive behaviour therapy for adolescents with chronic fatigue syndrome: Randomized controlled trial. *British Medical Journal, 330*(7481), 14–17.

Sturges, J.W. & Sturges, L.V. (1998). In vivo systematic desensitization in a single-session treatment of an 11-year-old girl's elevator phobia. *Child and Family Behavior Therapy, 20*(4), 55–62.

Sudi, K., Ottl, K., Payerl, D., Baumgartl, P., Tauschmann, K. & Muller, W. (2004). Anorexia athletica. *Nutrition, 20*(7–8), 657–661.

Sullivan, M.J.L., Bishop, S.R. & Pivik, J. (1995). The Pain Catastrophizing Scale: Development and validation. *Psychological Assessment, 7*(4), 524–532.

Sumpter, R.E. & McMillan, T.M. (2005). Misdiagnosis of post-traumatic stress disorder following severe traumatic brain injury. *British Journal of Psychiatry, 186*, 423–426.

Sun, L., Zhao, Z.Y., Li, L. & Cheng, H.Y. (2004). Preschool children's lead levels in rural communities of Zhejiang province, China. *International Journal of Hygiene and Environmental Health, 207*(5), 437–440.

Super, C.M., Herrera, M.G. & Mora, J.O. (1990). Long-term effects of food supplementation and psychosocial intervention on the physical growth of Columbian infants at risk of malnutrition. *Child Development, 61*, 29–49.

Suppes, T., Baldessarini, R.J., Faedda, G.L. & Tohen, M. (1991). Risk of recurrence following discontinuation of lithium treatment in bipolar disorder. *Archives of General Psychiatry, 48*(12), 1082–1088.

Surma-aho, O., Niemela, M., Vilkki, J., Kouri, M. et al. (2001). Adverse long-term effects of brain radiotherapy in adult low-grade glioma patients. *Neurology, 56*(10), 1285–1290.

Sussman, S., Dent, C.W., Simon, T.R., Stacy, A.W. et al. (1995). Immediate impact of social influence-oriented substance abuse prevention curricula in traditional and continuation high schools. *Drugs and Society, 8*, 65–81.

Svartberg, M., Stiles, T.C. & Seltzer, M.H. (2004). Randomized, controlled trial of the effectiveness of short-term dynamic psychotherapy and cognitive therapy for cluster C personality disorders. *American Journal of Psychiatry, 161*(5), 810–817.

Swearington, C.E., Moyer, A. & Finney, J.W. (2003). Alcoholism treatment outcome studies, 1970–1998: An expanded look at the nature of the research. *Addictive Behaviors, 28*, 415–436.

Swedo, S.E. & Leonard, H.L. (1994). Childhood movement disorders and obsessive-compulsive disorder. *Journal of Clinical Psychiatry, 55*, 32–37.

Swedo, S.E., Rapoport, J.L., Leonard, H.L., Lenane, M. & Cheslow, D. (1989). Obsessive-compulsive disorder in children and adolescents: Clinical phenomenology of 70 consecutive cases. *Archives of General Psychiatry, 46*, 335–341.

Swift, R.M. (1999). Medications and alcohol craving. *Alcohol Research and Health, 23*(3), 207–213.

Swift, W., Hall, W. & Teesson, C. (2001a). Characteristics of DSM-IV and ICD-10 cannabis dependence among Australian adults: Results from the National Survey of Mental Health and Wellbeing. *Drug and Alcohol Dependence, 63*(2), 147–153.

Swift, W., Hall, W. & Teesson, C. (2001b). Cannabis use and dependence among Australian adults: Results from the National Survey of Mental Health and Wellbeing. *Addiction, 96*(5), 737–748.

Swindle, R.W., Cameron, A.E., Lockhart, D.C. & Rosen, R.C. (2004). The psychological and interpersonal relationship scales: Assessing psychological and relationship outcomes associated with erectile dysfunction and its treatment. *Archives of Sexual Behavior, 33*(1), 19–30.

Swonger, A.K. & Constantine, L.L. (1983). *Drugs and therapy: A handbook of psychotropic drugs* (2nd ed.). Boston: Little, Brown.

Symon, J.B. (2005). Expanding interventions for children with autism. *Journal of Positive Behavior Interventions, 7*, 159–173.

Symons, F.J., Thompson, A. & Rodriguez, M.C. (2004). Self-injurious behavior and the efficacy of naltrexone treatment: A quantitative synthesis. *Mental Retardation and Developmental Disabilities Research Reviews, 10*(3), 193–200.

Szelenberger, W., Niemcewicz, S. & Dabrowska, A.J. (2005). Sleepwalking and night terrors: Psychopathological and psychophysiological correlates. *International Review of Psychiatry, 17*, 263–270.

Szostak, C., Lister, R., Eckhardt, M. & Weingartner, H. (1995). Dissociative effects of mood on memory. In R.M. Klein & B.K. Doane (Eds.), *Psychological concepts and dissociative disorders*. Hillsdale, NJ: Lawrence Erlbaum.

Tagliaferri, F., Compagnone, C., Korsic, M., Servadei, F. et al. (2006). A systematic review of brain injury epidemiology in Europe. *Acta Neurochirurgica, 148*, 255–268.

Tagliaro, F., Battisti, Z., Smith, F.P. & Marigo, M. (1998). Death from heroin overdose: Findings from hair analysis. *Lancet, 351*(9120), 1923–1925.

Tallis, S., Davey, G.C.L. & Capuzzo, N. (1994). The phenomenology of non-pathological worry: A preliminary investigation. In G.C.L. Davey & F. Tallis (Eds.), *Worrying: Perspectives on theory assessment and research*. Chichester: Wiley.

Tam, S.F. & Man, W.K. (2004). Evaluating computer-assisted memory retraining programmes for people with post-head injury amnesia. *Brain Injury*, 18(5), 461–470.

Tanda, G., Pontieri, F.E. & DiChiara, G. (1997). Cannabinoid and heroin activation of mesolimbic dopamine transmission by a common mu 1 opioid receptor mechanism. *Science*, 276(5321), 2048–2050.

Tannock, R. (1998). Attention deficit hyperactivity disorder: Advances in cognitive, neurobiological and genetic research. *Journal of Child Psychology and Psychiatry*, 39, 65–99.

Tarrier, N. (2006). An introduction to case formulation and its challenges. In N. Tarrier (Ed.), *Case formulation in cognitive behaviour therapy*. Hove: Routledge.

Tarrier, N., Barrowclough, C., Vaughn, C., Bamrah, J.S. et al. (1988). The community management of schizophrenia: A controlled trial of a behavioral intervention with families to reduce relapse. *British Journal of Psychiatry*, 153, 532–542.

Tarrier, N. & Wykes, T. (2004). Is there evidence that cognitive behaviour therapy is an effective treatment for schizophrenia? A cautious or cautionary tale? *Behaviour Research and Therapy*, 42, 1377–1401.

Tarullo, L.B., Richardson, D.T., Radke-Yarrow, M. & Martinez, P.E. (1995). Multiple sources in child diagnosis: Parent–child concordance in affectively ill and well families. *Journal of Clinical Child Psychology*, 24, 173–183.

Taylor, C.T., Laposa, J.M. & Alden, L.E. (2004). Is avoidant personality disorder more than just social avoidance? *Journal of Personality Disorders*, 18(6), 571–594.

Taylor, J., Malone, S., Iacono, W.G. & McGue, M. (2002). Development of substance dependence in two delinquency subgroups and nondelinquents from a male twin sample. *Journal of the American Academy of Child and Adolescent Psychiatry*, 41(4), 386–393.

Taylor, P.J. & Gunn, J. (1999). Homicides by people with mental illness: Myth and reality. *British Journal of Psychiatry*, 174, 9–14.

Taylor, S. & Cox, B.J. (1998). Anxiety sensitivity: Multiple dimensions and hierarchic structure. *Behaviour Research and Therapy*, 36(1), 37–51.

Tazaki, M. & Landlaw, K. (2006). Behavioural mechanisms and cognitive-behavioural interventions of somatoform disorders. *International Review of Psychiatry*, 18, 67–73.

Teasdale, J.D. (1988). Cognitive vulnerability to persistent depression. *Cognition and Emotion*, 2, 247–274.

Teasdale, J.D., Segal, Z.V. & Williams, J.M.G. (1995). How does cognitive therapy prevent depressive relapse and why should attentional control (mindfulness) training help? *Behaviour Research and Therapy*, 33(1), 25–39.

Teasdale, J.D., Segal, Z.V., Williams, J.M.G., Ridgeway, V.A., Soulsby, J.M. & Lau, M.A. (2000). Prevention of relapse/recurrence in major depression by mindfulness-based cognitive therapy. *Journal of Consulting and Clinical Psychology*, 68, 615–623.

Telch, M.J., Lucas, J.A., Schmidt, N.B., Hanna, H.H. et al. (1993). Group cognitive-behavioral treatment of panic disorder. *Behaviour Research and Therapy*, 31(3), 279–287.

Telch, M.J., Schmidt, N.B., Jaimez, T.L.N., Jacquin, K.M. & Harrington, P.J. (1995). Impact of cognitive-behavioral treatment on quality-of-life in panic disorder patients. *Journal of Consulting and Clinical Psychology*, 63(5), 823–830.

Temple, N. (2002). A critical enquiry into the psychoanalytic theories and approaches to psychosomatic conditions. *International Journal of Psychoanalysis*, 56, 11–15.

Terrell, F. & Terrell, S.L. (1984). Race of counselor, client sex, cultural mistrust level, and premature termination from counseling among black clients. *Journal of Counseling Psychology*, 31, 371–375.

Tezzi, A., Duckworth, M.P. & Adams, H.E. (2001). Somatoform and factitious disorders. In H.E. Adams & P.B. Sutker (Eds.), *Comprehensive handbook of psychopathology* (3rd ed.). New York: Kluwer.

Thapar, A. & Rice, F. (2006). Twin studies in pediatric depression. *Child and Adolescent Psychiatric Clinics of North America*, 15(4), 869&.

Thara, R., Henrietta, M., Joseph, A., Rajkumar, S. & Eaton, W.W. (1994). 10-year course of schizophrenia: The Madras Longitudinal Study. *Acta Psychiatrica Scandinavica*, 90(5), 329–336.

Thase, M.E., Greenhouse, J.B., Frank, E., Reynolds, C. et al. (1997). Treatment of major depression with psychotherapy or psychotherapy-pharmacotherapy combinations. *Archives of General Psychiatry*, 54, 1009–1015.

Thase, M.E. & Kupfer, D.J. (1996). Recent developments in the pharmacotherapy of mood disorders. *Journal of Consulting and Clinical Psychology*, 64, 646–659.

Thase, M.E., Trivedi, M.H. & Rush, A.J. (1995). MAOIs in the contemporary treatment of depression. *Neuropsychopharmacology*, 12(3), 185–219.

Theodor, L.H. & Mandelcorn, M.S. (1973). Hysterical blindness: Case report and study using a modern psychophysical technique. *Journal of Abnormal Psychology*, 82(3), 552–553.

Thomas, H. (1996). A community survey of adverse effects of cannabis use. *Drug and Alcohol Dependence*, 42(3), 201–207.

Thompson, C.K., Kearns, K.P. & Edmonds, L.A. (2006). An experimental analysis of acquisition, generalization, and maintenance of naming behaviour in a patient with anomia. *Aphasiology*, 20, 1226–1244.

Thompson, G.O.B., Raab, G.M., Hepburn, W.S., Hunter, R., Fulton, M. & Laxen, D.P.H. (1989). Blood-lead levels and children's behaviour: Results from the Edinburgh lead study. *Journal of Child Psychology and Psychiatry*, 30, 515–528.

Thompson, M.G., McInnes, R.R. & Willard, H.F. (1991). *Genetics in medicine* (5th ed.). Philadelphia: Saunders.

Thompson, S.H., Corwin, S.J. & Sargent, R.G. (1997). Ideal body size beliefs and weight concerns of fourth-grade children. *International Journal of Eating Disorders*, 21(3), 279–284.

Thoresen, C.E. & Mahoney, M.J. (1974). *Behavioral self-control*. New York: Holt, Rinehart & Winston.

Thorpe, S.J. & Salkovskis, P.M. (1995). Phobic beliefs: Do cognitive factors play a role in specific phobias? *Behaviour Research and Therapy*, 33(7), 805–816.

Thorpe, S.J. & Salkovskis, P.M. (1997). The effect of one-session treatment for spider phobia on attentional bias and beliefs. *British Journal of Clinical Psychology*, 36, 225–241.

Tiefer, L. (2006). Female sexual dysfunction: A case study of disease mongering and activist resistance. *PLOS Medicine*, 3(4), 436–440.

Tienari, P., Wynne, L.C., Laksy, K., Moring, J. et al. (2003). Genetic boundaries of the schizophrenia spectrum: Evidence from the Finnish adoptive family study of schizophrenia. *American Journal of Psychiatry*, 160, 1587–1594.

Tierney, A.J. (2000). Egas Moniz and the origins of psychosurgery: A review commemorating the 50th anniversary of Moniz's Nobel Prize. *Journal of the History of Neuroscience*, 9, 22–36.

Tiggemann, M. (2003). Appearance and social comparison processing in response to music videos. *Australian Journal of Psychology*, 55, 65.

Tiggemann, M. & Pickering, A.S. (1996). Role of television in adolescent women's body dissatisfaction and drive for thinness. *International Journal of Eating Disorders*, 20(2), 199–203.

Tiggemann, M. & Slater, A. (2004). Thin ideals in music television: A source of social comparison and body dissatisfaction. *International Journal of Eating Disorders*, 35(1), 48–58.

Tillfors, M., Furmark, T., Ekselius, L. & Fredrikson, M. (2001). Social phobia and avoidant personality disorder as related to parental history of social anxiety: A general population study. *Behaviour Research and Therapy*, 39(3), 289–298.

Timko, C., Moos, R.H., Finney, J.W. & Lesar, M.D. (2000). Long-term outcomes of alcohol use disorders: Comparing untreated individuals with those in Alcoholics Anonymous and formal treatment. *Journal of Studies on Alcohol, 61*(4), 529–540.

Tinklenberg, J.R. (1971). A clinical view of the amphetamines. *American Family Physician, 5*, 82–86.

Titone, D., Holzman, P.S. & Levy, D.L. (2002). Idiom processing in schizophrenia: Literal implausibility saves the day for idiom priming *Journal of Abnormal Psychology, 111*(2), 313–320.

Toal, F., Murphy, D.G.M. & Murphy, K.C. (2005). Autistic-spectrum disorders: Lessons from neuroimaging. *British Journal of Psychiatry, 187*, 395–397.

Tolin, D.F., Abramowitz, J.S., Brigidi, B.D., Amir, N. et al. (2001). Memory and memory confidence in obsessive-compulsive disorder. *Behaviour Research and Therapy, 39*(8), 913–927.

Tolin, D.F., Woods, C.M. & Abramowitz, J.S. (2003). Relationship between obsessive beliefs and obsessive-compulsive symptoms. *Cognitive Therapy and Research, 27*, 657–669.

Tomasson, K., Kent, D. & Coryell, W. (1991). Somatization and conversion disorders: Comorbidity and demographics at presentation. *Acta Psychiatrica Scandinavica, 84*(3), 288–293.

Tonn, R.T. & Obrzut, J.E. (2005). The neuropsychological perspective on autism. *Journal of Developmental and Physical Disabilities, 17*, 409–419.

Torgersen, S. (1986). Genetics of somatoform disorders. *Archives of General Psychiatry, 43*, 1085–1089.

Torgersen, S., Kringlen, E. & Cramer, V. (2001). The prevalence of personality disorders in a community sample. *Archives of General Psychiatry, 58*, 590–596.

Torgersen, S., Lygren, S., Oien, P.A., Skre, I. et al. (2000). A twin study of personality disorders. *Comprehensive Psychiatry, 41*(6), 416–425.

Torrey, E.F. (1991). A viral-anatomical explanation of schizophrenia. *Schizophrenia Bulletin, 17*, 15–18.

Torrey, E.F. (2001). *Surviving schizophrenia: A manual for families, consumers and providers* (4th ed.). New York: HarperCollins.

Torrey, E.F., Miller, J., Rawlings, R. & Yolken, R.H. (1997). Seasonality of births in schizophrenia and bipolar disorder: A review of the literature. *Schizophrenia Research, 28*(1), 1–38.

Tost, H., Vollmert, C., Brassen, S., Schmitt, A., Dressing, H. & Braus, D.F. (2004). Pedophilia: Neuropsychological evidence encouraging a brain network perspective. *Medical Hypotheses, 63*(3), 528–531.

Touchette, E., Petit, D., Paquet, J., Tremblay, R.E., Boivin, M. & Montplaisir, J.Y. (2005). Bedwetting and its association with developmental milestones in early childhood. *Archives of Pediatrics and Adolescent Medicine, 159*, 1129–1134.

Tracey, S.A., Chorpita, B.F., Douban, J. & Barlow, D.H. (1997). Empirical evaluation of DSM-IV generalized anxiety disorder criteria in children and adolescents. *Journal of Clinical Child Psychology, 26*, 404–414.

Tramonta, J. & Stimbert, V.E. (1970). Some techniques of behavior modification with an autistic child. *Psychological Reports, 27*(2), 498.

Treatment for Adolescents with Depression Study Team (2004). The treatment for adolescents with depression study (TADS): Short-term effectiveness and safety outcomes. *Journal of the American Medical Association, 292*, 807–820.

Trillenberg, P., Lencer, R. & Heide, W. (2004). Eye movements and psychiatric disease. *Current Opinion in Neurology, 17*(1), 43–47.

Troop, N.A. (1998). Eating disorders as coping strategies: A critique. *European Eating Disorders Review, 6*(4), 229–237.

True, W.R., Xian, H., Scherrer, J.F., Madden, P.A.F. et al. (1999). Common genetic vulnerability for nicotine and alcohol dependence in men. *Archives of General Psychiatry, 56*(7), 655–661.

Trull, T.J., Sher, K.J., Minks-Brown, C., Durbin, J. & Burr, R. (2000). Borderline personality disorder and substance use disorders: A review and integration. *Clinical Psychology Review, 20*(2), 235–253.

Trull, T.J., Widiger, T.A., Useda, J.D., Holcomb, J. et al. (1998). A structured interview for the assessment of the five-factor model of personality. *Psychological Assessment, 10*(3), 229–240.

Trzesniewski, K.H., Donnellan, M.B., Moffitt, T.E., Robins, R.W., Poulton, R. & Caspi, A. (2006). Low self-esteem during adolescence predicts poor health, criminal behaviour, and limited economic prospects during adulthood. *Developmental Psychology, 42*, 381–390.

Tsai, L.Y. (1987). Pre-, peri- and neonatal factors in autism. In D.E. Berkell (Ed.), *Autism: Identification, education and treatment*. Hillsdale, NJ: Lawrence Erlbaum.

Tsai, L.Y. & Ghaziuddin, M. (1997). Autistic disorder. In J.M. Weerner (Ed.), *Textbook of child and adolescent psychiatry*. Washington, DC: American Psychiatric Association.

Tsuang, M.T., Bar, J.L., Harley, R.M. & Lyons, M.J. (2001). The Harvard Twin Study of Substance Abuse: What we have learned. *Harvard Review of Psychiatry, 9*, 267–279.

Tsuang, M.T., Lyons, M.J., Meyer, J.M., Doyle, T. et al. (1998). Co-occurrence of abuse of different drugs in men: The role of drug-specific and shared vulnerabilities. *Archives of General Psychiatry, 55*(11), 967–972.

Tu, G.C. & Israel, Y. (1995). Alcohol consumption by Orientals in North America is predicted largely by a single gene. *Behavior Genetics, 25*(1), 59–65.

Tucker, K.A., Robertson, K.R., Lin, W., Smith, J.K. et al. (2004). Neuroimaging in human immunodeficiency virus infection. *Journal of Neuroimmunology, 157*(1–2), 153–162.

Tulett, F., Jones, F. & Lavender, T. (2006). Service practitioner and referrer perspectives of a primary care-based mental health consultation service. *Clinical Psychology Forum, 166*, 19–23.

Turner, C.M. (2006). Cognitive-behavioural theory and therapy for obsessive-compulsive disorder in children and adolescents: Current status and future directions. *Clinical Psychology Review, 26*, 912–938.

Turner, J.A., Manci, L. & Aaron, L.A. (2006). Short- and long-term efficacy of brief cognitive behavioural therapy for patients with chronic temporomandibular pain disorder: A randomized, controlled trial. *Pain, 121*, 181–194.

Turner, R.J. & Wagonfeld, M.O. (1967). Occupational mobility and schizophrenia. *American Sociological Review, 32*, 104–113.

Turner, S.M., Beidel, D.C., Dancu, C.V. & Keys, D.J. (1986). Psychopathology of social phobia and comparison to avoidant personality disorder. *Journal of Abnormal Psychology, 95*(4), 389–394.

Turner, S.M., Hersen, M. & Heiser, N. (2003). The interviewing process. In M. Hersen & S.M. Turner (Eds.), *Diagnostic interviewing* (3rd ed.). New York: Wiley.

Tyler, K.A., Cauce, A.M. & Whitbeck, L. (2004). Family risk factors and prevalence of dissociative symptoms among homeless and runaway youth. *Child Abuse and Neglect, 28*(3), 355–366.

Uhl, M. & Sachs, H. (2004). Cannabinoids in hair: Strategy to prove marijuana/hashish consumption. *Forensic Science International, 145*(2–3), 143–147.

UKATT Research Team (2005). Effectiveness of treatment for alcohol problems: Findings of the randomized UK alcohol treatment trial (UKATT). *British Medical Journal, 331*, 541.

UK Government Statistics (2005). www.statistics.gov.uk/cci/nugget.asp?id=866; retrieved November 2006.

UK National Institute for Clinical Excellence (NICE) (2004). *Self-harm: The short-term physical and psychological management and secondary prevention of self-harm in primary and secondary care*. London: NICE.

UK National Treatment Agency for Substance Abuse (2002). *Models of care for the treatment of drug abusers*. London: Department of Health.

Ullman, L.P. & Krasner, L. (1975). *A psychological approach to abnormal behaviour* (2nd ed.). Englewood Cliffs, NJ: Prentice-Hall.

Unal, F. & Pehlivanturk, B. (2004). Comorbid psychiatric disorders in 201 cases of encopresis. *Turkish Journal of Pediatrics, 46*, 350–353.

Ungless, M.A., Whistler, J.L., Malenka, R.C. & Bonci, A. (2001). Single cocaine exposure in vivo induces long-term potentiation in dopamine neurons. *Nature, 411*(6837), 583–587.

US Bureau of the Census (1997). *Statistical abstract of the United States* (117th ed.). Washington, DC: US Government Printing Office.

US Department of Health and Human Sciences (1994). *National survey results on drug use from the monitoring and future study, 1975–1993*. Rockville, MD: National Institute on Drug Abuse.

Ustun, T.B., Ayuso-Mateos, J.L., Chatterji, S., Mathers, C. & Murray, C.J.L. (2004). Global burden of depressive disorders in the year 2000. *British Journal of Psychiatry, 184*, 386–392.

Ustun, T.B., Bertelsen, A., Dilling, H., van Drimmelen, J. et al. (1996). *ICD-10 casebook: The many faces of mental disorders. Adult case histories according to ICD-10*. Washington, DC: American Psychiatric Press.

Vacha-Hasse, T., Kogan, L.R., Tani, C.R. & Woodall, R.A. (2001). Reliability generalization: Exploring variation of reliability coefficients of MMPI clinical scale scores. *Educational and Psychological Measurement, 61*, 45–49.

Vajda, F.J.E. & Solinas, C. (2005). Current approaches to management of depression in Parkinson's disease. *Journal of Clinical Neuroscience, 12*, 739–743.

Van Baar, A. (1990). Development of infants of drug dependent mothers. *Journal of Child Psychology and Psychiatry, 31*, 911–920.

Van Boeijen, C.A., van Oppen, P., van Balkom, A.J.L.M., Visser, S. et al. (2005). Treatment of anxiety disorders in primary care practice: A randomized controlled trial. *British Journal of General Practice, 55*, 763–769.

Van de Beek, D., de Gans, J., Spanjaard, L., Weisfelt, M. et al. (2005). Clinical features and prognostic factors in 696 adults with bacterial meningitis. *Neurology, 64*(6), A408–A408, Suppl. 1.

Van de Beek, D., de Gans, J., Spanjaard, L., Weisfelt, M., Reitsma, J.B. & Vermeulen, M. (2004). Clinical features and prognostic factors in adults with bacterial meningitis. *New England Journal of Medicine, 351*(18), 1849–1859.

Van de Beek, D., Schmand, B., de Gans, J., Weisfelt, M. et al. (2002). Cognitive impairment in adults with good recovery after bacterial meningitis. *Journal of Infectious Diseases, 186*(7), 1047–1052.

Van den Hout, M. & Kindt, M. (2003). Phenomenological validity of an OCD-memory model and the remember/know distinction *Behaviour Research and Therapy, 41*(3), 369–378.

Van den Oord, E.J., Boomsma, D.I. & Verhulst, F.C. (1994). A study of problem behaviors in 10- to 15-year-old biologically related and unrelated international adoptees. *Behavior Genetics, 24*, 193–205.

Vandereycken, W. & van Deth, R. (1994). *From fasting saints to anorexic girls: The history of self-starvation*. New York: New York University Press.

Van der Linden, G.H., Stein, D.J. & van Balkom, A.J.L.M. (2000). The efficacy of the selective serotonin reuptake inhibitors for social anxiety disorder (social phobia): A meta-analysis of randomized controlled trials. *International Clinical Psychopharmacology, 15*, S15–S23.

Van Furth, E.F., van Strien, D.C., Martina, L.M.L., Vanson, M.J.M. et al. (1996). Expressed emotion and the prediction of outcome in adolescent eating disorders. *International Journal of Eating Disorders, 20*(1), 19–31.

Van Griensven, F., Chakkraband, M.L.S., Thienkrua, W., Pengjuntr, W. et al. (2006). Mental health problems among adults in tsunami-affected areas in southern Thailand. *JAMA: Journal of the American Medical Association, 296*, 537–548.

Van Ommeren, M., Sharma, B., Komproe, I., Poudyal, B.N. et al. (2001). Trauma and loss as determinants of medically unexplained epidemic illness in a Bhutanese refugee camp. *Psychological Medicine, 31*(7), 1259–1267.

Van Oppen, P. & Arntz, A. (1994). Cognitive therapy for obsessive-compulsive disorder. *Behaviour Research and Therapy, 32*(1), 79–87.

Van Tijen, N.M., Messer, A.P. & Namdar, Z. (1988). Perceived stress of nocturnal enuresis in childhood. *British Journal of Urology, 81*, 98–99.

Vasey, M.W. (1993). Development and cognition in childhood anxiety: The example of worry. In T.H. Ollendick & J.R. Prinz (Eds.), *Advances in clinical child psychology* (Vol. 15). New York: Plenum.

Vasey, M.W. (1995). Social anxiety disorder. In A.R. Eisen, C.A. Kearney & C.E. Schaefer (Eds.), *Clinical handbook of anxiety disorders in children and adolescents*. Northvale, NJ: Aronson.

Vasey, M.W. & Borkovec, T.D. (1992). A catastrophizing assessment of worrisome thoughts. *Cognitive Therapy and Research, 16*(5), 505–520.

Vasterling, J.J., Duke, L.M., Brailey, K., Constans, J.I. et al. (2002). Attention, learning, and memory performances and intellectual resources in Vietnam veterans: PTSD and no disorder comparisons. *Neuropsychology, 16*(1), 5–14.

Veale, D., Gournay, K., Dryden, W., Boocock, A. et al. (1996). Body dysmorphic disorder: A cognitive behavioural model and pilot randomized controlled trial. *Behaviour Research and Therapy, 34*(9), 717–729.

Veitch, E. (2008). Assessment in clinical neuropsychology. In G.C.L. Davey (Ed.), *Clinical psychology*. London: Hodder.

Verdellen, C.W.J., Keijsers, G.P.J., Cath, D.C. & Hoogduin, C.A.L. (2004). Exposure with response prevention versus habit reversal in Tourette's syndrome: A controlled study. *Behaviour Research and Therapy, 42*(5), 501–511.

Verdoux, H., Gindre, C., Sorbara, F., Tournier, M. & Swendsen, J.D. (2003). Effects of cannabis and psychosis vulnerability in daily life: An experience sampling test study. *Psychological Medicine, 33*(1), 23–32.

Verhulst, F.C., Vander Lee, J.H., Akkerhuis, G.W., Sanders-Woudstra, J.A.R. et al. (1985). The prevalence of nocturnal enuresis: Do DSM-III criteria need to be changed? *Journal of Child Psychology and Psychiatry, 26*, 989–993.

Vidaeff, A.C. & Mastrobattista, J.M. (2003). In utero cocaine exposure: A thorny mix of science and mythology. *American Journal of Perinatology, 20*(4), 165–172.

Viglione, D.J. (1999). A review of recent research addressing the utility of the Rorschach. *Psychological Assessment, 11*, 251–265.

Villano, L.M. & White, A.R. (2004). Alternative therapies for tobacco dependence. *Medical Clinics of North America, 88*(6), 1607&.

Visser, S. & Bouman, T.K. (2001). The treatment of hypochondriasis: Exposure plus response prevention vs. cognitive therapy. *Behaviour Research and Therapy, 39*(4), 423–442.

Vitousek, K. & Manke, F. (1994). Personality variables and disorders in anorexia nervosa and bulimia nervosa. *Journal of Abnormal Psychology, 103*(1), 137–147.

Vlaeyens, J.W.S., Kole-Snijders, A.M.J., Rotteveel, A.M., Rusenik, R. & Heuts, P.H.T.G. (1995). The role of fear of movement/(re)injury in pain disability. *Journal of Occupational Rehabilitation, 5*(4), 235–252.

Voegtlin, W.L. & Lemere, F. (1942). The treatment of alcohol addiction: A review of the literature. *Quarterly Journal of the Study of Alcohol, 2*, 717–803.

Vohs, K.D., Bardone, A.M., Joiner, T.E., Abramson, L.Y. & Heatherton, T.F. (1999). Perfectionism, perceived weight status, and self-esteem interact to predict bulimic symptoms: A model of bulimic symptom development. *Journal of Abnormal Psychology, 108*, 695–700.

Volkmar, F.R., Szatmari, P. & Sparrow, S.S. (1993). Sex differences in pervasive developmental disorders. *Journal of Autism and Developmental Disorders, 23*(4), 579–591.

Volkow, N.D., Chang, L., Wang, G.J., Fowler, J.S. et al. (2001). Association of dopamine transporter reduction with psychomotor impairment in methamphetamine abusers. *American Journal of Psychiatry, 158*(3), 377–382.

Volkow, N.D., Wang, G.J., Fischman, M.W., Foltin, R.W. et al. (1997). Relationship between subjective effects of cocaine and dopamine transporter occupancy. *Nature, 386*(6627), 827–830.

von Aster, M., Kucian, K., Schweiter, M. & Martin, E. (2005). Dyscalculia in children. *Monatsschrift Kinderheilkunde, 153*(7), 614&.

von Gontard, A., Hollmann, E., Eiberg, H., Benden, B., Rittig, S. & Lehmkuhl, G. (1997). Clinical enuresis phenotypes in familial nocturnal enuresis. *Scandinavian Journal of Urology and Nephrology, 183*, Supplement, 11–16.

von Sydow, K., Lieb, R., Pfister, H., Hofler, M., Sonntag, H. & Wittchen, H.U. (2001). The natural course of cannabis use, abuse and dependence over four years: A longitudinal community study of adolescents and young adults. *Drug and Alcohol Dependence, 64*(3), 347–361.

Vredenburg, K., Flett, G.L. & Krames, L. (1993). Analog versus clinical depression: A critical reappraisal. *Psychological Bulletin, 113*, 327–344.

Wacker, D.P., Steege, M.W., Northrup, J., Sasso, G., Berg, W., Reimers, T., Cooper, L., Cigrand, K. & Donn, L. (1990). A component analysis of functional communication training across three topographies of severe behavior problems. *Journal of Applied Behavior Analysis, 23,* 417–429.

Wade, T.D., Bulik, C.M., Sullivan, P.F., Neale, M.C. & Kendler, K.S. (2000). The relation between risk factors for binge eating and bulimia nervosa: A population-based female twin study. *Health Psychology, 19*(2), 115–123.

Wagle, A.C., Wagle, S.A., Markova, I.S. & Berrios, G.E. (2000). Psychiatric morbidity in Huntington's disease: The current view. *Neurology, Psychiatry and Brain Research, 8*(1), 5–16.

Wagner, G., Fugl-Meyer, K.S. & Fugl-Meyer, A.R. (2000). Impact of erectile dysfunction on quality of life: Patient and partner perspectives. *International Journal of Impotence Research, 12*(4), S144–S146.

Wahlberg, K.E., Wynne, L.C., Hakko, H., Laksy, K. et al. (2004). Interaction of genetic risk and adoptive parent communication deviance: Longitudinal prediction of adoptee psychiatric disorders. *Psychological Medicine, 34*(8), 1531–1541.

Wahlberg, K.E., Wynne, L.C., Keskitalo, P., Nieminen, P. et al. (2001). Long-term stability of communication deviance. *Journal of Abnormal Psychology, 110,* 443–448.

Wakefield, A.J., Murch, S.H., Anthony, A., Linnell, J. et al. (1998). Ileo-colonic lymphonodular hyperplasia, non-specific colitis and autistic spectrum disorder in children: A new syndrome? *Gastroenterology, 114*(4), A430–A430 G1753.

Wakefield, J.C. (1997). Diagnosing DSM-IV. Part I. DSM-IV and the concept of disorder. *Behaviour Research and Therapy, 35,* 633–649.

Wakschlag, L.S., Pickett, K.E., Kasza, K.E. & Loeber, R. (2006). Is prenatal smoking associated with a developmental pattern of conduct problems in young boys? *Journal of the American Academy of Child and Adolescent Psychiatry, 45,* 461–467.

Waldinger, M.D. & Schweitzer, D.H. (2005). Retarded ejaculation in men: An overview of psychological and neurobiological insights. *World Journal of Urology, 23,* 76–81.

Waldman, I.D. & Gizer, I.R. (2006). The genetics of attention deficit hyperactivity disorder. *Clinical Psychology Review, 26,* 396–432.

Waldman, I.D. & Rhee, S.H. (2002). Behavioral and molecular genetic studies. In S. Sandberg (Ed.), *Hyperactivity and attention disorders of childhood* (2nd ed.). New York: Cambridge University Press.

Waldron, H.B., Slesnick, N., Brody, J.L., Turner, C.W. & Peterson, T.R. (2001). Treatment outcomes for adolescent substance abuse at 4- and 7-month assessments. *Journal of Consulting and Clinical Psychology, 69*(5), 802–813.

Walker, C., Thomas, J. & Allen, T.S. (2003). Treating impulsivity, irritability, and aggression of antisocial personality disorder with quetiapine. *International Journal of Offender Therapy and Comparative Criminology, 47*(5), 556–567.

Walker, H. & Buckley, N. (1968). The use of positive reinforcement in conditioning attending behavior. *Journal of Applied Behavior Analysis, 1,* 242–252.

Walker, L.E.A. (2000). *The battered woman syndrome* (2nd ed.). New York: Springer.

Walkup, J.T., Labellarte, M.J. & Ginsburg, G.S. (2002). Fluvoxamine for the treatment of anxiety disorders in children and adolescents. *New England Journal of Medicine, 344*(17), 1279–1285.

Wall, T.L., Shea, S.H., Chan, K.K. & Carr, L.G. (2001). A genetic association with the development of alcohol and other substance use behaviour in Asian Americans. *Journal of Abnormal Psychology, 110,* 173–178.

Wall, T.L., Shea, S.H., Luczak, S.E., Cook, T.A.R. & Carr, L.G. (2005). Genetic associations of alcohol dehydrogenase with alcohol use disorders and endophenotypes in white college students. *Journal of Abnormal Psychology, 114*(3), 456–465.

Wallace, C., Mullen, P.E. & Burgess, P. (2004). Criminal offending in schizophrenia over a 25-year period marked by deinstitutionalization and increasing prevalence of comorbid substance use disorders. *American Journal of Psychiatry, 161*(4), 716–727.

Wallesch, C.W. & Johannsen-Horbach, H. (2004). Computers in aphasia therapy: Effects and side-effects. *Aphasiology, 18*(3), 223–228.

Wallin, M.T., Wilken, J.A. & Kane, R. (2006). Cognitive dysfunction in multiple sclerosis: Assessment, imaging and risk factors. *Journal of Rehabilitation Research and Development, 43,* 63–71.

Walling, M., Andersen, B.L. & Johnson, S.R. (1990). Hormonal replacement therapy for postmenopausal women: A review of sexual outcomes and related gynecologic effects. *Archives of Sexual Behavior, 19*(2), 119–137.

Walsh, B.T., Wilson, G.T., Loeb, K.L., Devlin, M.J. et al. (1997). Medication and psychotherapy in the treatment of bulimia nervosa. *American Journal of Psychiatry, 154*(4), 523–531.

Walsh, R.A. & McElwain, B. (2002). Existential psychotherapies. In D.J. Cain & J. Seeman (Eds.), *Humanistic psychotherapies: Handbook of research and practice.* Washington, DC: American Psychological Association.

Walters, E.E. & Kendler, K.S. (1995). Anorexia nervosa and anorexia-like syndromes in a population-based female twin sample. *American Journal of Psychiatry, 152*(1), 64–71.

Wang, P.S., Demler, O. & Kessler, R.C. (2002). Adequacy of treatment for serious mental illness in the United States. *American Journal of Public Health, 92*(1), 92–98.

Warburton, D.M. (1992). Smoking within reason. *Journal of Smoking-Related Disorders, 3,* 55–59.

Ward, E., King, M., Lloyd, M., Bower, P. et al. (2000). Randomized controlled trial of non-directive counselling, cognitive-behaviour therapy, and usual general practitioner care for patients with depression. I. Clinical effectiveness. *British Medical Journal, 321,* 1383–1388.

Ward, K.E., Friedman, L., Wise, A. & Schulz, S.C. (1996). Meta-analysis of brain and cranial size in schizophrenia. *Schizophrenia Research, 22*(3), 197–213.

Ward, T., Hudson, S.M., Johnston, L. & Marshall, W.L. (1997). Cognitive distortions in sex offenders: An integrative review. *Clinical Psychology Review, 17,* 479–507.

Wardle, J. & Johnson, F. (2002). Weight and dieting: Examining levels of weight concern in British adults. *International Journal of Obesity, 26*(8), 1144–1149.

Ware, J., Jain, K., Burgess, I. & Davey, G.C.L. (1994). Factor analysis of common animal fears: Support for a disease-avoidance model. *Behaviour Research and Therapy, 32,* 57–63.

Ware, M.A., Adams, H. & Guy, G.W. (2005). The medicinal use of cannabis in the UK: Results of a nationwide survey. *International Journal of Clinical Practice, 59*(3), 291–295.

Waring, M. & Ricks, D. (1965). Family patterns of children who become adult schizophrenics. *Journal of Nervous and Mental Disease, 140,* 351–364.

Warner, L.A., Kessler, R.C., Hughes, M., Anthony, J.C. & Nelson, C.B. (1995). Prevalence and correlates of drug use and dependence in the United States: Results from the National Comorbidity Study. *Archives of General Psychology, 52,* 219–229.

Warner, R., Taylor, D., Powers, M. & Hyman, J. (1989). Acceptance of the mental illness label by psychotic patients: Effects on functioning. *American Journal of Orthopsychiatry, 59,* 398–409.

Warren, S.L., Schmitz, S. & Emde, R.N. (1999). Behavioral genetic analyses of self-reported anxiety at 7 years of age. *Journal of the American Academy of Child and Adolescent Psychiatry, 38*(11), 1403–1408.

Warwick, H.M.C. (1995). Assessment of hypochondriasis. *Behaviour Research and Therapy, 33,* 845–853.

Warwick, H.M.C. & Marks, I.M. (1988). Behavioral treatment of illness phobia and hypochondriasis: A pilot study of 17 cases. *British Journal of Psychiatry, 152,* 239–241.

Watanabe, H., Kawauchi, A., Kitamori, T. & Azuma, Y. (1994). Treatment system for nocturnal enuresis according to an original classification system. *European Urology, 25*(1), 43–50.

Watkins, P.C., Mathews, A., Williamson, D.A. & Fuller, R.D. (1992). Mood-congruent memory in depression: Emotional priming or elaboration. *Journal of Abnormal Psychology, 101*(3), 581–586.

Watson, D. (2005). Rethinking the mood and anxiety disorders: A quantitative hierarchical model for DSM-V. *Journal of Abnormal Psychology, 114,* 522–536.

Watson, J.B. & Rayner, R. (1920). Conditioned emotional reactions. *Journal of Experimental Psychology, 3*, 1–14.

Watts, F.N. & Sharrock, R. (1984). Questionnaire dimensions of spider phobia. *Behaviour Research and Therapy, 22*, 575–580.

Wearden, A.J., Tarrier, N. & Barrowclough, C. (2000). A review of expressed emotion research in health care. *Clinical Psychology Review, 20*, 633–666.

Webster, J.S., McFarland, P.T., Rapport, L.J., Morrill, B. et al. (2001). Computer-assisted training for improving wheelchair mobility in unilateral neglect patients. *Archives of Physical Medicine and Rehabilitation, 82*(6), 769–775.

Wechsler, D. (2004). *Wechsler Preschool and Primary Scale of Intelligence: Third UK Edition* (WPPSI-III UK). London: Harcourt Assessment.

Weems, C.F., Pina, A.A., Costa, N.M., Watts, S.E. et al. (2007). Predisaster trait anxiety and negative affect predict posttraumatic stress in youths after Hurricane Katrina. *Journal of Consulting and Clinical Psychology, 75*, 154–159.

Weiden, P.J. & Olfson, M. (1995). Cost of relapse in schizophrenia. *Schizophrenia Bulletin, 21*(3), 419–429.

Weintraub, D., Morales, K.H., Moberg, P.J., Bilker, W.B. et al. (2005). Antidepressant studies in Parkinson's disease: A review and meta-analysis. *Movement Disorders, 20*(9), 1161–1169.

Weisman, A. (1997). Understanding cross-cultural prognostic variability for schizophrenia. *Cultural Diversity and Mental Health, 3*, 3–35.

Weisman, A.G., Nuechterlein, K.H., Goldstein, M.J. & Snyder, K.S. (2000). Controllability perceptions and reactions to symptoms of schizophrenia: A within-family comparison of relatives with high and low expressed emotion. *Journal of Abnormal Psychology, 109*(1), 167–171.

Weissman, M.M., Bland, R.C., Canino, G.J., Faravelli, C. et al. (1996). Cross-national epidemiology of major depression and bipolar disorder. *JAMA: Journal of the American Medical Association, 276*(4), 293–299.

Weissman, M.M., Bland, R.C., Canino, G.J., Faravelli, C. et al. (1997). The cross-national epidemiology of panic disorder. *Archives of General Psychiatry, 54*(4), 305–309.

Weisz, J.R., Suwanlert, S., Chaiyasit, W. & Walter, B. (1987). Epidemiology of behavioral and emotional problems among Thai and American children: Parent reports for ages 6–11. *Journal of the American Academy of Child and Adolescent Psychiatry, 26*, 890–897.

Welch, S.L., Doll, H.A. & Fairburn, C.G. (1997). Life events and the onset of bulimia nervosa: A controlled study. *Psychological Medicine, 27*(3), 515–522.

Welch, S.L. & Fairburn, C.G. (1994). Sexual abuse and bulimia-nervosa: 3 integrated case-control comparisons. *American Journal of Psychiatry, 151*(3), 402–407.

Wellings, N., Wilde, E. & McCormick, E. (Eds.) (2000). *Transpersonal psychotherapy*. Thousand Oaks, CA: Sage.

Wells, A. (1997). *Cognitive therapy of anxiety disorders*. Chichester: Wiley.

Wells, A. (1999). A metacognitive model and therapy for generalized anxiety disorder. *Clinical Psychology and Psychotherapy, 6*, 86–95.

Wells, A. (2006). Cognitive therapy case formulation in anxiety disorders. In N. Tarrier (Ed.), *Case formulation in cognitive behaviour therapy*. Hove: Routledge.

Wells, A. (2006b). Metacognitive model of worry and generalized anxiety disorder. In G.C.L. Davey & A. Wells (Eds.), *Worry and its psychological disorders: Theory, assessment and treatment*. Chichester: Wiley.

Wells, A., Clark, D.M. & Ahmad, S. (1998). How do I look with my mind's eye: Perspective taking in social phobic imagery. *Behaviour Research and Therapy, 36*(6), 631–634.

Wells, A. & Papageorgiou, C. (1998). Relationships between worry, obsessive-compulsive symptoms and meta-cognitive beliefs. *Behaviour Research and Therapy, 36*(9), 899–913.

Wenzlaff, R.M., Klein, S.B. & Wegner, D.M. (1991). The role of thought suppression in the bonding of thought and mood. *Journal of Personality and Social Psychology, 60*(4), 500–508.

Wenzlaff, R.M. & Wegner, D.M. (2000). Thought suppression. *Annual Review of Psychology, 51*, 59–91.

Werry, J.S. (1996). Pervasive developmental, psychotic, and allied disorders. In L. Hechtman (Ed.), *Do they grow out of it? Long-term outcomes of childhood disorders*. Washington, DC: American Psychiatric Press.

Wesnes, K. & Warburton, D.M. (1983). Smoking, nicotine and human performance. *Pharmacology and Therapeutics, 21*(2), 189–208.

Wessely, S. (1992). Measurement of fatigue and chronic fatigue syndrome. *Journal of the Royal Society of Medicine, 85*, 189–190.

Westen, D., Novotny, C.A. & Thompson-Brenner, H. (2004). The empirical status of empirically supported psychotherapies: Assumptions, findings, and reporting in controlled clinical trials. *Psychological Bulletin, 130*, 631–663.

Westheimer, R.K. & Lopater, S. (2002). *Human sexuality: A psychosocial perspective*. Baltimore: Lippincott Williams & Wilkins.

Westreich, L., Heitner, C., Cooper, M., Galanter, M. & Guedj, P. (1997). Perceived social support and treatment retention on an inpatient addiction treatment unit. *American Journal on Addictions, 6*(2), 144–149.

Wetterberg, L. (1999). Melatonin and clinical application. *Reproduction Nutrition Development, 39*(3), 367–382.

Wetzel, C., Bents, H. & Florin, I. (1999). High-density exposure therapy for obsessive-compulsive inpatients: A 1-year follow-up. *Psychotherapy and Psychosomatics, 68*(4), 186–192.

Whalen, C.K. & Henker, B. (1998). Attention-deficit/hyperactivity disorder. In T.H. Ollendick & M. Hersen (Eds.), *Handbook of child psychopathology* (3rd ed.). New York: Plenum.

Whaley, A.L. (1997). Ethnicity/race, paranoia, and psychiatric diagnoses: Clinician bias versus sociocultural differences. *Journal of Psychopathology and Behavioral Assessment, 19*, 1–20.

Whaley, A.L. (1998). Racism in the provision of mental health services: A social-cognitive analysis. *American Journal of Orthopsychiatry, 68*, 47–57.

Whaley, A.L. (2004). Ethnicity/race, paranoia, and hospitalization for mental health problems among men. *American Journal of Public Health, 94*(1), 78–81.

Whelan, E. & Cooper, P.J. (2000). The association between childhood feeding problems and maternal eating disorder: A community study. *Psychological Medicine, 30*(1), 69–77.

Whiffen, V.E. & MacIntosh, H.B. (2005). Mediators of the link between childhood sexual abuse and emotional distress. A critical review. *Trauma Violence and Abuse, 6*, 24–39.

While, D., Kelly, S., Huang, W.Y. & Charlton, A. (1996). Cigarette advertising and onset of smoking in children: Questionnaire survey. *British Medical Journal, 313*(7054), 398–399.

Whittal, M.L., Agras, W.S. & Gould, R.A. (1999). Bulimia nervosa: A meta-analysis of psychosocial and pharmacological treatments. *Behavior Therapy, 30*, 117–135.

Widiger, T.A. (1997). Mental disorders as discrete clinical conditions: Dimensional versus categorical. In S.M. Turner & M. Hersen (Eds.), *Adult psychopathology and diagnosis* (2nd ed.). New York: Wiley.

Widiger, T.A. (2001). Social anxiety, social phobia, and avoidant personality. In R. Crozier & L.E. Allen (Eds.), *International handbook of social anxiety: Concepts research and interventions relating to the self and shyness*. New York: Wiley.

Widiger, T.A., Cadoret, R., Hare, R., Robins, L. et al. (1996). DSM-IV antisocial personality disorder field trial. *Journal of Abnormal Psychology, 105*(1), 3–16.

Widiger, T.A. & Clark, L.A. (2000). Toward DSM-V and the classification of psychopathology. *Psychological Bulletin, 126*, 946–963.

Widiger, T.A. & Corbitt, E.M. (1993). Antisocial personality disorder: Proposals for DSM-IV. *Journal of Personality Disorders, 7*(1), 63–77.

Widiger, T.A. & Corbitt, E.M. (1997). Comorbidity of antisocial personality disorder with other personality disorders. In D. Stoff, J. Breiling & J.D. Maser (Eds.), *Handbook of antisocial behavior*. New York: Wiley.

Widiger, T.A. & Samuel, D.B. (2005). Diagnostic categories or dimensions? A question for the Diagnostic and Statistical Manual of Mental Disorders: Fifth Edition. *Journal of Abnormal Psychology, 114*, 494–504.

Widiger, T.A. & Simonsen, M.D. (2005). Alternative dimensional models of personality disorder: Finding a common ground. *Journal of Personality Disorders*, 19, 110–130.

Widiger, T.A. & Trull, T.J. (1993). Borderline and narcissistic personality disorders. In P.B. Sutker & H.E. Adams (Eds.), *Comprehensive handbook of psychopathology* (2nd ed.). New York: Plenum.

Widom, C.S. & Maxfield, M.G. (1996). A prospective examination of risk for violence among abused and neglected children. *Annals of the New York Academy of Sciences*, 794, 224–237.

Wielgus, M.S. & Harvey, P.D. (1988). Dichotic listening and recall in schizophrenia and mania. *Schizophrenia Bulletin*, 14, 689–700.

Wiens, A.N., Montague, J.R., Manaugh, T.S. & English, C.J. (1976). Pharmacological aversive counterconditioning to alcohol in a private hospital: One-year follow-up. *Journal of Studies on Alcohol*, 37(9), 1320–1324.

Wiersma, D., Nienhuis, F.J., Slooff, C.J. & Giel, R. (1998). Natural course of schizophrenic disorders: A 15-year follow-up of a Dutch incidence cohort. *Schizophrenia Bulletin*, 24(1), 75–85.

Wilhelm, S. (2000). Cognitive therapy for obsessive-compulsive disorder. *Journal of Cognitive Psychotherapy*, 14, 245–260.

Williams, G., King, J., Cunningham, M., Stephan, M., Kerr, B. & Hersh, J.H. (2001). Fetal valproate syndrome and autism: Additional evidence of an association. *Developmental Medicine and Child Neurology*, 43(3), 202–206.

Williams, J.M.G. & Scott, J. (1988). Autobiographical memory in depression. *Psychological Medicine*, 18(3), 689–695.

Williams, L.M. (1995). Recall of childhood trauma: A prospective study of women's memories of child sexual abuse. *Journal of Consulting and Clinical Psychology*, 62, 1167–1176.

Williams-Gray, C.H., Foltynie, T., Lewis, S.J.G. & Barker, R.A. (2006). Cognitive deficits and psychosis in Parkinson's disease: A review of pathophysiology and therapeutic options. *CNS Drugs*, 20(6), 477–505.

Willick, M.S., Milrod, D. & Karush, R.K. (1998). Psychoanalysis and the psychoses. In M. Furer, E. Nersessian et al. (Eds.), *Controversies in contemporary psychoanalysis: Lectures from the faculty of the New York Psychoanalytic Institute*. Madison, CT: International Universities Press.

Willig, C. (2001). *Introducing qualitative research in psychology: Adventures in theory and method*. Buckingham: Open University Press.

Wills, T.A., Duhamel, K. & Vaccaro, D. (1995). Activity and mood temperament as predictors of adolescent substance use: Test of a self-regulation mediational model. *Journal of Personality and Social Psychology*, 68(5), 901–916.

Wills, T.A., Sandy, J.M. & Yaeger, A.M. (2002). Stress and smoking in adolescence: A test of directional hypotheses. *Health Psychology*, 21(2), 122–130.

Wilsnack, S.C., Vogeltanz, N.D., Klassen, A.D. & Harris, T.R. (1997). Childhood sexual abuse and women's substance abuse: National survey findings. *Journal of Studies on Alcohol*, 58(3), 264–271.

Wilson, B.A., Emslie, H., Quirk, K. & Evans, J. (1999). George: Learning to live independently with Neuropage. *Rehabilitation Psychology*, 44, 284–296.

Wilson, B.A., Emslie, H., Quirk, K., Evans, J. & Watson, P. (2005). A randomized control trial to evaluate a paging system for people with traumatic brain injury. *Brain Injury*, 19(11), 891–894.

Wilson, E.J., MacLeod, C., Mathews, A. & Rutherford, E.M. (2006). The causal role of interpretive bias in anxiety reactivity. *Journal of Abnormal Psychology*, 115, 103–111.

Wilson, G.D. (1987). An ethological approach to sexual deviation. In G.D. Wilson (Ed.), *Variant sexuality: Research and theory*. Baltimore: Johns Hopkins University Press.

Wilson, G.T. (1978). Aversion therapy for alcoholism: Issues, ethics, and evidence. In G.A. Marlatt & P.E. Nathan (Eds.), *Behavioral assessment and treatment of alcoholism*. New Brunswick, NJ: Center for Alcohol Studies.

Wilson, G.T., Eldredge, K.L., Smith, D. & Niles, B. (1991). Cognitive-behavioral treatment with and without response prevention for bulimia. *Behaviour Research and Therapy*, 29(6), 575–583.

Wilson, G.T., Fairburn, C.G. & Agras, W.S. (1997). Cognitive-behavioral therapy for bulimia nervosa. In D.M. Garner & P.E. Garfinkel (Eds.), *Handbook of treatment for eating disorders* (2nd ed.). New York: Guilford Press.

Wilson, G.T., Fairburn, C.C., Agras, W.S., Walsh, B.T. & Kraemer, H. (2002). Cognitive-behavioral therapy for bulimia nervosa: Time course and mechanisms of change. *Journal of Clinical and Counselling Psychology*, 70, 267–274.

Wilson, G.T. & Lawson, D.M. (1976). The effects of alcohol on sexual arousal in women. *Journal of Abnormal Psychology*, 85, 489–497.

Wilson, G.T., Loeb, K.L., Walsh, B.T., Labouvie, E. et al. (1999). Psychological versus pharmacological treatments of bulimia nervosa: Predictors and processes of change. *Journal of Consulting and Clinical Psychology*, 67(4), 451–459.

Wilson, G.T. & Pike, K.M. (1993). Eating disorders. In D.H. Barlow (Ed.), *Clinical handbook of psychological disorders*. New York: Guilford Press.

Wilson, G.T. & Shafran, R. (2005). Eating disorders guidelines from NICE. *Lancet*, 365, 79–81.

Wilson, J.J. & Gil, K.M. (1996). The efficacy of psychological and pharmacological interventions for the treatment of chronic disease-related and non-disease-related pain. *Clinical Psychology Review*, 16(6), 573–597.

Wilson, M. (1984). Female homosexuals' need for dominance and endurance. *Psychological Reports*, 55, 79–82.

Winblad, B., Kilander, L., Eriksson, S., Minthon, L. et al. (2006). Donepezil in patients with severe Alzheimer's disease: Double-blind, parallel-group, placebo-controlled study. *Lancet*, 367(9516), 1057–1065.

Windle, M. & Searles, J.S. (Eds.) (1992). *Children of alcoholics: Critical perspectives*. New York: Guilford Press.

Wink, P. (1996). Narcissism. In C.G. Costello (Ed.), *Personality characteristics of the personality disordered*. New York: Wiley.

Wittchen, H.U. & Hoyer, J. (2001). Generalized anxiety disorder: Nature and course. *Journal of Clinical Psychiatry*, 62, 15–21.

Wladman, I.D. & Gizer, I.R. (2006). The genetics of attention deficit hyperactivity disorder. *Clinical Psychology Review*, 26, 396–432.

Wolf, M., Bally, H. & Morris, R. (1996). Automaticity, retrieval processes, and reading: A longitudinal study in average and impaired readers. *Child Development*, 57, 988–1000.

Wolf, S. (2000). Schizoid personality in childhood and Asperger syndrome. In A. Klin, F.R. Volkmar et al. (Eds.), *Asperger syndrome*. New York: Guilford Press.

Wolfe, D.A. & McEachran, A. (1997). Child physical abuse and neglect. In E.J. Marsh & L.G. Terdl (Eds.), *Assessment of childhood disorders*. New York: Guilford Press.

Wolpe, J. (1958). *Psychotherapy by reciprocal inhibition*. Stanford, CA: Stanford University Press.

Wolpert, C.M., Donnelly, S.L., Curraro, M.L., Hedges, D.J. et al. (2001). De novo partial duplication of chromosome 7p in a male with autistic disorder. *American Journal of Medical Genetics*, 105(3), 222–225.

Wolraich, M.L., Wilson, D.B. & White, J.W. (1995). The effect of sugar on behavior or cognition in children: A meta-analysis. *Journal of the American Medical Association*, 274, 1617–1621.

Wonderlich, S.A., Swift, W.J., Slotnick, H.B. & Goodman, S. (1993). DSM-III-R personality disorders in eating disorder subtypes. *International Journal of Eating Disorders*, 9(6), 607–616.

Woodruff-Borden, J., Morrow, C., Bourland, S. & Cambron, S. (2002). The behavior of anxious parents: Examining mechanisms of transmission of anxiety from parent to child. *Journal of Clinical Child and Adolescent Psychology*, 31(3), 364–374.

World Health Organization (2004). *Global status report on alcohol*. Geneva: World Health Organization Department of Mental Health and Substance Abuse.

World Health Organization (2006). www.who.int/substance_abuse/facts/cocaine/en/; retrieved February 2008.

World Health Report (2002). *Reducing risks, promoting healthy life*. Geneva: World Health Organization.

Worrel, J.A., Marken, P.A., Beckman, S.E. & Ruehter, V.L. (2000). Atypical antipsychotic agents: A critical review. *American Journal of Health-System Pharmacy, 57*(3), 238–255.

Wortman, C.B. & Brehm, J.W. (1975). Responses to uncontrollable outcomes: An integration of the reactance theory and the learned helplessness model. In L. Berkowitz (Ed.), *Advances in social psychology*. New York: Academic Press.

Wu, P., Bird, H.R., Liu, X.H., Fan, B. et al. (2006). Childhood depressive symptoms and early onset of alcohol use. *Pediatrics, 118*(5), 1907–1915.

Wykes, T. & van der Gaag, M. (2001). Is it time to develop a new cognitive therapy for psychosis – Cognitive remediation therapy (CRT)? *Clinical Psychology Review, 21*, 1227–1256.

Wylie, A.S., Scott, R.T.A. & Burnett, S.J. (1995). Psychosis due to skunk. *British Medical Journal, 311*(6997), 125.

Yager, J. (2002). Using email to support the outpatient treatment of anorexia nervosa. In R.C. Hsiung (Ed.), *E-therapy: Case studies, guiding principles, and the clinical potential of the internet*. New York: W.W. Norton.

Yalom, I.D., Green, R. & Fisk, N. (1973). Prenatal exposure to female hormones: Effect on psychosexual development in boys. *Archives of General Psychiatry, 28*(4), 554–561.

Yellowlees, P.M. (2002). Clinical principles of professional ethics for e-therapy. In R.C. Hsiung (Ed.), *E-therapy: Case studies, guiding principles, and the clinical potential of the internet*. New York: W.W. Norton.

Young, J.E., Klosko, J. & Weishaar, M.E. (2003). *Schema therapy: A practitioner's guide*. New York: Guilford Press.

Young, J.T. (2004). Illness behaviour: A selective review and synthesis. *Sociology of Health and Illness, 26*, 1–31.

Youth Risk Behavior Surveillance, United States (1997). www.cdc.gov/mmwR/preview/mmwrhtml/00054432.htm; retrieved January 2008.

Yui, K., Ikemoto, S., Ishiguro, T. & Goto, K. (2000). Studies of amphetamine or methamphetamine psychosis in Japan: Relation of methamphetamine psychosis to schizophrenia. Neurobiological mechanisms of drugs of abuse: Cocaine, ibogaine, and substituted amphetamines. *Annals of the New York Academy of Sciences, 914*, 1–12.

Zahn-Waxler, C. (1993). Warriors and worriers: Gender and psychopathology. *Development and Psychopathology, 5*, 79–89.

Zajicek, J., Fox, P., Sanders, H., Wright, D. et al. (2003). Cannabinoids for treatment of spasticity and other symptoms related to multiple sclerosis (CAMS study): Multicentre randomized placebo-controlled trial. *Lancet, 362*(9395), 1517–1526.

Zanarini, M.C., Frankenburg, F.R., Dubo, E.D., Sickel, A.E. et al. (1998). Axis I comorbidity of borderline personality disorder. *American Journal of Psychiatry, 155*(12), 1733–1739.

Zanarini, M.C., Frankenburg, F.R., Reich, D.B. et al. (2000). Biparental failure in the childhood experiences of borderline patients. *Journal of Personality Disorders, 14*(3), 264–273.

Zanarini, M.C., Williams, A.A., Lewis, R.E., Reich, R.B. et al. (1997). Reported pathological childhood experiences associated with the development of borderline personality disorder. *American Journal of Psychiatry, 154*(8), 1101–1106.

Zatzick, D.F., Marmar, C.R., Weiss, D.S., Browner, W.S. et al. (1997). Posttraumatic stress disorder and functioning and quality of life outcomes in a nationally representative sample of male Vietnam veterans. *American Journal of Psychiatry, 154*(12), 1690–1695.

Zayfert, C. & Becker, C.B. (2007). *Cognitive behavioral therapy for PTSD*. New York: Guilford Press.

Zeiss, A.M., Lewinsohn, P.M., Munoz, R.F. (1979). Nonspecific improvement effects in depression using interpersonal skills training, pleasant activity schedules, or cognitive training. *Journal of Consulting and Clinical Psychology, 47*(3), 427–439.

Zermann, D.H., Kutzenberger, J., Sauerwein, D., Schubert, J. & Loeffler, U. (2006). Penile prosthetic surgery in neurologically impaired patients: Long-term followup. *Journal of Urology, 175*(3), 1041–1044.

Zeskind, P.S. & Ramsay, C.T. (1981). Preventing intellectual and interactional sequelae of fetal malnutrition: A longitudinal, transactional, and synergistic approach to development. *Child Development, 52*, 213–218.

Zhang, L., Beatriz, M.D., Abreu, C., Seale, G.S. et al. (2003). A virtual reality environment for evaluation of a daily living skill in brain injury rehabilitation: Reliability and validity. *Archives of Physical Medicine and Rehabilitation, 84*, 1118–1124.

Zhang, Z.F., Morgenstern, H., Spitz, M.R. et al. (1999). Marijuana use and increased risk of squamous cell carcinoma of the head and neck. *Cancer Epidemiology Biomarkers and Prevention, 8*(12), 12, 1071–1078.

Zhou, J.N., Hofman, M.A., Gooren, L.J.G. & Swaab, D.F. (1995). A sex difference in the human brain and its relation to transsexuality. *Nature, 378*(6552), 68–70.

Zigler, E. & Hodapp, R.M. (1991). Behavioral functioning in individuals with mental retardation. *Annual Review of Psychology, 42*, 29–50.

Zigman, W.B., Schupf, N., Sersen, E. & Silverman, W. (1995). Prevalence of dementia in adults with and without Down syndrome. *American Journal of Mental Retardation, 100*, 403–412.

Zimmerman, J. & Grosz, H.J. (1966). 'Visual' performance of a functionally blind person. *Behavior Research and Therapy, 4*, 119–134.

Zimmerman, M., Rothschild, L. & Chelminski, I. (2005). The prevalence of DSM-IV personality disorders in psychiatric outpatients. *American Journal of Psychiatry, 162*, 1911–1918.

Zimmermann, G., Favrod, J., Trieu, V.H. & Pomini, V. (2005). The effect of cognitive behavioral treatment on the positive symptoms of schizophrenia spectrum disorders: A meta-analysis. *Schizophrenia Research, 77*(1), 1–9.

Zoccolillo, M. (1993). Gender and the development of conduct disorder. *Development and Psychopathology, 5*, 65–78.

Zola, S.M. (1998). Memory, amnesia, and the issue of recovered memory: Neurobiological aspects. *Clinical Psychology Review, 18*(8), 915–932.

Zucker, K.J. & Bradley, S.J. (1995). *Gender identity disorder and psychosexual problems in children and adolescents*. New York: Guilford Press.

Zucker, K.J., Finegan, J.A.K., Deering, R.W. & Bradley, S.J. (1984). Two subgroups of gender-problem children. *Archives of Sexual Behavior, 13*(1), 27–39.

Zucker, K.J., Wild, J., Bradley, S.J. & Lowry, C.B. (1993). Physical attractiveness of boys with gender identity disorder. *Archives of Sexual Behavior, 22*(1), 23–36.

Zvolensky, M.J. & Eifert, G.H. (2001). A review of psychological factors/processes affecting anxious responding during voluntary hyperventilation and inhalations of carbon dioxide-enriched air. *Clinical Psychology Review, 21*, 375–400.

Zwirs, B.W.C., Burger, H., Buitelaar, J.K. & Schulpen, T.W.J. (2006). Ethnic differences in parental detection of externalizing disorders. *European Child and Adolescent Psychiatry, 15*, 418–426.

Zygmunt, A., Olfson, M., Boyer, C.A. & Mechanic, D. (2002). Interventions to improve medication adherence in schizophrenia. *American Journal of Psychiatry, 159*(10), 1653–1664.

Illustration Sources and Credits

The editors and publisher gratefully acknowledge the permission granted to reproduce the copyright material in this book.

9   Focus Point 1.2, photo © PA Photos.

14   Figure 1.2   Photo Researchers/Science Photo Library.

14   Plate 1.1   www.CartoonStock.com.

23   Figure 1.4   Watson, D. (2005). Rethinking the mood and anxiety disorders: A quantitative hierarchical model for DSM-V. *Journal of Abnormal Psychology, 114*, 522–536.

34   Figure 2.1   Form completed by the author; Original © The Psychological Corporation

36   Figure 2.2   Science Museum/Science and Society Picture Library.

36   Figure 2.3   Reprinted by permission of the publishers from Henry A. Murray, Thematic Apperception Test, Card 12 F, Cambridge, Mass.: Harvard University Press, Copyright © 1943 by the President and Fellows of Harvard College, © 1971 by Henry A. Murray.

37   Research Methods Box 2.1, Figure 1 from Kimble, M.O., Kaufman, M.L., Leonard, L.L., Nestor, P.G. et al. (2002). Sentence completion test in combat veterans with and without PTSD: Preliminary findings. *Psychiatry Research, 113*, 303–307.

38   Plate 2.1   Wechsler Adult Intelligence Scale, 3rd edition (WAIS-III). Copyright © 1997 by Harcourt Assessment, Inc. Reproduced with permission. All rights reserved.

38   Plate 2.2   Paul Barker/AFP/Getty Images.

40   Plate 2.3   TEK Image/Science Photo Library.

41   Figure 2.4   *top* © Photo Create/Shutterstock; *bottom left* Du Cane Medical Imaging Ltd/Science Photo Library; *bottom right* Science Photo Library.

41   Figure 2.5   Dr Harry Chugani and Dr Michael Phelps, UCLA School of Medicine, Los Angeles, CA.

42   Focus Point 2.1, Figures 1–4 from Nock, M.K. & Kurtz, S.M.S. (2005). Direct behavioural observation in school settings: Bringing science to practice. *Cognitive and Behavioral Practice, 12*, 359–370.

44   Figure 2.6   Piasecki, T.M., Hufford, M.R., Solham, M. & Trull, T.J. (2007). Assessing clients in their natural environments with electronic diaries: Rationale, benefits, limitations, and barriers. *Psychological Assessment, 19*, 25–43.

49   Figure 2.7   Dallos, R. & Stedmon, J. (2006). Systemic formulation: Mapping the family dance. In L. Johnstone & R. Dallos (Eds.), *Formulation in psychology and psychotherapy*. London: Routledge.

50   Activity Box 2.1, cognitive model of panic disorder from Wells, A. (2006). Cognitive therapy case formulation in anxiety disorders. In N. Tarrier (Ed.), *Case formulation in cognitive behaviour therapy*. Hove: Routledge.

60   Activity Box 3.2, model of panic disorder from Clark, D.M. (1986). A cognitive approach to panic. *Behaviour Research and Therapy, 24*, 348–351.

65   Figure 3.1   Author's own data.

66   Plate 3.1   www.CartoonStock.com.

67   Focus Point 3.2, photo © AP/PA Photos.

70   Activity Box 3.3, cartoon, www.CartoonStock.com.

73   Figure 3.2   Huppert, J.D., Schultz, L.T., Foa, E.B. & Barlow, D.H. (2004). Differential response to placebo among patients with social phobia, panic disorder, and obsessive-compulsive disorder. *American Journal of Psychiatry, 161*, 1485–1487.

74   Plate 3.2   PA/Topfoto.

76   Figure 3.3   Bledisoe, R., Smith Myles, B. & Simpson, R.L. (2007). Use of a story intervention to improve mealtime skills of an adolescent with Asperger syndrome. *Autism, 7*, 289–295.

78   Research Methods Box 3.1, Figure 1 from Abrahamsson, K.H., Hallberg, L.R. & Carlsson, S.G. (2007). Ambivalence in coping with dental fear: A qualitative study. *Journal of Health Psychology, 7*, 653–664.

93   Plate 4.1   The Kobal Collection/The Picture Desk.

104   Figure 4.1   Ludman, E.J., Simon, G.E., Tutty, S. & von Korff, M. (2007). A randomized trial of telephone psychotherapy and pharmacotherapy for depression: Continuation and durability of effects. *Journal of Consulting and Clinical Psychology, 75*, 257–266.

104   Plate 4.2   Image Source/Getty Images.

106   Focus Point 4.1, photo Iconica/Getty Images.

108   Figure 4.2   Clark, D.M., Ehlers, A., Hackmann, A., McManus, F. et al. (2006). Cognitive therapy versus exposure and applied relaxation in social phobia: A randomized controlled trial. *Journal of Consulting and Clinical Psychology, 74*, 568–578.

123   Plate 5.1   *top* Glowimages/Getty Images; *bottom* Photo © Adam Gryko/Shutterstock.

125   Activity Box 5.1 *top left* Photo © John Bell/Shutterstock; *top right* Photo © Sharyn Young/Shutterstock; *middle left* Photo © Kristian Sekulic/Shutterstock; *middle right* Photo © Mateusz Drozd/Shutterstock; *bottom left* Getty Images/David de Lossy; *bottom right* Photo © An Nguyen/Shutterstock.

127   Plate 5.2   *(from left to right)* Photo © Dmitrijs Mijejevs/Shutterstock; Photo © Philip Lange/Shutterstock; Photo © Holger W/Shutterstock; Photo © M.I.K.E./Shutterstock.

127   Plate 5.3   Photo by Stephen Dagadakis; courtesy of Hunter Hoffman (spider2007a6008in.jpg).

131   Figure 5.2   Perowne, S. & Mansell, W. (2002). Social anxiety, self-focussed attention, and the discrimination of negative, neutral and positive audience members by their non-verbal behaviours. *Behavioural and Cognitive Psychotherapy, 30*, 11–23.

133   Case History 5.1, files photo, Rackermann/istockphoto.com.

135   Figure 5.3   Rapee, R.M., Brown, T.A., Antony, M.M. & Barlow, D.H. (1992). Response to hyperventilation and inhalation of 5.5 percent carbon dioxide-enriched air across the DSM-III-R anxiety disorders. *Journal of Abnormal Psychology, 101*(3), 538–552.

138   Figure 5.4   Clark, D.M. (1986). A cognitive approach to panic. *Behaviour Research and Therapy, 24*, 348–351.

141   Plate 5.4   Pearls Before Swine © Stephan Pastis/Dist. by United Feature Syndicate, Inc.

142   Figure 5.5   Mogg, K., Bradley, B.P., Williams, R. & Mathews, A. (1993). Subliminal processing of emotional

144   Figure 5.6   information in anxiety and depression. *Journal of Abnormal Psychology, 102*(2), 304–311.

144   Figure 5.6   UK National Institute for Clinical Excellence.

147   Plate 5.5   Avik Gilboa/WireImage/Getty Images.

150   Figure 5.7   Salkovskis, P.M., Wroe, A.L., Gledhill, A., Morrison, N., Forrester, E., Richards, C., Reynolds, M. & Thorpe, S. (2000). Responsibility attitudes and interpretations are characteristic of obsessive compulsive disorder. *Behaviour Research and Therapy, 38,* 347–372.

151   Figure 5.8   Clark, D.M., Ball, S. & Pape, D. (1991). An experimental investigation of thought suppression. *Behaviour Research and Therapy, 29*(3), 253–257.

160   Plate 5.6   © Benjamin Lowy/Corbis.

175   Plate 6.1   Photo © Galina Barskaya/Shutterstock.

176   Plate 6.2   Photo by Colin Atherton, University of Sussex.

179   Figure 6.2   Davidson, R.J., Pizzagalli, D., Nitschke, J.B. & Putnam, K. (2002). Depression: Perspectives from affective neuroscience. *Annual Review of Psychology, 53,* 545–574, figure 1. Reprinted with permission.

182   Plate 6.3   Harley Schwadron.

188   Figure 6.4   UK National Institute for Clinical Excellence.

189   Treatment in Practice Box 6.1, *Beating the Blues,* © Ultrasis UK Ltd.

190   Plate 6.4   The Kobal Collection/The Picture Desk.

197   Focus Point 6.2, photo Janine Wiedel Photolibrary/Alamy.

198   Plate 6.5   © Lynn Goldsmith/CORBIS.

199   Focus Point 6.3, suicide note © 2000/7 Forensic Linguistics Institute (F.L.I.). All rights reserved.

208   Focus Point 7.1, Figure 1, Taxi/Getty Images.

209   Focus Point 7.1, Figure 2, Grunnitus Studio/Science Photo Library.

211   Plate 7.1   www.CartoonStock.com.

213   Focus Point 7.2, photo, IBL/Rex Features.

225   Figure 7.2   reproduced by permission of Monte S. Buchsbaum, Mount Sinai School of Medicine.

226   Focus Point 7.5, photo, Dr R. Dourmashkin/Science Photo Library.

230   Focus Point 7.7, photo © Ron Hilton/Shutterstock.

231   Figure 7.3   Reprinted from Corcoran, R., Cahill, C. & Frith, C.D. (1997). The appreciation of visual jokes in people with schizophrenia: A study of 'mentalizing' ability. *Schizophrenia Research, 24*(3), 319–327. Copyright © 1997. Published by Elsevier B.V.

238   Plate 7.2   Cardiff Libraries and Information Service.

245, 521, 564   A Week in the Life of a Clinical Psychologist, diary photo, istockphoto.com.

246   Plate 7.3   David Hoffman Photo Library.

249   Figure 7.4   NICE, *Clinical algorithms and pathways to care* (December 2002).

250   Activity Box 7.2, article by Oliver James, *The Guardian,* Saturday 22 October, 2005.

259   Plate 8.1   Dave Benett/Getty Images Entertainment/Getty Images.

260   Figure 8.1   www.who.int/substance_abuse/facts/cocaine/en/.

266   Focus Point 8.1, photo © Quayside/Shutterstock.

267   Plate 8.2   www.CartoonStock.com.

270   Focus Point 8.2, photo, Photofusion Picture Library/Alamy.

272   Focus Point 8.3, photo © Pritmova Svetlana/Shutterstock.

273   Figure 8.4   www.statistics.gov.uk/cci/nugget.asp?id=866.

274   Focus Point 8.4, photo © Brett Mulcahy/Shutterstock.

275   Plate 8.3   Bubbles Photolibrary/Alamy.

277   Figure 8.5   www.drugabuse.gov/researchreports/cocaine/cocaine3.html.

277   Plate 8.4   © Bettmann/CORBIS.

278   Focus Point 8.5, photo, Darrin Jenkins/Alamy.

280   Focus Point 8.6, photo, Al Pereira/Michael Ochs Archives/Getty Images.

282   Focus Point 8.7, photo, Sakki/Rex Features.

284   Plate 8.5   Pictorial Press Ltd/Alamy.

285   Focus Point 8.8, photos, *top* Digital Vision/Getty Images; *bottom* © Scott Houston/Sygma/Corbis.

289   Focus Point 8.10, photo, Darrin Jenkins/Alamy.

289   Client's Perspective Box 8.2, photo, Maciej Wojtkowiak/Alamy.

292   Focus Point 8.11, photo, Everynight Images/Alamy.

293   Plate 8.6   www.CartoonStock.com.

312   Plate 9.1   courtesy of the Advertising Archives (p. 312); © Comic Company 1998–2007 (p. 313).

313   Activity Box 9.1, photo © Yegor Korzh/Shutterstock.

317   Figure 9.1   after Currin, L., Schmidt, U., Treasure, J. & Jick, H. (2005). Time trends in eating disorder incidence. *British Journal of Psychiatry, 186,* 132–135.

317   Plate 9.2   Peter Brooker/Rex Features.

318   Case History 9.1, illustration reproduced from *Understanding Eating Disorders,* BMA Family Doctor Books.

322   Plate 9.3   Victoria and Albert Museum, London, UK/The Bridgeman Art Library.

323   Plate 9.4   © ABACA/PA Photos.

325   Figure 9.2   after Jacobi, C., Hayward, C., de Zwaan, M., Kraemer, H.C. & Agras, W.S. (2004). Coming to terms with risk factors for eating disorders: Application of risk terminology and suggestions for a general taxonomy. *Psychological Bulletin, 130,* 19–65.

327   Plate 9.5   Brian Rasic/Rex Features.

328   Plate 9.6   www.CartoonStock.com.

328   Figure 9.3   Forbes, G.B., Adams-Curtis, L.E., Rade, B. et al. (2001). Body dissatisfaction in women and men: The role of gender-typing and self-esteem. *Sex Roles, 44*(7–8), 461–484.

329   Figure 9.4   Stice, E. (2001). A prospective test of the dual-pathway model of bulimic pathology: Mediating effects of dieting and negative affect. *Journal of Abnormal Psychology, 110,* 124–135.

337   Figure 9.5   Fairburn, C.G. (1997). Eating disorders. In D.M. Clark & C.G. Fairburn (Eds.), *The science and practice of cognitive behaviour therapy.* Oxford: Oxford University Press.

345   Activity Box 10.1, photo © AP/PA Photos.

348   Plate 10.1   Art Shay/Time and Life Pictures/Getty Images.

357   Figure 10.1   Rosen, R., Shabsigh, R., Berber, M., Assalian, P. et al. (2006). Efficacy and tolerability of vardenafil in men with mild depression and erectile dysfunction: The depression-related improvement with vardenafil for erectile response study. *American Journal of Psychiatry, 163*(1), 79–87.

357   Plate 10.2   www.CartoonStock.com.

362   Figure 10.2   Moore, R.A., Edwards, J.E. & McQuay, H.J. (2002). Sildenafil (Viagra) for male erectile dysfunction: A meta-analysis of clinical trial reports. *BMC Urology, 2.*

367   Focus Point 10.2, photo, Housewife/Hulton Archive/Getty Images.

374   Research Methods Box 10.1, Figure 1, Gannon, T.A. (2006). Increasing honest responding on cognitive distortions in child molesters: The bogus pipeline procedure. *Journal of Interpersonal Violence, 21*(3), 358–375.

378   Plate 10.3   AFP/Getty Images.

385   Focus Point 10.4, photo, Peter Treanor/Alamy.

392   Plate 11.1   *top* The Kobal Collection/The Picture Desk; *bottom* Rank, courtesy of Aquarius.

396   Plate 11.2   www.CartoonStock.com.

404   Plate 11.3   Gesellschaft der Musikfreunde, Vienna, Austria/The Bridgeman Art Library.

406   Plate 11.4   www.CartoonStock.com.

407   Focus Point 11.2, photo, Jim Dandy/Stock Illustration Source/Getty Images.

413   Focus Point 11.3, photo, Tim Macpherson/Stone/Getty Images.

415   Figure 11.1   Lahey, B.B., Loeber, R., Burke, J.D. & Applegate, B. (2005). Predicting future antisocial personality disorder in males from a clinical assessment in childhood. *Journal of Consulting and Clinical Psychology, 73*, 389–399.

417   Figure 11.2   Data from Blair, R.J.R., Jones, L., Clark, F. & Smith, M. (1997). The psychopathic individual: A lack of responsiveness to distress cues? *Psychophysiology, 34*(2), 192–198.

418   Research Methods Box 11.1, Figures 1 and 2 from Birbaumer, N., Viet, R., Lotze, M., Erb, M. et al. (2005). Deficient fear conditioning in psychopathy: A functional magnetic resonance imaging study. *Archives of General Psychiatry, 62*(7), 799–805.

421   Case History 11.3, photo © PA Photos.

428   Figure 11.3   Arntz, A. (1999). Do personality disorders exist? On the validity of the concept and its cognitive-behavioral formulation and treatment. *Behaviour Research and Therapy, 37*, S97–S134.

429   Treatment in Practice Box 11.2, *Dead Man Walking* film poster, Everett Collection/Rex Features.

438   Focus Point 12.1, photo, PA/Topfoto.

446   Plate 12.1   www.CartoonStock.com.

449   Plate 12.2   Mary Evans Picture Library.

451   Figure 12.2   Warwick, H.M.C. (1995). Assessment of hypochondriasis. *Behaviour Research and Therapy, 33*, 845–853.

452   Activity Box 12.1, Pain Anxiety Symptoms Scale © Lance McCracken.

454   Research Methods Box 12.1, PET scan from Halligan, P.W., Athwal, B.S., Oakley, D.A. & Frackowiak, R.S.J. (2000). Imaging hypnotic paralysis: Implications for conversion hysteria. *Lancet, 355*(9208), 986–987.

457   Treatment in Practice Box 12.1, photo, Oscar Burriel/Science Photo Library.

466   Plate 13.1   Tyler Hicks/Getty Images News/Getty Images.

469   Focus Point 13.1, photo © Jean Schweitzer/Shutterstock.

476   Figure 13.1   DePrince, A.P. & Freyd, J.J. (2004). Forgetting trauma stimuli. *Psychological Science, 15*, 488–492.

478   Focus Point 13.2, both photos © AP/PA Photos.

495   Plate 14.1   Ronald Grant Archive.

502   Figure 14.4   Tucker, K.A., Robertson, K.R., Lin, W., Smith, J.K. et al. (2004). Neuroimaging in human immunodeficiency virus infection. *Journal of Neuroimmunology, 157*(1–2), 153–162. Copyright © 2004. Reprinted with permission from Elsevier BV.

504   Plate 14.2   © Gary Hershorn/Reuters/Corbis.

505   Plate 14.3   Illustration from *Massachusetts Medical Journal*, 1868.

506   Figure 14.5   Morris, P.L.P., Robinson, R.G., Andrezejewski, P., Samuels, J. & Price, T.R. (1993). Association of depression with 10-year poststroke mortality. *American Journal of Psychiatry, 150*(1), 124–129.

509   Figure 14.6   Blennow, K., de Leon, M.J. & Zetterberg, H. (2006). Alzheimer's disease. *Lancet, 368*, 387–403.

515   Treatment in Practice Box 14.1, virtual reality kitchen from Zhang, L., Beatriz, M.D., Abreu, C., Seale, G.S. et al. (2003). A virtual reality environment for evaluation of a daily living skill in brain injury rehabilitation: Reliability and validity. *Archives of Physical Medicine and Rehabilitation, 84*, 1118–1124. Copyright © 2003 Elsevier.

516   Treatment in Practice Box 14.2, photos from Smania, N., Girardi, F., Domenicali, C., Lora, E. & Aglioti, S. (2000). The rehabilitation of limb apraxia: A study in left-brain-damaged patients. *Archives of Physical Medicine and Rehabilitation, 81*(4), 379–388. Copyright © 2000 Elsevier.

536   Figure 15.1   Mental Health of Children and Adolescents in Great Britain, 1999 ONS Survey.

541   Activity Box 15.1, photo, image100/Alamy.

544   Plate 15.1   Reuters/Franck Revel.

546   Plate 15.2   www.CartoonStock.com.

547   Figure 15.2   Krol, N., Morton, J. & De Bruyn, E. (2004). Theories of conduct disorder: A causal modelling analysis. *Journal of Child Psychology and Psychiatry, 45*, 727–742.

551   Focus Point 15.1, photo © PA Photos.

562   Figure 15.3   www.dri-sleeper.com/treatment.htm.

564   Treatment in Practice Box 15.2, photo, Jennifer Harrison.

578   Figure 16.1   Shaywitz, S.E. (2003). *Overcoming dyslexia: A new and complete science-based program for reading problems at any level.* New York: Alfred A. Knopf.

578   Plate 16.1   Will and Deni McIntyre/Science Source, National Audubon Society Collection/Photo Researchers, Inc. Reproduced with permission.

587   Plate 16.2   *top left* Stock Connection Distribution/Alamy; *bottom left* Wellcome Images; *top and bottom right* Genetics Centre/Wellcome Images.

591   Focus Point 16.2, photo, Taxi/Getty Images.

592   Plate 16.3   FASawareUK.

595   Plate 16.4   Alix/Phanie/Rex Features.

603   Activity Box 16.1, photo, Saturn Stills/Science Photo Library.

DVD MATERIAL

Case study videos © University of Sheffield and Dr Stephen Peters. Used with permission. These case studies are part of the *Differential Diagnosis in Psychiatry* series produced by the University of Sheffield, UK. The series is available from Films for the Humanities and Sciences in the USA and the University of Sheffield in the UK and the rest of the world.

Clinical Training Video © University of Leeds and Canterbury Christ Church University. Used with permission.

Every effort has been made to trace copyright holders and to obtain their permission for the use of copyright material. The publisher apologizes for any errors or omissions in the above list and would be grateful if notified of any corrections that should be incorporated in future reprints or editions of this book.

Author Index

Subject Index